C000205818

NEWCASTLE UNITED
The Ultimate Who's Who 1881-2014

By Paul Joannou

**NEWCASTLE
UNITED**

AN OFFICIAL PUBLICATION

NEWCASTLE UNITED
The Ultimate Who's Who 1881-2014

This Who's Who is dedicated to
The Men Who Made United,
in particular William Armstrong Coulson,
regarded as the club's founder and
the captain of Stanley Football Club in 1881.

First published November 2014 in Great Britain by
N Publishing, part of St James Ventures Ltd

Bolam White House, Belsay, Newcastle upon Tyne, NE20 0HB, England

Text & Data © 2014 Paul Joannou.
Design © 2014 N Publishing & Team Digital Limited

ISBN 978-0-9568156-1-3

DESIGN & LAYOUT
Paul Joannou and Dave Hewson & Simon Arbon,
Team Digital Limited, Team Valley Trading Estate, Gateshead.

PRINTED & BOUND BY
Elanders Limited, Merlin Way, New York Business Park, North Tyneside.

Photographs & Illustrations are courtesy of: Newcastle United FC Archive, P Joannou Archive as well as the Newcastle Chronicle & Journal. Many of the photographs reproduced are from original material in the archives of Newcastle United FC who also retain the rights to official photocall pictures from the modern era taken by the official photographer. We have been unable to trace the sources of all illustrations used, but any photographer involved is cordially invited to contact the publisher in writing providing proof of copyright of any individual photograph.

JACKET ILLUSTRATIONS
Front & rear cover: Some of the Men Who Made United over more than 130 years.

■ *Frank Hudspeth receiving the FA Cup from HRH Duke of York after United's 2-0 victory over Aston Villa in the 1924 Final at Wembley.*

NEWCASTLE UNITED

The Ultimate Who's Who 1881-2014

CONTENTS

TOP 10 Appearances League & Cup Fixtures

1	Lawrence, Jimmy	GK	496
2	Hudspeth, Frank	FB	472
3	Given, Shay	GK	463
4	Clark, Frank	FB	456
5	McCracken, Bill	FB	432
6	McMichael, Alf	FB	431
7	Craig, David	FB	411
8	Mitchell, Bobby	OL	408
9	Shearer, Alan	CF	404
10	Milburn, Jackie	CF	397

TOP 10 Goalscorers League & Cup Fixtures

1	Shearer, Alan	CF	206
2	Milburn, Jackie	CF	200
3	White, Len	CF	153
4	Gallacher, Hughie	CF	143
5	Macdonald, Malcolm	CF	121
6	Beardlsey, Peter	Fwd	119
7	McDonald, Tom	IL	113
8	Mitchell, Bobby	OL	113
9	Harris, Neil	CF	101
10	Robson, Bryan	Fwd	97

400 GAMES 200 GOALS

405 ▶	206	Shearer, Alan
(All games)		Centre-forward
494 ▶	238	Milburn, Jackie
(All games)		Centre-forward

Bob Moncur

"To wear those famous black-and-white stripes is one of the greatest feelings you can have."

NEWCASTLE UNITED

Captain BOB

An epic drama with a cast of thousands and more than 130 years of history – that is the Newcastle United Story. The names and faces change, but the stage remains constant, and it has been my privilege to play a central role on that great stage for part of what is a never-ending play.

In the 50 years and more since I arrived at St James' Park as a raw Scottish hopeful, I have seen the club from many perspectives, as a youth player, a reserve, first-teamer – included captain – and commentator. To the present day when at the age of 69 I am privileged to be part of Newcastle United's corporate relations team.

The history of this famous club has over the years been told in many different ways, and as official club historian, Paul Joannou has previously produced substantial portions of that history, including the marvellous first part of the club's Ultimate project; *Newcastle United: The Ultimate Record*.

Now Paul has brought years of research and labour to worthy fruition with *Newcastle United: The Ultimate Who's Who*, in which everyone who has played their part, both major and minor, is duly recorded and honoured.

Almost 1,800 biographies stretching across the full spectrum of players, managers, backroom staff and administrators dating back to when United's roots were planted in 1881 provides an unprecedentedly comprehensive catalogue of the club's leading personalities and more. Not only players, managers and coaches, but also directors – how many colourful characters have occupied the St James' Park boardroom! – are given their rightful place in this book.

For myself, to have been part of this rich tapestry is at once a source of pride and humility. Before I was even born, illustrious greats such as Colin Veitch, Stan Seymour and Hughie Gallacher trod the famous turf and donned the famous stripes. Joe Harvey, Cup-winning captain of the Fifties, was the manager under whom I played as United won promotion in 1965 and the Inter Cities Fairs Cup in 1969, and to have been skipper of the side on that memorable night in Budapest – Joe's birthday, June 11th – remains a source of eternal pride for me. That is the last major trophy the club has won – a distinction I would rather not have maintained for so long – but surely for a club of this magnitude the next silverware cannot be far away.

To play for Newcastle United is to become part of the fabric of not only a football club, but also of a region which is unrivalled for its passion and support. And many famous, fabulous players decorate the tableau. From the thrilling excitement of Malcolm Macdonald to the glorious accomplishments of Alan Shearer, the speed and power of Jackie Milburn and the aerial strength of Wyn Davies, many and varied have been the great Magpies goalscorers.

United's panoply of greats extends to such special talents as Peter Beardsley, whom I had with me when I was manager at Carlisle United, and Tony Green, the Scottish international of the 1970s whose brief career was so cruelly cut short by injury. The full-back partnership of David Craig and Frank Clark, who made my job alongside them so much easier when we came through together in the Sixties, and the silky skills of the late Alan Suddick, were all factors in the club's development in that era.

The book includes every player to play senior football for the club. All the famous and well known names are included of course, yet also many players not to get the break at the right time, or be unluckily injured. And during my time colleagues like John Markie and Colin Clish managed only a handful of games between them, yet both went onto have solid careers elsewhere.

Bobby Moncur holds the Inter Cities Fairs Cup on the 40th anniversary of United's victory.

And football is littered with injury victims. Apart from Tony Green, I recall Geoff Allen especially, a winger who could have gone to the very top.

Paul Joannou has extended the players' histories to take in their later careers, uncovering some fascinating postscripts tracing those who became doctors and dentists, landlords and entrepreneurs, and adopted so many other remarkable occupations.

We should never forget the trainers and coaches, either, for they too have played a significant part. Such men as Dave Smith, Keith Burkinshaw, Joe Richardson and Benny Craig set the template for those who followed.

Figures of distinction populated the boardroom: Lord Westwood, Stan Seymour, Fenton Braithwaite, Alderman McKeag, though to the recent times of Sir John Hall, Freddy Shepherd, Derek Llambias and present owner Mike Ashley.

In the later years of the 20th Century and early years of the 21st Century, club facilities have also changed dramatically, from terraces to all-seater stadia, and from open training fields to state-of-the-art academies. It certainly seems a long time ago that we players jogged from St James' Park up Barrack Road to Hunter's Moor for training on a windswept and uncultivated patch of grass! Now the club's emerging apprentices have every example of five-star facilities to help them make the grade.

Football has changed hugely in the 50 years and more since I first played; and as time goes by the memories and personalities of the past become ever more remote. That is why a book such as *The Ultimate Who's Who* is so valuable, laying in stone as it does a permanent and indispensable record.

For generations ahead, this volume will take its place as a benchmark of its genre, a touchstone of tradition, a marvellous and definitive work of reference in Newcastle United's already comprehensive library.

■ United's squad at the Rhyl Marine Hydro Hotel during 1908. Directors Oliver and Bell have the company of several waitresses on the balcony.

In a work of this magnitude I am most indebted to many, many people during a period of almost 35 years. I have been determined over that time to produce the definitive story of Newcastle United. Together with the club's official Millennium History, *United:The First 100 Years & More* as well as *The Ultimate Record* and now *The Ultimate Who's Who...* I am delighted that task has been completed for posterity. This book completes the trilogy, a comprehensive volume of all those individuals who contributed to making Newcastle United.

For much of the opening years of Newcastle United's origins factual information is very scarce. Reporting of football in local newspapers was brief and devoid of hard information. Gradually though, the association code gained column inches albeit conflicting match reports, teams, goalscorers and attendances were frequent in differing newspapers. Notes on individual players and officials were scant, with the formal approach then being not to give Christian names and only initials. This all added to the problems of unravelling biographies of Newcastle's early personalities.

Apart from the local Tyneside press, notably the Daily Journal, Daily Chronicle and Tyneside Echo, extensive reference has also been made to contemporary newspapers from other parts of the region. There were other good sources of information like rare volumes of the Northern Athlete and Northern Gossip magazine.

Over the three decades of research Newcastle upon Tyne Central Library's Local Studies Department has been a priceless as well as a core point of inquiry and their staff are duly thanked. Similarly the Local Studies Departments at Gateshead, Sunderland, Darlington and Middlesbrough libraries together with the Tyne & Wear Archives Service at the Discovery Museum in Newcastle (where the Northumberland FA archives are housed) have also been an invaluable source of research. Mention must also be made of the excellent archive facilities at the Woodhorn Northumberland Museum in Ashington. Staff at all these locations have shown unfailing courtesy and assistance. Their help is much appreciated. Visits have also been made to the National Archives in London and Edinburgh, as well as the Mitchell Library in Glasgow.

Acknowledgement is also made to the many authors and fellow historians of hundreds of historical football volumes together with the multitude of web-based club and research sites covering the English and Scottish game which have been reviewed, too many to schedule in a bibliography. Past study of Newcastle United's official Minute books from the earliest times has provided much original information, while Jordan Tinniswood's extensive research notes, Before They Were United, were a point of reference, and since he has been of help unravelling various queries on those early days.

The staff at the National Football Museum in Manchester and Preston, Peter Holme, Alex Jackson and Gordon Small are acknowledged for their assistance and determination to provide the country with a central archive. The ENFA (English National Football Archive), set up by Tony Brown has also been a first-class point of research as has the Scottish player data-base created by John Litster.

A special note of thanks to John Allan, 'Newcastle John' to all on Tyneside, who has been a valued assistant in unearthing information on Newcastle's footballers over the past couple of years. His enthusiasm has been unrivalled. Scottish football historian Andy Mitchell, past press officer at the Scottish FA and now with UEFA, has assisted greatly on the many players with links north of the border. Martin O'Connor of Worcester has kindly passed on much of his pre-war research from the archives of the Football Association and Football League.

Any book of this nature would not be complete had the very players, managers, coaches and officials themselves not been consulted. In those 30-odd years I have been in touch with many of those who actually pulled on Newcastle's famous colours. In addition, countless relatives of those players have been in touch, not only from the UK, but from Europe, Africa, Asia, Australia and North America. Their personal memories and family archives have been especially invaluable in producing this book. Thanks to all.

Over time I have gathered hundreds of illustrations of United's personalities from earliest years; press photographs, vintage postcards and cigarette cards, and where individual images were difficult to find, newspaper cuttings. The club's official archive has provided many images while in the modern era, Newcastle United's in-house photography department has been invaluable, notably official photographers Ian Dobson, Ian Horrocks and Serena Taylor. Magpie enthusiast and United photograph collector Adrian Clark has helped enormously, loaning images to scan and copy.

Former club director Kenneth Slater who for over 30 years was at the heart of St James' Park has provided an insight to the many personalities he worked alongside. Mike Bolam of nufc.com, another life-long United supporter has given encouragement and continually sent snippets on the never-ending player movement trail.

The following individuals and organisations have also assisted in the trawl for information for this Who's Who over the last few years: A Armstrong, A Candlish, T Carder, P Coates, E Curry, J Cross, P Days, J Diamond, M Dix, L Donnelly, G Dykes, J Edminson, M Edmondson (The Back Page), C Fraser, M Gibson, B Greenbank, P Macnamara, R Mason (Sunderland AFC), B Milne, I Nannestad, D Potter, I Rigby, WH Swann, R Talbot, P Tully, AJ Turnbull, I Weller, D Wherry.

My thanks to the directors and staff of Newcastle United for their agreement to publish the Ultimate project on the Club's behalf. Stuart Middlemiss at Newcastle United has been supportive of the project while Mark Hannen and Tony Toward at St James' Park have assisted enthusiastically as has Anthony Marshall, publication editor.

Designers Dave Hewson and Simon Arbon at Team Digital, first involved in producing Newcastle United publications back in 1994 including and continuing for 13 seasons on the official Matchday Programme, has provided a first-class product along with Tyneside printers Elanders.

Finally, thanks to Bob Moncur for his Foreword; a steadfast Scot, one with black-and-white blood who epitomises everything worthy about Newcastle United, and not least a wonderful defender and skipper, one of the very best to have worn the famous stripes.

The men who made UNITED

FA CUP FINAL 1924, Wembley – United v Aston Villa

The official *Newcastle United: The Ultimate Who's Who* has been an ongoing historical project for over 35 years with the aim of providing comprehensive profiles of those men – and two women – who have shaped the club since the pioneering days on Victorian Tyneside. Apart from being an essential reference text to dip into when information on a particular player is required, it is urged that readers take time to discover about all of the *Men Who Made United* – from A-Z, all 400 pages and around 1,800 players, managers, trainers, coaches and backroom staff, as well as directors and officials. It may take a while, but the tales of those individuals who fashioned the Magpies over more than 130 years are thoroughly intriguing. The heroes, the villains, the vaguely recalled, the completely forgotten; names much-loved, much-derided and many frequently honoured. They have fashioned Newcastle United and created what is a very special Toon heritage.

Newcastle's first title winning squad in 1905, sponsored on this vintage postcard by Oxo.

CATEGORISATION

Included in this *Ultimate Who's Who* are all the personalities since formation of the club in November 1881. For the period from 1881-82 to the end of season 2013-14, all first-team players, managers, as well as those behind the scenes are profiled. A photograph is included of the majority although several Victorian characters and officials remain frustratingly difficult to unmask. All data is correlated up to the close-season of 2014 including participation in the 2014 World Cup in Brazil and the club's pre-season matches of 2014-15. At the end of Section 1, a 'New Arrivals' supplement is included profiling additions to the squad during the opening transfer window, players to make their debut as the new season unfolds. The Who's Who is categorised as follows:

SECTION 1: Senior Players (Appearances in 'First-class' fixtures)

Detailed biographies are included for every player to have appeared in senior football for Newcastle United and their pioneers, Stanley FC and Newcastle East End FC, since 1881. Senior football is designated by an appearance (including substitute outings) in any of the following competitions:

- Northern League, Football League, Premier League (including Test Matches, Play-Offs & void matches).
- FA Cup (including Qualifying games, the 1945-46 FA Cup competition & void matches), Football League Cup.
- European fixtures; UEFA Champions League, UEFA European Cup Winners Cup, UEFA Cup, UEFA Europa League, Intertoto Cup, Inter Cities Fairs Cup & Anglo-Italian Cup.
- Texaco Cup, Anglo-Scottish Cup, FA Charity/Community Shield, Sheriff of London Charity Shield, Full Members Cup including later sponsored tournaments (Simod Cup & Zenith Data Systems Cup) and the Mercantile Credit Centenary Trophy.
- Wartime football; League & Cup fixtures 1918-19, 1939-40 to 1945-46.
- Northumberland & Durham Challenge Cup & Northumberland Challenge Cup fixtures 1882-83 to 1889-90 (when a first-eleven was fielded).

SECTION 2: Senior Players (Appearances in 'Other' fixtures)

Abridged biographies are included for United personalities to have only made an appearance (including as substitute) in any supplementary first-team match and who was not selected for a first-class appearance. This includes the many pioneer players who took part during the formative years of Stanley and East End before league competition flourished and when a multitude of friendlies were played each season. Included are also those players who have not taken part in a first-eleven fixture but who reached the substitute's bench without being called to take the field. Matches include:

- Other first-eleven fixtures including semi-competitive games, miscellaneous and local competitions such as the Coronation Cup and Newcastle & Sunderland Hospitals Cup, all friendlies, overseas tour matches, testimonials, & sundry charity, benefit or invitation tournaments.
- Substitute non-appearance in first-class fixtures or other secondary games.

For several matches over the years a *Newcastle United XI* opposed certain teams, with the make-up of the side being far from the regular senior eleven. A judgement has been taken to classify these matches into either 'first-eleven' or 'reserve' fixtures, dependent on the number of first-teamers included. Appearances in these *Newcastle United XI* matches are included at the end of Section 2, while in addition, on occasion a combined *Newcastle United & Sunderland XI* has been fielded; appearances in these games are also added. Outings in abandoned matches or fixtures classed as 'reserve' matches as well as modern 'Behind Closed Doors' games are not included. Also not included is the Football League's centenary tournament at Wembley in 1988 when games were not the full 90 minutes in duration.

SECTION 3: Managers

Comprehensive biographies are included of all United's managers since the appointment of Andy Cunningham in 1930. Detailed is the manager's debut and total number of matches each was fully in charge of the Magpies, including periods as a caretaker-manager. Where managers were also players, biographies can be found in the Player Section.

SECTION 4: Coaching & Support Staff

Pen-pictures are included for individuals appointed to support either the Manager or Board of Directors in terms of playing affairs, including:

- Assistant Manager & Director of Football.
- Trainers & Coaches; first-eleven, reserve team, Academy leaders as well as senior coaches to the youth team.
- Senior physiotherapists.

Not included is the wider backroom staff, especially relevant in modern football when at times a substantial team of fitness and medical staff have been appointed. Also not incorporated are youth team coaches below senior youth level, before and after the introduction of the Newcastle United Academy when at times the club fielded several junior sides of varying age groups. Where support staff were also players, biographies can be found in the Player Section unless stated.

SECTION 5: Directors & Officials

All those individuals are profiled to have served the club at Board of Director level including Chairmen as well as other modern posts. Included are the pioneering Committee men of Stanley and East End during the years before the club turned professional in 1890 and then were managed by a Board. Information from this era is scarce and therefore a few gaps exist in the listing.

Many of Newcastle United's early officials during the Victorian era on the face of it were men with only surnames and initials. However, to a historian's delight two surviving club Share Ledgers started in 1890 when East End became a limited company and running into the 1900s, give important data; full names, addresses and occupations. Fortunately the census of 1891 tied to the same era and as a result the majority of Newcastle's original Committee and Directorate have been traced.

Ownership of the club over United's history has largely been one of a shareholding. In the modern era the club has been owned by two organisations; Cameron Hall (Sir John Hall and family) and St James Holdings (Mike Ashley). Biographies are included for the following United positions:

- Chairmen & Directors 1890 to date, including PLC status appointments 1996 to 2007.
- President & Committee members 1881 to 1890.
- Club Secretary, Chief-Executive & Managing Director.
- Honorary Club President & Sole-Owner.

Not included are non-Board appointments, Associate Directors or the like, or Vice-Presidents, nor are Assistant Secretaries, Financial Secretaries, all posts which have existed over the years.

Research

Piecing together information from numerous sources and identifying a career from birth to death (where applicable) is in many ways like a huge jig-saw. Gathering data on the biographical history of Newcastle United began at the end of the Seventies. Since the original *Newcastle United Who's Who* was produced in 1983, then something of a pioneering club who's who, only the second ever produced on a British club, followed by the much more detailed and comprehensive 512 page *The Black'n'White Alphabet* in 1996 (right), research on the Beautiful Game has moved substantially. The arrival of the internet and with it a vast

electronic world-wide knowledge base has become available. This coupled with an explosion of historical books on football, and especially club titles, since 2000, has given a rich source of new data, although it has to be noted that much information found via the world-wide-web does need checked and verified with a good secondary source.

Football research has also been hugely supplemented by the game's archives at the National Football Museum in Manchester and Preston, as well as The Scottish Football Museum at Hampden Park where original League and Association registration ledgers are held. The creation of the English National Football Archive (ENFA) has also been a huge bonus in research, while the popularity of genealogy has seen a profusion of various family-history type sites with a wealth of official national records. Invaluable data is now available covering birth, death, probate records, as well as census information and military service. Electronic technology and sites such as Ancestry and Scotland's People has made access to such files easy and priceless. All of this has supplemented the already first-class Local Studies Department at Newcastle Central Library where the regional data-base is exceptional.

Over the period of compilation, hundreds of former Newcastle stars have been contacted, now many sadly to have passed away. But their story has been recorded for posterity and facts established such as Harry McMenemy's blood link to Lawrie McMenemy or Tom Finney's stay in the North East with United during World War Two.

Descendents of United's stars have been in touch from all over the world; relations of Albert Shepherd, Jock Peddie and Tom Watson in the States, Bill McCracken in Australia, as well as an endless list of relatives from the UK, always pleased to receive confirmation their grandfather or distant cousin played for Newcastle United and relate their kin's life story.

Great care has been taken to eradicate errors and disparity. Many checks and cross-checks have been completed. In the compilation of the vast amount of biographical information, including so many facts and figures, anomalies and discrepancies have been found. Football writing in the past has been prone to error, many carried through the years from volume to volume. Most have been investigated and resolved. However, it is inevitable that with material stretching back to the Victorian era, there remains frustrating inconsistency or a new slice of information which cannot be fully confirmed. On occasion within the text, where there is only a probability of this being accurate it is noted in [square brackets]. In a book with so much factual detail in the near 1,800 life stories, inevitably a few inaccuracies will slip the net.

The story of United's personalities is never-ending and a life-time could be spent researching Newcastle United's great and good. There are still a handful of the club's early personalities who are difficult to trace; contemporary newspapers being at times scant and notoriously contradictory. Gaps remain to be filled, and no doubt interesting tales to unearth.

Newcastle United: The Ultimate Record

The companion text to this book, *The Ultimate Record*, contains core summaries of players, managers, coaches and directors. All data is cross-referenced between the two books, although certain new and updated information relating to player names and initials is included here.

Stanley, East End & Newcastle United

The early years of development of Newcastle United saw the club born as Stanley FC in November 1881, changing their name to Newcastle East End during October 1882 and then to Newcastle United in December 1892. Throughout the Who's Who when a player has joined the club in these pioneering years, the name of the club at the time has been used. So when Alec White joined the club during 1884, he joined East End, although in essence he joined Newcastle United. For ease of reference STANLEY, EAST END and UNITED are shown in capitals within each biography.

Birth & death data

A review of the birth and death particulars for the majority of United's personalities has been undertaken through contact with family members and ancestry research web-sites. Some gaps remain, especially from early years. Where birth and death particulars have only been part traced, details follow the practice of official government registration data; by showing the birth or death period in yearly quarters; Q1, Q2, Q3 and Q4, eg Quarter 1 refers to the period January to March of the year in question.

There are discrepancies which occur surrounding the players actual 'birthplace' with conflicts to his actual 'residence', a frustration to historians. For example a player who resided say in the village of Longhorsley in Northumberland may have been actually born in the nearest local hospital, in Alnwick or Morpeth. His birth registration could show either and noted over time as either location.

A similar quandary sometimes exists with actual dates of birth. The celebrated Jack Rutherford has been recorded throughout the last century as being born on the 12 October; however research with the Rutherford family actually reveals this is his baptism date and not his actual birth date. Church records confirm he was born four days earlier on 8 October. In addition registration details rely on individuals noting the correct day of birth or death, on occasion minor anomalies exist.

Conflicts occur with birth dates and age details recorded in the club's official Player Registers at the time of signing and relayed to the press, being noted in player profiles for decades, sometimes wrongly. Perhaps some white lies were told to ensure a deal was finalised, who knows.

Names

In the pioneering Victorian era, differences are evident in the reporting of player names. Many of United's earliest players are often identified with variances. For instance Alex Sawyers is noted also as Sawers, and with the initial A or G, while Gibbons has P, PE or G! Even players changed their name. Jock Sorley arrived on Tyneside under the name of McSorland, while he also used McSorley, although his birth certificate notes Sorley. The use of the Scottish prefix of 'Mac' and 'Mc' causes problems too with the differing spelling of players names contained in many sources of information. Examples such as MacFarlane/Macfarlane/McFarlane or MacKenzie/Mackenzie/McKenzie are typical. It becomes almost impossible to determine the correct usage when the player's own autograph also uses the different spellings, as is the case with Roddie McKenzie/MacKenzie.

There are a few instances where the true identity of a player has yet to be ascertained. These are restricted to a mere handful. In season 1894-95 two appearances were made by a player called Hynd or Haynes, which may be the same player or two different individuals. During wartime football in 1918-19, Jack Doran was at St James' Park, a player to later have a good career elsewhere. He is noted in the club's ledgers but in newspaper reports some of his four games are identified as a player called 'Johnson' who is not recorded in the club's team line-up. It is probable that Doran played under a pseudonym as he may not have been properly registered at the time.

The influx of many players from around the globe has added a new dimension, with care needed to understand their full name. Nation custom at times utilise a surname as their 'first' name and vice-versa, such as Emre (Emre Bolozoglu). Footballers from a Latin background often use a 'playing-name' rather than their own family name as in the case of Xisco (Franciso Tejada Jimenez) and Mirandinha (Francisco Ernandi Lima da Silva) (pictured right). In these cases their alphabetical entry in the Who's Who uses the playing-name used, eg Emre or Xisco.

Professionalism

When Stanley and East End first kicked off on Victorian Tyneside, the game was largely amateur, but rapidly becoming a paid occupation, part-time at first, then full-time, legal or illegal. Under-the-counter arrangements to break the rules soon became rife and in England professionalism was part legalised in the game during 1885, although Scotland held out for some while. Consequently many Scots headed to the North of England to be paid for playing football. Early footballers held full-time occupations, many in traditional industries of Tyneside; platers, riveters, joiners and miners.

Newcastle East End's official Minutes in March 1891 record the wage structure for players as; *10 shillings (50p) for 1 match, plus 5 shillings (25p) extra for each match after, plus 5 shillings (25p) win or draw*. By season 1891-92 wages had increased to £1 per match, win or draw and 15 shillings (75p) a loss. In 1893 it was noted in *Athletic News* that the average wage was £3 during the week in the season. A maximum wage rule was introduced during 1901 and a strict wage cap became the norm for 60 years. Players received Benefits for loyal service of five year and 10 year periods. In 1901 the maximum wage was £4 per week, by 1922 it was £8 per week and in 1953 £15 per week.

Several players supplemented their football wages with part-time and second jobs, sometimes against the rules of their club. United's Johnny Campbell was sacked because he took over the running of the Darnell pub during 1898. In the immediate post-war years many Newcastle United footballers were engaged in occupations essential to the country's economy after conflict, notably working at one of the many local pits. The likes of Jack Milburn, Len Shackleton and Len White were really part-time footballers for a large proportion of their younger playing days with the club.

As the game developed, and if the player's profile was big enough, advertising deals were the norm; United's Edwardian players were linked to Oxo, Jack Milburn had a deal with a boot retailer in Gateshead and with Quaker Oats. Later of course sponsorship was to explode into lucrative contracts.

A PFA arm-band from the Edwardian era.

For much of football's history clubs held the reigns on player movements and contracts, being all-powerful and dictatorial. Newcastle's players were heavily involved in the creation and rise of the PFA union with Colin Veitch and Jimmy Lawrence both leading advocates of the cause.

Footballers were branded by one side of the game's divide as "Soccer Slaves" for a long period. Frank Brennan battled against Newcastle's hierarchy in 1955, taking his cause to the TUC. But football was changing as society moved with the times towards the end of the Fifties. The maximum wage rule was broken in 1961, then at £20 per week. At St James' Park Ivor Allchurch quickly became United's highest earner at £60 per week. United's George Eastham took on the antiquated authorities and won a landmark High Court judgement giving freedom at the end of a contract.

Thereafter footballers largely held the upper hand and wages escalated rapidly, especially so when television became such a big economic factor on the dawn of the Premier League during 1992 and the landmark 'Bosman' ruling in 1995 gave footballers much control over their own destiny.

In the player movement section of each biography, for later years where the term 'free' has been used, it does not necessarily indicate the club offloaded that player at the end of his contract. It could also mean that the player in question invoked his right to move to another club on what has been termed a 'Bosman free', the club losing the opportunity of gaining a transfer fee. While professionalism has been the norm, occasionally the club signed players who wished to retain an amateur status. But these were a rarity and in 1974 the FA dropped the term 'amateur'.

Wartime Football

Following the closure of Football League action at the end of the 1914-15 programme, Newcastle United took little part in the game during the First World War. They did not enter any first-eleven organised competition between 1915-16 and 1918, despite the existence of regionalised competitions in other parts of the country. The North East was left with only friendly games between a handful of clubs and local contests. In January 1919 the Northern Victory League was formed to celebrate the Armistice and end of the Great War. Players to appear in these senior friendlies and the Northern Victory League are included in this Who's Who.

Wartime match team-sheet for the Tyne Wear Tees Cup final against Darlington in 1943-44.

During World War One in Scotland, football continued in a similar peacetime manner when south of the border the game largely closed down. Many United players appeared in the Scottish game during this period when still formally registered with Newcastle, although their contracts had been suspended at the end of the 1914-15 season. As parent clubs still held their registration, these players are noted as a 'wartime guest/loan' for the particular club to retain consistency.

The Football League programme of 1939-40 was only three games old when war was declared and the competition terminated. Friendly matches were quickly organised until a regional league system was introduced around the country, initially into 13 localised areas. Newcastle took part in all competitions, including the Football League War Cup which was competed on a north and south basis, with a regional and combined final, the knock-out tournament including a qualification system linked to league results. A Football League North and Football League South soon developed, while there were also local cup tournaments such as the Tyne-Wear-Tees Cup.

Many young local footballers were used while the guest system also operated sanctioned by the game's authorities. If footballers were back in their native region of the North East, or for other factors, maybe stationed at military barracks, they often turned out in United's colours. There were many seasoned and noted professionals to guest for the Magpies during both World Wars; names such as Steve Bloomer and Stan Mortensen. In wartime Britain during both conflicts many footballers served in the country's armed forces (with several being killed) or were engaged in reserved occupations such as coal-mining or in armament factories.

Appearances & Goals

A summary for appearances (including substitute appearances) & goals for each player is shown split into the various competitions. Void appearances and goals, such as the annulled FA Cup contest with Nottingham Forest in 1974 and the abandoned 1939-40 season, are added in parenthesis. Abandoned fixtures are not included.

For those players not to have figured in a first-class match, but who have been selected in 'Other Fixtures', appearances & goals are grouped for such secondary games. Data from such miscellaneous fixtures is incomplete, notably for the pre-1892 era and certain Continental tours. Statistics published are for traced matches. Games played 'Behind Closed Doors' in modern years are not included, so players such as Pablo Paz (2000-01) and Chris Carr (2003-04) do not qualify for inclusion.

When player appearances and goals are noted within the text of each biography, they generally refer to league and cup matches combined, ie all senior appearances (including wartime and substitute appearances), and not just league fixtures unless specifically noted.

Although the occasional substitute was recorded in early or later friendly matches, senior league and cup action only permitted the use of substitutes from season 1965-66 and initially only when a player had been injured. The rules for the use of substitutes were soon eased and greatly expanded during the 1990s and after, to such an extent that now in the Premier League three players can be used from a bench from a selected seven. Totals for substitute appearances are shown in parenthesis in each summary record.

Player Debuts

The player's debut for Newcastle United is noted and is the first senior league or cup outing for the club, inclusive of any substitute appearance. Unless stated debuts are for league fixtures. Where a player has made an earlier debut than his senior bow, for instance in a subsidiary competition such as wartime or Texaco Cup game, this is additionally shown in parenthesis.

Honours

A comprehensive list of player, manager and backroom staff honours is included at the end of each biography, although in the abridged profiles of players with secondary appearances, these are within the narrative. All details are for the individual's full career and not just for his period with Newcastle United. Years noted represent the football season; ie 1952-53 is shown as *1953*. So even if a player won a single international cap in the early part of that season, say August 1952, this would be notated as *1 Eng cap 1953*, ie the 1952-53 season. There are certain inconsistencies such as European Super Cup finals, where on occasion the game was played in the following year than the actual labelled final, eg the 1982 Super Cup being played in January 1983. The protocol as listed by UEFA has been used, ie using the tournament year, of 1982, and not when the game was played.

Jack Fairbrother's FA Cup medal from United's victory in 1951.

Players who have taken part in various league competitions as title winners are noted in the honours section. Generally if a footballer made 10 or more appearances in the season they are recognised without any suffix, however if he only had a marginal part in the success, ie less than 10 appearances, the number of games he played is shown as, *FL champs 1956 (2 app)*. Usually players with 10 or more appearances received a medal, although in many instances other players were given such mementoes with specially struck medals by the club with permission of the league in question. The same criterion applies to promotion winning seasons.

Runner-up placings in the principal league competitions are not generally noted, except when as a Newcastle United player, ie for the Premier League seasons 1995-96 and 1996-97, the only two years the Magpies have concluded the campaign in second position.

In England the four-tier league structure is included throughout. It should be remembered that before the introduction of the Football League's lower division structure with the start of the Third Division North & South (later Divisions 3 & 4) in 1921, the principal league competition outside of the Football League umbrella was the Southern League. This can be classed as an equivalent competition and included for a period such teams as West Ham United, Tottenham and Southampton. Title wins are added for this competition up to 1921. Where traced senior league honours are also included for Scotland and both Northern Ireland and the Republic of Ireland, as well as for foreign leagues. Generally other lower league competitions are not included.

Readers should also note that in both England and Scotland the titles of divisions have changed over time, notably with the introduction of the Premier League both north and south of the border. The arrival of the Premier League in England for season 1992-93 resulted in the Football League renaming their three divisions; Division Two became Division One and so on. Then in 2004 Division One became The Championship which meant Division Two (the old third-tier) became Division One and Division Three (the old fourth-tier) was renamed Division Two. Scotland went through similar changes at different times. This confuses matters considerably. Honours noted are as the league tiers in place at the time.

Football in Ireland split into two associations as the Twenties began, the first championship of the Republic (The League of Ireland) being contested for 1921-22 while the FA Ireland Cup (later the Free State Cup) began also. The game in Northern Ireland continued with the Irish League Championship and Irish FA Cup. Honours won in the Republic are notated as 'Eire' to avoid confusion with Northern Ireland and the All-Ireland pre-1921 period.

In terms of cup final appearances, only those players to have appeared in a final (including as a substitute) are noted, however non-playing substitutes are shown where identified, noted with a suffix, *FAC final (sub no app)*. In certain circumstances players who did not take part in the final but played in the preceding ties may have received an actual cup medal. In 1924 United's official Minutes record that apart from medals being given to non-playing Sandy Mutch and Tom Curry, "all Directors, Secretaries, Trainers and the Lord Mayor were each to receive a medal". The FA agreed to this proposal on the proviso the medal "could not be an exact replica of the winners' medals". These medal holders are not included.

All senior honours achieved by a player are built into each biography, including where traced are also senior foreign honours. Secondary competitions such as the Texaco Cup are not included, nor are non-league achievements except prestige annual awards and trophies; FA Amateur Cup, FA Vase and international appearances. Also added is the principal youth competition, the FA Youth Cup, where winners are noted, as are the FA Trophy and FL Trophy.

Many United names have been honoured by prestigious awards such as the Footballer of the Year as well as non-football honours; knighthoods, OBE, CBE and the like. All are included.

International & Representative Honours

All major representative appearances by a player, manager and backroom staff are included in the honours section. Footballers who have participated in the World Cup finals or Olympic Games are also shown; each would have received a 'participation medal'. Other national competition participation such as the European Championships or African Cup of Nations is not indicated unless the player reached the final of the competition. It should be noted that while the term 'cap' is universally utilised to indicate an international appearance, not every game played by a player actually results in a cap being issued. Totals include substitute appearances and it should be recognised that anomalies do exist in several non-UK based statistics. Generally appearances include both FIFA internationals and non-FIFA matches, with the most accurate being used.

Featured are the now long gone international trial fixtures which took place into the Twenties. These comprised combinations such as The Probable's v The Possible's, The North v The South, Amateurs v Professionals, England v The Rest, and in Scotland, games like Home Scots v Anglo Scots, Scotland 'A' v Scotland 'B'. All of these representative matches were one-step away from a full cap.

International caps for Scotland (Andy Aitken 1910) and England (Rob Lee 1996).

Unofficial international games are added, noted separately and form a variety of different fixtures, but all grouped as non-first-class. Included also in the honours roll are representative games for the FA XI. For the period up to 1961 these were important games for professional footballers, in some quarters described as international "trial fixtures" bringing players to the attention of England selectors and management. On many occasions when on tours abroad, England teams were under the banner of an FA XI.

Under-23 and Under-21 appearances are shown, while so too are Young England appearances, when for a period in the 1950s and 1960s, an annual pre-FA Cup final fixture took place. These appearances are added to the Under-23 totals. Generally, appearances for Services combinations, eg Army XI, are not included.

Newcastle's high-profile press conference when they unveiled the world record signing of Alan Shearer in 1996.

Career & Transfers

Each player's career movement is noted in consecutive order after school. For easy reference, the dates at the beginning of each biography, eg *1946-1949*, refer to the years the player joined and left United.

Throughout the book player transfer fees are scheduled as either official club fees or those amounts generally reported in the media. Throughout the last century and more, and especially so in modern football where transfers have become more and more complicated, clubs, including Newcastle United, have at times been reluctant to divulge exact transfer figures. When United secured Hughie Gallacher in 1925 it was initially reported as being a new national record fee of £10,000, then reduced to quoted amounts of both £7,000 and £6,500. In recent years most fees in Newcastle's transfer dealings have been officially released noted as "undisclosed" and such fees included are those generally used by the media or other club involved.

Fees shown do not generally include add-on amounts such as the league levy or agent's fees. Due to these factors, discrepancies do occur in the transfer amounts. In 1969 the purchase of Jimmy Smith was generally reported as being £100,000, the club's first six-figure transfer. Yet it appears the fee was more like £80,000, topped up with add-ons to a figure approaching £100,000. Alan Shearer's world record transfer purchase is circulated as a £15m fee, however the amount the deal actually cost United is more, at around £15.75m. Michael Owen's overall fee is around £16.8m rather than the publicised £16m.

United's Secretary writing out a transfer cheque in 1948.

In years past many players arrived at St James' Park from local clubs without any official transfer fee; sometimes amateurs turning professional with the Magpies. It was though the custom for the local club to request 'compensation' or a 'donation' from Newcastle as a result. Fees were given by United as an ex-gratia payment and these have been recorded in the club's records. These are shown in the player movement section of each biography as a transfer fee, usually minimal amounts varying from £5 or £10 upwards to £500.

After World War Two the country adopted a compulsory National Service system to which all youngsters in the age group 17 to 21 spent 18 months in the armed forces. Newcastle United had to release their up and coming stars and the player's career development was often disrupted at a key age with several losing opportunities to claim a regular place in United's first-team as a result. Certain players were loaned to other clubs during a period at perhaps an army barracks. National Service was abolished in 1960.

Within the career path of each player, school teams are not included although clubs out with school are, eg youth clubs (Wallsend Boys Club). Generally if a player appeared at local city or county level as a schoolboy, eg Newcastle Boys or Northumberland Boys, this is not scheduled.

Dates of joining and leaving United, and other clubs, have been cross-checked from several sources; Newcastle United official ledgers, Football League and Football Association records as well as Scottish archives. Discrepancies do occur, especially with dates noted in the press.

Transfer movements in places will differ slightly to the previous publication, *The Black'n'White Alphabet*, this is due principally to the use now of official Football League data, ie the date each player was registered to play for United with the ruling body. Transfer dates may have moved from those as announced in newspapers due to the time lag in the Football League registering the player. For example Joe Harris was reported as joining the Tynesiders during late September 1925, written in the club's official Player Ledger as 29 September 1925. However the registration was not completed until the following week in October 1925. It should also be noted that in some cases the player's eligibility to appear may have been even later, but these eligible dates have been ignored. Much later, in the modern game, transfer agreements are often publicised sometime before the actual deal is finalised, especially during the summer months when a pre-agreement is reached, say in April, but the formal paperwork is not completed until the player's existing contract expires, say into July.

On retirement, many players often scouted for various clubs around the country. Generally these appointments are not fully included due to the sometimes brief or part-time nature of attachments to clubs, or links to multiple clubs. Where players had a sustained period with a single club this is included where traced.

For United players who have also appeared in first-class cricket, in the County Championship, their career span is shown after the football career section with international and honours included. Minor County affiliation (to the like of Northumberland and, in the past, Durham) as well as club cricket is only referred to in the narrative of each biography.

Newcastle forward and England Test cricketer Harry Hardinge.

Loan & Guest Players

Loan deals for players have existed since early years. Where players have been at Newcastle United or elsewhere, periods are noted in the career movement section as *loan*, with the months joining and leaving the Magpies, and at other clubs, the season of the loan transaction.

Occasionally United fielded 'guest' players for non-competitive matches, or during wartime football when the practice was allowed due to the fact that many footballers were dispersed around the country away from their parent club. Guest Players who appeared in first-team matches are included in the Who's Who. During wartime football when the system was widespread, such players with United (and elsewhere) are noted with the season they appeared as a guest notated as *war-guest*. At other times, where the club invited particular players to wear United's shirt for a one-off or short-term appearance, these are shown with the month they played.

Cross Reference

Within the Who's Who various entries include a cross-reference to other biographies for family associations, eg Peter Withe will have a note regarding his brother Chris Withe who also played for the club. In these instances the reference (qv) is included, indicating that individual also has a biography.

Certain United personalities have served the club in more than one role, be it as a player and coach, and even manager as well as director. Biographical entries are included once only with a cross reference noted in other sections, eg Stan Seymour will be included as a senior player but also with notation in both manager and director sections.

Brothers George and Ted Robledo at St James' Park

Club & Country titles

The titles for football clubs are those used at the point in time, eg Birmingham City will be noted as that title from 1945 to date, and as Small Heath from 1888, and Birmingham from 1905 to 1945. Manchester United are referred to as Newton Heath up to 1902. The former Football League club of Loughborough is also commonly referred to as *Loughborough Town*, but their official title was Loughborough Athletic & Football Club and is notated as Loughborough. The exception is Sheffield Wednesday. Their title for many years was *The Wednesday*, but common practice throughout football was to call them Sheffield Wednesday. Additionally, for simplicity, Arsenal, Bournemouth and Brighton have been used rather than their full titles at various times. In Scotland the giants of Rangers and Celtic are not given the prefix of 'Glasgow' as the city title does not form part of their official name.

The abbreviation in England and Scotland of 'FC' (Football Club) is not generally used in the club section of each biography. However, for overseas clubs, titles are used with the classification such as 'AC' (Athletic Club) or 'SC' (Sport Club), generally the title expressed as being used in that particular country, eg *FC Barcelona* or *SS Lazio*, as well as *Sporting Clube* and *Internazionale*, rather than the anglicised Sporting Lisbon and Inter Milan.

Foreign clubs also note the country of origin as do player birth-places. Usually the country noted is the title of the nation at the time the player was either born or played football, eg Temuri Ketsbaia was born in Georgia when it was part of the USSR and therefore it is noted he was born in the USSR, and later played for an independent Georgia at national level.

Ex-League clubs

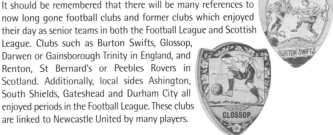

It should be remembered that there will be many references to now long gone football clubs and former clubs which enjoyed their day as senior teams in both the Football League and Scottish League. Clubs such as Burton Swifts, Glossop, Darwen or Gainsborough Trinity in England, and Renton, St Bernard's or Peebles Rovers in Scotland. Additionally, local sides Ashington, South Shields, Gateshead and Durham City all enjoyed periods in the Football League. These clubs are linked to Newcastle United by many players.

Non-League clubs

The non-league structure in England has historically been an important source of footballers and hundreds of Newcastle players derived from the various leagues around the country, locally strong competitions like the North Eastern League, Northern Alliance and Northern League. Teams such as North Shields Athletic, Blyth Spartans and Hebburn Argyle, as well as the many colliery welfare clubs of the past in the Northumberland and Durham coalfield. In modern football the non-league pyramid has now become an important port of call for many of those younger players to have failed to make the grade at St James' Park.

South Shields FC in 1922 featuring Alf Maitland and boss Jimmy Lawrence, two United stalwarts as well as 'keeper Ernie Hoffman. Links with local clubs have always been strong.

Scottish Junior football is not as the name suggests a grade of the sport for youngsters, the term 'Junior' generally being the equivalent of the English non-league scene. Newcastle have acquired many a player from such Junior and other semi-professional clubs, renowned combinations like Ashfield from Glasgow, Rutherglen Glencairn, Shotts Bon Accord and Clachnacuddin of Inverness.

During the years before 1950 top clubs had every so often formal but normally unofficial links with other clubs, notably non-league sides, and were known as 'nursery clubs'. Newcastle created arrangements with several neighbouring teams. In 1947 it was recorded in the club's Minutes that Throckley FC was a nursery. Tottenham Hotspur were associated with Northfleet and Ivor Broadis appeared for them, while Wolves had a bond with Bournemouth where Joe Harvey spent some time.

Reserve Football

While there is a long list of United players who only recorded a handful of games for the club in senior action, these footballers would have also played many fixtures for the Magpies at reserve level. Prior to 1970, and especially so before World War Two, the standard of reserve football was exceptional, maybe even equivalent to the present-day Football League third-tier or Conference game. Bob Dennison noted during the 1930s: "When we played Villa Reserves who included five internationals coming to the end of their career, there were 30,000 people in St. James' Park."

Schools, Youth & Junior classification

Over decades the rules and regulations of clubs signing youngsters has changed, at times substantially. In days before World War Two there were no Academies, Youth Training Schemes or Apprentice structure. If lads were under 17 years of age, they joined a club's 'Groundstaff' as an amateur player until they were old enough to sign a contract. These youngsters did a variety of jobs from cleaning toilets to painting railings….with the odd bit of football thrown in. Roy Bentley described his experience on the groundstaff of Bristol Rovers as "helping to maintain the pitch, to sweep the terraces clean, and be a general dog's body". He added that he "wouldn't see a football until Saturday" and when at Bristol City his main role as a young footballer "involved looking after the club's horse"! There was as a similar practice for young players who were employed by the club as 'Office Boys'. Arnold Grundy joined the Magpies as a clerk and made his debut in Division Two during 1937.

United's junior line-up in July 1976. *Back row, left to right: Richley (chief-scout), Herd (coach), Robinson, Manners, Howes, Liddane, Baldwin, Barton, Mullen, Patterson, Armstrong, McFaul (coach). Front row: Robson, Bailes, Cooper, Scott, Mulgrove, Guy (K), Burn.*

The introduction of the first apprentice scheme for boys between 16 and 17 years of age in 1960 changed the face of player development and reduced the reliance on the non-league breeding ground. Thereafter various structures and formats have been set up. In the Seventies the schoolboy apprentice scheme was established which allowed schoolboys between the ages of 13 and 15 to be attached to a club.

The 'Youth Training Scheme' or 'YTS' arrived in 1984 when clubs received funds from the government for engaging teenagers. It was then changed to 'Youth Training' in 1990 and termed in football as 'Trainees'. During 1998 the 'Football Scholarship' scheme was introduced, and the idiom 'Scholars' was used.

The advent of the Centre of Excellence (CoE) concept during the Eighties (at Newcastle in 1985) and then the Premier League Academies (Newcastle in 1999) saw juvenile footballers attached to major clubs including at Newcastle United. Senior clubs could not sign schoolboys until they were 14 years-old but through the CoE scheme they were allowed to coach boys from an earlier age without any commitment being given by either party. At the same time though, kids were still playing for local youth clubs, including some prominent and successful organisations around Tyneside; Wallsend Boys Club, Walker Central and Cramlington Juniors.

The FA Premier League started its own Academy League structure and then during the summer of 2012 reserve and junior football at the highest level was revamped with the introduction of a club Professional Development Squad and the creation of Under-21 competitions.

Over the border in Scotland, rules at school and youth level have been different again. Scotland adopted an 'S Form' or 'Provisional' classification for lads under the age of 16 years old.

It has been difficult at times to ascertain when players moved from one category to another, eg associated schoolboy to apprentice to full-time professional. On occasion players were also part-time and never went through a junior development programme. Throughout the Who's Who the following categorisation has been used;

- Amateur/groundstaff (noted as *amat*); youngsters prior to any professional contract or purely amateur status.
- School/CoE/Academy/Youth/YTS/Apprentice (noted as *jnr*); the player's first link with the club.
- Professional (noted as *prof*); the player's first professional contract with the club.

An example of how youngsters developed through the ranks at various stages is recorded in the Football League registration archive for Alan Duffy. He first joined United on schoolboy forms in December 1964, became an amateur with the Magpies during July 1965, then signed an apprentice deal over a year later during September 1966. Finally in March 1967 Alan became a fully fledged professional footballer.

In international football the various age levels for schools and youth internationals have also varied over time. The Who's Who honours schedule within each biography does not attempt to classify any caps into age-levels. If a player has appeared for his country at any school or youth level below Under-21 stage, it is noted as *Eng sch-youth app*.

Football Style

It should be remembered that over the years tactics and style of football have changed. A centre-half who played in the 1900s had a different role to that of a centre-half of the Premier League years, while inside-forwards of the past are now known as midfielders, or second strikers.

Football can be divided into largely three eras with evolved tactical formations. Prior to 1925 the field of play was split into a 2-3-5 formation; two full-backs acting solely as defenders and rarely crossing the half-way line; three half-backs working both as creators and spoilers; and five forwards consisting of two wingers who usually stuck hard to their touchline, one centre-forward with two inside men alongside.

An important change in the offside law in 1925 led to the role of the centre-half being altered and, to a lesser extent, that of the inside-forwards. The two full-backs were now supported by a centre-back, the previous midfield role of the centre-half becoming a defensive one. The inside-forwards now often dropped into midfield to assist the under strength wing-half backs and the line-up became now 3-2-5.

Continental football's growing impact and England's World Cup victory in 1966 saw changes made with wingers becoming midfielders and full-backs starting to overlap down the flank. Tactical systems of 4-4-2 and 4-3-3 were deployed which, as the decades evolved to the modern era, became at times more intricate with further variations such as 4-4-1-1 or 4-1-4-1 on the field of play.

Manager, Trainer, Coach & Support staff

For many decades Newcastle United had no manager as such, and even when the club first appointed Andy Cunningham in 1930, his power was much restricted. The Board oversaw team affairs with a Director Selection Committee while football captaincy up to World War One, was in many respects more like a cricket role. It was a responsible and involved appointment with few outright managers, teams being run by an administrative Secretary and Directors with a trainer (rather than a coach) being appointed to keep players fit. One description of the day described old-style trainers in the era without managers as "quasi-NCO figures and, in addition to maintaining the players fitness, their main function was to keep an eye on them and make sure they kept out of mischief".

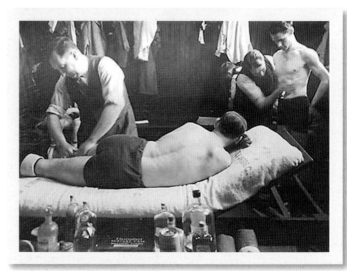

United's dressing-room before a game during 1939; trainer Norman Smith prepares the players with a rub-down.

Abbreviations

A full list of abbreviations can be found at the end of the book.

Players to have appeared in senior football (including as substitute) for Newcastle United and their pioneers, Stanley FC and Newcastle East End FC, since 1881 comprising league and cup matches, as well as wartime fixtures (see Introduction for further classification).

The Who's Who includes all individuals up to the end of the 2013-14 season, in addition at the end of Section 1, a 'New Arrivals' supplement is added profiling acquisitions at the start of the 2014-15 season to make their debut as the new programme unfolded.

The joy of professional football at the top level; Alan Shearer is mobbed at Old Trafford after netting the winner in United's FA Cup semi-final against Sheffield United during 1998.

A

ABEID-HAMDANI Mehdi 2011-date

Midfield
6'1"
b. Montreuil (Paris), France 6 August 1992

Career: Thiais (Fr) 1999/UJA Alfortville (Fr) 2002/
RC Lens (Fr) 2003/UNITED trial May 2011, pmt July
2011 (St Johnstone loan 2012-13)(Panathinaikos (Gr)
loan 2013-14).

*One of United's French contingent during the modern
era, Mehdi Abeid joined United as a teenage recruit in
the close-season of 2011 following an impressive trial
period at St James' Park. The young Frenchman first
stepped into United's Benton training complex some six weeks before as a rising and
talented midfielder, having represented his country at Under-16, Under-17 and Under-
18 level. With Lens since he was aged 11, Abeid was never given an opportunity in their
first eleven and looked for a new start at the end of season 2010-11. Favouring a central
midfield role, Newcastle's management made sure they signed the tall, athletic and
energetic player who was able to work from box-to-box in midfield. Mehdi was soon
courted by the country of his parents, Algeria, being called up to their Olympic
qualification squad at Under-23 level. He appeared for United's first eleven in the 2011-
12 pre-season fixtures and then deputized for Cabaye but then was sent out on loan to
Scotland and Greece when he wasn't able to claim a regular place in Newcastle's strong
first-team squad. With Panathinaikos he enjoyed a good 2013-14 campaign, winning
the Greek Cup and qualifying for the Champions League. His younger brother Walid
Abeid was on trial at Gallowgate during season 2012-13.*

Appearances & Goals:
Debut v Nottingham Forest (a) 20 September 2011 (FLC)
FAC: 2 app 0 gls
FLC: 1 app 0 gls
Euro: 1(1) app 0 gls
Total: 4(1) app 0 gls

Honours:
Fr sch-youth app/4 Alg u23 app 2011-date/Gr Cup winner 2014.

ACUNA Clarence William Donoso 2000-2003

Midfield
5'8"
b. Rancagua (Chile), 8 February 1975

Career: O'Higgins (Ch) jnr, prof July
1994/Universidad de Chile 1997/UNITED trial
Aug 2000, pmt Oct 2000 £954,000 to Sept
2003 free/FK Lyn (Nor) briefly/CA Rosario
Central (Arg) Jan 2004/CD Palestino (Ch)
Sept 2005/Union Espanola (Ch) 2006/
Deportes Concepcion (Ch) July 2007/Union
Espanola (Ch) July 2008/ Deportes La Serena
(Ch) Jan 2010/Retired Sept 2010/O'Higgins
(Ch) Technical Director to July 2014.

*Like Christian Bassedas who arrived in the
same close-season of 2000, Clarence Acuna
was a respected footballer in his own country,
winning titles with Universidad before
moving to the other side of the world for a
near £1m fee. Capped over 60 times for Chile,
Acuna impressed in the Copa America and
was destined for a move to Europe despite
being banned for testing positive for drugs (a medication for asthma) following an
international fixture with Peru in April 2000. The 25-year-old settled quickly on Tyneside
and found a place in season 2000-01 and in several of the following season's fixtures.
An honest professional with lots of endeavour, the short but stocky Chilean broke up
play in midfield, the spoiler in seasons 2000-01 and 2001-02 for a period alongside
playmakers such as Solano and Dyer. He had an accurate pass-count, characteristic of
international players and was much heralded as following in the footsteps of United's
Chilean FA Cup winning Robledo brothers. Out of action with injury during 2002-03,
Clarence though failed to win a regular slot in United's large and talented squad despite
his harrying play, and frustrated at the lack of opportunity headed back to South
America in 2004. He made his senior debut as a 15-year-old in Chile and captained his
country on occasion. On retirement he acted as an advisor for the O'Higgins club
in Chile.*

Appearances & Goals:
Debut v West Ham United (a) 28 October 2000
PL: 35(11) app 6 gls
FAC: 6(2) app 1 gl
FLC: 3(1) app 0 gls
Euro: 0(1) app 0 gls
Total: 44(15) app 7 gls

Honours:
61 Ch caps 1995-2004/WdC 1998/Ch Lg champs 1999, 2000/Ch Cup winner 1998, 2000.

ADAM George 1896-1897

Left-half
5'10"
b. Ayrshire

Career: Kilmarnock March 1889/Norton Park
1889/ Cowlairs cs 1892/Kilmarnock Oct 1894/
UNITED Feb 1896/Hebburn Argyle July 1897/
Southern League football 1899/ Darlington
St Augustine 1903.

*A good young prospect who arrived at St James'
Park after impressing United's officials with
some splendid displays north of the border in
Ayrshire as part of Kilmarnock's rise to become
a member of the Scottish League. George was
deputy to the powerful Jimmy Stott for most of his stay on Tyneside and had little
opportunity to claim a regular first-team place.*

*(Note: Certain contemporary press reports note his name both as Adam and Adams,
but official records confirm Adam.)*

Appearances & Goals:
Debut v Loughborough (a) 7 March 1896
FL: 13 app 1 gl
Total: 13 app 1 gl

AGNEW William Barbour 1902-1904

Left-back
5'8"
b. New Cumnock, near Kilmarnock, 30 December 1880
d. Moffat, 19 August 1936

Career: Afton Lads (New Cumnock)/Kilmarnock Nov
1900/UNITED May 1902 £200/Middlesbrough June
1904 £150/Kilmarnock Sept 1906 £150/Sunderland
May 1908/Falkirk Sept 1910 to 1912/Third Lanark
trainer Aug 1913/East Stirlingshire Sept 1913/
Falkirk April 1914.

*But for the eminent names of Carr, McCombie and
McCracken, William Agnew would have had a far more
fruitful stay at St James' Park. A defender of the finest
pedigree, he was well built and brave in combating attacks. Although described as a
touch slow, one comment in 1902 noted that "his tackling and clean kicking are of the
highest class". Bill operated in both full-back roles during his career and was the first of
only a handful of men to appear for all three of the North East's major clubs after the
pioneering era; Boro (73 app) and Sunderland (28 app). Blond-haired, Agnew made a
big name for himself during his second spell at Kilmarnock when he was capped by his
country. His parents gave him the Christian name of their earlier son who had died
tragically aged only six weeks old in 1879.*

Appearances & Goals:
Debut v Stoke (h) 6 September 1902
FL: 43 app 0 gls
FAC: 1 app 0 gls
Total: 44 app 0 gls

Honours:
3 Scot caps 1907-08/2 SL app 1907-08/Scot trial app 1908.

AIREY Philip John 2006-2012

Striker
5'11"
b. Newcastle upon Tyne, 14 November 1991

Career: UNITED jnr 2006, prof Jan 2011 (Hibernian loan 2011-12)(Gateshead loan 2011-12)/ Spennymoor Town trial Aug 2012/Blyth Spartans Aug 2012 (Whitley Bay loan 2013-14)/ Newcastle Benfield July 2014.

Phil Airey was part of the Newcastle United Academy set-up since an early age, starting as a full-back or in midfield but then mainly as a striker. Graduating to the reserve eleven in 2008-09 he soon impressed, especially during the following season but then was sidelined with knee ligament trouble. Raised in Acklington and schooled in Amble, Phil supported the club as a youngster and has a tattoo to prove the point. The Geordie made a recovery from injury and pushed his way into the first-team squad, promoted by new boss Alan Pardew for the FA Cup visit to Stevenage in January 2011. Strong and direct, Airey had spirit and got onto the pitch in place of Peter Lovenkrands to make his senior debut. A tall centre-forward with ability in the air and on the ground, he was able to make and take chances in United's reserve and junior teams but following that debut rarely was given the opportunity to claim a place in Newcastle's first eleven. Airey spent a short period at Easter Road with Hibernians on loan during 2011-12 playing a single Scottish Premier League fixture.

Appearances & Goals:
Debut v Stevenage (a) 8 January 2011 (FAC)
FAC: 0(1) app 0 gls
Total: 0(1) app 0 gls

AITKEN Andrew 1895-1906

Half-back
5'8"
b. Ayr, 27 April 1877
d. Ponteland, near Newcastle upon Tyne, 15 February 1955

Career: Elmbank/Ayr Thistle/Ayr Parkhouse 1894/ UNITED June 1895 (Kilmarnock loan 1898-99)/ Middlesbrough player-manager Oct 1906 £500/Leicester Fosse Feb 1909, becoming player-manager April 1909/ Dundee player May 1911/Kilmarnock June 1912/ Retired due to injury Jan 1913/Gateshead Town manager June 1913/Arsenal scout.

One of early football's most prominent players, Andy Aitken was known as 'Daddler'. He was well respected for his drive, stamina, attacking ability and head play; a central midfielder who always supported his forwards, Aitken took part in United's inaugural First Division game during 1898 and skippered the side on many occasions. He was only a youngster when he first appeared for the Magpies, but quickly made an impression scoring a hat-trick for the club when only a teenager against Notts County. Andy became a tremendous asset to the club during their rise to become Football League Champions. One biography of the day noted Aitken as being, "of the bustling type", while another recorded he was, "lean, lissom, artistic in method and touch". Colleague Alex Gardner once said: "He may lack physique, but for clever headwork and terrier-like persistency he would be hard to beat." Aitken was extremely adaptable too and is arguably the club's most versatile player of all time, operating in every position except goalkeeper for Newcastle. He was also often capped by Scotland, and led out his country too being skipper on the day of the fateful Ibrox disaster in 1902. When at both Boro and Leicester he operated in a secretary-manager role in addition to playing, being quite an undertaking in any era of the game. A former grocer's boy, Aitken was a player above the ordinary, one of the elite in football before World War One. He later became a publican for a time, residing on Tyneside to his death. Andy was related to Alex Gardner by marriage; the two United stars wed sisters who were Tiller-trained dancers, performing as The Lunelle Sisters.

Appearances & Goals:
Debut v Loughborough (h) 7 September 1895 (1 goal)
FL: 316 app 31 gls
FAC: 33 app 8 gls
Total: 349 app 39 gls

Honours:
14 Scot caps 1901-11/1 unoff Scot app 1902/Scot trial app 1901-12/FL champs 1905, 1907 (3 app)/FAC final 1905, 1906/FL div 2 prom 1898.

AITKEN Robert Sime 1990-1991

Midfield
6'0"
b. Irvine, 24 November 1958

Career: Ayr Utd BC/Celtic BC/Celtic jnr 1972, prof June 1975/UNITED Jan 1990 £500,000/St Mirren player-coach Aug 1991 £150,000 /Aberdeen asst-player-manager June 1992 £100,000, becoming manager Feb 1995 to Nov 1997/Maldives Islands coach to March 1998/ Al-Shabab (Kuwait) coach 1997-98/Leeds Utd asst-coach Sept 1999 to May 2003/Aston Villa asst-manager June 2003, becoming caretaker-manager July to Aug 2006/Scotland asst-manager Jan 2007/Birmingham City asst-manager Nov 2007/Al-Ahli (UAE) asst-manager July 2010, becoming Sporting Director April 2011.

After 667 senior games for Celtic, Scotland's captain Roy Aitken arrived on Tyneside as something of a veteran, but with inspirational qualities United's side needed at the time. Nicknamed 'Roy', the 31-year-old commanded respect and had a remarkable debut for the Magpies, leading the side to a terrific 5-4 victory over Leicester after being 4-2 behind. Big and tough, Roy never shirked from a challenge and was far more skilled on the ball than many critics gave him credit for. Aitken mainly operated in midfield for United, but also appeared in central defence, and his whole-hearted displays almost took the Black'n'Whites to promotion during 1989-90, United failing in the Play-Offs. A regular for Scotland, he led his country in the 1986 World Cup finals and was indispensable to Celtic, lifting trophy after trophy at Parkhead including a Scottish double in 1977 and 1988, Celtic's centenary year. He was though, a fiery player at times, once sent-off in a Scottish Cup final, and by the time he joined the Magpies had become something of a victimised player in his native country. With a change in manager Aitken was discarded by United's new boss, Ossie Ardiles, when perhaps his vast experience was exactly what Newcastle's young side needed. Also known as 'The Bear', Roy represented Great Britain schools at basketball before concentrating on a career in football. In between coaching appointments Aitken operated as a player agent.

Appearances & Goals:
Debut v Leicester City (h) 13 January 1990
FL: 56 app 1 gl
FAC: 6 app 0 gls
FLC: 2 app 0 gls
Others: 1 app 0 gls
Total: 65 app 1 gl

Honours:
57 Scot caps 1980-92/WdC 1986, 1990/1 unoff Scot app 1990/16 Scot u21 app 1977-85/Scot sch-youth app/SL champs 1977, 1979, 1981, 1982, 1986, 1988/SC winner 1977, 1980, 1985, 1988, 1989/SC final 1984/SLC winner 1983, 1996(m)/SLC final 1977, 1978, 1984, 1987, 1993.

AITKEN William John 1920-1924

Outside-right
5'9"
b. Peterhead, 2 February 1894
d. Dunston, Gateshead, 9 August 1973

Career: Kirkintilloch Harp 1914/Kirkintilloch Rob Roy 1915/Kilsyth Rovers/Queen's Park Sept 1916/Rangers Aug 1918/Port Vale loan cs 1919, pmt Oct 1919/ UNITED May 1920 £2,500/Preston North End June 1924 £1,000/ Chorley Sept 1926/Norwich City Dec 1926 £175/Bideford Town player-trainer Sept 1927/ Juventus (It) c1929/AS Cannes (Fr) player-manager Oct 1930/Stade Reims (Fr) manager 1934/FC Antibes (Fr) 1937/Retired and returned to Tyneside 1939/ Brussels (Belg) player-trainer c1946/SK Brann (Nor) player-trainer 1948/Retired c1950.

A

A typical winger of his day, clever and fast, good enough to appear in the Anglo-Scots versus Home Scots fixtures, Billy Aitken appeared in Glasgow for amateurs Queen's Park (63 app) then professionally with Rangers (21 app). Aitken scored plenty of goals over the border, but he struggled to find the net in England where he concentrated on being a provider. With the Magpies, Billy had his best season during 1920-21 when Newcastle ended in fifth position in the First Division table. Described at the time as a "masterly ball manipulator", Aitken was strongly framed and took the eye on the field. The Scot lost his place in United's side during the first half of the 1924 FA Cup winning season when he found both Jimmy Low and Willie Cowan ahead of him in team selection. Aitken left St James' Park for Deepdale soon after the trophy arrived on Tyneside. Eventually moving across the Channel, to France, Aitken took part in the very first all-France professional championship contest in season 1932-33, narrowly losing the national Play-Off to Lille, lifting also the Coupe de France in a productive stay on the Cote d'Azur. Something of a runner too, in 1929 he won the Morpeth sprint and also took part in the prestigious Powderhall Run, while during World War Two he was employed at the giant Vickers Armstrong factory alongside the Tyne. His many years on the Continent saw Billy fluent in French and Italian and, when he finally called a halt to his long career in the game, took up the role of representative at a North East based wine and spirit merchant. He travelled Europe and resided on Tyneside to his death. It is recorded that the Scot possessed a fiery temperament as a player; once, when starved of the ball during a game, when it finally came to him, he kicked it out of the Gallowgate stadium in disgust!

Appearances & Goals:
Debut v West Bromwich Albion (h) 28 August 1920
FL: 104 app 10 gls
FAC: 6 app 0 gls
Total: 110 app 10 gls

Honours:
Scot trial app 1920-21/Fr Lg champs (Gp B) 1933/Fr Lg champ Play-Off final 1933/Fr Cup winner 1932.

ALBERT Philippe Julien Marie Claude 1994-1999

Centre-half
6'3"
b. Bouillon (Belgium), 10 August 1967

Career: Dematter (Belg)/Standard Bouillon (Belg)/ RSC Charleroi (Belg) 1986 £12,000/KV Mechelen (Belg) cs 1989/RSC Anderlecht (Belg) cs 1992/UNITED Aug 1994 £2.65m (Fulham loan 1998-99)/RSC Charleroi (Belg) July 1999 £600,000, becoming asst-manager/Retired due to injury Oct 2000.

Established Belgian international Philippe Albert had been a long term target of Newcastle United and during the 1994 World Cup finals in the USA, Kevin Keegan saw Albert stand out as a special talent and a player who could take the ball from the back line and use it purposefully. Within weeks of the Magpies' boss returning from the States, Albert became a United player. Cool and confident on the ball, he was a defender who could attack with menace in the Continental fashion, striding forward from the middle of defence with style. A tough and no-nonsense defender too, Albert possessed an exquisite left-foot and much of Newcastle's passing game started from his vision at the back. A European thoroughbred, he appeared for his country in two World Cups, Albert immediately took to the Geordie way of life and became a crowd favourite at St James' Park in his No 27 shirt, indeed having his own terrace song to the tune of Rupert the Bear. The Belgian was just starting to take the Premiership by storm when an unfortunate training mishap forced him onto the sidelines for over six months with a cruciate ligament injury. Dangerous at free-kicks and corners, Albert could hit a venomous shot and returned to help Newcastle's assault of the Premier League crown, twice runner-up in a black-and-white shirt. Among the goals too, his inspired chip from outside the box to beat Manchester United's Peter Schmeichel in 1996 has now gone down in Geordie folklore. More injury caused the Belgian to be on the sidelines again, eventually being forced to quit playing after seven operations on his right knee. One of four footballing brothers in his home country, Philippe was still a teenager when he won his first cap for Belgium and was brought up in the Ardennes, being Flemish speaking with a good command of English. Philippe settled back in Belgium near Baulet where he became a television pundit as well as working in a fruit and vegetable supply business. Albert often returns to Tyneside where he is received with much warmth.

Appearances & Goals:
Debut v Leicester City (a) 21 August 1994
PL: 87(9) app 8 gls
FAC: 7(1) app 1 gl
FLC: 11(1) app 2 gls
Euro: 18(3) app 1 gl
Others: 1 app 0 gls
Total: 124(14) app 12 gls

Honours:
41 Belg caps 1987-97/WdC 1990, 1994/PL runner-up 1996, 1997/FL div 2 champs 1999/FAC final 1998 (sub no app)/Belg Lg champs 1993, 1994/Belg Cup winner 1994/Belg Cup final 1991, 1992/Belg PoY 1992.

ALDERSON John Thomas 1913-1919

Goalkeeper
6'0"
b. Crook, Co Durham, 28 November 1891
d. Sunderland, 17 February 1972

Career: Crook Town / Shildon Athletic/ Middlesbrough amat July 1912/Shildon Ath/ UNITED Feb 1913 £30/Crystal Palace May 1919 £50/ Pontypridd July 1924/Sheffield Utd May 1925/Exeter City May 1929/Torquay Utd player-trainer Nov 1930/ Crook Town March 1931/Worcester City Sept 1931 to April 32/Crook Town trainer 1932 to May 1934.

John Alderson became a noted, consistent goalkeeper who made his name away from Gallowgate. Known as Jack to football fans, a reserve to Jimmy Lawrence at St James' Park, he also had tough competition from two other professional 'keepers at Gallowgate in Syd Blake and William Mellor. As a consequence he moved on following World War One, being stationed in London when in the services, Alderson signed for Crystal Palace where he quickly became something of a legend appearing over 200 times for the Eagles, part of the side which entered Football League action then lift silverware in their first season of senior football. Alderson was noted for his ability to stop penalty-kicks; he once saved two spot-kicks in the same match and Jack was good enough to play for England, even though he was out of the top division. His talent was not un-noticed by bigger clubs, Alderson went onto have a fine period with Sheffield United in Division One, totalling 133 games for the Blades. Once retired from the game, Jack became a farmer residing in the North East.

Appearances & Goals:
Debut v Woolwich Arsenal (h) 25 January 1913
FL: 1 app 0 gls
Total: 1 app 0 gls

Honours:
1 Eng cap 1923/FL div 3 champs 1921/1 SnL app 1920/1 WsL app 1925.

ALDERSON Stuart 1965-1967

Outside-right
5'9"
b. Bishop Auckland, 15 August 1948

Career: Evenwood Jnrs/Evenwood Town 1963/ UNITED August 1965 £50/York City June 1967 free to cs 1968/Ashington 1969/Wear Valley FC/West Auckland Town Sept 1970 becoming asst-manager 1980 then General Manager to date.

Stuart Alderson was a teenage debutant for United, unexpectedly thrown into league action at a time of poor results when the Magpies were struggling to steer away of relegation from the First Division. A rival of Bryan Robson at St James' Park, Alderson found it difficult to cope with the rigours of a relegation dog-fight and he quickly returned to Central League soccer. It was 'Pop' Robson who soon flourished in the Magpie line-up, and Alderson drifted onto the non-league scene after a stint at York City where he claimed 20 appearances. Stuart then began a long association with West Auckland Town. For over 40 years he served the club in various capacities, Alderson receiving the Northern League's Arthur Clark Memorial Trophy in recognition of his "substantial unpaid efforts and dedication" to local football.

Appearances & Goals:
Debut v Burnley (h) 10 September 1966
FL: 3 app 0 gls
FLC: 1 app 0 gls
Total: 4 app 0 gls

ALLAN Edward M 1900-1901

Left-back
5'9"
b. Montrose, 31 August 1875

Career: Montrose/Dundee Wand Sept 1896/Millwall Ath Oct 1899/UNITED May 1900/Dundee May 1901/ Watford July 1902 (Edinburgh St Bernard's loan 1902-03)/Dundee cs 1903 to c1905.

Purchased from London club Millwall for the start of the 1900-01 season, Ned Allan was deputy to Dave Gardner and Charles Burgess and found it difficult to make a first-team place his own at Gallowgate. He did turn out in four games for the club, as well as in several friendlies, but was released during the summer of 1901. When in the capital, Allan took part in Southern League Millwall's giant-killing run to the FA Cup semi-final of 1900. Newcastle were suitably impressed with the Scot in this headlining performance and brought him north to Tyneside. For a period was skipper of Watford.

(Note: Although certain press reports spell his name Allen, records at the FA, FL and SFA confirm Allan.)

Appearances & Goals:
Debut v Stoke (h) 15 September 1900
FL: 4 app 0 gls
Total: 4 app 0 gls

ALLAN Richard 1897-1898

Outside-right
5'8"
b. Scotland

Career: Motherwell Sept 1893/Preston North End Feb 1894/Motherwell May 1895/Chorley Sept 1895/Dundee May 1896/UNITED May 1897/Bristol St George May 1898/Bristol Rovers March 1899/ Thames Ironworks Nov 1899 (Ayr loan 1902-03)/ Stockport Co Aug 1903 £15/Stalybridge Rovers July 1904.

A very businesslike forward who rarely wasted the ball, Dicky Allan was a regular in United's successful promotion side during 1898. Along with Willie Wardrope, he was one of the chief providers for centre-forward Jock Peddie that season, but was discarded for the Magpies debut in the First Division. At the start of his career, Allan scored on his debut for Preston but totalled just two games for the Lilywhites beginning a ground-hopping career which saw him settle at only West Ham United, taking part in their first season in Southern League football after reforming from the Thames club. At that time and when out of the Football League, he was still registered as a player with Newcastle United.

Appearances & Goals:
Debut v Walsall (a) 11 September 1897
FL: 24 app 4 gls
FAC: 5 app 0 gls
Total: 29 app 4 gls

Honours:
FL div 2 prom 1898/Scot trial app 1897.

ALLAN Stanley James E 1908-1911

Inside-forward
5'10"
b. Wallsend, 28 December 1886
d. Wallsend, 4 May 1919

Career: Wallsend/North Shields Ath/Sunderland amat/UNITED June 1908 £10/West Bromwich Albion May 1911 £150/Nottingham Forest June 1912 to May 1913/Worcester City Oct 1914.

A fringe player at St James' Park, James Allan began his career as a half-back, but ended playing at either inside or centre-forward. Commonly known as Jack, he joined United after a short period on Wearside without getting into first-team action. Allan was fast, strong and of the old fashioned bustling breed. He had a

good scoring run during season 1908-09 as a stand-in for Albert Shepherd, when he scored six goals in ten games following his debut, playing a small part in the Magpies' title winning season. Moving to the Hawthorns, Allan was again unable to command a regular place although he helped Albion to the 1912 FA Cup final, appearing in the semi-final replay. Allan retired from top-level football due to ill-health when at Forest and became a school-teacher. He only totalled a handful of games at all his senior clubs; 16 with United, 20 at Albion and 22 at Forest. Jack joined the Royal Army Medical Corps on the outbreak of war in 1914 and served throughout the hostilities, only to tragically die aged 32 of pneumonia, within two weeks of his safe return to Tyneside.

Appearances & Goals:
Debut v Leicester Fosse (h) 5 September 1908
FL: 15 app 5 gls
Others: 1 app 1 gl
Total: 16 app 6 gls

Honours: FL champs 1909 (9 app).

ALLCHURCH Ivor John MBE 1958-1962

Inside-forward
5'10"
b. Plasmarl, Swansea, 16 December 1929
d. Swansea, 9 July 1997

Career: Plasmarl Jnrs/Swansea Town amat May 1947, prof 1948 (Shrewsbury Town loan 1948-49) (Wellington loan 1949-50)/ UNITED Oct 1958 £28,000/Cardiff City Aug 1962 £15,000/ Swansea Town July 1965 £6,500/Worcester City July 1968 /Bishoptown/Haverford West player-manager May 1969/ Pontardawe Ath/Retired April 1980.

One of the finest inside-forwards to appear in post-war football, Ivor Allchurch was a distinguished schemer who played either on the right or left, and who turned out in over 700 first-class games. A goalscorer too, Allchurch was deadly within shooting range and he scored over 250 goals. Establishing himself as a player of special ability with Swansea and Wales, Ivor moved into the big-time at a late age, when 28 years old, and to the First Division when he joined Newcastle for a new club record fee. A gentleman on the field with a complete repertoire of skills, he played with panache and possessed a hypnotic body swerve, as well as a deceiving turn of speed. Matt Busby once remarked: "He vies with the greatest of all time, yet he has the modesty that becomes him." Ivor stroked the ball around with precision and grace, and was the king of the long pass as well as having the gift of threading a telling ball into his attackers, linking with Len White with menace for United over three seasons. Well balanced, he had the touch of a master both in skill and that special aptitude to make time for himself on the field. Netting twice on his debut for the Black'n'Whites, immediately Ivor charmed the St James' Park crowd and became a favourite on Tyneside, yet his time at Gallowgate was destined to be during a period of decline for United, and Allchurch couldn't stop the club slipping into the Second Division in 1961. He also ran into trouble with the club's infamous hierarchy at the time being refused permission to turn out for Wales and over an unfavoured selection tactic of playing in the centre-forward role. Ivor held the record for international appearances for his country for many years, his younger brother Len, was also a Welsh international, while another brother, Sid, appeared for the Welsh at amateur level. Allchurch was awarded the MBE for his services to the game in 1966 while he was United's top paid star at £60 per week after the abolition of the maximum wage. Moving back to Wales, Allchurch eventually returned to the Swans where he clocked up a total of 503 senior games (192 goals) over 13 seasons, a grand servant to that club. He later resided in Bishopton on the Gower Peninsula playing and coaching local football into his 50th year when employed as a storeman in a stationary warehouse. As a teenager and before he became a noted footballer, Ivor worked for a period as a fish porter and at a local steel works. A residential street is named after Allchurch in Newcastle's West End and a statue of the celebrated Welshman is located outside Swansea's Liberty Stadium.

Appearances & Goals:
Debut v Leicester City (h) 11 October 1958 (2 goals)
FL: 143 app 46 gls
FAC: 8 app 4 gls
FLC: 3 app 1 gl
Total: 154 app 51 gls

Honours:
68 Wales caps 1951-66/WdC 1958/4 WsL app 1951-54/1 Wales & Ireland comb app 1956/Wales sch-youth app/WsC winner 1950, 1964, 1965, 1966/WsC final 1956, 1957/ FL Legend/MBE 1966.

ALLEN Geoffrey Barry 1962-1974, 1979-1981

Outside-left & Coach
5'7"
b. Walker, Newcastle upon Tyne, 10 November 1946

Career: UNITED jnr May 1962, prof April 1964/ Retired March 1970 due to injury, becoming asst-coach to June 1974/Gateshead coach 1974/North Shields manager Nov 1977/UNITED asst-coach July 1979/ Mansfield Town coach July 1981 to Jan 1983.

A down to earth Geordie from the Scrogg Road area of Walker, Geoff Allan was a most unlucky player with injuries. But for a persistent cruciate ligament problem he would have no doubt made a big name for himself in United's First Division and Fairs Cup side. It was in the club's very first European fixture against Feyenoord during September 1968 that Allan made headlines. He very much destroyed the Dutch giants with a brilliant display of wing play, but a few weeks later was on the treatment table with a bad leg injury following a rash tackle from behind in a league match against Nottingham Forest. Geoff was sidelined for a long period eventually making a comeback during April 1969 against Sheffield Wednesday at St James' Park, but his return lasted a matter of minutes. After 17 months on the sidelines the injury wrecked his career when still only 23 years old and he was given a testimonial during 1971 (10,000). Allen was one of the youngest ever players to appear for the club when he made his debut during the club's Second Division season of 1963-64. Rosy-cheeked, following a period in non-league he later returned to Gallowgate as coach. Geoff afterwards settled in the Mansfield area, employed for motorised crane manufacturer Fassi UK.

Appearances & Goals:
Debut v Norwich City (h) 25 April 1964
FL: 22 app 1 gl
FAC: 1 app 0 gls
FLC: 1 app 0 gls
Euro: 2 app 0 gls
Total: 26 app 1 gl

Honours:
FL div 2 champs 1965 (1 app)/Eng sch-youth app.

ALLEN John 1898-1901

Centre-forward
5'10"
b. Bishop Auckland

Career: Bishop Auckland/UNITED amat Jan 1898/ Bishop Auckland 1898/ Manchester Utd May 1904/ Bishop Auckland Aug 1907/West Auckland Aug 1909.

A well-built youngster, John Allen was an eager teenager when he arrived at St James' Park offered a chance to impress by club directors who had been taken by his form for noted amateurs Bishop Auckland. He deputised at centre-forward for the established Jock Peddie during the club's first promotion campaign in 1897-98, but apart from that single appearance for the black-and-whites, he was always considered a reserve and played out his Magpie career in United's Northern Alliance side. Allen was signed as an amateur from the Bishops illegally, without their permission, and United were censored and fined, with secretary Frank Watt suspended for a period. Allen meanwhile had his Football League registration documents with the Magpies cancelled in March 1898, although it appears he remained with the club for a period as an amateur. Returning to

Bishop Auckland, he was a regular scorer and a key figure as they lifted the Northern League title in 1899, 1901 and 1902. He also took part in their FA Amateur Cup victory over Lowestoft Town at Filbert Street during 1900, reaching another final two years later. Allen made another big-time move when he joined Manchester United at the end of season 1903-04, totalling 35 games at Old Trafford.

(Note: Various newspaper and official records note his surname as both Allan and Allen, and also John and Jack.)

Appearances & Goals:
Debut v Darwen (h) 15 January 1898
FL: 1 app 0 gls
Total: 1 app 0 gls

Honours:
FL div 2 prom 1898 (1 app)/FAAC winner 1900/FAAC final 1902.

ALLEN John William Alcroft 1931-1934

Centre-forward
5'10"
b. Newburn, Newcastle upon Tyne,
31 January 1903
d. Burnopfield, Co Durham,
19 November 1957

Career: Prudhoe Castle May 1920/ Leeds Utd Feb 1922/Brentford Aug 1924/Sheffield Wed March 1927 £750/UNITED June 1931 £3,500/ Bristol Rovers Nov 1934 £200/ Gateshead Aug 1935 £100/ Ashington cs 1936/Retired Feb 1936.

An aggressive, bustling leader with a deadly left-foot shot Jack Allen had made his name with Brentford in the lower divisions. Although during the early years of his career Allen was described as "clumsy" and "awkward", he had an eye for goal and soon flourished. Jack arrived back on his native Tyneside after plundering 85 senior goals in only 114 league and cup games for Sheffield Wednesday. He was the Owls' leading goalscorer for two years in succession as the Tykes twice lifted the Championship trophy, netting over 30 goals in each campaign. Despite his outstanding strike-rate Jack was replaced at Hillsborough and jumped at the chance of moving to his home-town club. Yet during his early months at St James' Park, Jack struggled and failed to live up to his big billing, but slowly the Tynesider found his form and by the time United set on a Wembley FA Cup run during 1932, Allen was the Magpies' danger man. He netted seven crucial goals, including two in the famous 'Over the Line' final with Arsenal, the first being the highly controversial equaliser which earned him immortality in football history. Jack had also been involved in another contentious cup goal in the 1930 semi-final for Sheffield Wednesday against Huddersfield. His brother Ralph, turned out for Brentford and Charlton Athletic, and Jack remained in the North East after retirement becoming a noted publican at The Travellers Rest in Burnopfield to his death. His daughter, Anne Darling OBE, became High Sheriff of Tyne & Wear while Jack's grandsons both became noted barristers, Paul Darling QC a co-owner of Derby winner Motivator in 2005.

Appearances & Goals:
Debut v Liverpool (h) 29 August 1931
FL: 81 app 34 gls
FAC: 9 app 7 gls
Others: 1 app 0 gls
Total: 91 app 41 gls

Honours:
FL champs 1929, 1930/FL div 2 champs 1924 (2 app)/FAC winner 1932.

ALLEN Malcolm 1993-1995

Striker or Midfield
5'8"
b. Deiniolen, near Caernarfon, 21 March 1967

Career: Deiniolen/Llanberis 1982/Watford jnr July 1983, prof March 1985 (Aston Villa loan 1987-88)/ Norwich City Aug 1988 £175,000/Millwall March 1990 £400,000/ UNITED Aug 1993 £300,000/Retired due to injury Dec 1995/Gwynedd Council coach and development officer July 1996/Aberystwyth Town Jan 1997/Stevenage Borough coach Feb 1997 & player for Colney Heath 1997-98/Molesey asst-manager Dec 1999 to cs 2000, resigning as a player Nov 2000 to Jan 2001/ Edgeware Town player-asst-manager March 2001/ Letchworth Town coach/ Tottenham Hotspur asst-coach c2005.

Rejected by Watford and then Manchester United as a trialist, Malcolm Allen received another chance at Vicarage Road and carved out a decent career in the game. Making his Football League debut in November 1985, he made only four senior appearances under Graham Taylor's guidance before being called up by Wales as a teenager for his international debut. Skilful on the ball with a sure pass and shot, Allen arrived at Gallowgate as cover for the injured Peter Beardsley as United embarked on their inaugural season in the Premier League. He made a good start in a black-and-white shirt looking a prized buy. The Welshman found the net with confidence, able to shield the ball well and link with colleagues. But Malcolm was then badly injured and found himself on the sidelines for almost a year with a knee ligament problem, this after a lengthy spell out of action when at Carrow Road. By the time he returned to fitness, Allen found several multi-million pound stars at St James' Park ahead of him for a first-team place. Malcolm unluckily then had an injury relapse, which forced him to leave the game, aged only 28 after seven operations on his knee. Raised speaking the Welsh language, Malcolm worked in PR and took a post as a Wales FA coach and later with several non-league clubs. Allen developed a career as a television presenter for the Welsh speaking Sgorio channel and newspaper columnist. He produced his autobiography in his native tongue and confirmed that for a period a drink problem almost ruined his life. Malcolm's younger brother Gavin appeared for the Welsh Under-21 side and for Stockport County.

Appearances & Goals:
Debut v Tottenham Hotspur (h) 14 August 1993
PL: 9(1) app 5 gls
FLC: 3 app 2 gls
Total: 12(1) app 7 gls

Honours:
14 Wales caps 1986-94/1 Wales B app 1991/Wales sch-youth app/1 FL app 1993

ALLON Joseph Ball 1981-1987

Centre-forward
5'11"
b. Gateshead, 12 November 1966

Career: UNITED jnr July 1981, prof Nov 1984/ Swansea City Aug 1987 free/Hartlepool Utd loan Oct 1988, pmt Nov 1988 £12,500/Chelsea Aug 1991 £300,000 (Port Vale loan 1991-92)/Brentford Nov 1992 £275,000 (Southend Utd loan 1993-94)/ Port Vale March 1994/Lincoln City July 1995 £42,500/ Hartlepool Utd Oct 1995 £50,000/Retired due to injury Jan 1998/Leeds Utd asst-coach March 2007 to Feb 2008.

As a youngster, blond-haired Joe Allon scored almost 120 goals for United's reserve and junior sides in less than 150 games, and even overshadowed Paul Gascoigne in the same Magpie line-up as Newcastle's kids won the FA Youth Cup. An 18-year-old debutant who should really have been given a better chance in the club's senior line-up, he rivalled two other centre-forwards, Cunningham and Whitehurst, both of whom registered mediocre records in a Magpie shirt. Dogged by a knee injury at a crucial time in his United career, Allon was released by manager Willie McFaul as a 20-year-old, even though he was the club's overall top scorer in each of the previous three seasons. Joe earned a second opportunity in the big-time, this time with Chelsea after becoming the most potent striker in the Fourth Division during 1990-91 with 28 goals. Again though his chances were limited and he drifted around the lower divisions for the remainder of his career, but always grabbing goals. Allon ended his career after recurring knee problems with a more than respectable total of 135 goals in 361 senior outings, notably at Swansea and Hartlepool where he grabbed 79 goals in 194 games. Despite his travels, Joe was a United man through and through and once remarked: "When I bleed, I bleed black and white." Residing in the North East, Allon worked in the media and in 2004 set up Player Inc, a company organising talk-ins and celebrity appearances. His brother Paul appeared for non-league Whickham in the 1981 FA Vase final.

Appearances & Goals:
Debut v Stoke City (h) 1 December 1984
FL: 9 app 2 gls
FLC: 1 app 0 gls
Total: 10 app 2 gls

Honours:
Eng sch-youth app/FAYC winner 1985/FL div 4 prom 1988, 1991/PFA ToS (d4) 1991.

AMALFITANO Romain 2012-2014

Midfield
5'9"
b. Nice (France), 27 August 1989

Career: AS Cannes (Fr) 1998/LB Chateauroux (Fr) 2005/Evian TG (Fr) July 2009 free/Stade Reims (Fr) July 2010/UNITED July 2012 (Dijon FC (Fr) loan 2013-14)/Dijon FC (Fr) July 2014.

The success of Newcastle's raid on French football during the modern era, bringing to Tyneside the likes of Cabaye and Ben Arfa, saw United attract another talented Gallic footballer to the North East in the close-season of 2012, Roman Amalfitano. Although not as established as previous buys, 22-year-old Amalfitano was rated highly as an attacking midfielder with much promise. With Reims, he showed ability on the ball and helped the red-and-whites secure promotion to Liga 1 in 2011-12. The Frenchman was never immediately going to gain an automatic slot in the Magpies' engine-room, and he spent most of his first season in England on the fringe, gaining occasional run-outs in Europa League fare. Without making any impact Amalfitano returned to France in the summer of 2014. Romain has Italian parentage and can also play as a striker. His elder brother French international Morgan Amalfitano appeared as a regular for Marseille and joined West Bromwich Albion in 2013. His father was also a professional player in France.

Appearances & Goals:
Debut v Atromitos (a) 23 August 2012 (sub) (EL)
Euro: 1(4) app 0 gls
Total: 1(4) app 0 gls

Honours:
Fr div 2 prom 2012/Fr div 3 champs 2010.

AMBROSE Darren Paul Francis 2003-2005

Midfield
6'0"
b. Harlow, Essex, 29 February 1984

Career: West Ham United jnr 1995/Ipswich Town jnr July 2000, prof July 2001/UNITED March 2003 £2m/ Charlton Ath July 2005 £700,000 (Ipswich Town loan 2008-09)/Crystal Palace July 2009 free/Birmingham City July 2012 £250,000/Apollon Smyrnis (Gr) Jan 2014/Colchester Utd trial July 2014/Ipswich Town Sept 2014.

Hailed by Bobby Robson as an emerging 19-year-old and future England player who could take over from the highly popular Nobby Solano on the right of midfield, Darren Ambrose was perhaps plunged into United's battleground too quickly following his £2m move from Portman Road. Possessing a forceful shot and strong running, he followed the path of previous Ipswich finds to St James' Park, Kieron Dyer and Titus Bramble, the Essex-born midfielder was another bright prospect. Coached as a kid by ex-United player Colin Suggett, having gained a regular place in the Tractor Boys line-up for season 2002-03 Ambrose was watched by several top clubs before United made their move. He filled in across midfield in 2003-04 as cover to senior players during a busy campaign of domestic and UEFA Cup football and showed that he did have raw talent to reach the very top with the ability to hit a stinging shot at goal. Injury halted his progress though, out of action with ankle, knee and shin knocks. Selected ahead of Solano as the 2003-04 season developed, to many in and outside the inner sanctum of St James' Park he was never ready to replace the talented Peruvian, who hardly deserved demotion, and who was eventually shown the door. As a result a big void existed in United's play. Darren though had a chance to claim a place but was unluckily injured and too often in the treatment-room. As season 2004-05 got under way, Robson's departure signalled Darren's exit too, and as it happens Solano's return. Ambrose headed back to his homeland in South London, to Charlton Athletic and went onto have a solid career, largely in the second-tier, where he became a pivotal player for the Addicks and later Crystal Palace, totalling over 100 games for each club. Ambrose scored on his home debut for the Magpies, arriving

A

from the bench in the 88th minute of European action against Breda and promptly heading in a Robert cross. He is one of only two United players to have been born on a leap year date, February 29th (with W Stewart).

Appearances & Goals:

Debut v West Bromwich Albion (a) 11 May 2003 (sub)
PL: 18(19) app 5 gls
FAC: 0(2) app 0 gls
FLC: 1(1) app 0 gls
Euro: 8(7) app 1 gl
Total: 27(29) app 6 gls

Honours:

10 Eng u21 app 2003-07/Eng sch-youth app/FAYC winner 2001.

AMEOBI Foluwashola 1992-2014

Striker
6'2"
b. Zaria (Nigeria), 12 October 1981

Career: Walker Central BC/UNITED jnr 1992, prof Oct 1998 (Stoke City loan 2007-08)/Gaziantep BBK (Trk) Aug 2014.

Although born in Nigeria, Foluwashola Ameobi – Shola to all – was raised in Newcastle from the age of five and was soon in United's sights as a footballer, part of the School of Excellence set-up when 11 years old, then with the new Academy when still with Walker Boy's Club. Ameobi had ability and was quickly handed a YTS contract in July 1995 developing rapidly thereafter. Tall, leggy and with skill on the ball, he made his senior debut in season 2000-01 when injury forced Carl Cort on to the sidelines, famously squaring up to Denis Wise against Chelsea at Gallowgate. He became an England Under-21 regular and had a bright future, tipped to go to the very top, although his laid back style and inconsistency frustrated many, as Shola once admitted, fans have "sung my name, booed me, cheered me, jeered me". Despite all, Ameobi served the Black'n'Whites for the majority of his career and on occasion displayed the special qualities which some thought would bring him full international recognition for England. Under Sir Bobby Robson's guidance, his ability to cause problems in the box was evident in not only domestic football, but also in the Champions League and UEFA Cup. He netted 34 goals over a four season period between 2002 and 2006 and was destined to become, if not Alan Shearer's replacement, a first-rate support striker for the Magpies. He survived several managerial changes at Gallowgate and was constantly in and out of the first choice line-up due to injury and that inconsistency with some noting a lack of a ruthless streak on the field. Shola remained a popular character on Tyneside and despite a persistent and long term hip joint injury claimed almost 400 appearances for the club. With a nice touch of the ball and some audacious trickery at times, he could hit the ball with precision and power. Ameobi did exceptionally well in white-hot derby fixtures with Sunderland. Only Jack Milburn has scored more than Shola's eight goals. He was in line for that England call up during August 2004 but a back injury forced him out of contention for a squad place, however he reached full international level for Nigeria in 2012 and experienced the World Cup of 2014 in Brazil while Ameobi can boast that he scored a Champions League goal in the Camp Nou against Barcelona during December 2002. Two younger brothers have been in the ranks at St James' Park as well; Sammy (qv) and Tomi Ameobi, Sammy appearing in the same Premier League line-up as Shola in 2010-11. Against Morecambe during 2013, both brothers were on the United score-sheet. His sister was also an athlete of note on Tyneside. Shola marked his departure with a harsh sending off against Liverpool then appeared in the World Cup in Brazil.

Appearances & Goals:

Debut v Chelsea (h) 9 September 2000 (sub)
FL/PL: 167(145) app 53 gls
FAC: 11(8) app 3 gls
FLC: 10(5) app 8 gls
Euro: 31(20) app 15 gls
Total: 219(178) app 79 gls

Honours:

9 Ng caps 2013-date/WdC 2014/19 Eng u21 app 2001-04/FL ch winner 2010/FL prom 2008 (6 app).

AMEOBI Samuel Oluwaseyi Jesutoromo 2006-date

Midfield
6'3"
b. Newcastle upon Tyne, 1 May 1992

Career: Walker Central BC 2002/UNITED jnr 2006, prof July 2010 (Middlesbrough loan 2012-13).

The younger brother of Shola Ameobi (qv) and with United since a kid with the club's Academy, Sammy Ameobi rapidly became something of a crowd favourite before he had even made an impact in the game. Indeed, when the younger Ameobi appeared in a pre-season friendly at Darlington, such were the joyous scenes that the game had to be stopped for a period due to the crowd getting out of control. Tall and leggy like his older brother, Sammy was soon to follow Shola into United's senior eleven, making his debut also against Chelsea almost 11 years later. He forced his way with an unorthodox style into Alan Pardew's first-team squad for the 2011-12 season, the campaign he also reached the England Under-21 set-up. Operating on the left flank as a midfielder-cum-striker of the new breed, the Tynesider looked awkward and gangly, but was out of the ordinary with vision and trickery, gifts which could see him make the top level if he could master his erratic form. Sammy first played alongside his brother in United's first eleven against Chelsea, one of only a handful of pairs of siblings to have done so in senior action for the club. The following season of 2012-13 saw the young Ameobi break into United's squad but just as he was making an impression with cameo appearances from the bench, injury put him out of action for the last months of the season. Sammy returned strongly for 2013-14 when his quick-feet on the ball impressed many. He also has appeared for the Nigerian Under-20 side, the country of his parents, before he had graduated to United's senior team. A third brother, Tomi, also was on Newcastle's books but failed to appear in the first-eleven.

Appearances & Goals:

Debut v Chelsea (a) 15 May 2011 (sub)
FL/PL: 6(23) app 0 gls
FAC: 1 app 0 gls
FLC: 2(3) app 2 gls
Euro: 4(1) app 0 gls
Total: 13(27) app 2 gls

Honours:

5 Eng u21 app 2012-date/2 Ng u20 app 2011.

ANCELL Robert Francis Dudgeon 1936-1944

Left-back
5'10"
b. Dumfries, 16 June 1911
d. Monifieth, near Dundee, 5 July 1987

Career: Mid-Annandale Jnrs/St Mirren Feb 1930 (Queen of the South loan 1931-32)/UNITED Aug 1936 £2,750 (Carlisle Utd war-guest 1939-40) (Blackpool war-guest 1941-42)(Rochdale war-guest 1941-42)(Blackburn Rovers war-guest 1941-43)(Aberdeen war-guest 1941-44)(Derby Co war-guest 1943-44)(Burnley war-guest 1945-46)/ Dundee player-trainer Aug 1944 £150/Aberdeen player-trainer Jan 1949/Berwick Rangers player-manager Dec 1950 to April 1952/Dunfermline Ath manager May 1952/ Motherwell manager Aug 1955/Dundee manager March 1965/ Dundee asst-coach Sept 1968/Nottingham Forest scout Oct 1969.

Bobby Ancell was a great favourite with the St James' Park crowd in the years leading up to World War Two, this after breaking his leg when playing for Scotland against Wales only four months into his United career. Slightly-built, he was a sound and capable defender who contested for the ball with footballing skills and anticipation rather than brawn. Cool headed, he was likened to the famous inter-war full-back, Warney Cresswell in style, one of the elite of his day. Highly rated by many when skipper of St Mirren (210 app), Ancell was persuaded to join the Magpies by manager Tom Mather at Dumfries railway station when the pair underwent negotiations as the trains went by – and thwarting Sunderland's attempts to also secure his services. A quietly spoken Scot and described as a "gentleman", Bobby later became a noted manager north of the border, especially when in charge of Motherwell for a decade, where he created the 'Ancell Babes', a side which included Ian St John, much fancied by the Magpies. During

the war Bobby served in the RAF as a training instructor and guested for a number of clubs as he travelled around the country. Ancell resided alongside the River Tay, in Monifieth following retirement. He was originally a time-served compositor in the printing trade, his brother Charlie Ancell played with Queen of the South.

Appearances & Goals:
Debut v Barnsley (h) 29 August 1936
FL: 97 app 1 gl
FAC: 5 app 0 gls
War: 50 app 0 gls
Total: 152 app 1 gl
(Void FL: 3 app 0 gls)

Honours:
2 Scot caps 1937/1 Scot war app. 1940/1 unoff Scot app 1943/SC final 1934/ SL div 2 champs 1947/SL div 2 prom 1936. 1955(m)SLC final 1968(m)/FLN(WLg) champs 1942 (1 app).

ANDERSON Andrew Lyle 1908-1912

Outside-left
5'8"
b. Milton, Glasgow, 26 February 1885
d. Glasgow, 22 January 1969

Career: Ashfield/St Mirren Oct 1904/ UNITED May 1908 £350/Third Lanark May 1912 £100/Leicester Fosse July 1914/Abercorn Jan 1920.

Andy Anderson came to Tyneside with good reviews from his days in Paisley with St Mirren where he appeared on 129 occasions (38 goals). An unselfish winger who always played for the team, he performed well for United over three seasons. Anderson shared the wing berth with another noted Scot of the time, George Wilson, the pair often playing together at inside and outside-left as Newcastle lifted the title in season 1908-09. In days before substitutes, Andy was a travelling reserve for United's 1911 FA Cup final. On the fringe of a Scotland cap, Andrew was fast and direct rather than tricky. He had a decent spell with Leicester before returning north of the border.

Appearances & Goals:
Debut v Woolwich Arsenal (a) 12 September 1908
FL: 61 app 5 gls
FAC: 6 app 2 gls
Others: 1 app 0 gls
Total: 68 app 7 gls

Honours:
FL champs 1909/SC final 1908.

ANDERSON John Christopher Patrick 1982-1993

Right-back or Centre-half & Coach
5'11"
b. Dublin, 7 November 1959

Career: Stella Maris (Dublin)/West Bromwich Albion Nov 1977/Preston North End Aug 1979 £40,000/ UNITED trial Aug 1982, pmt Sept 1982 free/Retired due to injury Jan 1992/Berwick Rangers manager June 1992/UNITED asst-coach Sept 1992/Dunston Federation March 1993/Whitley Bay Dec 1993/ Dunston Federation 1994 to cs 1994/Later appearing in local Sunday football notably for Blakelaw SC and Walbottle Masons.

United received grand service from John Anderson following his arrival on a free transfer during the summer of 1982. Released by Gordon Lee at Preston after over 50 games, the Dubliner proved Newcastle's former boss wrong as he became a huge terrace favourite with his gutsy, never-say-die attitude on the field. Versatile at full-back, central defence or in the midfield anchor role, John had little of the finer skills on the ball, but was a workmanlike and honest professional respected by his team-mates. Consistent and reliable, he missed only one game during the Magpies' promotion campaign of 1983-84. Capped by Ireland, John missed out on the 1990 World Cup with the Republic, unable to make Jack Charlton's final 22-man squad. An ankle injury picked up in a testimonial match at Whitley Bay during 1988 troubled him for almost four

years and eventually forced him to quit after a decade at St James' Park. John had a well supported testimonial fixture in April 1992 (13,780) and later remained in the North East working for a local Rover dealership then for BBC Radio Newcastle where he became a popular member of the media covering United's ups and downs for more than 20 years. He also occasionally worked for Irish channel RTE. For a period, 'Ando' as he was known, assisted Newcastle Kestrels woman's football club as coach. Later he ran a family business, Hadrianshaul.com, a courier and tourist service for visitors to Hadrian's Wall in Northumberland. The son of a Dublin docker, Anderson played Gaelic football as a teenager and was also at Manchester United, Coventry, Wolves and West Ham for trials.

Appearances & Goals:
Debut v Blackburn Rovers (a) 1 September 1982 (sub)
FL: 285(16) app 14 gls
FAC: 14 app 0 gls
FLC: 17 app 1 gls
Others: 4(1) app 0 gls
Total: 320(17) app 15 gls

Honours:
16 Eire caps 1980-89/1 unoff Eire app 1984/1 Eire u21 app/Eire sch-youth app/FL div 2 prom 1984.

ANDERSON Ronald James 1940-1942

Inside-right
b. Fenham, Newcastle upon Tyne, 3 July 1922
d. Chatham, Kent, February 1984

Career: Newcastle YMCA 1938/Middlesbrough trial 1938-39/Bury Aug 1939 (UNITED war-guest 1940-42)(Millwall war-guest 1941-42)/Crystal Palace May 1947 to c1948.

Appearing as a schemer as well as in the Number 9 shirt for United, Ron Anderson hailed from the West End of the city and took part in a handful of fixtures in Newcastle colours when he returned home from Lancashire as the Second World War broke out. Scoring in one of his matches for the Geordies, against Bradford City during September 1941, once the fighting had ceased he resurrected his career at Gigg Lane managing only a few outings. Anderson then attempted a career at Selhurst Park but failed to make the Football League eleven.

Appearances & Goals:
Debut v Middlesbrough (h) 29 March 1941 (WC)
War: 3 app 1 gl
Total: 3 app 1 gl

ANDERSON Stanley 1963-1965

Right-half
5'10"
b. Horden, Co Durham, 27 February 1934

Career: Horden CW/Springwell Utd/Sunderland amat June 1949, prof Feb 1951/UNITED Nov 1963 £19,000/Middlesbrough player-coach Nov 1965 £11,500, becoming manager April 1966/ AEK Athens (Gr) coach Jan 1973/Panathinaikos (Gr) coach May 1974/Queens Park Rangers asst-coach, then asst-manager June 1974 to Nov 1974/Manchester City scout Dec 1974/ Doncaster Rovers manager Feb 1975/Bolton Wand coach Nov 1978, becoming manager Feb 1980 to May 1981/Occasional scout thereafter, including for Newcastle Utd 1988 to 1991.

A cultured, whole-hearted half-back, Stan Anderson was something of a legend at Roker Park during 447 senior outings over a decade – holding the Reds' match record for several years. Sunderland, Newcastle and Middlesbrough skipper, he made a total of over 550 appearances for the North East's three senior clubs. When 29 years old, Stan joined the Magpies in a shock move which stunned Wearside, the beginning of Joe Harvey's push to rejoin the First Division elite. Dignified, consistent and composed on the field, Stan was an experienced tactician for the Magpies. Anderson was a key purchase, and during the 1964-65 Second Division championship campaign the former England international became a driving force. A brilliant short-term buy, Anderson led the side by example and oozed class on the ball. Stan was a past captain of the England Under-23 line-up and travelled with the country's party to the 1962 World Cup finals in Chile, although always as second choice

to the likes of Moore, Robson, Clayton and Flowers. A former apprentice plasterer and plumber, Anderson was rejected by Middlesbrough as a youth, only to return as a veteran, while he was once sent-off when wearing the white shirt of England, in 1957, then a rarity in football. In his prime, he played cricket during the summer months to a good standard, for Horden CC in the Durham Senior League. Stan later resided in the Doncaster area.

Appearances & Goals:
Debut v Cardiff City (h) 9 November 1963
FL: 81 app 13 gls
FAC: 2 app 1 gl
FLC: 1 app 0 gls
Total: 84 app 14 gls

Honours:
2 Eng caps 1962/WdC 1962 (no app)/1 Eng B app 1957/5 Eng u23 app 1954-57/Eng sch-youth app/7 FA app 1954-62/FL div 2 champs 1965/FL div 2 prom 1964/FL div 3 prom 1967(m).

ANDERSON William Ronald 1946-1948

Goalkeeper
6'0"
b. Ponteland, near Newcastle upon Tyne, 20 September 1927
d. Co Durham, 1995

Career: Dinnington 1943/Throckley CW 1946/ UNITED amat October 1946 £25, prof Feb 1947/Annfield Plain cs 1948/Local soccer until retirement through injury 1953.

Bill Anderson was a miner in the local pits and impressed United's officials when appearing in the strong North Eastern League just after World War Two. He joined the St James' Park staff as an amateur and then part-time professional, having to compete with several other goalkeepers on United's books, notably Garbutt, Swinburne, Theaker and later Jack Fairbrother. Anderson was only 19 years old when he made his single appearance for the Magpies against Leicester. His brother Bob Anderson was also a goalkeeper, for Crystal Palace and both Bristol clubs during the Fifties. For many years Bill lived in Peterlee.

Appearances & Goals:
Debut v Leicester City (h) 19 April 1947
FL: 1 app 0 gls
Total: 1 app 0 gls

ANDERSSON Andreas Claes 1998-1999

Striker
6'0"
b. Stockholm (Sweden), 10 April 1974

Career: Hova IF (Swd) 1992/Tidaholms GIF (Swd) 1994/Degerfors IF (Swd) 1994/IFK Goteborg (Swd) July 1995 £250,000/AC Milan (It) July 1997 £1.6m/ UNITED Jan 1998 £3.6m/ AIK (Swd) Aug 1999 £2m, retiring due to injury Aug 2005 becoming asst-coach/Hova IF (Swd) 2006/Andrea Doria (Swd) 2010/IF Elfsborg (Swd) May 2011/Degerfors IF (Swd) sports manager 2006.

Andreas Andersson, a tall, blond-haired Scandinavian striker enjoyed a rapid rise to fame and fortune following a season with the IFK club of Gothenburg. Netting over 30 goals and impressing in the Champions League against AC Milan, that display earned a big move to the Italian giants during the summer of 1997. Yet Andersson was hardly to figure in the colours of the Rossoneri, on the sidelines as an understudy to Weah and Kluivert for much of his stay in Italy. Kenny Dalglish picked up the 23-year-old the following summer and brought him to Tyneside as a striker to be developed as a partner for Alan Shearer. Slimly built rather than a powerhouse, he liked to play a deep

role and at times Andreas showed neat and clever touches on the ball, often doing his best work outside the danger area. Rarely though was he a threat in the box and lacked the potency required for top level English football. Strikers are judged by their goals and Andreas did not have a good record of hitting the net, Andersson managed only four goals for the club over two seasons and with Ruud Gullit arriving as boss, eventually the more established Duncan Ferguson arrived in season 1998-99 and the Swede was offloaded. He was again a success in his native country totalling over 100 matches for Stockholm's AIK although a serious knee injury disrupted his progress. Likable, hardworking and a sincere footballer, Andersson was at both Liverpool and Birmingham City for trials during 1994. He scored twice on his international debut while his father and brother both played for Hova in Sweden.

Appearances & Goals:
Debut v Aston Villa (a) 1 February 1998
PL: 21(6) app 4 gls
FAC: 3(1) app 0 gls
Euro: 1 app 0 gls
Total: 25(7) app 4 gls

Honours:
42 Swd caps 1995-2003/WdC 2002/Swd B app/Swd u21 app/FA Cup final 1998/Swd Lg champs 1996/Swd Cup final 2001, 2002.

ANITA Vernon San Benito 2012-date

Midfield
5'6"
b. Willemstad (Curacao, Dutch Antilles), 4 April 1989

Career: CW Willemstad (Dutch Antilles) 1996/W Maarssen (Neth) 1997/Ajax (Neth) jnr 1999, prof March 2006/UNITED Aug 2012 £6.7m.

Developed through the renowned Ajax youth system which has produced many a top footballer, Vernon Anita moved to Tyneside as a 23-year-old in August 2012 for a fee of almost £7m. Having been with Ajax for 13 years, he looked forward to making a name for himself in arguably Europe's most competitive league. Small, mobile with good technical ability so prevalent with Dutch players, Anita became a regular of the Ajax squad in the Eredivisie during season 2008-09 and totalled 138 senior games, including much European experience. Vernon operated in midfield or at left-back for the Amsterdam giants and reached the Netherlands international side, making his debut during May 2010 against Mexico. He was included in the initial Dutch squad for the 2010 World Cup but was omitted for the final party. In midfield, Vernon shows lots of energy which made up for his lack of build, is neat on the ball and rarely gives up on a tackle. With family roots in the Caribbean, his family moved to Holland from the island of Curacao in 1997 when still an infant returning for a period as a youngster. Anita was eyed by several clubs and Newcastle added his versatile talent to the Gallowgate squad just before the 2012-13 campaign.

Appearances & Goals:
Debut v Tottenham Hotspur (h) 18 August 2012 (sub)
PL: 45(14) app 1 gl
FAC: 2 app 0 gls
FLC: 2 ap 0 gls
Euro: 9(2) app 1 gl
Total: 58(16) app 2 gls

Honours:
3 Neth caps 2010-date/5 Neth u21 app/Neth sch-youth app/Neth Lg champs 2011, 2012/Neth Cup winner 2010/Neth Cup final 2011.

APPLEBY Matthew Wilfred 1988-1994

Centre-half
5'10"
b. Middlesbrough, 16 April 1972

Career: Hartlepool Utd jnr 1987/Middlesbrough jnr/
Nunthorpe/UNITED jnr March 1988, prof May 1990/
Darlington loan Nov 1993, pmt June 1994 free/Barnsley
July 1996 £250,000/Oldham Ath Jan 2002/Darlington trial
July 2004, pmt March 2005/Whitby Town July 2006/
Retired cs 2008.

Matty Appleby was tracked as a youngster by both Middlesbrough and Hartlepool, and although he had periods at both clubs, Matty joined United's junior set-up. The Teesside youngster impressed manager Ossie Ardiles at a time of a youthful imprint on United's side at centre-back, or occasionally in midfield. With Benny Kristensen injured, Appleby was given an extended run in the club's Second Division back line. Assured on the ball, to an extent that he appeared at times too casual, Matty looked to be a good prospect until the intense pressure of a relegation fight in 1992 affected his form. When Kevin Keegan took control of affairs he was soon back in the reserves and following a bad ankle injury moved to Feethams. With Darlington (104 app), Matty appeared at Wembley in 1996 in an unsuccessful bid to gain promotion to Division Two then he reached the top flight as part of Barnsley's line-up. He was well-liked at Oakwell (163 app), quick-thinking and solid at the back, but injury disrupted his progress. Despite being shown the door by the Magpies, Appleby went onto amass 384 senior matches in his career. His younger brother, Richie (qv), was also given a contract by the Black'n'Whites and the pair appeared together in the Anglo-Italian Cup campaign of 1992-93. On leaving the game, Matty moved into the profession of a deep-sea commercial diver with his brother.

Appearances & Goals:
Debut v West Bromwich Albion (h) 27 October 1990
FL: 18(2) app 0 gls
FAC: 2 app 0 gls
FLC: 2(1) app 0 gls
Others: 2(2) app 0 gls
Total: 24(5) app 0 gls

Honours:
FL div 1 champs 1993 (3 app)/FL div 1 prom 1997.

APPLEBY Richard Dean 1989-1995

Midfield
5'9"
b. Middlesbrough, 18 September 1975

Career: UNITED jnr Nov 1989, prof Aug 1993 (Darlington
loan 1994-95)/Ipswich Town loan Nov 1995, pmt Dec
1995/Swansea City Aug 1996 free to cs 2001/Cambridge
Utd trial cs 2001/Kidderminster Harriers loan Nov 2001,
pmt Dec 2001/Hull City July 2002 to Jan
2004/Kidderminster Harriers Aug 2004/ Forest Green
Rovers Oct 2004 to May 2005/Llanelli March 2006 to
c2008.

An England youth international, Richie Appleby at one stage of his career at St James' Park looked to have a bright future. Possessing lovely skills, he was destined for the top and after appearing for the Magpies in Anglo-Italian fixtures, playing alongside his brother Matty (qv) against Bari and Cesena during the 1992-93 season (a rarity in the club's history), his early progress was rapid, despite a broken ankle. He operated on the wing, up front or in midfield for the club's junior and reserve teams, Appleby however lost his way and was overlooked by Kevin Keegan. The youngster was given another chance by Ipswich Town but again he could make little impression and moved to Wales for a new start. It was at the Vetch Field where Appleby made an impact and this despite suffering persistent hamstring injuries. Nevertheless Richie still made his mark in over 150 appearances for the Welsh club. Signed by manager Jan Molby at Swansea, Kidderminster and Hull, he settled into an attacking midfield role with an eye for a pot at goal, frequently hitting the net. On retiring he became a deep-sea diver with his brother.

Appearances & Goals:
Debut v AS Bari (a) 8 December 1992 (AIC)
Others: 2 app 0 gls
Total: 2 app 0 gls

Honours:
Eng sch-youth app/FL div 3 champs 2000/FL div 2 prom 2004.

APPLEYARD Willie 1903-1908

Centre-forward
5'10"
b. Caistor, near Cleethorpes, 16 November 1878
d. Newcastle upon Tyne, 14 January 1958

Career: Cleethorpes Town/Cleethorpes Rovers Nov 1900/
Grimsby Tradesmen/Grimsby Town trial March 1901,
prof July 1901/UNITED April 1903 £350/Oldham Ath
June 1908 £350, joint deal with F Speedie/Grimsby Town
Nov 1908/Mansfield Mechanics May 1909 to cs 1913.

A terror to goalkeepers, Bill Appleyard was a well-built striker, weighing over 14 stone who led United's forwards with much gusto during the early part of the Magpies' Edwardian dominance. In complete contrast to Newcastle's other more cultured players, Bill couldn't be classed as a brilliant stylist, but battled away up front and he was a clinical finisher in front of goal, especially on the right, his left being described as a "swinger". Big Bill was often on the score-sheet, claiming nine goals, the most by any player in a first-eleven match, in a friendly with Beaumaris during 1908, while he also netted five against Paris Athletique in 1905. Appleyard was the Black'n'Whites goal threat as the club lifted the title in both 1905 and 1907. With little frills, he also often aimed to put the then unprotected opposing 'keeper in the net as well as the ball, and was on several occasions involved in goalmouth skirmishes. One of 13 children, Bill had a difficult route to break into the game, his father having little time for the sport as he worked in the family fish merchant business, hence the nickname of 'Cockles'. He was once nearly killed in the quicksand of the Cleethorpes coast when collecting shellfish. Despite obstacles to his football career, Bill made his way with Grimsby Town as a late developer and when at his peak with the Magpies just missed an England cap, chosen as reserve for the international with Scotland in 1908. Bill was also a fine billiards player, being footballers' champion and occasionally gave exhibition displays around the North East. Appleyard registered Newcastle's first senior FA Cup hat-trick, against his old club Grimsby during 1908. After retiring from the game, he returned to Tyneside and worked as a labourer at the Vickers factory where he used his substantial muscle to shovel coal into the furniss. Bill lived in the city's Fenham district and was also for a short period a United scout as well as at various times running a fish shop and pub in the West End. Although press reports note that United had paid £700 for his services when he moved to St James' Park, an amount which would have been a new record sum, the fee was much less at £350.

(Note: Appleyard's birth documentation reveals he was registered as Willie and not William).

Appearances & Goals:
Debut v Blackburn Rovers (a) 18 April 1903
FL: 128 app 71 gls
FAC: 17 app 16 gls
Others: 1 app 1 gl
Total: 146 app 88 gls

Honours:
FL champs 1905, 1907/FAC final 1905, 1908.

ARCHIBALD JOHN 1922-1923

Goalkeeper
5'11"
b. Strathaven, Lanarkshire, 23 August 1895
d. 1967

Career: Stranraer Corinthians/Albion Rovers Nov
1912/Reading Aug 1919/Chelsea Jan 1920/Edinburgh
St Bernard's Aug 1921/UNITED April 1922 £200/
Grimsby Town May 1923 free/Darlington March
1927/Albion Rovers Aug 1928/East Stirlingshire
Nov 1928/Clydebank Feb 1929.

One journalist of the day described John as, "a goalkeeper of consummate coolness and marked ability". Purchased by United as a potential successor to the veteran Jimmy Lawrence, but after only a single appearance in the Black'n'Whites senior eleven, lost out to rivals Bill Bradley and Sandy Mutch. The Scot did well though at Blundell Park, being a regular for Grimsby over four seasons as he clocked up 121 matches. He was part of the Mariners' promotion winning team, but then fell out of favour in season 1926-27 being something of a scapegoat after a terrible defensive run. He was actually banned from the ground before moving to Darlington. During World War One Archibald served in Gallipoli and Egypt with the Royal Field Artillery.

Appearances & Goals:
Debut v Manchester City (h) 29 April 1922
FL: 1 app 0 gls
Total: 1 app 0 gls

Honours:
FL div 3(N) champs 1926.

A

ARENTOFT Preben 1969-1971

Midfield
5'7"
b. Copenhagen (Denmark), 1 November 1942

Career: Bronshoj BK (Den) jnr 1952, snr Jan 1961/ Morton Sept 1965/UNITED March 1969 £18,000/ Blackburn Rovers Sept 1971 £25,000/ Helsingborg IF (Swd) July 1974/Retired Nov 1974/ Bronshoj BK (Den) coach 1975-76/Helsingor IF (Den) coach 1977 to 1980/Stenlose BK (Den) coach 1981 to 1983/BK Friheden (Den) coach 1984-85/Gladsaxe Hero BK (Den) coach 1986-87/HGI Hillerod (Den) coach 1988-89/Brondby IF (Den) asst-coach 1990/ Ostykke (Den) coach 1991 to 1993.

A diminutive, but stocky midfield worker Preben Arentoft excelled in a close-marking role during United's first assault on European soccer. Known as 'Benny', he was one of the earliest of Newcastle's foreign imports and was an astute footballer, able to read the game well and perform to the team's benefit, rather than his own. Arentoft was a good athlete able to run and work for the full 90 minutes and although he may have lacked the finer skills, fitted perfectly into Newcastle's team-plan for a couple of seasons. Capped by his country, Arentoft left his largely amateur domestic football scene with several of his fellow countrymen in an attempt to carve out a future in Scotland, totalling 137 games at Cappielow. He was one of a few to succeed south of the border at the time. Arentoft netted in the 1969 Fairs Cup final for United, and later operated at full-back for Blackburn at Ewood Park. An educated man of many talents, Benny later was employed as a senior manager in day-care services by Copenhagen City Council, while he was also something of an art dealer and part-time journalist, as well as an accountant. He resides in Stenlose near Denmark's capital. Before moving to St James' Park, Benny had a week's trial period at Tottenham.

Appearances & Goals:
Debut v Tottenham Hotspur (a) 2 April 1969
FL: 46(4) app 2 gls
FAC: 3 app 0 gls
Euro: 10(1) app 1 gl
Total: 59(5) app 3 gls

Honours:
9 Den caps 1965-71/1 Den B app/Den sch-youth app/ICFC winner 1969/SL div 2 champs 1967.

ARMSTRONG Adam 2013-date

Centre-forward
5'8"
b. Newcastle upon Tyne, 10 February 1997

Career: Blue Star Jnrs/UNITED jnr 2013, prof Feb 2014.

Raised in the West End of Newcastle, Adam Armstrong attended Walbottle school and joined United's Academy at Under-10 level in 2006 quickly progressing to reserve level as part of the Under-21 development squad. At junior level Adam showed he was a quick finisher, able to use both feet when the chance comes his way. And he shined for England too, during 2013 hitting six goals in the space of a week for the Under-17 line-up against Gibraltar, Armenia and the Republic of Ireland in the European Championships. Boss Alan Pardew was impressed with his talent and rapid headway promoting the 17-year-old Armstrong to the senior squad during season 2013-14 and he sat on the bench for Premier League matches before making his debut as a substitute at Craven Cottage during March 2014. Armstrong is the type of striker with a trick to beat his man and is capable of exciting runs on goal.

Appearances & Goals:
Debut v Fulham (a) 15 March 2014 (sub)
PL: 0(4) app 0 gls
Total: 0(4) app 0 gls

Honours:
Eng sch-youth app.

ASKEW William 1990-1992

Midfield
5'6"
b. Great Lumley, Co Durham, 2 October 1959

Career: Lumley Jnrs/Middlesbrough Oct 1977 (Blackburn Rovers loan 1981-82)/Gateshead cs 1982/Hull City Oct 1982 free/UNITED March 1990 £150,000 (Gateshead loan 1991-92) (Shrewsbury Town loan 1991-92)/Gateshead cs 1992 free/Whitley Bay Oct 1994/Spennymoor Utd/Workington/ Darlington asst-coach & scout 1996.

Billy Askew was signed by Newcastle as a 30-year-old, manager Jim Smith seeing the North Easterner as a player to add guile and experience to the Magpie's midfield. A United supporter as a teenager who visited Wembley as a fan in 1974, it took him almost 13 years to fulfil his ambition of playing for the club. In that time he had been reserve for several years to David Armstrong at Ayresome Park, before making his name in the lower divisions with Hull City. Askew spent eight seasons in Tigers' colours totalling 300 games before moving to Tyneside. Blessed with bags of energy, he was the proverbial midfield dynamo; small, tenacious, neat on the ball with lots of stamina. With a sweet left-foot, Billy was past his best when he arrived at Gallowgate and was unlucky with niggling injuries to his hamstring, groin and calf which kept him out of first-team selection. After retiring from playing he ran a pub in Pelaw for a period before settling in a coaching role with Darlington, latterly at their Elite Development Centre then his own Youth Performance Centre in Billingham.

Appearances & Goals:
Debut v Blackburn Rovers (a) 24 March 1990
FL: 7(1) app 0 gls
Total: 7(1) app 0 gls

Honours:
Fl div 4 prom 1983/FL div 3 prom 1985/FLT winner 1984.

ASPRILLA Faustino Hernan Hinestroza 1996-1998

Striker
5'9"
b. Tulua (Colombia), 10 November 1969

Career: Estudiantes de Tulua (Col)/Deportivo Cali (Col) 1989/Atletico Nacional (Col) July 1990/Parma AC (It) cs 1992 £3m/UNITED Feb 1996 £7.5m/Parma AC (It) Jan 1998 £6m/SE Palmeiras (Brz) July 1999/Fluminense (Brz) 2000/Atlante (Mex) May 2001 to Dec 2001/ Atletico Nacional (Col) 2002/Al-Jazira Club (UAE) Sept 2002/ Universidad de Chile 2002 to July 2003/Tulua (Col) Sept 2003/Shanghai Shenhua (Chn) Feb 2004/Estudiantes (Arg) Feb 2004/Valle D'Aosta (It) 2004.

The record £7.5 million purchase of 26-year-old Colombian international Faustino Asprilla was surrounded in controversy, and at times, media hysteria. The on-off transfer from Italian club Parma was a drawn out affair and had more twists than a television soap opera, but in the end the flamboyant and highly talented South American arrived on Tyneside to link up with Ferdinand, and later Alan Shearer, to form United's strike-force. Manager Kevin Keegan was first attracted to his unique style and special ability a year earlier when he stood out for both Colombia and Parma, United's boss making the comment: "He is a one-off, a special player, a big-stage performer." Nicknamed 'The Black Arrow' in Italy, Asprilla could be explosive on the field and defenders knew he could destroy them, but with a sometimes volatile temperament, Asprilla immediately became the focus of tabloid headlines for both his brilliance on the ball creating and scoring goals, and his sometimes rash retaliation towards defenders who gave him a rough time. A unique entertainer, he specialised in an acrobatic somersault celebration on scoring which delighted supporters. Known as 'Tino' on Tyneside, he looked far from being a thoroughbred footballer, being leggy and loping in appearance, but Asprilla possessed frightening ability and balance, able to turn defenders in tight situations. Unorthodox in style, Tino had deceptive pace over a few yards and could call on an array

of extravagant ball skills. Able to speak only a few words of English on his arrival, it took Asprilla several months to settle in the North East and adapt to the Premier League game. A touch erratic, in the end he found the frantic English game something of a struggle, although on the European stage, was a match-winner, his crowning moment being a superb hat-trick in United's opening Champions League match against Barcelona during 1996. Both fabulous and frustrating, the South American was a player who split United's support down the middle and with Kenny Dalglish in charge, Tino was rarely first choice and he ended up returning to Italy and onto a chequered career around the world. The Colombian skippered his country on occasion and appeared in the World Cups of 1994 and 1998 as well as the 1992 Olympic Games and was a fans' hero with Parma as the Italian club challenged AC Milan at the top of Serie A. In the news throughout his career, for actions both on and off the pitch, although much of the sometimes adverse publicity was exaggerated, he was one of Keegan's personality signings which made Newcastle one of the most talked about clubs in the country. On leaving the game, Tino has been involved in various activities including breeding horses on his ranch, setting up his own football club in Colombia (Club Athletic Faustino Asprilla) and even a spot of nude male modelling! He also appeared in Colombian television celebrity reality shows as well as more conventional football programmes.

Appearances & Goals:

Debut v Middlesbrough (a) 10 February 1996 (sub)

PL: 36(12) app 9 gls

FAC: 1 app 0 gls

FLC: 2 app 0 gls

Euro: 11 app 9 gls

Others: 0(1) app 0 gls

Total: 50(13) app 18 gls

Honours:

57 Col caps 1993-2001/WdC 1994, 1998/OG 1992/PL runner-up 1996, 1997/Col Lg champs 1991/It Cup winner 1992/It Cup final 1995/ECWC winner 1993 (sub no app)/ECWC final 1994/UEFAC winner 1995, 1999/ESC winner 1993/ICC final 1999/LibC winner 1999/LibC final 2000/MerC final 1999/Col FoY 1991.

AULD John Robertson 1896-1906

Centre-half & Director

5'9"

b. Lugar, near Cumnock, 7 January 1862

d. Sunderland, 29 April 1932

Career: Kilmarnock/Lugar Boswell Thistle/Third Lanark 1883/Queen's Park Nov 1884/Third Lanark 1886/Queen's Park July 1887/Sunderland May 1889/UNITED amat Oct 1896 to June 1897 when he retired, becoming a United director to 1906.

A member of the famous Sunderland 'Team of all the Talents', John Auld arrived at St James' Park nearing the end of his career, into his thirties and as the first player to be transferred from Wear to Tyne once both clubs had entered top level league football. It was a controversial transaction, Auld moving to United as a reinstated amateur which meant no fee was due to the Reds, the press noting that the deal went ahead "after the childish hubbub of the Wearsiders". Auld played in the centre of midfield and was an expert at breaking up play in a spoiler role. Highly regarded in football, James Crabtree, one of the early greats, said of Auld that he possessed "infallible judgement". For a season he linked well, helping the Black'n'Whites fashion an eleven to push for promotion. He was in fact the first of three noted Sunderland players from their all conquering side to assist United in reaching the First Division, the others being Harvey and Campbell. The younger legs of Ghee or Ostler took his place as Auld moved into United's boardroom, the first, and one of only a handful of ex-players to do so at St James' Park. The Ayrshire product made over 100 appearances for Sunderland including being captain for their first Football League game. A shoe-maker by trade, his early transfer to Wearside is one of the best recorded. Auld received a £150 signing-on fee, £20 for turning professional, £300 in wages for two years, and financial assistance in establishing a boot and shoe shop. He resided in the Roker area of Wearside to his demise.

Appearances & Goals:

Debut v Manchester City (a) 17 October 1896 (1 goal)

FL: 14 app 3 gls

FAC: 1 app 0 gls

Total: 15 app 3 gls

Honours:

3 Scot caps 1887-89/1 unoff Scot app 1889/Scot trial app 1887/FL champs 1892, 1893, 1895 (4 app)/SC winner 1889.

BA Demba 2011-2012

Striker

6'2"

b. Sevres, Paris (France), 25 May 1985

Career: Montgaillard (Fr) 1992/AS Port Autonome du Havre (Fr) 1998/SC Frileuse (Fr) 2000/Montrouge CF (Fr) 2001/Olym Lyonnais (Fr) May 2004 trial/AJ Auxerre (Fr) Sept 2004 trial/Barnsley, Gillingham & Swansea City trial 2004/Watford Nov 2004/Amiens SC (Fr) trial May 2005/FC Rouen (Fr) July 2005/RE Mouscron (Bel) July 2006/TSG Hoffenheim (Ger) Aug 2007 £2.6m/West Ham Utd Jan 2011 £500,000/UNITED June 2011 free/Chelsea Jan 2012 £7m/Besiktas JK (Trk) July 2014 £4.7m.

Impressing in the Premier League during a short spell with West Ham United in season 2010-11, Demba Ba showed that he had the razor-sharp ability to be a threat in attack, this after being released by Watford earlier in his career and a string of trials. Although the Hammers were relegated, Ba grabbed seven goals in 13 games before looking for a new club during the close-season. After being turned down by Stoke City following a medical, in stepped the Magpies and captured the Senegalese for what was heralded by all as the signing of the season, for just agent and signing-on fees. Tall and athletic, Demba recovered from a badly broken leg during 2006-07 and had shined in the Bundesliga over three-and-a-half seasons with unfancied Hoffenheim, netting 40 goals in 103 matches and he was to display the same form in attack for United as the 2011-12 campaign opened. Once settled, Demba went on the rampage, striking a hat-trick in his first full outing at Gallowgate against Blackburn Rovers and bagging a sequence of 15 goals in 16 matches. Tall, lithe and with a true strike of the ball, he took the Number 19 shirt at Gallowgate and teamed up with the club's new Number 9, Papiss Cisse, also a Senegalese international. While that partnership never really clicked, Ba's own performances remained top-class prompting several clubs to be linked with him due to a 'buy-out' clause within the player's contract. He was snapped up by European Champions Chelsea yet was not a regular selection for the Blues, missing the Europa League victory and Ba fell down the pecking order when Jose Mourinho returned to Stamford Bridge. A confident character, Ba recorded an excellent 50% strike-rate on Tyneside at the very top level; 29 goals in 58 games, one of the best in United's history. He also holds the shortest surname in the club's annals.

Appearances & Goals:

Debut v Arsenal (h) 13 August 2011

PL: 51(3) app 29 gls

FLC: 2 app 0 gls

Euro: 1(1) app 0 gls

Total: 54(4) app 29 gls

Honours:

20 Seng caps 2007 to date/Ger div 2 prom 2008.

BABAYARO Celestine Hycieth 2005-2007

Left-back

5'9"

b. Kaduna (Nigeria), 29 August 1978

Career: Plateau Utd (Ng) Sept 1993/RSC Anderlecht (Belg) jnr Aug 1994, prof Sept 1995/Chelsea June 1997 £2.25m/UNITED Jan 2005 free to Dec 2007/LA Galaxy (USA) Jan 2008 free to March 2008/Portsmouth trial July 2008/Middlesbrough trial March 2010/Retired July 2010.

A highly experienced full-back to see plenty of top action for Anderlecht, Chelsea and at international level for Nigeria, Celestine Babayaro arrived at St James' Park during January 2005 when aged 26 and seemingly at the top of his playing career. It was a deal that appeared to be a good one for United, his know-how at the back giving the side a boost. An attacking full-back with a silky touch, Celestine had showed he was a first-class performer being fast and athletic. Babayaro however was far from a success on Tyneside after a bright opening. Initially making an impression on the European scene in Brussels with

B

Anderlecht and at the 1996 Olympic Games in Atlanta where he won a gold medal, at left-back he was a defender with poise and the ability in attack to make things happen down the left flank. A move to Stamford Bridge followed and Babayaro spent over seven seasons in Chelsea's blue, lifting silverware before being frozen out of Mourinho's eleven and replaced by Wayne Bridge. He joined a refashioned United squad under the leadership of Graeme Souness as a free transfer from the capital. Babayaro competed with Olivier Bernard for the left-back spot then took his place completely for season 2005-06. In that campaign the African displayed some good football giving polished displays. However, his form, and seemingly his attitude, plummeted after that, earning little respect from the Gallowgate faithful. Often on the sidelines injured, Babayaro left Tyneside as 2008 opened and he struggled to find another club, retiring from football two years later. At his peak, Celestine skippered Nigeria at the Olympics in 2000, yet was always a touch volatile, being sent home from the African Cup of Nations during 2004. He celebrated rare goals by performing a somersault and once broke his ankle at Chelsea in pre-season action as a result. Babayaro is the youngest player to appear in Champions League football, being just over 16 years of age when he turned out for Anderlecht in 1994. His brother, goalkeeper Emmanuel, also played for Nigeria. After retiring from the game Celestine went through financial difficulties for a period but now is involved with the development of the game in both Nigeria and Europe.

Appearances & Goals:
Debut v Yeading (a) 9 January 2005 (FAC)
PL: 45(2) app 0 gls
FAC: 7 app 1 gl
FLC: 3 app 0 gls
Euro: 11 app 0 gls
Total: 66(2) app 1 gl

Honours:
27 Ng caps 1996-2004/WdC 1998, 2002/OG 1996(gold), 2000/6 Ng u23 app/Ng sch-youth app/PL champs 1905 (4 app)/Belg Lg champs 1995/FAC winner 2000/FAC final 2002/ESC winner 1998/Belg YPoY 1995, 1996.

BAILEY John Anthony 1985-1988

Left-back
5'8"
b. Liverpool, 1 April 1957

Career: Holy Cross/Everton jnr/Blackburn Rovers jnr June 1973, prof April 1975/ Everton July 1979 £300,000/UNITED Oct 1985 £80,000/Bristol City Sept 1988 free/Retired Jan 1992/Everton asst-coach to April 1993/Sheffield Utd asst-coach March 1996 to 1997.

John Bailey turned out in over 200 games for Everton before heading for Tyneside. A clever defender who liked to attack down the flank, previously being a forward as a teenager, he was the joker of the dressing-room, possessing a typical Scouse sense of humour. John had one good season in United's ranks, in 1985-86, before losing his place to local lad Kenny Wharton. Lively and something of an extrovert, Bailey was a useful boxer too as a youngster, competing in the ABA championships. Before joining the Goodison set-up, John worked as a panel-beater and had been rejected by Everton as a kid, but when he returned to Goodison he shared in an era of much glory for the Blues alongside other future Magpies Kevin Sheedy and Paul Bracewell. Bailey was later involved with Everton on match-days, part of their hospitality service. He also did a spot of after-dinner speaking around Merseyside.

Appearances & Goals:
Debut v Aston Villa (a) 26 October 1985
FL: 39(1) app 0 gls
FAC: 1 app 0 gls
FLC: 1 app 0 gls
Total: 41(1) app 0 gls

Honours:
1 Eng B app 1981/1 FL app 1980/FL champs 1985/FL div 3 prom 1990/FAC winner 1984/FLC final 1984/ECWC winner 1985 (sub no app).

BAINBRIDGE Richard 1943-1944

Centre-forward
5'9"
b. Hebburn, 22 July 1923
d. Hebburn, 24 May 1999

Career: Hebburn St Aloysius/Reyrolle Jnrs/Reyrolle Works/Grimsby Town c1939 (Reyrolle Works war-guest 1943)(UNITED war-guest 1943-44)/Hartlepools Utd Aug 1945/Horden CW July 1948.

Richard Bainbridge was a pacy forward who graduated from the talented and successful Hebburn-based Reyrolle team of the 1940s and was spotted by Grimsby scouts who gave him a professional contract just before the Second World War began. Richard's senior debut was back on Tyneside, at Gallowgate against United in 1940. During the war years he was part of the Reyrolle Works' eleven which lifted the Durham Challenge Cup in 1943, this after defeating a powerful Sunderland Reserves line-up (including Raich Carter) in the semi-final, then Doxford Amateurs in the final. He earned a call-up from Newcastle United during season 1943-44 and although his only game for United was at centre-forward, he played across the attack in the Northern Combination side, both on the wing and in the inside channels. On the return of peacetime football, Bainbridge joined Hartlepool but didn't claim a first-team position at the Victoria Ground and moved into local non-league football. Away from football, he finished training at Reyrolle and worked in the Hebburn coke oven complex and as a machinist at the Tyneside based Bushing Company. A lifelong Newcastle United supporter, Richard later ran the family coal merchant's business.

Appearances & Goals:
Debut v Bradford Park Avenue (a) 11 September 1943 (FLN)
War: 1 app 0 gls
Total: 1 app 0 gls

BAIRD Ian James 1984-1985

Centre-forward
6'0"
b. Rotherham, 1 April 1964

Career: Bitterne Saints/St Mary's/ Southampton jnr July 1980, prof April 1982 (Cardiff City loan 1983-84)(UNITED loan Dec 1984 to Jan 1985)/Leeds Utd March 1985 £100,000/Portsmouth Aug 1987 £285,000/Leeds Utd March 1988 £185,000/ Middlesbrough Jan 1990 £500,000/Heart of Midlothian July 1991 £350,000/Bristol City July 1993 £295,000/Plymouth Argyle Sept 1995 £75,000/Brighton July 1996 £35,000/ Southampton asst-coach 1998/Instant Dict (HK) player-manager 1989-99/ spells with Salisbury City, Wimborne Town, Dorchester Town/Farnborough Town Aug 2000/Havant & Waterlooville June 2004, becoming manager Nov 2004/ Eastleigh manager Oct 2007 to Sept 2012.

Ian Baird was acquired on trial as a 20-year-old by Jack Charlton when United were searching for a target man to play up front alongside playmakers Waddle and Beardsley. A centre-forward with a big heart and battling instincts, however he failed to make a big impression during his limited stay at St James' Park. Baird lost his first game, by 4-0, he did though take part in a terrific New Year's Day 'derby' clash with Sunderland, won 3-1 by the Magpies. A touch fiery, Ian was often booked by referees and wasn't retained, United going for Reilly and Cunningham instead. But after returning to the Saints, he served all his clubs in a professional manner, especially Leeds over 192 appearances where he helped the Tykes to promotion and was recognised as Player of the Year during 1988-89. Ian was good at holding the ball up and his robust style fitted in well to the tactics of several of his clubs. Baird had a good spell with Boro as well and in Scotland with Hearts. Following a stint in the Far East he settled back in the UK, for a period as a player agent and running his own motor insurance business. Ian was also involved with a scaffolding company in Southampton as well as being a consultant at Midas Sports.

Appearances & Goals:
Debut v Aston Villa (a) 22 December 1984
FL: 4(1) app 1 gl
Total: 4(1) app 1 gl

Honours:
Eng sch-youth app/FL div 2 champs 1990/FL div 3 prom 1996.

BALMER John 1941-1942

Inside-right
5'10"
b. Liverpool, 6 February 1916
d. Liverpool, 25 December 1984

Career: Collegiate Old Boys 1934/Everton amat March 1935/Liverpool amat May 1935, prof Aug 1935 (Brighton war-guest 1940-41)(UNITED war-guest 1941-42)/Retired cs 1952.

An England wartime international in November 1939 and on the fringe of a full cap, Jack Balmer had a noted spell at Anfield, totalling 313 games, netting 111 goals. Liverpool skipper, he was a highly skilled goal-poacher who teamed up with former Magpie Albert Stubbins in the Reds' team which secured the title trophy in 1946-47. Tall and a great opportunist up front, he possessed a stinging shot, Balmer once struck three consecutive hat-tricks for Liverpool during November of that Championship winning season. Jack was joint top scorer with United's ex-centre-forward with 24 goals. During his short stay with United for season 1941-42, he first developed that marvellous understanding with Stubbins that was to serve Liverpool so well after the Second World War. Jack hailed from a footballing family, his uncles William and Robert both played for Everton.

Appearances & Goals:
Debut v Sheffield Wednesday (h) 25 December 1941 (FLN)
War: 6 app 1 gl
Total: 6 app 1 gl

Honours:
1 Eng war app 1940/FL div 1 champs 1947/FLN2(WLg) champs 1943.

BAMLETT Thomas 1901-1904

Right-back
5'10"
b. Kibblesworth, near Gateshead, 1880
d. Horden, 9 October 1913

Career: Kibblesworth Colliery/UNITED Feb 1901/West Ham Utd May 1904/West Stanley Oct 1905 to cs 1909/Later playing in local football, probably with Horden Ath 1911-12.

A local product, Tom Bamlett was a noted Tyneside footballer, but one who found it hard to break into United's developing side during the opening years of the century. Competition was fierce at the time with six or seven players challenging for the two full-back positions. Able to play on either flank, Bamlett moved to London to join Southern League West Ham in search of regular first-team football and appeared in the Hammer's inaugural match at Upton Park during September 1904 along with two other ex-United players, Matt Kingsley and Dave Gardner. After football, the Tynesider became a colliery blacksmith in the region. It is thought that Tom is related to pre-war referee and manager of Middlesbrough and Manchester United, Herbert Bamlett, also from the Kibblesworth area.

Appearances & Goals:
Debut v Notts County (a) 3 October 1901
FL: 2 app 0 gls
Total: 2 app 0 gls

BARBER Stanley 1925-1928

Left-half
5'10"
b. Wallsend, 28 May 1908
d. Newcastle upon Tyne, 18 April 1984

Career: Raby Old Boys/Wallsend/UNITED Sept 1925 £100/ Bristol City June 1928 £500/Exeter City June 1930 player-exch/Brighton May 1934 free/Wallsend c1935.

Constantly overshadowed at Gallowgate by Willie Gibson and Joe Harris, half-back Stan Barber was a good player nevertheless and displayed many a decent game for the club's strong reserve side during the inter-war years, matches supported with a regular 10,000 attendance. He was a key figure in the Magpies North Eastern League title victory in 1926 and when he received a call up to the senior line-up, never let the side down. Big, strong and rosy-cheeked, Barber was enthusiastic, a terrific worker in midfield and always a gentleman. Stan established himself at the other St James' Park in Exeter, taking part in a famous giant-killing FA Cup run during 1931 and clocking up 127 league and cup fixtures for the Grecians. Playing with an urge to get forward, however, after being noted as one of the best players in the lower divisions, Stan was dogged by illness and never recaptured his eye-catching form. He later returned to Tyneside.

Appearances & Goals:
Debut v Burnley (a) 31 March 1928
FL: 1 app 0 gls
Total: 1 app 0 gls

BARKER John 1891-1893

Inside-left
5'9"
b. South of England
d. Newcastle upon Tyne, 1925

Career: Drysdale (Newcastle)/Newcastle West End 1884 (EAST END guest 1886-87 & 1888-89)/EAST END Dec 1891/Trafalgar (Newcastle) cs 1893/Shankhouse 1893.

One of the most prominent of Tyneside's pioneer footballers, John Barker served both Newcastle West End and East End during their formative years on Victorian Tyneside. He was on the field for West End's very first FA Cup fixture in 1886 and he took part in their first FA Cup Proper tie against Grimsby Town during season 1889-90. Barker also reached three Northumberland Senior Cup finals (1886, 1887 and 1888) and when he exchanged allegiance to United's embryo club, took part in Newcastle's first season at St James' Park during 1892-93, appearing once in the Northern League fixture with Middlesbrough. Barker was also a noted cyclist, a popular sport during his day, appearing for the Clarion Bicycle Club while he played cricket for the Bath Lane, White Rose and West End clubs. John resided in the west of the city and after retiring he managed several pubs; The Turks Head and Albion Hotel included. Barker was also employed at a local factory and lost an eye in a work accident. A popular character on Tyneside, he has the distinction of being awarded a benefit match when with West End, staged at St James' Park against Sunderland during April 1891. A huge crowd for the day of between 5,000 and 6,000 turned up. John is also recorded as being the first man sent-off in a competitive match for the West Enders, during a feisty local derby with East End during 1889.

Appearances & Goals:
Debut v Newcastle West End (h) 6 February 1892 (NL) (2 goals)
NL: 6 app 2 gls
Total: 6 app 2 gls

BARKER Allan Michael 1972-1979

Left-back
5'10"
b. Bishop Auckland, 23 February 1956

Career: Bishop Auckland/UNITED jnr 1972, prof March 1973 (Tulsa Roughnecks (USA) loan cs 1978)/Gillingham Jan 1979 £65,000/Ferryhill Ath April 1980/Bishop Auckland/Hartlepool Utd Sept 1982/Bishop Auckland cs 1984/Whickham 1987.

A forceful, fierce tackling full-back who was a reserve to Alan Kennedy during most of his time at St James' Park. Micky Barker's best season was during the club's relegation from Division One in 1977-78, but he was eventually replaced by first, Kenny Mitchell, then new signing Ian Davies. Micky moved to the Priestfield Stadium in Kent where he had a solid if not spectacular career with Gillingham in 70 appearances and, on his return to the North East, also did well with

B

Hartlepool where he totalled 66 senior matches. Barker once walked out on United after a dispute over wages and worked in a garage for almost a year before returning to Gallowgate. After leaving football he ran The Castle public-house in Bishop Auckland and later opened a golf driving range and golf course, running his own company Castle Golf Ltd as well as other business interests around the County Durham area. He is one of four footballing brothers who hailed from Bishop Auckland and who all played for the famous non-league side.

Appearances & Goals:
Debut v West Ham United (a) 28 February 1975
FL: 21(2) app 0 gls
FAC: 4 app 0 gls
FLC: 1 app 0 gls
Others: 1 app 0 gls
Total: 27(2) app 0 gls

BARNES John Charles Bryan MBE 1997-1999

Midfield
5'11"
b. Kingston (Jamaica), 7 November 1963

Career: Bartex (Jm)/Stowe BC 1976/Sudbury Court Sept 1980/Watford July 1981/Liverpool June 1987 £900,000/UNITED Aug 1997 free/Charlton Ath Feb 1999/Celtic manager June 1999 to Feb 2000/ Jamaica manager Sept 2008/Tranmere Rovers manager June 2009 to Oct 2009.

As manager Kenny Dalglish refashioned the Magpies in season 1997-98, he brought two veteran internationals of Liverpool to Tyneside; John Barnes and Ian Rush. The duo's pedigree was second to none, but their best days were behind them. Nevertheless 33-year-old John Barnes gave United decent service for a season and still showed much of the talent which had made him a star on Merseyside and with England for a decade. Indeed, for much of the season he was United's best player. Taking a midfield role he had developed later into his career, John still occasionally got into the box and scored some important goals, an added bonus as both Shearer and Ferdinand were missing injured. Nicknamed 'Digger' (after a television Dallas character) he gave an injury depleted side experience during United's debut Champions League campaign, Barnes possessing all the know-how of his successful years with the Reds. Some 16 years before at the beginning of his football life with Watford, he totalled 296 games under Graham Taylor before moving to Anfield in a near £1m deal. Soon to flourish with England, making his debut when still 19, a spectacular solo goal against Brazil in the Maracana during 1984 set his career on the up. John went onto become a regular for England, taking part in the 1990 World Cup. Well-balanced and strong on the ball, Barnes possessed dazzling ability and showed he could finish clinically, often with self-made opportunities. He scored many special efforts in his 200-plus haul of goals during his career. The Jamaicans mazy runs past defenders were what supporters longed to see, and often with an end product unlike many other players of his kind. John was also a free-kick specialist, able to whip and curl the ball up and over a wall. The arrival of Ruud Gullit at Gallowgate as the 1998-99 campaign began saw Barnes outcast and when 35 years of age he moved to Charlton where he concluded his playing career before trying an unsuccessful stint as a manager. One of an elite band of players to have lifted the Footballer of the Year award twice, John was honoured with the MBE for his services to football during his short stay at St James' Park. With strong Caribbean roots, his father played football and was a colonel in the Jamaican army. When he was appointed as Military Attaché during 1976 based in London, the family moved to England and John was raised in the capital. After leaving the game, Barnes became Channel 5's football presenter for a period and is often seen as a media authority especially for overseas channels in the Middle East, Malaysia and South Africa. Barnes lives on the Wirral and often speaks on racism in sport. He took part in Celebrity Come Dancing during 2007 while at his peak as a player reached the top of the charts in 1990 with the England World Cup song; 'Rap, England, Rap.'

Appearances & Goals:
Debut v Wimbledon (h) 13 September 1997
PL: 22(5) app 6 gls
FAC: 3(2) app 0 gls
FLC: 3 app 0 gls
Euro: 5 app 1 gl
Total: 33(7) app 7 gls

Honours:
79 Eng caps 1983-96/WdC 1990/1 unoff Eng app 1988/2 Eng u21 app 1983/Eng sch-youth app/FL champs 1988, 1990/FL div 2 prom 1982/FAC winner 1989/FAC final 1984, 1988, 1996, 1998/FLC winner 1995/FoY 1988, 1990 (FWA)/PoY 1988 (PFA)/PFA ToS (d1) 1988, 1990, 1991/Eng HoF/FL Legend/FAYC winner 1982/MBE 1998.

BARR John W 1893-1894

Right-half
b. unknown

Career: Grantham Rovers/UNITED Aug 1893/Ashington June 1894/Southwick by 1896.

Half-back John Barr joined United during the summer months of 1893, just after the club had become members of the Football League. Captain of the Grantham side, he was described in the Newcastle Daily Chronicle as being "a well-built youth", noted to have plenty of weight and speed, although "he appears to be rather weak in kicking". Barr only appeared once for United, during the club's first league season in Division Two during 1893-94. A reserve to Bob Creilly, he had departed by the close-season of 1894. Barr was a travelling reserve when Newcastle took part in their first league outing at Arsenal.

Appearances & Goals:
Debut v Burton Swifts (a) 23 September 1893
FL: 1 app 0 gls
Total: 1 app 0 gls

BARRON James 1944-1945

Goalkeeper
5'10"
b. Burnhope, 19 July 1913
d. Newcastle upon Tyne, 15 September 1969

Career: Durham City/Blyth Spartans cs 1933/Blackburn Rovers March 1935 £100 (Bradford City war-guest 1941-42)(Gateshead war-guest 1941-42 & 1943-44) (Darlington war-guest 1943-44) (UNITED war-guest 1944-45)(York City war-guest 1944-45)/Darlington June 1946 to 1947.

Only appearing once for the Magpies, against Huddersfield Town at the end of 1944, Jim Barron had been the first choice 'keeper at Ewood Park before the outbreak of World War Two. Returning to his native region on essential work in the steel industry, he was called-up by Newcastle's officials due to the unavailability of another guest player, Dave Cumming of Middlesbrough. All told Barron totalled 83 games for Blackburn in a sound, if not spectacular run after recovering from a broken wrist early into his senior career. He helped lift the Second Division title in 1939 and reached the War Cup final for Rovers against West Ham the following year. Barron's son, Jim (junior), also a goalkeeper, appeared prominently for Nottingham Forest and Wolves during the 1960s and 1970s.

Appearances & Goals:
Debut v Huddersfield Town (a) 23 December 1944 (FLN)
War: 1 app 0 gls
Total: 1 app 0 gls

Honours:
FL div 2 champs 1939/WC final 1940.

BARROWCLOUGH Stewart James 1970-1978

Outside-right
5'7"
b. Barnsley, 29 October 1951

Career: Barnsley jnr March 1967, prof Nov 1969/UNITED Aug 1970 £33,000/ Birmingham City May 1978 exch deal with T Hibbitt & J Connolly/Bristol Rovers July 1979 £90,000, becoming player-coach July 1980/Barnsley Feb 1981 £50,000/Mansfield Town Aug 1983 free/ Frickley Ath 1984/Local Yorkshire football cs 1985/Grimethorpe Miners Welfare manager July 1995 to 1997/Frickley Ath manager July 2000 to Oct 2000/Barnsley asst-coach c2001 for a period.

Brought to Tyneside by Joe Harvey as an 18-year-old with only a handful of senior appearances to his name, Stewart Barrowclough had terrific potential as a lean, fast winger who could supply the crosses for Malcolm Macdonald. Being lightweight, at only nine stones when he arrived on Tyneside, the youngster had to wait almost six months before he got a real chance at Gallowgate and was afterwards frustrated at ot getting into the side, ready to leave in 1971-72 for pastures new. However, once established he was quick on the flank and could whip in a telling cross into the box. Although Barrowclough had a more than respectable career, Stewart perhaps never fulfilled his early expectations after being selected for England's Under-23 side. With United for eight seasons, he figured in the Magpies two runs to Wembley in 1974 and 1976 and could be a match-winner on his day. His omission from the FA Cup final line-up in 1974 was a controversial decision while under Gordon Lee he operated in midfield and the Yorkshireman had his best term as Newcastle finished fifth in the First Division and qualified for Europe in 1976-77. On hanging up his boots, 'Barra' as he was known, opened a florist and fruit business in his native town for a period but still retained an active interest in local football, guiding Grimethorpe to Wembley in the FA Carlsberg Pub Cup during 1996. Barrowclough was later employed with Rexham Glass as a technician. Stewart's son, Carl, also appeared for Barnsley.

Appearances & Goals:
Debut v Blackpool (h) 29 August 1970 (sub)
FL: 201(18) app 21 gls
FAC: 14(7) app 2 gls
FLC: 14(3) app 1 gl
Euro: 4 app 0 gls
Others: 27 app 4 gls
Total: 260(28) app 28 gls.
(Void FAC: 1 app 0 gls)

Honours:
5 Eng u23 caps 1973/FLC final 1976/FL div 3 prom 1981.

BARTLETT Thomas 1893-1894 & 1896-1897

Inside-left
5'10"
b. Tyneside

Career: St Thomas' (Newcastle)/Science & Art (Newcastle)/Arthur's Hill (Newcastle)/UNITED Sept 1893/Willington Ath Dec 1894/Walsall Town Swifts Sept 1895/Willington Ath 1895-96/UNITED May 1896/ Hebburn Argyle May 1897/Gateshead NER Aug 1899.

Given the nickname of 'Knocker' after his renowned foraging and bustling play; Tom Bartlett was a most popular reserve in United's ranks before the turn of the 19th century. He was a well known personality in local Tyneside soccer and in his limited appearances for United during the club's first league campaign did very well; the side winning all three games and Bartlett striking a marvellous hat-trick in a 5-1 victory over Lincoln City. Despite this success, he was always second choice to Joe Wallace and soon moved back into local competition. During 1893 Bartlett was selected for the Northumberland County side.

Appearances & Goals:
Debut v Notts County (h) 9 December 1893
FL: 3 app 3 gls
Total: 3 app 3 gls

BARTON David 1974-1983

Centre-half
6'0"
b. Bishop Auckland, 9 May 1959

Career: UNITED jnr Oct 1974, prof May 1977 (Blackburn Rovers loan 1982-83)(Darlington loan 1982-83)/Darlington July 1983 free/Retired due to injury March 1984/Blyth Spartans cs 1984/ Coundon 1985-86/Newton Aycliffe manager July 1990/Spennymoor Utd asst-manager 1993 to c1998.

A tall, gangling looking central defender, ideally built for the stopper's position, David Barton showed lots of promise during his early years with United and looked like developing into a fine centre-half. However, his progress was halted, not only by a succession of injuries but also by being part of a United line-up struggling to come to terms with Second Division football during the early Eighties. In his prime, David was positive at the back and tough in the tackle, a move to Blackburn though was wrecked by a badly twisted knee. Predictably nicknamed, 'Dick' in the dressing-room, he was replaced by Jeff Clarke in United's ranks and missed out on the Keegan led resurgence at Gallowgate. Barton served Darlington well for a

period, totalling 60 games, and after retiring was for many years a representative for Samuel Smith's Brewery living in County Durham. David was a regular Leazes Ender at St James' Park as a kid.

Appearances & Goals:
Debut v Leeds Utd (a) 2 January 1978
FL: 101(1) app 5 gls
FAC: 2(1) app 0 gls
FLC: 5 app 1 gl
Total: 108(2) app 6 gls

BARTON Joseph Anthony 2007-2011

Midfield
5'11"
b. Huyton, near Liverpool, 2 September 1982

Career: St Anne's/Everton jnr 1992/Liverpool jnr/ Manchester City jnr 1999, prof July 2001/UNITED June 2007 £5.8m/Queens Park Rangers Aug 2011 free (Fleetwood Town loan July 2012) (Olym Marseille (Fr) loan 2012-13).

Often to create news for non-footballing reasons, Joey Barton has also showed he is a terrific combative midfield player and by the same token made many headlines for his footballing ability. Born on the Huyton estate on Merseyside, after short periods with Everton and Liverpool, as well as a trial spell with Nottingham Forest, he quickly became a noted youngster in Manchester City's youth ranks. Making his senior debut during April 2003 and becoming a regular during the following season, however, Barton seemed to be a magnet for controversy, even at an early age. He ran into trouble at the old Maine Road ground on several occasions; notably in a fracas with City colleague Jamie Tundy and then was arrested and charged with the assault on another teammate, Ousmane Dabo. By that time Joey had reached the England side, pulling on his country's shirt during 2006-07, reinforcing the view that despite his misdemeanours, he was an exceptional footballing talent. Attack minded, Barton was a driving influence on the park. Somewhat remarkably to many, Newcastle decided to purchase the 24-year-old midfielder in the summer of 2007 for a substantial sum after over 150 games for City, even though he was due to appear in Court over previous charges as well as face FA discipline. Manager Sam Allardyce liked his footballing talent nevertheless, but on arrival he was injured immediately with a broken metatarsal and it took some time before he pulled on a Toon shirt on a regular basis. Barton was in trouble off the field again shortly after his move to Tyneside, arrested for an incident on Merseyside during December 2007. He was eventually convicted of assault and affray and was jailed for six months, serving 74 days of his sentence in Walton prison before he could once more attempt to resurrect his career with the Magpies. Some reckoned the club should have jettisoned the player at that stage, but Joey was given a second chance and to his credit largely controlled his often quick temper both on and off the field. In the process he won over United's support with consistently good performances on the pitch in a gutsy manner wearing the black-and-white shirt, despite more injury lay-offs. Playing a major role in the Magpies' 2009-10 promotion romp in the Championship, he then ran into a much publicised row with the club's directors which led to him being handed a free transfer and a move to newly promoted QPR in August 2011. At Loftus Road Joey helped the Londoners survive their first season back at the top, yet again though he made the news, sent off at the end of the campaign and receiving a lengthy 12-match ban; the second long sentence dished out by the FA on the player. Off the field, Barton was a slick operator with the media that had often condemned him, while through his own Twitter page Joey spoke his mind and frequently issued a stream of interesting comments on the game and life in general, every so often using quotes by the likes of George Orwell and philosopher Nietzsche. In 2013 he began studying for a philosophy degree at Roehampton University.

Appearances & Goals:
Debut v Tottenham Hotspur (h) 22 October 2007 (sub)
PL: 68(13) app 7 gls
FAC: 1 app 1 gl
FLC: 0(2) app 0 gls
Total: 69(15) app 8 gls

Honours:
1 Eng cap 2007/2 Eng u21 app 2004/FL ch winner 2010/FL ch prom 2014.

BARTON Warren Dean 1995-2002

Right-back
5'11"
b. Islington, London, 19 March 1969

Career: Leyton Orient jnr 1985/Leytonstone & Ilford (Dagenham & Redbridge) cs 1987/Maidstone Utd July 1989 £10,000/Wimbledon June 1990 £300,000/UNITED June 1995 £4m/Derby Co Feb 2002 £300,000/Queens Park Rangers Oct 2003, becoming player-coach/Wimbledon Feb 2004, retiring March 2004, becoming asst-coach/ Dagenham & Redbridge asst-coach 2004/ Queens Park Rangers, Wimbledon & Arsenal as a part-time coach/LA Galaxy (USA) asst-coach 2008/ San Diego Flash (USA) manager & co-owner Jan 2010/Los Angeles Blues (USA) General Manager & Technical Director Dec 2012.

Warren Barton became Newcastle United's most expensive purchase and Britain's costliest defender when he moved to Tyneside as a 26-year-old, although the club smashed the record only two days later in a week of spectacular acquisitions. Barton was rejected by former Magpie favourite, Frank Clark, when manager at Orient, then he caught the eye when turning out for Football League newcomers Maidstone United. The Magpies in fact tried to sign him back in 1990, but wouldn't pay the fee of £300,000 and he joined the Dons at Wimbledon instead. Blond-haired and confident on the ball, Barton was a good all round player also able to perform in midfield. He also loved to attack in the Newcastle mould of the time, but could also defend with resolve. During his time in South London the Cockney was picked by England at both 'B' and full level, although Warren's full debut for his country lasted barely half an hour, the international fixture in Dublin during 1995 being abandoned due to a riot. Having impressed United's boss Kevin Keegan he completed a move North after a persistent chase by the Black'n'Whites. During his rewarding stay on Tyneside, Warren took part in two FA Cup finals with the Magpies and finished twice as runner-up in the Premier League. Skipper on occasion, he also appeared in Champions League football. Warren trained with both Arsenal and Watford as a kid and worked in an accountant's office in the City's Embankment before moving into full-time football. Always communicative and a model professional, Barton was a PFA Committee member and was appointed Chairman in November 2003. On retiring from playing after over 500 senior games, Warren became involved in various activities from media work to scouting, running soccer schools and tours. He also opened a travel business for a while before heading for the States where he became a successful coach and studio analyst for the Fox Soccer channel.

Appearances & Goals:
Debut v Coventry City (h) 19 August 1995
PL: 142(22) app 4 gls
FAC: 19(3) app 0 gls
FLC: 12(0) app 1 gl
Euro: 20(2) app 0 gls
Total: 193(27) app 5 gls

Honours:
3 Eng caps 1995/3 Eng B app 1991-95/PL runner-up 1996, 1997/FL div 2 prom 2004 (3 app)/FAC final 1998, 1999(sub no app).

BASSEDAS Christian Gustavo 2000-2003

Midfield
5'10"
b. Buenos Aires (Argentina), 16 February 1973

Career: CA Velez Sarsfield (Arg) jnr 1984, prof 1991/ UNITED May 2000 £3.5m (CD Tenerife (Sp) loan 2001-02)/ CF Newell's Old Boys (Arg) June 2003/Retired playing Aug 2003/CA Velez Sarsfield (Arg) Sporting Director 2008.

The huge success of Nobby Solano in a black-and-white shirt prompted United to look at other players from South America during the latter years of the 1990s decade, culminating with a trio of signings made by Bobby Robson during the summer months of 2000. Christian Bassedas arrived on Tyneside with Daniel Cordone and Clarence Acuna, all in quick succession. Aged 27 and costing £3.5m, he was a consistent and top performer for Argentinean club Velez Sarsfield in more than 300 games, winning the

Primera Division on three occasions and capped for his country in midfield. It was hoped he could repeat that sort of form for United, and emulate the Peruvian Solano. Used to success, apart from league titles, also winning South America's equivalent of the Champions League and Super Cup, he had the pedigree being technically a good footballer without doubt. But Christian unluckily broke a bone in his foot as he prepared for the new season on a tour in the States and with this set back it took him three months to build up the fitness level to compete in the Premier League. Bassedas, although a neat and tidy link man, was never a hit. Lacking the pace for the Premier League, he was in and out of the side for two seasons as he tried to come to terms with the much faster and intense English game. With a first-class attitude, Christian was given opportunities in 2000-01, but rarely stamped any authority on games, only scoring once for the Magpies and hardly figured in the following campaign. Like both Cordone and Acuna, the South American soon moved on, United accepting all three deals had been in the end expensive failures, although the player and some judges noting he had hardly been given an extended run in the side. Bassedas tried football in Spain's La Liga briefly, then he returned to Argentina and following retirement as a player worked as a television commentator for Fox Sports. Bassedas moved back to Velez Sarsfield, guiding them to another title in Argentina during 2009 and 2011 as Sporting Director.

Appearances & Goals:
Debut v Bradford City (h) 1 November 2000 (FLC) (sub)
PL: 18(6) app 1 gl
FAC: 2 app 0 gls
FLC: 2(1) app 0 gls
Euro: 3(1) app 0 gls
Total: 25(8) app 1 gl

Honours:
22 Arg caps 1994-99/OG 1996(silver)/12 Arg u23 app/15 Arg u21 app/Arg Lg champs 1993, 1996, 1998/LibC winner 1994/ICC winner 1994.

BASSONG Sebastien Aymar Nguena 2008-2009

Centre-half
6'1"
b. Paris (France), 9 July 1986

Career: INF Clairfontaine (Fr)/FC Metz (Fr) 2003/ UNITED June 2008 trial, pmt July 2008 £1.5m/ Tottenham Hotspur Aug 2009 £8m (Wolverhampton Wand loan 2011-12)/Norwich City Aug 2012 free.

Newcastle brought the largely unknown Sebastien Bassong to Tyneside after a trial period during the summer of 2008. At 22 years of age, the tall defender was a bright, young centre-half with recently relegated French club Metz. Like many players in France, he was a graduate of the Clairefontaine school of football and appeared almost 100 times for Metz at first-team level. Sebastien impressed boss Chris Hughton and was signed permanently, soon being given an opportunity in the big-time of England's Premier League. Staring at left-back in a United shirt, he switched to centre-back and Bassong had an outstanding first season in 2008-09, even though United were relegated. Judges reckoned the Black'n'Whites had found a new star amongst the gloom. Thoughtful on the ball, quick in defence, as well as learning all the time, he was the preferred partner for another new signing, the Argentine Coloccini. Yet on the Magpies' demotion the lithe Bassong then fell into dispute over a new contract and he was one of the first to depart in the inevitable fire-sale. His rise in stature was noted by several clubs and he moved to Spurs for a hefty £8m fee in the close-season of 2009, the Magpies making a substantial profit on the £1.5m outlay. United lost a promising defender, but as the future showed, the Magpies got the best of the deal. Bassong started brightly at White Hart Lane but soon drifted out of first-team recognition as Harry Redknapp built a fine side. He was more often on the substitute's bench for the Londoners in the following years before he settled back with Chris Hughton at Carrow Road. In a Canaries shirt, Bassong revitalised his career and looked the same passable centre-half in Premier League action. Although born in Paris, he has appeared for his parent's country of Cameroon.

Appearances & Goals:
Debut v Coventry City (a) 26 August 2008 (FLC)
PL: 26(4) app 0 gls
FAC: 2 app 0 gls
FLC: 2 app 0 gls
Total: 30(4) app 0 gls

Honours:
15 Cam caps 2010-date/WdC 2010/2 Fr u21 app 2007-09.

BATEY Robert Norman 1942-1943

Half-back
5'9"
b. Greenhead, Northumberland, 18 October 1912
d. Chorley, 29 November 1988

Career: Greenhead South Tyne Rangers/Carlisle Utd amat Sept 1931, prof Sept 1932/Preston North End March 1934 (Liverpool war-guest 1940-41)(UNITED war-guest 1942-43) (Gateshead war-guest 1943-44) (Hartlepools Utd war-guest 1943-44)(Millwall war-guest 1943-44)(Southport war-guest 1943-44) (Barrow war-guest 1945-46)/Leeds Utd April 1946/ Southport June 1947 free/Annfield Plain player-trainer May 1948/Leyland Motors 1949/Chorley ass-player-trainer Sept 1952.

Prior to World War Two, Bob Batey was in and out of Preston North End's top-ranked side, yet he still topped over 100 matches and appeared at Wembley in the 1938 FA Cup final when the Lancastrians defeated Huddersfield to lift the trophy. A sturdy defensive figure in midfield, Batey was industrious and came into United's side during the spring of 1943 when serving in the RAF. His last game for the Black'n'Whites was a marvellous 5-5 draw with York City at Bootham Crescent. On leaving the game, Batey worked for Leyland Motors to his retirement in 1977.

Appearances & Goals:
Debut v Leeds United (a) 20 March 1943 (FLN)
War: 8 app 0 gls
Total: 8 app 0 gls

Honours:
FA Cup winner 1938.

BATTY David 1996-1998

Midfield
5'8"
b. Leeds, 2 December 1968

Career: Horse & Groom Sept 1978/Tingley Ath 1978/Pudsey Jnrs/Leeds City Boys/ Leeds Utd jnr 1983, prof Aug 1987/ Blackburn Rovers Oct 1993 £2.75m/ UNITED Feb 1996 £3.5m/Leeds Utd Dec 1998 £4.4m to Feb 2004 when he retired.

When David Batty's career became entangled in argument at Ewood Park following a long injury lay-off, Newcastle were alerted to the possibility of acquiring another international player to give the Magpies' flamboyant side added bite in midfield. The £3.5m deal was quickly concluded and Batty immediately slipped into the central anchor role, operating just in front of Newcastle's defence as a replacement for Barry Venison. David was an instant hit, both with his manager and the fans who warmed to his battling instincts and immaculate distribution of the ball. Although known for his robust tackling, ball-winning ability and the competitive edge to his game, Batty was a much better player than many critics gave him credit for. David kept the game simple and was composed on the ball, rarely wasting possession and could be an intelligent player too, linking and prompting his side forward. A former skipper of the Leeds youth side, David was in the first-team at Elland Road by the time he was 18 years old and went onto appear 373 times for Leeds in two spells. A down to earth Yorkshireman, David was very quickly a big personality with the Tykes, helping his local side to promotion and then to the Football League title in 1991-92. A regular in the England squad of the era, captaining the 'B' side, he was controversially sold to Blackburn in a deal that angered Leeds' supporters. An ankle injury and a near 12 month layoff robbed Batty of a second league winners' medal during 1994-95 with Blackburn, alongside Alan Shearer, before he settled on Tyneside. He was then involved in two more title races with the Black'n'Whites with his consistently good displays in a Toon shirt being the springboard for United's attacks. Sometimes fiery on the field, famously earlier in his career David had a much publicised fracas with teammate Graeme Le Saux.

With managers Keegan and Dalglish both departing, another change in boss at St James' Park led to his move back to Leeds. His second spell at Elland Road was dogged by an Achilles injury, while he was one of the England men to fail with a spot-kick against Argentina during the World Cup finals of 1998 in France. Residing on the outskirts of Leeds, Batty is an occasional football pundit on Radio Aire.

Appearances & Goals:
Debut v Manchester United (h) 4 March 1996
PL: 81(2) app 3 gls
FAC: 9 app 1 gl
FLC: 6 app. 0 gls
Euro: 15 app 0 gls
Others: 1 app 0 gls
Total: 112(2) app 4 gls

Honours:
42 Eng caps 1991-2000/WdC 1998/5 Eng B app 1990-92/7 Eng u21 app 1988-90/Eng sch-youth/FL champs 1992/PL champs 1995 (5 app)/PL runner-up 1996, 1997/FL div 2 champs 1990/FAC final 1998/PFA ToS (PL) 1994, 1997, 1998.

BATTY Ronald Robson 1944-1958

Left-back
5'8"
b. West Stanley, Co Durham, 5 October 1925
d. West Stanley, Co Durham, 25 July 1971

Career: East Tanfield CW/Quaking Houses Jnrs/UNITED amat Aug 1944, prof Oct 1945 £10/Gateshead March 1958 £510, becoming player-manager Oct 1958/Retired March 1960 and occasionally scouted for Bury.

A sound and able defender, especially impressive when under pressure, Ron Batty spent over a decade at St James' Park and was held in high esteem by his fellow professionals. Many colleagues considered Ron to be the best left-back at the club during the immediate post-war years. Fierce and hard as they come, Jack Milburn recalled Batty as a player, "who could cut wingers in two with his tackling". He was most unlucky with injuries, and missed out on both the 1951 and 1952 FA Cup finals, while he almost lost out again in 1955. Second choice to Alf McMichael that season, he received a call-up on the Irishman dropping out, only for Batty to break his wrist in the run up to Wembley; fortunately he still played, with his arm heavily strapped. For much of his time at Gallowgate Ron had to battle for the number three shirt with McMichael, but when Bobby Cowell was forced to call it a day, switched flanks and found a place at right-back for a period. When in charge of Gateshead, he was manager for much of the season during which the Tyneside club were controversially voted out of the Football League in 1960. Batty later resided in the Stanley area and was employed as an electrician at the Marley Hill Colliery. Ron's brother, Fred Batty appeared for Bradford Park Avenue.

Appearances & Goals:
Debut v Portsmouth (a) 2 October 1948
(v Bradford Park Avenue (a) 27 March 1946 (FLN))
FL: 161 app 1 gl
FAC: 20 app 0 gls
War: 1 app 0 gls
Others: 1 app 0 gls
Total: 183 app 1 gl

Honours:
FAC winner 1955.

B

BEARDSLEY Peter Andrew MBE 1983-87, 1993-97, 2001-date

Striker or Midfield
5'8"
b. Longbenton, Newcastle upon Tyne,
18 January 1961

Career: R Holmes YC/Wallsend BC
1972/Longbenton YC 1972/Cramlington Jnrs
1975/The Fusilier (Newcastle) 1977/Wallsend
BC 1977/Ashington 1978/Carlisle Utd Aug
1979/Vancouver Whitecaps April 1981
£220,000 (Carlisle Utd loan 1981-
82)(Manchester Utd loan 1982-83)/UNITED
Sept 1983 £120,000/Liverpool July 1987
£1.9m/Everton Aug 1991 £1m/UNITED July
1993 £1.5m/Bolton Wand Aug 1997
£450,000 (Manchester City loan 1997-
98)/Fulham loan 1997-98, 1998-99, pmt Nov

1998/Hartlepool Utd Dec 1998 to May 1999 when he retired/England asst-coach
July 1999 to Oct 2000/Melbourne Knights (Aus) Feb to April 2000/UNITED asst-
coach March 2001, thereafter in various roles, including Joint Caretaker-Manager
(Dec 2010), Development Manager Oct 2011 and asst-coach to date. Also appeared
as an occasional guest player for Ponteland as well as United's junior and reserve
teams.

*To many United supporters of the modern generation, Peter Beardsley is recognised
as the best player to have pulled on the black-and-white shirt. And without doubt
the locally born striker ranks with the most eminent of men to have played for the
club in its long history. Although Peter spent several of his most productive years
away from St James' Park, on Merseyside with Liverpool and Everton, he never lost
his passion for his native Tyneside and boyhood idols, Newcastle United. A brilliant
little player, slight of build, who in his role operating just behind the front strikers
proved devastating at both creating and scoring goals, Peter netted over 250 in his
career at club and international level. Possessing lovely ball skills, marvellous vision,
as well as tremendous stamina, enthusiasm and work-rate, above all Beardsley had
the special quality of finding the net with truly spectacular goals, over and over again.
Rarely did he convert a chance by ordinary means. Many came by stunning long range
shooting, splendid placement, precision timing or delightful dribbles. With over 100
goals registered for the Magpies, many were worthy of monthly or even season
awards, such were their quality. Beardsley was in fact on United's books in three spells,
being released by Bill McGarry as a teenager when at Gallowgate on trial during the
summer of 1979. He also had spells with Gillingham, Cambridge United, Burnley and
Oxford before he was picked up as an 18-year-old by former Newcastle skipper Bob
Moncur, manager at Carlisle, and Peter proceeded to make a name for himself at
Brunton Park, a gem in over 100 appearances among the rough and tumble of lower
division football. He developed further in the North American calypso and played a
mere single match (and subbed at that) of senior football in a five month trial at Old
Trafford before being released. Arthur Cox brought him back to the North East to
partner Kevin Keegan as Newcastle made sure they returned to Division One in
spectacular fashion during 1983-84. He was then 23 years old and Beardsley's
captivating brand of football soon matured and he became an England regular, an
effective partner to Gary Lineker. Peter once netted four goals for his country in an
unofficial match against Aylesbury, while he captained England as well as appearing
in two World Cups. But Peter clashed with United boss Jack Charlton and the club's
stagnation meant he was off to Anfield in search of trophies for a new British record
deal. Honours duly came and Beardsley was noted as one of the country's top
entertainers, yet following the arrival of new boss, Graeme Souness at Liverpool, he
moved across Stanley Park to Everton where he again became a crowd favourite. When
Beardsley was 32 years old, he made a dramatic return to St James' Park for £1.5m, a
fee which proved to be the bargain of the decade. Back alongside Kevin Keegan and
later Arthur Cox too, Peter led United's charge on the Premiership as he had a new
lease of life. Now an experienced head went with his all round ability and he skippered
the Magpies as they became a new force in the game. Beardsley perhaps displayed
the best football of his career at this time as the Magpies just missed out on the
Premier League title in 1996. Quick to see an opening and with a formidable football
brain, he delighted everyone who paid to see him play. The Tynesider was awarded
the MBE for his services to football during 1995 and just missed out on the Footballer
of the Year award in the previous year. One of only three United men to record a hat-
trick in a derby against Sunderland (on New Year's Day 1985), Beardsley was
nicknamed 'Pedro' by his colleagues. Peter was a match-winner supreme, a genius in
football boots and his testimonial in 1999 against Celtic saw a crowd of 38,733 turn
up at Gallowgate. Thereafter Peter remained on Tyneside, residing in Ponteland, a
much admired personality. During Christmas 1999 he once appeared in panto as 'King
Pedro of Gallowgate' in Sleeping Beauty.*

Appearances & Goals:
Debut v Barnsley (a) 24 September 1983 (sub)
FL/PL: 272(4) app 108 gls
FAC: 17 app 3 gls
FLC: 21 app 4 gls
Euro: 10 app 4 gls
Others: 2 app 0 gls
Total: 322(4) app 119 gls

Honours:
59 Eng caps 1986-96/WdC 1986, 1990/1 unoff Eng app 1988/2 Eng B app 1991-92/1
FL app 1988/FL champs 1988, 1990/PL runner-up 1996, 1997/FL div 2 champs 1999/FL
div 2 prom 1984/FL div 3 prom 1982/FAC winner 1989/FAC final 1988/PFA ToS (d1)
1987, 1988, 1990 (PL) 1994/Eng HoF/NU HoF/MBE 1995.

BEASANT David John W 1988-1989

Goalkeeper
6'4"
b. Willesden, London, 20 March 1959

Career: Old Uffintonians 1975/Legionnaires
1976/Edgeware Town 1976/Walthamstow
Avenue July 1978/Edgeware Town Sept 1978/
Wimbledon March 1979 £1,000/UNITED
June 1988 £850,000/Chelsea Jan 1989 £725,000
(Grimsby Town loan 1992-93)(Wolves loan
1992-93)/Southampton Nov 1993 £300,000/
Fulham gkp-coach Sept 1997/Nottingham Forest
loan Sept 1997, pmt Nov 1997 free/Portsmouth
Aug 2001/Tottenham Hotspur Nov 2001/

Portsmouth Jan 2002/ Bradford City Sept 2002/Wigan Ath Oct 2002/Brighton loan
Jan 2003, pmt Feb 2003/Wycombe Wand trial July 2003/Fulham Aug 2003 to
cs 2004 when he retired, becoming full-time gkp-coach, as well as Wycombe Wand
coach & N Ireland gkp-coach 2004 to 2005/Fulham gkp-coach April 2007/Later coach
at the Glenn Hoddle Academy/Bristol Rovers gkp-coach Aug 2012 for a period/
Occasional player, including for Greenford 2013/Stevenage gkp-coach June 2014.

*Dave Beasant became United's costliest player, along with fellow Wimbledon defender
Andy Thorn, when he moved north in the summer of 1988. Also Britain's most
expensive 'keeper at the time, Beasant had made headlines just prior to signing for
the Magpies by becoming the first man to save a penalty kick during a Wembley FA
Cup final, against Liverpool in a famous Wimbledon victory. As captain of the Dons,
he lifted the trophy and was a central figure in that club's rise from non-league
football to become an established Premiership club. Starting his working life as an
apprentice printer and having an ashes to glory footballing career, Dave was known
affectionately as 'Lurch' by his team-mates. He is one of the tallest players to turn
out for the Magpies and was a rare goalkeeper-skipper of the Magpies for the opening
weeks of the 1988-89 season. Dave reached the England squad with United, but had
left to join Chelsea (157 app) by the time he was called up to play for his country as
with the Magpies having both Tommy Wright and Gary Kelly in reserve, United cashed
in on Beasant when Jim Smith needed to rebuild the squad. Noted for sprinting yards
out of his goal to clear his lines like a centre-back, Beasant could be quite brilliant at
times, yet was prone to a costly and embarrassing lapse. The Londoner began his
career as a prolific scoring centre-forward in non-league before switching to between
the posts. Dave created a tremendous run on consecutive appearances, a record
bettered at the time by one man in the history of the game (Harry Bell) when he
totalled 394 games without a gap from August 1981 to October 1990. Consistent
over his long career, Beasant played on until he was 44 years old and amassed over
1,000 senior games, becoming Forest's oldest player in the process. On retirement,
apart from working as a goalkeeping coach, Beasant was also for a period an
'International Consultant and Talent Evaluator' in the States for the Virginia Chaos
club. He was also attached to the Midas Sports Management agency as a consultant.
His son Sam Beasant appeared for Woking and Stevenage.*

Appearances & Goals:
Debut v Everton (a) 27 August 1988
FL: 20 app 0 gls
FAC: 2 app 0 gls
FLC: 2 app 0 gls
Others: 3 app 0 gls
Total: 27 app 0 gls

Honours:
2 Eng caps 1990/WdC 1990 (no app)/7 Eng B app 1989-91/FL div 1 champs 1998/FL
div 2 champs 1989/FL div 4 champs 1983/FL div 2 prom 1986/FL div 3 prom 1984/FL
div 4 prom 1981/FAC winner 1988.

BEDFORD Henry 1930-1932 & 1937-1938

Inside-forward & Trainer
5'8"
b. Calow, near Chesterfield, 15 October 1899
d. Derby, 24 June 1976

Career: Grassmoor Ivanhoe (Chesterfield)/Nottingham Forest amat Oct 1918, prof Aug 1919/Blackpool March 1921 £1,500/Derby Co Sept 1925 £3,000/UNITED Dec 1930 £4,000/Sunderland Jan 1932 £3,000/Bradford Park Avenue May 1932/Chesterfield June 1933/Heanor Town player-trainer Aug 1934/UNITED trainer Oct 1937/Derby Co masseur May 1938/Belper Town manager Jan 1954/ Heanor Town manager March 1955 to March 1956.

Harry Bedford was a dashing and fearless centre-forward who scored more than 300 goals during his outstanding career between the two world wars. He arrived at St James' Park nearing the veteran stage of his playing days and was used largely out of position at inside-forward in a black-and-white shirt. However, Bedford still gave good short term service to the Magpies at a difficult time during the club's history in the aftermath of the controversial sale of Hughie Gallacher. An ex-miner, Harry never settled too well in the North East, at either Newcastle or Sunderland, but he came to the region with a formidable record for Blackpool and Derby. He had attracted national attention netting 118 goals in 182 league and cup matches for the Seasiders, being the league's leading scorer in both 1922-23 and 1923-24. There was a more strategic approach to his play up front rather than force, with dribbling runs with the ball and neatly placed shots often finding the net while Harry once scored four goals for the Football League against the Irish in 1924. Bedford was underrated in an era with a galaxy of noted strikers, but was especially admired at the Baseball Ground where he was the Rams' leading goal-getter for five years in in a row striking almost 30 a season and 152 in total. Forging a good relationship with ex-Magpie George Jobey as Derby boss, Harry was always immaculately turned out, both on and off the field. On retiring from playing, he had a brief stay back with the Black'n'Whites before taking over a pub, a licensee in Derby and for 23 years Bedford worked in the fire-service at the Rolls Royce plant in the Midlands. He was also masseur to Derbyshire County CC for a period. His uncles both played football too, Harry Turner (Chesterfield) and George Bedford (Leicester City).

Appearances & Goals:
Debut v Leicester City (h) 13 December 1930 (1 goal)
FL: 30 app 17 gls
FAC: 2 app 1 gl
Total: 32 app 18 gls

Honours:
2 Eng caps 1923-25/2 FL app 1925-26/Eng trial app 1925/FL div 2 prom 1926.

BEHARALL David Alexander 1993-2002

Centre-half
6'2"
b. Walker, Newcastle upon Tyne, 8 March 1979

Career: Walker Central BC/UNITED jnr June 1993, prof July 1997 (Grimsby Town loan 2001-02)/Oldham Ath loan Nov 2001, pmt March 2002 £150,000/Carlisle Utd Feb 2005 free/Port Vale trial/Stockport Co Feb 2006 to May 2006 when he retired.

A product of local football in Newcastle and a teenage colleague of Shola Ameobi at the Walker Central Boy's Club, centre-back David Beharall joined United as a kid at the Centre of Excellence and was fostered through the ranks, captain of the junior and reserve sides. Showing up well as a positive and committed player at that level of football, Dutch boss Ruud Gullit brought in the tall defender to the reckoning towards the end of the 1998-99 season as a replacement for Laurent Charvet, the young Tynesider doing well. With injuries to both Steve Howey and Nikos Dabizas, there was a chance that David would play in the 1999 FA Cup final, yet that did not materialise although the Geordie was part of the squad which travelled to Wembley. He was not favoured in the same way by Bobby Robson though, and David found it difficult to get a look in, never selected by the new boss. After a long lay-off due to a knee injury, Robson allowed Beharall to move down the football ladder and he joined Oldham in 2001. David had a decent spell at Boundary Park, totalling 78 appearances, while during his short stay with Grimsby was part of the Mariners' team which knocked Liverpool out of the League Cup during 2001. Before concluding his playing career with Stockport, David helped Carlisle regain their Football

League status by winning promotion from the Conference in season 2004-05. Afterwards Beharall opened a web-design company, Candid Sky, based in Oldham, his own Twitter account describing David as a "Technology Entrepreneur".

Appearances & Goals:
Debut v Everton (h) 17 April 1999
PL: 4(2) app 0 gls
Total: 4(2) app 0 gls

Honours:
FL div 2 champs 2006 (6 app).

BELL Anthony Wayne 1971-1975

Goalkeeper
6'0"
b. North Shields, 27 February 1955

Career: UNITED jnr Dec 1971, prof March 1973/ North Shields May 1975 free.

Tony Bell was one of first choice goalkeeper Willie McFaul's deputies during the Irishman's extensive dominance of the number one jersey. The young Tyneside product was called up only once, against Spurs, when his other rival for the 'keeper's position at Gallowgate, Martin Burleigh, was concluding a transfer to Darlington. Nineteen-year-old Bell found the Tottenham forwards on top form at White Hart Lane as Newcastle fell 3-0, Spurs netting all three of their goals in a six minute period. Tony had what could be described as an 'off day' as two of the goals were as a result of his nervous afternoon and in some reports one of the goals was recorded as a goalkeeper own-goal. He didn't get another chance in the Magpie senior line-up, Mick Mahoney being purchased before the season was out. Nevertheless, Bell proved to be a fine custodian between the posts in the local Northern League. He later resided in Monkseaton on the North East coast and for a period worked with a family business on fishing trawlers then afterwards for Maersk Containers, on supply ships for North Sea oil rigs.

Appearances & Goals:
Debut v Tottenham Hotspur (a) 7 December 1974
(v Southampton (a) 27 November 1974 (TC))
FL: 1 app 0 gls
Others: 1 app 0 gls
Total: 2 app 0 gls

BELL David 1930-1934

Right-half
5'11"
b. Gorebridge, Midlothian, 24 December 1909
d. Monkseaton, Whitley Bay, 16 April 1986

Career: Arniston Rangers/Musselburgh Bruntonians/ Wallyford Bluebell 1929/UNITED April 1930 £150/Derby Co June 1934 £700/Ipswich Town Oct 1938 £1,075/Retired May 1950.

Known as 'Daniel' and a deputy to the tenacious Roddie MacKenzie in United's squad, Scotsman Bell proved to have lots of promise in midfield when called upon. He was, though a victim of fate. When performing well and impressing United's team selection committee and manager Andy Cunningham, he seriously injured an ankle, then a cartilage, which left him sidelined for a long periods. Untiring and always in the thick of the action in the MacKenzie mould, Daniel departed following United's relegation from Division One and went onto have a good career at Portman Road, appearing in Ipswich Town's first ever league game during 1938. He totalled 236 games for the Suffolk club and played on until he was over 40 years old. After retiring from the game he worked for a period at crane manufacturers Ransome & Rapier in Ipswich, where his immense strength was renowned to his work-mates. He later lived in the Monkseaton area of Tyneside to his death.

Appearances & Goals:
Debut v Grimsby Town (a) 5 September 1931
FL: 21 app 1 gl
FAC: 2 app 0 gls
Others: 1 app 0 gls
Total: 24 app 1 gl

Honours:
Scot sch-youth app.

BELL Derek Stewart 1980-1983

Midfield
5'9"
b. Fenham, Newcastle upon Tyne, 19 December 1963

Career: UNITED jnr July 1980, prof Dec 1981/Retired due to injury Nov 1983/Eppleton CW/Newcastle Blue Star 1983-84/Gateshead Feb 1985/North Shields Feb 1988/Gateshead 1988/Bridlington Town June 1993/ Bishop Auckland 1993-94/Blyth Spartans/ Whitley Bay/Berwick Rangers player-coach June 1994/ Whitley Bay player-manager Feb 1995/Blyth Spartans player-asst-manager Nov 1995/ Durham City July 1996/Lemington SC (Newcastle) player-manager 1998 to Feb 1999/Ponteland March 1999/Durham City player-coach cs 1999/Newcastle Benfield 2002/Gateshead manager Nov 2002, becoming Director of Football Nov 2003, Deputy Chairman, then Chairman 2004 and Chief Executive July 2006 to 2008, afterwards a part-time coach for a period.

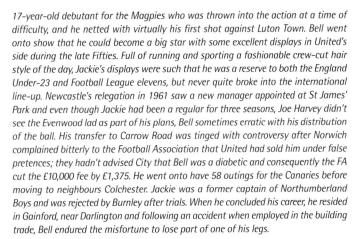

Derek Bell had an unfortunate time at St James' Park with injuries. Firstly, soon after turning professional he was in the treatment room for many weeks with a bad ankle knock, then after showing what he could do in senior action, picked up knee trouble which eventually forced him to quit the Football League scene. Bell was only 19 years of age when he made a mark and had showed he was a bright prospect, full of running in the middle of the field with plenty of stamina. After leaving full-time football, Derek was employed in a snooker and golf business then worked with the City of Newcastle's Housing Department. At the same time Derek continued a career in North East non-league soccer where he won two Northern Premier League titles with Gateshead, the club he held a long association with, eventually clocking up over 300 games and becoming Chairman and Chief Executive. During his days on the local beat, he was selected for the FA's England non-league squad in 1989 while his father was a player for Partick Thistle in Scotland. Derek left Gateshead to join Platinium4 Sports Ltd, a football agency.

Appearances & Goals:
Debut v Blackburn Rovers (a) 1 May 1982
FL: 3(1) app 0 gls
Total: 3(1) app 0 gls

BELL George William 1913-1920

Left-back
5'9"
b. Sunderland

Career: UNITED 1913, and again, amat 1918, prof May 1919/Malay Straits 1920.

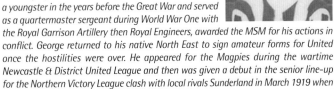

Able to play on both flanks in defence, George Bell was a youngster in the years before the Great War and served as a quartermaster sergeant during World War One with the Royal Garrison Artillery then Royal Engineers, awarded the MSM for his actions in conflict. George returned to his native North East to sign amateur forms for United once the hostilities were over. He appeared for the Magpies during the wartime Newcastle & District United League and then was given a debut in the senior line-up for the Northern Victory League clash with local rivals Sunderland in March 1919 when he deputised for Frank Hudspeth. On the club's books for the resumption of Football League action in season 1919-20, he couldn't break through and soon left the club.

Appearances & Goals:
Debut v Sunderland (a) 22 March 1919 (NVL)
War: 3 app 0 gls
Total: 3 app 0 gls

BELL John Russell 1956-1962

Left-half
5'8"
b. Evenwood, Co Durham, 17 October 1939
d. Gainford, Co Durham, 22 April 1991

Career: Evenwood Town/Burnley trial/UNITED jnr Oct 1956 £10, prof July 1957/Norwich City July 1962 £8,725/Colchester Utd May 1965/Gainford Town June 1966.

A former England Boys reserve who quickly developed through United's junior ranks, Jackie Bell was a fine attacking wing-half with a deadly shot. An apprentice plasterer, he was a

17-year-old debutant for the Magpies who was thrown into the action at a time of difficulty, and he netted with virtually his first shot against Luton Town. Bell went onto show that he could become a big star with some excellent displays in United's side during the late Fifties. Full of running and sporting a fashionable crew-cut hair style of the day, Jackie's displays were such that he was a reserve to both the England Under-23 and Football League elevens, but never quite broke into the international line-up. Newcastle's relegation in 1961 saw a new manager appointed at St James' Park and even though Jackie had been a regular for three seasons, Joe Harvey didn't see the Evenwood lad as part of his plans, Bell sometimes erratic with his distribution of the ball. His transfer to Carrow Road was tinged with controversy after Norwich complained bitterly to the Football Association that United had sold him under false pretences; they hadn't advised City that Bell was a diabetic and consequently the FA cut the £10,000 fee by £1,375. He went onto have 58 outings for the Canaries before moving to neighbours Colchester. Jackie was a former captain of Northumberland Boys and was rejected by Burnley after trials. When he concluded his career, he resided in Gainford, near Darlington and following an accident when employed in the building trade, Bell endured the misfortune to lose part of one of his legs.

Appearances & Goals:
Debut v Luton Town (a) 16 November 1957 (1 goal)
FL: 111 app 8 gls
FAC: 6 app 0 gls
Total: 117 app 8 gls

Honours:
FL div 4 prom 1966 (7 app).

BELL William 1942-1943

Goalkeeper
5'9"
b. Kilmarnock

Career: Shawfield Jnrs/Kilmarnock June 1939 (UNITED war-guest 1942-43) (Halifax Town war-guest 1943-44)/Ayr Utd cs 1946.

A Scottish junior international goalkeeper, Willie Bell also took part in the 1939 Scottish Junior Cup final before joining his local club, Kilmarnock. He was unfortunate to have been given his chance in professional football just before war was declared in the Scottish First Division during 1939-40. Although he lacked height for a 'keeper, being only 5'9" tall, Bell possessed good anticipation coupled with a steady pair of hands. A stylish custodian, his two games in United's colours both ended in victories, 3-1 at Leeds and 2-0 against Gateshead. He managed only a handful of outings for Killie.

Appearances & Goals:
Debut v Gateshead (h) 20 February 1943 (FLN)
War: 2 app 0 gls
Total: 2 app 0 gls

Honours:
Scot Jnr app/SJC final 1939.

BELLAMY Craig Douglas 2001-2005

Striker
5'8"
b. Cardiff, 13 July 1979

Career: Caer Castell/Bristol Rovers jnr/Canary Rangers/Norwich City jnr 1995, prof Jan 1997/Coventry City Aug 2000 £5m/UNITED June 2001 £6.5m (Celtic loan 2004-05)/Blackburn Rovers June 2005 £3.75m/Liverpool July 2006 £6m/West Ham Utd July 2007 £7.5m/ Manchester City Jan 2009 £14m (Cardiff City loan 2010-11)/Liverpool Aug 2011 free/Cardiff City Aug 2012 free/retired May 2014.

Much travelled and on occasion controversial, Craig Bellamy was a lightning fast and match-winning forward who formed a telling partnership with Alan Shearer for a period, one of the best pairings in Europe at the time. The Welshman started with Norwich City's nursery in Chepstow before heading for Carrow Road and as a teenager soon made a name for himself in the yellow shirt

of City as a fast and furious attacker able to strike the net. A regular during 1997-98, Coventry paid a club record fee for his services and he joined United from the Highfield Road club for £6.5m in June 2001 to replace Duncan Ferguson up front. At 22 years of age, he had a stuttering start at St James' Park but won over the fans and was soon lifting the PFA Young Player-of-the-Year award. He was also often at odds with referees, fellow teammates, managers and at times supporters. Despite Bellamy's volatile temperament the Welshman had ability to secure victory with devastating pace in attack, in a spiky and relentless style that unsettled defenders. Always hounding opponents, Craig possessed that extra gear which most strikers lacked. Over four seasons the pairing of Bellamy and Shearer, a pace and power combination, netted 142 goals and saw United compete at the top of the table as well as on the European stage in both the Champions League and UEFA Cup. Frequently on the sidelines at times with knee injuries since his days at Carrow Road, undergoing several operations, he was a difficult player to manage and while Sir Bobby Robson did that well, during season 2004-05 he was at odds with new manager Graeme Souness as well as with several dressing-room colleagues. He left Tyneside with acrimony, on a loan deal to Celtic in January of that season. Then Bellamy moved on again, to Blackburn Rovers in the summer of 2005 and thereafter pulled on the colours of Liverpool, West Ham United and Manchester City, all following big moves. And at each stadium he showed the cutting edge and match-winning ability to be the difference. Craig eventually moved back to his home city of Cardiff to wind down his much travelled playing career. He won over 70 caps for Wales, also being captain of his country on occasion, as well as leading out the Great Britain team during the London 2012 Olympics. Bellamy was just 16-years-old when he first played for the Welsh under-21 eleven, while aged 18, Craig is one of the youngest to appear for the full international side too. His son Ellis started a career on Cardiff's books and was called into the Wales youth set-up during 2012. Bellamy created a football academy to help disadvantaged youngsters in Sierra Leone under his own Foundation and once netted a hat-trick for United as an extra-time substitute, in all of 14 minutes, against Brentford during a League Cup tie in 2001.

Appearances & Goals:
Debut v Sporting Lokeren SNW (a) 14 July 2001 (ITC)
PL: 87(6) app 27 gls
FAC: 5 app 0 gls
FLC: 3(2) app 4 gls
Euro: 24(1) app 11 gls
Total: 119(9) app 42 gls

Honours:
78 Wales caps 1998-2013/8 Wales u21 app 1996-99/OG 2012/Wales sch-youth app/FL ch winner 2013/FAC final 2012/FLC winner 2012//SC winner 2005/CL final 2007 (sub no app)/YPoY 2002 (PFA).

BEN ARFA Hatem 2010-date

Striker or Midfield
5'11"
b. Clamart, Paris (France), 7 March 1987

Career: ASV Chatenay-Malabry (Fr) 1994/Montrouge CF (Fr) 1996/AC Boulogne-Billancourt (Fr) 1998/INF Clairefontaine (Fr) 1999 (FC Versailles (Fr) occasionally)/Olym Lyonnais (Fr) 2002, prof Aug 2004/Olym Marseille (Fr) July 2008 £10.5m/UNITED loan Aug 2010, pmt Jan 2011 £5.75m to date (Hull City loan 2014-15).

Of Tunisian decent, Hatem Ben Arfa has been described as both magical and maddening, entertaining and enigmatic. A highly talented striker-cum-midfield player, Ben Arfa settled at Gallowgate during August 2010, initially on a loan deal, following a drawn out transfer saga with Marseille. Born in the Parisian suburbs, Hatem like many top French footballers to move to England began at his country's Clairfontaine academy. His trickery and shooting power up front saw Hatem capped by France at under-16 level and earn a contract at French champions Lyon. He was a 17-year-old debutant at the Stade de Gerland and won five Ligue 1 titles before moving to the Mediterranean coast to join Marseille for season 2008-09 in a substantial deal. A touch hot-tempered, Ben Arfa had his bust-ups at both Lyon and Marseille, but his skill and match-winning left boot were unquestioned, although like many of his kind, inconsistency was an obstacle in his game. He could play on either flank or as a support striker and in a black-and-white shirt soon displayed his brand of sometimes spectacular football, netting a top-class winner at Everton on his first full outing. With fine balance when on the ball and the skill to confound defenders, the Premier League looked to have a new star, but just as Ben Arfa started to make an impact he broke his leg in two places following a tackle from Manchester City's Nigel De Jong, during the opening minutes into his fourth match for the Magpies.

He was out for almost 12 months, although when on the sidelines United completed his permanent transfer for a fee of over £5m. Ben Arfa made a cautious return to action in the early months of 2011-12 often used a substitute, while he started to display cameo performances of that special ability; typically an eye-catching solo goal against Blackburn in FA Cup action in which he weaved past several players on a high speed dribble before sending a rocket shot past 'keeper Bunn. By the end of that programme Hatem had fully established himself in the side, always having the ability to strike goals of special quality which made plenty sit up and take notice, once more hitting a solo effort, this time against Fulham. Maturing as a footballer, his form prompted a recall to the French national side and United found they had another player with that special touch of flair and imagination to make things happen around the box. At times though continuing to be infuriatingly inconsistent, he found himself often selected on the bench instead of in the starting line-up and his relationship with the management deteriorated, as did his form and fitness during 2013-2014. His father appeared for the Tunisian national side.

Appearances & Goals:
Debut v Blackpool (h) 11 September 2010 (sub)
PL: 48(28) app 13 gls
FAC: 3 app 1 gl
FLC: 2(2) app 0 gls
Euro: 2(1) app 0 gls
Total: 55(31) app 14 gls

Honours:
13 Fr caps 2008-date/4 Fr u-21 app 2007/Fr sch-youth app/Fr Lg champs 2005 (9 app), 2006, 2007, 2008, 2010/Fr Cup winner 2008 (sub no app)/Fr LC winner 2010/Fr YPoY 2008.

BENNETT Albert 1965-1969

Striker
6'0"
b. Chester Moor, near Chester-le-Street, 16 July 1944

Career: Chester Moor CW Jnrs/UNITED amat 1960/ Rotherham Utd jnr May 1960, prof Oct 1961/UNITED July 1965 £27,500/Norwich City Feb 1969 £25,000/ Retired March 1971 due to injury/Bury St Edmunds player-manager July 1972/Sprowston Ath/Thurlton/ Yarmouth Town Oct 1979 to May 1981/Sprowston Ath/Carrow/Quebec Rovers/ Sprowston Thursday/Taverners (All East Anglian sides).

Albert Bennett caught the attention of several big clubs as a noted goal-poacher in three seasons of consistent scoring for Rotherham United; he netted 70 goals and had reached the England Under-23 line-up. Newcastle and Aston Villa led the chase to take the 21-year-old leggy striker into the First Division and Joe Harvey was the manager who succeeded, landing the player who was once on the Magpies' books as a teenage trialist after scoring 100 goals for Chester Moor. Curly-haired with a colourful, naturally jovial character, Albert became a popular footballer at Gallowgate forming a good understanding with Wyn Davies in season 1967-68 that led to the Black'n'Whites qualifying for Europe for the first time. Unfortunately by the time United played their first game, Bennett had undergone knee surgery following a clash with his own teammate, John Tudor, which saw him miss United's debut in the Inter Cities Fairs Cup, and worse, lose his place as partner to Davies, to Bryan Robson. United's first named substitute in 1965, Albert is also noted as being responsible for nicknaming Emlyn Hughes, 'Crazy Horse', during a 1967 United-Liverpool confrontation. Known as 'Ankles' himself, having to tape up his ankles following a broken ankle injury when appearing for the young England side, Bennett was mentioned in dialogue in the celebrated television programme, 'Auf Wiedershen Pet', Oz making reference to Albert as a "great centre-forward"! A former apprentice bricklayer, after quitting the professional scene when only 27 years old due to more knee handicaps when at Norwich, Albert had a succession of jobs including working for the prison service and running a catering business as well as even a joke shop on Lowestoft pier. Residing in Norfolk, he was a publican for several years then operated a taxi. Albert continued playing in local Norwich football for several years and managed Coleman's Mustard FC for a period.

Appearances & Goals:
Debut v Sheffield Wednesday (a) 28 August 1965
FL: 85 app 22 gls
FAC: 1 app 0 gls
FLC: 3 app 1 gl
Euro: 0(1) app 0 gls
Total: 89(1) app 23 gls

Honours:
1 Eng u23 app 1965/Eng sch-youth app.

B

BENNIE Robert Brown 1901-1904, 1930-1945

Right-back & Director

5'8"

b. Polmont, near Falkirk, 28 September 1873

d. Jesmond, Newcastle upon Tyne, 1 October 1945

Career: Airdrieonians/Heart of Midlothian/Royal Albert June 1895/St Mirren May 1896/UNITED May 1901 in a joint deal with R Orr/Retired due to injury cs 1904/Morpeth Harriers Sept 1904/UNITED director July 1930 to 1943.

An honest player and a thoroughly professional individual, Bob Bennie had impressed United after five seasons of consistent play in St Mirren's line-up (84 app). Although dogged with a persistent knee complaint which eventually forced his retirement, Bennie was a good all round sportsman too. He was local golf and bowls champion and later became a successful Tyneside entrepreneur. Uncle of the famous Airdrie and Scotland player of the same name during the Twenties, Bob also had four brothers who played the game north of the border. He was a regular choice for the Magpies in season 1901-02, one writer of the day described him as a footballer who "tackles in a strong forcible manner, and is a good, clean kicker." But due to those knee problems he lost his place to firstly, local lad, James Tildesley, then to Scottish international Andy McCombie when he arrived for a record fee. Bennie, himself, just missed out on a cap for his country appearing in a trial game during 1901-02. Over 25 years after leaving United as a player, he returned to the fold as a director. Bennie lived in the Jesmond area of the city to his death and for a period before the First World War was a publican at the Collingwood Arms in Newcastle.

Appearances & Goals:

Debut v Blackburn Rovers (a) 7 September 1901

FL: 33 app 0 gls

FAC: 4 app 0 gls

Total: 37 app 0 gls

Honours:

Scot trial app 1902.

BENSON Robert William 1902-1904

Right-back

5'9"

b. Whitehaven, 9 February 1883

d. Islington, London, 19 February 1916

Career: Dunston Villa April 1902/Shankhouse May 1902/Swalwell/UNITED Nov 1902 £150/ Southampton Sept 1904 £150/Sheffield Utd May 1905 £150/Woolwich Arsenal Nov 1913 to cs 1915.

A young miner when he was at St James' Park, Bob Benson developed his talent away from Tyneside, especially noted for his displays at Bramall Lane for Sheffield United where he made 285 outings, being skipper for a period. With competition for United's full-back positions extremely fierce during the early years of the new century, Bob Benson had a difficult task breaking into the Newcastle side. After famous international Andy McCombie had been purchased from Sunderland, Benson's opportunities were limited to a single game and it was no surprise when he was transferred south. Yet, the Cumbrian proved a point to Newcastle's directors when he developed into a bold defender who represented his country. He was something of a heavyweight full-back, at over 14 stone and was described by one biography of the day as being, "a terror to opposing forwards". Fair-haired and once also described as a "splendid specimen of a footballer", Bob adopted a curious strategy with penalty kicks in which it is recorded he ran almost half the length of the pitch before walloping the ball as hard as he could towards goal! At the age of only 33, Benson met a tragic end. Working at a munitions factory in Woolwich, he had given up football during the First World War, but during February 1916 had gone to watch the Arsenal versus Reading fixture. With the Gunners a man short, Benson volunteered to fill-in for his old club. Hardly fit for such a challenge after working long shifts at the factory, he became dizzy on the field and had to depart for the dressing-room. Within a matter of minutes he died in trainer George Hardy's arms from a heart-attack due to a longstanding condition. Benson was buried in an Arsenal shirt.

Appearances & Goals:

Debut v Liverpool (a) 7 March 1903

FL: 1 app 0 gls

Total: 1 app 0 gls

Honours:

1 Eng cap 1913/Eng trial app 1913/1 FL app 1910/3 unoff Eng app 1910.

BENTLEY Roy Thomas Frank 1946-1948

Inside-right

5'11"

b. Shirehampton, Bristol, 17 May 1924

Career: Portway/Shirehampton Jnrs/Bristol Rovers amat May 1938/Bristol City amat July 1938, prof Aug 1941 (Shell Mex FC war-guest)(Hartlepool Utd war-guest)(Liverpool war-guest, under a pseudonym) (Gateshead war-guest 1945-46)/ UNITED June 1946 £8,500/Chelsea Jan 1948 £12,500/Fulham Sept 1956 £8,600/Queens Park Rangers June 1961/Reading manager Jan 1963 to Feb 1969/Swansea Town manager August 1969 to Oct 1972/Thatcham Town manager 1973 to 1976/ Reading secretary Aug 1977 to Feb 1984/Aldershot secretary Jan 1985 to 1986.

When Roy Bentley joined United immediately after the Second World War, he became the most expensive player signed from the lower divisions. He was almost an unknown, Stan Seymour, however saw a rich talent in the slightly-built youngster and received a glowing report from ex-teammate Bobby Hewison, then boss of City. Starting off at Bristol Rovers as an office-boy, Roy possessed vision and thought on the ball as well as the natural ability to find the net. The 22-year-old began with a flourish in a Magpie shirt, netting twice on his debut and 22 goals in his first season displaying a style of play that was perfect for the team game; keeping the ball moving and always looking to retain possession. However, he was also frequently laid low through ill heath when in the North East and it was said he could never get used to the harsher climate. Leaving for Chelsea during United's promotion season, once back in the south, Bentley became a huge personality in the game. He was inventive and unorthodox in method, and when operating at centre-forward became one of the first roving leaders, popping up all over the park to confound defenders. Often raiding from the flanks, Roy packed a tremendous shot in his right-foot and was, despite his slight build, supreme in the air. He scored goals on a regular basis at Stamford Bridge and Bentley skippered the Blues to their first Championship victory during 1954-55, top scorer in the title success with 22 goals. He was their leading scorer for eight consecutive seasons and all told scored 150 goals in 367 games for the Londoners, one of Chelsea's all-time greats. His stay at the Bridge was not all roses though, Roy going on strike over his contract and was forced out of the Blues' camp. Bentley also recorded an impressive record for England too, scoring nine times in only 12 internationals, including a hat-trick for his country in season 1954-55, while he also represented Great Britain. He appeared as well in the England side that lost so infamously to the USA in the 1950 World Cup. Bentley was a player who attracted the crowds, one of the elite of the glorious Fifties era. During World War Two Bentley served aboard destroyers, for a time on hazardous convoy duty in the Atlantic. On retirement Roy settled in the Reading area, becoming secretary at Shrivenham golf club for a lengthy period to 1992. His father was a noted rugby player appearing for the Bradford Northern club.

Appearances & Goals:

Debut v Millwall (a) 31 August 1946 (2 goals)

FL: 48 app 22 gls

FAC: 6 app 3 gls

Total: 54 app 25 gls

Honours:

12 Eng caps 1949-55/WdC 1950/2 Eng B app 1949-50/3 FL app 1949-55/1 FA app 1953/GB app 1956/FL champs 1955/FL div 2 prom 1948, 1959/FL div 4 prom 1970(m).

BERESFORD John 1992-1998

Left-back

5'6"

b. Sheffield, 4 September 1966

Career: Manchester City jnr April 1983, prof Sept 1983 (Finn Harps loan 1984–85)/Barnsley Aug 1986 free/Portsmouth March 1989 £300,000/UNITED June 1992 £650,000/Southampton Feb 1998 £1.3m (Birmingham City loan 1999-2000)/Retired due to injury May 2000/ Ossett Town June 2001/Alfreton Town Feb 2002/Halifax Town July 2002/ Worksop Town/Occasional local football in Yorkshire.

When John Beresford made the long trip from Portsmouth to Tyneside, he quickly became one of the Magpies most consistent players. With an attacking flair from his left-back position, he immediately was a hit with the Gallowgate crowd as the Magpies lifted the Division One crown. The Yorkshireman had almost signed for

Liverpool before heading to team up with Kevin Keegan, but once the Anfield deal fell through due to a medical, the Magpies stepped in and neither club nor player regretted the move. It was with Barnsley that Beresford became a first-team regular after being shown the door at Maine Road by Billy McNeill, and following over 100 games for Pompey, including their run to the FA Cup semi-final (missing a spot-kick in a penalty shoot-out), had become hot property. A former England youth skipper, John was included in both Graham Taylor's and Terry Venables' England squads and was on the fringe of a full cap, on the bench as substitute in 1995. A gutsy defender with a cultured left-foot, the full-back was always comfortable on the ball and committed to United's cause. Nicknamed 'Bez', he spent almost six years on Tyneside and once described his stay at St James' Park as a "dream", an influential part of the Entertainers line-up. John also tasted Champions League football with United, finding the net more than once, before moving back to the south coast with Southampton following a fall-out with new boss Kenny Dalglish over a rotation selection policy. After a cruciate ligament knee injury wrecked his senior career when aged 33, John then set up a fantasy football site, entered the media, became a director for BBJ Northern shop-fitting company and regularly was seen at St James' Park in a hospitality role. With Southampton and Liverpool for trials as a schoolboy, John's father appeared for Notts County and Chesterfield while his cousin Mitch Ward appeared for Sheffield United and Everton. His son Billy Beresford was on the Blades books and joined Scunthorpe in 2012.

Appearances & Goals:
Debut v Southend United (h) 15 August 1992
FL/PL: 176(3) app 3 gls
FAC: 17(1) app 1 gl
FLC: 17 app 0 gls
Euro: 14(1) app 4 gls
Others: 3 app 0 gls
Total: 227(5) app 8 gls

Honours:
2 Eng B app 1994-95/Eng sch-youth app/FL div 1 champs 1993/PL runner-up 1996, 1997/PFA ToS (d1) 1993, (d2) 1992.

BERNARD Olivier Jimmy Wilfred 2000-2005, 2006-2007

Left-back
5'9"
b. Paris (France), 14 October 1979
Career: Olym Lyonnais jnr (Fr) 1998/UNITED Sept 2000 £45,870 (Darlington loan 2000-01)/ Southampton Jan 2005/Birmingham City trial cs 2005/Bolton Wand trial cs 2005/Rangers Sept 2005 free/Sheffield Utd trial July 2006/UNITED Sept 2006 free to June 2007/Toronto (Can) trial May 2008/Retired due to injury 2008/ Durham City owner & Chairman Dec 2013.

As a teenager Olivier Bernard found it hard to fully break into the Lyon first-team picture, the French club during the first decade of the Millennium dominating Le Championnat. As a result, Bernard looked elsewhere to develop his career, heading to the North East at the start of the 2000-01 season, a move which triggered a long-running dispute between United and the French authorities over the transfer; some years later United being forced to pay a modest amount after debates within FIFA, the French Courts and European Court of Justice. Small but stocky with a powerful frame and tenacious with it, Olivier was handed the left-back role, replacing Robbie Elliott for season 2002-03 after a year of largely coming off the bench and a period learning the English way at Darlington. He was something of a revelation, a real find and did not look out of place in a star-studded United eleven. Manager Bobby Robson liked his tough application and forays down the left flank, linking with fellow countryman Laurent Robert to good effect. Bernard was the manager's first choice and his career looked like going all the way to the top. He reached the fringe of a full international call-up at the start of the 2004-05 season, just missing out on final selection, then injury in that season, followed by a change in boss, halted the Frenchman's rise. In dispute with the club over contract terms, Graeme Souness selected his experienced new purchase Babayaro ahead of him and Bernard was soon looking for a new club. The Frenchman headed for Southampton and a spiral downwards from the heights of the Champions League in a black-and-white shirt. Injury and illness did not help, Bernard tried to raise his game at Ibrox

and he returned to St James' Park in 2006, but was not fit and not the same player. He soon quit the game struggling with a hip injury. Later Olivier went into business in Newcastle, opening a fast-food outlet in 2008 as well as coaching in the region and working in the football media. At the end of 2013, Bernard acquired Northern League club Durham City with the aim of developing the Citizens into a major feeder base for the North East's senior teams.

Appearances & Goals:
Debut v Sporting Lokeren SNW (h) 21 July 2001 (sub) (ITC)
PL: 82(20) app 6 gls
FAC: 5 app 0 gls
FLC: 6 app 0 gls
Euro: 26(6) app 0 gls
Total: 119(26) app 6 gls

Honours:
Fr sch-youth app.

BERTRAM William 1920-1921

Inside-left
5'7"
b. Brandon, Co Durham, 31 December 1897
d. Crossgate, Co Durham, 27 October 1962
Career: Browney Colliery/Durham City amat 1919/ UNITED April 1920 £150/Norwich City May 1921 £150/ Leadgate Park Aug 1922/ Durham City Jan 1923/ Rochdale May 1925/ Accrington Stanley Oct 1931.

Never able to break fully into United's senior line-up during the immediate years following World War One, Willie Bertram appeared in the last three games of the 1919-20 season. An accomplished player nevertheless, a schemer with a good touch on the ball, in the same mould as future star, Terry Hibbitt. His career began with Durham City's Northern Victory League side before joining United but, it was with a second spell at Durham, during their Football League days that Bertram became a noted star at that level. He made 105 appearances in an attacking midfield role as City competed with the likes of Wolves and Grimsby. Willie then moved to Rochdale and had a fine spell over six seasons at Spotland, totalling over 200 matches for the Lancashire club, netting frequently in their colours, 74 senior goals. A pocket dynamo in midfield, Bertram served in the Durham Light Infantry during the war, and on retiring from the game returned to County Durham where he became a publican. His younger brother George started at Durham City too and pulled on the colours of several clubs including Brentford and Fulham.

Appearances & Goals:
Debut v Manchester City (h) 17 April 1920
FL: 3 app 0 gls
Total: 3 app 0 gls

BEST Jeremiah 1919-1920

Outside-left
5'9"
b. Mickley, Northumberland, 23 January 1901
d. Darlington, 10 February 1975
Career: Mickley/South Shields Nov 1919/Mickley CW Dec 1919/UNITED Dec 1919 £100/Leeds Utd July 1920 £100/ North Eastern League football, probably Mickley 1921/ Providence Clamdiggers (USA) Sept 1924/New Bedford Whalers (USA) 1925/Fall River Marksmen (USA) Nov 1929/Pawtucket Rangers (USA) Sept 1930/New Bedford Whalers (USA) 1930/Clapton Orient Aug 1931/Darlington Oct 1933/Hull City Oct 1936/Hexham cs 1937.

Jerry hailed from a local footballing family of which several relations graced the Football League and non-league circuit during the inter-war years, notably Sunderland's Bobby Best. A fast winger with good control, Best rivalled Alex Ramsay for a season as a youngster with lots of promise, but United's management only gave him two opportunities to impress during the first season after the First World War. A versatile player, operating at centre-forward and inside-left too, Jerry moved on soon after and was very popular at Feethams scoring 80 goals in 124 games for Darlington. With the Quakers, Best became one of the first winners of the Third Division (North) Cup in 1934 and during the following season he netted 34 goals in only 37 outings. He later resided in that area, and was one of several inter-war players to sample North America's early experiments with association football, totalling impressive stats of 135 goals in a little over 230 games over seven seasons. Best had appeared in Leeds United's first ever Football League fixture during 1920. Apart from his direct football relatives, United's Bobby Hewison (qv) married into the Best family, and Joe Wilson (qv) was also part of the wider clan. It was quite a family steeped in local football.

Appearances & Goals:
Debut v Blackburn Rovers (h) 6 March 1920
(v Hartlepools Utd (h) 11 January 1919 (NVL))
FL: 2 app 0 gls
War: 1 app 0 gls
Total: 3 app 0 gls

Honours:
FL div 3(N) Cup winner 1934.

BEST Leon Julian Brendan 2010-2012

Striker
6'1"
b. St Anne's, Nottingham,
19 September 1986

Career: Lourdes Celtic (Dublin)/Notts Co jnr/ Southampton 2004 (Queens Park Rangers loan 2004-05)(Sheffield Wed loan 2005-06) (Bournemouth loan 2006-07) (Yeovil Town loan 2006-07)/Coventry City July 2007 £650,000/UNITED Feb 2010 £1.5m/Blackburn Rovers July 2012 £3m (Sheffield Wed loan 2013-14)(Derby Co loan 2014-15).

Capped by the Republic of Ireland, 23-year-old striker Leon Best was brought to St. James' Park by boss Chris Hughton during February 2010 to boost the club's striking options. Born and raised on a tough St Anne's Estate in Nottingham with an Irish background, having lived in Dublin as a youngster, Best was part of the Southampton eleven alongside Bale and Walcott which lost the 2005 FA Youth Cup final. Making his senior bow as a teenager against the Magpies in 2004, his career though stuttered with the Saints yet moving to Coventry he more frequently showed good form in the sky-blue shirt of City; 23 goals in 104 games. On Tyneside, Leon was soon dubbed with the nickname of 'Geordie Best' by the Toon crowd and when fit, and on a run of games, was a deadly striker in the box at times. Injury though did not help Leon, out when a United player for lengthy spells due to ankle and medial ligament problems. Deemed not quite good enough by some to be a top Premiership striker, including United's management when he was transfer-listed, Best's goals per game ratio remained sound. Netting 10 in 46 outings in black-and-white colours was a decent record, and this return won over many United fans that had been less than impressed when he first pulled on the shirt. His positional sense in the box was good and Leon was a battler for the high ball. Although he had a run in the side as United returned to the Premier League for season 2010-11, Best was always destined to be replaced by manager Alan Pardew, who soon brought in both Ba and Cisse. He moved to relegated Blackburn but was unfortunate to suffer a cruciate injury and was to miss the majority of the 2012-13 season.

Appearances & Goals:
Debut v Cardiff City (h) 5 February 2010
FL/PL: 31(11) app 10 gls
FAC: 3 app 0 gls
FLC: 1 app 0 gls
Total: 35(11) app 10 gls

Honours:
7 Eire caps 2009-date/1 Eire u21 app 2009/Eire sch-youth app/FL ch winner 2010.

BETTON Alexander 1931-1934

Centre-half
6'0"
b. New Tupton, Derbyshire, 28 November 1903
d. Scarborough, 19 July 1965

Career: New Tupton Ivanhoe/Chesterfield May 1926/ Scarborough June 1929/UNITED Jan 1931 £500/ Stockport Co June 1934 £600 to c1935 when he retired due to injury/Scarborough trainer cs 1936, later becoming asst-trainer to c1964.

Within a few short weeks of showing up well in Scarborough's FA Cup success during 1930-31, Alec Betton made the leap from Midland League football obscurity to the big-time. He had lifted the league title with Boro in 1930 and was a solid non-league defender, a very effective left-back or stopper who possessed long legs and a powerful frame. On Tyneside Betton was seen very much as a centre-back who replaced Dave Davidson after the Magpies' Wembley success in 1932. Alec was commanding in the air and for a season with United, 1932-33, few centre-forwards got the better of him. Yet the following campaign saw United fail to survive a relegation fight and Betton lost his place. Biographies of the era note Alec as an honourable and sporting defender, who on Tyneside never received credit from his critics. Betton had been a former pit-boy in Derbyshire and later was associated with Scarborough for over 25 years behind the scenes. His brother Fred was on Chesterfield's books for a period.

Appearances & Goals:
Debut v West Ham United (a) 26 January 1931
FL: 61 app 1 gl
FAC: 2 app 0 gls
Total: 63 app 1 gl

BEYE Habib 2007-2009

Right-back
6'0"
b. Suresnes, Paris (France), 19 October 1977

Career: Paris St-Germain (Fr) jnr 1997/RC Strasbourg (Fr) cs 1998/Olym Marseille (Fr) Aug 2003 £2.1/UNITED Aug 2007 £2m/ Aston Villa Aug 2009 £3m/Doncaster Rovers loan Nov 2011, pmt Feb 2012 to July 2012.

At Marseille's Stade Velodrome, Habib Beye was skipper and recognised as one of the best full-backs in Le Championnat. Born in a fashionable suburb of Paris with a Senegalese background, Habib clocked up almost 150 games for the Provence giants and had played European football on a regular basis; including against United in the UEFA Cup semi-final of 2004. One of a large group of players from France to serve United in the modern era, he moved to Gallowgate as a 29-year-old for the start of the 2007-08 season for what looked a bargain fee of £2m. Described as a "pure athlete", Habib was upright and classy on the ball at right-back, he took over from Stephen Carr and was an impressive performer during his debut season, quick to make forays into the opponents' defensive heart. Badly injured with a reckless tackle by Wigan's Lee Cattermole as the following season got underway, Beye was in the treatment room for three months. He returned to see the Black'n'Whites in dire trouble at the wrong end of the table then picked up a hamstring injury. Like many in that 2008-09 season, his form suffered as relegation came closer and closer. With United facing Championship level football, several high wage earners were off-loaded during the close-season of 2009 and Beye moved to Villa Park but surprisingly rarely figured in the claret-and-blue. His career nose-dived in England and he was released by the Midland club, finding a place at struggling Championship club Doncaster Rovers where his agent was involved in the managerial set-up. At the height of his career Habib collected 35 caps and reached the World Cup quarter-final with the Senegalese Lions in 2002. Returning to France, Beye entered the media, notably with Canal+ commentating of Premier League and Ligue 1 fixtures.

Appearances & Goals:
Debut v Derby County (a) 17 September 2007 (sub)
PL: 49(3) app 1 gl
FLC: 2 app 0 gls
Total: 51(3) app 1 gl

Honours:
35 Seng caps 2001-08/WdC 2002/Fr Cup winner 2001/Fr Cup final 2006, 2007/FLC final 2010 (sub no app)/UEFAC final 2004.

BIGIRIMANA Gael 2012-date

Midfield
5'9"
b. Bujumbura (Burundi), 22 October 1993

Career: African Tigers (Ugd) c2002/Coventry City jnr 2004, prof cs 2011/UNITED July 2012 £1m.

Gael Bigirimana arrived in England during 2004 as an 11-year-old, a refugee with his family from war-torn Burundi, and having spent some time living in Uganda. Settling in the Midlands, as a raw kid he landed at Coventry City's training ground door without boots or kit and asked for a trial; remarkably the youngster impressed and earned a contract. Bigirimana was encouraged and coached by Sky Blue's staff he responded quickly. Gael soon became part of the first-team squad and made his senior debut when 17 years of age during August 2011 in Championship action. Making an impact over season 2011-12, the Black'n'Whites watched him, stepping in with a bid of around £1m to the struggling Midlanders during the summer of 2012. Small and full of energy in midfield, the teenager soon received a call-up to United's Europa League games, taking the central anchor role in Newcastle's midfield. Nicknamed 'Little Cheick' at St James' Park, being a player of similar style to Cheick Tiote, the African showed much potential with a mature temperament for such an inexperienced youngster. He was born on the shores of Lake Tanganyika.

Appearances & Goals:
Debut v Atromitos (a) 23 August 2012 (EL)
PL: 3(10) app 1 gl
FAC: 1 app 0 gls
FLC: 1(1) app 0 gls
Euro: 8(2) app 0 gls
Total: 13(13) app 1 gl

Honours:
Eng sch-youth app.

BILLINGTON Hugh John Richard 1940-1941

Centre-forward
5'9"
b. Ampthill, Bedfordshire,
24 February 1916
d. Luton, 1988

Career: Luton Cocoa Works/Chapel St Methodists/ Waterlows/Luton Town May 1938 (UNITED war-guest 1940-41)(York City war-guest 1943-44)/ Chelsea March 1948 £8,000/Worcester City Aug 1951/Retired April 1953.

Hugh Billington was a potent centre-forward just coming to his peak when the Second World War began. He was especially prominent for Luton Town where in all first-eleven games (including wartime) he grabbed 150 goals in only 160 matches. Billington also showed up well after the Second World War when he appeared in the blue shirt of Chelsea. With a record of 32 goals in 90 appearances for the Stamford Bridge club, Hugh ended his long career on a high note. Having a terrific shot, he collected many of his goals from long range efforts and during his brief period at St James' Park also had a first-class tally. Not of big build, Billington was only 5'9", but was strong, fast and deadly with his shooting. Consequently he caused all sorts of problems for defenders.

Appearances & Goals:
Debut v Bradford Park Avenue (a) 26 October 1940 (FLN) (1 goal)
War: 4 app 3 gls
Total: 4 app 3 gls

BIRD John Charles 1975-1980

Centre-half
6'0"
b. Rossington, near Doncaster, 9 June 1946

Career: Doncaster Utd/Doncaster Rovers March 1967/Preston North End March 1971 £6,000/ UNITED Aug 1975 cash-exch for A Bruce/ Hartlepool Utd May 1980 free, becoming player-coach cs 1983 and manager Oct 1986/York City manager Oct 1988 to Oct 1991/Doncaster Rovers coach 1992/Halifax Town manager Feb 1994 to March 1996.

The purchase of John Bird was clouded in controversy when Preston officials sold their star player and captain against the wishes of their manager, Bobby Charlton. The famous ex-England player resigned in protest, yet Bird arrived at St James' Park nevertheless and took time to settle in the First Division, finding the transition from the lower divisions a handful at first. With almost 200 games for Preston to his name, he had a torrid debut at Maine Road; United losing 4-0, but the Yorkshireman quickly came to grips with Newcastle's defence. Bird eventually replaced Glenn Keeley at centre-half and on occasion looked a solid defender, especially during season 1978-79 following United's relegation from Division One. Often sidelined through injury however, John was replaced by the arrival of Stuart Boam and the development of local youngster David Barton. He concluded his career with Hartlepool in 155 matches, John took part in two title winning sides without qualifying for medals with Doncaster and Preston. Following a period as a boss in the lower divisions, Bird turned his back on the game to concentrate on his pastime of sketching and painting which he used as relaxation when a player. John became an accomplished artist, setting up his own studio and gallery, Era Prints, based in Bawtry near his home town of Doncaster.

Appearances & Goals:
Debut v Manchester City (a) 30 August 1975
FL: 84(3) app 5 gls
FAC: 4 app 1 gl
FLC: 4 app 0 gls
Euro: 1(1) app 0 gls
Others: 2 app 0 gls
Total: 95(4) app 6 gls

Honours:
FL div 3 champs 1971 (7 app)/FL div 4 champs 1969 (9 app).

BIRKETT Ralph James Evans 1938-1941

Outside-right
5'9"
b. Newton Abbot, Devon, 9 January 1913
d. Torquay, 8 July 2002

Career: Dartmouth Utd/Torquay Utd amat Aug 1929, prof March 1930/Arsenal April 1933 £1,588/Middlesbrough March 1935 £5,900/UNITED Aug 1938 £5,900 to 1941 (Darlington war-guest 1939-40, 1945-46)(Fulham war-guest 1940-41) (Chester war-guest 1941-42) (Middlesbrough war-guest 1941-42) (Chelsea war-guest 1942-43)(Reading war-guest 1942-43)(Torquay Utd war-guest 1945-46).

Ralph Birkett was an outstanding schoolboy prospect, proficient at football and cricket in his native Devon. He was introduced to the senior game as a 17-year-old at Torquay and soon attracted the attention of major clubs, including the team of the era, Arsenal. A regular scorer from the wing during his entire career, by the time Ralph appeared for the Magpies he had built a reputation as a quality First Division player. Signing for United when they were rebuilding to make a push to return

B

to Division One, Birkett was re-united at St James' Park with his former Arsenal international colleague and close friend, Ray Bowden. Stan Seymour had envisaged that the pairing was to be United's cutting edge, but the Second World War put a swift end to such plans. Possessing a powerful shot, being direct and fast, the ever-cheerful Ralph was capped when at Ayresome Park and was extremely popular on Teesside making just over 100 appearances and scoring 36 goals. He had formed an exciting forward line at Middlesbrough alongside Wilf Mannion and George Camsell and when he joined United supporters of Boro were dismayed. During the Second World War Ralph served as an Army PT instructor, and although he was in India for a time, Birkett also played for several clubs as a guest when stationed in England. After conflict Ralph ran a pub in Thornaby, the Oddfellows Arms, before setting up a haulage business in the South West. For many years Birkett resided in Brixham, Devon.

Appearances & Goals:
Debut v Plymouth Argyle (h) 27 August 1938 (1 goal)
FL: 23 app 3 gls
FAC: 3 app 0 gls
War: 39 app 12 gls
Total: 65 app 15 gls
(Void FL: 1 app 0 gls)

Honours:
1 Eng cap 1936/1 Eng war app 1941/2 FL app 1936-37/Eng trial app 1936/FL champs 1934, 1935 (4 app).

BIRNIE Edward Lawson 1898-1905

Half-back
5'10"
b. Sunderland, 25 August 1878
d. Southend, 22 December 1935

Career: Sunderland Seaburn/UNITED June 1898/ Crystal Palace May 1905/Chelsea Aug 1906 £100/ Tottenham Hotspur July 1910/Mulheim (Ger) player-trainer Aug 1911/Newcastle City Oct 1911//Rochdale July 1912/Leyton player-manager July 1914/ Newcastle City during World War One/Sunderland asst-trainer & chief scout Aug 1919/Rochdale trainer June 1921/Southend Utd manager Jan 1922 to May 1934/Germany coaching/Newcastle City player-manager 1926.

Newcastle United's utility reserve player during the early years of the century, Ted Birnie played in six different positions for the Magpies during his 20 games. His opportunities in the First Division were spread over six seasons; included were full-back, outside-left, centre-forward and in his more accustomed midfield role. Ted was a key figure in United's Northern League title winning sides of 1903, 1904 and 1905, while he never let Newcastle's first-team down when called upon. Described in press reports as a "cultured player", Birnie looked leisurely at times, had good command of the ball and was an intelligent player who rarely wasted possession. After leaving St James' Park he became an exemplary skipper of Crystal Palace during their Southern League days then had a good spell at Stamford Bridge where he became a tremendous asset to Chelsea's promotion side as they reached the top level for the first time, clocking up 108 games for the Pensioners, before his playing career was disrupted by a broken leg. Birnie was also noted as one of Southend's most successful managers, being in charge in Essex for over a decade. During his early career the Wearsider represented Northumberland on more than one occasion when training as an engineer in the North East.

Appearances & Goals:
Debut v Notts County (h) 17 September 1898
FL: 19 app 0 gls
FAC: 1 app 0 gls
Total: 20 app 0 gls

Honours:
FL div 2 prom 1907.

BLACK Neville 1947-1953

Inside-left
5'11"
b. Pegswood, Northumberland, 19 June 1931
d. [Pegswood], Northumberland, August 2004

Career: Pegswood/UNITED amat Nov 1947, prof Sept 1949/Exeter City Jan 1953 £250/Rochdale July 1953 to cs 1956/Ashington.

Neville Black's only appearance with senior company was in the 1952 FA Charity Shield clash against Manchester United at Old Trafford when George Hannah was injured. A tall inside-forward who was described as having "great promise", Black possessed a turn of speed that troubled defenders. Following his debut the local press remarked that Stan Seymour had, "a fatherly talk with the lad and gave him an expert critique". Due to the mass of stars at St James' Park though during that era, Neville never reached the first-eleven again, although he did well at Rochdale claiming 63 senior appearances, a regular in their Third Division line-up for three seasons.

Appearances & Goals:
Debut v Manchester United (a) 24 September 1952 (CS)
Others: 1 app 0 gls
Total: 1 app 0 gls

BLACKBURN Maurice David 1938-1941

Inside-right
5'5"
b. Prudhoe, Northumberland, 13 November 1920
d. Newcastle upon Tyne, 4 April 1996

Career: Backworth/Chopwell CW/UNITED amat Oct 1938 to Aug 1941.

A local pit-worker at Chopwell, Maurice Blackburn was unlucky to be spotted by the club playing for his colliery side just prior to the outbreak of World War Two. Joining the club as an amateur, the diminutive schemer appeared for the Black'n'Whites in wartime football, scoring on his debut against Leeds during June 1940. Blackburn didn't resume his career on the cessation of hostilities in 1945, although it appears he did some scouting for Exeter City. He resumed work in the region's coalfield after the Second World War.

Appearances & Goals:
Debut v Leeds United (a) 8 June 1940 (FLN) (1 goal)
War: 12 app 1 gl
Total: 12 app 1 gl

BLACKBURN Robert 1906-1908

Outside-right
5'8"
b. Edinburgh, 26 November 1882

Career: St Johnstone/Heart of Midlothian Jan 1902/Raith Rovers July 1903/Hamilton Acc Aug 1904/Leith Ath June 1905/UNITED May 1906 free/Aberdeen July 1908/Grimsby Town May 1909 to May 1910.

As one contemporary report noted, Robert Blackburn possessed, "speed, dash and cleverness". He was a deputy to the great Jackie Rutherford at Gallowgate, gaining a call-up to senior action on three occasions in 1906-07 as the Magpies lifted the league crown, and twice in 1907-08. Blackburn performed well in the club's reserve side which picked up the North Eastern League title in both of those seasons, but the small and stocky Caledonian did not have much hope in displacing United's immense wall of international talent at St James' Park. He packed a stinging shot and moved back to Scotland to appear for Aberdeen. His record north of the Cheviots was decent; 95 matches and 26 goals in senior football.

Appearances & Goals:
Debut v Sheffield Wednesday (a) 3 September 1906
FL: 5 app 0 gls
Total: 5 app 0 gls

Honours:
FL champs 1907 (3 app)/SL div 2 champs 1906.

BLACKETT Francis Brindley 1887-1892

Forward
b. St Peter's, Newcastle upon Tyne, 18 January 1869

Career: EAST END June 1887 to Jan 1892/Also North Sands Rovers guest 1888 & Raby Rovers between 1885 and 1890.

One of five Blackett brothers, four to play local football for Newcastle East End as United's pioneers developed the club on Victorian Tyneside. Frank was born and bred in the club's birthplace of St Peter's alongside the River Tyne. He is recorded to have first appeared for the club in the Temperance Festival on the Town Moor during June 1887. He became a regular with East End Swifts in various forward-line positions and graduated to the senior line-up for season 1887-88. Blackett took part in the club's Northern League campaign of 1889-90. By season 1891-92 he was turning out for East End Amateurs (the club's reserve side) until they were disbanded in January. Frank also played cricket locally like many early footballers, appearing for Raby Rovers CC. He was a boilermaker by trade. Frank's brother William (qv) also played senior football for the club, while John Blackett (qv) turned out in friendly action and the youngest of the family, Joseph, was in the reserve ranks before moving south to earn a level of success with Wolves.

Appearances & Goals:
Debut v Auckland Town (a) 21 December 1889 (NL)
NL: 2 app 0 gls
Total: 2 app 0 gls

BLACKETT William 1883-1890

Forward or Half-back
b. St Peter's, Newcastle upon Tyne, 21 July 1866

Career: EAST END Oct 1883 (appeared occasionally for Raby Rovers 1885-86)/ Barrow Nov 1888/EAST END again by Feb 1889 to 1890.

Capped a number of times for the Northumberland side when inter-county football was an important representative fixture in the region, William Blackett was a well respected player, also appearing for a select Newcastle & District eleven which faced up to The Corinthians in 1887. He served East End at wing-half with honour for six years, his first appearance being against Prudhoe Rovers in 1883 going on to total over 70 matches in all games. William then became a regular over seasons between 1885-86 to 1887-88, appearing in plenty of friendly matches for East End. Raised in the Byker district like so many of the club's early players, he was a waterman on the Tyne. Blackett left the area for a short spell, perhaps working away, when he appeared for Barrow. William was the most prominent of the Blackett brothers locally, although the youngest Joseph made headlines elsewhere notably with Wolves. Blackett played cricket in the summer months for Priory Park and St Luke's.

Appearances & Goals:
Debut v South Bank (a) 15 October 1887 (FACQ)
NL: 1 app 0 gls
FAC: 1 app 0 gls
Total: 2 app 0 gls

BLACKHALL Raymond 1972-1978

Right-back
5'9"
b. Ashington, 19 February 1957

Career: UNITED jnr March 1972, prof Aug 1974/Sheffield Wed Aug 1978 £20,000/IK Tord (Swd) free July 1982/Mansfield Town Oct 1982 to May 1983/Carlisle Utd trial cs 1984/Blyth Spartans Sept 1984.

Nicknamed 'Bomber', Ray Blackhall was developed by Newcastle United through the junior sides and broke initially into the first-eleven during season 1974-75 and more permanently in 1976-77. He was a tough tackling defender who liked to go forward and who improved rapidly the more he played in United's First Division side. Ray was also given a midfield role for the Black'n'Whites and was often on call as substitute on the bench. Released after relegation to the Second Division in 1978, Blackhall then flourished under the guidance of Jack Charlton at Hillsborough where he made 140 outings for Sheffield Wednesday,

being a regular when The Owls regained their Second Division status in season 1979-80. After leaving the game Blackhall worked for a period in the steel industry before deciding to head south and join the Metropolitan Police, becoming part of the Diplomatic Protection unit in Kensington until retirement from the force.

Appearances & Goals:
Debut v Arsenal (a) 18 March 1975
FL: 26(11) app 0 gls
FAC: 5(1) app 2 gls
FLC: 0(1) app 0 gls
Euro: 1 app 0 gls
Others: 1(1) app 0 gls
Total: 33(14) app 2 gls

Honours
FL div 3 prom 1980.

BLACKLEY John Henderson 1977-1979

Centre-half
5'10"
b. Westquarter, near Falkirk, 12 May 1948

Career: Bo'ness Utd/Gairdoch Utd/Hibernian June 1965/UNITED Oct 1977 £100,000/Preston North End July 1979 free/Hamilton Acc Oct 1981, becoming player-manager Oct 1982/ Hibernian asst-manager May 1983, becoming manager Oct 1984 to Nov 1986/Cowdenbeath manager Oct 1987/ Dundee asst-manager Sept 1988, becoming caretaker-manager May to Aug 1991 and asst-manager again/ St Johnstone coach Nov 1993/Dundee Utd asst-manager Sept 1998/Plymouth Argyle coach Sept 2002/Sheffield Wed coach Sept 2004 to Oct 2006/Swindon Town coach Nov 2006/Plymouth Argyle coach 2008 to Oct 2009/Stirling Albion asst-manager Jan 2011 to Dec 2011/ Thereafter working in development coaching roles in Scottish football and as a Scottish Premier League delegate.

In over a decade operating on the Scottish beat, John Blackley was recognised as one of Scotland's most accomplished players. Able to read the game, John was cool and assured, a skilful centre-half but tough and robust as well, who liked to play alongside a big partner in the middle of the back four. Blackley had the ability to set attacks moving with accurate distribution and the vision of a midfield player. On several occasions during the Seventies decade the Scot had been linked with big moves south of the border, including with United's boss Joe Harvey, before he eventually moved to England after more than ten years and over 400 games for Hibs, being purchased by one of Harvey's successors, Richard Dinnis at a time of crisis at St James' Park. By then he was 29 years old and reaching the end of his playing career and he displayed an almost casual and arrogant approach to the game which gave United's back-line a touch of class. The Scot was a first-class organiser in defence and at St James' Park United fans likened to his play almost immediately, voting him Player of the Year. But his undoubted talent was unable to halt a United slide which saw the club drop into the Second Division and thereafter Blackley was more often than not found in the treatment room. Nicknamed 'Sloop' north of the border after a Beach Boys hit song; he took part in Scotland's World Cup quest during 1974 and skippered the Under-23 side. Moving into a coaching role, he teamed up with Scotland colleague Paul Sturrock at several clubs for a lengthy period.

Appearances & Goals:
Debut v Derby County (h) 8 October 1977
FL: 46 app 0 gls
FAC: 5 app 0 gls
FLC: 1 app 0 gls
Total: 52 app 0 gls

Honours:
7 Scot caps 1974-77/WdC 1974/4 Scot u23 app 1970-71/1 SL app 1972/SLC winner 1973/SLC final 1969, 1975, 1986(m)/SC final 1972.

B

BLAKE Sydney 1905-1906, 1909-1914

Goalkeeper
5'10"
b. Whitley Bay, 1883
d. Coventry, 1929 (Q3)

Career: Willington Ath/Whitley Ath Oct 1904/UNITED Jan 1905/Queens Park Rangers May 1906/Whitley Ath Sept 1907/North Shields Ath March 1908/UNITED May 1909 £30/ Coventry City May 1914 free/Retired 1918/Coventry City trainer cs 1920 to c1922.

Although Syd Blake made his United debut at outside-left, he later changed his role into that of a goalkeeper and became a trustworthy and secure custodian. Unfortunately, during his stay with Newcastle United Syd had internationals in Albert Gosnell and Jimmy Lawrence as rivals in both positions and found getting chances in the senior team limited during his two spells at Gallowgate. Blake's best season with United was during 1911-12 when Lawrence was injured for 10 games. He tried his luck in the Southern League with QPR and Coventry City, during both clubs pre-Football League days. Syd settled in the Midlands and was Coventry's trainer after World War One. He once faced three penalty kicks for United against Manchester City during January 1912; and wasn't beaten, saving two, the other going wide!

Appearances & Goals:
Debut v Notts County (a) 14 April 1906
FL: 14 app 0 gls
FAC: 1 app 0 gls
Total: 15 app 0 gls

BLANTHORNE Robert 1908-1910

Centre-forward
6'1"
b. Neston, Cheshire, 8 January 1884
d. Rock Ferry, Cheshire, March 1965

Career: Rock Ferry/Birkenhead/Liverpool Nov 1905/ Grimsby Town Oct 1907/UNITED May 1908 £350/ Hartlepools Utd Dec 1910 free/Tranmere Rovers July 1912.

Signed as a replacement for the popular Bill Appleyard during the summer of 1908, Bob Blanthorne had cruel luck in United colours. On his very first appearance, and as it turned out his only outing, he broke his leg and was out of action for almost a year. The new arrival collided with Bradford City right-back Campbell and sustained a double fracture during the second-half of the match at Gallowgate. It was a bad break and ruined his career albeit his single match for the Geordies was in the title winning season. Bob had impressed United's directors after grabbing 21 goals in 33 matches for the Mariners, including five in one FA Cup match against Carlisle. Well built in the Appleyard mould, he stood over six feet tall and was a most assertive leader who could have become quite a star in a black-and-white shirt. After his injury Blanthorne was never the same marksman again, and by the time he was nearing fitness, United had completed the signing of England leader Albert Shepherd. He tried to resurrect his career at both Hartlepool and Tranmere without luck; being injured again wearing 'Pool's blue-and-white. When Bob started out in the game, he was working as a bricklayer and playing as a defender rather than a striker. He only appeared twice for Liverpool before moving to Grimsby.

Appearances & Goals:
Debut v Bradford City (h) 2 September 1908
FL: 1 app 0 gls
Total: 1 app 0 gls

Honours:
FL champs 1909 (1 app).

BLYTH Thomas Hope 1896-1898

Centre-forward
6'0"
b. Seaham Harbour, near Sunderland, 16 October 1876
d. Ryhope, near Sunderland, 16 December 1949

Career: Durham University/UNITED 1896/Sunderland Nomads/UNITED Jan 1897/ Hebburn Argyle May 1898/Later became Old Bedens (Sunderland) coach & Durham FA referee.

Thomas Blyth only had a brief stay with Newcastle United during the years leading up to the turn of the century. As understudy to top scorer Richard Smellie in United's Second Division team for season 1896-97, he was once called upon to lead the Magpies' attack. He did well, netting a goal in Newcastle's 2-1 victory over now defunct club, Burton Swifts in front of 4,000 at St James' Park. While he was on United's books, Blyth was training to become a teacher and attended the Universities of London and Durham. For many years he later was a chemistry master in Sunderland at the Bede School. Apart from his teaching profession, Blyth was also a Sunderland councillor, Freemason and keen sports enthusiast, as well as a life governor of Sunderland Orphanage. During World War One Blyth fought at Arras and Ypres as a signaller in a siege battery. Nicknamed 'Tosh' he lived on Wearside to his death.

Appearances & Goals:
Debut v Burton Swifts (h) 27 March 1897 (1 goal)
FL: 1 app 1 gl
Total: 1 app 1 gl

BOAM Stuart William 1979-1981

Centre-half
6'1"
b. Kirkby in Ashfield, near Mansfield, 28 January 1948

Career: Kirkby BC/Mansfield Town July 1966/Middlesbrough June 1971 £50,000/UNITED Aug 1979 £140,000/Mansfield Town player-manager July 1981 to Jan 1983/Hartlepool Utd March 1983/Guisborough Town player-manager Aug 1983/Occasional scout, including for Newcastle Utd 1989-90.

For eight years Stuart Boam had been the linchpin of Middlesbrough's defence at a time when the Teesside club possessed a fine side. Tall and commanding at centre-half, Boam was a formidable defender who alongside Willie Maddren was respected in First Division company. He appeared 393 times for the Reds and was once tipped for an England cap. When he headed the short journey north to join United, Stuart was over 31 years old, but still helped give a shaky Magpie back four experience and stability for two seasons in their bid to climb out of Division Two. Able to dominate a centre-forward and rugged with it, he was a born leader, Boam captaining all his clubs. He also possessed neat skills on the ball for a defender. After having been turned down by Nottingham Forest as a teenager, Stuart was recommended to his home town club, Mansfield by former United pre-war star Sammy Weaver. A former toolmaker, Boam proceeded to make a big name for himself with the Stags (215 app), and later managed the club too. Stuart afterwards resided in Kirkby and was employed as a manager for Kodak, later running a local newsagency and convenience store.

Appearances & Goals:
Debut v Chelsea (h) 1 September 1979
FL: 69 app 1 gl
FAC: 5 app 0 gls
FLC: 3 app 1 gl
Total: 77 app 2 gls

Honours:
FL div 2 champs 1974.

BODIN Paul John 1991-1992

Left-back
6'0"
b. Cardiff, 13 September 1964

Career: Chelsea amat 1981/Newport Co jnr 1981, prof Jan 1982/Cardiff City Aug 1982/Merthyr Tydfil Aug 1985/Bath City Aug 1985/Newport Co Jan 1988 £15,000/ Swindon Town March 1988 £30,000/Crystal Palace March 1991 £550,000 (UNITED loan Dec 1991 to Jan 1992)/ Swindon Town Jan 1992 £225,000/Reading July 1996 free (Wycombe Wand loan 1997-98)/Bath City player-manager April 1998, becoming manager June 1998 to May 2001/ Swindon Town asst-coach cs 2001, becoming caretaker-manager April 2011 and then Head of Coaching & Youth Development to June 2013.

Newcastle's supporters only saw a fleeting glimpse of Welsh international Paul Bodin during a month's loan deal during season 1991-92. He was tried by manager Ossie Ardiles for six games but, despite showing some exciting attacking ideas down the left touchline, wasn't offered a permanent deal. Returning to Crystal Palace, he quickly rejoined Swindon Town where he made his mark and displayed all his best football, being a regular for the Robins in almost 300 games. Bodin netted many goals in his career, several from the penalty spot, including the last-minute winner to gain the Wiltshire club promotion to the top flight in a thrilling 4-3 Wembley Play-Off victory over Leicester City in May 1993. He did, however, miss one crucial spot-kick for Wales in a World Cup qualifying tie during 1994 against Romania. His son Billy appeared for the Welsh Under-21 side when with Swindon.

Appearances & Goals:
Debut v Port Vale (h) 7 December 1991
FL: 6 app 0 gls
Total: 6 app 0 gls

Honours:
23 Wales caps 1990-95/1 Wales u21 app 1983/Wales sch-youth app/FL div 1 prom 1993/FL div 2 champs 1996/FL div 2 prom 1990 (later annulled)/FL div 3 prom 1983/PFA ToS (d2) 1991, 1996.

BOGIE Ian 1982-1989

Midfield
5'7"
b. Walker, Newcastle upon Tyne, 6 December 1967

Career: Wallsend BC/UNITED jnr Jan 1982, prof Dec 1985/ Preston North End Feb 1989 cash-exch for G Brazil/ Millwall Aug 1991 £145,000/Leyton Orient loan Oct 1993, pmt Dec 1993/Port Vale March 1995 £50,000/ Kidderminster Harriers Aug 2000 free/UNITED FiC coach Sept 2001/Bedlington Terriers Nov 2001 to cs 2004 when he retired/Walker Central manager cs 2004/Gateshead asst-manager cs 2006, becoming manager May 2007 to Dec 2012/Stockport Co manager March 2013 to Aug 2013/UNITED Academy part-time asst-coach 2014.

One of several bright young hopefuls that were developed through the club's youth policy during the Eighties, Ian Bogie was a midfield find with a sure touch on the ball and an eye for opening up defences in the mould of Paul Gascoigne, whom he had followed through the ranks. The media in fact dubbed the local lad, the new Gazza, but Bogie never lived up to that unfair billing. Small and stocky, he showed United's fans nice skills on his limited outings, but didn't stamp his authority on the game. Perhaps Ian was released too early by Newcastle as manager Jim Smith rarely gave youth a chance, many considering he should have been given an extended run in the side rather than the odd game and a handful of substitute run-ons. Bogie afterwards had a sound, if not spectacular, career in the lower divisions. He did well at Preston (91 app) and especially with Port Vale (181 app) where he was a midfield anchor for several seasons. During his period back on Tyneside after retiring as a player, Ian looked after the Tyne Metropolitan College coaching programme for a period and spent nearly five years as Gateshead boss.

Appearances & Goals:
Debut v Luton Town (a) 30 August 1986
FL: 7(7) app 0 gls
FAC: 1(2) app 0 gls
FLC: 0(1) app 0 gls
Others: 3(1) app 1 gl
Totals: 11(11) app 1 gl

Honours:
Eng sch-youth app/FAYC winner 1985 (sub no app)/PFA ToS (d2) 1994.

BOLTON Hugh 1905-1906

Inside-right
5'8"
b. Port Glasgow, 15 November 1879

Career: Clydeville/Port Glasgow Jnrs/Port Glasgow Ath April 1902 (Rangers loan 1903-04)/UNITED May 1905/Everton Jan 1906/Bradford Park Avenue Dec 1908/Morton Sept 1910/Glentoran 1912 to 1915/ Johnstone 1916.

Before moving to Tyneside Hugh Bolton was a regular in midfield for Port Glasgow's Scottish First Division line-up over three seasons and totalled 72 matches. Yet he appeared only once for United, during the 1905-06 season, as stand-in for established schemer Jimmy Howie. The young Scot was to be quickly picked up by United's main rivals during the Edwardian era, Everton, and amazingly faced the Magpies not only on his first appearance for the Merseysiders, but then in the same season's FA Cup final when he assisted Everton to victory. Hugh went onto become a favourite at Goodison Park turning out on 87 occasions for the Blues and always had an eye for the goal. Bolton could strike the ball hard and placed it accurately and netted 34 goals for Everton. He made a second successive FA Cup final appearance for the Toffees in 1907 but lost that final to Sheffield Wednesday.

Appearances & Goals:
Debut v Sheffield United (a) 2 December 1905
FL: 1 app 0 gls
Total: 1 app 0 gls

Honours:
FAC winner 1906/FAC final 1907.

BOOTH Curtis Thomas 1913-1920

Inside-left
5'11"
b. Gateshead, 12 October 1891
d. Amsterdam (Netherlands), 29 October 1949

Career: Wallsend Elm Villa/Choppington Utd/Wallsend Elm Villa/UNITED Nov 1913 £15 (Leeds City war-guest 1915-16)/Norwich City Sept 1920 £800/Accrington Stanley player-manager June 1923 to May 1924/SC Erfurt (Ger) June 1925/VfR Wormatia (Ger) trainer 1932 to 1934//Racing Club de Paris (Fr) 1934 to 1935/ Turkish FA head-coach Sept 1936/Later coaching on the Continent in the Netherlands and Egypt.

Curtis Booth was a popular local forward in North Eastern League soccer who earned a contract at St James' Park before the outbreak of the First World War. He was unfortunate to have just made the breakthrough at Gallowgate in season 1914-15 when the hostilities stopped his eye-catching progress. Booth served with the Durham Light Infantry and was injured fighting at Villers-Bretouneux near Amiens, but, once recovered he started brightly in the Magpies' side during the first season after peace was restored. One biography noted that Curtis "enjoyed the cut and thrust of the game" and was "fast, tricky, strong and able". Vying for the inside-forward position with another local product, Andy Smailes, he lost out and moved south to conclude his playing days with Norwich City and Accrington, where he was Stanley's first manager in the Football League. On his debut for the Lancashire club he had to retire after only 20 minutes due to a knee ligament problem, and he didn't play again. Booth later was a respected coach overseas, residing in the Netherlands to his death. He was known as Tommy later in his career.

Appearances & Goals:
Debut v Sheffield Wednesday (h) 9 September 1914
FL: 34 app 6 gls
War: 8 app 5 gls
Total: 42 app 11 gls

B

BOTT Wilfred E 1934-1936

Outside-right
5'7"
b. Featherstone, near Pontefract, 25 April 1907
d. Hastings, July 1992

Career: Yorkshire Main CW/Edlington CW/Doncaster Rovers March 1927/Huddersfield Town March 1931 £1,000/UNITED Dec 1934 £1,000 plus T Lang/Queens Park Rangers May 1936 £750 to 1941 (Aldershot war-guest 1939-40)(Brighton war-guest 1939-40)(Chelsea war-guest 1939-40)/Colchester Utd July 1946/Guildford City Oct 1946/Lancaster City c1947.

One joining United, Wilf Bott made immediate headlines with Newcastle United by striking a marvellous hat-trick on his first outing in a black-and-white shirt during a New Year's Day holiday fixture against Bury at Gallowgate. A flier, he was very fast and always willing to cut in from his wing berth and fire a shot at goal. With outstanding displays for Huddersfield over three-and-a-half seasons, totalling 26 goals in 115 games, including an important role in the Terriers' First Division runners-up spot during season 1933-34, Bott had caught the attention of several clubs. His 14 goals from the flank in 1933-34 prompted United to bring him to Tyneside due to that sort of goal scoring ability. He replaced the ageing Jimmy Boyd in United's side, but after only two seasons moved on, to join QPR where he became a terrace favourite, again grabbing goals from the wing, this time 42 in 102 appearances including war fixtures. During wartime football, Wilf represented the FA against the RAF.

Appearances & Goals:
Debut v Bury (h) 1 January 1935 (3 goals)
FL: 37 app 11 gls
FAC: 7 app 4 gls
Total: 44 app 15 gls

Honours:
1 FA app 1941.

BOTTOM Arthur Edwin 1958

Inside-right
5'10"
b. Sheffield, 28 February 1930
d. Sheffield, 18 April 2012

Career: Sheffield YMCA/Sheffield Utd amat May 1946, prof April 1947/York City June 1954/UNITED Feb 1958 £4,500/Chesterfield Nov 1958 £5,000/Boston Utd cs 1960/Alfreton Town 1960 to 1965.

Purchased during a time of crisis at St James' Park, Arthur Bottom gave excellent short term service to United when they were fighting to remain in the First Division during season 1957-58. He switched from the Third Division to the top level to good effect coming into the Magpies side when they were 19th in the table and immediately made an impact netting a brace of goals on his debut and five more for the rest of the season in only eight games. Bottom linked with Len White up front and effectively saved United from the drop. A battling, aggressive striker, with sometimes a short fuse, he was strong and forceful in attack and a legendary figure at Bootham Crescent, being York's goal-getter during their FA Cup exploits in the mid-Fifties. Arthur led the line when the Tykes reached the FA Cup semi-final in 1955 and faced the Black'n'Whites. They very nearly caused a huge upset by reaching Wembley and Bottom's display against United greatly impressed the club's directors. He possessed explosive shooting, scoring 105 goals in 158 senior outings for York and was the Third Division North's leading marksman in 1954-55 with 31 goals; still a club record for York, and he netted another eight goals in the FA Cup. Bottom was not favoured at Gallowgate by new boss Charlie Mitten and when United signed Welsh maestro Ivor Allchurch, Arthur found himself frozen out as the White-Eastham-Allchurch trio came together. He was unfortunate and moved on, although his tremendous goal-a-game record perhaps deserved better. Once a ball-boy at Bramall Lane; Bottom appeared on a handful of occasions as the Blades won promotion in 1953. After his football days, Arthur worked as a silversmith at a cutlery firm in Yorkshire and lived in his home town.

Appearances & Goals:
Debut v Everton (a) 22 February 1958 (2 goals)
FL: 11 app 10 gls
Total: 11 app 10 gls

Honours:
FL div 2 champs 1953 (6 app).

BOUMSONG Jean-Alain Somkomg 2005-2006

Centre-half
6'3"
b. Douala (Cameroon), 14 December 1979

Career: US Palaisau (Fr) 1993/Le Havre AC (Fr) 1995/Auxerre (Fr) July 2000/Rangers July 2004 free/UNITED Jan 2005 £8m/Juventus (It) Aug 2006 £3.26m/Olym Lyonnais (Fr) Jan 2008 £2m/Panathinaikos (Gr) July 2010 £800,000 to cs 2013 when he retired.

A substantial Graeme Souness purchase to replace Jonathan Woodgate during the January 2005 transfer window, Newcastle's boss went back to his former club Rangers to spend £8m on the 25-year-old French centre-half Jean-Alain Boumsong. Ironically only a matter of six months earlier, Newcastle's previous boss Bobby Robson was reported to have been offered the international defender on a free when the player was out of contract but chose to pass on the deal. Outstanding in the Scottish game, Jean partnered either Andy O'Brien, Titus Bramble, or later, Craig Moore, at the heart of the Black'n'Whites rearguard. Boumsong at times looked the cool and collected player he had shown in France, notably over 150 games for Auxerre where he tasted Champions League football. However, often he was caught, out of position, or left for dead by the pace and power of opponents in the Premier League. A gentleman and a highly intelligent one with a degree in mathematics, a series of lapses at the back were costly and Boumsong suffered at the hands of the media, with the intense television scrutiny of his defending proving to be somewhat cruel. A regular choice for a season-and-a-half, Jean was unfairly the scapegoat as United struggled in 2005-06 and moved back to the Continent during the close-season of 2006 when he joined demoted Italian giants Juventus, Newcastle taking a sizable £5m loss on what ended an expensive deal. In French football, where he had began his career after moving from Africa when 14 years of age, Boumsong won Le Championnat and the Coupe de France. He was capped by his country on 27 occasions including being involved in the 2006 World Cup final on the bench, before moving to Greece to win further domestic honours. On his retirement Jean-Alain worked on French television also co-owning a five-a-side centre in Paris. His cousin, David Ngog, signed for Liverpool and also appeared for Bolton, while his younger brother, Yannick Boumsong, turned out for Auxerre and CSKA Sofia.

Appearances & Goals:
Debut v Yeading (a) 9 January 2005 (FAC)
PL: 44(3) app 0 gls
FAC: 7 app 0 gls
FLC: 1 app 0 gls
Euro: 4 app 0 gls
Total: 56(3) app 0 gls

Honours:
27 Fr caps 2003-09/WdC final 2006 (sub no app)/21 Fr u21 app 1999-2002/Fr sch-youth app/SL champs 2005/Fr Lg champs 2008/It div 2 champs 2007/Fr Cup winner 2003, 2008/Gr Cup winner 2010.

BOWDEN Edwin Raymond 1937-1939

Inside-forward
5'10"
b. Looe, Cornwall, 13 September 1909
d. Plymouth, 23 September 1998

Career: Looe/Plymouth Argyle amat cs 1926, prof June 1927/Arsenal March 1933 £7,000/UNITED Nov 1937 £5,000/Retired Sept 1939.

A forward full of grace and style, Charlie Buchan noted Ray Bowden was, "a great player with the ball". Making his name in the fabulous Arsenal side of the Thirties, Bowden dovetailed so well with Joe Hume in the Gunners' line-up that they formed England's right flank too. He arrived at St James' Park late into his career, in a bid to revitalise a Magpie eleven who, up to his arrival, had made hard work of getting out of the Second Division. Having a presence on the field and appearing at both inside-left or right, despite being sidelined with injury as well as illness, Bowden certainly inspired United when he was in the mood, but like many of the stylish greats, lacked consistency. Of a rather frail physique, mild-tempered and a gentleman on the field, Ray oozed class and could turn a game with a single pass being unselfish with the ball. Ray grew up in a Cornish fishing village, as a teenager worked as a clerk in Plymouth and as a junior footballer scored 10 goals in one game and 100 in a season for Looe. He was immediately snapped up by his local club Argyle during the mid-Twenties. With the

Pilgrims he bagged almost 90 goals in 153 games and at Arsenal 48 in 138 matches, Bowden also scored a hat-trick on the very last day of his senior career, netting three for United against Swansea Town just prior to war being declared. Bowden was still registered with United for season 1945-46 but didn't return to action. He later ran sports outfitters business in Plymouth.

Appearances & Goals:
Debut v Southampton (h) 6 November 1937
FL: 48 app 6 gls
FAC: 4 app 0 gls
Total: 52 app 6 gls
(Void FL: 3 app 3 gls)

Honours:
6 Eng caps 1935-37/2 FL app 1935-36/1 unoff Eng app 1935/9 FA app 1931/Eng trial app 1937-38/FL champs 1933 (7 app), 1934, 1935, 1938/FL div 3(S) champs 1930/FAC winner 1936.

BOWMAN John 1893-1894

Outside-right
b. Scotland

Career: Dundee East End/UNITED Aug 1893 to 1894.

John Bowman played his early football alongside the Tay, with Dundee East End, one of the pioneer clubs of the present Dundee FC. He left for Tyneside just after they merged with Dundee Our Boys to form the new club and had been a regular at the Carolina Port ground during 1892-93. He was described in the Newcastle press on his arrival as being one of the best forwards on Tayside. John appeared only once for the Magpies, but in the historic inaugural Football League meeting with Arsenal that took place in the capital and ended in a 2-2 draw. Bowman did not stay in the North East long, leaving before United's first league season, 1893-94, was completed. He was a reserve for established forwards Crate and Quinn.

Appearances & Goals:
Debut v Woolwich Arsenal (a) 2 September 1893
FL: 1 app 0 gls
Total: 1 app 0 gls

BOWYER Lee David 2003-2006

Midfield
5'9"
b. Poplar, London, 3 January 1977

Career: Aztec Jnrs/Senrab Jnrs/Charlton Ath jnr, prof April 1994/Leeds Utd July 1996 £3.25m/West Ham Utd Jan 2003 £100,000/UNITED July 2003 free/West Ham Utd June 2006 £250,000/Birmingham City loan Jan 2009, pmt July 2009 free/Ipswich Town July 2011 free to June 2012.

One of group of talented former Leeds United players to serve Newcastle United in modern years, Lee Bowyer rediscovered his eye-catching play on Tyneside only in patches. A slightly-built midfielder who was strong in the tackle and resilient, qualities which had made him an exciting player at Elland Road for seven seasons. Reaching the Champions League semi-final with the Tykes and captain of England's under-21 side, Bowyer joined the Magpies after a short deal with West Ham United as part of the club's transfer activity during the summer of 2003, despite the fact he had been branded as something of a problem player after several incidents of ill-judgement and indiscipline. But Lee was determined to atone for past errors and recovering from an ankle injury when with the Hammers, as well as having to serve a lengthy UEFA ban received when playing for Leeds, the feisty attacking midfielder was a regular with the Magpies for three campaigns winning over much of United's support with gutsy performances. Competing for places with the likes of Speed, Dyer, Jenas and Solano, as well as Viana, Butt, Emre, Parker, and another Leeds player James Milner, Newcastle's management had plenty of talent to choose from. Bowyer gave the added option of a player always willing to do battle with opponents and also get into the box and test the 'keeper. Preferring a central role in midfield, but often played on the flank, Lee's best season was 2004-05 when he grabbed seven goals in Premier League and European action. Often to be embroiled in controversy during his career both on and off the field, he

was sent-off on four occasions in a Magpie shirt and was infamously involved in the St James' Park punch-up with teammate Kieron Dyer against Aston Villa during April 2005, all captured on television to a bemused audience. Earlier, with Charlton he became one of the first footballers to fall foul on the FA's drug-buster policy, and then when at Elland Road, Lee was charged with grievous bodily harm and race allegations along with colleague Jonathan Woodgate. Hull Crown Court cleared Bowyer of both charges after a controversial retrial in 2001 amidst huge publicity; a two-year ordeal. He was brought up on the mean streets of London's East End and was a product of the Senrab club, to have developed such other stars as Terry, Defoe, Wilkins and Sol Campbell. Bowyer then became a teenage star with Charlton before embarking on his career of fame and sometimes notoriety. His cousin Mark Noble also appeared for West Ham. On retirement from the game, Bowyer took time out and being a first-rate golfer attempted to qualify for the Open Golf Championship in 2012.

Appearances & Goals:
Debut v Leeds United (a) 17 August 2003
PL: 61(18) app 6 gls
FAC: 3(1) app 1 gl
FLC: 1(1) app 0 gls
Euro: 11(2) app 4 gls
Total: 76(22) app 11 gls

Honours:
1 Eng cap 2003/13 Eng u21 app 1996-2000/Eng sch-youth app/FL ch prom 2009/FLC winner 2011/PFA ToS (d1) 1996.

BOYD James Murray 1925-1935

Outside-right
5'10"
b. Possilpark, Glasgow, 29 April 1907
d. Bournemouth, 22 March 1991

Career: Springburn Hibs/Petershill/Edinburgh St Bernard's Oct 1924/UNITED May 1925 £600/Derby Co May 1935 £1,000/Bury Jan 1937/Dundee Sept 1937/ Grimsby Town July 1938 £200 (St Mirren war-guest 1939-40) (Hamilton Acc war-guest 1941-42)(Morton war-guest 1941-42)(Leyton Orient war-guest 1943-44)(Brighton war-guest 1943-44)/ Retired March 1947 and coached in Sweden/ UNITED scout Aug 1949/Middlesbrough scout Dec 1958.

Jimmy Boyd had a consistent if not headlining career at St James' Park. Never the flamboyant type, but a thoroughly professional team-man who ran up and down the right wing supplying accurate crosses. He was noted for his penetrating far post ball and ability to snatch a goal himself. Moving to Tyneside as a teenager, the youngster played a small part in the club's 1927 title victory, then during season 1931-32, Boyd grabbed 23 goals from the wide position and was a key player in the Magpies' run to FA Cup glory. A regular for United over six seasons after taking over from Tommy Urwin, he spent a decade on Tyneside. Always immaculately turned out, on and off the pitch, during his early career Jimmy was the subject of a legal test case over the signing of amateur players by senior clubs (St Bernard's) in Scotland. Boyd was something of a dressing-room joker and kept United's Thirties stars smiling with a stream of humorous pranks. Afterwards a Physical Education instructor, he scouted for both United and Boro in Scotland when he worked for Glasgow Corporation's Education & Welfare department. In later life when he settled on the south coast, Jimmy became an expert indoor bowls player and represented England. He lived into his eighties, residing in Westbourne.

Appearances & Goals:
Debut v Cardiff City (a) 20 September 1926
FL: 198 app 58 gls
FAC: 16 app 5 gls
Others: 1 app 1 gl
Total: 215 app 64 gls

Honours:
1 Scot cap 1934/FL champs 1927 (2 app)/FAC winner 1932.

B

BOYES Walter Edward 1942

Outside-left
5'4"
b. Killamarsh, Derbyshire, 5 January 1913
d. Sheffield, 16 September 1960

Career: Woodhouse Mills Utd/West Bromwich Albion Feb 1931/Everton Feb 1938 £6,000 (UNITED war-guest 1941-42)(Middlesbrough war-guest 1941-42)(Brentford war-guest 1942-43)(Clapton Orient war-guest 1942-43) (Sunderland war-guest 1942-43)(Millwall war-guest 1942-43)(Leeds Utd war-guest 1942-44)(Aldershot war-guest 1944-45) (Preston North End war-guest 1944-45) (Manchester Utd war-guest 1944-45)(Wrexham war-guest 1944-45)(Linfield war-guest)(Crook Town war-guest)/Notts Co player-trainer Aug 1949/Scunthorpe Utd player Aug 1950/Retford Town player-manager 1953/Hyde Utd manager 1958/Swansea Town trainer 1959 to May 1960.

Wally Boyes was a distinguished pre-war England international winger who won three caps for his country and appeared twice for the Football League side. A splendid little player, at only 5'4" tall (although reports vary from 5'3" to 5'6"), Wally was strong, tricky and always able to score goals as well as create openings. He often dazzled the crowd, although sometimes criticised for being too intricate than direct. Few full-backs could totally master him and the fair-haired winger appeared on 76 occasions for Everton before and after World War Two and took part in the Goodison club's title success in 1938-39. He also reached the FA Cup final with West Bromwich Albion in 1935, a day at Wembley which saw him find the net. Boyes clocked up 165 games for the Baggies scoring 38 goals. An errant traveller during the war, Boyes landed at Gallowgate during February and March 1942 and took the place of Charlie Woollett on the left touchline. He was later a sports master at a Sheffield school during the Fifties.

Appearances & Goals:
Debut v Middlesbrough (h) 28 February 1942 (FLN)
War: 2 app 0 gls
Total: 2 app 0 gls

Honours:
3 Eng caps 1935-39/1 Eng unoff app 1936/2 FL app 1936-39/FL champs 1939/FAC final 1935.

BRACEWELL Paul William 1992-1995

Midfield
5'8"
b. Heswall, Cheshire, 19 July 1962

Career: Stoke City jnr Sept 1978, prof Feb 1980/Sunderland June 1983 £225,000/Everton May 1984 £250,000/Sunderland loan Aug 1989, pmt Sept 1989 £250,000/UNITED June 1992 £250,000/ Sunderland player-coach May 1995 £50,000/Fulham Oct 1997 £75,000, becoming player-coach May 1998, then manager May 1999 to March 2000/Halifax Town manager Oct 2000 to Aug 2001/FA coach Jan 2002 to Jan 2004/Walsall asst-manager Feb 2004 to May 2004.

When Kevin Keegan made a transfer swoop for 30-year-old Sunderland captain, Paul Bracewell during the summer of 1992, both Tyne and Wear were stunned. Bracewell had just led the Roker side out at Wembley in the FA Cup final and was the cornerstone of the Red's line-up. But United's boss pulled off a marvellous deal, bringing the highly experienced England midfielder to Gallowgate to provide the Magpies' new side with a bargain-priced anchor man who could dictate play from the middle of the field. Having a steadying influence, Paul's gritty determination knitted perfectly with his simple yet efficient distribution of the ball. It was at Goodison Park that Bracewell found most success, in an enterprising midfield alongside Reid, Steven and fellow United colleague Kevin Sheedy, the foursome being the engine room behind Everton's success. Unlucky to appear in four FA Cup finals and lose them all, Paul was also unfortunate to undergo over a dozen operations during his career, including a cancer scare at St James' Park. Bracewell though was resilient and always bounced back to prove a welcome asset at all his clubs and despite the injury lay-offs totalled over 700 senior games; 270 for Sunderland and 146 for Everton. One of his bad injuries came at St James' Park when Billy Whitehurst clattered into him when playing for Everton in 1986; as a result he was out of action for almost 20 months. Cool and composed, he was a vital cog in the resurgence of Newcastle United during seasons

1992-93 and 1993-94. On leaving the professional scene Bracewell went into business setting up a concept to roll-out a chain of football academies, 'Complete Football', opening the first complex in Gosforth before selling his stake in the company.

Appearances & Goals:
Debut v Southend United (h) 15 August 1992 (1 goal)
FL/PL: 64(9) app 3 gls
FAC: 6(2) app 0 gls
FLC: 3(1) app 1 gl
Others: 2 app 0 gls
Total: 75(12) app 4 gls

Honours:
3 Eng caps 1985-86/13 Eng u21 app 1983-85/FL champs 1985/FL div 1 champs 1993, 1996/FL div 2 champs 1999/FL div 2 prom 1990/FAC final 1985, 1986, 1989, 1992/ECWC winner 1985/PFA ToS (d2) 1998.

BRADLEY George Joseph 1938-1946

Right-half
6'0"
b. Maltby, South Yorkshire, 7 January 1917
d. West Surrey, 8 December 1998

Career: Maltby Hall Old Boys/Rotherham Utd March 1937/UNITED Nov 1938 £820 (Hull City war-guest 1940-41)(Bradford City war-guest 1941-42)(Rotherham Utd war-guest 1943-45)(Arsenal war-guest 1944-45)/Millwall Sept 1946 £1,000/Guildford City Aug 1950.

George Bradley had the making of a decent player when he stood in for the established Jimmy Gordon, after being spotted by United scouts playing well for Rotherham during season 1937-38. Bradley though was one of a group of youngsters to have their careers in the game ruined by the outbreak of the Second World War. He lost his best footballing years to the hostilities and by the time the Yorkshireman had returned to St James' Park as peace was restored, George found a new generation of youngsters ahead of him. Moving to Millwall, he did well at The Den appearing on nearly 100 occasions for the Lions. The Yorkshireman was noted as being a hard and tough player with an uncompromising attitude on the field – even in training. Bradley afterwards resided in the Guildford area; George served with the RAF during the war and saw action in Belgium and France.

Appearances & Goals:
Debut v Blackburn Rovers (a) 19 November 1938
FL: 1 app 0 gls
War: 20 app 1 gl
Total: 21 app 1 gl

BRADLEY Robert 1926-1929

Right-back
5'10"
b. Washington, 16 September 1906
d. Carlisle, 18 February 1934

Career: Washington CW/Bishop Auckland/ UNITED amat Nov 1926, prof March 1927 £100/Fulham July 1929 £125/Tunbridge Wells Rangers June 1930/Carlisle Utd Aug 1932 to his death.

An amateur player at Gallowgate for a time, Robert Bradley arrived on the staff with a big reputation playing for the famous non-leaguers Bishop Auckland. Understudy to Alf Maitland during his stay on Tyneside, Bradley was chosen for a single Football League appearance before moving to Craven Cottage. He later became a noted servant to Carlisle United displaying a battling and combative style in defence. Bradley was skipper of the side when he died suddenly aged only 27. Bob made 75 appearances prior to his untimely death which occurred shortly after playing for the Cumbrians at Chester. Complaining of stomach pains he travelled back to his lodgings and the following morning was found dead in his bed. A post-mortem determined death was from natural causes.

Appearances & Goals:
Debut v Leicester City (h) 7 April 1928
FL: 1 app 0 gls
Total: 1 app 0 gls

BRADLEY William 1914-1927

Goalkeeper
6'0"
b. Wardley, Gateshead, 1 March 1893
d. North Shields, 20 June 1960

Career: Dunston Wed/Felling NER/Fatfield Albion/ Jarrow Caledonians Oct 1911/Portsmouth March 1912 £100/ Jarrow June 1913/UNITED April 1914 £300 (Gainsborough Trinity war-guest 1915)(Leeds City war-guest 1915-16) (Scotswood war-guest 1915-16)/Ashington May 1927 to Feb 1929/North Shields Feb 1930, becoming a director to March 1933.

A goalkeeper who gave United fine service before and after the First World War, Bill Bradley returned to the North East after a short stay with Pompey in the Southern League. He was reserve to Jimmy Lawrence as a youngster then claimed the 'keeper's jersey for himself during the early years of the Twenties. As United embarked on a Wembley FA Cup run in 1924, Bill found himself second choice again, this time to the veteran Sandy Mutch who had been signed from Huddersfield. Bradley looked like missing out on a medal until Mutch was injured in the last league fixture before heading for Wembley and unluckily was sidelined for the final. In stepped Bill Bradley to play the game of his life against Aston Villa as United lifted the trophy. Tall and thin, Bradley could be a commanding goalkeeper on his day; he afterwards served Ashington during their Football League years. He joined the Tank Corps during the Great War and later ran a profitable hen ranch on Tyneside for a period. For many years he resided in North Shields later opening a newsagents business near the railway station.

Appearances & Goals:
Debut v Preston North End (h) 1 November 1919
(v Middlesbrough (h) 29 March 1919 (NVL))
FL: 133 app 0 gls
FAC: 10 app 0 gls
War: 4 app 0 gls
Total: 147 app 0 gls

Honours:
FAC winner 1924.

BRADSHAW Darren Shaun 1989-1992

Centre-half
5'11'
b. Sheffield, 19 March 1967

Career: Sheffield Wed jnr/Grimsby Town trial//Matlock Town 1986 (Chesterfield trial Aug 1987)/York City Nov 1987 £2,000/UNITED loan Aug 1989, pmt Sept 1989 £10,000/Peterborough Utd Aug 1992 free (Plymouth Argyle loan 1994-95)/Blackpool Oct 1994 £65,000/ Rushden & Diamonds Oct 1997 free/Stevenage Borough Feb 2001/Worksop Town cs 2001 to cs 2004/Belper Town 2004, becoming manager briefly/Retired due to injury.

Tall and pacy, Darren Bradshaw possessed ideal qualities for the central defender's position. Although a bright prospect as a teenager, a broken leg at Hillsborough ruined his early career, but he received a chance of top football again when he was recommended to United by his former boss at York, Bobby Saxton then assistant-manager at St James' Park. Darren was initially on loan at Gallowgate as a 22-year-old and impressed manager Jim Smith during a month's trial earning a full-time contract. The blond-haired Bradshaw was never a regular in United's line-up, competing with Scott and Matty Appleby at centre-half, as well as Stimson and Neilson at full-back, but he was versatile, appearing on the right or left of defence and was used as cover across the back line. At Peterborough, Bradshaw was appointed captain and totalled over 80 games, while he suffered an Achilles injury which affected his later career. His younger brother, Carl appeared with both Sheffield clubs, Manchester City and Norwich. After being released by Sheffield Wednesday as a teenager, Darren took a job cleaning power station boilers before getting a second chance in the game at York.

Appearances & Goals:
Debut v Swindon Town (a) 30 December 1989
(v Oldham Athletic (h) 28 November 1989 (FMC))
FL: 33(6) app 0 gls
FAC: 2(1) app 0 gls
FLC: 3 app 0 gls
Others: 2 app 0 gls
Total: 40(7) app 0 gls

Honours:
Eng sch-youth app.

BRADY Garry 1998-2001

Midfield
5'10"
b. Glasgow, 7 September 1976

Career: Celtic BC 1988/Tottenham Hotspur jnr, prof Sept 1993/UNITED July 1998 £650,000 (Norwich City loan 1999-2000, 2000-01), free Jan 2001/China briefly/Portsmouth trial Feb 2001, pmt June 2001/ Kilmarnock Jan 2002/ Walsall trial July 2002/Dundee trial Aug 2002, pmt Sept 2002/St Mirren June 2006/ Brechin City July 2011 to cs 2013.

Tottenham Hotspur received £650,000 for the services of midfielder Garry Brady when Kenny Dalglish decided to bring the Scot to Gallowgate during the summer of 1998. In an sour dispute with Tottenham's management and on the fringe of the Spurs eleven, Brady managed only one start and 11 games all told in the their line-up, the deal was something of a gamble for United. Brady needed a new start after almost 18 months out of action through injury and fellow Glaswegian Dalglish gave him the opportunity. Soon though his countryman departed and Brady had to show new manager Ruud Gullit he had something to offer. A playmaker with energy and accurate distribution of the ball, he was given opportunities in 1998-99, with a dozen outings either in the starting line-up or from the bench. A player who could get forward to join the attack, however, an ankle injury did not assist Garry's progress. Gullit preferred the international quality of Speed, Solano, Lee and Hamann, as well as Temuri Ketsbaia and Brady headed to Norwich on loan then to Portsmouth before making an impression in Scotland. He made over 100 appearances for Dundee and did well in the black-and-white colours of St Mirren too where he reached 100 games once more. Garry's brother, Darren Brady, turned out notably for Livingston and Raith Rovers.

Appearances & Goals:
Debut v Everton (a) 23 November 1998 (sub)
PL: 3(6) app 0 gls
FAC: 2(1) app 0 gls
Total: 5(7) app 0 gls

Honours:
Scot sch-youth app/SC final 2003/SLC final 2010.

BRAMBLE Titus Malachi 2002-2007

Centre-half
6'2"
b. Ipswich, 31 July 1981

Career: Ipswich Town jnr June 1997, prof Aug 1998 (Colchester Utd loan 1999-2000)/UNITED July 2002 £6m/Wigan Ath July 2007 free/Sunderland July 2010 £1m to June 2013/Ipswich Town trial July 2013/ West Ham Utd trial July 2103.

Joining United's squad as a 21-year-old emerging talent from Ipswich Town, Titus Bramble cost a substantial fee of £6m for a player who had only been a regular for two seasons, totalling 62 games for the Portman Road club. Described as a young colossus, Bramble though had much potential as a stopper who it was hoped could be developed into a steadfast and dominant centre-back. Built like a proverbial tank, he possessed all the physical attributes for the centre-back role being positive in the air, full-blooded in the tackle and quick for such a big man. He also could spray the ball around with long diagonal balls. A succession of United managers tried to nurture Titus, while a multitude of partners at the back hardly helped his development on Tyneside. Newcastle received two things on the field from Bramble; often brilliant and commanding displays as the focal point of the defence, but alas prone to calamitous moments which at times cost a goal. All in charge tried to eliminate that lack of concentration which ultimately stopped him being a Premier League stalwart. It was a frustrating defect in his play which ended his five-year stay at Gallowgate, Titus moving to Wigan Athletic during 2007. Thereafter he moved back to the region as a Sunderland player, again often impressing, but just as often to have what was termed that infuriating 'Bramble moment'. He skippered the red-and-whites for a period and was a favourite of Steve Bruce when boss of the Latics and Black Cats. Off the field, during and after his days at St James' Park, Titus also found himself making headlines in the press for the wrong reasons. Unable to find a decent opportunity after leaving Wearside, Bramble opened an Academy of Football Excellence and began coaching youngsters. His brother Tes appeared prominently for Southend and Stockport as well as being an international footballer for Montserrat.

Appearances & Goals:
Debut v NZ Zeljeznicar (a) 14 August 2002 (CL)
PL: 96(9) app 3 gls
FAC: 8 app 0 gls
FLC: 5 app 0 gls
Euro: 38(1) app 4 gls
Total: 147(10) app 7 gls

Honours:
10 Eng u21 app 2001-03.

BRANDER George Milne 1952-1954

Outside-left
5'9"
b. Aberdeen, 1 November 1929
d. Scotland, 1996

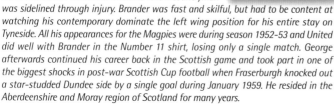

Career: Aberdeen East End/Bury Oct 1949/ Aberdeen East End/Raith Rovers Oct 1949/UNITED March 1952 £1,850/Stirling Albion Jan 1954 £750/ Arbroath/ Fraserburgh c1957/Huntly/Elgin City 1959.

George Brander pulled on the shirt of the great Bobby Mitchell on a few occasions when his fellow countryman was sidelined through injury. Brander was fast and skilful, but had to be content at watching his contemporary dominate the left wing position for his entire stay on Tyneside. All his appearances for the Magpies were during season 1952-53 and United did well with Brander in the Number 11 shirt, losing only a single match. George afterwards continued his career back in the Scottish game and took part in one of the biggest shocks in post-war Scottish Cup football when Fraserburgh knocked out a star-studded Dundee side by a single goal during January 1959. He resided in the Aberdeenshire and Moray region of Scotland for many years.

Appearances & Goals:
Debut v Derby County (h) 1 November 1952
FL: 5 app 2 gls
Total: 5 app 2 gls

BRAYSON Paul 1993-1998

Striker
5'7"
b. Newcastle upon Tyne, 16 September 1977

Career: Walker Central BC/UNITED jnr 1993, prof Aug 1995 (Swansea City loan 1996-97)/Reading March 1998 £100,000/ Cardiff City July 2000 free/Cheltenham Town Aug 2002/ Northwich Victoria Aug 2004/York City Aug 2004 (Gateshead loan 2004-05)/Northwich Victoria 2005/York City June 2007/ Gateshead Jan 2008/Newcastle Blue Star June 2008/Durham City June 2009/Blyth Spartans Aug 2009/Harrogate Town July 2011/Bedlington Terriers July 2012.

Paul Brayson had scored over 100 goals in reserve and junior football during his early two seasons on United's staff and was rated as a huge prospect. Nicknamed 'Brassy', the Tyneside youngster was soon given a fast-track within the corridors of St James' Park to get into the first-team squad. Although small and boyish-looking, he possessed the natural touch of a striker in front of goal. Direct, quick over a short distance, and thoughtful up front, Paul had been a regular at the FA's training complex in Lilleshall and also reached his country's youth line-up. He received a call-up to the first-team as an 18-year-old for a League Cup tie during 1995-96, but that's as far as Brayson got in the Magpies' team, never being given another opportunity, apart from a single outing from the bench. He moved down the league ladder and had a decent career thereafter, including taking part in an archetypal FA Cup tie when non-leaguers Northwich faced Sunderland during 2005-06. He did well with the Bluebirds, 20 goals in 94 appearances hitting the net on 15 occasions during their promotion campaign of 2000-01. Later Paul played for a long period back in the North East and was a noted striker at non-league level grabbing 60 goals for Blyth. Brayson was brought up in the shadows of the old Gallowgate pylons in Stanhope Street and once netted eight goals for the Magpies in a match against Hartlepool juniors.

Appearances & Goals:
Debut v Bristol City (h) 4 October 1995 (FLC)
FLC: 1(1) 0 gls
Total: 1(1) 0 gls

Honours: Eng sch-youth app/1 Eng C app 2007/FL div 3 prom 2001.

BRAZIL Gary Nicholas 1989-1990

Striker
5'11"
b. Tunbridge Wells, 19 September 1962

Career: Crystal Palace jnr Sept 1978/Sheffield Utd Aug 1980 free (Port Vale loan 1984-85)/ Preston North End Feb 1985 £20,000 (Mansfield Town loan 1984-85)/UNITED Feb 1989 £250,000/ Fulham loan Sept 1990, pmt Nov 1990 £110,000, becoming asst-coach Jan 1996/ Cambridge Utd trial Aug 1996/Barnet Sept 1996 free/Slough Town Feb 1997 to cs 1998 when he retired playing/Fulham asst-coach Jan 1998/ Notts Co asst-coach May 1998, becoming asst-manager Aug 1999, then manager Oct 1999 to May 2000, and again Oct 2001 to Jan 2002, becoming Director of Youth May 2002, then asst-manager/Doncaster Rovers coach May 2004/FA coaching staff cs 2004/ Fulham Academy manager Jan 2007 to Nov 2010/PL staff 2011/Nottingham Forest asst-coach June 2012, becoming Academy Manager and caretaker-manager March 2014 to May 2014 when he returned to the Academy.

At Newcastle as the Black'n'Whites struggled, initially to stay in the top level, then to get out of the Second Division, Gary Brazil was often named as substitute and was never given an extended opportunity in either attack or midfield. A player with good skills and guile rather than force, Gary was restricted in his Gallowgate career by a damaged back disc and out of action for a lengthy period. In his 27 games for the Magpies, Brazil started only eight fixtures, and when fit perhaps should have been given a chance by managers Willie McFaul and Jim Smith. Captain of Preston when he joined United, he had netted 72 goals for the Deepdale club in 202 appearances and was recognised one of the top players in the lower divisions. Becoming frustrated at the lack of first-team action on Tyneside, Gary moved south and was an instant hit at Craven Cottage. He quickly became a favourite and totalled over 250 outings for the Thames outfit. During the early part of his career, Gary took part in Sheffield United's promotion from Division Three, and once he had finished playing found a career in coaching, notably with Notts County where he operated in various roles for over five years.

Appearances & Goals:
Debut v Coventry City (a) 11 February 1989
FL: 7(16) app 2 gls
FAC: 0(1) app 0 gls
FLC: 1(1) app 1 gl
Others: 0(1) app 0 gls
Total: 8(19) app 3 gls

Honours
FL div 4 champs 1982 (1 app)/FL div 3 prom 1984/FL div 4 prom 1987.

BRENNAN Frank 1946-1956

Centre-half
6'3"
b. Annathill, near Coatbridge, 23 April 1924
d. Newcastle upon Tyne, 5 March 1997

Career: Coatbridge St Patricks 1940/ Airdrieonians amat Feb 1941/UNITED May 1946 £7,500 (Hartlepool Utd guest 1951)/ North Shields March 1956 free, becoming coach/British Council coach, including in Singapore and Trinidad/North Shields manager April 1967/Darlington coach Dec 1970, becoming manager Aug 1971 to Dec 1971/South Shields coach Feb to Oct 1972/ Thailand coaching Jan to April 1974.

A tremendous centre-half for Newcastle United, Frank Brennan is rated the best to have played for the Magpies in over a century of football. Known as the 'Rock of Tyneside', he was cool-headed, steady and tough, a no nonsense defender who formed a terrific bond with Geordie supporters for a decade. Having impressed for the Scotland side in 1946, United won the transfer scramble for his signature and it proved to be one of Stan Seymour's finest captures for the club. A towering 6'3" tall, weighing over thirteen-and-a-half stone and wearing size 11 boots; he was fast for such a big man and possessed all the necessary attributes for combat with the opposition. Frank relished a duel with the many big-name centre-forwards of his era and often came out on top, being the king-pin to United's defence as they first, won promotion, then lifted the FA Cup two years in succession. By the time the Black'n'Whites reached Wembley again in 1955, new boss Livingstone wanted younger blood while Brennan also had become entangled in a dispute with the club's hierarchy, an unsavoury affair which saw his wages cut and led to protest meetings, speeches at the Trade Union Congress and the Scot's eventual departure from the first-class game. Brennan later travelled the world as a coach for the British Council and then successfully led North Shields to Wembley. For many years he ran a sport outfitters business close to St James' Park, the source many reckoned of his dispute with supremo Seymour who had a rival outlet. Frank retired to live in Whitley Bay, a well known and liked figure in the region. During his early days in Scotland, Frank worked at a local pit then a brick works while at Gallowgate he was employed as an electrical engineer at Hartley Main Colliery during the late 1940s. Frank was famous on Tyneside for a huge appetite, and such was his football reputation with the Magpies that a street was named after him in the city's West End; Brennan Close.

Appearances & Goals:
Debut v Millwall (a) 31 August 1946
FL: 318 app 3 gls
FAC: 29 app 0 gls
Others: 2 app 0 gls
Total: 349 app 3 gls

Honours:
7 Scot caps 1947-54/3 unoff Scot app 1946-47/FAC winner 1951, 1952/FL div 2 prom 1948/FAAC winner 1969(m)/NU HoF.

BRIDGES Michael 2004

Striker
6'1"
b. North Shields, 5 August 1978

Career: Wallsend BC/UNITED jnr 1989/Sunderland jnr May 1995, prof Nov 1995/Leeds Utd July 1999 £5.6m (UNITED loan Jan 2004 to May 2004)/Bolton Wand June 2004 free/Sunderland loan Sept 2004, pmt Dec 2004/Bristol City Aug 2005 free/Carlisle Utd Nov 2005 free/Hull City Aug 2006 £350,000 to June 2009 (Sydney (Aus) loan 2007-08)(Carlisle Utd loan 2008-09)/MK Dons Aug 2009/Newcastle Jets (Aus) Sept 2009, retiring in April 2011, becoming development-coach, then re-instated as a player 2012 to cs 2014.

Michael Bridges arrived back on his native Tyneside following a career frustrated by injury. As he was emerging with Sunderland and Leeds United in the 1990s, the Geordie striker was destined to become one of England's brightest stars. A teenage debutant for the Wearsiders, Michael was first struck down by a knee injury and at Elland Road suffered a shattered ankle, then Achilles and more knee injuries. Bridges was in the treatment room for many months at an age when his career should have been flourishing and never really recaptured the incisive forward play he had showed when he won his young England caps during seasons 1996-97 to 1999-2000. Tall and pacy, Michael was stylish on the ball and had a natural eye for a goalscoring opportunity. During January 2004 Bobby Robson gave the Tyneside lad an opportunity to show at only 25 years of age he still had something to offer football at the top level despite his set-backs. Joining the club he supported as a youngster, Michael was delighted to have joined the Magpies noting: "It's everything I've ever wanted." Given few opportunities in the black-and-white striped shirt, however, Michael never looked like claiming a regular place in Robson's side and wasn't retained at the end of the season. Bridges made his senior debut with the red-and-whites of Wearside in season 1995-96, and registered 113 games (23 goals) before he moved to the Premiership for a big fee in 1999 joining a Leeds United line-up seemingly on the brink of much success under David O'Leary. As a youngster Bridges had been at Newcastle's School of Excellence for almost five years before joining Sunderland. Michael headed to Australia to end his playing career in 2011 with Newcastle Jets. Afterwards he moved into coaching with the Aussie club also opening a wine-bar on the Pacific coast of the country as well as a pundit for Fox Sports.

Appearances & Goals:
Debut v Leicester City (h) 7 February 2004 (sub)
PL: 0(6) app 0 gls
Euro: 1(2) app 0 gls
Total: 1(8) app 0 gls

Honours:
3 Eng u21 app 1997-2000/Eng sch-youth app/1 FL app 1998/FL ch winner 2005/FL div 1 champs 1996, 1999/FL ch prom 2008 (7 app)/FL div 2 champs 2006.

BRITTAIN Martin 1994-2006

Midfield
5'8"
b. Cramlington, 29 December 1984

Career: UNITED jnr 1994, prof Sept 2003 to cs 2006 free/Trial at various clubs cs 2006; Coventry City, Brighton, Hull City, Kilmarnock/Ipswich Town Aug 2006 free (Yeovil Town loan 2006-07)/Luton Town trial July 2007/Carlisle Utd trial cs 2007, pmt Aug 2007/Walsall trial Jan 2008/Toronto (Can) trial March 2008/Kidderminster Harriers trial Aug 2008/Gateshead June 2009/Celtic Nation (Carlisle) July 2012/North Shields Sept 2012/Blyth Spartans Sept 2012/Bedlington Terriers Nov 2012/Ashington Jan 2014.

From the Cramlington area, Martin Brittain was attached to the Newcastle United's Academy since he was nine years of age. An attack minded midfielder and for at time, as a full-back, Brittain took part in the Magpies' junior FA Premier League under-17 trophy victory in 2002, via a Play-Off against Manchester United. Like many home developed midfielders in modern years Martin had a tough, if not impossible, task of dislodging a whole array of talent in the Magpies squad, namely Dyer, Butt, Bowyer, Jenas and Milner as well as the rising N'Zogbia and Darren Ambrose. Brittain reached contention himself in season 2003-04 when Bobby Robson used him twice from the bench, while the following term Martin was in the dug-out almost a dozen times but not called upon by new boss Graeme Souness. At the end of that season he was allowed to move on and he struggled to cement a place in the Football League, eventually moving into the local non-league scene.

Appearances & Goals:
Debut v Valerenga IF (h) 3 March 2004 (sub) (UEFAC)
PL: 0(1) app 0 gls
FAC: 1 app 0 gls
FLC: 0(2) app 0 gls
Euro: 0(4) app 0 gls
Total: 1(7) app 0 gls

BROADIS Ivan Arthur 1953-1955

Inside-right
5'9"
b. Isle of Dogs, London, 18 December 1922

Career: Golders Green/Finchley/Northfleet Utd/Finchley/Tottenham Hotspur amat Aug 1939/(Millwall war-guest 1940-41) (Manchester Utd war-guest 1942-44) (Tottenham Hotspur war-guest 1944-46) (Blackpool war-guest 1944-45)(Carlisle Utd war-guest 1944-45)(Distillery (Belfast) war-guest 1944-45)(Bradford Park Avenue 1944-45)/Millwall amat Dec 1945/Carlisle Utd player-manager Aug 1946/Sunderland Jan 1949 £18,000/Manchester City Oct 1951 £25,000/UNITED Oct 1953 £17,500/Carlisle Utd player-coach July 1955 £3,500 (Third Lanark guest 1956)/Queen of the South June 1959/Retired playing cs 1961.

Ivor Broadis was a creative, fast thinking inside-forward who possessed a lethal shot yet, although a well respected player during the Fifties, he never seemed to fit in too well at Gallowgate. That was perhaps due to a poor relationship with the club's Board and skipper Jimmy Scoular. He spoke out at times noting that players were being treated as "second-class citizens" and once was quoted as saying: "I know what people say about me. That I'm hard to please. That I'm a rebel. Better to speak your mind than be a slave." Known commonly as 'Ivor' although christened Ivan, he arrived at St James' Park to boost United's creative ability on the field and rivalled fellow international Reg Davies for the Number 8 shirt. Broadis made headlines on his home debut, laying on a goal in the opening minute then going onto score twice at Gallowgate. At times Ivor showed a mastery in everything he did and appearing in the 1954 World Cup finals, he had an excellent record in an England shirt grabbing eight goals in 14 appearances. However, after displaying some good form during United's FA Cup run in 1955, Ivor was left out of the Wembley line-up and moved on within weeks of the Magpies victory. During the Second World War he was a commissioned officer, a Dakota navigator with a Transport Command squadron, while he also played for a number of sides on service, doing especially well with Spurs netting 38 goals in 83 games. On peace being restored, Broadis became, at 23 years of age, the youngest player-boss around when appointed at Brunton Park and later sold himself to Sunderland. He always had a close tie with Carlisle though, where he had been stationed during the war, and by the time he had retired and had completed a second spell with the Cumbrians, Broadis had clocked up over 250 games for the club. Afterwards Ivor became a sports journalist, initially on Tyneside with The Journal, then back in Cumbria with the Cumberland News as well as the Evening News & Star. Broadis settled on the outskirts of Carlisle.

Appearances & Goals:
Debut v Sheffield United (a) 31 October 1953
FL: 42 app 15 gls
FAC: 9 app 3 gls
Total: 51 app 18 gls

Honours:
14 Eng caps 1952-54/WdC 1954/3 FL app 1952-53/FLS(WLg) champs 1945 (7 app)/4 FL div 3(N) app 1956-58.

BROADY Percy Kent 1942-1946

Half-back
5'10"
b. Port Clarence, Stockton, 2 January 1924
d. Middlesbrough, November 1987

Another player to have his career halted by Hitler's invasion of Europe, Percy Broady was spotted in local football by United's excellent scouting network in the North East at the time, joining the Magpies during May 1942. After a year in the second-eleven, he was given an opportunity in the club's wartime Football League North side. Percy made his senior debut in an amazing 5-5 draw against York City during May 1943. Although he resigned for the Magpies as an amateur in May 1944, becoming a professional the following year during May 1945 in readiness for normal action, that absorbing encounter with the Minstermen was his only outing for the club's first eleven. With a long list of midfield talent ahead of him for a place in Newcastle's team, Broady wasn't retained and was released in 1946.

Appearances & Goals:
Debut v York City (a) 1 May 1943 (FLN)
War: 1 app 0 gls
Total: 1 app 0 gls

BROCK Kevin Stanley 1988-1994

Midfield
5'9"
b. Middleton Stoney, near Bicester, 9 September 1962

Career: Oxford Utd May 1979/Queens Park Rangers Aug 1987 £260,000/ UNITED Dec 1988 £300,000 to June 1994 (Cardiff City loan 1993-94)/ Cambridge Utd trial July 1994/Stockport Co trial Sept 1994/Marlow 1994/ Stevenage Borough Nov 1994/Yeovil Town Feb 1995/Rushden & Diamonds cs 1995/ Oxford City Aug 1996 player-asst-coach/Banbury Utd player-manager cs 1999 to 2007/Woodford Utd coach Jan 2008/Ardley Utd manager cs 2008.

Although a much sought after schoolboy star, courted by a string of big clubs including Manchester United, Everton and Spurs, Kevin Brock preferred to sign for his home town side, Oxford United. He developed quickly, playing in a friendly when he was still at school, then in the Third and Fourth Divisions. He assisted Oxford in their rise to the top level as well as becoming the first lower division player for many years to be selected by an England side, appearing for the Under-21 eleven. His manager Jim Smith, rated Brock's delicate skills and football brain in midfield highly and took the slightly framed player with him to Loftus Road and then onto St James' Park when he was appointed boss. At Gallowgate for five seasons, Kevin was a regular over four of those years and at times looked a very good player always liable to find the net. At a lean time, Brock's cultured play was held in high regard. He just missed out on promotion in the Play-Offs during

1990 when he had his best season for United. However, Brock was also often on the sidelines through injury or illness during the latter period of his career with the Magpies and maybe lacked the determination to reach the very top. He wasn't part of either Ossie Ardiles' or Kevin Keegan's plans and was handed a free transfer. Before that, Brock appeared in a handful of matches during the club's title winning season in 1993 and once ended in goal for United against Birmingham City. With Oxford Kevin totalled over 300 senior games; Brock was also a noted local cricketer.

Appearances & Goals:
Debut v Wimbledon (h) 10 December 1988
FL: 137(10) app 14 gls
FAC: 11 app 1 gl
FLC: 7 app 1 gl
Others: 7(1) app 1 gl
Total: 162(11) app 17 gls

Honours:
4 Eng u21 app 1984-86/2 Eng B app 1988-90/Eng sch-youth app/FLC winner 1986/WsC winner 1994/FL div 1 champs 1993 (7 app)/FL div 2 champs 1985/FL div 3 champs 1984/PFA ToS (d3) 1984.

BROUGHTON John Robert 1882-1890

Goalkeeper, Forward & Committee
b. Darrington, near Pontefract, June 1865
d. Newcastle upon Tyne, June 1921

Career: Rosewood Oct 1882/EAST END cNov 1882 to 1890, Committee 1883 to 1885-86.

One of the Rosewood FC squad which were amalgamated with Byker neighbours Newcastle East End late in 1882 as Newcastle United's pioneers developed their footballing base. Broughton was a teenager, barely 17 years old, like many of East End's early footballers, when he first appeared for the side during season 1882-83 and he remained with the club for a lengthy period. John became the East Enders regular 'keeper but also played outfield on occasion. Broughton also served on East End's committee before a Board of Directors had been formed, certainly for season 1883-84 to 1885-86, but also probably before and after. He was also a Northumberland FA committee man. John resided in Byker Bank and later Wilfred Street, he was a brass finisher by trade while his brother Fred Broughton (qv) also played for East End. Later John was recognised as a fine bowls player for the Newcastle Armstrong Club and sat on the local Temperance Committee during the mid-1880s. By 1911 he was working for the Tyne Tees Shipping Company.

Appearances & Goals:
Debut v Darlington (h) 7 September 1889 (NL)
NL: 3 app 0 gls
FAC: 2 app 0 gls
Total: 5 app 0 gls

BROWN Alan 1981-1982

Striker
5'11"
b. Easington, Co Durham, 22 May 1959

Career: Easington Jnrs/Sunderland jnr, prof Sept 1976 (UNITED loan Nov 1981 to Jan 1982)/Shrewsbury Town July 1982/Doncaster Rovers March 1984 £35,000 to cs 1986 when he retired due to injury.

Arriving at St James' Park from Wearside on an eight week trial deal, Alan Brown quickly made an impression on United's supporters forming a fruitful partnership with Imre Varadi. He was a bustling front man who put himself about and with his devastating pace was a considerable handful for defenders. However, to the surprise of many, the blond-haired striker was not retained by Newcastle and returned to Roker Park amidst controversy, some claiming he was injured with back and hamstring problems, whilst others noted that United had no cash to purchase him at the £100,000 asking price. Later in the season United brought David Mills to Tyneside as his replacement. Brown had been a 17-year-old debutant for Sunderland, while the Black Cats had also just pipped United for his signature from school. Alan totalled 25 goals in 127 senior games for the red-and-whites and moved from Wearside eventually, serving Shrewsbury and Doncaster, claiming another 27 goals in his career. Brown was later employed in the prison service, an officer at Durham Prison. His son, Chris Brown, was also on Sunderland's books as well as turning out for Doncaster and Preston.

Appearances & Goals:
Debut v Chelsea (a) 7 November 1981
FL: 5 app 3 gls
Total: 5 app 3 gls

Honours:
FL div 2 prom 1980/FL div 4 prom 1984 (9 app).

BROWN Ernest Charles 1945-1947

Inside-forward
5'6"
b. South Shields, 3 February 1921
d. 1976

Career: South Shields Ex-Schoolboys/South Shields/UNITED Dec 1945 (South Shields loan 1946-47)/Southend Utd Feb 1947 part exch-deal/Hartlepools Utd Jan 1951 to c1952/Whitburn/Later becoming a Blackpool scout.

Ernie Brown was given a trial at Gallowgate by Stan Seymour after impressing in South Shields' ranks at the end of the Second World War. The Tyneside-born schemer did enough to earn a contract and his highlight in a black-and-white shirt occurred when he netted twice in a 3-0 victory at Leeds during April 1946. A rival to Ernie Taylor, he found it hard to establish himself in United's senior squad once Football League action began for season 1946-47. Brown moved south to Southend as part of the deal that brought Joe Sibley to St James' Park, but made only a handful of appearances in Essex before heading for Hartlepool.

Appearances & Goals:
Debut v Everton (a) 2 March 1946 (FLN)
War: 12 app 4 gls
Total: 12 app 4 gls

BROWN Henry 1906-1907

Inside-left
5'8"
b. Northampton, November 1883
d. Basingstoke, 9 February 1934

Career: St Sepulchre's Northampton)/Northampton Town May 1902/West Bromwich Albion Nov 1903 £200/Southampton April 1905/UNITED July 1906 £380/Bradford Park Avenue Oct 1907 £250/Fulham April 1908/ Southampton Oct 1910/Woolston Sept 1913.

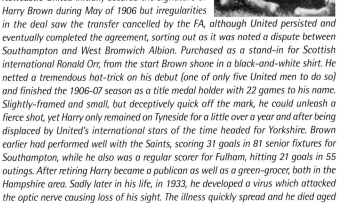

Newcastle United initially secured the signature of Harry Brown during May of 1906 but irregularities in the deal saw the transfer cancelled by the FA, although United persisted and eventually completed the agreement, sorting out as it was noted a dispute between Southampton and West Bromwich Albion. Purchased as a stand-in for Scottish international Ronald Orr, from the start Brown shone in a black-and-white shirt. He netted a tremendous hat-trick on his debut (one of only five United men to do so) and finished the 1906-07 season as a title medal holder with 22 games to his name. Slightly-framed and small, but deceptively quick off the mark, he could unleash a fierce shot, yet Harry only remained on Tyneside for a little over a year and after being displaced by United's international stars of the time headed for Yorkshire. Brown earlier had performed well with the Saints, scoring 31 goals in 81 senior fixtures for Southampton, while he also was a regular scorer for Fulham, hitting 21 goals in 55 outings. After retiring Harry became a publican as well as a green-grocer, both in the Hampshire area. Sadly later in his life, in 1933, he developed a virus which attacked the optic nerve causing loss of his sight. The illness quickly spread and he died aged 50 within a few months.

Appearances & Goals:
Debut v Birmingham (a) 8 September 1906 (3 goals)
FL: 24 app 8 gls
Others: 1 app 2 gls
Total: 25 app 10 gls

Honours:
FL champs 1907.

BROWN Joseph 1919

Centre-forward
5'10"
b. probably Tyneside

Joe Brown was a striker who deputised for Curtis Booth in United's forward-line during the Northern Victory League programme of 1919. Scoring on his only appearance for the Magpies against Scotswood, Brown wasn't offered a full-time contract once Football League action started later in the same year. He also appeared for Durham City during the region's gala to mark the end of the Great War.

Appearances & Goals:
Debut v Scotswood (a) 18 January 1919 (NVL) (1 goal)
War: 1 app 1 gl
Total: 1 app 1 gl

BROWN Malcolm 1983-1985

Right-back
6'2"
b. Salford, 13 December 1956

Career: Bury jnr cs 1973, prof Dec 1975/Huddersfield Town May 1977 free/UNITED July 1983 £100,000/ Huddersfield Town June 1985 £45,000/Rochdale Feb 1989/Stockport Co July 1989/Rochdale Aug 1991 free to cs 1992 when he retired due to injury.

Malcolm Brown was rated as the best defender in the lower divisions when he was purchased by Arthur Cox for a big fee. He was part of a double full-back signing along with John Ryan, both players arriving in an effort to boost Newcastle's promotion campaign for 1983-84. As it turned out, Brown missed the whole of that wonderful Keegan-inspired season and he didn't make his debut for fully twelve months due to a snapped Achilles tendon injury sustained in training, and this after not missing a fixture for the Terriers in 259 games, a five year record! A cheerful and resilient personality, Brown bounced back to become a regular in United's return to Division One, however, that bad injury affected his fitness and Malcolm later admitted it took him fully three years to regain top form. As a result he was not part of new boss Jack Charlton's plans, and surprisingly was allowed to return to Leeds Road during the summer of 1985 for a knock-down price. With the Terriers, Brown appeared in more than 400 matches for the Yorkshire club over nine seasons. At 6'2" and over 13 stone he was a powerful defender, one of the tallest full-backs to appear for the Magpies. After a knee injury brought an end to his career, Brown settled in the Greater Manchester area and ran a driving school, MBM; Malcolm Brown Motoring.

Appearances & Goals:
Debut v Leicester City (a) 25 August 1984
FL: 39 app 0 gls
FAC: 2 app 0 gls
FLC: 4 app 0 gls
Total: 45 app 0 gls

Honours:
FL div 4 champs 1980/FL div 3 prom 1983/FL div 4 prom 1974 (1 app), 1991/PFA ToS (d3) 1981, 1982, 1983, (d4) 1980, 1991.

BROWN Noel William 1907-1908

Outside-right
b. Newcastle upon Tyne, 25 December 1884

Career: Walker Parish/Newcastle Bohemians/UNITED Dec 1907/Newcastle Bohemians loan 1908-09, pmt c1909 to c1911.

Joining Newcastle United as an amateur from local football over the Christmas period of 1907 after showing up well for the Bohemian's club, Noel Brown deputised for England international Jackie Rutherford in the Magpies senior line-up only once, during season 1907-08. That wasn't a pleasing afternoon for United as Villa won 5-2 on Tyneside during the Black'n'Whites preparations for the FA Cup final and when the club rested several star names. Brown still did well in reserve ranks and was part of the Magpie eleven which lifted the Northumberland Senior Cup in 1909 by defeating Newburn. He returned to Bohemians, at the same time being registered with United and turning out for the second-string on occasion. Brown was employed as a marine engineer.

Appearances & Goals:
Debut v Aston Villa (h) 8 April 1908
FL: 1 app 0 gls
Total: 1 app 0 gls

B

BROWNLIE John Jack 1978-1982

Right-back
5'10"
b. Caldercruix, Lanarkshire,
11 March 1952

Career: Pumpherston Jnrs 1968/Hibernian Aug 1968/UNITED Aug 1978 cash-exch deal for R Callachan/ Middlesbrough July 1982 £30,000 (Vasalunds IF (Swd) loan 1983-84)/ Hartlepool Utd Aug 1984 free/Berwick Rangers Aug 1985/ Blyth Spartans Jan 1986/Ashington player-coach 1986/Cowdenbeath asst-manager Nov 1987, becoming manager 1988 to May 1992/Clyde asst-manager cs 1992/Meadowbank Thistle manager Dec 1993 to Feb 1994/Clyde asst-manager 1994 to Sept 1996/East Stirlingshire manager April 1997/Raith Rovers asst-coach Jan 1998 to June 1999/Arbroath manager Sept 2000 to Oct 2003/East Stirlingshire coach 2006, becoming asst-manager, then caretaker-manager Feb 2008 to March 2008.

Right-back John Brownlie was a highly respected player on the Scottish beat, like his international colleague at Easter Road, John Blackley, who also made the journey over the border to sign for the Magpies. At his peak during the early Seventies, Brownlie was out of action for over a season with a badly broken leg in 1973 and took a while to reach the impressive form that had made him a target of nearly every top English club. By the time John had signed for the Magpies, he was back to his best and wanted a crack at English football after 10 years with Hibs. Brownlie became a favourite of United's fans very quickly, showing glimpses of a quality player in an ordinary Magpie eleven. He was always willing to surge forward in the modern style and could pack a cracking shot. With his permed hair style, fashionable in the Eighties, John was Newcastle's most exciting player during season 1979-80. An injury saw him out of the reckoning for a long period, then a dispute with the club over terms resulted in the Scot departing just as the Magpies were ready to take off; Brownlie heading for Middlesbrough as Kevin Keegan was set to sign for Newcastle. After concluding his playing career, Brownlie worked in various capacities in the lower Scottish leagues, as well as being employed as a materials co-ordinator at a factory near Stirling. Living in Central Scotland near Linlithgow, John was capped by Scotland before his 20th birthday, whilst his elder brother appeared for Partick Thistle and son Paul was on the books of Raith and Arbroath. Latterly Brownlie has been scouting in Scotland, part of Terry Butcher's back-room team.

Appearances & Goals:
Debut v Cambridge United (a) 2 September 1978
FL: 124 app 2 gls
FAC: 7(1) app 1 gl
FLC: 4 app 0 gls
Total: 135(1) app 3 gls

Honours:
7 Scot caps 1971-76/5 Scot u23 app 1972-76/1 SL app 1972/SLC winner 1973/SLC final 1975/SC final 1972/SL div 2 prom 1992(m).

BRUCE Alexander Robert 1974-1975

Striker
5'8"
b. Dundee, 23 December 1952

Career: Dundee jnrs/Preston North End jnr April 1968, prof May 1970/UNITED Jan 1974 £150,000/ Preston North End Sept 1975 cash-exch for J Bird/Wigan Ath asst-player-manager Aug 1983 free/ Retired as player April 1985.

After striking 22 goals for Preston in seasons 1972-73 and 1973-74, Alex Bruce was purchased for one of Newcastle's biggest fees and in the middle of United's 1974 FA Cup run to Wembley. Being cup-tied with the Deepdale club, he rarely received an opportunity in Joe Harvey's first eleven that season, and afterwards found it almost impossible to break the Macdonald-Tudor front combination. Neither tall nor powerfully built, the

flame-haired Bruce relied on positional play and quick-thinking to convert a goal chance. Preferring a striker role, United considered he could do a job in a deeper position, but that never worked. Alex returned to Preston without reaching double figures in any of his three seasons at St James' Park, and although he won an Under-23 cap for his country when on United's books, has to be recognised as an expensive flop, although he was hardly given a chance to claim a place. Bruce though, found his touch again with the Lilywhites being the Third Division's leading goal getter during 1977-78 and on seven occasions their top scorer, in total hitting 171 goals in over 400 matches, not far off Tom Finney's club record. Alex afterwards resided in that town and was employed running a leisure centre later becoming Operations Manager, overseeing all leisure facilities for South Ribble Borough Council. Bruce scored in Newcastle's Texaco Cup final success over Southampton in 1975 and was initially developed as a kid by Arthur Cox at Deepdale.

Appearances & Goals:
Debut v Southampton (a) 5 February 1974
FL: 16(4) app 3 gls
Others: 4 app 1 gl
Total: 20(4) app 4 gls

Honours:
1 Scot u23 app 1974/FL div 3 prom 1978.

BULLOCH Hugh Cairns 1935-1936

Centre-half
5'11"
b. Larkhall, Lanarkshire, 2 June 1908

Career: Royal Albert Ath/Morton Jan 1931/Portadown 1933/UNITED Nov 1935 £1,325/New Brighton Sept 1936 free/Portadown player-manager Dec 1937/New Brighton May 1938 to Sept 1939/Portadown 1939/Aircraft Utd 1941/Resumed with Portadown 1947.

A report of the day noted Hugh Bulloch as, "one of the outstanding players in Irish league football". A centre-back who could turn defence into attack, Bulloch impressed United manager Tom Mather and directors Oliver and Rutherford when playing in the Irish Gold Cup semi-final during 1935. Having played in 57 games on the Scottish beat, he captained Portadown to success in the competition and Newcastle quickly brought him to Tyneside to compete for the centre-half position alongside Dave Davidson and former England captain, Tony Leach. With a receding hairline, Bulloch showed an unyielding approach and was whole-hearted in his play, however, was unfortunate to pick up an injury soon after making his debut for the Magpies and, once recovered, never regained his place. He later did well on Merseyside with New Brighton, an inspiration to their defence in 100 matches during the club's Football League days. Hugh was also skipper of the Rakers.

Appearances & Goals:
Debut v Nottingham Forest (h) 30 November 1935
FL: 5 app 0 gls
Total: 5 app 0 gls

Honours:
NI GC winner 1935.

BURGESS Charles Millar 1900-1901

Right-back
5'10"
b. Montrose, 20 November 1873
d. Massachusetts (USA), 21 May 1960

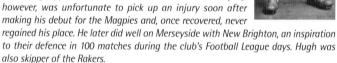

Career: Montrose 1888/Dundee June 1895/Millwall Ath May 1898/UNITED May 1900/Portsmouth May 1901/Montrose July 1903 to c1904 when he switched sports to become a golf professional.

Scot Charles Burgess was a tall, powerful and robust defender who appeared as a regular during the 1900-01 season. Having started playing the game with Montrose as a 15-year-old, joining his brother in the Links Park line-up, Charles had played a lot of football by the time he arrived on Tyneside. Although performing consistently, Burgess was never a favourite of the Tyneside fans and it is recorded he received some characteristic terrace abuse during his short stay at St James' Park.

As a consequence he moved after one season to appear successfully in the Southern League, then in the days before the formation of the Third and Fourth Divisions. One pen-picture during 1903 noted that he, "tackles with extreme resolution, and will take the risk of rushing among a crowd of players to get the ball". Burgess had been a keen golfer from his teenage years and on returning to the Scottish coastal town of Montrose in 1903, took up the sport on the links course seriously, becoming a well known and expert golfer. Charles was appointed professional at the Royal Albert club moving to the States around 1909 to begin an illustrious career as a golf instructor. Known as Chay Burgess then, he was highly respected and played against and taught some of the great names of his era, many celebrities taking lessons from him including the likes of Bing Crosby. Burgess also coached Harvard University soccer team into the Twenties and retired as the Woodland club's golf pro in 1939 after 30 years of service. He lived near Boston to his death.

Appearances & Goals:
Debut v Nottingham Forest (h) 1 September 1900
FL: 30 app 0 gls
FAC: 1 app 0 gls
Total: 31 app 0 gls

Honours:
1 SnL app 1899/SnL champs 1902.

BURKE Richard John 1946-1947

Right-back
5'10"
b. Ashton under Lyne, 28 October 1920
d. Blackpool, 4 January 2004

Career: Droylsden/Blackpool amat cs 1937, prof Nov 1937 (Portsmouth war-guest 1940-42)/UNITED Dec 1946 £3,250/Carlisle Utd Aug 1947 £1,350 to May 1949/Ashton Utd 1953.

Starting his career with Blackpool prior to the outbreak of the Second World War, Dick Burke had made his debut in the Football League as a teenager against Manchester United only a matter of months before his contract was cancelled due to Hitler's advances in Europe. Consequently Dick's promising career was ruined and he didn't return to Bloomfield Road action for over five years, until 1945 after serving in the Royal Navy. In the transitional 1945-46 programme, Burke's displays caught the eye of Stan Seymour's scouting network and he signed for the Magpies to add a touch of experience to the club's young squad. He rivalled one of those kids, Bobby Cowell, for a season before Cowell showed he was to become a star of the future. A competent rather than brilliant defender, Burke travelled across the Pennines and continued to appear for Carlisle for two seasons (79 app) before moving into non-league football.

Appearances & Goals:
Debut v Plymouth Argyle (h) 7 December 1946
FL: 15 app 0 gls
FAC: 2 app 0 gls
Total: 17 app 0 gls

BURLEIGH Martin Stewart 1968-1974

Goalkeeper
5'11"
b. Willington, Co Durham, 2 February 1951

Career: Willington/UNITED amat Nov 1967, trial Oct 1968, pmt Dec 1968/Darlington Oct 1974 £8,000/Carlisle Utd June 1975/Darlington Aug 1977/Hartlepool Utd Oct 1979 £8,000 to May 1982/Bishop Auckland Nov 1982/Spennymoor Utd July 1983 to Dec 1983/Langley Park 1984.

Deputy to Irish international Willie McFaul, goalkeeper Martin Burleigh began his career at St James' Park following good displays in the Northern League. After waiting four years to gain possession of United's green jersey, the unlucky Burleigh fractured a finger in a clash with Southampton's Mick Channon. In his few appearances for the club Martin showed that he was a good last line of defence to call upon and a goalkeeper who could command his area. However

difficulty keeping his weight to an acceptable level, coupled with McFaul being at his peak during the early Seventies, meant Burleigh's future was likely to be elsewhere. Martin fell into dispute with boss Joe Harvey and walked out on the club in August 1974 when he considered joining the RAF. He was replaced by Mick Mahoney and he moved to Feethams then to the Victoria Ground. With Darlington he registered 112 matches while at rivals Hartlepool totalled 96 games. He was on the substitute's bench for United's 1970-71 European campaign, Burleigh later resided in Ferryhill, employed in the decorating trade.

Appearances & Goals:
Debut v Leeds United (a) 26 December 1970
FL: 11 app 0 gls
Others: 4 app 0 gls
Total: 15 app 0 gls

BURNS Michael Edward 1974-1978

Striker or Midfield
5'7"
b. Preston, 21 December 1946

Career: Preston North End 1964/Chorley/Skelmersdale Utd amat 1965/Blackpool May 1969/UNITED July 1974 £170,000/Cardiff City player-coach Aug 1978 £72,000/Middlesbrough Sept 1978 £72,000, becoming asst-coach July 1981 to Nov 1982/PFA Education Officer Feb 1984, later becoming Chief Executive of the FL & PFA's Educational & Vocational Training Society, based in Manchester, to Feb 2004.

When Micky Burns joined the staff in the close-season of 1974 following impressive figures at Blackpool of 72 goals in 218 matches, he became United's most expensive signing next to Malcolm Macdonald. Only 5'7" tall, but full of trickery and the natural touch of a goalscorer in front of the posts, Burns netted a stunning effort on his first appearance at St James' Park during a Texaco Cup match against Middlesbrough. In a marvellous solo run from the half-way line he went past several defenders before slipping the ball in the net. A versatile forward, he operated on the wing initially, however Burns' relationship with Joe Harvey started poorly, the player once refusing to play in a Central League match for the reserve side. It wasn't until Gordon Lee took over that the player flourished. Intelligent and thoughtful with the ball, he then became more of an out and out striker, operating just behind the front runners, and he often found the net as United reached Wembley in 1976 and qualified for Europe the following season when he scored 17 goals in the Number 9 shirt. Quick off the mark and difficult to stop when in full flow, Burns relished that free role up front. He was a central figure in the so-called players' revolt that ended with Richard Dinnis being given the manager's job, and on Dinnis' departure, Burns left quickly along with many of the side. An educated individual, holding a degree in economics, Micky exchanged a teaching career to sign for Blackpool after being recognised as one of the top amateur players in the country. On retiring from the game, Burns was a key promoter of the Youth Training Scheme (YTS) and football's links with the community, becoming an important member of the PFA's staff in Manchester for a lengthy period.

Appearances & Goals:
Debut v Coventry City (h) 17 August 1974
(v Sunderland (a) 3 August 1974 (TC))
FL: 143(2) app 39 gls
FAC: 17 app 5 gls
FLC: 14 app 4 gls
Euro: 4 app 0 gls
Others: 11 app 3 gls
Total: 189(2) app 51 gls

Honours:
1 Eng amat app 1969/FAAC final 1967/FLC final 1976/FL div 2 prom 1970.

B

BURNS Michael Thomas 1927-1936

Goalkeeper
5'10"
b. Leeholme, Co Durham, 7 June 1908
d. Newcastle upon Tyne, September 1982

Career: Chilton CW/UNITED Sept 1927 £100/
Preston North End July 1936 £400/Ipswich Town
May 1938 (Norwich City war-guest 1939-40)
(Crook Town war-guest 1940-41)/Retired playing
May 1952.

*After once being converted to a forward for
conceding too many goals, Mick Burns developed
into a steady goalkeeper to serve Newcastle for
nine seasons. At a time when the Magpies had
three or even four senior 'keepers on the books,
Burns had a constant challenge to be recognised
as a first choice, although he turned out on 30
occasions in season 1928-29, his best term.
He initially battled with Willie Wilson for the position, then international 'keeper Albert
McInroy as well as Norman Tapken. When Burns joined Preston he quickly found himself
thrust into the biggest game of his life, as stand-in for Harry Holdcroft in the 1937 FA
Cup final against Sunderland. He later played for many years with Ipswich Town, being
on the field for the East Anglians' inaugural match in the Football League during 1938.
A dependable last line of defence and thoroughly professional, curly-haired Mick's
career spanned all of four decades, his last game being recorded during season 1951-
52 when he was almost 44 years old. Following retirement from the game, Burns
returned to Tyneside where he was a caretaker at a Roman Catholic school in
Newcastle.*

Appearances & Goals:
Debut v Blackburn Rovers (h) 1 October 1927
FL: 104 app 0 gls
FAC: 3 app 0 gls
Others: 1 app 0 gls
Total: 108 app 0 gls

Honours:
FAC final 1937.

BURRIDGE John 1989-1991, 1993-1996

Goalkeeper & Coach
5'11"
b. Great Clifton, near Workington, 3 December 1951

Career: Workington Town jnr April 1967, prof Jan
1970/Blackpool April 1971 £20,000/Aston Villa Sept
1975 £75,000 (Southend Utd loan 1977-78)/Crystal
Palace March 1978 £65,000/ Queens Park Rangers
Dec 1980 £200,000/ Wolverhampton Wand Aug
1982 £75,000 (Derby Co loan 1984-85)/Sheffield Utd
Oct 1984 £75,000/Southampton Aug 1987 £30,000/
UNITED Oct 1989 £25,000 (Falkirk loan 1991-92)/
Hartlepool Utd trial July 1991/Hibernian Aug 1991
free/Barrow cs 1993/UNITED Aug 1993 part-time
player & part-time gkp-coach to 1996/Scarborough
Oct 1993/Lincoln City Dec 1993/Enfield Feb
1994/Aberdeen March 1994/Barrow Sept 1994/Dunfermline Ath Oct 1994/
Dumbarton Nov 1994/Falkirk Nov 1994/Manchester City Nov 1994/Notts Co Sept
1995/Witton Albion Oct 1995/Darlington Nov 1995/Grimsby Town Dec 1995/
Northampton Town Jan 1996/Gateshead Jan 1996/Durham City March 1996/
Gateshead March 1996/Queen of the South March 1996/Purfleet March 1996/
Leeds Utd part-time gkp-coach 1996 to 1998/Blyth Spartans Aug 1996/Scarborough
Dec 1996/Durham City March 1997/Blyth Spartans player-manager March 1997 to
May 1998/Oman FA gkp-coach July 1998/Al-Ain coach (UAE) 2006/Oman FA coach
to Jan 2011/Singapore FA gkp-coach Feb 2014.

*John Burridge has undergone a remarkable career in the game, appearing for more
than 30 different clubs in a long playing span of almost 30 years. He started as a
teenager with then Football League side Workington and made his Football League
debut in May 1969 and since has appeared throughout England and Scotland in over
900 senior matches, later during his career becoming something of an emergency
call-out 'keeper, filling in for clubs with a goalkeeping problem. His last senior outing
was over 28 years later in November 1997, for Blyth against Blackpool in the FA Cup
when he was almost 46 years of age. Always superfit, Burridge lived for playing
football. He was agile and brave, and ever an extrovert, entertaining supporters with*

*brash warm up routines. Being added to Newcastle's roster when almost 38 years
old, at the time the club's oldest post-war player, John always had United as one of
his favourite clubs since supporting them as a boy, and he later returned to become
Kevin Keegan's goalkeeping coach. This after being handed a free transfer by Ossie
Ardiles, although winning the club's Player of the Season award for the previous 1990-
91 campaign. Confident and dedicated as they come, John possessed an infectious
personality in the dressing-room and has been a popular player at all his venues. Ex-
teammate Andy Gray colourfully described him in one book Foreword as being an
"oddball, crazy, madcap, looney, eccentric". Known the nation over as 'Budgie', he
unusually appeared for Manchester City against United in season 1994-95 when on
the Magpies' staff, while he was also sub for the Black'n'Whites when aged over 40
during the previous season. Burridge lived in Durham for many years and his son
played for the Wasps and Great Britain at ice-hockey. During the summer of 1998
John moved overseas following a court appearance for retailing counterfeit goods in
a business enterprise. He settled in the Middle East, coaching in the region, afterwards
becoming a television presenter and columnist living in Muscat. He was at that time
involved in a serious traffic accident when on a cycle, being hit and dragged by a car;
he was badly injured with one leg left disabled. John was brought up in a rugby area
of Cumbria and played for England schools at the sport.*

Appearances & Goals:
Debut v Reading (h) 4 October 1989 (FLC)
FL: 69 app 0 gls
FAC: 7 app 0 gls
FLC: 4 app 0 gls
Others: 4 app 0 gls
Total: 84 app 0 gls

Honours:
FLC winner 1977/FL div 2 champs 1979/FL div 2 prom 1983/FL div 4 prom 1978
(6 app)/SLC winner 1992/PFA ToS (d2) 1983.

BURTON Alwyn Derek 1963-1973

Centre-half
5'11"
b. Chepstow, Monmouthshire, 11 November 1941

Career: Bulwark BC Sept 1957/Chepstow Town/
Newport Co Dec 1958/Norwich City March 1961
£11,000/UNITED June 1963 £37,500/Retired due to
injury 1973.

*Impressing manager Joe Harvey in several displays for
Norwich against the Black'n'Whites, including a 5-0
FA Cup hammering by the Canaries during 1963, 21-
year-old Ollie Burton became one of United's costliest
purchases at the time after recording 73 games at
Carrow Road. Signed as a wing-half, the Welshman eventually operated as a defensive
centre-half stopper when football's style changed in the aftermath of the 1966 World
Cup. He was a versatile player for the Magpies, Burton also played at right-back, in
midfield and even at centre-forward. Ollie took time to settle in the North East failing
to live up to his big price tag at first and Burton didn't gain a permanent position in
United's side until Newcastle had returned to the First Division during 1965. With
rivals like Anderson, Iley, Thompson and later, Moncur and McNamee, Ollie always
had stiff competition at Gallowgate. But he did hold the Number 5 shirt during the
club's Inter Cities Fairs Cup success. Characterised by auburn hair, Burton was a tough
footballer, but one who could play a bit too. He also possessed a tremendous drive
which rarely was used to its full potential at Gallowgate. On United's books for ten
years, he was unlucky with injuries throughout his career, a knee problem after a clash
with his own 'keeper Willie McFaul in January 1972 later forcing his early retirement.
A well supported testimonial took place in May 1973 (35,873) and afterwards Burton
returned to Norfolk often watching Norwich at Carrow Road. He was employed in
public relations for firstly Rothmans, then brewers Hurlinam before concentrating on
a catering business, The Sandwich Basket, in Diss. Burton became the first Newcastle
substitute to enter the field in September 1965 against Northampton, while he also
was the first sub to score for the club two years later when he netted facing Lincoln.
Ollie is also much remembered for hitting two screaming spot-kicks at Roker Park
against Sunderland during December 1967.*

Appearances & Goals:
Debut v Derby County (h) 24 August 1963
FL: 181(7) app 6 gls
FAC: 9 app 0 gls
FLC: 7(1) app 2 gls
Euro: 18(1) app 0 gls
Others: 5 app 0 gls
Total: 220(9) app 8 gls

Honours:
9 Wales caps 1963-72/5 Wales u23 app 1961-65/Wales sch-youth app/FL div 2 champs
1965 (2 app)/FLC winner 1962/ICFC winner 1969.

BUSBY Vivian Dennis 1971-1972

Striker
6'0"
b. High Wycombe, Buckinghamshire,
19 June 1949

Career: Terries (High Wycombe)/Wycombe Wand July 1966/Luton Town Jan 1970 (UNITED loan Dec 1971 to Feb 1972)/Fulham Aug 1973 £25,000/Norwich City Sept 1976 £50,000/Stoke City Nov 1977 £50,000 (Sheffield Utd loan 1979-80)/Tulsa Roughnecks (USA) £30,000 March to Nov 1980/Blackburn Rovers Feb 1981 £40,000/ York City player-coach Aug 1982, becoming asst-manager 1984/Sunderland asst-manager May 1987/ Manchester City scout Dec 1991/ Hartlepool Utd manager Feb 1993 to Nov 1993/Afterwards a scout for several clubs including Southampton and West Bromwich Albion/Sheffield Utd asst-coach Dec 1995/ Everton asst-coach June 1997/ Ethnikos Piraeus (Gr) asst-manager Aug 1998/Fulham asst-coach Dec 1999/Swindon Town asst-coach 2000, becoming Head of Youth/York City asst-manager Sept 2004, becoming caretaker-manager Dec 2004 to Feb 2005/ Gretna Academy Director 2005/Workington coach and asst-manager Sept 2007 to Oct 2011/Also a spell as Sheffield Wed "Girls & Womens football co-ordinator".

A former goalscoring partner to Malcolm Macdonald at Luton, Viv Busby was unfortunate that his short loan period at St James' Park at a time of injury absentees, coincided, firstly, with a lay off due to influenza, then with the club's biggest humiliation in their modern history, a defeat at Hereford United in the FA Cup. The tall and silky striker was available at £50,000 and had scored for United in his first two outings, consequently finding himself in the line-up which ran out at Edgar Street on that fateful February afternoon during 1972. That infamous defeat was never going to help Viv's chances of a contract at Gallowgate and although Busby didn't play badly during his sojourn north, he was sent back to Kenilworth Road. He proceeded to prove that he was a useful, if not brilliant, striker elsewhere, notably at Fulham and QPR, grounds where he had trials earlier as a teenager. At Craven Cottage he scored 38 goals in 155 outings and Busby was part of the Londoner's FA Cup giant-killing side, scoring some crucial goals during their run to Wembley. On retiring from the playing side of the game, Busby fashioned out a career as a coach and assistant-manager, club-hopping to various ports of call around the country. Viv battled against leukaemia later during his football career and moved to the Costa del Sol to reside in 2011. His younger brother, Martyn, also appeared for QPR as well as Burnley and Portsmouth.

Appearances & Goals:
Debut v West Bromwich Albion (a) 11 December 1971 (1 goal)
FL: 4 app 2 gls
FAC: 1 app 0 gls
Total: 5 app 2 gls

Honours:
FL div 2 prom 1979/FL div 3 prom 1970 (9 app)/FL div 4 champs 1984 (3 app)/FAC final 1975.

BUTLER Joseph William 1958-1965

Left-back
5'7"
b. Newcastle upon Tyne, 7 February 1943

Career: UNITED jnr Aug 1958, prof Sept 1960/ Swindon Town Aug 1965 £5,500/Aldershot Aug 1976/ Whitney Town 1978.

Small in stature, Joe Butler was one of the club's early youth products developing alongside the likes of Bob Moncur, Frank Clark and David Craig. A ninety minute worker, he appeared for United's reserve and junior sides at both full-back and wing-half, but it was at left-back that he was selected for all his senior appearances during season 1963-64. Butler stood in for George Dalton, but saw Frank Clark leap ahead of him to take over Dalton's role in time for the Magpies promotion to Division One. Joe was transferred to Swindon where he became a noted servant to the Robins, totalling 428 games in

---

a versatile fashion; in midfield, attack or in defence. He showed lots of courage and determination, and was part of the famous Swindon side that reached Wembley as a Third Division club during 1969 and defeated the mighty Arsenal. Joe later settled in Wiltshire and ran a taxi firm in Swindon.

Appearances & Goals:
Debut v Manchester City (a) 4 April 1964
FL: 3 app 0 gls
FLC: 1 app 0 gls
Total: 4 app 0 gls

Honours:
FL div 3 prom 1969/FLC winner 1969.

BUTT Nicholas 2004-2010

Midfield
5'10"
b. Gorton, Manchester, 21 January 1975

Career: Boundary Park Jnrs/Manchester Utd jnr July 1991, prof Jan 1993/UNITED July 2004 £2m (Birmingham City loan 2005-06) to June 2010/South China AA (HK) Dec 2010 to May 2011 when he retired playing/Manchester Utd asst-coach Oct 2012.

One of Manchester United's 'Golden Generation' at Old Trafford, Nicky Butt graduated through the Reds' youth system together with David Beckham, Paul Scholes, Ryan Giggs and the Neville brothers. Following almost 400 games and nearly 12 seasons as a professional for Alex Ferguson's side as a midfield competitor with grit and resolve, a period in which he won just about everything including the heralded treble in 1999, Nicky moved to Tyneside in a £2m deal during the summer of 2004. Bobby Robson wanted Butt to replace Gary Speed in the central anchor role and to compliment his many attacking players in the squad. His career in a black-and-white shirt though did not begin too well with Robson moving on and Souness arriving as boss, the season ending with humiliation in the FA Cup semi-final at the hands of his old club Manchester United, a game in which Nicky was well below par. Butt's time with the Magpies looked over and he was loaned to Birmingham City for a the complete 2005-06 season, yet to his credit Nicky put the opening months at Gallowgate behind him and was determined to make an impact and show the Geordie public he was no flop. Returning for season 2006-07 under new boss Glenn Roeder, his battling performances, a mix of a tigerish streak and neat, thoughtful distribution, won over the Toon Army and Nicky went onto total over 170 games for the Magpies. After six seasons as a Newcastle player and when 35 years old, Butt was released following United's relegation from the Premier League. He effectively called a halt to his admirable career, although he then briefly appeared in the Far East. Sometimes fiery on the field, especially during his younger days, he was once sent off in Toon colours after only 133 seconds on the Gallowgate pitch, coming on as substitute then immediately being ordered off in a clash with a Hapoel opponent during 2004. After performing well in the 2002 World Cup in Japan-Korea, the celebrated Pele judged Nicky as his "player of the tournament". Butt unusually made his debut at St James' Park when a Newcastle player, not playing for the Magpies, but for England, against Ukraine in August 2004. He skippered the Magpies on occasion during his stay on Tyneside.

Appearances & Goals:
Debut v Middlesbrough (a) 14 August 2004
PL: 121(13) app 5 gls
FAC: 10 app 0 gls
FLC: 6(2) app 0 gls
Euro: 15(4) app 0 gls
Total: 152(19) app 5 gls

Honours:
39 Eng caps 1997-2005/WdC 2002/7 Eng u21 app 1995-97/Eng sch-youth app/PL champs 1993 (1 app), 1994 (1 app), 1996, 1997, 1999, 2000, 2001, 2003/FL ch winner 2010/FAC winner 1996, 2003, 2004/FAC final 1995/FLC final 2003 (sub no app)/ CL winner 1999/ICC winner 1999/PFA ToS (PL) 1998/FAYC winner 1992.

C

CABAYE Johan 2011-2014

Midfield
5'9"
b. Tourcoing, near Lille (France),
14 January 1986

Career: US Tourcoing 1992/Lille OSC jnr July 1998, prof cs 2004/UNITED June 2011 £4.3m/ Paris St-Germain (Fr) Jan 2014 £19m.

Having been a key figure in Lille's French double winning triumph of 2010-11, Yohan Cabaye made the move to Tyneside as part of Alan Pardew's rebuilding strategy during the close-season of 2011. The 25-year-old French star was seen as an influential link man. In midfield and part of the French international set up, Cabaye patrols the centre of the field with vision and a cool assurance. A compactly built footballer, good on the ball who can pick out a pass, force the play as well as track back and defend, he also possesses a potent shot, striking several picture goals. Very quickly Johan adapted to the rigours of the Premier League and equally as swiftly became a Toon Army favourite, the crowd appreciating his effort and stand-out ability. With first-class technical ability, he rarely wastes a pass, and is never shy to tackle; Cabaye became United's playmaker, at his best when moving forward although at the start of the 2013-14 season was criticised over his stance when a big transfer was on the cards. That exit speculation continued, yet Cabaye remained the fulcrum of United's midfield, the most important player in the Magpie line-up. However, the lure of France's top club PSG and with it Champions League football was too great, Cabaye moving to Paris in January 2014 with United inevitably cashing in with a substantial profit. With Lille from a teenager, he registered 253 games netting 39 goals for the Les Dogues over seven seasons and experienced the top level of European football.

Appearances & Goals:
Debut v Arsenal (h) 13 August 2011
PL: 76(3) app 17 gls
FAC: 2 app 0 gls
FLC: 2(1) app 1 gl
Euro: 7(2) app 0 gls
Total: 87(6) app 18 gls

Honours:
34 Fr caps 2011-date/WdC 2014/15 Fr u21 app/Fr sch-youth app/Fr Lg champs 2011, 2014/Fr Cup winner 2011/Fr LC winner 2014.

CACAPA (Da Silva) Claudio Roberto 2007-2009

Centre-half
6'0"
b. Lavras (Brazil), 29 May 1976

Career: Clube Atletico Mineiro (Brz) 1996/Olym Lyonnais loan Jan 2001, pmt cs 2001 £4m/ Al-Rayyan SC (Qt) July 2007/UNITED Aug 2007 free, to cs 2009/Cruzeiro EC (Brz) 2009/Evian (Fr) Jan 2011/Avai (Brz) July 2011/Retired Jan 2012/ Brazil asst-coach Nov 2013.

In the fashion of many Brazilian footballers, Claudio Da Silva used the playing-name of 'Cacapa' throughout his career. One of new manager Sam Allardyce's first imports, the vastly experienced tall and athletic Brazilian was brought to Gallowgate as a short-term move to give United's suspect rearguard both quality and all the expertise the defender had shown at the top with Lyon. Although not too well known to the ordinary supporter in England, Cacapa was much respected in both Brazil and especially France. At 31 years of age and past his peak, the Brazilian centre-back still had the touch of a master footballer and he shared the defending role in the 2007-08 season with fellow imports David Rozehnal, Abdoulaye Faye and local product Steven Taylor. Although he could be a no-nonsense stopper, he was steady and calm at the back and appeared in over 150 games for the French club, several as captain. He had many games in the Champions League too and was part of the team which lifted six French titles when at the Stade de Gerland. A groin strain saw him on the sidelines on Tyneside though and the following season he was much less used at Gallowgate as United made a shock exit from the Premier League. The South American departed in the summer of 2009 to wind down his career and begin coaching, later looking after his country's under-15 squad. Cacapa holds dual nationality of Brazil and France.

Appearances & Goals:
Debut v Aston Villa (h) 18 August 2007 (sub)
PL: 20(5) app 1 gl
FAC: 2 app 1 gl
FLC: 2 app 0 gls
Total: 24(5) app 2 gls

Honours:
3 Brz caps 2000-01/1 unoff Brz app/Fr Lg champs 2002, 2003, 2004, 2005, 2006, 2007 (6 app)/Fr LC winner 2001/CC winner 1997.

CAHILL Thomas 1951-1955

Left-back
5'9"
b. Glasgow, 14 June 1931
d. Spain (on holiday), 27 January 2003

Career: Vale of Leven/Fulham briefly/ UNITED Dec 1951 £750/Barrow Aug 1955 to cs 1965/Vickers Sports.

Having played well in front of watching United scouts in the Scottish non-league football, Tommy Cahill was given an opportunity to join the Magpies, but very much as a reserve. He was third choice at left-back behind Ron Batty and Alf McMichael, two tremendous servants to the club, and therefore was given very limited opportunity in Newcastle's first-team. A dogged fighter in defence, Cahill did very well at Holker Street over nine seasons, being fledgling boss Joe Harvey's first signing as he began his career in management. In Barrow's Football League side, the Scot went on to take part in 307 outings for the west coast outfit in a consistent style and good enough to appear for the divisional select eleven. Cahill retired and lived in Barrow, his son Tommy appeared for United's juniors during the early Seventies without making the grade.

Appearances & Goals:
Debut v Cardiff City (h) 25 December 1952
FL: 4 app 0 gls
Total: 4 app 0 gls

Honours:
FL div 3(N) app 1957.

CAIE Alexander 1901-1903

Right-half
5'10"
b. Torry, near Aberdeen, 25 June 1877
d. Lowell, Massachusetts (USA), 17 November 1914

Career: Victoria Utd (Aberdeen) Aug 1894/ Woolwich Arsenal Feb 1897/Bristol South End May 1897/Bristol City April 1898/Millwall Ath March 1900/UNITED May 1901/Brentford May 1903/ Motherwell July 1904 £30/ Westmount (Can)/Sons of Scotland (Can)/Rosedale (Can) to death.

A well-built, powerful half-back at over 13 stones, Alex Caie was versatile enough to play in most outfield positions during his career and in four different roles for Newcastle. Apart from right-half, Caie also operated at left-half, centre-forward and inside-left. With a splendid shot in his repertoire, he arrived from London after a fine spell with Bristol City (114 app 64 goals) to take over the role of Tommy Ghee following consolidation in the First Division at the turn of the century. Fiery and robust on the field, it was said that due to his rough play against Mickley in one United match, the entire population of the Northumberland pit village was roused against him! He was effective for a season, in 1901-02, but when Alex Gardner landed on Tyneside, Caie moved on and eventually emigrated to North America where he worked as a fireman in a manufacturing plant. Alex was later killed following a railway accident in the States, hit by a train when only 37 years old. Known as 'Big Sandy', Colin Veitch once noted Caie as being, "hard as nails" and "stout of heart." Born overlooking the Bay of Nigg, he started with the pioneers of the Aberdeen club before heading to London. Caie once appeared between the posts for Newcastle in a friendly contest against Rangers.

Appearances & Goals:
Debut v Notts County (a) 3 October 1901
FL: 31 app 1 gl
FAC: 4 app 0 gls
Total: 35 app 1 gl

CAIRNS Thomas 1914-1917

Inside-left
5'10"
b. Newcastle upon Tyne, 1895
d. Arras (France), 13 October 1917

Career: Chopwell Villa/Newcastle City April 1914/
UNITED Sept 1914 £20 to death in 1917.

Tom Cairns was one of the many who tragically sacrificed their lives during the First World War. He was one of the first of United's players to respond to Lord Kitchener's call for men to arms, joining the Royal Field Artillery and reaching the rank of corporal. Serving in the 61st Trench Mortar Battery around Arras, he fell fighting in the trenches of France and is remembered on the Arras memorial at Pas de Calais commemorating almost 35,000 allied soldiers who died. Raised in Chopwell, Cairns earned a good reputation playing in the local Northern Combination League and was signed by the Magpies just before the Great War erupted. Tommy deputised for Curtis Booth for the concluding fixture of the 1914-15 season, the last before war enforced a close-down to football, and played his part in a fine 3-0 victory over Aston Villa. Tom was one of five United players in the club's 1915 squad who died in the hostilities.

Appearances & Goals:
Debut v Aston Villa (h) 28 April 1915
FL: 1 app 0 gls
Total: 1 app 0 gls

CAIRNS William Hart 1933-1944

Centre-forward
5'9"
b. Newcastle upon Tyne,
7 October 1914
d. Grimsby, 9 January 1988

Career: Holborn Rangers/Stargate
Rovers/UNITED May 1933 £25
(Chester war-guest 1940-41)
(Liverpool war-guest 1940-41)
(Mansfield Town war-guest 1941-42)
(Nottingham Forest war-guest 1941-42)(Chesterfield war-guest 1942-43)
(Notts Co war-guest 1942-43)/
Gateshead Nov 1944 free (Sunderland
war-guest 1945-46)/Grimsby Town
May 1946/Retired cs 1954, becoming
Grimsby Town asst-coach to 1959.

Thrustful and bustling, Billy Cairns did well for Newcastle in the years leading up to the Second World War. Getting a chance in the senior line-up after relegation in 1934, he firstly partnered Jack Smith, then took over in the leader's shirt to good effect. During season 1936-37 he grabbed 16 goals, while in the campaign before war, Billy hit the net on 20 occasions. Big hearted, one Thirties scribe noted him as, "a high spirited, hell for leather, shoot on sight centre-forward, determined to score no matter the risk". He was strong and hard to push off the ball, while Cairns was always a danger in the air. He twice scored four goals in a single game for the Magpies, and once netted five against Halifax Town during the wartime programme of 1939-40. After a record season at Redheugh Park with Gateshead when he scored 42 goals, Billy started the post-war section of his career with Grimsby when a 34-year-old, yet made up for the war years with a remarkable period at Blundell Park despite his age. Cairns didn't retire from the game until he was almost 40, appearing for the other black-and-whites with distinction. He found the net 129 times in 231 senior games for Grimsby and was skipper of the Mariners for a period. His younger brother Jackie Cairns played for Hartlepool, his father and grandfather were noted runners on Tyneside, while Billy can claim to be the first Magpie centre-forward to actually wear the now famous Number 9 shirt, this when numbers were introduced in 1939. For a period he returned to Tyneside, then spent the rest of his life in Cleethorpes, a noted publican at The Freeman Arms for 30 years.

Appearances & Goals:
Debut v Bury (h) 1 January 1935
FL: 87 app 51 gls
FAC: 3 app 2 gls
War: 21 app 13 gls
Total: 111 app 66 gls
(Void FL: 2 app 1 gl)

CALDER Henry 1889-1890

Full-back
b. Lanarkshire, Scotland

Career: Drumpellier 1884/Albion Rovers 1886/EAST END Nov 1889 to c1891/
Sunderland 1891 to c1892.

Having appeared for three seasons for Coatbridge side Albion Rovers in Scotland's Central Belt, Calder was an experienced player when he arrived on Tyneside late in 1889, one of many Scots to head over the border at the time to help develop the game in the North East. He no doubt caught the eye of East End's committee men when the Scottish club visited the region on mini-tours in 1886-87 and 1888-89 and his move to England was noted in Albion Rovers' history at a time when "poaching" was taking place by English teams. On Calder's debut for East End against Morpeth Harriers in a friendly he was described as a "capital defender" and the Scot performed with credit for a short while in East End's blue shirts. He didn't see first-team action with Sunderland while back in Scotland he represented Lanarkshire at county level.

Appearances & Goals:
Debut v Auckland Town (a) 21 December 1889 (NL)
NL: 9 app 0 gls
Total: 9 app 0 gls

CALDER Neil Alexander 1940-1944

Goalkeeper
5'10"
b. Tyneside

Career: Ryton Jnrs/UNITED amat May 1940, prof Jan 1943 to c1944.

Joining United from Tyneside junior club Ryton, Neil Calder pulled on the goalkeeper's jersey on only one occasion for the Magpies, for a meeting against Leeds United during season 1942-43 in the wartime Football League North. The youngster had a harrowing baptism in senior company as the Tykes fired seven goals past the debutant. He failed to impress and spent his short stay with the club in United's wartime reserve league with Tom Swinburne and Ray King taking the first-team role between the posts when peace was restored.

Appearances & Goals:
Debut v Leeds United (a) 30 January 1943 (FLN)
War: 1 app 0 gls
Total: 1 app 0 gls.

CALDWELL Steven 1997-2004

Centre-half
6'3"
b. Stirling, 12 September 1980

Career: North Broomage Hearts/UNITED jnr June 1997, prof Oct 1997 (Blackpool loan 2001-02)(Bradford City loan 2001-02)(Leeds Utd loan 2003-04)/Sunderland June 2004 free/Burnley Jan 2007 £400,000/Bolton Wand trial July 2010/Wigan Ath Aug 2010/Birmingham City July 2011 free/Toronto (Can) May 2013.

Steven Caldwell, the elder of two footballing brothers from Stirling, arrived at Gallowgate during the summer of 1997 and within 12 months his younger brother Gary was alongside him in United's junior ranks. Caldwell had already caught the eye of boss Kenny Dalglish, being on trial briefly at Blackburn when the Scottish legend was in charge at Ewood, but it was Kevin Keegan who first brought him to Gallowgate, for a trial in April 1996 when Steve was still at school. The slender Caldwell reached the fringe of United's first-team in season 1998-99 but he didn't make his senior debut until the autumn of 2000 when he was regularly on United's bench. In his first full Premier League outing, a derby against Sunderland, Caldwell was outstanding and won the man-of-the-match award. With competition fierce for the two centre-back positions, Caldwell had to tussle for a place with Bramble, Marcelino, Goma, Dabizas, O'Brien as well as new signing Jonathan Woodgate. Steven did get a run in the Magpie eleven during mid-season of 2002-03, then again for a handful of games in the following programme, but he began to be impatient and a touch impetuous due to his lack of progress. Although tall at 6'3" and being good in the air, his reading

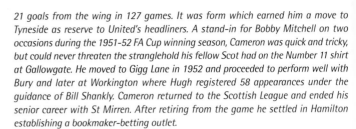

of the game and distribution of the ball was not quite up to Premier League needs and Bobby Robson released Caldwell. He dropped down a division when he moved to Wearside, but found a regular place with Sunderland and with the natural urge to shout out commands on the field became the Black Cats skipper for a period. He led the Wearsiders to promotion, although then quickly was relegated, and promoted again. Always committed, he also led Burnley to promotion. Caldwell has captained his country at Under-21 and B level and played alongside his brother Gary for Scotland at full international level. The siblings never managed to appear for United together in a first-team match apart from a testimonial outing, although the pair teamed up at club level for a short period at Wigan. His father Tom appeared for East Stirling and at junior level in Scotland.

Appearances & Goals:
Debut v Manchester City (a) 30 September 2000 (sub)
PL: 20(8) app 1 gl
FLC: 3 app 1 gl
Euro: 1(5) app 0 gls
Total: 24(13) app 2 gls

Honours:
12 Scot caps 2001-11/3 Scot B app 2003-04/8 Scot u21 app 2001-02/Scot sch-youth app/FL ch winner 2005, 2007/FL ch prom 2009.

CALLACHAN Ralph 1977-1978

Midfield
5'10"
b. Edinburgh, 29 April 1955

Career: Tynecastle BC/Heart of Midlothian Sept 1971/UNITED Feb 1977 £100,000/Hibernian Aug 1978 cash-exch for J Brownlie/Morton Sept 1986/ Meadowbank Thistle Nov 1986/Berwick Rangers Sept 1988, becoming manager Aug 1990 to May 1992.

Scot Ralph Callachan can count himself unlucky to have landed at St James' Park at the wrong time. Following over 100 matches for Hearts, the transfer of the 21-year-old midfielder from Tynecastle was completed between the departure of Gordon Lee and the appointment of Richard Dinnis, and amidst rumours that he was actually signed by the directors, later bring confirmed Chief Scout Len Richley advised the Board to make the purchase. A midfield player with the typical vein of Scottish ball skills to the fore, Callachan was composed in possession and had a stylish look but never fitted into a relegation fight during season 1977-78. He wasn't given many opportunities by Dinnis and a persistent ankle injury did not help his chances. By the time Bill McGarry had taken over the hot-seat, Callachan had resigned himself to a return to Scotland. With Hibs, Ralph did well in over 250 games, as he had done on the other side of Edinburgh in Hearts' maroon. He was highly rated north of the border and served the capital's senior clubs for almost 15 seasons. Later Callachan went into business in Edinburgh running several pubs, notably The Sportsman's Bar in Musselburgh which he operated for over 20 years. Ralph afterwards became a taxi driver in the city.

Appearances & Goals:
Debut v Bohemians (a) 14 September 1977 (UEFAC)
FL: 9 app 0 gls
Euro: 2 app 0 gls
Total: 11 app 0 gls

Honours:
Scot sch-youth app/Scot amat app 1973/SL div 1 champs 1981/SC final 1976, 1979.

CAMERON Hugh Gibson 1951-1952

Outside-left
5'8"
b. Burnbank, near Blantyre, Lanarkshire, 1 February 1927

Career: Burnbank Ath/Clyde Nov 1946/Torquay Utd May 1948 free/UNITED April 1951 £4,500/ Bury March 1952 £500/Workington Nov 1953/ St Mirren Aug 1956 free to c1958.

Moving the long distance from Glasgow to Torquay, Hugh Cameron made a name for himself at Plainmoor in the Third Division South, scoring

21 goals from the wing in 127 games. It was form which earned him a move to Tyneside as reserve to United's headliners. A stand-in for Bobby Mitchell on two occasions during the 1951-52 FA Cup winning season, Cameron was quick and tricky, but could never threaten the stranglehold his fellow Scot had on the Number 11 shirt at Gallowgate. He moved to Gigg Lane in 1952 and proceeded to perform well with Bury and later at Workington where Hugh registered 58 appearances under the guidance of Bill Shankly. Cameron returned to the Scottish League and ended his senior career with St Mirren. After retiring from the game he settled in Hamilton establishing a bookmaker-betting outlet.

Appearances & Goals:
Debut v Liverpool (h) 3 November 1951
FL: 2 app 0 gls
Total: 2 app 0 gls

CAMPBELL Adam 2002-date

Striker
5'6"
b. North Shields, 1 January 1995

Career: Wallsend BC/UNITED 2002, prof July 2011 (Carlisle Utd loan 2012-13)(St Mirren loan 2013-14) (Fleetwood Town loan 2014-15).

A diminutive live-wire striker raised in Wallsend, Adam Campbell joined United as a kid during 2002 by way of the renowned Wallsend Boys Club football academy. The young Tynesider impressed boss Alan Pardew during the pre-season preparations for 2012-13, so much so he was elevated to the first-team squad for the Europa League Play-Off with Greek side Atromitos and made his debut as a 17-year-old, the club's youngest ever player in Continental action. With a clean and sure strike of the ball, many judges rated Campbell highly, being quick and elusive up front. Flame-haired, Campbell was selected by England at both Under-16 and Under-17 level. He spent periods on loan at both Carlisle and in Scotland with St Mirren gaining valuable experience.

Appearances & Goals:
Debut v Atromitos (a) 23 August 2012 (sub) (EL)
PL: 0(3) app 0 gls
Euro: 0(2) app 0 gls
Total: 0(5) app 0 gls

Honours:
Eng sch-youth app.

CAMPBELL John Middleton 1897-1898

Centre-forward
5'8"
b. Renton, Dunbartonshire, 19 February 1870
d. Sunderland, 8 June 1906

Career: Renton Union/Renton/Sunderland June 1889/UNITED May 1897, joint deal with J Harvey £40/Retired after dismissal Oct 1898.

An important member of Sunderland's famous 'Team of all the Talents' during the years before the turn of the Victorian century, Johnny Campbell was a magnificent forward in his day and at his peak was the Football League's leading goal-getter on three occasions in four seasons between 1892 and 1895. The Scot was a touch hefty for his 5'8" frame, noted as weighing "12 stone, even when perfectly fit". Yet Johnny was one of the country's most feared strikers, described as "the most dangerous centre of modern times". Stocky and bustling, he loved to take on player after player and all told the Scot netted 154 times in 215 league and cup games for the Wearside club and played a key role in the Reds lifting three Championship trophies. In one hot spell of goalscoring during 1892 he scored 13 goals in 14 matches for the Wearsiders. Campbell arrived at Gallowgate very much as a player of experience nearing the end of his career, but still with much to offer to a Magpie side aiming to join Sunderland in the First Division. And Johnny did his job in a first-class manner with his "do or die" attitude during

United's promotion year of 1898. As Newcastle's first programme in Division One opened, Campbell fell out of favour with United's directors after he decided to take-over the management of The Darnell public-house on Barrack Road with the aim of a career once he had retired. This was strictly against the Board's rules at the time and after a long running, controversial saga, the club dismissed the player when not yet 30 years of age. Campbell's impressive career was ended and he concentrated on a business in the licensing trade in the North East, notably at the Alnwick Castle then the Turf Hotel on Wearside. To many judges of his Victorian era it was a mystery why this potent centre-forward never played for his country, being on the fringe of international selection several times but never receiving the call to pull on the blue shirt of Scotland. Campbell has the distinction of being on the field for both Newcastle, and Sunderland's, inaugural First Division fixtures. His brother Robert Campbell was appointed Secretary at Roker Park in 1896. As a teenager Johnny won the Scottish Cup with Renton before following an exodus to the North East along with two of his Renton colleagues. He lived in the region and died at a young age, being only 36 years old.

Appearances & Goals:
Debut v Woolwich Arsenal (h) 4 September 1897 (1 goal)
FL: 26 app 10 gls
FAC: 3 app 2 gls
Total: 29 app 12 gls

Honours:
FL champs 1892, 1893, 1895/FL div 2 prom 1898/SC winner 1888/Scot trial 1896/North app 1893.

CAMPBELL (Sol) Sulzeer Jeremiah 2010-2011

Centre-half
6'2"
b. Plaistow, London, 18 September 1974

Career: Senrab Jnrs/Tottenham Hotspur jnr 1989, prof Sept 1992/Arsenal July 2001 free/ Portsmouth Aug 2006 free/Notts Co Aug 2009 free to Sept 2009/Arsenal Jan 2010 free/ UNITED July 2010 free to June 2011/ Retired May 2012.

With Newcastle making a quick return to Premier League football for season 2010-11, manager Chris Hughton needed a wise head and cover for the key centre-back positions. With Steven Taylor recovering from a bad injury, United were left with only Fabricio Coloccini and Mike Williamson. At 35-years-old, former England king-pin Sol Campbell was available, without a club since having an all too brief stint with Notts County. Having recently married a local girl, the daughter of property tycoon Sir Lawrie Barratt and set up home in Northumberland, he was an obvious choice as a short-term fix. For over a decade Campbell had been one of the country's foremost defenders, skipper of both Tottenham and Arsenal, totalling over 700 games for club and country. Comfortable on the ball and confident to stride forward from defence, Campbell was an high-class defender with little weakness and won two Premier League titles in an exemplarily career which had reached many highs and certain moments of controversy such as when he moved from White Hart Lane to neighbouring Highbury in 2001. His footballing knowledge was unquestioned, whether Sol could still compete for the Magpies in the pacy, frenetic world of the Premier League was debatable. With Hughton being replaced by Alan Pardew, he was used sparingly, Campbell only recording five starts in a Toon shirt. He departed during the summer of 2011 effectively ending his outstanding career in which he had made 315 appearances for Tottenham, 211 for Arsenal and played in three World Cups, as well as three European Championships. Sol also captained England during his fine international career. With a home in London as well, Campbell began a coaching career in a part-time role with Arsenal when taking his UEFA badges.

Appearances & Goals:
Debut v Chelsea (a) 22 September 2010 (FLC)
PL: 4(3) app 0 gls
FLC: 1 app 0 gls
Total: 5(3) app 0 gls

Honours:
73 Eng caps 1996-2007/WdC 1998, 2002, 2006/1 Eng B app 2006/1 unoff Eng app 1996/11 Eng u21 app 1994-96/PL champs 2002, 2004/FAC winner 2002, 2005 (sub no app), 2008/FL div 2 champs 2010 (1 app)/FLC winner 1999/CL final 2006/PFA ToS (PL) 1999, 2003, 2004.

CAMPBELL Thomas 1894-1895

Outside-right
b. probably Scotland

Career: Linthouse/UNITED April 1894 to 1895/ Linthouse 1896-97.

A former Northumberland County player, Tom Campbell arrived from Scotland having appeared in the Scottish Football Alliance for the Linthouse club of Govan in Glasgow. He was selected in the first two games of the 1894-95 Second Division campaign for United, but then was replaced and did not regain a first-team place. He returned to appear in Division Two north of the Cheviots.

(Note: Some sources have his surname spelt as 'Cambell', but official FA and FL record books note it as above.)

Appearances & Goals:
Debut v Darwen (a) 1 September 1894
FL: 2 app 0 gls
Total: 2 app 0 gls

CANNELL Paul Anthony 1972-1978

Striker
5'11"
b. Newcastle upon Tyne, 2 September 1953

Career: Montague & N Fenham BC/ Sunderland jnr/Whitley Bay Nov 1971/ UNITED prof July 1972 (Washington Diplomats (USA) loan cs 1976)/ Washington Diplomats (USA) Feb 1978 £40,000/ Memphis Rogues (USA) Nov 1979/Calgary Boomers (Can) 1980/ Detroit Express (USA) Jan 1981/ Washington Diplomats (USA) April 1981/North Shields Nov 1981/Mansfield Town Jan 1982/Berwick Rangers May 1983/Blyth Spartans Jan 1984 to April 1984/SC Vaux Jan 1986/Afterwards appearing occasionally for various local clubs in minor football.

As a teenager Paul Cannell was a much coveted prospect on Tyneside. A schoolboy star appearing for the city and county sides as well as England Boys, he was initially in Sunderland's junior ranks, but with an agreement to be released if the Magpies came for him, which they did in 1972. Cannell rose through United's reserve set-up quickly and was on the bench in United's League Cup final at Wembley in 1976. On the departure of Malcolm Macdonald to Arsenal in 1976 Paul was given a regular striker's role by manager Gordon Lee and the Geordie grabbed the chance. The dark and moustached Cannell was quick off the mark, performed well and grew in maturity, striking 13 goals alongside Alan Gowling and Micky Burns as Newcastle qualified for Europe in season 1976-77. Supporters took to him, a local lad doing well, but the internal strife which followed affected the young Tynesider and on the appointment of Bill McGarry, Paul was part of a mass clear-out. He decided to continue his career in North American football like many players at that time. Paul was a big hit in the States and Canada, appearing in the NASL alongside such world megastars as Pele, Eusebio, Best and Giorgio Chinaglia. He netted over 50 goals in that standard of football and enjoyed a star-spangled lifestyle for three years. As a teenager Cannell gave up a place at Durham University to study law, being persuaded to sign professional by Joe Harvey. On returning from the North American scene when it collapsed, he settled on Tyneside, employed for Vaux Brewery for a while before running Zoots nightclub and a publishing company. He later ran several pubs in the region including The Corner House, Edgefield Lodge and the Alexandra. During the late Seventies, comedian Jasper Carrott handed him the inventive rhyming slang expression of "Fucking Hell, Paul Cannell" which stuck in Geordie folklore.

Appearances & Goals:
Debut v Manchester City (a) 27 March 1974
(v Ayr Utd (h) 27 September 1972 (TC))
FL: 47(1) app 13 gls
FAC: 5 app 0 gls
FLC: 7(1) app 4 gls
Euro: 3 app 1 gl
Others: 5(1) app 2 gls
Total: 67(3) app 20 gls

Honours:
Eng sch-youth app/FLC final (sub no app) 1976.

C

CAPE John Phillips 1930-1934

Outside-right
5'8"
b. Carlisle, 16 November 1911
d. Carlisle, 6 June 1994

Career: Penrith/Carlisle Utd May 1929/UNITED Jan 1930 £1,750/Manchester Utd Jan 1934 £2,000/Queens Park Rangers June 1937/Carlisle Utd Aug 1939/Scarborough cs 1946/Carlisle Utd Oct 1946 to Feb 1947, becoming asst-trainer for a period.

Jackie Cape, a strong and rugged player, was in and out of the Magpies' line-up during his five season stay on Tyneside. Joining United as a teenage part-timer for a hefty fee from Carlisle, money which was used to construct a roof on the Brunton Park Scratching Pen, Cape had only appeared on a handful of occasions in senior action, but was seen as a bright prospect for future years. It was described at the time that "he would run like a deer" for the ball if it was pushed in front of him and Cape did at times realise his potential, but never quite consistently enough to become the big star many hoped for. A sturdy winger at nearly 13 stone, Cape was overshadowed by Jimmy Boyd at Gallowgate, yet had several memorable moments in a black-and-white striped shirt including scoring the single goal that defeated Chelsea when St James' Park's record attendance was set in 1930, and also a brace as the club recorded their biggest ever FA Cup scoreline, 9-0 against Southport. He also bagged a stunning treble in a 7-4 victory over Manchester United. Disappointed not to get into United's FA Cup final side during 1932, he did receive a specially minted winners' medal. It was the Old Trafford side Cape joined after his stint with Newcastle was over and with the Reds, as well as with QPR, he did well assisting Manchester United to promotion in 1936 and totalling 60 matches. He is noted as scoring one of the most important goals (and he made the other in a 2-0 victory) in the Reds' history; against Millwall on the last day of the season in 1934 which saw his club avoid relegation to the old Division Three North. Jackie was an apprentice electrician before he signed for the Magpies, a job he reverted to during the Second World War. After retiring from the game he resided in his home town for the rest of his life working as a driver. Cape's uncle, Jack Nixon, was a director of Carlisle United.

Appearances & Goals:
Debut v Leicester City (a) 18 January 1930
FL: 51 app 18 gls
FAC: 2 app 2 gls
Total: 53 app 20 gls

Honours:
FL div 2 champs 1936.

CARLTON William 1926-1929

Right-half
5'8"
b. Washington, Co Durham, 15 July 1907
d. Co. Durham, 1973 (Q4)

Career: Washington CW/UNITED Sept 1926 £20/Merthyr Town May 1929 free/West Stanley Sept 1930/Ashington Nov 1931/Annfield Plain Aug 1933/Bedlington Utd Jan 1934.

With Newcastle United at the time of their League Championship victory in 1927, dark-haired local youngster Billy Carlton was given few chances to impress due to the Magpies established stars. He was largely third choice for the right-half midfield position behind Joe Harris and Roddie McKenzie. Following brief outings in 1927-28, Carlton returned as a deputy during the next season, hitting the net against Sheffield United. He joined Welsh Division Three South club Merthyr where he had a good run of games at mainly right-back for a campaign. Carlton soon returned to the North East playing on the non-league circuit.

Appearances & Goals:
Debut v Liverpool (h) 3 December 1927
FL: 5 app 1 gl
FAC: 1 app 0 gl
Total: 6 app 1 gl

CARNEY Stephen 1979-1985

Centre-half
5'10"
b. Wallsend, 22 September 1957
d. Newcastle upon Tyne, 6 May 2013

Career: Dudley Jnrs/North Shields 1975-76/Blyth Spartans cs 1977/UNITED Oct 1979 £1,000 (Carlisle Utd on loan 1984-85)/Darlington July 1985 free (Rochdale loan 1985-86)/Hartlepool Utd March 1986 to May 1986/Tow Law Town Sept 1986/Blyth Spartans March 1987 to May 1991/Newcastle Blue Star (Newcastle RTM) manager 1992 to April 1996.

Plucked from the rough and tumble of non-league football with Blyth Spartans, Steve Carney arrived late onto the Football League circuit as a 22-year-old along with Alan Shoulder, after the pair had been instrumental in the Spartans' headlining FA Cup run to the Sixth Round draw in 1978. Carney was at his best when operating in the centre of United's defence where he partnered Jeff Clarke, and later Glenn Roeder. In United's promotion season of 1983-84 Steve was a revelation. Although not tall and powerful in the typical stopper mould, Carney was quick and possessed steely determination with a biting tackle, as well as a fiery streak which occasionally got him into trouble on the field. Carney also played at full-back and in midfield for United, but wasn't given a role by Jack Charlton in the Magpies' First Division line-up. As a youngster Steve was with West Bromwich Albion for a short spell, and he exchanged an electrician's job for that of a professional footballer when he signed for the Black'n'Whites. After leaving the game, Carney was involved in property development, Managing Director of English Homes in the North East, before setting up a fitness and health venture, Steve Carney Fitness based in Jesmond. He also ran a family business retailing children's clothing before his untimely death in 2013.

Appearances & Goals:
Debut v Fulham (h) 1 December 1979
FL: 125(9) app 1 gl
FAC: 9 app 0 gls
FLC: 6 app 0 gls
Total: 140(9) app 1 gl

Honours:
FL div 2 prom 1984.

CARR Edward Miller 1942-1945

Centre-forward
5'6"
b. Wheatley Hill, Co Durham, 3 October 1917
d. Huddersfield, June 1998

Career: Wheatley Hill CW/Arsenal amat Feb 1935 (Margate loan 1935-36, 1936-37), prof Aug 1937 (Hartlepools Utd war-guest 1939-40)(Bradford Park Avenue war-guest 1940-44)(UNITED war-guest 1942-45) (Middlesbrough war-guest 1942-43)(Darlington war-guest 1943-44)/Huddersfield Town Oct 1945/Newport Co Oct 1946/Bradford City Oct 1949/Darlington Aug 1953, becoming trainer July 1954, manager June 1960 to April 1964/Tow Law Town manager 1964/UNITED scout 1969 to 1971.

Eddie Carr was an ex-miner who after establishing himself as a promising striker at Highbury, returned to County Durham to work down the pits during the hostilities. Carr became, next to Albert Stubbins, Newcastle's most potent forward during the era, boasting an impressive 81% strike-rate of 57 goals in only 70 outings. Sturdy, but not tall at 5'6", following two seasons at Arsenal's nursery side of Margate, Eddie was deputy in the main to Ted Drake in London, but he had some excellent performances in the Gunner's star-studded line-up. Carr helped his side to the title in 1938 when he scored two of the goals which clinched the trophy. A knee operation just before the Second World War threatened his career, but after recovering Eddie joined the Magpies and on one occasion in the black-and-white stripes, hit six goals in an 11-0 thrashing of Bradford City during 1944. In post-war football Eddie continued scoring goals, for Newport (54 goals) and Bradford City (56 goals) before returning to his native County Durham to settle. As manager of Tow Law Town, he guided the Lawyers to a famous FA Cup victory over Mansfield Town in 1967.

Appearances & Goals:
Debut v Leeds United (h) 26 September 1942 (FLN) (1 goal)
War: 70 app 57 gls
Total: 70 app 57 gls.

Honours:
FL champs 1938.

Appearances & Goals:
Debut v Crewe Alexandra (h) 25 December 1895
FL: 4 app 0 gls
Total: 4 app 0 gls

Honours:
FL div 2 prom 1898 (2 app)/SL div 2 champs 1899 (6 app).

CARR Franz Alexander 1991-1993

Outside-right
5'7"
b. Preston, 24 September 1966

Career: Blackburn Rovers jnr Sept 1982, prof July 1984/Nottingham Forest Aug 1984 £100,000 (Sheffield Wed loan 1989-90)(West Ham Utd loan 1990-91)/UNITED June 1991 £250,000/Sheffield Utd loan, pmt Jan 1993 £180,000/Leicester City loan Sept 1994, pmt Oct 1994 £100,000/Aston Villa Feb 1995 cash-exch deal £250,000/AC Reggiana (It) trial Sept 1996, pmt Oct 1996 free/Everton trial Oct 1997/Bolton Wand Oct 1997/West Bromwich Albion Feb 1998 to April 1998/ Grimsby Town trial Aug 1998/Runcorn 1999/Pittsburg Riverhounds (USA) 2000, becoming coach to cs 2001.

Small, direct and a potential match-winner on the right-wing, Franz Carr had been a teenage star under Brian Clough at Nottingham Forest and played for England at school, youth and Under-21 level. Carr appeared on over 150 occasions for the Reds and took part in a League Cup run to Wembley, but perhaps lacked the necessary genuine craft to complement his exceptional pace to become a top quality forward. In and out of Forest's eleven, being left out of the 1991 FA Cup final side, he was picked up by Ossie Ardiles as a 24-year-old and for a time looked to be finding a level of consistency until a bad knee injury put him out of action for many months. Kevin Keegan was in charge by the time Carr was available for selection, but within a few weeks the mercurial forward who loved to hug the touchline saw Robert Lee purchased as his replacement and the winger was off to Bramall Lane. From then on it was a struggle to claim a regular place at any of his clubs, often being left in football's wilderness. Nicknamed 'Roadrunner' on Tyneside, he was a flier, and as a youngster, was good enough to be offered athletics' scholarship in the USA. Carr settled in Derbyshire opening a bistro in Nottingham, then becoming a player agent and consultant.

Appearances & Goals:
Debut v Charlton Athletic (a) 18 August 1991 (1 goal)
FL: 20(5) app 3 gls
FLC: 2(2) app 0 gls
Others: 3(1) app 0 gls
Total: 25(8) app 3 gls

Honours:
9 Eng u21 app 1987-88/Eng sch-youth app/FL div 1 champs 1993/FL div 2 prom 1991 (2 app)/FLC winner 1990.

CARR John Robert 1894-1898

Left-half
5'10"
b. Newcastle upon Tyne, 1875 (Q2)
d. [Newcastle upon Tyne, 22 February 1919]

Career: Science & Art (Newcastle)/UNITED Nov 1894/ Kilmarnock May 1898 £20/Tyneside minor soccer 1900.

A commendable Tynesider, Jack Carr was the son of a local councillor and made his first appearance for the Magpies in a 6-0 St James' Park victory over Crewe on Christmas Day 1895. A vigorous, efficient amateur, Jack was a stand-in for the powerhouse of Jimmy Stott at half-back and his handful of matches in the United first-team were spread over three seasons, including when United were promoted to the top level for the first time. Carr departed the scene to enter university in Glasgow when he also turned out for Kilmarnock, assisting in their Second Division title success just before the turn of the century. He later returned to his native North East, and became a well known player in local circles for many years. Carr ran a dental practice in Elswick, then at Brighton Grove in the West End of the city.

CARR John Thomas 1897-1922

Left-back
5'10"
b. Seaton Burn, Northumberland, 1878 (Q3)
d. Newcastle upon Tyne, 17 March 1948

Career: Seaton Burn/UNITED Oct 1897 becoming asst-trainer 1912/Blackburn Rovers manager Feb 1922 to Dec 1926.

Jack Carr was one of the most celebrated locals to perform for Newcastle United. He started as a left-half with United, then, on the arrival of Peter McWilliam in the senior side, moved to left-back where he displayed a physical and rugged style, typical of the day. Carr was a noted player, picked for England, who took part in a treble of league title wins with the Magpies as well as reaching three FA Cup finals. Sound and judicious in his football, Jack was also a fine cricketer appearing for the Northumberland County side on 14 occasions (1908-14) and the Benwell, Hendon, Birtley, Old Novos and South Northumberland cricket clubs. Carr spent the whole of his playing career with Newcastle and represented the club over 13 seasons totalling over 300 games. He was one of the team's most resilient characters, a tough Geordie with a hard-hitting edge to his game, a perfect contrast to many of the club's footballing artistes of the time. Tasting the role of manager when appointed the very first boss at Blackburn in 1922, however Jack didn't take to management too well, suffering embarrassing FA Cup defeats at Ewood Park although as the Rovers' history noted, he had "a monumental task" of rebuilding the club. A pipe smoker, Carr left the game and returned to Tyneside becoming a licensee. For many years he was a publican near the Greenmarket in Newcastle's city-centre.

Appearances & Goals:
Debut v Nottingham Forest (a) 2 December 1899
FL: 252 app 5 gls
FAC: 25 app 0 gls
Others: 1 app 0 gls
Total: 278 app 5 gls

Honours:
2 Eng caps 1905-07/Eng trial app 1907/1 FL app 1907/FL champs 1905, 1907, 1909/FAC winner 1910/FAC final 1905, 1906.

CARR Kevin 1976-1985

Goalkeeper
6'2"
b. Morpeth, 6 November 1958

Career: Burnley trial/UNITED trial Nov 1975, prof July 1976/Carlisle Utd July 1985 after loan period (Darlington loan 1986-87)(Middlesbrough loan 1986-87)/ Hartlepool Utd July 1987/Middlesbrough briefly cs 1988/Blyth Spartans Aug 1988/ Bedlington Terriers July 1989/ Gateshead 1990 to 1991.

Local product Kevin Carr spent almost 10 years with Newcastle after signing for the club following a trial at Burnley, given a contract by Gordon Lee. For a long time Carr was reserve to Mick Mahoney, then Steve Hardwick, but eventually proved to

C

new boss Arthur Cox he was a capable 'keeper. He earned the Number 1 jersey for himself during season 1980-81 when he was voted Player of the Year. Tall and agile, Kevin produced a level of sound goalkeeping for a period before a new rival appeared on the scene in the shape of Martin Thomas. Of a similar standard, Carr shared the custodian's role during Newcastle's promotion campaign in 1983-84, but eventually lost his place to the Welsh international. Kevin was especially good at penalty stops; saving eight for United. He also registered six clean sheets in a row during 1982, the best on record. But Carr left the club somewhat bitter, after nearly a decade of service, shown the door by a brief impersonal letter. When Kevin retired from the game he opened a trophy business for a time before joining the Northumbria Police during 1989 and becoming a detective in the North East. Kevin won a bravery award ten years later for catching two masked raiders in Bedlington. He also played football for the England Police XI in 1991.

Appearances & Goals:
Debut v Queens Park Rangers (a) 10 December 1977
FL: 173 app 0 gls
FAC: 13 app 0 gls
FLC: 9 app 0 gls
Total: 195 app 0 gls

Honours:
FL div 2 prom 1984.

CARR R 1890

Half-back
b. *unknown*

Career: Everton/Hebburn Argyle/EAST END Sept 1890 to cDec 1890.

Recorded as having a spell with Everton (although he did not appear in any senior fixture) Carr joined the club from Tyneside rivals Hebburn Argyle and graduated to East End's first eleven from reserve action during September 1890. That was for a trip to Teesside, his only outing for East End, a match which resulted in an 8-0 defeat on the Parade Ground. He appears to have drifted from the scene late in 1890 probably returning to local football on Tyneside. Carr was also a cricketer for Walker CC in 1886-87.

Appearances & Goals:
Debut v Middlesbrough Ironopolis (a) 20 September 1890 (NL)
NL: 1 app 0 gls
Total: 1 app 0 gls

CARR Stephen 2004-2008

Right-back
5'9"
b. Dublin, 30 August 1976

Career: Trinity Boys/St Kevin's/Stella Maris/ Tottenham Hotspur jnr 1992, prof Sept 1993/ UNITED Aug 2004 £1.5m to May 2008/ Birmingham City trial Feb 2009, pmt July 2009/ Retired May 2013 due to injury.

A £1.5m arrival for the 2004-05 season from Tottenham Hotspur where he had totalled 272 games as a regular over seven seasons, by that time Stephen Carr was an accomplished full-back at both club and international level. For the next three seasons the Irishman was first choice in the right-back berth, although injury forced him onto the sidelines on several occasions. Committed and full-blooded in a contest, Carr was also comfortable going forward always being attack-minded. He lost out to new arrival Habib Beye for season 2007-08 and Carr became somewhat disillusioned with life at St James' Park. He left Tyneside on a free transfer and after struggling to find a new contract at the time when clubs were cutting back playing staff levels, Stephen found himself out of action for a period. The Irishman though resurrected his career with Birmingham City, capitalising on a chance given to him by boss Alex McLeish. He helped the Blues to promotion and then skippered City to Football League Cup glory at Wembley in 2011, although did suffer relegation at the end of the same season. Carr though had shown again what a fine player he was. He played for almost a decade in the Republic of Ireland international side, captaining his country on occasion, and began his career with junior Dublin-based clubs before having trials at both Arsenal and Tottenham. Carr was unlucky to miss the World Cup of 2002 due to injury. Following three operations in 18 months, knee trouble forced his retirement during 2013, afterwards Carr moving to Spain to run a restaurant and night-spot in Marbella.

Appearances & Goals:
Debut v Middlesbrough (a) 14 August 2004
PL: 76(2) app 1 gl
FAC: 8 app 0 gls
FLC: 1 app 0 gls
Euro: 20 app 0 gls
Total: 105(2) app 1 gl

Honours:
44 Eire caps 1999-2008/1 Eire unoff app 2005/Eire B app/12 Eire u21 app/Eire sch-youth app/FL ch prom 2009/FLC winner 1999, 2011/PFA ToS (PL) 2001, 2003.

CARROLL Andrew Thomas 2004-2011

Centre-forward
6'3"
b. Gateshead, 6 January 1989

Career: Low Fell Jnrs/UNITED jnr 2004, prof July 2005 (Preston North End loan 2007-08)/Liverpool Jan 2011 £35m/West Ham Utd loan Aug 2012, pmt Aug 2013 £15.5m.

Born and raised in Gateshead as past United and England home-grown stars Chris Waddle and Paul Gascoigne had been, centre-forward Andy Carroll was attached to United's football nursery since he was a little over 10 years of age. Appearing for Low Fell Juniors as a kid, he joined the club's Academy set-up and was soon playing for the England youth side. Carroll made his senior Newcastle debut as a 17-year-old in European action against Palermo during November 2006 and then had a loan spell with Preston North End. The well built Geordie found a regular place in United's line-up as the club won the Championship trophy in 2009-10, netting 19 goals during the season all told. He was then rewarded with the iconic Number 9 shirt for Newcastle's return to Premier League competition. Tall at 6'3", powerful and rugged, apart from the physical side of his game no defender relishes facing, Andy is a danger in the air, can hold the ball up and has a work ethic so important in modern football. With a forceful shot on his left, at times Carroll can look awkward but has a deft touch on the ball. Likened by several judges to ex-United striker Duncan Ferguson, he became an England Under-21 player and despite some indiscretions off the pitch, reached the full England side in 2010. With characteristic long hair and pony-tail, the Tynesider soon became the new local hero, a centre-forward star in the making. He was the Magpies cutting edge as they made a swift return to the Premier League then started off in the same manner in the top flight. But after only a season-and-a-half of regular first-team action (and only half-a-season in the Premier League) was the subject of a huge £35m bid from Liverpool at the end of the January 2011 transfer window. A shock move to Merseyside was concluded, a record deal for both clubs, and the highest fee for any British player, Carroll went onto have a mixed beginning at Anfield, yet reached two Wembley cup finals and was part of England's Euro 2012 squad. With a part Scottish bloodline, Carroll had been called up for the Scotland Under-19 squad in 2007, but noted that he wanted to play for England. His stay at Anfield did not last long, with a change of management he moved to rejoin Sam Allardyce at Upton Park in London, although his appearances for the Hammers, and for England, were restricted due to a series of injuries.

Appearances & Goals:
Debut v Palermo (a) 2 November 2006 (sub) (UEFAC)
FL/PL: 57(23) app 31 gls
FAC: 3(5) app 2 gls
FLC: 0(1) app 0 gls
Euro: 0(2) app 0 gls
Total: 60(31) app 33 gls

Honours:
9 Eng caps 2011-date/5 Eng u21 app 2010/Eng sch-youth app/FL ch winner 2010/FAC final 2012/FLC winner 2012/PFA ToS (ch) 2010.

CARTWRIGHT Peter 1979-1983

Midfield
5'7"
b. Newcastle upon Tyne, 23 August 1957

Career: Dudley Welfare Jnrs/North Shields 1978/UNITED June 1979 £2,000 (Scunthorpe Utd loan 1982-83)/ Darlington March 1983 to cs 1984/ Blyth Spartans Sept 1984 to cs 1987 (Middlesex Wand tour combination in 1985 and 1986), rejoining Spartans Oct 1987 to 1988.

One of three bargain captures from the local non-league circuit around the same period, dark-haired Peter Cartwright, like Shoulder and Carney, gave Newcastle good short term service. A former trainee civil engineer, Peter turned his mind to professional football as a 21-year-old after an outstanding performance in the Northumberland Senior Cup final at St James' Park during 1979. He quickly burst onto the scene in Magpie colours, netting on his second outing in a derby with Sunderland at Roker Park. Short in height but with plenty of running and stamina, Cartwright was a midfield worker and became a regular for season 1979-80. His ability on the ball was always limited, but in the dog-fight to escape the Second Division, he performed with credit. Peter also had trials with Middlesbrough and Nottingham Forest before he ended up at Gallowgate. Back in local football after he left the Magpies, Cartwright was selected to the England non-league squad in 1985. During a spell at Feethams where he totalled 59 games, Peter became one of the quickest-ever substitutes to take the field, coming on after only five seconds of play against Chester in 1983. He later became a mathematics teacher in Blyth.

Appearances & Goals:
Debut v Charlton Athletic (a) 25 August 1979 (sub)
FL: 57(8) app 3 gls
FAC: 1 app 0 gls
FLC: 0(3) app 1 gl
Total: 58(11) app 4 gls

Honours:
FL div 4 prom 1983 (4 app).

CARVER Jesse 1936-1939

Centre-half
5'10"
b. Aigburth, Liverpool, 7 July 1911
d. Bournemouth, 29 November 2003

Career: Blackburn Rovers amat Dec 1927, prof June 1928/UNITED June 1936 £2,000/Bury April 1939 £850/Huddersfield Town asst-trainer 1945/RFC Xerxes (Neth) coach 1946/Netherlands national coach April 1947/Millwall coach Sept 1948/ Juventus (It) coach July 1949/Torino (It) June 1951/ AC Marzotto (It) coach 1951-52/West Bromwich Albion manager April 1952 to Dec 1952/SS Lazio (It) coach Dec 1952 to June 1953/Torino (It) coach July 1953 to June 1954/AC Roma (It) coach July 1954/ Coventry City manager June to Dec 1955/SS Lazio (It) coach Jan 1956 to June 1957/ Internazionale (It) coach July 1957 to June 1958/Sweden national coach cs 1958/ Tottenham Hotspur coach Oct 1958 to March 1959/Genoa (It) coach 1959-60/ SS Lazio (It) coach 1961/APOEL (Cy) coach 1962-63, and again 1969-70/ Also coached in Portugal and USA.

Jesse Carver made his Football League debut in 1930 and was developed as a youngster of note at Ewood Park having captained his country as a schoolboy in 1913. A sturdy and effective pivot in defence, he made 146 first class appearances for Blackburn and was a keen student of the tactical game which later served him well during a long career as a distinguished coach. Joining Newcastle as part of a rebuilding process, Carver was a regular for two seasons in the Black'n'Whites' side, before a near disastrous fall into Division Three North saw his place taken by the up and coming Jimmy Denmark. War ended his playing career and then the Merseyside started on a quite remarkable career on the Continent, especially in Italy where he became something of a legend. Over two seasons with Juventus, he guided the Turin Zebras to the Italian title during his first season in 1949-50 before falling out with the club's President in the following campaign. Yet his success made him a much wanted coach in Italy and elsewhere. In Continental style he hopped from club to club, including help rebuild the Torino squad in 1951 after the fateful Superga air crash. Jesse also had brief stays back home, at one time when he joined Coventry he was recognised as, "the highest paid manager in the Football League". But his footballing brain and methods were too ahead of their time in England, and it was throughout Europe that Carver was revered the most. A cheerful but strict character, he was dubbed the "Iron Sergeant" in Italy for his qualities of discipline and motivation. During his long coaching career he took part in both the World Cup, in 1958 as assistant to Sweden's manager George Raynor, and as boss himself leading the Dutch in the Olympic Games of 1948. As a teenager, Jesse started out as a butcher's assistant while he also was a champion weight lifter. During the Sixties, Carver returned to England to retire, living in Bournemouth past his 90th year.

Appearances & Goals:
Debut v Barnsley (h) 29 August 1936
FL: 70 app 0 gls
FAC: 6 app 0 gls
Total: 76 app 0 gls

Honours:
Eng sch-youth app/OG 1948(m)/It Lg champs 1950(m)/Cy Cup winner 1963(m).

CASEY Thomas 1952-1958

Left-half
5'8"
b. Comber, Northern Ireland,
11 March 1930
d. Nailsea, near Bristol, 11 January 2009

Career: Comber/Clara Park (Belfast)/ Belfast YMCA 1944/East Belfast 1946/ Bangor 1947/Leeds Utd May 1949/ Bournemouth Aug 1950/UNITED Aug 1952 £7,000/Portsmouth July 1958 £8,500/Bristol City March 1959 £6,000/ Gloucester City player-manager July 1963/Inter Roma (Can) c1965, later becoming trainer/ Swansea Town trainer July 1965 to Oct 1966/ Ammanford Town player-manager 1966/ Distillery (Belfast) player-manager Jan 1967 to Oct 1968/Everton asst-coach 1968, becoming caretaker-manager Jan 1972/ Coventry City coach July 1972/Grimsby Town manager Feb 1975 to Nov 1976/ KR Reykjavik (Ice) manager May to Aug 1977/Harstad IL (Nor) manager late 1977/ Also managing the Northern Ireland youth side.

A human dynamo on the field, Tommy Casey was a 90-minute man with lots of stamina and endeavour. Brought up on in the Shankill Road area of Belfast, Casey caught the eye of United's scouting network with some fine performances during 68 games for Bournemouth in the lower divisions. He wasn't stylish or fancy on the ball, but effective in his midfield destroyer's role and was always willing to have a shot at goal, something of a sharp-shooter. Tenacious and full of vigour, Casey was the iron-man of Northern Ireland's noted 1958 World Cup line-up that reached the quarter-finals in Sweden. Recommended to the Magpies by former stalwart, Bill McCracken, Casey spent six seasons in United's squad, his best campaigns being 1952-53, 1955-56 and 1956-57. A rival to Charlie Crowe, he stepped into his contemporary's place for the 1955 Wembley showpiece following Crowe's unfortunate injury. The Irishman was quite a traveller during his career and following four seasons of regular action with Bristol City (137 app) entered coaching and scouting in various capacities for over 20 years. When Casey quit football, he was later self-employed as a fishmonger in Portbury near Bristol. He retired in 1997 and resided in Nailsea, Casey appeared over 400 times in senior football.

Appearances & Goals:
Debut v Burnley (a) 6 September 1952
FL: 116 app 8 gls
FAC: 16 app 2 gls
Others: 2 app 0 gls
Total: 134 app 10 gls

Honours:
12 NI caps 1955-59/WdC 1958/NI FA tour app 1953/NI sch-youth app/ FA Cup winner 1955.

C

CASSIDY Thomas 1970-1980

Midfield
5'11"
b. Belfast, 18 November 1950

Career: Glentoran/UNITED Oct 1970 £25,000 (Lusitano & Rangers (SA) loan cs 1976)/ Burnley July 1980 £30,000 to May 1983/ APOEL (Cy) Nov 1983, becoming manager June 1985 to Nov 1988/Gateshead commercial manager Oct 1990 to May 1991/Gateshead manager Nov 1991 to Nov 1993/Glentoran manager June 1994/Ards manager Nov 1997/Sligo Rovers manager Nov 1999 to June 2001, also assisting the Northern Ireland side part-time/Workington manager Oct 2001/Newcastle Blue Star manager Sept 2007 to March 2008/Whitby Town manager Oct 2010 to Oct 2011/Blyth Spartans manager Dec 2011 to Oct 2012.

Tommy Cassidy burst onto the Ulster football scene by netting a hat-trick as a teenager for Glentoran in the City Cup final during 1969. Newcastle quickly pounced to bring him to Tyneside but after being signed by Joe Harvey as a player of promise, Irish international Tommy Cassidy took some time to find a regular place in Newcastle's side. At one point during 1972-73 he was transfer listed for not focusing on football, but the Irishman knuckled down to become a valuable member of the Geordies' squad. When he did earn a position in the side, Cassidy showed he had subtle skills on the ball for a well built man. He could go past opponents with a feint and dummy and had the ability to thread passes through the defence to create a goalscoring opportunity. At the peak of his form as United headed for Wembley in 1974 and 1976, and as the Magpies qualified for Europe, Tommy linked well in a midfield alongside the likes of Terry Hibbitt and Tommy Craig and was skipper of the Magpies for a handful of games. Appearing for the Irish in the 1982 World Cup in Spain, Cassidy spent a decade at St James' Park and was always liable to find the net from the edge of the box. During his period on Tyneside he also had a spell in South Africa appearing for the Lusitano and Rangers clubs, and at the end of his playing career signed off on a high with Burnley, helping the Clarets to the Third Division title and recording 98 appearances for the Turf Moor club. He managed non-league clubs for periods, having a successful and lengthy stay with Workington spanning nearly 300 games. In between football appointments Tommy also ran a newsagency in the Newcastle suburbs, a trophy business and worked for local radio. At one stage during Cassidy's period in Cyprus, he was banned from the game by UEFA after allegations and accusations against those who ran the game in that country. Before joining United, Cassidy had trials with Manchester United, Tommy was highly regarded in his native Northern Ireland, featured as a player on a Belfast wall mural alongside Best, Blanchflower and Dougan.

Appearances & Goals:
Debut v Southampton (a) 7 November 1970
FL: 170(10) app 22 gls
FAC: 22(1) app 1 gl
FLC: 17(2) app 3 gls
Euro: 3 app 0 gls
Others: 13(1) app 2 gls
Total: 225(14) app 28 gls

Honours:
24 NI caps 1971-82/WdC 1982/FAC final 1974/FLC final 1976/FL div 3 champs 1982/NI Lg champs 1970/NI Cup winner 1996(m)/NI GC winner 1994(m)/Cy Lg champs 1986(m)/Cy Cup winner 1984/Cy Cup final 1986(m).

CHALMERS William 1928-1931

Inside-right
5'9"
b. Bellshill, Lanarkshire, 25 July 1904
d. Hampshire, 1980 (Q3)

Career: Clydesdale Wand/Bellshill Ath Aug 1920/Queen's Park Dec 1920/Rangers May 1924/UNITED March 1928 £2,500/Grimsby Town June 1931 £1,000/Bury June 1932/Notts Co June 1936/Aldershot June 1938, becoming trainer during World War Two and acting manager/Ebbw Vale manager June 1943/Juventus (It) coach cs 1947/Bury asst-trainer Sept 1949 to cs 1951.

Willie Chalmers was an elegant player who always looked to have the ability to reach the very top of the game. One of the many finds by amateurs Queen's Park in Glasgow, United's Andy Cunningham claimed he was "among the best inside-forwards who have prevailed upon to leave Scotland". Hailing from the same Scottish town as Hughie Gallacher, Chalmers helped Rangers (19 app) to the Scottish title in both 1925 and 1928. He followed the famous centre-forward to St James' Park and played alongside his more famous contemporary in United's eleven. Scoring on his debut, in a 5-1 defeat, a goal direct from a corner, Willie performed well during season 1928-29 netting eight goals in 19 appearances when he delighted the Newcastle crowd with flashes of brilliance. Possessing a light physique, Chalmers was a crafty schemer, who perhaps lacked the bite and determination to succeed. After moving into the lower divisions, he became a big favourite with the fans at Gigg Lane and registered 104 games and 26 goals for the Shakers. When coaching in Italy, he was remarkably succeeded on the Juventus coaching staff by another United player, Jesse Carver, this after guiding Juve to a fourth place finish in the Scudetto.

(Note: Another Billy Chalmers at Queen's Park had a parallel career, WS Chalmers (Man United, Hearts), often their paths in football are confused.)

Appearances & Goals:
Debut v Leicester City (h) 7 April 1928 (1 goal)
FL: 41 app 13 gls
FAC: 1 app 0 gl
Total: 42 app 13 gls

Honours:
SL champs 1925, 1928 (1 app)/SL div 2 champs 1923.

CHAMBERS Colin John 1972-1978

Outside-left or Midfield
5'9"
b. North Shields, 1 October 1957

Career: UNITED jnr Oct 1972, prof July 1976 to May 1978/Whitley Bay cs 1978/Bishop Auckland 1980/ Ashington c1981/Alnwick Town 1983/Blyth Spartans 1984/Bedlington Terriers 1986/ Seaham Red Star/ Eppleton/Morpeth Town c1990/ thereafter appearing in minor local football to 2003.

Colin Chambers was one of Gordon Lee's youngsters thrown into a controversial Anglo-Scottish Cup meeting with Ayr United during September 1976. United's boss fielded a reserve line-up to show that he wanted no part in the much derided competition and Chambers was part of a side that fell 3-0, being substituted after 75 minutes. As a consequence Newcastle were heavily censored and fined. Skipper of United's juniors and a handful in midfield, Colin did get another opportunity in a friendly contest, but couldn't claim a league or cup debut for the Magpies, or for any other senior team. Chambers afterwards resided in Forest Hall in Newcastle and was involved in local football before moving to Morpeth in Northumberland. He worked as a joiner for North Tyneside Council until retiring. As a teenager, he had trials at various clubs before joining the Magpies.

Appearances & Goals:
Debut v Ayr United (a) 15 September 1976 (ASC)
Others: 1 app 0 gls
Total: 1 app 0 gls

CHANDLER Albert 1925-1926

Right-back
5'10"
b. Carlisle, 15 January 1897
d. Carlisle, 28 January 1963

Career: Dalston Black Reds (Carlisle)/Derby Co Aug 1919/ UNITED June 1925 £3,250/Sheffield Utd Oct 1926 £2,625/ Mansfield Town cs 1929/Northfleet Nov 1929/ Manchester Central Feb 1930/Holme Head (Carlisle) cs 1930/Queen of the South cs 1931 to 1933-34.

At times, Bert Chandler could be a steady defender who displayed moments of brilliance not usually associated with full-backs during the inter-war years. Appearing on 183 occasions for Derby, he was especially noted for a sliding tackle but, after taking over from Billy Hampson for the 1925-26 season, lost his place to Alf Maitland as the Magpies went onto lift the title the following term.

During his stay at Bramall Lane in 77 games at the top level, Chandler was censored due to financial irregularities over payments of Player Union subs and ultimately blacklisted by the Football League; his registration was "to be refused" by any club and although signed by Mansfield the ban meant he never appeared for the Stags. As a result he was unable to continue a career in senior football. Bert faithfully and gallantly served in both world wars, commissioned in the Machine Gun Corps, Chandler returned to football after surviving a gas attack in the trenches of Northern France. Bert later resided in Carlisle.

Appearances & Goals:
Debut v Bolton Wanderers (a) 29 August 1925
FL: 33 app 0 gls
FAC: 3 app 0 gls
Total: 36 app 0 gls

Honours:
FL champs 1927 (4 app).

CHANNON Michael Roger 1982

Striker
6'0"
b. Orcheston, Wiltshire, 28 November 1948

Career: Shrewton Utd/Southampton jnr March 1964, prof Dec 1965/Manchester City July 1977 £300,000/ Cape Town City (SA) 1978/Southampton Sept 1979 £200,000/Caroline Hill (HK) cs 1982/Durban City (SA) 1982/UNITED Sept 1982 free/Bristol Rovers Oct 1982/ Norwich City Dec 1982/Portsmouth Aug 1985 to May 1986/Finn Harps Oct 1986/Retired 1987 then continued with a variety of clubs in Australia and New Zealand including Blockhouse Bay (NZ), Kelston (NZ) and Newcastle KB Raiders (Aus).

Mike Channon was recognised as one of the top strikers in Division One during the Seventies and early Eighties era, finding the net over 300 times, including 21 goals for England when he played on many occasions alongside Kevin Keegan. It was the Keegan link which brought him to Tyneside during the opening weeks of the 1982-83 season. With his career drawing to a close, 33-year-old Channon teamed up with his former Saints colleague in a trial deal but, although Mick scored on his debut in a local derby with Middlesbrough, he lacked match sharpness and wasn't retained by manager Arthur Cox. As it turned out, Channon gave good service to Norwich afterwards, grabbing 25 goals in 112 games. Developing alongside Ron Davies at The Dell, Channon was a potent attacker, able to hold the ball up and possessing vision and the natural awareness to find the net. Tall and well-balanced, with pace and control to run at defenders, he holds the Saints' goalscoring record of 223 league and cup strikes in 596 games. Remembered for his windmill goal celebration style, Mick twice captained his country, and after leaving the game became a celebrated racehorse trainer at Lambourn, then at the historic West Ilsley Stables in Newbury. Channon gained his own racing license and developed a career as a much rated trainer, a regular top-six finisher in flat racing.

Appearances & Goals:
Debut v Middlesbrough (h) 8 September 1982 (1 goal)
FL: 4 app 1 gl
Total: 4 app 1 gl

Honours:
46 Eng caps 1973-78/1 unoff Eng app 1976/9 Eng u23 app 1971-72/3 FL app 1973-77/FAC winner 1976/FLC winner 1985/PFA ToS (d1) 1974, (d2) 1975, 1976, 1977.

CHARD William 1886-1890

Goalkeeper
b. Bombay (India), c1863
d. Gateshead, 1920 (Q4)

Career: Newcastle Association 1885/EAST END Dec 1886 (Gateshead Association guest 1885-87) to c1890.

Billy Chard was East End's first choice goalkeeper for two seasons following a move from the Newcastle FA club to Chillingham Road during December 1886. Taking over from McClen between the posts, after appearing in friendly action Billy made his senior bow for East End in Newcastle's very first FA Cup fixture, a meeting with South Bank on Teesside during 1887. He later became a noted referee in the region as the

game of football developed rapidly. Chard was also a proficient cricketer and played for several clubs including Dunston CC and North Eastern CC. He was noted as a "big hitter" in the summer game. Billy appeared for Northumberland County at trial level in both sports. Chard was born in India when his father was serving in the Empire with the Royal Artillery, for a period also living at the Woolwich garrison.

Appearances & Goals:
Debut v South Bank (a) 15 October 1887 (FACQ)
FAC: 1 app 0 gls
Total: 1 app 0 gls

CHARVET Laurent Jean 1998-2000

Right-back or Centre-half
5'11"
b. Beziers (France), 8 May 1973

Career: SC St Thiberien (Fr)/Agde (Fr)/AS Beziers (Fr)/UMS Montelimar (Fr)/AS Cannes Aug 1991 (Chelsea loan 1997-98)/UNITED July 1998 £515,000/Manchester City Oct 2000 £1m to Oct 2002/Ipswich Town trial Dec 2002/ FC Sochaux Jan 2003 to Aug 2004.

A versatile Frenchman able to operate in midfield, at full-back or in a central defender's role, Laurent Charvet was brought to Tyneside during the summer of 1998 by Kenny Dalglish after an extended loan period at Chelsea during 1997-98. Strongly built with short-cropped hair, he was favoured by Ruud Gullit and became a regular in the Dutchman's Magpie line-up during the following season, and walked out at Wembley as United appeared in the 1999 FA Cup final. Thoughtful with the ball and quick as well as powerful, Laurent on occasion looked an accomplished footballer but was inconsistent. The following year he was rarely in contention and when new boss Bobby Robson arrived he preferred others. Charvet did get into the side for the start of 2000-01 but was discarded as the campaign developed when he moved to wear the sky-blue of Manchester City. He later returned to France and played out his career at the Stade Auguste Bonal, home of United's one-time European opponents Sochaux-Montbeliard. Having made his name with Cannes as an attacking full-back over three seasons, Laurent ran into dispute with the Cote D'Azur club and joined Chelsea in a five month loan deal...ending up on the bench in a European final for the Blues in Stockholm against Stuttgart. On retiring from playing, Charvet became a director with the Principality Group, a company based in London engaged in sports management.

Appearances & Goals:
Debut v Charlton Athletic (h) 15 August 1998
PL: 37(3) app 1 gl
FAC: 6 app 0 gls
FLC: 3 app 0 gls
Euro: 4 app 0 gls
Total: 50(3) app 1 gl

Honours:
Fr sch-youth app/FL div 1 champs 2002 (3 app)/FAC final 1999/ECWC winner 1998 (sub no app).

CHILTON Allenby C 1943

Centre-half
6'1"
b. South Hylton, Sunderland, 16 September 1918
d. Southwick, Sunderland, 15 June 1996

Career: Hylton Colliery Jnrs/Seaham Colliery 1934/Liverpool amat Sept 1938/Manchester Utd Nov 1938 (Cardiff City war-guest 1941-42)(UNITED war-guest 1942-43)(Charlton Ath war-guest 1943-44) (Airdrieonians war-guest 1943-44)(Hartlepools Utd war-guest 1944-45)(Middlesbrough war-guest 1944-45) (Reading war-guest 1945-46)/Resumed with Manchester Utd 1946/Grimsby Town player-manager March 1955 to April 1959/Wigan Ath manager May to Dec 1960/ Hartlepools Utd scout 1961, becoming manager July 1962 to May 1963.

C

A key defensive figure for Manchester United after the Second World War, Allenby Chilton was recognised as one of the finest players of his time, tough at the back, yet highly creative with the ball. A tall and powerful pivot, he claimed over 400 games for the Old Trafford club, many as captain and recorded 179 consecutive appearances (1951-55) to create a club record. Appearing for England, he secured both the title and FA Cup with Manchester United, as well as lifting wartime honours for the Reds as he did at Charlton too. As player-boss of Grimsby, he took the Mariners to the Third Division North title in 1956. Playing in the last two games of the 1942-43 season for Newcastle, Chilton served with the Durham Light Infantry and was wounded after the Normandy landings at Caen. On retiring from football following a distinguished career, Allenby later ran a retail business and worked at a steelworks. He returned to his native Wearside, residing in Seaburn. Chilton was destined to become a boxer during his teens before football took over making his senior debut for Manchester United on the day before war was declared in September 1939.

Appearances & Goals:

Debut v Gateshead (h) 26 April 1943 (FLN)
War: 2 app 0 gls
Total: 2 app 0 gls.

Honours:

2 Eng caps 1951-52/1 Eng unoff app 1955/FL champs 1952/FL div 3 champs 1956(m)/FAC winner 1948/FLN(WLg) champs 1942/FL WC(S) winner 1944/FL WC(N) final 1945.

CHOPRA Michael Rocky 1993-2006

Striker
5'9"
b. Gosforth, Newcastle upon Tyne, 23 December 1983

Career: Montague & N Fenham BC/UNITED jnr July 1993, prof Jan 2001 (Watford loan 2002-03) (Nottingham Forest loan 2003-04)(Barnsley loan 2004-05)/Cardiff City July 2006 £500,000/Sunderland July 2007 £5m/Cardiff City loan Nov 2008, pmt July 2009 £3m/Ipswich Town June 2011 £1.5m/Blackpool July 2013 to June 2014/Kerala Blasters (Ind) Aug 2014.

With Newcastle United as an eight-year-old schoolboy, Michael Chopra was a regular international at schools and youth level, captaining the young England line-up. Graduating from United's Academy to the reserves and eventually to the fringe of Bobby Robson's first eleven, he was small and quick with an eye for goal in the mould of strikers Gary Lineker and Jermaine Defoe. The Tynesider was much heralded to become a top home-grown poacher and after successful loan stints with Watford and then Barnsley in which he grabbed 17 goals during season 2004-05, Michael showed he could hit the net in senior company, albeit a level below the Premier League. However Chopra never quite achieved the high expectation in Toon colours after making his breakthrough during seasons 2002-03 and 2003-04. Michael had at first very little hope of dislodging Craig Bellamy as Alan Shearer's favoured partner, arguably the best combination in the Premiership, then faced a new challenge when Michael Owen arrived on the scene. Never given any kind of extended run in United's line-up, it was inevitable perhaps he would move on when he joined Cardiff City when 22 years old during the summer of 2006. The Tynesider became a first choice striker in tier-two, feared at Championship level, netting plenty of goals for the Bluebirds (63 in 159 games) and later Ipswich Town. Chopra played on the edge of the final third, on the back of defenders and had pace and good movement with what some called an "Owenesque-style". Michael also had a spell on Wearside with Sunderland, although went through a difficult period with a gambling addiction which affected him for much of his career, being found guilty in 2013 of betting irregularities by the British Horseracing Authority. From an ethnic background, Chopra was the first of Asian extraction to appear for Newcastle, and one of only a handful to play at the top level in English football. On his senior bow for United as an 18-year-old against Everton, he skied a spot-kick over the bar in a penalty shoot-out while in a hostile Tyne versus Wear derby with Sunderland on Wearside in 2006, he came off the bench to immediately find the net for the Magpies... after a mere 13 seconds on action. Chopra attended the same Gosforth school as Alan Shearer. In 2014 Michael joined the India Super League competition with Kerala Blasters.

Appearances & Goals:

Debut v Everton (h) 6 November 2002 (sub) (FLC)
PL: 7(14) app 1 gl
FAC: 1(1) app 1 gl
FLC: 1(2) app 0 gls
Euro: 1(4) app 1 gl
Total: 10(21) app 3 gls

Honours:

1 Eng u21 app 2004/Eng sch-youth app/PFA ToS (ch) 2007, 2010.

CISSE Papiss Demba 2012-date

Centre-forward
6'0"
b. Dakar (Senegal), 3 June 1985

Career: AS Generation Foot (Seng) 2002/Douanes Dakar (Seng) 2004/ FC Metz (Fr) July 2005 (AS Cherbourg loan 2005-06)(LB Chateauroux loan 2007-08)/SC Freiburg (Ger) Dec 2009 £1.32m/UNITED Jan 2012 £10.56m.

It took United all of 12 months to find a replacement for Andy Carroll following his record sale, Senegalese striker Papiss Cisse filling the iconic Number 9 shirt when he arrived on Tyneside during January 2012. Having made a name for himself with Bundesliga club Freiburg with a record of 39 goals in 65 games in which he netted 24 goals during 2010-11, Cisse made his debut on Tyneside against Aston Villa as an early sub for Leon Best (after only 13 minutes) and Newcastle's faithful saw their new centre-forward make an immediate impact. He scored a gem of a goal, chesting down a cross and striking a sweet half-volley into the top corner of the Gallowgate net. The St James' Park crowd took to the lively and energetic striker from the start, some fans considering he was a cross between the deadly and lightening fast Andy Cole and the tricky, unorthodox style of Tino Asprilla. With an excellent first touch, Cisse makes intelligent runs, works back and has the striker's instinct with a clean strike of the ball. As a bonus Papiss refreshingly plays his football with a smile rather than tantrums like some. He formed a dangerous front duo with fellow countryman Demba Ba (a No. 9 and No. 19 combination) and like Ba netted at ease in his opening salvo as a Newcastle player; 11 goals in his first 10 games, one of the best on record. In the process Papiss showed a fondness for hitting superlative goals, contenders for any goal-of-the-season award ultimately lifting the BBC's Match of the Day award for an amazing strike against Chelsea. Cisse's second and third seasons in 2012-13 and 2013-14 with United were not as successful with the striker struggling to recapture his previous devastating form in front of goal, netting only a sparse return in those two campaigns and often not being first choice in attack. His attempt to return to goalscoring form was curtailed when he broke a knee-cap towards the end of the 2013-14 season. Raised in the small town of Sedhiou, Cisse is a devout Muslim and French speaking. Before moving to the football stage he worked as an ambulance driver in Dakar and has captained his country's eleven. For a period his uncle was the official driver of the President of Senegal.

Appearances & Goals:

Debut v Aston Villa (h) 5 February 2012 (sub) (1 goal)
PL: 63(11) app 23 gls
FAC: 1 app 1 gl
FLC: 2(1) app 2 gls
Euro: 9(1) app 4 gls
Total: 75(13) app 30 gls

Honours:

30 Seng caps 2010-date.

CLARK Albert Henry 1948-1949

Right-half
5'10"
b. Ashington, 24 July 1921
d. Newcastle upon Tyne, 1977 (Q4)

Career: North Shields/UNITED Jan 1948 £850/North Shields March 1949 free/Morpeth Town player-coach Sept 1953.

Impressing United's manager George Martin following a series of good displays for North Eastern League club, North Shields, Albert Clark was given an opportunity to join the Magpies, albeit very much as a reserve to skipper Joe Harvey. He assisted Newcastle's second string to the Central League championship during 1948, but only managed a single appearance in the senior team before moving back to Appleby Park.

Appearances & Goals:

Debut v Sheffield United (h) 11 December 1948
FL: 1 app 0 gls
Total: 1 app 0 gls

CLARK Frank Albert 1962-1975

Left-back
6'0"
b. Highfield, near Gateshead,
9 September 1943

Career: Sunderland jnr 1958/Preston North End jnr/Highfield Utd/Crook Town Aug 1961/UNITED Nov 1962 £200/ Nottingham Forest May 1975 free/ Sunderland asst-manager July 1979 to April 1981/Nottingham Forest asst-coach Aug 1981/Orient asst-manager Oct 1981, becoming manager May 1983 and Managing Director Nov 1986/ Nottingham Forest manager May 1993 to Dec 1996/ Manchester City manager Dec 1996 to Feb 1998/LMA Executive, scout and football consultant/ Nottingham Forest Chairman Oct 2011 to July 2012 when he became a Forest ambassador to Jan 2013.

Frank Clark served his apprenticeship as a laboratory technician before signing professional terms for Newcastle United, this after declining a full-time career with Sunderland and Preston. He appeared as an amateur for Crook, where he reached Wembley in the FA Amateur Cup final, but Clark had a bad start at St James' Park, breaking his leg when a 19-year-old at Anfield in a reserve contest with Liverpool. However, Frank battled his way back and was handed the left-back shirt when George Dalton faded from the scene. In his first full season, when Clark was an ever-present, the Magpies lifted the Second Division trophy and for the next ten years the solid and dependable defender was an automatic choice for manager Joe Harvey totalling over 480 league and cup games, the most by any United outfield player in post-war football. Described by former skipper Stan Anderson as a "thinking man's footballer", he was neither flamboyant or volatile, Clark had the perfect temperament and simply shrugged off criticism from some sections of United's crowd who at times did not like his rather lacklustre style. With good positional sense in the back line, Frank was totally dedicated to United's cause appearing also at centre-half during his last three seasons. At the end of the 1974-75 campaign when Harvey resigned the manager's post, club skipper Clark was handed a controversial free transfer when aged almost 32, although many considered he still had much to offer the club. Clark moved to join Brian Clough at the City Ground and proceeded to win Championship, League Cup and European Cup honours in his 157 games. He then started a learning period in management and coaching eventually ending up back alongside the Trent in charge of Forest, where he led the Reds to an unbeaten run of 25 games in the Premier League. A fine local cricketer too, Frank Clark has never lost his affection for the Magpies although he lived away from the region in the Midlands for many a year and can be recognised as one of the club's finest servants. He was given a well supported testimonial fixture in 1976 (19,974). Clark has been involved in the League Managers Association for a lengthy period and was appointed Chief Executive in 1992. He also acted as a FA Premier League assessor and sat on various transfer and Premier League and Football League tribunals.

Appearances & Goals:
Debut v Scunthorpe United (a) 18 April 1964
FL: 388(1) app 0 gls
FAC: 25 app 0 gls
FLC: 19 app 1 gl
Euro: 23 app 0 gls
Others: 29(1) app 1 gl
Total: 484(2) app 2 gls
(Void FAC: 1 app 0 gls)

Honours:
1 FL app 1970/Eng sch-youth app/1 Eng amat app 1962/FL champs 1978/FL div 2 champs 1965/FL div 2 prom 1977/FL div 1 prom 1994(m)/FL div 4 prom 1989(m)/FAC final 1974/FLC winner 1978, 1979/EC winner 1979/ICFC winner 1969/FAAC winner 1962/MoY 1995 (LMA).

CLARK James Robinson 1921-1924

Inside-left
5'8"
b. Bensham, Gateshead, 20 October 1895
d. Gateshead, 16 September 1947

Career: Annfield Plain/Jarrow Aug 1921/UNITED Dec 1921 £350/Leeds Utd May 1924 £300/Swindon Town June 1925/Morton Dec 1926/Ashington March 1927/Shelbourne cs 1927.

The lesser known of the two JR Clarks on Newcastle's books at the same time, James was very much on the fringe of United's side, deputy to Tom McDonald as the club lifted the FA Cup in 1924. Scoring 20 goals for United's second string in season 1922-23, he was a key part of the Magpies' reserve side that won the North Eastern League title that year. He later appeared in Scotland and Ireland before returning to Tyneside but totalled only 37 games in English senior football at all his clubs. He pulled on Ashington's black-and-white colours during their Football League days before being badly injured against Stockport. Clark lived in the area to his death, for many years working at the Wright-Anderson steelworks in Gateshead.

Appearances & Goals:
Debut v Chelsea (h) 27 January 1923
FL: 11 app 2 gls
Total: 11 app 2 gls

CLARK John Robert 1923-1928

Inside-right
6'0"
b. Newburn, Newcastle upon Tyne, 6 February 1903
d. Newcastle upon Tyne, 1977

Career: Spencer's Welfare/Hawthorn Leslie/ Newburn Grange/Newburn/Prudhoe Castle/UNITED Feb 1923 £130/Liverpool Jan 1928 £3,000/Nottingham Forest July 1931 to May 1932/North Shields Aug 1932, becoming player-coach Sept 1937/Newburn by 1938.

A very popular Novocastrian figure between the two wars, famed for his entertainment quality, Bob Clark was a hefty forward, over 14 stone and once described as, "skilful but slow". Despite his lack of pace, he possessed a ferocious shot and formed a 'Little and Large' partnership alongside Hughie Gallacher for several seasons including part of the title winning campaign of 1927. The Tynesider used his big frame well and defenders didn't relish a meeting with this 6'0" giant of a man. Clark moved to Merseyside where he had one good season at Anfield during 1928-29 when they finished in fifth spot in the table. Earlier in his career, Newcastle United were reprimanded by the Football Association for playing Clark in a friendly match, in essence a trial outing, before the club had actually signed him. When he retired from the game, Bob remained on Tyneside, living in Newburn to his demise.

Appearances & Goals:
Debut v Huddersfield Town (h) 7 April 1923 (1 goal)
FL: 77 app 16 gls
Total: 77 app 16 gls

Honours:
FL champs 1927.

CLARK Lee Robert 1986-1997, 2005-2007

Midfield & Coach
5'8"
b. Wallsend, 27 October 1972

Career: Wallsend BC/UNITED jnr Dec 1986, prof Dec 1989/Sunderland June 1997 £2.5m/Fulham July 1999 £3m to June 2005/UNITED Aug 2005, becoming asst-coach June 2006/Norwich City asst-manager Nov 2007/Huddersfield Town manager Dec 2008 to Feb 2012/Birmingham City manager June 2012.

Associated with United since a 10-year-old at the club's Centre of Excellence, Lee Clark was a juvenile star who

C

became a regular for the England school and youth line-ups, skippering his country on many occasions. A Geordie teenager who swapped the terraces of St James' Park for the dressing-room and consequently became a supporters' hero; the local lad from Walker made a significant impact in football. Clark's ability in midfield, initially as a creator, later as an anchor-man, always placed him alongside previous stars Waddle, Beardsley and Gascoigne as the next in line of Tyneside favourites. With accurate passing, both short and long, and vision to open the game up, it was Ossie Ardiles' who gave Lee his first break, during season 1990-91. With short cropped hair, at times even shaven, it was though under Kevin Keegan that Clark flourished. He established himself during Newcastle's Division One title season in 1992-93 and played a leading role as an attack minded midfielder. He was Player of the Season and showed he was a footballer for the future being the only ever-present in that trophy winning year. The Tynesider developed and matured, but as a constant stream of big money buys arrived on Tyneside, Clark found himself frozen out and reluctantly moved on in search of regular football. He joined rivals Sunderland and helped the Wearsiders to promotion yet always retained his support for the Magpies despite wearing the red-and-white stripes. He made headline news when Lee followed United to the FA Cup final in 1999 and was famously pictured wearing a T-shirt displayed a derogatory message towards the Sunderland club's supporters. As a result he had to leave Wearside, for Fulham, yet at the same time his actions simply reinforced the strong bond he had with United's Toon Army. He did well for Fulham over six seasons, again winning promotion to the Premier League and recorded 178 games for the Londoners, captain at Craven Cottage. Lee then made a welcome return to Gallowgate as a 32-year-old and soon started on a road into management, often being tipped as a future United boss. During his first appointment, he guided Huddersfield to a 43-match unbeaten run during 2010 and 2011, a Football League record. Clark just missed a complete set of England honours for the national eleven, on the senior bench in 1997 under Glenn Hoddle's reign. Earlier in his career, Lee picked up the nickname of 'Gnasher' in the St James' Park dressing-room. His brother-in-law, Paul Baker, appeared prominently for Hartlepool.

Appearances & Goals:
Debut v Bristol City (a) 29 September 1990 (sub)
FL/PL: 161(56) app 24 gls
FAC: 16(2) app 3 gls
FLC: 17(1) app 0 gls
Euro: 3(5) app 0 gls
Others: 4 app 1 gl
Total: 201(64) app 28 gls

Honours:
11 Eng u21 app 1992-94/Eng sch-youth app/PL runner-up 1996, 1997/FL div 1 champs 1993, 1999, 2001/PFA ToS (d1) 1993, 1998, 1999, 2001.

CLARKE Jeffrey Derrick 1982-1987, 1988-1997

Centre-half & Coach
6'1"
b. Hemsworth, Yorkshire, 18 January 1954

Career: Manchester City jnr Aug 1971, prof Jan 1972/Sunderland June 1975 cash-exch deal/ UNITED Aug 1982 free (Brighton loan 1984-85)/ MKE Ankaragucu (Trk) cs 1987/Scarborough 1987/ Whitley Bay Feb 1988/UNITED community officer Nov 1988, becoming asst-coach cs 1993 to June 1997/Nissan coach & physio/Sunderland asst-physio Aug 1998/ Leeds Utd physio 2001/Dundee Utd physio Nov 2003 to date/Also played the occasional game in minor football, for Winlaton West End (1988).

A free transfer signing from Sunderland, 28-year-old Jeff Clarke arrived on Tyneside at the same time as the first Kevin Keegan bandwagon began. Blond-haired, he proved a marvellous capture, Clarke being an effective stopper at the heart of United's defence claiming the majority of high balls. Ideally built with composure and good distribution from the back line, he was part of the deal that took England centre-half Dave Watson to Manchester City from Roker Park. Jeff had several good seasons with the Reds totalling over 200 games, but missed out on both their promotion celebrations in 1976 and 1980 due to injury. Unluckily the same happened to the Yorkshireman at Gallowgate, sidelined for the Magpies' finale with a broken nose when Keegan, Beardsley, Waddle and Co regained the club's Division One status in 1984. Regaining fitness, Clarke played an important role in Newcastle's consolidation in the First Division during 1984-85 and 1985-86 before injury again saw him out of action. Jeff headed for a brief stay in Turkey, then on retirement returned to St James' Park to work his way up the coaching ladder, initially taking charge of the Magpies' reserve eleven. Clarke then qualified as a physiotherapist under a PFA scheme, earning a degree at Salford University and settled into a role in Scotland at Tannadice, physio to Dundee United. His son Jamie Clarke was on Sunderland's books for a period.

Appearances & Goals:
Debut v Queens Park Rangers (h) 28 August 1982
FL: 124 app 4 gl
FAC: 5 app 0 gls
FLC: 5 app 1 gl
Total: 134 app 5 gls

Honours:
Eng sch-youth app/FL div 2 champs 1976/FL div 2 prom 1980, 1984.

CLARKE Raymond Charles 1980-1981, 2004-2006

Centre-forward & Chief-scout
5'11"
b. Hackney, London, 25 September 1952

Career: Tottenham Hotspur jnr May 1968, prof Oct 1969/Swindon Town June 1973 £8,000/Mansfield Town Aug 1974 £5,000/ Sparta Rotterdam (Neth) July 1976 £80,000/Ajax (Neth) cs 1978/Club Brugge (Belg) July 1979/Brighton Oct 1979 £175,000/UNITED July 1980 £180,000/ Retired due to injury Aug 1981 becoming a prominent scout for various clubs including Rangers and Liverpool/Southampton asst-coach 1996 to cs 1997/Coventry City Euro scout 1997/Southampton chief-scout July 2002/UNITED chief-scout Nov 2004/ Celtic chief-scout Oct 2006/Portsmouth chief-scout Sept 2009/ Blackburn Rovers chief-scout Sept 2012.

Ray Clarke only took part in six months of action for Newcastle United following a transfer from the Goldstone Ground after a successful period in the Dutch and Belgian football. Clarke had made a reputation for himself as a dangerous leader with Mansfield netting 59 goals in 114 matches and was the Fourth Division's top goal-poacher during 1975. That earned him a move to the Continent and by the time he joined Ajax, was at the peak of his form, winning the double in the Netherlands. He netted 26 league goals for the Dutch giants in 1978-79 before moving across the border to Belgium where he also helped his side to the league title before returning to England. Ray moved to Tyneside as a replacement for Peter Withe, but never lived up to his billing. Not a power-packed centre-forward in the Newcastle United tradition, Clarke was quick and positive, relying on neat touches, lay-offs and positional play in the box. He was a former England schools trialist, and despite hitting plenty of goals at junior and reserve level never made the grade at White Hart Lane. Injured after only 18 matches with the Magpies, a knee problem forced his retirement from the game in 1981. Ray later became a hotelier on the Isle of Man until he returned to football and Clarke has since been an active scout for over 25 years, setting up a scouting network, Sportslive Recruitment and founding the PFSAA (Professional Football Scouts & Analysts Association) in 2011. Now Chairman of that group, he had a period back at Gallowgate for two years, brought in by his former Spurs colleague Graeme Souness to take charge of United's scouting network.

Appearances & Goals:
Debut v Sheffield Wednesday (a) 16 August 1980
FL: 14 app 2 gls
FAC: 4 app 1 gl
Total: 18 app 3 gls

Honours:
Eng sch-youth app/FL div 4 champs 1975/FAYC winner 1970/Neth Lg champs 1979/Neth Cup winner 1979/Belg Lg champs 1980/PFA ToS (d4) 1975.

CLIFTON Henry 1938-1946

Inside-forward
5'8"
b. Marley Hill, near Gateshead, 28 May 1914
d. Throckley, Newcastle upon Tyne, 17 October 1998

Career: Marley Hill/Lintz Colliery/Annfield Plain July 1932/ West Bromwich Albion amat Sept 1932/Scotswood Dec 1932/Chesterfield Aug 1933/UNITED June 1938 £8,500 (Chelsea war-guest 1940-41)/Grimsby Town Jan 1946 £2,500/Goole Town July 1949/Sutton Town Oct 1951 to cs 1952.

For a season Harry Clifton looked to be a buy of distinction in black-and-white colours. A record purchase, during 1938-39 he bagged 17 goals from either the inside-right or left positions and was set to be a focal point in the Mather-Seymour regeneration of Newcastle United. War put an end to that plan and all but ruined Clifton's football career. Harry's best years were lost to the conflict, but he did manage to appear for his country in a wartime international. Clifton had become hot property at Chesterfield, with 73 goals in 141 games, the pick of a group of North Easterners at Saltergate. He was an ebullient young pro and gave many bustling and tenacious displays as the Spireites won honours in 1935-36. He was highly regarded, described by one contemporary biography as being "a great stayer who snatches up every opportunity and turns seemingly unimportant attacks into deadly thrusts". Clifton was in the England party which travelled to face Germany during May 1938, Harry a reserve who along with the team had to give the Nazi salute in Berlin before kick-off. Within days of that experience he had signed for United. He had a lively sense of anticipation in the box and was an eye-catching player, special enough to be one of the great Jack Milburn's favourites as a lad. Clifton served in the army in the Middle East during the hostilities and on peace being restored during 1945, Clifton was United's club skipper but he was eased out of the St James' Park scene by the many developing youngsters, including Milburn. After football, Harry worked in the Chesterfield Tube Works and at Arkwright Colliery as well as being a steward at Saltergate before he returned to Tyneside. He resided in Throckley, a regular at the Bank Top Club for many years.

Appearances & Goals:
Debut v Plymouth Argyle (h) 27 August 1938 (1 goal)
FL: 29 app 15 gls
FAC: 6 app 2 gls
War: 42 app 27 gls
Total: 77 app 44 gls

Honours:
1 Eng war app 1940/FL div 3(N) champs 1936.

CLISH Colin 1959-1963

Left-back
5'11"
b. Hetton-le-Hole, Co Durham, 14 January 1944

Career: UNITED jnr June 1959, prof Jan 1961/ Rotherham Utd Dec 1963 £5,000/ Doncaster Rovers Feb 1968 exch deal/ Retired due to injury 1972/Gainsborough Trinity.

Stocky blond-haired defender Colin Clish, who developed alongside Bob Moncur and David Craig in United's talented Youth Cup winning side of 1962, was neat and tidy at his game and always tried to play football. Many considered Clish as the natural successor to the long serving Alf McMichael and he looked to have a bright future with the Magpies. He skippered the successful junior line-up but was unfortunate to soon afterwards have as a rival for the left-back spot in Frank Clark.

Manager Joe Harvey chose to nurture Clark as a potential First Division defender rather than Clish, and a transfer to Millmoor quickly followed. A twice broken leg eventually forced Colin to leave the Football League and he afterwards joined the British Transport Police becoming a railways detective in the Doncaster and Grantham area. Colin made his Magpie debut as a 17-year-old and appeared almost 150 times for Rotherham, and more than 100 for Doncaster in Division Three and Four. Clish was a fine cricketer, as a youth appearing at county level for Durham Colts and Durham Juniors.

Appearances & Goals:
Debut v Sheffield United (a) 2 October 1961 (FLC)
FL: 20 app 0 gls
FAC: 2 app 0 gls
FLC: 1 app 0 gls
Total: 23 app 0 gls

Honours:
FL div 4 champs 1969/FAYC winner 1962.

COLDWELL William 1887-1892

Half-back
b. Newcastle upon Tyne, 1869
d. [Newcastle upon Tyne, 1948]

Career: Cheviot/EAST END Sept 1887 to c1892.

William Coldwell was Byker club Cheviot's captain when they joined up with Newcastle East End in 1887. A strong midfielder at half-back, it was noted he was a reliable footballer who resided in East End's heartland, on Shields Road. A blacksmith in the district, he became East End Swifts (reserve XI) skipper and was elevated to senior action during season 1887-88. Coldwell was on the field when Newcastle played their very first FA Cup match against South Bank during 1887. By 1890-91 he was back in the second-string, a regular at that level. As with many of East End's early players, Coldwell also played cricket locally, for St Michael's CC and East End CC. He later remained in the Byker and Heaton area, employed as an insurance agent then at an engineering works.

Appearances & Goals:
Debut v South Bank (a) 15 October 1887 (FACQ)
NL: 1 app 0 gls
FAC: 4 app 0 gls
Total: 5 app 0 gls

COLE Andrew Alexander 1993-1995

Centre-forward
5'11"
b. Lenton, Nottingham, 15 October 1971

Career: Parkhead Acc (Nottingham)/ Emkals (Nottingham)/FA Lilleshall Academy 1985/Arsenal jnr Oct 1985, prof Oct 1989 (Fulham loan 1991-92)/ Bristol City loan March 1992, pmt July 1992 £500,000/ UNITED March 1993 £1.75m/ Manchester Utd Jan 1995 cash-exch deal for K Gillespie £7m/ Blackburn Rovers Dec 2001 £8m/ Fulham July 2004 free/ Manchester City July 2005 free/ Portsmouth Aug 2006 £500,000 (Birmingham City loan 2006-07)/ Sunderland Aug 2007 free (Burnley loan 2007-08)/Nottingham Forest July 2008/ Retired Nov 2008/MK Dons part-time asst-coach Aug 2009/ Huddersfield Town part-time asst-coach Aug 2009/Manchester Utd ambassador 2011.

With Jamaican parentage, Andy Cole was purchased by Kevin Keegan as a virtual unknown centre-forward who had lots of potential, being a graduate from the Lilleshall Academy and a player who had appeared for the England Under-21 side. Yet the 21-year-old Cole had not yet completed a full season in regular first-team action and many in football gasped at the club record fee Newcastle paid for the player. Keegan though had made a master signing as immediately the lithe and agile leader started to dominate the headlines over a short but quite amazing spell of 22 months at St James' Park. From his first showing at Gallowgate the goals started to flow in abundance and Cole became dubbed the most clinical hot-shot in the country as Newcastle regained their top-flight status. With devastating pace, astute positional sense and expert placement of his shot, Andy was simply lethal in the box and United's scintillating approach play, especially when paired with Peter Beardsley, made sure Cole had plenty of chances to find the net. In season 1993-94 his goals ratio for much of the campaign reached a tremendous 100% strike-rate, a goal a game, and he finished the year registering 41 goals in only 45 outings thereby smashing the long-standing club record held by Gallacher and Robledo. Not well built for the centre-forward's role, the whippet-like Cole became a cult figure in the tradition of the club's famous Number 9 heroes, yet the Nottingham-born star shunned publicity and didn't take to the limelight. Just as Andy was developing his raw talent further, into a certainty for an international cap and earning a place on the England substitute's bench, his manager decided to sell him to rivals Manchester United in a national record transfer valued at £7 million,

C

although the fee was later noted as £6.25m. It was a transaction which shocked the nation and Cole went onto become another hit at Old Trafford over eight seasons in which he amassed 122 goals, including scoring five in the Premiership match against Ipswich during March 1995. He won honours galore in a red Mancunian shirt, including the coveted treble during 1999, although his international career never quite took off. In his teens Andy was developed by George Graham at Arsenal, and while he shined in reserve football could never claim a place at Highbury. Next to the legendary Hughie Gallacher, Cole is the club's most deadly goalscorer with a career 81% strike-rate for the Magpies. Cole scored almost 300 goals all told while his son, Devante Cole, has appeared for England's youth side. In 1999 Andy released a record titled 'Outstanding' but failed to progress a music career and a year later he set up the Andy Cole Children's Foundation to help orphans in Zimbabwe. Apart from being part of Manchester United's PR team, Andy is involved in the media and in coaching.

Appearances & Goals:
Debut v Swindon Town (a) 13 March 1993 (sub)
FL: 69(1) 55 gls
FAC: 4 app 1 gl
FLC: 7 app 8 gls
Euro: 3 app 4 gls
Total: 83(1) app 68 gls

Honours:
15 Eng caps 1995-2002/1 Eng B app 1995/8 Eng u21 app 1992-94/Eng sch-youth app/1 FL app 1993/1 PL app 1994/PL champs 1996, 1997, 1999, 2000, 2001/FL div 1 champs 1991 (1 app), 1993/FL ch prom 2007 (5 app)/FAC winner 1996, 1999/FLC winner 2002/CL winner 1999/ESC final 1999/YPoY 1994 (PFA)/PFA ToS (PL) 2000.

COLLINS James 1888-1893, 1895-1897

Inside-right
5'9"
b. Scotland, 1872
d. Rochester, Kent, 2 January 1900

Career: Shawfield/EAST END Aug 1888/Newcastle West End guest April 1891, pmt cs 1891/UNITED May 1892/ Nottingham Forest July 1893/UNITED Aug 1895 £20/ Sheppey Utd Aug 1897/Chatham Utd May 1899 to death.

James Collins was a mobile and dangerous forward on the football field who assisted United and their pioneers during the very early years of the club's development, including the Tynesider's days in the Northern League. Coming to the region from north of the border as a Glasgow riveter to earn his living in the Tyne shipyards and in the emerging professional game of football, Collins was a versatile player appearing in both inside positions and on the wing for Newcastle. He was one of the best of the club's early finds from Scotland, described in the local press as invariably giving "splendid expositions of the game". Apart from his 91 senior outings, James recorded over 100 appearances in sundry fixtures scoring nearly 50 goals. Well known and admired in the region, he was gentlemanly off the park, yet could be an aggressive individual on it. The Scot had a decent spell with Forest after leaving Tyneside, playing on 44 occasions at the top level, scoring a hat-trick (4 goals) on his debut against Wolves in 1893. Sadly Collins died of tetanus after being injured when turning out for Kent club Chatham in a Southern League match against New Brompton (Gillingham) on Boxing Day 1899. He fell on a piece of flint and contracted lock-jaw. An obituary noted: "He was a quiet, inoffensive man, and many will miss him." James was part of East End's line-up for their very first fixture at St James' Park against Celtic during September 1892 while he also represented Northumberland during his stay in the North East. Collins skippered the East Enders during his stay at Chillingham Road in Heaton and James also tried his hand at baseball on Victorian Tyneside, a popular sport for a fleeting period. He was a 'catcher' for the Brunswick club in 1890.

Appearances & Goals:
Debut v Port Clarence (h) 6 October 1888 (FACQ)
NL: 41 app 7 gls
FL: 34 app 8 gls
FAC: 16 app 3 gls
Total: 91 app 18 gls
(Void NL: 2 app 2 gls)

COLOCCINI Fabricio 2008-date

Centre-half
6'0"
b. Cordoba (Argentina), 22 January 1982

Career: AA Argentinos Juniors (Arg) 1997/CA Boca Juniors (Arg) July 1998/AC Milan (It) July 1999 £6.6m (CA San Lorenzo (Arg) loan 2000-01) (Deportivo Alaves (Sp) loan 2001-02) (Atletico Madrid (Sp) loan 2002-03)(Villareal CF (Sp) loan 2003-04)/RC Deportivo La Coruna Jan 2005 £4.4m/UNITED Aug 2008 £10m.

The Black'n'Whites paid a substantial £10m to bring Argentinean international Fabricio Coloccini to St James' Park in August 2008, the biggest fee the club has paid for any defender. Having played most of his football in Spain, Coloccini was an experienced central defender since moving to Italy as a teenager and signing for AC Milan. He rarely figured for the Rossoneri (2 app) but being loaned out was a regular at Alaves, Atletico Madrid and Villareal, then Coloccini signed permanently for Deportivo La Coruna where he became a popular player. Early in his career Fabricio lifted the FIFA World Youth title then was part of the Argentina Olympic squad that won gold in Athens during 2004 going onto win over 30 caps for his country and taking part in the 2006 World Cup before moving to England. In the Premier League, at first the centre-back found the pace and power quite a test during his opening season of 2008-09, ending with United's relegation from the top sphere. Fabricio was though determined to remain at Gallowgate and show the Newcastle crowd he could be an asset. Like many players from abroad, after a season of acclimatisation, he settled in the North East and gradually began to show his ability. United's one season in the second level of football, in the Championship, saw confidence return and back in the Premier League few defenders showed a level of assured consistency, the South American being one of the best around, indeed he was included in the PFA Premier League team of the year for 2011-12. Skipper of United since 2011, although not with a big muscular frame, Coloccini's thoughtful reading of situations and timely interventions were a feature of his play. And his ability on the ball, in tight situations or moving out of the back-line, was much admired, showing excellent distribution to get United's moves started. With distinctive and lengthy curled hair, Fabricio became a solid favourite with the Toon faithful and earned a catchy stadium song to go with his cult popularity. His father Osvaldo played in top Argentinean football.

Appearances & Goals:
Debut v Manchester United (a) 17 August 2008
FL/PL: 190 app 4 gls
FAC: 7 app 0 gls
FLC: 8 app 1 gl
Euro: 5(2) app 0 gls
Total: 210(2) app 5 gls

Honours:
39 Arg caps 2003-date/WdC 2006/OG 2004 (gold)/Arg u20 app/FL ch winner 2010/Arg Lg champs 2001/CA final 2004/PFA ToS (PL) 2012, (ch) 2010.

CONNELL John 1896-1897

Inside-right
5'10"
b. Scotland

Career: St Mirren Sept 1894/Galston Dec 1895/UNITED Oct 1896/ Galston Aug 1897 to cs 1901.

John Connell was a noted Scot, fancied by Newcastle United's directors after several good displays in front of watching scouts. He had appeared on 33 occasions for Paisley's St Mirren before heading south and was described in Scottish Referee magazine as being, "a young player, smart and tricky". Taking the place of the veteran Collins during season 1896-97 as the Magpies attempted to gain promotion, Connell was a regular choice, but wasn't retained for the following year. He was good enough to represent Scotland in inter-league action during 1894-95 against the Irish.

Appearances & Goals:
Debut v Manchester City (a) 17 October 1896
FL: 24 app 3 gls
FAC: 1 app 0 gls
Total: 25 app 3 gls

Honours:
1 SL app 1895.

CONNELLY Edward John 1935-1938

Inside-left
5'8"
b. Dumbarton, 9 December 1916
d. Luton, 16 February 1990

Career: Rosslyn Jnrs (Fife)/UNITED March 1935 £90/Luton Town March 1938 £2,100/West Bromwich Albion Aug 1939 £4,150 (Dunfermline Ath war-guest 1941-42)(St Mirren war-guest 1941-42, 1942-43) (Luton Town war-guest 1945-46)/Luton Town April 1946/Leyton Orient June 1948 £2,000/Brighton Oct 1949 free/Cambridge Utd 1950/Retired c1951.

Eddie Connelly made his Football League debut with United as a teenager and was destined for a good career. Possessing heaps of talent, he was a marvellous ball-player, typical of the many celebrated Scots of his day. Bursting onto the scene in for the injured Harry McMenemy and on his day could be a match-winner. However, before he had left Tyneside the Scot was often criticised for overdoing the clever tricks, and for also occasionally losing his cool on the field. Connelly joined Luton to boost the Hatters attack when their star goal-getter, Joe Payne, moved to Chelsea. At Kenilworth Road Eddie became a firm favourite of supporters over two spells in which he totalled 98 matches (25 goals), while later in his career, when with West Bromwich Albion, he again was a popular star, however was once banned for life by the FA after being dismissed for wartime misdemeanours which were then punished heavily. Later he was reinstated and retired from soccer due to injury. Afterwards Connelly resided in Luton.

Appearances & Goals:
Debut v Walsall (a) 11 January 1936 (FAC) (1 goal)
FL: 25 app 8 gls
FAC: 5 app 1 gl
Total: 30 app 9 gls

CONNOLLY John 1978-1980

Outside-left
5'9"
b. Barrhead, near Glasgow, 13 June 1950

Career: Glasgow Utd 1966/St Johnstone Jan 1968/ Everton March 1972 £75,000/Birmingham City Sept 1976 £70,000/UNITED May 1978 exch deal/ Hibernian Sept 1980 free/Gateshead Feb 1982/ Blyth Spartans player-manager Nov 1982/ Gateshead Nov 1983/Whitley Bay manager Feb 1984 to Sept 1984/Later, Ayr Utd part-time coach 1995/Lemington SC (Newcastle) manager June 1997/Ashington manager 1998/Queen of the South manager May 2000/St Johnstone manager May 2004 to April 2005/Later becoming Dundee commercial manager as well as a Scottish based scout and Scottish Premier League match delegate.

Signed as part of Bill McGarry's rebuilding plans after Newcastle's relegation from Division One, John Connolly for a season looked to be an effective player in black-and-white striped kit. Linking well on the left wing and in midfield with United's strike-force of Peter Withe and Alan Shoulder, Connolly was prominent as the Magpies reached the top of the Second Division and looked as though they would regain their First Division place. But the team's good form vanished in the promotion run-in and with it went John's hope for a sustained period at Gallowgate while he suffered from a persistent thigh injury which needed lengthy treatment. The Scot could be described as an old-fashioned winger in style, he liked the ball at his feet, was tricky and always liable to cut inside and have a go at goal. Connolly had recovered from a twice broken leg at Goodison Park after making his name as a forward who had grabbed 55 goals at Muirton Park with St Johnstone. On Merseyside John enjoyed some good days in his 118 matches showing much of his talent in attack, Connolly possessing a neat body swerve and jink to beat his man. Reluctantly leaving the Magpies following a rift with the manager, after a spell on the North East non-league circuit, John worked for Vaux Breweries then returned to his native Scotland employed as an advertising manager for Golf Monthly magazine. As a manager Connolly was much admired for his work with Queen of the South; winning two trophies at Palmerston Park in Dumfries, the Scottish Division Two title and Scottish Challenge Cup. Afterwards Connolly was linked in Scotland with TSN, The Scouting Network, a world-wide football consultancy. His sons Stuart and Graeme both joined Ayr United.

Appearances & Goals:
Debut v Millwall (a) 19 August 1978
FL: 42(7) app 10 gls
FAC: 0(1) app 0 gls
FLC: 1 app 0 gls
Total: 43(8) app 10 gls

Honours:
1 Scot cap 1973/2 Scot u23 app 1971-73/SL div 1 champs 1981/SL div 2 champs 2002(m)/SLC final 1970/SCC winner 2002(m).

CONNOLLY J 1891-1892

Forward
b. unknown

Career: Stockton/EAST END Aug 1891/Newcastle West End Jan 1892 to cs 1892.

Arriving in Heaton from the Stockton club for the start of the 1891-92 season, Connolly operated across the forward-line for Newcastle East End and only appeared in a handful of pre-season fixtures. Yet he did register four goals during a friendly against Queen of the South Wanderers, before causing much controversy on Tyneside. His career with East End was short and colourful, being sent-off in the opening Northern League fixture against Darlington for striking an opponent. Leading the attack, Connolly had an altercation with an opponent and lost his cool, ordered from the field for hitting Waites the Quaker's defender. He was afterwards told by East End officials he would never play for the club again. As a result he was suspended for a lengthy period and soon Connolly moved across the city to St James' Park during January 1892 joining rivals West End, but found the club in a perilous financial state and didn't stay long.

Appearances & Goals:
Debut v Darlington (a) 19 September 1891 (NL)
NL: 1 app 0 gls
Total: 1 app 0 gls

CONNOR John 1942-1943

Left-back
b. Ashton under Lyne, 1 February 1914
d. Penrith, January 2000

Career: Mossley Methodists/Mossley 1932/ Bolton Wand Oct 1934 £325 (UNITED war-guest 1942-43)/Mossley 1946/ Tranmere Rovers June 1947 to 1949.

Making his Football League debut against Port Vale during February 1935, John Connor took part in 36 senior contests for Preston playing a small part in the Lilywhites promotion during that season. At St James' Park during the Second World War when stationed in the region, he stepped in for Doug Graham during November 1942, facing Gateshead in a double Football League North meeting. Connor helped United to a 7-4 victory over their Tyneside rivals in one of the derby clashes. Resuming his career with Tranmere after war, John totalled 48 matches for the Merseyside outfit.

Appearances & Goals:
Debut v Gateshead (a) 7 November 1942 (FLN)
War: 2 app 0 gls
Total: 2 app 0 gls

Honours:
FL div 2 prom 1935 (1 app).

COOK John 1918-1920

Inside-left
5'8"
b. Sunderland

Career: UNITED amat 1918, prof May 1919/
Scotswood April 1920.

Taking part in the Northern Victory League for Newcastle, John Cook recorded a single outing against Middlesbrough wearing United's centre-forward shirt although more often figuring in the inside-forward role in reserve football. He was offered a professional contract when peacetime soccer started once more for season 1919-20, but couldn't push for a First Division place and moved to local Tyneside soccer with the strong Scotswood outfit. During the Great War Cook served in the North Staffs Regiment and was awarded the DCM for his actions on the Continent.

Appearances & Goals:
Debut v Middlesbrough (h) 29 March 1919 (NVL)
War: 1 app 0 gls
Total: 1 app 0 gls.

COOPER Edward 1913-1920

Outside-right
5'8"
b. Walsall, 28 May 1891
d. Walsall, 7 July 1976

Career: Litchfield Phoenix/Stafford Rangers Oct 1911/
Glossop May 1912/UNITED March 1913 £1,375
(Grimsby Town war-guest 1917-18)(Bradford Park Avenue war-guest 1917-18)/Notts Co July 1920 £500 to cs 1921 free/
Stafford Rangers Nov 1921/Burton All Saints Aug 1923/
Cannock Town Aug 1925/Darlaston Sept 1926.

The First World War divided Ed Cooper's footballing career in two, like many unlucky footballers of his generation. Newcastle watched him in Glossop's Second Division line-up during 1912-13 and were impressed, bringing the winger to Tyneside as a potential replacement for the aging Jack Rutherford. He was a patient and talented deputy to Rutherford at Gallowgate, filling in for the famous England international during the years up to the outbreak of the Great War. His best turn-out was 1913-14 when Eddie totalled 14 games, while in the first season after peace was restored he made 11 appearances. By then Rutherford had departed, but Cooper was frustrated to find a new signing in Willie Aitken ahead of him for the first-team wing position. Despite this, Ed was a crowd pleaser with plucky displays on the touchline. During World War One, Cooper was with the West Yorkshire regiment in France.

Appearances & Goals:
Debut v Blackburn Rovers (h) 15 March 1913
FL: 45 app 2 gls
FAC: 1 app 0 gls
War: 10 app 2 gls
Total: 56 app 4 gls

COOPER Joseph 1952-1959

Half-back
5'7"
b. Gateshead, 15 October 1934

Career: Winlaton Mill/UNITED Sept 1952
£2,000 to 1959 free.

A part-time professional at St James' Park, Joe Cooper worked as a factory machinist at a Team Valley weaving company and found it extremely hard to secure a first-team place. Up against seasoned footballers and full-time professionals, he could play on either half-back flanks and deputised for two noted United skippers in Bob Stokoe and Jimmy Scoular during his lengthy period in reserve. Joe was 18 years of age when he made his debut against Preston, being elevated from Newcastle's third eleven when Stokoe fell down stairs the evening before the First Division clash. Cooper performed well against two

of the country's best forwards, Tom Finney and ex-United star Charlie Wayman. He also did well in a Tyne versus Wear derby when he matched Don Revie with much credit from the local press. The Tynesider though, was always destined for the shadow squad, and never managed more than two outings in any one season for the club.

Appearances & Goals:
Debut v Preston North End (a) 12 September 1953
FL: 6 app 0 gls
Total: 6 app 0 gls

COPELAND Edward 1939-1946

Outside-right
5'8"
b. Hetton-le-Hole, Co Durham, 19 May 1921
d. Newcastle upon Tyne, 12 July 2001

Career: Easington Jnrs/Hartlepools Utd Jan 1939/
Blackhall CW 1939/Easington CW/UNITED amat June 1939/Huddersfield Town 1942/UNITED prof Aug 1943/
Hartlepools Utd war-guest 1945-46, pmt cs 1946/
Stockton cs 1948/Spennymoor Utd c1949.

Briefly with United before the Second World War erupted, Ted Copeland returned to St James' Park and appeared on a regular basis for the club during season 1943-44. Rivalling a young Tommy Walker on the wing, Copeland was small and quick, while he could be a match-winner too. He netted twice as Newcastle defeated Gateshead 3-1 at Redheugh Park in a wartime derby match during December 1943. Copeland played for Hartlepools' senior line-up before, during and after the hostilities totalling 81 senior matches. After football, Eddie worked as a colliery electrician in the North East.

Appearances & Goals:
Debut v Bradford Park Avenue (h) 18 September 1943 (FLN)
War: 20 app 3 gls
Total: 20 app 3 gls

COPPINGER James 1998-2002

Midfield
5'7"
b. Guisborough, 18 January 1981

Career: Middlesbrough jnr 1991/Darlington jnr 1997/UNITED March 1998 £500,000 joint deal with P Robinson (Hartlepool Utd loan 1999-2000, 2000-01, 2001-02)(Queens Park Rangers loan 2000-01)/Exeter City Aug 2002 free/Doncaster Rovers July 2004 free (Nottingham Forest loan 2012-13).

As a 17-year-old teenager James Coppinger headed up the A1 from Darlington together with Quakers teammate Paul Robinson to join the Magpies in a double swoop. Both were purchased as players for the future, highly promising youngsters to get the opportunity on the big-time stage at St James' Park. Although slightly built at 5'7" tall, Coppinger showed at that age he had the vision and touch on the ball to be well suited to a midfield playmaker role, modelling his game somewhat on his Boro hero, Juninho. Fair-haired, James though had much competition at Gallowgate, not least an array of experienced international talent ahead of him all challenging for a first-team place. With the likes of Lee, Hamann, Speed, Ketsbaia and Solano, as well as Dyer, Georgiadis, Acuna and Bassedas in the reckoning, it was always going to be difficult if not impossible for Coppinger. He did get a brief look in during season 2000-01 as a 19-year-old, but after a loan period with Hartlepool, James moved permanently from the Premier League to Football League action with first Exeter then more successfully at Doncaster. James proceeded to become that playmaker just behind the front strikers with Rovers, albeit at a lower level of football. Spending over a decade in Yorkshire, Coppinger totalled over 400 games and was a key player in their rise through the divisions, in the second-tier Championship for a period. James netted the goal which secured the Division One title during 2013 for Doncaster. In the same year he was found guilty with Michael Chopra and others of betting irregularities on horse racing.

Appearances & Goals:
Debut v Tottenham Hotspur (h) 26 August 2000 (sub)
PL: 0(1) app 0 gls
Total: 0(1) app 0 gls

Honours:
Eng sch-youth app/1 Eng NG app 2004/FL div 1 champs 2013/FL div 1 prom 2008/
FLT winner 2007.

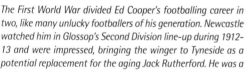

CORBETT Robert 1943-1951

Left-back
5'8"
b. Throckley, Newcastle upon Tyne,
16 March 1922
d. Newcastle upon Tyne, 30 September 1988

Career: Whorlton/Throckley Welfare/
UNITED amat Feb 1943, prof Aug 1943 £25/
Middlesbrough Dec 1951 £9,000/
Northampton Town £5,500 Aug 1957 to cs
1958/Brierley Hill manager for a period.

*Not always first choice at left-back for
Newcastle United, Bobby Corbett had stiff
competition for the first-team shirt in Doug
Graham, Benny Craig, Ron Batty and Alf
McMichael. But the Tynesider was an honest player who earned selection as the
Magpies reached Wembley in 1951. A former winger, Bobby switched to operate as a
full-back with pace, a player who loved to attack and who could cross an accurate
ball from the flanks. Corbett was one of Stan Seymour's youthful wartime products
along with Jack Milburn, Ernie Taylor and Bobby Cowell. Following an on-the-pitch
disagreement with skipper Joe Harvey at Burnden Park, Bobby soon afterwards moved
to Teesside to further his career and totalled almost 100 games for Boro. The Geordie,
who hailed from a local sporting family, and like many of his generation, from the
coal pits of the region, was a cheerful, happy character who always played his football
with a smile. On his retirement, Bobby lived in North Walbottle on Tyneside and was
involved his other sporting love, that of pigeons. It was said that when a player he
even occasionally took a basket of his prized birds on United away trips, to release
them and let them fly back home to Tyneside.*

Appearances & Goals:
Debut v Barnsley (h) 5 January 1946 (FAC)
(v Huddersfield Town (h) 9 October 1943 (FLN))
FL: 46 app 1 gl
FAC: 14 app 0 gls
War: 62 app 0 gls
Total: 122 app 1 gl

Honours:
FAC winner 1951/FL div 2 prom 1948 (4 app).

CORDONE Daniel Carlos 2000-2001

Striker or Midfield
5'9"
b. General Rodriguez, Buenos Aires (Argentina),
6 November 1974

Career: Velez Sarsfield (Arg) 1989/Racing Club de
Avellaneda (Arg) loan 1999, pmt 2000/UNITED June
2000 £500,000/AA Argentinos Juniors (Arg) July 2001
(CA San Lorenzo (Arg) loan 2002-03)/CA Argentino de
Merlo (Arg) 2005/CS Independiente Rivadavia (Arg)
2006/Deportivo Mutal Leandro (Arg) 2007/Deportivo
Tristan Suarez (Arg) c2008/Deportivo Mutal Leandro
(Arg) July 2010 to 2012 when he became coach.

*Daniel Cordone was spotted when United were watching fellow Argentinean Christian
Bassedas and in the first few games of his short Newcastle career, showed Magpie
fans that perhaps the Black'n'Whites had found a player with star quality in the
making. Scoring on his home debut against Derby County at the newly enlarged St
James' Park as the 2000-01 season began, the Argentinean forward found the net
again three days later on his next outing. Purchased as forward cover, he operated as
an attacking midfielder to support twin strikers Shearer and Cort, but Daniel got an
early opportunity up top when Cort was injured. Giving plucky and energetic displays,
he showed skill to convert chances with a perfect finish. Nicknamed 'Wolf' (or 'Lobo'
in Argentina) Cordone had a rock-star image and was characterised by long hair,
pony-tail, earrings and tattoos, he had spent 10 years with Velez Sarsfield alongside
Bassedas. He could take defenders on and for a short period gave the Magpies a new
dimension. Following that bright start though, Cordone rarely recaptured his opening
sparkling form. Nevertheless it could be said he did do well for his one and only season
in English football, however Daniel was totally out of the picture during preparations
for the 2001-02 programme, manager Robson releasing the South American during
the close season. Off the field misdemeanours did not help his career, in Argentina
Cordone appeared for a string of clubs and made the news for the wrong reasons,
once charged with "incitement" after scoring for Racing, then later failing drugs tests
and banned for two years.*

Appearances & Goals:
Debut v Manchester United (a) 20 August 2000
PL: 12(9) app 2 gls
FAC: 0(2) app 0 gls
FLC: 1(3) app 1 gl
Total: 13(14) app 3 gls

Honours:
CSA winner 2002/Arg div 3 champs 2007.

CORNWELL John Anthony 1987-1988

Midfield or Full-back
6'0"
b. Bethnal Green, London, 13 October 1964

Career: West Ham Utd jnr/Leyton Orient jnr July 1981,
prof Oct 1982/UNITED July 1987 £50,000/ Swindon
Town Dec 1988 £50,000/Southend Utd Aug 1990
£45,000 (Cardiff City loan 1993-94) (Brentford loan
1993-94)(Northampton Town loan 1993-94)/Retired
Aug 1994.

*A blond-haired utility player, John Cornwell operated
largely in midfield for United, but also on occasion at
full-back and in the centre of defence too. The Londoner joined the Magpies after 234
senior outings for Orient being a product of Frank Clark's local junior network. At
nearly 23 years of age, Cornwell had the opportunity to develop at a top club, but
found it difficult in a side which initially couldn't maintain a promotion challenge.
Having a biting tackle, his best season in United colours was during 1987-88 before
moving to Swindon a year later. Cornwell always gave 100% effort and he continued
to be a valued player in lower circles, notably with Southend where he totalled more
than 100 matches. Following retirement John managed public-houses in the South
East, including, The Reindeer, in the village of Black Notley. He also coached local sides
in the district.*

Appearances & Goals:
Debut v Southampton (h) 26 September 1987
FL: 28(5) app 1 gl
FAC: 1 app 0 gls
FLC: 3 app 0 gls
Others: 4(1) app 0 gls
Total: 36(6) app 1 gl

Honours:
FL div 2 prom 1990/FL div 3 prom 1991.

CORT Carl Edward Richard 2000-2004

Striker
6'4"
b. Southwark, London, 1 November 1977

Career: Wimbledon jnr, prof June 1996 (Lincoln City loan
1996-97)/UNITED July 2000 £7m/Wolverhampton Wand
Jan 2004 £1.6m/Leicester City Aug 2007 free/
UD Marbella (Sp) Feb 2008/Norwich City Dec 2008/
Wycombe Wand trial July 2009/Brentford Aug 2009 to
Jan 2011/Tampa Bay Rowdies (USA) Aug 2012.

*Carl Cort was the target of several clubs as he rapidly
developed in Wimbledon's Premier League eleven and
scored 25 goals for the Dons. Bobby Robson was keen on his ability, seeing the spritely,
tall striker as a good partner for Alan Shearer. A hefty fee of £7m brought the
22-year-old Cort to Tyneside for the start of the 2000-01 season and the leggy arrival
started well, scoring on his home debut after only three minutes against Derby.
Possessing a deft touch of the ball for such a gangly-looking player, he was
surprisingly better with the ball at his feet than in the air; Bobby Robson once
describing Cort as "slightly Bambi-esque". He was then unlucky to pick up a severe
hamstring injury, the start of recurring visits to the treatment room. A lengthy absence
followed, yet Cort again showed that when fit and on the field he was a danger. He
scored seven goals in 15 appearances in that first season and while Carl looked
ungainly at times, he was lively and had a presence in the box. Cort though was
struck with an injury-jinx and was out of action for another lengthy period with ankle*

and knee ligament problems. When he was eventually fit again, Craig Bellamy had established himself in United's side and Cort had to look elsewhere. One of several Robson high-value purchases which never produced the goods, in the final analysis Cort only managed 24 starts for the Magpies over three-and-a-half years, scant reward for such a big outlay. He moved to Wolves for a cut price £1.6m, United writing off over £5m on the original deal. At Molineux, Carl had his best return of goals, 32 all told for the Midlanders while his first full game for Wimbledon as a teenager was against the Magpies at St James' Park during September 1997, and he scored in the first minute. His brother Leon played prominently for Southend and Hull, the pair appearing together for the Guyana national side when Carl had a career renaissance in the States with Tampa Bay.

Appearances & Goals:
Debut v Manchester United (a) 20 August 2000
PL: 19(3) app 7 gls
FAC: 2 app 0 gls
FLC: 3 app 1 gl
Euro: 0(1) app 0 gls
Total: 24(4) app 8 gls

Honours:
6 Gy caps 2012-date/12 Eng u21 app 1999-2000.

COULSON William John 1971-1973

Midfield
5'10"
b. Newcastle upon Tyne, 14 January 1950

Career: Consett Town/North Shields 1970/UNITED Oct 1971/ Southend Utd Oct 1973 £15,000 (Aldershot loan 1974-75) (Huddersfield Town loan 1975-76)(Darlington loan 1975-76)/ North Shields June 1976/Hong Kong Rangers April 1978/ Urban Services (HK)/Caroline Hill (HK)/Kwong Wha (HK)/ Frankston City (Aus) c1982/Ringwood City Wilhelmina (Aus).

Fair-haired Billy Coulson grew up in the Benwell district of Newcastle and joined the club when he was working as a 21-year-old hod-carrier on a local building site. Coulson soon impressed many United supporters in a run of stirring displays for United's Central League side during season 1971-72. Able to get forward and become an extra striker, Coulson earned a first-team call up for a Texaco Cup semi-final meeting with Derby County in December of that season. He again played well and indications were at the time that Joe Harvey had found a gem from the local non-league scene. But Coulson suffered a cartilage injury and wasn't given a further opportunity, although he was on the subs bench in Football League matches. Nicknamed 'Coco' on Tyneside, he headed to Southend and totalled over 50 games before moving to Hong Kong then Australia where he played alongside several famous names, Martin Chivers and Martin Peters included. Billy lived in Melbourne for 20 years working for a period with Woolworths, then moved to the Australian east coast settling in appropriately, Newcastle, New South Wales. During 2001 he sold his house and bought a mobile caravan, touring Australia extensively. As a young footballer on Tyneside, Billy had a three month spell with Chelsea as an amateur, as well as trials at Burnley and Blackburn, before getting his chance at St James' Park.

Appearances & Goals:
Debut v Derby County (h) 8 December 1971 (TC)
Others: 1 app 0 gls
Total: 1 app 0 gls

COUPE Joseph 1888-1891

Half-back
b. Lancashire, c1869

Career: Blackburn Olympic/EAST END April 1888 to c1891.

A former Blackburn Olympic half-back, Joseph Coupe signed for East End near the end of the 1887-88 season and made a good impression on Tyneside totalling over 40 first-team matches for Newcastle's pioneers. He represented Northumberland in March 1889 and also appeared for the Newcastle & District combination side. Well-built and somewhat robust, contemporary reports made the comment that Coupe always "made his presence felt" on the field. By season 1890-91 Joe was more often than not in East End's reserve eleven, captain of the club's second-string. Although he registered only six first-class games, Coupe totalled over 40 miscelleanous fixtures as well. Coupe was a schoolmaster and resided at Tynemouth Road in Byker.

Appearances & Goals:
Debut v Elswick Rangers (a) 21 September 1889 (NL)
NL: 4 app 0 gls
FAC: 2 app 0 gls
Total: 6 app 0 gls

COWAN John 1967-1973

Midfield
5'10"
b. Belfast, 8 January 1949

Career: Crusaders amat/UNITED Feb 1967 £300/ Drogheda Utd player-manager Aug 1973/Darlington Aug 1975/Lusitano (SA) coach July to Sept 1976/Queen of the South Nov 1976/Scarborough 1976 to 1977.

The dark-haired, slimly-built John Cowan was rarely given an opportunity to show his stylish ability in United's first eleven after moving to Tyneside as a youngster. Although capped by Northern Ireland against England at Wembley when in United's Central League side, John only appeared in the Magpies' midfield during two seasons of the seven he was on the St James' Park staff. Nicknamed 'Seamus' by his colleagues, he was out of action with a bad knee injury for a long period, a knock which eventually forced him to quit senior football when only 27 years old. After a mere 11 games for the Quakers, the Irishman retired from the game, John soon settling on Tyneside. He opened what was to be a successful trophy business in 1978, initially with former team-mate Jimmy Smith. He managed Trend Trophies and the business developed into a major concern involved in the design, manufacture and distribution of a wide range of sporting awards world-wide. Based in Killingworth, Cowan handed the enterprise to his son in 2008. John also married into the family of one of United's all-time-greats, Frank Brennan.

Appearances & Goals:
Debut v Burnley (a) 1 November 1969
FL: 6(3) app 0 gls
FLC: 0(1) app 0 gls
Total: 6(4) app 0 gls

Honours:
1 NI cap 1970/NI sch-youth app.

COWAN William Duncan 1923-1926

Inside-right
5'10"
b. Edinburgh, 9 August 1896
d. Newcastle upon Tyne, 24 January 1965

Career: Dalkeith Thistle/Tranent Jnrs/Dundee Jan 1920/ UNITED July 1923 £2,250/Manchester City May 1926 £3,000/St Mirren May 1927 £700/Harrogate Town 1928/Peebles Rovers March 1929/Northfleet Utd Nov 1929/North Shields Feb 1930/Hartlepools Utd Sept 1930/Darlington Oct 1930/Bath City July 1931/ Wolverston St Peter's c1933.

W. COWAN

A midfield creator who was an important cog during United's FA Cup victory in 1924, the tall, slim Billy Cowan was elegant and effective, the type of player who could make time and space for himself. Having impressed many scouts appearing for Dundee (79 app), especially in season 1922-23 as the Tayside club finished seventh in Division One, United's strong network north of the border acted to bring him to Tyneside. With ability in both feet, Cowan consequently filled in on the left side of the pitch too and possessing a potent shot which frequently tested the opposition's goalkeeper, he was always able to score goals. Billy was at the height of his form as United embarked on their Cup run during the 1923-24 season; his career peaked when he starred at Wembley for both United, and then a fortnight later for his country against England. His performances during the following campaign however dipped alarmingly, and, after being barracked by the Gallowgate crowd, Cowan was quoted as saying, "I would rather drop into minor football than remain here". The Scot soon departed, to Maine Road, being replaced by a fellow countryman Bob McKay as Newcastle began a title winning campaign. One pen-picture of the day noted Cowan as being, "a mazy dribbler with the leather", while another recorded, "A brainy, speedy player, with a deadly shot". Later in life Bill returned to Tyneside and resided in Gosforth to his demise.

Appearances & Goals:
Debut v Sheffield United (h) 8 September 1923
FL: 87 app 22 gls
FAC: 14 app 5 gls
Total: 101 app 27 gls

Honours:
1 Scot cap 1924/Scot trial app 1924/FAC winner 1924.

COWELL Robert George 1943-1956

Right-back
5'9"
b. Trimdon Grange, Co Durham, 5 December 1922
d. Newcastle upon Tyne, 11 January 1996

Career: Grange Home Guard/Trimdon/Blackhall CW (Shotton trial)/UNITED amat Aug 1943, prof Oct 1943 £45 (Gateshead war-guest 1945-46)/ Retired due to injury cs 1956/Whitley Bay manager Aug 1956 to Sept 1956.

A solid defender, brave and tremendously quick to make up lost ground, ex-miner Bobby Cowell dominated the Number 2 shirt at St James' Park for nearly a decade after being signed as a youngster during World War Two. Appearing in three seasons of wartime soccer, Cowell made his Football League debut for the Magpies in the remarkable Second Division fixture with Newport County at Gallowgate during 1946, a game that produced the record scoreline of 13-0. He saw off challenges from Craig, Burke and Fraser and made the right-back spot his own, playing in every one of the club's 25 FA Cup-ties which saw the trophy brought back to Tyneside on three occasions; one of a trio of United players to be in each winning side (with Milburn and Mitchell). Celebrated for off-the-line clearances, including a famous moment in the FA Cup final, Bobby was on the fringe of an England call-up and one of the few attacking backs of the era. Jackie Milburn once remarked that he "was the best uncapped full-back I've known". Friendly and modest, like many of his era, the quietly spoken Cowell was injured following a reckless tackle during a friendly on tour in Germany during the summer of 1955 in a match against Nuremberg. He was forced to quit the game prematurely when aged 33 with knee ligament damage. A very popular player with the grass-root fans, in 1956 Cowell was given a testimonial fixture which saw 36,240 turn up to give him a send-off. Afterwards he resided in Ponteland on Tyneside, frequently watching United's fortunes for the next 40 years. Although Bobby appeared over 400 times for the Black'n'Whites, he never found the net apart from when in friendly action.

Appearances & Goals:
Debut v Barnsley (h) 5 January 1946 (FAC)
(v Bradford Park Avenue (a) 11 September 1943 (FLN))
FL: 289 app 0 gls
FAC: 38 app 0 gls
War: 81 app 0 gls
Others: 1 app 0 gls
Total: 409 app 0 gls

Honours:
FL div 2 prom 1948/FAC winner 1951, 1952, 1955.

COYDE Norman 1936-1938, 1942-1943

Outside-right
5'8"
b. Wallsend, 2 January 1918
d. Newcastle upon Tyne, 11 April 1985

Career: Wallsend shipyard works/Sunderland 1935/ UNITED May 1936 free/North Shields May 1938 free/ Southend Utd 1939 (Gateshead war-guest 1941-42) (UNITED war-guest 1942-43).

A teenage friend of Albert Stubbins at Carville School, Norman Coyde first joined the St James' Park staff at the same time as his more famous colleague in 1936. Noted then as a "speedy, intelligent youth", however he couldn't break through United's pre-war ranks and moved south to try his luck with Southend United. An effervescent winger, Coyde wasn't a regular with the Shrimpers and he returned to Gallowgate for wartime action, the highlight of his United career was a goal in the amazing 6-6 draw with Gateshead on Christmas Day 1942. Illness curtailed his career

and later he did well at Appleby Park for North Shields. Norman was employed as a shipyard manager in Wallsend, where he started his working life back in the mid-Thirties. He was also an excellent golfer as well as local cricketer and resided in Walker to his death.

Appearances & Goals:
Debut v Middlesbrough (h) 21 November 1942 (FLN)
War: 7 app 1 gl
Total: 7 app 1 gl

CRAGGS John Edward 1964-1971, 1982-1983

Right-back
5'8"
b. Flinthill, Co Durham, 31 October 1948

Career: UNITED jnr April 1964, prof Dec 1965/ Middlesbrough Aug 1971 £60,000/UNITED Aug 1982 free/ Darlington Aug 1983 free to cs 1985 when he became asst-coach/Crook Town 1987/Hartlepool Utd asst-coach Dec 1988 to c1991, being caretaker-manager Nov 1989.

With United in two spells, John Craggs had an association with the Magpies which spanned eight seasons. Joining the club as a teenager during 1964, he was unfortunate to develop in the shadows of David Craig and, despite his long period at Gallowgate, infrequently received an opportunity. Overlapping with style and vision, his best returns were in 1968-69 and 1969-70, when Craggs also was involved in the club's European success, playing in the Fairs Cup semi-final against Rangers and on the bench in the final. But for Craig's tremendous consistency, John would have earned the right-back spot, yet had to depart the scene to make sure of regular Football League action. Former United skipper Stan Anderson, boss at Middlesbrough, knew all about Craggs and paid what was a sizable fee for a United fringe player. But it was money well spent. At Ayresome Park, John enjoyed a consistent period himself, appearing on 488 occasions, many as captain, during a decade with Middlesbrough. With a solid frame, calm assurance and a polished style on the ball, he rejoined United for a short period at the end of his career and appeared alongside Kevin Keegan in a Magpie shirt. John was only 17 when he first played for United, and 33 when he began his second spell. Craggs later resided in Yarm, then Eaglescliffe, and for a period worked as a car salesman in Redcar then ran a sports shop initially for Willie Maddren, then when it was taken over by the Sports Direct empire, for Mike Ashley, Newcastle United's later owner.

Appearances & Goals:
Debut v Everton (a) 1 October 1966
FL: 60(4) app 1 gl
FAC: 2 app 0 gls
FLC: 1(1) app 0 gls
Euro: 5 app 0 gls
Total: 68(5) app 1 gl

Honours:
Eng sch-youth app/FL div 2 champs 1974/ICFC winner 1969 (sub no app)/PFA ToS (d2) 1974.

CRAIG Albert Hughes 1987-1989

Midfield
5'8"
b. Glasgow, 3 January 1962

Career: Yoker Ath Aug 1980/Dumbarton Dec 1981/ Hamilton Acc Aug 1986 £10,000/UNITED Feb 1987 £100,000 (Hamilton Acc loan 1987-88)(Northampton Town loan 1988-89)/Dundee loan Dec 1988, pmt Jan 1989 free/Partick Thistle Aug 1992/Falkirk Dec 1995/ Stenhousemuir Aug 1998/Partick Thistle July 1999/ Retired May 2000.

C

Albert Craig joined United as a 25-year-old midfielder who had risen to headline back-page news in Scotland with a series of dramatic displays for Hamilton. In the space of a few short weeks, he netted four goals in a derby against Motherwell, scored again opposing Celtic, then turned in a super performance during a shock cup defeat of Rangers at the end of January 1987. Newcastle scouts were suitably impressed and paid a six-figure fee to bring the part-timer to Tyneside. Craig gave up his job in a friend's television shop and turned his attention to the big time in England. However, manager Willie McFaul's vision of Craig's ability to become a top class link man never materialised. Not able to come to terms with the pace of English First Division soccer and unlucky to break a collarbone when just finding his feet, Albert struggled and totalled just a handful of games for the Magpies. At a big financial loss to United, Craig eventually returned north of the border where he became a key player for Partick Thistle in 159 matches, always able to hit the net. He also reached the Scottish Cup final with Falkirk when they were beaten by Kilmarnock. At the start of his career Albert turned out on more than 150 occasions for Dumbarton. On leaving the Scottish game after 512 appearances north of the border, Craig worked for Royal Mail in the West of Scotland as a delivery driver. He was convicted of postal theft of more than £40,000 during 2005 and sentenced to 12 months in prison, all as a result of a chronic gambling addiction.

Appearances & Goals:
Debut v Luton Town (h) 7 February 1987
FL: 6(4) app 0 gls
FAC: 1(1) app 0 gls
Others: 2 app 0 gls
Total: 9(5) app 0 gls

Honours:
SL div 1 champs 1988 (6 app)/SL div 1 prom 1992/SC final 1997.

CRAIG Benjamin 1938-1982

Right or Left-back & Coach
5'7"
b. Leadgate, Co Durham, 6 December 1915
d. Newcastle upon Tyne, 18 January 1982
Career: Medomsley Jnrs/Leadgate/Ouston Jnrs/Eden Colliery 1932/Huddersfield Town Jan 1934/UNITED Nov 1938 £4,000 (Chelsea war-guest 1941-42)/ Retired July 1950, becoming asst-coach and asst-physio July 1979 to his death in 1982.

Benny Craig was a loyal servant to Newcastle United for over 43 years; a shrewd, sound-kicking full-back and a respected and likable character behind the scenes. Able to play on both flanks, Craig rivalled Joe Richardson for the defender's role before the war and after losing some of his best years to the fighting, returned to give United an experienced head in the Magpies' promotion line-up of 1948. On retirement Craig worked alongside his former rival, Richardson, for all of three decades in the inner corridors of St James' Park, a pairing which was at the very heart of the club. Benny coached Newcastle's FA Youth Cup success during 1962 and helped enormously in the development of future stars Craig, Moncur and Alan Suddick along with a host of other youngsters in the Magpies emerging junior set-up at the time. During the war he served with the Royal Artillery and spent most of his active service in the Mediterranean theatre including the landings at Anzio when he won the Military Medal. As a teenager Benny had trials with Sunderland and Arsenal before entering senior football at Leeds Road where he totalled over 100 games, being a regular in the Terriers line-up when they challenged for the title during 1935-36. He also earned a Wembley place in 1938 appearing in Huddersfield's FA Cup defeat by Preston. Craig was originally a brick moulder in Consett, and guested for Ayr United in a friendly during 1950, against the Magpies.

Appearances & Goals:
Debut v Blackburn Rovers (a) 19 November 1938
FL: 66 app 0 gls
FAC: 1 app 0 gls
War: 52 app 0 gls
Total: 119 app 0 gls
(Void FL: 3 app 0 gls)

Honours:
FL div 2 prom 1948/FAC final 1938.

CRAIG David James 1960-1978

Right-back
5'10"
b. Comber, Belfast, 8 June 1944
Career: Scunthorpe Utd jnr/Boy's Brigade/ UNITED jnr July 1960, prof April 1962/Blyth Spartans cs 1978 free/Retired Nov 1978, occasionally appearing in local football, including Dunston Mechanics 1983-84.

Recognised by many judges to be one of the best defenders in the game during the Sixties and Seventies, David Craig stands alongside the likes of McCracken, Hudspeth and Cowell as the club's most consistent full-back. Following an unhappy four month period at Scunthorpe as a kid, when Craig became homesick, he joined United's apprentice scheme as a raw teenager from Ulster. David settled far better on Tyneside where he had fellow Irishmen Dick Keith and Alf McMichael as senior professionals to help him adjust to a new way of life. The youngster rapidly caught the eye of Joe Harvey after he starred in the club's Youth Cup success during 1962. Craig was in many ways a complete footballer, dependable and able to recover quickly when in defence, intelligent and positive going forward. He also had a steady character which never gave his manager a problem. David was a thorough professional and is one of only nine individuals to total over 400 league and cup games for the Magpies. One of those players was Craig's partner for many a season, Frank Clark, a duo that served United well for 12 campaigns, the majority in the top flight. Had it not been for several injuries that kept Craig out of action, including both 1974 and 1976 Wembley appearances, the Irishman would have come close to Jimmy Lawrence's longstanding appearance record. Although sidelined for the 1974 FA Cup final with a dislocated elbow, he received a runners-up medal for appearing in eight of the previous fixtures en route to the final. A regular member for the Northern Ireland international squad, he was a one club man with the Black'n'Whites and a crowd of 21,280 attended his testimonial match in 1975 while David is the only United player to appear in both of the Magpies' European campaign's of 1968-71 and 1977-78. Craig later resided on Tyneside and ran a newsagency outlet as well as a heating company and for a while a milk business. He afterwards became a support worker with the Edward Lloyd Trust in Newcastle, helping adults with learning difficulties. His cousin Ron White was a noted left-back for Linfield.

Appearances & Goals:
Debut v Bournemouth (a) 6 November 1963 (FLC)
FL: 346(5) app 8 gls
FAC: 21 app 2 gls
FLC: 17(1) app 1 gl
Euro: 21 app 0 gls
Others: 23 app 1 gl
Total: 428(6) app 12 gls
(Void FAC: 1 app 1 gl)

Honours:
25 NI caps 1967-75/2 NI u23 app 1965-67/1 All-Irel app 1973/FL div 2 champs 1965/FAYC winner 1962/ICFC winner 1969.

CRAIG Derek Malcolm 1968-1975

Centre-half
6'0"
b. Ryton, near Gateshead, 28 July 1952
Career: Clara Vale Jnrs/UNITED jnr June 1968, prof Aug 1969 (San Jose Earthquakes (USA) loan cs 1975)/ Darlington Sept 1975/York City May 1980 to cs 1982/Brandon Utd Nov 1982.

Tall, slender centre-half Derek Craig was plunged into the senior line-up at a time of injury crisis at Gallowgate during season 1971-72. Regular centre-backs, Ollie Burton, Bob Moncur and John McNamee were sidelined, and new signing Pat Howard was cup-tied, so in stepped the untried Craig for a difficult League Cup tie at Highbury, home of the reigning League Champions, Arsenal. The evening went badly for the 19-year-old youngster, the Gunners netting four times and Craig didn't get another opportunity in Joe Harvey's line-up apart from a Texaco Cup outing. However, Derek became one of the most respected defenders in the Fourth Division appearing on 214 occasions for the Feethams club. When he left the game during the Eighties, Craig set up an insurance and financial consultancy business on Tyneside.

Appearances & Goals:
Debut v Arsenal (a) 6 October 1971 (FLC)
FLC: 1 app 0 gls
Others: 1 app 0 gls
Total: 2 app 0 gls

CRAIG Thomas Brooks 1974-1978, 1998-2006

Midfield & Coach
5'7"
b. Penilee, Glasgow, 21 November 1950

Career: Avon Villa/Drumchapel Amateurs Aug 1965/Aberdeen jnr June 1966, prof Nov 1967/Sheffield Wed May 1969 £100,000/UNITED Dec 1974 £110,000/ Aston Villa Jan 1978 £270,000/Swansea City July 1979 £150,000/Carlisle Utd March 1982 becoming asst-manager July 1982/ Hibernian player-coach Nov 1984 £6,000 to Dec 1986/Celtic coach Feb 1987, becoming asst-manager, chief-scout and later, head-of-youth to Oct 1994/Aberdeen asst-manager May 1995 to Nov 1997/ Scotland u21 part-time coach, then manager 1993 to Oct 1998/UNITED asst-coach April 1998 to Sept 2006, becoming caretaker-manager Aug 1998/Hibernian asst-manager Nov 2006, caretaker-manager Dec 2007 to Feb 2008/RSC Charleroi (Belg) asst-manager Dec 2008, becoming manager 2009 to April 2010/ St Mirren asst-manager July 2011, becoming manager May 2014.

During the early part of his career, ginger-haired Tommy Craig was courted by Celtic, Liverpool and West Ham United as a schoolboy and later became the most expensive teenager on record when he moved from Pittodrie to Hillsborough for a six figure sum. Short but stocky, Craig's undoubted potential somewhat stagnated with Sheffield Wednesday in over 200 games, a quality player in a team which slipped to the Third Division. It wasn't until he moved back to the top in black-and-white colours that the talent of Tommy Craig was fully realised. He was capped by Scotland when at St James' Park as he became an influential United player. Rivalling the popular, but injured Terry Hibbitt in Newcastle's midfield, Craig could have easily received a back-lash from United's support having replaced Hibbitt when he was eventually sold. But Newcastle fans liked the Scots' ability and he became a popular player himself. Although not blessed with pace, Tommy had an educated left foot, always prompting and probing when on the ball, while he could hit a short pass accurately and place a telling long ball which could win a match. He possessed a stinging drive too which brought Craig several picture goals and was also a penalty-kick expert. Replacing the sidelined Geoff Nulty as skipper of the Magpies' Wembley eleven in 1976, Craig also captained his national side at Under-21, Under-23 and youth level, while Tommy is one of only a select number of Scots to have appeared at every level of international football for his country. The internal strife which resulted in Richard Dinnis' managerial reign at Gallowgate, eventually led to Craig's departure for a record club fee to Villa Park. The move was not a success and Craig ended his playing career with 107 games for Carlisle, a successful period at Brunton Park. When at Swansea, Tommy scored one of the goals which took the Welshmen to the top flight during 1980-81 while his brother, John, also appeared for Aberdeen. Tommy later became a respected coach in Scotland returning to St James' Park for a lengthy spell, caretaker-boss for a single game in August 1998 when Kenny Dalglish departed.

Appearances & Goals:
Debut v Carlisle United (a) 26 December 1974
FL: 122(2) app 22 gls
FAC: 13 app 3 gls
FLC: 11 app 2 gls
Euro: 4 app 2 gls
Others: 5 app 0 gls
Total: 155(2) app 29 gls

In Charge: 1 game (joint caretaker)

Honours:
1 Scot cap 1976/9 Scot u23 app 1974-76/1 Scot u21 app 1977/Scot sch-youth app/FL div 2 prom 1981/FL div 3 prom 1982/FLC final 1976/SLC final 1985/WsC winner 1981.

CRATE Thomas 1891-1895

Forward
5'9"
b. Kilmarnock, 1872

Career: New Cumnock/Lanemark 1889/EAST END cs 1891/Hebburn Argyle Feb 1895/Blyth Town March 1895/ Seaton Burn 1896/Morpeth early 1897/Ashington April 1897.

Tom Crate landed on Tyneside from his native Scotland having learned the game in Ayrshire football. One of the club's foremost pioneers appearing in Newcastle's first game at St James' Park against Celtic, and United's Football League baptism with Arsenal. Additionally, Tom took part in East End's initial FA Cup Proper fixture with Nottingham Forest during 1892. Crate also has the distinction of netting the Tynesider's first goal in league action against the Gunners; although some sources credit the historic strike to Willie Graham after "a scrimmage" in the Londoner's box. Crate appeared in all five forward positions for United during Newcastle's three years of existence following East End's move from Heaton to St James' Park and including friendly outings, totalled over 100 games for the club. He was always able to find the net, scoring 12 goals in the inaugural 1893-94 Division Two programme. But the Scot left the club under a cloud, released after a dispute over wages. He continued his career in local football helping Ashington to the East Northumberland title during 1898. By the early years of the new century Crate was working as a coal miner back in New Cumnock.

Appearances & Goals:
Debut v Darlington (a) 19 September 1891 (NL)
FL: 39 app 14 gls
NL: 23 app 4 gls
FAC: 7 app 2 gls
Total: 69 app 20 gls

CRAWFORD James 1995-1998

Midfield
6'0"
b. Chicago (USA), 1 May 1973

Career: Bohemians (Dublin) 1991/UNITED trial, pmt March 1995 £75,000 (Rotherham Utd loan 1996-97)(Dundee Utd loan 1997-98)/Reading March 1998 £50,000/Shelbourne July 2000 free to Dec 2007/Sporting Fingal Feb 2008 to cs 2008 when he retired due to injury/Shamrock Rovers coach cs 2008, becoming manager Oct 2008 to 2009/FAI Development Officer.

One of the most promising young footballers in Dublin, Jimmy Crawford earned himself a full-time contract with Premiership Newcastle United after impressing manager Kevin Keegan during a trial period on Tyneside towards the end of the 1994-95 season. The 21-year-old could play wide or in a more conventional midfield role and quickly was handed a senior debut in the League Cup meeting with Bristol City. Before joining the Magpies, Crawford had a trial period at Villa Park in Birmingham, but that chance at the big-time vanished and he welcomed a second opportunity. Born in the States, he had moved to Ireland when aged six years old, Jimmy skippered United's reserve side and was a talented player, reaching the Republic of Ireland's squad during 1995-96, qualifying due to his parental background. Jimmy though picked up niggling injuries and was never going to be good enough to dislodge the wall of international talent ahead of him at Gallowgate. He made only three appearances for the Black'n'Whites, all from the bench, and moved on, to Reading, with reserve colleague Paul Brayson. More injuries restricted his progress in England and after only 28 games he settled back in Ireland where he was a highly successful player with Shelbourne over eight seasons. Later Crawford joined the FA of Ireland development staff.

Appearances & Goals:
Debut v Bristol City (h) 4 October 1995 (sub) (FLC)
PL: 0(2) app 0 gls
FLC: 0(1) app 0 gls
Total: 0(3) app 0 gls

Honours:
3 Eire u21 app/PL runner-up 1997 (2 app)/Eire Lg champs 2002, 2003, 2004, 2006/Eire YPoY 1994.

C

CREILLY Robert 1888-1895

Right-half
5'10"
b. Scotland, c1873
d. Heaton, Newcastle upon Tyne, 9 April 1907

Career: Dunmore/EAST END Aug 1888 (North Eastern guest 1889-90)/Hebburn Argyle Aug 1895 to 1897, later with other local sides.

Like his team-mate Tom Crate, Scot Bobby Creilly was a stalwart of the Newcastle East End side that dominated the local scene and eventually saw off the challenge of West End to become Tyneside's premier club. He also appeared in Newcastle United's first fixture at St James' Park and saw action in their first Football League tussle as well as East End's inaugural gallant run to the early rounds of the FA Cup Proper. Looking more like a boxer, he was tough and uncompromising at half-back, Creilly was also a touch fiery and temperamental, once in 1894 suspended for two weeks for using bad language on the field to officials, while in 1891 he stormed off the field due to his colleagues' lack of effort! A versatile individual and although he generally operated in midfield, Creilly also turned out in other roles, including goalkeeper for East End. Apart from his senior matches for the club, Bobby appeared in numerous other non-competitive games, another 130-odd fixtures. He was selected for the Northumberland County side during those early Victorian years and was a well known figure on Tyneside. Later in life the Scot ran into hard times during the Edwardian era, noted as being in, "destitute circumstances". Records show that Newcastle United forwarded a gift of five guineas to help him out but during March 1905 he was, "removed to Coxlodge hospital", then a well known sanatorium in Newcastle. Sadly he died when only into his thirties. On his death the Northern Gossip magazine noted that in his day he was "a fine half-back, fearless and a man who never shirked his work."

(Note: Some sources have his surname spelt, Crielly, but official records show Creilly.)

Appearances & Goals:
Debut v Port Clarence (h) 6 October 1888 (FACQ)
FL: 54 app 1 gl
NL: 52 app 5 gl
FAC: 17 app 0 gls
Total: 123 app 6 gls
(Void NL: 2 app 2 gls)

CROPLEY Alexander James 1980

Midfield
5'8"
b. Aldershot, 16 January 1951

Career: St Bernard's BC/Edina Hibs (Edinburgh)/ Hibernian July 1968/Arsenal Dec 1974 £150,000/Aston Villa Sept 1976 £125,000 (UNITED loan Feb to March 1980)/Toronto Blizzard (Can) July 1981/ Portsmouth Sept 1981/Hibernian Sept 1982/Retired May 1985.

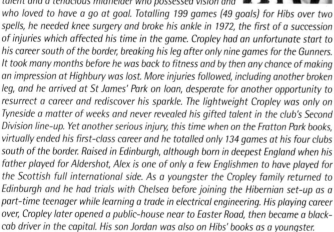

One of Scotland's big money exports south of the border, Alex Cropley had proved with Hibs that he was an exciting talent and a tenacious midfielder who possessed vision and who loved to have a go at goal. Totalling 199 games (49 goals) for Hibs over two spells, he needed knee surgery and broke his ankle in 1972, the first of a succession of injuries which affected his time in the game. Cropley had an unfortunate start to his career south of the border, breaking his leg after only nine games for the Gunners. It took many months before he was back to fitness and by then any chance of making an impression at Highbury was lost. More injuries followed, including another broken leg, and he arrived at St James' Park on loan, desperate for another opportunity to resurrect a career and rediscover his sparkle. The lightweight Cropley was only on Tyneside a matter of weeks and never revealed his gifted talent in the club's Second Division line-up. Yet another serious injury, this time when on the Fratton Park books, virtually ended his first-class career and he totalled only 134 games at his four clubs south of the border. Raised in Edinburgh, although born in deepest England when his father played for Aldershot, Alex is one of only a few Englishmen to have played for the Scottish full international side. As a youngster the Cropley family returned to Edinburgh and he had trials with Chelsea before joining the Hibernian set-up as a part-time teenager while learning a trade in electrical engineering. His playing career over, Cropley later opened a public-house near to Easter Road, then became a black-cab driver in the capital. His son Jordan was also on Hibs' books as a youngster.

Appearances & Goals:
Debut v Wrexham (a) 9 February 1980
FL: 3 app 0 gls
Total: 3 app 0 gls

Honours:
2 Scot caps 1972/3 Scot u23 app 1972-74/FLC winner 1977/SLC winner 1973/SLC final 1975.

CROSSON David 1970-1975

Right-back
5'9"
b. Bishop Auckland, 24 November 1952

Career: UNITED jnr Nov 1970, prof Nov 1972/Darlington Aug 1975 free/Crook Town cs 1980/Rapid Tasmania (Aus) c1981, becoming coach/Glenorchy Knights (Aus) coach/Tasmania State (Aus) coach.

A junior development, blond-haired David Crosson was stand-by for David Craig over two seasons, during 1973-74 and 1974-75. On his first outings in the senior eleven, he faced Birmingham City in the space of a few days during October 1973. Well built and strong tackling, he deputised ably when asked, but was never going to become anything but a reserve in United's Division One line-up. He also often appeared as a midfield enforcer in the Magpies' Central League side and with Darlington totalled 146 senior matches. Crosson later emigrated to Australia to continue his football career and became a noted player and coach in Tasmania, captaining the Tasmanian State team during the 1980s. He lived for a period in the gloriously named Mermaid Waters on the Gold Coast of Queensland.

Appearances & Goals:
Debut v Birmingham City (a) 30 October 1973 (FLC) (sub)
(v Birmingham City (a) 22 October 1973 (TC))
FL: 6 app 0 gls
FLC: 0(1) app 0 gls
Others: 3 app 0 gls
Total: 9(1) app 0 gls

CROWE Charles Alfred 1943-1957

Left-half
5'8"
b. Walker, Newcastle upon Tyne,
30 October 1924
d. North Shields, 27 February 2010

Career: Wallsend St Luke's/Heaton & Byker YC/UNITED amat Aug 1943, prof Oct 1944 £10/Mansfield Town Feb 1957/Retired cs 1958/Whitley Bay manager Aug 1958 to Jan 1960/FA staff coach to 1967.

Charlie Crowe was a tenacious, hard-working wing-half who never gave up the challenge in United's cause for all of 13 seasons. Crowe arrived at St James' Park as a youngster during the Second World War and was developed alongside the likes of Jackie Milburn and Bobby Cowell. Growing up in the Battlefield and Shieldfield area of the city and an apprentice pattern-maker at the Parsons engineering works in Walker, Crowe was a Geordie at heart. Working at the Burradon Colliery when at Gallowgate during the Forties, although he appeared as a regular in 1945-46, Charlie broke his ankle and didn't find a position in Newcastle's first-class line-up until season 1949-50, being a mainstay of the Magpies Central League title victory in 1948. Crowe had tough competition for senior action, with firstly Norman Dodgin and Doug Wright as rivals, then Ted Robledo and Tommy Casey. A player who rarely took the headlines, Crowe got on with the rough and tumble in the middle of the field as a spoiler of the opposition's tactics and winner of the ball, while he was also used to good effect as a man-marker. He unluckily missed out on the 1955 FA Cup victory at Wembley due to an ankle injury picked up at White Hart Lane only a week before the final. United captain for a spell, he qualified as a FA coach under Walter Winterbottom when on the club's books. Crowe afterwards resided in Longbenton and became a licensee at The North Star for a spell, also working at a local construction merchant and the giant Civil Service complex in the city as an Accommodation Officer. A warm and witty character, he often was seen back at St James' Park, a United supporter all his life. At one point during his career he was appointed manager of Cairo side Zamelek, only for the Arab-Israeli conflict to erupt and prevent him taking up the position.

Appearances & Goals:
Debut v Barnsley (h) 5 January 1946 (FAC)
(v Middlesbrough (h) 7 October 1944 (FLN))
FL: 178 app 5 gls
FAC: 14 app 1 gl
War: 24 app 1 gl
Total: 216 app 7 gls

Honours:
1 FL(N) app 1958/1 FA app 1956/FL div 2 prom 1948 (2 app)/FAC winner 1951.

CROWN Lawrence 1926-1927

Left-back
6'0"
b. Fulwell, Sunderland, 25 February 1898
d. Newcastle upon Tyne, 6 July 1984

Career: Furness Ath/Sunderland All Saints/Redcar/ South Shields April 1922/UNITED March 1926 £2,750/ Bury May 1927 £750/Coventry City July 1928/Retired cs 1931.

Known as Lawrie to his colleagues, Crown was a steadfast and gentlemanly character who had built up a fine reputation in 90 games at Horsley Hill, during the days of Football League soccer at South Shields. Tall and powerful, Crown always played the game fairly and was deputy to Frank Hudspeth for a year before moving to Gigg Lane. Later, when at Coventry, Lawrie was appointed captain and was a regular for three seasons totalling 117 appearances. After retiring from the game Crown returned to his earlier occupation as a draughtsman in the Wear shipyards and later resided in Wideopen.

Appearances & Goals:
Debut v Huddersfield Town (h) 6 March 1926
FL: 2 app 0 gls
Total: 2 app 0 gls

CRUMLEY Robert Walker 1903-1906

Goalkeeper
5'11"
b. Lochee, Dundee, 1875
d. Lochee, Dundee, 1949

Career: Lochee Utd/UNITED May 1903/Dundee April 1906 £50/Darlington Aug 1911/Dundee Sept 1912/Arbroath Oct 1913 to 1914/Later, Dundee Utd trainer Sept 1926.

Bob Crumley gained recognition when in the army with the Gordon Highlanders, lifting the Army Cup, but on joining the Geordies the dominance of fellow Scot, Jimmy Lawrence in United's goal meant he had few opportunities in Newcastle's senior eleven. Bob did though, take part in the Magpies' title winning season during 1904-05 as well as reserve success in the Northern League, North Eastern League and the local Northumberland Senior Cup. He liked to fist the ball away in the style of the day, and later became a respected goalkeeper back in Scotland with Dundee. The Scot played alongside two other ex-United players, Macfarlane and Fraser, as the Tay club lifted the Scottish Cup after defeating Clyde in a three game final. Crumley registered 152 games for the Dens Park club and was a revered character in the city, the last surviving member of the club's only Scottish Cup success. His brother James was also a custodian, for several clubs including Dundee Hibs, the forerunner of Dundee United, while his son, also James, pulled on a Darlington shirt during the Twenties. Before he became a professional footballer, Bob learned the trade of a tailor in Dundee. Serving as a Bombardier in World War One, he sadly went blind later in life. Bob's grandson, Jim Crumley, is a noted Scottish journalist and author.

Appearances & Goals:
Debut: v Sheffield Wednesday (a) 26 April 1905
FL: 4 app 0 gls
Total: 4 app 0 gls

Honours:
FL champs 1905 (1 app)/SC winner 1910.

CUMMING David Scott 1943-1945

Goalkeeper
5'11"
b. Aberdeen, 6 May 1910
d. Kirriemuir, Angus, 18 April 1993

Career: Woodside Thistle/Hall Russell Jnrs 1929-30/ Aberdeen June 1930/Arbroath June 1934/ Middlesbrough Oct 1936 £3,000 (UNITED war-guest 1943-45)/Partick Thistle 1948, retiring shortly afterwards.

A Scottish international goalkeeper, capped in season 1937-38, Dave Cumming was a regular with the Magpies during seasons 1943-44 and 1944-45 when he was occupied as a wartime driver between Tyneside and Teesside. Also winning a wartime cap for his country when at St James' Park during October 1944, Cumming was a hearty player with quick reflexes. Making headlines as part of Arbroath's promotion side during 1935, when he moved from Scotland to head for Teesside for £3,000, Dave was recognised as one of the most expensive 'keepers to cross the border. A good servant to Boro, he totalled 157 league and cup games (plus 118 in wartime) for the Ayresome Park side and actually appeared on several occasions for the Magpies against his registered club. The strapping Scot had a short fuse on the pitch at times, once in December 1946 he lost his cool and landed Arsenal's Les Compton with a smart right-hook, then immediately walked from the field before the referee could order him off! Dave retired from the game following a dislocated knee-cap.

Appearances & Goals:
Debut v Darlington (a) 20 November 1943 (FLN)
War: 56 app 0 gls.
Total: 56 app 0 gls.

Honours:
1 Scot cap 1938/1 Scot war app 1945/SL div 2 prom 1935.

CUMMINGS Henry 1918-1919

Outside-left
b. unknown

Career: UNITED amat 1918 to cs 1919.

Harry Cummings was a teenage footballer who took part in the club's 1918-19 Newcastle & District United League fixtures then was handed a single game for Newcastle during the celebratory Northern Victory League competition on the conclusion of World War One. Coming in for Alex Ramsay on the left wing, Cummings was blooded in a Tyne-Wear confrontation at Roker Park. United lost 2-1 to their rivals and Cummings wasn't offered terms during the summer months.

Appearances & Goals:
Debut v Sunderland (a) 22 March 1919 (NVL)
War: 1 app 0 gls
Total: 1 app 0 gls

CUMMINGS Robert Douglas 1954-1956. 1963-1965

Centre-forward
5'10"
b. Ashington, 17 November 1935
d. Blyth, 26 August 2008

Career: New Hartley Jnrs/Byth Spartans briefly cs 1954/ UNITED May 1954/Ashington Nov 1956 free/ Aberdeen Feb 1960 £2,000/ UNITED Oct 1963 £5,000/ Darlington Oct 1965 £3,500/ Hartlepools Utd Feb 1968 £2,500/ Port Elizabeth City (SA) June 1969/Bedlington Mechanics 1971.

Bobby Cummings was on the books at St James' Park on two occasions, firstly as a junior who didn't make the grade, then returning when nearly 28 years old, as a decent centre-forward who played his part in the club's Second Division title victory during 1965. Not big, nor powerfully built, nevertheless Bobby possessed fine positional sense, was good in the air and could find the net with important goals. He was a gutsy, determined player and always unselfish. Cummings later had an invaluable spell at Feethams, leading the Quakers to promotion for the first time ever and then did the same with Hartlepool, making a hat-trick of North East promotion successes. After leaving Gallowgate as a youngster in 1956, he impressed everyone by becoming Ashington's record goalscorer with 60 goals in 1958-59. Moving to Aberdeen and doing well in 86 games (49 goals), he once netted five goals against Clyde in the Scottish Cup. Cummings was targeted by United and had the odd experience of leading United's attack five days before his transfer to the Magpies, as a guest in Alf McMichael's testimonial fixture. He clinched the move back home after scoring a terrific goal. Bobby twice broke his leg during his career and was the epitome of a hard working professional who rarely took the headlines. He later lived in Blyth working at the Brentford Nylon factory for over 20 years.

Appearances & Goals:
Debut v Northampton Town (h) 26 October 1963
FL: 43(1) app 14 gls
FLC: 1 app 0 gls
Total: 44(1) app 14 gls

Honours:
FL div 2 champs 1965/FL div 4 prom 1966, 1968.

C

CUNNINGHAM Anthony Eugene 1985-1987

Centre-forward
6'2"
b. Kingston (Jamaica), 12 November 1957

Career: Lafayette/Kidderminster Harriers 1976/Stourbridge cs 1977/Lincoln City May 1979 £20,000/Barnsley Sept 1982 £85,000/Sheffield Wed Nov 1983 £100,000/Manchester City July 1984 £90,000/UNITED Feb 1985 £75,000/ Blackpool July 1987 £25,000/Bury July 1989 £40,000/Bolton Wand March 1991 £70,000/ Rotherham Utd Aug 1991 £50,000/Doncaster Rovers July 1993 free, becoming player-coach Nov 1993 and caretaker-manager Dec 1993/ Wycombe Wand March 1994 £5,000/ Gainsborough Trinity Sept 1994/Retired 1995.

Big Tony Cunningham very quickly became a crowd favourite at Gallowgate due to his splendid work-rate and attitude to the game, never shirking a challenge and never hiding from the action. Cheerful, tall and leggy, his skills on the ball were limited, yet Cunningham was still a handful in the lead role. Tony was never going to become one of Newcastle's great centre-forwards, but will be remembered as an honest striker at a time when manager Jack Charlton preferred to utilise a long ball game. Leaving the West Indies as a seven-year-old, Tony became an errant traveller; his career peaked with Lincoln City where he made his name scoring 42 goals in 148 appearances, and at Hillsborough where he also did well. His short stays with giants, Manchester City, Sheffield Wednesday and the Magpies, gave him a taste of top level football and by the time he was ready to hang up his boots, Cunningham had made almost 600 senior outings for 11 different senior clubs. An apprentice engineer when he started out in the game, at the end of his career Cunningham completed a business studies degree and concentrated on a career in law, employed as a legal executive in Lincoln, qualifying as a solicitor during 1999 and a partner with Andrew Jay & Co. His sons also had periods in football; Daniel was on the books of Notts County and Karl at Lincoln.

Appearances & Goals:
Debut v Manchester United (h) 9 February 1985
FL: 37(10) 4 gls
FAC: 1(1) app 0 gls
FLC: 2 app 2 gls
Total: 40(11) app 6 gls

Honours:
FL div 2 prom 1984/FL div 4 prom 1981, 1992.

CUNNINGHAM Andrew 1929-1935

Inside-right & Manager
6'0"
b. Galston, Ayrshire, 31 January 1891
d. Glasgow, 8 May 1973

Career: Galston Riverside Rangers 1906/Newmilns 1907/ Kilmarnock June 1909/Rangers April 1915 £800 (West Ham Utd war-guest 1915-19)/UNITED Feb 1929 £2,300, becoming player-manager Jan 1930, manager May 1930 to May 1935/Dundee manager June 1937 to May 1940.

One of the inter-war greats of Scottish football, Andy Cunningham appeared almost 450 times, scoring nearly 200 goals, for Rangers during the Ibrox club's Twenties heyday. Tall and golden-haired, he was a elegant inside-forward able to operate right or left with superb ball control, positional sense and passing ability, as well as a vicious shot that all goalkeepers feared. When Cunningham headed over the border for Tyneside he was into his 39th year and thought to be the oldest player to make his debut in the English League, aged 38 years 2 days. He arrived very much as United's first manager designate, quickly graduating to player-boss and then outright manager, although the club's directors still had a big say in team matters throughout his reign. As a boss it was noted Cunningham was very thorough in analysing his players' strengths and weaknesses, although he fell out with the club's biggest star, Hughie Gallacher. Scoring on his international debut and captain of Scotland, he was a fine tactician and great thinker on the game. Andy led the Magpies to Wembley victory, but alas to relegation and obscurity in the Second Division. After leaving football he

spent many years as a sports journalist with the Scottish Daily Express and was once noted as a player, having "the embodiment of all the virtues of the inside-forward", then as a manager as being "brainy, breezy and bowler-hatted". Cunningham was a touch superstitious like many footballers, he never once got ready for a game, as he said, "without leaving my left-boot to be fixed last". During World War One, Andy served as a Second Lieutenant Gunner in the Royal Field Artillery.

(Note: Although some sources note Andy having the Christian name of Nisbet or Nesbit, his birth records do not verify this.)

Appearances & Goals:
Debut v Leicester City (a) 2 February 1929
FL: 12 app 2 gls
FAC: 3 app 0 gls
Total: 15 app 2 gls

In Charge: 249 games
Debut v York City (h) 11 January 1930 (FAC)

Honours:
12 Scot caps 1920-27/Scot trial app 1921-24/10 Scot FA tour app 1927/10 SL app 1912-28/SL champs 1918 (4 app), 1920, 1921, 1923, 1924, 1925, 1927, 1928, 1929 (8 app)/SC winner 1928/SC final 1921, 1922/FAC winner 1932(m).

CURRY Thomas 1912-1929

Wing-half
5'8"
b. South Shields, 1 September 1894
d. Munich (Germany), 6 February 1958

Career: South Shields St Michaels/South Shields Parkside/ UNITED April 1912 £20 (Leeds City war-guest 1919)/ Stockport Co Jan 1929 free/Carlisle Utd trainer cs 1930/ Manchester Utd trainer June 1934 to his death.

A sergeant with the Royal Engineers in the Great War, Tom Curry was a good all-round player who served United well for 12 seasons after being spotted as a teenager in the Northern Alliance. At home in either right or left-half roles, Curry was a regular in United's line-up during the seasons immediately after World War One as the Tynesiders challenged for honours. Tom was good enough to be selected for the Football League eleven, showing much ability in both link play and foraging in midfield. He unluckily missed out though on the 1924 success at Wembley after playing in five of the games during the Magpies' FA Cup run. He then also couldn't find a place for much of the 1927 Championship campaign and had to be content to be on the sidelines as a reserve. A jovial figure, always with a joke to tell, Curry retired and entered the sphere of coaching, eventually becoming an important backstage aid to Matt Busby at Old Trafford during the 1940s and 1950s, but tragically was a victim of the Munich Air Disaster which claimed the lives of so many noted footballers in 1958.

Appearances & Goals:
Debut v Arsenal (a) 30 August 1919
(v Scotswood (a) 18 January 1919 (NVL))
FL: 221 app 5 gls
FAC: 14 app 0 gls
War: 13 app 0 gls
Total: 248 app 5 gls

Honours:
1 FL app 1920/OG 1948 (GB trainer)/FL champs 1927 (5 app).

CURRY William Morton 1953-1959

Centre-forward
5'9"
b. Walker, Newcastle upon Tyne, 12 October 1935
d. Mansfield, 20 August 1990

Career: UNITED jnr May 1953, prof Oct 1953/ Brighton July 1959 £13,000/Derby Co Oct 1960 £12,000/Mansfield Town Feb 1965 £10,000/ Chesterfield Jan 1968 £2,000 (Boston Utd loan 1968-69)/Worksop Town coach June 1969/ Boston Utd manager Feb 1971 to May 1976/ Sutton Town manager May 1977 to May 1980.

Very often wavy-haired Bill Curry looked the part in United's forward line, either at centre-forward or inside-left. Although not a big man, he was a danger in the air, quick on the floor with punch in the kill. A dour fighter, Bill would also battle hard for the ball and defenders always knew they had been in a contest. Curry was an outstanding product of Newcastle schools football and became the first United player to graduate from the club's new junior set-up, the N's. As a teenager he once netted eight goals for the kid's eleven in a FA Youth Cup victory. Like many players of his era, National Service affected his progress at Gallowgate, and just at a time when the Magpies were looking to replace Vic Keeble. He was away from the scene for long periods, but did get back to St James' Park, making a long 620 mile round trip from his barracks in Aldershot at every opportunity. He also appeared for the Army select eleven and scored five goals against the Navy in 1958. Curry has the distinction of appearing and scoring in the very first floodlight league match, against Portsmouth during 1956. Bill enjoyed some good spells for the club wearing the Number 9 shirt, grabbing six goals in six matches during 1957-58 and nine goals in nine outings in 1958-59. Curry also netted all five goals during a 5-0 romp against the British Olympic XI. Despite being the first Newcastle player to be chosen for the England Under-23 side, Bill was to be second choice to Len White at St James' Park when Curry was reaching an age when he needed first-team action. Bill moved on and scored goals at all his clubs, 76 with Derby and 57 at Mansfield. Cousin to George Luke (qv) who also appeared for the Magpies, the pair attended the same school in Walkergate. Leaving the game, Bill set up a window cleaning business in Mansfield.

Appearances & Goals:
Debut v Manchester United (a) 23 October 1954
FL: 80 app 36 gls
FAC: 8 app 4 gls
Total: 88 app 40 gls

Honours:
1 Eng u23 app 1958.

DABIZAS Nikolaos 1998-2004

Centre-half
6'1"
b. Ptolemaida, near Salonika (Greece), 3 August 1973

Career: Hermes-Amydeo (Gr)/Pontoio Verias (Gr) 1991/Olympiacos CFP (Gr) cs 1994/UNITED March 1998 £2.1 m/Leicester City Jan 2004 free/ RSC Anderlecht (Belg) trial cs 2005/AE Larissa (Gr) Aug 2005/Retired July 2011/Panathinaikos (Gr) Technical Director May 2013.

Moving from Greek giants Olympiacos to Tyneside towards the end of the 1997-98 season, Nikos Dabizas proceeded to wear the black-and-white shirt through six seasons at Gallowgate becoming a popular character in the North East. Boss Kenny Dalglish spent £2.1m for the international centre-half who had done it all in Piraeus as the likes of Darren Peacock, Philippe Albert and Steve Howey all moved out of favour. Nikos immediately shined, giving a commanding performance in the FA Cup semi-final against Sheffield United that saw the Magpies reach Wembley. At times he looked the part being positive, committed and with confidence on the ball. Yet at other times he was caught out by the sheer quality and tempo of Premier League forwards, yet he was not alone at that. Signalled out for criticism by Ruud Gullit who purchased three replacement centre-backs, Dabizas was favoured by Bobby Robson and resurrected his flagging career under the ex-England boss. Few could question his attitude and effort for the Magpies while Dabizas could also grab a goal at the other end of the field, dangerous at set plays to a flighted ball into the penalty area. In season 1999-2000 he scored five times, the most by any United centre-half and all told hit the net on 13 occasions for the Magpies. A cruciate ligament injury kept Nikos on the sidelines for much of the 2000-01 programme but he came back strongly for the following season, almost an ever-present. Eventually Jonathan Woodgate arrived to take his place and after six seasons Nikos moved back to Greece via Leicester City and had a successful swansong with provincial club Larissa, skippering them to Greek cup success and for a time alongside both Laurent Robert and Nobby Solano. He appeared in two FA Cup finals for the Magpies and captained Greece, in his country's squad when they lifted the European Championship in 2004, although he didn't play in the final. His brother also appeared as a professional in Greek football.

Appearances & Goals:
Debut v Coventry City (h) 14 March 1998 (sub)
PL: 119 (11) app 10 gls
FAC: 17(1) app 2 gls
FLC: 6 app 0 gls
Euro: 21(1) app 1 gl
Total: 163(13) app 13 gls

Honours:
70 Gr caps 1995-2005/ECh winner 2004 (sub no app)/17 Gr u21 app/Gr sch-youth app/Gr Lg champs 1997, 1998/Gr div 3 prom/FAC final 1998, 1999/Gr Cup winner 2007.

DALGLISH Paul Kenneth 1997-1999

Striker
5'9"
b. Glasgow, 18 February 1977

Career: Celtic jnr 1995/Liverpool Aug 1996/UNITED Nov 1997 free (Bury loan 1997-98)/Norwich City loan March 1999, pmt July 1999 £300,000/Wigan Ath loan March 2001, pmt Aug 2001/DC Utd (USA) trial April 2002/Burnley, Peterborough Utd & Preston North End trial cs 2002/Blackpool Aug 2002 free/Dallas Burn (USA) trial March 2003/Scunthorpe Utd loan March 2003, pmt cs 2003/Linfield July 2003 to Oct 2003/Modena (It) Jan 2004/Luton Town trial June 2005/Livingston Aug 2005/ Hibernian Jan 2006/Houston Dynamos (USA) Aug 2006/Wigan Ath & Ipswich Town trial Jan 2008/Leeds Utd trial Feb 2008/Kilmarnock Feb 2008 to cs 2008 when he retired/Later coaching in USA at Braveheart Academy (Houston) 2008/Houston Dynamo (USA) academy coach/Space City (USA) coach/Tampa Bay Rowdies (USA) manager Nov 2009 to Sept 2010/Dynamos Jnrs (USA) director in tandem with Austin Aztex (USA) coach Nov 2011/Real Salt Lake (USA) coach Jan 2014.

Born in Glasgow, Paul Dalglish followed his celebrated father and Kop hero Kenny Dalglish to Anfield. He joined the Liverpool junior set-up as a teenager but did not break past reserve level, moving to St James' Park when Dalglish senior was appointed boss. His father though soon departed, yet Paul was given an opportunity to impress by new boss Ruud Gullit. Direct and a forward who liked to run at defenders, he was part of the reckoning during the first half of the 1998-99 programme as the Dutch boss came to terms with the players he inherited. Unfair to compare him with his father, being of course one of the finest players of all time, although young Dalglish had the looks of Kenny, he never came close to displaying those very special talents. Paul did have his moments, and when he was capped by the Scotland Under-21 side it appeared his career was going to take off. But his opportunities in a black-and-white shirt were all too brief and he was frozen out as new faces arrived on Tyneside. Paul's best spells at his many ports of call afterwards were with Blackpool (31 app), Norwich (48 app), Wigan (36 app) and in Scotland with Livingston and Hibs. He roamed around the football circuit for several years, for a period leaving the game and having a slot on Sky TV, and had spells in the States, lifting the MLS Cup with Houston Dynamos in 2006 and 2007. He settled in Texas and became a football coach.

Appearances & Goals:
Debut v Coventry City (a) 19 September 1998 (sub)
PL: 6(5) app 1 gl
FLC: 2 app 1 gl
Total: 8(5) app 2 gls

Honours:
1 Scot B app 2002/7 Scot u21 app 1999-2000.

DALTON George 1958-1967

Left-half or Left-back
5'8"
b. West Moor, Newcastle upon Tyne, 4 September 1941

Career: UNITED jnr Aug 1958, prof Nov 1958/ Brighton June 1967 free/Birmingham City coach May 1970/Coventry City physio Jan 1976 to March 1999.

Highly thought of at St James' Park, at one stage of his United career George Dalton was tipped as an England player after a series of eye-catching displays in a black-and-white shirt during seasons 1962-63 and 1963-64. Cool-headed and with a constructive football brain for both defending and setting attacks going, Dalton was a popular character, but a clash with Leeds United's Johnny Giles in a match at Elland Road during Easter 1964 ruined his career. A badly fractured leg was the result of that tackle and Dalton was out of action for over a year and as a consequence George lost his place to the young and emerging Frank Clark. Dalton only appeared once more for the Magpies after that unfortunate injury and never displayed the same promise again, only wearing Brighton's blue shirt on 28 occasions. As a teenager he made his senior baptism as a half-back, a position George favoured during his early years in

D

Joe Harvey's first eleven. Dalton actually netted an own-goal on his debut after only six minutes of play at Filbert Street against Leicester City. After retiring he resided in the Midlands giving coaching and medical support to Coventry City behind the scenes for over 20 years before returning to his indigenous North East. His son, Paul, was on City's books for a period.

Appearances & Goals:
Debut v Leicester City (a) 11 February 1961.
FL: 85 app 2 gls
FAC: 2 app 0 gls
FLC: 7 app 0 gls
Total: 94 app 2 gls

DAVIDSON David Leighton 1930-1937

Centre-half
5'10"
b. Aberdeen, 4 June 1905
d. Tynemouth, 19 June 1969

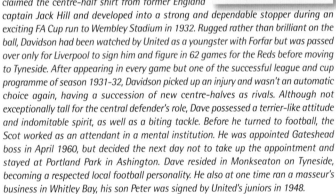

Career: Garthdee (Aberdeen)/Aberdeen Richmond/ Forfar Ath Aug 1927/Liverpool July 1928/UNITED Jan 1930 £4,000/Hartlepools Utd June 1937 £50/ Gateshead Oct 1937/Retired cs 1938/Whitley Bay manager 1945/Ashington manager 1955 to cs 1963.

After a slow start in United's ranks, Dave Davidson claimed the centre-half shirt from former England captain Jack Hill and developed into a strong and dependable stopper during an exciting FA Cup run to Wembley Stadium in 1932. Rugged rather than brilliant on the ball, Davidson had been watched by United as a youngster with Forfar but was passed over only for Liverpool to sign him and figure in 62 games for the Reds before moving to Tyneside. After appearing in every game but one of the successful league and cup programme of season 1931-32, Davidson picked up an injury and wasn't an automatic choice again, having a succession of new centre-halves as rivals. Although not exceptionally tall for the central defender's role, Dave possessed a terrier-like attitude and indomitable spirit, as well as a biting tackle. Before he turned to football, the Scot worked as an attendant in a mental institution. He was appointed Gateshead boss in April 1960, but decided the next day not to take up the appointment and stayed at Portland Park in Ashington. Dave resided in Monkseaton on Tyneside, becoming a respected local football personality. He also at one time ran a masseur's business in Whitley Bay, his son Peter was signed by United's juniors in 1948.

Appearances & Goals:
Debut v Huddersfield Town (a) 1 February 1930
FL: 128 app 0 gls
FAC: 16 app 0 gls
Others: 1 app 0 gls
Total: 145 app 0 gls

Honours:
FAC winner 1932.

DAVIDSON Thomas 1901-1903

Left-back
6'0"
b. West Calder, West Lothian, 1875
d. April 1949

Career: West Calder 1888-89/Dykehead June 1894/ Bury Dec 1894/Millwall Ath June 1900/UNITED May 1901/Brentford May 1903 to cs 1905/[Bathgate Aug 1906].

A tall and powerful looking defender, gritty and determined, Tom Davidson was a regular at left-back during the 1901-02 season. One description noted Davidson as, "strong as a lion, cool and reliable". He was a noted player in Bury's ranks, tallying 131 games at a time when the Lancashire club were a force at the top level, winning the FA Cup trophy in 1900 when the Shakers defeated Southampton convincingly by 4-0. Eventually though, Davidson lost his place at Gallowgate to new signing William Agnew and moved to the Southern League where he was skipper of Brentford. His brother Bob joined both Celtic and Manchester City without breaking through, also starting his career at Scottish club, Dykehead.

Appearances & Goals:
Debut v Sunderland (h) 28 September 1901
FL: 38 app 0 gls
FAC: 5 app 0 gls
Total: 43 app 0 gls

Honours:
FL div 2 champs 1895 (8 app)/FAC winner 1900.

DAVIES Alan 1985-1987

Midfield
5'8"
b. Manchester, 5 December 1961
d. Horton, near Swansea, 4 February 1992

Career: Mancunian Jnrs/Manchester Utd jnr Nov 1976, prof Dec 1978/UNITED July 1985 £50,000 (Charlton Ath loan 1985-86)(Carlisle Utd loan 1986-87)/Swansea City July 1987 free/Bradford City June 1989 £135,000/Swansea City Aug 1990 exch deal, to death.

Born in England of Welsh parents, Alan Davies had a meteoric rise to fame as one of Manchester United's modern 'Babes'. Developed at Old Trafford from a schoolboy, he started as a skilful outside-right later moving into a general midfield role. Davies was catapulted into the headlines when he was chosen in place of Steve Coppell for the 1983 FA Cup final. He played wonderfully well against Brighton as the Reds won the trophy after a replay. He was also capped by Wales, but just as his career was about to take off he unluckily broke an ankle and the chance to claim a regular position at the star-studded Old Trafford was lost. Following a long lay-off, Alan recovered to again become the star in another show-piece, this time the European Cup Winners Cup semi-final against Juventus but with names such as Arthur Graham then Jesper Olsen ahead of him, he only made 10 outings for the Mancunians and moved to Tyneside in the summer of 1985. At Gallowgate Davies only showed brief glimpses of his true capabilities and after further injury problems, soon moved into a lower grade of football, serving Swansea with note, in many games alongside Joe Allon. Davies was a regular choice in Wales, totalling 175 games being influential and efficient in midfield and attack. Tragically when 30 years of age, Alan Davies became overwhelmed by personal problems and committed suicide, being discovered dead in his car on the same day as he was due to play for the Swans against Cardiff in the Welsh Cup.

Appearances & Goals:
Debut v Southampton (a) 17 August 1985
FL: 20(1) app 1 gl
FLC: 2(1) app 0 gls
Total: 22(2) 1 gl

Honours:
13 Wales caps 1983-90/6 Wales u21 app 1982-83/Wales sch-youth app/FL div 2 prom 1986 (1 app)/FL div 4 prom 1988/FAC winner 1983/WsC winner 1989/PFA ToS (d4) 1988.

DAVIES Ellis Reginald 1951-1958

Inside-right or left
5'8"
b. Cymmer, Glamorgan, 27 May 1929
d. Perth (Australia), 9 February 2009

Career: Cwm Ath/Southampton 1948-49 amat/Southend Utd July 1949/UNITED April 1951 £9,000/Swansea Town Oct 1958 cash-exch deal for I Allchurch/Carlisle Utd June 1962 £4,000/Merthyr Tydfil July 1964/Kings Lynn player-manager Dec 1965 to Nov 1970/Bayswater Utd (Aus) player-coach 1971/Ascot Vale (Aus) player-coach/Balga (Aust) coach.

A slightly built inside-forward who played on both flanks to equal effect and who impressed United's scouts as he caught the eye playing for Southend in the Third Division South. Reg Davies possessed touches of real class and a burst of speed over ten yards that could prove devastating around the opposition's box. He had an inventive telling pass, but was a team-man first and foremost able to slot into a midfield or forward role. Reg had fellow international Ivor Broadis as his main rival at St James' Park and then saw two more noted players take over his role, George Eastham and Ivor Allchurch, as he moved to Wales. In United's side for eight seasons without ever being an automatic choice, Reg was somewhat underrated and Newcastle's 12th man for the 1952 FA Cup final and he unluckily missed out in 1955 too; although selected to play he developed tonsillitis and had to step down. Davies found a good home first at Swansea (128 app, 33 goals) where he sampled European football, then at non-league Kings Lynn, appearing for the Norfolk club over 200 times and having a successful period as manager. Reg emigrated to Australia in 1971, appearing for Western Australia against New Zealand at the age of 47 and playing on until his 50th year. As a former soprano choir boy, when a teenager with the Steffans Silver Singsters, he toured with the Great Britain choir and could have taken up a singing and show-biz career. But Reg's dream was to be on a pitch with the ball at his feet and entered the professional world of football.

Appearances & Goals:
Debut v Wolverhampton Wanderers (h) 6 October 1951 (1 goal)
FL: 157 app 49 gls
FAC: 13 app 1 gl
Others: 1 app 0 gls
Total: 171 app 50 gls

Honours:
6 Wales caps 1953-58/FL div 4 prom 1964/WsC winner 1961.

DAVIES Ian Claude 1979-1982

Left-back
5'8"
b. Bristol, 29 March 1957

Career: Fisons Sports (Bristol)/Cleveland Jnrs (Bristol)/ Norwich City jnr July 1973, prof April 1975 (Detroit Express (USA) loan cs 1978)/UNITED June 1979 £175,000/Manchester City Aug 1982 free (Bury loan 1982-83)(Brentford loan 1983-84)(Cambridge Utd loan 1983-84)/Carlisle Utd May 1984/Exeter City Dec 1984/ Yeovil Town 1984-85/Bath City cs 1985/Bury Town/Diss Town/Bristol Rovers Aug 1985/Swansea City Nov 1985 to Feb 1986/Gloucester City Nov 1987 to 1988.

Ian Davies had been Norwich City's youngest ever debutant at Carrow Road; 17 years and 29 days old, but by the time he joined United he had accumulated only 34 appearances for the Canaries. A defender full of potential though, and with a cultured left-foot, he was level-headed with an inclination to join the attack at every opportunity. Ian was a regular for two seasons and at his peak reached the full Welsh squad, on the substitute's bench twice, against the Republic of Ireland and England during 1979-80 without registering his international debut. After that however, Ian was discarded by Arthur Cox in favour of local talent Kenny Wharton. Perhaps lacking the pace and defensive bite to develop into a top-class player, Davies afterwards drifted around the Football League with little impact, recording all-told 187 games at senior level before moving to the non-league circuit. Davies returned to his native South West England, he was a fine cricketer too, on Somerset's books before heading on a career in professional soccer.

Appearances & Goals:
Debut v Oldham Athletic (h) 18 August 1979
FL: 74(1) app 3 gls
FAC: 1 app 0 gls
FLC: 6 app 1 gl
Total: 81(1) app 4 gls

Honours:
1 Wales u21 app 1978.

DAVIES Ronald Wyn 1966-1971

Centre-forward
6'1"
b. Caernarfon, 20 March 1942

Career: Caernarfon BC/Deiniolen/ Llanberis/Caernarfon Town 1958/ Wrexham amat Dec 1959, prof April 1960 £500/Bolton Wand March 1962 £20,000 plus player/ UNITED Oct 1966 £80,000/Manchester City Aug 1971 £52,500/Manchester Utd Sept 1972 £25,000/Blackpool June 1973 £25,000 (Crystal Palace loan 1974-75)/Stockport Co Aug 1975/Arcadia Shepherds (SA) May 1976/Crewe Alex Aug 1976/Bangor City Aug 1978 to May 1979.

Although the formidable figure of Wyn Davies never became one of the Magpies' goalscoring machines, his contribution to United's cause for five years as the club stormed Europe was immense, and it made him a cult hero on Tyneside. After a long chase and contest with Manchester City for his transfer from Second Division Bolton, where he had netted 74 goals in 170 games, Davies immediately became a crowd favourite. Lean and tall, he cost the Black'n'Whites a record fee and the big Welshman repaid the amount several times over. An ideal target man in the Number 9 shirt, Davies was noted for his considerable aerial menace, nicknamed 'Wyn the Leap' for his stunning jumping ability. He led United's line like few before or since, able to hold up the ball and bring his partners, notably Albert Bennett and Bryan Robson, into play. Davies created space for others and Robson in particular flourished as a top goal-getter. Wyn was able to soak up a physical battering by defenders, especially from Continentals who couldn't handle his presence at all. Davies was a brave player and on many occasions soldiered on even though in pain. Underrated with the ball at his feet, and his goal tally can only be regarded as modest, yet Wyn Davies will be recalled with esteem by every United supporter who witnessed his whole-hearted displays. He was a the key factor in United's Inter Cities Fairs Cup victory during 1969, and was the club's top goalscorer in European football for many years registering 10 goals in 24 games. The Welsh speaking Davies was also given the tag of 'The Mighty Wyn' or 'Welsh Flier' and before setting out on a football career Davies worked in a North Wales slate quarry. He ended his career with almost 700 senior matches to his name at club and international level. Legendary England goalkeeper Gordon Banks reckoned that his save from a Davies effort at the Victoria Ground, Stoke was even better than the much remembered World Cup stop from Pele in 1970. After retiring, Wyn settled in Bolton working for Warburton's bakery.

Appearances & Goals:
Debut v Sunderland (h) 29 October 1966
FL: 181 app 40 gls
FAC: 8 app 3 gls
FLC: 3 app 0 gls
Euro: 24 app 10 gls
Total: 216 app 53 gls

Honours:
34 Wales caps 1964-74/4 Wales u23 app 1963-65/Wales sch-youth app 1960/ICFC winner 1969/FL div 4 prom 1962.

DAY William 1962-1963

Outside-right
5'9"
b. South Bank, Middlesbrough, 27 December 1936

Career: Sheffield Wed amat 1953/South Bank/ Middlesbrough May 1955/UNITED March 1962 £12,000/ Peterborough Utd April 1963 £6,000/Cambridge Utd 1964/Retired 1965.

After a disappointing stay at Hillsborough as a kid, Billy Day gave up his apprenticeship in engineering to join a footballing career path with his local club. He soon was a popular winger at Ayresome Park scoring 21 goals in 131 league and cup matches for Middlesbrough, part of an attractive forward line containing Brian Clough and Alan Peacock. However, a broken leg meant he lost his place in the Reds' line-up and Billy moved up the North East coast to try his luck with the Magpies. A winger who tended to hug the touchline, Day's short period at St James' Park was not a productive one; he was overshadowed by the emerging talent of teenager Alan Suddick as manager Joe Harvey attempted to fashion a side to challenge for promotion. Former United goalkeeper Jack Fairbrother took Day to Peterborough during their early Football League years. Returning north after being laid low with pneumonia, Billy later became a bookmaker at Cleveland Park.

Appearances & Goals:
Debut v Scunthorpe United (h) 17 March 1962 (1 goal)
FL: 13 app 1 gl
FAC: 1 app 0 gls
Total: 14 app 1 gl

Honours:
1 FA app 1960.

D

DEBUCHY Mathieu 2013-2014

Right-back
5'10"
b. Fretin (France), 28 July 1985

Career: US Fretin (Fr) Sept 1992/OSC Lille (Fr) July 1993/UNITED Jan 2013 £5.5m/Arsenal July 2014 £11m.

After being a long-term transfer target of Newcastle United, French international Mathieu Debuchy arrived on Tyneside in the transfer window of January 2013. Aged 27, the French defender had caught the eye of many during the Euro 2012 Championships in Poland-Ukraine, appearing in the same French line-up as Yohan Cabaye. The right-back showed a willingness to surge forward, a frequent supply line for Les Bleus attack. An experienced player in the French league, Mathieu was a first-choice selection in 308 games over nine seasons with Lille, again alongside Cabaye as the Dragons lifted the French league and cup double in 2010-11. Debuchy added to the already substantial French presence on Tyneside, and quickly saw another four of his fellow countrymen join the squad before the transfer window had closed. Mobile and athletic, while Mathieu is always willing to be available in attack, Debuchy is a solid defender and quick to return to his defensive duties. After the World Cup in Brazil during the summer of 2014, Mathieu headed to London joining Arsenal in a big deal.

Appearances & Goals:
Debut v Norwich City (a) 12 January 2013
PL: 42(1) app 1 gl
FLC: 3 app 0 gls
Total: 45(1) app 1 gl

Honours:
25 Fr caps 2012-date/WdC 2014/Fr u21 app/Fr Lg champs 2011/Fr Cup winner 2011.

DE JONG Luuk 2014

Centre-forward
6'2"
b. Aigle (Switzerland), 27 August 1990

Career: SV DZC 68 (Neth)/De Graafschap (Neth) 2001/FC Twente (Neth) April 2009 £700,000/Borussia Monchengladbach (Ger) July 2012 £12.6m (UNITED loan Jan 2014)/PSV Eindhoven (Neth) July 2014 £4.3m.

Newcastle United had tracked the progress of Dutch international Luuk De Jong for some time before the Swiss-born striker joined the Magpies staff in the January 2014 transfer window. Having experienced an unproductive 18 months in Germany following a record move to Borussia-Park, 23-year-old De Jong needed a fresh start. Having tried to purchase him before, Alan Pardew had been impressed with his form in the Eredivisie with Twente, when he played alongside Chiek Tiote. Scoring 59 goals in 119 matches for the Enschede club, De Jong was prolific in front of goal in seasons 2010-11 and 2011-12, gaining a call-up to the Holland side during February 2011. A tall and quick centre-forward, Luuk possesses characteristic Dutch skills being neat and tidy on the ball. He became a rare Tyne versus Wear debutant for the Black'n'Whites, with Loic Remy suspended, De Jong was immediately thrown into the vitriolic atmosphere at the beginning of February and thereafter struggled to make an impact in the much faster and competitive Premier League where up front pace, power and punch was needed. Moving from Switzerland to Holland when he was only four years of age and settling in Doetinchem near Arnhem, his parents played volleyball professionally in the Netherlands, while his elder brother Siem (qv) also appeared for De Graafschap and later Ajax where he became skipper soon to join United. He was also part of the Dutch international squad alongside his brother.

Appearances & Goals:
Debut v Sunderland (h) 1 February 2014 (sub)
PL: 8(4) app 0 gls
Total: 8(4) app 0 gls

Honours:
7 Neth caps 2011-date/18 Neth u21 app 2009-13/Neth sch-youth app/Neth Lg champs 2010/Neth Cup winner 2011.

DENMARK James 1937-1946

Centre-half
6'1"
b. Shettleston, Glasgow, 30 May 1913
d. Gosforth, Newcastle upon Tyne, 31 January 1978

Career: Tollcross Clydesdale/Parkhead Jnrs/Third Lanark May 1931/UNITED June 1937 £2,550 (Middlesbrough war-guest 1941-42)/Queen of the South March 1946 £707/Ashington player-manager Nov 1948.

A big kicking stopper, very powerful in the air and in the tackle. Jimmy Denmark made a lasting impression on United's directors following commanding displays in Scottish football with Third Lanark. Appearing in almost 150 games for the Cathkin Park club, he was skipper of the Glasgow side and led them to the Scottish Cup final against Rangers during 1936. An inspiration on the field, he arrived at Gallowgate to rival Jesse Carver just prior to the Second World War so didn't have a sustained period to develop his career further. Jimmy was though an important factor in Newcastle's dramatic escape from relegation to the Third Division for the first time in 1938. Denmark was a defender who liked to get forward, unusual for a centre-half for that period.

Appearances & Goals:
Debut v Barnsley (h) 1 September 1937
FL: 51 app 0 gls
War: 51 app 0 gls
Total: 102 app 0 gls
(Void FL: 3 app 0 gls)

Honours:
SC final 1936/SL div 2 champs 1935.

DENNISON Robert Smith 1929-1934

Inside-left
6'0"
b. Amble, Northumberland, 6 March 1912
d. Margate, 19 June 1996

Career: Radcliffe Welfare Utd/UNITED May 1929 £10/Nottingham Forest May 1934 £1,400/Fulham June 1935/Northampton Town war-guest 1939-45, pmt Aug 1945 £450, becoming asst-coach, then manager March 1949/Middlesbrough manager (and secretary for a period) July 1954 to Jan 1963/Hereford Utd manager Dec 1963/Coventry City scout Dec 1967, becoming asst-manager Dec 1968, and various other roles including caretaker-manager March 1972 to retirement in 1978, later working as a part-time scout for Coventry until 1994.

From a large Scots family which settled in Northumberland, Bob Dennison joined United as a promising youngster who admitted later in life that he was, "just an ordinary player". Dennison had fierce competition for a first-team place at St James' Park and by the time he was ready for senior action had the immense talent of Harry McMenemy as a contemporary playmaker. Later moving to half-back, Bob turned out in seasons 1932-33 and 1933-34 before moving south in search of regular football. He suffered from an ankle injury at Forest and afterwards served Northampton well as both player (66 app) and manager, while Dennison was also in charge at Ayresome Park for eight-and-a-half seasons, the longest serving Middlesbrough boss. He introduced the likes of Brian Clough and Alan Peacock to Boro colours and was well respected on Teesside in a secretary-manager role of the old school. His son, Richard, was secretary at Coventry City, Port Vale and Gillingham, while his elder brother Jack, turned out for Coventry just after World War One. Following a long period with the Highfield Road club himself, Dennison settled in Kent, residing in Westgate on Sea near Thanet. He had 10 brothers and sisters who were all born in Scotland, Bob though was the only Englishman, raised a Northumbrian in Amble.

Appearances & Goals:
Debut v Sheffield United (h) 18 February 1933
FL: 11 app 2 gls
Total: 11 app 2 gls

Honours:
SnL div 1 champs 1965(m).

DESWART Walter Poole 1940-1941

Right-half
5'10"
b. Chester-le-Street, Co Durham, 14 January 1922
d. Co Durham, 1978 (Q4)

Career: Ouston Jnrs/UNITED amat March 1940 to 1941.

Of Belgian extraction, Walter Deswart was a big and powerful half-back who stood in for Jimmy Gordon for a North Regional League fixture with Grimsby Town during the early weeks of 1941. That away fixture was played at St James' Park due the threat of Luftwaffe air raids and Deswart didn't have a convincing afternoon as United fell 4-0.

Appearances & Goals
Debut v Grimsby Town (a) 11 January 1941 (FLN)
War: 1 app 0 gls
Total: 1 app 0 gls

DEVINE Joseph Cassidy 1930-1931

Inside-right or left
5'8"
b. Dalziel, Motherwell, 9 August 1905
d. Chesterfield, 9 May 1980

Career: Motherwell Watsonians/Cleland Jnrs/Bathgate Nov 1923/Burnley May 1925 £250/UNITED Jan 1930 £5,575/Sunderland Feb 1931 £2,597/Queens Park Rangers May 1933 £2,500/Birmingham City Jan 1935 £2,000/Chesterfield May 1937, becoming coach 1946 to cs 1950/Later coached in Iceland and scouted for Bristol City.

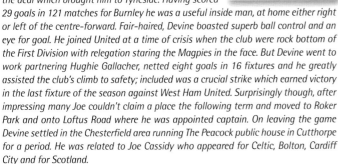

Joe Devine was a terrace favourite at Turf Moor before the deal which brought him to Tyneside. Having scored 29 goals in 121 matches for Burnley he was a useful inside man, at home either right or left of the centre-forward. Fair-haired, Devine boasted superb ball control and an eye for goal. He joined United at a time of crisis when the club were rock bottom of the First Division with relegation staring the Magpies in the face. But Devine went to work partnering Hughie Gallacher, netted eight goals in 16 fixtures and he greatly assisted the club's climb to safety; included was a crucial strike which earned victory in the last fixture of the season against West Ham United. Surprisingly though, after impressing many Joe couldn't claim a place the following term and moved to Roker Park and onto Loftus Road where he was appointed captain. On leaving the game Devine settled in the Chesterfield area running The Peacock public house in Cutthorpe for a period. He was related to Joe Cassidy who appeared for Celtic, Bolton, Cardiff City and for Scotland.

Appearances & Goals:
Debut v Huddersfield Town (a) 1 February 1930
FL: 22 app 11 gls
Total: 22 app 11 gls

DIATTA Lamine 2008

Centre-half
6'1"
b. Dakar (Senegal), 2 July 1975

Career: Toulouse (Fr) July 1998/Olymp Marseille (Fr) July 1999/Stade Rennais (Fr) Jan 2000/Olym Lyonnais (Fr) July 2004/AS St Etienne (Fr) Aug 2006 free/Besiktas JK (Trk) July 2007/UNITED trial Feb 2008, pmt March 2008 to May 2008/Stoke City trial Nov 2008/FC Sochaux (Fr) trial Nov 2008/Hamilton Acc March 2009/Al-Ahli SC (Qt) April 2009/ES Sahel (Tun) Jan to Sept 2011/Doncaster Rovers Dec 2011 to cs 2012.

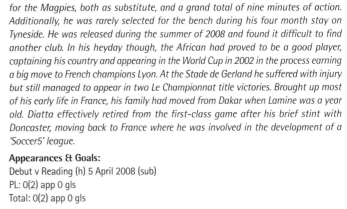

Senegal international defender Lamine Diatta had only a brief stay at St James' Park during season 2007-08. With a good track record for his country and in France, notably with Rennes where he totalled more than 140 games, the 32-year-old was brought into the United squad by boss Kevin Keegan to give cover to a rather threadbare central defence. He joined experienced defenders in Cacapa and Faye as options to partner Steven Taylor with new signing David

Rozehnal out of favour. Not having played regular football for some time it was a struggle for the centre-back and as a consequence Diatta only made two appearances for the Magpies, both as substitute, and a grand total of nine minutes of action. Additionally, he was rarely selected for the bench during his four month stay on Tyneside. He was released during the summer of 2008 and found it difficult to find another club. In his heyday though, the African had proved to be a good player, captaining his country and appearing in the World Cup in 2002 in the process earning a big move to French champions Lyon. At the Stade de Gerland he suffered with injury but still managed to appear in two Le Championnat title victories. Brought up most of his early life in France, his family had moved from Dakar when Lamine was a year old. Diatta effectively retired from the first-class game after his brief stint with Doncaster, moving back to France where he was involved in the development of a 'Soccer5' league.

Appearances & Goals:
Debut v Reading (h) 5 April 2008 (sub)
PL: 0(2) app 0 gls
Total: 0(2) app 0 gls

Honours:
40 Seng caps 2000-2008/WdC 2002/ACN final 2002/Fr Lg champs 2005, 2006.

DICKSON Charles 1894-1895

Outside-left
5'7"
b. Dundee

Career: Dundee Strathmore/Bolton Wand Jan 1892/Preston North End Feb 1894/Dundee Wand June 1894/UNITED Sept 1894 £5/Loughborough July 1895/Jarrow Aug 1896 to cs 1899.

Although fleet of foot, Charles Dickson did not get a look in at Bolton then was unable to gain a place in the fine Preston side which made a big imprint on the early days of Football League action, but when he joined United the Scot displayed vigour and zest up front. Noted as a "crack forward" he was adaptable in a wide or inside role. Dickson made a headlining beginning in a black-and-white shirt, netting on his debut then powering goals in each of his next three outings too. With United failing to gain promotion at the end of the 1894-95 season, he joined Football League newcomers Loughborough, and Willie Wardrope became his effective replacement. His transfer to United is recorded in detail in the club's Minutes; £5 went to agent Peter Allan, £5 to Dundee, the club that held his registration, while his wages were £2 per week with a £5 bonus.

Appearances & Goals:
Debut v Burslem Port Vale (a) 6 October 1894 (1 goal)
FL: 20 app 11 gls
FAC: 2 app 0 gls
Total: 22 app 11 gls

DILLON Kevin Paul 1989-1991

Midfield
6'0"
b. Sunderland, 18 December 1959

Career: Sunderland jnr/Birmingham City jnr June 1976, prof July 1977/Portsmouth March 1983 £200,000/UNITED July 1989 free/Sunderland trial cs 1991/Reading Aug 1991 free/Wycombe Wand trial Aug 1994/Brentford trial Sept 1994/Newbury Town 1994/Stevenage Borough Oct 1994/Yeovil Town Feb 1995, becoming asst-manager/ Fareham Town 1997/Reading scout, becoming asst-coach and asst-Academy director June 1998, coach June 2001 to May 2009, caretaker-manager Sept to Oct 2003/ Aldershot Town manager Nov 2009 to Jan 2011/Scouted for various clubs including Brighton and Watford.

With plenty of experience at gaining promotion into the First Division, Kevin Dillon joined United's staff approaching the end of a career that had seen him noted as one of Birmingham City's biggest prospects during an era when the St Andrews club held a respectable position in the top flight. The Wearsider developed through the Blues' ranks and was a 17-year-old debutant in 1977 alongside the likes of Trevor Francis and former United players; Hibbitt, Connolly and Howard. However, Dillon's early years

D

were clouded by his fiery streak, often being in trouble on and off the field. Totalling over 200 matches for City over six seasons, he holds the distinction of being sent-off at St James' Park, Ayresome Park and Roker Park in the North East. At his best, Kevin was a mobile and direct midfield player, always liable to find the net, scoring over 80 in his career, although during his spell with the Magpies, he found that his goalscoring touch deserted him. Brought to Tyneside to add steel and guile to the engine-room, Kevin's game flourished once Roy Aitken arrived in midfield at Gallowgate and during season 1989-90 when Newcastle missed promotion in the Play-Offs, the tall, slim Dillon had an effective campaign. He was captain of Jim Smith's side for a while, and later gave Reading a steadying influence when they reached Division One. The Wearsider had trials with Tottenham and a brief spell with his home town club before signing apprentice forms for Birmingham and embarking on his career of over 650 first-class games (Birmingham City 211 app, Portsmouth 257 app and Reading 119 app), while he once registered a hat-trick of penalties for Portsmouth against Millwall in 1986. After retiring from playing, Dillon gained a degree in Applied Management at Warwick University and operated as a qualified UEFA coach.

Appearances & Goals:
Debut v Leeds United (h) 19 August 1989
FL: 62(1) app 0 gls
FAC: 6(1) app 0 gls
FLC: 3 app 0 gls
Others: 3 app 0 gls
Total: 74(2) app 0 gls

Honours:
1 Eng u21 app 1981/Eng sch-youth app/FL div 2 champs 1994/FL div 3 champs 1983/FL div 2 prom 1980, 1987.

DIMOND Stuart 1943

Centre-forward
5'10"
b. Chorlton, Manchester, 3 January 1920
d. Didsbury, Manchester, November 2004

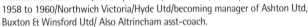

Career: Chesterfield/Manchester Utd amat May 1939, prof Nov 1939 (Distillery (Belfast) war-guest 1941-42)(UNITED war-guest 1942-43)(Notts Co war-guest 1943-44) (Leicester City war-guest 1943-44)(Swansea Town war-guest 1944-45) (Stockport Co war-guest 1944-45)/ Bradford City Sept 1945/ Winsford Utd Jan 1948/Mossley 1947-48/Ashton Utd/Mossley 1958 to 1960/Northwich Victoria/Hyde Utd/becoming manager of Ashton Utd, Buxton & Winsford Utd/ Also Altrincham asst-coach.

With the Royal Army Service Corps during the Second World War, Stuart Dimond appeared for several clubs as a guest player. Only appearing on a single occasion for United during March 1943, he played alongside Albert Stubbins in the leader's role for a home fixture against Leeds United. Dimond found the net in a terrific contest that ended 5-4 to the visitors. Unable to make the first-team at Old Trafford, Stuart entered first-class action with Bradford City, making a wonderful start by hitting four goals against Halifax Town during September 1945. However, Dimond managed only nine appearances in senior football then became a prominent figure in non-league circles in the North West for many years scoring over 200 goals for Ashton.

Appearances & Goals:
Debut v Leeds United (h) 27 March 1943 (FLN) (1 goal)
War: 1 app 1 gl
Total: 1 app 1 gl

DISTIN Sylvain 2001-2002

Centre-half
6'4"
b. Bagnolet, Paris (France), 16 December 1977

Career: Paris St-Germain (Fr) jnr/US Joue-Les-Tours (Fr) 1997/Tours (Fr) July 1998/FC Gueugnon (Fr) July 1999/Paris St-Germain (Fr) July 2000 (UNITED loan Sept 2001 to May 2002)/Manchester City July 2002 £4m (Mauritius XI guest June 2005)/Portsmouth July 2007 free/Everton Aug 2009 £5m.

With the Black'n'Whites central defensive options limited to Andy O'Brien and Nikos Dabizas, 23-year-old Frenchman Sylvain Distin arrived at Gallowgate on

a season loan deal from Paris giants, PSG. At 6'4" tall, Sylvain was quick to show manager Bobby Robson he could fill the gap in United's rearguard being fast and resolute as well as forceful in the air where his substantial frame was usually dominant. Making his debut from the bench in a terrific 4-3 victory over Manchester United, during season 2001-02 Distin quickly came to terms with the Premier League, a regular for most of the season alongside either Dabizas or O'Brien, but more often in a left-back role. There was much talk of a permanent deal for the defender but Distin and United could not agree terms and he looked elsewhere, moving to Manchester City and joining Kevin Keegan's squad, the Magpies losing out on a player who went onto become one of the best centre-backs in the Premier League over the following a decade and more. Newcastle instead turned to Titus Bramble, who arrived from Ipswich. Distin was a steady defender for City in 206 games and at Goodison Park where he totalled more than 150 matches, showing that the Magpies had made a big mistake not concluding a deal with the player. In between he helped Pompey lift the FA Cup under Harry Redknapp's leadership during 2008. Sylvain was on the fringe of international selection, but never received his senior call up for France. He was something of a late developer to the first-class scene, rising from the lower levels of football in France, but quickly prospered with PSG appearing in Champions League action before targeting a move to England.

Appearances & Goals:
Debut v Manchester United (h) 15 September 2001 (sub)
PL: 20(8) app 0 gls
FAC: 5 app 0 gls
FLC: 2 app 0 gls
Total: 27(8) app 0 gls

Honours:
FAC winner 2008/Fr LC winner 2000.

DIXON Edward Stanley 1913-1923

Inside-right
5'9"
b. Choppington, Northumberland, 26 May 1894
d. Bedlington, Northumberland, 13 August 1979

Career: Barrington Albion/UNITED amat Dec 1913, prof Feb 1914 £5/Blackburn Rovers March 1923 £1,100/Hull City May 1926 to cs 1930/ East Riding Amateurs.

A sturdy, talented inside-forward, extremely versatile across the forward line, Stan Dixon had his career at St James' Park divided by the First World War, playing for the club before and after the hostilities. After serving in the Engineers' Corps at the rank of sergeant, in season 1919-20 he commanded the inside-right position for the Magpies and was good enough to be reserve for both England and the Football League sides. Apart from that productive season, he struggled to claim a permanent place, although Stan always fitted smoothly into the team when called upon over the next three seasons. The highlight of his career with Newcastle was a stunning hat-trick against Chelsea during 1919 when United won 3-0 at Gallowgate. At Anlaby Road in Hull, Dixon made 107 appearances for the Tigers. When he retired Dixon became a cinema manager in Hull, later returning to his native Bedlington.

Appearances & Goals:
Debut v Liverpool (h) 1 April 1914
FL: 49 app 7 gls
FAC: 4 app 3 gls
War: 8 app 0 gls
Total: 61 app 10 gls

DIXON John Thomas 1941-1944

Inside-forward
5'10"
b. Hebburn, 10 December 1923
d. Sutton Coldfield, 20 January 2009

Career: Hebburn Boys Brigade/Spennymoor Utd 1940/ UNITED amat Oct 1941/Reyrolle Works 1942/UNITED prof May 1943 (Hull City war-guest 1944-45) (Middlesbrough war-guest 1944-45)(Sunderland war-guest 1944-45)/Aston Villa Aug 1944 to 1961 when he became asst-coach to 1967.

While Johnny Dixon failed to appear in league or cup football for the Black'n'Whites, he was to prove an exceptional footballer elsewhere, one of Aston Villa's finest post-war stars. A noted schoolboy player and part of an exceptional Reyrolle Works line-up alongside wartime colleague Ron Sales, he scored a brace on his United debut in December 1941, although the Magpies lost 4-2 at Hillsborough against Sheffield Wednesday. Dixon had his best season at St James' Park as a driving inside-forward during 1943-44 when he totalled 24 app (7 goals) and rivalled Ernie Taylor at Gallowgate during those wartime years. But Johnny lost out to the little schemer as peacetime approached. Released by the Magpies, he wrote to Aston Villa for a trial and succeeded in impressing the Midland club's officials. Settling and flourishing at Villa Park, Dixon developed into an inspirational leader, a dignified skipper of the Midland side when they lifted the FA Cup in 1957, a match in which he gave a tremendous display on the lush Wembley turf. A huge favourite with the club, Johnny appeared in 430 senior games for the claret-and-blues; he was an attack minded schemer, netting over 140 goals for Villa during 15 seasons. Dixon possessed a long stride in action and friendly personality. He later ran a hardware business in the Sutton area of the Midlands.

Appearances & Goals:
Debut v Sheffield Wednesday (a) 20 December 1941 (FLN) (2 goals)
War: 38 app 13 gls
Total: 38 app 13 gls

Honours:
FAC winner 1957/FL div 2 prom 1960.

DOCKING Stanley Holbrook 1934-1938

Inside-left
5'10"
b. Chopwell, near Gateshead, 13 December 1914
d. Newcastle upon Tyne, 27 May 1940

Career: Plessey Utd/Blyth Spartans/Chopwell Institute/Birtley/UNITED amat June 1934, prof Aug 1934 £5/Tranmere Rovers May 1938 £1,100 (Hartlepools Utd war-guest 1939-40).

A powerful, bustling forward and well built, at one stage weighing in at 14 stone, Stan Docking would invariably take the direct route for goal despite the number of defenders in his path. Being noticed when playing in the North Eastern League for Birtley, Stan packed a hot shot and was a big goal-getter with the Magpies' recently installed Central League side during the Thirties. In seasons 1936-37 and 1937-38 he was called-up for several first-team outings in midfield roles, but was never going to displace the established stars. When Docking moved to Merseyside, Newcastle inserted a clause in the transfer deal that if he helped Tranmere, "retain their place in Division Two", the Magpies would receive an extra £100. Rovers finished bottom in 1938-39 and United didn't get another penny. Docking died during the Second World War when serving as an aircraftsman in the RAF. Stan was on leave at his home in Whitley Bay when he contracted septicaemia and died suddenly of heart failure.

Appearances & Goals:
Debut v Fulham (h) 19 January 1935
FL: 21 app 3 gls
Total: 21 app 3 gls

Honours:
Eng sch-youth app.

DODDS John Thomas 1905-1908

Outside-right or left
5'9"
b. Hexham, October 1885
d. Hexham, March 1940

Career: Northern Star (Hexham)/UNITED trial Aug 1905, later pmt March 1906/Oldham Ath Aug 1908 £100/Heart of Midlothian June 1909 £50/ Reading Sept 1909/Darlington July 1910/ Merthyr Town July 1911/Barrow July 1913/ Stalybridge Celtic Feb 1914 to May 1915.

A local product, John Dodds deputised for international wingers Gosnell and Rutherford at St James' Park, making four of his five outings during the Tynesider's Football League title victory in 1906-07. He also took part in the club's reserve championship success in the North Eastern League during that same season, and again twelve months later. He was one of three Magpie players, Appleyard and Speedie being the others, who moved to Oldham during the summer of 1908. Dodds was unfortunate to pick up an injury in only his second game for the Latics, and, when fit,

sustained another knock. He only made eight appearances before trying his luck in Edinburgh with Hearts. The Hexham product enjoyed a good period with Merthyr's Southern League line-up which lifted silverware and won promotion, as well as enjoying a notable FA Cup run. When war broke out, Dodds enlisted during May 1915 in the celebrated Footballer's Battalion of the Middlesex regiment.

Appearances & Goals:
Debut v Woolwich Arsenal (h) 16 April 1906
FL: 5 app 0 gls
Total: 5 app 0 gls

Honours:
FL champs 1907 (4 app).

DODGIN Norman 1940-1950

Left-half
5'11"
b. Sheriff Hill, Gateshead, 1 November 1921
d. Teignbridge, Exeter, 9 August 2000

Career: Ouston Jnrs/Whitehall Jnrs/UNITED amat April 1940, prof Aug 1940/Reading June 1950 £5,000/ Northampton Town Sept 1951 £850/Exeter City Aug 1953, becoming player-manager to April 1957/ Yeovil Town manager June 1957/Barrow manager Sept 1957/Oldham Ath manager July 1958 to May 1960.

Norman Dodgin was a sound half-back and a player's player, always aiming to perform for the team. Tall and composed on the ball, he lost the best years of his career to the Second World War serving in the Durham Light Infantry, although he gained a lot of experience appearing in wartime soccer both at home and abroad, including in Italy where he caught the eye of AC Milan. A former bricklayer, Norman took part in United's promotion success during 1948 and was a regular in the club's initial season back in the First Division. He gave way to the younger Charlie Crowe during 1950 after a dispute with trainer Norman Smith. Dodgin hailed from a footballing pedigree; his brother, Bill, played for and managed a string of clubs, while he is uncle to Bill junior, who also appeared for and managed Football League sides. After quitting the game, Norman ran a newsagency in Dawlish, near Exeter.

Appearances & Goals:
Debut v Chesterfield (h) 3 September 1947
(v York City (a) 17 April 1940 (FLNE))
FL: 84 app 1 gl
FAC: 2 app 0 gls
War: 46 app 1 gl
Total: 132 app 2 gls

Honours:
FL div 2 prom 1948.

DOMI Didier Arsene Marcel 1998-2001

Left-back
5'10"
b. Sarcelles, Paris (France), 2 May 1978

Career: Pierrefitte (Fr)/Paris St-Germain (Fr) jnr 1992, prof July 1994/UNITED Jan 1999 £3.25m/ Paris St-Germain (Fr) Jan 2001 £3m/Leeds Utd Aug 2003 free/Portsmouth trial June 2004/RCD Espanyol (Sp) July 2004 free (Mauritius XI guest June 2005)/Olympiacos CFP (Gr) May 2006 to July 2010/New England Revolution (USA) Jan 2011 to July 2011 when he retired.

Although only 20 years old when he exchanged the Champs Elysee for the Bigg Market, Didier Domi was an established rising star with Paris St-Germain, in their line-up since a 17-year-old teenager. Manager Ruud Gullit saw much potential in the Frenchman as a raiding left-back who had the ability to reach the full national side. Fast, alert and confident, Didier at first settled quickly and rapidly showed he had the match-winning ability to rush forward and produce a decisive cross into the danger area. Taking part in the 1999 FA Cup final for the Magpies, he was unlucky to be sidelined with an ankle injury, losing career momentum as well as his place to rivals Hughes and Pistone. Then Didier

D

saw his mentor Ruud Gullit depart. Domi never had the same relationship with new boss Bobby Robson and his worth to the Magpies diminished. In season 2000-01 his career went off the rails, going missing in December, reported to a Muslim cult in Paris. Didier returned to PSG within weeks and for a period thereafter his football stock nose-dived. Making something of a return to the game in Spain and Greece, he again showed his undoubted talent, winning a string of honours with Olympiacos. His family hails from the Caribbean island of Martinique, Domi once suffered a freak injury when flying with United's squad to the States; breaking a rib when turbulence rocked the plane. After concluding his career with a short spell in Massachusetts, it was reported by the French media that he had become a resident in Qatar.

Appearances & Goals:
Debut v Chelsea (h) 9 January 1999
PL: 44(11) app 3 gls
FAC: 5(3) app 1 gl
FLC: 2(1) app 0 gls
Euro: 4 app 0 gls
Total: 55 (15) app 4 gls

Honours:
19 Fr u21 app 1998-2000/Fr sch-youth app/Gr Lg champs 2007, 2008, 2009/FAC final 1999/Fr Cup winner 1998/Fr LC winner 1998/Gr Cup winner 2008, 2009/ECWC final 1997/ESC final 1996.

DONALDSON Andrew 1943-1949

Centre-forward
6'0"
b. Newcastle upon Tyne, 22 March 1925
d. Peterborough, 20 June 1987

Career: South Benwell (Newcastle)/Vickers Armstrong Welfare (Newcastle)/UNITED amat Aug 1943, prof Sept 1943/Middlesbrough Jan 1949 £17,500/Peterborough Utd Aug 1951/Exeter City Sept 1953/Peterborough Utd cs 1955 to 1958.

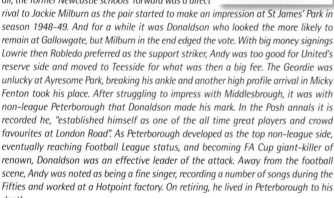

Tall and leggy, once described as being, "built like a greyhound", Andy Donaldson was the scoring force behind United's Central League title victory in 1948 when he netted 33 goals. Especially a danger in the air, the former Newcastle schools' forward was a direct rival to Jackie Milburn as the pair started to make an impression at St James' Park in season 1948-49. And for a while it was Donaldson who looked the more likely to remain at Gallowgate, but Milburn in the end edged the vote. With big money signings Lowrie then Robledo preferred as the support striker, Andy was too good for United's reserve side and moved to Teesside for what was then a big fee. The Geordie was unlucky at Ayresome Park, breaking his ankle and another high profile arrival in Micky Fenton took his place. After struggling to impress with Middlesbrough, it was with non-league Peterborough that Donaldson made his mark. In the Posh annals it is recorded he, "established himself as one of the all time great players and crowd favourites at London Road". As Peterborough developed as the top non-league side, eventually reaching Football League status, and becoming FA Cup giant-killer of renown, Donaldson was an effective leader of the attack. Away from the football scene, Andy was noted as being a fine singer, recording a number of songs during the Fifties and worked at a Hotpoint factory. On retiring, he lived in Peterborough to his death.

Appearances & Goals:
Debut v Leicester City (h) 19 April 1947
(v Huddersfield Town (a) 16 October 1943 (FLN))
FL: 19 app 6 gls
War: 12 app 3 gls
Total: 31 app 9 gls

Honours:
FL div 2 prom 1948 (5 app).

DONALDSON A 1893-1895

Inside-right
Debut v Newton Heath (h) 13 April 1895

A local player who joined United's staff during September 1893, little is recorded about Donaldson but he appeared for the Science & Art college team in 1888-89 and was on United's staff for both the 1893-94 and 1894-95 seasons. He initially reached the

first-team for a friendly match against Middlesbrough in September 1893 then gained an opportunity for the last two games of the Second Division campaign, including the club's record defeat, a 9-0 reverse at the Derby Turn ground, home of Burton Wanderers. On his debut against Newton Heath, he created an opportunity for Milne to score. Donaldson left Newcastle during the summer of 1895, possibly to Scottish club Linthouse where a Donaldson appeared during season 1895-96.

Appearances & Goals:
Debut v Newton Heath (h) 13 April 1895
FL: 2 app 0 gls
Total: 2 app 0 gls

DONALDSON Ryan Mark 2005-2012

Midfield or Forward
5'11"
b. Newcastle upon Tyne, 1 May 1991

Career: UNITED jnr 2005, prof Nov 2008 (Hartlepool Utd loan 2010-11)(Tranmere Rovers loan 2011-12) to June 2012 free/St Johnstone & Carlisle Utd trial cs 2012/Gateshead Aug 2012 free/ Cambridge Utd June 2013.

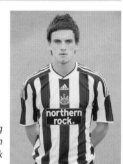

Ryan Donaldson was one of a group of promising youngsters who were on the fringe of the first-team squad as United entered a new era on promotion back to the Premier League in 2010. Donaldson was initially at United's Academy as a nine-year-old and joined the club from St Cuthbert's school as a striker. He earned international honours for his country at Under-17 and Under-19 level, scoring plenty of goals in a young England shirt. Appearing with the seniors in friendly action when a 17-year-old, the Geordie youngster reached United's bench at Old Trafford at the beginning of the 2008-09 season and a year later made his first start for the Magpies in a League Cup-tie at Peterborough. Ryan played a small part in United's promotion back to the Premier League during 2009-10 and looked to be a fine prospect. Lively and pacy, he hit the net regularly for United's junior and second teams, for a period alongside Andy Carroll. However, while his strike partner did break through into the big time, like many other local lads, Donaldson found it tough pushing his way into the Newcastle line-up and had a spell on loan at Hartlepool then Tranmere during 2011-12. Ryan was resourceful and mobile but his early promise with England and United's reserves was never fulfilled. He dropped back into midfield later into his career and joined Gateshead in the Conference. Later, when with Cambridge United, Ryan netted twice at Wembley as his club lifted the FA Trophy in 2014, then returned to the national arena for the Conference Play-Off against his former club Gateshead at the end of the season. His father, Ian Donaldson, had also turned out for Gateshead.

Appearances & Goals:
Debut v Leicester City (h) 31 August 2009 (sub)
PL: 0(2) app 0 gls
FAC: 0(2) app 0 gls
FLC: 2 app 0 gls
Total: 2(4) app 0 gls

Honours:
Eng sch-youth app/FL ch winner 2010 (2 app)/FAT winner 2014.

DONALDSON Robert Stone 1942-1947

Left-half
5'7"
b. South Shields, 26 February 1921
d. 19 June 1990

Career: South Shields Ex-Schoolboys/UNITED amat March 1942, prof Jan 1943/Hartlepools Utd July 1947, becoming trainer 1951/North Shields player-trainer.

Hard tackling and tenacious, Bobby Donaldson was a regular in United's wartime line-up for two seasons, during 1943-44 and 1944-45. Operating on both sides of the half-back line, he partnered Tot Smith. On the fringe of making United's Football League side during 1946-47, he joined Hartlepools during the close-season and proceeded to total 138 games for the Victoria Ground club. He was a crowd favourite on the Durham coast and later served the Poolies behind the scenes as part of the coaching staff. Donaldson started out in the same junior side in South Shields as Stan Mortensen and was for a period employed in a Tyneside shipping office then for Swan Hunter as a wages manager.

Appearances & Goals:
Debut v Gateshead (a) 4 April 1942 (FLN)
War: 87 app 2 gls
Total: 87 app 2 gls

DONNACHIE Joseph 1905-1906

Outside-left
5'9"
b. Kilwinning, Ayrshire, 18 December 1882
d. Chester, March 1967

Career: Rutherglen Glencairn 1902/Morton April 1904 (Albion Rovers loan 1904-05)/UNITED June 1905/ Everton Feb 1906/Oldham Ath Oct 1908 £250/Everton cs 1915 (Liverpool war-guest 1916-17)/Rangers March 1919 £800/Everton Aug 1919/Blackpool June 1920/ Chester player-manager cs 1921 to cs 1923 when he retired.

Smart and fast, as well as being bow-legged, Joe Donnachie was a Scot with much potential when he signed for the Magpies, but found it almost impossible to break into the club's near all international side. He did win reserve honours with the Black'n'Whites, yet Joe was forced to continue his career elsewhere and became an international player himself after some sterling displays for Oldham as they finished runners-up in the First Division. Totalling 238 senior games (21 goals) for the Latics, he played on both flanks, and although Joe liked to make mazy dribbles, he was direct and always liable to create an opening. With flair to produce the unusual, Donnachie had a good record with Everton as well, in two spells being a regular throughout the war years at Goodison Park. He also has the distinction of being one of only a handful of Roman Catholics to appear for Rangers during their first century of action. Donnachie was marvellously described by one Glasgow writer during his era as being, "cool, clever, and cuter than a basketful of monkeys". He later was publican at the Mariner's Arms Inn near Chester's Sealand Road stadium. His son, also Joe, was on Liverpool's books, but was killed in a wartime flying accident.

(Note: Joe was born as Joseph Donaghy, later changing his surname by the time he was living in Paisley.)

Appearances & Goals:
Debut v Birmingham (h) 9 September 1905
FL: 2 app 0 gls
Total: 2 app 0 gls

Honours:
3 Scot caps 1913-14/Scot trial app 1913-14/FL div 2 prom 1910.

DONNELLY John William 1918-1920

Outside-left
5'9"
b. Newcastle upon Tyne, 1902

Career: UNITED amat Aug 1918, prof May 1919/ Leadgate Park May 1920 free to Jan 1922.

A regular for the Magpies second eleven as the First World War came to a close in the local Newcastle & District United League during season 1918-19, John Donnelly earned a place in the opening games of the Northern Victory League competition during 1919. Scoring on his senior debut against Scotswood, John was a rival to Ed Cooper and Alex Ramsay on the wing. Donnelly was retained when a normal format of soccer reappeared in August 1919, but couldn't push his way through the wall of talent at Gallowgate and moved into the North Eastern League. He reached the Durham Senior Cup final with Leadgate Park during 1921.

Appearances & Goals:
Debut v Scotswood (a) 18 January 1919 (NVL) (1 goal)
War: 5 app 1 gl
Total: 5 app 1 gl

DORAN John Francis 1918-1919

Centre-forward
5'11"
b. Belfast 3 January 1896
d. Sunderland 7 January 1940

Career: St Wilfred's (Newcastle)/Gillingham Aug 1912/Gravesend Utd Oct 1912/North Shields Ath Dec 1912/Newcastle Empire 1913/ Coventry City May 1914/UNITED amat 1918/ Brentford Jan 1919/UNITED March 1919/ Norwich City May 1919/Brighton March 1920/ Manchester City Aug 1922 £1,050/Crewe Alex Jan 1924/Mid-Rhondda Utd July 1924/ Shelbourne Dec 1924/Fordsons cs 1925/Boston Town Aug 1925 to Oct 1927/Waterford Celtic.

Although born in Ireland, Jack Doran was brought up a Geordie after his family had moved to Northumberland. Appearing for the County side, this well built, tall and curly-haired striker was soon destined for a notable career in the game. Appearing for the Magpies in the 1918-19 District United League campaign, he made his senior appearance for the club in the Victory League derby contest with Sunderland during March 1919 when he found the net. But Doran wasn't recruited and he moved south to eventually find a place in Brighton's line-up. With a stinging shot, he scored 55 goals in only 85 games, form which saw him capped by Ireland. In one game for the Seagulls against Northampton during 1921 he grabbed five goals. A big move to Manchester City followed, but his stay at Maine Road wasn't a success and he later became a publican after leaving the game. During the First World War, Jack joined the Middlesex Footballer's Battalion when living in Newcastle, part of the Royal Army Ordnance Corps and won both the Military Medal and Distinguished Conduct Medal. He was though the victim of a gas attack on the Somme and Cambrai battlefield, and after settling in Sunderland, he died of a respiratory illness as a long-term consequence when 44 years old.

(Note: Newcastle United's official records show Doran appeared in four games; however local press reports suggest a player called Johnson may have replaced him in three fixtures. No record of Johnson exists which suggests he used a false name.)

Appearances & Goals:
Debut v Sunderland (a) 22 March 1919 (NVL) (1 goal)
War: 4 app 1 gl
Total: 4 app 1 gl

Honours:
3 Irel caps 1921-22.

DOUGLAS Angus 1913-1918

Outside-right
5'9"
b. Lochmaben, Dumfries, 1 January 1889
d. South Gosforth, Newcastle upon Tyne, 14 December 1918

Career: Castlemilk/Lochmaben Rangers/Dumfries Feb 1906 (Kilmarnock loan 1905-06)(Raith Rovers loan 1907-08)/Chelsea May 1908/UNITED Oct 1913 £1,100 to demise in 1918.

A former clerk in the Sheriff's office in Dumfries, Angus Douglas became a great favourite at Stamford Bridge for five seasons recording 103 games. He was an entertainer on the field, fast and clever on the ball, and by accounts, being notably handsome, especially liked by the Londoner's female contingent of fans. With Jackie Rutherford's departure, Douglas was purchased to replace one of Tyneside's best admired players of the era, and to the Scot's credit he fitted into the right-wing position well. The First World War, however, ended his footballing career and after surviving the fighting on the Continent, Angus returned to Tyneside, only to fall a victim of the influenza pandemic. Being invited to rejoin the Magpies staff at the end of 1918, Douglas died after contracting pneumonia when only 29 years of age.

Appearances & Goals:
Debut v Burnley (a) 1 November 1913
FL: 49 app 2 gls
FAC: 7 app 0 gls
Total: 56 app 2 gls

Honours:
1 Scot cap 1911/FL div 2 prom 1912.

D

DOWSEY John 1924-1926

Inside-right
5'11"
b. Willington, Co Durham, 1 May 1905
d. Costock, Nottinghamshire, 27 October 1942

Career: Hunswick Villa/UNITED amat March 1924, prof June 1924 £10/West Ham Utd May 1926 £250/Carlisle Utd Aug 1927/Sunderland Dec 1927/Notts Co Feb 1929/Northampton Town Nov 1931/Nuneaton Town Aug 1934.

A noted forward in Tyneside's non-leagues, John Dowsey was given a chance by Newcastle's directors just after the club had lifted the FA Cup in 1924. Known as 'Jack', he never threatened his senior professionals in United's colours and only made a handful of appearances during season 1925-26, standing in for Roddie MacKenzie while he was also tried at centre-forward in a friendly encounter. Dowsey however, was still a threat in reserve soccer as United's second string lifted the North Eastern League title. He netted 54 goals over two seasons for the club before the Hammers took him to East London, but again the Durham lad found it difficult to claim first-team football, making just a single appearance for the Upton Park outfit before moving on again. Jack found a permanent place with Notts County (103 app), winning the Third Division title, and with the Cobblers, Northampton Town (95 app) where he dropped back to play a wing-half role.

Appearances & Goals:
Debut v Tottenham Hotspur (h) 14 November 1925
FL: 3 app 0 gls
Total: 3 app 0 gls

Honours:
FL div 3(S) champs 1931.

DRYDEN John R 1932-1934

Outside-left
5'9"
b. Broomhill, Northumberland, 21 August 1908
d. Ashington, 16 September 1975

Career: United Bus Service FC/Pegswood Utd/Ashington 1930/UNITED Sept 1932 £175/Exeter City May 1934 free/Sheffield Utd May 1935 free/Bristol City July 1936/ Burnley May 1938/Peterborough Utd Aug 1939 (Aberdeen war-guest 1941-44)(York City war-guest 1941-42)(Arbroath war-guest)/Later becoming Ashington trainer and manager during 1950s.

Jackie Dryden was only allowed to leave St James' Park because of the special talent of Tommy Pearson on the wing. Dainty on his feet, Dryden possessed skill and pace, being a deputy to Tommy Lang before Pearson emerged. The Northumbrian moved to Exeter's St James' Park, then to Bramall Lane where he enjoyed a headlining start in the red-and-white of Sheffield United. Dryden scored four goals in his opening four games for the Blades during 1935-36, yet after that form deserted him and he totalled only 19 outings. During World War Two Dryden served in the RAF in Scotland and frequently assisted Aberdeen, part of their line-up which won the North East League Cup and Mitchell Cup during season 1942-43. From a footballing family, his brother Henry was on United's staff during 1937-38 while, a cousin Jackie Bell turned out for Middlesbrough and Walsall. His father, Amble-born Billy Dryden was with Clapton Orient. It is recorded he was linked to the famous Milburn clan as well.

Appearances & Goals:
Debut v Leeds United (h) 14 January 1933 (FAC)
FL: 5 app 1 gl
FAC: 1 app 0 gls
Total: 6 app 1 gl

DUFF Damien Anthony 2006-2009

Outside-left or Midfield
5'9
b. Ballyboden, Dublin, 2 March 1979

Career: Leicester Celtic/Lourdes Celtic 1994/ St Kevin's Boys/Blackburn Rovers jnr 1995, prof March 1996/Chelsea July 2003 £17m/UNITED July 2006 £5m/Fulham Aug 2009 £4m/ Melbourne City (Aus) June 2014.

At the peak of his career, Irishman Damien Duff was a surging and effective winger in Jose Mourinho's Chelsea line-up which lifted the Premier League title in seasons 2004-05 and 2005-06. Commanding a substantial £17m fee, a Chelsea record, when he moved to Stamford Bridge from Blackburn Rovers during 2003 following an impressive World Cup in Korea-Japan, Duff was both tricky and fast, a penetrating forward who could operate on either flank and deliver a telling cross, often to cut in and have a go at goal himself. A regular for the Republic of Ireland side for over a decade and one of the select few to reach a century of caps, after much success with Chelsea he was out of action with knee and Achilles injuries and his career lost momentum. Newcastle pounced to secure the 27-year-old's signature for what was a much reduced fee of £5m in the close-season of 2006. It looked a good deal for the Magpies, manager Glenn Roeder's star acquisition to compete with Charles N'Zogbia on the left flank of midfield. Yet following his three year period at Gallowgate, the Magpies perhaps never saw the best of the talented forward from Dublin. Always working hard for the cause and willing to track back into defence, Damien had a good opening spell in 2006-07 and also operated on occasion on the right and as a wing-back, but suffered from more injury woe on Tyneside; a knee injury, then calf problems and a severe foot complaint keeping him out for several months. Duff joined Fulham on the Magpies' relegation in 2009 as the club reduced their wage bill. Moving back to West London, he enjoyed a productive period at Craven Cottage, totalling over 150 games and played a major role in the Londoners reaching the Europa League final during 2010. Duff clocked up more than 220 games for Blackburn and 125 for Chelsea.

Appearances & Goals:
Debut v FK Ventspils (a) 10 August 2006 (UEFAC)
FL/PL: 61(8) app 5 gls
FAC: 5 app 1 gl
FLC: 2(1) app 0 gls
Euro: 8(1) app 0 gls
Total: 76(10) app 6 gls

Honours:
100 Eire caps 1998-2012/WdC 2002/1 Eire B app 1998/Eire sch-youth app/PL champs 2005, 2006/FL ch winner 2010 (1 app)/FL ch prom 2001/FLC winner 2002, 2005/EpL final 2010/PFA ToS (d1) 2001.

DUFFY Alan 1964-1970

Striker
5'6"
b. Stanley, Co Durham, 20 December 1949

Career: UNITED amat 1963, jnr Dec 1964, prof March 1967/ Brighton Jan 1970 £8,000/Tranmere Rovers March 1972/ Darlington Aug 1973 to cs 1974/Consett 1975/Pelton Fell 1976, becoming coach to 1985.

A product of Newcastle's excellent Sixties junior set-up, Alan Duffy climbed through the ranks to reach senior status alongside Alan Foggon and Keith Dyson. At the time he was described as "one of the most exciting prospects ever to emerge from North East junior football". Although not tall or powerful, Duffy was a quick and nimble striker, who was a reserve to Bryan Robson. As a teenager Alan was noted as a future star, but unlike his two more famous contemporaries in the junior ranks, Duffy didn't claim many appearances and was transferred to the south coast at the Goldstone Ground where he enjoyed a couple of seasons in the first-team, totalling 54 games. He later appeared on 33 occasions for Tranmere and 25 times for Darlington in Division Four. His grandfather Albert Bell pulled on the shirt of Leeds United and Accrington Stanley. Duffy later resided in his native Stanley.

Appearances & Goals:
Debut v Manchester United (a) 21 September 1968
FL: 2(2) app 0 gls
Total: 2(2) app 0 gls

Honours:
Eng sch-youth app/FL div 3 prom 1972 (9 app).

DUFFY Christopher Francis 1906-1908

Outside-left
5'7"
b. Jarrow, 24 January 1884
d. Whitley Bay, 18 August 1971

Career: Jarrow/St Mary's College (Hammersmith)/ Brentford amat Jan 1905/ Jarrow May 1905/ Middlesbrough Oct 1905/ UNITED Aug 1906 free/Bury May 1908 £100/North Shields Ath July 1913/Bury Nov 1914 to cs 1915/Tyneside Electrical Eng 1916-17/ Leicester City Dec 1919/ Chester-le-Street Aug 1920.

Although born on Tyneside, Chris Duffy attended St Mary's College in Hammersmith gaining a first-class education. He was a noted amateur sportsman and turned to soccer after winning several prizes as a sprinter. Returning to his native North East, Duffy was purchased to give the Magpies cover on the wing and did a sound job, although he was rarely given much scope in the senior eleven. However, Chris appeared on seven occasions during the club's Football League trophy victory during season 1906-07 and when at Gigg Lane in the top-tier, Duffy held an automatic place totalling 155 games for the Shakers. Chris started a career in teaching when still a footballer with Bury, and on retirement became a tutor in the region, holding the position of Headmaster at St Aloysius School (Newcastle) and St Dominic's School (Durham).

Appearances & Goals:
Debut v Sheffield United (a) 8 December 1906
FL: 16 app 1 gl
Total: 16 app 1 gl

Honours:
FL champs 1907 (7 app).

DUFFY Robert McFarlane Davidson 1944-1945

Left-half
5'8"
b. Dundee, 19 April 1913

Career: Dundee St Josephs 1932/Lochee Harp 1933/ Celtic Oct 1935 (Dundee war-guest 1939-40) (Blackpool war-guest 1940-41)(Bradford City war-guest 1941-42)(Fulham war-guest 1941-42)(Hamilton Acc war-guest 1941-42)(Huddersfield Town war-guest 1941-43)(Rochdale war-guest 1942-43)(Dundee Utd war-guest 1943-44)(Port Vale war-guest 1944-45) (Swansea Town war-guest 1944-45)(UNITED war-guest 1944-45)(Leeds Utd war-guest 1945-46)/Resumed with Celtic 1945 to April 1947.

During the Second World War, Bertie Duffy worked as a physical trainer instructor for the RAF and travelled the country as a consequence. Duffy's football career followed him around, landing at various ports of call up and down the length of England and Central Scotland. He was a solid half-back, a reserve to Celtic's stars at Parkhead, and as a result Bertie managed only four games for the Glasgow club, including one match when the Hoops lifted the Scottish League title before war started. But he produced some good performances in wartime soccer which had several pundits tip him for a Scotland cap during 1944-45, the season he turned out for Newcastle. His debut for the Magpies against Hull resulted in a 7-0 victory.

Appearances & Goals:
Debut v Hull City (h) 4 November 1944 (FLN)
War: 21 app 0 gls
Total: 21 app 0 gls

Honours:
SL champs 1938 (1 app).

DUMAS Franck 1999-2000

Centre-half
5'11"
b. Bayeux (France), 9 January 1968

Career: PPT Caen (Fr)/SM Caen (Fr)/INF Vichy (Fr) cs 1985/SM Caen (Fr) cs 1987/Monaco (M/Fr) July 1992/UNITED June 1999 £500,000/Olym Marseille (Fr) Jan 2000 £1.25m (RC Lens (Fr) loan 2000-01)/ SM Caen (Fr) Sept 2001, retired playing July 2004, becoming coach then manager May 2005 to June 2012/AC Arles-Avignon (Fr) Sporting Director Feb 2013, then manager cs 2013.

Exchanging the idyllic and luxury lifestyle of Monte-Carlo for Tyneside, Frank Dumas was one of a succession of experienced central defenders from the Continent to land on Tyneside during the Premier League years in a bid to give the Black'n'Whites solidity at the back. He cost a modest £500,000 fee as an accomplished player in France, notably with Monaco where he appeared over 200 times, playing against United in the UEFA Cup. At the Stade Louis II, Dumas was a huge influence and he was rated as one of France's foremost uncapped players of his era. Franck did appear to know the job of defending, often assured as well as composed, but at 31 years of age did not cope to well with the pulsating force week in-week out of English top-level football. Preferring to operate behind a stopper centre-back, and also in the libero role, Dumas read the play well but was sidelined with injury after starting the 1999-2000 season alongside Alain Goma. Favoured by Ruud Gullit during his brief reign at St James' Park, his stay in the North East was to be just as short, new boss Bobby Robson looking elsewhere to shore up the Magpies' defence. As the new Millennium started, Frank moved back to the South of France, then joined his local club Caen. Franck appeared over 250 times for the Normandy outfit and then managed the side for seven years, a grand servant. Afterwards Dumas was often on French TV as an expert summariser.

Appearances & Goals:
Debut v Aston Villa (h) 7 August 1999
PL: 6 app 0 gls
Euro: 1 app 0 gls
Total: 7 app 0 gls

Honours:
Fr A & B app/6 Fr u21 app 1989-90/Fr Lg champs 1997/Fr div 2 champs 2010(m)/Fr div 2 prom 2004, 2007(m).

DUMMETT Paul 2008-date

Left-back
5'10"
b. Newcastle upon Tyne, 26 September 1991

Career: UNITED jnr July 2008, prof July 2010 (Gateshead loan 2011-12)(St Mirren loan 2012-13).

Raised in Gosforth with a Welsh blood-line, Paul Dummett joined the club's Academy set-up when he was only nine years old. The young full-back quickly showed his potential and was called up to the senior squad for pre-season friendlies at the beginning of 2011-12. Dummett moved to the Scottish Premier League to gain experience with St Mirren but injury to Danny Simpson gave the Tynesider a brief window to make his bow in a Magpie shirt, arriving back from his loan deal to take to the stage at the Amex Arena for a FA Cup tie with Brighton. The arrival of French international Mathieu Debuchy saw Paul return to the Greenhill Road stadium in Paisley to continue his football learning. That period in Scotland, during which Paul totalled 35 senior games, was very rewarding; Dummett appearing in the 2013 Scottish League Cup final with on-loan colleague Conor Newton. His arrival at Gallowgate at the end of the season as a medal winner saw the emerging Geordie push for first-team recognition across the back-line, in the process the athletic and aggressive full-back earning a call-up to the Welsh full squad in September 2013.

Appearances & Goals:
Debut v Brighton (a) 5 January 2013 (FAC) (sub)
PL: 11(7) app 1 gl
FAC: 0(1) app 0 gls
FLC: 2(1) app 0 gls
Total: 13(9) app 1 gl

Honours:
1 Wales cap 2014-date/4 Wales u21 app 2011-date/Wales sch-youth app/SLC winner 2013.

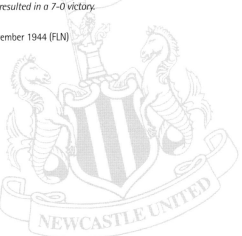

D

DUNCAN Adam Scott Mathieson 1908-1913

Outside-right
5'9"
b. Dumbarton, 2 November 1888
d. Helensburgh, 3 October 1976

Career: Dumbarton Oakvale/Dumbarton Corinthians/Clydebank Jnrs/Shettleston Jnrs/Dumbarton Nov 1905/UNITED March 1908 £150/Rangers May 1913 £600 (Manchester Utd war-guest 1918-19) (Celtic war-guest 1918-19)(Partick Thistle war-guest 1918-19)/ Dumbarton July 1919 (Cowdenbeath loan 1921-22, 1922-23)/ Dumbarton 1923/Retired cs 1923/Hamilton Acc manager July 1923/ Cowdenbeath manager July 1925 returning to Hamilton briefly, then back to Cowdenbeath Sept 1925/Manchester Utd manager June 1932/Ipswich Town manager Sept 1937, becoming secretary Aug 1955 to May 1958.

A distinguished personality of pre-war football, both as a player and as a manager, Scott Duncan was a swift, ball-playing winger, typical of his native breed. He could be intricate at dribbling, one biography described him as being, "one of the most stylish wingers in Britain". Although at St James' Park for six seasons, he took time to settle on Tyneside and spent the first few campaigns chiefly as a reserve, but he appeared in the club's Football League success in 1909 and really came into his own during season 1910-11 when his sparkling form saw him just miss a Scotland cap. Scott was twice on the stand-by roster for FA Cup finals with United, in 1908 and 1911. The son of a Dumbarton butcher, 'Archie', as he was known, worked in a solicitor's office as an articled student lawyer before heading to Tyneside. But with the stardom of football an option, Duncan dropped his legal studies to become a professional with the Magpies. During World War One he served as a signalling instructor in the Royal Field Artillery. He later became an outstanding manager on both sides of the border, taking Manchester United to promotion and developing into something of a legend at Portman Road, steering the then little known non-league side, Ipswich Town, into the Football League. Duncan had a long career in the game and lived into his nineties, residing in the Scottish resort of Helensburgh.

Appearances & Goals:
Debut v Everton (a) 4 April 1908
FL: 73 app 10 gls
FAC: 8 app 1 gl
Total: 81 app 11 gls

Honours:
Scot trial app 1910-11/FL champs 1909/FL div 2 champs 1936/FL div 3(S) champs 1954(m)/FL Long Service Award 1957.

DUNCAN John Gilhespie 1950-1953

Right-back & Centre-forward
5'11"
b. Glasgow, 10 December 1926
d. 1984

Career: Partick Avondale 1948/Ayr Utd April 1948/UNITED Nov 1950 £8,250/ Retired due to injury June 1953.

John Duncan was a versatile player who possessed an exciting talent. Purchased by United as a defender to be groomed for the future, Duncan made his early outings in Newcastle's colours at right-back, but when he was converted into the centre-forward's role, he created headlines by netting twice against Aston Villa then in the next fixture with Stoke grabbed another. Big-hearted and full of gusto, John was, however, soon afterwards sidelined with a badly wrenched knee injury and it took months of recuperation before he attempted a comeback. He did that as a goalkeeper at reserve level, but he struggled with the knee injury and it forced him to call a halt to his career. Duncan moved back to Ayr where he ran a haulage business.

Appearances & Goals:
Debut v Preston North End (a) 8 September 1951
FL: 5 app 3 gls
Others: 1 app 0 gls
Total: 6 app 3 gls

DUNS Leonard 1933, 1939-1942

Outside-right
5'9"
b. Newcastle upon Tyne, 26 September 1916
d. Ponteland, near Newcastle upon Tyne, 20 April 1989

Career: West End Albion/Newcastle West End/UNITED amat May 1933/Sunderland Sept 1933 (UNITED war-guest 1939-42)(Aldershot war-guest 1939-44) (Bristol City war-guest 1941-42)(Brentford war-guest 1941-42)(Reading war-guest 1941-42)(Notts Co war-guest 1942-43)(West Bromwich Albion war-guest 1943-44) (Lovell's Ath war-guest 1944-45)(Wrexham war-guest 1944-46)(Shrewsbury Town war-guest 1945-46)/ Resumed with Sunderland 1946/Ashington 1952, retiring May 1952.

A formidable player with Sunderland, Len Duns totalled 245 senior games for the Roker Park club, finding the net on 55 occasions. Raised in Newcastle's West End district, after being rejected by United as a youth, he showed the Magpies what a huge mistake they had made before the Second World War as Len went onto lift both the title and FA Cup in a red-and-white shirt when barely 20 years old. Duns netted five goals for the Wearsiders in their FA Cup run to Wembley during 1937. Although not a big footballer, Duns was strong and sturdy, a fast and direct winger who kept things simple, and scored plenty of goals, being often lethal if he gained a sight of goal. World War Two though ruined what would have been a much rewarding career, and perhaps international recognition. With the Royal Artillery during the hostilities, Duns guested for several clubs, including his rewarding spell with the Magpies on and off over three seasons. When peace was restored, the Tynesider returned to Roker Park for the immediate post-war seasons while he was also a prominent cricketer on the local scene. Len appeared for Benwell Hill CC for many years as a noted batsman, captain in 1954 and 1955 and amassed 1884 runs for the Newcastle club.

Appearances & Goals:
Debut v Hartlepools United (a) 21 October 1939 (FLNE)
War: 20 app 8 gls
Total: 20 app 8 gls

Honours:
FL champs 1936/FAC winner 1937.

DYER Kieron Courtney 1999-2007

Midfield
5'7"
b. Ipswich, 29 December 1978

Career: Whitton Sports BC/Ipswich Town jnr, prof Jan 1997/UNITED July 1999 £7m/ West Ham Utd Aug 2007 £7m (Ipswich Town loan 2010-11)/Queens Park Rangers July 2011 free/ Middlesbrough Jan 2013 free to July 2013 when he retired.

Possessing lightning pace over 10 to 20 yards that can win matches, Kieran Dyer spent eight seasons on Tyneside, and for much of the time was one of United's key assets. Every top modern side craves for his sort of speed in attack, and Dyer's surging runs from midfield gave United a cutting edge. Developed at Portman Road where he made 112 appearances, Ruud Gullit paid £7m for Dyer when he was 20 years old after becoming hot property as he found a regular place in the second-tier of English football and had progressed to the young England line-up. Small and slight, Kieron was destined for the top with ability on the ball and a direct focus. With plenty of energy, he quickly came to terms with the standard of the Premier League preferring the centre of midfield although he was often played in a wide role he disliked, at times to cause friction in the years to follow. Injuries never helped him, being out of action for lengthy periods, notably with hamstring and shin problems, but a fit Dyer was a bonus to United's team plan. Kieron was at his peak in 2002-03, 2003-04 and 2004-05, during the period as Craig Bellamy added the same sort of penetrating velocity in United's attack. He was rated among the best in the country and under Bobby Robson's management Dyer was influential in United's Champions League campaign. Often to make the wrong sort of headlines off the field, Dyer was also notoriously involved in the on-the-pitch altercation with Lee Bowyer at Gallowgate during 2005

and was remarkably booed by his own fans when playing for England at St James' Park during August 2004 after a public outburst when he refused to play in an unfavoured role; at times the Toon Army being fractious with Dyer despite his undoubted exciting ability. At this point his career didn't progress as it should have done and following more injury and illness during 2005 and 2006, the following year was to be Kieron's last in a black-and-white shirt. Now maturing as a person and player, he missed the early part of the 2006-07 programme but returned to help Glenn Roeder's side have a decent run in the UEFA Cup. Injury sidelined him again however, and Dyer moved south during the close-season of 2007, joining West Ham United. At Upton Park, his injury nightmare continued, breaking his leg soon after his debut. Dyer made just 17 starts over three seasons while having moved to QPR he quickly ended up on the sidelines once more after breaking his foot as further mishaps wrecked the latter years of his career. With England he won 33 caps, although Kieron only started eight internationals and most appearances were for short bursts from the bench. He was always seemingly on the fringe yet at times Dyer justified an extended run in his country's shirt, especially when on top form with United. He took part in the 2002 World Cup in Korea-Japan. On retirement in the summer of 2013 Kieran settled in Suffolk and began coaching youngsters in the region.

Appearances & Goals:

Debut v Aston Villa (h) 7 August 1999 (sub)

PL: 169(21) app 23 gls

FAC: 17(1) app 5 gls

FLC: 6(3) app 3 gls

Euro: 30(3) app 5 gls

Total: 222(28) app 36 gls

Honours:

33 Eng caps 2000-08/WdC 2002/3 Eng B app 1998-2007/11 Eng u21 app 1998-2000/Eng sch-youth app/PFA ToS (PL) 2003, (d1) 1998, 1999.

DYSON Keith 1965-1971

Striker

5'10"

b. Blackhill, Co Durham, 10 February 1950

Career: UNITED jnr Jan 1965, prof Aug 1968/Blackpool Nov 1971 cash-exch for A Green/Retired due to injury March 1976/ Lancaster City 1976/ Cleveland Cobras (USA) 1978/ Lancaster City 1979, becoming player-manager cs 1980 to 1982.

Choosing football rather than a place at Leeds University, Keith Dyson appeared for United's senior line-up as an 18-year-old. He was a highly thought of prospect, good enough for international recognition during season 1969-70 when he netted 12 goals for the Magpies. With ability to shield the ball and turn in confined spaces, Dyson created chances for himself in the box and could finish with accuracy. Dyson was calm with an ice-cool temperament and he could strike a ball cleanly. For a while Keith looked likely to develop into a top First Division striker appearing in several of the Magpies' European fixtures. But, like his teenage partner, Alan Foggon, the player never lived up to the early star billing and he moved to Bloomfield Road as part of the deal that brought Tony Green to Gallowgate. In five seasons with Blackpool, Keith grabbed 32 goals in 104 outings before a cruciate knee ligament injury at Southampton halted his senior career. Well qualified academically, Keith later took a computer science course at Lancaster University and emerged with a BSc. He afterwards worked for British Aerospace and British Telecom then began a career in insurance and financial management with Allied Dunbar, eventually returning to the North East, settling near Hexham.

Appearances & Goals:

Debut v Tottenham Hotspur (h) 28 September 1968

FL: 74(2) app 22 gls

FAC: 4 app 1 gl

FLC: 1(1) app 1 gl

Euro: 13(1) 2 gls

Others: 0(2) app 0 gls

Total: 92(6) app 26 gls

Honours:

1 Eng u23 app 1970/Eng sch-youth app.

EASTHAM George Edward OBE 1956-1960

Inside-right or left

5'8"

b. Blackpool, 23 September 1936

Career: Bispham Church/Highfield YC/ Ards amat April 1954, prof Sept 1956 (Distillery (Belfast) guest Jan 1956)/ UNITED May 1956 £9,000/ Arsenal Nov 1960 £47,500/Stoke City Aug 1966 £30,000 (Cleveland Stokers (USA) loan cs 1967)/Cape Town City (SA) player-coach 1970/Hellenic (SA) player-manager Feb 1971/Stoke City Oct 1971, becoming asst-player-manager Dec 1972 (part-time Hellenic (SA) player-manager 1972 to 1974)/Retired Feb 1975/East London Utd (SA) 1975/Stoke City manager March 1977 to Jan 1978/Dynamos (SA) manager 1978/Moroka Swallows (SA) manager 1980/Cape Utd (SA) Director of Scouting 2009.

A midfield master who linked with his colleagues through precision passing, George Eastham came from footballing stock; his father George, appeared for Bolton and England while uncle, Harry (qv), for Liverpool, as well as pulling on Newcastle's colours during wartime football. Blond-haired and slightly built almost to the point of looking frail, Eastham played alongside his father in Ulster for Ards as a 16-year-old before being spotted as a player with huge talent by United scout Bill McCracken. Stan Seymour quickly brought the 19-year-old to Tyneside, developing the youngster rapidly and he blossomed alongside the Welsh maestro Ivor Allchurch in midfield. Although he had an early set-back sustaining a broken leg during April 1957, Eastham recovered and could play equally well on the left or right showing a high level of technical know-how, pin-point passing and the ability to deliver the killer ball. George was a new star, however after becoming a regular for the young England side and certainty for a full cap, Eastham became embroiled in a series of quarrels with United's Board, then a major dispute with the Magpies; an unsavoury affair over, firstly money and a club-house, then eventually the basic right of a footballer to ply his trade wheresoever he chose. George stood up for his principles and, backed by the Players' Union, took football's antiquated authorities and rule-book, as well as Newcastle United, to the High Court and won a historic litigation battle to free, as the media then called footballers, the 'soccer slaves'. Having gone on strike, by the time the long legal process was resolved (in 1963), Eastham had been granted his wish to leave Newcastle, joining the Gunners for a club record fee and the second most expensive man in British football. At Highbury he was another success totalling 223 appearances for the Londoners, captain at Highbury for a period. United lost a special player, one who earned England recognition like his father, making the Eastham duo one of a handful of father and sons to appear for their country. George was included in both the 1962 and 1966 World Cup squads, but was more often than not a deputy for England. He retrospectively received a World Cup winners' medal for the 1966 tournament when FIFA agreed in 2007 to give non-playing members of the squad such medals. Eastham played on until he was over 37 years old, inspiring Stoke to Wembley success and their first major trophy victory in the League Cup final, a match in which he scored the winner. George registered 239 games for the Potters and later moved into coaching and management at the Victoria Ground. Before moving to Ireland as a teenager, George was an apprentice joiner and had trials with Blackpool and Bolton, then worked as a tool-maker in the Harland & Wolff shipyard. In 1978 Eastham emigrated to South Africa, to the Transvaal then Cape Town, and operated a sportswear company. He also coached youngsters for many years in South Africa being a noted opponent of Apartheid. For his services to the game he was awarded the OBE.

Appearances & Goals:

Debut v Luton Town (h) 6 October 1956

FL: 124 app 29 gls

FAC: 5 app 5 gls

Total: 129 app 34 gls

Honours:

19 Eng caps 1963-66/WdC 1962 (no app), 1966 winner (no app)/6 unoff Eng app 1961-66/1 FA app 1960/FA tour 1969/6 Eng u23 app 1960/3 FL app 1960-67/3 NIL app 1955-56/FLC winner 1972/NI GC winner 1955/OBE 1973.

E

EASTHAM Henry 1942

Inside-right
5'8"
b. Blackpool, 30 June 1917
d. Middlesbrough, September 1998

Career: Blackpool amat Sept 1933, prof July 1934/Liverpool Feb 1936 (Southport war-guest 1939-40)(New Brighton war-guest 1939-40) (Leicester City war-guest 1939-40)(Brighton war-guest 1940-44)(Bolton Wand war-guest 1941-42) (UNITED war-guest 1941-42)(Leeds Utd war-guest 1941-43) (Distillery (Belfast) war-guest 1943-44)(Blackpool war-guest 1944-45)/Resumed with Liverpool 1946/Tranmere Rovers May 1948 free/Accrington Stanley July 1953 to 1954/ Netherfield July 1955/Rolls Royce FC 1956 to 1958.

Uncle to Newcastle's George Eastham (qv), this member of the famous Eastham clan was noted for his excellent vision, control and accurate distribution of the ball. Harry Eastham was a craftsman on the field with a deft touch in the family tradition, like his England international brother George senior. Able to play anywhere in attack, Harry took part in a derby meeting with Sunderland for United during January 1942 when in the region on war duties and later assisted his parent club, Liverpool to the title trophy in 1947 alongside Albert Stubbins. He totalled 69 games for the Reds before moving across the Mersey where he clocked up over 150 matches for Tranmere. A knee injury halted his career, Eastham afterwards ran a pub near Bolton for a period.

Appearances & Goals:
Debut v Sunderland (h) 17 January 1942 (FLN)
War: 1 app 0 gls
Total: 1 app 0 gls

Honours:
FL champs 1947/FLN2(WLg) champs 1943 (1 app).

EDGAR David Edward 2002-2009

Centre-half or Full-back
6'2"
b. Kitchener, Ontario (Canada), 19 May 1987

Career: UNITED jnr 2002, prof Sept 2006/Burnley July 2009 £300,000 (Swansea City loan 2009-10, 2010-11)/Birmingham City June 2014 free.

Canadian-born David Edgar graduated from Newcastle's junior ranks to the club's senior bench in season 2006-07. The son of ex-goalkeeper Eddie Edgar (qv), he is one of only three father and son pairings to appear for the club. Thirty years after his father appeared between the posts for the Magpies, David made his debut at Bolton in Premier League action having moved from North America when Eddie, a coach in Canada, sent a group of youngsters to England. David was snapped up by United and settled with relations on Tyneside. Although more at home in central defence, he operated mainly at both right-back and left-back for United when called into senior action as a deputy. With several players fighting for the centre-back positions during his period at the club, Bramble, Moore, Taylor, Ramage, Rozehnal, Cacapa, Diagne-Faye and fellow youngster Paul Huntington, his development was going to have to be something special to claim a place. He did get opportunities during 2008-09 (13 app), the season in which he was included in the Canadian national squad for the first time. However, with new rivals in international defenders Coloccini and Bassong as well as United's relegation, it was little surprise when Edgar moved on. He signed for Burnley, a transfer which ran into a dispute between the two clubs. Edgar enjoyed a special 90 minutes in a Magpie shirt on his home debut; performing well against Manchester United and scoring an equaliser in the 2-2 draw on New Year's Day 2006. David's first six outings in first-team action for the Magpies were remarkably under no less than three different managers; Roeder, Allardyce and Keegan.

Appearances & Goals:
Debut v Bolton Wanderers (a) 26 December 2006
PL: 11(8) app 2 gls
FAC: 2 app 0 gls
FLC: 0(2) app 0 gls
Total: 13(10) app 2 gls

Honours:
22 Can caps 2011-date/Can u20 app/Can sch-youth app/FL ch prom 2014.

EDGAR Edward 1972-1976

Goalkeeper
5'11"
b. Jarrow, 31 October 1956

Career: UNITED jnr Sept 1972, prof Aug 1974/ Hartlepool Utd July 1976 free to March 1979/ North American football/Gateshead Jan 1980/ London City (Can) cs 1980/ Later coaching with University of Waterloo, Ontario (Can), at the Kitchener Minor Soccer School (Can) & London City (Can).

Ideally built for the goalkeeper's position, Eddie Edgar was reserve to Mick Mahoney in Gordon Lee's squad and only once was called upon to deputise for United's first choice custodian, and that in an important Sixth Round FA Cup tie. Immediately following the club's Football League Cup final defeat at Wembley in 1976, the Magpies travelled to the Baseball Ground to face Derby County with a long absentee list. At 19 years old, Edgar came into a patched up side at two hours notice and took part in a terrific match that United lost 4-2 to the reigning League Champions. Newcastle's boss then decided he needed another 'keeper, purchasing Roger Jones and discarded the young Edgar. Following 83 senior matches for Hartlepool at the lower level of football, Edgar quit the English circuit and appeared in Canada both as a 'keeper and as an outfield player. He settled in North America, in Kitchener near Toronto. His son David Edgar (qv) also appeared for the Magpies.

Appearances & Goals:
Debut v Derby County (a) 6 March 1976 (FAC)
FAC: 1 app 0 gls
Total: 1 app 0 gls

ELLIOT Robert 2011-date

Goalkeeper
6'3"
b. Greenwich, London, 30 April 1986

Career: Sittingbourne jnr/Erith Town/Charlton Ath jnr 2003, prof Jan 2005 (Bishops Stortford loan 2004-05) (Notts Co loan 2004-05)(Accrington Stanley loan 2005-06, 2006-07)/UNITED Aug 2011 £100,000.

Part of manager Alan Pardew's squad when he was in charge of Charlton Athletic, Rob Elliot made the move to Tyneside as the 2011-12 season began to rejoin his former boss and goalkeeper coach Andy Woodman, also at Gallowgate. At 25 years of age, Elliot became second-choice custodian behind Tim Krul as long-serving Steve Harper was loaned out to Brighton and eventually moved on. Rob totalled 109 games for the Addicks and also had spells with Notts County and Accrington Stanley on loan, helping the Reds to the Conference title in 2006. Starting in the non-league scene with Erith and Bishops Stortford, the tall, imposing goalkeeper made his debut for Charlton during April 2008 some five years after joining them as a teenager. He was the Londoners regular 'keeper in seasons 2008-09 to 2010-11. On Tyneside, Elliot was only handed sparse opportunities due to the brilliance of Krul, 21 starts in his three seasons so far. He did pull off acrobatic and important saves when in the Number 1 jersey and looked a more than competent goalkeeper reaching the full international squad of the Republic of Ireland.

Appearances & Goals:
Debut v Nottingham Forest (a) 20 September 2011 (FLC)
PL: 11(1) app 0 gls
FAC: 2 app 0 gls
FLC: 3 app 0 gls
Euro: 5 app 0 gls
Total: 21(1) app 0 gls

Honours:
1 Eire cap 2014-date/Eire sch-youth app/FL div 1 champs 2012 (4 app).

ELLIOTT David 1966-1971

Midfield
5'8"
b. Tantobie, Co Durham, 10 February 1945

Career: Wallsend Corinthians/Gateshead 1960/Sunderland jnr 1961, prof Feb 1962/UNITED Dec 1966 £10,000/Southend Utd Jan 1971/Newport Co player-manager April 1975 to Feb 1976/Bangor City player-manager cs 1976 to cs 1978/Newport Co Oct 1978/Caernarfon Town player-manager March 1980 to Feb 1981/Bangor City manager 1981 to Oct 1984.

During the festive period of season 1966-67 with United struggling to climb away from the First Division relegation zone, manager Joe Harvey made a critical decision to sell Alan Suddick in order to raise cash to purchase three players who effectively saved the Black'n'Whites hide. One of those men was Dave Elliott, a compact, chunky midfielder who had been on the fringe of the Sunderland side for several seasons appearing on 36 occasions. Having stamina and tackling ability, he boosted the Magpies' lightweight midfield. With his tigerish play in a spoiler's role, Elliott gave the club excellent service for a brief period, helping the club steer clear of the drop then on onto qualify for a European place for the first time. Although he appeared in Newcastle's opening European fixture against Feyenoord, he was replaced by Benny Arentoft in the midfield worker's role as Newcastle progressed in the Inter Cities Fairs Cup. Elliott moved to serve Southend well, clocking up 194 games for the Roots Hall club. Also a fine local cricketer, Elliott later resided in Anglesey, running a sports shop in Bangor. He had two spells in charge of the Welsh side and took the non-league club to the Northern Premier League title in 1982 then FA Trophy final. At the start of his career Elliott exchanged a job as a motor mechanic to join the Roker Park staff. Dave played his football despite a diabetic condition while his daughter, Louise Elliott, is a BBC Wales television and radio presenter.

Appearances & Goals:
Debut v Tottenham Hotspur (a) 31 December 1966
FL: 78(2) app 4 gls
FAC: 2(1) app 0 gls
FLC: 3 app 0 gls
Euro: 3(1) app 0 gls
Total: 86(4) app 4 gls

Honours:
FL div 2 prom 1964 (5 app)/FL div 4 prom 1972/WsC final 1978/FAT final 1984(m).

ELLIOTT Robert James 1988-1997, 2001-2006, 2008-2009

Left-back or Midfield & Coach
5'10"
b. Gosforth, Newcastle upon Tyne, 25 December 1973

Career: Wallsend BC/UNITED jnr May 1988, prof April 1991/Bolton Wand July 1997 £2.5m/UNITED July 2001 free/Sunderland Aug 2006 free/Leeds Utd Jan 2007 free/Hartlepool Utd July 2007 to cs 2008 when he retired/UNITED asst-coach July 2008 to June 2009/Later taking up a fitness coach role in both the UK and USA.

Robbie Elliott had trials with Manchester United and Southampton before the Magpies snapped him up from the renowned Wallsend Boy's Club. A 17-year-old debutant, Robbie was a versatile player with excellent distribution of the ball who appeared at full-back, in central defence and in midfield for United, always showing a cool and mature assurance on the field. Despite being dogged by serious injury in which he suffered from cruciate ligament, shin splints and medial ligament problems, the richly-talented Elliott bounced back to become an England Under-21 player, one to compete with Newcastle's big-name stars. Although Robbie had several good runs in the side, he was usually second-fiddle to John Beresford, but he enjoyed a good period in midfield as well where his hard, but fair, style of play was effective during 1996-97 as the Magpies finished in runners-up spot in the Premier League and entered Champions League football. Displaying an amusing 'funky-chicken' goal celebration, surprisingly to many, he was then sold to Bolton where, despite a broken leg on his home debut, the Tynesider recorded 103 games. Bobby Robson brought him back to Gallowgate as a 27-year-old and Elliott gave good service when the club again qualified for the Champions League in 2001-02. Injury again, however, saw Elliott on the sidelines before making a swansong wearing the black-and-white during 2004-05. In a fixture with West Ham United, along with Steve Watson, Robbie holds the distinction of being the youngest full-back pairing selected by the Magpies, both being 17 years of age. His elder brother, John, was also on United's books but released without breaking

through. Following a spell back on Tyneside developing a role as a Performance Coach and completing a degree course in Sports Science, Elliott took up a position in the States assisting the US Soccer national set-up as well as for sports giants Nike. Robbie splits his time between North America and his Tyneside home and also set-up the Robbie Elliott Foundation fund-raising venture during 2012.

Appearances & Goals:
Debut v Middlesbrough (a) 12 March 1991 (sub)
FL/PL: 126(16) app 11 gls
FAC: 12(4) app 0 gls
FLC: 9(1) app 0 gls
Euro: 17(2) app 1 gl
Others: 1 app 0 gls
Total: 165(23) app 12 gls

Honours:
2 Eng u21 app 1996/Eng sch-youth app/PL runner-up 1996 (6 app), 1997/FL ch winner 2007 (7 app)/FL div 1 prom 2001.

ELLISON Raymond 1966-1973

Right or Left-back
5'7"
b. Newcastle upon Tyne, 31 December 1950

Career: UNITED jnr July 1966, prof Oct 1968/Sunderland Feb 1973 £10,000/Torquay Utd July 1974 free/Workington Town July 1975/Gateshead Feb 1977/Tow Law Town/Whitley Bay player-coach June 1980/Alnwick Town manager Nov 1983 to 1984.

One of United's many home grown full-back discoveries during the Sixties and Seventies, Ray Ellison stood in for both David Craig and Frank Clark during the 1971-72 season and always gave a sound if not spectacular display. However, the emerging talent of Alan Kennedy and Irving Nattrass from the junior ranks saw Ellison surplus to manager Joe Harvey's requirements and the Tynesider headed for Roker Park where he was used again as full-back cover and only managed two appearances. Ray then moved to the South West with Torquay and afterwards turned out for the Reds of Workington on 64 occasions, at Borough Park when they were voted out of the Football League in 1977. Ellison later returned to the North East and became a taxi driver for a period, then a meat wholesaler.

Appearances & Goals:
Debut v Derby County (h) 2 October 1971
FL: 5 app 0 gls
FLC: 1 app 0 gls
Others: 1 app 0 gls
Total: 7 app 0 gls

EMRE (Belozoglu) 2005-2008

Midfield
5'8"
b. Istanbul (Turkey), 7 September 1980

Career: Gunesspor Jnrs (Trk) 1988/Zeytinburnuspor SK (Trk) March 1990/Galatasaray SK (Trk) 1995/Internazionale (It) July 2001 free/UNITED July 2005 £3.8m/Fenerbahce SK (Trk) July 2008/Atletico Madrid (Sp) June 2012 free/Fenerbahce SK (Trk) Jan 2013 free.

Small but well-built, Turkish international Emre Belozoglu (Emre being his Christian name, but also playing-name) was a noted footballer on the European scene when he moved to the North East as a 24-year-old from Milan giants Internazionale during the summer of 2005. He cost a £3.8m fee and was well-liked by boss Graeme Souness, a fan of Turkish football from his own days in that country. Emre had the ability in midfield to turn matches, a play-maker in a central role. Although never commanding an automatic spot in the Nerazzurri midfield, he spent three seasons at the San Siro totalling 108 games, taking part in Champions League action, including against United during 2002-03. Starting his career as a teenager with Galatasaray, where he followed Gheorghe Hagi, the talented Emre was a celebrated name in Istanbul, dubbed the "Maradona of the Bosporus". He first appeared for his country in 2000, and went onto to earn almost a

E

century of caps all told, being skipper on occasion. Having much technical acumen with the ball, in Toon colours the Turkish star was able to create and score goals, including a special derby winner against Sunderland, and showed up well in United's engine-room on several occasions. He was influential at times during 2005-06 and 2006-07, but all too often the Turk was on the sidelines injured. With a left-foot as good as any in a Toon shirt over modern times, Emre fell out of favour when Glenn Roeder took charge and moved back to Turkey, joining Istanbul's other foremost club Fenerbahce during the summer of 2008 where he once more became a huge favourite of the local crowd. At times over his career Emre was involved in controversy, banned from international football for a period after a controversial bust-up on the field when Turkey faced Switzerland during 2006, while he was twice involved in difficult racist allegations, in England following a United game at Everton, and in Turkey when playing for Fenerbahce. Emre missed the 2000 UEFA Cup final after being dismissed in the semi-final against Leeds.

Appearances & Goals:
Debut v RC Deportivo La Coruna (h) 3 August 2005 (ITC)
PL: 46(12) app 5 gls
FAC: 2(2) app 0 gls
FLC: 4(1) app 0 gls
Euro: 11(2) app 1 gl
Total: 63(17) app 6 gls

Honours:
91 Trk caps 2000-date/WdC 2002/12 Trk u21 app 1998-99/Trk sch-youth app/Trk Lg champs 1997 (1 app), 1998, 1999, 2000, 2011, 2014/Trk Cup winner 1999, 2000, 2012, 2013/It Cup winner 2005/ESC winner 2000, 2012/Trk PoY 2010.

ENGLISH Andrew 1940-1943

Centre-forward
b. Fawdon, Newcastle upon Tyne

Career: Coxlodge Jnrs/UNITED amat May 1940, prof Sept 1940 to 1943 (Gateshead war-guest 1942-43)/Gosforth & Coxlodge 1943.

Brought up in the northern suburbs of Newcastle, around Coxlodge and Fawdon, Andrew English worked as a brass fitter at a local engineering works, RB Charlton Ltd, on Tyneside and joined United's staff after scoring plenty of goals in junior league football for Coxlodge. A centre-forward who possessed dash and craft, Andrew had a good run in the club's side during season 1940-41 when he held the Number 9 shirt, with regular leader Albert Stubbins moving to inside-forward. English also assisted neighbours Gateshead during wartime football, but he never had a crack at the senior Football League scene when the post-war boom started in 1946.

Appearances & Goals:
Debut v Leeds United (h) 7 September 1940 (FLN)
War: 23 app 6 gls
Total: 23 app 6 gls

ENRIQUE (Sanchez Diaz) José 2007-2011

Left-back
5'11"
b. Valencia (Spain), 23 January 1986

Career: Levante UD (Sp) jnr 2002, prof 2004/ Valencia (Sp) cs 2005 (RC Celta Vigo loan 2005-06)/ Villareal July 2006/UNITED Aug 2007 £6.3m/ Liverpool Aug 2011 £7m.

Much like his Spanish speaking colleague Fabricio Coloccini, full-back Jose Enrique (Sanchez Diaz being his surname) needed a season to settle on Tyneside. An expensive import as an emerging defender at over £6m from Villareal, Enrique looked out of sorts to begin with as United struggled in the Premier League during season 2007-08 and 2008-09. However, as Jose settled to life on Tyneside and the English style of football, the Spaniard rapidly showed why he had been a promising talent in his native country. Strong on the ball and in the challenge, his productive sorties down the left flank were noticeable and set up many of United's attacking moves, while his partnership with Jonas Gutierrez was a feature of the Magpies' play. With excellent close control and the skill to slip past opponents, Enrique was hailed as one of the stars of the 2010 Football League Championship winning season, but then fell into dispute with the club's hierarchy over a new contract and was snapped up by Liverpool for a £7m fee as the Magpies returned to top level action. He was unlucky to miss most of the

2013-14 season due to injury as the Reds challenged for the Premier League title. In Spain, Jose was nicknamed 'El Toro' (the Bull) for his aggressive style of play and before he received a break in the game with first Celta Vigo, then at El Madrigal with Villareal, worked cleaning cars on the Costa del Azahar.

Appearances & Goals:
Debut v Barnsley (h) 29 August 2007 (FLC)
FL/PL: 111(8) app 1 gl
FAC: 6 app 0 gls
FLC: 4 app 0 gls
Total: 121(8) app 1 gl

Honours:
2 Sp u21 app/Sp sch-youth app/FL ch winner 2010/FAC final 2012/FLC winner 2012/PFA ToS (ch) 2010.

EVANS Reginald 1954-1959

Outside-left
5'9"
b. Consett, Co Durham, 18 March 1939

Career: West Stanley/UNITED jnr Oct 1954, part-time prof March 1956 £25, prof July 1957/Charlton Ath March 1959 exch for J Ryan/Ashington July 1960 to 1962.

A hard hitting forward who liked to raid from the wing, Reg Evans had tough competition for the Number 11 shirt at Gallowgate at the time, with no fewer than four rivals in McGuigan, Luke, Punton and the great Bobby Mitchell. Likened to another great, Tynesider Jimmy Mullen of Wolves, he was unfortunate to be injured on a tour of Ireland after just breaking into the United line-up. A damaged ankle hindered the rest of his St James' Park career and Evans tried his luck at The Valley after a swop deal with 'Buck' Ryan, but again he couldn't force his way into the first eleven on a regular basis totalling only 14 games in Second Division action. Evans returned to the region living in his native Consett and for over 30 years was employed by Newcastle Breweries at their complex, a mere goal-kick from St James' Park.

Appearances & Goals:
Debut v Wolverhampton Wanderers (a) 20 September 1958
FL: 4 app 0 gls
Total: 4 app 0 gls

EVANS Thomas John 1927-1929

Left-back
6'0"
b. Maerdy, Glamorgan, 7 April 1903

Career: Maerdy Sept 1923/Clapton Orient May 1924/United Dec 1927 £3,650/Retired due to injury May 1929/Clapton Orient June 1930 free/Merthyr Town July 1932.

The first Welsh international to appear for Newcastle United and only the second Welshman ever, Tom Evans was purchased as a replacement for the aging Hudspeth shortly after the Championship trophy was secured in 1927. A tall and athletic full-back, Tom was an exceptionally skilled defender who could fight for the ball and who had caught the eye in FA Cup ties for Orient, including against the Magpies during 1925-26. Evans though, didn't have the best of times at St James' Park being the target of sections of the crowd, perhaps being rushed into top level action too soon. Tom had atrocious luck with knee injuries throughout his career and was on the sidelines during most of his stay on Tyneside, eventually calling it a day during the close-season of 1929. However, he did make a comeback back in London, switching to a centre-half role, but Tom was never the same battling player again. He was nicknamed 'Con' by his team-mates; Evans registered 87 games for Clapton Orient.

Appearances & Goals:
Debut v Arsenal (a) 10 December 1927
FL: 13 app 1 gl
Total: 13 app 1 gl

Honours:
4 Wales caps 1927-28/WsL app 1932.

FAGAN William John 1942

Inside-left
5'10"
b. Inveresk, near Musselburgh, 20 February 1917
d. Wellingborough, 29 February 1992

Career: Balgonia Scotia/Wellesley Jnrs March 1934/
Celtic jnr June 1934, prof March 1935/Preston North
End Oct 1936 £3,500/Liverpool Oct 1937 £8,000
(Aldershot war-guest 1939-44)(Leicester City
war-guest 1940-41)(Northampton Town war-guest
1940-45)(Celtic war-guest 1941-42)(UNITED
war-guest 1942-43)(Chelsea war-guest 1943-44)
(Millwall war-guest 1944-45)(Reading war-guest 1944-45)(Crystal Palace war-guest
1945-46)/Resumed with Liverpool to 1951, becoming asst-trainer/Distillery (Belfast)
player-manager Jan 1952/Weymouth player-manager July 1952 to 1955.

*A Scotland wartime cap, Bill Fagan took part in two FA Cup finals, one either side of
war in 1937 and 1950. He was one of several Liverpool players to play for United
during wartime and then with Albert Stubbins in the Reds' title winning side of 1946-
47 while he also appeared in the War South Cup final for Chelsea, during one of his
many sojourns in the conflict. With United at the beginning of season 1942-43 when
stationed in the region, he was auburn-haired and well built; the Scot began as an
intelligent schemer who during his later days moved to a deeper half-back role in
midfield. With a bustling style, Fagan turned out for the Anfield club over 250 times
and scored more than 100 goals including wartime action. He was a very effective
player and was skipper of the Reds for a period. Bill later worked at a borstal in Dorset
while his uncle 'Jean' McFarlane appeared with Celtic and Middlesbrough.*

Appearances & Goals:
Debut v Bradford Park Avenue (h) 29 August 1942 (FLN)
War: 2 app 0 gls
Total: 2 app 0 gls

Honours
1 Scot war app 1945/1 Scot unoff app 1944/FL champs 1947/FL div 3(S) champs 1946
(3 app)/FAC final 1937, 1950/WC(S) final 1944/FLN2(WLg) champs 1943.

FAIRBROTHER Jack 1947-1952

Goalkeeper
6'0"
b. Church-Gresley, near Burton upon Trent,
16 August 1917
d. Titchmarsh, Northants, 17 October 1999

Career: Burton Town/Preston North End March
1937 (Blackburn Rovers war-guest 1939-
43)(Burnley war-guest 1940-41) (Chester war-
guest 1942-43)/ UNITED July 1947 £6,500/
Peterborough Utd player-manager June 1952/
Coventry City manager Dec 1953 to Oct 1954/
Israel FA national coach 1955 to March 1959/
Consett manager c1961/Gateshead manager
June 1962/Peterborough Utd manager Dec
1962 to Feb 1964.

*Jack Fairbrother was a tall, confident and stylish goalkeeper who made great studies
of positioning and the shooting styles of attackers during his career. He was also a
renowned humorist in United's dressing-room, always ready with a grin or a practical
joke and a most popular character. Unlucky to make his first senior appearance for
Preston in the aborted 1939-40 campaign just prior to the Second World War,
Fairbrother did not make his Football League debut until he was approaching 30 years
of age, having to be content with wartime soccer in which he was good enough to
appear for the Football League select team and in several representative wartime
fixtures. At Deepdale Jack took over from international Harry Holdcroft and was a
regular for the Lilywhites through the hostilities and as peace was restored, claiming
155 games. Settling at St James' Park, Jack replaced Garbutt and Swinburne and was
United's regular 'keeper over four seasons, a safe pair of hands who seldom made
spectacular stops, relying more on the examination of angles he had worked on
relentlessly. Fairbrother was an automatic selection in Newcastle's line-up until a
broken collar bone forced him out of the Magpie eleven allowing the younger Ronnie
Simpson to take his place. He was a safe custodian for Newcastle, some judges
considering he was good enough for an England cap during his heyday at the end of
the Forties. A former policeman during the war, for a time Jack wore white police
gloves on the field as a gimmick, Fairbrother left United with a touch of bitterness,
unable to reclaim his place and somewhat harshly shown the door. Afterwards, Jack
entered management and was a bright young manager until tragedy struck when he*

*was in charge at Highfield Road. Jack's wife was killed after a
domestic accident and he was left a widower with two young children.
A nephew of England and Everton player, George Harrison, his brother Tony
appeared for Burton Albion. Fairbrother later resided in Titchmarsh near
Kettering.*

Appearances & Goals:
Debut v Plymouth Argyle (h) 23 August 1947
FL: 132 app 0 gls
FAC: 12 app 0 gls
Total: 144 app 0 gls

Honours:
1 FL app 1942/FL div 2 prom 1948/FAC winner 1951/WC winner 1941/FLN(WLg) champs
1941.

FAIRHURST David Liddle 1929-1946

Left-back
5'8"
b. Blyth, 20 July 1906
d. Solihull, 26 October 1972

Career: Blyth Spartans/New Delaval Villa/UNITED
amat May 1924/Blyth Spartans/Walsall June 1927/
UNITED March 1929 £1,750 (Hartlepools Utd war-
guest 1939-40)(Wrexham war-guest 1943-44)/Retired
May 1946/Birmingham City trainer and later physio
July 1946 to c1960.

*Curly-haired Dave Fairhurst was a stout-hearted,
reliable defender rather than a flamboyant footballer.
He was at his best when under pressure, in the thick of
the action and for a decade served the Black'n'Whites
with credit. A former Tyneside pit lad and shipyard
worker, Dave had trials at St James' Park before moving
to sign for Walsall, but United brought him back to his
native North East after a spell in the Midlands where he showed his potential in 59
games for the Saddlers. Dave replaced Bob Thomson at left-back and became a regular
full-back as the 1930s began. During the Magpies' FA Cup run to Wembley in 1932
he was an ever-present and it wasn't until the Second World War approached, and
Dave was well into his thirties, that the club found a replacement. The sturdy frame
of Fairhurst reached the England side, while he occasionally appeared at right-back
as well as once taking to the wing when he was injured and still managed to net two
goals against Nottingham Forest during 1935. With Birmingham City for a long period
behind the scenes, he was part of the Blues' set-up as they became one of the first
English clubs to sample European football, facing Barcelona in the Fairs Cup during
1957-58. Dave retired and lived in Solihull to his death. From a family of footballers,
his father, Davy Fairhurst turned out for the Spartans also, while brother Bill did
likewise as well as appearing for Southport, Nelson, Hartlepool and Northampton.*

Appearances & Goals:
Debut v Derby County (a) 27 April 1929
FL: 266 app 2 gls
FA Cup: 18 app 0 gls
Others: 1 app 0 gls
Total: 285 app 2 gls

Honours:
1 Eng cap 1934/FAC winner 1932.

FARRIER Charles Surtees Greenfield 1918-1920

Outside-right
5'5"
b. Wallsend, 21 April 1894
d. Newcastle upon Tyne, 4 April 1982

Career: Close works XI/UNITED amat 1918, prof
May 1919/Ashington Aug 1920 free/Gateshead
to 1922.

*Lightly framed, fast and tricky on the ball, Charles
Farrier was a regular contender for the wing spot
in the club's local and Victory League competitions
during 1918-19. The Newcastle Daily Journal noted that he showed, "proof of his
qualification as an aspirant for a place on the First League team". By the time Division
One football had returned, Farrier earned a new contract for the 1919-20 season,*

F

however, the Tynesider didn't progress as expected and moved to Ashington. Charles was also a noted boxer and professional sprinter under the pseudonym of 'Charlie Bradley' and once topped the bill at St James' Hall. He was a favourite at the renowned Powderhall race meeting in Edinburgh and at the Victoria running track on Tyneside. Farrier was later employed at a local colliery and at Parson's Heaton complex in the city.

Appearances & Goals:
Debut v Hartlepools United (h) 11 January 1919 (NVL)
War: 7 app 0 gls
Total: 7 app 0 gls

FASHANU Justinus Soni 1991

Centre-forward
6'1"
b. Hackney, London, 19 February 1961
d. Shoreditch, London, 2 May 1998

Career: Shropham/Attleborough/Peterborough Utd/ Norwich City jnr Sept 1977, prof Dec 1978 (Adelaide City (Aust) loan cs 1980)/Nottingham Forest Aug 1981 £1m (Southampton loan 1982-83)/Notts Co Dec 1982 £150,000/Brighton June 1985 £115,000/ Retired due to injury 1986/Los Angeles Heat (USA) player-manager June 1986/ Edmonton Brickmen (Can) July 1988/Manchester City Oct 1989/West Ham Utd Nov 1989/Ipswich Town trial Feb 1990/ Leyton Orient March 1990/Southall player-coach March 1991/UNITED trial Oct 1991/ Leatherhead Town Nov 1991/Toronto Blizzard (Can) 1991/Torquay Utd Dec 1991, becoming asst-manager June 1992 to Jan 1993/ Motherwell Feb 1993/Airdrieonians Feb 1993/IFK Trelleborg (Swd) May 1993/Heart of Midlothian July 1993 to Feb 1994/ Toronto Blizzard (Can) March 1994/Maryland Mania (USA) coach 1994/Miramar Rangers (NZ) Oct 1996/Atlanta Ruckas (USA) 1997.

At one stage in his career, Justin Fashanu was one of the country's biggest names as he moved from Carrow Road to Brian Clough's Forest for £1 million, at a time when a seven figure transfer sum was rare. Hitting the headlines as Norwich City's leading marksman (40 goals in 103 app), winning BBC's Match of the Day's Goal of the Season award in 1980, his move to the big-time with the Garibaldi Reds was unproductive, Fashanu not seeing eye to eye with Forest's controversial boss. The tall, muscular striker never fulfilled the promising talent which earned him England Under-21 and 'B' honours, partly due to troublesome knee injuries which at one point forced him out of the game. He moved around from club to club trying to restart his career, eventually landing at St James' Park when almost 31 years old in a bid to resurrect his playing days at the top. Given a chance by Ossie Ardiles, his stay with United was short, only 11 days, and his deceptive skill and explosive shooting of ten years before had all but vanished. A former Barnado's Boy of African parents, Fashanu was a past schoolboy ABA heavyweight champion and before concentrating on a footballing career was a steel erector. His brother John also starred with Norwich then later for Wimbledon and England. Justin tragically committed suicide during 1998 when aged 37, being depressed and wanted by police. During 1990 he had been one of the very first in Britain to publically admit to being a gay footballer, and had to cope with an enormous media focus on his lifestyle.

Appearances & Goals:
Debut v Peterborough United (a) 29 October 1991 (FLC) (sub)
FLC: 0(1) app 0 gls
Total: 0(1) app 0 gls

Honours:
1 Eng B app 1980/11 Eng u21 app 1980-83/Eng sch-youth app.

FAYE Amdy Mustapha 2005-2006

Midfield
6'1"
b. Dakar (Senegal), 12 March 1977

Career: Monaco (M/Fr) jnr c1995/ES Frejus (Fr)/ Auxerre (Fr) July 1998/Portsmouth Aug 2003 £1.5m/UNITED Jan 2005 £2m/Charlton Ath Aug 2006 £2m (Rangers loan 2007-08)/Blackburn Rovers trial Jan 2008/Stoke City Aug 2008 £2m/Leeds Utd Sept 2010 to Jan 2011.

One of a wave of footballers to land in English football during modern years from the African continent, Amdy Faye settled on Tyneside as a central midfielder during the January 2005 transfer window. Having been an up and coming footballer with Auxerre over four seasons (94 app) he made an impression in England as part of Portsmouth's midfield. After 52 games at Fratton Park, Faye was a £2m signing by Graeme Souness to boost midfield and the first impression in Toon colours was good, the 27-year-old Senegal international showing the Tyneside public he was an accomplished anchor man, dominating the midfield in a FA Cup tie against Coventry City. He displayed composure on the ball and accurate short passing ability. But against inferior opponents such as the Sky Blues he was given time to dictate the play, in Premier League action it was a different story. Faye rarely looked at ease after that as he featured regularly in a black-and-white strip over the next season-and-a-half adding a defensive quality to the Magpies' middle line, although rarely advancing far up the pitch, usually found camped in and around the centre-circle making short link passes. He later moved to Stoke during 2008, being joined by his ex-United namesake Abdoulaye Faye, but never claimed a fixed place at the Britannia Stadium, making only 23 outings for the Potters. During November 2007 he was one of several men interviewed in connection with a major football corruption investigation into transfers, although no charges were progressed.

Appearances & Goals:
Debut v Coventry City (h) 29 January 2005 (FAC)
PL: 22(9) app 0 gls
FAC: 3 app 0 gls
FLC: 1(1) app 0 gls
Euro: 9 app 0 gls
Total: 35(10) app 0 gls

Honours:
31 Seng caps 2001-06/WdC 2002/ACN final 2002/Fr Cup winner 2003/UEFAC final 2008 (sub no app).

FAYE Diagne Abdoulaye 2007-2008

Centre-Half
6'2"
b. Dakar (Senegal), 26 February 1978

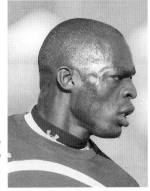

Career: ASEC Ndiambour (Seng) 1999/ ASC Jeanne D'Arc (Seng) 2001/RC Lens (Fr) July 2002 (FC Istres (Fr) loan 2004-05)/Bolton Wand Aug 2005 £750,000 after loan/UNITED Aug 2007 £2m/Stoke City Aug 2008 £2.25m/West Ham Utd July 2011 free/Hull City July 2012 free to June 2014.

Abdoulaye Diagne-Faye was tall, strong and positive in the challenge and joined the United bandwagon after a successful spell with Bolton (72 app). Although from Dakar, like his namesake Amdy Faye, at St James' Park during the same era, they are not related although the pair did play together for the Senegal national side. Sam Allardyce was Faye's boss at the Reebok and when Big Sam moved to Tyneside he saw Faye as the ideal commanding figure for the pivotal role in the Black'n'Whites defence and paid £2m to bring him to Gallowgate. Although he could also operate in midfield or at full-back, the Senegalese looked the part at the centre of the Magpies defence during much of season 2007-08, an effective partner alongside either Steven Taylor or Cacapa always showing accurate distribution of the ball. With Allardyce being replaced, Faye then became embroiled in something of a bust up with management at Gallowgate and headed for the Britannia Stadium at the start of the new 2008-09 season, United losing a defender who could have become a lynch-pin to United's rearguard. He spent three seasons in the Potteries, helping Stoke (84 app) to Premier League stability and the FA Cup final, later rejoining Allardyce at West Ham where he became a key part of the Hammers promotion to the top level.

(Note: There is some debate over his surname which may be Diagne-Faye, but he used Faye in English football.)

Appearances & Goals:
Debut v Derby County (a) 17 September 2007 (sub)
PL: 20(2) app 1 gl
FAC: 1 app 0 gls
FLC: 1 app 0 gls
Total: 22(2) app 1 gl

Honours:
35 Seng caps 2006-10/FL ch prom 2012, 2013/FAC final 2011 (sub no app).

Inside-left
5'8"
b. Grangetown, near Middlesbrough, 26 August 1910
d. Grangetown, near Middlesbrough, 5 March 1973

Career: Normanby Magnesite/Grangetown St Mary's/Whitby Utd 1928/South Bank/Whitby Utd Oct 1930/UNITED Dec 1930 £25/Notts Co June 1932 £500/Lincoln City June 1933 exch/ Stockport Co Feb 1934/Halifax Town Aug 1934/Chester May 1937/Darlington Feb 1938 to cs 1939/Ferryhill Ath committee Dec 1948.

A deputy to United schemer Harry McMenemy, Tommy Feeney made all his appearances for the Magpies during the club's FA Cup winning season of 1931-32. A popular reserve, the Teessider possessed neat skills, but also a temperament that could explode on the field at times. After leaving Gallowgate, Feeney proceeded to have a useful career in the Third Division North, markedly at the Shay Ground with Halifax where he appeared on 57 occasions and with Darlington, registering impressive statistics of 43 matches and 25 goals.

Appearances & Goals:
Debut v West Ham United (h) 30 January 1932
FL: 4 app 1 gl
Total: 4 app 1 gl

Outside-left
5'10"
b. Cleethorpes, 4 January 1936
d. Grimsby, 2 February 2011

Career: North Thoresby/Waltham (Grimsby) 1953/ Grimsby Town amat 1953, prof April 1954/ Everton March 1961 £18,500/UNITED March 1962 £3,000 plus G Heslop/Walsall July 1963 £5,000/ Lincoln City Jan 1964/ Boston Utd Jan 1966 to cs 1969/Skegness Town July 1969/Ross Group FC Sept 1970/ Empire Utd 1972-73/Deborah Lindsey 1977.

Tall, slim and direct, Jimmy Fell had a turn of speed which often frightened full-backs. One of the Mariner's finds during the late Fifties when he was working at the Courtaulds factory, he played on 174 occasions for Grimsby netting 35 goals before catching the attention of Everton. But it was at Blundell Park that Fell played his best football, although for a season with the Black'n'Whites, in 1962-63, he did look to be an effective winger, scoring 16 goals and becoming the Magpies top scorer in Second Division fare. But after this fine showing, Jimmy dropped out of favour with manager Joe Harvey and was replaced by Colin Taylor. When he retired, Fell returned to the Grimsby area and was employed in a leisure centre for over 20 years and back at Courtaulds as a colourist. His son, James (junior), began a Football League career with Grimsby too but failed to make the first-eleven. Both father and son speared together for Grimsby Sunday League team Deborah Lindsey during 1977.

Appearances & Goals:
Debut v Middlesbrough (a) 7 March 1962
FL: 49 app 16 gls
FAC: 2 app 0 gls
FLC: 2 app 1 gl
Total: 53 app 17 gls

Centre-forward
6'0"
b. Paddington, London, 8 December 1966

Career: Barandon Eagles/Harrow Club/ The Jaguars/Viking Sports/Southall 1983/Akna 1986/Hayes cs 1986/Queens Park Rangers March 1987 £30,000 (plus £590,000 when joined Newcastle) (Brentford loan 1987-88)(Besiktas JK (Trk) loan 1988-89)/UNITED June 1995 £6m/ Tottenham Hotspur Aug 1997 £6m/West Ham Utd Jan 2003 £200,000/Leicester City July 2003 free/ Bolton Wand July 2004 free/Reading Jan 2005 free to May 2005/Watford Sept 2005 free/Retired cs 2006/ Tottenham Hotspur asst-coach Nov 2008, becoming coach Jan 2014 to June 2014.

Prior to becoming United's record purchase at the time for a fee of £6 million, the tall and powerful Les Ferdinand was one of the most effective strikers in the Premiership, being fast, having a ferocious shot, as well as supreme authority in the air. After being tracked by Kevin Keegan for several months, he settled on Tyneside during the summer of 1995 from Queens Park Rangers with a record of 90 goals in 184 outings. He was the Magpies' long awaited replacement for Andy Cole, and the new Number 9 made an immediate impact, leading the line with drive and genuine menace. He became the spearhead to a United side bursting with attacking talent. Known as 'Sir Les' and capped by England, Ferdinand grabbed 29 goals as United just missed the Premiership crown with the striker receiving the Player of the Year award at the end of that campaign; the first Newcastle star to be awarded that prestigious honour. With an excellent all round game, judges considered Les alongside Alan Shearer as one of the most complete English strikers of his generation. Immensely popular on Tyneside, Ferdinand then found himself partnered by new signing Shearer for season 1996-97 and the £21m strike force showed they were the best in the business. Despite being a phenomenal success, United controversially sold the Londoner when a £6m bid from Spurs was lodged for the now 30-year-old during the summer of 1997. United's Chairman Freddy Shepherd later confirmed the sale was a mistake and "a great partnership was broken up". Les spent over five years at White Hart Lane (149 app 39 goals), subsequently appearing for West Ham United, Leicester, Bolton and Reading. During the early part of his career, he was something of a late developer in the first-class game; Ferdinand appeared on the capital's non-league scene reaching the FA Vase final before being picked up by QPR. However he did not blossom until Les had a successful spell in Turkey with Besiktas when he made a big impact in Istanbul netting 21 goals in 33 games, including the winning strike in the Turkish Cup final. He played on until nearing 40 years old while the Londoner worked in the media as well as being attached to his boyhood favourites Spurs as a specialist striker coach. He is a cousin of Rio and Anton Ferdinand while along with other United strikers Cole, Owen and Shearer, remains one of the Premier League's top goal scorers of all time. Les was awarded the MBE in 2005, far from Ferdinand's life-style before turning professional, when he had a number of jobs including those of decorator, shop-assistant, van driver and car cleaner. Brought up streetwise in Notting Hill of West Indian parents, Les was a first-class ambassador for all his clubs; always immaculately turned out and able to communicate with the media, very much a role model of a modern superstar. Ferdinand also is frequently a television expert summariser.

Appearances & Goals:
Debut v Coventry City (h) 19 August 1995 (1 goal)
PL: 67(1) app 41 gls
FAC: 4(1) app 2 gls
FLC: 6 app 3 gls
Euro: 4 app 4 gls
Others: 1 app 0 gls
Total: 82(2) app 50 gls

Honours:
17 Eng caps 1993-98/WdC 1998 (no app)/1 unoff Eng app 1996/1 Eng B app 1998/PL runner-up 1996, 1997/FLC winner 1999/FLC final 2002/FAV final 1986/Trk Cup winner 1989/PoY 1996 (PFA)/PFA ToS (PL) 1996/MBE 2005.

F

FEREDAY Wayne 1989-1990

Outside-left
5'9"
b. Warley, near Birmingham, 16 June 1963

Career: Queens Park Rangers jnr, prof Sept 1980/UNITED June 1989 £400,000/Bournemouth Nov 1990 £150,000/West Bromwich Albion loan Dec 1991, pmt Feb 1992 £60,000/Cardiff City March 1994 free/ Merthyr Tydfil 1995/Telford Utd Oct 1995 to Dec 1995/Later with Dorchester Town July 2001/Christchurch 2002.

It was during season 1980-81 that Wayne Fereday made a name for himself as a new teenage star at Loftus Road. He enjoyed an impressive first outing, netting twice on his Football League debut during 1980 as a 17-year-old, and Fereday developed well with QPR pulling on his country's shirt at Under-21 level. Lithe and extremely quick, one of the fastest players on the circuit, he appeared on almost 250 occasions for the Londoners before heading north to team up with his previous manager Jim Smith at St James' Park. Able to take on defenders and get in a dangerous cross, Wayne however, did not do his reputation justice, rarely showing his previous form on Tyneside. He admitted later that the move to Tyneside was a big mistake as he struggled to impress or have any rapport with the Geordie crowd. He also operated at full-back while Fereday was often on the sidelines through injury and Wayne soon headed back south as part of the deal that brought Gavin Peacock to Gallowgate. After leaving the first-class game, he resided in the Christchurch area of Dorset employed in several roles, latterly with the Cooke's Furniture store but also keeping in touch with the game covering fixtures for the Press Association and PFA as well as coaching youngsters in the south.

Appearances & Goals:
Debut v Leeds United (h) 19 August 1989
FL: 27(6) app 0 gls
FAC: 1 app 0 gls
FLC: 3(1) app 0 gls
Others: 1(2) app 0 gls
Total: 32(9) app 0 gls

Honours:
5 Eng u21 app 1985-86/1 FL app 1988/FL div 2 champs 1983 (5 app)/FL div 2 prom 1993/WsC final 1994.

FERGUSON Brian James 1979-1980

Midfield
5'11"
b. Irvine, Ayrshire, 14 December 1960

Career: Mansfield Town jnr 1977/UNITED Jan 1979/ Hull City Dec 1980 free/Goole Town Aug 1982 (Bridlington Trinity loan)/Southend Utd Aug 1983/ Chesterfield loan Oct 1984, pmt Dec 1984, becoming asst-coach to Dec 1988/Skegness Town cs 1989 becoming asst-manager 2003, and then manager.

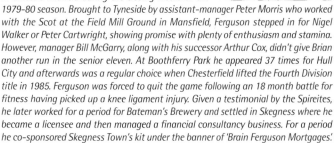

Youngster Brian Ferguson was handed an opportunity in United's midfield during the closing weeks of the 1979-80 season. Brought to Tyneside by assistant-manager Peter Morris who worked with the Scot at the Field Mill Ground in Mansfield, Ferguson stepped in for Nigel Walker or Peter Cartwright, showing promise with plenty of enthusiasm and stamina. However, manager Bill McGarry, along with his successor Arthur Cox, didn't give Brian another run in the senior eleven. At Boothferry Park he appeared 37 times for Hull City and afterwards was a regular choice when Chesterfield lifted the Fourth Division title in 1985. Ferguson was forced to quit the game following an 18 month battle for fitness having picked up a knee ligament injury. Given a testimonial by the Spireites, he later worked for a period for Bateman's Brewery and settled in Skegness where he became a licensee and then managed a financial consultancy business. For a period he co-sponsored Skegness Town's kit under the banner of 'Brain Ferguson Mortgages.'

Appearances & Goals:
Debut v Burnley (h) 7 April 1980 (sub)
FL: 4(1) app 1 gl
Total: 4(1) app 1 gl

Honours:
FL div 4 champs 1985.

FERGUSON Duncan Cowan 1998-2000

Centre-forward
6'4"
b. Stirling, 27 December 1971

Career: Carse Thistle 1988/Dundee Utd Feb 1990/ Rangers July 1993 £4m/Everton loan Oct 1994, pmt Dec 1994 £4.3m/UNITED Nov 1998 £8m/Everton Aug 2000 £4.75m/ Retired May 2006/Everton asst-coach Oct 2011, becoming coach Feb 2014.

Imposing Scot Duncan Ferguson may have cost United big money at £8m, and only stayed on Tyneside for less than two years, of which several weeks were on the sidelines through injury, nevertheless his talent as a centre-forward was not lost on United's knowledgeable supporters. They knew a top player and Ferguson was just that. Purchased by Ruud Gullit from Everton in November 1998, at 6'4" tall, the former Rangers and Dundee United star was in many ways a perfect partner for Alan Shearer up front, although no-one (apart from the manager) never quite knew if he was an actual replacement for Shearer. He began well on Tyneside, with a brace against Wimbledon and United's support took to him from the start. But then a groin injury struck after only five games and he just about missed the rest of the season, arriving back late on the scene as the Geordies headed for Wembley in the FA Cup. Ferguson wasn't quite fit, but ended up in Newcastle's eleven for both the semi-final and final of that run. With a physical presence, he was a menace in the air to any defence, yet for such a big man he possessed a delicate touch of the ball, able to control, hold and spot an opening. Ferguson knew where the goal was, hitting the net with several beauties in a Toon shirt including a stunning hooked volley against Manchester United. Like Shearer, Duncan was combative, and the duo for a short time had no equals in the Premier League. Although having a list of misdemeanours north of the border, culminating in a 12 match ban (later overturned by Court action) then being convicted for the on-pitch assault of Raith's John McStay when playing for Rangers and spending six weeks in Glasgow's Barlinnie Prison during 1995, on Tyneside Ferguson rarely gave his managers Gullit and Robson any trouble. Although he played more often in 1999-2000, the big Scot was injured again and moved back to Goodison Park where he enjoyed his football the most. The fiery Caledonian remains a legend at Gwladys Street, captain of Everton and totalling 273 games (72 goals) for the Blues. Due to his feud with the game's authorities north of the border, Ferguson only won a handful of caps for his country due to a self-imposed international exile, although the Scots were at the time desperate for a player of his ability up front. After leaving the game in 2006, Ferguson resided in the Balearic Islands involved in property development for a period before heading back to Merseyside and starting a coaching career. Duncan is related to Scotland defender Willie Cunningham and his brother-in-law is snooker player John Parrott.

Appearances & Goals:
Debut v Wimbledon (h) 28 November 1998 (2 goals)
PL: 24(6) app 8 gls
FAC: 6(2) app 3 gls
Euro: 2(1) app 1 gl
Total: 32(9) app 12 gls

Honours:
7 Scot caps 1992-97/6 Scot u21 app 1992-93/Scot sch-youth app/FAC winner 1995/FAC final 1999/SL champs 1994, 1995 (4 app)/SC final 1991, 1994.

FERGUSON Robert Burnitt 1953-1962

Left-back
5'10"
b. Dudley, near Newcastle upon Tyne, 8 January 1938

Career: Dudley/UNITED amat June 1953, prof May 1955/ Derby Co Oct 1962 £4,000/Cardiff City Dec 1965 £7,500/ Barry Town player-manager Dec 1968/Newport Co player-manager July 1969 £250, dismissed as manager Nov 1970, but remained as player until May 1971/Hereford Utd player-coach cs 1971/Ipswich Town asst-coach July 1971, becoming coach, asst-manager and manager Aug 1982 to May 1987/Al-Arabi SC (Kwt) manager June 1987/ Birmingham City asst-manager June 1989 to Jan 1991/

Colchester Utd coach April 1991/Coventry City scout 1991/Sunderland coach June 1992 to May 1993, being caretaker-manager Feb 1993/Later scout for a number of clubs including Sunderland until he retired 2011.

Bobby Ferguson's handful of appearances for the Magpies were spread over nine seasons, being an able stand-in for Irishman Alf McMichael when the noted international was at his peak. From a footballing background, both his father, Bobby, and uncle, Eddie, turned out in senior football, for West Bromwich Albion and Chelsea respectively while another uncle, Luke Curry, played for Bury. Although Ferguson made his debut as an 18-year-old, he was given little opportunity at St James' Park, being overtaken by the younger Colin Clish as the Sixties unfolded. Yet Ferguson grasped his chance at both Derby and Cardiff appearing in over 100 games at both the Baseball Ground and Ninian Park. Bobby tasted European football with the Bluebirds as Cardiff reached the European Cup Winners Cup semi-final. He later developed into a respected coach, notably at Portman Road as assistant to Bobby Robson for a lengthy period, replacing Newcastle's future boss when he took charge of England. A former England Boy's trialist and apprentice electrician at Seaton Burn pit, when on National Service with the Commando force, Ferguson represented the Army select eleven.

Appearances & Goals:
Debut v Manchester City (h) 7 April 1956
FL: 11 app 0 gls
FAC: 1 app 0 gls
Total: 12 app 0 gls

FERGUSON Shane Kevin 2007-date

Left-back
5'9"
b. Eglinton, near Londonderry, 12 July 1991

Career: Eglinton Eagles (Derry) 1997/Maiden City (Derry) 2001/UNITED jnr July 2007, prof June 2009 (Birmingham City loan 2012-13, 2013-14).

Raised in the historic walled city of Derry in Northern Ireland, Shane Ferguson pushed his way into contention for a first-team call-up as a teenager during season 2009-10 having greatly impressed United's manager and coaching staff. Supporters of junior and reserve fixtures gave glowing reports too and it was no surprise when he was blooded in the first-team for a Football League Cup-tie during August 2010. Slightly built but with quick feet and the bite of a terrier, Ferguson soon was in the reckoning for a Northern Ireland cap, having graduated quickly through his country's Under-21 ranks. Before he appeared in the Magpies' first-eleven Shane made his full debut against Italy during June 2009 when still not 18, considered to be one of United's youngest international players at 17 years 329 days old. Operating either on the left of midfield or as an attacking left-back, the young Ulsterman has the ability to go past opponents and deliver a telling cross, while he is quick to recover and track back into a defensive position. Under Lee Clark and Terry McDermott's guidance at St Andrews on loan, Shane was a regular in the Championship. As a schoolboy in Northern Ireland, he also played Gaelic football and was a noted player for his country at youth level, able to pursue that sporting career had he wished. But having travelled to the North East with his junior club, Shane was spotted by United's coaching staff as a genuine prospect, joining the Magpies along with another Maiden City youngster, Michael McCrudden.

Appearances & Goals:
Debut v Accrington Stanley (a) 25 August 2010 (FLC)
FL/PL: 7(16) app 0 gls
FAC: 0(1) app 0 gls
FLC: 3(1) app 0 gls
Euro: 3(1) app 0 gls
Total: 13(19) app 0 gls

Honours:
16 NI caps 2009-date/1 NI B app 2009/11 NI u21 app 2008-12/NI sch-youth app.

FERRIS Paul James 1981-1986, 1993-2006, 2009

Outside-left & Physio
5'8"
b. Lisburn, near Belfast, 10 July 1965

Career: Lisburn Jnrs/UNITED jnr Dec 1981, prof March 1983/Gateshead Sept 1986 free/Port Vale trial Oct 1986/ North Shields Feb 1988/Barrow Aug 1989/Whitley Bay Aug 1990/Retired Nov 1991/UNITED asst-physio Oct 1993 to Aug 2006, rejoining the club's medical team, April to May 2009.

Many United supporters who watched Paul Ferris play considered he should have been given an extended opportunity in the Magpies' first eleven instead of sitting on the substitutes' bench for long periods. Signing for Newcastle as a youth fresh from Ulster, Ferris was highly rated as a teenager and quickly reached the fringe of firstly, Arthur Cox's side, then Jack Charlton and Willie McFaul's team. He became the club's youngest ever debutant at the time, at 16 years 294 days old, but the management resisted selecting Ferris more than his one full match, although he came on as a replacement from the bench in 12 outings, and was named in the squad on many occasions without getting into the action. Fast and marauding on the flank, Paul had good control, but was unluckily one of those players who didn't get the break at the right time while he also received a bad medial knee ligament injury sustained in training which kept him on the treatment list for nine months. That injury subsequently forced him out of the first-class game when only 21 years of age and Ferris had a spell in a lower grade of football, tasting success at Wembley with Barrow and winning silverware with Whitley Bay. Ferris later returned to St James' Park following a period training in physiotherapy and working at Newcastle's Freeman Hospital, appointed by his former skipper Kevin Keegan, as assistant-physio. The Irishman spent over 22 years as a valued back-stage aide until he decided a change in career direction. Taking legal exams, Paul successfully qualifying as a barrister although he returned to Gallowgate briefly as part of Alan Shearer's set-up in 2009 then left the game once more. A man of many talents, he settled in Northumberland and penned a novel 'An Irish Heartbeat' during 2011 before becoming Managing Director of Speedflex, a performance gym in Jesmond.

Appearances & Goals:
Debut v Blackburn Rovers (a) 1 May 1982 (sub)
FL: 1(10) app 0 gls
FLC: 0(2) app 1 gl
Total: 1(12) app 1 gl

Honours:
NI sch-youth app/FAT winner 1990.

FIDLER Albert 1929-1930

Goalkeeper
5'11"
b. Newcastle upon Tyne, 1906 (Q4)

Career: Spen Black'n'White/Gosforth BL Swifts/ UNITED Aug 1929 £25/Walker Celtic Aug 1930/ Gosforth & Coxlodge BL cs 1931/Blyth Spartans trial Aug 1932/Retired due to injury Oct 1932/Newcastle Co-op 1935 to c1937Also appeared for Newburn.

A reserve guardian with Newcastle who had showed up well in local Tyneside football, Bert Fidler was third choice goalkeeper for a season at Gallowgate, behind Albert McInroy and Micky Burns. The Geordie was called upon on five occasions during the 1929-30 season at a time of injury crisis; he had the harrowing experience of conceding five goals on his debut at Upton Park against West Ham United. Fidler later returned to the local North East semi-professional scene and lifted the Newcastle Wednesday League title in 1935 with the local Co-op eleven.

Appearances & Goals:
Debut v West Ham United (a) 9 September 1929
FL: 5 app 0 gls
Total: 5 app 0 gls

FINDLAY John 1905-1906

Right-half
5'9"
b. Scotland
d. probably France, [20 September 1916]

Career: Leven Victoria/Nitshill Utd/UNITED May 1905/
Vale of Leven June 1906/Airdrieonians June 1909/
Vale of Leven Aug 1910.

Brought down to Tyneside from Scottish non-league football on the recommendation of the Newcastle's large scouting network north of the border, John Findlay deputised for Alex Gardner in United's formidable Edwardian line-up during season 1905-06. A midfielder with plenty stamina, the local press noted he was "a capable understudy" who was "cool and steady". Capped at junior level in Scotland, he returned north within a year and continued his career in the Scottish Second Division with Vale of Leven (75 app) and Airdrie (22 app). It is noted he died during the First World War, however details cannot be traced.

Appearances & Goals:
Debut v Bolton Wanderers (h) 23 December 1905
FL: 2 app 0 gls
Total: 2 app 0 gls

Honours:
Scot Jnr app.

FINLAY John 1909-1930

Left-half & Trainer
5'10"
b. Riccarton, Kilmarnock, 19 October 1882
d. Newcastle upon Tyne, 31 March 1933

Career: Kilmarnock Shawbank/Rangers March 1904/Airdrieonians June 1904/
UNITED May 1909 £775, retiring May 1927, becoming asst-trainer to 1930.

Known more commonly as 'Jock' on Tyneside, John Finlay was a grand servant to United for 14 seasons as a player. Shown the exit door by Rangers after just a single match, Finlay found a place with Airdrie and arrived at St James' Park as a talented player, a regular in over 150 games and part of the Diamonds line-up for five seasons when they challenged at the top of the Scottish First Division. During the years up to World War One, he was a largely a reserve to two great Scots, Peter McWilliam and Jimmy Hay, being twice reserve in FA Cup finals, in 1910 and 1911. Then, after peace was restored, Jock found a place himself in United's attractive side of the early 1920's. Popular in the dressing-room with what was called as a "dry Scotch humour", Finlay was described by one colleague as "a born leg puller". A team-man, Jock worked hard and rarely placed a pass astray on the field. He was on the fringe of a full Scotland cap, while he later gave the Magpies valuable service in the club's North Eastern League side by coaching youngsters. On leaving the game, Finlay went into business in Newcastle and on his death in 1933 it was recorded that his ashes were scattered from the top of Scafell in the Lake District.

(Note: Club ledgers indicate Finlay was born in 1892, however when birth records were checked, it has been discovered he was in fact 10 years older. Additionally, the careers of two other players John Findlay (qv) and reserve AJ Finlay, also to play for Airdrie during the same era, have at times become entangled in various sources of research.)

Appearances & Goals:
Debut v Blackburn Rovers (a) 4 September 1909
FL: 153 app 8 gls
FAC: 8 app 0 gls
War: 12 app 1 gl
Total: 173 app 9 gls

Honours:
1 SL app 1909/Scot trial app 1920.

FINNEY Thomas, Sir OBE CBE 1942

Outside-right
5'8"
b. Preston, 5 April 1922
d. Preston, 14 February 2014

Career: Preston North End amat May 1937, prof Jan 1940 (UNITED war-guest 1942-43) (Southampton war-guest 1942-43)(Bolton Wand war-guest 1942-43)/Resumed with Preston, retired April 1960, becoming a Preston director and later President/ Distillery (Belfast), briefly Sept 1963.

One of the most famous players in the English game and a football knight, Tom Finney pulled on the black-and-white shirt of Newcastle United for six games during the 1942-43 season. And on one occasion he scored a memorable hat-trick for the Magpies against Gateshead during November 1942 as United won an epic by 7-4. Winning 76 caps for his country, netting 30 goals, Finney was also selected on many occasions for the FA XI and Football League, while Tom was twice named Footballer of the Year. Slightly built, he was a genius with the ball at his feet and could play on the flank or through the centre-forward channel. Able to create and score, he showed in a consistent fashion the touch of the master he was. During World War Two, Finney served with the Royal Armoured Corps and saw action in Egypt with Monty's Eighth Army. Tom spent time in the north on training at Catterick and appeared for the Magpies during that period when a 20-year-old. As a youth Finney served as an apprentice plumber, hence his later nickname of the 'Preston Plumber', he developed rapidly as a player as the Fifties began, and was a one-club man at Deepdale for over 23 seasons and 472 games (210 goals), retiring when 38 years of age. Finney was associated with Preston for all of his adult life, later as the club's highly respected figurehead. He did have a brief stay in Belfast, appearing for Distillery in a European Cup clash with Benfica during 1963. Following a marvellous career ranked alongside the immediate post-war greats such as Matthews and Milburn, Finney settled in his native Preston running a plumbing and electrical business, also for a time a reporter for the News of the World, a magistrate and chairman of Preston Health Authority. Honoured with the Freedom of Preston, a statue of a celebrated picture catching Tom sliding on a wet surface, the 'The Splash', is located outside Deepdale. On his death in 2014 a civic funeral was held in Preston.

Appearances & Goals
Debut v Bradford Park Avenue (a) 5 September 1942 (FLN)
War: 6 app 3 gls
Total: 6 app 3 gls

Honours
76 Eng caps 1947-59/WdC 1950, 1954, 1958/2 Eng B app 1947-48/17 FL app 1948-56/10 Eng unoff & FA app 1945-61/FL div 2 champs 1951/FAC final 1954/WC winner 1941/FLN(WLg) champs 1941/FoY 1954, 1957 (FWA)/FL Long Service award 1961/FL Legend/Eng HoF/Freeman of Preston 1979/Knighted 1998, OBE 1961, CBE 1992.

FLANNIGAN David 1928-1929

Left-half
5'10"
b. Glasgow, 1906

Career: Kelty Rangers/Third Lanark March 1926/ UNITED June 1928 £2,500/East Stirlingshire loan May 1929, pmt Nov 1929 free/Arbroath July 1930/ Coleraine Aug 1931/Ballymena Utd Sept 1931/ Glenavon July 1932/Belfast Celtic/Ballymena Utd Nov 1933.

David Flannigan was, at 22 years of age, a much sought after half-back when United secured his signature from Glasgow club Third Lanark. Being a regular selection in the Third's line-up for seasons 1926-27 and 1927-28, he took part in a high standard of football in Scotland's First Division. Although possessing plenty of skill on the ball, Flannigan lacked the stamina and pace to succeed in the English league. He appeared on a handful of occasions during season 1928-29 as a stand-in for Joe Harris, but received few opportunities thereafter.

Appearances & Goals:
Debut v Aston Villa (a) 15 September 1928
FL: 3 app 0 gls
Total: 3 app 0 gls

FLEMING John BM 1911-1913

Centre-forward
5'9"
b. Slamannan, Stirlingshire, c1890
d. Yorkshire, 21 March 1916

Career: Bonnyrigg Rose/Edinburgh St Bernard's 1909/
UNITED April 1911 £250/Tottenham Hotspur May 1913
£300/Armadale cs 1915/Rangers Nov 1915 to demise.

*A bright and breezy Scot, John Fleming crossed the border
as a reserve to United's talented Edwardian side. He made
a great start in a black-and-white jersey, netting four
times on his debut during a tour match against Koln.
Fleming was given an opportunity during season 1912-13, tried along with several
others when Albert Shepherd was badly injured. Like many of his fellow countrymen,
Fleming had good skills and was described as a bustling forward with a good shot
but couldn't fill the leader's role on a regular basis. He was a deputy at White Hart
Lane too, while his brother, Bill, was also on Tottenham's books just prior to World
War One. Briefly with Rangers, John scored in the first minute of his debut for the
Ibrox club. Sadly, in the Great War Fleming sustained wounds in action at Ypres during
the Battle of Langemarck while serving with the Queen's Own Cameron Highlanders
in trench warfare on the Continent. It is noted he died at a military hospital in
Yorkshire.*

*(Note: Tottenham's annals note the player as being James Brown Montgomerie
Fleming but the player is John Fleming, facts being mixed up with another Scottish
war hero who died in the same era and who possessed the same initials of JBM
Fleming. Major James Brown Montgomerie-Fleming hailed from a notable Glasgow
family and had no football connection.)*

Appearances & Goals:
Debut v Tottenham Hotspur (a) 23 November 1912
FL: 4 app 0 gls
Total: 4 app 0 gls

FOGGON Alan 1965-1971

Striker
5'9"
b. West Pelton, Co Durham, 23 February 1950

Career: West Stanley/UNITED jnr Aug 1965,
prof Nov 1967/Cardiff City Aug 1971 £25,000/
Middlesbrough Oct 1972 £10,000 plus player/
Rochester Lancers (USA) April 1976/Hartford
Bi-Centennials (USA) June 1976/ Rochester
Lancers (USA) cs 1976/ Manchester Utd July
1976 £40,000/Sunderland Sept 1976 £25,000/
Southend Utd June 1977 £15,000 (Hartlepool
Utd loan 1977-78)/ Consett Aug 1978/
Whitley Bay.

*Alan Foggon was potentially a star find who had
developed through United's junior set-up during
the late Sixties. He was a 17-year-old debutant
at Highbury and for a while looked like solving
Newcastle's problem wing position when he hit
the First Division on a regular basis during season 1968-69. The teenager was a happy-
go-lucky kid when he burst onto the scene, perhaps characterising the era; he was
trendy with long flowing hair and had a somewhat untidy appearance on the field,
socks down and shirt outside his shorts. But Foggon also showed he had ability to
destroy defences with direct running at pace and he linked well with Wyn Davies and
Bryan Robson in United's attack. Alan could play wide or inside, and was on the fringe
of a regular place as the Magpies lifted the Inter Cities Fairs Cup, scoring a wonderful
goal as a substitute during the final in Budapest. He reached the young England set-
up and saw off more experienced rivals Jim Scott and Jackie Sinclair before losing his
way at Gallowgate through erratic form. Alan appeared for several clubs afterwards
and was a big hit at Boro under Jack Charlton, becoming Middlesbrough's top scorer
as the Teessiders were promoted to Division One with 19 goals and all told recorded
50 goals in 142 matches. He was a popular character at Ayresome Park, affectionately
nicknamed 'The Flying Pig' due to his 13 stone frame. A former England schoolboy
sprint champion, Foggon became a publican in Jarrow and Spennymoor and for a
period had a career with a security company on Tyneside. One of only a handful of
players who have turned out for the North East's three major clubs, wearing
Sunderland's red-and-white stripes on 10 occasions towards the end of his career,
Foggon walked out of the first-class game when only 28 years of age somewhat
disillusioned with professional football.*

Appearances & Goals:
Debut v Arsenal (a) 10 February 1968
FL: 54(7) app 14 gls
FAC: 4 app 0 gls
FLC: 1(1) app 0 gls
Euro: 10(3) app 2 gls
Total: 69(11) app 16 gls

Honours:
Eng sch-youth app/FL div 2 champs 1974/FL div 4 prom 1978/ICFC winner 1969/WsC
final 1972.

FORD David 1969-1971

Outside-left
5'7"
b. Sheffield, 2 March 1945

Career: Sheffield Wed amat Sept 1961, jnr
Jan 1962, prof Jan 1963/UNITED Dec 1969
cash-exch deal for J Sinclair/Sheffield Utd
Jan 1971 exch deal for J Tudor/Halifax Town
Aug 1973 to cs 1976.

*At the time of joining Newcastle United,
David Ford was the latest acquisition in an
attempt to find a consistent wide player to
give service to big Wyn Davies at centre-
forward. Having made a name for himself at
Hillsborough, being a key figure in
Wednesday's run to Wembley in 1966, Ford
had become one of football's most promising players until a fatal car accident
intervened. His fiancée was killed and David was badly hurt with knee and head
injuries and it took the England Under-23 player some time to recover. Stockily built
with powerful legs, Ford was quick and with potent shooting was always able to find
the net scoring 37 goals in 135 app for the Owls. However, at Gallowgate he only
gave the Tyneside crowd glimpses of the form he had shown in Wednesday's blue.
It wasn't long before he returned to Sheffield in a deal that saw 'keeper John Hope
also head for Bramall Lane and John Tudor arrive in the North East. Operating also in
midfield, he only pulled on the Blades' colours in 31 games before ending in Division
Three with Halifax Town (98 app). On retiring from soccer Ford ran a mechanical and
heating services business in his native city while he also had interests in the city's
Champs Sports Bar as well as the Cross Sythes pub in Totley. David remained
associated with the Owls, running the club's Executive Club for a period.*

Appearances & Goals:
Debut v Ipswich Town (h) 20 December 1969 (1 goal)
FL: 24(2) app 3 gls
FAC: 1(1) app 0 gls
Euro: 3 app 0 gls
Total: 28(3) app 3 gls

Honours:
2 Eng u23 app 1967/FL div 2 prom 1971/FAC final 1966.

FORD Joseph Charles 1931-1934

Centre-forward
5'5"
b. Canongate, Edinburgh, 20 September 1910
d. Leith, April 1951

Career: Rosewell Rosedale/UNITED May 1931 £40/
Partick Thistle Jan 1934/Leith Ath Feb 1934/Penicuik
Ath July 1935/Benford (Edinburgh) player & secretary.

*Joe Ford captivated United's reserve crowds with his
twinkling feet and audacious play in front of goal.
Much likened to Hughie Gallacher in style as well as
build, he was extremely popular on Tyneside and
nicknamed 'Hughie' after the recently departed centre-
forward hero. One of the smallest players ever to turn out for the club, Joe was
described as having, "the heart of a lion", and the ability to take on a whole defence.
With everything going well for the little Scot, hitting 20 goals in the North Eastern
League for the Magpies, including three hat-tricks, Joe came in for Jack Allen on his
debut against Grimsby. However, tragedy struck midway through the first-half when
Ford collided into goalkeeper Tommy Reid. He was carried from the field, albeit to a*

F

rousing and sympathetic reception, after sustaining a double fracture of his leg. And this after his landlady gave Joe a 'lucky rabbit's foot' to put in the stocking of his United strip for good luck! Ford took a long time to regain fitness and never recaptured his previous eye-catching form, or a place in the Magpies' first eleven. The Scot served in the Merchant Navy during the war, on hanging up his boots he spent a lengthy period in local football around Midlothian and was employed at the Holyrood Brewery of William Younger. Ford resided near to Easter Road and died of tuberculosis.

Appearances & Goals:
Debut v Grimsby Town (h) 16 January 1932
FL: 1 app 0 gls
Total: 1 app 0 gls

FORSTER Leslie James 1943

Outside-right
5'9"
b. Byker, Newcastle upon Tyne, 22 July 1915
d. Newcastle upon Tyne, June 1986

Career: Walker Celtic/Blackpool April 1936 £200 (UNITED war-guest 1942-43)(Gateshead war-guest 1942-45)/ York City Sept 1946/Gateshead Feb 1947 to 1948.

Born and bred in Byker, Leslie Forster took over the right wing position at St James' Park for a period during the spring of 1943. Having made his Football League debut for Blackpool during the season prior to war breaking out, his promising career was devastated by the hostilities and totalled only two senior games at Bloomfield Road. After war had ended he tried to make a go at a football career once more in the Third Division North, but managed only 10 outings with York and 15 for Gateshead before leaving the stage.

Appearances & Goals:
Debut v York City (a) 13 March 1943 (WC)
War: 3 app 0 gls
Total: 3 app 0 gls

FORSTER William Birkett 1932-1938

Right-back
5'7"
b. Walker, Newcastle upon Tyne, 28 May 1909
d. Whitley Bay, 23 February 1975

Career: Howdon British Legion/UNITED amat Sept 1932, prof Nov 1932 £25/Southend Utd Aug 1938 £150/Bristol Rovers July 1939.

A strong and thoughtful defender who had good positional sense, William Forster was reserve to Joe Richardson at St James' Park and never let the side down. Although deputising only occasionally, he was an important figure in the club's second eleven as they moved from local football into the stronger Central League featuring many top clubs from Northern England and the Midlands. On leaving his native Tyneside to further his career, Forster struggled to claim a place at both Southend and Bristol Rovers, totalling only nine matches at senior level.

Appearances & Goals:
Debut v Burnley (h) 8 February 1936
FL: 3 app 0 gls
Total: 3 app 0 gls

FOULKES William Isaiah 1951-1954

Inside or Outside-right
5'7"
b. Merthyr Tydfil, 29 May 1926
d. Hoole, Chester, 7 February 1979

Career: Cardiff City amat Feb 1945, prof June 1945/ Winsford Utd/Chester May 1948/UNITED Oct 1951 £11,500/Southampton Aug 1954 £5,000 cash-exch for T Mulgrew (Winsford Utd loan 1955-56)/Chester July 1956 £1,000/Hyde Utd July 1961.

Billy Foulkes was a compact, strong and stocky forward who had a dramatic rise to fame after joining United as a replacement for Ernie Taylor. He moved from the lower

leagues to St James' Park for a large fee and made his debut in the First Division within three days of his arrival. A week later came his first international outing against England, Billy scoring after four minutes with his first kick of the ball! Big in character, Foulkes complimented Jack Milburn well and continued making headlines for that 1951-52 season, ending a quite amazing six months by helping the Magpies lift the FA Cup at Wembley, an ever-present in United's cup run. At his peak during that campaign one commentator noted that he was "just as dangerous as a Matthews or a Finney when given the right ball". Billy possessed a stinging shot, was versatile, operating on the wing or at inside-forward, but after that bright opening the Welshman's face never quite fitted at Gallowgate. He moved to The Dell in a cash-exchange deal valued at £12,500 but suffered a back injury soon after and the Saints complained to the Football League requesting the transfer be reversed with the Magpies repaying £5,000. The dispute was ruled in Newcastle's favour to the annoyance of Southampton. Foulkes soon moved back to the Welsh border, serving Chester in a second spell. He was skipper of the blue-and-whites and amassed 326 matches (38 goals) over his two periods at Sealand Road. Bill resided in that city running a milk-bar in the tourist centre.*

Appearances & Goals:
Debut v Huddersfield Town (a) 13 October 1951
FL: 58 app 8 gls
FAC: 10 app 1 gl
Total: 68 app 9 gls

Honours:
11 Wales caps 1952-54/FAC winner 1952/WsC final 1958.

FOX Ruel Adrian 1994-1995

Outside-right
5'6"
b. Ipswich, 14 January 1968

Career: Whitton Utd 1980/ Ipswich Town jnr/ Norwich City jnr Oct 1983, prof Jan 1986/ UNITED Feb 1994 £2.25m/ Tottenham Hotspur Oct 1995 £4m/West Bromwich Albion Aug 2000 £200,000/Retired May 2002/Southend Utd trial Sept 2002/Whitton Utd player-coach Feb 2004 to 2008, becoming Chairman 2009, as well as, Montserrat head-coach Oct 2004 & Suffolk College coach Nov 2008.

Ruel Fox became the first of Newcastle United's multi-million pound men as they reinforced their position as one of the game's superclubs during 1994. Small, tricky and blessed with pace, Fox could be a handful for any defence and operated in the modern style, on the right or left-wing or in midfield. Rising to prominence in over 200 games as part of Norwich City's entertaining line-up which did well in the UEFA Cup, Ruel was an immediate hit with United's crowd, showing delightful ball skills as he gave service to Andy Cole in the box. Elevated to within a whisker of the full England set-up, winning 'B' honours, Fox also could be relied upon to grab goals, especially when cutting in from the touchline to hit a drive. However, the addition of David Ginola and Keith Gillespie to Kevin Keegan's international squad, meant Ruel could only claim a substitute's place as the 1995-96 season began. Fox wanted first-team action and moved to White Hart Lane for nearly double the fee Newcastle paid the Canaries. In London, Fox was again an inspiration at times and pulled on the cockerel shirt on 129 occasions. Descending from the Caribbean island of Montserrat, Fox later appeared for and coached their national side as well as acting as a talent scout. Ruel also ran a restaurant for a period and set up his own personal training business in Suffolk.

Appearances & Goals:
Debut v Wimbledon (a) 12 February 1994
FL: 56(2) app 12 gls
FAC: 5 app 0 gls
FLC: 3 app 1 gl
Euro: 4 app 1 gl
Total: 68(2) app 14 gls

Honours:
2 Eng B app 1994-95/2 Mnts caps 2004/PL runner-up 1996 (4 app)/FL div 1 prom 2002.

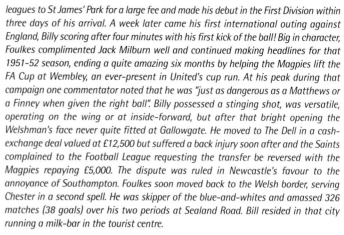

106

FOYERS Robert 1895-1897

Left-back
5'9"
b. Hamilton, Lanark, 22 June 1868
d. Glasgow, 16 August 1942

Career: Hamilton Palace Colliery/Burnbank Swifts c1888/ Edinburgh St Bernard's 1889/Heart of Midlothian Aug 1890/Edinburgh St Bernard's 1890/UNITED May 1895 £100/Edinburgh St Bernard's April 1897/Clyde June 1897 to Oct 1897/Wishaw Aug 1899/ Hamilton Acc Aug 1901/Adventurers Aug 1904.

Bob Foyers settled at Gallowgate from Scotland with a reputation of defensive expertise. An experienced international north of the border, he was appointed captain of United and showed a relentless and a shrewd attitude towards his game during season 1895-96. Short and well built, Bob was a touch temperamental and was often in trouble with Newcastle's hierarchy. He was stripped of the captaincy after "misconduct" in December 1895 and later censored for being, "worse for liquor"! Not surprisingly perhaps, he left the club soon after, replaced by White and Jackson. By profession, Foyers was a mechanical engineer, he was one of three brothers to appear for St Bernard's.

Appearances & Goals:
Debut v Loughborough (h) 7 September 1895
FL: 34 app 0 gls
FAC: 5 app 0 gls
Total: 39 app 0 gls

Honours:
2 Scot caps 1893-94/Scot trial app 1889-94/Scot Jnr app/SC winner 1895/SJC winner 1889, 1890.

FRANKS Albert John 1953-1960

Wing-half
5'10"
b. Boldon, Co Durham, 13 April 1936

Career: Jarrow Police/South Tyne Jnrs/Boldon CW/ Sunderland amat 1953/UNITED Dec 1953 £50/Rangers March 1960 £6,500 (Morton loan 1961-62)/Lincoln City Nov 1961/Queen of the South Jan 1964 free/ Scarborough player-manager June 1964 to Dec 1965.

A tall, powerful, barrel-chested half-back who operated equally well on the right or left side of the field, Albert Franks also possessed the stamina to last the hard slog of 90 minutes in the midfield battleground. An ex-police cadet and captain of the Durham youth side, Albert began his career at St James' Park as a stand-in for either Jimmy Scoular or Tommy Casey, but by season 1957-58 earned a place for himself. With a mighty long throw too, Franks proved an effective player for two seasons with progressive use of the ball. The arrival of Charlie Mitten as boss though saw him drop down the pecking order and signalled the end of his days at St James' Park. Albert moved to Scotland to sign for Rangers, one of only a few Englishmen to have joined the Ibrox club up to that time. Also a fine cricketer, Franks was unfortunate to be forced to spend 18 months of his time at Gallowgate on National Service, a period of this in Germany where he represented the RAF. Following his stay in Glasgow, Albert appeared for Lincoln (66 app) and Scarborough (55 app) before returning to his teenage pursuit of becoming a policeman. Joining the Durham Constabulary, Franks became a commended detective and served 22 years in the force while he also played for and managed the local police football eleven. Albert resided near Chester-le-Street and on retiring from the police force acted as a security consultant. With a Methodist background, Franks has been a lifelong teetotaller.

Appearances & Goals:
Debut v Luton Town (a) 16 February 1957
FL: 72 app 4 gls
FAC: 3 app 0 gls
Total: 75 app 4 gls

FRASER John 1899-1901

Outside-left
5'11"
b. Dumbarton, 10 November 1876
d. Stoke Newington, 1 October 1952

Career: Dumbarton Oct 1896/Motherwell Aug 1897/Notts Co Feb 1898 £70 (Morton loan 1898-99)/UNITED June 1899/St Mirren July 1901/Southampton May 1902/Dundee May 1905 to 1913/Chelsea scout 1919, becoming asst-manager to 1925, then scout once more to c1940.

Scot John Fraser was a workmanlike, courageous and lively outside-left who packed a thundering shot at goal. A hefty forward, tall and weighty for a wing man, but Fraser possessed good command over the ball. Known as 'Jack', he sported a finely manicured moustache in the fashion of the day and took over from the popular figure of Willie Wardrope at St James' Park. The winger had two good campaigns in a black-and-white shirt as the century closed, described in one contemporary biography as a "splendid dribbler", he was good enough to be on the fringe of an international call-up, reaching Scottish trial games. Fraser later became a firm favourite at The Dell, scoring a hat-trick on his debut for the Saints, while at the end of his playing career back in Scotland, he turned in brilliant performances for Dundee over 212 matches which earned him a Scottish Cup medal and eventually that Scottish cap he had been close to earlier in his career. With Chelsea for a lengthy period on retiring from playing football, Fraser was involved in negotiating the deal that saw Hughie Gallacher move from Tyneside to Stamford Bridge during 1930.

Appearances & Goals:
Debut v Everton (h) 9 September 1899
FL: 49 app 9 gls
FAC: 3 app 0 gls
Total: 52 app 9 gls

Honours:
1 Scot cap 1907/1 SL app 1902/Scot trial app 1901-07/SC winner 1910/SC final 1897/SnL champs 1903, 1904.

FRASER Robert 1947-1950

Right-back
6'0"
b. Glasgow, 23 January 1917
d. Newcastle upon Tyne, 11 April 2003

Career: Dunoon Ath/Ashfield/Hibernian Aug 1937 (Dumbarton war-guest 1939-40)/UNITED Jan 1947 £3,750/Retired July 1950, becoming a United scout.

Cool and versatile in defence, Bob Fraser appeared for United mainly at full-back, but also filled in at centre-half. After serving with the Glasgow Highlanders in Germany during the war and appearing in several wartime representative matches, Bob was purchased at a time of an injury pile-up and the experience Fraser held from pre-war football served United well, especially during the club's promotion success in 1947-48 when he totalled 20 games. A broken foot though put Bob out of action and eventually the younger Bobby Cowell replaced Fraser in United's side. After scouting for the club for a period, he concentrated on a stock-broking business as well as running a sports wholesale company on Tyneside, residing in Ponteland. Robert's brother, William, appeared for Partick Thistle.

Appearances & Goals:
Debut v Nottingham Forest (h) 1 January 1947
FL: 26 app 0 gls
FAC: 1 app 0 gls
Total: 27 app 0 gls

Honours:
FL div 2 prom 1948/Scot SnLC winner 1944.

F

FROST Arthur Douglas 1939-1946

Centre-forward
5'11"
b. Walton, Liverpool, 1 December 1915
d. North Sefton, near Liverpool, October 1998

Career: New Brighton amat July 1938, prof Aug 1938/UNITED March 1939 £2,515 (New Brighton war-guest 1939-42)(Wrexham war-guest 1941-43)(Southport war-guest 1942-44)(Tranmere Rovers war-guest 1942-46)/Resumed with United Jan 1946, but released/South Liverpool player-manager 1946.

Arthur Frost showed Newcastle United's scouts that he was a player with lots of potential when appearing for New Brighton's Football League outfit during season 1938-39. Frost was a much coveted 24-year-old as he grabbed 18 goals in 23 games, but by the time he had moved to Tyneside and quickly gained a chance in the Magpies' first-team, the Second World War had all but started and his footballing career was effectively ruined. Cool and intelligent in the leader's role, Frost played for the team in an unselfish way and once the hostilities began returned to the Merseyside area where he continued to bang in goals during wartime football. In 84 games for New Brighton, Arthur struck the net on no fewer than 65 occasions. On demob from the Lancashire Regiment late in 1945 and still registered as a Magpie player, Frost returned to St James' Park in an attempt to restart his career. Now 30 years old, he was given a trial but wasn't deemed good enough to compete with an eager group of new young players emerging at Gallowgate.

Appearances & Goals:
Debut v Sheffield Wednesday (h) 11 March 1939 (1 goal)
FL: 5 app 1 gl
Total: 5 app 1 gl

FULTHORPE George 1918-1919

Inside-left
5'10"
b. Tyneside

Career: Pandon Temperance 1918/UNITED Jan 1918/Pandon Temperance 1919.

George Fulthorpe was a local player who joined United's staff at the beginning of 1918, at a time when members of the Magpies' professional staff were scattered around the country due to war service. Fulthorpe scored on his debut for Newcastle, against Scotswood during January 1919 at the Novocastrians' ground alongside the Tyne, and continued to take part in the first half of the Northern Victory League programme. He was replaced once senior professionals Curtis Booth and Billy Hibbert had arrived back at St James' Park.

Appearances & Goals:
Debut v Scotswood (a) 18 January 1919 (NVL) (1 goal)
War: 6 app 1 gl
Total: 6 app 1 gl

FUMACA (Antunes) Jose Rodrigues Alves 1999-2000

Midfield
6'0"
b. Belem (Brazil), 15 July 1976

Career: AD Catuense (Brz)/West Ham Utd, Grimsby Town, Watford, SL Benfica (Ptg) all on trial 1998-99/ Birmingham City trial Dec 1998/Colchester Utd March 1999/Barnsley trial March 1999/Crystal Palace Sept 1999/UNITED trial Sept 1999, pmt Oct 1999 to May 2000 free/Real Zaragoza (Sp) trial March 2001/AD Catuense (Brz) 2001/America (Rio de Janeiro) (Brz) July 2001/Caxias (Brz) Jan 2002/ FC Koln (Ger) trial 2002/AD Catuense (Brz) July 2003/FK Drnovice (Cz) July 2005/Gornick Leczna (Pol) Jan 2006/ Turkiyemspor (Ger) Jan 2006/SC Paderborn (Ger) July 2006/SV Wilhelmshaven (Ger) Jan 2007/ Vereinslos (Ger) July 2007/Turkiyemspor (Ger) Jan 2008/Retired Aug 2008/FSV Hansa (Ger) asst-coach Oct 2009, returning as a player briefly March 2010, becoming coach cs 2012.

Brazilian midfielder Jose Antunes, known in the South American way by a playing-name of 'Fumaca', arrived in England during 1998 on a path to earn a contract in the professional game. Playing in the Brazilian Second Division, he was a trialist at several clubs with the slim midfielder earning short-term deals at Colchester and Crystal Palace. He managed a single game for Colchester in Division Two, against Manchester City when he was carried off after only 14 minutes, then three matches for the Eagles during 1999-2000. Despite many rejections, Fumaca was given a chance by the Magpies following a trial period, and described as a "box-to-box dynamo". Favoured by Robson's right-hand man Mick Wadsworth, supporters though were soon scratching their heads at why United took him on. Tall and slender, he looked the athlete, but on the pitch with the ball at his feet, he rarely displayed any of the usual Brazilian magic and did not develop as hoped, rarely showing his boss, or the fans, that he could claim a place in the first-team squad. Fumaca made a single full appearance in United's senior eleven against Tottenham and five brief substitute outings during 1999-2000. The South American never impressed. After nine months on Tyneside he moved on, trying his luck at a succession of clubs around Europe, eventually playing at a lower level of football in Germany.

Appearances & Goals:
Debut v Tottenham Hotspur (h) 28 November 1999
PL: 1(4) app 0 gls
FAC: 0(1) app 0 gls
Total: 1(5) app 0 gls

GALLACHER Hugh Kilpatrick 1925-1930

Centre-forward
5'5"
b. Bellshill, Lanarkshire, 2 February 1903
d. Gateshead, 11 June 1957

Career: Tannockside Ath 1919/Hattonrigg Thistle 1919/Bellshill Ath March 1920/Queen of the South Dec 1920/Airdrieonians May 1921/UNITED Dec 1925 £6,500/Chelsea May 1930 £10,000/Derby Co Nov 1934 £2,750/ Notts Co Sept 1936 £2,000/Grimsby Town Jan 1938 £1,000/Gateshead June 1938 £500 (York City war-guest 1939-40).

Hughie Gallacher is considered by many judges to be the greatest centre-forward of all time. Although only 5'5" tall, he was a handful for any defence possessing awesome strike power. Hughie could shoot with either foot, dribble with the ball, head, tackle, forage and also frequently lost his cool on the field. A record of netting a formidable total of 463 goals in 624 senior matches speaks for itself, while Gallacher is United's most potent attacker of all time with a strike-rate of over 82% in his 174 outings. Newcastle tracked the Scottish leader for many months before landing his signature for a new club record fee, and very nearly the biggest in the country at the time. Immediately Hughie took Tyneside by storm, hitting goals match after match and at the same time developing into one of the biggest cult figures Tyneside has witnessed. On, and off the field, where he became something of a playboy, Gallacher was worshipped by Magpie supporters, and when he skippered the club to the Football League title in 1927, bagging a season's record 39 goals in only 41 games, the Scot could do no wrong. Yet Hughie was a temperamental character, often in trouble with referees, directors and at times, the police, which just added to the amazing life story of this wizard of the leather. Gallacher struck 14 hat-tricks for the Magpies and is the fastest player to hit a century of goals. Although the Scot was the Magpies' top goal-getter in each of his five seasons with the club, his relationship with United's directors and new boss Andy Cunningham was never too healthy, and in the summer of 1930 Hughie was sold against his wishes to Chelsea for a vast fee to the outcry of Tyneside. Protests were many, and on his return to St James' Park with the Londoners for the first home fixture of the new season, Newcastle fans packed into Gallowgate to see their past idol. A record crowd of 68,386 was present with another 10,000 locked out and for the next decade and more Gallacher continued to be held in esteem. He made an impression on all his other clubs too, notably Airdrie (100 goals), when the Diamonds were next best to Rangers in Scotland, at Chelsea (81 goals) as well as Derby County (40 goals). A regular for Scotland for over ten years, he netted 23 goals for his country in only 20 games, while he was a star in the famous Wembley Wizards match during 1928. He also scored five goals for the Scottish League in one contest, one of four occasions he grabbed five in a game. Brother-in-law to United's George Mathison, after a long playing career, Gallacher retired on the outbreak of war, but often played in local representative fixtures, including for Bill Murray's Sunderland XI in aid of the Spitfire Fund during 1940. He settled in Gateshead employed in a number of roles from, sports journalist, once being banned from St James' Park for his outspoken remarks, to factory worker. Following a series of personal problems, Gallacher committed suicide throwing himself in front of the York to Edinburgh express train. The Newcastle Journal's headline noted, "Hughie of the Magic Feet is Dead". Football will never see another quite like 'Wee Hughie'. His sons, Hughie junior and Matty, both had opportunities in the Black'n'Whites junior ranks without making the grade while another son from an earlier relationship, Jackie Gallacher, appeared for Celtic (1943-51). Hughie is also related to another great name from the Bellshill area of Central Scotland, Matt Busby, being a second cousin.

Appearances & Goals:

Debut v Everton (h) 12 December 1925 (2 goals)

FL: 160 app 133 gls

FAC: 14 app 10 gls

Total: 174 app 143 gls

Honours:

20 Scot caps 1924-35/6 Scot unoff app 1935/1 Scot jnr app 1921/2 SL app 1925-26/Scot trial app 1925/FL champs 1927/SC winner 1924/Eng HoF/Scot HoF/FL Legend/NU HoF.

GALLACHER John Anthony 1989-1992

Outside-right

5'10"

b. Glasgow, 26 January 1969

Career: East Kilbride YC/Derby Co jnr 1985/ East Kilbride YC/Falkirk June 1987/UNITED June 1989 £100,000/Hartlepool Utd July 1992 free/ Falkirk March 1994/Kettering Town 1993-94/ Gateshead Aug 1994/Berwick Rangers 1994 to 1996.

Noted as a nephew of Alex Ferguson in one profile and a former schoolboy trialist at Manchester United, slimly built John Gallacher signed for the Magpies after only 16 outings in senior football for Falkirk. Being homesick and rejected at the Baseball Ground under Arthur Cox, Gallacher moved out of the full-time game to take on a career as an underwriter with Commercial Union until he received another chance at Brockville Park. His rise to the top was then meteoric as he played out of his skin in front of watching Newcastle officials, netting five goals in six games. Fast and direct and always able to find the net, Gallacher had a stunning beginning with United as season 1989-90 opened, showing match-winning potential down the flank. However, a stress fracture of his shin halted a blossoming career. The injury took many months to clear up and John was never the exciting find again and he drifted quickly out of the picture. Gallacher played on 23 occasions at the Victoria Ground for Hartlepool and later resided in the West End of Newcastle, employed as a supermarket manager. His son Owen joined United's Academy amd played for Scotland's Under-16 side during 2014.

Appearances & Goals:

Debut v Leeds United (h) 19 August 1989 (1 goal)

FL: 22(7) app 6 gls

FAC: 2 app 0 gls

FLC: 3 app 1 gl

Others: 3 app 1 gl

Total: 30(7) app 8 gls

GALLACHER Kevin William 1999-2001

Striker

5'8"

b. Clydebank, 23 November 1966

Career: Duntocher BC/Dundee Utd jnr July 1980, prof Sept 1983/Coventry City Jan 1990 £900,000/ Blackburn Rovers March 1993 £1.5m/UNITED Oct 1999 £700,000 to May 2001/Bolton Wand trial cs 2001/Preston North End Aug 2001/Sheffield Wed March 2002 to April 2002/Motherwell trial Aug 2002/ Huddersfield Town Aug 2002 to Oct 2002/ Blackburn Rovers part-time asst-coach 2003/ Darwen Director of Football March 2014.

Bobby Robson's first capture for Newcastle United, Kevin Gallacher arrived towards the end of a fine career as a somewhat bargain signing from Blackburn Rovers for £700,000 during the summer of 1999. During a short period of financial prudence at St James' Park in a more normal era of huge spending, the Scottish international proved an astute and excellent short-term purchase for the Magpies bolstering the manager's striking options over two seasons. Making a name for himself in 188 games wearing Dundee United's tangerine shirt when he reached the UEFA Cup final, Kevin moved south to score goals for Coventry City. Not big or brawny, Gallacher had pace and awareness in the box, as well as an intrepid attitude, while he always gave plenty of effort. Although often sidelined with bad injuries, recovering from four leg breaks, his determination made sure he came back fighting after set-backs. At Blackburn he was a favourite over eight seasons and registered a good record of 53 goals in over 150 matches, paired with Alan Shearer for a period until a leg fracture forced him onto the sidelines and saw him miss the majority of the Ewood club's Premier League title season. In a black-and-white shirt, Newcastle fans quickly recognised Kevin's wholehearted commitment on the field becoming an immediate favourite despite the fact he managed only six goals for the Toon. With a footballing pedigree few players can match, several of his family played the game to a high standard; his father Willie for Celtic, relatives John Divers senior and junior also for the Hoops while Tommy Gallacher played with Dundee with merit. Kevin's grandfather is Patsy Gallagher (Gallacher) a Celtic pre-war legend. On retirement, Gallacher entered the media as a freelance broadcaster and columnist, often returning to St James' Park as part of BBC's commentary team. He also coaches locally in the Lancashire area where he settled.

Appearances & Goals:

Debut v Middlesbrough (h) 3 October 1999

PL: 27(12) app 4 gls

FAC: 5(1) app 1 gl

FLC: 2 app 1 gl

Total: 34(13) app 6 gls

Honours:

53 Scot caps 1988-2001/WdC 1998/2 Scot B app 1990/7 Scot u21 app 1987-90/Scot sch-youth app/PL champs 1995 (1 app)/SC final 1987, 1988/UEFA Cup final 1987.

GALLACHER Patrick 1939

Inside-left

5'8"

b. Bridge of Weir, 21 August 1909

d. Greenock, 4 January 1992

Career: Linwood St Connels/Bridge of Weir/Sunderland amat Aug 1927, prof Sept 1928/Stoke City Nov 1938 £5,000 (UNITED war-guest 1939-40)(Morton war-guest 1939-40)(Notts Co war-guest 1940-41)(Dundee Utd war-guest 1941-42)(Leicester City war-guest 1942-43) (Brentford war-guest 1942-43)(Crystal Palace war-guest 1943-44)(Millwall war-guest 1943-44)(Luton Town war-guest 1943-45)/Weymouth player-manager.

Like Len Duns, forward colleague Patsy Gallacher was another noted Sunderland player from their successful pre-war side to appear in Magpie colours. A Scottish international schemer during 1934-35, Gallacher was a most effective forward. Winning title and FA Cup honours, he claimed 107 goals in 308 games for the Wearsiders, a regular and influential schemer for 10 seasons at Roker Park. Quick thinking on the ball, and always able to hit the net, his stay at Gallowgate was all too brief, only a single game against North East rivals Hartlepools United during October 1939. Gallacher served in the RAF during the war years and appeared for several clubs as a passing guest as well as Scotland representative matches during services football. After leaving the game Patsy entered business in London before returning to Scotland.

Appearances & Goals:

Debut v Hartlepools United (a) 21 October 1939 (FLNE)

War: 1 app 0 gls

Total: 1 app 0 gls

Honours

1 Scot cap 1935/FL champs 1936/FAC winner 1937.

G

GALLANTREE William Leslie 1931-1936

Outside-right
5'5"
b. East Boldon, Co Durham, 23 December 1913
d. Durham, 7 February 2006

Career: Harton Colliery Jan 1930/UNITED amat June 1931, prof Sept 1931 £20/Aldershot Town May 1936 free/Gateshead July 1937 to 1939.

Les Gallantree was a small, but a particularly sturdy winger who spent his time at St James' Park as deputy to first, Jimmy Boyd, then Wilf Bott and Tim Rogers. One biography of the day described Les as "small in stature, but strong and plucky". Les was direct and imaginative with the ball, he was unlucky to break his leg in 1935 during a Central League fixture which hampered his chances of a regular place in United's Second Division line-up. Following a spell down south, Les returned to join Gateshead's Third Division line-up for the seasons leading up to World War Two. The hostilities ended his footballing career and Gallantree then resided near Durham City employed as a cost accountant with a Sunderland-based timber company. His nephew, Colin Nelson, appeared for Sunderland at full-back.

Appearances & Goals:
Debut v Liverpool (a) 7 January 1933
FL: 9 app 2 gls
Total: 9 app 2 gls

GARBUTT Eric John Edward 1939-1951

Goalkeeper
5'11"
b. Scarborough, 27 March 1920
d. Billingham, 5 January 1997

Career: Middlesbrough amat 1937-38/Hartlepools Utd June 1938/Billingham Synthonia/ UNITED Jan 1939 £100/ Retired June 1951 due to injury.

Two serious injuries suppressed what would have been a fine career for Eric Garbutt. With plenty of stiff competition for places in United's ranks from Fairbrother and Swinburne, he firstly broke a hand during 1948, then a leg two years later which saw Garbutt out of action for many weeks and ultimately caused the premature conclusion to his career. At his best Eric was always alert with fine anticipation and he commanded respect from his colleagues, many noting the Yorkshireman as the pick of Newcastle's immediate post-war custodians. Garbutt served in the RAF during World War Two and later appeared on 17 occasions during the club's promotion campaign of 1947-48. After leaving the game, Eric was employed as a bus driver for the United Group around Teesside, residing in Billingham. His first senior outing for the Black'n'Whites against Sheffield United ended in a comfortable afternoon, a 6-0 victory.

Appearances & Goals:
Debut v Millwall (a) 31 August 1946
(v Sheffield United (h) 25 August 1945 (FLN))
FL: 52 app 0 gls
FAC: 1 app 0 gls
War: 1 app 0 gls
Total: 54 app 0 gls

Honours:
FL div 2 prom 1948.

GARDNER Alexander 1899-1910

Right-half
5'8"
b. Leith, 2 October 1878
d. Newcastle upon Tyne, 1 July 1921

Career: Leith Ivanhoe/Leith Ath Feb 1898/UNITED Nov 1899/Retired 1910/Blyth Spartans Feb 1911 briefly.

Although there were few midfielders better than Alex Gardner in football at the time, he remains the only one of United's Edwardian Greats not to appear for his country. A regular for the Black'n'Whites for almost a decade, his colleague Colin Veitch remarked that Alex was, "the best half-back who never got an international cap". Gardner reached Scottish trial fixtures but, to Tyneside's dismay, was always overlooked. Consistent throughout his long stay at St James' Park, the Scot perhaps didn't possess the brilliance of others around him, but he was a valuable asset and was a versatile player, starting off at inside-forward or outside-right, before switching to the heart of midfield just before United began to dominate the game in the mid-1900's. He specialised in the low, direct pass, forming a near telepathic understanding with Jack Rutherford on the right flank, a feature of United's play during that era. Captain of United on many occasions, Gardner broke his leg in 1909 during an FA Cup tie against Blackpool, an injury which closed his career although he attempted to play on in non-league with Blyth Spartans, but the injury was so severe he could not continue for long. In his early days with the Magpies, during November 1901, the Scot was out of action for a lengthy period recovering from scarlet fever, a killer virus during the early part of the century. Nicknamed 'Punky', he signed his name as, 'Alick' and later ran the Dun Cow public-house close to St James' Park.

Appearances & Goals:
Debut v Preston North End (h) 25 November 1899
FL: 279 app 22 gls
FAC: 34 app 4 gls
Others: 1 app 0 gls
Total: 314 app 26 gls

Honours:
Scot trial app 1900-06/FL champs 1905, 1907, 1909/FAC final 1905, 1906, 1908.

GARDNER Andrew 1902-1903

Outside-left
5'8"
b. Milton, Glasgow, 17 April 1877

Career: Kilbarchan Victoria/Kilbarchan Sept 1899/Clyde June 1900/Grimsby Town May 1901/UNITED Sept 1902/ Bolton Wand May 1903/Brighton June 1904/Queens Park Rangers May 1905/Carlisle Utd Aug 1906/Johnstone April 1908/ Carlisle Utd Jan 1909/Retired Oct 1912.

One of a trio of unrelated players with identical surnames at Gallowgate during the same era. The lesser known of the three, Andrew Gardner, was still a respected player at the turn of the century. He replaced the popular Richard Roberts on the left wing in United's side, but only appeared for two months in United's first eleven during season 1902-03 before another hugely favoured player, Bobby Templeton, arrived to take his place. Gardner settled in Carlisle after his playing days and was an innkeeper at the Crown Hotel for a period.

Appearances & Goals:
Debut v Liverpool (h) 8 November 1902
FL: 9 app 3 gls
FAC: 1 app 0 gls
Total: 10 app 3 gls

GARDNER Charles 1890-1892

Forward
b. Newcastle upon Tyne, c1872

Career: EAST END amat Jan 1890, prof April 1891 to Jan 1892/St Peter's Albion.

A mainstay for the club's reserve combination in season 1890-91, East End Swifts then East End Amateurs, Gardner found a place further up the ladder due to his sound performances, being good enough to represent Northumberland in County matches. He made his first-team debut in a friendly against Edinburgh University during April 1891 and soon was given a chance in Northern League action too. Charles though found it hard to maintain a senior place and never established himself as a permanent member of the first eleven. When the club's reserve outfit disbanded in January 1892, he appears to have left the club. Gardner also played cricket for the Guild of St John CC on Tyneside. Charles lived in Byker and worked as a riveter in the Tyne shipyards when he was with East End. He later became a boiler-maker.

Appearances & Goals:
Debut v Darlington (a) 4 April 1891 (NL)
NL: 3 app 0 gls
Total: 3 app 0 gls

GARDNER David Richmond 1899-1902

Left-back
5'8"
b. Glasgow, 31 March 1873
d. Longcliffe, near Matlock, 5 November 1931

Career: Wellpark Jnrs/Third Lanark Sept 1893/UNITED May 1899 £200/Grimsby Town May 1902 £250/West Ham Utd July 1904/Croydon Common Oct 1907, becoming player-manager Feb 1910, then trainer and occasional player to cs 1916/Leicester City trainer Aug 1919 to his demise.

A great favourite with the spectators, Dave Gardner was an intelligent as well as elegant defender, joining United following over 60 games for Third Lanark, a teammate of Jock Peddie in Glasgow. He was something of a gentleman on the field too, a rarity for a full-back in those years, and he always played to the crowd, possessing one trick of back-heeling the ball to fool his opponent that he used over and over again. Described in his era as being "a thoughtful player, as fast as most forwards", Gardner won a single cap for his country. He was on the fringe of more honours while Dave also captained United, and all his other senior clubs too. He also took part in West Ham's first game at Upton Park during September 1904 and totalled 80 games for the Hammers. Gardner died when playing golf alongside his Leicester colleagues during 1931.

Appearances & Goals:
Debut v West Bromwich Albion (a) 2 September 1899
FL: 76 app 2 gls
FAC: 2 app 0 gls
Total: 78 app 2 gls

Honours:
1 Scot cap 1897/1 Scot unoff app 1898/Scot trial app 1897-1900.

GARLAND Peter John 1992

Midfield
5'9"
b. Croydon, Surrey, 20 January 1971

Career: Croydon/Tottenham Hotspur jnr July 1987, prof July 1989/UNITED March 1992 £35,000/Charlton Ath Dec 1992 £35,000 (Wycombe Wand loan 1994-95)/Leyton Orient July 1996 free/Crawley Town May 1997/Dulwich Hamlet cs 2000/Croydon Dec 2000/Whyteleafe Aug 2002/ Erith Town/Greenwich Borough Dec 2004, becoming player-manager July 2006 to Nov 2006.

One of Kevin Keegan's earliest signings as manager of United, Peter Garland had never started a first-team fixture for Spurs, but had been on the bench on several occasions, joining the action once for Paul Gascoigne during 1991. When the former teenage international was given the opportunity to move to Gallowgate, the Londoner had the chance to impress and claim a regular position in United's developing side. Able to turn out at full-back or in midfield, Garland though, found he was again in the shadows never quite showing the form or fitness that warranted and extended run in United's line-up. Tenacious and mobile, he moved back to the capital and proceeded to have a decent career in London with Charlton where he claimed 63 outings before moving onto the non-league circuit.

Appearances & Goals:
Debut v Millwall (h) 18 April 1992 (sub)
FL: 0(2) app 0 gls
Others: 0(1) 0 gls
Total: 0(3) app 0 gls

Honours:
Eng sch-youth.

GARNHAM Alfred 1933-1939. 1942-1943

Left-half
5'9"
b. Birtley, Gateshead, 22 June 1914
d. Lanchester, Co Durham, 27 April 1998

Career: Fatfield Albion/Herrington CW/Birtley/UNITED amat May 1933, prof April 1934/Queen of the South Aug 1939 £500 (UNITED war-guest 1942-43)/West Stanley player-manager c1946/Retired 1950 due to injury.

A hearty local player who attempted to claim a first-team place in three different roles with United; left-back, left-half and right-half, Alf Garnham had two good seasons during 1935-36 and 1936-37, but was always recognised as a reserve afterwards. He was a dour performer, but one who never let the Magpies down. After retiring from the game he worked on Tyneside, later residing in Perkinsville near Chester-le-Street. During World War Two, Alf served with the RAF as a PT Instructor at bases in Uxbridge and Weston-super-Mare.

Appearances & Goals:
Debut v Norwich City (a) 7 December 1935
FL: 45 app 1 gl
FAC: 5 app 0 gls
War: 1 app 0 gls
Total: 51 app 1 gl

GARROW Herbert Alexander 1960-1963

Goalkeeper
6'3"
b. Troves, near Elgin, 24 January 1942

Career: Elgin Victoria 1957/Fochabers 1958/Chelsea trial Aug 1959/Elgin City trial 1959/UNITED Feb 1960 £1,150/Horden CW June 1963 free/South Shields 1965/Scarborough cs 1972/Retired cs 1974/Hartlepool Utd briefly Aug 1974/Bishop Auckland Sept 1978/ Newcastle Blue Star cs 1980 to 1982/Blyth Spartans & Whitley Bay briefly thereafter.

The son of a farmer, the tall and vastly built Bert Garrow, was at 6'3" and over 14 stone, one of the most powerfully framed players to have served the Magpies. Spotted playing Junior Cup football in Glasgow for his local club Fochabers, with Bryan Harvey, then Dave Hollins ahead of him in selection at St James' Park, as well as having Stuart Mitchell as a rival for the custodian's position, Garrow's opportunities in the senior eleven were limited. He deputised on four occasions, including in a 5-5 thriller with West Ham United during 1960. Although rated by Charlie Mitten, once new boss Joe Harvey arrived, Garrow dropped down the order and was discarded. The Scot could have joined former team-mate Bob Stokoe at Bury, but decided to become a part-time professional combining a vocation outside the game with football in the non-leagues. He played on until he was 40 years of age and did have a noted career in that circle of football being a well known and popular character in the north for over two decades. He also reached Wembley with Scarborough in 1973 and was given the Man of the Match accolade as the Seadogs lifted the FA Trophy. Appearing on 102 occasions for Boro, he showed at that level what a commanding goalkeeper he was. Taking a post in Newcastle's local authority Housing Dept, Garrow was for over 33 years employed with the City of Newcastle, later being appointed Principal Housing Officer before retirement. The Scot settled in the Tyne Valley at Ovingham, being at various times secretary, president and captain of Stocksfield Golf Club. Garrow married the daughter of United's ex-full-back and coach Benny Craig.

Appearances & Goals:
Debut v Blackburn Rovers (h) 26 November 1960
FL: 4 app 0 gls
Total: 4 app 0 gls

Honours:
FAT winner 1973.

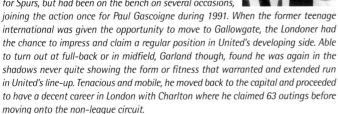

G

GASCOIGNE Paul John 1981-1988

Midfield
5'10"
b. Dunston, Gateshead, 27 May 1967

Career: Redheugh BC 1979/Dunston Jnrs/UNITED jnr June 1981, prof May 1985/Tottenham Hotspur July 1988 £2.3m (plus £350,000 later)/SS Lazio (It) May 1992 £5.5m/Rangers July 1995 £4.3m/ Middlesbrough March 1998 £3.45m/Everton July 2000 free/Burnley March 2002 free/DC Utd (USA) trial July 2002/Gansu Tianma (Chn) Jan 2003 to cs 2003/Wolves trial Oct to Nov 2003/Boston Utd player-coach July 2004/Kettering Town manager Oct to Dec 2005/Also assisted various clubs over short periods; Berwick Rangers (2002), Radcliffe Borough (2004), Algarve Utd (Ptg) (2005).

A phenomenon of the Nineties, Paul Gascoigne became the British game's biggest personality with a brand of entertainment on and off the field reserved only for a few gifted individuals. Raised in the Dunston and Teams area of Gateshead, Paul began his headlining career as the precocious young star of the Black'n'Whites FA Youth Cup victory in 1985. He quickly earned a place in Newcastle's senior eleven as a teenager who possessed an array of skills and flair that rapidly had the whole country taking notice. Gascoigne always wanted to be involved in the action, and added to his superb vision, passing, shooting and dribbling skills, was his strength and work rate as well as the ability to tackle, rare for his type of ball player, all of which turned him into almost a complete footballer. The only negative aspect of his game was the tendency to sometimes be rash, temperamental and even self-destructive. Known universally as 'Gazza', he developed into perhaps the second 'Clown Prince of Soccer', after Len Shackleton a generation before. Something of a loveable rascal, with colourful displays on the park and plenty of antics off it, Gascoigne became Tyneside's most famous son of the era and it was a huge disappointment when he left for London and White Hart Lane in a new British record deal during the summer of 1988. He flourished into a megastar under Terry Venables at Spurs (112 app) and became an England regular. Then, after a protracted transfer and fitness saga following a crippling self-inflicted cruciate knee injury collected in the 1991 FA Cup final, he eventually headed for Rome and Serie A giants Lazio. Dogged by injury throughout his career, Paul unluckily broke his leg with Le Aquile and underwent three operations. But he recovered from those long term setbacks to become a favourite at Ibrox with Rangers where he won an array of honours during his 104 games for the Glasgow club. Always the showman, keen to put a smile on the faces of supporters, Gascoigne won the prestigious BBC Television Sports Personality of the Year award in 1990. He also hit the record charts with a remake of the Geordie classic, Fog on the Tyne, while he was even preserved in wax at Madame Tussards. Once turned down as a kid by Ipswich Town, Southampton and Middlesbrough after trials, Paul wound down his playing career in a less than glamorous style and began a much publicised fight against drugs, alcohol and illness which would seriously affect him. His life spiralled downwards and Gascoigne was at various times arrested and detained, as well as spending periods in rehab clinics in an attempt to come to terms with a lifestyle away from the game.

Appearances & Goals:
Debut v Queens Park Rangers (h) 13 April 1985 (sub)
FL: 83(9) app 21 gls
FAC: 4 app 3 gls
FLC: 8 app 1 gl
Others: 2(1) app 0 gls
Total: 97(10) app 25 gls

Honours:
57 Eng caps 1989-98/WdC 1990/4 Eng B app 1988-90/13 Eng u21 app 1987-88/FL div 1 prom 1998 (7 app)/FAC winner 1991/FLC final 1998/FAYC winner 1985/SL champs 1996, 1997/SC winner 1996, 1997/SLC winner 1997/YPoY (PFA) 1988/Scot PoY 1996 (PFA)/Scot FoY 1996 (FWA)/BBC SPoY 1990/Eng HoF/FL Legend/PFA ToS (d1) 1988, 1991.

GASKELL Alec 1953-1954

Centre-forward
5'10"
b. Leigh, near Manchester, 30 July 1932
d. Bolton, 8 March 2014

Career: Plank Lane Jnrs 1944/Preston North End trial 1944/Manchester Road Jnrs 1946/Hindsford 1946/Blackburn Rovers amat Sept 1948/ Manchester Utd Jan 1949/Mossley trial 1950/ Southport amat Sept 1951, prof Nov 1952/UNITED Oct 1953 £5,000/ Mansfield Town June 1954 £3,500/Grantham July 1956/Tranmere Rovers June 1957 to cs 1958/Rhyl cs 1959/Wigan Rovers July 1959/Mossley 1960/ Winsford Utd Dec 1961/BICC Works XI (Leigh) player-manager 1962 to 1981.

One of the best strikers in the lower divisions, Alec Gaskell was purchased as a forward to be groomed into a star of the future at St James' Park, but in the end it was a deal that never bore fruit. With Southport he had showed menace in front of goal, striking 18 goals in 45 outings. Gaskell was given only one opportunity in United's first-team, a Boxing Day derby against Middlesbrough during season 1953-54 when he stood in for Jackie Milburn and Alan Monkhouse, both injured. Without making an impact at the top level, just as he had earlier done at both Ewood Park and Old Trafford, Gaskell returned to the lower sections of the football pyramid. Later Gaskell resided in Cheshire and worked in quality-control at the BICC complex in Leigh.

Appearances & Goals:
Debut v Middlesbrough (h) 26 December 1953
FL: 1 app 0 gls
Total: 1 app 0 gls

GAVILAN (Zarate) Diego Antonio 2000-2004

Midfield
5'9"
b. Asunción (Paraguay), 1 March 1980

Career: Cerro Porteno (Pg) jnr 1996, prof Jan 1998/UNITED Feb 2000 £2m (Estudiantes Tecos (Mex) loan 2001-02)(SC Internacional (Brz) loan 2002-03)/Udinese Calcio (It) Jan 2004/SC Internacional (Brz) July 2004/CA Newell's Old Boys (Arg) Dec 2005/ Gremio (Brz) Jan 2007/Flamengo (Brz) Dec 2007/ Portuguesa (Brz) June 2008 to Nov 2008/CA Independiente (Arg) Feb 2009/Club Olimpia (Pg) Jan 2010/Club Juan Aurich (Pu) Jan 2011/Independent FBC (Pg) Jan 2012.

Diego Gavilan was one of several largely unknown South American footballers brought to Tyneside during Bobby Robson's period in charge, all of who failed to make a big impact. Along with Cordone, Bassedas, Antunes and Acuna, the Paraguay international arrived from Cerro Porteno with glowing reports as an outside-right or midfielder who could make thing happen at the right end of the field. The first from Paraguay to appear in England's top flight, however Diego never came to terms with English football and failed to convince both the club's coaching staff and supporters he had the capability to make the grade. Nicknamed 'Sparrowhawk' or 'Pampero' (the horse that goes like the wind) in his native country, he was still 19 years of age when he arrived on Tyneside and was perhaps much too young to make such a move to the other side of the world and different way of life. With dark flowing hair and of slight build, Gavilan was handed sparse opportunities in the first eleven over his five seasons on the Gallowgate payroll, his best campaign being 1999-2000 when he claimed a mere two starts and four appearances from the bench. Newcastle cut their losses on the £2m capture, sending him on season loans during 2001-02 and 2002-03. Gavilan eventually joined Italian club Udinese permanently and continued his career in Central and South America where he had some success in Brazil, winning the Gaucho state title on three occasions. At the end of his playing days Diego returning to Asuncion where he started coaching. Although known as 'Gavilan', his surname is Zarate, his father, Antonio Gavilan, also played the game in Paraguay as did his uncle, Eladio Zarate.

Appearances & Goals:
Debut v Sunderland (a) 5 February 2000 (sub)
PL: 2(5) app 1 gl
FLC: 0(1) app 0 gls
Total: 2(6) app 1 gl

Honours:
43 Pg caps 1999-2006/WdC 2002, 2006 (no app)/Pg u20 app/Pg sch-youth app/CLib final 2007.

GAYLE Howard Anthony 1982-1983

Striker
5'11"
b. Toxteth, Liverpool, 18 May 1958

Career: Bedford (Liverpool)/Liverpool jnr June 1974, prof Nov 1977 (Fulham loan 1979-80)(UNITED loan Nov 1982 to Jan 1983)/Birmingham City loan Jan 1983, pmt June 1983 £50,000/Sunderland Aug 1984 £70,000/Dallas Sidekicks (USA) cs 1986/Stoke City March 1987/Blackburn Rovers July 1987 £5,000/Carlisle Utd trial Jan 1992/Wrexham trial March 1992/Halifax Town Aug 1992/Carlisle Utd trial Oct 1992/Accrington Stanley Sept 1993 to May 1995/Later becoming Tranmere Rovers asst-coach/Stoke City 'special inclusion officer' 2006.

An injury to Kevin Keegan led to the arrival of Howard Gayle on a loan transaction during the winter of 1982. One of Liverpool's shadow eleven, Gayle had only appeared on a handful of senior occasions for the Reds, but was still recognised as a potentially quality player, much like Kevin Sheedy who left Anfield and developed into one of the best. Gayle could operate in a wide role, or up front, as well as in midfield, and he caught the eye of many United supporters. However, while the Merseysider didn't do badly at St James' Park, he drifted in and out of games and manager Arthur Cox failed to be impressed. Howard possessed quick feet and pace to frighten defenders, could produce explosive shooting on occasion, as well as a hot temper. He later served Sunderland and Blackburn (144 app 34 goals) with credit. Howard played in one of Liverpool's European Cup semi-final ties, against Bayern Munich during 1981 and was sub in the final against Real Madrid without being called into action. On retiring, Gayle lived on Merseyside coaching local kids and was active in youth development and care programmes, including the Stanley House Youth Project. Howard was also strong supporter of anti-racism initiatives. He additionally covered the football scene for local radio on Merseyside.

Appearances & Goals:
Debut v Cambridge United (h) 27 November 1982
FL: 8 app 2 gls
Total: 8 app 2 gls

Honours:
3 Eng u21 app 1984/FL div 2 prom 1992 (4 app)/FLC final 1985/EC winner 1981 (sub no app).

GAYNOR Thomas 1990

Centre-forward
6'1"
b. Limerick, 29 January 1963

Career: Limerick Utd 1981/Shamrock Rovers cs 1982/Dundalk cs 1983/Limerick City cs 1984/Doncaster Rovers Dec 1986/Nottingham Forest Oct 1987 £25,000 (UNITED loan Nov to Dec 1990)/Millwall March 1993 to June 1993/Cork City Aug 1993/Athlone Town Oct 1995/Cork City Sept 1996/Athlone Town Jan 1997/Bohemians (Waterford) player-coach Feb 1997/St Patricks Ath 1997/Kilkenny City 1997/Limerick 1998/Kilkenny City Jan 1999, later becoming manager July 2007 to Sept 2007/Bohemians (Waterford) coach 2011/St Kevin's manager June 2012.

Tommy Gaynor arrived on Tyneside as an emergency replacement for striker Mark McGhee who was sidelined through injury. A tall Irishman, he had a good first touch and combined well up front, but like many of United's loan players never persuaded the club's management to immediately rush for the cheque-book. Tommy had made a name for himself at the Belle Vue Ground before being fancied by Brian Clough. With Forest he appeared in almost 80 matches for the Trent club in a gutsy style and was a favourite of supporters before heading for London and The Den. Returning to his native Ireland, Gaynor served several clubs in that country and for a period worked in the sportswear department of a local retail store in Nenagh, Tipperary. In Nottingham he is remembered with esteem, a street being named after him, Gaynor Court.

Appearances & Goals:
Debut v Watford (h) 24 November 1990
FL: 4 app 1 gl
Total: 4 app 1 gl

Honours:
2 EL app 1986/FLC winner 1989, 1990 (sub no app)/Eire Cup winner 1982, 1995/Eire PoY 1985.

GEORGIADIS George 1998-1999

Midfield
5'9"
b. Kavala, near Salonika (Greece), 8 March 1972

Career: Keravnos Krinides (Gr) amat/Doxa Drama (Gr) 1989/Panathinaikos (Gr) 1992/UNITED June 1998 £493,000/PAOK (Gr) Aug 1999 £300,000/Olympiacos (Gr) July 2003/Iraklis (Gr) July 2005/PAOK (Gr) Jan 2007 to c2008 when he became a coach and scout/Greece u21 manager Jan 2010/PAOK (Gr) Technical Director June 2012, being caretaker-manager May 2013 & March to May 2014.

A noted midfielder in Greek football, George (or Giorgios) Georgiadis appeared for top Athens club Panathinaikos, winning title and cup medals with the Shamrocks as well as reaching the Champions League semi-final in 1996. Earning over 60 caps for his national side, playing alongside United's other Hellenic import at the club during the same period, Nikos Dabizas, the midfielder was one of the best midfielders in Greek football and certainly worth a gamble at a modest fee of less than £500,000, due to an escape clause in his contract. With a quiet manner and compactly built, Georgiadis scored plenty of goals in the Alpha Ethniki of Greek league football and Kenny Dalglish saw him as a player who could adapt to the English game. However when Ruud Gullit took over, he rarely was considered. While Georgiadis was neat and efficient on the ball, and always professional, he lacked the energy and bite for the highly charged and pacy Premier League. Competing for a place in Newcastle's engine-room was no easy task with the likes of Speed, Solano, Lee, Hamann as well as fringe players such as Brady and McClen all eyeing selection. During season 1998-99 Georgiadis managed eight starts, enjoying a bit of FA Cup glory, netting in United's Sixth Round clash with Everton as the club headed for Wembley. Frustrated at a lack of opportunity, George returned to top provincial club PAOK after one season where he continued to be recognised as a first-rate player in his own country. As a youngster George lived in Germany from an early age before returning to the Salonika area. On retiring from the game, he became associated with his local club PAOK.

Appearances & Goals:
Debut v Manchester United (a) 8 November 1998
PL: 7(3) app 0 gls
FAC: 0(2) app 1 gl
FLC: 1 app 0 gls
Total: 8(5) app 1 gl

Honours:
62 Gr caps 1993-2004/ECh winner 2004 (sub no app)/Gr Lg champs 1995, 1996, 2005/Gr Cup winner 1993, 1994, 1995, 2001, 2003/Gr Cup final 1997, 1998, 2014(m)/ Gr FoY 1995.

GEREMI (Njitap Fotso) Sorele 2007-2010

Midfield
5'10"
b. Bafoussam (Cameroon), 20 December 1978

Career: RC Bafoussam (Cam) 1995/Cerro Porteno (Pg) Aug 1997/Genclerbirligi SK (Trk) Oct 1997/Real Madrid (Sp) July 1999 (Middlesbrough loan 2002-03)/Chelsea July 2003 £6.9m/UNITED July 2007 free/MKE Ankaragucu (Trk) Feb 2010 free/AE Larissa (Gr) Aug 2010 to Jan 2011.

By the time Cameroon midfielder Geremi landed on Tyneside during the close season of 2007, he was a highly rated footballer to have appeared at the very top level; playing in the World Cup, Olympic Games, African Cup of Nations, runs to the Champions League final and for such ranked clubs as Chelsea (109 app) and Real Madrid (70 app). After being part of Chelsea's squad as they twice lifted the Premiership trophy and were twice runners-up, he was brought to St James' Park by manager Sam Allardyce. At 28 years old Geremi was a first-choice during 2007-08, appointed captain, although once Allardyce departed subsequent managers had their doubts over his worth. In central midfield, he rarely tried the spectacular, rather linking play as an anchor-man. He scored only two goals for United and by 2009-10 as United struggled and were in dire need of someone with his experience to impose himself on matches, he was largely anonymous in the action, claiming only four starts as part of the side. After three seasons on Tyneside, for a player on such

G

high wages, it is doubtful if the club received value for money. But Geremi was not alone at this time with several expensive players underperforming. As United tumbled towards the Championship his days at St James' Park looked to be over and in limited opportunities on the pitch he received an element of criticism from the crowd. When the African retired from playing, Geremi returned to Cameroon (where he was one of 17 children) and during April 2012 was appointed as a special advisor to the President of the Player's Union. He was also part of the administrative team to develop a new professional league in Cameroon. A huge personality in his native country, Geremi captained the Indomitable Lions to the Olympic gold medal and is one of their most prominent sportsmen of all time. His father also played football for his country, while a cousin, Pierre Webo did likewise.

Appearances & Goals:
Debut v Bolton Wanderers (a) 11 August 2007
FL/PL: 38(11) app 1 gl
FLC: 4(1) app 1 gl
Total: 42(12) app 2 gls

Honours:
118 Cam caps 1997-2010/WdC 2002, 2010/OG 2000 (gold)/ACN winner 2000, 2002/ACN final 2008/Cam sch-youth/PL champs 2005, 2006/FL ch winner 2010 (7 app)/Sp Lg champs 2001/CL winner 2000 (sub no app)/ESC final 2000/WCC final 2000.

GHEE Thomas 1897-1920

Right-half & Trainer
5'11"
b. Kilmarnock, 27 July 1873
d. Newcastle upon Tyne, 12 September 1939

Career: Kilmarnock cs 1893/Darwen Jan 1894/Kilmarnock 1894/St Mirren Dec 1894/Kilmarnock April 1895/ St Mirren 1896/UNITED April 1897 £35/Retired 1902, becoming asst-trainer and backstage aide to 1920.

Close to international recognition, Tommy Ghee was said to have signed for United at a Paisley bar after United officials had been impressed with his play for St Mirren during season 1896-97, Ghee having swapped between Killie and the Saints over the previous seasons. The Scot helped United to promotion and took part in Newcastle's initial First Division match becoming one of the club's mainstays as they developed in the big-time. Skipper of the Magpies, Tommy was a whole-hearted character, a larger than life personality and a driving force on the field who possessed courage and tenacity; it was recorded he would, "stop the opposition at all costs". Ghee was tough and uncompromising, his rugged style linked perfectly with Jack Ostler and Jimmy Stott in midfield, a combination which served the Magpies with distinction. A fine all round sportsman, Ghee was proficient at both swimming and water-polo, then a popular pastime. Tommy later suffered from a leg injury which affected his walking. Once retired, he resided on Tyneside and assisted behind the scenes at Gallowgate for nearly 20 years, additionally looking after the player's billiard-room at St James' Park. His nephew Charlie McGill was a prominent player with Aberdeen during the 1930s, while his grand-daughter married United's Kenny Wharton (qv).

Appearances & Goals:
Debut v Woolwich Arsenal (h) 4 September 1897
FL: 134 app 4 gls
FAC: 10 app 1 gl
Total: 144 app 5 gls

Honours:
Scot trial app 1899/FL div 2 prom 1898.

GIBB Thomas 1968-1975

Midfield
5'10"
b. Bathgate, 13 December 1944

Career: Wallhouse Rose/Armadale Thistle/ Bathgate Utd/Bathgate Thistle May 1963/Partick Thistle May 1963/UNITED Aug 1968 £45,000/Sunderland June 1975 free/Hartlepool Utd July 1977 free to July 1979.

Tommy Gibb was purchased by boss Joe Harvey as a squad midfield player, having stood out for Partick Thistle in 153 games. He was a player to be groomed for the future. Yet the Scot grasped an early chance in a Magpie shirt due to injuries and proceeded to secure his midfield role for the next four seasons. In doing so Tommy created a club record, appearing in 171 successive games (Aug 1968 to Oct 1971). Slim with plenty of running power, Gibb was a terrific worker in the Magpie's blossoming European line-up. He did the simple things well on the ball, while he had the ability to make late, telling runs into the box. Tommy never really received the credit he deserved from fans on the terrace, sometimes being the victim of the boo-boys, yet was respected in the dressing-room by his colleagues. A key player as the Geordies won the Fairs Cup during 1968-69, Tommy played in all 12 games en route to the deciding match in Budapest. After leaving the game he returned to his native West Lothian where he managed a public house in Armadale for a while, then entered the haulage business. Gibb netted a well remembered 25-yard screamer on his home debut against Chelsea, while he assisted Sunderland when they lifted the Second Division crown in 1976.

Appearances & Goals:
Debut v Sheffield Wednesday (a) 14 August 1968
FL: 190(9) app 12 gls
FAC: 8(3) app 0 gls
FLC: 12 app 1 gl
Euro: 24 app 3 gls
Others: 17(6) app 3 gls
Total: 251(18) app 19 gls

Honours:
1 Scot u23 app 1968/FL div 2 champs 1976 (6 app)/FAC final 1974/ICFC winner 1969.

GIBBON P 1889-1890

Forward
b. unknown

Career: Bishop Auckland/EAST END April 1889 to cs 1890.

An effective forward Gibbon joined the Heaton set-up at Chillingham Road following a spell playing the game in the south of County Durham. His first outing for Newcastle East End was in a Tyne versus Wear meeting with Sunderland Albion during May 1889 and he became a customary selection in attack for the opening months of the 1889-90 Northern League campaign. Often on the score-sheet, for some unknown reason Gibbon fell out of favour and had lost his place by January and moved on during the close-season. It was recorded that he also played what was at the time the popular sport of baseball on Tyneside, for the City of Newcastle and Pelicans clubs.

Appearances & Goals:
Debut v Elswick Rangers (a) 21 September 1889 (NL)
NL: 8 app 3 gls
FAC: 2 app 2 gls
Total: 10 app 5 gls

GIBSON Colin Hayward 1948-1949

Outside-right
5'11"
b. Normanby, Yorkshire, 16 September 1923
d. Stourbridge, 27 March 1992

Career: Penarth Pontoons/Cardiff City Aug 1942 £10/ UNITED July 1948 £15,000/Aston Villa Feb 1949 £17,500/ Lincoln City Jan 1956 £6,000/Stourbridge July 1957/Cradley Heath Nov 1958/Stourbridge Aug 1959/Retired May 1960.

A dashing, blond, slimly-built forward, Colin Gibson played on the wing or at inside-forward with style and panache throughout the immediate post-war years. Newcastle were impressed with his sparkling performances for Cardiff City (in over 150 games) and brought him to Tyneside for what was then a near record fee. The former dockyard marine engineer, had one season wearing United's colours, 1948-49, before losing his place. But his was always a talent which many clubs admired and, after turning in two brilliant performances against Aston Villa, he moved to Birmingham soon after his five-star display, during February 1949. Becoming a crowd-pleaser with Villa he scored 26 goals in 167 games for the Claret-and-Blues and graduated into the England set-up. Gibson eventually retired to the Stourbridge area where he moved into the licensing trade, managing a succession of pubs in the Midlands. Colin was also an accomplished pianist and often entertained his colleagues when staying away in hotels.

Appearances & Goals:
Debut v Everton (a) 21 August 1948
FL: 23 app 5 gls
FAC: 1 app 0 gls
Total: 24 app 5 gls

Honours:
1 Eng B app 1949/1 FL app 1949/FA app 1949/FL div 3(S) champs 1947/FLSW(WLg) champs 1945.

GIBSON James 1959-1961

Centre-forward
6'0"
b. Belfast, 4 September 1940

Career: Linfield/UNITED Jan 1959 £6,000/Cambridge Utd July 1961 free/Luton Town Feb 1965 to 1966/Chicago Mustangs (USA)/University of Wisconsin (USA)/ Bavarian Soccer Club (USA)/Racine Soccer Club (USA).

A former Belfast shipyard electrician, Jimmy Gibson was recommended to Newcastle as a buy for the future by former hero, Jack Milburn, who played alongside the 18-year-old and rated the raw Irish youngster highly. The Ulster teenager moved to Tyneside after netting 18 goals in only nine league games for Linfield, Gibson was something of a full-blooded, tearaway type leader. Manager Charlie Mitten also had faith in the youngster, convinced he had found a star in the making. Gibson exploded in a black-and-white shirt, banging in five goals on his first outing against Doncaster Juniors, quickly netting four more goals, and then another hat-trick. He grabbed 13 goals in his first four outings. Strong and forceful, Jimmy though, only received a chance in United's first-team on two occasions, deputising for Len White and Bill Curry. He perhaps lacked guile, but Gibson did well when he moved into the Southern League with Cambridge United, hitting 35 goals during his first season and a haul of 105 goals all told. It was form which earned another chance in the Football League at Kenilworth Road, but that never worked out and Jimmy soon moved to play the game in Illinois and Wisconsin, USA.

Appearances & Goals:
Debut v West Ham United (h) 30 March 1959
FL: 2 app 1 gl
Total: 2 app 1 gl

GIBSON Robert James 1911-1912, 1918-1919

Outside-right
5'7"
b. Brownieside, near Alnwick, 2 May 1887
d. Fenham, Newcastle upon Tyne, 11 March 1958

Career: Newcastle East End/Scotswood Nov 1907/ North Shields Ath May 1908/Bury May 1908 £10/ Crystal Palace Aug 1909/Middlesbrough Aug 1910/ UNITED Aug 1911 £50/Lincoln City May 1912 £35/ Chesterfield Town Oct 1913/Third Lanark May 1914/ UNITED 1918 to 1919 (Scotswood war-guest 1919)/ Clydebank May 1919 (Dumbarton loan 1919-20)/ Durham City Oct 1919/Vale of Leven 1920 to 1922.

After appearing in most of Middlesbrough's First Division fixtures during season 1910-11, United brought the well travelled Northumbrian back to his native North East to act as cover to Jack Rutherford on the right wing. Gibson made only two outings in his single season with the Magpies before being transferred to Lincoln where he failed to make the grade. Afterward Robert continued his journey around the country, making a brief stop at St James' Park after World War One, appearing for the Geordies in the local Newcastle & District United League and Victory League competitions. He wasn't retained when the club's squad was finalised for the start of senior football again in August 1919. He was a joiner by trade when he joined the Magpies and was related to the Easton family, Steven Easten (later Sir Stephen) twice Lord Mayor of Newcastle and who operated a Tyneside construction company. Bobby was also a runner of note, taking part in the Powderhall meeting in Edinburgh, winning the celebrated sprint race in 1915 under an alias of WR Stevens.

Appearances & Goals:
Debut v West Bromwich Albion (h) 7 October 1911
FL: 2 app 0 gls
War: 1 app 0 gls
Total: 3 app 0 gls

GIBSON William Muir 1923-1929

Left-half
5'8"
b. Larkhall, Lanarkshire, 20 July 1896
d. Carluke, Lanarkshire, 14 September 1992

Career: Larkhall Thistle/Cadzow St Anne's/St Anthony's (Glasgow)/Ayr Utd Oct 1919/UNITED Nov 1923 £2,500/ Birmingham City trainer May 1929/Inverness Clacknacuddin player-trainer Nov 1932/Queen's Park trainer 1946 to cs 1963 when he retired.

A talented Scottish ball-player who possessed near perfect distribution in midfield, Willie Gibson hailed from a famous footballing pedigree. Son of the illustrious Neil Gibson of Rangers and Scotland, he had two other brothers of note in the game as well. After making an impression in Ayr United's First Division line-up, totalling 128 games, Gibson became a regular in the Magpies' line-up during season 1923-24 and was prominent in both United's FA Cup and League Championship victories of that era. Although appearing to be duck-footed, he proved an important link-man able to forage for the ball in defence, while he was quick to set up Newcastle's attack. After he retired from the game, Gibson spent lengthy periods at both Birmingham and Queen's Park as trainer, although for a period in the Thirties was seen back on Tyneside working as a baker. As a coach he was well respected, and described as immaculately dressed, even running onto the field to attend to injured players in a "lounge suit and soft felt hat"!

Appearances & Goals:
Debut v Preston North End (a) 17 November 1923
FL: 124 app 2 gls
FAC: 18 app 2 gls
Total: 142 app 4 gls

Honours:
FL champs 1927/FAC winner 1924.

GILFILLAN Robert Inglis 1959-1961

Centre-forward
5'9"
b. Cowdenbeath, 29 June 1938
d. Scotland, 8 November 2012

Career: Cowdenbeath Royals/Dundonald Bluebell 1955/Cowdenbeath June 1955/UNITED Oct 1959 £4,000/St Johnstone Jan 1961 £4,000/Raith Rovers March 1962/Southend Utd June 1963/Doncaster Rovers Nov 1965 £40,000/Northwich Victoria player-coach cs 1971/Retford Town c1972.

Bobby Gilfillan had an eye-catching record in the Scottish League at Cowdenbeath with 54 goals in 82 games during seasons 1957-58 and 1958-59 prompting United's scouts to note his name to United boss Charlie Mitten. Small and thin, Bobby arrived at Gallowgate when the Magpies were in trouble near the foot of the table as cover for Len White. He was immediately thrown into the relegation action but struggled to impose himself. Afterwards Gilfillan was only rarely handed the Number 9 shirt in senior action, yet had the odd good outing, netting twice in a 7-2 victory over Fulham. And when White was badly injured Gilfillan was overlooked and didn't get the call-up, moving shortly afterwards back to Scotland. He later had a good spell in the lower divisions at Roots Hall, scoring 35 goals in 70 matches, and at the Belle Vue Ground, a regular for six seasons, topping 200 games for Doncaster. Bobby was another player from a footballing family; his relations Willie and Jock Gilfillan both had decent careers in the game. Leaving football, he was for a period a sales manager for a Volvo dealership in Doncaster before he returned to his native Fife, living in Kelty. Bobby was afterwards a member of a Scottish skiffle group, the Red Hawks.

Appearances & Goals:
Debut v Bolton Wanderers (h) 24 October 1959
FL: 7 app 2 gls
Total: 7 app 2 gls

Honours:
FL div 4 champs 1966, 1969.

G

GILHOME Alan George 1939-1942, 1945-1946

Inside-right
5'7"
b. Whitley Bay, 8 July 1921
d. Monkseaton, near Whitley Bay, 21 September 1990

Career: Backworth/UNITED amat March 1939 to 1942/ Horden CW/UNITED amat Oct 1945/Bishop Auckland 1946/Whitley Bay 1951, becoming player-manager 1955 to cs 1956, then manager Sept 1956 to Jan 1957.

Alan Gilhome was a most useful schemer who joined United's ranks as a teenager just before the outbreak of World War Two. Having showed talent in local Tyneside football, United's boss Tom Mather signed the playmaker with the aim to nurture the youngster as a future star. But war ruined Gilhome's chances of a decent career in the game. Initially making his debut during season 1939-40, he appeared on 17 occasions for the Black'n'Whites during season 1940-41. On the restoration of peace, Alan moved to non-league football where he reached Wembley as part of Bishop Auckland's FA Amateur Cup runners-up team in 1950 against Willington. He was also a key member of Northern League title sides of 1950, 1951 and 1952. Gilhome afterwards became a noted player with Whitley Bay, totalling almost 250 appearances and winning more medals in the Northern Alliance and Northumberland Senior Cup. Alan later resided in Monkseaton, working as an insurance executive.

Appearances & Goals:
Debut v Leeds United (a) 8 June 1940 (FLNE) (1 goal)
War: 21 app 3 gls
Total: 21 app 3 gls

Honours:
FAAC final 1950.

GILLESPIE Keith Robert 1995-1998

Outside-right
5'10"
b. Larne, Northern Ireland, 18 February 1975

Career: NI Boys Brigade/West Bangor/St Andrew's BC/Rangers trial 1988/Manchester Utd part-time jnr 1988/Dungannon Swifts 1989/Linfield Colts 1989/Manchester Utd jnr 1991, prof Feb 1993 (Wigan Ath loan 1993-94)/UNITED Jan 1995 £1m/Blackburn Rovers Dec 1998 £2.35m (Wigan Ath loan 2000-01)/ Leicester City July 2003 free/Leeds Utd trial cs 2005/Sheffield Utd Aug 2005 (Charlton Ath loan 2008-09)/Leeds Utd Feb 2009/Bradford City March 2009/Ferencvaros TC (Hng) trial July 2009/Glentoran Aug 2009/Notts Co trial July 2010/Darlington trial Oct 2010, pmt Nov 2010 to Dec 2010/Longford Town March 2011 to cs 2013 when he retired.

Arriving in the North East as part of the dramatic multi-million pound deal that sent Andy Cole to Old Trafford, Keith Gillespie quickly showed the football world that he was no make-weight in the transaction. The young Northern Ireland international proved he had the ability to become a huge name in his own right. Fast and direct with a cutting edge to become a match-winner on the right touchline, Keith had greatly impressed manager Kevin Keegan before the Cole deal in a series of matches against the Magpies. Starring in United's successful side of 1995-96, Gillespie possessed balance and control on the ball and searing pace running at defenders, qualities which could destroy the opposition. Keith was rapidly endorsed as a crowd favourite, giving United a contrasting option on the flank to their other wide player, David Ginola, as the Magpies challenged for the Premier League trophy in 1995-96 and 1996-97. A former Youth Cup winner alongside other Fergie Fledglings as Beckham, Scholes, Giggs and Nicky Butt, he was a 17-year-old debutant at Old Trafford. Keith played for his country at every level, gaining his full cap when he was only 19 years of age. In the years which followed though, Gillespie failed to establish himself as one of the Premierships really big stars as had been hoped, although he still had sparkling periods, including when United defeated Barcelona in their Champions League debut at Gallowgate, a game in which he gave international full-back Sergi a torrid evening. Missing the Magpies 1998 FA Cup final due to a foot injury, the Ulsterman went onto have good spells with Blackburn (137 app) and Sheffield United (103 app). He also remained a fixture for the Northern Ireland side for over a decade. Keith noted he led a "colourful life" in football and occasionally found himself the subject of off the field headlines, notably in a fracas with Alan

Shearer when United were in Dublin, while he struggled to cope with flawed business investments and a gambling addiction. Keith confirmed in his autobiography that he squandered his £7m-plus earnings of his career. The Irishman was once sent-off for the Blades after less than a minute of being on the field as a substitute.

Appearances & Goals:
Debut v Sheffield Wednesday (a) 21 January 1995 (sub)
PL: 94(19) app 11 gls
FAC: 9(1) app 2 gls
FLC: 7(1) app 1 gl
Euro: 11(4) app 0 gls
Others: 0(1) app 0 gls
Total: 121(26) app 14 gls

Honours:
86 NI caps 1995-2009/1 NI u21 app 1994/NI sch-youth app/PL runner-up 1996, 1997/FL div 1 prom 2001/FL ch prom 2006/FLC winner 2002/NI LC winner 2010/FAYC winner 1992.

GILLESPIE William Blyth 1927-1929

Left-back
5'8"
b. Buckhaven, Fife, 29 October 1903

Career: Leven Rovers/Buckhaven Victoria 1918/ East Fife Sept 1921/UNITED May 1927 £1,500/ Bristol Rovers June 1929 free/St Mirren July 1930 free/East Fife Oct 1930/Distillery (Belfast) Aug 1932/ Bangor Aug 1935/East Fife 1936-37.

Scot Willie Gillespie crossed the border as a replacement for United's veteran defender Frank Hudspeth. He had just appeared in East Fife's 3-1 defeat at the hands of Celtic in the 1927 Scottish Cup final, and had been impressive throughout their run to Hampden Park as well as a key player for six seasons in the Fifers line-up. However, the Scot never quite excelled in English football and was replaced by another of his countrymen in Bob Thomson. Following a brief period at Eastville with Bristol Rovers, Gillespie continued to clock up games for East Fife, totalling over 250 games at Bayview Park. He enjoyed a good spell in Northern Ireland with Distillery over three seasons and 138 games.

Appearances & Goals:
Debut v Manchester United (h) 21 January 1928
FL: 9 app 0 gls
Total: 9 app 0 gls

Honours:
SC final 1927/NI Cup final 1933.

GILLESPY Thomas (Toby) 1893-1894, 1895-1898

Inside-right or left
5'8"
b. Tyneside

Career: Arthur's Hill (Newcastle) 1888/UNITED Sept 1893 to cs 1894/Hebburn Argyle 1894 to 1895/ UNITED Sept 1895 to cs 1898.

A local product, Toby Gillespy was signed as a professional following the disbandment of local club, Arthur's Hill, and just as United entered Football League soccer in 1893. A versatile forward who stepped into action on four occasions during United's inaugural Football League season, Gillespy afterwards returned to local football turning out for Hebburn Argyle, a home for several of United's pioneers. He later returned to St James' Park where he was part of the Northern Alliance title winning eleven at reserve level in 1898. The Tynesider was well respected locally, noted as being "speedy, tricky and effective" and "for a small player is exceedingly fast". The Northern Gossip correspondent wrote in 1896 that Toby "seemed to lay down and worship the leather".

(Note: Both spellings of Gillespy and Gillespie are used in various sources of information, he was commonly known as Toby rather than Thomas)

Appearances & Goals:
Debut v Lincoln City (a) 7 October 1893
FL: 4 app 0 gls
Total: 4 app 0 gls

GINOLA David Desire Marc 1995-1997

Midfield
6'0"
b. Gassin, Cote d'Azur (France),
25 January 1967

Career: St Maxime BC (Fr)/St Raphael (Fr) 1979/OGC Nice (Fr) 1982 to 1983/SC Toulon (Fr) 1985/Matra Racing (Fr) July 1988/Brest Armorique (Fr) July 1990/Paris St-Germain (Fr) Dec 1991/UNITED July 1995 £2.5m/ Tottenham Hotspur July 1997 £2m/Aston Villa Aug 2000 £3m/Everton Feb 2002/Retired May 2002.

The £2.5 million signing of David Ginola set United's fanatical Toon Army alight with expectation during the close-season of 1995. Born on the Mediterranean coast, near St Tropez, Ginola came to Tyneside as a player of experience with Paris St-Germain, having reached three European semi-finals, including the Champions League in 1994-95. He was one of the Continent's finest players, a flamboyant star with style and match-winning ability. His very persona knitted with United's vision of being a club with razzmatazz. Appearing in almost 400 senior games before crossing the Channel for England, Ginola was a virtuoso of the very highest quality, possessing marvellous balance and poise. A tall, elegant international winger-cum-midfielder with a near perfect physique, the Frenchman arrived on Tyneside with a reputation for being something of a pin-up star who could entertain but also deliver the goods, and it was hoped he would turn the Magpies into a trophy winning outfit. That didn't quite materialise, but Ginola made a huge impact on English football nevertheless, being in contention for the Player of the Year award at the end of the 1995-96 season as United lost the Premier League title by a narrow margin. Known as 'Il Magnifique' in France and possessing tremendous technique and style on the ball, he operated wide on the left and could use both feet to deliver telling crosses and passes. English defences learnt that they had only one way to stop Ginola, by hunting in packs of two or even three men to swamp his trickery. Largely overlooked by his own national side when on Tyneside following a fall-out as France failed to qualify for the World Cup, Ginola was at times erratic and didn't work back as much as some wanted, yet he could send the crowd roaring with delight with his special brand of skill in attack and an uncanny ability to race away with the ball in complete control. During the early part of his career, David quit football to concentrate on studying law in Nice, only to be given a second chance in the game with Toulon. Charming and articulate, with the looks of a film star, he also acted as a model for Italian fashion-house Nino Cerutti and for L'Oreal. Ginola had a strong rapport with manager Kevin Keegan, but the Frenchman did not have the same good relationship with his replacement. The arrival of Kenny Dalglish saw David soon join Tottenham in July 1997 and at White Hart Lane he continued to shine, lifting a rare double of the Player of the Year and Footballer of the Year awards during 1998-99. David was a huge hit in North London and made 127 outings (21 goals) for Spurs before moving on to Aston Villa and Everton at the end of his career in England. Ginola was frequently in the limelight, even later to enter the world of cinema as an actor (The Last Drop, 2005), as well as setting up a vin-yard and winery in Provence. He is often to be seen as part of the football media in the UK and France and is involved in much charity work for worthy causes. His father was also a semi-professional footballer in France.

Appearances & Goals:
Debut v Coventry City (h) 19 August 1995
PL: 54(4) app 6 gls
FAC: 4 app 0 gls
FLC: 6 app 0 gls
Euro: 6(1) app 1 gl
Others: 1 app 0 gls
Total: 71(5) app 7 gls

Honours:
17 Fr caps 1991-96/Fr B app 1992/8 Fr u21 app 1987-89/PL runner-up 1996, 1997/Fr Lg champs 1994/FLC winner 1999/Fr Cup winner 1993, 1995/Fr Cup final 1990/Fr LC winner 1995/Fr FoY 1993/PoY 1999 (PFA)/FoY 1999 (FWA)/PFA ToS (PL) 1996, 1999.

GIVEN Shay John James 1997-2009

Goalkeeper
6'1"
b. Lifford, Co Donegal (Eire), 20 April 1976

Career: Lifford Celtic/Celtic jnr Sept 1992/ Blackburn Rovers Aug 1994 (Swindon Town loan 1994-95, 1995-96)(Sunderland loan 1995-96)/ UNITED July 1997 £1.5m/Manchester City Feb 2009 £5.9m/Aston Villa July 2011 £3.5m (Middlesbrough loan 2013-14).

Only two players have worn United's shirt more in senior action than goalkeeper Shay Given. His 463 appearances for the club are bettered only by fellow custodian Jimmy Lawrence as well as Frank Hudspeth. Had it not been for a regime change at St James' Park and deterioration of the Magpies fortunes at the time, the Irishman would have no doubt passed Lawrence's longstanding record total. As it was following more than a decade at Gallowgate and when 32 years of age, Given moved during February 2009 for a reported £5.9m to Manchester City with a tinge of bitterness. Nevertheless, he had enjoyed huge popular support by the club's Toon Army during his rollercoaster period between the posts. The Irishman started his senior career at Parkhead with Celtic as a teenager, then Shay was an emerging goalkeeper at Blackburn Rovers when Kenny Dalglish was boss at Ewood Park. With Tim Flowers blocking his path at Blackburn, he was brought to Tyneside during the close-season of 1997 for £1.5m once his manager moved to Gallowgate and having showed his potential following successful loan spells with first Swindon, then Sunderland where he helped win promotion. Given was soon making an impression at Gallowgate and he became United's regular 'keeper for all of 12 seasons, with only the odd period exchanged with his long term rival Steve Harper. Always able to produce breathtaking saves, sound and agile, Shay developed into one of the Premier League's finest custodians. He took part in two FA Cup finals for the Magpies, one on the bench, and was just as much a match-winner as his forward colleagues on many occasions. The Irishman also featured in a succession of European ties with Newcastle, including Champions League action. Shay was recognised as one of the best stoppers in world football during the modern era, able to pull-off incredible saves and in a consistent manner too. Captaining his country and winning over a century of caps for the Republic of Ireland, he became one of the most respected footballers in the game and the club's most capped player; 82 appearances when on United's staff. No other player has appeared more for United in post-war football while Given was also a rare goalkeeper skipper of United on occasion. Before moving into the professional game, Shay earned a living as a teenager selling fruit and vegetables in Donegal and had trials at both Manchester United and Bradford City.

Appearances & Goals:
Debut v Sheffield Wednesday (h) 9 August 1997
PL: 354 app 0 gls
FAC: 34 app 0 gls
FLC: 12(1) app 0 gls
Euro: 62 app 0 gls
Total: 462(1) app 0 gls

Honours:
125 Eire caps 1996-2012/WdC 2002/1 Eire unoff app 2005/Eire u21 app/Eire sch-youth app/FAC winner 2011 (sub no app)/FAC final 1998, 1999 (sub no app)/FL div 1 champs 1996/FL div 2 champs 1996 (5 app)/PFA ToS (PL) 2002, 2006/Freedom of Co Donegal 2006.

GLASS Stephen 1998-2001

Midfield
5'9"
b. Dundee, 23 May 1976

Career: Crombie Sports/Aberdeen Oct 1994/UNITED July 1998 £650,000/Watford July 2001 free/Hibernian July 2003 free/Dunfermline Ath loan Jan 2007, pmt July 2007 to May 2010/St Mirren July 2010/Carolina Rail Hawks (USA) March 2011/Shamrock Rovers asst-manager Jan 2012, becoming caretaker-manager Sept 2012 to Nov 2012/Triangle FC (USA) asst-coach 2013 & North Carolina Alliance soccer academy.

G

Raised in Fintry, for three seasons Stephen Glass was recognised as one of the best forwards in Scottish football, being a teenage star as the Dons lifted the Scottish League Cup during 1996. With a deft touch of the ball and a talented left boot, the Aberdeen midfielder or flanker had totalled 130 games north of the Cheviots and was tipped for a full cap before his move to Tyneside for a tribunal set £650,000 fee, this after a protracted and disputed transfer deal. Operating either as a raiding left-winger of the old-school, or a modern wide midfielder, Glass showed he had ability, producing a handful of outstanding displays in a Magpie shirt during the first half of season 1998-99. Brought to Tyneside by Kenny Dalglish only to find his Scottish compatriot depart quickly, he was one of a few of the existing squad favoured by Ruud Gullit. Of slight build, he could whip in a telling cross and possessed a sure shot. But the physical rigour and pace of the English Premiership was a step up from football north of the border and a knee injury affected his progress. The Scot became a bit-part player for the following two campaigns and when his third boss on Tyneside, Bobby Robson assessed his playing squad at Gallowgate, he allowed Glass to depart to the second tier, replacing the left slot in midfield with French import Laurent Robert. With Watford, Stephen gained regular action for two seasons, part of the Hornets' line-up which reached FA Cup semi-final.

Appearances & Goals:
Debut v Liverpool (h) 30 August 1998 (sub)
PL: 24(19) app 7 gls
FAC: 3(4) app 0 gls
FLC: 3 app 0 gls
Euro: 2(3) app 0 gls
Total: 32(26) app 7 gls

Honours:
1 Scot cap 1999/3 Scot B app 1996-2003/11 Scot u21 app 1995-97/FAC final 1999/SLC winner 1996.

GLASSEY John Robert 1944

Inside-left
5'10"
b. Chester-le-Street, 13 August 1914
d. Durham, 10 July 1984

Career: Horden CW/Liverpool Jan 1934/Stoke City Feb 1938/Mansfield Town May 1939 (Hartlepools Utd war-guest 1939-40)(Third Lanark war-guest 1940-43)(Dundee Utd war-guest 1941-43)(Raith Rovers war-guest 1942-44)(UNITED war-guest 1943-44)/Stockton 1945/Horden CW/West Stanley Aug 1948/Blackburn Rovers scout.

Bobby Glassey only appeared occasionally at all his Football League clubs, although during his stay at Anfield did well for Liverpool, netting four goals in nine matches then was restricted due to a bad ankle injury. Arriving at St James' Park towards the end of the 1943-44 season, he stepped into Johnny Dixon's role at inside-forward for fixtures against Darlington and Sheffield United. Stationed in Scotland for a lengthy period during the war, he appeared frequently for Third Lanark, Raith and Dundee United.

Appearances & Goals:
Debut v Darlington (h) 25 March 1944 (WC)
War: 2 app 0 gls
Total: 2 app 0 gls

GODDARD Paul 1986-1988

Centre-forward
5'9"
b. Harlington, Middlesex, 12 October 1959

Career: Queens Park Rangers jnr Dec 1972, prof July 1977/West Ham Utd Aug 1980 £800,000/ UNITED Nov 1986 £415,000/Derby Co July 1988 £425,000/Millwall Dec 1989 £800,000/Ipswich Town Jan 1991 free, becoming coach May 1994, caretaker-manager Dec 1994, asst-coach 1995/ FA coaching staff 1997/Ipswich Town asst-coach cs 2000/West Ham Utd asst-manager July 2001 to Jan 2004.

Paul Goddard commanded record club fees when he joined West Ham, Newcastle and Millwall. Not a tall and powerful centre-forward in the traditional mould, Goddard was small, but knew how to control and shield the ball, and had the poacher's instinct in front

of goal. Developing through the ranks at Loftus Road where he started as a schoolboy, it was at Upton Park on the other side of London where Goddard really flourished. He appeared on 213 occasions for the Hammers, netted 71 goals and was a key man in West Ham's promotion and League Cup run during season 1980-81. However, a dislocated shoulder forced him to the sidelines and by the time Paul was fit again his place had been taken by Frank McAvennie. Newcastle jumped at the chance to bring the quality striker north and immediately Goddard repaid the Magpies hefty fee by netting 11 precious goals, including seven in seven consecutive games, which effectively saved the Magpies from the First Division trapdoor in 1987. Nicknamed 'Sarge' after his Boy's Brigade days, Goddard had a willingness to play for the team and had the knack of scoring important goals. He was admired by United's supporters, but for family needs, Paul returned south to continue his career and United lost a talented forward. Goddard has one of the shortest careers in an England shirt on record, all of 50 minutes, scoring on his only appearance as substitute against Iceland. Following periods coaching for Ipswich, West Ham and the England youth side, Paul was engaged with the Stellar sporting agency based in London. He also ran a holiday letting business for a period.

Appearances & Goals:
Debut v Leicester City (a) 8 November 1986
FL: 61 app 19 gls
FAC: 6 app 3 gls
FLC: 3 app 1 gl
Total: 70 app 23 gls

Honours:
1 Eng cap 1982/1 Eng B app 1985/8 Eng u21 app 1981-83/FL div 2 champs 1981, 1992/FLC final 1981/PFA ToS (d2) 1981.

GOLDING William 1944-1945

Goalkeeper
5'10"
b. Newcastle upon Tyne, 1922

Career: Burradon Welfare/UNITED Sept 1944 to 1945.

William Golding was a local goalkeeping talent signed by Newcastle as cover during season 1944-45. Stepping in for regular choice, on loan international 'keeper Dave Cumming of Middlesbrough, Golding had a debut to savour. He appeared at Ayresome Park in a Tyne-Tees derby and helped United to a convincing 8-2 victory. By the time United's professional custodians were returning to the fold at the end of the Second World War, Newcastle found they had no fewer than eight goalkeepers on the staff and as a consequence Golding was released.

Appearances & Goals:
Debut v Middlesbrough (a) 14 October 1944 (FLN)
War: 2 app 0 gls
Total: 2 app 0 gls

GOMA Alain Jean 1999-2001

Centre-half
6'0"
b. Sault (France), 5 October 1972

Career: RC Versailles (Fr) 1982/AJ Auxerre (Fr) jnr 1988, prof cs 1993/Paris St-Germain (Fr) cs 1998/UNITED July 1999 £4.75m/Fulham March 2001 £3.5m to cs 2006/ Al-Wakrah SC (Qt) 2007/retired cs 2009.

One of several French footballers to have pulled on the black-and-white striped shirt in the modern era of the game, Alain Goma became manager Ruud Gullit's answer to Newcastle's sometimes suspect and often criticised back-line. He joined the club as a 26-year-old for a near £5m fee during the summer of 1999, Goma was a strong-looking centre-back; tall, powerfully built and muscular with it. Capped by France, Alain had showed with Auxerre in nearly 200 games he had the winning mentality, playing alongside Stephane Guivarc'h. Gullit also acquired Spanish international Marcelino to play alongside Goma, another expensive Continental buy. That new partnership was never fruitful and while the Spaniard flopped alarmingly, at least Goma earned a degree of respect from the Geordie support due to his periods of effective defensive play. Alain was out injured though too often and was never really at the top of physical fitness with the Magpies. Soon after pulling on United's shirt he was sidelined for a long period with an Achilles tendon injury and subsequently only figured in runs of a dozen matches at most without dropping out. The Frenchman moved to Fulham towards the end of the 2000-01 season and spent six seasons at Craven Cottage, enjoying some injury-free periods, although still often in the treatment-room. Before retiring from the first-class scene he totalled 152 games for the Londoners. Goma then settled in London and set-up his own personal fitness company, Algofit, as well as being a director of a development company engaged in residential property in the capital. Goma was raised in the south of France, around Avignon, with family roots in Zaire.

Appearances & Goals:
Debut v Aston Villa (h) 7 August 1999
PL: 32(1) app 1 gl
FAC: 2 app 0 gls
FLC: 4 app 0 gls
Euro: 2 app 0 gls
Total: 40(1) app 1 gl

Honours:
2 Fr caps 1997-98/1 Fr A app 1996/17 Fr u21 app 1992-94/Fr sch-youth app/FL div 1 champs 2001 (3 app)/Fr Lg champs 1996/Fr Cup winner 1994, 1996.

GONZALEZ Ignacio Maria (Gatti) 2008-2009

Midfield
5'11"
b. Montevideo (Uruguay), 14 May 1982
Career: Danubio (Ugy) 2002 (AS Monaco (Fr) loan 2008)/Valencia (Sp) Sept 2008 (UNITED loan Sept 2008 to May 2009)(Levadiakos (Gr) loan 2009-10) (Levante (Sp) loan 2010-11)/Standard Liege (Belg) July 2011 (Hercules CF (Sp) loan 2012-13)/Club Nacional (Ugy) Aug 2013.

The arrival on a season-long loan deal of United's first Uruguayan, midfielder Gonzalez Gatti in the summer of 2008 brought with it headlining consequences. Manager Kevin Keegan did not want the player, the deal being concluded by others within the newly installed United regime and the relationship soon deteriorated fatally between club and manager. None of that of course was of the Valencia player's making. To make matters worse the international midfielder was injured on arrival, unable to be considered for selection until September and few could quite understand why the club brought him to Tyneside. Nicknamed 'Nacho', when fit, Gonzalez was included in the squad for the 2008-09 season, but managed only 38 minutes of football, wearing a senior United shirt in fleeting substitute appearances. Then he was sidelined again, out for the campaign with an Achilles injury. A grafter on the field rather than a creative entertainer, Gonzales had been part of Uruguay's World Cup squad in South Africa during 2010, alongside Louis Suarez. Gonzalez returned to Valencia at the end of his stint attached to Newcastle United and was immediately released to join La Liga strugglers Levante, the player remarkably not appearing once for Valencia since moving to the Mestalla arena at the start of 2008-09 then immediately being loaned to the Magpies. Gonzales moved to Belgian football for 2011-12 and back to Uruguay in 2013.

Appearances & Goals:
Debut v Hull City (h) 13 September 2008 (sub)
PL: 0(2) app 0 gls
Total: 0(2) app 0 gls

Honours:
18 Ugy caps 2006-date/WdC 2010/Ugy Lg champs 2004, 2007.

GOOD Curtis Edward 2012-date

Centre-half
6'2"
b. Melbourne (Australia), 23 March 1993
Career: Box Hill Utd (Aus)/Nunawding City (Aus) 2005/Australian Institute of Sport 2009/Melbourne Heart (Aus) jnr 2011, snr Feb 2011/UNITED trial April 2012, pmt Aug 2012 £400,000 (Bradford City loan 2012-13)(Dundee Utd loan 2013-14).

Newcastle made a surprise purchase of 19-year-old Aussie Curtis Good in 2012, a young defender who had showed much promise in his first season with top Australian club Melbourne Heart. Able to operate as a centre-back or left-back, Good soon went on loan with tier-four Bradford City during 2012-13 and enjoyed being part of the Tykes' headlining League Cup run to Wembley in which they defeated Premier League Arsenal and Aston Villa. Curtis appeared at Wembley in the final,

although experienced defeat to Swansea City. Additionally the Aussie helped in a small way as City secured promotion to Division One. That experience did much to acclimatise the youngster to English football and he benefited greatly from the loan deal. A regular member of the young Australian team, captaining the Socceroos Under-20 side, Good was selected as a Magpie substitute for a Premier League contest with Manchester City during March 2013, then got a run out in a friendly before making his Newcastle debut in a Football League Cup tie at Morecambe as the new 2013-14 season opened. He was elevated to the full Australia line-up in March 2014 and was included in his country's preliminary squad for the Brazil World Cup until a hip injury forced him out of contention. It was an unlucky knock which also saw Curtis miss Dundee United's Scottish Cup final. Good has family roots in Liverpool.

Appearances & Goals:
Debut v Morecambe (a) 28 August 2013 (FLC)
FLC: 1 app 0 gls
Total: 1 app 0 gls

Honours:
1 Aus cap 2014-date/Aus sch-youth app/FL div 2 prom 2013 (3 app)/FLC final 2013.

GOODWILL Thomas 1913-1916

Outside-left
5'7"
b. Bates Cottages, near Earsdon, Northumberland, 7 September 1893
d. Thiepval (France), 1 July 1916
Career: Bates Wand/Seaton Delaval 1913/UNITED May 1913 £100 to death.

A former teenage miner, Tommy Goodwill was the archetypal working-class hero. Graduating from local football, he gained a chance with the Black'n'Whites and made such an impression in the club's reserve eleven that he quickly succeeded Scottish international George Wilson on the left wing. He was a quick mover and could accurately cross the ball as well as being able to delight the crowd. Goodwill was hailed as a new star as he became a regular for United during the two seasons before the Great War halted football in 1915. Like so many of the game's players he volunteered for action on the Continent, signing up for one of the 'Pals' units, the 'Newcastle Commercials', the 16th Northumberland Fusiliers Battalion, along with United colleagues Dan Dunglinson and Stan Hardy. Sadly Goodwill and Dunglinson were both killed in the terrible opening Battle of the Somme. Their battalion was ordered to attack the fortress village of Thiepval and as the Commercials left the trenches at walking pace, Germans opened fire with machine-guns and shells; Goodwill being fatally hit by shrapnel. He was only barely into his twenties and fell a few yards from his team-mate who was also fatally wounded. It is thought that one of the figures on the Barras Bridge War Memorial of the Commercials in Newcastle features that of Tommy Goodwill. His name is engraved on the memorial at Thiepval, one of 73,412 men who have no known grave at that hamlet in Northern France.

Appearances & Goals:
Debut v Everton (h) 13 September 1913
FL: 52 app 4 gls
FAC: 8 app 2 gls
Total: 60 app 6 gls

GORDON James 1935-1945

Right-half
5'7"
b. Fauldhouse, West Lothian, 23 October 1915
d. Derby, 29 August 1996
Career: Forth Wand/Wishaw Jnrs/UNITED April 1935 £140/Middlesbrough Nov 1945 £3,500, becoming asst-coach cs 1955/Blackburn Rovers coach 1961/Derby Co coach cs 1969/Leeds Utd coach July 1974 to Sept 1974/Nottingham Forest coach Jan 1975/Retired May 1981.

Ex-miner Jimmy Gordon was one of the best players around during the immediate years before the Second World War broke out in 1939. Joining United after being the star of the 1935 Scottish Junior Cup semi-final in front of manager Andy

Cunningham, Jimmy was a polished wing-half, frequently tipped for Scottish caps during 1937 and 1938, but was unlucky to break his fibula when almost a certainty for his first call-up. Sure and effective and rarely flustered, Gordon was tenacious to the point that one colleague noted that he was, "the terror of forwards", while he also specialised in a long throw. Jimmy turned out for the Magpies often during the war, but was unable to command a first-team place at St James' Park after the hostilities due to rising youngsters. He headed for Ayresome Park where he continued to perform with distinction until his 38th year, and amassed 253 games for Boro, also having a period as skipper. It was on Teesside that the Scot first made contact with Brian Clough, Gordon becoming the third member of the celebrated Clough and Peter Taylor management team which lifted several trophies during the Seventies. A wise and enthusiastic aide, he once led Nottingham Forest out at Wembley in a League Cup final, a gesture and acknowledgment of the Scots' influence behind the scenes by Clough. Jimmy afterwards resided in Derby to his death.

Appearances & Goals:
Debut v Oldham Athletic (a) 27 April 1935
FL: 132 app 2 gls
FAC: 11 app 1 gl
War: 110 app 18 gls
Total: 253 app 21 gls
(Void FL: 1 app 0 gls)

GORRY Martin Christopher 1976-1978

Left-back
5'10"
b. Derby, 29 December 1954

Career: Barnsley jnr 1972, prof May 1973/UNITED Oct 1976 £50,000 (Stockport Co loan 1977-78)/Hartlepool Utd July 1978 free to cs 1980/Shildon Ath Oct 1980/ Later with Rotorua City (NZ) player-coach c1984 to c1990.

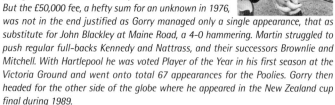

With less than a year of senior experience to his name, Martin Gorry was purchased by United manager Gordon Lee as a prospect to be developed into a First Division defender. Described as "one of the League's most promising young defenders", much was expected of the new arrival. But the £50,000 fee, a hefty sum for an unknown in 1976, was not in the end justified as Gorry managed only a single appearance, that as substitute for John Blackley at Maine Road, a 4-0 hammering. Martin struggled to push regular full-backs Kennedy and Nattrass, and their successors Brownlie and Mitchell. With Hartlepool he was voted Player of the Year in his first season at the Victoria Ground and went onto total 67 appearances for the Poolies. Gorry then headed for the other side of the globe where he appeared in the New Zealand cup final during 1989.

Appearances & Goals:
Debut v Manchester City (a) 26 December 1977 (sub)
FL: 0(1) app 0 gls
Total: 0(1) app 0 gls

GOSLING Daniel 2010-2014

Midfield
5'11"
b. Brixham, Devon, 1 February 1990

Career: Brixham Utd/Plymouth Argyle jnr 2006, prof Feb 2007/Everton Jan 2008 £1.3m/UNITED July 2010 (Blackpool loan 2013-14)/Bournemouth July 2014 free.

As an Everton youngster, Dan Gosling created headlines when he netted an extra-time winner for his club in a high-profile FA Cup meeting with rivals Liverpool during 2009. An energetic midfielder, he went onto make a brief appearance in that season's FA Cup final for the Toffees against Chelsea. A bright future awaited the Devon-born player, but in March 2010 he sustained a cruciate knee injury which put him out of action for nearly 12 months. Following 37 games for the Mersey club, he then ran into a contract dispute with the Goodison Park management, and in stepped the Magpies, signing Gosling when he was still recuperating from that injury during July 2010. Dan remained out of action for another long period, but made a comeback as part of United's side against Sunderland in January 2011, a rare derby debutant, albeit as a late substitute. He was first noticed when barely a teenager by Plymouth Argyle

as he played for his home-town side of Brixham United near Torquay. Gosling made an impact in the Championship tier, recorded his senior bow as a 16-year-old and he soon was recognised by England as a potential star of the future, earning caps at Under-17, Under-18 and Under-19 level. Dan then moved to the big-time during 2008 when he joined Everton as a teenager soon making his England Under-21 debut. When fully fit and in contention for a Newcastle place, Gosling found it difficult to get into United's line-up. He appeared on 16 occasions (13 from the bench) during 2011-12 but only nine times the following term, when he suffered from another injury.

Appearances & Goals:
Debut v Sunderland (a) 16 January 2011 (sub)
FL/PL: 5(19) app 1 gl
FAC: 0(2) app 0 gls
FLC: 4(1) app 0 gls
Euro: 3(2) app 0 gls
Total: 12(24) app 1 gl

Honours:
3 Eng u21 app 2010-12/Eng sch-youth app/FAC final 2009.

GOSNELL Albert Arthur 1904-1910, 1919-1921

Outside-left & Trainer
5'10"
b. Colchester, 10 February 1880
d. Norwich, 6 January 1972

Career: The Albion (Colchester) cs 1898/ Colchester Town/New Brompton Sept 1901/ Chatham Aug 1902/UNITED May 1904 £10/ Tottenham Hotspur July 1910 £100/Darlington June 1911/Port Vale May 1912 to cs 1913/ Newcastle City Sept 1913/UNITED asst-trainer 1919/Norwich City manager Jan 1921 to March 1926/Colchester Town trainer cs 1926.

A lively winger for a big man who weighed in at over 12 stone, Albert Gosnell boasted a consistent cross and good shot, but never got on too well with United's spectators, probably as a result of replacing their favourite, the flamboyant Bobby Templeton. Gosnell was exactly the opposite in style and character to Templeton. He was a steady player, reliable and thoroughly a team man. And he was, despite the problems encountered with the boo-boys, a very effective player for United as they won the title prize in 1904-05 and 1906-07. Bert's stock was on the rise and justified his England selection. By the time the Magpies had lifted their next title, two years later, Gosnell was only given a sparse run in the side and replaced, to many of the fans' delight, by another Scottish maestro, George Wilson. Gosnell had the best years of his career on Tyneside, after leaving the game he scouted and then became a licensee at The Raven in Norwich for a period.

Appearances & Goals:
Debut v Middlesbrough (h) 5 November 1904
FL: 106 app 15 gls
FAC: 18 app 3 gls
Others: 1 app 0 gls
Total: 125 app 18 gls

Honours:
1 Eng cap 1906/Eng trial app 1906/FL champs 1905, 1907, 1909 (5 app)/FAC final 1905, 1906.

GOUFFRAN Yoan 2013-date

Striker
5'10"
b. Villeneuve-St-Georges, Paris (France), 25 May 1986

Career: Red Star Paris 1992 (Fr)/SM Caen (Fr) jnr, prof July 2003/Bordeaux (Fr) June 2008 £5.7m/ UNITED Jan 2013 £2.1m.

Yoan Gouffran impressed manager Alan Pardew having played against United in the Europa League for Bordeaux and when a deal for Marseille's Loic Remy fell through switched his attention to the lean and fast Girondins player. At 26-years-old, the Frenchman settled on Tyneside as an experienced utility forward, able to play across the line and always likely to find the net, having scored 12 goals in season 2012-13 for his club Bordeaux before joining United. Lively and full of energy, Gouffran took to the fast pace of the Premier League and foraged up and down the field in a workmanlike manner. Ironically he then became a colleague of Remy at

Gallowgate in 2013-14 as Yoan became first-choice in attack and midfield ahead of Cisse, Ben Arfa and Gutierrez. With parents from the islands of Guadeloupe, Yoan developed as a young player with Caen in Normandy, making what was a big transfer move for nearly £6m to Bordeaux during 2008. He soon became a fixture in Les Girondins line-up and before his move to England had totalled 179 games, netting 40 goals. With his energetic and hardworking style, Gouffran became a favourite on Tyneside.

Appearances & Goals:
Debut v Aston Villa (a) 29 January 2013
PL: 45(5) app 9 gls
FAC: 1 app 0 gls
FLC: 3 app 1 gl
Total: 49(5) app 10 gls

Honours:
22 Fr u21 app/Fr Lg champs 2009/Fr div 2 prom 2007.

GOURLAY Archibald Murdoch 1988-1992

Midfield
5'8"
b. Greenock, 29 June 1969

Career: Gourock Utd 1981/Morton Sept 1985/UNITED March 1988 £50,000 (Morton loan 1989-90) (Gateshead loan 1991-92)/Motherwell April 1992 free/Gateshead/Linfield/Hartlepool Utd Sept 1994/ Whitley Bay 1994/Morpeth Town player-coach March 1995 to cs 1998/South Shields Aug 1998 becoming manager Dec 1998/Bedlington Terriers Feb 1999/ Birtley Town player-coach Oct 1999.

Archie Gourlay was still 18 years old when he joined Newcastle as a skilful forward from Scottish football. With only two games to his name in the senior game north of the border, Gourlay was clearly the unfinished article when he arrived on Tyneside, but possessed the look and style that prompted Ossie Ardiles to note him as, "one of the most talented players on our books". Archie never fulfilled his potential and was almost totally restricted to Central League football at Gallowgate and at one stage couldn't even get to train with the senior pool. Slightly built, he operated up front as well as in midfield and after leaving United played the game at a number of non-league clubs in the region. Gourlay was also employed as an advertising manager with Herald Newspapers in the North East. For a period he returned to Gallowgate as a Football in the Community coach during 2004 and 2005.

Appearances & Goals:
Debut v Luton Town (a) 3 December 1988 (sub)
FL: 2(1) app 0 gls
FLC: 0(2) app 0 gls
Total: 2(3) app 0 gls

GOWLING Alan Edwin 1975-1978

Striker
6'0"
b. Stockport, 16 March 1949

Career: Manchester University/Manchester Utd amat Aug 1965, prof April 1967/Huddersfield Town June 1972 £65,000/UNITED Aug 1975 £70,000/Bolton Wand March 1978 £120,000/ Preston North End Sept 1982 free/ Retired Aug 1983.

Gangling, awkward-looking front runner Alan Gowling never appeared overly skilful or even epitomised most fans idea of a footballer, but was nevertheless an extremely effective striker for the Magpies. A university graduate in economics, Gowling was a star youngster at Old Trafford, playing alongside established names like Charlton and Best, either in midfield or up front. He made his debut for the Reds when still an amateur student and had much talent, becoming skipper of the England Under-23 side. Following 87 games (21 goals) in United's shirt Alan moved to Leeds Road for a club record fee, but suffered two successive relegation seasons with Huddersfield as they plunged into the Division Four graveyard. His goalscoring record was still a good one, 61 for the Terriers, and it prompted Gordon Lee to rescue Gowling and place him alongside Malcolm Macdonald as Newcastle began the 1975-76 season. The partnership worked and Gowling ended up top scorer with 30 goals. A thoughtful player, he once described himself as "tall, lean and a glutton for work". His deceptive skill on the ground and power in the air proved a menace as United reached Wembley and afterwards qualified for the UEFA

Cup. A bust-up with the Magpies over the sacking of Richard Dinnis led to Gowling moving on, to Bolton for another record fee and at Burnden Park Gowling was a success again, recording 175 games for the Trotters. He later became Chairman of the PFA (1980-82) and was on the Management Committee from 1975 to 1984. He once scored four goals in a single match for both the Magpies and Manchester United, while he turned down a place at Cambridge University to turn professional at Old Trafford. On retiring from the game, Gowling entered business in Lancashire as General Manager for a chemical manufacturing company. He also kept a link with the game by becoming a local radio commentator covering Premier League matches in Lancashire as well as having a column in the Manchester Evening News for a period.

Appearances & Goals:
Debut v Ipswich Town (a) 16 August 1975
(v Sunderland (h) 6 August 1975 (ASC))
FL: 91(1) app 30 gls
FAC: 15 app 8 gls
FLC: 9 app 7 gls
Euro: 3 app 3 gls
Others: 4 app 4 gls
Total: 122(1) app 52 gls

Honours:
1 Eng u23 app 1972/Eng sch-youth app/Eng amat app/British Olympic app 1968/FL div 2 champs 1978 (8 app)/FLC final 1976.

GRAHAM Douglas 1940-1950

Left-back
5'10"
b. Ashington, 15 July 1921
d. Newcastle upon Tyne, 10 November 1993

Career: Barrington Utd/UNITED amat April 1940, prof Aug 1940 £20 (Middlesbrough war-guest 1941-42)/ Preston North End Nov 1950 £8,000/Lincoln City Dec 1951/St Gallen (Switz) player-coach July 1957/ Gateshead coach c1965.

A bricklayer and joiner at Barrington Colliery, Duggie Graham was converted from a centre-forward to a stylish defender and able to operate on the right or left flank. Graham was unfortunate to lose the best years of his career due to World War Two. Nicknamed 'The Duke' on account of his immaculate attire, Graham also played with class on the field able to read the game well. On the resumption of peacetime football, he was part of United's promotion eleven during 1948 and playing at top form until a bad injury put him out of the side. He also helped Lincoln to promotion, being skipper of the Imps; at Sincil Bank he gave City over five years splendid service totalling almost 200 outings. Graham married United coach, Norman Smith's daughter, while he was also an accomplished sprinter. He later resided in Newcastle and worked for a Tyneside car dealership.

Appearances & Goals:
Debut v Millwall (a) 31 August 1946
(v Bradford City (h) 8 June 1940 (FLNE))
FL: 71 app 0 gls
FAC: 3 app 0 gls
War: 90 app 1 gl
Total: 164 app 1 gl

Honours:
FL div 2 prom 1948/FL div 3(N) champs 1952.

GRAHAM John R 1901-1903

Outside-left
5'7"
b. Newcastle upon Tyne

Career: Workington Black Diamonds/UNITED Nov 1901/Bradford City Aug 1903 to cs 1905/Workington Aug 1905.

A stand-in for regular winger Richard Roberts during the 1901-02 season, John Graham was "quick witted and dexterous on the green" according to one Edwardian critic. But in Newcastle's ranks he was always recognised as a reserve, although Graham had a good spell with Bradford City as they entered Football League soccer during 1903. Over two seasons with the Bantams, he registered 59 appearances in Second Division fare.

Appearances & Goals:
Debut v Bury (h) 28 December 1901.
FL: 6 app 0 gls
Total: 6 app 0 gls

G

GRAHAM Samuel 1902-1905

Outside or Inside-right
5'6"
b. Galston, Ayrshire, 7 April 1878

Career: Galston Sept 1899/UNITED April 1902/ Norwich City May 1905/Kilmarnock May 1906/ Galston Aug 1907/Ayr FC Aug 1908 (Ayr Parkhouse loan 1909-10)/Ayr Utd Aug 1910 (Galston loan 1911-12, 1912-13) to 1916.

Sam Graham had an long career of over 20 years in the game as a player, never reaching great heights, but the Scot was a most dependable player especially in Ayrshire football where he was a well known figure. At St James' Park, Sam deputised for internationals Jack Rutherford, Ronald Orr and Jimmy Howie across the Magpies' forward line, and always fitted in adequately, although unjustly compared to his great contemporaries. He took part in United's title success during 1905 and won Northern League championship medals with the Novocastrians. He was also a member of the Galston side that lifted the Scottish Qualifying Cup in 1900.

Appearances & Goals:
Debut v Wolverhampton Wanderers (a) 1 November 1902
FL: 5 app 0 gls
FAC: 1 app 0 gls
Total: 6 app 0 gls

Honours:
FL champs 1905 (3 app).

GRAHAM William 1892-1899

Centre-half
5'10"
b. Dreghorn, Ayrshire, 12 January 1866
d. New Cumnock, Ayrshire, 12 March 1937

Career: New Cumnock/Preston North End 1888/Annbank cs 1889/Lanemark 1889-90/ UNITED July 1892 (Lanemark loan 1898-99) to Jan 1899 when he returned to Scotland.

One of the Magpies' earliest stalwarts, coal-miner Willie Graham arrived from Scotland as Newcastle East End had just completed their move from Heaton to St James' Park and to soon become Newcastle United. He appeared in the club's first fixture at the Barrack Road arena and then in the Northern League campaign for 1892-93. And the following season he was on the field for the Tynesider's debut in Football League soccer, becoming a regular during those formative years in Division Two. Graham was a tireless worker in the middle of the field and was an inspiration on the field. Captain of the club, he organised United's team plan and had a big influence on the side. When he left Gallowgate during 1899 it was without the club's permission following a dispute. From a large family of seven brothers, his more famous sibling, John Graham, also appeared for Preston. Both men took part in the Lilywhites' historic capture of the Football League title trophy during the inaugural season of competitive football in 1888-89. Willie played in the very first round of league fixtures that season, for Preston against Burnley and when he arrived on Tyneside from Annbank in Ayrshire some four years later, the local press described him as a "celebrated half back". His younger brother Hugh joined the Magpies in November 1898 from Lanemark but did not reach the first eleven.

Appearances & Goals:
Debut v Sheffield United (a) 24 September 1892 (NL)
NL: 10 app 2 gls
FL: 88 app 10 gls
FAC: 11 app 1 gl
Total: 109 app 13 gls

Honours:
FL champs 1889 (5 app).

GRAVER Andrew Martin 1947-1950

Centre-forward
5'10"
b. New Kyo, near Craghead, Co Durham, 12 September 1927
d. York, 18 January 2014

Career: Quaking House Jnrs 1942/Willington Ath 1945/Annfield Plain April 1947/UNITED Sept 1947 £50/Lincoln City Sept 1950 £5,000/ Leicester City Dec 1954 £27,600/Lincoln City July 1955 £14,000/Stoke City Nov 1955 £12,000/Boston Utd Sept 1957 £3,500/Lincoln City Oct 1958 £2,500/Skegness Town July 1961/Ilkeston Town July 1962/Retired due to injury Nov 1963/Lincoln City asst-coach June 1964 to Oct 1965, becoming a Lincoln scout.

A centre-forward with youthful enthusiasm and no little talent, after showing up well in the Northern League during season 1946-47, Andrew Graver found it difficult to break out of Newcastle's Central League side as the immediate post-war years unfolded. He was given only a single chance in United's senior eleven, as a 22-year-old stand-in for Jack Milburn, and he was injured in a collision with Manchester City 'keeper Bert Trautmann. But when he moved south in search of a regular first team place, Andy quickly developed into the most potent striker in the lower divisions. A household name in post-war football with Lincoln City, Graver holds the record aggregate scoring total for the Imps; 150 goals in 289 outings during three spells at Sincil Bank. During season 1951-52 when City won promotion, he was the Third Division North's leading scorer with 36 goals which included netting six in one fixture against Crewe. Unlucky to miss an England 'B' cap in 1952 due to injury, he was fast as well as direct. Andy was a leader who would chase anything that moved up front and a player who commanded club record fees when he moved to Filbert Street and then back to Lincolnshire. His big move to Filbert Street never worked out for Andy, apparently being purchased by the Foxes' directors rather than the manager and being given few chances. His father, Fred, turned out for Grimsby, Southend and Leeds during the inter-war years while his brother, Alf was also on Lincoln's books for a time. Later Andy resided near the cathedral city, in Bracebridge Heath, employed as a financial consultant with the Bank of Scotland for 15 years. He latterly moved to York where he died.

Appearances & Goals:
Debut v Manchester City (a) 21 January 1950.
FL: 1 app 0 gls
Total: 1 app 0 gls

Honours:
FL div 3(N) champs 1952.

GRAY Andrew Dunsmore 1920-1921

Outside-right
5'9"
b. Widdrington, near Newcastle upon Tyne, 6 January 1894
d. Newcastle upon Tyne, March 1981

Career: Jesmond Villa/UNITED Oct 1920 £10/Leadgate Park June 1921 free/South Shields cs 1921 to cs 1923 when he retired.

Local product Andrew Gray appeared mainly as a half-back in United's reserve side, but was called up to deputise on the wing for William Aitken during the 1920-21 season. Without pushing the senior players for their place at St James' Park, Gray later returned to local football before making a comeback in the Football League with South Shields. He made 37 appearances for the Tynesiders in Second Division and FA Cup action over seasons 1921-22 and 1922-23. Gray's father was Chairman of the Horsley Hill club for a period during the Twenties.

Appearances & Goals:
Debut v Aston Villa (h) 4 December 1920
FL: 2 app 0 gls
Total: 2 app 0 gls

GRAY Robert 1940-1945

Goalkeeper
5'0"
b. Newcastle upon Tyne, 14 December 1923

Career: Whitehall jnrs/UNITED amat April 1940
/Millwall war-guest 1941-42)/Gateshead 1942
/UNITED war-guest 1944-45)/Resumed with
Gateshead 1945 to 1959/Ashington/
North Shields cs 1959.

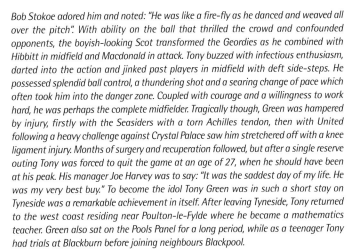

Bob Gray appeared between the posts on two occasions for United, once when on the club's books as an amateur during season 1939-40, the other during 1944-45 after he had signed for neighbours Gateshead. On his debut against Bradford City he became United's youngest player at 16 years 5 months 25 days old and appeared in a thrilling match which ended with a 4-3 defeat. Taking part as a regular in Newcastle's reserve side during 1940-41, Gray developed into an outstanding goalkeeper for the Redheugh Park club, one of the best in the lower divisions of the Football League during post-war soccer. Installed as first-choice in season 1947-48, he totalled over 450 senior matches for Gateshead, and was a tall, commanding custodian. It was a surprise to many that a top club didn't take him into First Division football such was his reputation. Bob was good enough to appear for the Football League North side during season 1956-57. Gray later resided in Whickham then in County Durham into his Nineties.

Appearances & Goals:
Debut v Bradford City (h) 8 June 1940 (FLNE)
War: 2 app 0 gls
Total: 2 app 0 gls

Honours:
FL(N) app 1957.

GRAY Thomas Davidson 1944

Right-half
b. Dundee, 21 August 1913
d. Dundee, 24 December 1992

Career: Morton/Dundee Aug 1944 (UNITED
war-guest 1944-45)/Arbroath Aug 1949, becoming
player-coach April 1955, then manager/Dundee Utd
manager March 1957 to Oct 1958/Later becoming
scout for several clubs including Rangers.

Briefly on Tyneside during the winter of 1944, Tommy Gray deputised for Donaldson and Gordon at right-half and took part in an absorbing derby tussle with Sunderland on Boxing Day in front of a 40,311 crowd at St James' Park. Just starting to make a name for himself at Dens Park, Gray figured in a 3-1 victory before heading back north. He proceeded to appear on over 100 occasions for Dundee before having a healthy spell as a player and manager at Arbroath over five seasons. His brother David turned out for Rangers, Preston and Blackburn.

Appearances & Goals:
Debut v Sunderland (h) 26 December 1944 (FLN)
War: 1 app 0 gls
Total: 1 app 0 gls

GREEN Anthony 1971-1973

Midfield
5'7"
b. Kinning Park, Glasgow, 13 October 1946

Career: Drumchapel Amateurs/Kirkintilloch
Rob Roy/Albion Rovers July 1964/Blackpool May 1967
£15,500/UNITED Oct 1971 £150,000 cash-exch for K
Dyson/Retired due to injury Dec 1973.

The all too brief career of Tony Green is fondly cherished by every Newcastle supporter who saw him play. With United in the relegation mire, Green landed on Tyneside from Blackpool as the most expensive Scot on record after becoming one of the hottest properties in the country. He made 137 appearances for Blackpool, many in a fruitful partnership with ex-Newcastle star Alan Suddick. His boss at Bloomfield Road, ex-United defender

Bob Stokoe adored him and noted: "He was like a fire-fly as he danced and weaved all over the pitch". With ability on the ball that thrilled the crowd and confounded opponents, the boyish-looking Scot transformed the Geordies as he combined with Hibbitt in midfield and Macdonald in attack. Tony buzzed with infectious enthusiasm, darted into the action and jinked past players in midfield with deft side-steps. He possessed splendid ball control, a thundering shot and a searing change of pace which often took him into the danger zone. Coupled with courage and a willingness to work hard, he was perhaps the complete midfielder. Tragically though, Green was hampered by injury, firstly with the Seasiders with a torn Achilles tendon, then with United following a heavy challenge against Crystal Palace saw him stretchered off with a knee ligament injury. Months of surgery and recuperation followed, but after a single reserve outing Tony was forced to quit the game at an age of 27, when he should have been at his peak. His manager Joe Harvey was to say: "It was the saddest day of my life. He was my very best buy." To become the idol Tony Green was in such a short stay on Tyneside was a remarkable achievement in itself. After leaving Tyneside, Tony returned to the west coast residing near Poulton-le-Fylde where he became a mathematics teacher. Green also sat on the Pools Panel for a long period, while as a teenager Tony had trials at Blackburn before joining neighbours Blackpool.

Appearances & Goals:
Debut v Everton (a) 30 October 1971
FL: 33 app 3 gls
FAC: 2 app 0 gls
Others: 3(1) app 0 gls
Total: 38(1) app 3 gls

Honours:
6 Scot caps 1971-72/Scot sch-youth app.

GREEN Stanley 1936-1945

Inside-forward
5'10"
b. Newcastle upon Tyne, 1915

Career: Heaton Stannington/Ashington/UNITED amat July 1936
(Grimsby Town war-guest 1944-45)/York City 1945 to c1946.

Tall and rangy, Stan Green appeared in United's Central League side during the years leading up to the outbreak of World War Two. Tenacious and good on the ball, he was a jovial character in United's dressing-room. Green deputised for Harry Clifton at inside-right, and for Jimmy Gordon in the right-half role during season 1939-40 before joining the RAF in 1941. On demob Stan was transferred to York City and made three appearances for the Minstermen in the FA Cup tournament during 1945-46.

Appearances & Goals:
Debut v York City (a) 17 April 1940 (FLNE)
War: 2 app 0 gls
Total: 2 app 0 gls

GREENER Ronald 1951-1955

Centre-half
5'11"
b. Easington, Co Durham, 31 January 1934

Career: Easington Colliery Jnrs/UNITED May 1951/
Darlington June 1955 free to cs 1967/Stockton.

Ron Greener made his inaugural appearance in United's line-up as a 19-year-old deputy for Frank Brennan and impressed everyone with a composed display. In fact Ron hardly put a foot wrong during his limited first-team outings, but had to be content to watch Brennan, then Stokoe and Paterson, dominate the Number 5 shirt at the centre of Newcastle's defence. He made up for the lack of opportunity with the Magpies by moving to Feethams where he proceeded to clock up a record total of matches for Darlington; more than 490 games over 12 seasons, and this despite the handicap of a broken leg. Greener performed with wholehearted endeavour for the Quakers and was recognised as an outstanding pivot in the lower divisions. When he retired from the game, he became a car salesman in Darlington and also had a stint running a petrol station. Ron was a regular watcher of the Quakers fortunes with a lounge named after him at the club's ground. When he joined United, Greener was working in the blacksmith's shop at his local colliery.

Appearances & Goals:
Debut v Charlton Athletic (h) 3 October 1953
FL: 3 app 0 gls
Total: 3 app 0 gls

Honours:
FL div 3(N) app 1957/FL div 4 prom 1966.

G

GREY Thomas J 1908, 1910-1919

Centre-half
5'11"
b. Newcastle upon Tyne, 5 March 1885
d. Corbridge, Northumberland, 31 March 1957

Career: Whitley Bay Ath/Morpeth WMC/Bedlington
Utd Jan 1907/Sunderland July 1907/Bedlington Utd
Oct 1907/UNITED Jan 1908 £70/Morpeth Harriers
May 1908/Morpeth Town Sept 1909/Knaresborough
1909-10/Blyth Spartans April 1910/UNITED amat
Oct 1910/Newcastle Bohemians 1919.

Tom Grey was a respected local player who had two spells with United, his latter stay just prior to World War One being more productive. The Tynesider was then an amateur on Newcastle's books, one of the best in the north, being capped for his country and taking part in the English Wanderers tour to Scandinavia, although he was very unfortunate to miss out on England's Olympic gold victory in Stockholm during 1912. A stout player who operated on the field when the centre-half position was mainly that of a midfielder, Tom was rarely hurried and was an intelligent footballer with the ball. He claimed only a single first-team appearance for the Magpies, replacing the injured Wilf Low during season 1913-14. An amateur with Sunderland too, he made a single appearance for the red-and-whites as well, while he was skipper at Blyth before returning to St James' Park in 1910. During World War One, Grey was one of several footballers to join up in the forces and he served with the Royal Engineers. Tom was raised in the Walker and Byker area of the city being the son of the publican at a hostelry on Shields Road before moving to Whitley Bay. He trained as a land surveyor and continued his profession when a footballer.

Appearances & Goals:
Debut v Aston Villa (a) 4 April 1914
FL: 1 app 0 gls
Total: 1 app 0 gls

Honours:
3 Eng amat app 1912-14.

GRIFFIN Andrew 1998-2004

Right-back
5'9"
b. Billinge, near Wigan, 7 March 1979

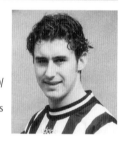

Career: Stoke City jnr April 1995, prof Sept 1996/
UNITED Jan 1998 £1.5m/Portsmouth July 2004 free
(Stoke City loan 2006-07)/Derby Co Aug 2007 £500,000/
Stoke City Jan 2008 £300,000/Reading loan Jan 2010,
pmt July 2010 £250,000 to June 2012/ Doncaster Rovers
Oct 2012/Retired cs 2014/Newcastle under Lyme
College coach 2014.

Full-back Andy Griffin was purchased by Newcastle United as a rising 18-year-old starlet to be developed for the future. Having made his senior debut for Stoke City in Division One as a 17-year-old, the terrier-like defender became a regular for the Potters and had made 64 appearances before he moved to the North East. Kenny Dalglish's scouting network produced glowing reports on his progress and the Magpies brought him to Tyneside for a £1.5m fee midway through the 1997-98 season. Aggressive and mobile at full-back, Andy joined the Gallowgate squad to compete for a place alongside firstly Barton and Domi, then Hughes and Bernard. Versatile on either the right or left berth, Andy preferred the right flank becoming a member of the first-team squad for all of seven seasons. Although often out injured, with groin and persistent back complaints, Griffin was outstanding in Newcastle's FA Cup semi-final victory over Tottenham during 1999 when he marked David Ginola out of the game. With fast and furious raids down the flank, Andy then had his best campaigns under Bobby Robson's influence in 2000-01 and 2002-03, when he figured on a regular basis during United's Champions League line-up, scoring a memorable goal against Juventus in 2002. Those frequent injuries though hampered his development, Andy never consistently producing form as he showed in European action. Griffin moved to Portsmouth and never reached such heights in the game again, although in his three spells with the Potters managed to claim 137 games for City.

Appearances & Goals:
Debut v West Ham United (h) 7 February 1998
PL: 63(13) app 2 gls
FAC: 6 app 0 gls
FLC: 8 app 0 gls
Euro: 14 app 1 gl
Total: 91(13) app 3 gls

Honours: 3 Eng u21 app 1999-2001/Eng sch-youth app/FL ch winner 2012 (9 app)/
FL ch prom 2008/FAC final 1999.

GRUNDY Arnold John 1935-1944

Left-half
5'8"
b. Whickham, near Gateshead, 19 September 1919
d. Colchester, March 1989

Career: Dunston CWS/UNITED amat Nov 1935, prof
Sept 1936 £5 (Liverpool war-guest 1940-41) (Fulham
war-guest 1940-41)(Southport war-guest 1942-
43)(Queen of the South war-guest)/Resumed with
United to May 1944 free.

Arnold Grundy was only 17 years old when he turned out for the Magpies, one of the youngest debutants on record. He was elevated to United's Second Division side in place of the injured Bill Imrie, but was never going to challenge the former Scottish international, or his successor Doug Wright, for the senior's jersey. Grundy was fast and like Imrie, tenacious while he started his career at St James' Park as an assistant in the club's offices, working part-time as a staff clerk. Inevitably, the outbreak of the Second World War virtually ended his professional career. He did try to gain a contract with United towards the end of the hostilities but wasn't retained.

Appearances & Goals:
Debut v Bradford City (h) 24 April 1937
FL: 2 app 0 gls
Total: 2 app 0 gls

GUIVARC'H Stephane Pierre Yves 1998

Striker
6'0"
b. Concarneau (France), 6 September 1970

Career: US Concarneau (Fr)/Stade Brest (Fr) jnr
Sept 1984, prof 1989/EA Guingamp (Fr) Dec
1991/AJ Auxerre (Fr) June 1995 (Stade Rennais (Fr)
loan 1996-97)/UNITED July 1998 £3.54m/ Rangers
Nov 1998 £3.5m/AJ Auxerre (Fr) June 1999 £3.4m/
EA Guingamp (Fr) July 2001/Retired May 2002 due
to injury/US Tregunc (Fr) coach May 2007,
becoming President Nov 2012.

In French domestic football, centre-forward Stephane Guivarc'h was a much respected goal-getter, rattling home more than 100 goals for notably Rennais and Auxerre, over 40 in season 1997-98 before he moved to Tyneside. That sort of strike-rate earned him a chance with Les Blues and he held the Number 9 shirt as France lifted the World Cup on home soil in 1998. Rubbing shoulders with some terrific footballers as the French roared impressively to the trophy, the likes of Zidane, Petite and Henry, however Guivarc'h was not in that exalted class. By then he had agreed to become a Newcastle United player, Kenny Dalglish sealing a deal for the Frenchman before the World Cup kicked off for a substantial £3.54m fee. Newcastle supporters waited his arrival with mixed opinion. Having just turned 28 years of age, he was a World Cup winner but wasn't one of the star-studded French line-up who had impressed during the television extravaganza. As the new 1998-99 season began, the new striker's mentor, Dalglish, quickly departed, and his successor, Ruud Gullit, had little time for Guivarc'h, having already criticised his lack-lustre performances as a television pundit covering the World Cup. A hard working striker but one without panache, he possessed a ferocious shot but the new manager soon demoted the Frenchman to train with the reserves and offloaded him to Rangers within only four months of the season's start, the Magpies recouping their outlay. Stephane only appeared on four occasions for United and while he was hardly given any chance at all, most fans and judges considered the club had done well to move him on at no loss. That was perhaps seen to be true as Guivarc'h also failed to make the grade in the lower level of football in Scotland clocking up only 19 games (7 goals). He moved back to France during 1999 and continued to increase his impressive tally of goals in Le Championnat before succumbing to a succession of knee injuries. Afterwards, Guivarc'h returned to his local region of Finistere and worked for Canal+ television as well as setting up a business designing and installing pools and spas. He also became involved with his local football club, US Tregun, eventually becoming the lower league side's President.

Appearances & Goals:
Debut v Liverpool (h) 30 August 1998 (1 goal)
PL: 2(2) app 1 gl
Total: 2(2) app 1 gl

Honours:
14 Fr caps 1998-2000/WdC winner 1998/Fr Lg champs 1996/Fr div 2 prom 1995/Fr div
3 prom 1994/SL champs 1999/SLC winner 1999/Fr Cup winner 1996 (sub no
app)/Legion d'Honneur 1998.

GUPPY Stephen Andrew 1994

Outside-left
5'11"
b. Winchester, 29 March 1969

Career: Colden Common/Southampton
1988/Wycombe Wand Sept 1989/UNITED Aug 1994
£150,000/Port Vale Nov 1994 £225,000/Leicester
City Feb 1997 £850,000/Celtic Aug 2001 £700,000/
Leicester City Jan 2004 to May 2004/Leeds Utd trial
cs 2004/Stoke City Sept 2004/Woking trial Nov
2004/Wycombe Wand Nov 2004/DC Utd (USA)
March 2005/Wycombe Wand trial July 2006/
Stevenage Borough Aug 2006/Rochester Rhinos
(USA) player-coach March 2008/Colorado Rapids
(USA) asst-coach Nov 2008 to Nov 2011/Sunderland
asst-coach March 2012 to April 2013/Eire asst-coach Nov 2013.

As a 25-year-old who had developed late onto the scene, Steve Guppy joined United after only one complete season as a full-time professional. Following a 10-week trial period at The Dell he hadn't made the grade, but progressed through the non-league ranks with Wycombe in 253 matches, a star of Wanderers' rise under Martin O'Neill from the Vauxhall Conference to Second Division football. Tall and slimly built, Steve proved direct and penetrating on the wing and was purchased by Kevin Keegan as cover, although he was steadily developing further. When Port Vale made an approach United accepted a profit on the deal, making his stay at Gallowgate one of the shortest on record, a mere four months. However the Magpies should have resisted the offer, as Guppy went onto rejoin O'Neill at Leicester and show his potential the more first-team games he played, reaching the England side during October 1999, ironically called up by his ex-boss Keegan. He helped win the League Cup for the Blues and possessed a magical left foot with a special ability to whip in a cross right into the danger area, reminiscent of Chris Waddle. Totalling 189 matches for the Foxes, Steve also had a spell in Scotland with Celtic and won more honours. An ex-bricklayer, Guppy's father was on West Bromwich Albion's books during the Fifties as a goalkeeper. His younger brother turned out for Aldershot Town.

Appearances & Goals:
Debut v Manchester United (h) 26 October 1994 (sub) (FLC)
FLC: 0(1) app 0 gls
Total: 0(1) app 0 gls

Honours:
1 Eng cap 2000/1 Eng B app 1998/1 Eng u21 app 1998/Eng semi-prof app 1993/FL div 3 prom 1994//FLC winner 2000/FLC final 1999/FAT winner 1993, 2007/SL champs 2002/SC final 2002 (sub no app)/PFA ToS (d3) 1994.

GUTHRIE Christopher William 1968-1972

Centre-forward
6'1"
b. Dilston, near Hexham, 7 September 1953

Career: UNITED jnr cs 1968, prof Jan 1971/Southend
Utd Nov 1972 £10,000/Sheffield Utd May 1975
£90,000/Swindon Town July 1977 £25,000/Fulham Sept
1978 £65,000/Millwall March 1980 £100,000 to
cs 1980/Retired due to injury March 1982/Witney Town
player-manager July 1982/Roda JC Kerkrade (Neth)
Nov 1982/Willem II (Neth) Dec 1982/Helmond Sport
(Neth) 1983/Seiko SA (HK) Feb 1984/Blyth Spartans
April 1985/RWD Molenbeek (Neth) Sept 1985/
Ashington commercial manager 1987/
UNITED kit-manager Feb 1989 to Oct 1993.

A schoolboy star, Chris Guthrie appeared for his country as a teenager, netting seven goals in six matches, and was a prominent goalscorer in United's junior and reserve elevens. Big and powerful, after making his debut as an 18-year-old, Guthrie was handed little opportunity to break the first choice strike force of Macdonald and Tudor at St James' Park and it was no surprise when he moved south to further his career. Chris returned to the big-time, commanding substantial fees after doing especially well with Southend (118 app 40 gls). The big striker was also prominent up front at Bramall Lane (79 app 23 goals). Younger brother of Ron Guthrie (qv), who was with the Magpies during the same era although the pair never appeared in United's first-team together, Chris rejoined United looking after the kit-room at St James' Park for a period. He also became an international fly fisherman, an active and noted tournament angler, later working for a fishing rod manufacturer in the region. Guthrie also coached youngsters on Tyneside. His son, Chris (junior), appeared for Sunderland and Gateshead.

Appearances & Goals:
Debut v Manchester United (h) 23 October 1971
(v Coventry City (a) 19 October 1971 (TC))
FL: 3 app 0 gls
Others: 1 app 0 gls
Total: 4 app 0 gls

Honours:
Eng sch-youth app.

GUTHRIE Danny Sean 2008-2012

Midfield
5'9"
b. Shrewsbury, 18 April 1987

Career: Aston Villa jnr/Manchester Utd jnr
2001/Liverpool jnr July 2002, prof Dec 2004
(Southampton loan 2006-07)(Bolton Wand loan
2007-08)/UNITED July 2008 £2.5m/Reading
July 2012 free.

Originally a youngster with Manchester United, Danny Guthrie joined the Liverpool junior set-up when he left school. Under the guidance of Steve Heighway at Melwood Academy, Danny won England caps at Under-15 to Under-19 level. He squeezed his way onto the senior Liverpool bench during season 2006-07, ironically one of seven appearances for the Reds coming at St James' Park. In search of regular action, he moved first to Southampton, then on a season-long loan deal to Bolton for 2007-08 where he was a regular in Premier League action as well is in the UEFA Cup, claiming 35 outings all told. His form that season prompted the Black'n'Whites to offer the 21-year-old a deal and he joined the Magpies in July 2008. Strong running, with good distribution from his favoured central midfield role, Guthrie tasted relegation during his first season with the club and was sidelined with a bad hamstring tear. But recovering, he then was a regular at Championship level and won a title winning medal with United in 2009-10. Having a strong shot when he was in range, Danny then competed for the engine-room of Newcastle's midfield as they returned to Premier League action but was never guaranteed a regular place, either through more injury problems or by selection, and headed for newly promoted Reading during the summer of 2012.

Appearances & Goals:
Debut v Manchester United (a) 17 August 2008
FL/PL: 81(11) app 7 gls
FAC: 5(1) app 0 gls
FLC: 6 app 2 gls
Total: 92(12) app 9 gls

Honours:
Eng sch-youth app/FL ch winner 2010.

GUTHRIE Ronald George 1962-1973

Left-back
5'10"
b. Burradon, Newcastle upon Tyne, 19 April 1944

Career: New Hartley Welfare Jnrs/UNITED jnr
May 1962, prof July 1963 £100/Sunderland Jan
1973 £15,000/Ashington June 1975 free/
Gateshead Utd 1975/Lusitano (SA) manager
July 1976/Blyth Spartans cs 1977/North Shields
Sept 1981 to 1982.

Although Ron Guthrie started out as a goalscoring outside-left or centre-forward, it was as a full-back with a biting tackle he is remembered. Guthrie possessed good distribution and was quick to recover, yet was unlucky to be second choice to Frank Clark during his near ten year spell with the Black'n'Whites. Occasionally used as a midfield power source too, Guthrie was part of United's Fairs Cup winning squad and enjoyed a lot of crowd support while many would have liked to see the chunky defender find a place in United's side. However, injury didn't help his cause at Gallowgate; Ron was

G

sidelined through two cartilage operations. But after his move to Sunderland he found better fortune, appearing on 81 occasions for the Wearsiders and being part of Bob Stokoe's team which lifted the FA Cup. Guthrie is one of only a few FA Cup winners to play in every round of the competition, including preliminary stages, a feat recorded when he was with Blyth Spartans. As part of the non-league clubs famous eleven that reached the Sixth Round draw in 1978, Guthrie enjoyed a twilight couple of years in the game. Following retirement, Ron settled in Killingworth on Tyneside and for a time was employed by department store Fenwick's as a despatch driver. His son David appeared for Northumberland at rugby.

Appearances & Goals:
Debut v Aston Villa (a) 20 August 1966
FL: 52(3) app 2 gls
FAC: 0(1) app 0 gls
FLC: 2 app 0 gls
Euro: 3(2) app 0 gls
Others: 3 app 0 gls
Total: 60(6) app 2 gls

Honours:
FAC winner 1973.

GUTIERREZ Jonas Manuel 2008-date

Midfield
6'1"
b. Roque Saenz Pena, near Buenos Aries (Argentina), 5 July 1983

Career: Estudiantes Jnrs (Arg)/Argentinos Jnrs (Arg)/River Plate Jnrs (Arg)/Velez Sarsfield (Arg) 1999/RCD Mallorca (Sp) July 2005 £3m/UNITED July 2008 £5m (Norwich City loan 2013-14).

When Jonas Gutierrez headed to Tyneside from the holiday island of Mallorca as a 24-year-old during the close-season of 2008, he had appeared on several occasions for the Argentina national side alongside the likes of Lionel Messi and Carlos Tevez, as well as teammate to be, Fabricio Coloccini. The transfer deal was the subject of a row between his club Real Mallorca, the player and United, the fee being eventually settled by the Court of Arbitration for Sport at £5m. Immediately the tall, long-haired left-winger made an impression in England showing expert close control of the ball going forward, coupled with a work ethic to track back few could match and which was invaluable to the team. Although Jonas often went past two or three defenders in a forward surge, during his early days he was often criticised for a lack of end product, be it a cross or shot at goal. However, the South American became a fixture in United's side, a rare bright spot at times as the club were relegated, then as a key factor in their quick promotion, to eventually become a noted Premier League performer. On the way Jonas also started to make an impact around the box with his final delivery, learning not to waste the ball and adding consistency to his previous erratic form in the danger area. Gutierrez was one of United's most reliable and top players as they made their mark in the Premier League once more during 2010-11 and 2011-12. He was also effective in central midfield and left-back, on occasion also used in those roles. He added to his international caps haul with United, appearing in the 2010 World Cup. Jonas was a regular on the left of midfield in Newcastle's line-up over much of his five seasons, a model of professionalism and rarely missing a game. Out of action for the start of the 2013-14 season, his place was taken successfully by Yoan Gouffran and Jonas moved on, rejoining Chris Hughton at Norwich. Handed the nickname of 'Spiderman' in Spain's La Liga, a result of donning the superhero mask when he scored a goal, the unusual celebration being once famously witnessed at St James' Park during 2009-10 against Barnsley.

Appearances & Goals:
Debut v Manchester United (a) 17 August 2008
FL/PL: 163(14) app 10 gls
FAC: 5(2) app 1 gl
FLC: 3(2) app 0 gls
Euro: 3(3) app 0 gls
Total: 174(21) app 11 gls

Honours:
22 Arg caps 2007-date/WdC 2010/Arg u20 app/FL ch winner 2010/Arg Lg champs 2005.

GUY Alan 1975-1979

Striker
5'10"
b. Jarrow, 8 September 1957

Career: UNITED jnr, prof Sept 1975 (Shrewsbury Town loan 1977-78)/Peterborough Utd March 1979 £10,000, joint deal with A Smith, to cs 1981/ Later North East non-league football.

A regular junior and Central League scorer for United, Alan Guy never quite possessed the needed craft and pace to perform at the highest level but can boast he pulled on the famous Number 9 shirt for the Magpies in an Anglo-Scottish Cup match. Following a handful of opportunities, and once Peter Withe was installed in the striker's role on Tyneside, Alan was transferred south to attempt a career in the Third and Fourth Division with Peterborough. Under the guidance of ex-Magpie coach Peter Morris at London Road, Guy was converted to a midfield player and had a short period of success. He netted twice on his debut for the Posh and totalled 59 games over seasons 1979-80 and 1980-81. He later returned to the North East to settle playing non-league football. Residing in Hebburn, he was later confined to a wheelchair due to knee and spinal problems which cut short his career.

Appearances & Goals:
Debut v Gillingham (a) 1 September 1976 (FLC)
FL: 3(1) app 0 gls
FAC: 2 app 0 gls
FLC: 1 app 0 gls
Others: 1 app 0 gls
Total: 7(1) app 0 gls

GUY Lewis Brett 1999-2005

Striker
5'11"
b. Penrith, 27 August 1985

Career: UNITED jnr 1999, prof Aug 2002/Doncaster Rovers trial Feb 2005, pmt March 2005 (Hartlepool Utd loan 2008-09)(Oldham Ath loan 2009-10)/MK Dons July 2010 (Oxford Utd loan Aug 2011-12)/St Mirren trial Jan 2012, pmt May 2012/Carlisle Utd July 2013/Gateshead July 2014.

A north country lad from Cumbria, Lewis Guy scored plenty of goals for the Black'n'Whites reserve and junior sides, notably when the club won the Academy League play-off in 2002. Dark haired, Guy was elevated to the senior squad for the start of the 2004-05 campaign after impressing in the pre-season warm-up games, on tour in the Far East when he scored six goals. He was given a solitary chance in Newcastle's senior shirt during season 2004-05, and that as substitute. The Cumbrian got onto the field in the UEFA Cup fixture with Sporting Lisbon, a Group clash during December. Despite his fine record in the second-string, Lewis never was close again to United's first eleven. Apart from the senior strikers, he also had Michael Chopra as a rival from the youth system, and Chopra became the preferred choice. Like many home-grown front men to have come through the ranks over the modern past, Guy moved to the lower divisions where he eked out a reasonable career. He enjoyed a good spell with Doncaster, totalling 186 games (24 goals).

Appearances & Goals:
Debut v Sporting Clube (h) 16 December 2004 (sub) (UEFAC)
Euro: 0(1) app 0 gls
Total: 0(1) app 0 gls

Honours:
Eng sch-youth app/FL div 1 prom 2008/FLT winner 2007.

HADDOCK Peter Murray 1976-1986

Centre-half
5'11"
b. Newcastle upon Tyne, 9 December 1961

Career: Cramlington Jnrs/UNITED jnr Oct 1976, prof Dec 1979 (Dunedin City (NZ) loan cs 1985) (Burnley loan 1985-86)/Leeds Utd July 1986 £45,000/ Retired due to injury July 1992.

Peter Haddock was an outstanding schoolboy prospect, playing alongside Peter Beardsley for South Northumberland Boys, and he earned an early opportunity in United's first eleven during season 1981-82. Composed on the ball with accurate distribution, he was a regular in defence but the arrival of Glenn Roeder and the emergence of Steve Carney saw Haddock relegated to the fringe of firstly, Arthur Cox's side, then Jack Charlton's. An underrated and unpretentious player, Peter moved on to join up with Leeds United and at Elland Road found a regular place as the Tykes won promotion back into Division One. He clocked up 146 matches for Leeds, a highly regarded defender and key part of their revival during the late 1980s. Injury, though, hampered his progress throughout his career and after an awkward fall in a Leeds versus Manchester United League Cup semi-final clash during 1991 was out of action with a knee problem for 18 months. Haddock returned only to play one reserve match before the injury forced his early retirement from the game. Later he returned to the North East and resided in North Tyneside. Suffering from an arthritis complaint, a legacy of his football career, Peter opened a sports memorabilia shop for a period, then had a bakery outlet, before becoming a postman, insurance salesman, security co-ordinator and courier for Royal Mail Parcelforce in the Blyth area. He is related by marriage to United's former player, and latter-day coach John Carver (qv).

Appearances & Goals:
Debut v Queens Park Rangers (a) 5 September 1981
FL: 53(4) app 0 gls
FLC: 3 app 0 gls
FAC: 5 app 0 gls
Total: 61(4) app 0 gls

Honours:
FL div 2 champs 1990/FL div 2 prom 1984 (3 app).

HAGAN Alfred 1919-1923

Inside-right
5'6"
b. Usworth, Co Durham, 11 November 1893
d. Sunderland, June 1980

Career: Washington CW/UNITED May 1919 £10/Cardiff City May 1923 £250/Tranmere Rovers July 1926 to cs 1927/ Later returning to North East local football notably with Usworth CW.

A former coal-miner, without having a great deal of height or build, Alf Hagan relied on his considerable ball skills which at times delighted the Tyneside crowd. A good reserve to have on the sidelines, Hagan appeared for United in both inside-forward roles, filling in for injured seniors during the immediate seasons after World War One. A pen-picture of the day noted Alf as being "dainty and zealous", while he was always capable of grabbing an opportunist goal. Hagan had a spell with Cardiff (9 app), then attempted to carve out a career at Prenton Park with Tranmere, however he stayed on Merseyside for only a season, making 12 appearances. He was the father of Jimmy Hagan, a noted player for Sheffield United and England during the mid 1950s. Alf served with the Northumberland Fusiliers during the hostilities. After his football career Hagan lived in the Washington area.

Appearances & Goals:
Debut v Manchester United (a) 20 December 1919 (1 goal)
(v Durham City (h) 12 April 1919 (NVL) (1 goal))
FL: 21 app 5 gls
War: 4 app 1 gl
Total: 25 app 6 gls

HAIDARA Massadio 2013-date

Left-back
5'10"
b. Trappes, near Paris (France), 2 December 1992

Career: La Verriere (Fr) 2002/FC Versailles (Fr) 2003/AC Boulogne-Billancourt (Fr) 2005/FC Nantes (Fr) jnr 2008, prof Jan 2011/UNITED Jan 2013 £2.5m.

Athletic and possessing first-rate technical skills with the ball, Massadio Haidara arrived on Tyneside as a 20-year-old defender with huge potential. Having made his senior debut for Nantes during 2010, his career was moving fast, recognised as a star of the future. He soon was given a chance in United's Europa League line-up and quickly showed the Toon Army he had the ability to succeed in the English game. Packing a powerful shot, fast with good anticipation and prompt with his tackles, the Frenchman of Senegalese decent could also move forward with confidence. His start as a Newcastle United player was a success but then was left in the treatment room following a reckless and foul tackle at Wigan during March 2013, an incident to create many headlines. Although appearing to recover quickly, Haidara suffered a set-back and was not fit for action until the autumn.

Appearances & Goals:
Debut v Metalist Kharkiv (a) 21 February 2013 (EpL)
PL: 5(10) app 0 gls
FAC: 1 app 0 gls
FLC: 1 app 0 gls
Euro: 4 app 0 gls
Total: 11(10) app 0 gls

Honours:
2 Fr u21 app 2012-date/Fr sch-youth app.

HAIR George 1943-1949

Outside-left
5'4"
b. Ryton, near Gateshead, 28 April 1925
d. Peterborough, 24 October 1994

Career: Spen Jnrs/UNITED amat April 1943, prof May 1943 £10/Grimsby Town Feb 1949 £6,000/ Peterborough Utd Aug 1951/Boston Utd cs 1956/ Spalding Utd cs 1957.

Claiming much local success before joining the Magpies, George Hair was a winger who could use both flanks, but who generally operated on the left for United. Recovering from a broken leg at St James' Park, the diminutive Hair appeared often during wartime league and cup football for the club. He became a Gallowgate favourite with his perky displays in seasons 1944-45 and 1945-46, but as peacetime football resumed was crowded out by the stylish Tom Pearson. Hair, a member of a then rare breed of footballer who wore contact lenses, was one of the club's influential figures as the Black'n'Whites' reserve side won the Central League trophy in 1948. A direct and alert winger with little of the tricky stuff, many on Tyneside considered United should not have sold him. Following a stay with Grimsby (70 app), Hair joined the ambitious and emerging non-leaguers Peterborough for the start of 1951-52 playing alongside both Jack Fairbrother and Andy Donaldson at London Road in the Midland League. After retiring from the game, George was heavily involved with the Northamptonshire FA, living in the Peterborough area to his death. His son, Michael, became a Football League linesman for a period.

Appearances & Goals:
Debut v Barnsley (h) 5 January 1946 (FAC) (1 goal)
(v Bradford Park Avenue (h) 9 September 1944 (FLN))
FL: 23 app 7 gls
FAC: 3 app 1 gl
War: 51 app 14 gls
Total: 77 app 22 gls

Honours:
FL div 2 prom 1948 (6 app).

HALE Kenneth Oliver 1956-1962

Inside-right
5'7"
b. Blyth, 18 September 1939

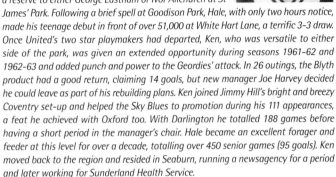

Career: Newsham BC/Everton jnr 1955/UNITED jnr, prof Oct 1956/Coventry City Dec 1962 £10,000/Oxford Utd March 1966 £5,000/Darlington May 1968 £5,000, becoming caretaker-manager Jan to March 1972/ Halifax Town player-coach Jan 1973 £500/ Hartlepool Utd manager June 1974 to Sept 1976.

Blond-haired, stockily-built, Ken Hale possessed good control and vision in midfield, being initially recognised as a reserve to either George Eastham or Ivor Allchurch at St James' Park. Following a brief spell at Goodison Park, Hale, with only two hours notice, made his teenage debut in front of over 51,000 at White Hart Lane, a terrific 3-3 draw. Once United's two star playmakers had departed, Ken, who was versatile to either side of the park, was given an extended opportunity during seasons 1961-62 and 1962-63 and added punch and power to the Geordies' attack. In 26 outings, the Blyth product had a good return, claiming 14 goals, but new manager Joe Harvey decided he could leave as part of his rebuilding plans. Ken joined Jimmy Hill's bright and breezy Coventry set-up and helped the Sky Blues to promotion during his 111 appearances, a feat he achieved with Oxford too. With Darlington he totalled 188 games before having a short period in the manager's chair. Hale became an excellent forager and feeder at this level for over a decade, totalling over 450 senior games (95 goals). Ken moved back to the region and resided in Seaburn, running a newsagency for a period and later working for Sunderland Health Service.

Appearances & Goals:
Debut v Tottenham Hotspur (a) 28 December 1957
FL: 30 app 15 gls
FLC: 1 app 0 gls
FLC: 4 app 1 gl
Total: 35 app 16 gls

Honours:
FL div 3 champs 1964, 1968.

HALL Alexander Noble 1907-1908

Centre-forward
5'10"
b. Aberdeen, 3 December 1880
d. Toronto (Canada), 25 September 1943

Career: Peterhead/Toronto Scots (Can) 1901/Galt (Can) 1904/ Petershill/Aberdeen Oct 1905/Peterhead Dec 1905/Edinburgh St Bernard's April 1906/UNITED April 1907 £200/ Dundee Feb 1908 £200/Portsmouth May 1910/ Motherwell May 1911/Dunfermline Ath Aug 1912 to 1919.

The son of an Aberdeen whaler, Sandy Hall was a stone-cutter by trade and joined the Magpies after his Edinburgh club, St Bernard's, had lifted the Second Division trophy. He soon impressed United's selection committee on a tour of Germany during the summer of 1907 when he netted no fewer than 10 goals in only three games, including a five-goal strike against Freiburg. But Hall found gaining a place in Newcastle's star-studded team difficult, only standing in occasionally for Bill Appleyard. Alex had a similar physique to Appleyard, he was powerfully built and could hit a rasping shot. Hall played all his games for United during season 1907-08 before moving to Tayside in search of regular action. At Dens Park, Sandy took part in Dundee's run to the Scottish Cup final during 1910, alongside three other ex-United men, but was unlucky not to be selected for the final. In 1912 Sandy saved a lad from drowning in Peterhead harbour and received bravery awards, while during the Great War he served initially as a gunner then with the embryo Tank Corps. Earlier in his career, Hall had a period in Canada and took part in the 1904 Olympic Games in St Louis, recorded in history as one of the earliest players to win gold, albeit only three club sides took part, including his, Galt FC. After World War One Sandy concluded his career and returned to Canada during 1923, living in Toronto where he worked at the city incinerator.

Appearances & Goals:
Debut v Sheffield Wednesday (a) 7 September 1907
FL: 6 app 2 gls
Total: 6 app 2 gls

Honours:
OG 1904 (gold)/SL div 2 champs 1907.

HALL Ernest 1933-1937

Centre-half
5'10"
b. Crawcrook, near Gateshead, 6 August 1916
d. Austria, 7 July 1944

Career: West Wylam CW Jnrs/UNITED amat Aug 1933, prof Sept 1933 £10/Brighton May 1937 £100/Stoke City July 1939.

A former policeman on Tyneside, Ernie Hall was United's second string centre-half, rivalling Dave Davidson and Tony Leach for the stopper's position in Newcastle's side. He was given scant openings to show his true worth, only turning out on two occasions during the 1935-36 Second Division programme, although he was a regular in the Magpies' Central League side at a time when games attracted crowds approaching 20,000 to St James' Park. On his debut for United he did well, the Newcastle Journal noting "his exhibition made a lasting impression". The Tynesider moved to the south coast to try his luck at the Goldstone Ground with Brighton. Again though he found claiming a regular spot hard and made only four appearances before heading to Stoke just as World War Two was to erupt. Hall joined the RAF and became a Pilot Officer and tragically was a victim of the conflict, killed in action when only 29 years of age. Stationed in Italy during 1944 as the Allies advanced towards Germany, he was part of a mission to Feuersbrunn airfield not far from Vienna when his Wellington bomber was shot down. He is remembered at Klagenfurt war cemetery in Austria and also on the Northumbria Police memorial in Ponteland. Ernie's brother, Tom Hall, was skipper of Coventry City and also appeared for Ashington.

Appearances & Goals:
Debut v Blackpool (h) 25 April 1936
FL: 2 app 0 gls
Total: 2 app 0 gls

HALL Fitz Benjamin 2010

Centre-half
6'4"
b. Leytonstone, London, 20 December 1980

Career: West Ham Utd jnr 1995/Barnet jnr 1997/Chesham Utd/Oldham Ath March 2002 £30,000/Southampton July 2003 £250,000/Crystal Palace Aug 2004 £1.5m/Wigan Ath June 2006 £3m/Queens Park Rangers Jan 2008 (UNITED loan Jan 2010 to May 2010)/Watford July 2012 free to cs 2013/Millwall trial Nov 2013/Watford Nov 2013.

Fitz Hall was a short-term loan signing during the 2009-10 season after an injury to Steven Taylor left the first choice centre-half on the sidelines, the QPR defender giving United defensive cover. With know-how and a cool head at the back, Hall was well travelled, appearing for nine clubs in a 13 year period. Tall at 6'4", and nicknamed 'One Size', he performed admirably during his few outings for the Magpies showing a calm and unhurried style and assisted the Toon to promotion in 2010. Returning to Loftus Road, he proceeded to repeat the feat with Rangers, appearing as the Londoners themselves lifted the Championship trophy during 2010-11, and all told almost 100 times for the Loftus Road side. Fitz then was part of Zola's Italian revolution at Vicarage Road and helped Watford make a bid for the Premier League. During the early part of his career Iain Dowie brought him out of the non-league scene to join Oldham from Chesham, managed by his brother Bob Dowie. He then had a good period at Selhurst Park in 81 games.

Appearances & Goals:
Debut v Cardiff City (h) 5 February 2010
FL: 7 app 0 gls
Total: 7 app 0 gls

Honours:
FL ch winner 2010 (7 app), 2011/PFA ToS (d2) 2003.

HALL Thomas 1913-1920

Centre-forward
5'9"
b. Newburn, Newcastle upon Tyne,
4 September 1891
d. Newcastle upon Tyne, 1978

Career: Newburn Grange 1908/Newburn Alliance Aug 1908/Sunderland Jan 1909/UNITED May 1913 £425 (Leeds City war-guest 1918-9)(Hartlepools Utd war-guest 1919)/Gillingham May 1920, becoming trainer Aug 1926.

A prolific goalscorer as a schoolboy and in the non-leagues on Tyneside, Tom Hall hailed from a large Newburn working-class family. He achieved a headlining first outing for the Magpies netting against his former club Sunderland in a Tyne-Wear derby at Roker Park, a fabulous goal skipping past two of his former colleagues before finding the net. Recording 30 games (8 goals) for the Wear club and part of the Reds' title winning side, Hall was a play anywhere forward; on the wing, at inside-forward or in the centre-forward's role, the position he favoured. Once netting five goals for United in a friendly against Alnwick during 1919, he was an industrious leader, possessing plenty of dash. Tom became a prolific scorer for the club's reserve side and, although an effective centre-forward, didn't quite grab enough goals in senior company when he deputised for Albert Shepherd just before, and just after World War One. Tom did appear on 207 occasions for Gillingham where he enjoyed a rewarding period, scoring 55 goals. His brother, Bertie, joined the club during the inter-war years, but didn't get a first-team outing before appearing for Hartlepools and Norwich City.

Appearances & Goals:
Debut v Sunderland (a) 6 September 1913 (1 goal)
FL: 54 app 15 gls
FAC: 4 app 1 gl
Total: 58 app 16 gls

Honours:
FL champs 1913 (1 app).

HALLIDAY Bruce 1976-1983

Centre-half
6'0"
b. Sunderland, 3 January 1961

Career: UNITED jnr Oct 1976, prof Jan 1979 (Darlington loan 1982-83)/Bury loan Nov 1982, cmt cs 1983/Bristol City Aug 1983/Hereford Utd June 1985/Bath City cs 1987/APIA-Leichhardt (Aus) 1989/Gateshead Aug 1990/Dunston Fed 1993/Blyth Spartans asst-manager July 1996 to March 1997/Mitchelton (Aus) asst-coach c2005.

Following a harrowing first outing for United when United fell 6-0 at Stamford Bridge, Bruce Halliday, who was tough and brisk at the heart of the defence, showed for a period that he was capable of developing into a top centre-half. Maturing quickly, the Wearsider impressed many for half-a-season during 1980-81, scoring the winner in the return fixture with Chelsea. However, loss of form as the following programme began, saw a fellow home-grown product, Peter Haddock take-over in defence and Halliday drifted into the shadows and moved down the leagues. Bruce did well with Bristol City, claiming 66 games and a regular anchor at the back as they won promotion, and then at Edgar Street, playing on 77 occasions for Hereford. He later returned to East Boldon to settle, playing and coaching local football (over 100 app for Gateshead) and was employed in the pensions and financial sector, turning his back on full-time soccer before he was 30 years of age. Halliday also operated a property company for a period and was part of the sports agency ISM Ltd. During 2004, Bruce moved back to Australia where earlier he had sampled life in the suburbs of Sydney with the APIA club. Halliday continued his successful career in financial management and during 2012 was appointed Business Development Manager for Vanguard Investments based in Queensland.

Appearances & Goals:
Debut v Chelsea (a) 25 October 1980
FL: 32 app 1 gl
FAC: 4 app 0 gls
FLC: 2 app 0 gls
Total: 38 app 1 gl

Honours:
FL div 4 prom 1984.

HALLIDAY William 1927-1928

Inside-left
6'1"
b. Dumfries, 14 November 1906
d. Dumfries

Career: Noblehill/Queen of the South Sept 1923/UNITED Nov 1927 £1,000/Third Lanark June 1928 free/Connah's Quay & Shotton Utd Aug 1929/Boston Town 1929-30/Exeter City May 1930/Gainsborough Trinity Sept 1932/Queen of the South Aug 1933/Hyde Utd Oct 1933/St Cuthbert Wand (Dumfries) 1934-35.

Brother of Sunderland idol Dave Halliday, Billy was a tall and powerful forward who joined the Magpies with an excellent reputation. However, unlike his brother the Scot couldn't adapt to the English game and made only a solitary appearance for the Magpies when he stood in for Tom McDonald at Filbert Street. Halliday, though, was a celebrated player for Queen of the South for almost three seasons before moving east to Tyneside, claiming 64 matches for the Doonhamers, netting 22 goals. On leaving the game, Billy resumed his trade as an electrician, residing in the Southern Uplands region around Dumfries until his death.

Appearances & Goals:
Debut v Leicester City (a) 26 November 1927
FL: 1 app 0 gls
Total: 1 app 0 gls

HAMANN Dietmar 1998-1999

Midfield
6'3"
b. Waldsassen, Bavaria (Germany), 27 August 1973

Career: Wacker Munich (Ger) amat/Bayern Munich (Ger) June 1989/UNITED Aug 1998 £4.5m/Liverpool July 1999 £7.5m/Bolton Wand July 2006 free/Manchester City July 2006 £400,000/Retired June 2009/MK Dons coach July 2010/Leicester City coach Feb 2011/ Stockport Co manager July 2011 to Nov 2011.

Part of Germany's World Cup line-up for the France 98 tournament, Dietmar Hamann was along with Stephane Guivarc'h, United's two headline purchases from that summer festival of football. At £4.5m Hamann, unlike his French colleague, was a huge success in England, although mainly in Liverpool's red rather than United's black-and-white. Nicknamed 'Didi', the 24-year-old German was an established star in his native country, lifting title and cup honours, as well as gaining much European experience. He quickly adapted to the Premier League, one of only a handful of his countrymen to have done so in modern football. Tall and slender, Hamann was a midfielder of quality and a most effective player, able to hit accurate long and short passes and with an engine to last the full 90 minutes. With Newcastle's status having slipped at the top level under Dalglish and Gullit, eyes of others were soon fixed on the German. Following an early injury set-back in Toon colours when he damaged ligaments, Didi confirmed his credentials, recording some fine displays including appearing for United in the 1999 FA Cup final, although he retired injured at half-time. He also netted the odd spectacular goal using strong shooting to good effect. Never really settling on Tyneside, nor working well with United's Dutch manager, Hamann was courted by Liverpool and a £7.5m offer at the end of his first campaign in English football of 1998-99 saw Hamann move to Anfield. United almost doubled their money, but had lost a player capable of much more as the following years were to show. Didi settled wonderfully well on Merseyside, unlike his time in the North East, and with the Reds he soon became an influence. Hamann was a regular for seven seasons, a driving force from the centre of midfield, more a holding player alongside Steven Gerrard. He was part of Liverpool's successful Champions League team in 2005 when the Reds made a dramatic comeback from being 3-0 behind in the Istanbul final. Occasionally skippering his country, the German appeared on 282 occasions in senior action for the Reds before stepping down a level when over 32 years old. During the course of his fine career Hamann admitted to a gambling problem, once losing an incredible £288,000 on a single bet. The German dabbled in management with Stockport briefly before joining the media band of ex-footballers. His father Wolfgang was coach at Wacker Munich and a brother Matthias was also a player, and later manager for a number of German clubs. Didi netted the last competitive goal scored at the old Wembley Stadium, for Germany against England...in the process ending Kevin Keegan's reign as national boss.

H

Appearances & Goals:
Debut v Charlton Ath (h) 15 August 1998
PL: 22(1) app 4 gls
FAC: 7 app 1 gl
FLC: 1 app 0 gls
Total: 30(1) app 5 gls

Honours:
59 Ger caps 1997-2005/WdC 1998, 2002 final/10 Ger u21 app/Ger sch-youth app/FAC winner 2001, 2006/FAC final 1999/FLC winner 2001, 2003/FLC final 2005/Ger Lg champs 1994, 1997/Ger Cup winner 1998/CL winner 2005/UEFAC winner 1996, 2001/ESC winner 2001, 2005.

HAMILTON David Stewart 1939-1946

Outside-right
5'7"
b. Carlisle, 8 February 1919
d. Zimbabwe, 18 October 1978

Career: Shawfield Jnrs/UNITED June 1939 £200 (Southampton war-guest 1943-44)(Fulham war-guest 1944-45)(Queens Park Rangers war-guest 1945-46)/Southend Utd May 1946 £100 to 1947.

Blond-haired winger Dave Hamilton had a most unfortunate career. Joining the United staff as a youngster full of promise, he had burst into the Black'n'Whites' senior team for the start of the 1939-40 season, quickly making an impact and forming a bond with the fans. But with only three games of the new campaign completed, Germany's invasion of Poland put a stop to the first-class game and Hamilton's senior games for Newcastle were expunged from the record book. More bad luck followed when he soon afterwards broke his leg in wartime football against Bradford Park Avenue and, by the time peace was restored five years later, Hamilton's career was in tatters. He did try and earn a contract with the Magpies during 1946, but found many younger players at Barrack Road ahead of him. He moved to the Southend Stadium but only played on four occasions for the Shrimpers. Yet, as a teenager, United saw Hamilton as a big star of the future. Standing out in the Scottish Junior Cup final, Stan Seymour immediately made a move to bring him to Tyneside and set Dave on a threshold of what could have been a brilliant career. Serving with the Black Watch, Tyneside Scottish regiment, during the war, Hamilton was one of the thousands of the British Expeditionary Force evacuated from Dunkirk in Operation Dynamo during 1940. David had an active wartime service, later as a glider pilot part of another famed wartime engagement, the huge airborne assault of 1944 to Arnhem in Operation Market Garden. Hamilton survived the war and he afterwards moved to Rhodesia, later to declare independence from Britain as Zimbabwe, employed in insurance with Norwich Union.

Appearances & Goals:
Debut v Nottingham Forest (a) 31 August 1939 (FLa)
War: 8 app 1 gl
Total: 8 app 1 gl
(Void FL: 2 app 1 gl)

Honours:
FLSN(WLg) champs 1946 (3 app).

HAMILTON Derrick Vivian 1997-2001

Midfield
5'11"
b. Bradford, 15 August 1976

Career: Queensbury Celtic/Bradford City jnr 1990, prof June 1994/UNITED March 1997 £1.375m (Sheffield Utd loan 1998-99)(Huddersfield Town loan 1998-99)(Norwich City loan 1999-2000) (Tranmere Rovers loan 2000-01)/Cardiff City July 2001 free/Grimsby Town loan March 2003, pmt July 2003 free/Barnet March 2004 free/Retired May 2004, later playing local football in the Bradford area, including for Campion FC.

Kenny Dalglish's first signing as United boss, Derrick Hamilton had impressed several judges when in the claret-and-amber colours of Bradford City during seasons 1995-96 and 1996-97. Known as 'Des', he was one of the brightest prospects in England's second-tier, Hamilton reaching England's Under-21 side as a energetic right-back or midfielder who had made his senior bow as a 17-year-old trainee and starred at Wembley as City won promotion in the Play-Off final. At 20 years of age, Hamilton joined United towards the end of the 1996-97 season for a £1.375m fee and was confined mainly to the bench for the remainder of the programme. Thereafter he was given a few outings the following campaign, a regular squad member but usually destined for the dug-out. A change in manager did not help his progress, although Hamilton gained Champions League experience playing against both PSV and Barcelona as United made their debut in the tournament. It was soon clear Des was not going to be able to push and challenge the likes of Speed, Solano, Lee and Hamann for a regular midfield slot and following less than two seasons on the club's books was sent out on loan and offloaded back to a lower level of football. Derrick moved in permanent deals to Cardiff and Grimsby, but never recaptured the form he had shown at Valley Parade in 105 matches. He left the senior game aged only 28, returning to the Bradford area where during 2011 he was appointed as a full-time 'Health Mentor' at Lister Primary School in Manningham, inspiring kids to be healthier and more active.

Appearances & Goals:
Debut v Hull City (h) 15 October 1997 (FLC) (1 goal)
PL: 7(5) app 0 gls
FAC: 1 app 0 gls
FLC: 1(1) app 1 gl
Euro: 2(1) app 0 gls
Total: 11(7) app 1 gl

Honours:
1 Eng u21 app 1997/1 FL app 1997/FL div 2 prom 1996, 2003 (6 app).

HAMPSON William 1914-1927

Right-back
5'9"
b. Radcliffe, near Bury, 26 August 1884
d. Congleton, 23 February 1966

W. HAMPSON

Career: Woolfold Wesleyans (Bury)/Ramsbottom Aug 1905/Bury Wesleyans/Bury May 1906/Rochdale Nov 1908/Norwich City July 1909/UNITED Jan 1914 £1,250 (Leeds City war-guest 1916-19)(Scotswood war-guest 1919)/South Shields Sept 1927, retired playing cs 1928/ Carlisle Utd manager March 1930 to May 1932/ Ashington manager July 1934 to May 1935/Leeds Utd manager July 1935 to May 1947, becoming chief scout/Norwich City scout Oct 1947/Northumberland FA schools coach.

Noted as one of the best full-backs in the Southern League, Billy Hampson was initially signed by United as cover to the club's noted full backs McCracken and Hudspeth, and consequently took time to find a regular place. Able to play on either side of defence, he showed fine consistency and eventually took over the right-back role for season 1922-23. Stan Seymour described him as "cool and brainy", Hampson was a stylish and steady defender who, for many years, was thought to be (at 41 years 8 months) the oldest footballer to have taken part in a FA Cup final during 1924, until his birth certificate was checked, revealing him to be two years younger! Billy played on for another two seasons in Newcastle's first-team after that victory at Wembley, but by the time the Magpies embarked on their title campaign in 1927 the veteran Hampson was to play only twice more for the club. He is the Magpies oldest player, aged 42 years 7 months 14 days, when he turned out against Birmingham during April 1927. Billy afterwards moved on, playing for another season with South Shields, and then to Carlisle where, as boss of Brunton Park, he discovered Bill Shankly. He also had a long spell in charge of Leeds United. During his early football career Hampson once appeared at centre-forward for then pre-Football League Norwich, and scored twice in a FA Cup giant-killing feat over Sunderland. Billy, whose two brothers, Tom and Walker, also played the game during the inter-war years, was an effective cricketer during the summer months. Both brothers had unsuccessful trials with the Magpies.

Appearances & Goals:
Debut v Sheffield Wednesday (a) 24 January 1914
FL: 163 app 1 gl
FAC: 11 app 0 gls
Total: 174 app 1 gl

Honours:
FL champs 1927 (2 app)/FAC winner 1924/WL champs 1918.

HANNAH George 1949-1957

Inside-left
5'8"
b. Liverpool, 11 December 1928
d. Sale, 5 May 1990

Career: Everton amat 1946-47/Linfield/
UNITED Sept 1949 £23,000 joint deal with
A McMichael/Lincoln City Sept 1957
£5,000/Manchester City Sept 1958 £10,000
plus player/Notts Co July 1964 £3,000/
Bradford City Oct 1965 £1,000/Retired May
1966.

Possessing lovely ball skills, the slender and rather frail looking George Hannah was a joy to watch when on form and could always hit a defence splitting pass. Only a little over nine stone in build, he possessed deceiving pace and was a one touch type of schemer. Slick on the ball with a quicksilver movement, but like many of his breed, Hannah was rarely an automatic choice at St James' Park, although he came into his own between 1952 and 1955 when George Robledo headed back to Chile. Hannah played a star role in the FA Cup final victory over Manchester City, scoring at Wembley. Having an accurate and sure drive, he was always liable to find the net and at one stage of his career was tipped in some quarters as sneaking an England cap. Discarded by United, Hannah joined the Maine Road set-up in 1958, and enjoyed his time with Manchester City (131 app), playing on until he was nearing 40 years old in his 20th season of action. As a teenager George moved to Ireland when serving with the Royal Ulster Rifles and was spotted, along with Alf McMichael, in Linfield's eleven. On leaving the game he ran a newsagency business in Fallowfield, Manchester for a decade, as well as working for British Telecom to his retirement in 1990.

Appearances & Goals:
Debut v Manchester City (h) 17 September 1949 (1 goal)
FL: 167 app 41 gls
FAC: 8 app 2 gls
Others: 2 app 0 gls
Total: 177 app 43 gls

Honours:
5 FA app 1958-64/7 FA tour app 1958/1 NIL app 1950/FAC winner 1955.

HARDINGE Harold Thomas William 1905-1907

Centre-forward
5'7"
b. Greenwich, London, 25 February 1886
d. Cambridge, 8 May 1965

Career: Eltham 1903/Tonbridge/Maidstone Utd 1904/UNITED May 1905/Sheffield Utd Dec 1907 £350/Woolwich Arsenal June 1913 £500/ Retired cs 1921/Tottenham Hotspur asst-coach 1935. (Kent county cricket 1902-33, Leicestershire coach 1934-39).

Harry Hardinge grabbed United's attention as a teenage forward when he scored plenty of goals for Maidstone, reportedly 70 goals over two seasons in the Kent leagues. He was a member of Newcastle's reserve side for most of his stay on Tyneside, influential as the North Eastern League title was secured in 1907 and 1908. Hardinge, though was better than that standard and later developed into a superb forward, full of tricks and good enough to win an England cap when at Bramall Lane. Nicknamed 'Wally', he stood in for big Bill Appleyard in black-and-white colours during the 1905-06 season and was on standby to appear in the 1906 FA Cup final with Rutherford doubtful. When Sheffield United took a gamble at his transfer, he quickly flourished as a free-scoring inside-forward and occasional leader of the attack. An intelligent and strong-willed character, sometimes at odds with authority, Harry could be brilliant on his day but is described in the Blades' annals as an "annoyingly inconsistent footballer". He had as many good outings as mediocre for the Tykes in his 154 appearances (46 goals), but showed enough quality to earn England recognition when at his peak during 1909-10 and 1910-11. His transfer to Arsenal was embroiled in dispute between club and player, an FA commission having to resolve matters. Hardinge also performed to the top level at cricket, being a right-hand batsman of distinction as well as a left-arm spin bowler. He appeared for Kent as a 16-year-old at their Tonbridge nursery during 1899 then became a noted player for over 25 years, appearing in 607 first class matches. Harry totalled 33,519 runs including 75 centuries (once hitting 263) and recorded 1,000 runs

in a season no fewer than 18 times. During 1921 Wally became a double England international when he appeared against Australia at Headingly. After leaving football he joined the well known sports outfitters and publishers, John Wisden, then worked for the Cement Marketing Board. Hardinge served as a Chief Petty Officer in the Royal Navy air force during World War One.

Appearances & Goals:
Debut v Sunderland (a) 2 September 1905
FL: 9 app 1 gl
Total: 9 app 1 gl

Honours:
1 Eng cap 1910/1 Eng Test (cricket) app 1921/County champs (cricket) 1909, 1910, 1913/Wisden Cricketer of the Year 1915.

HARDWICK Stephen 1976-1983

Goalkeeper
5'11"
b. Mansfield, 6 September 1956

Career: Chesterfield jnr, prof July 1974/UNITED Dec 1976 £80,000 (Detroit Express (USA) loan cs 1978)/ Oxford Utd Feb 1983 £15,000 (Crystal Palace loan 1985-86)(Sunderland loan 1987-88)/Huddersfield Town July 1988 free/Scarborough trial Aug 1991/ Kettering Town March 1992/Also appeared for Emley FC.

A former England youth and amateur international, Steve Hardwick followed a line of fine Chesterfield goalkeepers, in the path of the likes of Gordon Banks. As a teenage debutant with the Spireites, several clubs took notice of him and he became Newcastle's record goalkeeper purchase at the time following 44 games for Chesterfield. Hardwick graduated into his country's Under-21 squad when at St James' Park and following a brief spell in the States took over the Number 1 jersey from Mick Mahoney. He quickly matured and showed agility and confidence until a series of lapses made him, to certain sections of the crowd, something of a villain. Hardwick had ability for the occasional wonderful display, although his lack of consistency eventually cost him the first-team position to Kevin Carr. He assisted Oxford during their dramatic rise from the Third Division to Division One registering 196 appearances, including 158 matches consecutively, for the Headington club. Hardwick also did well with the Terriers, totalling 129 games for Huddersfield. By the time Steve had left the senior circuit had made almost 600 outings in league and cup football, including a short period with Sunderland when they were in the third-tier of English football. A keen club cricketer too, he was later involved with Yorkshire village side, Hoylandswaine, as a noted wicket-keeper. On retiring from football, he became their captain and later groundsman, living in the village near Barnsley.

Appearances & Goals:
Debut v Liverpool (a) 23 August 1977
FL: 92 app 0 gls
FAC: 4 app 0 gls
FLC: 3 app 0 gls
Euro: 2 app 0 gls
Total: 101 app 0 gls

Honours:
Eng sch-youth app/Eng amat app/FL div 2 champs 1985/FL div 3 champs 1984, 1988 (6 app).

HARDY Stanley 1911-1914

Inside-left
5'7"
b. Newcastle upon Tyne, April 1890
d. Gosforth, Newcastle upon Tyne, 29 March 1937

Career: Rutherford College (Newcastle)/UNITED Nov 1911 £20 to 1914/Nottingham Forest asst-secretary April 1927, becoming secretary May 1929 to Jan 1932.

Stan Hardy had no easy task to break into United's exceptional line-up during the years up to the First World War and was unfortunate to be coming to his prime just when his contract was suspended due to

the fighting on the Continent. A clever midfield player who was quick to break into attack, he soon joined Lord Kitchener's army, one of the club's first volunteers, signing for the Newcastle Quayside Commercials Pals battalion of the Northumberland Fusiliers during September 1914. Rising to the rank of lieutenant in the machine-gun corps, Stan was severely gassed in the trenches and had to retire from soccer as peacetime resumed. Related to the celebrated goalkeeper, Sam Hardy of Nottingham Forest, he later became involved in the administrative side of the game at the City Ground alongside the Trent. Stan afterwards returned to Tyneside and was a "traveller" with the James Deuchar company in Newcastle.

Appearances & Goals:
Debut v Sheffield United (h) 13 December 1913
FL: 3 app 1 gl
Total: 3 app 1 gl

HAREWOOD Marlon Anderson 2009

Striker
6'1"
b. Hampstead, London, 25 August 1979

Career: Nottingham Forest jnr July 1995, prof Sept 1996 (FC Haka (Fin) loan 1998)(Ipswich Town loan 1998-99)/West Ham Utd Nov 2003 £500,000/Aston Villa July 2007 £4m (Wolverhampton Wand loan 2008-09)(UNITED loan Sept to Dec 2009)/Blackpool trial Aug 2010, pmt Aug 2010 (Barnsley loan 2010-11)/Guangzhou (Ch) July 2011/Nottingham Forest trial Dec 2011/Sheffield Wed trial July 2012/ Barnsley Aug 2012 free/Millwall trial July 2013/ Bristol City Aug 2013 free/Hartlepool Utd Jan 2014 free.

At 6'1" tall and with a frame of a boxer, Marlon Harewood enjoyed an exceptional period with West Ham United during 2004-05 and 2005-06 under Alan Pardew's management as the Hammers won promotion and reached the FA Cup final, netting the winning goal in the semi-final over Middlesbrough. The Cockney scored 56 goals in 170 games for the Londoners and did well at Forest when he started his career, scoring an impressive 21 goals as they reached the Play-Offs, and 55 all told in 211 games, showing he had pace and an explosive finish. Out of the picture at Aston Villa after a big transfer to the Midlands fell flat, Harewood jumped at the opportunity to join United on a three month loan deal, even though he dropped a division. With Ameobi out injured, 30-year-old Marlon gave boss Chris Hughton options up front as a partner for Andy Carroll; either the small and quick Peter Lovenkrands or another big striker in Harewood. He may not have been the most athletic of players to have worn the black-and-white shirt for the club and was a bit rusty in terms of regular action, but Harewood's five goals in 15 appearances (six being from the bench) was a decent return for the Magpies as they stormed to the Championship title. He headed back to Villa Park at the end of 2009 and had in a small way helped United back to the Premier League. Leaving Villa permanently during the close-season of 2010, the Londoner thereafter struggled to gain a regular place in senior football.

Appearances & Goals:
Debut v Ipswich Town (a) 26 September 2009 (sub)
FL: 9(6) app 5 gls
Total: 9(6) app 5 gls

Honours:
FL ch winner 2009 (5 app), 2010/FL ch prom 2005/FL div 1 champs 1998 (1 app)/FAC final 2006/Fin Lg champs 1998/Fin Cup winner 1998.

HARFORD Michael Gordon 1980-1981, 1982

Centre-forward
6'2"
b. Sunderland, 12 February 1959

Career: Lambton Star BC (Sunderland)/Lincoln City July 1977/UNITED Dec 1980 £216,000/Bristol City Aug 1981 £160,000/UNITED March 1982 free briefly/Birmingham City March 1982 £100,000/Luton Town Dec 1984 £250,000/Derby Co Jan 1990 £480,000/Luton Town Sept 1991 £325,000/Chelsea Aug 1992 £300,000/Sunderland March 1993 £250,000/Coventry City July 1993 £200,000/ Wimbledon Aug 1994 £75,000, retired Aug 1998,

becoming coach, asst-manager June 2000/Luton Town coach May 2001 to May 2003, reinstated as coach and Director of Football Aug 2003 to Aug 2004 after a dispute/Nottingham Forest asst-manager Nov 2004, becoming caretaker-manager Dec 2004/Swindon Town asst-manager Jan 2005/Nottingham Forest asst-manager Feb 2005/Rotherham Utd manager April 2005 to Dec 2005/Colchester Utd asst-manager June 2006/Queens Park Rangers coach cs 2007/Luton Town manager Jan 2008 to Oct 2009/Queens Park Rangers asst-manager Dec 2009, becoming caretaker-manager Jan 2010 to Feb 2010/MK Dons asst-manager May 2012/ Millwall coach June 2013, becoming asst-manager.

A prolific scoring leader in the lower divisions with 45 goals in 126 games for the Imps, 21-year-old Mick Harford cost the Magpies a Fourth Division record fee when he moved back to his native North East. Tall and slim, as a target centre-forward, he was exceptional in the air and also possessed nice footwork for a big man. Yet during his brief eight-month stay on Tyneside under the management of Arthur Cox, Harford wasn't considered the man to replace the powerful play of Peter Withe and the manager quickly discarded his hidden potential. Mick moved to debt-stricken Bristol City for £160,000 but the Robins encountered difficulties with repayment of the transfer-fee instalments. Consequently, as part of his move to St Andrews, the Wearsider made a unusual return to Gallowgate en route for St Andrews enabling the Black'n'Whites to recoup monies owed. From then on Mick's career took off. Joining Luton Town, he developed into the very centre-forward Newcastle had been searching for, showing subtle flicks and lay-offs, well timed and often brave runs into the danger zone and ever dangerous going for a cross. Although hindered by knee operations, Harford totalled 217 games for the Hatters (92 goals) and gained England recognition before becoming an errant traveller during the latter days of his career, always being something of a thorn to the Magpies whenever he faced United. Scoring over 230 goals in his career, as a kid had trials at both St James' Park and Roker Park, eventually appearing briefly for his boyhood favourites on Wearside. Harford entered coaching and management in 1998, assistant to Joe Kinnear for periods, turning down an opportunity to join him at St James' Park in 2013.

Appearances & Goals:
Debut v Grimsby Town (a) 26 December 1980
FL: 18(1) app 4 gls
Total: 18(1) app 4 gls

Honours:
2 Eng caps 1988-89/1 Eng B app 1988/FLC winner 1988/FLC final 1989/FL div 2 prom 1985/FL div 4 prom 1981/FLT winner 2009(m).

HARKER Christopher Joseph 1953-1959

Goalkeeper
5'10"
b. Shiremoor, Newcastle upon Tyne, 29 June 1937
d. Darlington, 5 September 2014

Career: Backworth YC/Backworth Methodists 1952/UNITED amat 1952/West Allotment Celtic/UNITED amat Nov 1953, prof April 1955 (Consett loan 1958-59)/Aberdeen loan Nov 1959, pmt Dec 1959 £1,000/Bury Feb 1962 £3,000/ Grimsby Town June 1967/Rochdale July 1968 free/Darlington coach July 1970 to June 1971/Stockton player-manager 1971 to 1972.

After making his debut in United's first eleven, Chris Harker was unlucky to be called up for National Service with the Royal Engineers during which time he was involved in a serious road accident which kept him out of action. Harker missed the chance of claiming Ronnie Simpson's goalkeeper's jersey and was third choice behind Bryan Harvey and Stewart Mitchell at one stage. Following two seasons with Aberdeen, he was purchased by former colleague Bob Stokoe who rated the 'keeper and Harker became a regular custodian at Gigg Lane (197 app) then later at Spotland with Rochdale (97 app). When appearing for Bury, Chris was involved in the clash which led to the premature retirement of Brian Clough's playing career with a serious knee injury. A former shipyard fitter, Harker later resided in the Darlington area employed as a laboratory technician and caretaker at Hammersknott School as well as a maintenance joiner for Magnet in their local works.

Appearances & Goals:
Debut v Burnley (h) 28 April 1958
FL: 1 app 0 gls
Total: 1 app 0 gls

Honours:
FL div 4 prom 1969.

HARNBY Donald Reed 1942-1947

Right-back
5'11"
b. Kelloe, Co Durham, 20 July 1923
d. Stockton, 24 October 2009

Career: Hurworth/Darlington ATC/
UNITED amat 1942, prof May 1944 to June 1947
(Middlesbrough war-guest 1944-45)(Hull City
war-guest 1944-45)/York City Aug 1947/
Spennymoor Utd Oct 1947/Grimsby Town Sept
1949/Grimsby Borough Police May 1952/
Spennymoor Utd Nov 1953/Horden CW 1957 to
1959 when he retired/Ferryhill Ath trainer 1959
to 1964.

*Don Harnby was spotted by United when playing
a representative match for the Durham Air Training Corps. He joined United as an
amateur during the early years of the war, making his debut sometime later against
Gateshead during August 1944. Harnby was a strong tackler and rugged defender.
Filling in for the veteran Joe Richardson at right-back, he had a rival in Bobby Cowell
for the right-back shirt and ultimately Cowell was to win the race as preferred choice.
Don was a tall full-back who became a regular in the club's Central League line-up
for 1946-47 before moving to York and Grimsby where he totalled 37 outings. Later
Harnby spent a short time as a Grimsby policeman, also appearing for the police
football side, before returning to County Durham to work at a radio factory in
Spennymoor. Later Don moved to Stockton where he was employed as a welfare officer
in a district school education department then for the Local Authority Social Services
in the region.*

Appearances & Goals:
Debut v Gateshead (a) 26 August 1944 (FLN)
War: 8 app 0 gls
Total: 8 app 0 gls

HARPER Stephen Alan 1991-2013

Goalkeeper
6'2"
b. Easington, Co Durham, 14 March 1975

Career: Burnley jnr 1985/Seaham Red Star 1986/
UNITED amat Dec 1991, prof July 1993 (Bradford
City loan 1995-96)(Gateshead loan 1996-97)
(Stockport Co loan 1996-97)(Hartlepool Utd loan
1997-98)(Huddersfield Town loan 1997-98)
(Brighton loan 2011-12)/Hull City July 2013 free.

*Newcastle United's longest serving player of all time,
with service of 20 years, Steve Harper first donned a
Magpie goalkeeper jersey as a junior in December
1991, when at the club for a spell from local club
Seaham Red Star. Only 16 years-old then, Steve
appeared for United's Northern Intermediate side
before heading back to the non-league, and to
college, before turning down a place at John Moores University in Liverpool to return
to the club on a permanent deal during July 1993. Since then Harper was part of the
Magpie first-team set-up for 20 seasons, coinciding with the club's resurgence as
they joined the Premier League in 1993-94. During the early term of his lengthy period
with the club, he had 'keepers Pavel Srnicek, Shaka Hislop and Mike Hooper ahead of
him. Going out on loan, Harper appeared for Bradford City, Hartlepool and Huddersfield
Town where he showed he had the talent to succeed. Steve then contested a friendly
rivalry with Shay Given for the Number 1 spot in the side, won usually by the Republic
of Ireland legend. Harper though did claim a regular place at the end of the 1998-99
season and for season 1999-2000, while he was Newcastle's last line of defence in
the 1999 FA Cup final. Although he deputised for Given over the following seasons,
he also spent 420 matches on the subs bench. Steve stepped up when Given moved
on during 2009, becoming a safe and reliable custodian. Immensely popular with
Newcastle's support, many judges considered Harper would have been good enough
for an England cap had he enjoyed more regular first-team action. Tall at 6'2", with
ability to pull of the brilliant stop, he was consistently good as the club lifted the
Championship trophy during 2009-10 and recorded a new club record of keeping 21
clean sheets in that season. Steve then gave way to the much younger Tim Krul as
United returned to Premiership action and left the club when 38 years of age during
the summer of 2013. Harper captained United on rare occasions, and appeared in
Champions League football for the Magpies while he is related to pre-war forward*

*Jonathan Wilkinson (qv). Harper took part in 619 senior league and cup matches;
either in the team or on the bench and always as a model professional. The Easington
product started to qualify as a referee during his earlier days at Gallowgate, holding
an FA licence he took charge of local matches, while Steve also studied for a social
sciences degree, but found his Newcastle United commitments were too great to allow
him to continue. Harper was also a fine cricketer appearing in Durham league
competition. After two decades with United, Steve joined Hull City in the summer of
2013 and enjoyed a nostalgic charity testimonial fixture at St James' Park supported
by a 50,937 crowd.*

Appearances & Goals:
Debut v Wimbledon (h) 28 November 1998 (sub)
FL/PL: 149(8) app 0 gls
FAC: 9(1) app 0 gls
FLC: 12 app 0 gls
Euro: 17(3) app 0 gls
Total: 187(12) app 0 gls

Honours:
FL ch winner 2010/FL div 2 prom 1996 (1 app)/FAC final 1999, 2014 (sub no app).

HARRIS Albert 1935-1936

Outside-right
5'4"
b. Horden, Co Durham, 16 September 1912
d. Lincolnshire, May 1995

Career: Hetton Utd/Herrington Swifts/Hull City
May 1930/Blackhall CW cs 1931/UNITED March
1935 £100/Barnsley May 1936 £200/Darlington
Jan 1937/Scunthorpe & Lindsay Utd March 1939.

*Albert Harris was given a second chance at the
Football League scene after completing an
unsuccessful spell with Hull City. Known as 'Diddler'
to both colleagues and spectators, Albert reverted to local North East football with
the strong Blackhall Colliery line-up and caught the eye of manager Tom Mather with
penetrating displays on the wing. The Magpies added the short but sturdily built
outside-right to their squad for the 1935-36 season when he rivalled Wilf Bott. With
infinite courage and enthusiasm, Harris, who could operate on both touchlines and
was as fast as they come, did well on his limited opportunities and later impressed at
Feethams. He claimed 68 games for the Quakers and wound down his career in the
Midland League with Scunthorpe just as war erupted.*

Appearances & Goals:
Debut v Fulham (h) 28 September 1935 (1 goal)
FL: 12 app 4 gls
Total: 12 app 4 gls

HARRIS Joseph 1925-1931

Wing-half
5'8"
b. Glasgow, 19 March 1896
d. Glasgow, 29 October 1933

Career: Strathclyde Jnrs/Partick Thistle June 1913/
Middlesbrough March 1923 £4,200/UNITED Oct 1925
£750/York City June 1931 free to his demise.

*When he arrived at St James' Park nearing the end of his
career, Scottish international Joe Harris rivalled both Willie
Gibson and Roddie MacKenzie for the half-back role, being
equally effective on the right or left side of midfield.
Although no stylist, the tenacious Joe was dainty-footed
and recorded a handful of outings during the Magpies'
title success of 1927, including appearing in three crucial
matches of the season's finale. One of a large tartan clan
at Gallowgate at the time, Harris made a name for himself
in 241 games at Firhill for Partick Thistle as they
challenged with the best in Scottish football. He was also
a regular for Boro following a big move to Teesside, but then fell out of favour and
United stepped in for a player respected in the game. He always contributed on the*

H

field and was a consistent and commanding player at his peak. Joe became a regular immediately following United's title success and was a popular individual with the Geordie crowd. When still on York's books, Harris died when on a return visit to his native Glasgow, being only 37 years old. He suddenly took ill with leukaemia and died in Glasgow Infirmary.

Appearances & Goals:
Debut v Liverpool (a) 25 December 1925
FL: 149 app 2 gls
FAC: 8 app 0 gls
Total: 157 app 2 gls

Honours:
2 Scot caps 1921/Scot trial app 1921-24/FL champs 1927 (9 app)/SC winner 1921.

HARRIS Neil Lamont 1920-1925

Centre-forward
5'8"
b. Tollcross, Glasgow, 30 October 1894
d. Swindon, 3 December 1941

Career: Vale of Clyde/Partick Thistle June 1913 (Kilmarnock war-guest 1916-17)(Rangers war-guest 1916-17)(St Mirren war-guest 1917-18) (Fulham war-guest 1918-19)(Distillery (Belfast) war-guest 1918-19)/UNITED May 1920 £3,300/ Notts Co Nov 1925 £3,000/Shelbourne May 1927/Oldham Ath July 1927 £400/Third Lanark March 1929 £400/Burton Town player-manager 1929/Distillery (Belfast) manager May 1932/ Swansea Town manager July 1934/Swindon Town manager June 1939 and occasional wartime player 1939-40 to Aug 1940.

Brought up in the Shettleston area of Glasgow, Neil Harris was a daring centre-forward, possessing the born eye for an opening and packing a fearsome drive. He soon became a noted striker in Scotland with 92 goals in 162 matches for Thistle. At 5'8" tall, he was not a big leader, but showed he was a proven and prolific goalscorer throughout his career. Harris became one of only nine players to score over 100 league and cup goals for the Magpies. Yet 'Neilly' as he was known in football, wasn't an instant hit at Gallowgate, having a difficult early period on Tyneside despite striking the net. At one stage in February 1923 he was transfer listed at a modest £2,500 before finding a rich seam of form. That catapulted him to prominence as he led United to the FA Cup final with his goals during 1924, including scoring in the Wembley victory over Aston Villa. The Scot often produced electric dashes in attack while his aggressive style was awkward to play against, and he linked well with United's other FA Cup heroes, Seymour and McDonald. Father of John Harris, later Chelsea player and Sheffield United manager, Neil's brother Joshua also appeared for Chelsea as well as Leeds, Fulham and Wolves. Another son, Neil (junior), appeared for Swindon in 1940 at the time of his father's management.

Appearances & Goals:
Debut v West Bromwich Albion (h) 28 August 1920
FL: 174 app 87 gls
FAC: 20 app 14 gls
Total: 194 app 101 gls

Honours:
1 Scot cap 1924/Scot trial app 1924/3 Scot jnr app/FAC winner 1924/FAVC final 1919.

HARROWER James 1961-1962

Inside-right
5'9"
b. Alva, near Stirling, 18 August 1935
d. Stirling, 28 November 2006

Career: Sauchie Juveniles/Kilsyth Rangers/Sauchie Juveniles/Bo'ness Utd/Hibernian June 1954/Liverpool Jan 1958 £11,500/UNITED March 1961 £15,000/Falkirk Jan 1962 £3,115/St Johnstone Aug 1963/Albion Rovers July 1965/Alloa Ath Aug 1966 to Sept 1966/Sauchie 1968/Albion Rovers manager May 1969 to Nov 1969.

Jimmy Harrower possessed a good rapport with the Anfield crowd before heading for Tyneside after 105 games and 22 goals for the Reds over four seasons. A player who excited the supporters with his typical

Scottish talent, Jimmy was able to split a defence with a single pass, but could also be temperamental, often entering into conflict with opponents and officials. He arrived at Gallowgate during a season of relegation trouble and suffered some negative crowd reaction at the Barrack Road stadium; additionally he was alleged to have been purchased by director Stan Seymour rather than manager Charlie Mitten who did not want the player. As a consequence the small, but heavily-built inside-forward pulled on a Magpie shirt only six times and quickly drifted back to Scotland where he was always appreciated. Jimmy's grandfather and father both took the field for St Mirren. When he left the game, Harrower resided in his native Alva in Central Scotland.

Appearances & Goals:
Debut v Tottenham Hotspur (a) 22 March 1961
FL: 5 app 0 gls
FAC: 1 app 0 gls
Total: 6 app 0 gls

Honours:
1 Scot u23 app 1958/Scot sch-youth app.

HART William Robert 1940-1944

Right-half
5'9"
b. Tynemouth, 1 April 1923
d. North Shields, 25 March 1990

Career: Willington Quay/UNITED amat June 1940, prof Sept 1940 to 1944/ North Shields/Chesterfield March 1945/Bradford City May 1947 to cs 1949.

Bill Hart was described by one colleague as, "the ultimate terrier". A player who revelled in a contest, he was small and slim, a ball winning wing-half, tough as they come. In contention for a place during seasons 1939-40 to 1942-43, in the 1941-42 campaign Hart was chosen on 22 occasions for United across the half-back line, but wasn't retained when peace was restored and he moved to local football with North Shields. He was soon picked up by Chesterfield and made his Football League debut with the Spireites, before claiming 30 matches for Bradford City.

Appearances & Goals:
Debut v Bradford City (h) 8 June 1940 (FLNE)
War: 38 app 1 gl
Total: 38 app 1 gl

HARVEY Bryan Robert 1958-1961

Goalkeeper
6'0"
b. Stepney, London, 26 August 1938
d. Aylesbury Vale, Bucks, 31 March 2006

Career: March Town Utd/Wisbech Town 1956/ UNITED Sept 1958 £3,000 (New York Americans (USA) guest cs 1960)/Cambridge City June 1961/ Blackpool March 1962 £3,000/Northampton Town Oct 1963 £1,000/Kettering Town cs 1968 free to cs 1970.

Agile and with a commanding frame, Bryan Harvey was plucked out of non-league football as a 20-year-old and given the United First Division goalkeeper's shirt after impressing many in Wisbech Town's FA Cup runs during 1957 and 1958. Bryan took over from the injured Simpson and displaced second choice Stewart Mitchell. Sound if not brilliant, Harvey's form suffered though, like many of his colleagues, when the Magpies were stuck in a relegation battle during season 1960-61. Newcastle purchased Dave Hollins and Harvey moved on, turning down a move to Spain and Espanol for a club closer to his home, at non-league Cambridge City, a deal which at the time saw him earn more money than the maximum wage would have given him in the Football League. Harvey eventually resurfaced in senior company as a key part of Northampton's swift and dramatic rise from the Fourth Division to First Division. He registered 181 games for the Cobblers and later resided in Wooton near Northampton, employed as a chemical company manager.

Appearances & Goals:
Debut v Wolverhampton Wanderers (a) 20 September 1958.
FL: 86 app 0 gls
FAC: 4 app 0 gls
FLC: 1 app 0 gls
Total: 91 app 0 gls

Honours:
FL div 2 prom 1965.

HARVEY John 1897-1900

Inside-right & Trainer
5'5"
b. Scotland, 22 January 1867
d. Middlesbrough, 11 February 1940

Career: Renton 1888/Sunderland 1889/Clyde Jan 1891/Sunderland Sept 1892/UNITED May 1897 £40 in a joint deal with J Campbell/ Retired May 1899, becoming asst-trainer to c1900.

A member of the celebrated Sunderland 'Team of all the Talents', Johnny Harvey took part in over 100 games for the red-and-whites and was in the side during the Wearsiders' first Football League campaign as well as taking part in United's inaugural Division One fixture. Arriving at St James' Park very much as a personality of experience and guile, he joined the club at the same time as Sunderland colleague Johnny Campbell, also to play together at Renton. Harvey, like Campbell, was noted as one of the best players around who had not won an international cap. Nicknamed the 'Little Un', at only 5'5" tall, the diminutive Harvey became an influential figure as Newcastle gained promotion to the First Division. He played across the right flank of the forward line, occasionally taking the leader's role too. Later in life John resided on Teesside while working at the ICI complex.

(Note: Some sources record his surname as 'Harvie' although United and the Football League's archives note it as 'Harvey'.)

Appearances & Goals:
Debut v Woolwich Arsenal (h) 4 September 1897
FL: 30 app 8 gls
FAC: 5 app 2 gls
Total: 35 app 10 gls

Honours:
FL champs 1893, 1895 (6 app)/FL div 2 prom 1898.

HARVEY Joseph 1945-1955, 1962-1989

Right-half, Trainer & Manager
6'0"
b. Edlington, near Doncaster, 11 June 1918
d. Newcastle upon Tyne, 24 February 1989

Career: Edlington Rangers/Bradford Park Avenue May 1936/Wolverhampton Wand Nov 1936/Bournemouth May 1937/Bradford City July 1938 (Bradford Park Avenue war-guest 1941-2)(Watford war-guest 1942-43)(Aberdeen war-guest 1942-43)(Dundee Utd war-guest 1942-43) (Aldershot war-guest 1943-45)(York City war-guest 1943-45) (Hartlepools Utd war-guest 1944-45)/UNITED Oct 1945 £4,250, becoming player-trainer June 1953, trainer Jan 1954 & part-time Crook Town trainer March 1954 to April 1955/Barrow manager July 1955/Workington manager June 1957/UNITED manager June 1962 to April 1975, becoming chief scout as well as caretaker-manager Aug 1980 to Sept 1980, asst-manager cs 1984 to cs 1988, remaining associated with the club to his demise in 1989.

A devoted servant to the Magpies for most of his adult life, Joe Harvey was an inspiring captain during the club's post-war glory years, then a popular manager as Newcastle won promotion, lifted a European trophy and reached Wembley. As a player he was lean and strong, a tough, uncompromising wing-half who lacked finer skills but was at his best when the contest was at its most fierce. After being on Wolves' books as a youngster and sent to their nursery club, Bournemouth, Harvey was developed in the war leagues, totalling 126 games for Bradford City before Stan Seymour brought the Yorkshireman north to Tyneside as a vital cog in his new United machine. Having been a sergeant-major in the Royal Artillery as a PT instructor, Joe then became a driving force on the field for United, bellowing instructions all over the pitch as only he could. With a presence and a passion, he skippered the Football League line-up and is United's longest serving captain (over seven years) going onto lift the FA Cup twice for United, then additionally was a coach in another victory during 1955. After that success Joe concentrated learning the managerial skills in the backwaters of Cumberland. An unsuccessful applicant for the Newcastle manager's position when Charlie Mitten was appointed, he returned to Gallowgate as boss following relegation in 1961. Harvey proceeded to rebuild the club and brought the Magpies out of obscurity and into an entertaining period. With an eye for a talented player, his teams always bristled with star names like Wyn Davies, Malcolm Macdonald and Jimmy Smith. Described as a down-to-earth boss, direct and honest, he kept the

game uncomplicated and left most of the tactical discussion to his coaches. Many players had a strong rapport with the Yorkshireman-adopted-Geordie, noted as a man's man who had exceptional motivating qualities. While Joe won the Inter Cities Fairs Cup, Harvey always regretted not winning a major domestic trophy for United, and never wavered at the criticism thrown his way during his later days in charge of Gallowgate. In 1977 he was given a well deserved, though belated, testimonial (14,000) and, with nearly 40 years service to his name, remained an active personality at St James' Park right up to his death. Joe remains the club's longest serving boss, 13 years 10 days in charge. During 1951 he appeared once for Hartlepools in a Festival of Britain exhibition match, bringing the FA Cup to the Victoria Ground as a bonus, while at Crook, he returned to Wembley again to see the non-leaguers lift the FA Amateur Cup in 1954. A commemorative plaque marking Harvey's service with United is located at St James' Park.

Appearances & Goals:
Debut v Barnsley (h) 5 January 1946 (FAC)
(v Blackpool (h) 20 October 1945 (FLN))
FL: 224 app 12 gls
FAC: 23 app 0 gls
War: 33 app 1 gl
Others: 1 app 0 gls
Total: 281 app 13 gls

In Charge: 628 games
Debut v Cardiff City (a) 18 August 1962

Honours:
3 FL app 1948-52/FL div 2 champs 1965(m)/FL div 2 prom 1948/FAC winner 1951, 1952/FAC final 1974(m)/ICFC winner 1969(m).

HAY James 1911-1919

Left-half
5'8"
b. Woodside, near Annbank, Ayrshire, 9 February 1881
d. Ayr, 4 April 1940

Career: Woodside Annbank/Annbank White Brigade/ Annbank Jan 1899/Glossop trial March 1899/Annbank May 1899/Celtic trial May 1900/Ayr Jan 1902 (Annbank loan 1901-02)/Glossop Sept 1902/Annbank March 1903/ Celtic March 1903 £50 (Annbank loan 1902-03)/UNITED July 1911 £1,250 (Ayr Utd war-guest 1915-18)(Heart of Midlothian war-guest 1917-18)(Clydebank war-guest 1918-19)/Ayr Utd cs 1919, becoming player-trainer cs 1920/Clydebank 1921, retired 1922, becoming manager/ Ayr Utd manager June 1924 to Jan 1926/UNITED scout 1928.

To be the successor to the injured Peter McWilliam, United had to find an exceptional player and sandy-haired Jimmy Hay was just that. Captain of Celtic and Scotland, he was a naturally gifted midfielder, quick to support his attack and ever effective spoiling the opposition's play. Signing for the Magpies as a 30-year-old following a dispute over terms at Parkhead, Jimmy had been one of the mainstays of Celtic's all conquering side north of the border which lifted six titles in a row, recording 324 senior outings for the Hoops. Short and stocky, Jimmy was nicknamed 'The General' and 'The Man with the Iron Chest', or the more colloquial 'Dun' Hay; the broad-shouldered Scot was a powerful character on the park, mixing neat skills with anticipation and vigour. Never the quickest, but he was a noted tactician and leader on the field of play. Hay was a regular in the black-and-white striped jersey over four seasons up to World War One, and while he never lifted a trophy with the Magpies, still displayed his obvious qualities. He was conscripted into the Royal Field Artillery as a gunner and after the war became a somewhat controversial Scottish boss, often cynical of the game's administrators in his native country. Indeed, he was suspended sine-die for a period following a bribery scandal in which Hay accused directors, officials and referees of underhand dealings. As a teenager Hay had signed for Glossop, but his father refused to let the youngster move so far south. Hailing from a large family with a pit background, leaving school he worked down the local pit at Woodside. After Jimmy's footballing days were over Hay returned to his roots and settled in his native Ayrshire becoming an insurance agent.

Appearances & Goals:
Debut v Bolton Wanderers (a) 2 September 1911
FL: 132 app 8 gls
FAC: 17 app 0 gls
Total: 149 app 8 gls

Honours:
11 Scot caps 1905-14/6 SL app 1909-11/Scot trial app 1905-12/SL champs 1905, 1906, 1907, 1908, 1909, 1910/SC winner 1904, 1907, 1908, 1911/SC final 1909.

H

HAYNES 1894-1895

Left-back
b. unknown

Seemingly a local player, Haynes stepped into the full-back's role for one appearance during United's second season in the Football League for 1894-95. He remained for the programme with the club, but did not get another opportunity in the senior eleven. However, it is suspected that this player could well be United's goalkeeper John Hynd (qv). Research indicates that the club's reserve custodian may have taken the position in an emergency. The name of 'Haynes' appears in brief local reports of the match, but is not mentioned in club records or either the Football League or Football Association archives. The Newcastle Evening News of the day notes that Hynd actually "performed several times at full-back in his younger days".

Appearances & Goals:
Debut v Crewe Alexandra (a) 9 March 1895
FL: 1 app 0 gls
Total: 1 app 0 gls

HEARD Timothy Patrick 1984-1985

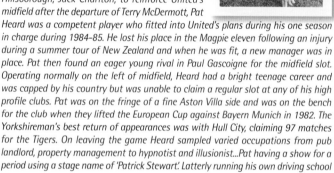

Midfield
5'10"
b. Hull, 17 March 1960

Career: Everton jnr June 1976, prof March 1978/ Aston Villa Oct 1979 £100,000/Sheffield Wed Jan 1983 £60,000/UNITED Sept 1984 cash-exch for J Ryan/Middlesbrough Aug 1985 £10,000/Hull City March 1986 £5,000/Rotherham Utd July 1988/ Cardiff City Aug 1990 free/Hull City Aug to Oct 1992/Hall Road Rangers 1993/Brunei national XI Jan 1994.

Brought to Tyneside by his previous boss at Hillsborough, Jack Charlton, to reinforce United's midfield after the departure of Terry McDermott, Pat Heard was a competent player who fitted into United's plans during his one season in charge during 1984-85. He lost his place in the Magpie eleven following an injury during a summer tour of New Zealand and when he was fit, a new manager was in place. Pat then found an eager young rival in Paul Gascoigne for the midfield slot. Operating normally on the left of midfield, Heard had a bright teenage career and was capped by his country but was unable to claim a regular slot at any of his high profile clubs. Pat was on the fringe of a fine Aston Villa side and was on the bench for the club when they lifted the European Cup against Bayern Munich in 1982. The Yorkshireman's best return of appearances was with Hull City, claiming 97 matches for the Tigers. On leaving the game Heard sampled varied occupations from pub landlord, property management to hypnotist and illusionist...Pat having a show for a period using a stage name of 'Patrick Stewart'! Latterly running his own driving school around Birmingham, he also works as a football pundit for Free Radio Birmingham.

Appearances & Goals:
Debut v West Ham United (h) 29 September 1984
FL: 34 app 2 gls
FAC: 2 app 0 gls
Total: 36 app 2 gls

Honours:
Eng sch-youth app/EC winner 1982 (sub no app)/ICC final 1982 (sub no app)/ESC winner 1982 (sub no app)/FL div 2 prom 1984 (5 app)/FL div 4 champs 1989/FL div 4 prom 1984 (5 app).

HEDLEY George H W 1906-1908, 1910-1911

Outside-left
5'11"
b. Earsdon, near Newcastle upon Tyne, c1887
d. South Northumberland, June 1945

Career: Whitley Bay Ath/UNITED amat March 1906, later trial Aug 1906, pmt amat Sept 1906/ Knaresborough cs 1908/Bradford City trial 1908/ Carlisle Utd Dec 1908/UNITED amat March 1910 to 1911.

George Hedley was a well known Tyneside player and handicap sprinter who was called up once into United's side as an eleventh hour replacement for Bert Gosnell.

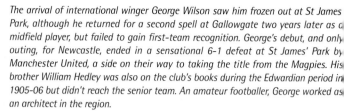

The arrival of international winger George Wilson saw him frozen out at St James Park, although he returned for a second spell at Gallowgate two years later as a midfield player, but failed to gain first-team recognition. George's debut, and only outing, for Newcastle, ended in a sensational 6-1 defeat at St James' Park by Manchester United, a side on their way to taking the title from the Magpies. His brother William Hedley was also on the club's books during the Edwardian period in 1905-06 but didn't reach the senior team. An amateur footballer, George worked as an architect in the region.

Appearances & Goals:
Debut v Manchester United (h) 12 October 1907
FL: 1 app 0 gls
Total: 1 app 0 gls

HEDLEY Richard 1894-1895, 1898-1899

Outside-right
b. Newcastle upon Tyne, 1873
d. Newcastle upon Tyne, 21 September 1908

Career: Marlborough (Newcastle)/Arthurs Hill (Newcastle)/Newcastle Albion/UNITED amat Aug 1894 to Oct 1894/Jarrow late 1894/UNITED Aug 1895/Hebburn Argyle 1896/UNITED 1898-99/Morpeth Harriers July 1899/ Jarrow Feb 1902.

One of many local league favourites to join United, once described as "spry and fearless" and "the pick of United's reserve forwards", Dickie Hedley was a ball dribbler of the day who loved to speed down the wing and take on defenders scoring plenty of goals in the process at local level. However, before the Tynesider was able to make an impression on the Football League scene, an unfortunate clash with Newcastle's hierarchy led to his departure. He was one of several amateur reserves who demanded payment and went on strike during 1894. Due to this industrial action the club disbanded the 'A' team and he was dismissed along with several of his colleagues, although Hedley made a brief appearance back at Gallowgate in 1898-99. He was again a popular forward in Newcastle's black-and-white stripes at reserve level. Dickie afterwards became seriously ill for a long period and died at a young age of 35 years old. His widow was given a benefit game at St James' Park.

Appearances & Goals:
Debut v Notts County (h) 22 September 1894
FL: 3 app 1 gl
Total: 3 app 1 gl

HEDWORTH Christopher 1980-1986

Centre-half
6'1"
b. Wallsend, 5 January 1964

Career: Wallsend BC/UNITED jnr Jan 1980, prof Jan 1982/Barnsley Aug 1986 free/Halifax Town Aug 1988 free/Blackpool Sept 1990 to cs 1992.

Chris Hedworth was a reserve defender who graduated through United's youth set-up under Arthur Cox to make the fringe of the club's senior team. Tall and slim, Hedworth was handed a debut during season 1982-83 as the Magpies won promotion, and then further outings in the First Division. However, Chris never looked likely to develop enough to become a top class defender and he moved to the lower divisions where he concluded his career. The dark-haired centre-back appeared on 30 occasions for Barnsley, clocked up 50 in Halifax colours then had 31 outings for Blackpool. He once ended up between the posts for United in a dramatic 8-1 defeat at Upton Park during season 1985-86; having taking over from the injured Martin Thomas, Chris also had to leave the field with a knock, leaving Peter Beardsley to end up United's 'keeper. On retirement from the game he returned to the North East region residing in the Whitley Bay area working for South Tyneside Council and at Longbenton College. Hedworth also spent a period living in New Zealand.

Appearances & Goals:
Debut v Leeds United (a) 30 October 1982 (sub)
FL: 8(1) app 0 gls
FLC: 1 app 0 gls
Total: 9(1) app 0 gls

Honours:
FL div 4 prom 1992 (4 app).

HELDER (Cristovao) Marino Rodrigues 1999-2002

Centre-half
5'11"
b. Luanda (Angola), 21 March 1971

Career: GD Estoril Praia (Ptg) 1989/SL Benfica (Ptg) 1992/Deportivo la Coruna (Sp) Jan 1997 £2.9m (UNITED loan Nov 1999 to May 2002)/SL Benfica (Ptg) May 2002 free/Paris St-Germain (Fr) Aug 2004/AE Larissa (Gr) cs 2005 to cs 2006 when he retired/GD Estoril (Ptg) manager July 2009 to Sept 2009/Portimonense SC (Ptg) asst-coach Jan 2011/SL Benfica (Ptg) B coach July 2013.

Portugal's 'Helder' Cristovao was a vastly experienced defender by the time he arrived at Gallowgate during the winter of 1999. Having spent five seasons in a successful Benfica and Deportivo line-up, winning caps for Portugal and appearing during Euro 1996 in England, the centre-back knew what the professional game was all about. Manager Bobby Robson admired his thoughtful play in defence, knowing the player from his time on the Continent. United needed defensive cover during season 1999-2000 with only Dabizas available as Dumas, Goma and Howey picked up injuries while Marcelino was far from convincing. Having just recovered from a long-term injury with Deportivo when he snapped a knee tendon, at 28 years of age, Helder gave the Magpies decent service for the rest of the season. Cool and composed, he also possessed a no-nonsense attitude and cleared the ball quickly when he needed to do so. Turning out on 229 occasions for the Lisbon Eagles, Helder also played a small part in Deportivo's very first La Liga title success during 1999-2000 before heading to Tyneside. On retiring, he was often engaged as an expert pundit with RTP, Portugal's main broadcaster.

Appearances & Goals:
Debut v Tottenham Hotspur (h) 28 November 1999
PL: 8 app 1 gl
FAC: 4 app 0 gls
Total: 12 app 1 gl

Honours:
35 Ptg caps 1992-2001/Ptg Lg champs 1994/Ptg Cup winner 1993, 1996, 2004 (sub no app)/Sp Lg champs 2000/Sp Cup winner 2002.

HENDERSON Duncan 1888-1891

Goalkeeper
b. probably Scotland

Career: Kilmarnock 1885/EAST END Aug 1888/Middlesbrough Ironopolis Oct 1889/EAST END again Nov 1889/Kilmarnock cs 1891 to Nov 1893.

Noted in Kilmarnock annals as a "custodian of merit", Duncan Henderson was the regular 'keeper for the Ayrshire club from 1885 to early 1887. He took over as first choice in Heaton for the start of the 1888-89 Northern League programme and appeared in East End's first Northern League match against Darlington during September 1889. First choice until October, he was replaced between the posts by Matt Scott. Apart from his first-class call-ups, Henderson appeared over 40 times for the club in friendly matches. He moved down the North East coast to join new breakaway Tees club Ironopolis but did not stay long.

Appearances & Goals:
Debut v Port Clarence (h) 6 October 1888 (FACQ)
NL: 5 app 0 gls
FAC: 4 app 0 gls
Total: 9 app 0 gls

HENDERSON Henry Burton 1943-1945

Outside-right
5'8"
b. Newcastle upon Tyne, 23 September 1923
d. Newcastle upon Tyne, 2 July 1997

Career: Throckley Welfare/UNITED amat Sept 1943, prof Oct 1943 to 1945.

Able to operate on both wings, Harry Henderson rivalled Eddie Copeland and Charles Woollett, as well as Tommy Walker, for the touchline position at St James' Park during wartime football. And he was often fourth choice having to appear in the club's reserve side in the Northern Combination League. But on his few outings in senior company, Henderson played well and provided several telling crosses which resulted in goals for Albert Stubbins. Harry was also a noted local cricketer, appearing for Northumberland in a span of 24 years (1947 to 1971). A first-class wicket-keeper and batsman, Henderson registered 264 matches for the County (2,426 runs, 475 victims) and set many records; recording six catches in an innings more than once, as well as taking nine victims from behind the stumps on one occasion. He played against the West Indies touring team during 1953 and was skipper of Northumberland on occasion.

Appearances & Goals:
Debut v Hartlepools United (h) 23 October 1943 (FLN)
War: 5 app 0 gls
Total: 5 app 0 gls

HENDERSON James 1919-1920

Inside-right
5'8"
b. Newcastle upon Tyne, 1895

Career: Scotswood/Cardiff City April 1913/Grimsby Town 1918-19/UNITED May 1919 £50/Scotswood 1920 free/Ashington June 1920/Scotswood Aug 1922/Spennymoor Utd Jan 1923/Annfield Plain cs 1923.

As a young Geordie, James Henderson was robbed of a career at Ninian Park due to the outbreak of the First World War, but after serving with the Lancashire Fusiliers and on the signing of the Armistice he started again as a Magpie player. Henderson showed enough talent in pre-season fixtures to be given the inside-right position for the opening game of the new 1919-20 campaign at Highbury, and went onto net Newcastle's first goal after the Great War had ended. Although smart and fast, he was replaced later in the season by Stan Dixon and afterwards appeared once for Ashington during their inaugural Football League season of 1921-22 when the Third Division North and South was introduced.

Appearances & Goals:
Debut v Arsenal (a) 30 August 1919 (1 goal)
FL: 6 app 1 gl
Total: 6 app 1 gl

HENDERSON John 1895-1896

Goalkeeper
6'0"
b. Lanarkshire
d. Burnbank, Lanarkshire, 4 July 1932

Career: Burnbank Swifts c1889/Motherwell June 1893/Burnbank Ath/Clyde June 1894/ UNITED May 1895/Clyde May 1896/Burnbank Swifts April 1897.

Described as being somewhat well-built and burley, goalkeeper John Henderson was acquired to take-over the custodian's position for the beginning of the 1895-96 Second Division season. Henderson came south from Scotland with a first-class record in Clyde's top level line-up during 1894-95 and he gave some sterling displays in the period he was with the club. However, some reports noted that he had, "given alarm to the dodgy hearted" on occasion and he was replaced by Charlie Watts within a year.

Appearances & Goals:
Debut v Loughborough (h) 7 September 1895
FL: 30 app 0 gls
FAC: 5 app 0 gls
Total: 35 app 0 gls

Honours:
SJC winner 1890.

H

HENDRIE John Grattan 1988-1989

Outside-right
5'7"
b. Lennoxtown, 24 October 1963

Career: Lennoxtown BC/St Flannan's Guild/Possil YC/Coventry City jnr June 1980, prof May 1981 (Hereford Utd loan 1983-84)/Bradford City July 1984 free/UNITED June 1988 £500,000/Leeds Utd June 1989 £600,000/Middlesbrough July 1990 £550,000/Barnsley Oct 1996 £300,000, becoming manager July 1998 to April 1999.

United's most expensive winger at the time, John Hendrie settled in the North East as one of Willie McFaul's purchases in an attempt to quieten the uproar over Paul Gascoigne's sale. A consistent forward with Bradford City, John had missed only a single game for the Bantams in four seasons and totalled 212 matches scoring an impressive 59 goals. Recognised as one of the best players out of the First Division, Hendrie was part McFaul's new side which unfortunately never blended together, although John himself was an individual success. Perceived as an out and out winger, Hendrie preferred an inside or central role and showed his best form in that position. Committed and exciting to watch on the field, having a knack of being able to take the ball with his back to goal then spin quickly, by the end of the 1988-89 season, relegation and a managerial change saw Hendrie move on. John headed back to Yorkshire, to Leeds United where he tasted success, as he did in six seasons at Ayresome Park for Boro (235 app 56 goals) as well as at Oakwell where he was a key member of a Barnsley unit which reached the Premier League. Despite often battling against injury set-backs, John was five times part of a promoted side, although twice relegated too. When starting out at Highfield Road with Coventry, his first job as a junior was to be ex-United full-back George Dalton's assistant in the physio room, while Hendrie was in Bradford City's team (with Peter Jackson) when the tragic Valley Parade fire disaster took place in May 1985. His older brother Paul appeared notably for Halifax and Stockport, his cousin Lee Hendrie reached the England side with Aston Villa. John's sons also entered football; Luke started a career with Manchester United and Jordan with Bradford City. He is also uncle of Callum Hendrie who was on Motherwell's books. On leaving football, Hendrie afterwards became a sport's law consultant with Blacks Solicitors in Yorkshire, acting also as a mediator for the Sports Dispute Resolution Panel. John was additionally involved in media work covering the game.

Appearances & Goals:
Debut v Everton (a) 27 August 1988
FL: 34 app 4 gls
FAC: 4 app 0 gls
FLC: 2 app 1 gl
Others: 3 app 0 gls
Total: 43 app 5 gls

Honours:
Scot sch-youth app/FL div 1 champs 1995/FL div 2 champs 1990/FL div 3 champs 1985/FL div 1 prom 1997/FL div 2 prom 1992/PFA ToS (d1) 1995, (d2) 1987, 1988.

HERD Alexander 1940-1941

Inside-forward
5'8"
b. Bowhill, Fife, 8 November 1911
d. Dumfries, 21 August 1982

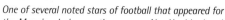

Career: Hearts of Beath/Hamilton Acc Nov 1928/Manchester City Feb 1933 (Manchester Utd war-guest 1939-40)(UNITED war-guest 1940-41)(Hamilton Acc war-guest 1941-45)(Chelsea war-guest 1944-45)(Middlesbrough war-guest 1945-46)(Stockport Co war-guest 1945-46)/Resumed with Manchester City 1946/Stockport Co March 1948 free to 1951.

One of several noted stars of football that appeared for the Magpies during wartime soccer. Alec Herd had an immensely successful period with Manchester City prior to the Second World War, reaching two FA Cup finals and playing a major part in their title victory of 1937. He claimed almost 400 games in all for the Maine Road club and netted 125 goals. A player who could cause menace to defences with late runs and pile-driver shots, Alec hailed from a footballing family. His brother Andrew was capped by Scotland when with Hearts, while his son, David appeared with credit for Manchester United and also for Scotland. Alex himself claimed a wartime cap in 1942 and appeared alongside his son for Stockport during

season 1950-51 when he continued in action until over 40 years of age. In Newcastle's ranks, Herd impressed on a short but productive stay; he netted three goals over the winter period of season 1940-41. After leaving the game, for several years Herd was a representative of an asphalt company.

Appearances & Goals:
Debut v Grimsby Town (h) 28 December 1940 (FLN) (1 goal)
War: 4 app 3 gls
Total: 4 app 3 gls

Honours:
1 Scot war app 1942/Scot trial app 1942/2 Scot unoff app 1943-44/FL champs 1937/FL div 2 champs 1947/FAC winner 1934/FAC final 1933.

HESLOP George Wilson 1958-1962

Centre-half
5'11"
b. Wallsend, 1 July 1940
d. Lytham St Annes, Lancashire, 16 September 2006

Career: Dudley Welfare Jnrs/UNITED jnr Aug 1958, prof Feb 1959/Everton March 1962 part-exch J Fell/Manchester City Sept 1965 £25,000 (Cape Town City (SA) loan 1971-72)/Bury Aug 1972 £3,000/Northwich Victoria player-manager Dec 1977/Bury coach June 1978 to June 1980/Macclesfield Town coach.

Tall, well-built and blond-haired, George Heslop made his debut for United in an 8-2 victory over one of his future clubs, Everton. George rivalled Bill Thompson as Bob Stokoe's replacement in United's side, but had little joy wearing a Magpie shirt and moved to Goodison Park where he struggled to displace Brian Labone. It was though, when he joined Manchester City that Heslop enjoyed considerable success being a rock in their defence as Joe Mercer and Malcolm Allison fashioned a marvellous line-up at Maine Road. Turning out on 204 occasions, he won title, cup and European medals, missing only a single game when the First Division Championship trophy was secured in 1968...ironically with a victory at where his career started, St James' Park. George was later a well-known publican in Manchester, at the Hyde Road Hotel (later the City Gates Hotel), the original home of the Light Blues as well as at the Royal George in Piccadilly and the Carters Arms, Wilmslow. Afterwards Heslop became a social worker in Blackpool, residing in Lytham St Annes.

Appearances & Goals:
Debut v Everton (h) 7 November 1959
FL: 27 app 0 gls
FAC: 1 app 0 gls
FLC: 4 app 0 gls
Total: 32 app 0 gls

Honours:
FL champs 1968/FL div 2 champs 1966/FLC winner 1970/ECWC winner 1970.

HEWARD Harold Aubrey 1931-1934

Left-half
5'8"
b. Hetton-le-Hole, Co Durham, 31 August 1910
d. Sutton, Surrey, June 1985

Career: Herrington CW Swifts/UNITED amat Oct 1931, prof March 1932 £20/Bradford Park Avenue Aug 1934 free/Hartlepools Utd July 1935/Yeovil & Petters Utd Oct 1936 to 1946.

Harry Heward was a whole-hearted player, splendid in the tackle and one not to make rash clearances. A ninety minute man, he never let the Magpies down when called upon to deputise for John Murray at half-back. Heward made all his outings for the Geordies during the 1932-33 season before moving to Second Division rivals Bradford Park Avenue. He afterwards totalled 30 games for Hartlepools before having a successful period with Yeovil. During his decade at the Huish ground, he was an influential schemer, turning out on 157 occasions, as well as many more games during the war. He worked at the Westland's factory in Somerset and returned to County Durham once peace had been restored.

Appearances & Goals:
Debut v Huddersfield Town (a) 11 February 1933
FL: 5 app 0 gls
Total: 5 app 0 gls

HEWISON Robert 1908-1914, 1919-1920

Right-half
5'8"
b. East Holywell, near Newcastle upon Tyne,
25 March 1890
d. Bristol, 1964 (Q2)

Career: East Holywell Villa/Whitley Ath/UNITED amat March 1908, prof July 1908 £10/Leeds City loan 1914, then pmt, becoming player-manager to Dec 1919/UNITED trial Dec 1919, pmt Jan 1920/ Northampton Town player-manager May 1920 £250/Queens Park Rangers player-manager May 1925 to May 1931/Bristol City manager March 1932 to March 1949/Gateshead manager May 1949 briefly/Guildford City manager/Bristol Rovers scout/Bath City manager May 1957/Retired 1961.

Steady midfield exponent Bob Hewison, despite several injuries, was developed into a solid but unspectacular professional and a loyal player who gave United grand service for three seasons before the outbreak of the Great War. Bobby began at St James' Park as a youthful rival to the renowned Colin Veitch, eventually replacing the Magpie stalwart. When Newcastle all but closed down during the First World War, Hewison teamed up with the Leeds City outfit and spent the war years appearing for the Tykes. Although he was unlucky to twice break his leg, Bob won wartime honours before he was embroiled in the Leeds City scandal that rocked football during 1919 and led to his club being expelled from the game. Returning to Gallowgate, and now aged almost 30, he was unable to find a first-team place and continued his career with Northampton Town, as player boss. Hewison became a character in football, later becoming once more involved in controversy at Ashton Gate when Hewison was suspended for the majority of season 1938-39 following an illegal payment inquiry. Characterised by suit and glasses, bank-manager style, Bob was nevertheless a respected manager by that time and in 1943 he was awarded the Football League's Long Service medal. Hewison also took charge of the League's representative side. During May 1947, Hewison was on the short-list for the United manager's job and was interviewed for the post.

Appearances & Goals:
Debut v Notts County (h) 8 October 1910
FL: 67 app 0 gls
FAC: 3 app 0 gls
Total: 70 app 0 gls

Honours:
WL champs 1918/SnL champs 1960(m)/FL Long Service medal 1943.

HEYWOOD Frederick 1900-1902

Inside-left
5'5"
b. Edgworth, Lancashire, 1879

Career: Turton/UNITED May 1900/Blackpool July 1902/Reading May 1903/Blackpool July 1904/ Oldham Ath May 1905/Darwen Aug 1906/Turton Nov 1908/Chorley June 1909/Hyde July 1911/Nelson Nov 1911/Hyde Sept 1912/Denton March 1914/ Altrincham Sept 1914/Denton Dec 1914.

A pygmy figure at inside-forward or centre-forward, the slightly-built and Lancashire-born Fred Heywood was full of cunning, a footballer who showed plenty of grit and determination. One account of his style of play noted that he had only one objective every time he received the ball, to make a bee-line for goal and Fred's snaky runs were a feature of his play. The Northern Gossip magazine described him as a player "full of resource and excels in tricky touches". When on Tyneside Heywood was due to wear United's shirt for the derby contest with Sunderland on Good Friday 1901, but the fixture was abandoned without a ball being kicked due to what has gone down in history as a notorious riot. Although Heywood only gained opportunities during one season for the Geordies, 1900-01, he later became a noted and well-travelled figure in Lancashire football. Fred held a regular slot in Blackpool's Second Division line-up during 1902-03 and totalled 37 games for the Seasiders.

Appearances & Goals:
Debut v Derby County (a) 16 February 1901
FL: 13 app 3 gls
Total: 13 app 3 gls

HIBBERT William 1911-1920

Inside-forward
5'8"
b. Golborne, near Wigan, 21 September 1884
d. Blackpool, 16 March 1949

Career: Golborne Jnrs/Newton-le-Willows/ Brynn Central May 1905/Bury May 1906/ UNITED Oct 1911 £1,950 (Bury war-guest 1915-16)(Arsenal war-guest 1916-17) (Sheffield Wed war-guest 1917-18)(Leeds City war-guest 1917-19)(Rochdale war-guest 1918-19) (Hartlepools Utd war-guest 1919) (Rotherham Co war-guest)/Bradford City May 1920 £700/ Oldham Ath May 1922 £500/ Bridgend Town manager May 1923/Fall River Marksmen (USA) player-trainer July 1923/Hamilton Steelworks (Can) Sept 1923/Saskatchewan Swastikas (Can) Oct 1923/ J & P Coats (Rhode Island, USA) Nov 1923 to 1926/Gimnastic de Tarragona (Sp) coach June 1927/Wigan Borough trainer May 1928/Burscough Rangers Feb 1930/Budapest FC (Hng) coach Aug 1930/Retired 1938.

Billy Hibbert cost United a new British record transfer fee when he moved from Lancashire to St James' Park being a nimble, enthusiastic and most skilful forward who featured in the inside positions as well as leading the attack. Hibbert worked as a collier then in an iron foundry before getting the chance to make his way as a footballer. He was soon impressing the football public at Gigg Lane with a catchy rhyme noting Hibbert as: "A clever player, there's no doubt...a tricky man to meet...who's so nimble on his feet." Not of big build, Hibbert possessed the goal-poacher's instinct and became one of the country's top strikers after topping Bury's scoring list for four years in a row during their Edwardian First Division years. He had a formidable stats record with the Shakers, 105 goals in 188 games and was purchased by United to replace the goalscoring talent of Albert Shepherd. Billy never quite lived up to his billing in terms of goals, yet was a popular player in a black-and-white shirt before and after the war. Capped by England and the Football League, he also took part in the FA's first tour of South Africa during 1910 when he scored an amazing 34 goals during the programme. Hibbert played at the top level until he was 38 years of age and bagged over 200 goals during his career and later travelled the Continent and North America teaching the game. Following retirement Billy settled in Blackpool and at his funeral during 1949, greats of football Frank Swift and Billy Meredith were pole-bearers. His brother Jack was also on Oldham's books for a period.

Appearances & Goals:
Debut v Blackburn Rovers (h) 21 October 1911
FL: 139 app 46 gls
FAC: 16 app 3 gls
War: 4 app 1 gl
Total: 159 app 50 gls

Honours:
1 Eng cap 1910/Eng trial app 1912-13/3 unoff Eng app 1910/3 FL app 1908-11/WL champs 1918.

HIBBITT Terence Arthur 1971-1975, 1978-1981

Midfield
5'7"
b. Bradford, 1 December 1947
d. Ponteland, near Newcastle upon Tyne,
5 August 1994

Career: Leeds Utd jnr April 1963, prof Dec 1964/UNITED Aug 1971 £30,000/Birmingham City Aug 1975 £100,000/UNITED May 1978 exch deal for S Barrowclough/Retired due to injury June 1981/Gateshead July 1981, becoming player-coach Jan 1983, manager April 1986/Durham City player 1986, becoming asst-manager Nov 1986 to May 1987.

One of United's best-ever bargain buys, Joe Harvey picked Terry Hibbitt up for a paltry fee from Don Revie's Leeds United squad at a time of rebuilding by Newcastle's boss. At the same time, Malcolm Macdonald arrived on Tyneside and the Hibbitt-Supermac

H

combination was to give the Magpies a new dimension. Small and frail-looking, yet perky and plucky, Terry possessed a sweet left foot and forged a great understanding from his midfield role with his centre-forward team-mate, providing accurate long-ball service to capitalise on Macdonald's pace. Hibbitt hailed from down-to-earth Yorkshire stock like his manager, and possessed a bubbly, and at times, fiery character; he was once described affectionately by Malcolm Macdonald as a "scallywag". Hibbitt was quickly adopted by United's supporters, every bit a hero as Macdonald was. On the fringe of an England call up as Newcastle reached Wembley in 1974, Terry was a competitor with a lion's heart and always urged his colleagues on. Injury and the arrival of new manager Gordon Lee saw him move on, many noting he was badly treated by United's new boss, but following a good spell at Birmingham (122 app) Hibbitt returned to the fold as captain for a second spell on Tyneside as Newcastle tried to reclaim their former top level status. Another knee injury forced his departure from the senior game, but Terry went onto lift the Northern Premier title with Gateshead during his 130 games and reach the FA's non-league England side. After quitting the game, he became a newsagent and milkman for a while before settling as manager of The Diamond pub in Ponteland on the outskirts of the city. An adopted Geordie, Terry Hibbitt tragically died of cancer when nearing 47 years old. His brother Kenny, another fine midfielder, appeared over 500 times for Wolves during the same era.

Appearances & Goals:
Debut v Crystal Palace (a) 14 August 1971
FL: 227(1) app 12 gls
FAC: 14 app 1 gl
FLC: 16 app 0 gls
Others: 33 app 5 gls
Total: 290(1) app 18 gls
(Void FAC: 1 app 0 gls)

Honours:
FA app 1982/FL champs 1969/FAC final 1974/ICFC winner 1968.

HIGGINS Alexander 1905-1919

Inside-forward
5'9"
b. Kilmarnock, 4 November 1885
d. Newcastle upon Tyne, 15 March 1939

Career: Belle Vue Jnrs/Kilmarnock 1904/UNITED July 1905 £250 (Hartlepools Utd war-guest 1915-16)(Hull City war-guest 1916-17) Kilmarnock Aug 1919/ Nottingham Forest June 1920/Jarrow player-manager Sept 1921/Norwich City Nov 1921/ Wallsend Dec 1922/Kilmarnock trainer 1924-25/FC Bern (Swtz) trainer 1925/Preston Colliery (North Shields) Nov 1926.

Sandy Higgins came to prominence during United's Football League title campaign of 1908-09 after being signed as a teenager from Scotland three seasons before. He was one of several versatile players to be groomed as stars of the future on United's books during their Edwardian heyday. Higgins quickly made an impact with senior company, netting all four goals on a tour match against Vienna in 1905-06. The Scot operated at either inside-forward position or at centre-forward and possessing a marvellous left-foot, he could ghost past defenders at ease, proving himself as a big-match player with an abundance of craft. A superb purveyor of passes, it was noted Sandy tended to be rather selfish at times when in possession, and never quite developed into the household name he perhaps should have become, although he was capped by Scotland and was still recognised as one of the best forwards around. Son of the famous Kilmarnock and Forest international of the same name, his younger brother Nicholas was with United between 1911 and 1913 without breaking through, tragically killed in World War One. Sandy missed the 1920 Scottish Cup final due to the death of his father a few hours before the match, however he was still given a medal. Serving in World War One with both the Yorkshire Regiment and Durham Light Infantry, the Scot was awarded the Military Medal and a citation for his actions. After retiring from the game, Higgins settled on Tyneside running a grocer's business in Byker as well as being employed as a publican in the city.

Appearances & Goals:
Debut v Aston Villa (h) 24 March 1906
FL: 126 app 36 gls
FAC: 24 app 5 gls
Total: 150 app 41 gls

Honours:
4 Scot caps 1910-11/Scot trial app 1910/FL champs 1907 (1 app), 1909/FAC winner 1910/FAC final 1911/SC winner 1920 (no app).

HIGGINS William 1898-1900

Centre-half
5'11"
b. Smethwick, near Birmingham, 1869

Career: Woodfield (Handsworth)/Albion Swifts/ Birmingham St George/Grimsby Town June 1892/Bristol City May 1897/UNITED May 1898/Middlesbrough May 1900/Newton Heath Sept 1901 to May 1902.

Purchased by United's directors in readiness for the Magpies' debut in the First Division, William Higgins appeared in the club's first ever Division One fixture against Wolves and was an experienced and steady head as Newcastle consolidated their newly found status. With a role in the centre of midfield, although he played at full-back and centre-forward for United as well, one contemporary report noted that he was a, "fearless player" and was especially regarded for sweeping passes to the wings as well as his stinging shots at goal. Higgins had made his name at Grimsby Town where he clocked up 149 games (35 goals), while he was the first captain of Bristol City, additionally skippering the Tynesiders too. In contention for international honours, Higgins was captain of Middlesbrough as well during his short period on Teesside. He is also recorded as being the first player to be sent-off in a Football League match for Boro.

Appearances & Goals:
Debut v Wolverhampton Wanderers (h) 3 September 1898
FL: 35 app 3 gls
FAC: 4 app 0 gls
Total: 39 app 3 gls

Honours:
1 FL app 1897.

HIGHMOOR George Wilfred 1942-1946

Outside-right
5'8"
b. Clara Vale, near Gateshead, 1 February 1923

Career: Clara Vale Jnrs/UNITED Sept 1942 (Halifax Town war-guest 1942-43) to 1946.

George Highmoor has the distinction of pulling on the shirt of the great Tom Finney for his three games as a Newcastle United player. A war-guest from Preston, Finney couldn't make the side for a trio of games during October 1942 and Highmoor stepped in to face Bradford City (two matches) and Gateshead. Finney returned the following week and Highmoor concluded his career with the Magpies' reserve line-up in the Northern Combination.

Appearances & Goals:
Debut v Bradford City (h) 24 October 1942 (FLN)
War: 3 app 0 gls
Total: 3 app 0 gls

HILL John Henry 1928-1931

Centre-half
6'3"
b. Hetton-le-Hole, Co Durham, 2 March 1897
d. Helensburgh, 14 April 1972

Career: Hetton Jnrs/Durham City amat Jan 1919, prof July 1919/Plymouth Argyle Sept 1920 £10/Burnley May 1923 £5,450/UNITED Oct 1928 £8,100/Bradford City June 1931 £600/Hull City Nov 1931, becoming manager April 1934 to Jan 1936, then scout 1948 to 1955.

Red-haired, tall and lanky, Jack Hill was one of the elite of the Twenties. Captain of England, as well as United and Burnley, he was a footballing centre-half, remembered for his stunning duels with Magpie legend, Hughie Gallacher. It was in fact Gallacher who recommended Hill to United's directors when they were searching for a powerful defensive pivot to replace Charlie Spencer. Making 198 outings for Burnley, he was considered by many, including Gallacher, to be the best in the country and Newcastle paid a club record fee when Jack moved back to his native North East, the

Magpies just beating off the challenge of Sunderland for his signature; indeed he was all set to join the Roker Park set-up until, as Jack recorded, an "eleventh hour" switch. He then faced the red-and-whites in a local derby on his debut, losing 5-2! Having began his career as a central midfielder with North Eastern League outfit Durham City and then 400 miles south at Plymouth during their first years in the Football League, he was always willing to move forward from the recently introduced stopper centre-half role with a constructive urge. Hill possessed quality distribution and was a towering figure on the field, in both personality and build. After a couple of seasons of good service as United struggled at the top level, Hill fell into dispute during 1930-31 with United's directors and new boss Andy Cunningham who wanted a younger man at the heart of defence. Hill was sidelined for weeks and led to his premature departure for a knock-down fee. A former teenage miner in the Durham coalfield, following a spell in management then a period with Scarborough running their pools and supporter department, Jack moved to Helensburgh on the west coast of Scotland to retire. Jack was also a keen cricketer in his younger days, appearing for Eppleton CC in the Durham Senior League while during World War One several of the Hetton Juniors side joined up together, including Hill, serving with the East Yorks Regiment in the Dardanelles and Salonika. A family press cutting reveals that he could well be related to celebrated Liverpool manager Bob Paisley, also born in Hetton.

Appearances & Goals:

Debut v Sunderland (a) 27 October 1928
FL: 74 app 2 gls
FAC: 4 app 0 gls
Total: 78 app 2 gls

Honours:

11 Eng caps 1925-29/3 FL app 1924-26/1 SnL app 1923/Eng trial app 1923-26/FL div 3(N) champs 1933.

HILL James Matthew 1957-1958

Inside-right
5'8"
b. Carrickfergus, 31 October 1935

Career: Carrickfergus YMCA/Carrick Rangers/Linfield 1953/UNITED July 1957 exch deal for J Milburn/Norwich City July 1958 £3,000/Everton Aug 1963 £25,000/Port Vale Oct 1965 £5,000/Derry City player-manager March 1968/Linfield manager Aug 1971 to May 1972/Carrick Rangers manager Nov 1988 to May 1991.

Following a sparkling display on his debut for the Magpies against Spurs, Jimmy Hill never blossomed into the player that had been promised at St James' Park following his arrival from Windsor Park as part of the transfer which saw Jack Milburn leave Tyneside, Hill being valued at £5,000. A rival to Gordon Hughes in season 1957-58, Hill was given a run during the first half of the programme, but then was replaced by his rival and remained in the Central League side during his short stay at Gallowgate. Jimmy moved to Carrow Road at the end of the season and claimed conspicuous success with Norwich, a key member of the Canaries noted FA Cup giant-killing runs and a goalscorer when City lifted the Football League Cup in 1961-62. Although some considered Hill a luxury, others reckoned he was a match-winner who possessed a ferocious shot. He scored 66 senior goals in 195 games when at his peak with Norwich and is described in City's annals as being "quick and clever with a magician's touch". Although Jim played mainly on the right of midfield, or on the right wing, for United, he spent a lot of his career at inside-left. Capped at every level for Northern Ireland, he was nicknamed 'Tiger'. Hill settled in his home town of Carrickfergus and ran a sports shop for many years.

Appearances & Goals:

Debut v Tottenham Hotspur (h) 31 August 1957
FL: 11 app 2 gls
Total: 11 app 2 gls

Honours:

7 NI caps 1959-64/2 NI B app 1958-60/6 NIL app 1955-69/NI sch-youth app/1 NI amat app 1953/FLC winner 1962/FL div 3 prom 1960/NI champs 1954, 1955, 1956/NIC final 1971.

HILLEY David 1962-1967

Inside-forward
5'9"
b. Glasgow, 20 December 1938

Career: Market Star Juveniles/Muirend Amateurs/Jordanhill College 1958/Pollock Jnrs April 1958/Third Lanark June 1958/UNITED Aug 1962 £40,000/S Mitchell/Nottingham Forest Dec 1967 £25,000/Highlands Park (SA) Nov 1970/Hellenic (SA) 1973/Scarborough Oct 1975/South Shields July 1976/Bedlington Terriers July 1977/Retired May 1978.

As Joe Harvey's replacement playmaker for the departed Ivor Allchurch, Dave Hilley cost United a big fee at the time as a player recognised as one of the best north of the border, unlucky not win a full Scottish cap. Dave began in the senior game when still a student in Glasgow and played alongside his brother Ian for Third Lanark. Following more than 150 games for the Cathkin Park club he made the move south. Chased by the Magpies for almost two years, dainty on the field and slightly built, the Scot took a period to bed into United's camp, but by the time Newcastle were to make a push to regain their First Division place during 1964, Hilley had settled into a schemer's role that was to be central to United's Division Two title success. With Scottish skills to the fore, Dave was a cunning footballer, capable of creating openings and was once described as being "mathematical in his passes of slide-rule precision". He was also able to hit the net on a regular basis, scoring 12 important goals during that trophy-winning season of 1964-65. An automatic choice on the team-sheet for five years, Hilley afterwards appeared for Forest in 98 games before having a successful spell in South Africa. He then experienced Wembley victory in the FA Trophy for Scarborough, alongside fellow Scot and ex-United 'keeper Bert Garrow. Dave later resided on Tyneside becoming a schoolteacher at Oakfield College in Newcastle's West End until retirement in 1996. He also reported on North East soccer for the Sunday Post for 20 years. Hilley was once fined by the Scottish FA for being part of a group which organised unsanctioned games in Spain's Costa Brava during 1962 when he guested for local side Lloret.

Appearances & Goals:

Debut v Cardiff City (a) 18 August 1962 (1 goal)
FL: 194 app 31 gls
FAC: 8 app 1 gls
FLC: 7 app 1 gl
Total: 209 app 33 gls

Honours:

2 Scot unoff app 1961-62/2 Scot u23 app 1961/1 SL app 1960/Scot sch-youth app/FL div 2 champs 1965/SLC final 1960/FAT winner 1976/SA Cup winner 1973.

HINDMARSH Edward 1942-1943

Half-back
5'10"
b. Castletown, Sunderland, 7 September 1922
d. Co Durham, 1997 (Q3)

Career: Hylton Jnrs/UNITED amat Aug 1942, prof Sept 1942 to Aug 1943/Sunderland Oct 1943/Carlisle Utd July 1945 to May 1947.

Eddie Hindmarsh made his debut in a thrilling wartime fixture with Leeds United during September 1942, a contest which ended in a 5-3 defeat for the Tynesiders. He appeared at both right-half and left-half during his brief period in the club's first-eleven. Attempting a career with his local club, Sunderland, Hindmarsh turned out in 19 games for the Wearsiders then found a home at Brunton Park for a season where he entered Football League and FA Cup contests and totalled 16 senior matches.

Appearances & Goals:

Debut v Leeds United (h) 26 September 1942 (FLN)
War: 6 app 0 gls
Total: 6 app 0 gls

HINDSON Gordon 1967-1971

Midfield
5'9"
b. Quaking Houses, Co Durham, 8 January 1950

Career: UNITED jnr Oct 1967, prof Aug 1968/Luton Town Oct 1971 £27,500 (Carlisle Utd loan 1975-76) (Blackburn Rovers loan 1975-76)/Hartford Bicentennials (USA) 1976/Evenwood Town cs 1976/Consett c1978, becoming coach Aug 1979/Spennymoor Utd Jan 1981/ Gateshead Nov 1981/Consett player-coach Jan 1984, becoming manager June 1984.

Gordon Hindson was a fast and determined midfield player who began at outside-left in United's junior and reserve set-up. He was on the fringes of United's first choice line-up during the club's earliest European campaigns but found it difficult to claim a place, his seven games for the Magpies being spread over four seasons. Gordon did well at Kenilworth Road, however, making almost 100 appearances, including a FA Cup victory at St James' Park during 1973. Following a broken ankle, he departed the Football League scene, afterwards serving local non-league sides with distinction. He assisted Gateshead when they lifted the Northern Premier League title during 1983. Hindson afterwards resided in the North East and was employed in management at Stanley, and later, Newburn leisure centres, then at the Crowtree complex in Sunderland.

Appearances & Goals:
Debut v Southampton (a) 15 February 1969
FL: 7 app 1 gl
Euro: 0(1) app 0 gls
Total: 7(1) app 1 gl

Honours:
FL div 2 prom 1974 (7 app).

HISCOCK Edward 1883-1889

Forward
b. Byker, Newcastle upon Tyne, 1866
d. Byker, Newcastle upon Tyne, 7 June 1939

Career: EAST END 1883 (Tyne Association guest 1884-85, Cheviot guest 1886-87, Raby Rovers guest 1887)/Barrow Benedict's Nov 1888/EAST END again 1889/ Pandon Temperance.

A crowd pleasing forward, a ball dribbler in the style of the day and once described in the local press as "amusing the spectators by his fine dodging". Known as 'Ned', the Geordie from Byker scored plenty of goals for United's pioneers and became the first Newcastle East End player to be selected for Northumberland during 1884 against Durham. Hiscock was nicknamed 'Cannonball' due to his potent shooting and he also registered the first hat-trick for East End in a first eleven match, claiming four goals in a 9-0 friendly victory over Hibernia during the same year. Ned was also the first man to claim three in a any competitive match, against Newcastle Association in the Tyne Charity Shield during 1885. Playing over 80 matches all told for the Heatonites (scoring 40 goals), his only first-class outing was in the club's debut FA Cup match against South Bank during 1887. From a family of footballers who served the club, Charles (qv) and Matt (qv) also pulled on East End's shirt. Hiscock was a riveter by trade in the Tyne shipyards and he later moved to the west coast, probably to work in the Barrow shipyards but returned to turn out for East End towards the end of the 1888-89 season. He played football to a veteran age, appearing for Pandon Temperance in the 1919 Northumberland Senior Cup final having twice lifted the trophy in his younger days. Hiscock also played cricket to a good standard, for East End CC and Raby Rovers CC.

Appearances & Goals:
Debut v South Bank (a) 15 October 1887 (FACQ)
FAC: 1 app 0 gls
Total: 1 app 0 gls

HISLOP Neil Shaka 1995-1998

Goalkeeper
6'4"
b. Hackney, London, 22 February 1969

Career: Howard University (USA)/Baltimore Blast (USA) May 1992/Reading July 1992 trial, pmt Sept 1992/UNITED Aug 1995 £1.575m/West Ham Utd July 1998 free/Portsmouth July 2002 free/West Ham Utd July 2005 free/FC Dallas (USA) July 2006 to Aug 2007 when he retired/Later becoming Quinnipiac University (USA) goalkeeping coach 2009 briefly.

Like most of Kevin Keegan's big money deals, Shaka Hislop had been a target for several months before the 6'4" goalkeeper arrived in Newcastle, the Black'n'Whites sealing the deal when a protracted move for Brad Friedel fell through. Considered the best guardian outside the Premiership at the time, Hislop was agile and safe in the air, and in many ways was very similar in style to his rival Pavel Srnicek. Although born in London of Caribbean parents, Shaka, whose name originates from a Zulu king, lived most of his early years in Trinidad. The son of a lawyer and magistrate, Hislop played teenage football and cricket alongside West Indian Test star Brian Lara, before moving to the USA where he studied and received a degree in mechanical engineering and robotics at a Washington university. Awarded a four-year football scholarship, he was spotted by Reading's ex-Magpie boss, Mark McGhee playing in a friendly contest for Baltimore Blast against Aston Villa at the NEC in Birmingham; Shaka turned on a stunning display and was given a chance in the Football League. Hislop rapidly became the Elm Park club's first choice, appearing on 126 occasions and helping the Royals to promotion, and then very nearly to the Premier League before Reading lost a Wembley Play-Off during 1995. Hislop is one of United's tallest ever players, while he pulled on size 11 boots and size 11 gloves! Shaka at times looked the part between the posts for the Magpies, and with a string of good displays reached both the England 'B' and full squads in 1998, sitting on the bench for an international with Chile at Wembley. He was part of the Newcastle squad to twice end as Premier League runners-up and was in the dug-out for United's 1998 FA Cup final defeat. Hislop became a regular with the Hammers and ended his career on a high; his final club game being the 2006 FA Cup final and last international for Trinidad & Tobago during the World Cup of 2006 in Germany. His brother Kona appeared for the Magpies' reserve eleven before attempting to begin a career elsewhere, notably at Hartlepool, while a nephew, Makan, also won caps for Trinidad. On leaving the game Shaka lived in the States, during 2008 joining the ESPN Soccernet sports team giving expert commentary and analysis. He also became the President of the Players' Association of Trinidad.

Appearances & Goals:
Debut v Coventry City (h) 19 August 1995
PL: 53 app 0 gls
FAC: 6 app 0 gls
FLC: 8 app 0 gls
Euro: 4 app 0 gls
Total: 71 app 0 gls

Honours:
26 TT caps 1999-2006/WdC 2006/1 Eng u21 app 1998/TT sch-youth app/PL runners-up 1996, 1997/FL div 1 champs 2003/FL div 2 champs 1994/FAC final 1998 (no app), 2006/PFA ToS (d1) 1995, 2003.

HOBAN Thomas 1884-1892

Forward
b. c1861
d. Newcastle upon Tyne, January 1908

Career: Newcastle Rangers Dec 1881/EAST END cs 1884 (Newcastle West End, Cheviot, Newcastle FA, Gateshead Association, St Silas all as a guest) to 1892/Hibernian Nov 1894.

A former Newcastle Rangers player when the trail-blazing club was based at St James' Park, Tommy Hoban gained several honours at representative level for both the Northumberland and Newcastle & District representative sides. He moved to Newcastle East End together with his colleague Alec White when Rangers folded, both players becoming cornerstones to the developing Heaton club. An outside-left of note, Hoban was a hugely popular character on Tyneside and totalled almost a century of games for United's pioneers in all fixtures, being also a regular scorer. The Northern Magpie magazine of the day humorously noted that he "has played since the days of stage coaches and is about as fast as one". Hoban liked to play to the crowd and another local periodical, Northern Athlete, described him as a "flashy left wing, but far too fond of gallery play". Tom was though a footballer who thrilled the Victorian supporters at times with his attacking ability, one of the club's first entertainers. Hoban succeeded Alec White as captain of East End in 1888 and was part of the East Enders line-up which made its debut in the FA Cup during 1887. By season 1891-92 he had lost his place in the first eleven, being skipper of East End Amateurs, the club's reserve combination. While he recorded only a handful of first-class outings, like many of his colleagues of that era, Tom played on numerous occasions for East End in the profusion of friendly and miscellaneous fixtures before serious league football took hold. Hoban totalled over 80 games and scored almost 40 goals for the club. Tommy also had a spell with Hibernian in Scotland and early in his career lifted the Northumberland & Durham Challenge Cup during 1883 with Rangers while Hoban took part in the first Northumberland Challenge Cup final of 1884 as well as the County's inaugural representative fixture.

Appearances & Goals:
Debut v South Bank (a) 15 October 1887 (FACQ)
NL: 1 app 0 gls
FAC: 4 app 1 gl
Total: 5 app 1 gl

HOCKEY Trevor 1963-1965

Outside-right
5'6"
b. Keighley, 1 May 1943
d. Keighley, 2 April 1987

Career: Keighley Central YC 1957/Bradford City jnr May 1958, prof May 1960/Nottingham Forest Nov 1961 £15,000/UNITED Nov 1963 £25,000/Birmingham City Nov 1965 £22,500/ Sheffield Utd Jan 1971 £50,000/ Norwich City Feb 1973 cash-exch deal/Aston Villa June 1973 £38,000/Bradford City June 1974 £12,500/ Athlone Town player-manager March 1976/San Diego Jaws (USA) April 1976/Las Vegas Quicksilver (USA) player-coach April 1977/San Jose Earthquakes (USA) player-coach June 1977/Stalybridge Celtic manager Aug 1977/ Ashton Utd 1977-78/Keighley Town manager Oct 1980.

During his early days as a footballer, the diminutive Trevor Hockey was an orthodox fast raiding outside-right, on his day a match-winner, but like many talented forwards, suffered inconsistency. A chirpy character, Trevor never quite established himself at St James' Park although played a part in the 1965 promotion season. He also occasionally appeared as a midfielder for the Magpies just when football was changing into the modern style. Moving on to the Midlands, during the Seventies Hockey modelled himself into a midfield general, tenacious and hardworking, and characterised by long hair and bushy beard, much changed from the clean-cut look when at Gallowgate. Becoming one of the personalities of that era, Trevor eventually racked up more than 600 senior games in a chequered and nomadic career, having an especially good period over six seasons with Birmingham City, skipper of the St Andrew's club during his 231 games. Relishing a battle on the field, he was charismatic and fiery, and, qualifying due to his father's nationality, good enough to win international honours for Wales, being the first to be sent-off for the Welsh, in 1973. An extrovert, Trevor once owned a blue suede-covered Triumph Herald car and played a pink piano in a rock group, cutting a record during 1968, 'Happy 'cos I'm Blue'. On retirement, Hockey for a time coached at Pontin's holiday centres, later ran the Lord Rodney pub in his home town, as well as for a period the Trevor Hockey Quicksilver Lottery and local soccer camps. He sadly collapsed and died when only 43 years old after playing five-a-side football at the Marley stadium in Keighley. His grandfather and father were noted rugby league players while Trevor played both union and league forms of the sport as a kid.

Appearances & Goals:
Debut v Cardiff City (h) 9 November 1963
FL: 52 app 3 gls
FAC: 2 app 0 gl
FLC: 2 app 0 gls
Total: 56 app 3 gls

Honours:
9 Wales caps 1972-74/FL div 2 champs 1965/FL div 2 prom 1971.

HODGES Glyn Peter 1987

Midfield
6'0"
b. Streatham, London, 30 April 1963

Career: Wimbledon jnr Feb 1979, prof Feb 1981/UNITED July 1987 £300,000/Watford Oct 1987 £300,000/Crystal Palace July 1990 £410,000/Sheffield Utd loan Jan 1991, pmt April 1991 £410,000/Derby Co Feb 1996 free/Golden Club (HK) Aug 1996/Hull City Aug 1997/Nottingham Forest Feb 1998 free/Scarborough Jan 1999/Retired due to injury Feb 1999/Total Network Solutions Aug 1999/ Barnsley coach Aug 2000, becoming caretaker-manager Oct to Nov 2001, manager Oct 2002 to June 2003/Wales u21 coach March 2004 & Blackburn Rovers asst-coach Sept 2004/Manchester City asst-coach June 2008 to Dec 2009/Fulham asst-coach Oct 2010/Queens Park Rangers Head of Coaching July 2012/Stoke City asst-coach July 2013.

Totalling 273 games for Wimbledon, Glyn Hodges, the Dons first ever full international, was a regular in the line-up which leapt from the Fourth Division to First Division alongside Dave Beasant. Making his debut as a 17-year-old, he was a left sided midfield player with a good touch and a stinging shot that frequently tested goalkeepers. However, despite his talents, the blond-haired Hodges only had a brief stay on Tyneside operating wide on the left, a position in which he was never comfortable. After a mere 86 days as a United player, manager Willie McFaul told the Welshman to train with the juniors and he was allowed to move back to London. Glyn later rejoined his Wimbledon manager Dave Bassett at Bramall Lane where he displayed his best football, registering 171 appearances for Sheffield United, at times being a delight to watch. His transfer to the Blades was in fact only sanctioned after fund raising by supporters' clubs.

Appearances & Goals:
Debut v Tottenham Hotspur (a) 19 August 1987
FL: 7 app 0 gls
Total: 7 app 0 gls

Honours:
18 Wales caps 1984-96/1 Wales B app 1991/5 Wales u21 caps 1983-84/Wales sch-youth app/FL div 4 champs 1983/FL div 1 prom 1996/FL div 2 prom 1986/FL div 3 prom 1984/FL div 4 prom 1981.

HODGSON Gordon Henry 1970-1974

Midfield
5'11"
b. Newcastle upon Tyne, 13 October 1952
d. Peterborough, 4 April 1999

Career: UNITED jnr Nov 1970, prof June 1971/ Mansfield Town May 1974 £8,000/Oxford Utd Sept 1978 £30,000/Peterborough Utd Aug 1980 £10,000/Kings Lynn cs 1982/March Town.

A schoolboy find by Newcastle United, Gordon Hodgson had the potential to become a big name at the top end of football's ladder. Exceptionally skilful, the Tynesider from the Benwell area of Newcastle developed quickly through the Magpies junior ranks to push hard for a first-team place, but the wall of quality players in front of him, men like Hibbitt, Smith, Cassidy and McDermott, proved unmoveable obstacles. Following a handful of games, plus many outings on the bench, Gordon moved down the league pyramid where he became one of the best players in the lower divisions, twice skippering Mansfield to promotion and appearing on 213 occasions for the Stags. He was also captain at Oxford (71 app) and did well with Peterborough (97 app). After leaving the game Gordon joined the police force in Peterborough reaching the rank of Detective Constable in the Cambridgeshire Constabulary. He died suddenly when 46 years of age when playing golf on the Thorpe Wood course near Peterborough.

Appearances & Goals:
Debut v Nottingham Forest (a) 8 April 1972
FL: 8(1) app 0 gls
FAC: 1 app 0 gls
Others: 1(2) app 0 gls
Total: 10(3) app 0 gls

Honours:
Eng sch-youth app/FL div 3 champs 1977/ FL div 4 champs 1975/PFA ToS (d4) 1975.

H

HODGSON Kenneth 1958-1961

Outside-right
5'10"
b. Newcastle upon Tyne, 19 January 1942
d. Macclesfield, 23 October 2007

Career: Montague & N Fenham YC/UNITED jnr Aug 1958, prof May 1959/Scunthorpe Utd Dec 1961 £3,000/ Bournemouth June 1964 £5,000/Colchester Utd July 1966 £4,000 (Chelmsford City loan 1969)/Poole Town July 1969/Eastern Suburbs (NZ) April 1974/Ringwood Town Feb 1979/Christchurch/Parley Sports.

As a teenager Ken Hodgson was a bright prospect, versatile across the forward-line, but who preferred the outside-right channel. After impressing Charlie Mitten when he netted 54 goals in youth leagues, Hodgson was given a contract at Gallowgate. Described as an 18-year-old who "oozes self-confidence", his chance for first-team action arrived during the 1960-61 season, a year of relegation strife for Newcastle, when he deputised Gordon Hughes. With the club's demotion at the end of the programme, Hodgson was not in the Magpies rebuilding plans and he moved to the Old Show Ground as part of the deal that brought Barrie Thomas north. He then began a decent career with Third and Fourth Division clubs as more of a strike partner, especially prominent with Scunthorpe where he scored 30 goals in 94 matches. He was unlucky when doing well for Colchester, fracturing a leg at Layer Road, then suffered another break in a comeback match during 1969, an injury which forced him out of senior football. Following a period in New Zealand, Ken afterwards returned to Tyneside becoming a branch manager for Amplivox Ultratone in Newcastle, distributing hearing-aid equipment. He later resided in Wilmslow.

Appearances & Goals:
Debut v Nottingham Forest (h) 14 January 1961
FL: 6 app 0 gls
FAC: 1 app 0 gls
Total: 7 app 0 gls

HOLLAND Christopher James 1994-1996

Midfield
5'9"
b. Whalley, near Clitheroe, 11 September 1975

Career: Preston North End jnr 1989, prof June 1992/UNITED Jan 1994 £100,000/Birmingham City loan Sept 1996, pmt Oct 1996 £600,000/ Huddersfield Town Feb 2000 £200,000/Boston Utd March 2004 free/Southport Jan 2007/Leigh Genesis July 2008/Fleetwood Town Nov 2008/ Burscough March 2009/Guiseley July 2009, becoming asst-manager Sept 2010 to Sept 2013.

Signed by Newcastle as a youngster to be developed for the future, Chris Holland hardly appeared in Preston North End's senior side, but had given United's management glimpses of his talented repertoire and prompted the club to pay £100,000. Such was his progress at St James' Park that Chris was appearing for England's Under-21 side within 18 months, a further progression through his country's ranks as Holland had already played for both the school and youth teams. And this after only receiving limited opportunities in the Magpies' midfield. Furthermore, Chris was even called up to train with the full England squad during December 1995. Much was expected of the youngster, he was labelled by some as the second 'Gazza', Holland possessing a striking resemblance and similar style on the field to the England star. Chris had a good touch on the ball and fed both short and long passes accurately. After impressing by creating two goals with telling crosses on his bow for United against Ipswich, during 1995 his blossoming career was disrupted and even threatened following an incident in a Newcastle nightclub; he was sprayed in the face with ammonia and hospitalised for five weeks in a fight to save the sight of his right eye. Chris recovered to play again, but couldn't break into United's side and he departed at a time when the Magpies let several fringe players go in a cash raising ploy to boost funds after the purchase of Alan Shearer. Holland moved to St Andrews and a career away from the Premiership limelight. He registered 84 games for the Brummies, 139 for Huddersfield and 99 for Boston. As a teenager, he was chased by Everton, Blackburn, Liverpool and Leeds as well as by the Magpies.

Appearances & Goals:
Debut v Ipswich Town (h) 23 March 1994
PL: 2(1) app 0 gls
FLC: 0(1) app 0 gls
Total: 2(2) app 0 gls

Honours:
10 Eng u21 caps 1995-97/Eng sch-youth app/1 FL app 1997/FL div 3 prom 2004 (3 app).

HOLLINS David Michael 1961-1967

Goalkeeper
6'0"
b. Bangor, Wales, 4 February 1938

Career: Merrow (Guildford) 1955/Brighton jnr Nov 1955, prof March 1956/UNITED March 1961 £11,000/Mansfield Town Feb 1967 £2,500 (Nottingham Forest loan 1969-70)/Aldershot July 1970 (Portsmouth loan 1970-71)/Romford Sept 1971 to 1972.

After joining United from Brighton as a replacement for Bryan Harvey, new goalkeeper Dave Hollins had a remarkable opening few weeks as a Newcastle player. He saved a penalty on his debut against the eventual Double winners, Spurs, then saw Chelsea plant six goals past him on his first appearance at St James' Park and finally witnessed United's relegation from Division One four weeks later. Agile and acrobatic, once being described as a "green-jerseyed panther", Hollins at times looked a wonderful goalkeeper making a string of breathtaking stops which earned him recognition on the international stage for Wales. But he failed to maintain such a high standard week in and week out and, following a dispute with new manager Joe Harvey over wages, the Magpies brought in Gordon Marshall as first choice between the posts. Hollins was transferred and he served Mansfield with distinction in 126 games, part of their FA Cup giant-killing line-up which reached the Sixth Round during 1968-69. Dave came from a well known footballing family, his father Bill was a 'keeper for Wolves, his brother John was a household name at Chelsea and another brother, Roy, also turned out for Brighton. Strangely, Dave and John played international football for different countries with John appearing for England. Additionally he related to television presenter Chris Hollins, who appeared for QPR and Charlton as a youth before making a career on the small screen on such shows as BBC Breakfast and Watchdog. After quitting the game, Dave settled in Guildford running a decorating business, while he also played bowls for the London Welsh club.

Appearances & Goals:
Debut v Tottenham Hotspur (a) 22 March 1961
FL: 112 app 0 gls
FAC: 3 app 0 gls
FLC: 6 app 0 gls
Total: 121 app 0 gls

Honours:
11 Wales caps 1962-66/2 Wales u23 app 1960-61/FL div 3(S) champs 1958 (3 app).

HOOPER Michael Dudley 1993-1996

Goalkeeper
6'3"
b. Bristol, 10 February 1964

Career: Mangotsfield Utd/Swansea City amat/Bristol City Nov 1983/Wrexham loan Feb 1985, pmt July 1985 £4,000/Liverpool Oct 1985 £40,000 (Leicester City loan 1990-91)/UNITED Sept 1993 £550,000 (Sunderland loan 1995-96)/Portsmouth July 1996, retiring soon afterwards due to injury.

Although purchased for £550,000 from Liverpool to become United's preferred goalkeeper, Mike Hooper was destined to be third choice behind Srnicek and Hislop. Following an initial run in United's Premiership line-up during 1993-94, the well built 6'3" red-haired goalkeeper lost form, confidence and his place to his Czech rival, Srnicek. And Hooper rarely received a look-in

afterwards. Prior to heading for Tyneside, Mike spent most of his career as reserve to Bruce Grobbelaar at Anfield, having a good season with Liverpool during 1988-89 (17 app) and registering 66 games all told for the Reds before joining the Magpies' staff. Mike experienced a major disappointment on Merseyside when he was left out of the Liverpool 1992 FA Cup final side in favour of Grobbelaar after appearing in several of the games between the semi-final and final. Hooper had a struggle to convince the Geordie masses he was worth the Number 1 shirt and suffered at the hands of sections of the crowd, but his career on Tyneside ended making headlines; in his final match against Tottenham Mike arrived on the field as a substitute following Srnicek's red-card and immediately saved the resultant penalty-kick. A keen ornithologist and fell walker, Hooper holds a degree in English Literature taken at Swansea University before he committed to a career in football. Mike had a short loan spell with United's arch rivals Sunderland in season 1995-96 and following a back problem left the game. He settled in County Durham reportedly having occupations from PE teacher, a Betterware salesman, to nightclub doorman.

Appearances & Goals:
Debut v West Ham United (h) 25 September 1993
PL: 23(2) app 0 gls
FAC: 3 app 0 gls
FLC: 2 app 0 gls
Total: 28(2) 0 gls

Honours:
Eng sch-youth app/FL champs 1988 (2 app).

HOPE George 1969-1975

Centre-forward
5'10"
b. Haltwhistle, Northumberland, 4 April 1954

Career: Workington trial/UNITED jnr April 1969, prof April 1972/Charlton Ath June 1975 free/York City loan Nov 1976, pmt Dec 1976 £1,000/Wezel Sport (Belg) May 1978 free/RRC Gent (Belg) 1982 to 1983.

On his home debut for Newcastle United, youngster George Hope made all the headlines, scoring the winner in a pulsating 3-2 victory over Manchester United; with a glorious 70th minute header. Growing up in the Tyne Valley and a Magpie supporter as a schoolboy, he stood in for the injured Malcolm Macdonald for three matches and did reasonably well, considering he was thrown into combat with experienced First Division defenders. George, though, had little chance to find a regular position when Supermac was fit, or to displace John Tudor, while a back injury hindered his progress, so the inevitable transfer soon followed. He didn't make an impression at The Valley, but did somewhat better with York City claiming 48 games. George had trials with Workington's Football League side before joining United's apprentice scheme. On leaving football, Hope was employed as a car salesman in York and later in Hull. George took the part of a referee in the television drama 'Playing the Field' during the late 1990s.

Appearances & Goals:
Debut v Leicester City (a) 10 November 1973
FL: 6 app 1 gl
Total: 6 app 1 gl

HOPE George 1943-1946

Inside-right
5'9"
b. Newcastle upon Tyne

Career: Scotswood/UNITED amat, prof March 1943 (Airdrieonians war-guest 1943-44) to 1946.

George Hope's only game in a black-and-white jersey was in a wartime Football League North contest against Hartlepools United at St James' Park during October 1943. A replacement for Johnny Dixon, he was only at Gallowgate during a brief spell at home on army leave. Hope was resigned by the club during the close season of 1945 but failed to break into the Magpies' senior eleven.

Appearances & Goals:
Debut v Hartlepools United (h) 23 October 1943 (FLN)
War: 1 app 0 gls
Total: 1 app 0 gls

HOPE John Williams March 1969-1971

Goalkeeper
6'0"
b. Shildon, Co Durham, 30 March 1949

Career: Darlington jnr 1964, prof May 1967/UNITED March 1969 £8,000/Sheffield Utd Jan 1971 exch deal for J Tudor (Preston North End loan 1973-74)/Hartlepool Utd July 1975/Stockton coach Oct 1980/Wingate manager July 1986/Whitby Town Oct 1988/Willington manager June 1989/Hartlepool Utd asst-coach Jan 1991/Darlington coach 1992.

John Hope was reserve to international goalkeeper Willie McFaul at St James' Park over a period which included United's early years of European football. Hope was on the bench for many of the club's Inter Cities Fairs Cup ties, including the final against Ujpesti Dozsa during 1969. Tall, strong and ideally built for the Number 1 shirt, on leaving Tyneside he found a regular slot with the Blades at Bramall Lane despite a number of knee operations. The long-haired custodian appeared on 71 occasions for Sheffield United. A quirk of his career saw Hope appear in all four divisions of the Football League over seven consecutive matches between 1966-67 and 1970-71 (for Darlington, Newcastle and Sheffield United). His father played local soccer for Shildon while John's offspring, Chris played with Scunthorpe, while Richard notably for Darlington and Northampton.

Appearances & Goals:
Debut v Manchester City (a) 5 May 1969
FL: 1 app 0 gls
Total: 1 app 0 gls

Honours:
ICFC winner 1969 (sub no app)/FL div 2 prom 1971.

HORSFIELD Arthur 1969

Striker
5'11"
b. Newcastle upon Tyne, 5 July 1946

Career: Montague & N Fenham YC/Middlesbrough jnr cs 1962, prof July 1963/UNITED Jan 1969 £17,500/Swindon Town June 1969 £17,000/Charlton Ath June 1972 £15,000/Watford Sept 1975 £20,000/Dartford Aug 1977, later becoming coach to 1979.

A former Newcastle city schoolboy star at both soccer and athletics, Arthur Horsfield grew up close to St James' Park on Stanhope Street. He was a Leazes End regular, but began his footballing career further down the east coast at Ayresome Park. Arthur was 22 years old when he returned to Tyneside as a stop-gap purchase when Albert Bennett was injured and had an unlucky opening for his home town club when he netted on his first outing at Manchester City after two-and-a-half minutes, only for the game to be abandoned due to heavy rain. Never too fast or flamboyant, Horsfield was nevertheless a good team player always able to strike the ball cleanly but wasn't kept by boss Joe Harvey, allowing the Tynesider to drop to a lower level of the game. Arthur did well at that grade of football where his wholehearted play and sure touch in front of goal made him an important player at all his ports of call. With Boro he made his debut as a teenager proceeding to turn out on 128 occasions, netting 56 times, including 22 goals when they won promotion during 1966-67, while at Charlton he appeared on 156 occasions, all of which were consecutive; a record for the Londoners. Horsfield was the Third Division's leading marksman during 1972-73 and when with Swindon Town, netted a hat-trick in the 1969 Anglo-Italian Cup final, twice helping to win the trophy for the Robins. Arthur concluded his career as a centre-half. He afterwards resided in Gravesend, for a period working as a postman, managing a social club then as a Depot Manager for Royal Mail's Parcelforce in Canterbury.

Appearances & Goals:
Debut v Southampton (a) 15 February 1969
FL: 7(2) app 3 gls
Euro: 1 app 0 gls
Total: 8(2) app 3 gls

Honours:
Eng sch-youth app/FL div 3 prom 1967, 1975.

H

HOTTIGER Marc 1994-1996

Right-back
5'10"
b. Lausanne (Switzerland),
7 November 1967

Career: FC Renens (Swtz) jnr, snr 1985/FC Lausanne-Sport (Swtz) 1988/FC Sion (Swtz) 1992/UNITED Aug 1994 £520,000/Everton March 1996 £700,000/FC Lausanne-Sport (Swtz) Aug 1997 £25,000/FC Sion (Swtz) Aug 1999/FC Echallens (Swtz) coach May 2002/Neuchatel Xamax (Swtz) asst-coach/Academy Director, Ohio (USA) 2007/Team Vaud, FC Lausanne-Sport (Swtz) Technical Director Jan 2009.

The first of Kevin Keegan's two signings from the 1994 USA World Cup stage, Marc Hottiger had stood out for Switzerland in that tournament and cost United what was a bargain fee for such an established international full-back. A regular in Newcastle's Premier League side for the 1994-95 programme, Marc could look back on his first season in England with much satisfaction. He showed a calm attitude and ability to link with the attack in the modern wing-back style, causing opponents problems down the right flank. Yet, despite a good start on Tyneside, he was perhaps not strong enough defensively and was squeezed out of contention for a first team place by the £4 million signing of Warren Barton, as well as the versatility of local lad Steve Watson. Hottiger was left on the sidelines and with his international place in danger due to lack of regular action, made a move to Everton, although that transfer was almost jettisoned by problems over a work permit. He only appeared on 18 occasions at Goodison Park and soon returned to Switzerland to rack up more than 150 games for both Lausanne and Sion. After Marc ran a Brad Friedel Premier Soccer Academy in Ohio, he became a noted coach around Lausanne, managing the youth development programme at Team Vaud. The French-speaking Hottiger could also play in midfield, on the wing, or in the centre of the defence, while he captained Switzerland during 1994 and scored the goal against Italy which sent the Swiss to the World Cup finals.

Appearances & Goals:
Debut v Leicester City (a) 21 August 1994
PL: 38(1) app 1 gl
FAC: 4 app 1 gl
FLC: 6(1) app 0 gls
Euro: 4 app 0 gls
Total: 52(2) app 2 gls

Honours:
63 Swtz caps 1989-96/WdC 1994/Swtz B app/PL runner-up 1996 (1 app)/Swtz Cup winner 1998.

HOUGHTON Frank Calvert 1948-1953

Wing-half
5'9"
b. Preston, 15 February 1926
d. Exeter, 19 August 1994

Career: Preston North End amat 1942/Derry City amat 1944/Linfield amat c1945/Harryville Amateurs 1946/Ballymena Utd amat 1946, prof Sept 1947/UNITED Jan 1948 £6,000/Released due to ill-health Aug 1953/Exeter City Aug 1953 asst-trainer, reinstated as a player Aug 1954, becoming player-trainer Oct 1955/Retired playing cs 1957.

Frank Houghton will always be remembered on Tyneside for his goals in the dying minutes against Sheffield Wednesday which virtually clinched United's promotion to the First Division during 1948. With a dramatic two-goal burst he became United's hero ending in hospital with a broken arm and thigh wound; when scoring the second he also collided with the opposition 'keeper and the post, being carried off to a huge ovation from the near 67,000 crowd. An honest, slightly-built, play anywhere individual, Houghton tragically lost the best years of his career due to injury and illness. Whilst serving in Omagh as a PT instructor with the Royal Ulster Rifles, Frank was spotted by the

Magpies as a 21-year-old and joined the club just as the Black'n'Whites were developing a fine set-up. Lion-hearted in every outing, Frank was a young rival to seniors Woodburn and Dodgin and his best season was during 1949-50 when he appeared on 34 occasions in a number of roles; right-half, inside-left and centre-forward. A year later during November 1950, Houghton was struck by illness after scoring a hat-trick in a Central League match at a wintry Derby. He contracted pneumonia which turned to pleurisy and tuberculosis, his weight at one stage dropping to only eight stones. Undergoing major surgery, as a result he missed almost three seasons, for a part of the time being sent to a Switzerland sanatorium in Davos to recuperate. Houghton was back and forward to the Swiss Alps over a two year period, supported financially by Newcastle United. His chance of stardom at Gallowgate was wrecked and he moved to the other St James' Park at Exeter to start coaching. Frank regained fitness to return to action once more, only to twice fracture his leg. Frank once remarked that "my career reads more like a medical chart". Houghton made a home for himself in Devon, becoming a well known bookmaker and appeared for an old-boys team he created, the Houghton Old Stars, during the Sixties. A modest and likable man, he was related to the famous trumpeter of the 1950's, Eddie Calvert, hence his middle name.

Appearances & Goals:
Debut v Leicester City (h) 31 January 1948
FL: 55 app 10 gls
FAC: 2 app 0 gls
Total: 57 app 10 gls

Honours:
FL div 2 prom 1948.

HOWARD Patrick 1971-1976

Centre-half
5'11"
b. Dodworth, Yorkshire, 7 October 1947

Career: Barnsley jnr April 1963, prof Oct 1965/ UNITED Sept 1971 £23,000/Arsenal Sept 1976 £50,000/Birmingham City Aug 1977 £40,000 (Portland Timbers (USA) loan 1978)/Bury July 1979 free to cs 1982/Later becoming a local coach in Lancashire.

A blond-haired, forceful stopper centre-half, Pat Howard quickly became a popular character at St James' Park following a bargain transfer from Barnsley. A solid defender at Oakwell in 201 games, he was purchased initially as a stand-in for the injured Bob Moncur, yet Pat's form in the heart of United's defence was so good that he eventually formed a commanding partnership with Moncur. Brian Clough once noted that Howard, at his peak in 1975, was one of the top five central defenders in the country. Described as "slick and fast with a crushing tackle", he appeared twice at Wembley for the Magpies; the Yorkshireman was rugged and uncompromising, and made up for a lack of the finer skills by reading the game and possessing an indomitable will to win. More than a few doubted the wisdom of his departure when he quickly followed Malcolm Macdonald to Highbury during 1976, branded something of a rebel with Supermac by new boss Gordon Lee. Howard remained only briefly in North London before serving Birmingham City (43 app) then concluded his senior career with Bury (137 app). Howard later worked as a Football in the Community officer around Manchester and also for the PFA's Education organisation. In 1988 he was Football Administrator for Salford Council's Academy of Football as well as conducting an FA School of Excellence in Manchester and being coach to the Old Grammarians. For a period he opened a snooker centre and sports shop in Bury while Pat was also an occasional radio summariser.

Appearances & Goals:
Debut v Wolverhampton Wanderers (h) 18 September 1971
FL: 182(2) app 7 gls
FAC: 22 app 1 gl
FLC: 19 app 0 gls
Others: 37 app 1 gl
Total: 260(2) app 9 gls
(Void FAC: 1 app 0 gls)

Honours:
FAC final 1974/FLC final 1976/FL div 4 prom 1968.

HOWDON Stephen 1941-1943

Inside-forward
5'10"
b. Prudhoe, 1 February 1922
d. Northumberland, 1998 (Q3)

Career: Ryton Jnrs/UNITED Aug 1941 to Dec 1943/Gateshead Nov 1944/ Hexham Hearts c1947.

On United's books for three seasons during the wartime leagues and an automatic choice in United's Northern Combination line-up, Howdon came into the Football League North side on an injury or unavailability of senior men. Operating at either inside-right or left, his debut was against Bradford City during August 1941. He later took part in peacetime football for Gateshead in the Third Division North as well as the FA Cup, totalling seven appearances during 1945-46 and 1946-47 with the Redheugh Park club.

Appearances & Goals:
Debut v Bradford City (h) 30 August 1941 (FLN)
War: 10 app 1gl
Total: 10 app 1 gl

HOWE Donald 1939

Inside-forward
5'8"
b. Outwood, Wakefield, 26 November 1917
d. Bolton, September 1978

Career: Whitehall Printeries/Bolton Wand amat 1933, prof Nov 1934 (UNITED war-guest 1939-40)(Norwich City war-guest 1940-42)/Resumed with Bolton 1945 to June 1953.

Don Howe had a remarkable single outing for Newcastle United, netting all of five goals against York City during October 1939 when the Magpies won 9-2. His Bolton colleague Ray Westwood was also in the line-up and netted a hat-trick. A quality all round footballer, Howe was a teenage debutant for Bolton and remained at Burnden Park all of his Football League career totalling 286 appearances, grabbing 35 goals. Skipper of the Trotters, he was somewhat lightweight, but a versatile and intelligent footballer, a grand club player. During the war he served with several of his Bolton teammates in the Wanderers' footballing 53rd Territorial Royal Artillery reaching the rank of sergeant-major. He was involved in the Dunkirk evacuation then saw action in Egypt and the Middle East with the Eighth Army subsequently taking part in the invasion of Italy and then the advance on Rome. Returning to Burnden Park on demob, he retired at the end of the 1952-53 season, although he took his FA coaching badges, Don left the game and afterwards worked for a paper merchant in Bolton.

Appearances & Goals:
Debut v York City (h) 28 October 1939 (FLNE) (5 goals)
War: 1 app 5 gls
Total: 1 app 5 gls

HOWEY Stephen Norman 1986-2000

Centre-half
6'2"
b. Sunderland, 26 October 1971

Career: Sunderland jnr/UNITED jnr June 1986, prof Dec 1989/Manchester City Aug 2000 £2m/ Leicester City July 2003 £300,000/Bolton Wand Jan 2004 free to May 2004/Sheffield Utd trial July 2004/New England Revolution (USA) Nov 2004/ Hartlepool Utd March 2005 to May 2005/Brandon Utd coach cs 2005 to Nov 2005/Crook Town manager Sept 2006 to Nov 2006/Middlesbrough asst-coach 2007/Bishop Auckland coach 2007/ Houghall College (Durham) & East Durham College coach 2007/Sunderland RCA coach July 2011.

Beginning his career as a 17-year-old debutant up front and continuing as an out and out striker over 30 games for the Magpies, Steve Howey's progress in that role had been destined to end up in the lower divisions like many of United's junior developments. But a crucial switch from attack into the heart of Newcastle's defence was made during 1991, initially by Ossie Ardiles, but positively by Kevin Keegan thereafter, and Howey's career took off. Installed in the pivot's role for the 1992-93 First Division title winning campaign, Steve showed that his height and build, as well as his pace, aggression and ball skills, were perfect qualities for the modern centre-back role. His ability to move forward with the ball, and distribute accurate passes fitted smoothly into Keegan's tactical plan. And as a bonus, Howey was always dangerous in attack where his original striker's instincts gave United's attack a boost at set pieces. Overcoming a troublesome groin injury which saw the Wearsider out of action after several operations, on and off, for over 12 months, Steve became a regular in Terry Venables' England squad, this after being selected on occasion for the Under-21 side, but unluckily having to withdraw because of injury. The Wearsider was unfortunate to pick up more injuries throughout his career, being sidelined with calf and Achilles tendon problems, missing the 1999 FA Cup final when injured in the semi-final, just when playing to top form. Steve also had to sit out the Euro 1996 international championships following a bizarre injury when running in a local forest, tearing ligaments when he stumbled. Captain of the Magpies occasionally, before moving to Manchester City during 2000, Howey had played under the guidance of no fewer than seven managers at St James' Park. He totalled over 100 games for the Sky Blues before winding down his career. Steve left the senior game to enter coaching, working in a number of roles around County Durham, as well as for Premier Skills in Africa, Asia and South America. Howey also became a FA Premier League match delegate for a period and was additionally an occasional television and radio broadcaster. His brother, Lee, appeared for Sunderland, Northampton and Burnley.

Appearances & Goals:
Debut v Manchester United (a) 13 May 1989 (sub)
FL/PL: 167(24) app 6 gls
FAC: 21(2) 0 gls
FLC: 14(2) 1 gl
Euro: 5(2) 0 gls
Others: 5 app 0 gls
Total: 212(30) app 7 gls

Honours:
4 Eng caps 1995-96/1 unoff Eng app 1996/PL runner-up 1996, 1997 (8 app)/FL div 1 champs 1993, 2002/FA Cup final 1998.

HOWIE James 1903-1910

Inside-right
5'10"
b. Galston, Ayrshire, 19 March 1878
d. Wandsworth, London, 13 December 1962

Career: Galston Ath/Kilmarnock May 1898 (Galston Ath loan 1900-01)/Kettering Town 1902 briefly/Bristol Rovers May 1902/UNITED May 1903 £300/Huddersfield Town Dec 1910 £675/ Queens Park Rangers manager Nov 1913 to March 1920/ Middlesbrough manager April 1920 to July 1923.

Recognised as one of the very best inside-forwards in the game during his era prior to World War One, Jimmy Howie was known as 'Gentleman Jim' and possessed a style that oozed finesse. Although never to be described as fast, he was a genius at creating opportunities and also taking chances himself from his midfield role, netting 82 goals for the Magpies during the Scots seven full campaigns at Gallowgate. A regular with Kilmarnock over four seasons before heading south, when in full flow with the ball Jimmy was described as possessing a peculiar hopping action and style in which he moved the ball from either foot. Howie linked to perfection with Jack Rutherford on United's right wing, an international pairing that had much to do with the club's three Championship trophy winning feats and their first FA Cup victory. Jimmy also took part in another three runs to the FA Cup final as runners-up and was an influential player in the club's great decade of being ranked the top side in the country. Howie could glide past opponents with the ball and delighted the crowd with flair and entertainment. After a successful stay on Tyneside, Howie appeared on 87 occasions for Huddersfield Town in Division Two. His younger brother David, was on Newcastle's books just prior to war during 1912-13 and 1913-14, but moved on to have a decent

H

career with Bradford Park Avenue. Following a spell in management, Jimmy resided in London running a tobacconist shop in Willesden.

Appearances & Goals:
Debut v Aston Villa (h) 2 September 1903
FL: 198 app 68 gls
FAC: 37 app 14 gls
Others: 2 app 0 gls
Total: 237 app 82 gls

Honours:
3 Scot caps 1905-08/1 SL app 1901/Scot trial app 1903-05/FL champs 1905, 1907, 1909/FAC winner 1910/FAC final 1905, 1906, 1908/SL div 2 champs 1899.

HUBBLE Leonard 1940-1946

Left-back
5'9"
b. Chester-le-Street, 8 June 1923
d. Durham, October 1994

Career: Horden CW Jnrs/UNITED amat Sept 1940, prof Sept 1941 (Middlesbrough war-guest 1943-44)(Leicester City war-guest 1944-45) (Charlton Ath war-guest 1944-45) to 1946/Later with Annfield Plain.

Playing alongside Tot Smith at Horden, Len Hubble made the same journey to St James' Park to join his former team-mate within United's ranks. Although he was on Newcastle's staff for five seasons, Hubble only managed two games in the first-eleven during 1941-42 and 1945-46, his debut being on Christmas Day 1941. He did though play many more games for United's second-string in the Northern Combination, but by the time peace was restored was overshadowed by Bobby Corbett at Gallowgate.

Appearances & Goals:
Debut v Sheffield Wednesday (h) 25 December 1941 (FLN)
War: 2 app 0 gls
Total: 2 app 0 gls

HUCKERBY Darren Carl 1995-1996

Striker
5'10"
b. Nottingham, 23 April 1976

Career: Notts Co jnr briefly/Lincoln City jnr June 1992, prof July 1993/UNITED Nov 1995 £450,000 (Millwall loan 1996-97)/Coventry City Nov 1996 £1.65m/Leeds Utd Aug 1999 £5.5m/Manchester City Dec 2000 £2.5m (Nottingham Forest loan 2002-03)/ Norwich City loan Sept 2003, pmt Dec 2003 £1m/ San Jose Earthquakes (USA) July 2008 to Sept 2009/ Norwich City asst-coach 2013-14.

On his limited opportunities in United's first eleven, Darren Huckerby greatly impressed both the Magpies' support and the club's management. Within a few short weeks the 19-year-old youngster had exchanged football in front of a handful of spectators with bottom division club Lincoln, to that of a packed audience at St James' Park, appearing alongside world stars like Ginola and Asprilla. Huckerby possessed pace, a body swerve to take him past opponents as well as control of the ball which tested defenders and, although slightly built, was fast and had a willingness to run at the opposition back four. Purchased as cover for Les Ferdinand, and as a player to develop for the future, Newcastle had to act quickly to secure his signature on the transfer form as Manchester United were also bidding for his raw talent. With Lincoln, Darren netted eight goals in 31 outings and had scored within five minutes of his senior baptism against Shrewsbury during 1994. Despite his undoubted potential when at Gallowgate, Huckerby soon found he had a difficult job grabbing a place in United's star-studded squad and with the club in need to replenish the coffers after Alan Shearer's world record purchase, he was allowed to leave only a year after heading north to Tyneside. The young striker went onto show the Magpies that they had made a mistake in not giving him an extended opportunity to prove himself. Although at times erratic, Darren proved a top forward over the next decade, especially with Norwich where he became a hugely popular player, scoring 48 goals in 203 matches reaching the fringe of an England cap. On hanging up his boots, Huckerby settled in Norfolk and set up his own charity, the Darren Huckerby Trust, supporting needy groups in the region. He also is involved in corporate hospitality at Carrow Road. As a kid, Darren was rejected by Notts County for being too small, his brother Scott was also on Lincoln's books.

Appearances & Goals:
Debut v Chelsea (h) 17 January 1996 (FAC) (sub)
PL: 0(1) app 0 gls
FAC: 0(1) app 0 gls
Total: 0(2) app 0 gls

Honours:
1 Eng B app 1998/4 Eng u21 app 1997/PL runners-up 1996 (1 app)/FL div 1 champs 2002, 2004.

HUDSON John 1940-1945

Outside-right
5'9"
b. Blaydon, 5 October 1921
d. Chesterfield, 14 January 2008

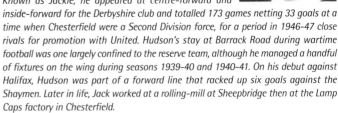

Career: Clara Vale Jnrs/UNITED trial May 1940, prof Aug 1940 to 1945/West Stanley 1945-46/Chesterfield Oct 1946 (Bangor City loan 1952-53)/Shrewsbury Town Sept 1953 £2,500/Buxton July 1955/Burton Albion Sept 1957.

John Hudson was a Tynesider who became a key figure in Chesterfield's ranks during the immediate post-war years. Known as Jackie, he appeared at centre-forward and inside-forward for the Derbyshire club and totalled 173 games netting 33 goals at a time when Chesterfield were a Second Division force, for a period in 1946-47 close rivals for promotion with United. Hudson's stay at Barrack Road during wartime football was one largely confined to the reserve team, although he managed a handful of fixtures on the wing during seasons 1939-40 and 1940-41. On his debut against Halifax, Hudson was part of a forward line that racked up six goals against the Shaymen. Later in life, Jack worked at a rolling-mill at Sheepbridge then at the Lamp Caps factory in Chesterfield.

Appearances & Goals:
Debut v Halifax Town (h) 29 May 1940 (FLNE)
War: 3 app 0 gls
Total: 3 app 0 gls

HUDSON Raymond Wilfred 1971-1978

Midfield
5'11"
b. Dunston, Gateshead, 24 March 1955

Career: UNITED jnr Dec 1971, prof March 1973 (Morton loan 1974-75)/Fort Lauderdale Strikers (USA) March 1978 £40,000/Brighton Oct 1983 to Nov 1983/ FC Union Solingen (WG) Jan 1984/Minnesota Strikers (USA) 1984/Edmonton Brickmen (Can) 1987, becoming player-coach 1989/Fort Lauderdale Strikers (USA) 1988/ Tampa Bay Rowdies (USA) 1990/Fort Lauderdale Strikers (USA) 1991, retired playing 1992/Hershey Wildcats (USA) coach 1992 to 1995, as well as Nova Southern University (USA) coach/Miami Fusion (USA) manager May 2000/DC Utd (USA) manager Jan 2002 to 2004.

Tall, lean and with abundant skill, blond-haired Ray Hudson developed through United's reserve structure to push for a place in the club's first-team just after the Magpies reached Wembley in 1974. With midfield places dominated by experienced seniors, Hudson didn't find it easy to get a regular opportunity but, according to many spectators, showed enough talent on his few outings to warrant an extended run. That never came and 'Rocky', as he was known, moved to the States as a 22-year-old where he found a stage to show off his skills. Hudson became a big star and displayed a brand of flamboyant football that would have graced the St James' Park field. Hudson was especially admired in Fort Lauderdale colours alongside the likes of George Best and Gerd Muller, appearing on more than 200 occasions (over 50 goals) during his two spells, reaching the Soccer Bowl in 1980. He also totalled over a century of games for Minnesota Strikers. Rocky remained in Florida as a Geordie ex-pat when he stopped playing, working in various jobs including cleaning swimming pools between coaching appointments. He was Miami's "Community Outreach Director" for a period, while he tasted some success as coach of Miami Fusion, guiding them to the Eastern Division title. Ray also began a career as a sports journalist eventually becoming a television commentator for Gol TV, a football channel in the sunshine state. He became very popular with a witty style, known for using "mind-blowing phrases" which have been collected into famous Hudson sound-bites. That's all a far cry from when Ray started work in a metalwork factory when trying to earn an apprentice deal at St James' Park.

Appearances & Goals:
Debut v Stoke City (h) 3 November 1973 (sub)
FL: 16(4) app 1 gl
FAC: 3 app 1 gl
FLC: 1 app 0 gls
Euro: 0(1) app 0 gls
Others: 4 app 0 gls
Total: 24(5) app 2 gls

HUDSPETH Francis Carr 1910-1929

Left-back
5'9"
b. Percy Main, Newcastle upon Tyne, 20 April 1890
d. Burnley, 8 February 1963

Career: Scotswood/Newburn/Clara Vale Jnrs/North
Shields Ath/UNITED March 1910 £100 (Hartlepools Utd
war-guest 1915-16)(Bradford Park Avenue war-guest
1915-19)(Leeds City war-guest 1916-17)/Stockport Co
Jan 1929/Crook Town Dec 1930 to Jan 1931 when he
retired/Rochdale trainer July 1933/Burnley asst-trainer
cs 1934/Retired 1945.

*With 472 senior games to his name (482 app in all
competitions), no player has appeared more for United
in an outfield position in league or cup football than
left-back, Frank Hudspeth. And only goalkeeper Jimmy
Lawrence can claim more matches for the
Black'n'Whites. Frank was a dependable defender, good
in all departments and a model of consistency over a
long career of nearly 19 years at St James' Park. No-one in over 130 years has more
service as a player other than Steve Harper. With his international colleague Bill
McCracken, Hudspeth forged the infamous offside trap which led to a change in the
rules of football; Frank having a tactical mind like McCracken and their joint defensive
game at a time of a two man back-line was a feature of United's play, McCracken
noting Frank was "the essence of reliability, always seeming to be on the very spot
required". The older and more experienced Hudspeth became, the better a player he
developed into. He was 34 when the Magpies won the FA Cup in 1924, almost 36
when he won his first England cap (the oldest debutant at the time, although he was
third choice to play), and 37 when he was an ever present in the club's title victory of
1927. United captain on many of his games for Newcastle, Frank was also something
of a penalty-kick expert, striking eight in season 1925-26 and 34 during his career
with the Magpies. The Tynesider also skippered England during a 1919 Victory
international against Wales. During the First World War, Frank served in the Royal
Navy as an able seaman. On hanging up his boots in 1931, he managed a billiard's
hall in Newcastle before moving to Lancashire. Hudspeth lived in Burnley to his death.*

Appearances & Goals:
Debut v Bradford City (h) 3 December 1910
FL: 430 app 34 gls
FAC: 42 app 3 gls
War: 10 app 1 gl
Total: 482 app 38 gls

Honours:
1 Eng cap 1926/1 unoff Eng app 1920/Eng trial app 1913-14/FL champs 1927/FAC
winner 1924.

HUGHES Aaron William 1995-2005

Centre-half or Right-back
6'0"
b. Magherafelt, Northern Ireland, 8 November 1979

Career: Coagh Utd/Lisburn BC/Dungannon
Swifts/Irish BB/UNITED jnr July 1995, prof July
1997/Aston Villa Aug 2005 £1.5m/Fulham July 2007
£1m/Queens Park Rangers Jan 2014 free/
Brighton July 2014 free.

*Not many British players can boast a teenage debut
in the famous Camp Nou against Barcelona, but
that's where Aaron Hughes first pulled on a
Newcastle United shirt in senior action. On the bench
for the Champions League clash with the Catalans
during 1997, illness to Philippe Albert saw Aaron*

*enter the action at half-time. In that break-through season Hughes appeared in the
Northern Intermediate League and Pontins League, then in the Champions League
and Premier League all in quick succession. Much coveted as a schoolboy player in
Ulster, Hughes joined the St James' Park set-up during 1995; the Magpies holding off
a challenge from Manchester United for the 15-year-old youngster after Hughes had
spent a short period at Old Trafford. Although not a strapping six-foot-plus defender,
Hughes was cool-headed and unflustered while he read the game well and following
that headlining debut held his own in a squad of superstars for six seasons. Operating
effectively at centre-back or right-back, Aaron was favoured by Bobby Robson and
fully broke through in season 1999-2000 as the new boss revitalised the Magpies,
Aaron showing versatility by playing across the back-line as well as occasionally in
midfield. Capped first by Northern Ireland during 1997-98, Hughes went onto skipper
his country and while he may not have been ranked with the very best defenders in
England's Premier League, was a more than decent and thoughtful professional. He
never gave his manager any difficulty on and off the pitch and was a regular in
United's defence, mainly at right-back, during a period when United were in the mix
for honours. After more than 270 games for the Magpies Aaron was allowed to depart
by new boss Graeme Souness. He joined Aston Villa during 2005 then onto Fulham
where he totalled nearly 250 matches for the Cottagers, including appearing in the
Londoner's Europa League final of 2010. Hughes spent nearly 17 years in the top flight
of football, one of the most underrated footballers on the circuit.*

Appearances & Goals:
Debut v FC Barcelona (a) 26 November 1997 (CL) (sub)
PL: 193(12) app 4 gls
FAC: 15(4) app 1 gl
FLC: 9(1) app 0 gls
Euro: 39(5) app 1 gl
Total: 256 (22) app 6 gls

Honours:
90 NI caps 1998-date/2 NI B app 1997-98/NI sch-youth app/FL ch prom 2014 (9
app)/EpL final 2010.

HUGHES Gordon 1956-1963

Outside-right
5'6"
b. Washington, 19 June 1936

Career: Fatfield Jnrs 1952/Easington Lane 1954/Tow
Law Town 1954/UNITED Aug 1956 £30/Derby Co Aug
1963 £12,000/Lincoln City March 1968 £6,000/
Boston Utd March 1971/Retired March 1972.

*Gordon Hughes was a part-timer, still working as a
Fatfield pit-lad, when he was introduced for his Football
League debut by United. He had been turned down by
Middlesbrough, Sunderland and Workington before
Newcastle took a chance with him, but the Magpies
soon realised they had made a good move and Gordon was quickly elevated to the
First Division stage. On his first outing against Manchester United, and against
England full-back Roger Byrne, the newcomer impressed, giving the top-rated defender
a difficult 90 minutes. He was extremely fast on the wing and could clock 100 yards
in 10 seconds, once described as a "head-down and full throttle-ahead little chap".
However, after impressing so well, Hughes unfortunately broke his leg in a friendly
against Morton and the injury kept him out of action for a long period. But Gordon
bounced back and over four seasons up to 1961 was a regular choice. Stocky with an
effervescent character and never-say-die spirit, he always possessed an eye for goal
and had a direct attitude towards playing the game. Later Hughes did well for Derby
(201 app) and for Lincoln (131 app) and in all recorded almost 600 senior matches
during his career. On leaving the game, Gordon joined the Rolls Royce company as an
engineering surveyor for 20 years. He returned to the North East and resided in Chester
Moor.*

Appearances & Goals:
Debut v Manchester United (h) 8 September 1956
FL: 133 app 18 gls
FAC: 9 app 2 gls
FLC: 1 app 0 gls
Total: 143 app 20 gls

H

HUGHES John 1932-1935

Left-half
5'8"
b. Tanfield, Co Durham

Career: Tanfield Lea Institute/UNITED May 1932 £20/Aldershot May 1935 free/Hartlepools Utd July 1937/Consett June 1938.

John Hughes came into Newcastle's first eleven during the 1933-34 season on an injury to John Murray, however with United struggling to survive a relegation battle, the ex-West Stanley miner could make little headway. Hughes spent another season with the Magpies, but travelled south the following summer where he completed his career in the lower divisions before the Second World War erupted. Hughes registered 53 games for Aldershot, his best return during his career, while he totalled 40 matches at the Victoria Ground for Hartlepool. A tireless and unselfish half-back, John had trials with Nottingham Forest before joining the Magpies.

Appearances & Goals:
Debut v West Bromwich Albion (h) 27 January 1934
FL: 5 app 0 gls
Total: 5 app 0 gls

HUGHES Joseph 1938-1943

Right-back
5'7"
b. Hetton-le-Hole, 1 September 1918

Career: Bishop Auckland/UNITED amat Aug 1938, prof Dec 1938 to 1943.

Developed through United's 'A' team, Joe Hughes was a young reserve at St James' Park during the Second World War who stood in for the experienced Joe Richardson at right-back during season 1942-43. His debut occurred against Bradford Park Avenue during August 1942, a 4-1 defeat.

Appearances & Goals:
Debut v Bradford Park Avenue (h) 29 August 1942 (FLN)
War: 2 app 0 gls
Total: 2 app 0 gls

HUGHES Thomas 1912-1914

Inside-left
5'7"
b. Wallsend, 1893
d. Ypres (Belgium), 23 May 1915

Career: Wallsend Park Villa March 1912/UNITED April 1912 £80/Jarrow June 1914 to his demise.

Local youngster Tom Hughes was given a brief taste of First Division football during the 1912-13 season in place of internationals James Stewart and George Wilson. Hughes was a small and compact schemer who until the outbreak of World War One, was making good progress within United's ranks. During the summer of 1914, Tom joined the Northumberland Fusiliers and soon headed to the Continent where, sadly, he was killed in action. He is remembered at the Menin Gate Memorial at Ypres, losing his life during the battle for the Belgian town, one of 54,896 names on the vast and poignant monument in Flanders.

Appearances & Goals:
Debut v Bradford City (a) 8 February 1913
FL: 2 app 0 gls
Total: 2 app 0 gls

HUGHES William John 1908-1910

Right-half
5'8"
b. Rhyl, 1889
d. Rhyl, 1955

Career: Rhyl Ath/UNITED March 1908/Huddersfield Town March 1910 £37/Oswestry Town July 1911/Norwich City June 1912/Halifax Town June 1913/Bradford City Jan 1914/Barrow June 1914/Halifax Town Jan 1915/Rhyl Ath Oct 1919 becoming trainer & groundsman.

Newcastle United's first Welshman, Jack Hughes was spotted when the Magpies were on what was called "special" FA Cup training in his native North Wales resort of Rhyl. More at home in attack, he appeared for the first-team only once, as a last minute replacement at right-half. By all accounts Hughes was a stalwart all-round athlete, reports noting he, "showed really promising form alike in attack and defence".
During World War One he served in the army and was awarded the Military Medal, although the Welshman suffered the consequences of exposure to mustard gas for the rest of his life. Hughes later returned to Rhyl, assisting the Welsh club in various capacities, including groundsman. As the coxswain of the local lifeboat, he was a well known personality in that town while Jack also operated a fishing boat.

Appearances & Goals:
Debut v Everton (a) 4 April 1908
FL: 1 app 0 gls
Total: 1 app 0 gls

HUNT Andrew 1991-1993

Centre-forward
6'0"
b. Thurrock, Essex, 9 June 1970

Career: Ashill Hearts/Norwich City trial 1989/Kings Lynn 1989/Kettering Town Aug 1990/UNITED Jan 1991 £210,000/West Bromwich Albion loan March 1993, pmt May 1993 £100,000/Charlton Ath July 1998 free to May 2001 when he retired due to injury, but returned Oct 2003 trial to Nov 2003/Kings Lynn 2003/Kettering Town 2003.

In a surprise transfer, Andy Hunt exchanged the non-league scene of the Vauxhall Conference with Kettering Town for the big-time set-up of St James' Park. Tall and awkward to play against and good in possession, Hunt proved to be a consistent goalscorer in both reserve and first-team football for the Tynesiders. Andy had started to develop a good partnership with Mick Quinn before a broken ankle halted his progress, and by the time he was fit again Gallowgate was very much a different place with Sir John Hall and Kevin Keegan in charge. Hunt couldn't break into the new-look United squad and was picked up by West Bromwich Albion. He proceeded to be a regular striker at the Hawthorns, starting his career in the Midlands with a sparkling hat-trick on his home debut and proceeding to net 85 goals in 240 games for the Baggies. Hunt also did well with Charlton (94 app), but was sidelined by a mystery illness, later diagnosed as a post-viral fatigue syndrome which forced him out of the game. Disillusioned with football, Andy moved abroad afterwards and started a new life in the exotic landscape and climate of Belize. He settled on the edge of a jungle river and created popular tourist attractions; the Jungle Dome and Green Dragon Adventure Travel. He also occasionally turned out for his local football team, Banana Bank FC. At the beginning of his football career, Andy began as a centre-half, playing in three trial appearances for Norwich City's reserve eleven and gave up his job in computer systems to turn professional as a 20-year-old. Due to his grandparent's bloodline, he was in 2000 lined up to be included in Austria's national squad, but illness forced him out of contention.

Appearances & Goals:
Debut v Watford (a) 9 March 1991 (sub)
FL: 34(9) app 11 gls
FAC: 2 app 2 gls
FLC: 3 app 1 gl
Others: 3 app 0 gls
Total: 42(9) app 14 gls

Honours:
FL div 1 champs 2000/FL div 2 prom 1993/PFA ToS (d1) 2000.

HUNTER Isaac 1918-1919

Left-half
5'10"
b. Heddon, near Newcastle upon Tyne, c1893
Career: UNITED 1918/Motherwell May 1919/Ashington Aug 1919 briefly/
Newburn March 1920.

When the First World War came to a close, regions marked the Armistice with football celebration competitions. Isaac Hunter appeared in the opening fixture of the Northern Victory League against Hartlepools United at St James' Park during January 1919. That turned out to be his only senior outing for the Magpies, his place taken by noted Scot, Jock Finlay. Hunter nevertheless was a regular in the club's local District League side for season 1918-19. Isaac headed for non-league football with Ashington then to Scotland where he appeared on three occasions for Motherwell's Division One line-up in 1919-20.

Appearances & Goals:
Debut v Hartlepools United (h) 11 January 1919 (NVL)
War: 1 app 0 gls
Total: 1 app 0 gls

HUNTER James Alton 1919, 1924-1925

Left-back
5'8"
b. Balfron, Stirlingshire, 5 July 1898
Career: UNITED 1919/Motherwell Aug 1919 briefly/
Forth Rangers/Falkirk Dec 1919/UNITED Jan 1924
£3,500/Heart of Midlothian trial July 1925/
New Bedford Whalers (USA) May 1925 to 1930.

United purchased James Hunter, who was a regular with Falkirk (145 app) earning Scottish League XI honours as cover to the aging Frank Hudspeth whose career in 1924 was thought to be coming to an end. But United's veteran continued for several seasons and James had to be content to perform in the club's reserve side for the most part. He was also at St James' Park briefly immediately after World War One, Newcastle keeping tracks of his progress back in Scotland before making the move to sign him permanently. Hunter was a tactful defender who at times had a controversial career, firstly signing for Motherwell without permission of the Magpies who held his registration. The club reported Motherwell to the Inter-League Board and Hunter then become embroiled in a disagreement with Newcastle's directors. Consequently he was transfer listed at such a high fee that no one would sign him and as a result, Hunter emigrated to North America and continued his footballing career in the States. He served New Bedford Whalers in Massachusetts for a lengthy period, appearing on over 150 occasions for the club. He also teamed up with his country's touring side during 1927 and was a regular as the Scots played around North America.

Appearances & Goals:
Debut v Tottenham Hotspur (h) 26 January 1924
FL: 10 app 0 gls
FAC: 2 app 0 gls
Total: 12 app 0 gls

Honours:
2 SL app 1923-24/13 unoff Scot app on tour 1927.

HUNTER James Boyd 1941

Outside-right
5'9"
b. Dunfermline, 12 July 1910
d. Ilkeston, June 1976
Career: Wheeldons Utd 1928/Stanton Ironworks 1929/
Ilkeston Utd 1930/Fulham trial 1932/Ripley Town cs 1934/
Mansfield Town amat Nov 1934, prof Feb 1935/Plymouth
Argyle Nov 1935 £500/Preston North End July 1939
(Mansfield Town war-guest 1939-43)(Nottingham Forest
war-guest 1940-41)(UNITED war-guest 1941-42)
(Blackburn Rovers war-guest 1943-44)(Plymouth Argyle
war-guest 1945-46)(Aldershot war-guest 1945-46).

An established pre-war winger or inside-forward, Jimmy Hunter was born a Scot, but raised in Derbyshire after his family moved in search of work. And during World War Two, Hunter found himself aiding the war effort at Wallsend, employed in the shipyards for a period as an electrician. Taking part in the early months of the 1941-42 Football League North programme, he later appeared for several clubs on his travels around the country but did not see senior action after World War Two. Hunter totalled 98 games for Plymouth during the Thirties.

Appearances & Goals:
Debut v Bradford City (h) 30 August 1941 (FLN)
War: 8 app 0 gls
Total: 8 app 0 gls

HUNTINGTON Paul David 2002-2007

Centre-half
6'3"
b. Carlisle, 17 September 1987
Career: Yewdale Pegasus BC/UNITED jnr 2002, prof July
2005 (Plymouth Argyle trial Aug 2006)/Leeds Utd Aug
2007 £500,000/Stockport Co Sept 2009/Yeovil Town July
2010 free/Preston North End July 2012.

Although more comfortable at centre-half, Carlisle-born Paul Huntington rarely was given a chance in his favoured role at Gallowgate. On the fringe of Newcastle's team plan, Huntington was tall and lithe, being handed a few outings during the winter months of 2006-07, albeit out of position at either right-back or left-back and very occasionally in the centre of defence. Used as cover across the back line, few centre-backs have developed through United's ranks to become a regular selection in the club's modern history, only Aaron Hughes and Steven Taylor, and Huntington was destined for a career at a lower level of football like many predecessors. Paul joined Leeds United, but following a bright start, he failed to win a regular place at Elland Road, lost confidence and picked up a bad groin injury which needed surgery. 'Hunty' though, recaptured his form with Yeovil Town during 2010-11 and 2011-12 in Division One, becoming skipper at Huish Park. Paul moved closer to his Cumbria home when he joined Preston in the summer of 2012.

Appearances & Goals:
Debut v Blackburn Rovers (a) 9 December 2006 (sub)
PL: 10(1) app 1 gl
FAC: 2 app 0 gls
FLC: 1 app 0 gls
Euro: 1(1) app 0 gls
Total: 14(2) app 1 gl

Honours:
Eng sch-youth app.

HUTCHINSON Robert 1918-1920

Inside-left
5'9"
b. Gosforth, Newcastle upon Tyne, 22 December 1894
d. Gosforth, Newcastle upon Tyne, 4 August 1971
Career: Palmers Works (Jarrow)/Gosforth/Palmers
Works/St Mirren 1914/UNITED amat 1918, prof May
1919/Ashington May 1920/Nelson May 1922/
Stockport Co Jan 1924/Chesterfield May 1924/
Barrow June 1925/New Bedford Whalers (USA)
1926-27/Hartford Americans (USA) 1927-28/also
with, Springfield Babes (USA)/Fall River Marksmen
(USA)/Newark Skeeters (USA)/Darlington March 1928/West Stanley Sept 1928/
Gosforth & Coxlodge BL Sept 1930.

Bob Hutchinson had an unlucky spell with Newcastle United. Apart from having his early footballing career ruined by World War One, he underwent cartilage surgery in 1919 which cost him an opportunity to push for a place at St James' Park at a crucial time when openings were available as a new post-war squad was assembled. Hutchinson's single appearance came in a Northern Victory League clash with Scotswood, a deputy for Ed Dixon, and the Geordie moved to appear in Ashington's first season as a the Football League club. He established himself as a good player at Portland Park being fast and resourceful and in 1922 headed for Lancashire, joining another of the now ex-Football League sides, Nelson, where he took part in the Blues' Third Division North title success during 1922-23 and claimed 64 appearances for the Pennine club.

Appearances & Goals:
Debut v Scotswood (h) 15 March 1919 (NVL)
War: 1 app 0 gls
Total: 1 app 0 gls

Honours:
FL div 3(N) champs 1923.

H

HUTCHISON Duncan 1929-1932

Centre-forward
5'7"
b. Kelty, Fife, 3 March 1903
d. Dundee, 12 December 1973

Career: Leathens Heatherbell/Rosewell
Rosedale/Dunfermline Ath Oct 1925/
Dundee Utd July 1927 free/UNITED Aug
1929 £4,050/Derby Co March 1932
£3,100 joint deal with R Hann/Hull City
July 1934/Dundee Utd June 1935 exch
deal/Retired Aug 1939/
Dundee Utd director March 1953 to 1972,
becoming Chairman Nov 1963 to June
1965.

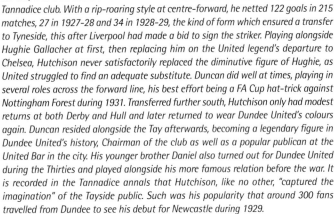

*Duncan Hutchison, nicknamed 'Hurricane
Hutch' after a dare-devil silent film star of
his era, was a household name with the
Tannadice club. With a rip-roaring style at centre-forward, he netted 122 goals in 215
matches, 27 in 1927-28 and 34 in 1928-29, the kind of form which ensured a transfer
to Tyneside, this after Liverpool had made a bid to sign the striker. Playing alongside
Hughie Gallacher at first, then replacing him on the United legend's departure to
Chelsea, Hutchison never satisfactorily replaced the diminutive figure of Hughie, as
United struggled to find an adequate substitute. Duncan did well at times, playing in
several roles across the forward line, his best effort being a FA Cup hat-trick against
Nottingham Forest during 1931. Transferred further south, Hutchison only had modest
returns at both Derby and Hull and later returned to wear Dundee United's colours
again. Duncan resided alongside the Tay afterwards, becoming a legendary figure in
Dundee United's history, Chairman of the club as well as a popular publican at the
United Bar in the city. His younger brother Daniel also turned out for Dundee United
during the Thirties and played alongside his more famous relation before the war. It
is recorded in the Tannadice annals that Hutchison, like no other, "captured the
imagination" of the Tayside public. Such was his popularity that around 300 fans
travelled from Dundee to see his debut for Newcastle during 1929.*

Appearances & Goals:
Debut v Manchester United (h) 31 August 1929
FL: 40 app 16 gls
FAC: 6 app 5 gls
Total: 46 app 21 gls

Honours:
SL div 2 champs 1929.

HUTTON Thomas Osborne 1939-1942

Full-back
5'11"
b. Ryton, near Gateshead, 10 September 1922
d. Blackburn, December 2004

Career: Sleekburn Welfare/UNITED amat 1939, prof
June 1940 to 1942/Red Rose (Army, Lancashire)/
Accrington Stanley Nov 1944/Carlisle Utd Aug 1947/
Rochdale Aug 1949/Nelson Feb 1950/Tranmere Rovers
Aug 1950/Chorley player-trainer Aug 1951.

*Described as, "sound rather than spectacular", Tom
Hutton was a hardworking defender, tall and solid, who
could also play at half-back. A joiner by trade, he came
into United's wartime Football League North team as a
replacement for Jimmy Denmark at centre-half for a
Christmas Day meeting with Middlesbrough in 1940. All
Tom's appearances with the club were during that 1940-41 season, but then he soon
joined the army and later had a decent career in the lower divisions during immediate
post-war football appearing on 45 occasions for Carlisle.*

Appearances & Goals:
Debut v Middlesbrough (h) 25 December 1940 (FLN)
War: 3 app 0 gls
Total: 3 app 0 gls

HYND John 1894-1895

Goalkeeper
b. Scotland

Career: Cowdenbeath 1889/UNITED Nov 1894/Cowdenbeath Aug 1895 to cs 1900.

*Goalkeeper Jock Hynd replaced United's regular custodian Ward for two months over
the winter of 1894-95, during Newcastle's second Football League season. Following
a run of nine successive games, Ward regained his place after Hynd conceding eight
goals in defeats at the hands of Burton Swifts and Woolwich Arsenal. The Scot joined
the Magpies after noteworthy reports landed at St James' Park following his excellent
displays in the East of Scotland versus West of Scotland contest north of the border.
Jock also showed up well playing for the Fife representative team and appeared in
two Fife Cup winning sides for Cowdenbeath. One local reporter described John as
being a sound player and having "always given proof of having his head screwed on
right"! Hynd stayed with the club for only one season, while he also operated as a
full-back and it is suspected he appeared in this role for the club under the press
reported name of "Haynes" (qv).*

Appearances & Goals:
Debut v Grimsby Town (a) 1 December 1894
FL: 9 app 0 gls
Total: 9 app 0 gls

ILEY James 1962-1969

Left-half
5'11"
b. South Kirkby, Yorkshire, 15 December 1935

Career: Moorthorpe St Josephs BC/Pontefract/
Sheffield Utd amat March 1951, June 1953/
Tottenham Hotspur Aug 1957 £16,000/
Nottingham Forest July 1959 £16,000/UNITED
Sept 1962 £17,000/Peterborough Utd player-
manager Jan 1969 to Sept 1972/Cambridge Utd
scout Oct 1972/Barnsley manager April 1973/
Blackburn Rovers manager April 1978/Luton Town
scout Oct 1978/Bury manager July 1980 to
Feb 1984/Exeter City manager June 1984 to
April 1985/Scout for various club including
Charlton Ath and Luton Town.

*A former colliery lad at Frickley pit and brought up around the South Kirkby and
South Elmsall districts of Yorkshire before turning professional, Jim Iley made his
Football League debut as a 17-year-old part-timer with Sheffield United. He quickly
reached the first-team and began to be noticed, earning a move to White Hart
Lane where he won England honours before returning north after having difficulty
settling in the capital, although still recording 66 games for Spurs. By the time he
arrived at St James' Park, Iley was an experienced wing-half who was destined to
become the cornerstone in the Number 6 shirt alongside Stan Anderson, influential
in the Magpies' promotion line-up during 1964-65. Balding on top, Jim was in
many respects a complete player, possessing good control, versatility, tremendous
shooting ability, consistency and a team attitude on the field. Skipper of United
before, and after Anderson's leadership, Iley was a driving force in midfield, always
able to be a danger around the box; he netted a screamer from 20 yards against
Bolton Wanderers which sent United back into the First Division. A regular for six
seasons, after taking part in Newcastle's first European match on the bench, he
moved on when he was 33 years old, wanting to further his playing days rather
than take a coaching job at St. James' Park. Iley later proved he could manage
clubs on a limited budget, although he had a turbulent period of only 172 days at
Ewood Park. On leaving the game Iley resided in the Bolton area, for a while running
an Italian restaurant in Chorley. During his time at Bramall Lane, where he totalled
112 matches, Jim once missed two penalty kicks in the same match during 1956-
57. His brother-in-law is Sheffield United and England winger, Colin Grainger, while
his grandfather appeared for Crook Town.*

Appearances & Goals:
Debut v Plymouth Argyle (h) 8 September 1962
FL: 227(5) app 15 gls
FAC: 9 app 0 gls
FLC: 7 app 1 gl
Euro: 0(1) app 0 gls
Total: 243(6) app 16 gls

Honours:
1 Eng u23 app 1958/2 FL app 1956-59/1 FA app 1962/FL div 2 champs 1965.

IMRIE William Noble 1934-1938

Right-half
5'11"
b. Methil, Fife, 4 March 1908
d. Windygates, near Methil, Fife,
26 December 1944

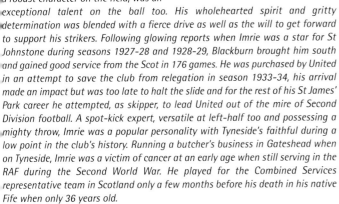

Career: Kirkcaldy Jnrs/East Fife jnrs/ Dunnikier Jnrs/St Johnstone May 1927/ Blackburn Rovers Sept 1929 £4,775/UNITED March 1934 £6,500/Swansea Town July 1938 £2,500/Swindon Town July 1939 £800/East Fife Nov 1939 (Raith Rovers war-guest 1942-43).

The red-haired Bill Imrie was a burley, powerful figure, who, apart from being a robust character on the field, was an exceptional talent on the ball too. His wholehearted spirit and gritty determination was blended with a fierce drive as well as the will to get forward to support his strikers. Following glowing reports when Imrie was a star for St Johnstone during seasons 1927-28 and 1928-29, Blackburn brought him south and gained good service from the Scot in 176 games. He was purchased by United in an attempt to save the club from relegation in season 1933-34, his arrival made an impact but was too late to halt the slide and for the rest of his St James' Park career he attempted, as skipper, to lead United out of the mire of Second Division football. A spot-kick expert, versatile at left-half too and possessing a mighty throw, Imrie was a popular personality with Tyneside's faithful during a low point in the club's history. Running a butcher's business in Gateshead when on Tyneside, Imrie was a victim of cancer at an early age when still serving in the RAF during the Second World War. He played for the Combined Services representative team in Scotland only a few months before his death in his native Fife when only 36 years old.

Appearances & Goals:
Debut v Sheffield United (a) 17 March 1934
FL: 125 app 24 gls
FAC: 3 app 0 gls
Total: 128 app 24 gls

Honours:
2 Scot caps 1929/WsC final 1938.

INGLIS John 1893-1894

Outside-left
b. Scotland

Career: Dalmuir Thistle/UNITED Oct 1893/Duntocher Harp Dec 1894 to cs 1897.

John Inglis arrived on Tyneside during October 1893 from the Dalmuir Thistle club near Clydebank on a trial deal as United entered the Football League for the first time during season 1893-94. He didn't remain in Newcastle long, appearing on three occasions as a stand-in for Quinn. The Newcastle Daily Chronicle recorded "he had a splendid reputation" and "he showed up some smart doings". Nevertheless, the Magpies did not retain the Scot and he moved back north of the border to Clydebank.

Appearances & Goals:
Debut v Notts County (a) 14 October 1893
FL: 3 app 0 gls
Total: 3 app 0 gls

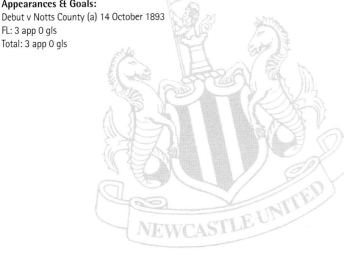

INNERD Wilfred Lawson 1900-1905

Centre-half
5'9"
b. Newcastle upon Tyne, 1878 (Q4)
d. Newcastle upon Tyne, 24 June 1967

Career: Wallsend Park Villa 1899/UNITED May 1900/Crystal Palace May 1905/Shildon Ath June 1909/Newcastle City Aug 1910 to cs 1913.

Chiefly a reserve to Andy Aitken at St James' Park, Wilf Innerd responded to a call-up for First Division action in season 1900-01 and once during the Black'n'Whites Football League championship winning campaign of 1904-05. He also aided the club's second string lift the Northern League title on three occasions before he moved south. Wilf found a place in the Crystal Palace side which did well in both the Southern League and FA Cup as giant-killers, including leading the Eagles in the Londoner's famous success on Tyneside against the Magpies during January 1907. Innerd totalled 133 senior games for Palace, a key figure in midfield during their formative years. The Tynesider took over as skipper in London from another ex-United man, Ted Birnie, but was badly injured in a big FA Cup match against Wolves during January 1909 and never really recovered, moving into the non-league scene back north. Innerd settled in the North East following his retirement and lived well into his eightieth year, residing in Heaton and working for many years at the Robert Sinclair cigarette works near St James' Park.

Appearances & Goals:
Debut v Liverpool (a) 30 March 1901
FL: 3 app 0 gls
Total: 3 app 0 gls

Honours:
FL champs 1905 (1 app)/SnL div 2 champs 1906.

IRELAND Stephen James 2011

Midfield
5'8"
b. Cobh, Co Cork, 22 August 1986

Career: Cobh Ramblers 1994/Manchester City jnr 2001, prof Sept 2004/Aston Villa Aug 2010 cash-exch for J Milner (UNITED loan January to April 2011)/Stoke City loan Sept 2013, pmt Jan 2014.

During season 2008-09 as a Manchester City player, Stephen Ireland was one of the Premier League's top performers showing a drive and thrust from midfield, continually making things happen for the Sky-Blues. The Irishman looked to have the football world at his feet, however City boss Mark Hughes was replaced by Roberto Mancini and his bourgeoning career came to a halt. After almost 180 games (23 goals) he found himself part of the huge £24m deal which took ex-Magpie James Milner to City, with Ireland heading to Villa Park, the Irishman being valued at £8m in the transaction. In the Midlands, Stephen found himself out of the reckoning in Gerard Houllier's Villa line-up and when Newcastle came calling during the January transfer window to enhance their attacking options, Villa were eager to send him out on loan. He arrived at Gallowgate somewhat reluctantly, but with a chance to impress and get his career back on track. Unfortunately the shaven-headed and talented midfield man never got going in a Toon shirt. Hardly fit when he arrived, he soon picked up a knee injury, then a thigh strain and ankle problem, and was on the sidelines more often than not. It took Ireland more than three months to make his United bow; the Irish international only recording two fleeting appearances, both as substitute during April 2011, a total of 49 minutes of action on the field. As a consequence supporters never saw the real Stephen Ireland and he headed back to the Midlands still in need of a career boost. As a youngster, Ireland suffered from Osgood-Schlatter disease, but still managed to become a noted schoolboy star having a number of trials with top English clubs.

Appearances & Goals:
Debut v Manchester United (h) 19 April 2011
PL: 0(2) app 0 gls
Total: 0(2) app 0 gls

Honours:
6 Eire caps 2006-08/1 Eire u21 app 2005/ Eire sch-youth app.

J

JACKSON Darren 1986-1988

Striker
5'7"
b. Edinburgh, 25 July 1966

Career: St Bernard's BC/Melbourne Thistle/
Broxburn Ath/Meadowbank Thistle May 1985/
UNITED Oct 1986 £240,000/Dundee Utd Nov 1988
£200,000/Hibernian July 1992 £400,000/Celtic
July 1997 £1.5m (Coventry City loan 1998-99)/
Dalian Wanda (Ch) Feb 1999/Heart of Midlothian
March 1999 £300,000/Livingston Jan 2001/
St Johnstone July 2001 free/Clydebank Jan 2002/
HK Malaysia cs 2002, retiring soon afterwards/
Partick Thistle part-time asst-coach Sept 2012/
Dundee Utd asst-coach Feb 2013.

*Darren Jackson was given a chance by Newcastle
after scoring 19 goals as a part-time professional
in his first season with Meadowbank. Slight of
build, but fast and eager for the ball, Jackson was moved around from position to
position at St James' Park, operating as a striker, in midfield or even at full-back.
Always having the potential to succeed, reaching the Scotland Under-21 squad when
with the Magpies, Darren perhaps wasn't developed in the manner to get the best
out of the player during his stay on Tyneside. Released too hastily back north to
Scotland by new boss Jim Smith, a move he reluctantly agreed too, Jackson indeed
realised his potential by becoming a regular for the Scots at full international level
and playing in the World Cup during France 98. He was recognised as one of Scotland's
top strikers being a success at both Tannadice and Easter Road, then later at Parkhead
where he won a title medal. By the end of his career in Scotland Jackson had totalled
over 500 games and netted 141 goals. After halting his career, Darren worked as a
player agent for a period with the FIFA registered Inspire Sports Management
company.*

Appearances & Goals:
Debut v Arsenal (h) 18 October 1986 (sub)
FL: 53(16) app 7 gls
FAC: 5 app 1 gl
FLC: 5 app 1 gl
Others: 4 app 0 gls
Total: 67(16) app 9 gls

Honours:
28 Scot caps 1995-99/WdC 1998/1 Scot B app 1995/SL champs 1998/SL div 1 champs
2001 (9 app)/SC final 1991/SLC final 1994.

JACKSON James 1897-1899

Left-back
5'9"
b. Cambuslang, Glasgow, 15 September 1875

Career: Hamilton Acc/Elmstown Rosebuds (Aus)/
Newton Thistle/Cambuslang 1896/Rangers May 1896/
UNITED April 1897/Woolwich Arsenal May 1899
£40/Leyton player-manager May 1905/West Ham Utd
Nov 1905/Rangers May 1906 (Port Glasgow Ath loan
1908-09)(Hamilton Acc loan 1909-10)/Morton May
1910/Abercorn Sept 1911 to 1919.

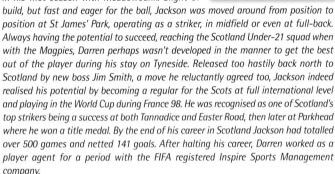

*A steadfast and clever defender, perhaps a decade ahead
of his time as a tactician, fair-haired James Jackson was
an eye-catching player. He was a rock in United's defence as the Magpies reached
promotion to Division One via the Test Matches during 1898. When Jackson was only
two years old, his parents emigrated to Australia from Clydeside and the youngster
was to learn the Aussie rules version of the game before returning to Scotland in his
teens and taking up the association code back in Glasgow. After assisting greatly in
Newcastle's consolidation as a force in the game, James moved to Arsenal where he
became a noted captain of the Gunners, appearing on 204 occasions, also leading
the Londoners into the First Division. A strict teetotaller, Jackson ran a sports outfitters
business outside Highbury too and after leaving the game he became a blacksmith in
Greenock. His two sons played football as well; one, a past skipper of Liverpool, the
distinguished Reverend James Jackson, while Archie appeared for Sunderland and
Tranmere. Australian Test cricketer, Archibald Jackson was a nephew.*

Appearances & Goals:
Debut v Woolwich Arsenal (h) 4 September 1897
FL: 62 app 1 gl
FAC: 6 app 2 gls
Total: 68 app 3 gls

Honours:
Scot trial app 1905/FA trial app 1902/FL div 2 prom 1898, 1904.

JACKSON Peter Allan 1986-1988

Centre-half
6'1"
b. Shelf, near Bradford, 6 April 1961

Career: Bingley Jnrs/Sheffield Utd trial 1976/Burnley jnr
1976/Bradford City jnr July 1977, prof April 1979/
UNITED Oct 1986 £250,000/Bradford City Sept 1988
£290,000/Huddersfield Town Sept 1990 free/Chester loan
Sept 1994, pmt Nov 1994/Halifax Town Aug 1997/
Huddersfield Town manager Oct 1997 to May 1999, then
again, June 2003 to March 2007/Lincoln City manager
Oct 2007 to Sept 2009/Bradford City manager Feb 2011
to Aug 2011.

*As captain of Bradford City, Peter Jackson was a great favourite at Valley Parade, a
17-year-old debutant and skipper when 18, totalling almost 400 senior games for
the Bantams. He was a strong character and an inspiration on the field; positive,
commanding in the air and able to battle for the ball. Jackson continued his bond
with the fans when he landed at Gallowgate, being a popular character with United's
black-and-white army of support right up to the day he left the region in a return
transfer to his home town club. A committed and durable centre-back, Peter was
Player of the Year during his first season with Newcastle and his move back to
Yorkshire after two seasons surprised many on Tyneside, at the time losing his place
and, as he later confirmed, being too eager to leave Gallowgate. At the time Peter
was both Bradford's record sale, and purchase. Jackson was captain of City when the
Valley Parade fire disaster occurred in 1985, while he once scored two own-goals in a
Newcastle versus Manchester United clash during 1987. In between his management
appointments, Jackson worked as a player agent, with local radio in Yorkshire, and
created a company with his wife caring for the elderly, Caremark Calderdale, based in
Halifax.*

Appearances & Goals:
Debut v Aston Villa (a) 25 October 1986
FL: 60 app 3 gls
FAC: 6 app 0 gls
FLC: 3 app 0 gls
Others: 3 app 0 gls
Total: 72 app 3 gls

Honours:
FL div 3 champs 1985/FL div 3 prom(m) 2004/FL div 4 prom 1982.

JEFFREY Harry 1892-1895

Right-back
5'9"
b. Newcastle upon Tyne, March 1867
d. Newcastle upon Tyne, 16 February 1930

Career: Drysdale (Newcastle)/Newcastle West End
c1888 (Boundary & Newcastle Wed occasionally)/
Drysdale (Newcastle) 1890/Sunderland amat 1890/
Third Lanark amat 1890/Newcastle West End 1890/
EAST END April 1892/Retired due to injury 1895/
South Shields June 1897.

*One of the club's earliest personalities, Harry Jeffrey
was a regular for rivals Newcastle West End and on
joining East End took part in the club's debut at St James' Park against Celtic and
then the Tynesider's first ever Football League encounter at Arsenal. Strong-tackling,
he was something of a controversial character within the ranks, once suspended for
two weeks for being, as the club's Minutes of Meetings note, "a non trier", while he
also received a month's ban for playing in the close-season without permission. It
was reported in September 1894 that, due to a fracas, he "will not be seen upon the
team again". Jeffrey also sustained a bad leg injury in January 1895 when at
Gallowgate which was serious enough to force him to quit the top-class scene.*

Against Sunderland he was carried from the field with a knee-cap injury and dislocated ankle. It was noted that Harry was "very ill" for a lengthy period and the serious mishap kept him out of action for over two years, ultimately forcing him to play at a lower level in the Northern Alliance. Noted by one biography of his day as a, "stylish and scientific exponent of the game", Harry scored Newcastle's first recorded penalty kick in senior action, against Walsall Town Swifts during March 1894. Jeffrey also captained Northumberland, as well as West End, and played cricket for the Drysdale, Boundary and Bath Lane clubs. He resided during his later years in Stanhope Street near to St James' Park.

Appearances & Goals:
Debut v Sheffield United (a) 24 September 1892 (NL)
NL: 7 app 0 gls
FL: 45 app 3 gls
FAC: 3 app 0 gls
Total: 55 app 3 gls

JEFFREY Michael Richard 1993-1995

Midfield
5'11"
b. West Derby, Liverpool, 11 August 1971

Career: San Paulo (Liverpool), Stoke's (Liverpool)/ Bolton Wand jnr 1984, prof Feb 1989/Doncaster Rovers loan March 1992, pmt May 1992 (Nottingham Forest trial July 1993)/UNITED Oct 1993 £85,000/ Rotherham Utd June 1995 £100,000/Fortuna Sittard (Neth) Dec 1995 £205,000/Kilmarnock July 1999/ Grimsby Town trial July 2000, pmt Aug 2000 free (Scunthorpe Utd loan 2001-02) to cs 2002.

Mike Jeffrey had trials with Sheffield Wednesday and Liverpool before an extended opportunity came his way at Burnden Park in Bolton. He was released though and it was with Doncaster that Jeffrey caught the eye of Kevin Keegan as he appeared in Divisions Three and Four. Totalling over 50 matches for Rovers, he was signed in a deal that saw David Roche move to Belle Vue. Mike became a fringe player in Keegan's squad which established the club as one of the powers of the Premier League. Like so many of United's reserves in that era, it was almost impossible for Jeffrey to break through an array of international talent ahead of him. Only rarely given a first-eleven outing, the Merseysider always performed with credit in a role either in midfield, or just behind the Magpies' main striker. Finding his way to Dutch football, Mike was a regular with Fortuna, claiming over 100 appearances playing alongside Mark van Bommel for a period. After he left football, Jeffrey returned to Merseyside and worked in a family car sales business.

Appearances & Goals:
Debut v Tottenham Hotspur (a) 4 December 1993
PL: 2 app 0 gls
FLC: 1 app 1 gl
Euro: 0(2) app 0 gls
Total: 3(2) app 1 gl

Honours:
Neth Cup final 1999.

JENAS Jermaine Anthony 2002-2005

Midfield
5'11"
b. Nottingham, 18 February 1983

Career: Clifton All Whites/Nottingham Forest jnr June 1999, prof Feb 2000/UNITED Feb 2002 £5m/ Tottenham Hotspur Aug 2005 £7m (Aston Villa loan 2011-12)(Nottingham Forest loan 2012-13)/ Queens Park Rangers Jan 2013.

Jermaine Jenas was recognised as a star of the future when Sir Bobby Robson brought the youngster to Tyneside during February 2002. Almost 19 years of age and having completed only 39 games in Forest's senior line-up, and in a tier below the Premier League, he was untried but his talent and potential was such that he commanded a fee of £5m, one of the most expensive teenagers in the game at that time. Tall and slim, Jenas was a mobile and brisk link-man in midfield, the raw newcomer quickly showing the Tyneside public he could live up to his glowing early reviews and perhaps replace the recently departed Rob Lee's box-to-box play. Becoming a regular in Robson's powerful engine-room during season

2002-03, 'JJ' as he was nicknamed, matured quickly and steadily added experience to his game over three seasons, so much so that he pushed his way into England reckoning. Confident and always wanting the ball in midfield, Jenas though never took the next big step in a black-and-white shirt; to become one of the Premier League's elite. His career stagnated somewhat at Gallowgate and once Robson departed, Jermaine was sold to Tottenham as the 2005-06 campaign got underway. He famously claimed he could not cope with living in a "gold-fish bowl" on Tyneside. Moving to White Hart Lane for a £7m fee, in North London Jermaine again showed at times he could live with the best in his 200-plus games, claiming a place in the England squad, but he was often sidelined with injury and lost his position as Harry Redknapp created a first-rate Spurs line-up. Jenas headed for Villa Park on a season-long loan deal but where he again was out of action for many months with a bad Achilles injury and eventually landed back with Redknapp at QPR. Unlucky with knocks after he left Gallowgate, Jermaine suffered a cruciate injury in April 2014 and found himself once more on the sidelines. Jenas appeared at every level for his country, captain of the youth and Under-21 side. He also skippered United when he was only 21 years of age. Jenas is a cousin of Jermaine Pennant, also to have a decent career in football during the same era, while his father had a short period on Forest's books.

Appearances & Goals:
Debut v Southampton (h) 9 February 2002 (sub)
PL: 86(24) app 9 gls
FAC: 6(1) app 1 gl
FLC: 3 app 1 gl
Euro: 28(4) app 1 gl
Total: 123(29) app 12 gls

Honours:
21 Eng caps 2003-10/WdC 2006 (no app)/2 Eng B app 2006-07/9 Eng u21 app 2002-04/Eng sch-youth app/FLC winner 2008/FLC final 2009/FL ch prom 2014/YPoY (PFA) 2003.

JOBEY George 1906-1913

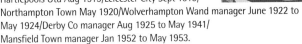

Wing-half
5'10"
b. Heddon-on-the-Wall, near Newcastle upon Tyne, 12 July 1885
d. Chaddesden, Derby, 9 March 1962

Career: Throckley Villa/Morpeth Harriers Jan 1906/ UNITED May 1906 £10/Woolwich Arsenal May 1913 £500/Bradford Park Avenue June 1914 (Hamilton Acc war-guest 1915-16)(Arsenal war-guest 1918-19)/ Hartlepools Utd Aug 1919/Leicester City Sept 1919/ Northampton Town May 1920/Wolverhampton Wand manager June 1922 to May 1924/Derby Co manager Aug 1925 to May 1941/ Mansfield Town manager Jan 1952 to May 1953.

One the prominent names of pre-war soccer, perhaps not as a player, but as a manager George Jobey was a well known and respected figure for over 30 years. The Tynesider made his first appearance for United in the Magpies' League Championship winning celebration game at the close of the 1906-07 season and after recovering from a cartilage injury was for the next six campaigns a squad player, operating in any half-back role as well as at centre-forward. Described by one colleague at Gallowgate as being "a man of great strength of character" and "of iron temperament", George won a title medal in 1909 and was selected for the 1911 FA Cup final as a replacement for the injured Albert Shepherd. It was related that he was a player of the purest footballing type and the reason he didn't play more for the Magpies was because he lacked an aggressive streak, rarely tackling for the ball. Zealous and dependable, with a tactical mind, it was little surprise that he entered management after World War One, becoming especially noted for his work at the Baseball Ground. He took Derby to promotion, then to a whisker of the title, the Rams twice becoming runners-up in 1930 and 1936. Jobey was a wheeler and dealer in the transfer market and attracted an impressive list of names to his club, including Hughie Gallacher, but in 1941 was suspended for life (later lifted) after a FA Inquiry into the financial dealings of the Rams; it was found that illegal bonus payments and signing on fees had been paid to many of the stars Jobey purchased. George holds the distinction of scoring the very first goal at Highbury in 1913, later in the game being carried off injured on a so-called milk-cart! He later resided in Derby for the rest of his life.

Appearances & Goals:
Debut v Bolton Wanderers (a) 20 April 1907
FL: 47 app 2 gls
FAC: 6 app 0 gls
Total: 53 app 2 gls

Honours:
FL champs 1907 (1 app), 1909/FL div 2 prom 1926(m)/FL div 3(N) champs 1924(m)/FAC final 1911.

J

JOHNSEN Ronny Jean 2004-2005

Centre-half
6'2"
b. Sandefjord (Norway), 10 June 1969

Career: Semi IF (Nor)/Stokke IL (Nor) 1987/EIK Tonsberg (Nor) 1989/FK Lyn (Nor) Jan 1992/Lillestrom SK (Nor) Jan 1994/ Besiktas JK (Trk) Jan 1995/ Manchester Utd July 1996 £1.2m/FC Schalke (Ger) trial 2002/Aston Villa Aug 2002 free to cs 2004/ UNITED Sept 2004 free to Jan 2005/ Valerenga IF (Nor) Feb 2005/Retired Nov 2008.

When Norwegian international defender Ronny Johnsen joined the Black'n'Whites just as the 2004-05 season had started, he had all but retired from the game and was out of contract. Aged 35, the experienced centre-back was without a club having left Aston Villa some three months before. Manager Graeme Souness needed a cool and influential player to boost his threadbare defensive options with Jonathan Woodgate having being sold to Real Madrid and only Hughes, O'Brien and Bramble available. Johnsen filled a gap until United could buy in the January window, bringing Jean-Alain Boumsong to Tyneside. Having become a noted defender in Turkey with Besiktas, he then made a move to Old Trafford to replace Steve Bruce. Ronny was an influential player for the Reds in 150 appearances being at the peak of his career, Johnson winning the treble in 1999 with Manchester United. Often sidelined through injury, the gritty Scandinavian certainly possessed the know-how but on Tyneside took time to get match fit and in the end only turned out on five occasions for the Magpies, being one of the oldest players to record his debut for the club (aged 35 years 4 months). A key figure in the Norway side for more than a decade, he was nicknamed the 'Norwegian Beckenbauer'. After retiring from playing, Ronny set up a property company in Norway and also became involved in the Uni-Bet business as a high profile front man. He is also a Manchester United club ambassador and expert commentator for Norwegian television.

Appearances & Goals:
Debut v Norwich City (h) 27 October 2004 (FLC)
PL: 3 app 0 gls
FLC: 2 app 0 gls
Total: 5 app 0 gls

Honours:
62 Nor caps 1992-2008/WdC 1998/PL champs 1997, 1999, 2000 (3 app), 2001/FAC winner 1999/CL winner 1999.

JOHNSON Henry 1932-1937

Left-back
5'10"
b. Walker, Newcastle upon Tyne, 8 August 1913
d. Nottingham, 1976

Career: Walker Park/UNITED amat Oct 1932, prof Aug 1933/ Port Vale June 1937/Hartlepools Utd June 1938/Reyrolle cs 1939.

Hard and fierce, typical of many full-backs of the inter-war era, Harry Johnson was a stand-in for Joe Richardson, with Fairhurst switching to right-back, and collected all his senior outings during the 1935-36 season. Johnson moved from Gallowgate in the close-season of 1937 and proceeded to appear on 21 occasions for Port Vale then 27 times for Hartlepools, both in the Third Division North. His elder brother had a spell on Chelsea's books during the Twenties and turned out for Wigan and Darlington. Harry's son, Alec Johnson, was a first-class county cricketer with Notts (1963-74), also appearing for both Northumberland and Durham.

Appearances & Goals:
Debut v Hull City (a) 13 April 1936
FL: 5 app 0 gls
Total: 5 app 0 gls

JOHNSON Peter Edward 1980-1983

Left-back
5'10"
b. Harrogate, 5 October 1958

Career: York City trial/Middlesbrough jnr, prof Oct 1976/ UNITED Oct 1980 £60,000 (Bristol City loan 1982-83)/ Doncaster Rovers March 1983/Darlington Aug 1983/ Whitby Town Sept 1985/Crewe Alex Oct 1985/ Whitby Town Jan 1986/Exeter City March 1986/ Southend Utd Aug 1986/Gillingham Aug 1989/Southend Utd Aug 1990 trial/Peterborough Utd Oct 1991 to Jan 1992/Later becoming Southend Utd asst-coach.

Twenty-two-year-old Peter Johnson arrived on Tyneside as a replacement for Ian Davies and as Arthur Cox's first purchase for the Magpies. He impressed everyone during his opening games for the club, looking assured and always wanting to get forward from his left-back position. But after three months he eventually lost his place to a revitalised Davies and never saw first-team action again. Moving into the lower divisions, Peter found regular action at Southend (151 app) and Darlington (108 app). In his much travelled career Johnson registered 460 senior matches winning promotion on three occasions.

Appearances & Goals:
Debut v Watford (h) 1 November 1980
FL: 16 app 0 gls
FAC: 4 app 0 gls
Total: 20 app 0 gls

Honours:
FL div 3 prom 1992/FL div 4 prom 1985, 1987.

JONES Roger 1976-1977

Goalkeeper
5'11"
b. Upton upon Severn, 8 November 1946

Career: Portsmouth jnr Aug 1963, prof Nov 1964/Bournemouth May 1965 £5,000/Blackburn Rovers Jan 1970 £30,000/UNITED March 1976 joint deal with G Oates £100,000/Stoke City Feb 1977 free/ Derby Co July 1980 £25,000 (Birmingham City loan 1981-82)/York City Aug 1982 £5,000 to May 1985, becoming asst-coach/Sunderland asst-coach Nov 1988 to May 1993/Later becoming Swindon Town kit-manager 2000.

With a reputation as one of the top 'keepers in the lower divisions during his era, Roger Jones followed United's new manager Gordon Lee from Ewood Park to Tyneside. Capped by the young England line-up when with Bournemouth, Jones went onto break Blackburn's goalkeeper appearance record with 272 games (subsequently topped by future United coach Terry Gennoe) once saving two spot-kicks in a single fixture for Rovers. Although showing excellent judgement and a mighty throw or kick out, Jones was unlucky with injuries. He was dogged by wrist, knee and shoulder knocks at St James' Park, his shoulder injury being severe enough that United refused to pay Blackburn the previously agreed fee. Considered to be a touch injury prone, he lost his place on Tyneside to Mick Mahoney and was allowed to leave once Gordon Lee had departed. Despite being freed by the Black'n'Whites, Roger confounded everyone at Gallowgate by playing on for another eight years, including good spells with Stoke City, Derby and York. All told Jones amassed almost 800 senior outings in his career and was skipper of the Minstermen when they won the Fourth Division title. Following a brief spell as a coach, he concentrated on a decorating business in the Potteries. He returned to the game as Swindon's kit-manager in 2000 and remained for over a decade with the Robins, also running a hostel for the club's young players.

Appearances & Goals:
Debut v West Ham United (h) 13 March 1976
FL: 5 app 0 gls
Others: 2 app 0 gls
Total: 7 app 0 gls

Honours:
2 Eng u23 app 1968/FL div 3 champs 1975/FL div 4 champs 1984/FL div 2 prom 1979/PFA ToS (d3) 1974, 1975, (d4) 1984.

JULIUSSEN Albert Laurence 1944

Inside-right
6'0"
b. Blyth, 20 February 1920

Career: Blyth Spartans/East Cramlington Jnrs/ Huddersfield Town Oct 1938 (Blyth Spartans war-guest 1939-40)(Bradford Park Avenue war-guest 1939-40)(Mossley war-guest 1939-40)(North End Jnrs Dundee) war-guest 1941)(Dundee Utd war-guest 1941-45)(UNITED war-guest 1943-44)/Dundee Aug 1945 £2,000/Portsmouth March 1948 £10,500/ Everton Sept 1948 £10,500/Consett player-manager/ Berwick Rangers Aug 1951/Dundee Utd 1953/Brechin City Dec 1953.

Of Scandinavian extraction and the son of a Norwegian fisherman, Albert Juliussen was brought up in Northumberland and was a feared striker during wartime football, especially for Dundee United, then for their city rivals at Dens Park in the years after World War Two. A terrace favourite with a shoot-on-sight policy, he had a great left foot and possessed deadly goal-poaching, netting almost 100 for Dundee United and over a century goals for their neighbours in three years. That explosive record saw him move south to Portsmouth for a big fee of £10,500, but Juliussen never quite recaptured his deadly form south of the border and his equally high profile move to Goodison Park ended in failure, Everton placing such a high fee on his head with no takers that he decided to move back to the North East with Consett. The former Northumberland Boys player took to the St James' Park field on a single occasion during season 1943-44, facing Hartlepools United. Once in two successive Scottish League fixtures during March 1947 he found the net no fewer than 13 times; seven goals against Dunfermline and six against Alloa! During the hostilities Bert served with the Black Watch regiment stationed in Perth. He was a regular selection for the many strong wartime representative matches, hitting the target on six occasions for the Scottish Command in a match against the Army during 1942 and seven times against the RAF in 1945.

Appearances & Goals:
Debut v Hartlepools United (h) 11 March 1944 (WC)
War: 1 app 0 gls
Total: 1 app 0 gls

Honours:
Scot trial app 1942/SL div 2 champs 1947/FLN (WLg) champs 1945 (1 app).

KADAR Tamas 2007-2012

Centre-half
6'1"
b. Veszprem (Hungary), 14 March 1990

Career: Zalaegerszegi TE (Hng) 2004/Bolton Wand trial 2007/UNITED trial Dec 2007, pmt Jan 2008 (Huddersfield Town loan 2010-11) to June 2012/ Portsmouth trial July 2012/Roda JC (Neth) Aug 2012 free/Diosgyori VTK (Hng) loan 2013-14, pmt June 2013.

One of several young players brought to Tyneside from the Continent as part of a development programme to find first-team regulars, Tamas Kadar was spotted in Hungary playing with the Zalaegerszegi club near the Slovenian and Austrian border. Arriving at St James' Park as a 17-year-old, he operated at centre-back or full-back for the Magpies. A Hungarian Under-21 international, he was to graduate to his country's full squad during May 2008 and receive his first cap in February 2012 against Lithuania. However, Kadar was never able to claim a regular spot in United's eleven. After playing in several friendly matches for the Black'n'Whites and reaching the first-team bench in December 2008, he broke his leg during a Tyne versus Wear reserve derby at Eppleton, then when fit suffered a bad hamstring tear. Tamas did fill vacant slots during the 2009-10 Championship winning season, deputising in the back line, but rarely got close to regular Premier League action, having to be satisfied with the occasional selection for the substitute's bench. He moved to Holland in 2012, but was rarely in the manager's plans at Kerkrade for Roda.

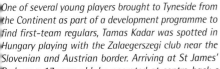

Appearances & Goals:
Debut v Huddersfield Town (h) 26 August 2009 (FLC)
FL/PL: 6(7) app 0 gls
FAC: 2 app 0 gls
FLC: 3 app 0 gls
Total: 11(7) app 0 gls

Honours:
15 Hng caps 2012-date/16 Hng u21 app/Hng sch-youth app/FL ch winner 2010.

KARELSE John 1999-2003

Goalkeeper
6'3"
b. Kapelle (Netherlands), 17 May 1970

Career: W Welmeldinge (Neth)/AGOW Apeldoorn (Neth)/NAC Breda (Neth) 1985/ UNITED Aug 1999 £750,000 (Denizlispor (Trk) trial Aug 2000) to May 2003/AGOW Apeldoorn (Neth) June 2003/Retired July 2004, later becoming NAC Breda (Neth) gkp-coach, then asst-coach July 2005 and joint-caretaker-manager Sept 2010, becoming manager 2011 to Oct 2012.

A lengthy servant in the Dutch Eredivisie with NAC Breda, John Karelse was rated highly by fellow countryman Ruud Gullit when United's new boss decided he needed to advance his goalkeeping cover for the start of the 1999-2000 season, even though the club had three experienced custodians in Given, Harper and Perez. Spending £750,000 on the tall and composed 'keeper, the 29-year-old filled in while Shay Given was out injured. John deputised and ended up conceding seven goals, including a taxing debut against Southampton at The Dell, seeing four goals go past him in only 20 minutes, turning the game after Newcastle had led by a single goal. Karelse had impressive stats in Holland, a consistent last line of defence, but John rarely got an opportunity following his opening for the Magpies. He was fated to be third choice behind Given and Harper and after three seasons on the sidelines he returned to the Netherlands. Back in the Dutch league he continued where he had left off before his sojourn to England, becoming coach and later manager at the Rat Verlegh stadium in Breda where he had totalled over 400 senior games.

Appearances & Goals:
Debut v Southampton (a) 15 August 1999
PL: 3 app 0 gls
Total: 3 app 0 gls

Honours:
5 Neth u21 app/Neth sch-youth app.

KEATING Albert Edward 1923-1925

Inside-right
5'9"
b. Swillington Common, near Leeds, 28 June 1902
d. Fenham, Newcastle upon Tyne, 18 October 1984

Career: Prudhoe Castle/UNITED Jan 1923 £130/ Bristol City Nov 1925 £650/Blackburn Rovers May 1928/Cardiff City Feb 1931/Bristol City Nov 1932/ North Shields July 1933/Throckley Welfare cs 1935.

Bert Keating was a consistent reserve goalscorer for United; not one perhaps blessed with cultured ball talents, but who had the football brain to get into dangerous positions around the danger zone making sure he could find the net. Bert was a versatile player and deputised for Cowan and Clark in the schemer's role, as well as for Neil Harris at centre-forward. On a close-season tour with the Magpies during 1924 he netted two goals against Barcelona and in the Barcelona Cup challenge against Everton. He later did exceptionally well at Ashton Gate, poaching 54 goals in 104 outings, a willing poacher when Bristol City won promotion during season 1926-27. Keating did well at Ninian Park too, scoring 26 goals in only 48 games for Cardiff. His brother Reg, was on United's books without getting into the senior eleven and was a much travelled forward of the same era, replacing his brother in the Bluebirds' line-up in Wales. After retiring, Keating became a local referee, running a tobacconists and grocer's business in Newcastle.

Appearances & Goals:
Debut v Huddersfield Town (h) 9 February 1924
FL: 12 app 3 gls
Total: 12 app 3 gls

Honours:
FL div 3(S) champs 1927.

K

KEEBLE Victor Albert William 1952-1957

Centre-forward
6'0"
b. Colchester, 25 June 1930

Career: King George YC (Colchester) 1945/Colchester Casuals 1945/Arsenal amat, jnr July 1946/Colchester Utd amat May 1947, prof Sept 1950/UNITED Feb 1952 £15,000/ West Ham Utd Oct 1957 £10,000/Retired due to injury 1960/Colchester Utd development manager 1968/Chelmsford City secretary & development manager 1968, becoming general manager/Retired 1994.

An ex-rugby player as a teenager, Vic Keeble's form for Football League newcomers Colchester United greatly impressed Newcastle's celebrated scout Bill McCracken during the early part of season 1951-52 when he registered an impressive 17 goals. Keeble grabbed 65 goals in 81 matches all told in non-league and senior competitions at Layer Road and earned a contract at St James' Park, signing for the club when he was six months into his National Service in the army. A persistent and exuberant leader, not pretty to watch yet certainly effective and who often mixed it with opposing defenders on the field. Keeble was a menace in the air and as one enthusiast once remarked "would even take a penalty with his head"! Nicknamed 'Camel' by his colleagues, he was deputy to Jackie Milburn or George Hannah at inside-forward during his early days at Gallowgate, but when Milburn moved to outside-right, Vic took over the Number 9 shirt and had two brilliant seasons in 1954-55 and especially during 1955-56 when he claimed 29 goals. He once netted four times against Huddersfield Town and included was a run to Wembley in which Keeble found the net on five occasions. A back complaint stalled his United career and he soon afterwards joined the Upton Park set-up, Vic proceeding to be a key factor in West Ham's return to the First Division, totalling 49 goals in 80 senior games for the Hammers. Keeble retired aged 29 due to the same prolapsed disc injury and worked for a local newspaper before concentrating on a long period in charge of administration for Chelmsford City. Vic had a spell working for the Essex Chronicle and Colchester Express before retiring. Residing in Essex, his son, Chris joined the Ipswich Town staff in 1995 and later appeared for Colchester United like his father. Vic once scored a 12 minute hat-trick for the U's against Plymouth during March 1951.

Appearances & Goals:
Debut v Chelsea (a) 12 March 1952
FL: 104 app 56 gls
FAC: 16 app 11 gls
Others: 1 app 2 gls
Total: 121 app 69 gls

Honours:
FAC winner 1955/FL div 2 champs 1958.

KEEGAN Joseph Kevin OBE 1982-1984, 1992-1997, 2008

Striker & Manager
5'8"
b. Armthorpe, near Doncaster,
14 February 1951

Career: Enfield House YC/Pegler's Brass Works 1966/Lonsdale Hotel/Scunthorpe Utd jnr Dec 1967, prof Dec 1968/ Liverpool May 1971 £33,000/SV Hamburg (Ger) June 1977 £500,000 (Cape Town City & Cape Town Spurs (SA) guest cs 1978)/Southampton July 1980 £400,000/UNITED Aug 1982 £100,000/Retired May 1984/UNITED manager Feb 1992 to Jan 1997/Fulham Chief Operations Officer Sept 1997, becoming manager May 1998/England manager Feb 1999 to Oct 2000/ Manchester City manager May 2001 to March 2005/UNITED manager Jan 2008 to Sept 2008.

When Kevin Keegan first joined United during the summer of 1982, the whole of Tyneside was set alight with Keegan-mania. Newcastle were languishing in the Second Division at the time, and manager Arthur Cox saw the former England skipper, and one of the game's superstars, as the man to lead the Magpies back to Division One. Keegan was from Geordie stock, his father hailed from Hetton-le-Hole, while his grandfather Frank Keegan was a past mine disaster hero at West Stanley. Kevin took immediately to Tyneside and its supporters and with his unique charisma, a special bond between player and fan resulted and helped significantly in revitalising Tyneside's fortunes. Being rejected as a youngster after trials at Coventry, the dynamic Keegan developed into a world-class star at Liverpool (323 app, 100 goals), netting twice as the Anfield club lifted the FA Cup at the expense of United in 1974. He was an influential figure for England too, skippering his country 31 times and scoring 21 goals during his 63 appearances. Operating up front, or in midfield, Kevin possessed control, awareness, the ability to create and combine with others, as well as a deadly finish. He had lots of courage, was a hard worker on the pitch and importantly was a winner, hating to lose at anything he did. Keegan appeared on almost 800 occasions in senior football netting 274 goals. As captain, he guided Newcastle to promotion then announced his retirement, afterwards employed in television and promotion work, residing for much of the time in Marbella. Then, with the Magpies in a dire predicament during 1992 as a club takeover came to its head, he was appointed manager at St James' Park, his first taste of the football hot-seat. Teaming up with new Chairman, Sir John Hall, the powerful duo started to turn Newcastle United into one of the country's mega-clubs. Keegan again acted as a catalyst and United's fans rallied to the call. His judgement as a manager was first-class and Kevin fashioned a series of celebrated line-ups packed with players comfortable on the ball and who wished to play the game in a flamboyant manner. The First Division title was secured in style and then the Premiership crown was only narrowly missed, Keegan's side finishing as runners-up in 1996. Newcastle had been transformed into a club to rival Manchester United as England's finest. Following the huge disappointment of not securing that first Premier League trophy, Keegan was even more determined as the 1996-97 season began, and showed it by spending over £15m, a new world record fee, for Alan Shearer. Yet in the background the conversion of the club into a PLC was to have a detrimental effect on United's boss, as did the mounting pressure to succeed. Just when everything seemed to be looking good, United surging to the top of the table by November, he ran into disagreement with the club's Board over the strategic way forward for the club and Keegan resigned during January 1997. The news was a monumental shock. Keegan's legacy as a boss over a near five-year period was exceptional. Kevin had perhaps achieved more than any other manager in United's history. Returning to St James' Park as the Pied Piper Geordies were to happily follow in their thousands, he rescued the club from the brink of the old Third Division, rapidly secured promotion to the Premiership in style, built a marvellous side dubbed 'The Entertainers' which missed glory by a whisker, and made finishes of 3rd, 6th, 2nd and 2nd elevating the name of Newcastle United alongside some of Europe's biggest clubs. He moved on to take charge of Fulham, Manchester City and England with mixed success before Keegan renewed his special bond with the Toon Army, brought back 11 years later in January 2008, to a very different St James' Park under new ownership. Gallowgate was not quite the same, with Keegan and the new regime unable to create a working relationship and he departed after less than 12 months in charge during September 2008. An acrimonious dispute followed and that was Keegan's last job in football management, afterwards entering the media as a television presenter with ESPN. Kevin Keegan remains arguably United's finest ever signing, both as a player and as a manager. During his younger days, Keegan was also a successful pop singer, recording three singles during the Seventies while during his periods away from the game he developed and opened a Soccer Circus concept in Glasgow during 2006. For his services to football during his playing career, he was awarded the OBE.

Appearances & Goals:
Debut v Queens Park Rangers (h) 28 August 1982 (1 goal)
FL: 78 app 48 gls
FAC: 3 app 0 gls
FLC: 4 app 1 gl
Total: 85 app 49 gls

In Charge: 272 games
Debut v Bristol City (h) 8 February 1992

Honours:
3 Eng caps 1973-82/WdC 1982/1 unoff Eng app 1976/5 Eng u23 app 1972/1 Euro XI app 1983/FL champs 1973, 1976, 1977/PL runners-up 1996(m)/FL div 1 champs 1993(m), 2002(m)/FL div 2 champs 1999(m)/FL div 2 prom 1984/FAC winner 1974/FAC final 1977/EC winner 1977/EC final 1980/UEFAC winner 1973, 1976/ESC final 1977/WG Lg champs 1979/FoY 1976 (FWA), 1982 (PFA)/PFA ToY 1983, 1984/PFA ToS (d1) 1976, 1977, 1982, (d2) 1983, 1984/EFoY 1978, 1979/WG FoY 1978/Eng HoF/FL Legend/OBE 1982.

KEELEY Glenn Matthew 1974-1976

Centre-half
6'2"
b. Barking, Essex, 1 September 1954

Career: Ipswich Town jnr July 1970, prof Aug 1972/ UNITED July 1974 £70,000/Blackburn Rovers Aug 1976 £30,000 (Birmingham City loan 1982-83) (Everton loan 1982-83)/Oldham Ath Aug 1987 £15,000 (Colchester Utd loan 1987-88)/Bolton Wand Sept 1988 to April 1989/ Chorley Aug 1990/Colne Dynamoes 1990/ Clitheroe 1991/Chester City 1992/ Lancashire FA at Bolton Community coach 1997/Colne coach 2000/Football Development Officer for the English Federation of Disability c2001/Bolton Council Football Development Officer Feb 2005, becoming 'Get Into Football' officer at Bolton Community Leisure Trust Nov 2010.

Arriving at Gallowgate as a 19-year-old defender who was destined for the top, Glenn Keeley had only totalled a mere five senior games for Ipswich when United signed him for a substantial fee. However, manager Joe Harvey recognised potential to develop in Glenn who had stood out in youth internationals and Ipswich Town's FA Youth Cup victory. Keeley replaced Magpie skipper Bob Moncur and, although he made a few costly errors, as all youngsters do, Glenn was developing well, reaching the England Under-23 squad until a change in management saw new boss Gordon Lee discard him in favour of Aidan McCaffery. Keeley did, though, gain a place in the Black'n'Whites Wembley visit during 1976, but was transferred soon after, to Blackburn where he proceeded to have an exceptional stay at Ewood Park. Keeley spent 11 seasons with Rovers, many as captain, and clocked up 419 games being something of a cult figure to local supporters as he bonded effectively with future United coach Derek Fazackerly in Rovers' defence. His transfer from Tyneside afterwards resulted in court proceedings and a FA Inquiry between United and Blackburn. Keeley only played 30 minutes of football for Everton when on loan, being sent-off in a derby with Liverpool. Glenn's brother, Andy, turned out for both Sheffield United and Tottenham. On retirement Keeley managed a pub in Leyland, took a degree in sports rehabilitation at Salford University, later also lecturing in Sports Studies at Trafford College between 2003 and 2005 before becoming a football development officer. During 2012 he joined the Blackburn Trust with an aim of supporters taking control of the Ewood club.

Appearances & Goals:
Debut v Coventry City (h) 17 August 1974
v Sunderland (a) 3 August 1974 (TC))
FL: 43(1) app 2 gls
FAC: 8 app 0 gls
FLC: 10 app 2 gls
Others: 11 app 0 gls
Total: 72(1) app 4 gls

Honours:
Eng sch-youth app/FLC final 1976/FL div 3 prom 1980/FAYC winner 1973.

KEEN Errington Ridley Liddell 1926-1930

Left-half
5'8"
b. Walker, Newcastle upon Tyne, 4 September 1910
d. Fulham, London, July 1984

Career: Nuns Moor (Newcastle)/UNITED jnr 1926, prof Sept 1927/Derby Co Dec 1930 exch deal for H Bedford/Chelmsford City player-manager May 1938/ Colchester Utd Nov 1938/Hereford Utd player-manager July 1939 (Notts Co war-guest 1940-44) (Rochdale war-guest 1940-41)(Everton war-guest 1941-42)(Fulham war-guest 1941-42)(Millwall war-guest 1942-43)(Liverpool war-guest 1942-43)(Lincoln City war-guest 1943-44)(Charlton Ath war-guest 1943-44)/Leeds Utd Dec 1945/ Bacup Borough July 1946/Hull City Nov to Dec 1946/Egypt national coach 1947-48/ Denmark coach 1948/IFK Norrkoping (Swd) 1949/Besiktas (Trk) coach cs 1949 to 1950/Later coaching in Hong Kong.

A promising youngster with the club's Swifts team at St James' Park, Errington Keen, generally known as 'Ike', played only once in the first eleven, as deputy for Jimmy Naylor. That outing was against Derby County and the Rams were suitably impressed with Keen's potential that their ex-United boss George Jobey soon afterwards took him to the Baseball Ground. It was to the Magpies' regret that the blond-haired Keen developed into a marvellous half-back, talented on the ball and always driving forward, although tending to sometimes dally in defensive situations. The Tynesider was capped by England and played on 237 occasions for Derby, runner-up in the top-flight during 1935-36 with County. After retiring from the game, Ike coached for a few years, including guiding the Egypt national side to the 1948 Olympics in London. He then went into business in Derby, but later was declared a bankrupt when his company collapsed. He was related to James Keen (qv), who was also on United's books a few years earlier, and to Sam Graham of Hartlepools.

Appearances & Goals:
Debut v Derby County (h) 18 October 1930
FL: 1 app 0 gls
Total: 1 app 0 gls

Honours:
4 Eng caps 1933-37/Eng trial app 1933/1 FL app 1937/FLN2 champs (WLg) 1943.

KEEN James Frederick 1922-1923

Outside-left
5'7"
b. Walker, Newcastle upon Tyne,
27 November 1895
d. Darlington, September 1980

Career: Walker Celtic/Bristol City April 1920/ UNITED May 1922 £100/Queens Park Rangers May 1923/Hull City July 1924/Darlington June 1925/ Wigan Borough Aug 1925/Walker Celtic Oct 1926.

Uncle of England international 'Ike' Keen, James was a product of the Welbeck Road School in Newcastle's Walker district like his nephew and as a teenager before World War One worked in the Tyne shipyards. A noted professional sprinter in the region, he was extremely fast, the proverbial 'flier' on the touchline. Keen, who could operate on either flank, was only given an opportunity twice during season 1922-23 as reserve on either flank to Jimmy Low and Stan Seymour. He later had one good season with QPR, selected 32 times in their 1923-24 Third Division South campaign.

Appearances & Goals:
Debut v Birmingham (h) 6 September 1922
FL: 2 app 0 gls
Total: 2 app 0 gls

K

KEERY Stanley 1952-1957

Half-back
5'7"
b. Derby, 9 September 1931
d. Crewe, 7 March 2013

Career: Blackburn Rovers amat/Wilmorton/Shrewsbury Town Aug 1952/UNITED Nov 1952 £8,250/Mansfield Town May 1957 £2,500/Crewe Alex Oct 1958 to 1965.

Small, stocky and a tenacious midfielder who was an able stand-in during United's mid-Fifties era, Stan Keery's 20 outings were spread over five seasons, mainly as deputy to either George Hannah or Jimmy Scoular. Having something of a meteoric rise from basement football to the FA Cup winners, Keery perhaps had the misfortune that the Magpies' staff did not really decide his best role. He also appeared at centre-forward where he was a solid worker who foraged tirelessly for every kind of ball. At Gresty Road in Crewe, Stan became a key figure playing 282 matches for the Railwaymen. He later resided in that town, employed firstly as a bookmaker, and then for the Rolls Royce company in the accounts department for almost 19 years. He also coached a local Sunday league team in Crewe for several years.

Appearances & Goals:
Debut v Preston North End (a) 24 January 1953
FL: 19 app 1 gl
FAC: 1 app 0 gls
Total: 20 app 1 gl

Honours:
FL div 4 prom 1963.

KEIR Matthew 1893-1894

Outside-right
b. Old Kilpatrick, near Dumbarton, 23 February 1871

Career: Dalmuir Thistle/UNITED Oct 1893 to 1894.

Matt Keir was a lively Scot who arrived on Tyneside during the autumn of 1893 from Dalmuir Thistle on Clydeside as Newcastle entered the Football League competition. Making only a single appearance, as a replacement for Quinn, he sustained an injury on his debut against Notts County and wasn't selected again. Keir returned north of the border before the season was concluded.

Appearances & Goals:
Debut v Notts County (a) 14 October 1893
FL: 1 app 0 gls
Total: 1 app 0 gls

KEITH Richard Mathison 1956-1964

Right-back
6'0"
b. Belfast, 15 May 1933
d. Bournemouth, 28 February 1967

Career: Boy's Brigade/33rd Old Boys/Linfield amat, prof 1950 (Distillery (Belfast) guest Jan 1956)/ UNITED Sept 1956 £9,000/Bournemouth Feb 1964 £3,300/Weymouth Aug 1966 to his death.

A one time tinsmith, Dick Keith arrived on Tyneside as one of the most promising youngsters to come out of Ulster in the period immediately after World War Two. Performing in front of Stan Seymour at Windsor Park, he played out of his skin for Linfield and earned a move to England. Dick took over the role of the retired Bobby Cowell and was immediately handed a debut against Manchester United. He was an instant success and thereafter became a regular for seven seasons, partnering his fellow Irishman, Alf McMichael at full-back. It was an accomplished duo, one that also appeared at international level, including during Northern Ireland's positive World Cup campaign of 1958. Keith had a cool, assured manner on the field and attempted to play football from defence whenever possible. His polished style served the Magpies well, being captain of the club as his period at St James' Park came to an end following relegation in 1961.

Moving to Dean Court, Dick concluded his first-class career with Bournemouth and afterwards appeared for non-league Weymouth. He was tragically killed when only 33 years of age following an accident in a builder's merchants where he was employed as a warehouse supervisor. When dismantling an automatic garage door, Dick's skull was fractured and died soon afterwards.

(Note: Although certain sources have his middle name as Mathewson, United's official player ledger notes it as Mathison, having crossed out the former, while family history data also confirm this.)

Appearances & Goals:
Debut v Manchester United (h) 8 September 1956
FL: 208 app 2 gls
FAC: 11 app 0 gls
FLC: 4 app 0 gls
Total: 223 app 2 gls

Honours:
23 NI caps 1958-62/WdC 1958/1 NI B app 1958/4 NIL app 1956/NI sch-youth app/N Lg champs 1954, 1955, 1956/NI Cup winner 1953/NI FoY 1956.

KELLY David Thomas 1991-1993

Centre-forward
5'11"
b. Birmingham, 25 November 1965

Career: West Bromwich Albion jnr 1980/ Alvechurch/Walsall Dec 1983/West Ham Utd Aug 1988 £600,000/Leicester City March 1990 £300,000/UNITED Dec 1991 £250,000/ Wolverhampton Wand June 1993 £750,000/ Sunderland Sept 1995 £900,000/Tranmere Rovers Aug 1997 £300,000/Sheffield Utd July 2000 free/ Motherwell July 2001 free/Stoke City trial Dec 2001/Mansfield Town Jan 2002 free/ Derry City July 2002/Retired Sept 2002/ Tranmere Rovers asst-manager Oct 2002/ Sheffield Utd asst-manager cs 2003/ Preston North End asst-manager Sept 2004/Derby Co asst-manager July 2007 to Nov 2007/Nottingham Forest asst-manager Jan 2009 to June 2011/Walsall asst-manager Jan 2013/Nottingham Forest asst-manager Feb 2013 to March 2014.

Hugely impressive during United's last gasp battle to avoid relegation from Division Two in season 1991-92, David Kelly netted 11 vital goals and then proceeded to become the club's top goal-getter with 24 strikes when they earned promotion twelve months later. Not a spectacular striker, but a player's player, honest with lots of effort, deceivingly quick around the penalty area and able to take a chance on the ground or in the air. Kelly burst onto the scene as a teenager with Walsall, after converting 26 goals in season 1986-87 attracted the attention of top clubs and he moved to Upton Park. Kelly had his ups and downs at both West Ham, and later Leicester, but flourished under Kevin Keegan's inspirational management at Gallowgate. Alongside Gavin Peacock and later Andy Cole, Kelly became a successful front-line pivot before being surprisingly discarded as the Magpies entered the Premier League. Kelly was disappointed when he was allowed to leave, but United's boss had the plan to combine Cole with the finer skills of Peter Beardsley. Kelly netted a hat-trick in his last match against former club Leicester City, while he also grabbed three on his debut for the Republic of Ireland against Israel. In a lengthy career of almost 800 games and over 250 goals, David skippered Tranmere at Wembley in 2000 and as a coach was closely associated with boss Billy Davies at a number of clubs. Before turning professional at Fellows Park, David had trials with Wolves as well as Southampton and worked at the Cadbury's plant in the Black Country while Kelly appeared in the World Cup finals in the USA during 1994. Always popular with the Toon Army, he received what is a rare, stirring reception as a Sunderland player when playing for the red-and-whites in a derby against United.

Appearances & Goals:
Debut v Port Vale (h) 7 December 1991
FL: 70 app 35 gls
FAC: 5 app 1 gl
FLC: 4 app 2 gls
Others: 4 app 1 gl
Total: 83 app 39 gls

Honours:
26 Eire caps 1988-98/WdC 1990 (no app), 1994/1 Eire unoff app 1993/3 Eire B app 1990-95/Eire u21 & u23 app/FL div 1 champs 1993, 1996/FL div 3 prom 1988, 2002/FLC final 2000/Eire Cup winner 2002/PFA ToS (d3) 1987.

KELLY Dominic 1938-1946

Centre-half
6'1"
b. Sandbach, Cheshire, 23 June 1917
d. Croydon, 20 October 1982

Career: Selsdon Wand/Sandbach Ramblers/Leeds Utd amat 1933, prof Sept 1935/UNITED Nov 1938 £1,165 (Hereford Utd war-guest 1945-46) to March 1946 when he retired due to injury.

A well built centre-half of Irish decent, Dom Kelly was purchased after only a handful of games for Leeds to rival Jimmy Denmark for the stopper's position. An uncomplicated player at the back, he cleared his lines swiftly and was a powerful defender. But joining the Magpies just prior to the outbreak of World War Two, the 21-year-old saw his St James' Park career halted quickly when hostilities were declared. Kelly entered the army, serving in the Middle East with the Royal Signals where he appeared in many service fixtures. A great humorist, he returned to Gallowgate on peace being restored in an attempt to earn a new contract, but having suffered ligament damage when in the services, he struggled to reach fitness. The injury ended his career and Kelly joined the Newcastle police force during 1946 where he quickly rose to be part of the CID on Tyneside. His career in the force though deteriorated when he was demoted following a dispute, then he was discharged in 1957 following a conviction for theft. During the years after war, Dom also played cricket in the region, a strong batsman, good enough to represent Northumberland in the Minor Counties Championship during 1948. He also played club cricket for Benwell and the force side. On leaving the police, Kelly had a number of jobs on Tyneside from debt collector to office worker but his life quickly spiralled downhill being jailed in 1960 for embezzlement. A marriage break up saw Kelly move to London as the Sixties opened and he again went from job to job, at times sleeping rough in the capital, occasionally in more trouble with the police. Working as a porter at the small Winton's Hotel during 1968, Kelly had an altercation with the manager, was sacked, and took revenge by setting fire to the hotel on Christmas Eve. Tragically a young Spanish maid was killed in the fire which gutted the building. Kelly was arrested, then charged with manslaughter and arson. He was tried and in June 1969 was convicted and sent to prison for five years.

Appearances & Goals:
Debut v Coventry City (h) 4 February 1939
FL: 1 app 0 gls
War: 8 app 0 gls
Total: 9 app 0 gls

KELLY Gary Alexander 1981-1989

Goalkeeper
5'10"
b. Fulwood, Preston, 3 August 1966

Career: St Cecilia's (Longridge)/UNITED jnr Oct 1981, prof June 1984 (Blackpool loan 1988-89)/Bury loan Oct 1989, pmt Nov 1989 £75,000 (West Ham Utd loan 1993-94)/Oldham Ath Aug 1996 £10,000/Northwich Victoria cs 2002/Sheffield Utd March 2003 to May 2003/Leigh RMI Sept 2003, retired 2004, becoming asst-manager to Nov 2004.

Gary Kelly has a marvellous football pedigree; his brother Alan Kelly (jnr) was also a goalkeeper, for Sheffield United, while his father, Alan Kelly (snr), was a noted 'keeper for Preston and the Republic of Ireland. Graduating from the ranks during 1986 at St James' Park, Gary lifted the FA Youth Cup with the Magpies and claimed the Number 1 goalkeeper's shirt for season 1987-88 displacing Martin Thomas. As United reached eighth position in the First Division, Kelly showed he was an agile guardian, a good shot stopper, once saving two penalty kicks against Chelsea in February 1988. But his lack of height perhaps cost him a senior place in the top division and he was replaced by record purchase Dave Beasant. With Bury, Gary recorded nearly 300 matches, despite being on strike for a period over a wages dispute, and with Oldham, Gary also totalled a respectable number of games, 263 outings for the Latics. He once appeared for a Republic of Ireland line-up at Under-23 level and faced his brother in the Northern Ireland goal, while he achieved a similar unusual feat when Newcastle rival, Ulsterman Tommy Wright, was capped and faced Kelly across the field. Gary was unlucky not to win a full cap for the Republic, being on the bench in 1999-2000. Later in his career Kelly took a Business Studies degree, as well as earning a UEFA coaching licence. Kelly settled in his native Lancashire coaching local youngsters.

Appearances & Goals:
Debut v Wimbledon (h) 20 September 1986
FL: 53 app 0 gls
FAC: 3 app 0 gls
FLC: 4 app 0 gls
Others: 2 app 0 gls
Total: 62 app 0 gls

Honours:
1 Eire B cap 1990/1 Eire u23 app 1989/8 Eire u21 app/Eire sch-youth app/FL div 3 prom 1996/FAYC winner 1985/PFA ToS (d3) 1995.

KELLY John 1933-1935

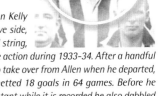

Centre-forward
5'8"
b. Hetton-le-Hole, Co Durham, 2 March 1913
d. Hetton-le-Hole, February 2000

Career: Hetton Jnrs/Burnley Oct 1930/UNITED April 1933 exch deal with T Miller/Leeds Utd Feb 1935 £1,150/Birmingham City Jan 1938/Bury May 1939 (Hartlepools Utd war-guest 1939-40).

Reserve to Jack Allen at St James' Park, John Kelly was an entertaining player in United's reserve side, scoring almost a goal a game for the second string, 22 in the club's first season of Central League action during 1933-34. After a handful of senior outings, John was given a chance to take over from Allen when he departed, but soon moved to Elland Road where he netted 18 goals in 64 games. Before he turned to football, Kelly was a butcher's assistant while it is recorded he also dabbled as a part-time magician.

Appearances & Goals:
Debut v Derby County (h) 9 September 1933
FL: 5 app 1 gl
Total: 5 app 1 gl

KELLY Peter Anthony 1973-1981

Right-back
5'7"
b. East Kilbride, 6 December 1956

Career: Fernhill Ath/UNITED jnr Aug 1973, prof July 1974/Retired due to injury June 1981/London City (Can) June 1981/Gateshead 1982/Dunston Fed briefly 1988, later having a period as Redheugh BC coach.

Blond-haired Peter Kelly was spotted by Newcastle's officials in a schoolboy trial at Skegness, this after he had been to Old Trafford during 1972. A pacy, attacking full-back, the Scot came into his own on the departure of Irving Nattrass and seemed destined for a long run in the Number 2 shirt following his teenage debut. During season 1978-79, Peter showed he could develop into perhaps another Nattrass, showing vivacious and entertaining bursts forward and the ability to cause danger in attack. He was selected for the Scottish Under-21 squad during 1976 but then tragedy struck for the young defender. Tearing his medial and cruciate ligament against Luton, the injury was serious enough to keep him sidelined for nine months, then unluckily he damaged the knee again and had carbon fibre ligaments inserted, a revolutionary operation which wasn't a complete success. As a result his knee was unstable and eventually caused his retirement from first-class football when approaching 25 years of age. Kelly was later part of the Gateshead side which lifted the Northern Premier League championship in 1983. He afterwards ran a newsagency business on Tyneside for 18 years, for a period with ex colleague Terry Hibbitt. Kelly also ran a sandwich business before becoming a support teacher at Castle View Academy in Sunderland.

Appearances & Goals:
Debut v Chester (h) 4 December 1974 (FLC)
FL: 31(2) app 0 gls
FLC: 3 app 0 gls
Euro: 1 app 0 gls
Others: 1 app 0 gls
Total: 36(2) app 0 gls

K

KELLY William Bainbridge 1911

Inside-right
5'9"
b. Newcastle upon Tyne, 1890 (Q4)
d. Newcastle upon Tyne, 19 April 1920

Career: Benwell Adelaide (Newcastle)/Balmoral (Newcastle)/Blaydon Utd/North Shields Ath May 1909/Watford Aug 1910/UNITED May 1911 £200/ Manchester City Nov 1911 £405/Blyth Spartans Aug 1913/Rochdale July 1914 to cs 1915.

Bill Kelly joined Newcastle's staff as a 20-year-old with a noted reputation in local football with the North Shields Athletic club, a strong North Eastern League side. That form gave him a chance in the Southern League with Watford, but he soon returned to Tyneside. Kelly started the 1911-12 season as a first choice, a replacement for the injured Shepherd, but dropped back to the reserve line-up once expensive signing Billy Hibbert arrived on Tyneside. Kelly was still a useful reserve and he later did well on his return to the region with Blyth Spartans following a stint with Manchester City where he appeared sparsely in Division One, although grabbing goals at reserve level. He settled in his native Newcastle to concentrate on business interests in the region. Kelly died early, being only 30 years of age.

Appearances & Goals:
Debut v Bolton Wanderers (a) 2 September 1911
FL: 6 app 0 gls
Total: 6 app 0 gls

KELSEY William John 1906-1908

Goalkeeper
5'11"
b. Boldon, Co Durham, 1887 (Q2)
d. Durham, 1952 (Q4)

Career: Boldon Jnrs/Boldon Star/UNITED Dec 1906/Boldon Colliery Nov 1908 to c1915.

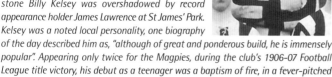

Like all reserve goalkeepers on United's books during the early years of the twentieth century, the thirteen-stone Billy Kelsey was overshadowed by record appearance holder James Lawrence at St James' Park. Kelsey was a noted local personality, one biography of the day described him as, "although of great and ponderous build, he is immensely popular". Appearing only twice for the Magpies, during the club's 1906-07 Football League title victory, his debut as a teenager was a baptism of fire, in a fever-pitched derby with Sunderland, a 2-0 defeat at Roker Park. He returned to Boldon after United purchased Tom Sinclair as preferred reserve to Lawrence.

Appearances & Goals:
Debut v Sunderland (a) 20 March 1907
FL: 2 app 0 gls
Total: 2 app 0 gls

Honours:
FL champs 1907 (2 app).

KENNEDY Alan Philip 1971-1978

Left-back
5'10"
b. Sunderland, 31 August 1954

Career: UNITED jnr July 1971, prof Sept 1972/ Liverpool Aug 1978 £330,000/Sunderland Sept 1985 £100,000/Hartlepool Utd Aug 1987/ Husqvarna FF (Swd) Sept 1987/ Hartlepool Utd Oct 1987/K Beerschot VAV (Belg) Nov 1987/ Grantham Town 1987-88 briefly/Sunderland 1987-88 briefly/Wigan Ath Dec 1987/ Northwich Victoria July 1988 to Dec 1988/ Colne Dynamoes Aug 1988 briefly/Enfield July 1989 to Dec 1989/ Wrexham March 1990 to Dec 1990/ Morecambe March 1991/Netherfield player-manager cs 1991 to Aug 1992/Radcliffe Borough July 1992/Netherfield Nov 1993/ Barrow July 1994 to June 1996.

Another of United's many self developed full-backs of renown, Alan Kennedy rapidly became a terrace favourite once he had tasted first-team action as a teenager. Brave and tough in the tackle, he never shirked at a 50-50 ball and possessed a natural instinct to break forward with direct runs at the opposition's box in a marauding style which had the crowd roaring in appreciation. Alan appeared in the 1974 FA Cup final as a 19-year-old after only a handful of senior outings and afterwards replaced Frank Clark in the left-back berth, giving United four years of quality service. Capped at Under-23 and 'B' level with United, he was also selected for a full England place during March 1975, but a knee injury prevented his appearance and he didn't get another chance to play for his country for almost a decade. By that time Kennedy had moved onto Liverpool, quitting Gallowgate after relegation in 1978. In 359 senior games for the Reds, Alan won plenty of honours, including two European Cups, netting winners in both finals against Real Madrid and Roma (in a penalty shoot-out). Nicknamed affectionately 'Barney Rubble' on Merseyside, he is one of the English game's leading medal winners, claiming over 10 major titles from his time at Anfield. Alan almost rejoined the Magpies in 1985, but chose Roker Park instead and was subsequently relegated to the third-tier with Sunderland. Leaving the Football League scene during 1990, Alan played on in non-league football, becoming a local coach and radio personality on Merseyside as well as an accomplished after-dinner speaker. His brother Keith Kennedy (qv) also played for the Magpies during the same era, both raised in the family home of Shiney Row with differing Newcastle and Sunderland allegiance. As a teenager Alan recovered from Osgood-Schlatter disease, suffering from a bone growth in both knees.

Appearances & Goals:
Debut v Stoke City (h) 10 March 1973
FL: 155(3) app 9 gls
FAC: 21(1) app 0 gls
FLC: 16 app 0 gls
Euro: 2 app 0 gls
Others: 16(1) app 1 gl
Total: 210(5) app 10 gls
(Void FAC: 0(1) app 0 gls)

Honours:
2 Eng caps 1984/7 Eng B app 1978-80/6 Eng u23 app 1975-76/FL champs 1979, 1980, 1982, 1983, 1984, 1986 (8 app)/FAC final 1974/FLC winner 1981, 1982, 1983, 1984/FLC final 1976/WsC final 1990/EC winner 1981, 1984/ESC final 1978, 1984/ICC final 1981 (sub no app), 1984.

KENNEDY Keith Vernon 1968-1972

Left-back
5'7"
b. Sunderland, 5 March 1952

Career: UNITED jnr Aug 1968, prof July 1970/Bury Oct 1972 £3,000/Mansfield Town Aug 1982 free/Barrow cs 1983/Morecambe 1985 to 1988/Netherfield/Colne Dynamoes.

Small but stocky and the elder of the two Kennedy brothers on United's books during the Seventies, Keith was the first to show. He claimed a Football League debut against Nottingham Forest in season 1971-72, but it was his younger brother Alan (qv) who excelled in the same position, leap-frogging over Keith to replace Frank Clark as the preferred left-back. Keith departed to a lower grade of football at Gigg Lane where he became a solid defender and a model of consistency, turning out in almost 500 games for the Shakers. He showed a gritty determination, being one of the very best in the lower divisions for a decade. After leaving the game Kennedy ran a greetings card business, residing near Bury in Greenmount. His son, Tom Kennedy, appeared as a left-back as well, for Bury, Rochdale, Barnsley and Leicester.

Appearances & Goals:
Debut v Nottingham Forest (a) 8 April 1972
FL: 1 app 0 gls
Total: 1 app 0 gls

Honours:
FL div 4 prom 1974/PFA ToS (d3) 1978.

KERR Brian 1997-2004

Midfield
5'10"
b. Motherwell, 12 October 1981

Career: Hibernian jnr 1994/UNITED jnr June 1997, prof Nov 1998 (Coventry City loan 2002-03, 2003-04)(Livingston loan 2003-04)/ Motherwell June 2004 free/Hibernian June 2007 to Sept 2008/Brighton, Oldham, Hamilton Acc, Livingston & Toronto (Can) all on trial late-2008/ Inverness Cal Thistle Jan 2009 free/Dundee July 2009 free/Arbroath July 2011 free.

Auburn-haired Brian Kerr was in the mix for midfield selection during season 2000-01 after graduating through United's youth system. He appeared in pre-season tour games during July 1999 and was neat and tidy at passing and linking play, as well as gritty and dogged. Kerr preferred a central role in midfield, but a twice dislocated shoulder stalled his career path with the Magpies. He moved to Motherwell during the summer of 2004 and proceeded to carve out a decent career in Scotland in over 250 games. He was first capped by his country during August 2002 when still at Gallowgate and played three times in the Scots' blue jersey.

Appearances & Goals:
Debut v Coventry City (a) 6 September 2000 (sub)
PL: 4(5) app 0 gls
FAC: 0(2) app 0 gls
Euro: 1(1) app 0 gls
Total: 5(8) app 0 gls

Honours:
3 Scot caps 2003-04/3 Scot B app 2003-06/1 unoff Scot app 2002/14 Scot u21 app 2003-04/Scot sch-youth app.

KERRAY James Ridley 1962-1963

Inside-forward
5'9"
b. Stirling, 2 December 1935

Career: Denny/Dunipace Rovers/Dunipace Jnrs/Raith Rovers Aug 1956/Dunfermline Ath Feb 1960 £2,000/Huddersfield Town Aug 1960 £8,000/UNITED Feb 1962 £10,000 plus L White/Dunfermline Ath April 1963 £3,000/St Johnstone June 1964 £6,250/Stirling Albion March 1966 £6,000/Falkirk Jan 1968 to cs 1969/Buxton/Ossett Town.

Jimmy Kerray could operate in either inside position and started at St James' Park alongside Ivor Allchurch as a replacement for George Eastham after several players had failed to adequately filled the schemer's role. A rather temperamental player, Kerray struggled to make a big impact on Tyneside at a time of rebuilding after relegation, although he netted plenty of goals in Scottish football and had been Denis Law's successor at Huddersfield. At Leeds Road the Scot claimed 13 goals over two seasons and alerted the Magpies, while his record of nearly 100 goals north of the border was evidence of his ability in front of the posts. At his best Kerray was a mobile forward, attacking from midfield and possessing a nice touch of the ball, his game being full of neat lay-offs and flicks with a potent shot. However, while he frequently dazzled he also often faded from the game, once noted as producing "a lot of eye-catching running without eye-catching success". Jimmy had trials at both Sunderland and Dundee before starting his football career with Raith. He later resided in the Huddersfield area, working for ICI and coaching local sides before moving back to his home of Stirling and living in Deanston.

Appearances & Goals:
Debut v Southampton (h) 10 February 1962 (1 goal)
FL: 38 app 10 gls
FAC: 1 app 0 gls
FLC: 1 app 0 gls
Total: 40 app 10 gls

KETSBAIA Temuri 1997-2000

Striker or Midfield
5'9"
b. Gali (USSR/Georgia), 18 March 1968

Career: Dinamo Sukhumi (USSR) 1986/Dinamo Tbilisi (USSR/Grg) Aug 1987/Anorthosis Famagusta (Cy) May 1991/AEK (Gr) June 1994/UNITED June 1997 free/Wolverhampton Wand Aug 2000 £900,000 to May 2001/Dundee Oct 2001/Anorthosis Famagusta (Cy) July 2002, becoming player-manager Jan 2004, manager June 2007 to April 2009/Olympiacos (Gr) manager May 2009 to Sept 2009/Georgia national manager Nov 2009.

Newcastle United manager Kenny Dalglish used a new transfer ruling to the club's total benefit when he landed established Georgian international Temuri Ketsbaia who had been one of the Greek league's top players. The £4 million rated midfielder moved from AEK Athens to Tyneside during the summer of 1997 on a free transfer after his contract had expired and the Magpies reaped the reward of the controversial Bosman ruling. With over 20 caps for his country at the time, the shaven head of Ketsbaia decided to join the Black'n'Whites after considering offers from several top European sides in Germany, Spain and Italy. With a football brain and non-stop engine, Temuri had little hesitation in selecting St James' Park, seeing the Premiership and Newcastle United as the place to be. With plenty of energy and an attacking urge from his midfield role, the Georgian national started his footballing career as a striker and made his mark in the old Soviet football network with the respected Dinamo Tbilisi club. Winning honours in his home country he moved abroad on the breakup of the USSR, to Cyprus and Greece, teaming up with AEK Athens in 1994. Although unpredictable and inconsistent, he was fast on and off the ball, and his weaving, penetrating runs from midfield gave United's side a boost, in the process becoming a new personality of the Premiership. Ketsbaia wasn't always an automatic choice, when on song he was an effective player, but was often frustrated at not getting into the starting line-up; none more so than against Bolton Wanderers during January 1998 when he arrived from the bench and netted a crucial goal then, as is now referred to, he 'did a Ketsbaia' with a bizarre celebration by kicking and attacking the advertising hoarding at the Gallowgate End in pure frustration. A popular character on Tyneside, many considered he was given a bit of a raw deal at St James' Park, and he left at the end of the 1999-2000 season after taking part in two FA Cup finals for the Magpies. Later Ketsbaia started a career as a coach, becoming his country's manager in 2009.

Appearances & Goals:
Debut v Sheffield Wednesday (h) 9 August 1997
PL: 41(37) app 8 gls
FAC: 8(8) app 4 gls
FLC: 1(1) app 0 gls
Euro: 7(6) app 2 gls
Total: 57(52) app 14 gls

Honours:
52 Grg caps 1994-2003/FAC final 1998, 1999/Gr Cup winner 1996, 1997/Gr Cup final 1995/Cy Lg champs 2005, 2008(m)/Cy Cup winner 2003, 2007(m)/Cy Cup final 1994/Grg Lg champs 1990, 1991/Grg FoY 1990, 1997.

KETTLEBOROUGH Keith Frank 1966

Midfield
5'8"
b. Rotherham, 29 June 1935
d. Sheffield, 2 November 2009

Career: Rotherham YMCA 1951/Grimsby Town trial 1953/Rotherham Utd Dec 1955/Sheffield Utd Dec 1960 £15,000/UNITED Jan 1966 £22,500/Doncaster Rovers player-manager Dec 1966 £12,000, being dismissed as manager May 1967, remaining a player/ Chesterfield Nov 1967 £6,000/Matlock Town player-coach Aug 1969, retired due to injury, becoming manager Nov 1971 to Oct 1972.

K

Keith Kettleborough was a wise short term purchase by manager Joe Harvey at a time when Newcastle were struggling to steer clear of the First Division relegation zone. Thirty years old and possessing a wealth of experience, the balding Kettleborough had an immediate impact on United's midfield, during his debut laying on both goals against West Ham to ensure the Black'n'Whites collected two needy points. His ability as a deep lying link-man, with accurate short and long passes, transformed the Magpies' performances and further valuable points were picked up to escape the drop. The Geordie fans took to Keith, appreciating his craft and skill which shone through as much as his unmistakable bald plate. Earlier during his career when showing top form with Sheffield United in 183 matches, Kettleborough was called up for England training during 1965 and 1966, part of Alf Ramsey's 'shadow squad'. Keith was also a fine club cricketer in Yorkshire, appearing for Rotherham Town CC and being a consistent run maker. Kettleborough lived in Wickersley near Rotherham and for a while ran a milk business before becoming a sports coach and clerk of works at Birkdale Prep School in Sheffield to his retirement during 1998.

Appearances & Goals:
Debut v West Ham United (h) 8 January 1966
FL: 30 app 0 gls
FAC: 2 app 0 gls
FLC: 1 app 0 gls
Total: 33 app 0 gls

Honours:
FL div 2 prom 1961.

KHIZANISHVILI Zurab Nodarovch 2009

Centre-half
6'2"
b. Tbilisi (USSR/Georgia), 6 October 1981

Career: Dinamo Tbilisi (Grg) cs 1998/Norchi Tbilisi (Grg) cs 1999/Lokomotivi Tbilisi (Grg) 2000/Arsenal, West Ham Utd & Fulham trial 2001/Dundee March 2001/Rangers June 2003 free/Blackburn Rovers loan Aug 2005, pmt April 2006 £500,000 (UNITED loan Sept 2009 to Dec 2009)(Reading loan 2009-10, 2010-11)/Kayserispor (Trk) June 2011 free to May 2014/Dinamo Tbilisi (Grg) cs 2014.

An experienced Georgian international of over 90 caps, Zurab Khizanishvili had played alongside Toon favourite Temuri Ketsbaia for his country and enjoyed success at Ibrox with Rangers. Brought to St James' Park from Blackburn Rovers on loan during the first half of the 2009-10 season as short-term cover across the back four, Zurab did his job in a satisfactory way, although at almost 28 years old he was at the wrong end of his career, at times lacking pace when matched against younger strikers. Khizanishvili stood in for Fabricio Coloccini during the autumn programme and was an adequate replacement as Newcastle headed towards the Championship league title. The Georgian, like Ketsbaia before him, had began his career with his country's top club before moving to Britain in an attempt to earn a contract. After trials at several clubs, he received a break with Dundee in Scotland and was so impressive that a move to Rangers followed, later being signed by Sam Allardyce for Blackburn. His father, Nodar Khizanishvili, appeared for the Soviet Union as a top defender.

Appearances & Goals:
Debut v Ipswich Town (a) 26 September 2009
FL/PL: 6(1) app 0 gls
Total: 6(1) app 0 gls

Honours:
93 Grg caps 1999-date/3 Grg u21 app 1999-2000/Grg sch-youth app/FL ch winner 2010 (7 app)/SC final 2003/SLC winner 2005 (sub no app)/Scot YPoY (SFWA) 2003.

KILCLINE Brian 1992-1994

Centre-half
6'2"
b. Nottingham, 7 May 1962

Career: Notts Co jnr 1978, prof April 1980/Coventry City June 1984 £60,000/Oldham Ath Aug 1991 £400,000/UNITED loan Feb 1992, pmt March 1992 £250,000/Swindon Town Jan 1994 £90,000/ Mansfield Town Dec 1995 free, becoming asst-coach/Halifax Town Oct 1997/Altrincham player-coach cs 1998 to Sept 1998/Later Huddersfield Town part-time asst-coach as well as coaching minor sides Noctorum Nomads, Cartworth Moor, Thongsbridge Utd.

One of the first tasks Kevin Keegan undertook on his appointment as boss of the Magpies was to tighten United's defence and give the side much needed leadership and character through the purchase of 29-year-old Brian Kilcline. Nicknamed 'Killer', and with the looks of a shaggy-haired marauding Viking, the powerful defender slipped into the heart of the defence showing a rugged, yet composed style at centre-half as the club foiled the Second Division trapdoor. His experience as captain did much to ensure Newcastle survived and then blossomed in 1992-93, although by that time he had made way for the emerging Steve Howey. Keegan noted that Brian "more than any other single player helped Newcastle United to stay up". It was at Coventry though that Kilcline had the best spell of his career making 211 appearances and skippering the Sky Blues to FA Cup victory. Although he perhaps was short of the finer skills, Brian led by example and was an outstanding defender, always grabbing his share of goals, netting over 50, before he headed for Tyneside. Born of Irish parents, Kilcline was a personality of the English game, characterised by his long hair, walrus moustache, and at Gallowgate, a ponytail; he was quite simply a fearsome sight to strikers. When he retired from the game at the end of the Nineties, Brian began refurbishing property, doing most of the work himself, then with his wife, the pair headed back-packing through India and Australasia, and a worthwhile book 'The Lion, The Witch & The Rucksack' related their adventure. He also completed a sailing course, gaining his skipper's ticket and also self-renovated a villa in the Algarve, letting it out for holiday breaks. When in the UK, Brian does some local coaching and media work, residing in Holmfirth in the Pennine hills.

Appearances & Goals:
Debut v Barnsley (h) 22 February 1992
FL/PL: 20(12) app 0 gls
FAC: 1(2) app 0 gls
FLC: 3(2) app 0 gls
Others: 5 app 0 gls
Total: 29(16) app 0 gls

Honours:
2 Eng u21 app 1983/FL div 1 champs 1993/FL div 2 prom 1981/FAC winner 1987.

KING George 1946-1948

Centre-forward
6'0"
b. Radcliffe, near Amble, Northumberland, 5 January 1923
d. Ely, 10 February 2002

Career: UNITED Aug 1946/Hull City March 1948 £750/ Port Vale April 1949/Barrow Feb 1950/ Bradford City Jan 1952 £3,000/Gillingham Oct 1952/Kings Lynn June 1954/Ely City player-manager June 1955.

Powerfully built at 6'0" and weighing over 13 stones, George King arrived at St James' Park after serving in the RAF and catching the eye in services games. With competition for forward positions fierce at Gallowgate just after the war, King had limited opportunities and was sidelined with injuries. Up against the likes of Milburn, Donaldson, Stobbart and Bentley, George had to be content with two outings during season 1946-47. Yet had King received a little bit of luck all young players need, his debut could have catapulted him onto a different career route. At White Hart Lane the big striker could easily have grabbed a hat-trick, but the chances went astray, then soon after was injured and out of action. King was left to scrape a career around the lower leagues, notably at Holker Street where he netted 38 goals for Barrow in 87 matches. One of three footballing brothers, goalkeeper Ray King (qv), was on United's books at the same time, and Frank King with Everton. George later resided in Cambridgeshire becoming a chiropodist once his days in charge of the local side Ely City had ended. He led the Robins to the First Round of the FA Cup in 1956-57 while during World War Two, King had a narrow escape onboard a troop ship which was torpedoed by a German U-boat. A good all-round sportsman, George was proficient as a cricketer and runner, and good enough to once play snooker star Steve Davis in an exhibition match.

Appearances & Goals:
Debut v Tottenham Hotspur (a) 14 September 1946
FL: 2 app 0 gls
Total: 2 app 0 gls

Honours:
FL div 3(N) prom 1949 (1 app).

KING John 1913-1920

Inside-forward
5'7"
b. Dykehead, Lanarkshire, c1894

Career: Renfrew/Shotts Utd/Partick Thistle April 1910/
UNITED June 1913 £600 (Dykehead war-guest 1915-
16)(Third Lanark war-guest 1915-16)(Motherwell war-
guest 1916-17)(Partick Thistle war-guest 1917-18)
(Hibernian war-guest 1918-19)/Resumed with UNITED
1919/Dykehead loan Feb 1920, pmt cs 1921/Clydebank
loan Oct 1921, pmt Feb 1922 £500 to 1926.

*Following good reports from scouts north of the border,
United's officials were impressed with the ball skills and
potent striking ability of slightly-built John King. With
Partick Thistle he became one of the hottest properties on
the Scottish beat, selected for inter-league fixtures and on
the verge of a full cap. Newcastle moved quickly to bring
King to Tyneside, although having a respectable record he
never hit it off with United's then critical crowd and rivalled Dixon and Smailes for
either of the schemer's channels. Once described as "a trier all the time", despite his
small stature he once played an entire game as a goalkeeper for United in 1915, after
selected 'keeper Bill Mellor was injured in the pre-match warm up. King took the shirt
and kept a clean sheet, United drawing the game 0-0 with Tottenham Hotspur. During
World War One, John served in the Scottish Rifles and played on occasion in the
Scottish leagues throughout the hostilities.*

Appearances & Goals:
Debut v Blackburn Rovers (a) 1 September 1913
FL: 54 app 8 gls
FAC: 7 app 2 gls
Total: 61 app 10 gls

Honours:
1 SL app 1913/Scot trial app 1913.

KING Raymond 1941-1946

Goalkeeper
6'1"
b. Radcliffe, near Amble, Northumberland,
15 August 1924
d. Bangkok (Thailand), 19 July 2014

Career: Amble ATC/Amble 1940/UNITED amat 1941,
prof April 1942 £10 (Wrexham war-guest)
(Wolverhampton Wand war-guest)(Chester war-guest
1944-45)/Leyton Orient Oct 1946 free/Amble
1947/Ashington 1948/Port Vale May 1949/Boston Utd
player-manager July 1957 £2,500/Poole Town
manager 1960/ Sittingbourne manager 1963/Oxford Utd trainer 1963 to 1965/
Southampton & Coventry scout/Luton Town youth manager Nov 1971, becoming
asst-physio to Dec 1973.

*Ray King was a promising heavyweight boxer in the army during the Second World
War, and was also highly rated as a goalkeeper by Newcastle, joining the Magpies as
a youngster and turning out in wartime football for United. He shared the Number 1
shirt with Tom Swinburne during season 1945-46 and received the nod for the
important two-legged FA Cup tie with Barnsley. King was a brave, but unlucky player
having a persistent problem with his wrists, initially suffering a break when guesting
for Chester and saving a Tommy Lawton spot-kick. With United, Ray broke his wrist
again when attempting to punch the ball clear, instead striking the crossbar; he played
on for all of 12 matches without realising the extent of the injury which ultimately
led to his release from Gallowgate. Then with Orient he fractured his other wrist,
remarkably the fourth break up to demob in 1947. Despite this recurring wrist
weakness, King bounced back to become a noted 'keeper in the lower divisions with
Port Vale, an important member of their 'Iron Curtain' defence, in a side which was
hailed as FA Cup giant-killers when they reached the semi-final during 1954. Ray
clocked up 275 games for Vale, he was capped at 'B' level for his country and was
reserve for the full side without getting a full cap. Brother of United's George King
(qv), Ray's second and elder brother, Frank (also a goalkeeper) appeared for Everton
and Derby. After retiring from the game, he resided in the Poole area and when out of
the football worked in sales, as a decorator as well as being a sports master and PE
instructor at the giant US Air Force base at Brize Norton for a period. King also started
a physiotherapist practice and later returned to his native Northumberland coastline
and settled in Amble practising Shiatsu, a form of physio treatment. King was also a
keen local cricketer and played the game wherever he lived. In later life he moved to
Thailand, living with his son.*

Appearances & Goals:
Debut v Barnsley (h) 5 January 1946 (FAC)
(v Sunderland (h) 25 May 1942 (FLN))
FAC: 2 app 0 gls
War: 31 app 0 gls
Total: 33 app 0 gls

Honours:
1 Eng B app 1954/2 FA app 1955/6 FA tour app 1956/FL div 3(N) champs 1954.

KINGHORN William John Darroch 1942

Outside-left
b. Strathblane, Stirlingshire, 27 February 1912
d. Liverpool, 1977 (Q1)

Career: Kirkintilloch Rob Roy/Pollock 1934-35/
Queen's Park Sept 1936/Liverpool April 1938
(Leicester City war-guest 1939-40)(Brighton
war-guest 1940-44)(Manchester City war-guest
1941-42)(UNITED war-guest 1941-42)(Leeds Utd
war-guest 1942-43)(Blackburn Rovers war-guest
1944-45)(Burnley war-guest 1944-45)/Resumed
with Liverpool 1945 to cs 1946.

*One of several personalities from Anfield to wear the black-and-white stripes during
wartime football, Billy Kinghorn had just established himself in Liverpool's ranks as
war clouds hovered across the nation in 1939. A past Scottish amateur international
winger with Queen's Park, Kinghorn joined the Merseyside club with a career in top
football at his feet. War though, stopped all that and he made only 19 appearances
for the Reds in first-class football. In the North East for a period during the war years,
he stepped in for Charles Woollett on the wing in each of his outings for United.*

Appearances & Goals:
Debut v Sheffield United (a) 14 March 1942 (FLN)
War: 2 app 0 gls
Total: 2 app 0 gls

Honours:
4 Scot amat app 1937-38.

KINGSLEY Matthew 1898-1904

Goalkeeper
5'11"
b. Turton, Lancashire, 1875
d. Atherton, Lancashire, 27 March 1960

Career: Edgeworth/Blackburn Rovers 1893/Turton/
Darwen May 1895/UNITED April 1898/West Ham Utd
May 1904 £50/Queens Park Rangers May 1905/
Barrow Sept 1906/Rochdale Oct 1907 to cs 1908.

*United's first capped England player when on the St James'
Park staff, Matt Kingsley took over the custodian's role
during season 1898-99, Newcastle's initial campaign in
Division One. Brought up in the twin communities of Turton
and Edgeworth, Kingsley joined the Magpies after 75
games for Darwen when they were a Second Division side. He was a Newcastle regular
for six seasons before Jimmy Lawrence arrived on the scene. Efficient at his game,
Matt was noted for his fisted clearances in the style of the day, and also for a habit
of continually swinging his arms to and fro as he was waiting for the action.
Somewhat hefty at 14 stones, Kingsley took part in the club's debut in the First
Division while the goalkeeper twice netted when playing in friendlies; against
Brampton in 1899 and Coventry during 1900. Matt was noted as the country's most
reliable custodian in 1901, when with the Hammers during 1904-05 he was once sent-
off for kicking a Brighton player, causing a crowd invasion and much debate. His
cousin was on the books of Bolton and Manchester City. Kingsley later resided in the
Blackburn area working as a foreman steamer in a bleach works.*

Appearances & Goals:
Debut v Wolverhampton Wanderers (h) 3 September 1898
FL: 180 app 0 gls
FAC: 9 app 0 gls
Total: 189 app 0 gls

Honours:
1 Eng cap 1901/Eng trial app 1901/3 FL app 1901-02.

K

KINSELLA John 1897

Inside-left
b. unknown

Career: [Dundee Harp July 1893/Dundee Hibs Oct 1894/Chatham March 1896]/Darwen Sept 1896/UNITED Feb 1897 to cs 1897.

Purchased from rival Second Division outfit Darwen mid-way through the 1896-97 season as a player with good pedigree, John Kinsella stood in for established names on two occasions as the club were striving to join the First Division. Despite being chaired by the critics, he was not held in esteem by the team committee and had departed by the summer. Kinsella had played alongside 'keeper Matt Kingsley in Lancashire. It is suspected he had a spell in Scotland after leaving Tyneside.

Appearances & Goals:
Debut v Walsall (h) 6 March 1897
FL: 2 app 0 gls
Total: 2 app 0 gls

KIRKCALDY James William 1904-1907

Left-half
5'10"
b. Newcastle upon Tyne, 8 November 1885
d. 1913

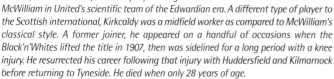

Career: Westwood/Northern Temperance (Newcastle)/UNITED Nov 1904 to May 1907 when he returned to local football/Kilmarnock trial Nov to Dec 1908/Huddersfield Town April 1909/Kilmarnock Nov 1909/Benwell Adelaide (Newcastle) c1910 to cs 1911.

A reserve player of remarkable stamina and appetite for the ball, James Kirkcaldy was a deputy to the great Peter McWilliam in United's scientific team of the Edwardian era. A different type of player to the Scottish international, Kirkcaldy was a midfield worker as compared to McWilliam's classical style. A former joiner, he appeared on a handful of occasions when the Black'n'Whites lifted the title in 1907, then was sidelined for a long period with a knee injury. He resurrected his career following that injury with Huddersfield and Kilmarnock before returning to Tyneside. He died when only 28 years of age.

Appearances & Goals:
Debut v Aston Villa (h) 24 March 1906
FL: 11 app 1 gl
Total: 11 app 1 gl

Honours:
FL champs 1907 (3 app).

KIRKMAN Alan John 1963

Inside-left
5'10"
b. Bolton, 21 June 1936
d. Bolton, 14 January 2011

Career: Bacup Borough/Manchester City amat 1954, prof Feb 1956/Rotherham Utd March 1959 £4,000/UNITED Sept 1963 £12,300/Scunthorpe Utd Dec 1963 £10,000/Torquay Utd July 1965/Workington Jan 1967 £1,700/Netherfield player-manager Sept 1968/Rossendale Utd 1970, retired 1972, becoming manager/Horwich RMI manager 1978 to Oct 1985 (in 2 spells).

Alan Kirkman scored twice on his debut for Manchester City and found the net on a regular basis for Rotherham, including a goal in the very first Football League Cup final during 1961. His record for the Millers was first-class, 63 goals in 170 games, form which had several clubs taking note of his ability in attack. Sturdy and able to snap up the opportunist goal, he joined Newcastle as part of manager Joe Harvey's rebuilding plans, albeit as a second choice after United's boss failed to land his colleague at Millmoor, Albert Bennett (who later did join United as well). Kirkman failed to settle on Tyneside and after a handful of outings was soon on the treatment table and his stay at Gallowgate is one of the shortest on record, moving to the Old Show Ground at Scunthorpe within four months of his arrival. On leaving the senior game, Alan lived in Bolton and was for a long period in charge of non-leaguers Horwich. He was also employed as transport manager for a local haulage company.

Appearances & Goals:
Debut v Southampton (a) 18 September 1963
FL: 5 app 1 gl
Total: 5 app 1 gl

Honours:
FL div 4 prom 1966/FLC final 1961.

KITSON Paul 1994-1997

Striker
5'10"
b. Murton, Co Durham, 9 January 1971

Career: Leicester City jnr July 1987, prof Dec 1988 (VS Rugby loan 1987-88)/Derby Co March 1992 cash-exch deal £1.35m/UNITED Sept 1994 £2.25m/West Ham Utd Feb 1997 £2.4m (Charlton Ath loan 1999-2000)(Crystal Palace loan 2000-01)/Brighton Aug 2002 free to May 2003/Rushden & Diamonds Sept 2003 free/St Alban's City trial Aug 2004/Aldershot Town Aug 2005/Rushden & Diamonds player-coach Jan 2006/Retired cs 2006, later becoming Spennymoor Town President June 2009.

For much of his stay at St James' Park, Paul Kitson was on the sidelines, often on the substitute's bench. Purchased for a big fee prior to the shock departure of Andy Cole, the Durham-born striker initially slipped into Cole's position at centre-forward, although not an out and out striker. Yet, Kitson performed with credit in season 1994-95, giving 100% effort and finding the net on 12 occasions in 31 full games. But the former Derby County star couldn't claim a place in the Magpie line-up once United had signed internationals Shearer, Ferdinand, Ginola and Asprilla. A product of Leicester's junior ranks, he made his debut as a teenager during season 1989-90 and went onto appear on 62 occasions for the Filbert Street club. A lean, nimble striker who was at his best feeding off a target man, Kitson was sharp around the box and worked hard, chasing and harrying defenders, a style appreciated by a Newcastle crowd always willing to applaud endeavour. Paul developed into a young England player under the guidance of Arthur Cox at the Baseball Ground where he totalled 131 games (49 goals) and he again found Cox an influence during his stay at Gallowgate. Leaving the Magpies, Kitson struggled with injury at both West Ham and Brighton, only registering 91 games over six seasons. Paul was a schoolboy trialist at Ipswich, however was not given a chance at Portman Road. He settled back in County Durham, for a period running a company developing and installing home entertainment systems.

Appearances & Goals:
Debut v Aston Villa (a) 1 October 1994 (sub)
PL: 26(10) app 10 gls
FAC: 6(1) app 3 gls
FLC: 3(2) app 1 gl
Euro: 0(1) app 0 gls
Total: 35(14) app 14 gls

Honours:
7 Eng u21 app 1991-92/Eng sch-youth app/PL runners-up 1996 (7 app), 1997 (3 app)/FL div 1 champs 2000 (6 app).

KLUIVERT Patrick Stephan 2004-2005

Striker
6'2"
b. Amsterdam (Netherlands), 1 July 1976

Career: ASV Schellingwoude (Neth)/Ajax (Neth) jnr 1984, prof 1990/AC Milan (It) July 1997 free/FC Barcelona (Sp) Sept 1998 £9m/UNITED July 2004 free/Valencia (Sp) June 2005 free/PSV Eindhoven (Neth) Aug 2006/OSC Lille (Fr) Aug 2007 to May 2008 when he retired/AZ (Alkmaar)(Neth) asst-coach July 2008/Brisbane Roar (Aus) coach Jan 2010/FC Twente (Neth) asst-coach June 2011, becoming also Netherlands asst-coach July 2012 to July 2014.

Patrick Kluivert was one of Europe's foremost players of his generation who enjoyed much success and plenty of controversy on and off the field during a headlining career, notably with Ajax (95 app, 49 goals), Barcelona (255 app, 120 goals) and for his country Holland. A dazzling player at his peak, being tall, lithe and exceptionally skilled on the ball, he faced the Magpies on three occasions in Barca colours and received respected adulation from the Geordie crowd each time. When his stay at the Camp Nou came to a conclusion during the summer of 2004 the Black'n'Whites were in the queue to offer him a crack at the Premier League. Joining the Magpies at the end of his glittering career which saw the Dutchman win an array of honours (including the Champions League when only 18 years of age) and not least becoming his country's most deadly marksman with 40 goals, Newcastle acquired Kluivert on a free, but with a substantial wage package in a reported £6m deal. The Magpies enjoyed attack options in 2004-05 of either Kluivert or Bellamy, or both, to play alongside Alan Shearer. Newcastle fans drooled at the prospect and the club had high hopes they had pulled off a massive coup. But that was not to be. Like many stars in the closing stages of their prime, Patrick picked up several niggling injuries and only managed 25 starts out of a possible 57 games, but still managed to show some of the brilliance in his locker; ability to hold the ball, turn quickly, set up chances with astute flicks or lay-offs, and hit the net. The Dutchman appeared in the UEFA Cup run and took the Magpies to the semi-final of the FA Cup with match winning goals against Chelsea and Tottenham. But to many his focus was elsewhere, either enjoying his final big pay-day and Newcastle nightlife or planning his career after football. Still, Tyneside saw a brief glimpse of one of modern football's finest before he moved back to the Continent in the summer of 2005 following only 10 months in the North East. Kluivert appeared in short periods for Valencia, PSV and Lille then began a coaching career. He is also a UEFA ambassador, while his father was also a professional footballer. His sons Justin and Quincy both joined the Ajax Academy.

Appearances & Goals:
Debut v Middlesbrough (a) 14 August 2004 (sub)
PL: 15(10) app 6 gls
FAC: 3(1) app 2 gls
FLC: 2 app 0 gls
Euro: 5(1) app 5 gls
Total: 25(12) app 13 gls

Honours:
79 Neth caps 1995-2004/WdC 1998/Neth sch-youth app/Neth Lg champs 1995, 1996, 2007/It Cup final 1997/Sp Lg champs 1999/CL winner 1995/CL final 1996/ESC winner 1995/WCC winner 1995/Neth YPoY 1995.

KNOX Thomas 1965-1967

Outside-left
5'9"
b. Glasgow, 5 September 1939

Career: St Francis Juveniles/East Stirlingshire jnr Sept 1957, prof June 1960/Chelsea June 1962 £5,000/UNITED Feb 1965 £10,000/Mansfield Town March 1967 £5,000/ Third Lanark 1966-67/ Northampton Town Nov 1967 £5,000/St Mirren June 1969/Hillingdon Borough Feb 1970/Tonbridge June 1972.

Tommy Knox followed his teammate at East Stirling, Eddie McCreadie, to Chelsea as a Scot with plenty of promise. While McCreadie blossomed in London, Knox didn't make an impression at Stamford Bridge. He played a bit-part in the Blues' promotion during 1962-63 then was given another opportunity when he arrived on Tyneside during United's Second Division trophy winning season of 1964-65. Arriving to rival the enigma of Trevor Hockey and Alan Suddick, the Glaswegian again found it hard to claim a regular place and after a brief run in each of the next two seasons, was discarded to join Mansfield. A tricky winger, rather than one with searing pace, Knox totalled 36 games for the Stags and afterwards had a spell with the Cobblers at Northampton. He briefly appeared for Third Lanark during their very last season of existence before liquidation in 1966-67.

Appearances & Goals:
Debut v Leyton Orient (a) 20 February 1965
FL: 24(1) app 1 gl
FLC: 1 app 0 gls
Total: 25(1) app 1 gl

Honours:
FL div 2 prom 1963 (6 app), 1965 (9 app).

KOENEN Fransiscus Leonardus Albertus 1980-1981

Midfield
5'8"
b. Waalwijk (Netherlands), 4 November 1958

Career: SV Hatert (Neth)/Nijmegen EC (Neth)/ Oldham Ath trial cs 1980/UNITED trial, pmt Aug 1980 £80,000/Exeter City trial 1981/ SV Hatert Jan 1981 free/De Treffers (Neth) 1982-83/KFC Diest (Belg) 1983/Vitesse SBV (Neth) 1984/De Treffers (Neth) 1986-87/GVV Veenendaal (Neth) 1988 to 1991/SV ARC (Neth) coach 1991/GVV Veenendaal (Neth) coach 1993 to 1995/VV de Batavan (Neth) coach 1997/VV Germania (Neth) coach 2004/ VV Rood Wit coach 2006/GVV Veenendaal (Neth) coach July 2008/RKH VV (Neth) coach June 2010.

After a short trial period at St James' Park, Dutchman Frans Koenen earned a contract showing neat skills on the ball and a sweet left foot from his midfield position. But the pace and rigours of Second Division English football was never suited to his style and after the opening weeks of the 1980-81 season the sturdily-built Koenen was dropped and selected more often than not for the Central League line-up. He picked up a knee injury which did not help his progress on Tyneside, nor did a change in management when Arthur Cox arrived at St James' Park. A past skipper of the Dutch Under-21 eleven, Frans returned to the Netherlands on a free transfer when he couldn't find another Football League side. He went onto have a lengthy career in the Low Countries as a player, notably with Veenendaal side GVV where he totalled over 100 games, and then coach with several minor clubs.

Appearances & Goals:
Debut v Sheffield Wednesday (a) 16 August 1980
FL: 11(1) app 1 gl
FLC: 2 app 0 gls
Total: 13(1) app 1 gl

Honours:
Neth u21 app.

KRISTENSEN Bjorn 1989-1993

Centre-half
6'1"
b. Malling (Denmark), 10 October 1963

Career: Belder (Den)/Malling (Den)/Horsens FS (Den)/ AGF Aarhus (Den) jnr 1982, prof Feb 1983/UNITED March 1989 £260,000 (Bristol City loan 1992-93)/ Portsmouth March 1993 £120,000/Aalborg BK (Den) July 1995 free/Aarhus Fremad (Den) 1997/AGF Aarhus (Den) commercial development director.

A respected and gifted player, Bjorn Kristensen appeared in over 200 games for top Danish side AGF before he moved across the North Sea. Capped by Denmark and known as 'Benny', the Dane showed United's supporters he was a composed defender who liked to use the ball and surge forward. Also able to play at full-back or in midfield, he was a likable character in the dressing-room and possessed plenty of experience, playing in the European Cup for his Danish club. Benny could also be a danger in attack with a stinging shot. Following two seasons as a regular with the Magpies, he suffered a serious knee-cap injury which put him on the treatment table for a long period, and at a crucial time during the Keegan led resurgence. When he was fit again, Kristensen wasn't part of the new manager's plans and he rejoined Jim Smith at Fratton Park claiming 90 games over three seasons. At the end of his career Benny played with Aalborg in the Champions League before moving into a new career in Denmark. Although he coached locally and worked for sports company Hummel as well as in the media for radio 100FM, Kristensen set up a head-hunter recruitment firm and in 2012 joined staff agency Assessit in Aarhus. He was also a councillor in that town for a time.

Appearances & Goals:
Debut v Aston Villa (h) 8 April 1989
FL: 71(11) app 4 gls
FAC: 6 app 0 gls
FLC: 3 app 0 gls
Others: 6(1) app 1 gl
Total: 86(12) app 5 gls

Honours:
20 Den caps 1987-93/12 Den u21 app/Den sch-youth app/Den Lg champs 1986/Den Cup winner 1987, 1988.

K

KRUL Timothy Michael 2005-date

Goalkeeper
6'3"
b. Den Haag (Netherlands), 3 April 1988

Career: Hvv RAS (Den Haag)/ADO Den Haag jnr 1998/ UNITED July 2005 (Falkirk loan 2007-08) (Carlisle Utd loan 2008-09).

Joining United as a 17-year-old youngster from Dutch football in the summer of 2005, Tim Krul worked his way through the club's ranks to challenge senior 'keepers Shay Given and Steve Harper. Making his debut in a difficult UEFA Cup match in Sicily and producing a wonderful display of shot stopping, Given's move to Manchester City gave the tall and agile Dutchman a real opportunity to press for a first-team place. Following United's return to the Premier League after a season's absence, Tim overtook Steve Harper as first-choice and became a regular selection for season 2011-12 and thereafter Krul quickly showed to a world-wide audience that he was a top 'keeper in the making, producing a series of stunning saves and consistency to go with his acrobatics between the posts. He also reached the full Dutch side in that landmark season, this after skippering his country's Under-21 line-up. Out of action for periods with knee and shoulder problems, Krul has become a much coveted talent. As a junior with the Magpies, Tim once saved a spot-kick in a FA Youth Cup match then went onto score in a penalty shoot-out. During the World Cup in Brazil, Krul made headlines in another penalty spectacular, this time at the very highest level. Coming on as a sub in the last minute of extra-time during Holland's quarter-final against Costa Rica, specifically for a penalty shoot-out, he ended up the hero saving two of the five kicks to help Holland win 4-3 on penalties.

Appearances & Goals:
Debut v Palermo (a) 2 November 2006 (UEFAC)
FL/PL: 119(3) app 0 gls
FAC: 6 app 0 gls
FLC: 9 app 0 gls
Euro: 8 app 0 gls
Total: 142(3) app 0 gls

Honours:
6 Neth caps 2011-date/WdC 2014/12 Neth u21 app/Neth sch-youth app/FL ch winner 2010 (3 app).

KUQI Shefki 2011

Striker
6'2"
b. Vucitrn (Yugoslavia/Kosovo), 10 November 1976

Career: KF Trepca (Sb)/KaPa-51 (Fin) 1991/MiKi (Fin) 1992/MP (Fin) 1994/ HJK (Fin) 1997/FC Jokerit (Fin) 1999/ Wolves trial Nov 2000/Stockport Co Jan 2001 £300,000/Sheffield Wed Jan 2002 £700,000/ Ipswich Town loan Sept 2003, pmt Nov 2003/ Blackburn Rovers July 2005 free/Crystal Palace Aug 2006 £2.5m (Fulham loan 2007-08)(Ipswich Town loan 2007-08)/TuS Koblenz (Ger) July 2009/ Swansea City Jan 2010 (Derby Co loan 2010-11)/ UNITED Feb 2011 free to June 2011/Oldham Ath Aug 2011 free/Hibernian Aug 2012 free to Jan 2013/FC Honka (Fin) manager Feb 2014.

When United concluded the record sale of Andy Carroll during January 2011 it was on the last day of the mid-season transfer window. As a result the Magpies were left short of striking talent, made worse by an injury to Shola Ameobi. Without a club, Shefki Kuqi breezed into Gallowgate as cover for the remainder of the 2010-11 programme. At 34 years old and with an interesting career, the Albanian-born but naturalised Finn, was a hugely likable character but rarely got a sniff of Premier League action with United. Not match-fit, he was kept on the bench for most of his stay, only to be used in dire need. Kuqi was called upon for fleeting moments of action as he appeared on six occasions from the bench for either Ameobi or Best. Capped over 60 times for Finland, at the high point of his career, the striker was an old fashioned centre-forward of the bustling style, powerful and gutsy. During his first period in England, Shefki impressed at Edgeley Park, then also at Hillsborough. Kuqi was also a firm favourite with Ipswich, recording 32 goals in 92 games. That strike-rate earned crack at the Premier League with Blackburn Rovers. He possessed a famous goal celebration too, diving full-length arms outstretched, but never witnessed in Magpie colours. United's deal was always a quick-fix for boss Pardew and Shefki left at the end of the season, going onto join Oldham Athletic and Hibs in a much travelled and varied career which saw the striker appear in the Champions League for Finnish side HJK. When 13 years old, Shefki's family had been granted asylum in Finland having fled Albania before the Balkan war erupted. His younger brother, Njazi Kuqi also played the game for several clubs in the UK, including Dundee and Birmingham. He is also a cousin of Daut Kuqi, another professional footballer. Shefki settled back in Finland, coaching the game, working for the media and noted as an ambassador for a sports betting company.

Appearances & Goals:
Debut v Blackburn Rovers (a) 12 February 2011 (sub)
PL: 0(6) app 0 gls
Total: 0(6) app 0 gls

Honours:
62 Fin caps 2000-10/8 Alb caps/FL ch winner 2011 (2 app)/Fin Lg champs 1997/Fin Cup winner 1998/Fin LC winner 1998.

LACKENBY George 1950-1956

Right-back
6'0"
b. Newcastle upon Tyne, 22 May 1931
d. Wallsend, 3 April 2004

Career: UNITED jnr May 1950, prof Oct 1950/ Exeter City Dec 1956 £1,500/Carlisle Utd July 1957 exch deal/Gateshead July 1959/ Hartlepools Utd Aug 1960/Ashington cs 1963 to c1965.

Tall and strong, George Lackenby was a play anywhere defender, who made his debut at right-half, then had to wait another four seasons before he gained an extended run in the side. He appeared extensively at right-back during the 1955-56 programme as a temporary replacement for the injured Bobby Cowell and was tenacious on the field, revelling in a conflict and at times stirred the crowd with his biting tackles, described in the press as showing an "aggressive form of defence". Once Dick Keith arrived for the 1956-57 season George found himself surplus to requirements and he moved to join Exeter City then to Carlisle where he appeared on 49 occasions. After experiencing demotion from the Football League with Gateshead (44 app), Lackenby moved to the Victoria Ground in Hartlepool and appeared almost 100 times before heading into non-league football. He later resided in Wallsend.

Appearances & Goals:
Debut v Tottenham Hotspur (a) 29 December 1951
FL: 19 app 0 gls
Others: 1 app 0 gls
Total: 20 app 0 gls

LAIDLAW James A 1900-1901

Outside-left
5'11"
b. Kirkhope, Selkirkshire, c1876

Career: Uphall Dec 1893/Burnley 1895 briefly/Leith Ath June 1896/UNITED Aug 1900 £10/Woolwich Arsenal Aug 1901/Broxburn April 1902/Bathgate August 1902/ Broxburn Shamrock Oct 1903.

The purchase of Jimmy Laidlaw was surrounded in controversy. United were fined a guinea (£1.05) and censored by the Football Association after approaching the player in Edinburgh without the permission of his registered club, Burnley, who apparently had signed for on a brief trip south from Central Scotland. Nevertheless, the Scot joined the Gallowgate staff and proceeded to become a useful utility forward for the 1900-01 season. Having played as a dangerous forward with the Leith club in the Scottish Second Division, scoring an impressive 40 goals in 60 games, he deputised for fellow Scots, Fraser and Macfarlane at either inside-left or on the wing as the Magpies challenged strongly for league title silverware. In London with Arsenal, Laidlaw had only three outings, but netted twice and made his debut in a capital derby meeting with Tottenham.

Appearances & Goals:
Debut v Stoke (h) 15 September 1900
FL: 10 app 3 gls
FAC: 1 app 0 gls
Total: 11 app 3 gls

LANG Thomas 1926-1934

Outside-left
5'7"
b. Larkhall, near Motherwell, 3 April 1906
d. Cleland, near Motherwell, 12 May 1988

Career: Larkhall Thistle/UNITED Oct 1926 £110/
Huddersfield Town Dec 1934 exch for W Bott/
Manchester Utd Dec 1935 exch deal/Swansea
Town April 1937 £550/Queen of the South Aug
1938 (Queen of the South war-guest 1940-41,
1942-43)(Motherwell war-guest 1940-41)(Albion
Rovers war-guest 1941-42)(Hamilton Acc war-
guest 1942-43)(Burnbank Ath war-guest 1943-
44)/Ipswich Town Oct 1946/Retired June 1947,
becoming Ipswich Town trainer for a period.

*Tommy Lang was signed by United while he was
still working on his father's fruit farm in
Lanarkshire. He was a noble little winger who was
an ideal team player. Following in the wake of Stan Seymour at outside-left, Lang
proved to be a splendid replacement. He had deft footwork with the ball, was accurate
with his crosses and possessed a style that saw him cut in from the flank to have a
shot at goal. United's official programme notes once described Lang in the words of
Kipling: "He's little but he's wise, he's a terror for his size." Tommy was a regular for
the club over seven seasons, and during 1931-32, the year of FA Cup glory, he was an
ever-present; in United's semi-final victory over Chelsea, Lang made one goal and
scored another to take Newcastle to Wembley. When Tommy moved to Old Trafford,
the Scot played a small part in their Second Division title success during 1935-36
while at Ipswich, Lang continued on as one of the game's veterans, turning out for
the Portman Road club as a 41-year-old during April 1947. His younger brother, James
Lang, appeared for Halifax Town.*

Appearances & Goals:
Debut v Cardiff City (a) 24 September 1927
FL: 215 app 53 gls
FAC: 14 app 5 gls
Others: 1 app 0 gls
Total: 230 app 58 gls

Honours:
FAC winner 1932/FL div 2 champs 1936 (4 app).

LARNACH Michael David 1977-1978

Striker
5'9"
b. Lybster, Caithness, 9 November 1952

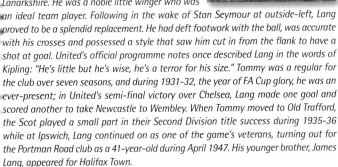

Career: East Stirlingshire 1971/Campsie Black Watch
(Stirling)/Clydebank July 1972/UNITED Dec 1977
£100,000/Motherwell Aug 1978 £70,000/Ayr Utd
Sept 1980 £30,000/Stenhousemuir Aug 1983/
Clydebank Nov 1983/Kilbowie coach c1986.

*Bill McGarry, after being recently installed as United's
boss, signed Mike Larnach in a bid to boost the
Magpies' shot-shy attack. Larnach, having plundered
29 goals for Clydebank in season 1976-77 and 76 up to that time for the Bankies,
along with Mark McGhee, were both purchased for large fees, and without apparently
being watched by Newcastle's boss. Larnach started the better of the pair in a black-
and-white shirt but, thrown into a relegation fight, the young Scot quickly faded and
was more often than not appearing in Central League football and destined for a
quick return north of the border. Mike holds an unhappy hat-trick serving United,
Clydebank and Motherwell when all three clubs were relegated. With Clydebank in
two spells, Larnach was a celebrated name at the Kilbowie Park ground increasing his
goals tally to over a century and registering 327 games. In the far north of the
country, Mike had a brief stay with Everton for trials and although Larnach's career
never took off in England, his record of 121 goals over 450 matches in Scotland is a
good one. He later worked in Central Scotland, at the giant petro-chemical plant in
Grangemouth as a power engineer.*

Appearances & Goals:
Debut v Liverpool (h) 31 December 1977
FL: 12(2) app 0 gls
Total: 12(2) app 0 gls
Honours:
Scot sch-youth app/SL div 2 champs 1976/SL div 1 prom 1977.

LAUGHTON Dennis 1973-1975

Centre-half
5'11"
b. Dingwall, Ross & Cromarty, 22 January 1948

Career: Ross Co/Morton Sept 1967/UNITED Oct 1973
£20,000/Retired due to injury June 1975/
Whitley Bay c1980.

*Dennis Laughton impressed United's officials when
appearing for Morton against the Black'n'Whites during
the Texaco Cup tournament, even when he netted an
own-goal at St James' Park in the deciding leg, although
he had scored at the 'right end' in Greenock. Moving to
Cappielaw from Highland football, Dennis spent seven
seasons with the Clyde club (100 app) and joined Newcastle as a reserve defender. He
was tall and positive, but was always going to be a stand-in to the likes of Bob
Moncur. Laughton also operated in midfield to add steel to the creative heart of the
side and, after picking up a bad knee injury, later moved to Gibraltar for a period
before returning to Tyneside where he became a Whitley Bay hotelier for a time. He
was later then employed for UK Plant in the region.*

Appearances & Goals:
Debut v Birmingham City (a) 8 December 1973
FL: 7 app 0 gls
FLC: 0(1) app 0 gls
Others: 1(1) app 0 gls
Total: 8(2) app 0 gls

LAVERICK J 1894

Full-back
5'9"
b. Tyneside

Career: Trafalgar/UNITED Jan 1894/Hebburn Argyle 1894 to c1897.

*A tough tackling defender, Laverick appeared in both full-back positions for United
during their earliest Football League seasons of 1893-94 and 1894-95. A reserve
signing from local football, he deputised for Rodgers and Jeffrey before moving to
Hebburn Argyle in 1894 where he remained for two seasons alongside the Tyne.
Laverick was part of a strong Hebburn line-up in the Northern Alliance.*

Appearances & Goals:
Debut v Northwich Victoria (h) 13 January 1894
FL: 4 app 0 gls
Total: 4 app 0 gls

LAW John Alfred 1937-1944

Left-back
5'8"
b. Felling, Gateshead, 24 January 1917
d. Sheriff Hill, Gateshead, 4 November 1986

Career: Washington Colliery/UNITED amat Aug 1937
to May 1944 free.

*With a robust style, John Law came into United's side
as a replacement for Bobby Ancell for a wartime
clash with York City during April 1940. One
commentator noted him as "a nippy full-back and
strong tackler". Law was on the brink of his Football League debut for United just
before the outbreak of the Second World War, his prospering career though was
wrecked by the hostilities. Law worked for George Angus and Company in Newcastle
during the conflict, and appeared frequently for the club in the Magpies' reserve eleven.*

Appearances & Goals:
Debut v York City (a) 17 April 1940 (FLNE)
War: 1 app 0 gls
Total: 1 app 0 gls

NEWCASTLE UNITED
The Ultimate Who's Who 1881-2014
169

L

LAW John H 1893-1894

Outside-left
b. Scotland

Career: [Clyde 1891]/Rangers Jan 1892/Bootle
Aug 1892/Everton 1893 briefly/UNITED Nov 1893 to
cs 1894/[Clyde Sept 1894/Arthurlie/Thornliebank
cs 1895].

*Newcastle's directors brought John Law to Tyneside
following a brief stay on Merseyside in an effort to
improve a flagging attack during the club's first ever
Football League season in 1893-94. Registered with
Rangers, the Scot joined the Magpies after a delay sorting
his transfer papers out due to the fact that he had
already joined Everton. Obtaining a release from Goodison Park, he quickly impressed
and the Newcastle Daily Journal noted that he had, "showed himself to be a splendid
exponent of the game". However, after a brief flurry of action over a few weeks, Law
lost his place and returned to Scotland. It is likely he is the footballer who appeared
with Clyde and other Scottish clubs.*

Appearances & Goals:
Debut v Walsall Town Swifts (a) 26 December 1893
FL: 8 app 2 gls
FAC: 2 app 0 gls
Total: 10 app 2 gls

LAWRENCE James 1904-1922

Goalkeeper
5'10"
b. Glasgow, 16 February 1885
d. Glasgow, 21 November 1934

Career: Partick Ath/Glasgow Perthshire (Hibernian
loan 1903-04)(Distillery (Belfast) loan 1903-04)/
UNITED July 1904/South Shields manager May 1922
to Jan 1923/Preston North End manager Feb 1923/
Karlsruhe (Ger) manager Aug 1925 to 1931/ Stranraer
director, becoming Chairman Sept 1933 to demise.

*In 14 seasons as first choice goalkeeper, the durable
and consistent Jimmy Lawrence amassed a record 496
senior outings for United, 507 in all competitive game.
He took part in all of the Magpies' Edwardian success;
one of only three players to do so (with Rutherford and
Veitch). Lawrence caught the eye of several clubs when appearing for Possilbank club
Glasgow Perthshire and arrived on Tyneside to replace Charlie Watts between the
posts. He initially gained the first-eleven goalkeeper's shirt when Watts was injured
during 1904, and kept it without any real rival until 1922! A student of the game's
tactics and something of an intellectual joker in the dressing-room, Lawrence was at
the very heart of United's great Edwardian line-up, an influential character on and
off the field. In the style of the day for a goalkeeper, Jimmy rarely caught the ball but
fisted away clearances and was always liable to make a stunning save, yet also a
costly error, two of which occurred in FA Cup finals; one writer of the day noted he
tended "to be nervy on big occasions". Always attempting to raise spirits, he was cool,
confident and extremely popular, both with Geordie supporters and his colleagues
while he had a liking for Tyne versus Wear matches; saving four penalties in derby
clashes. A keen politician of the game too, Jimmy was a leading figure in the Players'
Union at a time when the organisation was struggling to take-off. On the
Management Committee for several years, the Scot was appointed Chairman during
September 1921 to the summer of 1922 and was an outspoken voice against the
establishment in the Football Association and Football League headquarters. Lawrence
was a household name during the years up to World War One, taking part in the
Magpies' three successful title winning sides and five runs to the FA Cup final. Moving
to the Continent when he left Tyneside following a brief spell in charge of South
Shields, Jimmy led Karlsruhe to the regional title in his first season then followed that
success with other trophies in 1928, 1929 and 1931 as German football developed.
He afterwards lived in Stranraer, Chairman of the club to his sudden death in 1934.*

Appearances & Goals:
Debut v Manchester City (h) 1 October 1904
FL: 432 app 0 gls
FAC: 64 app 0 gls
War: 9 app 0 gls
Others: 2 app 0 gls
Total: 507 app 0 gls

Honours:
1 Scot cap 1911/Scot trial app 1911-12/1 Scot jnr app/FL champs 1905, 1907, 1909/FAC
winner 1910/FAC final 1905, 1906, 1908, 1911/NU HoF.

170

LEACH Thomas 1934-1936

Centre-half
5'10"
b. Wincobank, near Sheffield, 23 September 1903
d. Owston Ferry, near Gainsborough, 30 January 1968

Career: Retford Town/Blackburn Wesleyans/Wath
Ath/Rotherham Co trial May 1922/Liverpool Dec
1923 trial/Tankerton Utd/Sheffield Wed Oct 1925
£150/UNITED June 1934 £1,100/Stockport Co July
1936 £300/Carlisle Utd Feb 1937 exch deal/Lincoln
City Sept 1938 to cs 1939.

*A personality player, one of the big names of the
early Thirties era, Thomas Leach arrived at
Gallowgate as a vastly experienced international campaigner who had served Sheffield
Wednesday with distinction; 260 league and cup games over eight seasons in which
he helped the Owls to two First Division titles, alongside United striker Jack Allen.
With an iron frame and broad shoulders, he was appointed captain of the Magpies,
Leach being the pivot around which United's management planned to rebuild their
new side following relegation in 1934. Fast with an attacking urge from the back, for
a season that plan unfolded, Leach marshalling the Geordies, but in 1935-36, 'Tony'
as he was known, lost his place and moved down the football ladder. When at Carlisle
during season 1936-37 Leach was involved in scandal when he accepted incentives
from a director of Stockport and was banned for four weeks and heavily fined. At the
beginning of his career, as a Yorkshire pit-worker, Leach started the game as a centre-
forward and was rejected after trials at Liverpool and Rotherham County. Once retired
from football, Tony worked as a builder in the Hull area.*

Appearances & Goals:
Debut v Nottingham Forest (a) 25 August 1934
FL: 51 app 2 gls
FAC: 2 app 0 gls
Total: 53 app 2 gls

Honours:
2 Eng caps 1931/1 FL app 1931/FL champs 1929, 1930/FL div 3(N) champs 1937.

LEAVER Phillip Henry 1977-1982

Centre-half
5'10"
b. Wirksworth, Derbyshire, 19 October 1961

Career: UNITED jnr June 1977, prof July 1980/
Whitley Bay July 1982 free/Newcastle Blue Star
1983/North Shields Aug 1985/Washington Nov
1985/Blyth Spartans Nov 1985/Durham City/
Consett coach/later Crook Town coach June 2001.

*Locally brought up in the North East although born in
Derbyshire, Phil Leaver developed through United's junior
sides across the back four positions and earned a debut
in a League Cup tie during the last days of Bill McGarry's
reign as boss. With Arthur Cox installed as a new
manager, Leaver rivalled Kenny Mitchell and Bruce Halliday, two other United
youngsters, but didn't impress the new regime and was given a free transfer,
afterwards serving top local clubs as a player and coach. Leaver later took up teaching.*

Appearances & Goals:
Debut v Bury (h) 27 August 1980 (FLC)
FLC: 1 app 0 gls
Total: 1 app 0 gls

LEE Raymond 1943-1944

Goalkeeper
5'11"
b. unknown

*Ray Lee joined United as an amateur during September 1943, and remained one of
the club's goalkeepers for the 1943-44 wartime season. He was third choice 'keeper
behind Dave Cumming and Ray King, Lee appearing twice for the Novocastrians in
senior company. His debut was an absorbing thriller against Hartlepools United at
the Victoria Ground during October 1943 which ended in a 5-4 defeat for the Magpies.*

Appearances & Goals:
Debut v Hartlepools United (a) 30 October 1943 (FLN)
War: 2 app 0 gls
Total: 2 app 0 gls

LEE Robert Martin 1992-2002

Midfield
5'11"
b. Plaistow, London,
1 February 1966

Career: Pegasus (Havering) 1973/Sovereign (Havering)/ Park Heath/ Hornchurch 1981/ Charlton Ath amat, prof July 1983/UNITED Sept 1992 £700,000/Derby Co Feb 2002 £400,000/West Ham Utd Aug 2003 free/Oldham Ath Nov 2004 to Dec 2004/Wycombe Wand March 2005 to June 2006 when he retired.

During United's period of dramatic revival in the 1990s one player stood out as an influential figure, Robert Lee. Joining the Gallowgate set-up as a 26-year-old, Lee contributed hugely in the whole success story. And at £700,000, the Londoner proved to be perhaps United's best value-for-money signing in that era. After appearing on almost 350 occasions for Charlton Athletic in which he netted more than 60 goals, Lee was rated one of the best players outside the top division and was often tipped for a move to a bigger stage. With United, Rob was given that platform and he very quickly became one of the best performers in the new Premiership too. He first played an important role on the right wing, showing match-winning ability as Newcastle won the First Division title being very strong in possession, able to withstand tackles and shield the ball, as well as turn quickly. Lee then switched to a more conventional midfield role as United started life in the Premier League. Rob's worth to Newcastle became immense as he developed into a terrific box-to box midfielder. The Londoner was consistent, full of energy and work-rate, and showed considerable panache at linking up front and finding the net with either stinging drives or placement shots as he ghosted into the penalty box. He once scored an astonishing goal that never was against Brentford during March 1993; a 62 yard effort from within his own half which caught the Bee's 'keeper stranded, only for the referee to rule it out for offside! Lee was elevated to the England squad and scored on his debut for his country against Romania and at that time was, according to his manager, Kevin Keegan, the best all round midfielder in the country. Lee registered a marvellous hat-trick in the UEFA Cup against Antwerp, the first Magpie player to score three goals in European football. Additionally, one of his goals in that tie in Belgium is also the quickest on record in a European fixture for the club, after only 50 seconds. Brought up in London's East End with Tyneside blood, his grandmother hailing from Jarrow, before turning professional with Charlton, Rob had trials at West Ham and Spurs and worked as a shipping clerk as well as being a turnstile operator at The Valley. Although he was ostracised during Ruud Gullit's short term of office, Rob Lee was one of the club's 'blue-chip' players as they were termed, a model professional within the corridors of St James' Park. He served the club for 10 seasons until aged 36 and was given a testimonial against Athletic Bilbao during 2001 (18,189). Lee was skipper of the side at Wembley in the FA Cup final of 1998, as well as twice being runners-up in the Premier League and he appeared in the Magpies' first Champions League match. On leaving the game, Lee worked in the media and created a wealth management business based in London. He remains one of the club's finest midfield players of all time. His sons, Oliver and Elliot, both started a career with West Ham's Academy.

Appearances & Goals:
Debut v Middlesbrough (h) 23 September 1992 (FLC)
FL/PL: 292(11) app 44 gls
FAC: 27 app 5 gls
FLC: 22(1) app 3 gls
Euro: 27 app 4 gls
Others: 1 app 0 gls
Total: 369(12) app 56 gls

Honours:
21 Eng caps 1995-99/WdC 1998/1 Eng B app 1994/2 Eng u21 app 1986-87/PL runners-up 1996, 1997/FL div 1 champs 1993/FL div 2 prom 1986/FAC final 1998, 1999/PFA ToS (PL) 1996.

LEEK Kenneth 1961

Centre-forward
5'10"
b. Ynysybwl, near Pontypridd, 26 July 1935
d. Daventry, Northants, 19 November 2007

Career: Pontypridd YC 1950/Ynysybwl Jnrs c1951/ Northampton Town amat Aug 1951, prof Aug 1952/ Leicester City May 1958 £10,000/UNITED June 1961 £25,000/Birmingham City Nov 1961 £23,000/ Northampton Town Dec 1964 £9,000/Bradford City Nov 1965 £9,500/Rhyl Town player-coach Aug 1968/ Merthyr Tydfil/Ton Pentre Feb 1970/Retired June 1970.

Ken Leek arrived on Tyneside following Newcastle's relegation from the First Division as a new leader to replace the injured Len White. He made an immediate impact, netting a hat-trick on his first appearance, in a friendly against Aarhus. With a reputation as a more than useful goal-getter, Leek had been top scorer at Filbert Street, but had been controversially dropped on the morning of their 1961 FA Cup final, despite the fact that he had scored in every round to Wembley. Totalling 111 games (43 goals) for the Foxes, as a front runner with a robust style, Ken was looking to a new start at St James' Park. Sometimes played out of position at Gallowgate, to United's disappointment the Welshman never settled in the North East and he moved on after only four months of the season. He returned to the Midlands where he found the net on a regular basis at St Andrews over 120 matches, scoring twice in Birmingham's League Cup final victory during 1963 when he led the line with zest and opportunism. Ken totalled almost 200 goals in his career, 49 of which came in the two seasons after leaving United. Once retired, he was employed for the Ford Motor Company in Daventry, residing in the Northampton area. As a teenager, Leek worked in the South Wales mines before gaining a chance with Northampton Town. His grandson, goalkeeper Karl Darlow joined Newcastle in August 2014 from Nottingham Forest.

Appearances & Goals:
Debut v Walsall (h) 23 August 1961
FL: 13 app 6 gls
FLC: 1 app 0 gls
Total: 14 app 6 gls

Honours:
13 Wales caps 1961-65/WdC 1958 (no app)/1 Wales u23 app 1958/FLC winner 1963/FL div 2 prom 1965.

LEIGHTON William Alexander 1931-1938

Inside-right
5'9"
b. Walker, Newcastle upon Tyne, 8 December 1914
d. Southend, 1981 (Q4)

Career: Meldon Villa/Walker Park/UNITED amat July 1931, prof Feb 1932 £25/Southend Utd May 1938 £1,000 (Ekco Sports player-manager c1940)/Colchester Utd 1945 to 1946.

Well-built, but possessing a dainty touch on the ball, Billy Leighton made his debut for the Magpies during season 1932-33. A reserve to Harry McMenemy and Jimmy Richardson, he spent the next five years trying to find a permanent position in the side, but was always recognised as a second choice. Leighton enjoyed good runs during seasons 1934-35 (15 app) and 1936-37 (16 app) when his expert passing ability showed up well for a period in Second Division fare. He stepped down a division in an attempt to find regular first-team action, but war intervened and halted his progress, although he continued to appear for Southend during the hostilities.

Appearances & Goals:
Debut v Chelsea (h) 4 February 1933
FL: 39 app 8 gls
FAC: 1 app 0 gls
Total: 40 app 8 gls

L

LENNOX Malcolm 1895-1898

Outside or Inside-left
5'9"
b. Glasgow, 6 April 1874

Career: Cathkin Ath/Glasgow Perthshire/UNITED Oct 1895/
New Brompton July 1898/Third Lanark April 1901/
Morton Oct 1902.

*A Trojan individual and described as, "a splendid player",
Malcolm Lennox was spotted in the highly respected
Glasgow local football scene. Joining United during the
club's drive to get out of Division Two for the first time,
Lennox helped the Black'n'Whites to build a side that
succeeded and was a regular in the forward line for two seasons. Always willing to
work hard, Malcolm could also frequently get on the score-sheet, netting 13 goals
during his first season of 1895-96. However, by the time Newcastle were pushing for
promotion two years later, he was replaced by Sunderland's veteran John Harvey and
Lennox moved south. In Gillingham's pioneering side, New Brompton, Malcolm was
an ever-present in their Southern League outfit until a badly broken leg sustained in
a stormy derby match with Sheppey United put him out of action for part of 1899.
The injury was serious enough to make sure he was sidelined for a lengthy period,
moving back to Scotland in a bid to resurrect his career.*

Appearances & Goals:
Debut v Darwen (a) 9 November 1895
FL: 46 app 16 gls
FAC: 3 app 1 gl
Total: 49 app 17 gls

Honours:
FL div 2 prom 1898 (4 app).

LEWIS David Jenkin 1944

Outside-right or left
5'7"
b. Merthyr Tydfil, 2 February 1912
d. Llanharan, near Bridgend, 4 August 1997

Career: Gellifaelog Amateurs/Swansea Town amat
Sept 1930, prof Oct 1930/Bury May 1936/Crystal Palace
Oct 1937/Bristol Rovers Feb 1938/Bath City 1938
(Blyth Shipyard war-guest)(UNITED war-guest 1943-44)
(Llanelli war-guest)(Aberaman war-guest).

*Although club records note David Lewis being on Swansea's staff when he guested for
Newcastle, research indicates the player was actually with Bath City when he arrived
at St James' Park as a wartime guest and probably still registered with the Swans.
Twice capped by Wales during 1933 when he was earlier at the Vetch Field, Lewis was
a lightweight on the wing possessing a rasping shot and was, when on top form, quite
a handful with his tricky style. Despite being hampered by knee problems, Lewis
appeared with credit for Swansea on 125 occasions. He was known as 'Dai' and
nicknamed 'Jinky', during the Second World War he served with the Welsh Regiment
as a training instructor and spent a period in the North East. David appeared once for
the Magpies, against Gateshead at Redheugh Park. After the war, Lewis continued his
career in Welsh football and was later employed by ICI and as a postman in Swansea.*

Appearances & Goals:
Debut v Gateshead (a) 29 January 1944 (FLN)
War: 1 app 0 gls
Total: 1 app 0 gls

Honours:
2 Wales caps 1933/1 WsL app/WsC winner 1932.

LIDDELL Robert 1903-1911

Right-half
5'8"
b. Blaydon, near Newcastle upon Tyne, May 1877

Career: Heaton Rothbury/Westwood/UNITED amat Oct 1903,
prof May 1904 £10/Millwall Ath June 1911 £150 to 1915.

*United's reserve team skipper, Bob Liddell stepped in for half-
back stars Colin Veitch, Alex Gardner and Peter McWilliam on
and off over five seasons, including during the Magpies' title
victories in 1906-07 and 1908-09. Stocky and a power on the
field, he was also an expert penalty taker and when in the*

---

*capital with Millwall, was good enough to be chosen for the Southern League select
eleven. Liddell had a rewarding period alongside the Thames, totalling 138 appearances
for the Londoners. After World War One, Bob returned to Tyneside.*

Appearances & Goals:
Debut v Wolverhampton Wanderers (a) 17 March 1906
FL: 14 app 2 gls
Total: 14 app 2 gls

Honours:
4 SnL app 1914-15/FL champs 1907 (1 app), 1909 (5 app).

LIGHTFOOT Lawrence 1943-1946

Outside-left
5'9"
b. Waterhouses, Co Durham, 1923

Career: Waterhouses Home Guard/UNITED amat July 1943, prof Sept 1943/
Consett July 1946.

*Operating at both outside-left and occasionally outside-right, Lawrie Lightfoot shared
the Number 11 shirt with Charles Woollett during the Football League North wartime
season of 1943-44. His debut occurred in a tussle with Bradford Park Avenue in
September 1943, and although he was on Newcastle's staff to the end of the conflict,
it was Woollett and later Tommy Pearson, as well as George Hair, who pushed him
out of the reckoning and into local non-league football. It is noted he later worked in
a chemist's shop in Crook.*

Appearances & Goals:
Debut v Bradford Park Avenue (a) 11 September 1943 (FLN)
War: 10 app 0 gls
Total: 10 app 0 gls

LINDSAY Duncan Morton 1930-1931

Centre-forward
5'10"
b. Cambuslang, Glasgow, 21 March 1903
d. Ashton under Lyne, 29 November 1972

Career: Cambuslang Bluebell Juv 1922/St
Anthony's 1923/Cambuslang Rangers 1924-25/East
Fife Aug 1925/Cowdenbeath April 1926 (Heart of
Midlothian guest briefly, May 1930)/UNITED May
1930 £2,700/Bury May 1931 £525 (Ashton National
loan 1933-34)/Northampton Town trial Feb 1934/
Hurst March 1934/Hartlepools Utd July 1934/
Barrow July 1935/York City Oct 1935/Ashton
National July 1936/Hurst March 1938/Retired c1945.

*One of manager Andy Cunningham's replacements for Hughie Gallacher, fellow Scot,
Duncan Lindsay was a good player but like all other strikers at Gallowgate at the
time, was never on the same level as the immortal Gallacher. Sturdy and although
not a six-footer, Lindsay had created plenty of headlines north of the border, once
netting six goals for Cowdenbeath against Renfrewshire side, Johnstone in 1928, and
he scored over 90 senior goals all told for the Fifers in four seasons. Groomed by ex-
United player Scott Duncan at Cowdenbeath, United's scouts watched him on several
occasions and brought the quick and tenacious striker into the First Division where
he had an excellent, if short career in a black-and-white striped jersey. Given the
centre-forward's shirt for part of the 1930-31 season, Lindsay grabbed 12 goals in 19
games, good statistics by anyone's standards. But he fell out of favour and moved to
Bury where he continued his good strike-rate as he did with every club he appeared
for, netting over 250 senior goals during his career. After the Second World War,
Lindsay settled in Ashton under Lyne being employed with British Rail, part of the
team which rebuilt the London to Manchester line then working as a signalman. He
also assisted the local Droslyden club for many years. His cousin, Duncan Colquhoun,
appeared for a number of clubs, notably Southport.*

Appearances & Goals:
Debut v Sheffield Wednesday (a) 30 August 1930
FL: 19 app 12 gls
Total: 19 app 12 gls

LINDSAY James 1899-1900

Right-back
5'10"
b. Stockton on Tees, 28 August 1880
d. Manchester, 30 July 1925

Career: Stockton St John's/Jarrow 1898/UNITED amat April 1899/Burnley July 1900/Bury April 1901 to cs 1911 when he retired.

Employed as a blacksmith when on United's books as an amateur, Jimmy Lindsay, as could be expected of his trade, was a strong, tough and well-built defender. Brother of Billy Lindsay (qv), who was on United's staff at the same time, he was deputy to his elder brother at St James' Park and received few opportunities in the club's first eleven, either in league and cup action, or in friendlies. However, at Gigg Lane with Bury, Lindsay became a noted player, captain of the Shakers in the top flight and when they lifted the FA Cup during 1903. Appearing 271 times for the Lancashire club over nine seasons, he was a rock at the back. Marshalling Bury's defence with top-class ability, Jimmy ensured his team did not concede a goal on reaching the final, and then in the concluding game they romped home with a record 6-0 win against Derby County. Lindsay was also celebrated as something of a penalty-king, lashing spot-kicks home with ferocious power in many of his 29 goals for the club. On retirement, Jimmy became a licensee running The Eagle & Child public-house in Bury.

Appearances & Goals:
Debut v Glossop North End (a) 14 April 1900
FL: 2 app 0 gls
Total: 2 app 0 gls

Honours:
FAC winner 1903.

LINDSAY William Archibald 1898-1900

Right-back
5'11"
b. Stockton on Tees, 10 December 1872
d. Luton, 27 February 1933

Career: Stockton St John's 1888/Stockton 1888/Everton April 1893/Grimsby Town May 1894/UNITED Feb 1898 £150/Luton Town May 1900/Watford May 1903/
Luton Town April 1907/Hitchin Sept 1907 to May 1909.

A past captain of Grimsby Town, Billy Lindsay caught the eye of United's directors with his tenacious defending qualities, described by the Victorian press as a "powerful back". Appearing on 120 occasions for the Mariners, Lindsay moved to Tyneside and took part in the club's run-in to promotion, including the Test Match series, during 1898, and then became an automatic choice for the next two campaigns. Reliable and honest, Billy led United out for the Magpies' debut in Division One against Wolves and was captain for part of that historic first season in the top flight. At Luton he was also skipper and was at times a controversial character, once spotted at Kempton Races when he should have been playing for the Hatters! His younger brother, James (qv), was also on Newcastle's books during the same era. After leaving the game, Lindsay resided in Luton to his death.

Appearances & Goals:
Debut v Lincoln City (h) 26 February 1898
FL: 61 app 1 gl
FAC: 1 app 0 gls
Total: 62 app 1 gl

Honours:
FL div 2 prom 1898 (9 app)/SnL div 2 champs 1904.

LITCHFIELD Eric Brimley 1937-1943

Outside-right
5'8"
b. West Derby, Liverpool, 21 September 1920
d. Cape Town (South Africa), 23 July 1982

Career: Bedford Town/UNITED amat July 1937, prof Feb 1939 to 1943 (Hartlepool Utd war-guest 1939-40)(Leeds Utd war-guest 1941-42)(Reading war-guest 1942-43)(Millwall war-guest 1942-43)(York City war-guest 1943-44)(Northampton Town war-guest 1943-44).

The son of a clergyman, Eric Litchfield was a young budding star on United's books before the outbreak of the Second World War. Recognised as a "promising talent", he took part in Central League football, but his career was torn apart by the five year conflict. His two senior wartime fixtures for the Magpies occurred during seasons 1939-40 and 1942-43 before he served in South Africa during the war. As a guest player for Northampton, he once scored four goals in a 9-1 victory over Nottingham Forest. A former cricketer for Northumberland (1942-43), in 1951 Eric emigrated, moving back to South Africa where he became a sports journalist and later assistant Sports Editor on the Rand Daily Mail.

Appearances & Goals:
Debut v Huddersfield Town (a) 11 November 1939 (FLNE)
War: 2 app 0 gls
Total: 2 app 0 gls

LITTLE John 1927-1928

Right or Left-back
5'8"
b. Dunston, Gateshead, 18 September 1904
d. Southport, 5 July 1988

Career: Leeholme Jnrs/Shildon Ath/Crook Town 1926/UNITED Jan 1927/Southport May 1928 free/Chester April 1933/Le Havre AC (Fr) player-trainer Sept to Nov 1935/Northampton Town Jan 1936/Exeter City May 1938 to 1939 (Southport war-guest 1939-40, 1940-41)/Fleetwood Hesketh/High Park.

John Little was employed as a fitter and mechanic in a local Tyneside colliery when he joined United's staff during the club's Football League title winning season of 1926-27. Known as 'Jack', he was a reserve to Alf Maitland and Tom Evans at St James' Park and played in both full-back roles before moving in an attempt to gain regular first-team action. Little developed into one of the lower divisions best equipped defenders, serving Southport especially well during their Football League years. He was in the Sandgrounders eleven when they met the Magpies in the 1932 FA Cup, a three game tussle which ended with a 9-0 United victory. Jack clocked up 251 senior appearances in a sure and fearless manner for Southport before and during the war. After a period in local Lancashire football, he resided in the west coast resort employed at a local gas works for almost 30 years.

Appearances & Goals:
Debut v Cardiff City (a) 24 September 1927
FL: 3 app 0 gls
Total: 3 app 0 gls

L

LITTLE Richard 1912-1919

Right-back
5'8"
b. Ryton, near Gateshead, 30 May 1895

Career: Clara Vale Jnrs/Jarrow Croft/UNITED May 1912 £50/Hamilton Acc Aug 1919 £100 (Cowdenbeath loan 1921-22)/Motherwell June 1922/Morton June 1929/ Dunfermline Ath Oct 1930/Glentoran Jan 1933/ Newry Town 1933-34.

A product of Tyneside's junior leagues, Little was recognised as a "stout little performer" by the media of the day. A good man to have in reserve, Dick was an expert penalty taker in United's reserve side and he performed in a brave and honest manner whenever called upon to deputise for household names, McCracken or Hudspeth. But in the main, Little had to be content with North Eastern League football and, due to the First World War, didn't get much opportunity to sample senior football elsewhere until he joined Motherwell where he proceeded to clock up more than 150 games. During the hostilities Dick served as an able seaman in the Royal Navy.

Appearances & Goals:
Debut v Liverpool (a) 26 December 1912
FL: 3 app 0 gls
War: 4 app 1 gl
Total: 7 app 1 gl

Honours:
[NI Cup winner 1933].

LITTLEFAIR James 1900-1904

Outside-left
5'8"
b. Cambo, Northumberland, March 1876
d. Wideopen, near Newcastle upon Tyne, 16 June 1958

Career: Allendale Park/Burradon Ath/UNITED April 1900/Burradon Ath Sept 1904 to cs 1909.

The local newspaper correspondent of the day wrote that Jim Littlefair was, "a dainty little winger", a player who had been quite a handful in Tyneside football at the turn of the century. A former colliery lad, raised in Burradon, he was given a chance by United's directors, but only managed two outings, both in season 1900-01 as a stand-in for Fraser and Niblo. Jim did, however, pick up medals with United's reserve eleven as they lifted the Northumberland Senior Cup and Northern Alliance silverware during seasons 1900- 01 and 1901-02. On leaving the game, Littlefair returned to the pit where he had worked as a youngster, becoming traffic manager at Burradon Colliery and later Seaton Burn mine. He was for 33 years secretary of Burradon Working Men's Institute, residing in Wideopen.

Appearances & Goals:
Debut v Sheffield Wednesday (h) 6 April 1901
FL: 2 app 0 gls
Total: 2 app 0 gls

LIVINGSTONE Archibald 1935-1938

Inside-right
5'8"
b. Pencaitland, Lothian, 15 November 1915
d. Edinburgh, 12 August 1961

Career: Musselburgh Lewisvale c1932/Ormiston Primrose/Dundee/UNITED May 1935 £35/Bury June 1938 £500 (Rochdale war-guest 1939-40) (Leeds Utd war-guest 1941-42)(York City war-guest 1942-43)(Liverpool war-guest 1942-43) (Wrexham war-guest 1942-45)(Middlesbrough war-guest 1942-43)(Accrington Stanley war-guest 1944-45)(Brentford war-guest 1944-45)(Fulham war-guest 1944-45)/Everton May 1946/Southport June 1947 £1,000/Glenavon player-coach Aug 1948/Dundee 1949 to 1950/Worksop Town.

Although more at home in the inside-right berth, Archie Livingstone was an entertaining footballer who appeared in both inside channels for United, as well as at centre-forward. Small and tricky, with a lovely body swerve on the ball, Livingstone joined United after a spell as an apprentice slater in Scotland and had a good run in Newcastle's first-eleven during season 1936-37 when he totalled 15 matches. But St

James' Park was over-spilling with competition at the time, and Archie rivalled the likes of Harry McMenemy and Ed Connelly to start with, then Jimmy Richardson and Stan Docking, while by the time England international Ray Bowden had arrived, the Scot was resigned to a move elsewhere to further his career. During the Second World War Archie served with the Lancashire Fusiliers as a PT Instructor as well as working in an aircraft factory, and curiously his footballing career blossomed during this time when he was able to guest for a number of clubs in wartime football. Packing a tremendous shot, during 1943 he bagged seven goals in a single match for Wrexham against Tranmere. In that year he also appeared for the Scotland Army XI against England. Following the conflict, Livingstone resided back in his native Lothian, returning to his pre-football trade of a slater and plasterer in the Ormiston area.

Appearances & Goals:
Debut v Sheffield United (a) 23 November 1935 (1 goal)
FL: 33 app 5 gls
Total: 33 app 5 gls

Honours:
FLN2(WLg) champs 1943 (1 app).

LOCKEY James C 1895-1899

Right-back
5'10"
b. Newcastle upon Tyne, 4 January 1874
d. Ashington, 31 July 1955

Career: St Thomas' (Newcastle)/Caxton (Newcastle)/ Trafalgar (Newcastle)/Willington Ath/UNITED July 1895/Grimsby Town Feb 1899/UNITED May 1899 briefly/New Brompton June 1899/Gravesend Utd Aug 1900/New Brompton June 1901/Sittingbourne Aug 1902/Grays Utd Aug 1903/Sittingbourne July 1904/Hebburn Argyle cs 1906.

James Lockey was hugely successful at juvenile level but didn't make a big impression on the Football League circuit with either United or with Grimsby, but he was recognised as a celebrated local character on Tyneside, before and after his spell at St James' Park. A Northumberland County player, Lockey stood in for Billy Lindsay in the controversial Test Matches during United's promotion to Division One during 1898, but only received a single opportunity in the First Division before being transferred south. A biography from 1902 noted "he is a sure kick, and can always be relied upon" while another recorded he "shines best when severely pressed". Prior to signing professional, Jim was a brass finisher by trade.

(Note: Some sources including the FA and Football League registers spell his surname Lockie, however the club's official record notes, Lockey.)

Appearances & Goals:
Debut v Stoke (a) 23 April 1898 (FL Test Match)
FL: 3 app 0 gls
Total: 3 app 0 gls

Honours
FL div 2 prom 1898 (2 app).

LOCKIE Alexander James 1940

Centre-half
5'10"
b. South Shields, 11 April 1915
d. [South Shields], 25 March 1974

Career: South Shields YMCA Jnrs/South Shields St Andrew's YC/Reyrolles/Sunderland Sept 1935 (North Shields war-guest 1939)(UNITED war-guest 1940-41)/Notts Co Sept 1946 to c1947/South Shields manager.

Tall, strong and commanding in the air, Alex Lockie was described by a colleague as being able to "tackle like a tank". A draughtsman in a Tyne shipyard during the war, he was a regular for Sunderland in 1938-39, but then appeared only occasionally for the red-and- whites after war was declared, totalling 50 games all told for the Wearsiders. He moved to the other Magpies in Nottingham on peacetime football being restored and totalled 26 games for County. His single outing in United's eleven was as deputy to Jimmy Denmark for a trip to face York City in November 1940.

Appearances & Goals:
Debut v York City (a) 23 November 1940 (FLN)
War: 1 app 0 gls
Total: 1 app 0 gls

LOGAN James 1895-1896

Centre-forward
5'9"
b. Troon, Ayrshire, 24 June 1870
d. Loughborough 25 May 1896

Career: Ayr FC 1889/Sunderland Aug 1891 (Ayr FC loan 1891-92)/Aston Villa Oct 1892 £30/Notts Co Sept 1893 £15/Dundee March 1895/UNITED Sept 1895/Loughborough Jan 1896 £10 to death.

James Logan holds a celebrated place in football's history, being one of only a handful of players to have grabbed a hat-trick in an FA Cup final, for Notts County against Bolton during 1894. His performance on that day was outstanding; one writer of the day noting that he gave "one of the most wonderful exhibitions ever given by an individual in a big game". A prolific and cunning goal-getter before the turn of the century, the Scot failed to claim a regular place in Sunderland's emerging side due principally to illness, but managed to score goals for Villa and especially Notts County where he registered 37 in only 56 games. Twice a bit-part player in Championship winning squads, the stocky Logan started his days wearing a Newcastle shirt in devastating mood, netting in each of his first four games with his brand of direct running for goal. But he quickly fell out of favour, never getting on too well with the club's directors, and Logan moved on within a few months of his debut. Sadly, only two years after his moment of glory in the country's biggest game, he died when only 25 years of age after appearing for Loughborough against Newton Heath in April 1896. Without kit, which failed to turn up, Jimmy played in torrential rain in his own clothes and had to wear the same attire afterwards. Known for being vunerable to ill-health, he developed a chill which turned into pneumonia and claimed his life, a sudden and shock demise at the time. Logan also scored on his debut for Scotland, his only cap for his country. The roadway leading to Loughborough FC's ground at The Dome is named after him, James Logan Way. His brother, Peter Logan, turned out for Bradford City, and appeared against United in the FA Cup final of 1911.

Appearances & Goals:
Debut v Loughborough (h) 7 September 1895 (1 goal)
FL: 7 app 5 gls
FAC: 2 app 3 gls
Total: 9 app 8 gls

Honours:
1 Scot cap 1891/Scot trial app 1891/FL champs 1892 (2 app), 1894 (4 app)/FAC winner 1894.

LORMOR Anthony 1985-1990

Centre-forward
6'1"
b. Ashington, 29 October 1970

Career: North Shields/Wallsend BC/UNITED jnr July 1985, prof Feb 1988 (Norwich City loan 1988-89)/ Lincoln City Jan 1990 £25,000 (Halifax Town loan 1993-94)/Peterborough Utd July 1994 free/ Chesterfield Dec 1994 free/Preston North End Nov 1997 £130,000 (Notts Co loan 1997-98)/Mansfield Town July 1998 £20,000/Hartlepool Utd Aug 2000 £30,000 (Shrewsbury Town loan 2001-02)/ Kettering Town & Halifax Town trials July 2002/ Telford Utd Aug 2002/Retired due to injury Jan 2003/Sutton Town player-coach Dec 2003/Heanor Town Dec 2005/Sutton Town coach & commercial manager 2006/Teversal coach 2007, also becoming Chesterfield commercial manager and Mansfield Town commercial manager July 2007 to July 2008/Derby Co Account Executive July 2008, becoming Group Sales Executive Feb 2013/Chesterfield kit-manager June 2013.

Tony Lormor made his debut for the Magpies when still on a youth training scheme at Gallowgate, standing in for Brazilian international Mirandinha. Tall and slim, Anth, as he was also called, always looked to have the potential to succeed when he pulled on a Magpie shirt in junior and Central League football, and after scoring on his first two full appearances for the club, against Oxford and Portsmouth, was set for a bright future. Yet, after that headlining opening he rarely received a chance and as a 19-year-old Lormor had to be content to further his career at Sincil Bank. A centre-forward in the traditional mould, Anth rattled in 34 goals for Lincoln and was their leading scorer during his first three seasons, while he netted in Chesterfield's Play-Off final at Wembley in 1994-95, scoring 45 goals for the Spireites over 134 appearances. Lormor had recovered from a serious knee injury which wrecked his progress at Lincoln, but was dogged with further injuries. During 2000 he was part of

a PFA initiative aimed at fast-tracking players into becoming referees, Lormor reaching a lower level of football as an official. Leaving the game for a spell, the Northumbrian worked with Barclays Bank for a period as a financial advisor and at IBA in the East Midlands before returning to the game in a commercial role with Derby County and then returned to the Spireites.

Appearances & Goals:
Debut v Tottenham Hotspur (h) 23 January 1988 (sub)
FL: 6(2) app 3 gls
Total: 6(2) app 3 gls

Honours:
FL div 3 prom 1995, 1998 (7 app).

LOUGHLIN James William 1924-1927

Centre-forward
5'10"
b. Darlington, 9 October 1905
d. Darlington, 16 February 1954

Career: Alliance Jnrs/Darlington St Augustine's/ Darlington Railway Ath/UNITED Nov 1924 £125/ West Ham Utd May 1927 £650/Coventry City Jan 1929 £1,300/Dolphin (Dublin) cs 1931/Bray Unknowns Aug 1931/Worcester City Oct 1931/ Northwich Victoria cs 1932/Darlington July 1933 to 1934.

A former blacksmith, Jimmy Loughlin joined the Magpies at the same time as teammate Ossie Park, both stand-out players with the Darlington RA side in the Northern League. He filled in for Neil Harris and Hughie Gallacher on occasion during the seasons between United's FA Cup victory in 1924, and the club's title success three years later. In fact Jimmy turned out in four games of that League Championship winning season, but was always recognised as a talented reserve able to find the net in an opportunist way. He struck five goals in seven games during season 1925-26 before being picked up by West Ham where he again failed to gain a regular spot. Jimmy was, though, an instant success with Coventry, during season 1929-30 when he poached 29 goals, at the time a club record. All told Loughlin's strike-rate with City was first-class; 39 goals in 65 senior matches, however he was sidelined with a bad injury at the peak of his career when 25 years of age. Jimmy's career was effectively over, going out on loan to a series of clubs in an effort to regain fitness.

Appearances & Goals:
Debut v Huddersfield Town (a) 27 December 1924
FL: 12 app 5 gls
Total: 12 app 5 gls

Honours:
FL champs 1927 (4 app).

LOVENKRANDS Peter Rosenkrands 2009-2012

Striker
5'11"
b. Horsholm (Denmark), 29 January 1980

Career: Lillerod IF (Den) 1985/AB Copenhagen (Den) Feb 1998/ Rangers June 2000 £1.3m/FC Schalke 04 (Ger) May 2006 free/ UNITED Jan 2009 free to June 2009, rejoining Aug 2009/ Birmingham City July 2012 free to cs 2014.

By the time 28-year-old Danish striker Peter Lovenkrands joined the United set up at the start of 2009 he was an experienced player having won more than 20 caps for Denmark and served Rangers with distinction over six seasons. Winning the Scottish Premier League title and Scottish Cup medals at Ibrox during a spell in which he scored over 50 goals in his 180 appearances, Peter had been tipped to join the Magpies earlier when he headed for Scotland from Denmark in 2000. Manager Bobby Robson wanted to bring the Dane to Tyneside at that time, however the player decided to join the Glasgow giants. Not big or muscular, but a forward with pace and who ran the channels, he possessed a natural goal-poacher's instinct around the box. Although often selected on the flank in Scottish football he reverted to his more favoured role supporting a front striker at St James' Park. During Newcastle's trophy winning campaign of 2009-10, Peter grabbed 13 league goals (16 all told), a first-class support striker to Andy Carroll. Moving down the pecking order as the Black'n'Whites returned to the Premier League, Peter moved to Birmingham City where he played for Lee Clark. His elder brother Tommy Rosenkrands also appeared for AB Copenhagen and later St Johnstone.

Appearances & Goals:
Debut v Manchester City (a) 28 January 2009 (sub)
FL/PL: 47(28) app 22 gls
FAC: 2(1) app 3 gls
FLC: 6(1) app 4 gls
Total: 55(30) app 29 gls

Honours:
22 Den caps 2002-date/WdC 2002/12 Den u21 app 1998-2001/Den sch-youth app/FL ch winner 2010/SL champs 2003, 2005/SC winner 2002/SLC winner 2002, 2003, 2005 (sub no app)/Den Cup winner 1999.

LOW James 1921-1928

Outside-right
5'6"
b. Elgin, 9 March 1894
d. Elgin, 5 March 1960

Career: Bishopmill Utd/Elgin City/Edinburgh University/Heart of Midlothian Aug 1912/Elgin City 1919/Rangers March 1920/UNITED Oct 1921 £1,300 to May 1928/Buckie Thistle 1928-29.

Jimmy Low was once splendidly described at the time as "a dapper outside-right whose pluck and skill is out of all proportion to his inches". A fine, diminutive winger, who was a signed as a reserve initially but quickly took over from fellow Scot Billy Aitken in United's side. A regular over four seasons before Tommy Urwin entered the fray, in that period Low helped win the FA Cup for the Magpies. Sturdy and consistent without ever being flamboyant, Low had his differences with Newcastle's management during his period on Tyneside, twice failing to turn up for fixtures and by the time the 1927-28 season had got underway, his stock with the club was at a low point. He refused to play for the second string in the Northumberland Senior Cup final and United reported the Scot to the FA and placed him on the transfer list. Before FA officials sat to hear the dispute between player and club, Jimmy left Tyneside and returned to Elgin, where he had been brought up. The disciplinary committee sat in his absence and suspended Low, effectively ending his senior footballing career. On leaving school Jimmy had moved from his home in Moray to enter university in Edinburgh, an agricultural under-graduate. He was spotted by Hearts playing college football and soon became part of a good line-up at Tynecastle, totalling 83 games for the Maroons. During World War One, Low was commissioned with the Seaforth Highlanders, being initially part of a celebrated group of Hearts' players that joined up together in the 16th Royal Scots, known as McCrae's Battalion of which five players were killed in the conflict. He survived the Battle of the Somme but was twice wounded in the fighting and took sometime to recover and re-enter football. On retirement following a brief spell in Highland football, Jimmy remained in the Elgin area of Scotland. He is related to Colin Low, Lord Low of Dalston, for a long period President of the European of Blind Union and Chairman of the Royal National Institute of Blind People.

(Note: The Sports Budget Who's Who of 1925 records Jimmy being born in the Ayrshire town of Kilbirnie. This is an error as registration documents and local roll-calls note he was born and bred in Elgin where he started his career in football.)

Appearances & Goals:
Debut v Middlesbrough (h) 3 December 1921
FL: 108 app 8 gls
FAC: 13 app 1 gl
Total: 121 app 9 gls

Honours:
2 SL app 1915/FAC winner 1924/FL champs 1927 (2 app).

LOW Wilfred Lawson 1909-1933

Centre-half & Trainer
5'11"
b. Aberdeen, 8 December 1884
d. Newcastle upon Tyne, 30 April 1933

Career: Abergeldie/Montrose trial/Aberdeen Aug 1904/UNITED May 1909 £800 exch deal for J Soye (Hartlepools Utd war-guest 1915-16) (Fulham war-guest 1916-19)(Rotherham Co war-guest) retired cs 1924, becoming asst-trainer and later groundsman to his demise.

Although known as 'The Laughing Cavalier', Wilf Low was grim in his methods, a robust destroyer of the opposition. After his move from Aberdeen to Tyneside, the Magpies never once had reason to regret enlisting the services of this wholehearted Scot. With 118 games to his name with the Dons, Low became the hero of many a contest. A big, strapping centre-half who operated in midfield, then before the advent of the defensive pivot, Wilf's job was to protect the defence and he did it in an uncompromising fashion. One pen-picture of the day described Low as of "best Aberdeen granite with a particular fondness for crushing centre-forwards"! He was level-headed, unrelenting and tough, yet as one other critic remarked, was "an ornament to the game". Skipper of the club, Wilf is placed high in Newcastle's appearance ranking, and after he hung up his boots, looked after the Newcastle Swifts junior eleven before taking charge of St James' Park. He resided in Leazes Terrace, overlooking the stadium until his untimely death, the victim of a road accident in the city. His brother Harry appeared for Sunderland (228 app), while his son Norman turned out for Liverpool and Newport, and was on the field when United recorded their famous record 13-0 victory over the Welshmen in 1946. Another member of his family appeared in the game with credit; a cousin William served Aberdeen and Barnsley. During the First World War the Scot was enlisted as a sergeant with the Royal Engineers.

Appearances & Goals:
Debut v Bolton Wanderers (h) 1 September 1909
FL: 324 app 9 gls
FAC: 43 app 0 gls
War: 11 app 0 gls
Total: 378 app 9 gls

Honours:
5 Scot caps 1911-20/Scot trial app 1920/FAC winner 1910/FAC final 1911.

LOWERY Jeremiah 1946-1952

Goalkeeper
5'9"
b. Newcastle upon Tyne, 19 October 1924
d. Southwold, Suffolk, 1 October 2007

Career: Leicester City amat 1945/CA Parsons Ath 1945/Bradford City trial 1946/UNITED amat 1946, prof June 1947 £10/Lincoln City March 1952 £750/ Peterborough Utd July 1954 £300/Barrow June 1956/ Crewe Alex July 1958/Wisbech Town 1959 becoming asst-coach.

Jerry Lowery was born in the shadow of St James' Park, in Sutton's Dwellings on Barrack Road and was a Newcastle United supporter from boyhood. Following service in the Royal Navy as a stoker during the war, he impressed several scouts as a 21-year-old in local football and the Magpies fought hard to secure his signature at the end of World War Two. But joining the Gallowgate staff, Jerry found it equally hard to claim the 'keeper's jersey during the immediate peacetime seasons. With severe competition for the one senior place, Lowery found Jack Fairbrother in top form and his chances were limited to a handful over two seasons and he had to be satisfied with the goalkeeper's position in the club's Central League line-up, winning the reserve title during 1948. Lowery also figured at centre-forward for Newcastle in reserve football, playing against Blackburn and Huddersfield during 1950-51. Joining Lincoln, Jerry was a regular selection, claiming over 50 games before heading for the non-leagues and joining up with the Posh, ironically taking over from Jack Fairbrother. Not tall for a 'keeper, Jerry was a good shot-stopper and he also served Barrow to good effect over

90 games in the Third Division North. After retiring, Lowery ran a window-cleaning business then became a Cheshire Homes attendant at Hovendon House in Fleet. He later resided in Peterborough and then Beccles in Suffolk.

Appearances & Goals:
Debut v Huddersfield Town (a) 11 April 1950
FL: 6 app 0 gls
Total: 6 app 0 gls

LOWERY William 1893-1895
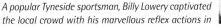

Goalkeeper
5'10"
b. Tyneside

Career: Gateshead Ass/Trafalgar (Newcastle) 1892/ Gateshead NER/Blyth FC/UNITED Sept 1893 to 1895 when he returned to local Tyneside football, appearing for Newcastle East End, Newcastle Wednesday and Heaton Wednesday/UNITED Sept 1896 briefly.

A popular Tyneside sportsman, Billy Lowery captivated the local crowd with his marvellous reflex actions in an era of usually ponderous and somewhat weighty goalkeepers. Described by the press of the day as "the best goalkeeper hereabouts", he joined United for the club's Football League debut in season 1893-94. Lowery took over the custodian's role for Newcastle's first home fixture, a 6-0 victory over Arsenal, and became United's first choice goalkeeper for the remainder of the programme before being replaced by Ward for the majority of season 1894-95. He afterwards returned to non-league football in the city, briefly being attached to United again in 1896.

Appearances & Goals:
Debut v Woolwich Arsenal (h) 30 September 1893
FL: 28 app 0 gls
FAC: 2 app 0 gls
Total: 30 app 0 gls

LOWES Thomas 1910-1914
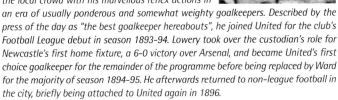

Inside-forward
5'6"
b. Walker, Newcastle upon Tyne, 9 April 1892
d. Newcastle upon Tyne, 20 November 1973

Career: Walker Church Jnrs/Walker Celtic/ Gosforth & Coxlodge BL/Wallsend Park Villa/ UNITED Sept 1910 £25/Coventry City June 1914 £50/Nuneaton Town June 1920/Caerphilly Town Aug 1921/Newport Co July 1922/Yeovil & Petters Utd player-trainer Aug 1926, becoming manager July 1928 to cs 1929/Barrow trainer Sept 1931, becoming manager 1932/Walsall manager April 1937 to Sept 1939/Arsenal scout 1945/ Norwich City scout 1961 to 1972.

At Gallowgate Tommy Lowes was an understudy to the stars, a rival to Sandy Higgins or Jock King at either inside-right or left. Although a good solid player, he was never to reach the heights of brilliance, except on one mini-run for the Tynesiders during 1911-12 when he netted in three successive fixtures, including a derby with Sunderland. Lowes also bagged four goals for United against South Shields in a friendly match during 1912-13. However, Lowes did well with Welsh club, Newport, totalling 125 games and 41 goals, and also with Yeovil where he brought much guile to the non-leaguers, netting 39 times in his first season. Once he had retired Tommy developed into one of the shrewdest men to be found in the backrooms of football. For over 40 years he was linked with several clubs as a manager, coach or scout, and when based in the North East discovered such stars as Johnny Hancocks (Wolves) and John Barnwell (Arsenal). He also found legendary goalkeeper Bert Williams.

Appearances & Goals:
Debut v Preston North End (a) 23 December 1911
FL: 16 app 3 gls
Total: 16 app 3 gls

LOWRIE George 1948-1949

Centre-forward
5'9"
b. Tonypandy, Glamorgan, 19 December 1919
d. Bristol, 3 May 1989

Career: Trehod Ex-schoolboys/Tonypandy 1933/Swansea Town amat Aug 1936, prof Jan 1937/Preston North End Dec 1937 cash-exch deal/Coventry City June 1939 £1,750 (Nottingham Forest war-guest 1940-41)(Bristol City war-guest 1940-41)(Northampton Town war-guest 1941-42)(Lincoln City war-guest 1943-44)/UNITED March 1948 £18,500/Bristol City Sept 1949 £10,000/ Coventry City Feb 1952/Lovells Ath July 1953 to 1955-56.

When he joined the Magpies, George Lowrie was the club's record signing and at a fee of £18,500, the third most expensive purchase in the game. Introduced to senior football as a 17-year-old by Swansea's ex-United leader Neil Harris, the Welshman boasted a tremendous scoring record in wartime football, netting 74 goals for Coventry. Then, in season 1946-47 and the opening months of 1947-48, he crashed home another 47 goals, thereby forcing United to act to capture his undoubted goal prowess. Also to operate at inside-left as well, George also netted a headlining hat-trick for Wales against England at Wembley in 1943. With slick black hair, Lowrie possessed a terrific shot and also a willingness to do the fetching and carrying, being rated very highly throughout the country. Arriving at St James' Park to boost United's promotion chances, the Welshman began well, but was quickly injured as the following 1948-49 season began and was out of action for six months. Turning his knee against Chelsea, he suffered a cartilage tear and needed surgery. By the time he was fit again, George Robledo and George Hannah had entered the action for United and Lowrie was surplus to requirements. At Ashton Gate he also had cruel luck with injury, a broken leg almost finishing his career. George was later employed for a confectionary firm, residing for a period in Suffolk before settling in Bristol.

Appearances & Goals:
Debut v Southampton (a) 13 March 1948
FL: 12 app 5 gls
Total: 12 app 5 gls

Honours:
4 Wales caps 1948-49/9 Wales war app 1942-46/FL div 2 prom 1948 (5 app).

LUALUA Kazenga 2005-2011

Midfield
5'7"
b. Kinshasa (Zaire/DR Congo), 10 December 1990

Career: UNITED jnr 2005, prof July 2006 (Doncaster Rovers loan 2008-09)/Brighton loan Feb 2010 to March 2010, again Aug 2010, pmt Nov 2011.

Some ten years younger than his brother Lomana LuaLua (qv) and born in the Democratic Republic of Congo, Kazenga LuaLua quickly showed in United's junior side he had similar crafty and elusive skills to his older relation. Operating usually on the left of midfield, often as an out and out winger, LuaLua found a place in United's substitutes dug-out during season 2006-07 when barely 16 years old; had he entered the field, he would have become the club's youngest ever debutant. Kazenga waited a year for his senior bow though and received a senior call-up in FA Cup action against Stoke City after appearing in friendly matches. He was a bright prospect for the future and was loaned to Brighton to gain much needed experience. Kazenga enjoyed success under Gus Poyet's management as the Seagulls won promotion to from the third-tier of football and began a new era at their recently constructed Amex Arena. LuaLua though sustained a broken leg, yet recovered to shine again, going on a second loan spell with Brighton; a permanent deal being concluded for the player during November 2011. Kazenga followed his elder brother into the Congo international squad during March 2008 when only 17 years of age while he also started to mimic Lomana's celebrated somersault goal celebration.

Appearances & Goals:
Debut v Stoke City (a) 6 January 2008 (FAC) (sub)
FL/PL: 0(8) app 0 gls
FAC: 0(4) app 0 gls
FLC: 3 app 0 gls
Total: 3(12) app 0 gls

Honours:
FL ch winner 2010 (1 app)/FL div 1 champs 2011.

L

LUALUA Lomana Tresor 2000-2004

Midfield or Forward
5'8"
b. Kinshasa (Zaire/DR Congo), 28 December 1980

Career: Leyton Orient trial/Leyton College/
Colchester Utd Sept 1998/UNITED Sept 2000 £2.25m
(Portsmouth loan 2003-04)/Portsmouth July 2004
£1.2m/Olympiacos (Gr) Aug 2007 £2.8m/Al-Arabi SC
(Qt) July 2008/Olympiacos (Gr) Dec 2009/AC Omonia
(Cy) July 2010/Birmingham City, Brighton, Sheffield
Wed & Hartlepool Utd, all on trial Aug-Sept 2011/
Blackpool Oct 2011/Karabukspor (Trk) May 2012/
Caykur Rizespor (Trk) Jan 2014.

Lomana LuaLua showed many scintillating skills in the lower divisions with Colchester United which had supporters at Layer Road drooling at his flair in attack. Soon top clubs were alerted and he was given a chance at the Premier League when Bobby Robson sanctioned his move north at the start of the 2000-01 season when 19 years of age. Described as a "superkid with dazzling trickery and blinding pace", it was something of a chancy buy, but a fee of £2.25m was worth risking, and would be a bargain if his raw talent could be harnessed in the correct way. Although the Congolese player had much to learn, he did have the special brand of ability up front which could turn games and delight fans. Audacious at times with the ball, Lomana possessed a good shot and enjoyed a rapport with United's crowd who wanted him to succeed. Like many players at Premiership clubs, he was on the very fringe on first-eleven selection and found it frustrating. With Shearer and Bellamy the undoubted first choice front pairing, with Ameobi and Cort also in support, and Robert in a wide role, LuaLua was in and out of the side, rarely getting an extended run from the start in any of his four seasons with the Magpies. LuaLua made no less than 67 cameo appearances from the substitute's bench; his best consecutive run in United's side was a handful of games at the end of 2001-02 and the start of 2002-03. With a power-packed shot, Lomana had his moments in Toon colours, scoring spectacular goals against Lokeren, TSV Munich and Bayer Leverkusen in European football. LuaLua became frustrated at being on the periphery and moved on in search of regular action during 2003-04, finding a place in Pompey's line-up. Appearing for Congo in the African Nations Cup, Lomana skippered his country on occasion, while as a teenager he had been a top-class gymnast (developing a spectacular goal celebration in athletic gymnastic style) and was rejected by Orient after trials. He then spent two years studying as a student of the Performing Arts aiming for a career in music, but was spotted playing locally for the college and headed for his big chance in football. His younger brother Kazenga (qv) came through Newcastle's Academy, although ended up in the same position as Lomana of having to move from Tyneside to secure a more certain place. Two cousins, Tresor Kandol and Yannick Bolasie, also found a career in the professional game.

Appearances & Goals:
Debut v Charlton Athletic (h) 23 September 2000 (sub)
PL: 14(45) app 5 gls
FAC: 0(7) app 0 gls
FLC: 2(3) app 0 gls
Euro: 5(12) app 4 gls
Total: 21(67) app 9 gls

Honours:
31 Congo caps 2002-13/Gr Lg champs 2008/Cy Cup winner 2011.

LUKE George Thomas 1950-1953, 1959-1961

Outside-left
5'8"
b. Newcastle upon Tyne, 17 December 1933
d. Newcastle upon Tyne, 23 March 2010

Career: Walker Central/UNITED jnr Sept 1950, prof Dec
1950/Hartlepools Utd Oct 1953 free/UNITED Oct 1959
£4,000/Darlington Jan 1961 £2,500/South Shields c1964.

A product of Walkergate schools, George Luke spent his entire football career in the North East, including two spells at St James' Park as a United player. His first period, as a youngster, was totally overshadowed by the skill and consistency of Scottish international Bobby Mitchell,

although he did show up well occasionally, scoring on his home debut and making three other goals against Everton in an 8-2 romp. A cruciate ligament injury did not help his progress, but by the time the small and chunky Luke had served Hartlepool with distinction (68 goals in 205 games) he was able to show he had something to offer the top flight. Indeed, in season 1959-60 George took over from the great Scottish maestro on the left wing and looked a penetrating forward at times. However, Newcastle's relegation trauma during the following season led to Luke's departure for a second time, but once more he displayed fine form with the region's other lower division club, Darlington, where he totalled 72 games. On retirement George resided in Newcastle, running a furnishings business in Forest Hall. He was cousin to United centre-forward Bill Curry, both playing in the same school team before joining Newcastle's youth set-up.

Appearances & Goals:
Debut v Fulham (a) 17 October 1959
FL: 27 app 4 gls
FAC: 2 app 0 gls
Total: 29 app 4 gls

Honours:
FL div 3(N) app 1958.

LUQUE Albert Martos 2005-2007

Forward
6'0"
b. Terrassa, near Barcelona (Spain), 11 March 1978

Career: FC Barcelona (Sp)/RCD Mallorca (Sp)
1997 (Malaga CF (Sp) loan 1999-2000)/
RC Deportivo La Coruna cs 2002 £10m/UNITED
Aug 2005 £11.4m/Ajax (Neth) Aug 2007 £2m/
Malaga CF (Sp) loan Aug 2008, pmt July 2009
free to Jan 2011.

If one player was to be labelled as the most expensive disappointment in United's history arguably Albert Luque would be at the top of the list. Only two footballers have cost the Magpies more; Alan Shearer and Michael Owen. Almost unheard of in England, Luque cost Newcastle all of £11.4m when he was captured from Deportivo La Coruna during the summer of 2005, part of a near £30m spending spree which never produced results. Manager Graeme Souness later made the comment he was not the man who brought him to Tyneside, prompting speculation he was purchased by the Chairman. Nevertheless he joined United's expensive and highly paid squad for the 2005-06 season with a YouTube clip of some of his goals in La Liga giving Newcastle supporters a glimpse of what he could do on the field. That looked impressive, Albert enjoying a period of some success with Real Mallorca and Deportivo when he reached the Spanish national side following a run of form which produced plenty of goals, including during a run to the Champions League semi-final. But the 27-year-old Luque rarely shined wearing a black-and-white shirt. In his defence, Albert was rarely given an extended opportunity as either a front striker or wide-raider during his two seasons on Tyneside. The dark-haired Spaniard only managed eight starts in his first season, and less in his second, a mere six, mainly utilised in the UEFA Cup rather than Premier League. He never had too much luck either, tearing his hamstring in only his second game for United and being out for 12 weeks. Then he found a new manager was in charge, with Glenn Roeder having little time for the Spaniard. Luque was on the bench or on the treatment table more often than not and the Geordies lost out heavily on the deal, allowing Luque to move to Ajax for a cut price fee after just 24 months and a mere 14 games from the kick-off, as well as a goal tally of just three strikes. Playing alongside Luis Suarez in Amsterdam, afterwards Luque did not enjoy much success elsewhere, having a period with Malaga before retiring from the game. Luque became a television pundit while he admitted in an interview that he never really wanted to join the Magpies, but came for the substantial money being offered.

Appearances & Goals:
Debut v Manchester United (h) 28 August 2005
PL: 6(15) app 1 gl
FAC: 1(2) app 0 gls
FLC: 1 app 0 gls
Euro: 6(3) app 2 gls
Total: 14(20) app 3 gls

Honours:
17 Sp caps 2002-06/WdC 2002/OG 2000 (silver)/13 Sp u21 app 1998-2000/2 Sp u23 app 2000/3 Catalonia app 2002-07.

MAGUIRE Gavin Terence 1991

Centre-half
5'10"
b. Hammersmith, London, 24 November 1967

Career: Northwood 1983/Queens Park Rangers Oct 1985 (Tampa Bay Rowdies (USA) guest June 1986)/Portsmouth Jan 1989 £225,000 (UNITED loan Oct 1991)/Millwall March 1993 £115,000 (Scarborough loan 1993-94) to May 1994/Harrow Borough/Northwood Sept 1997/Hillingdon Borough briefly.

Arriving from Portsmouth for a short one month's loan deal with Newcastle United, Gavin Maguire stepped into the heart of the Black'n'Whites defence with the aim to impress both manager Ossie Ardiles and the fans. He did well on his first outing against Leicester showing a competitive instinct and skill on the ball. However, after two more appearances and a knee injury, United sent him back to Fratton Park without an offer of a contract, Ardiles giving young Matty Appleby an extended run-out in his place. During his few weeks on Tyneside, Maguire did manage to play for his country as a Newcastle player in the European Championship qualification matches. With Pompey, he played on 108 occasions until he fell out with boss Jim Smith and moved on, Maguire quitting senior football in 1994 at an early age of 26 after persistent injuries. He then travelled the USA for a year before returning to work as a personal fitness trainer. Unusually for an ex-footballer, Gavin trained to be a hairdresser and opened a salon, 'Pure Unisex' in Somerton.

Appearances & Goals:
Debut v Leicester City (h) 12 October 1991
FL: 3 app 0 gls
Total: 3 app 0 gls

Honours:
7 Wales caps 1990-92/1 Wales B app 1991.

MAHONEY Michael James 1975-1978

Goalkeeper
5'11"
b. Bristol, 25 October 1950

Career: Bristol City prof Aug 1968/Torquay Utd loan, pmt Aug 1970 £5,000/UNITED March 1975 £25,000/Chicago Sting (USA) Nov 1978 £40,000/California Surf (USA) May 1979/Los Angeles Lasers (USA) 1982, becoming coach June 1986/Later with San Bernardino (USA) 1995.

After totalling 167 games for Torquay, rated one of the very best custodians in the lower divisions, Mick Mahoney became first choice goalkeeper at St James' Park on the retirement of Willie McFaul in season 1975-76. And for two years Mahoney displayed fine consistency and a string of wonderful saves, notably winning BBC's Match of the Day's Save of the Season award for one such effort against Ipswich during 1975. Agile and popular, Mick was the club's 'keeper as Gordon Lee's side won their way through to a League Cup final in 1976 but, by the time Lee had departed and Richard Dinnis had been installed as boss, Mahoney's form deteriorated. Newcastle slumped and tumbled towards the Second Division and new manager Bill McGarry did not rate Mahoney highly. Mick was part of an exodus of players and went overseas to try his luck in the USA. He played for several years in that grade of soccer, appearing in indoor football when in his forties. Residing in Running Springs, near Los Angeles, Mahoney remained across the Atlantic for almost 25 years, working for a brewery as a delivery driver as well as coaching part-time. He returned to the UK in 2002, settling in his native Bristol, for a period working for Royal Mail. On one occasion when playing for the Magpies against Aston Villa in 1976, Mahoney was credited with a rare occurrence of a goalkeeper's own-goal.

Appearances & Goals:
Debut v Everton (h) 12 April 1975
FL: 108 app 0 gls
FAC: 12 app 0 gls
FLC: 13 app 0 gls
Euro: 2 app 0 gls
Others: 3 app 0 gls
Total: 138 app 0 gls

Honours:
FLC final 1976.

MAITLAND Alfred Edward 1924-1930

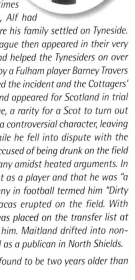

Right-back
5'10"
b. Leith, 8 October 1894
d. Leicester, 22 December 1981

Career: Leith Ath/Benwell Adelaide/South Shields amat Jan 1919, prof July 1919/Middlesbrough May 1923 £4,000/UNITED Oct 1924 £1,000/Jarrow May 1930 free/Northfleet Utd Nov 1930/Salisbury City player-manager Aug 1933 to May 1935/Shirley Town player-manager 1935-36.

Starting his career with United as an understudy to Frank Hudspeth at left-back, Alf Maitland switched to the right-back role and found a permanent position in United's Division One title season of 1926-27. Dashing and fearless, yet sometimes rather erratic according to contemporary reports, Alf had started playing football with Leith in Scotland before his family settled on Tyneside. He joined South Shields for the Northern Victory League then appeared in their very first Football League fixture during August 1919 and helped the Tynesiders on over 150 occasions. Once, in 1922, he was offered a bribe by a Fulham player Barney Travers to throw the Shields versus Fulham clash; Alf reported the incident and the Cottagers' striker was banned for life. The highly-rated Maitland appeared for Scotland in trial games during 1923 and also for the Football League, a rarity for a Scot to turn out for the English at such a level. Alf was something of a controversial character, leaving Middlesbrough for Gallowgate after a bust up, while he fell into dispute with the Magpies too. Along with Hughie Gallacher, he was accused of being drunk on the field when on tour in Hungary and in 1930 parted company amidst heated arguments. In later life he admitted that he was a bit too petulant as a player and that he was "a tough lad". He played the game with gusto and many in football termed him "Dirty Maitland", the Scot often joining in when any fracas erupted on the field. With disputes simmering between player and club, Alf was placed on the transfer list at such a high fee that no other top club would buy him. Maitland drifted into non-league soccer, later residing in Leicester after a spell as a publican in North Shields.

(Note: On checking birth and death registers, Alf is found to be two years older than previously published, born in 1894 not 1896.)

Appearances & Goals:
Debut v Everton (a) 25 December 1924
FL: 156 app 0 gls
FAC: 7 app 0 gls
Total: 163 app 0 gls

Honours:
Scot trial app 1923/1 FL app 1923/FL champs 1927.

MAKEL Lee Robert 1987-1992

Midfield
5'10"
b. Washington, 11 January 1973

Career: Springwell Jnrs/Hilda Park Jnrs/UNITED jnr Feb 1987, prof Feb 1991/Blackburn Rovers July 1992 £160,000 (plus £28,000 from subsequent move)/Huddersfield Town Oct 1995 £300,000/Heart of Midlothian March 1998 £75,000 (Portsmouth loan 1999-2000)/Motherwell trial Aug 2001/Bradford City trial Aug to Sept 2001/Livingston trial Dec 2001, pmt May 2002/Plymouth Argyle June 2004/Dunfermline Ath Jan 2005/Livingston June 2006/Ostersunds FK (Swd) player-coach April 2008/East Fife Feb 2009/Ostersunds FK (Swd) player-coach June 2009/Cowdenbeath Feb 2011, becoming asst-manager June 2012.

Only slightly-built at 10 stone, blond-haired Lee Makel was a lightweight midfielder who possessed a good touch on the ball and a silky style. He was given a first opportunity as an 18-year-old in the Zenith Data Cup, then a few outings in league action during the reign of Ossie Ardiles and his youthful set-up. However, the Argentinean's departure and the new batch of talent brought together by Kevin Keegan saw Makel very much a promising reserve. Kenny Dalglish at Blackburn had been impressed with his ability as well as attitude, and purchased his talent to

M

compete for a place at Ewood Park. But Lee again found he was second or third choice, although he did appear in the European Champions League with Rovers during season 1995-96. Moving to Huddersfield, Makel was given a regular slot, totalling 79 games for the Terriers, and was good enough to appear for the Football League eleven before becoming a consistent midfielder in Scottish football, recording over 250 appearances north of the border. For a period Lee set up a talent spotting football school in the Borders, his younger brother, Gavin Makel, appeared in the television hit Byker Grove and several Catherine Cookson dramas.

Appearances & Goals:
Debut v West Bromwich Albion (a) 4 May 1991 (sub)
(v Nottingham Forest (a) 21 November 1990 (sub) (FMC))
FL: 6(6) app 1 gl
FLC: 1 app 0 gls
Others: 0(1) app 0 gls
Total: 7(7) app 1 gl

Honours:
1 FL u21 app 1996/SL div 2 champs 2012 (3 app)/SLC winner 2004/SLC final 2006.

MALCOLM Walter Grant Lees 1957-1960

Outside-right
5'8"
b. Musselburgh, near Edinburgh, 25 October 1940
Career: Dalkeith Thistle/UNITED Nov 1957 £800/ Raith Rovers July 1960 £500/Airdrie June 1962 to April 1963 free/Scottish junior football 1963.

An 18-year-old debutant for the Magpies, Grant Malcolm made what was described as a "promising right wing display" when he first pulled on a black-and-white shirt. Malcolm played well on his only appearance against Nottingham Forest, despite an early knock that needed his ankle heavily bandaged. Standing in for Gordon Hughes, Grant afterwards rarely got close to another first team outing and returned over the border to conclude his career in Scotland, appearing on 27 occasions for Raith but more prominently in non-league football. He resided in the East Lothian area, near the capital, Edinburgh.

Appearances & Goals:
Debut v Nottingham Forest (h) 10 October 1959
FL: 1 app 0 gls
Total: 1 app 0 gls

Honours:
Scot sch-youth app.

MANNERS Peter John 1975-1979

Midfield
5'10"
b. Sunderland, 31 July 1959
Career: UNITED jnr Aug 1975, prof July 1977/Seiko SA (HK) Dec 1979 to March 1980/Blyth Spartans March 1981/Bedlington Terriers Sept 1983/Seaton Delaval 1985.

The slimly framed Peter Manners shone in Central League football for the Magpies and deserved his promotion to the senior side during the latter stages of the 1978-79 season. Coming in for Mick Martin, he showed plenty of running ability and potential, but like many fringe players wasn't given a sustained opportunity and he moved to the Far East for a year before returning to the region to appear in local football. Manners later joined the Northumbria Police for a period.

Appearances & Goals:
Debut v Bristol Rovers (h) 2 May 1979
FL: 2 app 0 gls
Total: 2 app 0 gls

MARCELINO Elena Sierra 1999-2003

Centre-half
6'2"
b. Gijon (Spain), 26 September 1971
Career: Sporting Gijon (Sp) 1986/RCD Mallorca (Sp) Jan 1996 £200,000/UNITED July 1999 £5.07m/ Polideportivo Ejido (Sp) Jan 2003 free/Retired 2004.

Ruud Gullit's answer to Newcastle's defensive frailty, Spanish centre-back Marcelino had enjoyed conspicuous success in a Real Mallorca side which reached the European Cup Winners Cup final at Villa Park towards the end of the 1998-99 season. A thoughtful defender, Marcelino had been a late developer in top football, his stock rising significantly as the Mallorca side reached that final as well as third spot in La Liga. His progress was such that Elena was also part of the Spanish international set-up. Marcelino tended to read situations at the back rather than tackle with force and was held in high esteem in his native country. Newcastle's first Spanish player, the signing though was an enormous flop for Newcastle United, and an expensive one at that, costing the Black'n'Whites all of nearly £10m including paying-up his substantial wages when he left. During season 1999-2000 Marcelino began his short United career as it was to continue; injured on his debut at Aston Villa. He was in and out of the line-up and when Bobby Robson took charge he was given a brief opportunity to shine as the winter of 2000 arrived. But Newcastle's boss preferred both Goma and Hughes to the Spaniard. Marcelino thereafter languished in United's squad, a forgotten man for almost two years and his career went into rapid decline. He was famously on the sidelines for several weeks with a finger injury; Newcastle struggled to offload him until a cut-price deal was completed with Spanish second-tier Polideportivo Ejido, the Magpies effectively writing-off their substantial outlay. Marcelino had started only 19 of a possible 178 matches during his spell on Tyneside. When he decided to quit playing, he became a registered FIFA agent based in Gijon, during March 2008 appointed for a period Liverpool's 'Spanish scout'. Marcelino also worked for Television Espanola and with Sky, covering La Liga games, while his son reached Spain's youth squad during 2007.

Appearances & Goals:
Debut v Aston Villa (h) 7 August 1999
PL: 15(2) app 0 gls
FAC: 2(1) app 0 gls
Euro: 2 app 0 gls
Total: 19(3) app 0 gls

Honours:
5 Sp caps 1999-2000/Sp div 2 prom 1997/Sp Cup final 1998/ECWC final 1999.

MARIC Silvio 1999-2000

Forward
5'9"
b. Zagreb (Yugoslavia/Croatia), 20 March 1975
Career: NK Lokomotiva (Cr)/Dinamo Zagreb (Cr) 1990 (HNK Segesta (Cr) loan 1994-95)/UNITED Feb 1999 £3.585m/FC Porto (Ptg) July 2000 £2m/Dinamo Zagreb (Cr) cs 2001 free/ Panathinaikos (Gr) June 2003 free/Dinamo Zagreb (Cr) cs 2005 to cs 2006 when he retired.

Like Mark Viduka, Croatian striker Silvio Maric was one of several talented players to catch the eye in a bright Zagreb squad during the mid to late 1990s, playing against United in the Champions League during 1997. Part of an outstanding Croatian national side too, he was tracked by several top clubs and cost Newcastle almost £3.6m, new manager Ruud Gullit viewing the 23-year-old quick and nimble support-striker as a player to develop as a partner to Alan Shearer, or as an attack-minded midfielder. He had ability to twist and turn with the ball; however, the dark-haired Maric only scored two goals for the Magpies and rarely showed enough to warrant a place in United's line-up. With Duncan Ferguson absent, Silvio was given a run during season 1998-99 but afterwards was more frequently on the bench, and when he did get the odd chance to impress appeared to freeze in front of goal, once being brushed aside by a focused Shearer as a chance was converted. It was no surprise when Silvio was sold to Porto in 2000, Newcastle taking a somewhat heavy transfer loss of £1.5m. Maric settled back in Croatia, working in the football media and often seen as a television pundit, being something of a celebrity in his native country. He also set-up a football academy in Zagreb.

Appearances & Goals:
Debut v Everton (h) 7 March 1999 (FAC)
PL: 12(11) app 0 gls
FAC: 1(3) app 0 gls
FLC: 1 app 0 gls
Euro: 3 app 2 gls
Total: 17(14) app 2 gls

Honours:
19 Cr caps 1997-2003/WdC 1998/20 Cr u21 app 1994-97/FAC final 1999/Cr Lg champs 1993, 1996, 1997, 1998, 2003, 2006/Cr Cup winner 1994, 1996, 1997, 1998, 2002/Cr YFoY 1997.

MARKIE John 1960-1964

Right-half
5'10"
b. Bo'ness, West Lothian, 16 December 1944

Career: Bathgate St Mary's/UNITED jnr Aug 1960, prof April 1962 (Hartlepool Utd trial May 1963)/ Falkirk May 1964 free/Clyde Oct 1976/ Stenhousemuir June 1977 to 1978/Dundee asst-coach.

A past captain of Scotland schoolboys, John Markie was a bright prospect in United's junior ranks along with the likes of Bob Moncur, David Craig and Bryan Robson. He helped to secure the club's first ever FA Youth Cup victory and manager Joe Harvey handed the Scot a debut during the 1963-64 season. That first outing did not go too well, the local press noting it has been "a miserable debut" as United lost 3-2 with the young Markie being kicked-out of the action. But his inclusion was always going to be a stop-gap move and within weeks the headline signing of England international Stan Anderson from Roker Park meant John's career development was blocked. He was released and returned to Central Scotland where he served Falkirk with distinction. Over 12 seasons Markie totalled in excess of 400 games and twice helped the Bairns to promotion. He was an outstanding servant at Brockville operating mainly in the centre-back shirt, being a teammate of Alex Ferguson for Falkirk for a period.

Appearances & Goals:
Debut v Northampton Town (h) 26 October 1963
FL: 2 app 0 gls
Total: 2 app 0 gls

Honours:
Scot sch-youth app/FAYC winner 1962/SL div 2 champs 1970, 1975.

MARSHALL Gordon 1963-1968

Goalkeeper
6'1"
b. Farnham, Surrey, 2 July 1939

Career: Balgreen Rovers/Dalkeith Thistle 1956/ Heart of Midlothian July 1956/UNITED June 1963 £18,500/Nottingham Forest Oct 1968 £17,500/ Hibernian April 1969 £2,500/Celtic July 1971 free/ Aberdeen Jan 1972/Arbroath June 1972 to July 1975/Newtongrange Star player-coach Aug 1975/ Arbroath Nov 1975/Newtongrange Star player-coach Feb 1980 to May 1981.

Although born in deepest England when his father was stationed in Aldershot with the Gordon Highlanders regiment, Gordon Marshall was raised in Edinburgh with a distinctive Scots' accent. An outstanding schoolboy goalkeeper, he was picked up by Hearts and quickly was elevated to the senior ranks. A tall and commanding 'keeper, he made a big name for himself at Tynecastle, making his first appearance as a 17-year-old against the Magpies in a friendly at St James' Park during 1956. Marshall hardly missed a fixture over six seasons and claimed 268 first-team matches, earning title and cup medals in Scotland. Not one to unduly leap around his area, rather being safe and consistent between the posts, he was also chosen to represent England's Under-23 line-up and on several occasions United watched his progress. When Newcastle ran into a wages dispute with first-choice goalkeeper, Dave Hollins, they moved to sign Marshall for what was then a hefty fee, a record for a goalkeeper moving across the border. Remembered for his bravery at rushing at forward's feet

and all-green outfit, Gordon was an ever-present as the Magpies lifted the Second Division title, and a regular as they re-established their position in Division One. Losing his place, he was on the bench for Newcastle's first European fixture then moved south joining Forest, too hastily as he later admitted, then concluded his career back in Scotland. From a sporting family, his eldest son Gordon senior appeared for Celtic and for Scotland, while his younger offspring, Scott, pulled on Arsenal and Southampton colours and was a member of his country's youth World Cup side in 1989. Additionally, his daughter and grand-daughter both appeared nationally at basketball. Marshall played at European Cup level with Hearts as well as for Celtic, and after a long playing career eventually settled in Edinburgh, running a newsagency and barber's business close to the capital's famous Princes Street thoroughfare on West Maitland Street. When he signed for Hearts as a teenager, Gordon was working as a clerk at the North British Rubber Mill, while he was once selected for the Scotland eleven to face the Army, until officials found out he was actually born in England.

Appearances & Goals:
Debut v Derby County (h) 24 August 1963
FL: 177 app 0 gls
FAC: 6 app 0 gls
FLC: 4 app 0 gls
Total: 187 app 0 gls

Honours:
1 Eng u23 app 1960/FL div 2 champs 1965/SL champs 1958, 1960/SLC winner 1959, 1960, 1963/SLC final 1962.

MARSHALL Terence William James 1958-1961

Outside-right
5'7"
b. Whitechapel, London, 26 December 1935

Career: Leyton Orient amat 1956/Wisbech Town/ UNITED Dec 1958 £7,000 to June 1961 free/Boston Utd 1961/Wisbech Town Dec 1962/Hastings Utd 1962/Bexley Utd/Later, Canvey Island manager 1975.

Initially tried at centre-forward in the absence of both Len White and Bill Curry during season 1958-59, Terry Marshall was played out of position being an out and out winger, and rarely made an impact. Catching the eye of United's scouts playing non-league football for Wisbech when he stood out during a FA Cup run, Terry was the target of several Football League clubs and United's manager Charlie Mitten paid a large sum for the untried forward. A rival and second choice to Gordon Hughes on the flank, Marshall never developed in the way Mitten had hoped and was handed a free transfer after three seasons on Tyneside. Returning to semi-professional football, Terry was a noted non-league forward in the south. He later resided on the Channel coast and worked in the printing trade for a period then organised functions in the South East.

Appearances & Goals:
Debut v West Ham United (a) 27 March 1959
FL: 5 app 1 gl
Total: 5 app 1 gl

MARSHALL Thomas 1886-1889

Forward
b. unknown

Career: Pembroke [College]/Tyne Association/Jesmond/ EAST END Nov 1886/Pembroke [College] during 1888-89.

A forward who had made his way into Tyneside pioneering football from what is suspected, Pembroke College at either Oxford or Cambridge at a time when the district's first club Tyne Association had brought the game to the community. When the Tyne club was dissolved in 1886 he joined East End and became a regular player during season 1886-87, his senior debut taking place as Newcastle appeared in the FA Cup for the first time on a wet, dismal day against South Bank on Teesside. Although Marshall appeared only once in senior competitive football, he totalled over 30 outings for the club in the profusion of friendlies at the time.

Appearances & Goals:
Debut v South Bank (a) 15 October 1887 (FACQ)
FAC: 1 app 0 gls
Total: 1 app 0 gls

M

MARTIN Dennis William 1977-1978

Midfield
5'11"
b. Edinburgh, 27 October 1947

Career: Kettering Town 1965/West Bromwich Albion July 1967 £5,000/Carlisle Utd July 1970 £22,222/ UNITED Oct 1977 £40,000/Mansfield Town March 1978 £25,000/ Aarhus Fremad (Den) 1979/Kettering Town cs 1980 to 1983/Corby Town.

Initially a winger, Dennis Martin developed at The Hawthorns after being purchased from non-league football then at Carlisle, he was converted into an effective midfield player who could regularly get forward. Martin was thinly framed with a neat, skilful touch on the ball and clocked up 324 games for the Cumbrians, always being able to hit the net, scoring 65 goals. Described as a "wiry winger", he stood out at Brunton Park and was purchased by beleaguered boss Richard Dinnis for United when the club were struggling to avoid relegation from the First Division. Martin was given a place in the senior eleven and scored a memorable goal at Old Trafford on his debut, but with results not improving, after two months he was axed by new manager Bill McGarry and destined to spend the rest of his Gallowgate career in the reserves. He was a member of Carlisle's successful team when they topped the First Division during 1974. Dennis later resided in Kettering being employed in insurance, moving to Spain for a period.

Appearances & Goals:
Debut v Manchester United (a) 15 October 1977 (1 goal)
FL: 9(2) app 2 gls
Total: 9(2) app 2 gls

Honours:
FL div 2 prom 1974.

MARTIN Michael Paul 1978-1983, 1987-1990

Midfield & Asst-coach
6'0"
b. Dublin, 9 July 1951

Career: St Vincents/Reds Utd/Home Farm/Greenfield/Home Farm/Bohemians (Dublin) 1968/Manchester Utd Jan 1973 £25,000/West Bromwich Albion loan Oct 1975, pmt Dec 1975 £30,000/UNITED Dec 1978 £100,000 to cs 1983/ Wolverhampton Wand Sept 1983 briefly/Vancouver Whitecaps (Can) May 1984/Willington Ath Nov 1984/Cardiff City Nov 1984/Peterborough Utd Jan 1985/Rotherham Utd Aug 1985/Preston North End Sept 1985/UNITED chief-scout Nov 1987, becoming asst-coach to Oct 1990/Celtic coach June 1991 to June 1993.

An effective midfield player for United, tall and graceful on the ball, Mick Martin captained both the Magpies and the Republic of Ireland during his career. Son of Con Martin, a noted Republic of Ireland international, Mick exchanged a sports manager's job in Ireland to enter the professional game at Old Trafford. The Irish youngster appeared on 46 occasions of the Reds, then was a regular with the Baggies in 111 matches. Solid, honest and dependable, Martin began slowly at St James' Park, injured with a medial ligament knock which forced him on the sidelines for 10 months; an absence which many noted cost United promotion during 1979-80. Recovering fitness, he had to show fans he was worth his place again, Martin settling as part of the side to win over Newcastle's supporters with consistent displays in midfield, rarely to hit a pass astray; his performances during seasons 1981-82 and 1982-83 even prompted the crowd to nickname him 'Zico' after the Brazilian ace. Despite a strong following from the terraces, Mick was discarded just as Arthur Cox's side was to embark on an entertaining season which ended in promotion. Martin was left to move around the country, and even to North America, to continue his football career. He eventually arrived back on Tyneside and was, for a short time assistant-boss to caretaker Colin Suggett during a transitional period in management during October 1988. On leaving the game, the popular Irishman resided on Tyneside, going into business in the region, for a period running betting outlets and a sports shop then a family concern, Mick Martin Workwear & Promotions Ltd based in Swalwell, supplying workwear, leisure and promotional goods. He also became a local radio pundit covering United's matches as well as frequent commentator on Irish broadcasts. Mick also scouts for the Republic of Ireland FA and at times works as a match-day host at St James' Park. Martin is one of only a handful of players to have been sent-off in a FA Cup semi-final, when playing for West Bromwich Albion against Ipswich during 1978.

Appearances & Goals:
Debut v Crystal Palace (a) 2 December 1978
FL: 139(8) app 5 gls
FAC: 10 app 1 gl
FLC: 6 app 0 gls
Total: 155(8) app 6 gls

Honours:
52 Eire caps 1972-83/1 unoff Eire app 1972/1 Eire u23 app 1973/3 Eire amat app 1971/2 All Ireland app 1973, 1979/1 EL app 1972/FL div 2 champs 1975 (8 app)/FL div 2 prom 1976.

MARTINS Obafemi Akinwunmi 2006-2009

Centre-forward
5'8"
b. Lagos (Nigeria), 28 October 1984

Career: Soccer Warriors (Ng) 1998/FC Ebedi (Ng) 1998/ AC Reggiana (It) 2000/ Internazionale (It) 2001 £507,000/UNITED Aug 2006 £10.14m/VfL Wolfsborg (Ger) July 2009 £9m/Rubin Kazan (Rs) July 2010 £6.65m (Birmingham City loan 2010-11)/Levante UD (Sp) Sept 2012/ Seattle Sounders (USA) March 2013.

A chunky, solidly-built striker, Obafemi Martins proved to be a very potent attacking option, yet to the frustration of many, usually only in flashes. Joining the Magpies for a big transfer fee of over £10m during the close season of 2006, although not a tall player at 5'8" he had pace and a ferocious shot. A teenage debutant for Inter, he was never an automatic choice at the San Siro, although he did well over nearly five years, totalling 134 games (49 goals) and did make an appearance as substitute against United in the Champions League during 2002-03. Oba welcomed the opportunity of more frequent senior action at St James' Park, with Glenn Roeder seeing the exciting Nigerian the ideal player to take over from Shearer in attack. He scored 17 goals during his debut season of 2006-07 and netted several wonderful goals in a black-and-white shirt; a thunderous shot on the run at White Hart Lane included made headlines, as did his trademark somersault celebration. With an effective spring-loaded leap for the ball in the air for such a small man, Martins initially looked the part as he took over the coveted Number 9 shirt, but he was inconsistent and somewhat moody, on occasion seemingly not up for the contest or showing the work ethic required to make it at the highest level. Despite having the goods in his locker, perhaps in a better Newcastle side he would have accomplished more, but in the end most at Gallowgate were content to see him depart after relegation during the close-season of 2009. With United cutting the wage bill, he headed for Germany with a respectable 35 goals to his name in a Magpie shirt. His form continued in the same manner elsewhere, later moving to Russia, Spain and the USA. Martins made a brief return to England when he had a short loan period with Birmingham City, scoring the winning goal from the bench with his first touch in the 2011 Football League Cup final at Wembley. He skippered his country on occasion, while Oba's elder brother Oladipupo played for FK Partizan and his younger brother, John Abiou, also appeared for his country.

Appearances & Goals:
Debut v Aston Villa (a) 27 August 2006
PL: 76(12) app 28 gls
FAC: 2 app 0 gls
FLC: 4(1) app 1 gl
Euro: 7(2) app 6 gls
Total: 89(15) app 35 gls

Honours:
38 Ng caps 2004-12/WdC 2010/FLC winner 2011/It Lg champs 2006/It Cup winner 2005, 2006/Rs Cup winner 2012.

MARVEAUX Sylvain James 2011-date

Midfield
5'8"
b. Vannes (France), 15 April 1986

Career: AS Menimur (Fr) 1992/Vannes OC (Fr) 1999/ Stade Rennais (Fr) jnr 2001, prof June 2006/ UNITED July 2011 free (EA Guingamp (Fr) loan 2014-15).

Although he was overlooked by Liverpool when a deal appeared to be all but completed, 25-year-old Sylvain Marveaux was picked up by the Magpies as part of a French influx during the summer months of 2011. An experienced player with Rennais, registering 118 matches and scoring 20 goals, slightly-built, neat and tidy on the ball with good technique in the style of players to have been developed through the French system, Marveaux had to wait to get a first-team run in United's side, being sidelined for a long period with a recurring groin injury. Having a gifted left foot, he operated on the left flank of midfield and once fit for the 2012-13 season, showed the Tyneside public he was a talented player, able to open up defences with either a jinking surge, or penetrating ball into the box. The more Marveaux played, he seemed to grow accustomed to the energy levels and pace of the English game which were a handicap to the Frenchman. Yet he was overlooked for season 2013-14, on the sidelines for much of the campaign seemingly at odds with his manager at times. Raised in Brittany, as a teenager, Sylvain quit a university place to take up football at the Stade de la Route de Lorient. His brother Joris appeared for Montpellier.

Appearances & Goals:
Debut v Scunthorpe United (a) 25 August 2011 (FLC)
PL: 13(25) app 1 gl
FAC: 0(1) app 0 gls
FLC: 6 app 0 gls
Euro: 9(3) app 1 gl
Total: 28(29) app 2 gls

Honours:
11 Fr u21 app 2006-08/Fr sch-youth app.

MATHIE Alexander 1993-1995

Centre-forward
5'10"
b. Bathgate, 20 December 1968

Career: Gairdoch Utd BC/Celtic BC 1981/Celtic May 1987/Morton Aug 1991 £75,000 (Port Vale loan 1992-93)/UNITED July 1993 £275,000/Ipswich Town Feb 1995 £500,000/Dundee Utd Oct 1998 £700,000 (Preston North End loan 1999-2000)/ York City Sept 2000 free/Pickering Town 2003/ Spennymoor Utd manager May 2003 to Sept 2003/ West Auckland Town manager Nov 2003 to Sept 2004/Pickering Town manager 2004 to Jan 2007.

Newcastle first attempted to purchase Alex Mathie early during 1992, but the move fell through. Yet Kevin Keegan, persistent with all his transfer targets, tried again and clinched the deal almost twelve months later. A Parkhead product, Mathie only appeared rarely for Celtic in senior action, moving to Morton in search for regular football. There he became a prolific scorer and was top goal-getter in two seasons netting over 40 times; the Cappielaw side eventually cashed in when the Magpies took an interest. The strongly-framed, pacy Mathie arrived at Gallowgate with much to learn. As Andy Cole's deputy, the Scot had a memorable debut for the Geordies, scoring a spectacular volley and making another goal in a 4-2 victory over Sheffield Wednesday. Gaining regular action was difficult at St James' Park though. Mathie was more often than not on the bench, yet he developed his game further and by the time he left for Portman Road, again in search of first-team soccer, was a much improved player. Alex became an Ipswich Town favourite and was a regular on the score sheet in Division One, holding a place in Portman Road folklore by striking a first-half hat-trick against rivals Norwich during 1998. He totalled 132 games for Ipswich, netting 47 goals, and by the time he had concluded his career had registered over 400 senior appearances and more than 100 goals. Mathie for a while was a BBC Radio Suffolk pundit and then resided in York, working for Royal Mail as a delivery driver and occasional radio summariser and commentator.

Appearances & Goals:
Debut v Sheffield Wednesday (h) 13 September 1993 (sub) (1 goal)
PL: 3(22) app 4 gls
FLC: 2(2) app 0 gls
Total: 5(24) app 4 gls

Honours:
FL div 2 champs 2000.

MATHISON George 1926-1933

Right-half
5'9"
b. Walker, Newcastle upon Tyne, 24 November 1909
d. Gateshead, 19 April 1989

Career: Walker Celtic/UNITED amat May 1926, prof Dec 1926/Lincoln City March 1933 £675/ Gateshead Aug 1934/Burnley May 1937/ Hartlepools Utd Jan 1938/Blyth Spartans cs 1938/ Walker Celtic 1938.

A fair-haired teenage star on Tyneside during the mid-Twenties and raised in the Welbeck Road area of the city, George Mathison was a much coveted schoolboy international (capped in 1924) who eventually signed for the Magpies. With a cool poise at half-back, George rivalled the tenacious Roddie MacKenzie for half-back places at Gallowgate, and with the exception of a spell during season 1929-30, was usually second choice. Only filling in on injury, Mathison had to be content with North Eastern League soccer where he assisted United to the second-string championship trophy. After a spell with Lincoln, he moved to Gateshead's Football League outfit and gave the Redheugh Park club good service in almost 100 games. Failing to make an impact at Turf Moor, George tried to claim a place with Hartlepool but was selected for senior action only once. George was the legendary Hughie Gallacher's brother-in-law and played with, and against, the famous Scottish leader. On retirement from football, Mathison resided in Low Fell, Gateshead.

(Note: Although United's player ledger at the time of signing notes George being born on 20 December 1909, death registration documents show he was born on 24 November 1909).

Appearances & Goals:
Debut v Bury (a) 19 January 1929
FL: 20 app 0 gls
FAC: 2 app 0 gls
Total: 22 app 0 gls

Honours:
Eng sch-youth app.

MEEK Joseph 1939-1942

Inside-forward
5'6"
b. Hazlerigg, near Newcastle upon Tyne, 31 May 1910
d. Hazlerigg, near Newcastle upon Tyne, 17 September 1976

Career: Burradon/Newcastle Co-op/Seaton Delaval cs 1926/Bedlington Utd July 1927/Liverpool trial March 1928/Stockton c1929/Middlesbrough amat Jan 1931/South Shields (Gateshead) Feb 1931/Bradford Park Avenue Oct 1934/Tottenham Hotspur March 1936/Swansea Town Feb 1939 (UNITED war-guest 1939-42)(Lincoln City war-guest 1940-42) (Middlesbrough war-guest 1940-41)(Southport war-guest 1940-41) (Grimsby Town war-guest 1941-42)(Nottingham Forest war-guest 1941-42) (Burnley war-guest 1945-46)(Rochdale war-guest 1945-46)/Retired 1945.

When a teenager working down the local pit a young Joe Meek was rejected by Liverpool after a trial for being too small at 5'6", the Tynesider though developed into a fine footballer and a character of the inter-war years. Recovering from a mine accident which damaged his left foot, as a consequence he was forced to play more

M

with his right as a goalscoring inside-forward. The Geordie had a productive period with South Shields at the time when they moved up-river on the Tyne to create a new base at Gateshead. Meek registered 144 games for the club during their Football League years scoring an impressive 55 goals. He went onto have two good seasons for Spurs, scoring a hat-trick on only his second outing during March 1936 and claimed 51 appearances all told. From the outskirts of Newcastle, he returned home on the declaration of war and when in the services with the RAF pulled on the United shirt twice, netting in each of his matches against Hartlepools and Leeds. On leaving the game, Joe resided on Tyneside to his death.

Appearances & Goals:
Debut v Hartlepools United (a) 21 October 1939 (FLNE) (1 goal)
War: 2 app 2 gls
Total: 2 app 2 gls

MEGSON Gary John 1984-1986

Midfield
5'10"
b. Manchester, 2 May 1959

Career: Frampton Rangers 1971/ Parkway Jnrs 1973/Mangotsfield Utd 1975/Plymouth Argyle jnr Aug 1975, prof May 1977/Everton loan Dec 1979, pmt Feb 1980 £250,000/Sheffield Wed Aug 1981 £108,500/Nottingham Forest Aug 1984 £170,000/UNITED Nov 1984 £110,000/ Sheffield Wed loan Dec 1985, pmt Jan 1986 £65,000/Manchester City Jan 1989 £250,000/ Norwich City July 1992 free, becoming asst-manager Jan 1994/Lincoln City July 1995 free/ Bradford City asst-manager Aug 1995/ Shrewsbury Town Sept 1995/Norwich City manager Dec 1995/Blackpool manager July 1996/Stockport Co manager July 1997/Stoke City manager

July 1999 to Nov 1999/West Bromwich Albion manager March 2000 to Oct 2004/Nottingham Forest manager Jan 2005 to Feb 2006/Leicester City manager Sept 2007/Bolton Wand manager Oct 2007 to Dec 2009/Sheffield Wed manager Feb 2011 to Feb 2012.

Gary Megson headed for St James' Park following a controversial and short four month stay with Nottingham Forest in which manager Brian Clough did not give the player a first-team outing. Newcastle stepped in, and Gary ended up on Tyneside, rejoining Jack Charlton, his previous manager at Hillsborough where he had totalled 286 games in a consistent fashion. Ginger-haired, Megson had wholehearted commitment; he was a gritty link-man, a player to pass the ball short or long, but who rarely tried anything spectacular. During Charlton's one season reign at Gallowgate during 1984-85, Megson found a place in the side, but moved on quickly when a change in the hot seat occurred. An abrasive tackler and once described as a "top-flight journeyman", he enjoyed a well travelled career and can count himself as being one of the most unlucky players of his era, reaching three FA Cup semi-finals, in 1980, 1983 and 1986, but finding himself on the losing side on each occasion. Gary's father was Don Megson, a formidable defender for Sheffield Wednesday and England.

Appearances & Goals:
Debut v Southampton (a) 24 November 1984 (sub)
FL: 21(3) app 1 gl
FAC: 2 app 1 gl
FLC: 1(1) app 0 gls
Total: 24(4) app 2 gls

Honours:
FL div 1 prom 2002(m), 2004(m)/FL div 2 prom 1984, 1989, 1997(m)/PFA ToS (d2) 1984.

MELLOR William Gladstone 1914-1920

Goalkeeper
6'0"
b. Stockport, 3 April 1886
d. Nelson, Lancashire, August 1969

Career: Barrow (rugby) 1905/Barrow May 1907/ Carlisle Utd 1908/Norwich City May 1910/ UNITED Jan 1914 £765 to cs 1920.

A former rugby player in Barrow at three-quarter before switching to soccer, Bill Mellor rose to the attention of Newcastle director's when playing for then Southern League club, Norwich City. He was a noted custodian at the Canaries' old Nest ground, and after 73 matches headed for the north to settle on Tyneside. Signed as a planned replacement for Jimmy Lawrence, the frustrated Mellor had to watch on the sidelines as United's veteran Scottish 'keeper continued to perform at the highest level of consistency. Mellor had to wait in reserve, both before and after the First World War, and never received the opportunity to grasp the first-team jersey between the posts. He was once described as, "a risk taker, but classy nonetheless".

Appearances & Goals:
Debut v West Bromwich Albion (h) 17 January 1914
FL: 23 app 0 gls
FAC: 2 app 0 gls
War: 1 app 0 gls
Total: 26 app 0 gls

METCALF Arthur 1909-1912

Inside-right
5'8"
b. Seaham, near Sunderland, 8 April 1889
d. Liverpool, 9 February 1936

Career: St George's (Sunderland)/Herrington Swifts/ Hebburn Argyle Aug 1908/North Shields Ath Oct 1908/UNITED April 1909 £100/Liverpool May 1912 £150/Stockport Co Aug 1918/Swindon Town June 1920/Accrington Stanley June 1922/Aberdare Ath June 1923/Norwich City July 1925 to 1926.

A player who claimed a high profile on Tyneside for his positive play in local football, stockily-built Arthur Metcalf earned a professional contract with United. He soon became a more than adequate replacement for internationals Howie and Stewart in the club's line-up being clever and thoughtful, although somewhat daring with rushes on goal according to contemporary reports. Metcalf was transferred to Anfield in 1912 where he was part of Liverpool's FA Cup final side just prior to the First World War. He grabbed 28 goals in 63 games for the Reds, an excellent 45% goal-ratio, and was a forceful as well as opportunist goalscorer throughout his career, the Lancashire Daily Post making a declaration on Arthur's ability: "A likable man who knew the whole alphabet of the game." Later, as skipper of Accrington, Metcalf occupied all five forward positions while he turned out on 79 occasions for Aberdare when they fielded a Division Three South eleven. His brother, George, was a fringe player with Sunderland and Huddersfield Town. Arthur became ill following working as a gateman at Anfield and died at a relatively young age of 46 years.

Appearances & Goals:
Debut v Bradford City (a) 9 March 1910
FL: 12 app 2 gls
Total: 12 app 2 gls

Honours:
FAC final 1914.

MILBURN John Edward Thompson 1943-1957

Centre-forward
5'11"
b. Ashington, 11 May 1924
d. Ashington,
9 October 1988

Career: Welfare
Rangers/REC Rovers/Hirst
East Old Boys/Ashington
YMCA/Ashington ATC/
UNITED amat, then prof,
both Aug 1943 (Sheffield
Utd war-guest 1944-
45)(Sunderland war-guest
1944-45)/ Linfield player-
manager June 1957 cash-
exch deal for J Hill/Yiewsley
Nov 1960, becoming
player-manager Dec 1960/
Carmel College
(Wallingford) coach 1962/
Ipswich Town manager
Jan 1963 to Sept 1964.

John Edward Thompson Milburn was nationally and internationally known as 'Wor Jackie'. A Geordie idol for over a decade as well as for many a year after he ceased to wear the black-and-white shirt, in an era of wonderful centre-forwards Milburn was recognised as one of the best. Possessing devastating pace, a former pro-sprinter with the apt initials of JET, he had a lethal shot in either foot. Jackie was especially remembered for the ability to swivel in tight situations to power a drive towards the net. Noted for his many spectacular goals, the Northumbrian relished the big match atmosphere and created headlines over and over again with breathtaking efforts, notably in the 1951 and 1955 FA Cup finals, his latter 45 second header being one of the quickest ever in a Wembley final for many years. He also netted in every round of the 1951 FA Cup run to Wembley (8 goals). Joining United as a youngster during the war, Jack had worked as a kitchen-boy, store-lad and pit apprentice before starting his St James' Park career on the right wing. Continuing working part-time at local collieries during the Forties, he also played in all other forward roles during his long career with United, equally as well as in the famous Number 9 shirt. Milburn could join expertly in approach play while he showed tremendous control when running at speed with the ball. He also possessed a much heralded sliding tackle that took the ball from opponents. Milburn is second to Alan Shearer with 200 senior goals for the club while no other United player has scored more than his 238 goals in all competitions for the Magpies. He is also credited (with Shearer) as scoring United's fastest ever goal, after eight to 10 seconds against Cardiff during 1947, and is one of only two players (with Shearer again) to record over 400 appearances and 200 goals in competitive matches for the club. Jack also once netted six goals for Newcastle against Alberta when on tour of North America during 1949. In the reckoning for an England place, it was to Tyneside's anger that he won only half of the caps he should have done. Appearing in the ill-fated 1950 World Cup finals, Jack grabbed three for his country against Wales and twice netted hat-tricks for the Football League eleven. On leaving United, the Northumbrian became as popular in Northern Ireland, appearing for Linfield in European Cup football and scoring 155 goals in only three-and-a-half seasons; for a second time netting six times during a match, all in the second 45 minutes of a City Cup match against Crusaders during 1959. Jackie then sampled management at Portman Road, but was never cut out for that ruthless world. Always a genuine person, a gentleman of the highest order, he returned to Tyneside becoming a respected journalist for the News of the World, covering United's fortunes for over 20 years. A member of the famous Milburn and Charlton footballing family from the colliery terraces of Ashington, Jack was a modest individual and perhaps never quite realised how immense his standing was in the North East. Given a belated testimonial at St James' Park in 1967, an astonishing crowd of 45,404 welcomed the three-time FA Cup winner. And his death, due to cancer, was much lamented and was given nationwide media coverage when much of Newcastle came to a standstill for his funeral. Jack Milburn was the workingman's hero, Tyneside's favourite son. A character who always had time for his fellow Geordie on the street and who left an impression on everyone who saw him as a player, and everyone who met him as a man. Jack was made a Freeman of the City, the club's main stand is named after him and statue at St James' Park recognises his achievement to the region. In Ashington, another statue is located in the town centre while a main thoroughfare is named Milburn Road, near to his original home of Sixth Row. Another road is named Milburn Drive in Newcastle's West End.

Appearances & Goals:
Debut v Barnsley (h) 5 January 1946 (FAC) (2 goals)
(v Bradford City (a) 28 August 1943 (FLN))
FL: 353 app 177 gls
FAC: 44 app 23 gls
War: 95 app 37 gls
Others: 2 app 1 gl
Total: 494 app 238 gls
(Note: one unofficial 'Golden Goal' goal scored against Darlington during 1943 in a TTW Cup match not in totals)

Honours:
13 Eng caps 1949-56/WdC 1950/1 FA app 1954/3 FL app 1949-50/4 NIL app 1958-61/FAC winner 1951, 1952, 1955/FL div 2 prom 1948/NIL champs 1959, 1961/NIC winner 1960/NIC final 1958/NI GC winner 1958, 1960/NI FoY 1958/Eng HoF/NU HoF/FL Legend/Freeman of Newcastle upon Tyne.

MILBURN John Nicholson 1940-1946

Outside-left
5'7"
b. Crook, 15 September 1920
d. Crook, 18 May 2006

Career: Crook Town/Willington 1936/Witton Park 1937/Crook Town 1937/Brandon c1938/West Auckland 1938/Stanley Utd 1939/UNITED amat Oct 1940, prof Nov 1940 (Chelsea war-guest 1940-41) to 1946/Consett 1946/Annfield Plain 1946/ Spennymoor Utd 1947/Ushaw Moor 1948.

The first Milburn to play for Newcastle United and one hardly known to Magpie supporters. John Milburn pulled on the black-and-white shirt almost three years before 'Wor Jackie' stepped onto the turf, competing in the wartime home clash with Grimsby Town during December 1940. Not related to his more famous namesake and although known as Jack as well, he appeared mainly in the Northern Combination league for the club. That game against the Mariners was his only first-class outing, being second choice to Laurie Nevins for most of his period at St James' Park. Joining the RAF during World War Two, he worked as an Air Craftsman, an electrician on aircraft maintenance and during a period in London at RAF Henlow guested for Chelsea, alongside Sammy Weaver for the Blues. He also served in Egypt for two years and appeared for the British Services XI. Milburn later continued his trade as an electrician for the North Eastern Electricity Board and then with the local council. Residing in Crook, during his younger days, Jack was also a celebrated local runner in an era of popular professional racing.

Appearances & Goals:
Debut v Grimsby Town (h) 28 December 1940 (FLN)
War: 1 app 0 gls
Total: 1 app 0 gls

MILLER James 1888-1893

Right or Left-back
5'8"
b. Scotland

Career: Kilmarnock Dec 1885 to 1887/EAST END c1888 to cDec 1893/Hurlford Town 1894 to 1895.

A Northumberland County player, James Miller was once described as a "rattling good back". He was a noted player at Rugby Park for Kilmarnock being a strong and hard footballer, a regular in the side as Killie won the Ayrshire Cup for a third successive time in 1886. Also to appear for the Newcastle & District representative eleven, Miller was one of the pioneers of Tyneside football, he turned out for the East End club as captain when they were installed at Heaton and appeared in the Northern League as well as leading out the side for their first fixture at St James' Park against Celtic following the move across the city. At times a touch fiery, Miller is recorded as being the first East End (or United) player to be sent-off in a competitive match following a clash with future teammate John Barker in a West End derby meeting during 1889-90. Controversy tended to follow the Scot, he was involved in a bribery scandal during 1893 following a FA Cup meeting with Middlesbrough, although after an enquiry he

M

was publically exonerated. The Scot appeared at right-back during the club's final Northern League programme in 1892-93, and started in Newcastle's inaugural Football League season the following year. Miller took part in United's first senior match against Arsenal during 1893 but soon after was disciplined after declaring in November 1893 that he didn't like training and refused to turn up for action. The club suspended Miller and he never played senior football for Newcastle again. Yet James totalled almost 200 matches for the club once friendly and other fixtures are added to his first-class haul, a good servant to the early Newcastle United.

(Note: James Miller should not be confused with two other J Millers (qv) who also appeared for Newcastle East End at the same time).

Appearances & Goals:
Debut v Port Clarence (h) 6 October 1888 (FACQ)
NL: 50 app 0 gls
FL: 9 app 0 gls
FAC: 12 app 0 gls
Total: 71 app 0 gls
(Void NL: 3 app 0 gls)

MILLER John (1) 1889-1890

Forward
b. Scotland

Career: Kilmarnock area/EAST END August 1889 to Jan 1890.

One of three Millers, and two John Millers, hence the suffix of Miller (1), to appear for Newcastle East End in the early months of season 1889-90. All were unrelated, but all were Scots. Making his debut in the very first league fixture for the club, a Northern League clash against Darlington, he scored, as did Miller (2) while full-back James Miller was also in the side at Chillingham Road to make matters even more difficult for officials and journalists reporting on the game. As luck would have it, both John Millers moved on quickly as the season unfolded.

(Note: There are three J Millers recorded as playing in Scotland & England during this era, it is likely both of Newcastle East End's John Millers continued their career in Scotland.)

Appearances & Goals:
Debut v Darlington (h) 7 September 1889 (NL) (1 goal)
NL: 8 app 3 gls
FAC: 2 app 0 gls
Total: 10 app 3 gls

MILLER John (2) 1889

Forward
b. probably Glasgow

Career: Glasgow football/EAST END Aug 1889 to Oct 1889.

Unrelated to James Miller and John Miller (1) with Newcastle East End in the same season, John Miller (2), like his namesake, scored on his debut in the club's first Northern League fixture against Darlington. Although John showed up well in attack, scoring five goals in only six senior outings, he left Heaton after only two months during October.

Appearances & Goals:
Debut v Darlington (h) 7 September 1889 (NL) (1 goal)
NL: 5 app 4 gls
FAC: 1 app 1 gl
Total: 6 app 5 gls

MILLER William 1895-1897

Right-half
5'9"
b. Kilmarnock

Career: Kilmarnock Jan 1894 (Rangers loan 1894-95)/ UNITED June 1895 (Kilmarnock loan 1896-97) to June 1897/Jarrow July 1897.

For a season-and-a-half William Miller was a useful and reliable player in midfield. He had been noted as a man to watch after reaching the Scottish Cup semi-final with Kilmarnock and following a short stay at Ibrox, moved to Tyneside. Miller slipped into United's Second Division line-up without causing anyone alarm, except for one incident

recorded in the Club's official Minutes of Meetings. During December 1895 when at Lincoln for a match, he was accused of the theft from the dressing-rooms of two gold rings, a charge he admitted, and as a result he was suspended for 14 days. Not surprisingly, the Scot did not remain long at St James' Park afterwards, moving on loan back to Kilmarnock during February 1897 for the rest of the season.

Appearances & Goals:
Debut v Loughborough (h) 7 September 1895
FL: 42 app 2 gls
FAC: 6 app 0 gls
Total: 48 app 2 gls

MILLS David John 1982, 1983-1984, 1995-2008

Midfield & Chief-scout
5'8"
b. Whitby, 6 December 1951

Career: Middlesbrough jnr June 1968, prof Dec 1968/West Bromwich Albion Jan 1979 £516,720 (UNITED loan Jan to May 1982)/ Sheffield Wed Jan 1983 £34,327/UNITED Aug 1983 cash-exch deal for I Varadi/ Middlesbrough player-coach June 1984 to May 1986/Darlington trial Aug 1986/ Whitby Town player-coach May 1987/Whitby Town Aug 1988/Dorman's Ath (Teesside) April 1994/ Middlesbrough asst-coach then scouting for various clubs/UNITED scout Nov 1995, becoming chief-scout Oct 2006 to April 2008/ Middlesbrough chief-scout April 2008/Leicester City scouting co-ordinator cs 2009/Hull City scouting co-ordinator cs 2010/Leicester City scouting co-ordinator 2011.

On Newcastle United's staff in two spells as a player, then later as a scout for over a decade, David Mills had long been fancied by Magpie officials during his playing career. As a youngster he had trials at both Everton and Manchester United, but began his career on Teesside. David had his ups and downs at Boro, overcoming a back injury which threatened his career, but he flourished under Jack Charlton's management. Making a name for himself as an unselfish striker or midfield player who loved to get forward, Mills was good enough to reach the England squad during 1974. Raised in Robin Hood's Bay, the Yorkshireman had an impressive record at Ayresome Park of 111 goals in 398 senior games. He became Britain's most expensive player when he moved to The Hawthorns, but only did moderately well with West Bromwich Albion after his big move, turning out in 77 matches. Hard working, challenging and jostling defenders, he possessed a deft touch, a football brain and the natural ability to find the net in front of goal, David almost moved to Gallowgate during 1976 in a double swoop with Graeme Souness, but Gordon Lee's deal fell through and he had to wait for another six years before he did pull on the black-and-white shirt. And then, following an extended loan deal, United couldn't raise enough cash to buy him at £100,000, only for the player to return at a cut price. During the 1983-84 promotion campaign Mills acted as a utility forward, on the bench more often than not, but always an experienced head to call upon and who scored some crucial goals in that successful season. After suffering with a persistent Achilles injury Mills quit the game and was employed as a sales executive with a printing group based in Bishop Auckland as well as becoming a sports journalist for The People newspaper. During January 1988 he was seriously injured in a fatal car accident on Tyneside and took many months to recover his health, having to undergo several plastic surgery operations. A good local cricketer too, Mills scored the goals which took both United (against Huddersfield in 1984) and Boro (in 1974) to promotion. For over 20 years Mills has acted as a talent spotter, with an extended period back at Gallowgate.

Appearances & Goals:
Debut v Norwich City (h) 30 January 1982 (1 goal)
FL: 33(6) app 9 gls
FLC: 0(2) app 0 gls
Total: 33(8) app 9 gls

Honours:
8 Eng u23 app 1974-76/FL div 2 champs 1974/FL div 2 prom 1984.

MILNE William J 1894-1895, 1897-1898

Outside-right
5'9"
b. Newcastle upon Tyne, 1873 (Q1)
d. Newcastle upon Tyne, 10 January 1951

Career: Bedlington/Science & Art (Newcastle) 1892/
Rutherford College (Newcastle)/UNITED trial Nov 1893,
then again Dec 1894/Sunderland Nov 1895/UNITED
1897/Hexham Hearts May 1898.

The son of Newcastle United director and chairman,
George T Milne (qv), William was a good all round
sportsman, celebrated at cricket as well as football.
Milne was an auspicious local cricketer who represented
the Northumberland County side on 22 occasions (1894-1908). For the Magpies, he
appeared in the schemer's role, as well as outside-left or right and was described as
"graceful". Milne was a regular player in the club's reserve side but only occasionally
was given a first-team call-up, in part, to maintaining "an untarnished amateur
status" and a professional career outside football. He was one of several second-
string men to go on strike over during season 1894-95 and was dismissed. Later
rejoining the Magpies, Milne played once during the Novocastrians' promotion to
Division One during 1897-98. Known as Willie, he was employed with Newcastle
Corporation Health Department as a clerk and lived in the city's Elswick district. His
two brothers, James and George (junior), were also top-class sportsmen. George was
on United's books during 1903-04 and 1904-05, while James had a spell in United's
'A' side as well. All three brothers were respected cricketers for Benwell CC and George
was especially talented, represented the County on 152 occasions (1901-1928).

Appearances & Goals:
Debut v Walsall Town Swifts (a) 29 December 1894
FL: 6 app 1 gl
Total: 6 app 1 gl

Honours:
FL div 2 prom 1898 (1 app).

MILNER James Philip 2004-2008

Midfield
5'9"
b. Horsforth, Leeds, 4 January 1986

Career: Rawdon Jnrs/Leeds Utd jnr 1997,
prof Feb 2003 (Swindon Town loan 2003-
04)/UNITED July 2004 £3.5m (Aston Villa loan
2005-06)/Aston Villa Aug 2008 £12m/
Manchester City Aug 2010 cash-exch £24m.

At the time of his debut in top-flight action
with Leeds United, James Milner became the
second youngest player to appear in the
Premier League at only 16 years of age, then
quickly was the youngest ever scorer when he
netted against Sunderland in 2002. He soon
became a regular selection at such a tender
age, a star of the future and when Leeds
imploded during 2003-04, Newcastle quickly
acted to secure his burgeoning talent for £3.5m, bringing the now 18-year-old Tyke
north to Tyneside. Possessing the maturity of a player with more like 300 outings to
his name, Milner was versatile and operated on either flank, or in midfield and always
gave full commitment and effort to the cause, being perhaps the ideal modern forward
with a willingness to track back. Having already appeared on 54 occasions at the top
for Leeds, James continued to develop in a Toon shirt under first Bobby Robson. He
really came into his own during season 2006-07 when no-one played more for the
club as United had an extended run in the UEFA Cup. Hardworking down either flank,
he possessed a match-winning cross into the box. James was a flourishing young
Magpie, a regular for England's Under-21 line-up (skippering the side and winning a
record haul of caps) and destined for a regular place in the full side, yet Milner's sale
to Aston Villa just after the start of the 2008-09 campaign was very much against
boss Kevin Keegan's wishes who saw him as an integral part of his rebuilding process.
That started an unsavoury episode in the club's history which saw manager and
masters at loggerheads. Not surprisingly Milner blossomed at Villa Park, quickly
becoming a fixture in the England squad, so much so he became the target of Arab
billions as Manchester City became determined to acquire his talent. City paid a
staggering £24m for Milner and in a star-studded squad, James became something
of a model professional, at times content to spend time on the City bench as they
challenged Manchester United, Chelsea and Arsenal as the country's strongest side.

Appearances & Goals:
Debut v Middlesbrough (a) 14 August 2004
PL: 72(22) app 6 gls
FAC: 5(3) app 2 gls
FLC: 6 app 1 gl
Euro: 17(11) app 2 gls
Total: 100(36) app 11 gls

Honours:
48 Eng caps 2010-date/WdC 2010, 2014/46 Eng u21 app 2004-09/Eng sch-youth
app/Eire sch-youth app/PL champs 2012, 2014/FAC winner 2011 (sub no app)/FAC final
2013/FLC winner 2014 (sub no app)/FLC final 2010/YPoY (PFA) 2010/PFA ToS (PL) 2010.

MIRANDINHA (da Silva) Francisco Ernandi Lima 1987-1990

Centre-forward
5'8"
b. Fortaleza, Ceara (Brazil), 2 July 1959

Career: SC Maguary (Brz) 1973/
Ferroviario AC (Brz) 1976/AA Ponte
Preta (Brz)1978/ Palmeiras Sao Joao
(Brz) 1979/Botafogo (Brz) 1980/Club
Nautico (Brz) 1983/ Portuguesa (Brz)
1984/Crezeiro EC (Brz) 1985 (Santos
(Brz) loan 1985)/SE Palmeiras (Brz)
1986/UNITED Sept 1987 £575,000/
Palmeiras (Brz) loan July 1989, pmt
Feb 1990 £150,000 (CF Belenenses
(Ptg) loan 1990-91)/Corinthians (Brz)
March 1991/ Fortaleza EC (Brz) 1991/
Shimiza S-Pulse (Jap) 1992/Shonan
Belmare (Jap) 1993 to 1994. Manager
or coach to a number of clubs:
Palmeiras Sao Joao (Brz) 1995/
Fortaleza EC (Brz) 1995/ Ferroviario AC
(Brz) 1996/Hajer (SAr) Sept 1998/

Goiania EC (Brz) 1999/CA Rio Negro (Br) 1999/Al-Raib Dured (SAr) 2000/Nacional
(Brz) 2000/CA Rio Negro (Brz) 2001/Flamengo-PI (Brz) 2002/Hajer (SAr) 2002/SC
River Plate (Brz) 2003/Kedah (Mal) Jan 2004/Cascavel (Brz) 2005/Libermorro (Brz)
Nov 2005/CA Rio Negro (Brz) 2006/Libermorro (Brz) 2008/Aracati EC (Brz) 2008/
Fortaleza EC (Brz) 2009/Hajer (SAr) 2009/Parnahyba SC (Brz) 2010/Ceara SC (Brz)
Nov 2010/SC Maguary (Brz) by 2012.

From a family of eight children, as a youngster Mirandinha had worked down a salt
mine and left his birthplace of Fortaleza on the edge of the Amazon jungle in northern
Brazil to discover fame and fortune around the world. Using the playing-name of
'Mirandinha' after a popular footballer of Sao Paulo, he was the first Brazilian to take
to the field at the top level in England when the South American became United's
record purchase. Manager Willie McFaul brought the 28-year-old international centre-
forward to England with a reputed scorecard of netting almost 300 goals in Brazil.
The owner of a pig farm in Sao Paulo, the deal was a fascinating one, but speculative
and risky, in the end deemed to fail miserably. Small with explosive pace over 10 yards
and nicknamed 'Mira', he packed a powerful shot and did reasonably well during his
first year on Tyneside in 1987-88 with 13 goals, rarely producing the traditional
Brazilian magic, yet being effective, the highlight being two goals at Old Trafford
during September 1987. A selfish player like many centre-forwards, he could be
electrifying and frustrating in the same dash for goal. Many United players found
Mira difficult to play alongside, although at times he enjoyed some fabulous link play
with the emerging Paul Gascoigne. John Hendrie was to say in his biography: "He was
so greedy with the ball that you needed two balls on the pitch - one for him and
another for the rest of the team." However, during the following campaign, Newcastle
were locked into a relegation battle, and Mira was not the type of player for a grim
contest on the field. He clashed with new manager Jim Smith who let the South
American depart at a big loss to the club, and at one stage following a dispute over
money, United's boss was quoted in the local press as saying: "He can rot in Brazil."
Mirandinha was nevertheless a popular character on Tyneside, chirpy and somewhat
tempestuous. He returned to his home country and had the best spell of his career
with Palmeiras in Sao Paulo, scoring a recorded 61 goals in 140 outings for the
Alviverde. Following a nomadic playing career, Mira had an equally well travelled
coaching path; he was in charge of a number of lower level Brazilian clubs year after
year. He also began a scouting programme, sending players to Europe and was Brazil's
World Cup 2014 ambassador for his local region of Ceara, helping preparations for

M

the tournament. During 2013 Mira also developed a football museum at the new Castelao stadium in Fortaleza where he hosts visitors. His eldest son, Hernandes da Silva, appeared for Utrecht in Holland for a period, while another son, Diego, played football in Brazil and had trials in England.

(Note: There are two players named Mirandinha to play and coach in Brazil at the same time and care is needed to distinguish between the pair.)

Appearances & Goals:
Debut v Norwich City (a) 1 September 1987
FL: 47(7) app 20 gls
FAC: 4(1) app 1 gl
FLC: 4 app 2 gls
Others: 3(1) app 1 gl
Total: 58(9) app 24 gls

Honours:
4 Brazil caps 1987/OG 1984/1 FL app 1988.

MITCHELL David Stewart 1991

Centre-forward
6'1"
b. Glasgow, 13 June 1962

Career: Enfield/Adelaide City (Aus) 1980/Rangers Nov 1981/Sydney City (Aus) 1983/Rangers Aug 1983/Seiko SA (HK) March 1985/Sydney City (Aus)/Eintracht Frankfurt (Ger) Dec 1985/ Feyenoord (Neth) July 1987/Chelsea Jan 1989 £200,000 (NEC (Nijmegen) (Neth) loan 1989-90) (UNITED loan Jan 1991 to Feb 1991)/Swindon Town July 1991 £30,000/Altay SK (Trk) July 1993 £20,000/Millwall Oct 1993/Selangor (Mal) July 1995/Sydney Olympic 1995, becoming player-coach/Sydney Utd player-coach 1997/Parramatta Power (Aust) manager 1999 to 2001/Later Sarawak FA (Mal) coach 2005/St Aloysius College, Sydney (Aus) coach 2006/Perth Glory (Aus) coach 2006, becoming manager Nov 2007, then Director of Football Oct 2010 to March 2011. Also part-time Australia u23 coach 2007-08.

Although born in Scotland, Dave Mitchell was brought up in Australia, raised in Adelaide from a young age. He eventually paid his own expenses to return to his native Glasgow to appear in trials at Ibrox, suitably impressing Rangers' officials to earn a contract. Big and strong at centre-forward, he totalled 45 matches for the Gers showing pace and an awkward bustling style up front. Mitchell landed on Tyneside after a spell in Germany and Holland then two years with Chelsea where his progress was hampered by a leg injury. At Gallowgate he was only given two chances to win over manager Jim Smith. Scoring on his debut was a good start, but not enough however and Mitchell was sent back to Stamford Bridge. Moving to Swindon, Mitchell did well in the Robins' line-up, claiming 24 goals in 80 games, before continuing on his globe-trotting football adventure. He qualified to play for Australia, being a regular at international level and later becoming a noted coach. One of the Aussie's earliest footballers to make his mark in the senior game, Mitchell was honoured by the Football Federation of Australia with a 'Distinguished Roll of Honour' award.

Appearances & Goals:
Debut v Blackburn Rovers (h) 12 January 1991 (1 goal)
FL: 2 app 1 gl
Total: 2 app 1 gl

Honours:
44 Aus caps 1981-93/OG 1988/Aus sch-youth app/FL div 1 prom 1993/FL div 2 champs 1989 (6 app)/SLC winner 1985.

MITCHELL Ian John 1970-1971

Outside-left
5'9"
b. Falkirk, 9 May 1946
d. Broughty Ferry, near Dundee, 2 April 1996

Career: Woodburn Ath/Dundee Utd amat July 1962, prof May 1963/UNITED July 1970 £50,000/Dundee Utd Oct 1971 exch deal for A Reid/Falkirk Oct 1973 free/ Brechin City July 1974 to retirement in 1977.

Although a respected player on the Scottish beat, Ian Mitchell never fulfilled his potential when he crossed the border as the Seventies opened. His record over two spells

of 127 goals for Dundee United in 301 matches are statistics only bettered by only a handful of other players at Tannadice. But Ian found the different energy between English and Scottish football too much to handle, his ball playing skills on the wing or in midfield, being swamped by quick tackling First Division defenders. Ian later confessed he had a tough challenge with fitness, pace and defenders acumen down south as compared to Scottish football. Liking to beat his man with a jink and piece of trickery rather than speed, Mitchell perhaps wasn't given an extended run in United's side. He had one excellent display in a Magpie shirt, against Ipswich during January 1971 when he hit the net with a special volley, but Mitchell couldn't claim a regular place and he quickly returned to the Tay club where he continued to impress north of the Cheviots. When courted as a schoolboy international in 1961, the Scot turned down a string of top clubs, including Manchester United, Liverpool, Spurs and Rangers, and became a regular with Dundee when only 16 years old. As Ian concluded his footballing career, he entered business in Dundee retailing cash registers and business supplies. He also coached local Tayside youth sides until his early passing when he was almost 50 years of age.*

Appearances & Goals:
Debut v Pecsi Dozsa (a) 4 November 1970 (ICFC) (sub)
FL: 2(1) app 0 gls
FAC: 1 app 1 gl
Euro: 0(1) app 0 gls
Total: 3(2) app 1 gl

Honours:
2 Scot u23 app 1967/5 Scot amat app 1963/Scot sch-youth app.

MITCHELL Kenneth 1973-1981

Left-back or Centre-half
5'11"
b. Sunderland, 26 May 1957

Career: UNITED jnr Sept 1973, prof April 1975 (Morton loan 1976-77)(Tulsa Roughnecks (USA) loan cs 1978)/ Darlington Aug 1981/Workington cs 1982 to Sept 1982/Seaham Red Star Aug 1983/Kuusysi Lahti (Fin) 1984/Seaham Red Star cs 1985 to Oct 1985/Gateshead Sept 1986/Newcastle Blue Star Dec 1986/Humbleton & Plains Farm 1988/North Shields 1989/Seaham Red Star March 1990.

Kenny Mitchell was all set to start work in a new job at a local Sunderland shipyard before United handed him a full-time chance at St James' Park. Originally a centre half, then an out and out striker, Kenny Mitchell was converted into firstly, a useful utility player, then a competent left-back and later back to a central defender. Always eager to move forward and have a crack at goal, Mitchell was a regular choice in season 1978-79 and had a good run in Arthur Cox's Magpie line-up during 1980-81. When he left England in 1984 to join up with top Finnish club Kuuysi Lahti, the Wearsider appeared in European football and helped lift the local championship. Tall and fair-haired, he won a FA Sunday Cup medal appearing for Wearsiders Humbledon & Plains Farm in the final at St James' Park during 1988. After leaving senior football Kenny settled back in his native Sunderland, at times coaching local clubs.

Appearances & Goals:
Debut v Manchester City (h) 16 February 1977
(v Ayr United (a) 15 September 1976 (ASC))
FL: 61(5) app 2 gls
FAC: 5 app 0 gls
FLC: 0(1) app 0 gls
Others: 1 app 0 gls
Total: 67(6) app 2 gls

Honours:
Fin Lg champs 1984.

MITCHELL Robert Carmichael 1949-1961

Outside-left
5'11"
b. Glasgow, 16 August 1924
d. Newcastle upon Tyne, 8 April 1993

Career: Market-Star Jnrs (Glasgow)/Boys Brigade 1942/Third Lanark June 1942/UNITED Feb 1949 £17,000 /Third Lanark guest May 1956)/Berwick Rangers June 1961 free/Gateshead player-manager May 1963 to Feb 1966.

Along with Jack Milburn and Frank Brennan, Bobby Mitchell was the darling of the Tyneside crowd during the club's marvellous immediate post-war years. First catching Newcastle director Stan Seymour's attention when scouting two Partick Thistle players in 1948, Mitchell mesmerised United's supremo with a sparkling display and he soon after signed for the club. Costing United a record fee for a winger, yet the Scot was worth every penny spent, winning three FA Cup winners' medals with the Magpies. Known throughout football as 'Bobby Dazzler', he was tall and willowy, Mitchell was never the speedy type in the wide position, instead being famed for his immaculate ball control as well as wing wizardry; able to turn opponents inside-out in tight situations, feinting one way, then going the other to pass his full-back...and often waiting for the defender to recover and then beat his man yet again! All left-footed, one writer of the day described Mitchell as being "wonderfully balanced" and tricky as a conjurer". With a cool temperament on the pitch, Bobby could send over accurate crosses and he also scored many an important goal for Newcastle, especially in FA Cup ties, over 100 all told in a career which spanned 13 seasons at St James' Park. Always able to raise his game for the important fixture, he thrilled the crowd with magic footwork and ball skills, no other player has appeared more as a forward for the Black'n'Whites than Mitchell's 410 games, while he stands alongside only three players in United's history to reach 400 appearances and score 100 goals. He scored on his Scotland debut, Bobby would have won far more international honours but for Liverpool's Billy Liddell while Mitchell, who was brought up in the shadows of Hampden Park, was the Scottish League's top goal-getter in 1946-47 (22 goals). Operating most of his career in the Number 11 shirt, the Glaswegian did have a spell at left-half during his latter seasons under Charlie Mitten. He was given a testimonial fixture in 1961 and a 40,993 crowd turned up, clear evidence of the affection in which Mitchell was held by United's fans. Retiring during 1966, Bobby became a noted Tyneside celebrity, a publican for many years in Jesmond (The Cradlewell) and Heaton (The Lochside). Living in Backworth to his demise, Mitchell served in the Royal Navy during World War Two, as a telegraphist in the Mediterranean and Pacific.

Appearances & Goals:
Debut v Sunderland (h) 5 March 1949
FL: 367 app 95 gls
FAC: 41 app 18 gls
Others: 2 app 0 gls
Total: 410 app 113 gls

Honours:
2 Scot caps 1951/1 unoff Scot app 1956/2 SL app 1947-49/FAC winner 1951, 1952, 1955/NU HoF.

MITCHELL Stewart Anderson 1953-1963

Goalkeeper
5'10"
b. Glasgow, 3 March 1933

Career: Benburb 1953/UNITED Sept 1953 £1,050/ Third Lanark June 1963 £2,500 to April 1965 free.

Stewart Mitchell's 48 games for United were spread over seven campaigns, with 1958-59 being his best campaign with 11 outings as the club's senior goalkeeper. A reserve to Ronnie Simpson and Bryan Harvey for the majority of his stay on Tyneside, as well as later to Dave Hollins, the Scot at one stage had a long spell as United's third team 'keeper. Stewart was unfortunate to break his finger when he had claimed the guardian's shirt on an injury to Simpson. Mitchell's transfer back to Scotland was part settlement of a match arranged with Third Lanark at the time of the Dave Hilley transaction; a game which in fact never took place. Mitchell later resided in Hamilton employed as a manager engaged in financial advice with Sun Life in Glasgow.

Appearances & Goals:
Debut v Preston North End (a) 4 September 1954
FL: 45 app 0 gls
FAC: 3 app 0 gls
Total: 48 app 0 gls

MITCHELL Thomas Morris 1920-1926

Outside-left
5'7"
b. Tudhoe, Co Durham, 30 September 1899
d. York, 22 November 1984

Career: Parkside Utd/East Chevington Rovers/ Tudhoe Utd/Spennymoor Utd/UNITED May 1920 £100/Leeds Utd Oct 1926 £785/York City Sept 1931, becoming manager March 1937 to Feb 1950/ Norway FA coach c1945/Later becoming FA coach in Yorkshire & York City director cs 1961 to cs 1969.

Tom Mitchell was lithe, fast on the wing and hugged the touchline in the style of the day. Having a good record with Spennymoor, the Magpies picked him up as the Twenties decade began and he became a direct rival to Stan Seymour for the outside-left berth. Tom held the position for much of season 1921-22, but then saw the legendary Seymour hog the limelight thereafter, although Mitchell always was on hand to deputise over the next four seasons. He was good enough to represent the FA select eleven, and was a target of several clubs before he moved to Elland Road in 1926. Mitchell became a popular character in Yorkshire, totalling 152 senior games for Leeds and later assisting York City in various capacities, captain of their noted FA Cup giant-killing run to the Sixth Round during 1938. He is described in the Minstermen's annals as "one of the most influential figures in City's history". On retiring Tom remained associated with the game, an FA coach looking after Yorkshire schools and a City director. He was also a licensee at The Peacock public-house next to Elland Road for several years, while for a period opened a sports shop in York, this after having a similar outlet in Whitley Bay. For part of the war, Mitchell served in the RAF as a pilot officer and on peace was stationed afterwards predominantly in Norway where he coached for the Norwegian FA.

Appearances & Goals:
Debut v Chelsea (a) 5 February 1921
FL: 60 app 5 gls
FAC: 1 app 0 gls
Total: 61 app 5 gls

Honours:
FA app 1924/FL div 2 prom 1928.

MITTEN John 1958-1961

Outside-left
5'9"
b. Davyhulme, Lancashire, 30 March 1941

Career: Mansfield Town amat Jan 1958/UNITED amat Sept 1958 (Whitley Bay loan 1958-59), prof Sept 1960/ Leicester City Sept 1961 free/Manchester Utd trial April 1963/Coventry City Aug 1963 free/Plymouth Argyle Jan 1967 £5,000/Exeter City July 1968/Bath City Aug 1971/Trowbridge cs 1972/ Sidmouth Town/Tiverton Town player-manager 1978 to 1981. (Leicestershire County cricketer 1961 to 1963).

John Mitten, the eldest son of United manager Charlie Mitten, and brother to Charles junior who appeared for United's reserves and entered senior football with Halifax in 1965, was a noted schools and youth player, who turned out for his country several times at that level. He showed the sort of promise on the wing that prompted many to claim he was destined to develop into a player as good as his father. But Mitten never became such an exciting and penetrating player and perhaps suffered because of his father's reputation. At St James' Park John made his debut as a 17-year-old amateur and had the misfortune of failing with a penalty on his first outing, surprisingly being handed the spot-kick during an atrocious period of misses by the Magpies. After that headlining start, Mitten showed coolness and maturity for such a youngster as he filled in on the left wing on a handful of occasions each season during his father's reign on Tyneside. He scored twice against Bolton when still an amateur, showing a destructive turn of pace and dangerous left-foot shot, just like his father. But when Mitten senior was sacked, his son also headed out of Gallowgate. John then moved south, doing well at both Highfield Road (41 app) and notably with Exeter (116 app). A natural sportsman, he also excelled at cricket, on the Notts staff before appearing for Leicestershire (14 app) as a right-hand bat and wicket-keeper. John played for Lancashire too without starting a senior fixture. On retiring from the

M

game, Mitten resided in the South West, also assisting his father in a sporting promotion business. His son, John junior, signed for Coventry during the 1990s.

Appearances & Goals:
Debut v West Bromwich Albion (h) 22 November 1958
FL: 9 app 3 gls
FLC: 1 app 0 gls
Total: 10 app 3 gls

Honours:
Eng sch-youth app/FL div 2 champs 1967/FL div 3 champs 1964 (4 app).

MOLE George 1900

Centre-forward
5'9"
b. Stockton on Tees, December 1878
d. Co Durham, 1957 (Q3)

Career: Stockton St John's/UNITED Jan 1900/Burnley July 1900 to cs 1902/South Bank.

After moving to St James' Park from local football on Teesside, George Mole deputised once for Sandy Macfarlane during season 1899-1900. Although he found the net on his debut against Preston in a 4-1 defeat, the small but stocky striker quickly departed, trying his fortune at Turf Moor where he recorded 12 games, netting on three occasions. Known as 'Barney', one of Mole's goals for Burnley was in a 7-0 FA Cup hammering of Manchester United.

Appearances & Goals:
Debut v Preston North End (a) 31 March 1900 (1 goal)
FL: 1 app 1 gl
Total: 1 app 1 gl

MONCUR Robert 1960-1974

Centre-half
5'10"
b. Perth, 19 January 1945

Career: Perth Life Boys/Uphall BC/ Tynecastle BC/UNITED jnr Oct 1960, prof April 1962/Sunderland June 1974 £30,000/Carlisle Utd player-manager Nov 1976, becoming manager Sept 1977/ Heart of Midlothian manager Feb 1980/ Plymouth Argyle manager June 1981 to Sept 1983/Hartlepool Utd manager Oct 1988 to Dec 1989.

Bobby Moncur was one of Newcastle United's finest captains and a superb central defender who marshalled the Magpies during the club's European success and then run to Wembley in 1974. A likable Scot off the field, Moncur was a rugged and determined player on it. As a past Scotland schoolboy captain, he was raised in Perth then from nine years of age at Kirkliston near Edinburgh. Bob began his career on Tyneside when 15 years old as an attacking half-back or inside-forward scoring in United's FA Youth Cup victory over Wolves in 1962. But the Scot struggled to claim a first-team place during his first five years with the club and almost departed for a small fee when 22 years old. Moncur though was determined to turn an average career into a great one and during season 1965-66, Bob began to concentrate on a central defender's role. Soon he was to dominate the centre-half position as the team's key figure at the back for the next eight seasons. Able to read the play which made up for a lack of pace, few were better in the country during the late 1960s and early 1970s. United's most capped Scot, Bobby also skippered his country and was rated highly by several top names in football, including

Sir Matt Busby who once said: "He is a splendid captain and leader of men." Dedicated to the Black'n'Whites' cause, he led Newcastle to a marvellous European victory in 1969, netting a stunning hat-trick over the two legged final with Ujpesti Dozsa, the pinnacle of an outstanding career in the game. Before joining the Gallowgate set-up, Bob had trials with Manchester United, Preston and Wolves while he ended his playing days at Roker Park where he was Bob Stokoe's skipper and led Sunderland to promotion, totalling 101 games for the red-and-whites before moving into management. Following a spell in charge of clubs at opposite ends of the country, he returned to Tyneside opening a squash club for a period and working with Newcastle United in an insurance business as well as hospitality, later becoming a club ambassador and having his own corporate suite at St James' Park. He also for a while was a local radio commentator and Director of Corporate Events at Ardwark Manor hotel and golf complex near York. An accomplished sailor, Bob additionally set up a sailing school on the Tyne, later having a company in the Caribbean sailing a catamaran based in St Vincent. A Royal Yachting Association master and instructor, Moncur has taken part in the Round Britain and Fastnet races, as well as Trans-Atlantic and south-north crossings, while he also competed in the Tall Ships race in 1995. He excelled at most sports, winning the footballer's golf championship. Bob lives in Low Fell, Gateshead and was honoured as a Freeman of the town.

(Note: Although publicised as becoming Whitley Bay coach in 1984, he did not take up the appointment.)

Appearances & Goals:
Debut v Luton Town (a) 30 March 1963
FL: 293(3) app 3 gls
FAC: 17 app 0 gls
FLC: 10 app 0 gls
Euro: 22 app 4 gls
Others: 15 app 2 gls
Total: 357(3) app 9 gls
(Void FAC: 1 app 1 gl)

Honours:
16 Scot caps 1968-72/1 unoff Scot app 1971/1 Scot u23 app 1968/Scot sch-youth app/FAC final 1974/FL div 2 champs 1965, 1976/ICFC winner 1969/SL div 1 champs 1980(m)/FAYC winner 1962/NU HoF/Freeman of Gateshead 2009.

MONKHOUSE Alan Thompson William 1953-1956

Centre-forward
5'10"
b. Stockton on Tees, 23 October 1930
d. Teesside, February 1992

Career: Thornaby/Millwall Aug 1950/UNITED Oct 1953 £11,500/York City June 1956 £4,000/ South Shields July 1957/Stockton.

Spotted playing for the army when on National Service, Alan Monkhouse made his debut for Millwall as a teenage amateur and quickly developed into a good striker in the lower divisions recording 23 goals in 69 games for the Lions. He never settled in London though and, eager to return north, he was delighted to join the Magpies, even though he was not guaranteed a place in United's forward line. Rivalling Milburn, Keeble and occasionally Len White, before his move to wear the Number 9 shirt, Monkhouse was a robust and effective leader in attack. Described by a colleague as "a strong, bustling old-fashioned centre-forward", he perhaps wasn't pretty to watch, but the Teessider's record of 11 goals in 23 matches in a black-and-white shirt was first-class and with United fighting off relegation during season 1953-54, Monkhouse took the weight off Newcastle's playmakers. He struggled to gain the support of United's fans on occasion, more used to seeing polished players, but did win over many doubters after a hat-trick against Sheffield United. Alan became something of a hero after striking two crucial goals in a FA Cup tie with Nottingham Forest the following season, although he missed out on both the semi-final, and final line-ups in 1955. On leaving the game, Alan settled back in Teesside, a caretaker for a local school near Norton.

Appearances & Goals:
Debut v Cardiff City (h) 7 November 1953
FL: 21 app 9 gls
FAC: 2 app 2 gls
Total: 23 app 11 gls

MOONEY Edward (Peter) 1917-1927

..ght or Left-half

..7"

.. Walker, Newcastle upon Tyne, 22 March 1897

.. [Newcastle upon Tyne, 1955 (Q1)]

Career: Walker Celtic/UNITED amat 1917, prof Aug
..919/Hull City June 1927 £500/ Scunthorpe &
..ndsey Utd Aug 1928/ Shildon/Northfleet Utd
..rial/Walker Celtic 1930/Local Tyneside football.

.. versatile midfielder, Edward Mooney was
..omething of a utility player for United over eight
..easons immediately following World War One. He
..arned a contract having impressed playing for
..nited's junior club, Newcastle Swifts. Operating as a
..egular at left and right-half, as well as centre-half, in
..he days before a pivot defender, Mooney was a popular
..ocal lad who had graduated to the top from being a Tyneside
..hipyard worker. Cheery and always to give the side total effort, he was known as
..Peter' (although it has not been ascertained if this was a Christian name or a
..ickname), had a broad Geordie accent and in many ways was a true son of the Tyne.
..fter taking part in United's FA Cup victory in 1924 and appearing on three occasions
..uring the title success in 1926-27, Mooney was transferred to Humberside; a move
..nged with controversy after Hull noted the player was unfit and claimed a reduction
..n the fee. A Football League committee considered the matter and judged in
..ewcastle's favour. Following a long career in local football, Mooney later was a
..teward in a Washington social club. Peter is related to James Bradford who appeared
..or Hartlepool as well as to Bernard Bradford of Hull and Walsall. He is a great-uncle
..o television and music star, Jimmy Nail.

Appearances & Goals:

.ebut v Huddersfield Town (h) 31 January 1920 (FAC)

.L: 121 app 3 gls

.AC: 14 app 1 gl

.otal: 135 app 4 gls

Honours:

.L champs 1927 (3 app)/FAC winner 1924.

MOONEY Thomas 1936-1944

.utside-left

.7"

.. Tollcross, Glasgow, 31 October 1910

.. Carluke, Lanarkshire, 15 December 1981

Career: Kirkmuirhill/Stonehouse Violet/Royal
..lbert/ Larkhall Thistle/Celtic May
..929/Airdrieonians 1932/UNITED Oct 1936 £2,650
..Airdrieonians war-guest 1940-43)(Albion Rovers
..var-guest 1943-44)(Dumbarton war-guest
..944-45)/Morton 1944.

.om Mooney was in great demand by English clubs
..ollowing a string of good displays for Airdrie in over
..150 games and also for the Scottish League side. A
..ootballer who could delight the crowd, he was
..direct and possessed a terrific shot that became his
..allmark. Tommy wore only size four boots, but
..ould hit the ball with stinging power towards the net. Famed for his hard driven cross
..oo, one cigarette card pen-picture of him during the Thirties noted: "He is, perhaps
..nore of an individualist than a combining player, but is nevertheless a real match-
..vinner." Another description of Mooney likened him to a past United and Scotland
..reat, noting he was a "will o'the wisp, reminiscent of Bobby Templeton". Mooney was
..apidly becoming an exciting talent at St James' Park just as war loomed, but his
..lossoming career like many others during that era was shattered in September 1939
..n the outbreak of the Second World War. After leaving the game, Tom settled in the
..Airdrie area of Central Scotland.

Appearances & Goals:

.ebut v Leicester City (h) 10 October 1936

.L: 75 app 17 gls

.AC: 5 app 2 gls

.otal: 80 app 19 gls

.void FL: 1 app 0 gls)

Honours:

. SL app 1934-36.

MOORE Craig Andrew 2005-2007

Centre-half

6'1"

b. Canterbury, Sydney (Australia), 12 December 1975

Career: North Star (Aus)/Australian Institute of
Sport/Rangers Sept 1993 free/Crystal Palace Oct 1998
£800,000/Rangers March 1999 £1m/Borussia
Monchengladbach (Ger) Jan 2005/UNITED July 2005
free/Queensland Roar (Aus) July 2007/AO Kavala (Gr)
Jan 2010, retiring March 2010/Federation Football
Australia advisor and ambassador.

Seasoned Australian international centre-back Craig
Moore was one of several defenders to land at Gallowgate
in an effort to fill a longstanding gap in United's team-plan. Having spent a decade at
Ibrox in two spells with Rangers (over 250 app), Moore had moved to the Bundesliga
with Borussia Monchengladbach during 2005 but did not settle in the Rhineland and
ran into a dispute with the club. Newcastle boss Graeme Souness brought him back to
the UK as a free agent during the summer of 2005. With over 50 caps to his name in
a fine career, Moore did show the experience and know-how at the back, and gave
United's rear-line a steadying influence, but at 29 years old, not surprisingly perhaps,
was not the quickest and was caught out at times by the Premier League's top-level
marksmen. Captain of Australia in both the Olympic Games and World Cup, Craig had
to wait a lengthy period for his Newcastle debut, out of action with a hamstring tear.
He made his bow during March and gave an assured display helping United to end the
season on a high. The following programme of 2006-07 saw Moore begin as first-
choice centre-back but another injury put him out of action in November when looking
the competent player he certainly was. One of the most prominent footballers in
modern times from Australia, he was inducted into the Aussie Hall of Fame. On retiring
from the game, Moore returned to Sydney and became an advisor to the Football
Federation of Australia, a mentor to up and coming stars as well as team advisor and
ambassador to Australia's 2014 World Cup squad. He also worked in the football media.

Appearances & Goals:

Debut v Chelsea (a) 22 March 2006 (FAC) (sub)

PL: 25 app 0 gls

FAC: 0(1) app 0 gls

FLC: 1 app 0 gls

Euro: 3(1) app 0 gls

Total: 29(2) app 0 gls

Honours:

52 Aus caps 1995-2010/WdC 2006, 2010/OG 2004/11 Aus u23 app/Aus sch-youth app/SL
champs 1994 (1 app), 1995, 1996, 1997, 1999 (8 app), 2000, 2003, 2005 (3 app)/SC
winner 2000, 2002, 2003/SC final 1998 (sub no app)/SLC winner 1997, 2003.

MORAN Paul 1991

Centre-forward

5'10"

b. Enfield, London, 22 May 1968

Career: Tottenham Hotspur jnr July 1984,
prof July 1985 (Portsmouth loan 1988-
89)(Leicester City loan 1989-90)(UNITED
loan Feb 1991) (Southend Utd loan 1990-
91)(Cambridge Utd loan 1992-93)/
Peterborough Utd July 1994/Enfield Feb
1996 free/Boreham Wood 1998-99/
Kingsbury Town 1999/Hertford Town April
2000/Hendon 2000-01/East Thurrock Utd
2001-02/Boreham Wood 2002-03/
Kingsbury Town 2002-03/Potters Bar Town
player-coach 2002-03, becoming player-
manager to 2005/Nazeing coach 2012.

Paul Moran, nicknamed 'Sparrow' at White Hart Lane, was a slightly-built, play
anywhere striker who found it difficult to break into the Spurs first eleven, although
gaining plenty appearances from the substitute's bench, claiming almost 50 outings
all told. Arriving on Tyneside in a bid to solve United's goalscoring problems, Paul
Moran did not have the happiest of debuts for the Magpies. He missed a glorious
chance at St James' Park to make a name for himself against Wolves, and manager

M

Jim Smith didn't give him another opportunity. Moran attempted to carve out a career at several clubs, but didn't gain a contract before landing at London Road, Peterborough. He afterwards played and coached with several non-league teams around north London, working for the Press Association at matches and at times as a decorator.

Appearances & Goals:
Debut v Wolverhampton Wanderers (h) 23 February 1991
FL: 1 app 0 gls
Total: 1 app 0 gls

Honours:
FL div 3 prom 1991 (1 app).

MORDUE Thomas 1925-1926

Centre-forward
5'7"
b. Horden, Co Durham, 22 June 1905
d. Sunderland, 1975 (Q4)

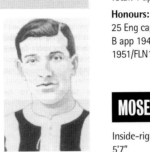

Career: Herrington Swifts/Hull City Sept 1923/Horden Ath 1924/UNITED Nov 1925 £150/Sheffield Utd Sept 1926 £500/ Hartlepools Utd Sept 1928 £100 to April 1931/Shotton CW Aug 1931/Horden CW cs 1932.

Known as 'Tucker' and from a celebrated local footballing family in County Durham, Tom Mordue proved to be a sturdy and aggressive little centre-forward. Gaining a chance only in season 1925-26 as Hughie Gallacher's deputy, Mordue performed admirably and was always well liked by supporters, whether in senior action or playing for the club's well supported reserve side. He bubbled with enthusiasm and later gave Hartlepool grand service in almost 104 games (27 goals). At the Victoria Ground, Tom played alongside other members of his family, Billy and Jack. Another relation was Jack Mordue of Sunderland and England fame who totalled almost 300 games for the Wearsiders while his brother-in-law was James Ashcroft, another England player. Like many of this celebrated family from County Durham, he was a formidable 'Fives' or handball player as well, a popular sport in the Durham coalfield at the time.

Appearances & Goals:
Debut v Sheffield United (h) 9 December 1925 (1 goal)
FL: 5 app 2 gls
Total: 5 app 2 gls

MORTENSEN Stanley Harding 1943

Centre-forward
5'10"
b. South Shields, 26 May 1921
d. Blackpool, 22 May 1991

Career: South Shields Ex-Schoolboys/Blackpool amat April 1937, prof May 1938 (Huddersfield Town war-guest 1941-43)(UNITED war-guest 1942-43) (Bath City war-guest 1942-44)(Aberdeen war-guest 1942-44)(Swansea Town war-guest 1942-43) (Sunderland war-guest 1943-44)(Heart of Midlothian war-guest 1943-44)(Arsenal war-guest 1944-46)(Watford war-guest 1945-46) Resumed with Blackpool 1946 (Distillery (Belfast) guest Oct 1954)/Hull City Nov 1955 £2,000/Southport Feb 1957/Bath City July 1958 to May 1959/Lancaster City Nov 1960/Retired March 1962/Blackpool manager Feb 1967 to April 1969.

Capped on 25 occasions for England, Stan Mortensen is one of Tyneside's most famous sons, recognised as one of the most dangerous forwards during the immediate post-war era. A legend at Bloomfield Road, he teamed up with Stanley Matthews to form an electrifying attack. With a tremendous burst of speed and deadly marksmanship, Stan was a lion-heart in the Number 9 shirt for Blackpool and England over a ten seasons. He scored a hat-trick in the 1953 FA Cup final and netted 226 goals in 359 matches for the Seasiders, plus a further 86 goals in wartime football for the club. He additionally recorded 23 goals for his country (one of the best goals-per-games ratios at 92%) including striking four on his debut in Lisbon. Apart from appearing for the England 'B' and wartime side, as well as Football League eleven, Mortensen also took to the field for Wales in a war international during 1943. Reaching another two Wembley finals in 1948 and 1951 (against Newcastle), on his single appearance for the Black'n'Whites, Stan netted twice in a resounding 9-0 defeat of Leeds in January 1943. The Magpies made a bid to sign the emerging Tynesider soon after war ended,

discussions on a cash-exchange deal with Len Shackleton taking place during May 1947, but negotiations fell through. At his peak as the early Fifties unfolded, 'Morty' as he was known, became an explosive goal-getter. In one spell during 1950-51 he hit 15 goals in 11 consecutive First Division matches. Stan possessed courage, was quick in thought and movement and packed a deadly shot. On leaving the game, Mortensen ran a card shop on Blackpool's Golden Mile and additionally owned sports and betting outlets. For a period he was a local councillor in Blackpool too, as well as sitting on the Pools Panel for many years. During the war years he served in a Wellington bomber and twice survived death; once when a parachute jump went wrong, and then in a plane crash near Lossiemouth in Scotland. Before embarking on a road to fame with Blackpool, Stan worked as a butcher's delivery boy and in the Tyneside docks cleaning scrap. A statue of Mortensen is located at Bloomfield Road.

Appearances & Goals:
Debut v Leeds United (h) 23 January 1943 (FLN) (2 goals)
War: 1 app 2 gls
Total: 1 app 2 gls

Honours:
25 Eng caps 1947-54/WdC 1950/3 Eng war app 1945-46/1 Wales war app 1943/2 Eng B app 1947-48/2 FA app 1945-51/5 FL app 1947-51/FAC winner 1953/FAC final 1948, 1951/FLN1(WLg) champs 1943 (3 app), 1944/FLN(WLg) champs 1942/Eng HoF/FL Legend.

MOSES George 1939-1946

Inside-right
5'7"
b. High Spen, Co Durham, 11 September 1920
d. Scarborough, 20 June 1987

Career: UNITED Aug 1939 (Aberdeen war-guest 1943-44)(Port Vale war-guest 1944-45)/Hartlepools Utd Aug 1946 to cs 1947.

Although slightly-built, George Moses clocked up nine games for the Magpies and had an excellent record of netting six goals. Scoring on his debut against Darlington at Feethams during the early weeks of wartime football, he was a fast, blond striker who played in a traditional centre-forward's role or as a schemer, quick to support the attack. An apprentice engineer in one of Scotswood's armaments factories at the start of the war, he later served in Bomber Command, as a flight lieutenant and had a distinguished service record. Moses joined Hartlepools for the 1946-47 Football League programme and totalled 21 games in first-class football.

Appearances & Goals:
Debut v Darlington (a) 4 November 1939 (FLNE) (1 goal)
War: 9 app 6 gls
Total: 9 app 6 gls

MOWAT Arthur (Archibald) 1891-1893, 1898-1900

Outside-right
5'8"
b. Hebburn, c1875
d. North Shields, 25 July 1924

Career: Wallsend Celtic/Wallsend Park Villa/EAST END 1891 to 1893/Wallsend Park Villa 1894/Hebburn Argyle July 1896/UNITED May 1898/Lincoln City June 1899/ UNITED May 1900/Prudhoe early Sept 1900/Seghill late Sept 1900.

A well known local personality during the years at the turn of the century, Archie Mowatt had three spells attempting a senior career with United, but managed only a single outing described when he joined the Magpies as a "young strapping player of great promise, he is very fast and a good shot at goal". Standing in for Joe Rogers during season 1898-99, he was nevertheless very popular with United's reserve spectators and was a key figure when Hebburn Argyle lifted the Northern Alliance trophy in 1897. He managed nine senior games for Lincoln City in between his spells with United. Mowatt was also a proficient racing cyclist, during an era when the sport was very popular in the North East. Archie was later employed in the Tyne shipyards by 1901, while as a 17-year-old teenager he was charged with "gaming" when playing cards on a Sunday in a public place at Wallsend, being fined along with three friends.

(Note: Various reports and registers have his surname as both Mowat and Mowatt, but more likely to be the former. He was born as Arthur, using his father's Christian name of Archibald, or Archie.)

Appearances & Goals:
Debut v Sheffield Wednesday (h) 17 December 1898
FL: 1 app 0 gls
Total: 1 app 0 gls

MUIR Andrew 1887-1892

Forward
b. Hartlepool, 1867 (Q3)

Career: Heaton Association 1884/Heaton Rovers 1884/Jesmond 1884/Elswick Leather Works 1885/Cheviot 1885/EAST END Sept 1887 to 1892/Victoria Wednesday.

Living on the Byker-Heaton border on Shields Road and a marine-engine fitter, Andrew Muir was a prolific goalscorer for East End at times, once claiming five goals in the record Northumberland Challenge Cup fixture with Point Pleasant during January 1888, yet amazingly he wasn't top scorer on the day, White grabbing seven in the 19-1 victory. Muir also hit four in the same competition against Ovingham during February 1889. He was originally one of the committee members at the Cheviot club in Byker when they merged with East End during 1887. Muir was a popular local sportsman totalling almost 40 games for the Heaton club in all matches and his older brother William Muir (qv) also played for East End, at times in the same line-up. Andrew was also a proficient cricketer turning out for Newcastle YMCA CC, North Eastern CC, Science & Art CC and Wesley Empress CC. All of Muir's senior outings for the club came in Newcastle's first season of FA Cup action.

Appearances & Goals:
Debut v South Bank (a) 15 October 1887 (FACQ)
FAC: 4 app 1 gl
Total: 4 app 1 gl

MUIR William 1885-1889

Forward
b. Hartlepool, c1864

Career: Tyne Association/Newcastle Rangers 1882/Heaton Rovers 1884/ Heaton Association 1884/EAST END cs 1885 (Newcastle Wednesday guest 1886)/ Rangers (SA) May 1889.

William Muir was brother of Andrew Muir (qv), also residing in the east of the city. He was raised on Teesside until his family moved to Heaton and originally started playing the game with flag bearers of the sport, Tyne Association and the Newcastle Rangers club. Described in census data as a "ship joiner", he was a cricketer too, skipper of East End CC and later appearing for West Elswick CC. William became a noted footballer during those early days, selected for Northumberland and the Newcastle & District select combination, while Muir registered both of East End's goals in their first ever FA Cup match against South Bank during October 1887. Although he only played one senior game for the club in an era before league action, he appeared in many local competition and friendly matches, totalling over 40 outings, often amongst the goals. William decided to emigrate to South Africa during 1891 to take up a prominent position in athletics. Muir was handed a gold scarf-pin as a token of his time with both East End football and cricket clubs. He later skippered Rangers of Johannesburg, a well known South African football team.

Appearances & Goals:
Debut v South Bank (a) 15 October 1887 (FACQ) (2 goals)
FAC: 1 app 2 gls
Total: 1 app 2 gls

MULGREW Thomas 1952-1954

Inside-right
5'6"
b. Motherwell, 13 April 1929

Career: Cleland/Morton/Northampton Town July 1949/UNITED Oct 1952 £9,000/Southampton Aug 1954 £12,500 joint deal with W Foulkes/Aldershot Aug 1962/Andover Aug 1965.

Quick to rise to prominence from the lower divisions, Tom Mulgrew was gritty and spirited, a player with purpose, having confidence on the ball with neat skills and characteristic solo dashes into the box. He showed up well during his early games in a Newcastle shirt during season 1952-53, setting up two goals with subtle passes on his debut and prompting one report to note he was "a real top-notcher". Those early impressive weeks on Tyneside even triggered speculation of a Scotland cap for the new recruit. At Gallowgate though, Mulgrew always had stern competition of international quality rivals for the inside-right berth, first from Reg Davies and then Ivor Broadis. As a consequence he

moved to The Dell as part of a joint deal (Mulgrew being valued at £7,000) in an attempt to play regular league football. He immediately made an impression, netting after only 15 seconds of his first appearance against Brentford, the fastest goal ever scored at the old Saints' stadium. Level-headed, Mulgrew became a crowd favourite with Southampton, scoring 100 goals over eight seasons and totalling 325 matches. Later Tom resided in Northampton, employed at a local steel factory, playing football for the works side.

Appearances & Goals:
Debut v Blackpool (a) 8 November 1952
FL: 14 app 1 gl
FAC: 1 app 0 gls
Total: 15 app 1 gl

Honours:
FL div 3 champs 1960.

MULGROVE Keith Arnold 1974-1980

Left-back
5'9"
b. Haltwhistle, Northumberland, 21 August 1959

Career: UNITED jnr Dec 1974, prof July 1977/Barrow cs 1980 free/Blyth Spartans March 1981/Consett 1982.

On the fringe of United's first-team pool during season 1978-79, Keith Mulgrove was a reserve to either John Brownlie or Kenny Mitchell at full-back. His one and only senior outing was as substitute at the Goldstone Ground when he came into the action for Colin Suggett. Being released by manager Bill McGarry, Mulgrove later moved into non-league football. He afterwards worked at Blenkinsop pit near Greenhead, then as a postman in the Tyne Valley. Mulgrove resides in his home town of Haltwhistle.

Appearances & Goals:
Debut v Brighton (a) 30 December 1978 (sub)
FL: 0(1) app 0 gls
Total: 0(1) app 0 gls

MULLEN James 1942-1943

Outside-left
5'10"
b. Newcastle upon Tyne, 6 January 1923
d. Wolverhampton, 23 October 1987

Career: Wolverhampton Wand amat June 1937, prof Jan 1940 (Leicester City war-guest 1940-41)(UNITED war-guest 1942-43)(Darlington war-guest 1943-46) (Reading war-guest 1942-43)(Middlesbrough war-guest 1945-46) Resumed with Wolves 1946/ Bromsgrove Rovers May 1960.

One of several celebrated Tynesiders to appear for the club during the war years, Jimmy Mullen joined the Wolves groundstaff straight from St Aloysius School in Newcastle and rapidly developed into a top winger. An England schools player and captain of Newcastle and Northumberland Boys, he could well have become a United player had his parents not moved south, but it was a Molineux that Jimmy fully realised his special schoolboy talent, making his debut as a teenager. With jet-black hair, he was tall, fast moving with a long stride, Mullen spent all of 23 seasons pulling on the gold shirt for Wolves, totalling almost 490 senior matches and scoring 112 goals, plus nearly another 100 wartime fixtures. Newcastle did try and bring him back to Tyneside, entering negotiations with Wolves during 1948 over a possible exchange for Andy Donaldson, but the deal fell through. A PT instructor with the Royal Armoured Corps during the hostilities, Jimmy partnered Jack Milburn during 'Wor Jackie's' United debut, and his displays as a guest when stationed at Catterick for Newcastle were as eye-catching as everything else in his career. Playing 12 times for England, Mullen won three titles and the FA Cup with Wolves, together with Football League, 'B' and wartime honours. Jimmy has the distinction of being England's first ever 'capped' substitute, against Belgium in 1950, when he came on for Milburn. He was awarded a Football League Long Service medal and on retiring from football Mullen opened a sports shop in Wolverhampton.

M

Appearances & Goals:
Debut v Sunderland (a) 5 December 1942 (FLN)
War: 15 app 4 gls
Total: 15 app 4 gls

Honours:
12 Eng caps 1947-54/WdC 1950, 1954/3 Eng war app 1943-46/3 Eng B app 1949-50/1 FL app 1954/2 FA app 1947-51/Eng sch-youth app/FL champs 1954, 1958, 1959/FAC winner 1949/FL WC winner 1942/FL Long Service medal 1961.

MULVEY Michael 1887-1891

Forward
b. Shettleston, Glasgow 3 July 1869

Career: Drumpellier Aug 1886/Motherwell/Darlington St Augustine Aug 1887/ EAST END Nov 1887 to April 1891/Gateshead NER Sept 1891/Grantham Rovers Jan 1892/Carfin Shamrock briefly Oct 1892/Celtic Oct 1892/Dundee Harp July 1893.

From the West of Scotland, Michael Mulvey was still a teenager when he arrived on Tyneside following a short spell in Darlington with St Augustine. A dispute erupted between East End and the Saints, the fixture between the two sides being cancelled because of his transfer to Tyneside as the 1887-88 season was underway, his stay with Darlington being ambushed by the Newcastle club. Versatile at wing-half or on the wing, as well as at centre-forward, Mulvey quickly made an impact and was referred to in the style of the day in the local press as being the "East End Dodger". He was a fine acquisition despite the animosity with Darlington and the Scot appeared for the Northumberland County line-up during his stay in the region. For almost four seasons the Glaswegian was a dangerous striker for East End, playing alongside fellow Scots McInnes, Sorley and Collins. Apart from his first-class record, Mulvey hit more than 30 goals in 80-odd sundry fixtures, topping a century of games for the club. Later into his career Mulvey joined Celtic for a brief period during 1892-93. He made four appearances and scored four goals for the Glasgow giants before heading to Tayside to turn out for the Dundee Harp club, soon to be suspended by the Scottish FA for failing to pay debts.

Appearances & Goals:
Debut v Sunderland (a) 17 November 1888 (FACQ)
NL: 29 app 5 gls
FAC: 6 app 1 gl
Total: 35 app 6 gls
(Void NL: 1 app 1 gl)

MURRAY John James 1932-1936

Left or Right-half
5'9"
b. Saltcoats, Ayrshire, 10 August 1908

Career: Saltcoats Victoria/Rangers Sept 1928/ UNITED July 1932 £2,500/Albion Rovers Nov 1936 £300.

An ex-plumber turned footballer, Jimmy Murray was a teammate of United's first manager, Andy Cunningham, at Rangers before joining his former colleague at St James' Park. A reserve at Ibrox claiming only a handful of outings in the senior line-up, he possessed wholehearted endeavour and Cunningham considered he could do a good job for United as he rebuilt a side. Murray operated in any position for United in midfield, appearing in different roles on a regular basis during his four seasons on Tyneside. As the Magpies' skipper on occasion, Murray was a consistent and intelligent performer for the club during a lean period in Newcastle's history.

Appearances & Goals:
Debut v Middlesbrough (h) 31 August 1932
FL: 92 app 10 gls
FAC: 4 app 0 gls
Total: 96 app 10 gls

MUTCH Alexander 1922-1958

Goalkeeper
5'10"
b. Inverurie, Aberdeenshire, 13 August 1884
d. Newcastle upon Tyne, 16 September 1967

Career: Inverurie Loco Works/Aberdeen June 1906/Huddersfield Town May 1910 £400/UNITED July 1922 £850/Retired due to injury 1924, becoming St James' Park groundsman May 1926 until his retirement in July 1958.

Alexander Mutch was one of the characters of Gallowgate for many a decade. Known as 'Sandy' and a former Aberdeen shipyard worker, Mutch made a name for himself after assisting Huddersfield when they entered Football League soccer during 1920, taking part in the Terriers' inaugural match. He became one of the country's most respected goalkeepers, totalling 25 games for the Leeds Road side over eight seasons. One of his last games for the Tykes was in the 1922 FA Cup final, then soon after headed for Tyneside to become a rival to Bill Bradley as United's 'keeper. Alex was by then a veteran, almost 38 years old. He became one of Newcastle's oldest ever debutants and, when over 39, one of the most senior to appear for the Magpies. During season 1923-24, Mutch held the custodian's shirt and would have appeared at Wembley in the FA Cup final for United but for an ironic injury sustained against Aston Villa. With many of United's Cup side rested for the league fixture just prior to the final, Mutch was one of only two regulars to appear at Villa Park, but he was carried off with a twisted knee and cartilage damage which forced him to miss the final. Mutch retired soon after due to that knee injury, but continued an association with the Geordies for another 34 years as groundsman and back-stage personality, Jack Milburn once noting, "the players thought the world of him". The name of Mutch was further linked with the club when his son, Alex junior (qv) was appointed assistant-trainer, later becoming United's physio to his death in 1987 and with Newcastle for over 50 years.

Appearances & Goals:
Debut v Everton (h) 26 August 1922
FL: 36 app 0 gls
FAC: 7 app 0 gls
Total: 43 app 0 gls

Honours:
FL div 2 prom 1920/FAC winner 1922/FAC final 1920.

MYERS James 1940-1941

Inside-right
5'9"
b. Co Durham, 1922

Joining the St James' Park staff as an amateur in August 1940 from the Ferryhill Athletic club, Jimmy Myers turned professional during April 1941 and was another player whose career never took off after being a promising junior. War service restricted him to a single game for the Magpies, during May 1941 against Leeds on Tyneside, a scoring debut for the teenager.

Appearances & Goals:
Debut v Leeds United (h) 3 May 1941 (FLN) (1 goal)
War: 1 app 1 gl
Total: 1 app 1 gl

McBAIN Thomas 1932

Centre-forward
5'9"
b. Whifflet, Lanarkshire, 1902

Career: Whifflet Emerald/UNITED Feb 1932
45/Carlisle Utd Oct 1932 to May 1934/
Glenavon cs 1934/Carlisle Utd asst-trainer to 1950.

Tom McBain, a frequent Scottish junior goalscorer, caught the attention of many top clubs as the thirties era opened. United brought him to England, but the small leader who possessed more than a trick or two found it difficult to break into the Magpies' first eleven. McBain stood in once for Jack Allen during season 1931-32, then went onto serve Carlisle United well, firstly as a player in 44 matches, then behind the scenes for several years. His debut and single outing for the Black'n'Whites resulted in a 6-0 defeat at Fratton Park.

Appearances & Goals:
Debut v Portsmouth (a) 16 April 1932
FL: 1 app 0 gls
Total: 1 app 0 gls

McCAFFERY Aidan 1972-1978

Centre-half
5'11"
b. Jarrow, 30 August 1957

Career: UNITED jnr Sept 1972,
prof Jan 1975/ Derby Co Aug
1978 £60,000/Bristol Rovers
Aug 1980 £75,000 (Bristol City
loan 1981-82) (Torquay Utd
loan 1984-85)/Exeter City July
1985 free/Hartlepool Utd Feb
1987/ Whitley Bay cs 1987
/Carlisle Utd asst-player-coach
Jan 1988, becoming manager
April 1991 to Sept 1992/Later
scouted for Bristol Rovers and
coached Florida College (USA).

Recommended to United, by then schoolteacher and former international athlete, Brendan Foster, Aidan McCaffery was a bright teenage star, appearing for the Magpies as a 17-year-old, his debut being in a thrilling 5-4 defeat at Portman Road. A former England youth captain, Aidan was initially second choice to Glenn Keeley, but the Tynesider was handed the Number 5 shirt for the 1976-77 season and on many occasions looked a solid defender alongside Geoff Nulty as United qualified for Europe. He showed the potential to reach the top, but during the club's turmoil and relegation mire the following season, Aidan was one of several youngsters to suffer. He had a series of rows with Newcastle's management and was released to join the squad at the Baseball Ground. After a reasonable spell with Derby, McCaffery made 224 senior outings over five seasons with Bristol Rovers, a solid and reliable defender at that level. He was also skipper at Eastville and once during 1984 in a match against Southend he had the misfortune to swallow his tongue after a collision, the swift action of the club physio saving his life. After a spell as Carlisle's boss, McCaffery joined the Northumbria Police.

Appearances & Goals:
Debut v Ipswich Town (a) 15 March 1975
FL: 57(2) app 4 gls
FAC: 5 app 1 gl
FLC: 3(1) app 0 gl
Euro: 3 app 0 gls
Total: 68(3) app 5 gls

Honours:
Eng sch-youth app.

McCALL William 1948

Outside-left
5'6"
b. Glasgow, 14 November 1920

Career: Bridgeton Waverley/Blantyre Victoria/Hamilton
Acc Jan 1944/Aberdeen prof May 1945 (Chelsea war-guest
1945-46)/UNITED Jan 1948 £8,400/Motherwell Dec 1948
£5,500/Third Lanark Sept 1950 £3,000/Worcester City
Jan 1953/Arbroath Aug 1953 to April 1954 free.

Willie McCall had lifted the Scottish Cup before he arrived at St James' Park as part of the cash and exchange deal that saw the popular Tommy Pearson head for Aberdeen. A compact, forceful winger, diminutive and direct in the traditional style of flankers, McCall took part in the Black'n'Whites' run-in to secure promotion during 1948. But he was then replaced by firstly George Hair, then Bobby Mitchell, when Newcastle reclaimed their First Division status. A most popular player in the Granite City, he allegedly left the Dons under controversy after a row over smoking before fixtures, then still popular with footballers. Leaving Tyneside, McCall had short, but productive spells at both Motherwell and Third Lanark. Afterwards, Willie settled in his native Glasgow, employed by the Marley Tile Company for many years.

Appearances & Goals:
Debut v Brentford (a) 17 January 1948
FL: 16 app 4 gls
Total: 16 app 4 gls

Honours:
FL div 2 prom 1948/SC winner 1947.

McCLARENCE Joseph P 1904-1908

Centre-forward
5'10"
b. Newcastle upon Tyne, 1885 (Q3)

Career: Northcote/Wallsend Park Villa/UNITED Feb 1904
£20/Bolton Wand March 1908 £350/Bradford Park
Avenue Nov 1908/Distillery (Belfast) cs 1911 to 1913.

An incessant and dashing goalscorer in reserve football for the Tynesiders, Joe McClarence performed creditably whenever called upon in first-team action. He filled in for noted forwards, Appleyard and Orr, covering their absence well, and always was capable of striking goals himself, claiming 13 in his limited opportunities, while in friendly action he once netted four against St Mirren. Joe was reserve for United's 1905 FA Cup final and took a small part in two of United's title successes, during 1904-05 and 1906-07, before moving to Bolton and onto Bradford where he continued to bag goals, netting 33 in 68 senior matches for the Park Avenue club. McClarence also did well with Belfast's Distillery claiming 30 goals in 73 matches. He unusually was also a dentist when playing football, later concentrating on that profession and settling in Belfast into the 1940s.

Appearances & Goals:
Debut v Blackburn Rovers (h) 3 December 1904 (1 goal)
FL: 30 app 13 gls
FAC: 2 app 0 gls
Total: 32 app 13 gls

Honours:
FL champs 1905 (6 app), 1907 (5 app)/FL div 2 champs 1909 (7 app).

Mc

McCLEN James David 1994-2005

Midfield
5'8"
b. Newcastle upon Tyne, 13 May 1979

Career: Cramlington Jnrs/UNITED jnr cs 1994, prof July 1997 (Motherwell loan 2000-01)/Carlisle Utd Aug 2005 to Dec 2005 free/Bristol City trial Jan 2006/Shrewsbury Town trial Feb to April 2006/ Miami (USA) trial May 2006/Blyth Spartans 2006/ Kidderminster Harriers June 2006 (Bedlington Terriers loan 2006-07)/Hamilton Acc Jan 2007 free to March 2007/Motherwell trial cs 2007/Gateshead Aug 2007/Newcastle Blue Star Jan 2008/Barrow trial cs 2009/Morpeth Town Aug 2009/Pattaya Utd (Th) Sept 2009/West Allotment Celtic Jan 2010/Hebburn Town Oct 2010 to 2013.

Raised in Cramlington, Jamie McClen joined United's School of Excellence set-up when only 10 years of age. Having trials with Hearts, Manchester City, Everton and Leeds, the young midfielder signed schoolboy forms with the Magpies in 1993. Not tall at 5'8", but solidly-built, the dark-haired link-man was a tireless worker in the engine-room of the field. Manager Ruud Gullit liked his all-round capabilities as well as ability to get forward and when Des Hamilton moved out on loan, McClen moved up a level and got a chance. Jamie crept into contention in season 1998-99 and during the following campaign under Bobby Robson he deputised on three occasions in both the Premier League and UEFA Cup. McClen also got on the field from the bench several times. With the special talent of Solano, Speed and Dyer as well as new men Acuna and Bassedas ahead of him for midfield places, he stood little chance of progressing. Like the majority of Newcastle's modern home-grown products, McClen was destined to find a career elsewhere and at a lower level of football. Following three years of frustration on the fringe, at the start of the 2005-06 campaign Jamie was signed by Carlisle after almost 16 years attached to the Black'n'Whites. He struggled to get into the Cumbrians first-eleven, claiming only five outings, and his stay at Gay Meadow resulted in a similar outcome, only totalling four games for Shrewsbury. He then moved around the non-league scene in the North East becoming a mental health worker in Northumberland. McClen's brother Steven was also a junior with Newcastle, but wasn't retained.

Appearances & Goals:
Debut v Tottenham Hotspur (h) 5 April 1999
PL: 7(7) app 0 gls
FAC: 3 app 1 gl
Euro: 0(5) app 0 gls
Total: 10(12) app 1 gl

Honours:
FL div 2 champs 2006 (2 app).

McCOLL Robert Smyth 1901-1904

Centre-forward or Inside-left
5'9"
b. Glasgow, 13 April 1876
d. Glasgow, 25 November 1959

Career: Benmore/Queen's Park Jan 1894 (Edinburgh St Bernard's guest 1901-02)/UNITED Oct 1901 £300/ Rangers Sept 1904/Queen's Park Nov 1907/Retired 1910.

Known as the 'Prince of Centre-forwards' during his era at the turn of the century, Bob McColl was a slightly-built forward with lightning fast acceleration and reflexes. He became a nationally known figure after netting three hat-tricks for Scotland in a sequence of only five games and registering an overall total of 13 goals in 13 internationals. Included was a special treble against England during 1900. As an amateur McColl was the doyen of Scottish football and many were surprised when he moved to Tyneside and turned professional. The local press reported United had signed "the smartest dribbler and goalscorer in Scotland". At Gallowgate, McColl was recognised as an important factor in the club's fast developing classical Edwardian side; Colin Veitch was to say he "set the standard" while the Evening Chronicle's Nikodemus wrote he was a "compound of philosopher, scientist and artist". A firm believer in team play, possession football and "minimum effort for maximum result", Bob was hugely popular and scrupulously fair on the field. With the touch of a master on the ball, many wrote of his talent. Waverley in the Scottish Daily Record noted Bob was "speedy

and lion hearted, he would chase anything" and "had an uncanny swerve tha completely deceived the opposition and could shoot with terrific force with eithe foot". McColl had positional awareness, snapped up a chance quickly and was als one of the first to utilise curl on the ball, described as hitting the ball "so that i flight took on a banana-like curve". In a Newcastle shirt, McColl at times showed h brilliance, but was frequently a marked man on the field. He left Tyneside to hea back to Scotland just before the club's Edwardian Masters era was set to begin, hugely successful period he did much to create. McColl captained his country an later went onto net six goals for Queen's Park in a single match against Port Glasgov Athletic. His brother Tom McColl (qv) also had a spell with Newcastle at the sam time mainly as a reserve, although he did play alongside his famous brother in friendl outings for the seniors during 1902-03. Possessed of an astute brain, the Scot also a this time went into business in Glasgow (with the £300 signing-on fee from Newcastle with his brother and founded the RS McColl confectionary and later newsagency chai which currently has nationwide convenience outlets, some of which still bear his nam although the family sold the business to Cadbury in 1933. For many years he wa nicknamed 'Toffee Bob' and was an enthusiastic supporter of local football in Glasgov setting up the RS McColl Cup.*

Appearances & Goals:
Debut v Manchester City (h) 9 November 1901 (1 goal)
FL: 64 app 18 gls
FAC: 3 app 2 gls
Total: 67 app 20 gls

Honours:
13 Scot caps 1896-1908/1 SL app 1901/Scot trial app 1896-1905/SC final 1900 1905/Scot HoF.

McCOMBIE Andrew 1904-1950

Right-back & Trainer
5'10"
b. Dingwall, 30 June 1876
d. North Shields, 28 March 1952

Career: Inverness Thistle 1893/Sunderland Feb 1899/ UNITED Feb 1904 £700/Retired April 1910, becoming asst-trainer and trainer Jan 1928 to cs 1930, then general assistant to retirement in 1950.

During his long service with the club, Andy McCombie was a rare defender who allied brawn with brain and no-one has served the club longer than his 46 years 3 months and 27 days at St James' Park. Equally competent on either flank, he was tough, but had a skilful touch and was described as being "cool, yet alert, familiar with every possible phase of attack, a past master in the art of feeding from the rear, and a judicious tackler". Andy was an automatic choice for five seasons with Sunderland, totalling over 160 games including helping to bring the title trophy t Wearside. The Highlander moved the short distance to Gallowgate at the peak of hi career for what was a world record £700 fee, but amidst rows between himself an Sunderland over a payment of £100 as a 'gift' or 'loan' to start a business when h first moved to Wearside. Both an FA Inquiry and Court heard the case and judged i McCombie's favour, a decision that rocked Sunderland as it was classed as an illega 'under the counter' payment resulting in several officials being fined and suspende by the FA. Thereafter he became something of a figure of hate to Wearsiders McCombie partnered fellow international Jack Carr in United's rearguard and was key figure in two Football League Championship victories for the club, as well as bein on the fringe of another as a veteran in 1909. Later, he was also involved as backstage aide when the Magpies won their fourth title in 1927. As a playe McCombie was an influential committee member of the early Player's Union. And became a United shareholder and resided in North Shields to his death, devoted t Newcastle's cause to his last day.

Appearances & Goals:
Debut v Notts County (h) 13 February 1904
FL: 113 app 0 gls
FAC: 18 app 0 gls
Total: 131 app 0 gls

Honours:
4 Scot caps 1903-05/Scot trial app 1901-04/FL champs 1902, 1905, 1907, 1909 (1 app)/FAC final 1905, 1906.

McCORMACK Cecil John 1945

Centre-forward
5'8"
b. Newcastle upon Tyne, 15 February 1922
d. Canada, 1995

Career: Newburn/Gateshead amat 1938, prof Sept 1941 (Sunderland war-guest 1941-42)(York City war-guest 1942-43)(UNITED war-guest 1944-45)(Chester war-guest 1944-46)(Manchester City war-guest 1945-46)(Middlesbrough war-guest 1945-46)(Ipswich Town war-guest 1945-46)(Aldershot war-guest 1945-46)/Resumed with Gateshead 1946/Middlesbrough April 1947/Chelmsford City November 1948 £7,000/Barnsley July 1950 £7,000/Notts Co Nov 1951 £20,000/King's Lynn cs 1956/Polish White Eagles (Can) Sept 1957 to 1962.

Gateshead's Cec McCormack filled in the Number 9 role for Albert Stubbins once during April 1945 and was one of several post-war celebrities to have pulled on Newcastle's shirt during the hostilities. Classy and of slight-build at centre-forward, McCormack proved to be a first rate opportunist who scored goals at all his clubs. During the war leagues he netted over 100 times for Gateshead as he thrilled spectators at Redheugh Park. Then with Barnsley the quick-thinking and quick-silver McCormack became the Second Division's top marksman in season 1950-51 with 33 goals, a post-war club record; registering 46 in all first-eleven games. A potent threat up front, he once netted five times in a single fixture against Luton for the Tykes. After a £20,000 deal took him to Notts County, Cec found the net on 36 occasions in only 85 games, another noted achievement. McCormack grew up on Scotswood Road in Newcastle, born above a newsagent's shop and as a teenager he served as an apprentice fitter at the nearby Vickers Armstrong works. McCormack was one of the early Wallsend Boy's Club lads and served with the RAF in the Second World War. He later emigrated to Canada, returning to his trade for De Havilland in Toronto. He also appeared for a Canadian Select XI later in his career.

Appearances & Goals:
Debut v Bolton Wanderers (a) 21 April 1945 (FLWC)
War: 1 app 0 gls
Total: 1 app 0 gls

McCORMACK James Henry 1942-1947

Outside-right
5'8"
b. Spennymoor

Joining United in April 1942 from local junior football, Jim McCormack was associated with the Magpies for five years as an amateur, not leaving St James' Park until the end of the 1946-47 season. He was always recognised as a reserve, only taking part in two games of the wartime Football League North competition, yet he played well on each occasion; firstly in a 3-3 draw with York City during October 1942 when he found the net, then in a 5-4 defeat at Leeds later in the season.

Appearances & Goals:
Debut v York City (h) 17 October 1942 (FLN) (1 goal)
War: 2 app 1 gl
Total: 2 app 1 gl

McCORMACK John Andrew 1906-1908

Centre-half
5'10"
b. Linwood, Renfrewshire

Career: Johnstone March 1906/UNITED March 1906 £25/Everton April 1908 £250/Johnstone Aug 1908/Millwall Aug 1909/Johnstone May 1910/Dumbarton Harp July 1913/Johnstone Dec 1914.

A stand-in for the elegant talent of Colin Veitch in United's Edwardian star-studded line-up, John McCormack only gained a run out in midfield during season 1907-08. He was a regular fixture in the Magpies' second eleven, winning the North Eastern League title twice in 1907 and 1908. At Goodison Park, the Scot didn't appear in Everton's first-eleven and moved back to Renfrew, rejoining Johnstone then in the Scottish League.

Appearances & Goals:
Debut v Sheffield United (h) 26 December 1907
FL: 2 app 1 gl
Total: 2 app 1 gl

McCRACKEN William Robert 1904-1923

Right-back
5'11"
b. Belfast, 29 January 1883
d. Hull, 20 January 1979

Career: Broadway Thistle/Distillery (Belfast) Dec 1900/UNITED May 1904 £50 (Distillery (Belfast) war-guest 1917-18)(Fulham war-guest 1918-19)/(Bradford Park Avenue war-guest 1918-19)/Hull City manager Feb 1923 to May 1931/Gateshead manager Sept 1932/Millwall manager May 1933 to March 1936/Aldershot manager Feb 1937 to Nov 1949/UNITED scout Sept 1951 to c1962/Watford scout to Jan 1978.

A celebrated figure of the game, Bill McCracken is recognised as perhaps the greatest and most colourful full-back to wear a United shirt. With a superb tactical mind, Bill perfected the offside game with expert positional play so well that he frustrated the opposition, and supporters, to an extent that in 1925 football's authorities had to change the rules. His tactical ploy, so cleverly delivered along with Billy Hampson or Frank Hudspeth, was even put on film in 1920, McCracken demonstrating the infamous offside trap on a silent reel. A player much loved on Tyneside, but the target of abuse elsewhere, receiving as Ivan Sharpe wrote "more cheers and jeers than any other footballer" and who was "belauded or condemned". McCracken was a controversial personality, often in dispute with the game's authorities, whether his country's FA over international payments (when he was suspended for a decade), or eyeball to eyeball with referees. Indeed his transfer to St James' Park ended in an FA Inquiry amidst rumours of illegal approaches and underhand payments when Bill was chased by several clubs, allegations the player strenuously denied and which were proved unfounded. Despite all the rant and rave over McCracken, the Irishman was a formidable opponent, Sharpe describing him as being "very alert, could leap, run, tackle and head the ball well". Together with Hudspeth, his colleague for many years, Bill recorded service of almost 19 years as a player for the Magpies, a record for many decades until Steve Harper surpassed it. An exuberant Irishman, he was captain of the club as well as of Ireland, and had arrived on Tyneside as a 21-year-old when still working as a joiner, starting as second choice to Andy McCombie or Jack Carr on either flank. The Irishman eventually took over the right-back spot and helped Newcastle to three titles and three FA Cup finals and is one of only nine players to pass 400 games for the Geordies. Bill represented both United and Ireland when over 40 years of age. Cousin of Robert McCracken, Crystal Palace and Ireland, Bill was an active scout for almost three decades after he left management and recommended many names to become stars of the game. Irish writer Malcolm Brodie saw McCracken in later life as having a "bubbling, mischievous sense of humour and a keen, penetrating mind". He died nine days short of his 96th birthday, a character of the game with a capital C.

Appearances & Goals:
Debut v Woolwich Arsenal (h) 3 September 1904
FL: 377 app 6 gls
FAC: 55 app 2 gls
War: 10 app 0 gls
Others: 2 app 0 gls
Total: 444 app 8 gls

Honours:
15 Irel & NI caps 1902-23/1 unoff Irel app 1903/2 Irel war app 1919/5 IL app 1902-04/1 FL app 1918/1 unoff FL app 1914/FL champs 1905, 1907, 1909/FAC winner 1910/FAC final 1908, 1911/IL champs 1903/IC winner 1903/IC final 1902/FA Long Service medal 1978/FL Legend/NU HoF.

Mc

McCREERY David 1982-1989

Midfield
5'7"
b. Belfast, 16 September 1957

Career: Ashfield BC/Manchester Utd amat Sept 1972, prof Oct 1974/Queens Park Rangers Aug 1979 £200,000/Tulsa Roughnecks (USA) March 1981 £225,000 joint deal/UNITED Oct 1982 £75,000/Sundsvaal (Swd) June 1989/Heart of Midlothian Sept 1989 free, becoming asst-coach/Hartlepool Utd player-coach Aug 1991, becoming asst-manager to June 1992/Coleraine Sept 1992/Carlisle Utd player-manager Oct 1992 to June 1993, then player to July 1994/Hartlepool Utd manager Oct 1994 to April 1995/Barnet scout 1995/Blyth Spartans consultant Sept 1995/CA Boca Juniors (Arg) UK representative 2003 to 2011/Magway (Bm) Technical Director & manager Jan 2011/Sabah State FA (Mal) Director & manager July 2012 to July 2013.

A vastly underrated midfielder, full of fire and determination, David McCreery became United's anchor man as the club won promotion in 1984. A product of the Old Trafford nursery, David was in Manchester United's line-up at 16 years of age and turned out twice at Wembley in cup finals when barely out of his teens. A perpetual substitute for the Reds, coming off the bench on over 50 occasions in his 110 matches, he left in search of regular action and performed his battling style for QPR and in the States calypso. Returning to England, McCreery joined Arthur Cox's exciting team at Gallowgate, linking perfectly with Terry McDermott in midfield, once noting, "my job is to win the ball and give it to somebody else". He carried out that role very effectively, without fuss or drama, always going in where it hurt and occasionally coming out of a tackle worse for wear; once against Bolton needing 60 stitches in a nasty leg gash. He was a perfect foil to the silky skills of Keegan, Beardsley and Waddle in United's side while McCreery was a regular for his country, taking part in the 1982 and 1986 World Cup finals. After leaving the game, David resided in Hepscott in Morpeth and ran a hospitality company, worked for Olscher Sports as well as being a consultant in the formation of the MLS, the new American soccer organisation. He also ran a welding company in Consett for a period while continuing his links to football in both Argentina and Malaysia.

Appearances & Goals:
Debut v Leeds United (a) 6 October 1982 (FLC)
FL: 237(6) app 2 gls
FAC: 10(1) app 0 gls
FLC: 15 app 0 gls
Others: 3 app 0 gls
Total: 265(7) app 2 gls

Honours:
67 NI caps 1976-90/WdC 1982, 1986/1 NI u21 app 1978/NI sch-youth app/FL div 2 champs 1975 (2 app)/FL div 2 prom 1984/FAC winner 1977/FAC final 1976 (sub no app).

McCULLOCH Alexander 1908

Centre-forward
5'9"
b. Leith, April 1887
d. 1962

Career: Bonnyrigg Rose Ath/Leith Ath April 1907/Middlesbrough Sept 1907/UNITED Feb 1908 £200/Brentford cs 1908/Bradford Park Avenue Nov 1908 £50/Swindon Town 1909 (Reading 1910-11)/Coventry City Oct 1912/Raith Rovers June 1913/Alloa Ath Oct 1915/Broxburn Utd 1916/Dunfermline Ath March 1917/Heart of Midlothian Aug 1918 to Feb 1919/Lincoln City July 1919/Bargoed Town Aug 1920/Merthyr Town Nov 1920/Llanelli Aug 1921/Dundee Hibernian March 1922/Gala Fairydean Sept 1922.

Alex McCulloch arrived at St James' Park as a youngster and became an errant traveller during his long career, never settling at any club for very long. Deputy to Alf Common at Boro, he was reserve to another noted centre-forward at Gallowgate in Bill Appleyard. Alex stood in once for Big Bill in a United shirt but didn't get another opportunity and was confined to Newcastle's North Eastern League eleven during his ten months on Tyneside. McCulloch later appeared at inside-forward for Hearts in the Scottish Victory Cup final during 1919; his club losing to St Mirren before a 60,000 crowd at Celtic Park.

Appearances & Goals:
Debut v Preston North End (h) 11 March 1908
FL: 1 app 0 gls
Total: 1 app 0 gls

Honours:
SVC final 1919.

McCURDIE Alexander H 1889-1892

Half-back
b. Gartmore, Perthshire, c1865

Career: Clydebank c1888/EAST END Jan 1889/Newcastle West End Jan 1892 to cs 1892.

A big favourite on Tyneside, Alec McCurdie joined East End from Clydebank with Joe McKane as 1889 opened and operated in midfield with distinction during the years up to the historic move by the Heaton club to St James' Park. Noted as a boiler-maker and living in lodgings in Heaton with Scottish colleagues Collins, Creilly and Miller, he appeared for the Northumberland County side, Alec was transferred to West End in January 1892 a few months before they became defunct. The Newcastle Daily Chronicle of the day made the compliment towards McCurdie that in the region "few finer lads have graced the football field". Alec totalled almost 100 games for East End in all matches and was awarded a benefit match during April 1893. After his period on Tyneside, he returned to Clydeside and by 1901 was working as a marine boiler-maker living in Old Kilpatrick.

Appearances & Goals:
Debut v Darlington (h) 7 September 1889 (NL)
NL: 29 app 1 gl
FAC: 5 app 0 gls
Total: 34 app 1 gl
(Void NL: 3 app 0 gls)

McCURLEY John 1927-1930

Inside-forward
5'8"
b. Kelty, Fife, 17 March 1906
d. Morpeth, 20 January 1969

Career: Kelty Rangers/Third Lanark Oct 1926/UNITED Dec 1927 £2,500/East Fife Aug 1930/Cowdenbeath June 1933 to 1938.

A relentless midfield worker, able to play on either flank, John McCurley was a reserve to Bob McKay and Stan Seymour during his early days on Tyneside. He was then given an extended run during season 1928-29 and he performed well in the inside-left role when Tom McDonald was injured. However, when his fellow countryman was fit again, 'Jock' as he was commonly known, stepped down and had to be content to act as a stand-in for any forward position, as well as at half-back, when the chance came his way. With Third Lanark, McCurley was good enough to represent the strong Glasgow city select combination, which prompted Newcastle to take a keen interest and bring him to Tyneside. McCurley totalled 286 games in Scottish football, especially prominent with Cowdenbeath where he made over 100 outings.

Appearances & Goals:
Debut v Blackburn Rovers (a) 14 January 1928 (FAC)
FL: 43 app 8 gls
FAC: 2 app 0 gls
Total: 45 app 8 gls

McDERMID Robert 1894-1897

Left or Right-back
5'7"
b. Bonhill, Dunbartonshire, 1870

Career: Renton Thistle/Renton/Newcastle West End 1887/Sunderland cs 1888 (Newcastle West End guest 1888-89 & 1889-90)/Sunderland Albion 1890/Accrington cs 1890/Burton Swifts 1891/Stockton 1892/Lincoln City April 1893/Renton July 1893/Dundee Wand 1894/UNITED Nov 1894 £15/Hebburn Argyle Feb 1897/Wormsley Jan 1898/ South Shields Sept 1899.

ob McDermid was a popular and early disciple of the game, especially in the North
ast where he served on Wearside as well as with United's Victorian rivals, Newcastle
West End, while he appeared for Northumberland County too, as well as for
unbartonshire and Durham. On his day a reliable and occasionally brilliant defender,
e was comfortable on the right or left side of the field. Appearing at St James' Park
or the West Enders when they lifted the Northumberland Senior Cup during 1888,
McDermid became a regular for two seasons when United became established as a
ootball League club during 1894-95 and 1895-96. Described as a "player devoid of
ll bravado", he preferred "to show his worth by deeds". Bob took part in Sunderland
lbion's campaign in the Football Alliance during 1889-90, the breakaway Wear club
inishing in third spot. He later became a publican in South Shields also working as a
oiler-maker in a steel works.

Note: Some sources spell his surname McDermidd, but club Minute books note it as,
McDermid as does family history data.)

Appearances & Goals:
Debut v Burton Wanderers (h) 10 November 1894 (1 goal)
L: 56 app 2 gls
AC: 8 app 0 gls
otal: 64 app 2 gls

McDERMOTT Terence 1973-74, 1982-84, 1992-98, 2005-08

Midfield & Asst-Manager
9"
. Kirkby, Liverpool, 8 December 1951

Career: Bury jnr 1968, prof Oct 1969/UNITED Feb
1973 £25,000/Liverpool Nov 1974 £170,000/
UNITED Sept 1982 £100,000 to Sept 1984/Cork
City Jan 1985 to March 1985/APOEL (Cy) July
1985 to cs 1987/UNITED asst-manager Feb 1992
to Aug 1998 (caretaker-manager Jan 1997)/
Celtic asst-coach July 1999 to Feb 2000/UNITED
asst-manager Jan 2005, becoming asst-coach &
scout June 2006 to Sept 2008/Huddersfield Town
asst-manager Dec 2008 to Feb 2012/Birmingham
City asst-manager June 2012 to Feb 2014.

Serving the club over four separate periods, Terry McDermott was first purchased for
a bargain fee as a 21-year-old midfielder with potential, then signed again after the
Merseysider had won everything on offer as a player of special talent with Liverpool
and England. Slightly-built and full of running, the Merseysider showed enough in
101 games for the Shakers to prompt a move to the North East and McDermott
developed quickly at Gallowgate during season 1973-74. His progress was rapid and
he impressed the Reds' management after his displays for the Magpies in an FA Cup
run to Wembley facing Liverpool in the final. A clash with boss Joe Harvey led to his
departure to Anfield and Terry was coached into one of the best link men on show,
totalling 322 games and 75 goals as Liverpool became the finest in Europe. He was
good at short and long passing, and had vision and the willingness to make late
penetrating runs into the box. He was also capable of always striking a spectacular
goal, several of which helped earn Liverpool trophies, including three European Cups.
Returning to Gallowgate as a 30-year-old, Terry teamed up with Kevin Keegan to lead
the club back to Division One, but again fell out with the management, only to return
as Keegan's so called 'buffer' in 1992. One of the games top medal winners, he picked
numerous major honours as a player, while as Kevin Keegan's lieutenant and closest
confidant became a success on the sidelines too, going onto work alongside Dalglish,
Souness, Roeder as well as Allardyce at St James' Park, before becoming Lee Clark's
right-hand man as he started on a managerial career. His two sons, Neale and Greg,
both started their careers at Gallowgate before moving on. McDermott still resides
on Tyneside, in Ponteland.

Appearances & Goals:
Debut v Manchester United (a) 17 March 1973 (sub)
FL: 129(1) app 18 gls
FAC: 12 app 3 gls
FLC: 7 app 2 gls
Others: 18 app 0 gls
Total: 166(1) app 23 gls
(Void FAC: 1 app 1 gl)

In Charge: 2 games (joint caretaker)

Honours:
25 Eng caps 1978-82/WdC 1982 (no app)/1 Eng B app 1978/1 Eng u23 app 1974/FL
champs 1976 (9 app), 1977, 1979, 1980, 1982, 1983 (2 app)/FL div 2 prom 1984/FAC
final 1974, 1977/FLC winner 1981, 1982/FLC final 1978/Cy Lg champs 1986/Cy Cup
final 1986/EC winner 1977, 1978, 1981/UEFA Cup winner 1976 (sub no app)/ESC winner
1977/ESC final 1978/ICC final 1981/FoY 1980 (FWA)/PoY 1980 (PFA)/PFA ToS (d1) 1980.

MACDONALD Malcolm Ian 1971-1976

Centre-forward
5'11"
b. Fulham, London, 7 January 1950

Career: Barnet/Forest Row/Knowle
Park Jnrs 1967/Tonbridge July
1967/Crystal Palace cs 1968/Fulham
Aug 1968 £1,750/Luton Town July
1969 £17,500/UNITED May 1971
£185,000 (Lusitano (SA) loan cs
1975)/Arsenal Aug 1976 £333,333
(Djurgardens IF (Swd) loan cs 1979)/
Retired due to injury Aug
1979/Fulham commercial executive
Sept 1979, becoming manager Nov
1980, then manager & director Aug
1981 to April 1984/Huddersfield
Town manager Oct 1987 to May
1988/South Kinson, briefly April
1990.

Known nationwide as 'Supermac',
Malcolm Macdonald was a phenomenon of the Seventies decade and hero worshipped
on Tyneside. Built like a middle-weight boxer, he was a brash and colourful centre-
forward who lived for hitting the ball into the back of the net. His style of play meant
excitement, crashing goals from all distances and all angles. Macdonald had
devastating pace, packed a mighty shot and was deceivingly good in the air too. Born
near to Craven Cottage, his father played as an amateur for Hull City and later for
Blyth Spartans, Malcolm had a good upbringing at Sloane Grammar School before
starting on a football path at Crystal Palace. Initially a full-back, Bobby Robson moved
him into attack but he was released by both Palace and then Fulham before making
his name with Luton Town as the Hatters climbed from the lower divisions. Possessing
verve and confidence, Macdonald arrived on Tyneside for a record fee after bagging
58 goals for Luton. At once the Cockney was taken to by the Gallowgate faithful,
striking a headlining hat-trick on his home debut against Liverpool. A huge personality
in the region for five years, both on and off the field, Macdonald appeared in two cup
finals for the Black'n'Whites, however departed after several publicised disagreements
with new manager Gordon Lee. He continued to find the net at Highbury, claiming 57
goals for Arsenal before a knee complaint early into the 1978-79 season caused
persistent problems. Having three operations, the injury forced his retirement at only
29 years of age, a complaint which affected him for many years afterwards until he
underwent major surgery in 1997 to replace the knee joint. Macdonald was the First
Division's leading goal-poacher in 1974-75 (21 goals) and 1976-77 (25 goals). He
scored a club total of 258 goals in 480 games, a 54% strike-rate, while he once hit
five goals for England at Wembley against Cyprus during 1975 to equal an
international scoring record. Malcolm is also credited with scoring Newcastle's fastest
ever goal; after only four seconds in a friendly against St Johnstone when he
unleashed a shot straight from the kick-off. On his retirement from playing, the
Londoner looked like developing into an astute manager at Fulham before a series of
personal problems led to Macdonald's departure from the game. After running pubs
in Worthing and then in Berwick, as well as working in the media, Malcolm, always
thoughtful and articulate, moved to Milan in 1991 employed in sporting
telecommunications for the Sullivan empire. For a period he was also a football agent,
assisting in bringing Brazilian, Mirandinha to Gallowgate. Recovering from an alcohol
addiction, he settled on Tyneside becoming a local radio broadcaster with Century,
Real Radio and other local stations as well as a newspaper columnist for the Evening
Chronicle. For several years Malcolm formed part of the Three Legends media team
covering North East football.

Appearances & Goals:
Debut v Crystal Palace (a) 14 August 1971
FL: 187 app 95 gls
FAC: 22 app 14 gls
FLC: 18 app 12 gls
Others: 29(1) app 17 gls
Total: 256(1) app 138 gls
(Void FAC: 1 app 0 gls)

Honours:
14 Eng caps 1972-76/4 Eng u23 app 1972-73/1 FL app 1972/FL div 3 prom 1970,
1982(m)/FAC final 1974, 1978/FLC final 1976/PFA ToS (d1) 1974/FL Legend/NU HoF.

Mc

McDONALD John (George M) 1895-1899

Inside-left
5'10"
b. England

Career: Glasgow Perthshire 1893/Ashfield 1894/UNITED Oct 1895/
Lincoln City Nov 1899/St Mirren Jan 1900.

A recruit from Scottish non-league football, a star with Ashfield, one of the leading sides north of the border, McDonald arrived at the same time as two other Scots, Lennox and McKnight. A reserve forward, deputising for William Miller and Andy Aitken during season 1895-96, he also operated at inside-right and centre-forward. McDonald, although noted as originally being born in England, had reached the Scotland junior international ranks when with Ashfield. After leaving Tyneside, he only made two appearances for Lincoln before moving back to Scotland with St Mirren. John's first action for the Magpies was to act as a linesman in United's reserve fixture against Gateshead NER!

(Note: Although some sources have the player as George M McDonald, local records note John.)

Appearances & Goals:
Debut v Leicester Fosse (h) 1 January 1896
FL: 6 app 2 gls
Total: 6 app 2 gls

Honours:
2 Scot jnr app.

McDONALD John 1912-1914

Outside-left
5'8"
b. Wemyss, Fife, 1886
d. 1943

Career: Wemyss Harp/Vale of Wemyss/Raith Rovers July 1902/Rangers Jan 1907 £100/Liverpool May 1909/ UNITED May 1912 £650/Raith Rovers June 1914/ Dundee Aug 1914/Raith Rovers Sept 1919 to 1921.

John McDonald was a well-known player in Liverpool's ranks for three seasons during which time he played almost 80 games and was a runner-up in the title race during 1910 before heading for the North East. He took over the outside-left berth when fellow Scot, George Wilson moved to a schemer's role and, although he enjoyed a good season in 1912-13, afterwards became second choice to emerging local lad, Tommy Goodwill. John was sometimes a touch temperamental, once failing to turn up for a United fixture against Derby in 1913 when he was fined a week's wages. During the early part of McDonald's career, he was a star of Raith's Scottish Qualifying Cup success in 1907, form which earned him a big move to Ibrox. His Scottish Cup final appearance during 1909 was the occasion of a notorious Hampden Park riot when no trophy was awarded to either participant, Rangers or Celtic. Before moving south from Fife, John worked as a coal-miner.

Appearances & Goals:
Debut v Bolton Wanderers (a) 2 September 1912 (1 goal)
FL: 31 app 4 gls
FAC: 5 app 0 gls
Total: 36 app 4 gls

Honours:
Scot trial app 1910/SC final 1909/SQC winner 1907.

McDONALD Neil Raymond 1982-1988

Midfield & Right-back
5'11"
b. Willington Quay, near Newcastle upon Tyne,
2 November 1965

Career: Wallsend BC/Carlisle Utd Jan 1980/UNITED jnr July 1982 £10,000, prof Feb 1983/Everton Aug 1988 £525,000/Oldham Ath Oct 1991 £500,000/ Bolton Wand July 1994 free/Preston North End Nov 1995 £40,000, becoming asst-coach/Bolton Wand asst-coach 2000, becoming coach/Crystal Palace asst-manager June 2005/Ajax (USA) youth camp coach 2005/Carlisle Utd manager June 2006 to Aug 2007/Ostersunds FK (Swd) manager Sept 2007/

Lincoln City asst-manager Nov 2007/Leeds Utd coach Feb 2008/Blackburn Rovers asst-manager Dec 2008 to Dec 2010/West Ham Utd asst-manager June 2011.

At one stage Neil McDonald became Newcastle's youngest ever debutant aged 16 years 326 days when he appeared against Barnsley. An England schoolboy player, he was a much coveted youngster with as many 29 clubs chasing him as a teenager. Neil came into United's side at a time of injury crisis and after only five reserve and junior matches to his name following a move back to Tyneside from Brunton Park. He performed with maturity and to the team's requirements and deserved an extended run, an opportunity he grasped to earn a regular position in midfield, and later at full-back, for the next six seasons. With a strong shot, at one stage Neil was tipped for an England cap, but his progress drifted after a big money move to Goodison Park. He did well at times in Everton's blue, totalling 124 games, but at Oldham and Bolton where he broke his leg, his promising career levelled to the ordinary. A past skipper of the England youth side, Neil was Kevin Keegan's boot-boy at Gallowgate while his father, James, appeared for the Magpie's junior team during the Fifties. During his coaching career, McDonald often teamed up with Sam Allardyce, but wasn't part of his managerial team when the former Bolton boss moved to Gallowgate.

Appearances & Goals:
Debut v Barnsley (h) 25 September 1982
FL: 163(17) app 24 gls
FAC: 10(1) app 1 gl
FLC: 12 app 3 gls
Others: 3 app 0 gls
Total: 188(18) app 28 gls

Honours:
5 Eng u21 app 1987-88/Eng-sch app/FL div 3 champs 1996/FL div 1 prom 1995 (4 app)/FL div 2 prom side 1984/FAC final 1989.

McDONALD Robert Roderick 1988-1989

Centre-forward
6'3"
b. Hull, 22 January 1959

Career: Hull City jnr 1974, prof Jan 1977 (Sportclub Cambuur (Neth) loan 1979-80)/FC Wageningen (Neth) Aug 1980 £19,000/Tilburg Willem II (Neth) cs 1981/Groningen (Neth) June 1982 £75,000/PSV Eindhoven (Neth) cs 1985 (Sporting Clube (Ptg) loan 1986-87)(Groningen (Neth) loan 1986-87)(Racing Jet (Neth) loan 1987-88)(Ikast (Den) loan 1987-88)/ Wimbledon trial 1988/UNITED Nov 1988 £150,000 /Besiktas JK (Trk) Aug 1989 £60,000/BV Veendam (Neth) March 1990/FC Emmen (Neth) asst-coach 1992/Zwolle (Neth) asst-coach 1993/Dovo

(Neth) coach 1997/De Graafschap (Neth) manager Oct 1999 to Nov 2000/Ajax Capetown (SA) manager 2001/Cambuur (Neth) coach 2002/WoG (Neth) coach 2003/Sligo Rovers manager Nov 2006 to March 2007/AS Trencin (Slv) coach 2007/W De Meern (Neth) coach 2008/W Dovo (Neth) technical manager, becoming coach July 2010 to July 2012.

After leaving Humberside to try his luck in the Netherlands, Rob McDonald eventually developed into a potent striker, with his big frame always a handful on the Continent. He had excellent spells with Groningen and with PSV, when he was a regular as the Dutch side won the league championship during 1986. He was unlucky then to be injured in a clash with a 'keeper when playing to top form and his opportunity for a sustained place in the PSV line-up was lost. In total McDonald netted over 100 goals in Holland and for a spell appeared alongside Ruud Gullit as well as experiencing European Cup and UEFA Cup football. With that pedigree, Rob returned to England and to St James' Park to give United's somewhat lightweight attack a boost. With a good touch of the ball, he showed a Dutch awareness; Rob started well but then missed chances and suffered the frustration of certain sections of the crowd. The pace and fiery nature of English soccer never suited his style and he headed across the Channel again within a few months. Living in the Netherlands for over 30 years, his game suited Dutch football, being nicknamed 'Mister One Touch' in Holland. After a lengthy period coaching lesser clubs in that country and elsewhere, McDonald set up a coaching head-hunting business during 2011. He also acted as a motivational speaker in the Netherlands.

Appearances & Goals:
Debut v Millwall (a) 19 November 1988
FL: 6(4) app 1 gl
FAC: 1(3) app 0 gls
Others: 1 app 1 gl
Total: 8(7) app 2 gl

Honours:
Neth champs 1986.

McDONALD Thomas Henry 1921-1931

Inside-left
5'8"
b. Inverness, 25 September 1895
d. Newcastle upon Tyne, 7 July 1969

Career: Inverness Thistle/Rangers Sept 1919/
Inverness Thistle Sept 1919/Rangers Oct 1919/
UNITED March 1921 £2,000/York City May
1931 free/Goole Town Aug 1933/York City
asst-trainer Aug 1934/Usworth Colliery Oct
1936.

Tom McDonald was one of the mainstays of
United's league and cup success during the
entertaining period of the Twenties. Forming an
excellent and feared understanding with firstly,
Stan Seymour, then with fellow countryman, Hughie
Gallacher, on the left flank of Newcastle's attack, McDonald
was an unselfish link man and a thorough professional. While always thinking of the
side's outcome first and foremost, he made sure he netted plenty of goals too, over a
century for the club in 10 seasons. A reserve for Scotland, he missed out on a full cap
by a whisker, appearing in three trial fixtures, but always being one of the unfortunate
not to be selected. A softly spoken Highlander, Tom was modest, yet is recognised in
Newcastle's history as one of the most consistent players, season after season. Blessed
with craft and guile, one contemporary biography noted his style as "possessing skilful,
constructive play and accurate marksmanship". McDonald served in the Royal Horse
Artillery during World War One, and after leaving the game settled in Newcastle's
West End suburb being employed at the Vickers Armstrong works as an engineer's
time-keeper. For many years he also looked after the Gallowgate press-box as a club
steward.

Appearances & Goals:
Debut v Middlesbrough (a) 5 March 1921
FL: 341 app 100 gls
FAC: 26 app 13 gls
Total: 367 app 113 gls

Honours:
Scot B app 1924/Scot trial app 1922-25/FL champs 1927/FAC winner 1924.

McDONOUGH Darron Karl 1992-1994

Midfield
5'11"
b. Antwerp (Belgium), 7 November 1962

Career: Oldham Ath jnr Dec 1977, prof Jan 1980/Luton
Town Sept 1986 £87,000/UNITED March 1992 £80,000/
Retired due to injury April 1994.

Well-framed, aggressive and positive with the ball, 29-
year-old Darron McDonough joined United's staff as a
utility player, able to play in defence or midfield.
However, the Belgian-born player was unlucky with
injuries, picking up a leg knock which ruled him out of
selection for long periods, this on top of being sidelined
at Kenilworth Road with cartilage and ligament problems. Darron had started his
career alongside Mick Quinn in Oldham's ranks, clocking up 200 games for the Latics
before moving to Luton. McDonough again performed well at that level, giving the
middle of the park ball-winning steel. He recorded 127 appearances for the Kenilworth
Road club, but unluckily missed the Hatters' League Cup final in 1988 due to an injury
sustained in the team's final training session before heading for Wembley. McDonough
was hoping for a fresh start on Tyneside, but after a series of problems both on and
off the field, he was forced to quit the scene at the end of the 1993-94 season due to
a snapped Achilles sustained in a reserve match. Although from the Continent, Darron
was brought up a Mancunian and on retirement he settled in Greater Manchester
running his own joiner and building business near Oldham, as well as helping with
the family sandwich and tea-shop.

Appearances & Goals:
Debut v Grimsby Town (a) 21 March 1992
FL: 2(1) app 0 gls
Total: 2(1) app 0 gls

Honours:
FLC final 1989.

MACFARLANE Alexander 1898-1901

Centre-forward or Inside-left
5'8"
b. Glasgow, 6 August 1878
d. Preston, 22 December 1945

Career: Baillieston Jnrs 1893/Airdrieonians March
1895/Arsenal Nov 1896/Airdrieonians Aug 1897/UNITED
Oct 1898 £30/Dundee Nov 1901/Chelsea April 1913 to
May 1916/Dundee manager March 1919 to Dec 1924/
Charlton Ath manager May 1925/Dundee manager
Dec 1927/Charlton Ath manager June 1928 to
Dec 1932/Blackpool manager July 1933 to July 1935.

Alex Macfarlane was an industrious worker with a stout
heart and had the ability to play across the frontline. Released by Arsenal, they missed
picking up a fine player, Newcastle appreciated his qualities and he gave the club
good service. Known as 'Sandy' and regarded as a purist on the field, he appeared in
all five attacking roles and was a regular in the Magpies' combination for three
seasons at the turn of the century. One biography in the Edwardian press noted he
was: "A brilliant inside-left with great command of the ball, and a player who never
forgets that he has a partner." Macfarlane fell out of favour on the arrival of Ronald
Orr and the emergence of Colin Veitch, but the Scot went onto have a marvellous
career back in Scotland with Dundee. He played on 333 occasions for the Dens Park
club scoring 71 goals and took part in their Scottish Cup victory as well as reaching
his country's national side. As a manager, twice in charge of Dundee, Sandy was a
highly respected personality of the inter-war era, noted as a tactician extraordinaire
and described as a "relentless perfectionist". In later life he moved to London but
during the Second World War saw his home destroyed in the Blitz; the Scot headed
north to see out the war in Preston where he died just as the hostilities ended.

(Note: Various sources spell his surname in different ways as is the case with many
of the Scottish Macs; documents at Register House in Edinburgh confirms it should
be Macfarlane.)

Appearances & Goals:
Debut v Preston North End (a) 29 October 1898
FL: 84 app 17 gls
FAC: 2 app 0 gls
Total: 86 app 17 gls

Honours:
5 Scot caps 1904-11/Scot trial app 1906/3 SL app 1904-11/SC winner 1910/FL div 3(S)
champs 1929(m).

McFAUL William Stewart 1966-1988

Goalkeeper, Coach & Manager
5'10"
b. Coleraine, 1 October 1943

Career: Coleraine Rangers/Coleraine 1960/
Linfield cs 1963/UNITED Nov 1966 £7,000
/Retired 1975, becoming asst-coach, coach
Jan 1977, caretaker-manager (twice), Nov
1977 & Aug to Sept 1985, then manager
Sept 1985 to Oct 1988/Coleraine manager
June 1990 to Jan 1992/Northern Ireland
asst-manager March 1994, as well as a
local coach in Ulster for the Northern
Ireland FA/ Guam national coach Dec 1999
to 2004/ Northern Ireland FA coach 2004
& Omagh Town coach Nov 2004 to June
2005/Later scouting for Norwich City.

After being on Tyneside for two weeks on trial in his teens during 1960, Willie McFaul
eventually signed for the club after a sparkling display for his club, Linfield against
the Magpies six years later, even though he saw seven goals flash past him!
Nevertheless, McFaul had still shown he was an acrobatic 'keeper with good reflexes
and potential to develop into a First Division guardian. Exchanging life as a part-time
footballer with a job in a joiner's shop, he took some time to settle, being reserve to
Gordon Marshall, but the likable Irishman was established as first choice for the start
of the 1968-69 season, coinciding with the club's march on Europe. For the next seven
campaigns Willie was an automatic selection and, despite a lack of height, was

Mc

recognised as one of the First Division's best goalkeepers. McFaul is fondly remembered for three stunning saves in key matches; against Burnley in the FA Cup semi-final, a penalty stop in the Inter Cities Fairs Cup semi-final with Rangers, and a spectacular tip over against Ujpesti Dozsa during the 1969 final. He appeared in every one of United's 24 European ties during the club's early years of action, while McFaul also scored against Pecsi Dozsa, in a penalty shoot-out. A part of the Northern Ireland squad for several years, he was unlucky to be around the international scene when Pat Jennings commanded the 'keeper's position. On Joe Harvey's resignation in 1975, Willie turned to coaching, being appointed caretaker boss twice (in 1977 and 1985) before claiming the hot-seat for himself. For a while his management appeared to work, but costly purchases at the start of the 1988-89 season took time to blend, and ultimately flopped. With United sliding towards a relegation fight, he wasn't given time to reverse the decline and was dismissed. McFaul soon returned to his native Northern Ireland and continued to be involved in football in the province, before spending almost five years on the West Pacific island of Guam, developing the small country's football side, once suffering a 19-0 defeat by Iran in World Cup qualifiers. McFaul is related to the Hunter footballing family from Ulster; Vic and Allan, as well as Barry, who was in United's reserve ranks from 1986-88.

Appearances & Goals:
Debut v Liverpool (h) 12 November 1966
FL: 290 app 0 gls
FAC: 22 app 0 gls
FLC: 18 app 0 gls
Euro: 24 app 0 gls
Others: 32 app 0 gls
Total: 386 app 0 gls
(Void FAC: 1 app 0 gls)

In Charge: 148 games
Debut v Southampton (a) 17 August 1985

Honours:
6 NI caps 1967-74/3 NI amat app 1962-63/NI sch-youth app/FAC final 1974/NIL champs 1966/NIC final 1966/ICFC winner 1969.

McGARRY Ronald James 1962-1967

Centre-forward or Inside-forward
5'9"
b. Whitehaven, 5 December 1937

Career: Lowca Amateurs/Whitehaven (rugby league)/ Workington amat Dec 1958, prof June 1960/Bolton Wand Feb 1962 £10,000/UNITED Dec 1962 £17,500/ Barrow March 1967 £3,500/South Coast Utd (Aus) 1968/Bulli FC (Aus) player-coach 1969/Balgownie Rangers (Aust) player-coach 1970/Barrow Sept 1970 to 1971/Gateshead player-manager 1972 to 1973/ Minor Tyneside football.

Ron McGarry was a tough, bustling striker who was purchased to replace Jimmy Kerray as Joe Harvey was building a side to push for promotion out of Division Two. Versatile in the Number 9 shirt, or in both inside-forward positions, McGarry was a stocky forward, possessing a powerful physique. He took punishment from defenders, but was always able to dish out a fair share of retribution, both in terms of goals and physical retaliation; hence his nickname of 'Cassius', after an infamous fracas with Swansea's Mike Johnson in which McGarry was sent-off. Ron was especially prominent during the Magpies' Second Division title victory in 1965, hitting the net with 16 efforts, the side's top goal-getter as he led the line with much vigour and verve. According to his manager, Ron was a "Robledo type of player", but wasn't quite good enough for United's Division One line-up and moved to Barrow. Always buoyant and a laugh-a-minute character, McGarry even had calling cards printed which he handed to opposing defenders noting 'Have Goals Will Travel' after a contemporary western television programme! McGarry was a coal-face worker at Lowca pit as a teenager, playing the rugby code before joining the Army on National Service. He was spotted by then Workington boss Joe Harvey at Longtown Camp and quickly made an impression at Borough Park (105 app, 32 goals), earning a move to Bolton where he played alongside Wyn Davies for a period. During a spell in Australia, Ron guided his Bulli FC side to five trophies. McGarry later settled on Tyneside, becoming for a while a bookmaker, then a newsagent, always retaining his witty personality.

Appearances & Goals:
Debut v Cardiff City (h) 15 December 1962
FL: 118(3) app 41 gls
FAC: 6 app 3 gls
FLC: 5 app 2 gls
Total: 129(3) app 46 gls

Honours:
FL div 2 champs 1965/FL div 4 prom 1967.

McGHEE Mark Edward 1977-1979, 1989-1991

Striker
5'10"
b. Glasgow, 20 May 1957

Career: Cumbernauld Burgh/Bristol City jnr 1973/Celtic jnr May 1975/Morton July 1975/UNITED Dec 1977 £150,000/Aberdeen March 1979 £80,000/SV Hamburg (Ger) May 1984 £285,000/Celtic Nov 1985 £200,000/ UNITED July 1989 £200,000/IK Brage (Swd) April 1991/Reading player-manager May 1991, retired playing 1993/Leicester City manager Dec 1994/ Wolverhampton Wand manager Dec 1995 to Nov 1998/Hartlepool Utd asst-coach Oct 1999/Millwall manager Sept 2000/Brighton manager Oct 2003 to Sept 2006/Motherwell manager June 2007/Aberdeen manager June 2009 to Dec 2010/Bristol Rovers manager Jan 2012 to Dec 2012/Scotland FA scout, becoming Scotland asst-coach Jan 2013.

An extremely clever forward, Mark McGhee possessed marvellous close control and the match-winning ability to weave his way past two or three defenders on one run. He was at Gallowgate in two spells, firstly as a 20-year-old youngster signed from the Scottish Second Division after scoring four goals in front of United officials, then later into his playing career when McGhee had proved himself one of the best strikers in the business. Mark's early period at Newcastle was not a happy one. At the club as a raw kid, he had shown flashes of the brilliance which was to follow, but was in many ways a victim of the Magpies' relegation and internal strife. Moving back north, he linked up with manager Alex Ferguson at Aberdeen and developed into an unorthodox goal-poacher, able to hold the ball up, link well and finish with deadly accuracy from the tightest of chances. At Pittodrie Mark enjoyed a golden period, he won domestic and European honours, scoring 100 goals, and earned a big move to, at the time, top German club Hamburg. Jim Smith brought the Scot back to Tyneside as a 32-year-old and he teamed up with Mick Quinn for the 1989-90 season and, thanks to a 61 goal partnership, the Black'n'Whites almost gained promotion, losing in the Play-Offs. McGhee showed his true worth in that season displaying at times remarkable close control of the ball but when Ossie Ardiles arrived he was one of the veterans released. Afterwards Mark started on a managerial ladder that had its ups and downs, winning promotion but also being shown the door. Mark was a trainee Architect before moving into full-time football and although he was turned down by Celtic as a trialist, the Parkhead club later paid out a hefty sum to sign him.

Appearances & Goals:
Debut v Leeds United (a) 2 January 1978
FL: 86(11) app 29 gls
FAC: 8(1) app 6 gls
FLC: 5(1) app 1 gl
Others: 3 app 0 gls
Total: 102(13) app 36 gls

Honours:
4 Scot caps 1983-84/1 Scot u21 app 1981/FL div 2 champs 1994(m), 2001(m)/FL div 2 prom 2004(m)/SL champs 1980, 1984, 1986, 1988/SL div 1 champs 1978/SC winner 1982, 1983, 1984, 1988, 1989/SLC final 1980, 1987/ECWC winner 1983/ESC winner 1983/Scot PoY 1981 (PFA).

McGOUGH Richard 1914-1917

Centre-half
5'9"
b. Carlisle, 1893 (Q3)
d. Feuchy, near Arras (France), 18 April 1917

Career: Carlisle Utd 1912/UNITED Dec 1914 £100 (Portsmouth loan 1914-15) to his death in 1917.

Youngster Richard McGough arrived at St James' Park from Carlisle United's pre-league outfit. Once scoring a goal from his own half for the Cumbrians, he was a compact and skilful midfielder showing Newcastle directors he was worth an opportunity. McGough operated in the middle of the park in the old fashioned centre-half role and deputised for Wilf Low in Newcastle's first-eleven during season 1914-15 before he joined up to do battle in World War One in October 1915. Richard was registered as a United footballer when he was killed in action serving as a bombardier in the Royal Garrison Artillery on a siege battery; his name is remembered at the Feuchy British Cemetery, Pas de Calais.

Appearances & Goals:
Debut v Middlesbrough (h) 10 March 1915
FL: 2 app 0 gls
Total: 2 app 0 gls

McGRATH John Thomas 1961-1968

Centre-half
6'0"
b. Manchester, 23 August 1938
d. Middleton, Manchester, 25 December 1998

Career: Bolton Wand amat June 1953/Miles Plating Swifts (Manchester)/Bury Oct 1955/UNITED Feb 1961 £24,000 plus R Stokoe/Southampton Feb 1968 £30,000 (Brighton loan 1972-73)/Southampton asst-coach Sept 1973/Port Vale manager Dec 1979 to Dec 1983/Chester manager Jan 1984 to Dec 1984/Preston North End manager June 1986 to Feb 1990/Halifax Town manager Oct 1991 to Dec 1992/ Canadian FA Technical Director for youth coaching 1996 for a period.

An immense tower of strength during the club's Second Division Championship victory in 1965, John McGrath was recognised as the cornerstone of the success along with fellow half-backs Anderson and Iley. Yet McGrath's early years in the North East were of mixed fortune. Arriving after 158 games for Bury with a good pedigree as the Shaker's skipper in the Third Division, and as something of a ball-playing central defender, John struggled to settle, was often injured and in his first season the Magpies were relegated. McGrath went on the transfer list for a while but then changed his game style, becoming a more rugged and physical centre-half in the traditional mould; as a result he was successful for three campaigns, before and after promotion. Always enduring stiff competition for places during his eight seasons on Tyneside, McGrath eventually lost out to the double rivalry of Ollie Burton and John McNamee, not to mention club skipper, Bobby Moncur. John headed for The Dell where he appeared on 195 occasions for the Saints winning a Football League cap, and then entered the rocky occupation of football management in the game's basement. After four jobs in charge, he called it a day, concentrating in a career of entertainment as a noted after-dinner speaker, full of football tales and witty anecdotes. McGrath resided in Greater Manchester and often worked for the media in the Manchester area until his untimely death on Christmas Day 1998.

Appearances & Goals:
Debut v Leicester City (a) 11 February 1961
FL: 169(1) app 2 gls
FAC: 5 app 0 gls
FLC: 6 app 0 gls
Total: 180(1) app 2 gls

Honours
2 Eng u23 app 1961/1 unoff Eng app 1969/1 FL app 1969/2 FA app 1960-61/FL div 2 champs 1965/FL div 3 champs 1961/FL div 4 prom 1983(m), 1987(m).

McGUIGAN John Joseph 1958-1962

Inside or Outside-left
5'8"
b. Motherwell, 29 October 1932
d. [Hamilton], 2004

Career: Muirkirk Jnrs/Bo'ness Utd/St Mirren Nov 1953/Southend Utd May 1955 free/UNITED July 1958 £2,250 plus W Punton/Scunthorpe Utd Jan 1962 exch deal with B Thomas/Southampton Aug 1963 £10,000/Swansea Town March 1965 £6,500 to 1966.

A versatile and tricky forward, Johnny McGuigan was never perhaps given an extended run in one position during his stay at St James' Park. Originally moving to the deep south of England from Paisley where he had been a tiler for a fire-place manufacturer, McGuigan soon showed his neat Scottish skills with Southend in the Third Division South. A good return of 37 goals in 138 games had his name on several scouting reports, including that of maestro Bill McCracken, triggering United to give him a chance on Tyneside. He took the outside-left, inside-left and centre-forward shirts for United, starting off as a replacement for the aging Bobby Mitchell during season 1958-59. But the Magpies' veteran wing wizard claimed back his jersey and John was tried in a different role. McGuigan went through a difficult period during season 1961-62 when sections of the Geordie crowd started to criticise his displays; action which prompted the club Board to make an appeal to the fans to give the player a chance. The arrival of new manager Joe Harvey saw the end to the Scots' days on Tyneside, United's ex-skipper making room for new blood by releasing McGuigan along with several other players.

After he left the football scene, John became a licensee in Southampton, at The Swan Hotel, Woolston, for a period before returning to Scotland where he worked at the Rolls Royce plant at Hillington. John's father appeared for Motherwell during the inter-war years.

Appearances & Goals:
Debut v Everton (a) 30 August 1958 (1 goal)
FL: 50 app 15 gls
FAC: 3 app 1 gl
FLC: 2 app 1 gl
Total: 55 app 17 gls

McINNES James Sloan 1941

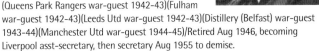

Left-half
5'9"
b. Ayr, 17 February 1912
d. Liverpool, 5 May 1965

Career: Glasgow University/Ardeer Recreation/Third Lanark Aug 1935/Liverpool March 1938 £5,500 (Brighton war-guest 1940-43)(York City war-guest 1941-42)(UNITED war-guest 1941-42)(Luton Town war-guest 1942-43)(Millwall war-guest 1942-43)(Queens Park Rangers war-guest 1942-43)(Leeds Utd war-guest 1942-43)(Distillery (Belfast) war-guest 1943-44)(Manchester Utd war-guest 1944-45)/Retired Aug 1946, becoming Liverpool asst-secretary, then secretary Aug 1955 to demise.

A talented wing-half, Jimmy McInnes was not only a fine player, totalling over 50 games for Liverpool, but also a highly educated man, holding a BSc gained at University. His intellect helped him to move from the playing side of the game into Anfield's management team after war had interrupted his career, although he still managed to total 82 games for the Reds in all senior matches. James became part of Liverpool's administrative team for almost 20 years, helping to rebuild the club during the days of Bill Shankly. During his early career the Scot reached the Scottish Cup final with Third Lanark, alongside Jimmy Denmark, before moving to Merseyside. During wartime Jimmy guested for a number of clubs and played his only game for United against Sheffield Wednesday on Christmas Day 1941. McInnes died in tragic circumstances, indirectly a result of the success at Liverpool he helped to create. Suffering from stress and overwork in advance of the club's 1965 FA Cup final and run to the European Cup semi-final, he committed suicide at Anfield just after the first-leg with Internazionale and victory at Wembley over Leeds United.

Appearances & Goals:
Debut v Sheffield Wednesday (h) 25 December 1941 (FLN)
War: 1 app 0 gls
Total: 1 app 0 gls

Honours:
SC final 1936/FLN2(WLg) champs 1943 (3 app).

McINNES Thomas Fair Macauley 1889-1891

Outside-left
5'6"
b. Bowling, Dunbartonshire, 8 July 1873
d. Dalmuir, Dunbartonshire, 1 December 1937

Career: Dalmuir Thistle/EAST END Dec 1889 (Newcastle West End guest Jan 1891)/Newcastle West End Aug 1891/Clyde Sept 1891/Nottingham Forest June 1892/Lincoln City Sept 1900/Port Glasgow cs 1904.

A potent outside-left during the Victorian era of football, Tommy McInnes served both of United's pioneer clubs when working as a riveter in the Tyne shipyards and became a distinguished player elsewhere. He was quickly an automatic choice for the East Enders and always a danger in attack usually alongside fellow Scot Mulvey. During his two seasons in East End colours, in all games, he bagged over 40 goals in a little over 50 outings. The Scot became the first player to register what could be called a 'league' hat-trick for the club when he grabbed three goals against West End in a Northern League derby during September 1890, a 7-1 victory. Still a teenager, Tom then went on to score the first ever FA Cup hat-trick for East End,

Mc

against Shankhouse during November 1890. McInnes was poached (with team-mate James Collins) by rivals West End the following January, although a dispute between the clubs saw the player remain in Heaton until the close-season. His stay at West End's St James' Park was short though, only appearing in practice matches and he moved back to Scotland with Clyde as the 1891-92 season began. McInnes, who was later included in Scotland trial matches, joined Nottingham Forest in June 1892 and proceeded to perform with much credit over seven seasons, totalling 195 senior games (57 goals), regarded as one of the best wingers in the Football League. Tom played in the Reds' inaugural Football League fixture (against Everton) and reached the 1898 FA Cup final with Forest, gaining a winners' medal before being transferred to Lincoln City in 1900. Described as a Scottish "Little'un" being "tricky" and having a "fine shot" who "plays the combination game to a nicety", he eventually settled back in his native Clydeside, working for a period at the Singer sewing-machine factory.

(Note: There has been much confusion over McInnes, as another player of the same name appeared for Notts County, Everton and Luton during the same era. He was born in Glasgow in the same year. However contemporary records and extensive family history research show that the Newcastle player is linked to Nottingham Forest and that he did not play for Scotland, instead the Notts County forward being capped.)

Appearances & Goals:
Debut v Darlington (a) 11 January 1890 (NL) (1 goal)
NL: 21 app 12 gls
FAC: 3 app 4 gls
Total: 24 app 16 gls
(Void NL: 2 app 2 gls)

Honours:
Scot trial app 1897-98/FA Cup winner 1898.

McINROY Albert 1929-1934

Goalkeeper
5'11"
b. Walton-le-Dale, Lancashire, 23 April 1901
d. Houghton-le-Spring, 7 January 1985

Career: Upper Walton 1919/Coppull Central/ High Walton Utd 1919/Preston North End amat 1921/ Great Harwood/Leyland Motors Nov 1922/Sunderland May 1923 £100/UNITED Oct 1929 £2,750/Sunderland June 1934 £250/Leeds Utd May 1935/Gateshead June 1937 to 1939/Stockton and other North East clubs as an occasional war-guest.

Albert McInroy showed remarkable consistency over a long period between the two world wars, form which made him one of the best 'keepers in the game at the time. Capped by his country and described as "one of the smartest and most daring in England", he made his name at Roker Park after a topsy-turvy early career when he played part-time and worked for the Leyland Rubber Works and as a packer for the Preston Co-op. Albert developed into a safe, sound pair of hands, totalling 227 games for the Wearsiders before switching to the Tyne and United when Micky Burns was injured. Exuding confidence, he was a fabulously witty character and a central figure during the Black'n'Whites journey to Wembley in 1932, one of the stars of the Magpies' semi-final victory over Chelsea that year. However, after being the Magpies' regular goalkeeper for five seasons, McInroy fell into dispute with the club's directors over a benefit payment and was handed a transfer, returning to Sunderland where he always felt at home. On retiring soon after the Second World War, Albert settled in the North East, for many years a publican in Newcastle, Gateshead and eventually Houghton-le-Spring. Like many old-time footballers, McInroy liked to smoke, his boss Andy Cunningham recording that he had "just one wee whiff" of a cigarette at the last moment before leaving the dressing-room. At one time during season 1933-34 at Newcastle he broke a collar-bone then sustained a poisoned finger, a serious complaint which necessitated talk of amputation. Thankfully, surgery was averted, although Albert was out of action for a long period, a critical loss for the Magpies as they were relegated from Division One.

Appearances & Goals:
Debut v Sheffield United (a) 5 October 1929
FL: 143 app 0 gls
FAC: 17 app 0 gls
Total: 160 app 0 gls

Honours:
1 Eng cap 1927/Eng trial app 1925/FAC winner 1932.

McINTOSH Alexander 1941

Inside-forward
5'10"
b. Dunfermline, 14 April 1916
d. Cannock, Staffordshire, 21 December 1965

Career: Kirkford Jnrs/Hearts of Beath/St Mirren Aug 1934/Hearts of Beath 1935/Raith Rovers Sept 1935/Folkestone Aug 1937/Wolverhampton Wand Oct 1937 (UNITED war-guest 1940-41) (Watford war-guest 1941-42)(Raith Rovers war-guest 1942-43)(Morton war-guest 1943-44) (Cardiff City war-guest 1943-44)/Birmingham City Jan 1947/Coventry City Feb 1948/Kidderminster Harriers cs 1949/Hednesford Town 1951/Bilston cs 1951.

Alex McIntosh lost the best years of his career to the war era. As fighting broke out, the Scot was a regular in the Wolves side that had just completed a Football League and FA Cup runners-up double. At 23 years of age he would have looked forward to a period at the top level of the game, but instead, McIntosh was stationed in the army at various points around the country, including at Netherwitton near Morpeth with the 2nd Battalion Bucks Regiment. Consequently he was attracted to St James' Park as a guest and appeared in United's League War Cup challenge during 1941, scoring three goals in a run which ended at the semi-final stage of the competition. McIntosh did well in the knock-out cup, winning the competition with Wolves the following season.

Appearances & Goals:
Debut v Rochdale (h) 15 February 1941 (FLWC) (1 goal)
War: 3 app 2 gls
Total: 3 app 2 gls

Honours:
FAC final 1939/FL div 2 champs 1948 (9 app)/FL WC winner 1942.

McINTOSH Robert Anderson 1920-1924

Right-half
6'0"
b. Dundee, 1 August 1892
d. Dundee, 9 January 1952

Career: Thistle/Fairfield (Dundee)/Dundee May 1912 (Motherwell war-guest 1917-19)/UNITED July 1920 £1,250/Stockport Co Oct 1924 £500 to 1925.

A tall, slimly-built link-man, calm and assured, Robert McIntosh rarely became flustered even in the most heated contest. He moved to England after good reports from scouts in Scotland as he totalled 180 games for Dundee in which he was a popular skipper at Dens Park. A feisty player who liked to take no prisoners on the field, once after a spicy meeting with Celtic which was abandoned, Bob was attacked by Hoops' fans after he had flattened a Celtic player with a robust tackle. On Tyneside, McIntosh immediately became a first-team midfielder and was an automatic choice for three seasons up to 1923-24 but then lost his place just as Newcastle were to embark on a run to Wembley. With Tom Curry and Edward Mooney both pressing for his position, United's directors allowed the Scot to depart for Edgeley Park.

Appearances & Goals:
Debut v West Bromwich Albion (a) 4 September 1920
FL: 101 app 2 gls
FAC: 2 app 0 gls
Total: 103 app 2 gls

McINTYRE Edward Patrick 1900-1906

Right or Left-half
5'8"
b. Newcastle upon Tyne, 1881 (Q4)
d. Newcastle upon Tyne, 21 February 1928

Career: Caxton (Newcastle)/Allendale Park/UNITED May 1900/Fulham May 1906/Plymouth Argyle Aug 1907/ Portsmouth July 1909/Arsenal c1910 briefly/West Stanley Sept 1910/Hartlepools Utd Feb 1911/South Shields May 1911/Ashington Dec 1911/South Shields Parkside Oct 1912/Gateshead Town July 1913/Newcastle City Oct 1914.

A deadly shot in Newcastle's 'A' team and recognised as a penalty expert, Teddy McIntyre usually appeared at centre-forward for the Magpies' reserves, but in senior action only once turned out in his true position. He deputised in midfield for United's internationals and appeared twice in the Novocastrian's title winning season of 1904-05. A servant for six years, he won Northern League and Northern Alliance honours, and was given a club benefit game as a token of his loyal service. McIntyre moved on to Craven Cottage, where he helped Fulham lift the Southern League trophy. However, during his spell with Plymouth, McIntyre was involved in controversy which led to him being arrested and charged following a dispute with his trainer, Nicholas Wallis, over a game of cards during 1909. Returning from a FA Cup match with Derby, McIntyre ended up in a fight, breaking the trainer's jaw, who afterwards died as a result of the clash. At the trial, a jury acquitted McIntyre of the manslaughter charge, but his reputation was tarnished and he soon moved into non-league football. He was part of the Newcastle City club which for a brief period tried to rival Newcastle United and had made an audacious attempt to join the Football League in 1912. The Tynesider was also a noted athlete and local runner who won contests in the so called "Morpeth Olympic Games" at the turn of the century.

Appearances & Goals:
Debut v Everton (h) 1 April 1903 (1 goal)
FL: 6 app 1 gl
Total: 6 app 1 gl

Honours:
FL champs 1905 (2 app)/SnL champs 1907 (5 app).

McKANE Joseph 1889-1895

Left-half
5'10"
b. Scotland, c1869

Career: Clydebank/EAST END Jan 1889/Blyth Feb 1895/Clydebank Utd Nov 1895.

A riveter in the Tyne shipyards, Joe McKane was a tough competitor, quick to the tackle and a hard working forager who creditably assisted United and their pioneers, Newcastle East End, during the club's formative years. He totalled over 200 games when non-competitive fixtures are added to his senior outings. Arriving in Newcastle from Clydeside at the same time as another noted Scot, Alec McCurdie, Joe appeared in East End's first FA Cup Proper fixture against Nottingham Forest during season 1891-92, then also took part in the inaugural match at St James' Park following the East Enders' move from Heaton. McKane was also on the field for the Geordie's Football League baptism a year later and was an ever-present in that historic campaign. A mainstay of the side at that time alongside Bobby Creilly, he once forced United to take to the field with only ten men at Middlesbrough after he had inadvertently missed the train south.

Appearances & Goals:
Debut v Darlington (a) 11 January 1890 (NL)
NL: 44 app 0 gls
FL: 41 app 0 gls
FAC: 11 app 0 gls
Total: 96 app 0 gls
(Void NL: 3 app 0 gls)

McKAY Robert 1926-1928

Inside-right
5'6"
b. Govan, Glasgow, 2 September 1900
d. 1977

Career: Parkhead White Rose/Vale of Clyde/ Parkhead/Neilston Victoria/Morton Sept 1921/ Rangers June 1925 £1,750/UNITED November 1926 £2,750/Sunderland Oct 1928 exch deal for R Thomson/Charlton Ath Dec 1930 £1,220/Bristol Rovers Nov 1932 £350/Newport Co June 1935 to cs 1936/Dundee Utd manager July 1939 to Oct 1939/Ballymena Utd manager 1946 to 1949/Charlton Ath scout.

An expert schemer, Bob McKay made a name for himself in Morton colours, totalling over 150 games in Greenock and a key figure in their Scottish Cup triumph.
He had a marvellous, though short, period with United after netting in the very first minute of his debut then going on to record a scintillating hat-trick. Continuing to strike goals throughout his career, the diminutive McKay went onto grab another headlining treble for the Magpies soon after; three goals within an amazing five-minute spree against Derby in 1927. McKay was a smart and proficient exponent on the park and a great tactician too, described in one pen-picture of the day as "a bundle of tricks and a clever pattern weaver". The Scot could turn on the exhibition stuff when he was in the mood, once in a derby match against Sunderland he scored a gem following a mazy run past half-a-dozen Sunderland men before unleashing a cross shot into the net. Bob arrived on Tyneside two months into the 1926-27 season and made a big impact on the side, being one of the reasons the Geordies went on to climb from seventh place to lift the title that year. But a season later, after reaching the Scotland line-up with United, he fell out of favour and moved the short distance to Roker Park where he again gave good short term service, 17 goals in 51 matches. Totalling almost 600 senior outings in his career, McKay played in all four home countries during a much-travelled period as a player. On retirement, Bob ran a billiards saloon in Glasgow and coached local youth sides around his district of Shettleston.

Appearances & Goals:
Debut v West Bromwich Albion (h) 6 November 1926 (3 goals)
FL: 62 app 21 gls
FAC: 4 app 1 gl
Total: 66 app 22 gls

Honours:
1 Scot cap 1928/1 SL app 1926/FL champs 1927/FL div 3(S) Cup winner 1935/SC winner 1922.

McKAY William 1895-1897

Centre-forward
5'10"
b. Scotland

Career: Rangers/UNITED June 1895 to 1897.

William McKay was described as a "scientific player" of high reputation in Scotland. Although not being able to command a regular place at Ibrox, he impressed Newcastle's directors when Rangers visited St James' Park in a friendly contest during March 1895. The Glasgow giants won 5-2 and afterwards McKay quickly became a Magpie player. A versatile forward and a utility player during season 1895-96, he appeared at half-back and at inside-right for the club too.

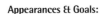

Appearances & Goals:
Debut v Loughborough (h) 7 September 1895
FL: 18 app 6 gls
FAC: 3 app 1 gl
Total: 21 app 7 gls

Mc

McKELLAR David Norwood 1986

Goalkeeper
6'1"
b. Ardrossan, Ayrshire, 22 May 1956

Career: Kilwinning Rangers Oct 1971/Ipswich Town jnr Sept 1972, prof March 1974 (Colchester Utd loan 1975-76) (Peterborough Utd loan 1975-76)/Dundee Utd May 1976 to April 1977 free/Ardrossan Winton Rovers July 1977/Derby Co April 1978 £2,500/Brentford Sept 1980 £25,000/Happy Valley AA (HK) 1983/Carlisle Utd Aug 1983/Hibernian Aug 1985 (Manchester City loan 1985-86)(UNITED loan Feb 1986 to May 1986)/Hamilton Acc June 1986 £10,000, becoming player-coach July 1987/ Dunfermline Ath Jan 1988 £10,000 (Hartlepool Utd loan 1988-89)/Carlisle Utd loan Oct 1988, pmt Nov 1988/Kilmarnock March 1990 £20,000/Rangers Aug 1991 £20,000 to cs 1992/Kilbirnie Ladeside/Largs Thistle manager 1993/Indian FA national youth coach c1994/Petershill Jnrs manager 1994 to 1995/Irvine Meadow manager 1996.

David McKellar was an emergency signing by the Black'n'Whites towards the end of the 1985-86 season after an injury to first choice goalkeeper Martin Thomas. A widely travelled and experienced 'keeper, McKellar had been a youth star, winning international honours and helping Ipswich lift the prestigious FA Youth Cup. His potential was perhaps never fully realised and the Scot drifted from club to club, enjoying good spells with Derby, Brentford and Carlisle where he played on 172 occasions and was outstanding for the Cumbrians as they just missed promotion to the top flight in season 1983-84, contenders with the Magpies that season. He concluded his nomad senior career with Scotland's finest side at the time, Rangers, as understudy to Andy Goram for a period. Although moving around the country, McKellar still totalled almost 400 top-class matches in his career. Dave settled in Glasgow, later working in child protection for Social Services.

Appearances & Goals:
Debut v Ipswich Town (h) 15 March 1986
FL: 10 app 0 gls
Total: 10 app 0 gls

Honours:
Scot sch-youth app/FAYC winner 1973.

MACKENZIE Roderick R 1922-1935

Right-half
5'7"
b. Inverness, 22 May 1901
d. Inverness, 25 March 1953

Career: Inverness Thistle/Clacknacuddin/UNITED trial Sept 1922, pmt Oct 1922 £100/Gateshead Aug 1935/Reading briefly 1937.

Following the likes of McCombie and McWilliam from Inverness, Roddie MacKenzie signed for United after a month's trial. As dour and as tough as they come, he was a hero on several occasions for Newcastle during his 12 seasons in the Magpies' first-eleven. Establishing a place for himself during 1924-25, the Scot became the side's engine-room in the middle of the field; tenacious and big hearted, it was recorded that he would "tackle anything that moves". Roddie was an inspiration to his team-mates and tended to raise his game when in a big match atmosphere, relishing the contests with star names. One such duel, season after season fondly recalled, was the meeting with Arsenal's Alex James; in one clash Roddie is noted to have spectacularly flattened the great international to the floor in front of Highbury's main stand. A Football League title and FA Cup winner with the Black'n'Whites, he was also in the side when relegation stunned Tyneside during 1934. Then at the veteran stage of his career, MacKenzie lost his place and moved the short distance to Redheugh Park. He later resided on Tyneside before moving back to the Highlands. It is possible he is related to the United boardroom dynasty of the same name, but this has not been confirmed.

(Note: Various contemporary sources spell his surname both McKenzie and MacKenzie; even his autograph uses both.)

Appearances & Goals:
Debut v Huddersfield Town (h) 7 April 1923
FL: 238 app 6 gls
FAC: 18 app 1 gl
Total: 256 app 7 gls

Honours: FL champs 1927/FAC winner 1932.

McKERRELL Daniel 1941

Outside-left
5'6"
b. Blantyre, Lanarkshire

Career: Bedlay Jnrs/Shawfield 1935/Hamilton Acc Aug 1936/ Falkirk April 1937/East Fife loan April 1938, pmt Dec 1938 (UNITED war-guest 1941-42)(Middlesbrough war-guest 1941-42)/Resumed with East Fife/Carlisle Utd March 1946.

Known as Danny, the Scot had a swift rise to fame just prior to war being declared in 1939. Joining East Fife, initially on loan due to an injury crisis, he made a dramatic debut in the Scottish Cup semi-final replay against St Bernard's during April 1938 and ended up scoring the winner in a 2-1 triumph. Then the fast and intricate Scot took part in the Hampden Park victory over Kilmarnock, netting the first and last goals in a replayed final which the Fifers won 4-2. McKerrell became an overnight hero in the Fife town of Methil and it was a great pity the fighting to soon erupt halted a bright career for the small and plucky winger. Billeted in the North East when on RAF service, the darting forward came into United's wartime side during the early part of the 1941-42 season.

Appearances & Goals:
Debut v Bradford City (a) 6 September 1941 (FLN)
War: 2 app 0 gls
Total: 2 app 0 gls

Honours:
SC winner 1938.

McKINNEY William E 1956-1965

Right-back
6'0"
b. Newcastle upon Tyne, 20 July 1936

Career: Wallsend Rising Sun/Wallsend St Luke's/UNITED May 1956 £50/Bournemouth Aug 1965 £2,750/ Mansfield Town July 1966 free/Wellington Town July 1968/Retired due to injury 1969.

Born and raised in Newcastle, Bill McKinney was employed as a panel-beater before signing full-time professional forms at St James' Park. A full-blooded, mean and solid full-back, he often left forwards knowing they had been in a physical battle. McKinney was a deputy to Dick Keith during the late 1950s and found it difficult to claim a regular place in the side, his 94 outings for the club being spread over eight seasons. A spot-kick expert, Bill had a good term in season 1960-61 (25 games) the year, alas, when United were relegated. However, by the time Irish international Keith had left the scene, McKinney, who was captain of Newcastle on occasion, then had the young David Craig as a rival. McKinney was released and concluded his career in the lower divisions, registering 59 games for Mansfield. When on National Service during 1959, he turned out for the Army eleven. After leaving football Bill resided in Dawley near Telford, reverting to his pre-football occupation with GKN Sankey before retiring in 1997.

Appearances & Goals:
Debut v Tottenham Hotspur (a) 28 December 1957
FL: 85 app 6 gls
FAC: 7 app 1 gl
FLC: 2 app 1 gl
Total: 94 app 8 gls

Honours:
FL div 2 champs 1965 (2 app).

McKINNON Robert 1984-1986

Left-back
5'11"
b. Glasgow, 31 July 1966

Career: East Kilbride YC/Rutherglen Glencairn/UNITED Nov 1984/Hartlepool Utd Aug 1986 (Manchester Utd loan 1990-91)/Motherwell Jan 1992 £150,000/FC Twente (Neth) July 1996/Heart of Midlothian July 1998 free (Hartlepool Utd loan 1998-99)(Carlisle Utd loan 1999-2000)/Clydebank Aug 2000/Bellshill Ath player-coach 2002, retired playing cs 2002, becoming asst-manager.

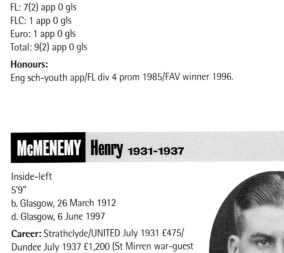

In his only outing for the Magpies, youngster Rob McKinnon stood in for Kenny Wharton in a tough away fixture at White Hart Lane. The Scot suffered, along with the rest of his defence, as Spurs inflicted a heavy 5-1 defeat. McKinnon didn't last the 90 minutes and never reached the first-team again, being transferred to Hartlepool not long afterwards. However, the ginger-haired Scot developed enormously at the Victoria Ground as he clocked up just short of 300 games and on his return to Scotland with Motherwell was established as one of the best defenders north of the border possessing flair to get forward. Rob eventually received a call up to his country's side too, and was capped at both full and 'B' level. On retirement, he joined the family business in Paisley, running an Iveco commercial truck dealership and repair centre, McKinnon & Forbes.

Appearances & Goals:
Debut v Tottenham Hotspur (a) 7 September 1985
FL: 1 app 0 gls
Total: 1 app 0 gls

Honours:
3 Scot caps 1994-95/3 Scot B app 1994-96/FL div 4 prom 1991/PFA ToS (d4) 1990.

McLAUGHLIN Hugh 1889-1890

Half-back or Forward
b. unknown

Career: Sunderland c1888/EAST END Nov 1889 to Dec 1890.

A versatile player who appeared in both defence and attack, Hugh McLaughlin was a regular in Sunderland's pre-league side during season 1888-89 and took part in the FA Cup qualifying meeting for the Wearsiders against East End that campaign. An experienced footballer with the more advanced Sunderland club, he appeared for the Durham County side too. On joining the Heaton club, McLaughlin became captain of the side but it was noted in the local press he became unreliable on occasion. During December 1890 the player did not turn up for the trip to face Middlesbrough, it was recorded that he would "unlikely to play for the club again". Club officials carried that report through and McLaughlin wasn't selected again.

(Note: Spelling of the player's surname varies between McLaughlin and McLauchlan.)

Appearances & Goals:
Debut v Elswick Rangers (h) 14 December 1889 (NL)
NL: 11 app 4 gls
FAC: 3 app 0 gls
Total: 14 app 4 gls

McLEAN David John 1974-1978

Midfield
5'7"
b. Newcastle upon Tyne, 24 November 1957

Career: UNITED jnr July 1974, prof Nov 1975/Carlisle Utd loan March 1978, pmt May 1978 free/Darlington Aug 1979 free/Scunthorpe Utd July 1986 £7,000/ Hartlepool Utd loan March 1987, pmt July 1988 free/ Whitley Bay Aug 1988/Esh Winning/Brigg Town cs 1989 to cs 1996 when he retired, becoming coach and later manager cs 2004 to Oct 2007.

One of a bright crop of youngsters who developed through United's junior side, David McLean was an outstanding schoolboy player. A past England school and youth forward, he received an opportunity in the senior team as an 18-year-old at the end of the 1975-76 programme. Standing in for Rocky Hudson, the auburn-haired midfielder had neat

skills and was a compact, tidy player. Although troubled by ankle injuries, he was on the fringe of Newcastle's side for three seasons, which included taking part and being on the bench for the UEFA Cup ties of 1977-78. His form though and prospects as a Magpie player nose-dived when the club were relegated. With Darlington, the Tynesider totalled 337 games, an inspiration and skipper to the Quakers when they won promotion during 1984-85. At the end of his career David, as captain, lifted the FA Vase trophy at Wembley for Brigg Town, serving the Lincolnshire non-leaguers for over 10 years. He was employed as a production supervisor for a furnishings business in Scunthorpe, residing in nearby Scotter.

Appearances & Goals:
Debut v Sheffield United (a) 19 April 1976 (sub)
FL: 7(2) app 0 gls
FLC: 1 app 0 gls
Euro: 1 app 0 gls
Total: 9(2) app 0 gls

Honours:
Eng sch-youth app/FL div 4 prom 1985/FAV winner 1996.

McMENEMY Henry 1931-1937

Inside-left
5'9"
b. Glasgow, 26 March 1912
d. Glasgow, 6 June 1997

Career: Strathclyde/UNITED July 1931 £475/ Dundee July 1937 £1,200 (St Mirren war-guest 1939-40)(Gateshead war-guest 1942-43)(York City war-guest 1943-44)(Halifax Town war-guest 1943-44).

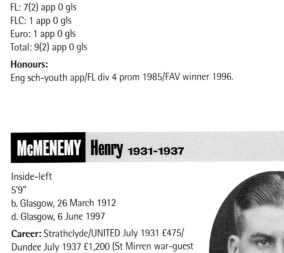

A cultured, highly-skilled competitor, Harry McMenemy excelled on the ball and had the ability to strike a telling pass quickly and accurately. An ex-bricklayer who was chased by several top clubs before United won the race; Harry arrived at St James' Park as a teenager, but won a position in the Magpies' side almost immediately. He showed much skill and craft, and quickly became a terrace favourite. His first season coincided with Newcastle's run to Wembley and McMenemy had a substantial influence on that success. Although dogged by injury after his first two successful seasons in a United shirt, he was also captain of the club for a period. Tipped on more than one occasion for a full Scotland cap, Harry was most unlucky, sustaining an injury and having to drop out of his country's side when selected to play in 1933. He was from a large family of noted footballers and it was, ironically, his brother John of Motherwell, who took his place in that Scotland fixture against Wales. Harry's father was the famous 'Nap' McMenemy of Celtic fame, while another brother, Frank, turned out for Northampton. He is also distantly related to celebrated manager Lawrie McMenemy, as well as United coach, Chris McMenemy (qv). During World War II Harry was twice wounded in action inside a week, being shot during the fighting at Arnhem. He recovered in a Manchester hospital and after the conflict Harry lived and worked in Glasgow.

(Note: His father, Nap McMenemy was born with the surname of McMenamin, as was Harry. But both used the name of McMenemy during their football careers as did the rest of the sporting family. Harry appears to have reverted to his registered name when he left the game.)

Appearances & Goals:
Debut v Grimsby Town (a) 5 September 1931
FL: 138 app 34 gls
FAC: 10 app 1 gl
Others: 1 app 2 gls
Total: 149 app 37 gls

Honours:
FAC winner 1932/Scot sch-youth app.

Mc

McMICHAEL Alfred 1949-1963

Left-back
5'8"
b. Belfast, 1 October 1927
d. Bangor, Co Down, 7 January 2006

Career: Wolfhill REC Jnrs 1942/
Cliftonville 1942/Linfield Oct 1945/
UNITED Sept 1949 joint deal with
G Hannah £23,000/South Shields player-
manager June 1963 free to Feb
1969/Bangor (NI) manager
Oct 1971 to 1972.

*Alf McMichael was for a long time United's
most capped player, captain of both club
and country. Possessing excellent
positional sense, he was studious at his job
and tended to raise his game against the
better wingers and for the big occasion,
Stanley Matthews once noting that
McMichael was "one of the best left-backs
I have ever played against". Never too fancy on the ball, Alf landed on Tyneside as a
youngster along with another noted United Fifties star, George Hannah. He took over
from Bobby Corbett and was a regular for 14 seasons, always showing a cool and
composed manner. The Irishman was unlucky to miss two of the club's three FA Cup
final appearances; in 1951 when he slipped in training and broke a wrist, and then in
1955 when he had ligament trouble. Later during his United career, McMichael
partnered fellow Irishman Dick Keith, a duo that also featured on the international
scene, including on the 1958 World Cup stage. One of only nine players to total over
400 matches for Newcastle, McMichael once netted an own-goal after only 32
seconds against West Bromwich Albion during 1951. The Irishman was given a well
supported testimonial in 1963 (24,175). After he left the soccer circuit, Alf settled in
Bangor, County Down, and was employed as a brewery representative then at the
Harland & Wolff shipyard in Belfast to retirement.*

Appearances & Goals:
Debut v Manchester City (h) 17 September 1949
FL: 402 app 1 gl
FAC: 25 app 0 gls
FLC: 4 app 0 gls
Others: 2 app 0 gls
Total: 433 app 1 gl

Honours:
40 NI caps 1950-60/WdC 1958/Rest of UK app 1952/NI FA & tour app/NI junior app/8
NIL app 1947-50/FAC winner 1952/NIL champs 1949/NIC winner 1948.

McNAMEE John 1966-1971

Centre-half
6'0"
b. Coatbridge, 11 June 1941

Career: Bellshill Ath/Celtic Aug 1959/Hibernian
April 1964/UNITED Dec 1966 £26,000/Blackburn
Rovers Nov 1971 £15,000 to June 1972/Morton
July 1973 (Hartlepool Utd loan 1973-74)/
Lancaster City 1974/ Workington Town manager,
and non-contract player, June 1975 to Dec 1975/
Carlisle Utd asst-coach.

*Big John McNamee was purchased by manager
Joe Harvey to add steel to United's flagging
defence during a relegation dog-fight during
season 1966-67; the cast-iron defender
proceeding to do his job with credit. A burley
centre-half, gritty and determined, McNamee
loved to challenge the many big name centre-forwards of the era and he became
something of a cult figure during his five years with the club. United's supporters
quickly took to John, if not for his pure footballing skills, which were limited, then for
his reputation as a hard-man stopper. That player-supporter bond was further
strengthened when 'Big John' netted a late equalising goal in a white-hot derby at
Roker Park during 1967, then saw him swing on the cross-bar in celebration; a
moment which has become embedded in Tyne versus Wear folklore. Part of the*

*Black'n'Whites celebrated European squad which lifted silverware in Budapest during
1969, by coincidence on his birthday, McNamee had been turned down by Manchester
United as a teenager, but then joined Celtic and established himself in Scotland. By
the time he crossed the border though, he had lost his place at Parkhead to Billy
McNeil and was a favourite with Hibs, while his rugged style had made him a marked
man by opposing fans and also, to a degree, by referees. Quite a character, John was
once booked for arguing and manhandling Frank Haffey, his own Celtic goalkeeper. A
popular footballer with Blackburn Rovers as well, after his career closed, McNamee
resided in the Lake District, in Cockermouth working as a postman, until a serious
accident in his post-van during 1988 forced him onto invalidity pension.*

Appearances & Goals:
Debut v Tottenham Hotspur (a) 31 December 1966
FL: 115(2) app 8 gls
FAC: 6 app 0 gls
FLC: 1 app 0 gls
Euro: 7(1) app 0 gls
Total: 129(3) app 8 gls

Honours:
Scot sch-youth app/SC final 1963/ICFC winner 1969 (sub no app).

McNEE John 1894-1895

Outside or Inside-left
5'4"
b. Renton, Dunbartonshire, c1867

Career: Renton Wand/Renton c1886/Bolton Wand Sept
1889 £100/Kingsland (Norfolk) player-coach cs 1893/
UNITED Sept 1894/Gateshead NER player-trainer Oct 1895/
Watford Oct 1897 to May 1900/Fulham Aug 1901 to c1902.

*John McNee, known also as Jack, Jock and even Jimmy, was
for a period a member of the famous Renton combination, a
team from the edge of Loch Lomond that competed in the
English FA Cup during season 1886-87. McNee was in the
side then, and he also took a prominent role when Renton lifted the Scottish Cup
during 1888 by a record 6-1 scoreline. Small and tricky, perhaps one of the original
traditional Scottish wingers, John was on the field when his club were crowned
unofficial 'Champions of the World' in May 1888 after that Scottish Cup win and
victories over English clubs, West Bromwich Albion and Preston. A true pioneer of the
game, he moved to Bolton where he was a regular, making 96 appearances (25 goals)
before heading for Tyneside when United were after new forward blood in their bid to
establish the club as a Football League side. McNee started well in the Novocastrians'
line-up, netting on his first two outings, but after a season faded from the scene,
although for a time he was regarded as a "great favourite at St James Park" by the
Daily Journal. At Watford, McNee became the Hornets' first captain at Cassio Road
as they developed into a professional club.*

Appearances & Goals:
Debut v Burslem Port Vale (a) 6 October 1894 (1 goal)
FL: 21 app 4 gls
FAC: 2 app 0 gls
Total: 23 app 4 gls

Honours:
Scot trial app 1887/SC winner 1888/SnL div 2 champs 1900.

McNEIL Matthew Alexander 1949-1951

Centre-half
6'3"
b. Glasgow, 28 July 1927
d. Kirkintilloch, 23 April 1977

Career: Hibernian Aug 1945/UNITED Dec 1949 £6,400/
Barnsley Aug 1951 £10,500/Brighton July 1953 £7,000/
Norwich City March 1956 £3,000/Cambridge Utd July
1957.

*Vastly built centre-half Matt McNeil was ideally
structured for the pivot's role in the heart of defence at
6'3" tall and over 12 stones, but always played second
fiddle to Frank Brennan at Gallowgate. Being tall and
rangy, he was a dominating figure and not surprisingly,
Matt was a master in the air, positive and tough, but*

his games for Newcastle were restricted to the 1950-51 season and he moved to Oakwell for a sizable fee when Matt decided he had to change clubs to further his career. The Scot did well over two seasons in Barnsley's Division Two line-up, claiming 70 games, before he was picked up by Brighton then Norwich where he made 44 appearances for the Canaries. McNeil later resided in his native Kirkintilloch near Glasgow to his early death of cancer.

Appearances & Goals:
Debut v Middlesbrough (a) 25 December 1950
FL: 9 app 0 gls
FAC: 2 app 0 gls
Total: 11 app 0 gls

McPHILLIPS William Pearson 1930-1938

Goalkeeper
6'1"
b. Musselburgh, 8 June 1910
d. York, November 1992

Career: Musselburgh Bruntonians/UNITED July 1930 £20/Guildford City June 1938 free/Bradford City June 1939 £170 (Hartlepools Utd war-guest 1939-40).

Tall, thinly-built and a confident goalkeeper, Bill McPhillips was on United's staff for almost eight years. 'Scots Wullie', as he was nicknamed in the dressing-room, made his debut during the Magpies' relegation season in 1933-34 but was always considered second choice to either Micky Burns, Norman Tapken or Tom Swinburne. However, the Scot did serve the club well whenever called upon, his 34 games spread over five campaigns. He left the club following a dispute over contract terms and moved into non-league football.

Appearances & Goals:
Debut v Liverpool (h) 1 January 1934
FL: 33 app 0 gls
FAC: 1 app 0 gls
Total: 34 app 0 gls

McQUADE George 1942-1945

Inside-forward
5'9"
b. Scotland, 1918

Career: Annan Ath/UNITED amat May 1942, prof Aug 1942 (Heart of Midlothian war-guest 1943-45)/Queen of the South Oct 1945.

Although wartime football curtailed normal sporting activity, United's scouting network still operated, and with notable success. George McQuade was of many finds during the war years, spotted when playing for Annan in the south of Scotland. An inside-forward, he was blooded on the wing as a replacement for Charlie Woollett for an end of season derby fixture with Sunderland during May 1942. The Scot though didn't get another opportunity in Newcastle's colours. He moved back to the Solway coast, joining Queen of the South where he displayed top form to his new supporters by netting a hat-trick on his debut against Aberdeen.

Appearances & Goals:
Debut v Sunderland (h) 25 May 1942 (FLN)
War: 1 app 0 gls
Total: 1 app 0 gls

McTAVISH John Kay 1912-1913

Inside-right
5'9"
b. Govan, Glasgow, 7 June 1885
d. Falkirk, 4 April 1944

Career: Ibrox Roselea/Fairfield Ath/Petershill/Falkirk June 1905/Oldham Ath June 1910/Tottenham Hotspur Jan 1911/UNITED April 1912 £650/Partick Thistle June 1913 £500/York City 1914-15/Goole Town Feb 1915 (Falkirk war-guest 1917-18)(Heart of Midlothian war-guest 1917-18)/East Fife cs 1919/Bo'ness 1919-20/Falkirk Sept 1920/Dumbarton Oct 1920/East Stirlingshire Aug 1921/Dumbarton c1922/Retired 1924.

An excellent ball-player, John McTavish came to prominence at Falkirk in more than 150 appearances when he partnered Scottish legend Jock Simpson in many matches and earned an international call-up. Following a spell with Spurs where he totalled over 40 senior games, McTavish arrived at St James' Park after the Magpies had chased him a year earlier but found a fee of £1,500 killed any deal. Newcastle persisted though and eventually succeeded in bringing him to Barrack Road for less than half that amount. His younger brother Robert was also at White Hart Lane, the two playing in the same line up during 1911. In a black-and-white shirt, John had one good season for the club during 1912-13, before heading back to Scotland where he totalled over 350 senior outings (64 goals). Also known as 'Jock', he died in Falkirk during 1944, collapsing on a local bus.

Appearances & Goals:
Debut v Blackburn Rovers (a) 27 April 1912
FL: 34 app 6 gls
FAC: 5 app 1 gl
Total: 39 app 7 gls

Honours:
1 Scot cap 1910/Scot trial app 1910/2 SL app 1907-08.

McVAY Thomas Lloyd 1939-1941

Goalkeeper
5'9"
b. North Shields, 10 October 1922
d. Haltwhistle, Northumberland, 22 January 1995

A former England schoolboy international goalkeeper, capped against Ireland in 1937, Tom McVay signed for United as an amateur during March 1939, then as a professional soon after in July. Tom however just had a few short months on Newcastle's Football League payroll before all contracts were cancelled on the outbreak of the Second World War. Before joining the RAF, he had one outing in Tom Swinburne's position, against Leeds during June 1940 when he was only 17 years of age, one of the youngest on record for the Magpies.

Appearances & Goals:
Debut v Leeds United (a) 8 June 1940 (FLNE)
War: 1 app 0 gls
Total: 1 app 0 gls

Honours:
Eng sch-youth app.

McWILLIAM Peter 1902-1911

Left-half
5'9"
b. Inverness, 21 September 1879
d. Redcar, 1 October 1951

Career: Heatherley (Inverness)/Inverness Thistle/Albion Rovers/Inverness Thistle 1899/UNITED Aug 1902 £10/Retired cs 1911 due to injury/Tottenham Hotspur manager Dec 1912/Middlesbrough manager Jan 1927 to March 1934/Arsenal scout cs 1934/Tottenham Hotspur manager April 1938/Retired June 1942.

Peter McWilliam was one of the most influential players during Newcastle's formidable Edwardian heyday. Known as 'Peter the Great', the Scot arrived at Gallowgate after heading south to work as a short-hand writer and to become a part-time footballer. He was in fact hijacked by United officials at Newcastle Central Station when he was on his way to Sunderland for trials and to meet an old friend, full-back Andy McCombie. Captured by the Magpies, Peter placed his planned office career to one side and focussed on professional football. He was a raw, but talented schemer to begin with, who actually struggled to claim a first-team place at St James' Park. But Peter came into his own after colleagues persuaded United's directors to give him a chance, and the club never looked back. Newcastle won the title in McWilliam's first full season and he rapidly developed thereafter as a half-back of exceptional quality. He had a famous body swerve which fooled opponents and characterised his game while Peter was described when at his peak as "the finest half-back in Britain" who possessed a "natural

N

command of the ball". Playing with delicacy and distinction, as well as a masterly ease, McWilliam had an acute mind for the tactical side of the game like many of United's celebrated figures of that period. He didn't tackle too often, but his passes were crisp and precise while he always urged his team-mates forward. Also nicknamed 'Pat', the Scot was a huge crowd favourite on Tyneside for seven eventful seasons before a knee ligament injury, sustained when playing for Scotland wrecked his career. Captain of the Scots in a game against Wales at the new Ninian Park, he was injured in a collision for the ball, some reports noting he gashed his knee on the poor surface which still contained debris from the building works and rubbish tip on which the pitch was built. That devastating set-back only galvanised Peter to develop as a master manager too. As boss of Spurs especially, he maintained a high standard of football, always coaching his line-up to play football in the Newcastle style; a passing, possession game. When he guided the Londoners to FA Cup victory, he became one of only a few men to have both managed and played for a FA Cup winning side. For his commitment to soccer Peter was awarded the Football League's Long Service medal in June 1939. On retirement McWilliam resided in Redcar to his death. His son Peter (junior) had a prominent career with the Civil Service in India and was the founder of the McWilliam School in north Bengal. He also played football for Alipurduar Town in Bengal.

(Note: Some sources record his birth in Inveravon, research confirms he was born in Inverness.)

Appearances & Goals:
Debut v Middlesbrough (h) 18 October 1902
FL: 199 app 11 gls
FAC: 41 app 1 gl
Others: 2 app 0 gls
Total: 242 app 12 gls

Honours:
8 Scot caps 1905-11/Scot trial app 1905-06/FL champs 1905, 1907, 1909/FL div 2 champs 1920(m), 1927(m), 1929(m)/FAC winner 1910, 1921(m)/FAC final 1905, 1906, 1908/FL Long Service medal 1939.

NAPIER Christopher Robin Anthony 1965-1966

Centre-forward
6'0"
b. Dunblane, near Stirling, 26 September 1943
Career: Blackpool amat May 1960, prof Nov 1960/ Preston North End June 1963 £2,000/Workington July 1964/UNITED Nov 1965 £17,500/Brighton Sept 1966 £8,500/Blackburn Rovers Aug 1972 £15,000 to May 1974 free/Durban Utd (SA) 1974/East London Utd (SA) 1975/Durban City (SA) 1976-77/ Virginia Utd (SA) coach.

Known as 'Kit' and a prolific scorer in the lower divisions with Workington having bagged 31 goals in 72 games, 22-year-old Christopher Napier signed for Joe Harvey's side at a time when the Black'n'Whites were desperate for goals and just having a bid for Welsh international leader Wyn Davies rejected. Tall and slim, Napier was purchased as a promising striker, hopefully to be developed as a First Division leader who could save United a hefty fee in the transfer market. Although Kit was good with the ball at his feet possessing control with a strong shot, he wasn't quick enough for top level football and the plan never materialised. After a handful of run-outs in the senior team, Harvey went back for Davies and Napier was transferred to Brighton. On the south coast, Kit was a big success at the Goldstone Ground, firing home 30 goals during season 1967-68 to record a new post-war scoring record for the Seagulls. Showing a subtle touch and fine positional awareness up front, he went onto appear on 291 occasions with a first-class return of 99 goals all told and was once described as being a player who could be frustrating yet brilliant. Napier afterwards played and resided in South Africa where he entered the motor trade, becoming a director with Kempster Ford in Durban. He was a regular on the pro-am golf circuit in South Africa and is related to Scotland cap Charlie Napier as well as Kilmarnock's George Napier.

Appearances & Goals:
Debut v Blackpool (h) 6 November 1965
FL: 8 app 0 gls
Total: 8 app 0 gls

Honours:
FL div 3 prom 1972.

NATTRASS Irving 1967-1979

Right-back
5'10"
b. Fishburn, Co Durham, 12 December 1952
Career: UNITED jnr 1967, prof July 1970/ Middlesbrough Aug 1979 £475,000/ Retired due to injury June 1986.

Cool and refined, Irving Nattrass began his first-team career for United in midfield, then took over from David Craig at right-back and concluded his period with the club in central defence where he read the game almost to perfection. A product of United's junior structure, Nattrass oozed confidence and was sure and positive, with constructive use of the ball to get his forwards moving. Becoming Newcastle skipper, he was destined to reach full international level before a series of cruel injuries kept him out of action, mishaps that were to follow him for the rest of his career. Irving suffered hairline fractures with Boro and had several operations due to knee problems which eventually halted his career. Nattrass missed the 1974 FA Cup run and later England's tour of South America during 1977 when he was a certainty for his first international appearance. With Newcastle relegated in 1978 and the Bill McGarry style of management not to his liking, Irving's obvious talent was too good for Second Division football and he soon moved back to the top division, signing for Middlesbrough in a record deal. A craftsman in defence, although he served Boro well, in 221 games over seven seasons, perhaps Nattrass would have earned that England opportunity had he joined a more high profile club, Spurs also challenging for his signature at the time. Nattrass suffered relegation three times, once with United and twice with Boro, yet on each occasion stood out as the classy player he was. Remaining in the North East after retiring and settling in Whitley Bay, Irving concentrated on developing a retail clothing business, running a series of outlets in the region from 1978 to 2012.

Appearances & Goals:
Debut v Derby County (h) 27 March 1971 (sub)
FL: 226(12) app 16 gls
FAC: 23 app 1 gl
FLC: 22 app 3 gls
Euro: 4 app 0 gls
Others: 25(1) app 2 gls
Total: 300(13) app 22 gls

Honours:
1 Eng u23 app 1976/FLC final 1976.

NAYLOR James 1930-1932

Right-half
5'10"
b. High Crompton, Lancashire, 2 March 1901
d. Shaw, near Oldham, 31 August 1983
Career: Shaw Parish Church/Shawside (Oldham)/ Oldham Ath amat May 1920, prof Oct 1922/ Huddersfield Town Dec 1928 £3,750/UNITED July 1930 £4,000/Manchester City Oct 1932 £500 (Oldham Ath loan 1932-33)/Macclesfield Town Feb 1934/Nelson Aug 1935/Wigan Ath Aug 1937/ Retired cs 1938.

Although Jimmy Naylor operated mainly on the right side of midfield for United, he was also efficient at left-half. His home debut against Chelsea coincided with St James' Park's record attendance, and Naylor recalled he had to hold onto a police horse's tail as he was guided to the dressing-room through the packed crowds! After a good first season at Gallowgate and being in the travelling party as 12th man for the 1932 FA Cup final, injury blighted his time with the Magpies. At his peak, Naylor was on the fringe of a full England call-up, a splendid attacking player who often produced majestic footwork on the ball and precision passing ability. As a teenager Jimmy worked at a local cotton mill before joining Oldham where he quickly developed as a footballer. He read the game well and was a star of the Latics for almost eight years, totalling 257 senior games. Jimmy was a hugely popular character at Boundary Park before joining Huddersfield during 1928. At Leeds Road, Jimmy assisted the Terriers when they reached Wembley in 1930 just before heading for Tyneside. On leaving the game, he returned to his native Lancashire where he spent the rest of his life, a housing manager for Crompton District Council. Naylor was also a noted Lancashire League cricketer for Crompton and Milnrow cricket clubs.

Appearances & Goals:
Debut v Sheffield Wednesday (a) 30 August 1930
FL: 30 app 0 gls
FAC: 2 app 0 gls
Total: 32 app 0 gls

Honours:
Eng trial app 1929/FAC final 1930.

NEALE Duncan Frederick 1959-1963

Right-half
5'8"
b. Portslade, near Brighton, 1 October 1939

Career: West Ham Colts/Woodford YC/Ilford 1957/ UNITED amat May 1959, prof June 1959/Plymouth Argyle Aug 1963 £12,000/Plymouth City cs 1970 to 1971/Plymouth Argyle asst-coach 1971 & non-contract player to 1972/Bodmin Town/Liskeard Ath/Saltash Utd.

Duncan Neale was plucked from the Isthmian League with Ilford and, after a season of transition, he gained a regular place in First Division football for the start of the 1960-61 season. A fine attacking player in midfield who showed non-stop enthusiasm, the fair-haired, stocky Neale is noted especially for two memorable goals on his debut for the Magpies against Fulham; hitting the net twice in eight minutes as United swamped the Londoners 7-2. Duncan was one of Charlie Mitten's "kittens" as the manager's new young players were termed, he scored Newcastle's first ever goal in the Football League Cup, against Colchester during 1960. But that season ended in relegation for the Novocastrians, and his form suffered. A new boss in the shape of Joe Harvey arrived soon after, and Neale became one of many players off-loaded in a rebuilding plan. With Plymouth over seven seasons, Duncan took part in 166 matches operating also at full-back, centre-half and inside-forward, rarely failing to give 100% on the field. After football, he ran a building and property business in the South West, residing in Landulph, Cornwall. As a lad, Duncan had the chance to join Chelsea but he decided to concentrate on studies and college as a trainee accountant, while he was also unlucky not to be selected for the GB Olympic squad before turning professional. His father Harry was on Clapton Orient's books.

Appearances & Goals:
Debut v Fulham (h) 24 August 1960 (2 goals)
FL: 88 app 8 gls
FAC: 6 app 3 gls
FLC: 4 app 1 gl
Total: 98 app 12 gls

NEILSON Alan Bruce 1989-1995

Centre-half
5'11"
b. Wegburg (West Germany), 26 September 1972

Career: Watford & Aston Villa trial/UNITED trial, jnr Aug 1989, prof Feb 1991/ Southampton June 1995 £400,000/Fulham Nov 1997 £250,000/Grimsby Town Oct 2001/Luton Town Feb 2002 free to May 2005/Tamworth Dec 2005/Salisbury City Feb 2007/ Luton Town & Barnfield College cs 2007 part-time coach/ Luton Town asst-coach June 2008, becoming coach Jan 2009, then asst-boss to Feb 2013, being on three occasions caretaker-manager; Oct 2009, March to April 2012 & Feb 2013/ Cambridge Utd coach Dec 2013.

Born on a British military base in West Germany while his father served in the RAF as a warrant-officer, Alan also lived in Cyprus, Scotland and Lincolnshire before writing to United for a trial. His hopeful letter was answered positively and he went onto successfully earn a contract with the Magpies. A full-back or central defender, Neilson gained experience during season 1991-92 under Ossie Ardiles, but a medial ligament injury knocked his progress and then he had to be content as a squad player when Kevin Keegan started to bring expensive stars to Gallowgate. Eligible for Wales due to being born on a UK overseas complex (and therefore could choose any of the home nations), Alan was capped at Under-21 and full level while in the Magpies' reserve

line-up. Neilson rarely performed badly for United when called upon to deputise, but he had little option to move on in search of a regular place. Having decent periods with Fulham (39 app) and Luton (63 app), Neilson was part of five promotion squads, but on each occasion couldn't claim a permanent role in the side. Alan is a past captain of United's junior and second eleven, skippering the reserves to the Division Two championship in 1995, while he also led out the Welsh Under-21 side. With local roots, his father hailed from Bishop Auckland and his grandfather, Joseph Neilson from Fawdon, was a noted local player on Tyneside.

Appearances & Goals:
Debut v Watford (a) 9 March 1991 (sub)
FL/PL: 35(7) app 1 gl
FLC: 4 app 0 gls
Others: 4 app 0 gls
Total: 43(7) app 1 gl

Honours:
5 Wales caps 1992-97/2 Wales B app 1992-94/7 Wales u21 app 1993-94/FL div 1 champs 1993 (3 app), 2001 (3 app), 2005 (9 app)/FL div 2 champs 1999 (4 app)/FL div 3 prom 2002 (8 app).

NELSON James 1930-1935

Right-back
5'8"
b. Greenock, 7 January 1901
d. Barry, Glamorgan, 8 October 1965

Career: St Paul's (Belfast)/Glenarm (Belfast)/Crusaders 1919/Cardiff City Aug 1921/UNITED Aug 1930 £7,000/ Southend Utd June 1935 £250 to May 1939/Ekco Sports (Southend) 1939 to 1945/UNITED scout June 1948.

Jimmy Nelson started his career as a forward, moved to centre-half, and finally ended up as a reliable and inspirational right-back of distinction. Club captain when United lifted the FA Cup during 1932; Jimmy was recognised as one of the classiest full-backs of the inter-war era, capped by Scotland and a member of the renowned Wembley Wizards combination in 1928. Although born a Scot, Nelson was brought up in Northern Ireland and worked as a boiler-maker in the shipyards before moving to Wales and signing for Cardiff. At Ninian Park he was part of a fine City team that reached the FA Cup final twice, bringing the trophy back to Wales for the first time in 1927. Possessing rare powers of anticipation, Newcastle's boss Andy Cunningham regarded Nelson highly and brought him to Tyneside after 270 games for the Bluebirds and for what was a big fee of £7,000 in 1930. A regular during four campaigns, he was noted as being "ice-cool and never flustered" and a "sturdy, clean-kicking full-back". On the club's relegation in 1934 and now into his thirties, Jimmy moved south and continued to perform well with his final club, Southend in 81 games. He afterwards became a well known publican at The Spread Eagle near Roots Hall and later in Cardiff at The Greyhound. Residing in Penarth, his brother David was also on Cardiff's books while Jimmy's son Tony, appeared for Newport and Bournemouth as an amateur international, while son-in-law, Stan Montgomery, played for both Southend and Cardiff too. Nelson has the dubious distinction of being the first Cardiff City player sent-off in the Football League.

Appearances & Goals:
Debut v Sheffield Wednesday (a) 30 August 1930
FL: 146 app 0 gls
FAC: 13 app 0 gls
Others: 1 app 0 gls
Total: 160 app 0 gls

Honours:
4 Scot caps 1925-30/Scot trial app 1928/Irish Alliance app/FAC winner 1927, 1932/ FAC final 1925/WsC winner 1923, 1927, 1928, 1930.

NESBIT Anthony 1982-1987

Midfield
5'7"
b. Sunderland, 28 January 1968

Career: UNITED jnr May 1982, prof
Feb 1986 to Sept 1987 free/Seaham
Red Star/Brandon Utd/ Seaham
Rovers.

*A former schoolboy international
player, Tony Nesbit was introduced
into top class soccer by manager
Willie McFaul having tasted success
by winning the prestigious English
Schools Trophy in 1984 and after
coming through the ranks alongside
the likes of Paul Gascoigne as the
Magpies lifted the FA Youth Cup. The
slightly-built youngster reached the
substitutes' bench during season 1986-87 when the Magpies were struggling at the
bottom of the First Division table. Nesbit had good ball control, and was a workhorse
of a player, described as "tough tackling" and an "out and out competitor". But due
to his slight height and build, Tony was always going to find it tough in the midfield
battleground. He quickly faded from the scene and was released the following summer
when he started to play local football although was forced to quit the game due to
a knee injury. Nesbit later joined the Northumbria Police, stationed in the Wearside
district and residing in Cleadon.*

Appearances & Goals:
Debut v Charlton Athletic (a) 6 December 1986 (sub)
(v Everton (a) 3 December 1986 (sub) (FMC))
FL: 1(2) app 0 gls
Others: 0(1) app 0 gls
Total: 1(3) app 0 gls

Honours:
Eng sch-youth app/FAYC winner 1985.

NESBITT John 1955-1959

Centre-half
6'2"
b. Washington, 24 September 1933
d. Dusseldorf (West Germany), 4 October 1978

Career: Ashington/South Shields/
UNITED Dec 1955 £10 to cs 1959.

*John Nesbitt possessed the perfect physique and
temperament for the important role at the centre of the
defence. Big and tough, he joined United after being
released from the Coldstream Guards, but his three-
season career was almost totally restricted to Central
League football as an understudy to Bob Stokoe and Bill
Paterson. Appearing when both his rivals were in the treatment-room during season
1957-58, Nesbitt also once took over Ronnie Simpson's goalkeeper's jersey during a
close-season tour. With Simpson not available and no other 'keeper in the party, John
wore the Number 1 shirt for the entire fixture with Romanians, Petrolul Ploesti during
May 1958, a 3-2 defeat. On leaving football he was employed by German airline
Lufthansa and resided in Dusseldorf.*

Appearances & Goals:
Debut v Sheffield Wednesday (h) 25 September 1957
FL: 3 app 0 gls
Total: 3 app 0 gls

NEVIN George William 1925, 1928-1930

Left-back
5'11"
b. Lintz, Co Durham, 16 December 1907
d. Sheffield, 1973 (Q1)

Career: Lintz Colliery/Dipton Utd/UNITED Aug 1925/
Sunderland amat March 1926/White-le-Head
Rangers/UNITED trial Oct 1928, pmt Dec 1928 £100/
Sheffield Wed June 1930 free/Manchester Utd Dec
1933 £1,000/Sheffield Wed March 1934 £500/Burnley
May 1935/Lincoln City May 1937/Rochdale June
1939/Ouston Utd 1939-40.

*Cool under pressure and able to challenge strongly for the ball, George Nevin operated
in both full-back roles for United's second eleven. He stepped in for regular defender
Bob Thomson and was a thoroughly reliable reserve. A former miner in the Durham
coalfield, Nevin was robust and solid at over 12 stone, but found it no easy task to
claim a permanent position at any of his clubs. His total Football League career record
reached a modest 48 matches, and only once did he manage a long run in the first-
eleven, that with Burnley during season 1935-36 (21 app). His father Ralph played
the game to a good standard for Gateshead and Exeter, while three uncles also figured
prominently in football as well. His nephew, John Nevin turned out for Crewe and
Barrow and his son David was on Sheffield Wednesday's books at reserve level.*

Appearances & Goals:
Debut v West Ham United (a) 9 September 1929
FL: 6 app 0 gls
Total: 6 app 0 gls

NEVINS Laurence 1938-1947

Outside-left
5'7"
b. Gateshead, 2 July 1920
d. Gateshead, 1972 (Q2)

Career: UNITED amat Aug 1938, prof Sept 1940
(Middlesbrough war-guest 1940-45)(Dundee Utd
war-guest 1941-44)(Queens Park Rangers war-guest
1944-45)/Resumed with United cs 1945/Brighton
June 1947 free/Hartlepools Utd March 1948 to cs 1949.

*In between duty as a submariner during World War Two,
Laurie Nevins pulled on the black-and-white colours
during three wartime seasons from 1939-40. A regular in 1940-41 when he totalled
30 games, Nevins showed he could be an effective left winger, quick and with a telling
cross. But war ruined his career and on returning to St James' Park in 1945 somewhat
older, at 25 years of age, he found he had no fewer than eight other outside-lefts as
rivals. He was released and Nevins only briefly tasted Football League action with
Brighton (5 app) and Hartlepools United (19 app). On leaving the game he settled on
Tyneside.*

Appearances & Goals:
Debut v Bradford City (h) 8 June 1940 (FLNE)
War: 33 app 5 gls
Total: 33 app 5 gls

NIBLO Thomas Bruce 1898-1902, 1907-1908

Outside or Inside-forward
5'9"
b. Dunfermline, 24 September 1877
d. Walkergate, Newcastle upon Tyne, 30 June 1933

Career: Cadzow Oak 1893/Hamilton Acc 1894/
Linthouse Aug 1896/UNITED March 1898 £90
(Middlesbrough loan 1899-1900)/Aston Villa Jan
1902/Nottingham Forest May 1904/Watford May
1906/UNITED Aug 1907/Hebburn Argyle player-
manager Aug 1908/Aberdeen Dec 1908/ Raith Rovers
Aug 1909/Cardiff City Dec 1910 £10/Blyth Spartans
February 1911/Newcastle City July 1911/Fulham
Nov 1915/Isle of Wight football 1919.

A rare and stylish ball dribbler, Tom Niblo possessed a splendid, and occasionally brilliant, "dandy left foot". During two spells with United he displayed his versatility, especially on the right or left flanks, by appearing in all five forward positions. One contemporary report noted he was "a genuine worker, who is smart in seizing opportunities" and the Villa News & Record noted that he was "a capital forward full of 'go' from start to finish". As with many talented footballers, the Scot's only deficiency was his inconsistency, and the tendency to take on too many players instead of parting with the ball. Nevertheless he was good enough to be selected for his country in 1903-04 when with Aston Villa where he totalled 51 games. Stocky and powerful, Niblo's son Alan spent a time on United's books without breaking through, while his grandson, Alan junior, captained Wolverhampton Wanderers' reserve side. Wounded during World War One, on his retirement, Tom settled on Tyneside becoming a publican for a period. When making his way as a young footballer at St James' Park in 1901, he was described in census records as a boiler-maker.

Appearances & Goals:
Debut v Loughborough (a) 11 April 1898
FL: 60 app 4 gls
Total: 60 app 4 gls

Honours:
Scot cap 1904/Scot trial app 1903-04/FL div 2 prom 1898 (1 app).

NICHOLSON Benjamin 1905-1907

Left-back
5'11"
b. Ashington, 1884
Career: Annfield Plain June 1904/White-le-Head Swifts Feb 1905/Morpeth Harriers Aug 1905/UNITED Oct 1905/Luton Town June 1907/West Stanley Aug 1908/Annfield Plain July 1910/White-le-Head Rangers Nov 1911/Dipton Utd Dec 1914.

Local lad Ben Nicholson joined the club's staff as a reserve half-back who could also stand-in at full-back. A consistent player for the second-eleven, Ben's stay on the Gallowgate staff was confined to Northern League and North Eastern League football apart from one outing in the senior team as a deputy to Jack Carr. That occurred in season 1906-07 against Manchester City, a 1-1 draw during the year Newcastle lifted their second title trophy. Following a short period with Luton, where he couldn't claim a place either, Nicholson returned to the region and continued in non-league football.

Appearances & Goals:
Debut v Manchester City (a) 16 February 1907
FL: 1 app 0 gls
Total: 1 app 0 gls

Honours:
FL champs 1907 (1 app).

NICHOLSON Gary Anthony 1976-1981

Outside-left
5'8"
b. Hexham, 4 November 1960
Career: UNITED jnr Sept 1976, prof Nov 1978/ Mansfield Town Aug 1981 £25,000/York City July 1984 £10,000/Halifax Town July 1985/Blyth Spartans cs 1987/Whitley Bay June 1988/North Shields 1989/ Guiseley/Gateshead Dec 1993/RTM Newcastle March 1994/Later with local Tyneside clubs including Lemington Labour Club 2001.

Lightly framed, fair-haired, Gary Nicholson graduated from United's junior set-up where he had proved himself as a prolific goalscorer from the wing. Although second choice to the experienced John Connolly, many at St James' Park expected the young Tynesider to develop quickly and become a noted player. However, following a handful of Second Division outings spread over three seasons, Nicholson never made the big leap from being a potential star on the sidelines. He moved to the Field Mill stadium and proceeded to total 132 games for Mansfield and then 68 for Halifax. Later in his career Gary became a respected player in local North Eastern soccer. He also worked for a period for the Fenwick's department store in Newcastle.

Appearances & Goals:
Debut v Cambridge United (h) 22 November 1978
FL: 7(5) app 0 gls
FAC: 1 app 0 gls
FLC: 3 app 0 gls
Total: 11(5) app 0 gls

NICHOLSON William Edward OBE 1943-1944

Right-half
5'9"
b. Scarborough, 26 January 1919
d. Potters Bar, London, 23 October 2004
Career: Scarborough Young Liberals/Scarborough Working Men's Club/Tottenham Hotspur amat March 1936 (Northfleet Utd loan 1937-38) Tottenham Hotspur prof Aug 1938 (Hartlepools Utd war-guest 1939-40)(Manchester Utd war-guest 1939-40)(UNITED war-guest 1942-44) (Sunderland war-guest 1942-43)(Middlesbrough war-guest 1942-43)(Fulham war-guest 1942-43) (Darlington war-guest 1944-45)(Crook Town war-guest)/Resumed with Tottenham 1946, retired playing 1954, assisting Eng u23 team/Tottenham Hotspur trainer Dec 1955, becoming asst-manager Aug 1957, manager Oct 1958 to Sept 1974/West Ham Utd scout & managerial consultant Oct 1974/Tottenham Hotspur managerial consultant July 1976, becoming President July 1991/Also was Cambridge University & Pegasus coach during early 1950s.

One of post-war footballs most eminent figures, Bill Nicholson travelled around the North East when serving in the Durham Light Infantry as a training instructor during wartime soccer and guested for all the region's clubs. A biting tackler, initially as a full-back, but later more often at wing-half, Bill pulled on United's black-and-white colours over two seasons. On peacetime he quickly established himself in the fine Spurs' line-up that won the Second Division championship in 1950. He then went onto lift the title at White Hart Lane, and earn an England cap (scoring with his first touch after 19 seconds of his only appearance against Portugal) together with 'B' and Football League honours. Once his solid playing career as a rugged half-back was concluded after 356 games for Spurs (including wartime), Nicholson moved into management in North London, leading Tottenham to a succession of trophies, a record unrivalled by few, and in an entertaining style to please all. He served Tottenham for over 50 years and was in charge for 823 matches and as a truly remarkable servant to the North London club took part in winning 10 major trophies as either a player or manager, including what was in 1961, a rare Football League title and FA Cup double. A legend at White Hart Lane, the roadway leading to the stadium is named 'Bill Nicholson Way'. For his services to the game Bill was awarded the OBE.

Appearances & Goals:
Debut v Middlesbrough (h) 10 April 1943 (FLN)
War: 19 app 0 gls
Total: 19 app 0 gls

Honours:
1 Eng cap 1951/WdC 1950 (no app)/4 Eng B app 1948-50/1 FL app 1950/FA app 1948/FL champs 1951, 1961(m)/FL div 2 champs 1950/FAC winner 1961(m), 1962(m), 1967(m)/FLC winner 1971(m), 1973(m)/ECWC winner 1963(m)/UEFAC winner 1972(m)/UEFAC final 1974(m)/Eng HoF/Freedom of Haringey Council 1998/OBE 1975.

NOBLE Peter 1964-1968

Striker
5'8"
b. Sunderland, 19 August 1944
Career: Consett/UNITED Nov 1964 £1,000/ Swindon Town Jan 1968 £8,000/Burnley June 1973 £40,000/Blackpool Jan 1980 £25,000 to May 1983.

A painter and decorator from Consett, Peter Noble joined United as a part-timer to begin with and at St James' Park operated mainly as a striker, although he also claimed an odd game in midfield, a position in which he later earned a solid reputation. Suffering from medial and lateral knee

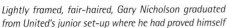

N

ligament injuries during his early years on Tyneside, being on the sidelines for several months, he was advised to quit the game by boss Joe Harvey. But Noble would have none of that and he battled back to fitness and although his knee was never quite the same he went onto enjoy a long career of almost 700 games. As the Magpies battled to steer away from the relegation zone during seasons 1965-66 and 1966-67, Noble was drafted in to replace Ron McGarry in a search for goals. And the Wearsider gave the club good short term service by netting seven valuable strikes and helped to retain United's First Division place. The arrival though, of Albert Bennett and Wyn Davies, as well as the emergence of Bryan Robson, meant Peter was transferred south. With Swindon he reached Wembley during 1969, a famous giant-killing run by the Robins which ended in a major upset when Arsenal were felled. Following 256 games (80 goals) for Swindon, Noble then served Burnley with distinction as a hardworking and versatile midfield player able to play up front or in defence. He played over 300 matches for the Turf Moor club, a regular for seven seasons. And he always grabbed goals, 17 for Burnley in season 1975-76 and 80 for the Turf Moor club all told, including many from the penalty spot. Dangerous in the air for his small build and able to get into the right spot in the box, he once netted four goals in a single fixture against Norwich. Peter played on until he was nearly 39 years of age and on hanging up his boots, he ran a sportswear business in Burnley, Peter Noble Sport Ltd, for nearly 20 years.

Appearances & Goals:
Debut v Chelsea (a) 25 September 1965
FL: 22(3) app 7 gls
Total: 22(3) app 7 gls

Honours:
FLC winner 1969/FL div 3 prom 1969.

NOLAN Kevin Anthony Jance 2009-2011

Midfield
6'0"
b. Liverpool, 24 June 1982

Career: Bolton Wand jnr 1997, prof Jan 2000/ UNITED Jan 2009 £4m/West Ham United July 2011 £4m.

For many of his nine seasons as a Bolton player, Kevin Nolan was a leading character in a line-up which consistently surprised football pundits. Under the guidance of Sam Allardyce, the Merseysider frequently impressed in Bolton's white shirt, often a match-winner in his 345 games with runs into the box from midfield. Tall and powerfully built, the 26-year-old Nolan moved to St James' Park for a £4m fee in the January 2009 transfer window and was soon an influence on the Magpies too. Although part of the side which suffered relegation in 2009, he was an inspiration during the promotion success a year later, in the process lifting the Championship trophy. From his central midfield role Kevin was also a potent goal threat, having scored 50 goals for Bolton, he continued scoring with the Magpies, grabbing 17 league strikes in that title winning campaign. Although appearing to lack pace and sometimes energy, Nolan had the know-how to ghost into dangerous positions in and around the box at the right time to support the attack, while he on occasion operated as a second striker with much cunning and guile. He was appointed skipper for United's return to the Premier League and entered United folklore by converting a hat-trick as he led the Magpies to a 5-1 victory over Sunderland in October 2010. Sometimes outspoken, the Merseysider teamed up once more with Allardyce at West Ham United, sold by United when 29 years old as the club refashioned their squad for the start of a new era during the summer of 2011. He performed admirably for the Hammers, again guiding his club to promotion and then continuing to hit goals at the highest level, and in the process showing the Magpies he perhaps should have been retained as a valuable squad member.

Appearances & Goals:
Debut v Sunderland (h) 1 February 2009
FL/PL: 84(1) app 29 gls
FAC: 3 app 0 gls
FLC: 1(2) app 1 gl
Total: 88(3) app 30 gls

Honours:
1 Eng u21 app 2003/Eng sch-youth app/FL ch winner 2010/FL ch prom 2012/FL div 1 prom 2001/FLC final 2004/PFA ToS (ch) 2010.

NULTY Geoffrey Owen 1974-1978

Midfield or Centre-half
5'10"
b. Prescot, Lancashire, 13 February 1949

Career: Stoke City July 1967/Burnley July 1968 free/UNITED Dec 1974 £120,000/Everton July 1978 £45,000/ Retired March 1980 due to injury, becoming Everton asst-manager/ Preston North End asst-manager Dec 1981 to Dec 1983.

Although never described as one of United's headlining stars, Geoff Nulty was a dedicated professional, steady and solid, who fitted into Newcastle's line-up in a manner which held the respect of all his team-mates. Joining the Magpies following 153 senior matches for Burnley where he was influential as the Lancashire club went from the Second Division to the upper levels of the First Division and within a whisker of the FA Cup final; defeated by United in 1974, Nulty hitting the woodwork in that semi-final meeting. He was a utility man at both Turf Moor and St James' Park, having begun his career as a full-back. Then he switched up front before settling in midfield, having a marker or destroyers' role. At Gallowgate Geoff also moved into the centre of the defence where he won the admiration of supporters too. Centre-half was perhaps Nulty's best position and under the leadership of Gordon Lee, and later Richard Dinnis, Geoff became an important figure. He was captain of the side that reached Wembley and then Europe, although he unfortunately missed the League Cup final appointment because of a broken jaw. Soon afterwards the turmoil in which the club found itself as the 1977-78 season began was instrumental in Nulty's move to his native Merseyside to rejoin his former boss Gordon Lee at Goodison Park. The bond between player and manager was strong and, on Nulty's retirement, he was appointed Lee's assistant at both Everton and Preston. Forced to quit the game following only 38 matches for the Toffees due to a bad knee injury sustained in a derby clash with Liverpool, at one stage he considered legal action against Jimmy Case who had inflicted what was a horror tackle. Holder of an Open University degree, Nulty afterwards dealt in property development in the North West, running an entrepreneurial business engaged in renting and refurbishing commercial and residential units, as well as being a sub-postmaster for 15 years.

Appearances & Goals:
Debut v Carlisle United (a) 26 December 1974
FL: 101 app 11 gls
FAC: 10 app 1 gl
FLC: 10 app 2 gls
Euro: 2 app 0 gls
Others: 4 app 0 gls
Total: 127 app 14 gls

Honours:
FL div 2 champs 1973.

N'ZOGBIA Charles Jacob 2004-2009

Midfield or Outside-left
5'9"
b. Harfleur (France), 28 May 1986

Career: Le Havre AC 1997/UNITED trial July 2004, pmt Sept 2004 £200,000/Wigan Ath Feb 2009 £6m/ Aston Villa July 2011 £9.5m.

United's scouting network on the Continent highlighted the emerging talent of Charles N'Zogbia when an 18-year-old with French Second Division club Le Havre during 2004. With several other clubs alerted, the Magpies acted quickly to secure his signature in a move to Tyneside, although the transfer was embroiled in controversy and animosity between the two clubs. Le Havre complained bitterly and resulted in a long drawn out dispute which was only settled by the Court for Arbitration in Sport some time later during July 2007. By then N'Zogbia was very much a Newcastle United player, a teenager to be groomed into a Premier League star. At either outside-left or in midfield, Charles was highly thought of by manager Bobby Robson and fast-tracked to the senior line-up. Swift, direct and with ability to both go past opponents and have a crack at goal, the Frenchman made his debut for United in 2004-05 and became a regular for contention as 2005 opened, an eventual replacement for Laurent Robert. N'Zogbia scored six goals in his break-through campaign of 2005-06 and looked to be a major find. At times fiery, N'Zogbia became frustrated and somewhat impulsive as he learned his way, especially when out of the side for periods which caused friction. His talent was unquestioned, tipped to add to his Under-21 caps for France, and he enjoyed more good seasons for the Black'n'Whites in 2006-07 and 2007-08. With Robson departing, subsequent new managers Souness and Roeder however struggled to get the best out of Charles and he fell out with Joe Kinnear, a famous row over the pronunciation of his surname which saw him move on. The Frenchman claimed he wanted a bigger club then moved to Wigan Athletic for £6m. Yet N'Zogbia developed further with the Latics (90 app) and went onto pull on his country's shirt in a full international and joined Aston Villa during 2011. But he was still to show consistency in attack, although always capable of a match-winning run and strike at goal. His career was disrupted by a long-term Achilles injury in 2013 and 2014. Charles has one of the shortest ever debuts as a United player; on the field as a substitute for all of 20 seconds without touching the ball against Blackburn during September 2004 before the full-time whistle was blown. His cousin is tennis player Jo-Wilfred Tsonga.

Appearances & Goals:
Debut v Blackburn Rovers (h) 11 September 2004 (sub)
PL: 86(32) app 9 gls
FAC: 8(2) app 0 gls
FLC: 7(1) app 1 gl
Euro: 13(5) app 1 gl
Total: 114(40) app 11 gls

Honours:
2 Fr caps 2011-date/13 Fr u21 app 2008-10/Fr sch-youth app.

OATES Graham 1976-1978

Midfield
6'2"
b. Bradford, 14 March 1949

Career: Tong Street (Bradford)/Manningham Mills/Bradford City jnr Nov 1969, prof Feb 1970/Blackburn Rovers June 1974 exch deal/UNITED March 1976 joint deal with R Jones/Detroit Express (USA) March 1978 £40,000/California Surf (USA) 1981/Bradford City Jan 1982 briefly/Lidget Green/ Dudley Hill Ath player-manager/Scarborough 1987/Gainsborough Trinity manager 1988/Later appearing for local Bradford clubs.

Graham Oates was purchased by his mentor Gordon Lee towards the end of the 1975-76 season as a player who could fill either a defender or midfield role. His United career began with a much publicised own-goal, within four minutes on his first full home outing against Leeds, Oates sending a 25-yard back-pass into the net. Tall and well-built, Graham had an uphill struggle at Gallowgate after that; he was never taken to heart by Geordie supporters, either when operating in defence, or in the centre of the field where he was drafted in to add some height and grit. Rarely using his physique to his advantage in midfield, he was cool and composed, but was ultimately a target of sections of the crowd who appreciated neither his role nor his effect on the side. Oates though, had a good record at Bradford City (175 app 21 gls) and Blackburn (91 app 11 gls), winning a Third Division title medal at Ewood Park. During his period in the States he also coached the Bloomfield Hills Andover school team during 1978 and 1979. He later operated a joinery business in his native West Yorkshire and continued playing for local sides when past 50 years of age.

Appearances & Goals:
Debut v Manchester United (h) 20 March 1976 (sub)
FL: 26(10) app 3 gls
FLC: 3 app 0 gls
Others: 4 app 0 gls
Total: 33(10) app 3 gls

Honours:
FL div 3 champs 1975.

OBERTAN Gabriel Antoine 2011-date

Outside-right
6'1"
b. Pantin, Paris (France), 26 February 1989

Career: CMS Pantin 1997/Paris FC 2002/Paris St-Germain 2003/INF Clairefontaine 2004/Bordeaux jnr 2005, prof 2006 (FC Lorient loan 2008-09)/Manchester Utd July 2009 £3m/UNITED Aug 2011 £3m.

On the fringe of Manchester United's senior line-up for most of his first two years in English football, Gabriel Obertan made the move to join the Magpies in a bid to play regular Premier League action. Costing United £3m at the start of the 2011-12 season, the fast raiding outside-right, began his career with local junior clubs around Paris before being inducted into the French way of football at the Clairefontaine academy. The Frenchman had scouts watching him in Bordeaux colours as he performed with much result in 79 games, a regular in Les Girondins when a teenager. Gabriel was purchased by Sir Alex Ferguson as a promising 20-year-old forward, one for the future, but he rarely got a look in at Old Trafford due to the array of talent at the club. He appeared on 28 occasions (13 starts) for the Reds, including Champions League action before making the switch to Tyneside. Obertan though found he couldn't hold down a regular position at St James' Park either, displaying a lack of penetration and consistency down the right touchline. He was often on the fringe of action and rarely showed his true worth in black-and-white stripes, finding it difficult to impress the watching supporters who often became frustrated by his play.

Appearances & Goals:
Debut v Arsenal (h) 13 August 2011 (sub)
PL: 22(18) app 1 gl
FAC: 2(1) app 0 gls
FLC: 1(3) app 0 gls
Euro: 8 app 1 gl
Total: 33(22) app 2 gls

Honours:
11 Fr u21 app 2009-11/Fr sch-youth app/PL champs 2011 (7 app)/Fr Lg champs 2009.

O'BRIEN Alan 2001-2007

Outside-left
5'10"
b. Sallynoggin, Dublin, 20 February 1985

Career: UNITED jnr July 2001, prof April 2002 (Carlisle Utd loan 2005-06)/Hibernian July 2007 £200,000/Swindon Town July 2009 free/Yeovil Town Aug 2011 free/St Mirren trial Jan 2012/Gateshead Feb 2012/Hungerford Town Aug 2012/Bedlington Terriers Oct 2012.

Raised in the Killiney district of Dublin with Tyneside connections, winger Alan O'Brien was what could be termed in old-style football terms as a 'speed-merchant'. Extremely fast on the left touchline, O'Brien developed through the club's junior and reserve structure and showed he had a cutting edge to cause havoc to defences. Newcastle gave the 20-year-old flying winger an opportunity in senior action from the bench during season 2005-06 at the time of managerial change. At the top level of football pace can make the difference, but coupled with that attribute is needed vision and awareness, as well as consistency. Blond-haired, O'Brien arguably lacked those added requirements, notably racing away head down rather than looking up. Although fleetingly used in the following season, he picked up injuries (including a broken leg) and drifted from contention at St James' Park to a lower level of football; firstly to Hibs (53 app) in Scotland then to Swindon Town (40 app), in tier-three of Football League action. Alan appeared for the Republic of Ireland when still in United's reserve side while he played a small part in Carlisle winning silverware during 2006.

Appearances & Goals:
Debut v Mansfield Town (h) 7 January 2006 (sub) (FAC)
PL: 1(4) app 0 gls
FAC: 0(3) app 0 gls
Euro: 0(1) app 0 gls
Total: 1(8) app 0 gls

Honours:
5 Eire caps 2007/1 Eire B app 2007/Eire u21 app/Eire sch-youth app/FL div 2 champs 2006 (5 app).

O

O'BRIEN Andrew James 2001-2005

Centre-half
6'2"
b. Harrogate, 29 June 1979

Career: Leeds Utd jnr/Bradford City jnr 1994, prof Oct 1996/UNITED March 2001 £2m/ Portsmouth July 2005 £2m/Bolton Wand Aug 2007 £2m/Leeds Utd loan Oct 2010, pmt Jan 2011 free to June 2012/Vancouver Whitecaps (Can) Aug 2012 free.

Andy O'Brien became a consistent performer at centre-back with Bradford City over a period of 150 games in the second-tier, then Premier League, in five seasons of action. His form prompted Bobby Robson to add the Yorkshire-born defender to his options towards the end of the 2000-01 season in a £2m transfer. At 21 years old, O'Brien had a fabulous start to his Newcastle career, making his debut against his former club, then in his fourth outing netting a winner against Sunderland on Wearside during April 2001 to write himself into a popular terrace musical ditty. Although not powerful looking, O'Brien was quick and mobile at centre-half and as the new season began was a regular choice as Newcastle searched for a solid rearguard and central partnership. Andy teamed up with Titus Bramble or Nikos Dabizas as United competed well at the top of the Premier League and in European action. While United's back line was never totally assured, O'Brien held his own with whole-hearted displays, always with a professional attitude. He was a regular over four seasons and totalled more than 150 games for the Magpies before falling out of favour when new boss Graeme Souness arrived. He wanted a more commanding centre-half and Andy moved on, heading for Portsmouth. When at Elland Road Andy had a difficult period and suffered from depression before moving to Canada for a fresh start. With parents from near Limerick, he was capped by the Republic of Ireland, although very much a Yorkshireman, Andy was part of the squad which took part in the 2002 World Cup in Japan & Korea. He once scored an own-goal for United in a FA Cup match against Peterborough during 2002, then scored again in the same match, this time at the correct end of the field.

Appearances & Goals:
Debut v Bradford City (a) 31 March 2001
PL: 114(6) app 6 gls
FAC: 7(3) app 1 gl
FLC: 4(1) app 0 gls
Euro: 32(5) app 0 gls
Total: 157(15) app 7 gls

Honours:
26 Eire caps 2001-07/WdC 2002 (no app)/1 unoff Eire app 2005/8 Eire u21 app/1 FL u21 app 1999/FL div 1 prom 1999.

O'BRIEN Patrick George 1894-1895

Right-back
5'11"
b. Edinburgh, 1873

Career: Broxburn Shamrock/Hibernian 1891-92/Middlesbrough Ironopolis 1892-93/ Sheffield Utd June 1894/UNITED Dec 1894/Edinburgh St Bernard's June 1895/ Hebburn Argyle May 1896 to 1898.

From early reports, Pat O'Brien appears as one of the pluckiest players ever to set foot on the Leazes pitch. The Scot made a good early impression at St James' Park during the club's second programme of Football League action in 1894-95. An energetic mover described as a "dashing player", Pat gloried in the sometimes mass charges at goal during those pioneer days of the game, but faded after playing in different roles up front and at full-back. With Hebburn Argyle, O'Brien helped lift the Northern Alliance championship during 1896-97 with a string of vital goals. He remained on Tyneside afterwards and by 1905 was laid low with illness and in "destitute circumstances". It is recorded in the club's Minutes of Meetings that Newcastle United helped him out by giving him five guineas.

Appearances & Goals:
Debut v Walsall Town Swifts (h) 22 December 1894
FL: 10 app 2 gls
FAC: 2 app 0 gls
Total: 12 app 2 gls

O'BRIEN William Francis 1988-1994

Midfield
6'1"
b. Dublin, 5 September 1964

Career: Cambridge Boys (Dublin) 1978/Stella Maris 1979/Bohemians (Dublin) amat 1981/Shamrock Rovers Sept 1983/Manchester Utd Oct 1986 £90,000/UNITED Nov 1988 £300,000/ Tranmere Rovers Jan 1994 £350,000/ Cork City player-coach cs 1999/ Bohemians (Dublin) player-coach Oct 2000, becoming asst-player-manager June 2001, retired playing Jan 2002, to Dec 2003/Shamrock Rovers asst-manager Jan 2004/Cork City coach 2006/Bohemians (Dublin) coach Feb 2008/Hibernian asst-manager Nov 2011 to June 2012/Eire Under-21 coach 2013 briefly/PFA Ireland coach 2013.

Known commonly as Liam, injury twice halted O'Brien's bright progress in United's line-up over the six seasons he was on Tyneside. Although tall and powerfully framed, Liam O'Brien wasn't a physical player, but more a talented pass-master with a languid style and perhaps, had he used his vast frame to more effect, would have reached the very top. Operating best in an anchor role for the Black'n'Whites, when in the mood the Irishman could dominate a game and spray passes all over the field. He also packed a stinging shot which occasionally found the net with a spectacular goal. It was caretaker boss Colin Suggett who brought the Irishman to Tyneside after he had failed to claim a regular spot at Old Trafford in 37 games during Alex Ferguson's early years in charge. O'Brien was also in and out of Newcastle's line-up until Ossie Ardiles and Kevin Keegan arrived, while he was also absent due to a broken leg (sustained playing international football) and knee ligament trouble. On an injury to Paul Bracewell, Liam stepped in to become a driving force behind the club's Division One victory in 1993, being forever remembered for his match-winning free-kick at Roker Park against Sunderland in 1992, his second strike for United on Wearside. The Irishman could always produce something special and enjoyed a lengthy run in the side until another injury put him on the sidelines and Bracewell returned. Newcastle's elevation to the Premier League, together with an influx of stars, meant Liam moved to Tranmere where he made 214 appearances. During the early part of his career, O'Brien worked as a fitter and welder, and experienced European Cup football with Shamrock. His grandfather appeared for Shamrock too and brother Mick had a spell on Luton's books while his son Conor played for Bohemians. During 1987 Liam was sent-off within 85 seconds of a First Division clash for Manchester United against Southampton, one of the quickest dismissals on record, while in 1994 he missed a penalty in a League Cup semi-final shoot-out that would have earned Tranmere a place at Wembley.

Appearances & Goals:
Debut v Millwall (a) 19 November 1988
FL/PL: 131(22) app 19 gls
FAC: 12(2) app 1 gl
FLC: 9 app 1 gl
Others: 9 app 1 gl
Total: 161(24) app 22 gls

Honours:
16 Eire caps 1986-97/1 Eire u23 app 1989/2 EL app 1986/Eire sch-youth app/FL div 1 champs 1993/EL champs 1984, 1985, 1986/Eire Cup winner 1985, 1986/Eire YPoY 1986.

O'NEIL Leslie Arthur 1961-1965

Inside-left
5'7"
b. Hartford, near Blyth, 4 December 1943

Career: New Hartley Jnrs/Blyth Spartans cs 1961/ UNITED amat Oct 1961, prof Nov 1961 £200/ Darlington Jan 1965 free/Bradford City March 1970 £8,000/Carlisle Utd May 1972 £6,000 to May 1976/ Queen of the South Aug 1977/Penrith manager/ Carlisle Utd, becoming asst-coach/Workington manager Oct 1989 to July 1991/Swindon Town coach 1991, becoming chief-scout to Sept 1998/Wycombe Wand chief-scout/Various scouting appointments before appointed Blackpool chief-scout.

A young pit worker in the Northumberland coalfield, Les O'Neil was given very little amplitude during his days at St James' Park. A teenager who started on the left wing, he was fast with a jinking manner, shining in the Magpies' FA Youth Cup victory during 1962. But while some of his colleagues in that successful line up graduated to a regular position in United's side, Moncur and Craig included, O'Neil picked up an injury and was discarded. His single appearance was against Pompey as a 19-year-old at inside-forward during season 1963-64, a tough debut as United fell by 5-2 and Les finished the game with double-vision after a clash of heads. Unluckily Les was then injured in a reserve match, tearing ankle ligaments. Being out of action for 11 months, his opportunity in United's first-eleven disappeared as Joe Harvey considered his fitness level was not good enough for the top level. Moving into the lower divisions, Les battled his way back. He eventually developed into a bustling and busy midfielder always probing, an important player at Bradford City (103 app) and to both Darlington (202 app) and Carlisle in promotion years. He was an influential figure for the Cumbrians in 184 games as they reached the First Division. Les ended his career with almost 500 senior outings to his name and later resided in Carlisle then Lytham St Anne's. For a decade he ran a milk round in Carlisle before becoming a respected scout in the game.

Appearances & Goals:
Debut v Portsmouth (a) 19 October 1963
FL: 1 app 0 gls
Total: 1 app 0 gls

Honours:
FL div 2 prom 1974/FL div 4 prom 1966/FAYC winner 1962.

O'NEIL Thomas Henry 1942-1948

Right-back
5'9"
b. Spennymoor, 5 January 1925
d. Newport, April 1978

Career: Spennymoor Utd 1942/UNITED amat Aug 1942, prof Sept 1942 (Leeds Utd war-guest 1943-44)/Resumed with United cs 1945/ Newport Co April 1948 £150/Spennymoor Utd July 1949.

A young rival to Joe Richardson during his early seasons at Gallowgate, Tom O'Neil managed only one wartime game in United's senior eleven, against Huddersfield Town during September 1942, a four-goal defeat. Failing to earn a contract at Gallowgate after the Second World War, he moved to Wales for a small fee of £150 in attempt to catch Football League action with Newport in Division Three South, yet O'Neil was unfortunate to break his leg which restricted his first-class record to nine matches. He later resided in the South Wales town to his death.

Appearances & Goals:
Debut v Huddersfield Town (h) 19 September 1942 (FLN)
War: 1 app 0 gls
Total: 1 app 0 gls

O'NEILL Michael Andrew Martin 1987-1989

Midfield or Striker
5'11"
b. Portadown, 5 July 1969

Career: Chimney Corner/Coleraine cs 1984/UNITED Oct 1987 £100,000/Dundee Utd Aug 1989 £350,000/ Everton trial July 1992/Middlesbrough trial July 1992/Hibernian Aug 1993 £250,000/Coventry City July 1996 £300,000 (Aberdeen loan 1997-98)(Reading loan 1997-98)/Wigan Ath Sept 1998 £100,000/St Johnstone Aug 2000/Portland Timbers (USA) April 2001/Clydebank Nov 2001/Boston Bulldogs (USA) May 2002/Glentoran July 2002/Ayr Utd July 2004, retired playing 2005/Cowdenbeath asst-manager Aug 2005/Brechin City manager April 2006/Shamrock Rovers manager Dec 2008/Northern Ireland manager Dec 2011.

Michael O'Neill made the journey from Ulster to Tyneside as an 18-year-old whizz-kid, destined by some of the misguided media to become the 'new George Best'. When he joined United, the transfer created a new record fee from a Northern Ireland club. O'Neill was very much a raw talent, indeed he was still studying for his GCE 'A' levels, but quickly he made a big impact on the First Division scene, soon elevated from the

reserve ranks after netting a hat-trick for the second-string. Joining the forward-line alongside Paul Gascoigne and Paul Goddard, O'Neill's intricate style and ball skills knitted with those of Gazza and the press claims of a 'new George Best' appeared to be a real possibility. He was United's Player of the Season in 1987-88 netting 13 goals in 22 full games. But then the Irishman was struck by illness and injury, losing form dramatically as United slid down the table to suffer relegation. After being in and out of the side over the following campaign he was transferred to Scotland, seemingly a discovery lost. O'Neill did resurrect his career north of the border, especially when he moved to Easter Road and later with Wigan where he rediscovered much of the talent which had delighted the Tyneside crowd for a season. His playing career returned respectable totals of 391 club matches and 65 goals. Before becoming a noted young manager, O'Neill, who studied for an Open University mathematics degree, started a career with a mortgage comparison business. Michael then built a good side at Shamrock to headline with a Europa League run during 2011-12, earning the chance of managing his country's national side.

Appearances & Goals:
Debut v Luton Town (a) 7 November 1987 (sub)
FL: 36(12) app 15 gls
FAC: 3(2) app 1 gl
FLC: 2 app 0 gls
Others: 2(1) app 1 gl
Total: 43(15) app 17 gls

Honours:
31 NI caps 1988-97/2 NI B app 1994-99/1 NI u23 app 1989/1 NI u21 app 1994/NI sch-youth app/SLC final 1994/EL champs 2010(m), 2011(m)/NIL champs 2003/NI LC winner 2003/FLT winner 1999.

ONYEWU Oguchialu Chijioke 2007

Centre-half
6'4"
b. Clemson, Washington DC (USA), 13 May 1982

Career: Sherwood (USA)/Clemson University Tigers (USA) 2000/FC Potomac (USA)/FC Metz (Fr) March 2002 (RAA Louvieroise (Belg) loan 2003)/Standard Liege (Belg) loan Jan 2004, pmt July 2004 (UNITED loan Jan to July 2007)/AC Milan (It) July 2009 free (FC Twente (Neth) loan 2010-11)/Sporting Clube (Ptg) June 2011 free/Malaga CF (Sp) Aug 2012/ Queens Park Rangers Oct 2013 free/Sheffield Wed Jan 2014 free to May 2014.

Manager Glenn Roeder found himself with a defensive gap as the 2006-07 season began. Injury to both Moore and Ramage saw United's manager look for a loan deal. During the January transfer window in came the strapping 6'4" tall USA international centre-back Oguchialu Onyewu, nicknamed 'Guchi'. Raised in the Silver Spring and Olney suburbs near the capital Washington DC, the powerful defender moved from States college football to Europe during 2002 when 19 years of age. Onyewu made an impact with Standard Liege, winning the Belgian title in both 2008 and 2009. However, in United's colours he found that Premier League football is a step up from Pro League in Belgium and while Guchi did have good attributes, notably in the air, he was caught out by top-class strikers in the best league in world football. With a Nigerian background, the American moved back to Belgium and carried on his career around Europe. He gained another opportunity at making a career in one of games toughest competitions, in Serie A, when he joined AC Milan during 2009. Yet he hardly played for the Rossoneri over the coming months in Lombardy due to a serious ruptured knee tendon injury. Onyewu became a regular for Team America taking part in two World Cups, a cornerstone to their defence.

Appearances & Goals:
Debut v Fulham (a) 3 February 2007
PL: 7(4) app 0 gls
Total: 7(4) app 0 gls

Honours:
69 USA caps 2005-date/WdC 2006, 2010/USA sch-youth app/Belg Lg champs 2008, 2009/Belg Cup winner 2011.

O

ORR (Gunion) Ronald Guiness 1901-1908

Inside-right or left
5'5"
b. Bartonholm, Ayrshire, 6 August 1876
d. Bartonholm, Ayrshire, 21 March 1924

Career: Kilwinning Eglinton 1896/St Mirren July 1898/
UNITED May 1901 joint deal with R Bennie/Liverpool
April 1908 £350/Raith Rovers Jan 1912/South Shields
March 1913 (Fulham war-guest 1916-19).

*Small in stature, but, at eleven-and-a-half stone, not
a lightweight, chunky forward Ronald Orr appeared
equally well in both inside roles. Having played with
clever, constructive play in St Mirren's line-up, top
scorer at Love Street, he moved over the border at the
end of the 1900-01 season. Possessing a power drive, he became a regular in United's
side at the turn of the century and grabbed plenty of goals for the Magpies, on one
occasion scoring four times during 1901 against Notts County. Appearing in two title
campaigns, Orr was an important link-man; a player not to take many headlines, but
who dovetailed nicely with the finer skills of McWilliam and Rutherford in midfield,
and fed off Bill Appleyard to perfection when up front. Surprisingly perhaps, the Scot
was excellent in the air too; able to leap for high balls despite his 5'5" height, yet Orr
always had trouble in gaining the affection of United's fans. For several seasons he
was the unfortunate individual they picked on if performances dipped, and Ronald
moved to Anfield as a direct result of crowd barracking. He soon made United suffer,
a regular scorer against the Magpies. Orr again performed well for Liverpool over three
seasons, claiming 38 goals in 112 games. Raised in the villages of Bartonholm and
Kilwinning, after retirement from the game, he returned to Ayrshire.*

*(Note: The Sportsman's Yearbook of 1905 claimed he was also with Glossop before
moving to Tyneside, however, this contemporary report is confused with another Scot,
William Orr, in action during the same period. Research into Orr's birth and death
reveals he was born as Ronald Guiness Gunion, with his middle name being that of
his mother's family of McGuiness. He later changed his surname to Orr, to be the
same as his father, as confirmed by his death certificate; Ronald Orr Gunion.)*

Appearances & Goals:
Debut v Blackburn Rovers (a) 7 September 1901
FL: 160 app 61 gls
FAC: 20 app 9 gls
Total: 180 app 70 gls

Honours:
2 Scot caps 1902-04/Scot trial app 1902-06/FL champs 1905, 1907/FAC final 1906.

OSBORNE Frederick 1940

Inside-forward
6'0"
b. Rotherham, 29 August 1915
d. Lincolnshire, 2004 (Q2)

Career: Thurnscoe Victoria 1934/Aston Villa April 1937
(UNITED war-guest 1940-41)(Middlesbrough
war-guest 1942-43)/Coventry City Dec 1946/
Denaby Utd 1948 to 1955.

*Fred Osborne was a tall and leggy schemer who was on
the fringe of the Villa side just as war was declared.
A regular scorer, grabbing almost 100 goals, for the
claret-and-blues' second-string during 1937-38 and
1938-39, war halted his promising progress. He briefly
appeared for United during the wartime season of
1940-41 when in the region on duty in the services, a
Christmas Day clash with Middlesbrough. Fred returned to Villa Park on peace being
restored but couldn't claim a place, joining neighbours Coventry. But he was again
unable to push his way to senior action and moved to non-league football. Osborne
later resided in Yorkshire and was employed by ICI. During World War Two he saw
action in France, Holland and Germany as part of the nation's forces.*

Appearances & Goals:
Debut v Middlesbrough (h) 25 December 1940 (FLN)
War: 1 app 0 gls
Total: 1 app 0 gls

OSTLER John 1896-1900

Centre-half
5'10"
b. Newarthill, near Motherwell, 1873
d. Prestonpans, East Lothian, 1958

Career: Motherwell Nov 1893/Bury April 1895/
Motherwell Aug 1895/UNITED Dec 1896 joint deal
with T Stewart £200 (Middlesbrough loan
1899-1900)/Retired cs 1900.

*Jack Ostler had gained much experience as Bury
won the Division Two title during 1894-95. He was to take that knowledge into
United's dressing-room and at centre-half formed the backbone, along with Stott and
Ghee, to Newcastle's first promotion side during 1897-98. A dominating and
unyielding personality in the centre of United's midfield, Jack was an important
character in United's consolidation as a top side. He took part in the club's inaugural
fixture in the First Division against Wolves. On leaving the game Ostler returned to
Lanarkshire working in a local colliery, later moving to Lothian where he was employed
at Rosewell pit.*

Appearances & Goals:
Debut v Grimsby Town (a) 26 December 1896
FL: 71 app 2 gls
FAC: 7 app 0 gls
Total: 78 app 2 gls

Honours:
FL div 2 champs 1895/FL div 2 prom 1898.

OWEN Michael James 2005-2009

Striker
5'8"
b. Chester, 14 December 1979

Career: Hawarden Pathfinders/
Mold Alexander jnrs/Hawarden
Rangers/St David's Park/Liverpool jnr
(FA Lilleshall Academy 1991-92), prof
Dec 1996/Real Madrid Aug 2004
cash-exch deal £10m/ UNITED Aug 2005
£16m/Manchester Utd July 2009 free to
June 2012/Stoke City Sept 2012
free to May 2013 when he retired.

*One of world football's biggest names of
recent times, Michael Owen sensationally
joined United at the end of August 2005
from Real Madrid for a club record £16m fee, and a substantial wage. It looked as
though United had pulled off another major coup, signing one of the world's best
strikers at the peak of his career, 25 years old and with much to offer. Around 16,000
turned up at Gallowgate to welcome him to Tyneside as the star signing was paraded
to the media, shades of Alan Shearer's arrival nearly a decade before. As a schoolboy
Owen had been linked with a number of clubs on trial, including Manchester United,
Arsenal and Chelsea before becoming a graduate of the FA's Lilleshall centre.
A teenage star with Liverpool and England, he scored almost 200 goals before a
headlining transfer to the Bernabeu in 2004. Small at 5'8" tall with a predatory touch
and explosively quick to get away from the last line of defence, Owen though was
often sidelined with injury throughout his career. After impressing in a Toon shirt
alongside his former England colleague Shearer, netting seven goals in 10 outings, he
was missing with a broken metatarsal then suffered a cruciate injury playing for his
country and was out of action for over 12 months, only to return and end up on the
treatment table again with hernia, thigh and ankle problems. All told, Owen's
expensive stay on Tyneside was a letdown, although his goals to games ratio is not
at all bad; 30 in 79 outings. When fit and on the field he was effective, but all too
often Owen was on the injured list. In the end a combined outlay of transfer fee and
wages of around £40m was never justified. Skipper under Kevin Keegan's management,
he departed on the Magpies' relegation joining Manchester United on a free transfer
in July 2009 where he was once more often in the hands of the medical team. On his
day though Michael was up there with the best as his scoring record more than
demonstrates; over 250 senior goals including 40 for England in 89 appearances.
Winning medals at Anfield and Old Trafford, he occasionally skippered his country
and became one of England's youngest players when he made his debut during 1998
as an 18-year-old, the year he became BBC's Sports Personality of the Year. Back in
1995, Michael had made his first big headline at St James' Park, netting for England*

choolboys against Scotland. On retiring during the summer of 2013 having been nable to hold down a regular place at either Manchester United or Stoke, Owen oncentrated on his race-horse stable complex in his native Cheshire as well as a nedia position with the BT Sport channel. Michael's father Terry Owen appeared for verton and Chester.

ppearances & Goals:
ebut v Fulham (h) 10 September 2005
L: 58(13) app 26 gls
AC: 5 app 1 gl
LC: 2(1) app 3 gls
otal: 65(14) app 30 gls

Honours:
9 Eng caps 1998-2008/WdC 1998, 2002/2 Eng B app 2006-07/1 Eng u21 app 998/Eng sch-youth app/PL champs 2011/FAC winner 2001/FLC winner 2001 (sub no pp), 2003, 2010/CL final 2011 (sub no app)/UEFA Cup winner 2001/ESC winner 001/FAYC winner 1996/WFoY 2001/EFoY 2001/YPoY (PFA) 1998/BBC SPoY 1998/Eng loF/PFA ToS (PL) 1998/PL PoY 1998/PL ToD.

OWENS Melvyn 1973-1977

eft-back
'10"
. Durham, August 1957

Career: Crook Town/UNITED jnr 1973, prof July 1975/ Crook Town cs 1977 free to c1982.

A junior product of Gordon Lee's management at St James' Park, Mel Owens signed schoolboy forms for the Magpies luring 1973 and once an apprentice developed quickly to he fringe of Newcastle's first-team squad. Selected for the ll fated and controversial trip to face Ayr United in the nuch maligned Anglo-Scottish Cup during September 976, Owens had to fight a rearguard action for most of he evening as the Geordie's weakened line-up fell by three goals. The England youth nternational then appeared in a friendly against Hibs but failed to make the grade fterwards and drifted out of professional football.

Appearances & Goals:
Debut v Ayr United (a) 15 September 1976 (ASC)
Others: 1 app 0 gls
Total: 1 app 0 gls

Honours:
Eng sch-youth app.

PAILOR Robert 1914-1915

Centre-forward
5'10"
b. Stockton, 7 July 1887
d. Hartlepool, 24 January 1976

Career: St Oswald's (Hartlepool)/West Hartlepool Oct 1906/Wingate Albion Nov 1907/West Hartlepool Nov 1907//West Bromwich Albion Oct 1908/UNITED May 1914 £1,550/Retired due to illness June 1915/Hartlepools Utd April 1916, becoming asst-manager Jan 1919 to Feb 1921, then director.

Bob Pailor signed for Newcastle after an impressive strike-rate of a goal every two games for Albion, claiming 47 in 92 senior fixtures. He had three excellent seasons at the Hawthorns and helped the Midland club to the Second Division title in 1911 and to the FA Cup final a year later when he scored an extra-time semi-final winner. The well-built Teessider possessed pace and agility at centre-forward which made him a handful in the box, but he never quite settled in the Midlands and wanted a move back north, returning to live in West Hartlepool a year before his transfer to Tyneside. Pailor was a most unlucky footballer. Firstly he signed for the Magpies just as war clouds hovered over the nation, then following a severe collision with the Chelsea keeper during 1915 had a diseased kidney removed and suffered illness. The former miner had to leave the first-class level and call it a day when war forced a sporting closedown. He afterwards resided in Hartlepool, employed as a bookmaker. Even away from the glare of football, fortune deserted Bob too. Later in life he had to give up his betting license when his sight faded and eventually he went blind. His brother Tom

was for a long period a director of Hartlepool as well as Mayor of the town on four occasions. Both Bob and Tom are very much embedded in the history of the 'Pool, the brothers taking a keen interest in sport in the district.

Appearances & Goals:
Debut v West Bromwich Albion (h) 2 September 1914
FL: 11 app 2 gls
FAC: 5 app 3 gls
Total: 16 app 5 gls

Honours:
FL div 2 champs 1911/FAC final 1912.

PANCRATE Fabrice 2009-2010

Outside-right
6'1"
b. Paris (France), 2 May 1980

Career: CS Louhans-Cuiseaux (Fr) 1999/EA Guingamp (Fr) 2000/Le Mans (Fr) 2002/Paris St-Germain (Fr) Aug 2005 £2m (Real Betis (Sp) loan 2006-07)(FC Sochaux (Fr) loan 2007-08) to July 2009/Sheffield Utd trial 2009/ UNITED Nov 2009 free to May 2010/Hannover 96 (Ger) trial Sept 2010/Leicester City trial Nov 2010/AE Larissa (Gr) Feb 2011/FC Nantes (Fr) July 2011 to cs 2014.

During a period of restricted transfer spending following relegation from the Premier League, Newcastle brought in several cut-price, free or loan players to replace a number of highly paid stars who went through the exit door during the summer of 2009. Fabrice Pancrate was one, a cost nothing forward from PSG who, following over 100 appearances in the French capital, was looking for a new start and chance to impress. An outside-right who could cut-in to join the strike force, 29-year-old Pancrate had failed to win a deal at Bramall Lane, but sufficiently impressed Chris Hughton and earned a short-term deal with the Magpies. With tidy ball skills, Pancrate looked good during his first few outings, able to slip past defenders with swerve and acceleration. And when he netted a gem of a goal against Watford, expertly taking the ball into the box before walloping it home, an effort that screamed into the Leazes net, most thought Newcastle had found a new star. However that was his only strike, the Frenchman rarely stamping his presence on a match after that. Fabrice was only selected to start on eight occasions, rivalling another player of similar inconsistency in Wayne Routledge, more often than not the pair exchanging places on and off the bench. Pancrate was not retained at the end of the Championship winning campaign and eventually moved back to France becoming a regular with FC Nantes.

Appearances & Goals:
Debut v Swansea City (h) 28 November 2009 (sub)
FL: 5(11) app 1 gl
FAC: 3 app 0 gls
Total: 8(11) app 1 gl

Honours:
FL ch winner 2010/Fr Cup winner 2006 (sub no app).

PAPAVASILIOU Nicodemos 1993-1994

Midfield
5'8"
b. Limassol (Cyprus), 31 August 1970

Career: Apollon Limassol (Cy) 1980/Arsenal trial 1986/Oldham Ath cs 1987/OFI (Gr) July 1988/ UNITED trial Feb 1993, pmt July 1993 £125,000/Genoa (It) trial July 1994/OFI (Gr) Dec 1994 £25,000/Apollon Limassol (Cy) 1995/Anorthosis (Cy) July 2000/Olym Nicosia (Cy) July 2001/Enosis NP (Cy) Jan 2002/KSK Beveren (Bel) trial July 2002/APOEL (Cy) Sept 2002/Retired playing 2003/APEP Pitsilia (Cy) coach 2005, then manager 2006/Olym Nicosia (Cy) manager 2008/ OFI (Gr) manager 2009/Olym Nicosia (Cy) manager Nov 2009 to June 2010/Doxa Katokopia (Cy) manager 2010/Enosis NP (Cy) manager 2011/Olym Nicosia (Cy) manager Feb 2012/Apollon Limassol (Cy) manager Sept 2012/Ermis Aradippou (Cy) manager Sept 2014.

A one-time Arsenal trialist as a teenager, Niki Papavasiliou was the first player to sign for the club from Mediterranean waters. Relentlessly pursued by manager Kevin Keegan, he impressed in a brief trial period with the club as a small, compact midfield player with an infectious work-rate and no little skill with his left foot. He was described once as a "little buzz bomb" on the field who could cover every blade of grass. After a bright opening in United's colours as the Premier League was encountered for the first time, Papavasiliou lost his place and then was injured in a reserve fixture which put him on the sidelines for a long period. By the time the likable Cypriot was fit, a pack of players were fighting for the midfield positions and Niki was destined to be down the list. With national service looming in his native country, the Cypriot returned to Greece to continue his football career. At the time of joining the Magpies, he was much fancied by Monaco, while his spell at Boundary Park fell foul of a work permit although he was at Oldham for 12 months. He was so keen to obtain a chance at Gallowgate that he paid his own air fare to Tyneside. Papavasiliou became a respected figure in football on the island of Cyprus, coaching and managing several clubs. He also opened his own academy near Limassol.

Appearances & Goals:

Debut v Tottenham Hotspur (h) 14 August 1993
PL: 7 app 0 gls
Total: 7 app 0 gls

Honours:

38 Cy caps 1991-99/Cy u21 app/Cy sch-youth app/Cy Cup final 1998/Gr Cup final 1990.

PARK John (Bluey) 1936-1945

Outside-right
5'9"
b. Douglas Water, near Lanark, 7 October 1913
d. Glasgow, January 2002

Career: Douglas Water Thistle/Partick Thistle trial 1931/Douglas Water Thistle 1932/Hamilton Acc April 1933 (Nithsdale Wand loan 1933-34)/UNITED April 1936 £1,800 (Chester war-guest 1939-40) (Hartlepools Utd war-guest 1939-40)(Wrexham war-guest 1940-41)(Hamilton Acc war-guest 1940-41)(Stranraer war-guest)(Third Lanark war-guest 1940-43)(Albion Rovers war-guest 1943-44)/Queen of the South Nov 1945 to c1946.

John Park caught the eye of United's scouts when on top form with Hamilton as season 1935-36 unfolded, during a sequence of games netting 13 goals in 13 outings in the Scottish First Division. A rival to Ehud Rogers on the right wing when he joined United, Park took over the role for the 1937-38 season and at times looked a great prospect. A former Scotland schoolboy player in 1932, he was robust and enthusiastic, the Scot's methods being not always ultra scientific, but he demonstrated that he could be a problem to the opposition. With his bustling style, Park also figured in the centre-forward shirt for United before the Second World War all but ended his senior football career, although he did appear for various clubs as a wartime guest. John worked in Motherwell's steelworks during the hostilities and remained employed there to his retirement. Since leaving St James' Park he lived in Lesmahagow near Lanark and was also known as Jack.

(Note: John confirmed a middle name of 'Bluey' but official documents don't reflect this. He signed his name JB Park on occasion.)

Appearances & Goals:

Debut v Bradford Park Avenue (a) 14 September 1936
FL: 60 app 11 gls
FAC: 1 app 1 gl
War: 12 app 2 gls
Total: 73 app 14 gls

Honours:

Scot sch-youth app.

PARK Oswald 1924-1931

Centre-half
5'11"
b. Darlington, 7 February 1905
d. Co Durham, 1957 (Q1)

Career: Cockerton St Mary's/Cockerton Jnrs/Darlington Railway Ath/UNITED Nov 1924 £125 (Connah's Quay & Shotton Utd loan 1929-30 & 1930-31)/Northampton Town May 1931 free/Hartlepools Utd July 1934/North Shields July 1937/Hartlepools Utd Nov 1937 player-trainer/Consett player-manager Feb 1938.

Clever and versatile, Ossie Park began his career as a midfield player operating in the centre of the field, but on the advent of the stopper centre-half changed his role into that of a defensive pivot. As deputy to Charlie Spencer, he appeared on five occasions as the Black'n'Whites lifted the Football League crown in 1927, then gained an extended run the following season. However, United directors didn't see Park as a long term replacement for the aging Spencer, and he was overlooked when the Magpies splashed out heavily on England centre-half Jack Hill during 1928. Falling out with the club's hierarchy, he then spent a long period on loan with Cheshire League outfit Connah's Quay before moving to Northampton. Ossie did well in two spells with Hartlepools and totalled 123 games, captain at the Victoria Ground for a period. He later resided in County Durham.

Appearances & Goals:

Debut v Bolton Wanderers (a) 29 August 1925
FL: 42 app 0 gls
FAC: 1 app 0 gls
Total: 43 app 0 gls

Honours:

FL champs 1927 (5 app).

PARKER Scott Matthew 2005-2007

Midfield
5'9"
b. Lambeth, London, 13 October 1980

Career: FA Lilleshall Academy/Charlton Ath jnr April 1996, prof Oct 1997 (Norwich City loan 2000-01/ Chelsea Jan 2004 £10m/UNITED June 2005 £6.5m/West Ham Utd June 2007 £7m/ Tottenham Hotspur Aug 2011 £5m/Fulham Aug 2013.

Highly respected at all his clubs as a midfielder with energy and vigour, Scott Parker looked to be a first-class purchase when he moved north from Chelsea during the summer of 2005 for a £6.5m fee, part of a big spending spree by boss Graeme Souness. Unable to get regular action in Jose Mourinho's all-conquering Blues line-up, making only 19 starts, at 24 years of age Parker was set to become Newcastle's pivotal player in the engine room of the side. Able to win the ball, distribute accurately and get from box to box for 90 minutes, Scott looked the part alongside Bowyer and Solano in the Magpie midfield. Appointed skipper for the start of the 2006-07 season when Alan Shearer retired, Parker excelled in protecting his back four, blocking, tackling and breaking up the opposition play, while he possessed good vision going forward. However the Londoner never settled in the North East, and although giving 100% match after match surprisingly never hit it off with sections of the Newcastle crowd who disliked his custom at the time of often going back and sideways rather than looking forwards. Injury and illness didn't help him on Tyneside and Parker returned to the capital after only two seasons at Gallowgate, joining West Ham (129 app) where his game-plan flourished even though he was part of a Hammers' team heading for relegation. Moving to Tottenham, Scott resurrected his England career, even skippering his country during 2012, and showed that he was the complete midfielder, proving the Newcastle doubters very much wrong in their evaluation of the player. Playing his best football in the capital, during his early days Parker appeared on 145 occasions for Charlton. As a young teenager he once took part in a television advert for McDonalds, showing off his ball-juggling skills.

Appearances & Goals:

Debut v Deportivo La Coruna (h) 3 August 2005 (ITC)
PL: 54(1) app 4 gls
FAC: 3 app 1 gl
FLC: 4 app 1 gl
Euro: 9(2) app 0 gls
Total: 70(3) app 6 gls

Honours:

18 Eng caps 2004-13/12 Eng u21 app 2001-02/Eng sch-youth app/PL champs 2005 (4 app)/FL div 1 champs 2000/FL ch prom 2012 (4 app)/FL div 1 prom 1998 (3 app)/FoY 2011 (FWA)/YPoY 2004 (PFA)/PFA ToS (PL) 2012.

PARKINSON Andrew James 1978-1979
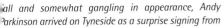

Striker
6'0"
b. Johannesburg (South Africa), 5 May 1959

Career: Highlands Park (SA)/Dynamos Utd (SA)/UNITED March 1978/Peterborough Utd Aug 1979 free/ Philadelphia Fury (USA) cs 1980/Montreal Manic (Can) 1981/Fort Lauderdale Strikers (USA) Nov 1982/Team America (USA) Jan 1983/New York Cosmos (USA) 1983/Chicago Sting (USA) March 1985/Tacoma Stars (USA) 1985/Fort Lauderdale Strikers (USA) 1988.

Tall and somewhat gangling in appearance, Andy Parkinson arrived on Tyneside as a surprise signing from South African soccer where manager Bill McGarry had plenty of contacts. With Newcastle on their way down into the Second Division, it was hoped that Parkinson would prove to be an awkward and effective striker, able to cause mayhem in and around the box. But the youngster, fresh from a sun-soaked landscape, failed to make an impact on his three outings as substitute, although he did possess nice touches on the ball. He moved on quickly, trying his luck with Peterborough by following his coach at Gallowgate, Peter Morris, but he lasted only a season at London Road recording 18 games, walking out on the Posh to conclude an unhappy period in the Football League. Parkinson then headed to North America where he enjoyed a successful career as a noted striker, netting 73 goals in just over 200 matches. He gained USA citizenship and appeared for the national side, Team America during May 1984. Andy was afterwards for a time employed at a Porsche dealership in Orlando.

Appearances & Goals:
Debut v Manchester United (h) 11 March 1978 (sub)
FL: 0(3) app 0 gls
Total: 0(3) app 0 gls

Honours:
2 USA caps 1984.

PARR Jack 1944

Left-back
6'1"
b. Derby, 21 November 1920
d. Littleover, Derbyshire, 28 November 1985

Career: Long Eaton/Holbrook St Michaels/Derby Co amat Dec 1937, prof March 1938/(Notts Co war-guest 1940-44)(Cardiff City war-guest 1941-42) (Lincoln City war-guest 1941-42)(Mansfield Town war-guest 1941-42)(Nottingham Forest war-guest 1943-44)(UNITED war-guest 1943-44)/Resumed with Derby Co 1945/Shrewsbury Town July 1953/ Gresley Rovers Aug 1956/Burton Albion June 1957/ Belper Town May 1958, becoming player-coach.

Always a steady and reliable player, Jack Parr was a solid, tall and 13 stone full-back who registered 134 senior appearances for Derby and 116 for Shrewsbury. He was unlucky to miss the 1946 FA Cup final because of a broken arm, after playing in every round to Wembley. In the North East on wartime service during season 1943-44, he appeared against Sheffield United for the Magpies in an important War Cup match at Bramall Lane. With a cultured style at the back, Parr was selected for the England 'B' side to face the Army during 1946-47.

(Note: Although most sources have Parr's death as 28 November 1985, death registers note this earlier in Q3 1985.)

Appearances & Goals:
Debut v Sheffield United (a) 1 April 1944 (WC)
War: 1 app 0 gls
Total: 1 app 0 gls

Honours:
1 Eng B app 1947/FLN2(WLg) champs 1945.

PATERSON Thomas A 1950-1952

Outside-left
5'8"
b. Lochore, Fife, 3 April 1927

Career: Raith Rovers Jan 1946/Lochgelly Albert July 1946/Leicester City March 1948/UNITED June 1950 £2,500/Watford July 1952 £750/ Berwick Rangers July 1955/Retired due to injury cs 1957.

A play-anywhere forward, Tom Paterson preferred an inside role, but was generally picked in the outside-left position for Newcastle. Paterson wasn't a regular at either Filbert Street (17 app) or St James' Park, stepping in on only two occasions for Mitchell and Hannah, but he did have a good run in senior football at Vicarage Road. Tom totalled 48 appearances for Watford before moving to the Scottish League with Berwick. After being forced to quit the game due to a knee injury, he later settled in Sheriff Hill, Gateshead.

Appearances & Goals:
Debut v Middlesbrough (a) 25 December 1950
FL: 2 app 0 gls
Total: 2 app 0 gls

PATERSON William Alexander Kennedy 1954-1958

Centre-half
6'1"
b. Kinlochleven, Argyll, 25 February 1930
d. Inverness, 2002

Career: Inverness Thistle/Ransome & Marles/Doncaster Rovers March 1950/UNITED Oct 1954 £22,250/ Rangers July 1958 £3,500/Morton Nov 1962 free/ Cheltenham Town 1963/Caledonian (Inverness) 1966/ Hamilton Steelers (Can) to 1970.

Purchased as a 24-year-old by United's directors for a then large fee of £22,250, Bill Paterson was in for a rough ride at St James' Park. Bestowed with the hugely popular Frank Brennan's shirt when the Scottish international was at the time in dispute with the club, Paterson looked anything but a commanding centre-half during his early days at Gallowgate. A stylish footballer who believed that defenders should also play attractive football, he was a totally different type of player to the physical Brennan and supporters did not take to the big Highlander. Even Paterson himself made the comment that, "I appeared a misfit". Bill's form plummeted, losing all the confidence that had earned him international recognition as skipper of the Scotland 'B' side after displaying commanding authority in 120 matches wearing Doncaster's colours in Second Division fare. United's support hardly gave him a chance and as Paterson tried harder and harder to win over the fans, his form just went from bad to worse. With the crowd against him it was no surprise when he left Tyneside. However, the powerfully built Scot returned to the big time at Ibrox, regaining his honour in 116 appearances for Rangers, part of their side that won several trophies in the early years of the Sixties. He also appeared in the final of the European Cup Winners Cup during 1961 when Rangers were defeated by Fiorentina. On leaving the game, Paterson became a publican and hotelier in various locations from Goole, Tadcaster, Hythe and Inverness. He retired to live in the Highlands to his death.

Appearances & Goals:
Debut v Tottenham Hotspur (h) 16 October 1954
FL: 22 app 1 gl
FAC: 5 app 1 gl
Total: 27 app 2 gls

Honours:
1 Scot B app 1954/SL champs 1961/SC winner 1960/SLC winner 1961, 1962 (first game)/ECWC final 1961.

P

PATON Harry D 1921-1922

Inside-right
5'8"
b. Larkhall, near Motherwell, 23 May 1897

Career: Larkhall Thistle/Queen's Park Dec 1917/
Motherwell Aug 1918/Clydebank Aug 1919/ UNITED
May 1921 £410/St Mirren Nov 1922 £600 to 1927.

*Harry Paton was a nimble player, well known to
Scottish fans and regarded as a good prospect during
the immediate post-war years. Following two
seasons of regular action with Clydebank in which he
scored 26 goals, he joined the Magpies' growing band
of Scotsmen. Paton took an active part in Newcastle's
1921-22 programme, but wasn't retained for the following
year. With St Mirren Harry was again described as "promising",
but only appeared sparsely for the Paisley club. Having paid out a sizable fee of £600,
they complained to Newcastle that Paton was unfit and the dispute went to the
International League Board for judgement. Paton's career then stalled, being registered
with the Saints but playing little active part in football over four years.*

Appearances & Goals:
Debut v Huddersfield Town (a) 27 August 1921
FL: 13 app 2 gls
Total: 13 app 2 gls

PATTEN John Thomas 1892-1936

Outside-right & Asst-secretary
5'9"
b. Newcastle upon Tyne, 1871
d. Newcastle upon Tyne, 11 January 1961

Career: Trafalgar (Newcastle) c1880/Newcastle West End/
UNITED May 1892/Hebburn Argyle 1897 to 1898/
UNITED asst-secretary & reserve manager July 1897 to
cs 1936/Northumberland FA member 1903-1947,
becoming secretary 1929 to 1947.

*John Patten was one of Tyneside's foremost pioneers. Once called a "typically blunt
Geordie", he was associated with the West End club before their liquidation in 1892,
and then joined East End in readiness for their development into Newcastle United.
As a player, Patten was chiefly a reserve operating on the right flank in Northern
Alliance football, still good enough to be capped by Northumberland. He was elevated
to Football League status only once, during the club's inaugural season in a fixture
against Ardwick, now Manchester City. On retiring from the playing side of the game,
'Jack' as he was commonly known, then concentrated on the game's administration
in the region. Firstly he acted for United behind the scenes, for many years in charge
as secretary of the Magpies' second string in the North Eastern League. He later
became involved with the County association and served the Northumberland FA for
over 40 years. He was also a member of the FA Council while Patten additionally
refereed and ran the line in reserve games. In a biography published during 1958, Jack
was described affectionately as "the grand old man of Tyneside football". Patten lived
in the High Heaton district of Newcastle into his nineties, a staunch United enthusiast
to his final day.*

Appearances & Goals:
Debut v Ardwick (a) 21 October 1893
FL: 1 app 0 gls
Total: 1 app 0 gls

PATTINSON Daniel 1900-1902

Inside-left
5'10"
b. Newcastle upon Tyne

Career: Malcolm Jnrs (Newcastle)/Rutherford College
(Newcastle)/Willington Ath/UNITED July 1900/Local football
cs 1902, being still registered with United until 1905.

*Youthful forward Dan Pattinson followed the track of Colin
Veitch to United, from Rutherford College and Malcolm Juniors
in the Heaton district of Newcastle. Although Pattinson played
well and netted on his debut as a reserve to Veitch, he wasn't
given another opportunity in senior company. After two seasons
of Northern League football, Dan returned to local soccer.*

Appearances & Goals:
Debut v Nottingham Forest (a) 19 March 1902 (1 goal)
FL: 1 app 1 gl
Total: 1 app 1 gl

PATTISON Matthew Joseph 2000-2008

Midfield
5'9"
b. Johannesburg (South Africa), 27 October 1986

Career: Redheugh BC/UNITED jnr 2000, prof July
2003/Norwich City loan Nov 2007, pmt Jan 2008/
Mamelodi Sundowns (SA) Aug 2009 to Dec 2011/
Leeds Utd & Hibernian trial Jan 2012/Santos (SA)
Feb 2012/Bidvest Wits (SA) June 2012/
MK Dons trial July 2014/Birmingham City trial Aug
2014/Hibernian trial Aug 2014.

*A South African by birth, Matty Pattison moved to
Tyneside when he was 11 years of age when his
Tyneside parents returned to the North East. When
at Redheugh Boys Club in Gateshead, he stood out above the other youngsters and
was given an opportunity at Newcastle's Academy during 2000. Glenn Roeder, in
charge of United's junior development then, rated Matty highly and when the former
Magpie skipper was appointed caretaker boss, then full-time manager, Pattison was
part of his plans. A stocky and aggressive player, he had an all-action style in the
central midfield role and came back from two cruciate knee injuries shortly after
getting into the first-team picture in a friendly against Celtic during 2004. Prompting
and probing in midfield, he rarely gave the ball away and was handed his debut during
2005-06 becoming a member of the first-team squad the following season. He was
never a regular, but often Pattison was on the bench, selected to play from the start
on four occasions. Capped by South Africa during season 2010-11 and in contention
for a place in his country's 2012 World Cup squad, a bright future beckoned for Matty,
however Roeder's departure also saw Pattison move on. Just missing out on a place
in the South African final selection, he rejoined Roeder at Carrow Road where he
appeared on 55 occasions but left after Norwich suffered relegation. Pattison headed
back to Johannesburg and was then managed by two former world stars, Hristo
Stoichkov and Johan Neeskens.*

Appearances & Goals:
Debut v Everton (h) 25 February 2006 (sub)
PL: 4(6) app 0 gls
FAC: 2 app 0 gls
Euro: 0(3) app 0 gls
Total: 6(9) app 0 gls
Honours:
2 SA caps 2011/1 unoff SA app.

PAYNE Lee John 1988-1989

Outside-left
5'10"
b. Luton, 12 December 1966

Career: Luton Town 1982/Hitchin Town 1985/
Dunstable/Barnet 1987/Leicester City trial Sept
1988/UNITED Sept 1988 £25,000/Reading
March 1989 £30,000/Veendam (Neth) 1990
£60,000/BVO Emmen (Neth) c1991 £110,000/
Gateshead July 1993 to Sept 1993/SC Veendam
(Neth) 1994/Retired due to injury 1996.

*After being rejected by a number of clubs
following trials due to an asthma complaint,
then at Kenilworth Road because of a knee
problem, Lee Payne tried to make a comeback in
senior football with Leicester during a trial period at Filbert Street. His sparkling form
alerted Magpie officials after the 21-year-old forward played well against United in
a Central League fixture. Manager Willie McFaul took a chance with £25,000 to bring
him north, the Irishman's last purchase as Newcastle boss. Exchanging his job as a
finishing foreman on a construction site, had Payne been a success at St James' Park,
he would have been recognised at the time as the most expensive transfer from non-
league football. He needed to total a certain number of appearances for United to
earn his previous club another £100,000. Unfortunately the fast and livewire winger*

idn't get past seven matches for the Magpies and new manager Jim Smith released ee to join Reading where he totalled 37 games before moving to Holland. With otably Veendam, Payne enjoyed a successful period in Dutch football with over 100 utings until a succession of knee injuries curtailed his progress. Injury forced him ut of action in 1996, for a period afterwards acting as a European scout for West lam under Glenn Roeder. He then continued scouting and developed a successful areer as a registered player agent based in Holland and Spain as well as a period in razil (where he linked with his ex-colleague Mirandinha). Payne later joined the Full ontract Law team based in the UK during 2012 as Head of Football Agency. It was ecorded that he was distantly related to Luton's legendary centre-forward Joe Payne although Lee cannot confirm this) while his father was an amateur goalkeeper with unstable and later boss at a number of non-league sides in the south.

Appearances & Goals:
ebut v Middlesbrough (h) 26 October 1988
L: 6(1) app 0 gls
otal: 6(1) app 0 gls

PEACOCK Darren 1994-1998

entre-half
'2"
. Bristol, 3 February 1968

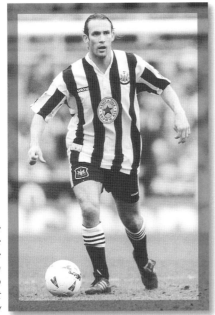

areer: Bristol City/Bristol
overs 1984/ Newport Co jnr cs
984, prof Feb 1986/ Hereford
Jtd March 1989 free/Queens
ark Rangers Dec 1990
350,000/UNITED March 1994
2.7m/Blackburn Rovers July
998 free (West Ham Utd loan
000-01) (Wolverhampton
Vand loan 2000-01)/ Retired
lue to injury Dec 2000/
ancaster City manager April
013.

Darren Peacock became the
ountry's most expensive
lefender at £2.7m and the
Magpies' record purchase when
ie moved from Loftus Road to
Gallowgate during 1994. That
eadline move was a far cry
rom his early days in the game with struggling Welsh club Newport County. Apart
rom being out of action for almost 17 months with a broken leg which needed a
bone graft, County's severe financial problems meant that Darren was handed a free
transfer when the club folded. Moving to Hereford, Peacock battled away in football's
basement and quickly established himself as a commanding stopper in the lower
divisions before being captured by QPR and developed further at Loftus Road as a top
flight defender. Tough and committed with the talent to use the ball well, Kevin Keegan
made a persistent chase to land the player and gave United's attack minded line-up
a touch of grit and stability in defence to blend with the side's entertainment value.
Although at first United's supporters had to be convinced he was a top rated player,
Darren's steely and determined performances during season 1994-95 won over the
fans and thereafter he became a popular character in United's squad of superstars.
Characterised by his long flowing hair and pony-tail, Peacock totalled 143 matches
at Loftus Road and was rejected as a youngster at both Bristol City and Rovers. His
career went full circle when he suffered a bad neck and spine injury after a collision
with the 'keeper during a Wolves versus Fulham match. This knock, on top of knee
injuries, saw Darren call it a day in 2000. Following his retirement, Darren spent a
period in Spain and Portugal engaged in property development before being appointed
ancaster City manager for the 2013-14 season.

Appearances & Goals:
Debut v Norwich City (h) 29 March 1994
PL: 131(2) app 2 gls
FAC: 11 app 0 gls
FLC: 13(1) app 2 gls
Euro: 16(1) app 0 gls
Others: 1 app 0 gls
Total: 172(4) app 4 gls

Honours:
PL runners-up 1996, 1997/WsC winner 1990.

PEACOCK Gavin Keith 1990-1993

Midfield or Striker
5'8"
b. Welling, London, 18 November 1967

Career: Queens Park Rangers jnr April 1983, prof Nov 1984/Gillingham loan Oct 1987, pmt Dec 1987 £40,000/Bournemouth Aug 1989 £210,000/ UNITED Nov 1990 £450,000 cash-exch deal with W Fereday/Chelsea Aug 1993 £1.25m/Queens Park Rangers Nov 1996 £1m (Charlton Ath loan 2001-02)/Retired July 2002.

Much courted as a schoolboy in London, Gavin Peacock joined Jim Smith's QPR but had to move into the lower divisions to find regular action. Heading to Tyneside when almost 23 years old, Gavin flourished in a Newcastle shirt and was United's outstanding player up front during season 1991-92, the year the club very nearly tumbled into the old Division Three. A hit with the fans, had it not been for Peacock's menace in attack, the Magpies may well have been doomed before Kevin Keegan arrived to rescue the side. Always able to fire home quality strikes from midfield as well, Gavin was recognised as a Premier League player, good at controlling the ball, with vision and a sure drive when in a scoring position. He almost departed to Middlesbrough as Keegan took total control, but he changed his mind when the Hall-Keegan duo swung into action. Until a hamstring injury put him out of the selection frame, the past England schools and youth player had taken a major role in the Magpies' First Division title success during 1992-93. Gavin's twisting runs and quick turns were in demand, and after family issues led to an expressed wish to return south, United agreed a deal with Chelsea on what was termed compassionate grounds. Brought up with a footballing pedigree and a Tyneside blood-line, his father Keith Peacock had a long career with Charlton, while he was also in charge of the Gills while Gavin was based in Kent. His debut for United resulted in a remarkable 5-4 defeat at Filbert Street; the following season on the same ground, Peacock was the saviour as Newcastle scrambled a win which ensured First Division survival. He ended his United career also against the Foxes, in a celebration 7-1 romp at Gallowgate following promotion. Peacock then benefited from being part of a good Chelsea line-up over three-and-a-half seasons and 134 games before returning to QPR where he increased his statistics at Loftus Road to over 200 outings. With a respectable overall career total of 632 games and 135 goals, Gavin then moved into the much expanding football media, a BBC presenter of Football Focus and Match of the Day. However, during 2008 Peacock, a devoted Christian, left the game to concentrate on his faith. Gavin moved to Canada to study divinity, earning a theology degree at Ambrose Seminary and becoming Home Missionary at Calvary Grace Church in Calgary on the edge of the Canadian Rockies. Gavin described himself on his Twitter account as a "Lover of Christ, husband, father, pastor, preacher". His son Jake became a Muay Thai fighter and martial arts competitor.

Appearances & Goals:
Debut v Leicester City (a) 1 December 1990
FL: 102(3) app 35 gls
FAC: 6 app 2 gls
FLC: 6 app 5 gls
Others: 3 app 4 gls
Total: 117(3) app 46 gls

Honours:
1 FL app 1993/Eng sch-youth app/FL div 1 champs 1993/FAC final 1994/PFA ToS (d1) 1993.

PEARCE Stuart MBE 1997-1999

Centre-half or Left-back
5'10"
b. Hammersmith, London, 24 April 1962

Career: Queens Park Rangers trial/Wealdstone 1977 & Dynamo Kingsbury Kiev (Hull City trial 1979)/Coventry City Oct 1983 £25,000/ Nottingham Forest June 1985 £240,000, becoming player-manager Dec 1996 to May 1997/UNITED July 1997 free/West Ham Utd Aug 1999 free/Manchester City player-coach July 2001, retired becoming asst-coach May 2002, then coach July 2004, caretaker-manager March 2005, manager May 2005 to May 2007/Also England u18 coach July 1999, England u21 part-time manager Feb 2007, becoming full-time July 2007 to June 2013, as well as England coach Jan 2008, caretaker-manager Feb to May 2012 (GB Olympic coach 2012)/ Nottingham Forest manager July 2014.

P

When 35-year-old Stuart Pearce joined the Magpies he was one of the veterans of the Premiership, yet the powerful and inspirational defender still had plenty to offer the Magpies. An outstanding professional for club and country, superbly fit and enthusiastic as any of his younger team-mates, Pearce was signed by Kenny Dalglish after Nottingham Forest had been relegated. He arrived on Tyneside on a free transfer and proved a good piece of business by United's management. Newcastle acquired a highly knowledgeable full-back with an intelligent football brain and one who was tough as they come with an unbeatable will to win. Also operating at centre-half effectively, he was just what Newcastle's defence needed, being a commanding influence. A late developer in the senior game, Stuart was a part-time player with Wealdstone in 242 games until he was 21 years old. Then he received a break with Coventry before being picked up by Nottingham Forest. At the City Ground since 1985, Pearce developed into something of a legend in Forest's red shirt by the time he departed during July 1997, 12 years later. Skipper of the club, he reached three Wembley finals and totalled 522 outings for the Reds as well as netting almost a century of goals; a formidable goalscoring record for a defender, having the ability to hit the net with ferocious free-kicks. An England cult figure as well, winning 78 caps, Pearce led his country out on occasion and displayed a rousing attitude every time he pulled on the Three Lions shirt; once described as showing "power, passion, pride, presence and pure commitment". Famously nicknamed 'Psycho' after his no-nonsense tackling and trademark clenched-fist salute, Pearce gave United much needed experience at the back and with his dangerous crossing ability and stunning shooting also reinforced Newcastle's creative options. During his short stay at Gallowgate Stuart captained the Magpies and became a popular character on Tyneside until he was marginalised by Ruud Gullit. But it wasn't the end of Stuart's playing career as he enjoyed a swansong at West Ham, returning to England duty when 37 years old before moving into coaching, notably with the England set-up. A street is named after him in Nottingham and Pearce returned to manage Forest during the summer of 2014.

Appearances & Goals:
Debut v Sheffield Wednesday (h) 9 August 1997
PL: 37 app 0 gls
FAC: 7 app 0 gls
FLC: 2 app 0 gls
Euro: 5(1) app 1 gl
Total: 51(1) app 1 gl

Honours:
78 Eng caps 1987-2000/WdC 1990/OG GB 2012(m)/1 Eng unoff app 1996/1 Eng u21 app 1987/FL div 1 champs 2002/FL div 1 prom 1994/FAC final 1991, 1998/FLC winner 1989, 1990/PFA ToS (d1) 1988, 1989, 1990, 1991, 1992/Eng HoF/MBE 1998.

PEARS William 1936-1941

Right-half
5'7"
b. Willington, Co Durham, 15 November 1918
d. Durham West, July 1992

Career: Crook Town/UNITED Sept 1936 £50 to Sept 1941.

Starting his career as an inside-forward, Billy Pears stood in for Jimmy Gordon at half-back during the 1938-39 season. A product of Durham schools football and an international at that level in 1933, he was a gritty midfielder who knitted determination with a fair degree of skill. However, Billy's development as a Football League player was cut short just when he was making an impact in the club's Central League eleven. War began soon after his senior outings and Pears joined the army for the duration of the hostilities, a blossoming career in the game over.

Appearances & Goals:
Debut v Bury (a) 15 April 1939
FL: 2 app 0 gls
Total: 2 app 0 gls

Honours:
Eng sch-youth app.

PEARSON James Findlay 1978-1980

Striker
5'10"
b. Falkirk, 24 March 1953

Career: Gairdoch Utd/St Johnstone amat June 1969, prof March 1970/Everton July 1974 £100,000/UNITED Aug 1978 £75,000/Retired due to injury Feb 1980/Barrow April 1980/Gateshead Nov 1981/North Shields player-manager June 1983/Gateshead July 1984/Workington Oct 1984/Whitley Bay coach Aug 1985, becoming manager Nov 1985/Blyth Spartans coach Nov 1985 to May 1988/North Shields manager June 1988 to Feb 1989/Gateshead asst-manager 1989 to May 1990.

A slimly-built, fair-haired Scot, Jim Pearson was able to play as a front runner or a midfield schemer. Skilful and with deft touches, at the peak of his career with St Johnstone and Everton, he was always liable to find the net. Jim made his debut as a 17-year-old in the Scottish League and a record of 54 goals in 148 outings alerted the Goodison Park club who snapped him up for a six figure sum. Pearson had misfortune with persistent knee injuries in both Scotland and England, but he still managed moments of brilliance in his 121 matches (19 goals) for the Merseysiders, part of the Toffees' Wembley squad for the 1977 League Cup final. Arriving on Tyneside as part of Bill McGarry's rebuilding plans, knocks continued at St James' Park and Jim was more often in the treatment room than on the pitch, eventually leaving the senior game due to more knee problems. He is remembered at Gallowgate for a crucial League Cup penalty shoot-out miss against rivals Sunderland during 1979 but also for a handful of quality strikes for the Black'n'Whites. Despite the spot-kick setback, Pearson was a respected professional, who later guided local non-league side Blyth to the Northern League title on two occasions. With a friendly demeanour, after leaving the game, Jim worked in insurance, then for sportswear giants Nike, based in Washington where he boosted the brand in the English game. Becoming the company's Head of Football, he remained with Nike for 14 years before taking up a lucrative appointment as Sports Consultant to the Sultan of Brunei during 1997. Pearson later returned to the UK and in 2000 set-up JJB Sports indoor football centres, then developed his own Soccarena complex in Durham. Pearson also worked for Lotto Sports as a brand manager, and for Northumberland County Council helping disadvantaged kids with activity projects while he has been a football consultant for law firms Blacks in Leeds and Last, Cawthra & Feather in Bradford. Residing in Ponteland, for a time Jim hosted corporate tables at St James' Park, then at Goodison Park and is an after-dinner and function speaker. Keeping fit, after leaving football Pearson has completed several Great North Runs.

Appearances & Goals:
Debut v Millwall (a) 19 August 1978
FL: 11 app 3 gls
FAC: 0(1) app 0 gls
FLC: 2 app 1 gl
Total: 13(1) app 4 gls

Honours:
6 Scot u23 app 1974-76/Scot sch-youth app/FLC final 1977.

PEARSON Stanley Clare 1941-1942

Inside-forward
5'9"
b. Salford, 11 January 1919
d. Alderley Edge, Cheshire, 17 February 1997

Career: Adelphi Lads Club/Manchester Utd amat 1935, prof May 1936 (Grimsby Town war-guest 1939-40) (Middlesbrough war-guest 1940-41)(Brighton war-guest 1941-43)(UNITED war-guest 1941-42)(Distillery (Belfast) war-guest 1942-43)(Queens Park Rangers war-guest 1943-44)(Folkestone war-guest)/Resumed with Manchester Utd 1946/Bury Feb 1954 £4,500/Chester Oct 1957, becoming manager April 1959 to Nov 1961/Prestbury manager 1962.

Stan Pearson was an inside-forward of immense power and who could create and hit goals season after season. Capped on eight occasions by England, he was an influential player in Manchester United's FA Cup success in 1948 (scoring a hat-trick in the semi-final) and then title victory during 1952 (when he was top scorer). He was also four times runner-up in the title race with the Reds. His service of nearly 18 years and record of 149 goals in 345 games (plus another 53 goals in wartime football) at Old Trafford is evidence enough of his contribution, while Stan also grabbed five goals in his limited appearances for his country, as well as a hat-trick for the Football League side. Later also serving Bury with distinction in 129 games (57 goals), he was a classy forward able to spray the ball around and a deadly finisher, one of the very best footballers in England during the immediate post-war years. Dark-haired, Pearson was stationed in Shildon with the South Lancashire Regiment for a period and landed at St James' Park for a few games during season 1941-42. He afterwards served with his regiment in Burma and India. Over a long career, Stan played on until he was over 40 years of age and later ran a newsagency business in Prestbury.

Appearances & Goals:
Debut v Sheffield Wednesday (a) 20 December 1941 (FLN)
War: 5 app 0 gls
Total: 5 app 0 gls

Honours:
5 Eng caps 1948-52/1 Eng B app 1948/2 FL app 1942-52/FA tour app 1953/FL champs 1952/FL div 2 prom 1938/FAC winner 1948/WsC final 1958/FLN(WLg) champs 1942 (7 app).

PEARSON Thomas Usher 1933-1948

Outside-left
5'8"
b. Edinburgh, 6 March 1913
d. Edinburgh, 1 March 1999

Career: Murrayfield Amateurs/Heart of Midlothian trial 1933/UNITED March 1933 £35 (Heart of Midlothian war-guest 1940-41)(Blackburn Rovers war-guest 1940-44)(Bolton Wand war-guest 1940-41)(Tottenham Hotspur war-guest 1941-42)(Birmingham City war-guest 1942-43)(Liverpool war-guest 1942-43)(Blackpool war-guest 1943-45)(Stoke City war-guest 1944-45)(Walsall war-guest 1944-45)/Resumed with United/Aberdeen Feb 1948 cash-exch deal with W McCall/Retired cs 1953/Aberdeen coach 1959, becoming manager Nov 1959 to Feb 1965/UNITED scout June 1967.

Tommy Pearson was a loyal servant to Newcastle United for over a decade and but for the Second World War would probably have also become a noted international star for Scotland. The skilful Pearson relied on immaculate ball control and skills; he was especially noted for magical runs on the touchline which featured bamboozling body-swerves and double-foot shuffles, as well as crowd pleasing nut-megs. Arriving on Tyneside having worked in the bacteriology lab of Edinburgh's public-health unit, when on the football pitch he was a key player as Murrayfield lifted the Scottish Amateur Cup. Pearson was quick to develop through United's ranks; he was unorthodox and became a regular for the Magpies in six peacetime seasons, oozing class and showing verve and sparkle on the flank. Tommy though fell out of favour, being dropped by the club on the same day as he was selected for the Scotland side to meet England at Wembley in 1947. Some directors, and supporters, considered he held onto the ball too long, others reckoned he was unfairly treated during the 1947-48 promotion campaign. Branded a troublemaker by certain sections of the management, allegations according to team-mates that were far from the truth. He left Tyneside with a sour taste; Len Shackleton later noting he received "shabby treatment" from the club. Although Pearson was reaching the veteran stage, his departure to Aberdeen opened another door and he became associated with the Dons for over 30 years, as player, coach and manager. He afterwards was a sports journalist for the Scottish Daily Mail for a period and returned to the city of his birth, Edinburgh, where he opened a jewellery business as well as continuing his passion for golf, being a first-class amateur golfer, once in his earlier days competing in the Open Championship at St Andrews. Tom is the only player to have appeared for both England and Scotland in international football, turning out for the English in emergency during a wartime fixture on Tyneside as a late replacement for Eric Brook. When he made his debut in his country's blue shirt, Pearson was over 34 years of age. Serving in the RAF during the war, Tommy was always guaranteed a match on his travels around the country, notably at Ewood Park (78 app) while he helped Blackpool to the 1944 wartime cup final. His father Tommy senior was with Hearts, while an uncle, Harry Pearson appeared for Arsenal without making the grade.

Appearances & Goals:
Debut v Arsenal (a) 14 October 1933
FL: 212 app 46 gls
FAC: 16 app 6 gls
War: 49 app 8 gls
Total: 277 app 60 gls
(Void FL: 2 app 2 gls)

Honours:
2 Scot caps 1947/1 Eng war app 1940/1 SL app 1948/1 FL app 1942/FL div 2 prom 1948/FLN2(WLg) champs 1943 (1 app)/FLN1(WLg) champs 1944 (2 app)/WC(N) final 1944.

PEART John George 1912-1913

Centre-forward
5'11"
b. South Shields, 3 October 1888
d. Paddington, London, 3 September 1948

Career: South Shields Adelaide Aug 1905/Treharris amat 1906/Sheffield Utd May 1907/Stoke June 1910 £50/UNITED March 1912 £600/Notts Co Feb 1913 £600 (Barnsley war-guest 1915-18)(Croydon Common war-guest 1915-16)(Leeds City war-guest 1916-19) (Chesterfield war-guest 1916-17)(Rochdale war-guest 1918-19)/Birmingham Nov 1919/Derby Co Jan 1920 £2,000/Ebbw Vale player-manager Aug 1920/Port Vale Jan 1922/Norwich City July 1922/Rochdale player-manager Feb 1923/Retired playing May 1924/Bradford City manager July 1930/Fulham manager May 1935 to his demise.

One of football's most travelled personalities of his era, Jack Peart was a central figure of the game for over 40 years, a player of expert ability and, as a manager, a shrewd judge. Only briefly at Newcastle as one of Albert Shepherd's replacements, the Tynesider was a strong leader with a bustling style. A skilled craftsman in attack, Jack made a name for himself netting 31 goals in only 21 games for Stoke during their non-league days. Peart appeared at every level of the Football League, as well as in the Southern and Welsh Leagues, and always he scored goals. Leaving United to drop a division when he joined Notts County, he scored 28 goals in 30 games as the other black-and-whites lifted the Second Division title. Totalling 52 goals for County all told and then 71 for Leeds City, he remained a feared striker. Jack was also often injured, once dubbed, "the most injured man in football". He broke his leg twice and fractured his arm, at St James' Park being out of action for several weeks as well. As a manager, the secretary-manager type of the old school, he took Fulham to the FA Cup semi-final during his 13 years in charge at Craven Cottage. Jack also fashioned a side to eventually take the Londoners into the First Division, only to die before his task was achieved.

Appearances & Goals:
Debut v Middlesbrough (h) 16 March 1912
FL: 17 app 6 gls
Total: 17 app 6 gls

Honours:
1 FL app 1914/3 SnL app 1912/FL div 2 champs 1914/WLg champs 1918/FL Long Service medal 1945.

PEDDIE John Hope 1897-1902

Centre-forward
5'11"
b. Glasgow, 21 March 1877
d. Detroit (USA), October 1928

Career: Cathkin Ath/Benburb/Third Lanark June 1895/UNITED trial Sept 1897, pmt Nov 1897 £135/Manchester Utd June 1902/Plymouth Argyle May 1903/Manchester Utd May 1904/Heart of Midlothian Jan 1907/5th King's Own Scottish Borderers Sept 1908/Vickers Works (Can) 1915.

After shining in a friendly match for Third Lanark against United during April 1897, United kept a close eye on Glaswegian Jock Peddie who showed goal prowess by grabbing over 25 goals in less than 50 games at Cathkin Park. It wasn't long before he was on Tyneside and immediately the free-scoring poacher started to belt home goals in a black-and-white shirt. Peddie was a potent attacker, often scoring from distance, having a shot of colossal power, reckoned to be the hardest ever seen at St James' Park during those late Victorian days, even once shaking the goal net pegs loose with one terrific shot against Loughborough during 1898. Perhaps Jock can be regarded as United's first centre-forward hero figure, contemporary reports noting he was extremely popular with supporters, having what can be regarded today as a cult following. His power in attack was the difference between Newcastle staying in Division Two, or tasting the top level for the first time in 1898, Peddie top scorer for the Geordies as they won promotion. At times moody, nonchalant and rebellious, the Scot appeared in the club's inaugural First Division fixture, but was often was in trouble with the club's hierarchy for a number of misdemeanours; refusing to play, being absent from training and ultimately being suspended sine-die in 1900 (later lifted). Peddie though could always claim to be doing his job on the field, 76 goals in 136 games is a fine record by any footballers' standard. By the time he had left to Old Trafford, many moaned at his departure. Jock scored more goals for Manchester United, 58 in 121 matches, and was on the verge of a Scottish cap on five occasions in trial contests boasting a strike-rate of 53% for his two English clubs. After a period with the pioneers of Queen of the South (King's Own Scottish Borderers), Peddie eventually emigrated to North America where he spent the rest of his life. Moving to Montreal in 1914, he was employed with the Canadian Vickers shipbuilding company as a shipyard store-keeper, later moving to Detroit in the mid-Twenties.

Appearances & Goals:
Debut v Newton Heath (a) 13 November 1897
FL: 126 app 71 gls
FAC: 10 app 5 gls
Total: 136 app 76 gls

Honours:
Scot trial app 1896-1906/FL div 2 prom 1898, 1906.

PENMAN William Salmond Thomson 1963-1966

Inside-left
5'10"
b. Coaltown of Wemyss, Fife, 7 August 1939

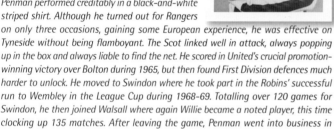

Career: Novar Star 1955/St Andrews Swifts 1956/Rangers June 1958/St Andrews Utd 1959/Rangers 1960/ UNITED April 1963 £11,500/Swindon Town Sept 1966 £9,800/Walsall Aug 1970 £6,000/Dundalk May 1973/ Cheltenham Town manager 1973/Seattle Sounders (USA) 1974.

As Newcastle challenged for the Second Division title in seasons 1963-64 and 1964-65, Willie Penman performed creditably in a black-and-white striped shirt. Although he turned out for Rangers on only three occasions, gaining some European experience, he was effective on Tyneside without being flamboyant. The Scot linked well in attack, always popping up in the box and always liable to find the net. He scored in United's crucial promotion-winning victory over Bolton during 1965, but then found First Division defences much harder to unlock. He moved to Swindon where he took part in the Robins' successful run to Wembley in the League Cup during 1968-69. Totalling over 120 games for Swindon, he then joined Walsall where again Willie became a noted player, this time clocking up 135 matches. After leaving the game, Penman went into business in Walsall employed for a sports company as a sales agent.

Appearances & Goals:
Debut v Charlton Athletic (h) 3 April 1963 (1 goal)
FL: 62(1) app 18 gls
FAC: 2 app 0 gls
Total: 64(1) app 18 gls

Honours:
FL div 2 champs 1965/FL div 3 prom 1969/FLC winner 1969/SJC winner 1960.

PEPPITT Sydney 1941

Outside-right
5'9"
b. Hanley, Stoke on Trent, 8 September 1919
d. Stoke on Trent, 25 December 1992

Career: Stoke City amat Sept 1934, prof Sept 1936 £10 (Middlesbrough war-guest 1940-41)(UNITED war-guest 1941-42)(Linfield war-guest 1941-42)(Millwall war-guest 1943-44)(Queens Park Rangers war-guest 1945-46)/ Resumed with Stoke City 1946/Port Vale May 1950 £4,000/Worcester City 1951 to 1953.

A former England schools player in 1934, Syd Peppitt appeared twice during wartime football for the Magpies, in a double header with local rivals Sunderland during the autumn of 1941. Attending the same school in Hanley as the legendary Stanley Matthews, Peppitt developed through Stoke's ranks alongside the maestro, making his Football League debut as a 17-year-old. He was a versatile forward, appearing

across the front line and was highly rated in the years just before the Second World War. In the Potteries he was regarded "as another Matthews", but the war ruined what could have been a headlining career. By the time he had left the Victoria Ground in 1950, Syd had totalled 161 matches for Stoke, netting 60 goals, still a first-rate return. Although normally an outside-right, he played in the number 11 shirt on the opposite touchline in both games for United.

Appearances & Goals:
Debut v Sunderland (h) 25 October 1941 (FLN)
War: 2 app 0 gls
Total: 2 app 0 gls

Honours:
Eng sch-youth app/NIC winner 1942/FL div 3(S)(WLg) champs 1946 (1 app).

PERCH James Robert 2010-2013

Centre-back or Midfield
5'11"
b. Mansfield, 28 September 1985

Career: Drezden Colts (Mansfield)/Norwich City jnr/Nottingham Forest jnr, prof Nov 2002/UNITED July 2010 £1.5m/Wigan Ath July 2013 £700,000.

Purchased by manager Chris Hughton following Newcastle's promotion back to the Premier League in the summer of 2010, James Perch at 24 years of age had gained experience over six seasons of regular action in Nottingham Forest's line-up, usually in a defensive role. With over 200 games to his name and having been a rival to the Black'n'Whites in the promotion race, Perch found himself on the fringe of selection during his opening months on Tyneside. Quick into the tackle, he was booked in his first five outings wearing Magpie colours then rarely got a look in as United started a new era at the top and it appeared that recently installed boss Alan Pardew, as well as the fans, saw Perch surplus to requirements. But the player refused to be discarded and knuckled down to work hard at his game and show he was worth a place in United's squad. Used ostensibly as a utility player across the back-line or in a midfield holding role when called upon, James gave a series of committed displays in 2011-12, often showing a composed and cool head. Deputising for skipper Coloccini, or slipping into the full-back or midfield berths, he won over the Toon support following a five-star performance in central defence against a star-studded Liverpool attack led by Andy Carroll. During the summer of 2013, Perch moved back to the Championship when he joined relegated Wigan Athletic.

Appearances & Goals:
Debut v Manchester United (a) 16 August 2010
PL: 41(24) app 1 gl
FAC: 3 app 0 gls
FLC: 4 app 0 gls
Euro: 8(1) app 0 gls
Total: 56(25) app 1 gl

Honours:
FL div 1 prom 2008.

PHILLIPSON Thomas William 1919-1921

Centre-forward
5'8"
b. Ryton, near Newcastle upon Tyne, 31 October 1898
d. Wolverhampton, 19 November 1965

Career: Winlaton/Scotswood May 1914/UNITED Dec 1919 £500/Swindon Town May 1921 £500/Wolverhampton Wand Dec 1923 £1,000/Sheffield Utd March 1928 £2,600/ Bilston Utd player-manager July 1930/Walsall Aug 1931 to May 1932.

A broad-shouldered, compact centre-forward, Tom Phillipson was noted for his first time shooting and crowd rousing sprint in a chase. Phillipson was a schoolboy star on Tyneside, recorded as scoring no fewer than 14 goals (out of 15) in a single fixture, and getting another 10 in his next

T.W.PHILLIPSON

match! Capped by England as a lad during 1913 and at St James' Park when the club was overflowing with potential stars, Tom was a promising talent in United's reserve side. However, he never quite grasped the opportunity he was given at Gallowgate immediately after the Great War and had to prove his worth elsewhere. Developing into a forceful goal-getter, he showed in first-team action with Swindon he could be a threat in nearly 100 appearances and reached his peak at Molineux, signed by his fellow Geordie and ex-United player, George Jobey. With Wolves, Tom cracked home 111 goals in only 159 games, netting a club record 37 league and cup goals during season 1925-26. He was a huge favourite in the Midlands town, once scoring 23 goals in 13 consecutive games, and five against Bradford City, as well as four against Barnsley. The Tynesider also did well at Bramall Lane, boosting his career total to over 160 goals. One retirement, Phillipson settled in Wolverhampton, entering local business and politics. A pillar of the establishment, Tom became Lord Mayor in 1938 for an extended period. During World War One he served as a sergeant in the West Yorkshire Regiment in Russia.

Appearances & Goals:
Debut v Everton (a) 24 January 1920
FL: 14 app 4 gls
FAC: 1 app 0 gls
Total: 15 app 4 gls

Honours:
Eng sch-youth app/FL div 3(N) champs 1924.

PINGEL Frank Mortensen 1989

Centre-forward
6'1"
b. Risskov (Denmark), 9 May 1964

Career: IHF Aarhus (Den)/Skovbakken (Den)/AGF Aarhus (Den) jnr 1984, prof July 1987/UNITED Jan 1989 £260,000/Brondby IF (Den) July 1989 £200,000/1860 Munich (Ger) Sept 1991 £250,000/Brondby IF (Den) cs 1992/Bursaspor (Trk) July 1993/Fenerbahce SK (Trk) June 1994 £300,000/Lille OSC (Fr) 1995/Aarhus Fremad (Den) Sept 1995 to June 1997/Herning Fremad (FC Midtjyland) (Den) coach 2001/AGF Aarhus (Den) masseur & physio Jan 2006 to March 2008.

A well-travelled striker, Frank Pingel was 24 years old when he joined United to team up alongside Brazilian, Mirandinha in a cosmopolitan-looking Magpie attack. Strong and physical, Pingel was a one-time boxing champion in Denmark. However, manager Jim Smith only briefly tried his overseas strike force during the 1988-89 season, before Frank became the target of a frustrated Gallowgate crowd. He soon moved back to his native country where the Dane developed into a useful centre-forward, firstly winning domestic championship honours and international caps before heading for the Bundesliga and for Turkey, where he became a popular character. Frank boasts a good record in a Danish shirt, netting five goals in his 11 international matches. He afterwards settled back in Denmark, working as an administrator for AGF and a stadium inspector, later training to become a physio.

Appearances & Goals:
Debut v Aston Villa (a) 14 January 1989 (sub)
FL: 13(1) app 1 gl
Total: 13(1) app 1 gl

Honours:
11 Den caps 1992-94/Den Lg champs 1990, 1991/Den Cup winner 1988.

PISTONE Alessandro 1997-2000

Left-back
5'11"
b. Milan (Italy), 27 July 1975

Career: ASD Alcione (It) 1984/AC Milan jnr (It) 1986/Aldini (It)/Vicenza (It) jnr April 1992, prof Aug 1995 (Bologna (It) loan 1993-94)(AS Solbiadese (It) loan 1993-94)(AC Crevalcore (It) loan 1994-95)/Internazionale (It) Nov 1995 £1.5m/UNITED July 1997 £4.3m (AC Venezia (It) loan 1998-99)/Everton July 2000 £3m to May 2007/Middlesbrough trial Aug 2007/ Watford trial Sept 2007/RAEC Mons (Bel) Dec 2007 to cs 2008 when he retired due to injury/ Later, AS Varese (It) asst-coach.

One of the brightest prospects in Italy's Serie A, Alessandro Pistone was almost 22 years old when he arrived on Tyneside during July 1997 for a £4.3m fee. A talented defender able to operate in the centre of the defence, or at left-back as well as in a wing-back role, Pistone had been a target of the Magpies for a considerable period. A change in management at the San Siro alerted United that he may be available and the player was delighted to move to the Premiership. A previous captain of the Italian Under-21 side, he was tipped for a full call-up for his country and gained experience at the highest level, both in Italian football and in European competition. Alessandro helped Inter reach the UEFA Cup final in 1997 before deciding to relocate to England. Showing the ability to move fast in attack and in recovery, he was cultured on the ball and naturally right-footed, but who played more often than not on the left flank. Pistone could be exciting when going forward and quickly became a favourite of the Geordie crowd, during 1997-98 providing plenty of attacking bursts down the left touchline. However once Kenny Dalglish departed and Ruud Gullit took over, his second season on Tyneside proved a disaster. He was rarely given a chance by the new manager along with other seasoned professionals, and had to wait until Bobby Robson arrived before his career got back on course. Then when playing to top form, Pistone was unlucky to break his leg in a Tyne versus Wear clash during February 2000, flattened by a late tackle by Gavin McCann. At Goodison Park his stay was similar to that at Gallowgate, having a couple of good campaigns in 2003-04 and 2004-05 before two knee injuries kept him on the sidelines for several months. He still managed to register 117 games for the Toffees before moving to Belgium where an Achilles tendon injury forced him to retire. His father Ernesto Pistone played football in France, while Alessandro took part in the 1996 Olympics in Atlanta. Following retirement Pistone returned to Lombardy and set up a specialised catering business and a restaurant in the Farinami district of Milan. He was also a keen card player, at times part of the Italian poker circuit.

Appearances & Goals:
Debut v Sheffield Wednesday (h) 9 August 1997
PL: 45(1) app 1 gl
FAC: 8 app 0 gls
FLC: 1(1) app 0 gls
Euro: 7 app 0 gls
Total: 61(2) app 1 gl

Honours:
11 It u21 app 1995-97/OG 1996/FAC final 1998/It div 2 prom 1995/UEFA Cup final 1997.

PORTER Leslie 1944-1946

Right-half
5'9"
b. Felling, Gateshead, 5 May 1923
d. Middlesbrough, November 2002

Career: Redheugh Steelworks/UNITED amat Feb 1944, prof Sept 1944/Hereford Utd Oct 1946/York City March 1949 £175 to 1953/North Shields June 1954.

Starting as a winger, Leslie Porter took part in three seasons of wartime football for Newcastle, making his debut during the 1943-44 campaign in a local Tyne versus Wear derby. A diminutive wing-half in midfield, it was with York City that he was elevated to the Football League scene in 1949, eventually totalling 38 games for the Tykes in the Third Division North.

Appearances & Goals:
Debut v Sunderland (h) 22 April 1944 (FLN)
War: 11 app 2 gls
Total: 11 app 2 gls

NEWCASTLE UNITED
The Ultimate Who's Who 1881-2014

P

PORTER William 1941-1943

Left-back
5'9"
b. Durham, 23 November 1923
d. Co Durham, 1975 (Q1)

Career: Shotton Colliery/UNITED amat March 1941, prof Sept 1942
(Horden CW loan)(Middlesbrough war-guest)/Hartlepools Utd Sept 1943 to cs 1947.

Billy Porter took part in a handful of Football League North fixtures during World War Two. At full-back or half-back he filled in during the 1942-43 season but moved to the Victoria Ground, Hartlepool in an attempt to secure a first-team place. He appeared in 29 wartime games for 'Pool and on peace being restored also managed to claim two matches in the FA Cup and in Division Three North.

Appearances & Goals:
Debut v Leeds United (h) 26 September 1942 (FLN)
War: 6 app 0 gls
Total: 6 app 0 gls

PRICE Arthur 1939-1945

Wing-half
5'6"
b. Rowlands Gill, near Gateshead, 12 January 1921
d. Gateshead, June 1995

Career: Spen Black & White/UNITED amat Aug 1939, prof Aug 1940/Consett Aug 1945 free/Leeds Utd amat Sept 1945, prof May 1946 (Newburn loan 1945-46) to cs 1947.

Red-haired and only 5'6" tall, Arthur Price was a compact and neat midfielder who played on either side of the field. He had two good seasons in United's wartime ranks, during 1940-41 and 1941-42, although he was registered with the club for five years, war service restricted his time in the region. Moving to Elland Road for a period, he worked as a maintenance engineer at Hebburn when with Leeds. Price was a regular in the 1945-46 wartime campaign then recorded seven games for the Tykes in senior football before concentrating on a career in engineering.

Appearances & Goals:
Debut v Halifax Town (h) 29 May 1940 (FLNE)
War: 43 app 1 gl
Total: 43 app 1 gl

PRIOR George Kenneth 1952-1954, 1956-1957

Outside-left
5'7"
b. Newcastle upon Tyne, 13 October 1932

Career: Cambois Jnrs/Sunderland amat 1950/ UNITED jnr, prof March 1952/Millwall May 1954 £100/ UNITED July 1956 £1,250/Berwick Rangers Jan 1957/ North Shields 1959/Horden Colliery 1963/Ashington cs 1964, becoming manager 1967/Alnwick Town manager Oct 1981 to cs 1984/ Afterwards coaching locally.

Ken Prior hailed from football stock, his father George appearing for Sheffield Wednesday, and his uncle, Jack for Sunderland and Grimsby. Additionally his brother-in-law was United full-back, Bobby Cowell. Prior had two spells at St James' Park in an attempt to break into the senior side, but on each occasion found the talent of Bobby Mitchell blocking his path for the Number 11 shirt. Ken was still a good footballer despite his lack of first team action on Tyneside, playing on 63 occasions for Millwall during his period in the Third Division South. Fast and accurate with his passes and crosses, his best season wearing the black-and-white jersey was during 1951-52 when he deputised for Mitchell on six occasions. Ken later settled in the North East, a prominent official in local football for over two decades and continuing to play football into his fifties. For a period he was a scout for Jack Charlton when boss at Ayresome Park and was employed as an electrician for the National Coal Board, living in Ashington.

Appearances & Goals:
Debut v Middlesbrough (h) 11 April 1952
FL: 10 app 3 gls
Total: 10 app 3 gls

PUDAN Albert Ernest 1906-1909

Left-back
5'11"
b. Canning Town, London 1881 (Q3)
d. Smithfield, London, 22 December 1956

Career: Clapton 1899/West Ham Utd cs 1900/Bristol Rovers July 1902/UNITED July 1906 £150/Leicester Fosse May 1909 £125/ Huddersfield Town secretary-manager Aug 1910/Leicester Fosse (player) April 1912/ Retired 1914/Leicester City director 1919 to Feb 1940 (Chairman 1929-31).

Known as 'Dick' throughout his career, Pudan was at his peak when on Tyneside, reaching the FA Cup final with the Magpies and appearing, albeit on only a handful of occasions, in United's title side of 1909. He was an excellent passer of the ball and possessed an intelligent footballing brain. Plucked from the Southern League at Bristol Rovers where he appeared in over 100 matches, Dick replaced England international Jack Carr for the 1907-08 season, but was himself replaced by Tony Whitson the following year. Pudan lost his place after an uncomfortable showing in that season's FA Cup final against Wolves, when really he should not have played at all, being bed-ridden a few days before the game with what was called, "a bout of boils". On leaving Tyneside, Pudan was in charge of Huddersfield Town when they entered Football League action, and later had a long spell as director, and Chairman for a period, at Filbert Street; one the first ex-players to reach the boardroom of a top club. He was also a successful businessman in the East Midlands running a hosiery manufacturing company Pudan & Burridge Ltd. Albert died when in London, at St Bartholomew's Hospital.

Appearances & Goals:
Debut v Blackburn Rovers (h) 26 October 1907
FL: 24 app 0 gls
FAC: 6 app 0 gls
Total: 30 app 0 gls

Honours:
FAC final 1908/FL champs 1909 (3 app)/SnL champs 1905.

PUGH Kevin John 1977-1982

Midfield
5'7"
b. Corbridge, Northumberland, 11 October 1960

Career: UNITED jnr Jan 1977, prof Oct 1978/Gateshead Aug 1982 free/Blyth Spartans 1982-83/Darlington Sept 1983/ Gateshead 1983/Sporting Charleroi (Belg) Aug 1984/RAA Louvieroise (Belg) June 1992/UBS Franks Borains (Bel) July 1996/Union Lower Sambre Auvelais (Bel) July 1997 to July 1999.

Talented teenager Kevin Pugh was chased by a host of clubs when a schoolboy on Tyneside, including Nottingham Forest, Aston Villa, Derby and United. Joining his local club, Pugh was sturdy and vigorous on the field. He made several headlines in reserve football for United and was frequently on the verge of a first-team call-up as the Eighties began. But Kevin had to be content with a single appearance for Newcastle, as a substitute for Imre Varadi during season 1981-82. When he was with Gateshead, Pugh helped win the Northern Premier League championship in 1983 and was called up for the England non-league squad. He later settled in Belgium and had a good career on the Continent, notably with the Zebra's of Sporting Charleroi. Kevin pulled on their black-and-white stripes almost 200 times, alongside Philippe Albert for a period. Pugh later resided in Belgium, running a coffee shop in Charleroi.

Appearances & Goals:
Debut v Chelsea (a) 7 November 1981 (sub)
FL: 0(1) app 0 gls
Total: 0(1) app 0 gls

PUNTON William Hamilton 1954-1958

Outside-left
5'9"
b. Glenkinchie, East Lothian, 9 May 1934

Career: Bredalbane/Portadown Aug 1953/
UNITED Feb 1954 £6,000/Southend Utd July
1958 cash-exch deal for J McGuigan/
Norwich City July 1959/Sheffield Utd Nov
1966 £7,500/Scunthorpe Utd Jan 1968
£3,000/Yarmouth Town player-coach June
1969, becoming manager May 1974/Diss
Town manager May 1990 to May 1995.

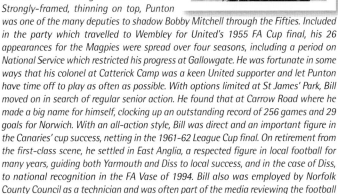

*Unorthodox in method, Bill Punton arrived
on Tyneside from Ireland after club scouts
saw him score four goals in one match.
Strongly-framed, thinning on top, Punton
was one of the many deputies to shadow Bobby Mitchell through the Fifties. Included
in the party which travelled to Wembley for United's 1955 FA Cup final, his 26
appearances for the Magpies were spread over four seasons, including a period on
National Service which restricted his progress at Gallowgate. He was fortunate in some
ways that his colonel at Catterick Camp was a keen United supporter and let Punton
have time off to play as often as possible. With options limited at St James' Park, Bill
moved on in search of regular senior action. He found that at Carrow Road where he
made a big name for himself, clocking up an outstanding record of 256 games and 29
goals for Norwich. With an all-action style, Bill was direct and an important figure in
the Canaries' cup success, netting in the 1961-62 League Cup final. On retirement from
the first-class scene, he settled in East Anglia, a respected figure in local football for
many years, guiding both Yarmouth and Diss to local success, and in the case of Diss,
to national recognition in the FA Vase of 1994. Bill also was employed by Norfolk
County Council as a technician and was often part of the media reviewing the football
scene around Norwich. He also became a popular Carrow Road match-day host.*

Appearances & Goals:
Debut v Manchester City (h) 3 April 1954
FL: 23 app 1 gl
FAC: 2 app 0 gls
Others: 1 app 0 gls
Total: 26 app 1 gl

Honours:
FLC winner 1962/FL div 3 prom 1960/FAV winner 1994(m).

PYKE George Woolston 1913-1922

Centre-forward
5'11"
b. Gateshead, 26 August 1893
d. Whitley Bay, 20 March 1977

Career: Rutherford College (Newcastle)/UNITED amat
March 1913, prof Nov 1913 £20 (Durham City war-guest
1918-19)(Scotswood war-guest 1919)/Blyth Spartans
Aug 1922 free to 1927/Local amateur football.

*An extremely popular character with supporters at
St James' Park immediately after World War One being
something of a local hero, George Pyke was one of many
budding forwards to attempt to claim a senior jersey in
those post-war seasons of 1919-20 to 1921-22. After netting
four goals in a first-eleven friendly against St Bernard's, he became
a serious challenger to Andy Smailes and then Neil Harris. However, George only
graduated to the first-eleven on a few occasions each campaign. But in reserve
football Pyke was a pleasure to watch; tall and a threat in attack, he ravaged North
Eastern League defences, once registering all five goals as Sunderland were felled 5-
2. Although good enough for Football League standard, George decided to remain in
the North East when it became obvious he wasn't going to get an extended
opportunity at Gallowgate. He joined Blyth and proceeded to net 136 goals for the
Spartans, many playing alongside his brother. During the First World War, George
joined up in October 1915 and served in the Middlesex Regiment, as part of the
acclaimed Footballer's Battalion. A corporal, Pyke survived the Somme offensive and
returned to the North East during 1918. On retiring he resided in Whitley Bay.*

Appearances & Goals:
Debut v Derby County (h) 24 September 1919
FL: 13 app 3 gls
Total: 13 app 3 gls

QUINN Charles 1893-1894, 1895-1896

Outside-right
b. Newcastle upon Tyne, c1875

Career: Local football/UNITED 1893/Manchester City Dec
1894/Trafalgar (Newcastle)/UNITED Aug 1895/Blyth July
1896/Gateshead NER Aug 1897/[Ashington Dec 1899].

*As Newcastle United entered the Football League in 1893,
Charlie Quinn was a regular in the club's forward line
during that historic first season. Appearing mainly on the
right wing, but also in the inside and outside-left
channels too, he was a consistent player for the
campaign, but afterwards fell out of favour. Quinn moved
to pastures new at the end of 1894, joining the newly
named Manchester City club but failed to gain a place.
He then headed back to his native Tyneside and rejoined
the Magpies for the 1895-96 season making the first-
eleven just once in that programme.*

Appearances & Goals:
Debut v Burton Swifts (a) 23 September 1893
FL: 24 app 5 gls
FAC: 2 app 0 gls
Total: 26 app 5 gls

QUINN Michael 1989-1992

Centre-forward
5'10"
b. Liverpool, 2 May 1962

Career: Nevites Close Jnrs/Huyton Boys/
Tranmere Rovers/Derby Co jnr July 1978/
Wigan Ath Sept 1979 free/Stockport Co
July 1982 free/Oldham Ath Jan 1984
£52,000/Portsmouth March 1986
£150,000/UNITED Aug 1989 £680,000/
Coventry City loan Nov 1992, pmt Dec
1992 £250,000 (Watford loan 1994-95)
(Portsmouth loan 1994-95)(Plymouth
Argyle loan 1994-95)/Hong Kong May
1995/PAOK (Gr) July 1995 to Feb 1996.

*A prolific goalscorer since he made an
impact with Wigan and Stockport in the
lower divisions, Mick Quinn moved north
from Fratton Park when at his peak aged
27 and having proved himself in the
Premier League, the fee decided by a
Football League tribunal. United were
forced to pay more than they wanted at £680,000 for the striker who had bagged 67
goals in 139 games for Portsmouth, but in the end the club had signed a player worth
every penny. The son of a Mersey docker, the chirpy Scouser immediately began to
repay his fee by hitting four goals on a dramatic debut for the club against Leeds,
then continued to bag a goal every second game for the Magpies. In his opening
season as Tyneside's new Number 9 hero, Quinn almost took United back into the
First Division with his goals, netting 36 all told in the campaign, the club just missing
out on promotion in the Play-Offs. He was the Football League's top striker in that
1989-90 campaign, and one of only a handful of Newcastle players to total over 30
goals in a single season. United supporters took to Quinn and his down-to-earth jovial
character from the start, and Mick loved the life-style of being top-dog on Tyneside.
Although a touch over fighting-fit on the field, the Toon crowd inventively came up
with a popular terrace melody: "He's fat, he's round, a number nine we've found, Micky
Quinn, Micky Quinn." An opportunist striker and nicknamed 'The Mighty Quinn', he
was expert at turning and finding the target in the tightest of situations and even
with his back to goal. Also the Second Division's top scorer in 1986-87 (22 goals) with
Pompey, Mick looked deceptively lazy in style, once described by manager Jim Smith
as, "an ugly duckling player", but Quinn possessed a deadly eye for goal when in the
danger zone. The Merseysider's career was also occasionally littered with controversial
moments, including a period of 21 days in Winchester Prison when with Pompey for
a motoring offence during January 1987. On the arrival of Kevin Keegan as boss at
Gallowgate, Quinn was sidelined with a long-term knee ligament injury (when scoring*

Q

against his former club Portsmouth) and once fit again was overlooked in favour of David Kelly and record purchase Andy Cole. At odds with Keegan on more than one occasion, he only appeared sparingly during United's 1993 promotion season and moved to Coventry. By the time he ended his domestic career, Quinn had totalled 263 senior goals in 588 matches, an excellent 45% strike-rate. A keen racehorse enthusiast, during July 1996 he joined Mick Channon's training complex in Hampshire as an assistant-trainer then set-up his own stables at Wantage in the summer of 1997. Mick also entered the media covering football, a popular face and voice on Sky and TalkSport. Quinn was once at Liverpool on trials as a youngster while his grandfather Luigi Silvano (Lew Sullivan) was a noted boxer on Merseyside. His younger brother Sean was on the books of Liverpool, Portsmouth and Oldham.

Appearances & Goals:
Debut v Leeds United (h) 19 August 1989 (4 goals)
FL: 112(5) app 59 gls
FAC: 7 app 4 gls
FLC: 7(2) app 0 gls
Others: 6(1) app 8 gls
Total: 132(8) app 71 gls

Honours:
FL div 1 champs 1993 (5 app)/FL div 2 prom 1987/PFA ToS (d2) 1987, 1990.

QUINN Wayne Richard 2001-2003

Left-back
5'10"
b. Hayle, Cornwall, 19 November 1976
Career: Sheffield Utd jnr, prof Dec 1994/UNITED loan Jan 2001, pmt Feb 2001 £1m (Sheffield Utd loan 2002-03)/ West Ham Utd loan Sept 2003, pmt Oct 2003 free (Walsall loan 2003-04) to June 2004/Plymouth Argyle trial Sept 2004/ Oldham Ath trial Dec 2004/Hayle Town 2005/Penzance player-asst-manager 2005/Hayle Town player-asst-manager April 2008, becoming manager/Falmouth Town March 2012/St Buryan/Newquay 2012-13/ Mousehole player-manager April 2013.

It was at the second attempt that full-back Wayne Quinn joined the Gallowgate set-up in 2001, a previous deal collapsing during 1998 due to a failed medical. Having appeared against the Magpies for Sheffield United in two high-profile FA Cup matches during 1997-98 and 1999-2000 (including a semi-final at Old Trafford), 24-year-old Quinn had showed enough in his displays for the Tykes that he had the potential to fill a somewhat problem left-back slot for Newcastle. With Italian Pistone departing, Andy Griffin injured and Didier Domi walking out, Quinn joined United for a £1m fee half-way through the 2000-01 season. It was a great opportunity for the Cornishman who in 179 games for the Blades showed he was comfortable on the ball but who perhaps lacked top-class defending know-how. Yet his all-round game was good enough to earn him an England 'B' cap. After some encouraging displays, groin and thigh injuries placed Quinn in the treatment room and veteran Robbie Elliott replaced him for the 2001-02 season then Olivier Bernard came on the scene and Quinn's chance at the big-time was lost. Wayne's career then went rapidly from the highs of the Premier League to football in the Cornwall Combination. Quinn was unable to secure another opportunity in senior football and returned to his indigenous West Country where he served local clubs for a decade.

Appearances & Goals:
Debut v Coventry City (h) 13 January 2001
PL: 14(1) app 0 gls
FAC: 0(1) app 0 gls
FLC: 1 app 0 gls
Euro: 6(1) app 1 gl
Total: 21(3) app 1 gl

Honours:
1 Eng B app 1998/2 Eng u21 app 1998.

RAFFERTY William Henry 1979-1980

Striker
5'11"
b. Glasgow, 30 December 1950
Career: Port Glasgow Rovers 1967/Coventry City July 1968/Blackpool Oct 1972 £40,000/Plymouth Argyle March 1974 £25,000/Carlisle Utd May 1976 £20,000/ Wolverhampton Wand March 1978 £125,000/ UNITED Oct 1979 £175,000/Portsmouth Dec 1980 £80,000/Bournemouth Feb 1984 £4,000/SC Farense (Ptg) July 1985/Louletano DC (Ptg) cs 1987/ Retired c1990/Carlisle Utd asst-coach to 1997.

Billy Rafferty arrived at St James' Park with a good scoring record both at Carlisle and Plymouth, where he formed a productive partnership with future England star, Paul Mariner. Netting 40 goals in 101 games for the Home Park club, he then became a favourite at Brunton Park before joining Wolves for a big fee. Rafferty made an uncertain start at St James' Park though, the ground he had made his senior bow for Coventry as a teenager, forming a strikeforce with Peter Withe and Bobby Shinton. After that, the Scot however, if only for a few weeks, did look as though he may become a noted striker. He was tall and leggy and able to cause trouble to defenders, but his relative success was short lived. Billy never scored enough goals over a sustained period for the Magpies and he moved south to Fratton Park where he was a central figure in Portsmouth's Third Division title victory. Rafferty netted over 40 times in 111 games for Pompey before concluding his first-class career on the south coast with Bournemouth then in Portugal. Billy settled in the Carlisle area where he ran a Health & Fitness club as well as Soccer Schools for youngsters and a corporate indoor league, Astro Soccer Sixes. His brother Stewart appeared in the Scottish League, notably for Motherwell and Dundee.

Appearances & Goals:
Debut v Cambridge United (h) 27 October 1979
FL: 34(5) app 6 gls
FAC: 1 app 0 gls
FLC: 2 app 2 gls
Total: 37(5) app 8 gls

Honours:
FL div 3 champs 1983/FL div 3 prom 1975/Ptg div 2 prom 1986, 1988/PFA ToS (d3) 1975.

RAINE James Edmundson 1903-1906

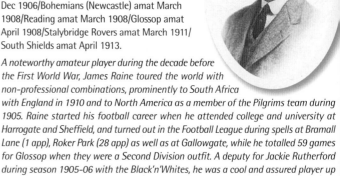

Outside-right
6'0"
b. Newcastle upon Tyne, 3 March 1886
d. Davos (Switzerland), 4 September 1928
Career: Trinity College (Harrogate)/Rydal Mount (Colwyn Bay)/Sheffield University/Scotswood 1903/ UNITED amat Nov 1903/Sheffield Utd amat July 1904/UNITED amat Aug 1904/Sunderland amat Dec 1906/Bohemians (Newcastle) amat March 1908/Reading amat March 1908/Glossop amat April 1908/Stalybridge Rovers amat March 1911/ South Shields amat April 1913.

A noteworthy amateur player during the decade before the First World War, James Raine toured the world with non-professional combinations, prominently to South Africa with England in 1910 and to North America as a member of the Pilgrims team during 1905. Raine started his football career when he attended college and university at Harrogate and Sheffield, and turned out in the Football League during spells at Bramall Lane (1 app), Roker Park (28 app) as well as at Gallowgate, while he totalled 59 games for Glossop when they were a Second Division outfit. A deputy for Jackie Rutherford during season 1905-06 with the Black'n'Whites, he was a cool and assured player up front, good enough to be a regular for his country, on the field for the very first England amateur international against France in 1906, a resounding 15-0 victory. James also took part in the prestige Amateurs versus Professionals showpiece in 1906-07. Raine was also a proficient cricketer (3 app for Northumberland County) and rugby player (for Percy Park), one of the region's finest sportsmen of the Edwardian era. He later settled in the Jesmond suburb of Newcastle, a successful businessman in the North East, Managing Director of an iron and steel manufacturer in Derwenthaugh. Raine served with the Durham Light Infantry with a rank of major during World War One while his uncle, Tom Raine, was also a celebrated amateur in the region, also playing cricket for Northumberland.

Appearances & Goals:
Debut v Middlesbrough (a) 3 March 1906
FL: 4 app 1 gl
Total: 4 app 1 gl

Honours:
10 Eng amat app 1907-11/2 unoff Eng app 1910/Eng trial app 1907/1 FL app 1908.

RAINNIE Alexander 1919-1920

Left-half
5'10"
b. Banff, 22 June 1891
d. Co Durham, 1965 (Q2)

Career: Dumbarton/South Shields amat Jan 1919/
UNITED May 1919/Darlington July 1920 £15/
Ashington Aug 1923 to June 1924.

*A stylish half-back, Alex Rainnie gave determined
performances for South Shields every time United's
directors watched him during the Northern Victory
League. Although not a youngster, he earned a
contract at St James' Park in the weeks immediately following the conclusion to the
competition, but found opportunities very limited, being one of several half-backs in
contention for a place. Alex never threatened first choice Jock Finlay, only once
deputising for the Scot, although he was chosen for the North Eastern select side to
play the Central League during 1921-22. Rainnie later appeared, again mainly as a
reserve, for Darlington (8 app) and for Ashington (1 app), in the Colliers earliest
Football League seasons as the Twenties unfolded. During the hostilities he served as
a Chief Petty Officer in the Royal Navy and remained in the Tyne reserve after the
hostilities. A Scot, the Rainnie family settled in Hebburn before the war, Alex working
as a shipwright.*

Appearances & Goals:
Debut v Everton (a) 24 January 1920
FL: 1 app 0 gls
Total: 1 app 0 gls

RAMAGE Peter Iain 1996-2008

Centre-half or Full-back
6'3"
b. Ashington, 22 November 1983

Career: Cramlington Jnrs/UNITED jnr cs 1996, prof July
2003/Queens Park Rangers June 2008 free (Crystal Palace
loan 2011-12)(Birmingham City loan 2011-12)/ Crystal
Palace Aug 2012 free (Barnsley loan 2013-14, 2014-15).

*The son of a local rugby player and referee, Peter Ramage
was raised in Berwick then moved to Whitley Bay and
started his career with United from school football when
he joined the club's Academy in 1996. Operating at mainly
centre-back in the Magpies' junior and reserves ranks,
manager Graeme Souness gave the emerging youngster a chance in United's line-up
as a reshuffle took place during season 2004-05 when Hughes, Butt and Jenas were
injured. He soon knew what the top level was all about, on his full debut facing Ryan
Giggs at Old Trafford in front of almost 68,000. Committed and rarely to shirk from a
challenge, Peter had a good run in the side during 2005-06 and 2006-07, usually at
right-back where he appeared most as a senior professional, but also at centre-back
and occasionally left-back when the boss had to patch up his rearguard. Tall and
slender, Ramage was sidelined with a hamstring tear, then a cruciate knee injury, and
didn't quite have the pure footballing ability to bring the ball out of defence in the
top-level of the Premier League. As a result he slipped down the pecking order on the
arrival of Sam Allardyce and Kevin Keegan as boss. Reluctantly he soon moved to
second-tier football, joining QPR in the summer of 2008 where he proceeded to help
the Londoners to promotion although he was again injured for much of that season.
Peter thereafter struggled to claim a defensive slot in Rangers' eleven and moved to
Birmingham City on a loan deal, finding a place at full-back under ex-United boss
Chris Hughton for a period before moving permanently to Crystal Palace.*

Appearances & Goals:
Debut v Olympiacos CFP (h) 16 March 2005 (sub) (UEFAC)
PL: 45(6) app 0 gls
FAC: 4(1) app 0 gls
FLC: 4(1) app 0 gls
Euro: 6(2) app 0 gls
Total: 59(10) app 0 gls

Honours:
FL ch winner 2011 (4 app).

RAMSAY Alexander Parrott 1918-1921

Outside-left
5'8"
b. Newcastle upon Tyne, 1899 (Q1)
d. Newcastle upon Tyne, 23 January 1957

Career: Spen Black'n'White Jnrs/Swalwell/UNITED
amat Dec 1918, prof May 1919 £100 (Hartlepools Utd
war-guest Jan 1919)/Queens Park Rangers June
1921/Aberaman Ath 1922.

*Alex Ramsay, who had been a gunner with the
Machine Gun Corps in France and Egypt during World
War One, made a big impact, firstly in the Northern
Victory League, then in the opening football programme
after peace had been restored. A regular on the wing during
season 1919-20, he was seen as a promising find, fast and direct
with an eye for an accurate cross. Although he was well liked by Newcastle's followers,
United's officials decided to bring in Stan Seymour from Morton as his replacement
and Ramsay left for London. With QPR, Alex only managed six outings in Division
Three South before moving to Wales. He once turned out for Hartlepool at Gallowgate
against his parent club when the visitors arrived a man short for the Northern Victory
League clash in January 1919. Ramsey afterwards resided in Newcastle, also with a
base in Alnmouth on the Northumberland coast.*

Appearances & Goals:
Debut v Liverpool (h) 4 October 1919
(v Middlesbrough (h) 29 March 1919 (NVL))
FL: 34 app 2 gls
FAC: 3 app 0 gls
War: 5 app 2 gls
Total: 42 app 4 gls

RAMSAY George (Andrew) 1890-1893

Goalkeeper
5'10"
b. Scotland

Career: Dundee Wand 1888/Dundee East End 1889/
EAST END 1890/Stockton May 1892/UNITED July
1893/Dundee Sept 1893/Dundonians April 1894.

*George Ramsay was Newcastle United's goalkeeper
for their very first Football League game against
Arsenal in 1893. That historic fixture was the only
first-class appearance the Scot made for the club,
although he took part in several of East End's
matches in friendlies before the Heaton outfit moved to St James' Park during the
summer of 1892. Ramsay departed the scene at a time of financial crisis when
directors gave players an ultimatum of taking a reduction in wages or finding a new
club. As a result the custodian headed north back to Dundee. He was described as
having, "height and weight" as well as being "remarkably sure in kicking out low shots".*

*(Note: The local press note both George and Andrew as his Christian name, however
Football League records show George.)*

Appearances & Goals:
Debut v Woolwich Arsenal (a) 2 September 1893
FL: 1 app 0 gls
Total: 1 app 0 gls

RANDALL Charles Edward 1908-1911

Inside-left
5'10"
b. Hobson, Burnopfield, Co Durham, 1884 (Q1)
d. Memetz (France), 27 July 1916

Career: Hobson Wand/UNITED April 1908 £5 (Huddersfield
Town loan 1908-09, 1909-10) (Castleford Town loan 1909-
10)/Woolwich Arsenal Sept 1911 £400/North Shields Ath
June 1914.

R

A robust forward, Charles Randall was quickly secured by United after scoring nearly 50 goals in one local amateur season. Randall made his debut during the Magpies' Football League title winning year of 1908-09, being brought back from a loan deal with then non-league Huddersfield Town. He was a popular character in the club's second string, on two occasions hitting trebles against rivals Sunderland in the North Eastern League programme of 1909-10. The following year he was with the seniors and in season 1910-11 claimed 16 outings, competing with internationals Sandy Higgins and George Wilson. But Randall found himself more often than not on the sidelines, or sent on loan to appear for the Terriers, and for neighbours Castleford; being part of the Huddersfield line-up when they eventually joined Football League action. Joining Arsenal, he clocked up 44 matches for the Gunners, again scoring a hat-trick against Sunderland, this time at the top level. Randall joined the Coldstream Guards when the Great War broke out and was a fatal casualty during the Battle of the Somme when only 32 years of age. He was killed fighting to clear a German trench complex called Dantzig Alley and is buried at that military cemetery in France.

Appearances & Goals:
Debut v Bradford City (a) 23 March 1909
FL: 18 app 6 gls
FAC: 1 app 0 gls
Total: 19 app 6 gls

Honours:
FL champs 1909 (1 app).

RANGER Nile 2008-2013

Striker
6'2"
b. Wood Green, London, 11 April 1991

Career: Barnet College/Crystal Palace jnr/ Southampton jnr 2007/Swindon Town trial cs 2008/ UNITED jnr July 2008, prof April 2009 (Barnsley loan 2011-12)(Sheffield Wed loan 2011-12) to March 2013 when he was released/Swindon Town Aug 2013 to May 2014/Blackpool Aug 2014.

Nile Ranger was raised in the Wood Green district of London and after having trials at both Crystal Palace and Tottenham, began his career at the St Mary's Stadium in Southampton. Without breaking into the senior eleven, Ranger was recognised as a talented striker who had much ability to develop. However, he went through a troubled period as a teenager in London and on the south coast and Ranger looked for a new start. Newcastle United offered the tall and slim forward that fresh beginning when he joined the club's Academy as a 17-year-old during July 2008. Nile quickly caught the eye during 2008-09 scoring 22 goals in junior and reserve ranks, being soon capped by England at youth level. Having good control of the ball, he could hold up play and possessed awareness of others around him, having that special football brain on the pitch. Ranger was elevated to first-team contention being used as a substitute during 2009-10 and 2010-11, his regular but brief appearances from the bench showing that the Londoner had a bright future. While his approach play was good, Nile though struggled in front of goal in first-team company, only scoring three times while he all too often made headlines off the pitch, and for the wrong reasons. At one point during 2012 Ranger had to answer no fewer than six charges by the FA and Courts for various offences and misdemeanours. His coach at Benton, Willie Donachie noted: "He is gifted with a physique and speed that if you weren't born with it, you can't give to somebody. Nile could be a really good player if his attitude was good." Unfortunately his approach was far from being good. Many supporters, although seeing Ranger had potential, considered that Newcastle should part company with a player seemingly unwilling to conform. He was loaned to Sheffield Wednesday where he assisted at the end of a promotion year for the Owls, scoring one of the goals which clinched elevation to the Championship. Eventually though, club and player parted company following more ill-discipline, Ranger leaving the United staff before the end of the 2012-13 season. Of his 62 appearances for the Magpies, he only started 12 matches.

Appearances & Goals:
Debut v West Bromwich Albion (a) 8 August 2009 (sub)
FL/PL: 5(46) app 2 gls
FAC: 1(4) app 0 gls
FLC: 5 app 1 gl
Euro: 1 app 0 gls
Total: 12(50) app 3 gls

Honours:
Eng sch-youth app/FL ch winner 2010/FL div 1 prom 2012 (8 app).

RANSON Raymond 1988-1993

Right-back
5'9"
b. St Helens, Lancashire, 12 June 1960

Career: Manchester City jnr 1974, prof June 1977/ Birmingham City Nov 1984 £15,000/UNITED Dec 1988 £175,000/Manchester City Jan 1993 free/ Reading July 1993 free to 1994/Witton Albion player-manager 1995 to Dec 1996/Later Coventry City Chairman Dec 2007 to March 2011.

Ray Ranson developed quickly as a youngster of note with Manchester City. A regular in the England Under-21 side, including several matches as skipper, Ray's career as a top player looked rosy until a City slump saw his fortunes nosedive. Relegated to the junior team by new manager Billy McNeill, Ranson moved to St Andrews after 235 games for the Light Blues and then to Tyneside following 158 matches for the Brummies when United were in need of experience and guile in defence. Ray had a difficult early period in a black-and-white shirt as United were relegated, but with accomplished displays, gradually won over the crowd who had been rather hasty in their criticism of the player. But then injury rocked his progress, Ray finding himself in the operating room with a pelvic injury and Achilles tendon problem. He missed over a year of action, and by the time he was back in training Kevin Keegan was in charge and a new batch of Magpie stars were in vogue. After playing a small part in the Magpies promotion season of 1992-93, it was a cue for Ranson's rather topsy-turvy career to take another turn. On leaving the first-class game he entered an insurance business based in Manchester and then made a huge success as a financial entrepreneur. He set up several companies, including REFF and R2 Asset Management and became involved in transfer rights investments within the game, a market which has lured investors from around the world. He also owned Prozone Sports Ltd for a period, a performance analysis company. With his success, Ranson first attempted to purchase Aston Villa and Manchester City as part of a consortium, then in December 2007 successfully acquired Coventry City.

Appearances & Goals:
Debut v Sheffield Wednesday (a) 26 December 1988
FL: 79(5) app 1 gl
FAC: 10 app 0 gls
FLC: 4 app 0 gls
Others: 3(1) app 0 gls
Total: 96(6) app 1 gl

Honours:
10 Eng u21 app 1980-81/Eng sch-youth app/FAC final 1981/FL div 2 prom 1985/FL div 1 champs 1993 (3 app)/FL div 2 champs 1994.

RAYLSTONE James 1888

Centre-half
b. probably Ayrshire, c1866

Career: Kilmarnock/Newcastle West End 1886 (EAST END guest 1887-88)/ EAST END cs 1888/Kidderminster Nov 1888/Sunderland 1889/ Sunderland Albion 1889/Newcastle West End Feb 1889/Rotherham Town cs 1890.

Noted in the local press as a "tough, uncompromising player", James Raylstone was an imposing character who served both Newcastle East End and West End after moving from Scotland with his younger brother. He appeared at St James' Park from 1886 to 1888 and was capped for Northumberland during that period. At centre-half he was also selected for his county when with East End, signing for the Chillingham Road outfit during the close season of 1888. Also operating at wing-half, Raylstone amassed over 100 games for the two Newcastle clubs in a belligerent style and was always able to notch a goal. He appeared in the West Enders first Northern League contest during 1889. Later moving to Wearside, he didn't see senior action for Sunderland, at the time rapidly developing into a top club. During April 1889 it was reported that James "narrowly escaped drowning" after falling into the water at South Dock in Sunderland. Unable to swim, a dock gateman and two river constables arrived to rescue him from his peril in the Wear.

Appearances & Goals:
Debut v Port Clarence (h) 6 October 1888 (FACQ) (1 goal)
FAC: 3 app 1 gl
Total: 3 app 1 gl

REAY Harry 1891-1893

Outside-right
5'11"
b. Co Durham, c1870

Career: Bedlington Burdon c1886/Gateshead/
Shankhouse Black Watch c1888/EAST END
cs 1891/Everton April 1893/ Southampton
St Marys May 1896/Sunderland Royal Rovers
March 1897/Bedlington.

*Harry Reay made a name for himself with one
of the North East's noted pioneer clubs,
Shankhouse Black Watch where he lifted the
Northumberland Challenge Cup and starred in
the final against Rendel. A fabulous winger on his
day, Reay thrilled Victorian crowds and by the time
he had joined Newcastle East End was one of the most
popular personalities of those early years. A reporter for
the Northerner & Athlete magazine recorded in 1893 that Harry was "simply
irresistible". Although he did not appear for United in the Football League, Reay took
part in the club's Northern League campaign during 1891-92 and 1892-93 after East
End moved across the city from Heaton to St James' Park. He also was on the field for
the Novocastrian's first FA Cup Proper fixture with Nottingham Forest. Harry once
scored five goals for United in a friendly against Scottish club, Annbank during March
1893; in fact he had another two efforts chalked off for, "hands" and "offside". Reay
stepped up to the top level with Everton, following a friendly contest with the
Merseysiders in which the forward performed with credit, celebrated Everton and
England international John Holt being hugely impressed and noting at the time, "Reay
is one of the finest forwards I have seen on a football field". At Goodison Park he was
chiefly a reserve, restricted by a severe knee injury although Harry took part in two
Combination titles and two Liverpool Cup finals. He managed just two senior games
before moving on and with Southampton featured in a single game against Kettering
before his knee gave way again, an injury which effectively ended his first-class career.*

Appearances & Goals:
Debut v Darlington (a) 19 September 1891 (NL)
NL: 24 app 9 gls
FAC: 6 app 5 gl
Total: 30 app 14 gls

REDHEAD William Sylvester 1954-1959

Left-half
5'8"
b. Newcastle upon Tyne, 10 October 1935
d. Northumberland Central, 2000 (Q3)

Career: Fatfield Jnrs/George Angus (Newcastle)/UNITED
Sept 1954/Gateshead Aug 1959 free/South Shields cs
1962/Gateshead c1963/Queen of the South May 1965
to 1967.

*At St James' Park for three seasons, Bill Redhead only
managed a single match for the Magpies, standing in for
Tommy Casey in midfield during 1956-57. He had a nerve-
shattering start with United, up against a Sheffield
Wednesday wing pair of Albert Quixall and Alan Finney on
the top of their form. Newcastle lost the contest 2-1, and
Redhead didn't get another chance in senior company. He
moved to Redheugh Park across the Tyne and took part in
Gateshead's last months as a Football League outfit (21 app) before concentrating
on local non-league soccer becoming recognised as a fine defender in those circles.
He completed his career with a spell in the Scottish League with Queen of the South.
Redhead later resided in Ponteland.*

Appearances & Goals:
Debut v Sheffield Wednesday (h) 29 December 1956
FL: 1 app 0 gls
Total: 1 app 0 gls

REED Frederick William Marshall 1919

Centre-half
5'10"
b. Scotswood, Newcastle upon Tyne, 10 March 1894
d. West Bromwich, 12 December 1967

Career: Scotswood Christian Endeavour/Newburn/
Wesley Hall/Benwell/Lintz Institute/West Bromwich
Albion amat Feb 1913, prof March 1913 (St Bernard's
war-guest 1916-17)(Lintz Institute war-guest 1919)
(UNITED war-guest 1919)(Durham City war-guest
1919)/Resumed with WBA cs 1919, retired July 1927
becoming trainer to 1950.

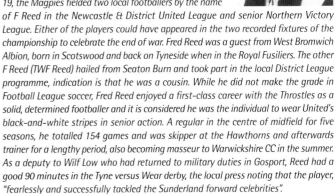

*Towards the end of the Great War, during season 1918-
19, the Magpies fielded two local footballers by the name
of F Reed in the Newcastle & District United League and senior Northern Victory
League. Either of the players could have appeared in the two recorded fixtures of the
championship to celebrate the end of war. Fred Reed was a guest from West Bromwich
Albion, born in Scotswood and back on Tyneside when in the Royal Fusiliers. The other
F Reed (TWF Reed) hailed from Seaton Burn and took part in the local District League
programme, indication is that he was a cousin. While he did not make the grade in
Football League soccer, Fred Reed enjoyed a first-class career with the Throstles as a
solid, determined footballer and it is considered he was the individual to wear United's
black-and-white stripes in senior action. A regular in the centre of midfield for five
seasons, he totalled 154 games and was skipper at the Hawthorns and afterwards
trainer for a lengthy period, also becoming masseur to Warwickshire CC in the summer.
As a deputy to Wilf Low who had returned to military duties in Gosport, Reed had a
good 90 minutes in the Tyne versus Wear derby, the local press noting that the player,
"fearlessly and successfully tackled the Sunderland forward celebrities".*

Appearances & Goals:
Debut v Sunderland (h) 25 January 1919 (NVL)
War: 2 app 0 gls
Total: 2 app 0 gls

Honours:
FL champs 1920 (1 app).

REID Dennis Alex 1971-1973

Midfield
5'8"
b. Glasgow, 2 March 1947
d. Canada, 1998

Career: Glasgow Perthshire/Rangers April 1963/
Dundee Utd July 1968 free/UNITED Oct 1971 exch
deal for I Mitchell/Morton loan Nov 1972, pmt
Oct 1973 £20,000/Dundee Utd Dec 1975/
Ayr Utd Oct 1976 £7,000/Retired due to injury 1977.

*Only appearing twice at Ibrox, Alex Reid was snapped
up by Dundee United and developed into one of the
best club players north of the border. He made a deep
impression on United manager Joe Harvey after displaying top form against the
Magpies in European ties for the Tannadice club during 1969. Ginger-haired, Reid had
a cultured left foot and could prompt and create from midfield, being very capable on
the ball but also a player who could turn to a spoiling role. Entering action in England
for season 1971-72, he found it a struggle to adapt to the much faster and
competitive First Division. Although the Scot showed flashes of excellent play, he was
always in and out of the Black'n'Whites line-up and quickly moved back north. Reid
continued to be a more than competent midfielder in Scotland, having three good
seasons with Morton before returning to Tannadice where he totalled 145 games
during his two spells there. A knee injury forced Alex to leave the game in 1977. He
later moved to Canada, residing in the Vancouver area. It was reported he was killed
in an accident during 1998.*

Appearances & Goals:
Debut v Nottingham Forest (h) 20 November 1971
FL: 15(8) app 0 gls
FAC: 0(2) app 0 gls
Others: 1 app 0 gls
Total: 16(10) app 0 gls

R

REID William 1895-1896

Right-half
5'10"
b. Rotherham

Career: Rotherham Town Nov 1894/UNITED Dec 1895 £20/Darwen July 1896/Attercliffe Sept 1898/Rotherham Town 1898-99/Barnsley May 1899 to cs 1900/Roundel Aug 1901/Rotherham Town cs 1903.

Billy Reid was signed after appearing on 37 occasions for the Rotherham Town club then in Division Two alongside United, and after his team had folded due to financial difficulties. He was elevated to the Magpies' first-eleven for two outings as a replacement for the injured Miller during season 1895-96, United's third season of Football League action, but did not enjoy a rewarding period in United's line-up. In his two games, Newcastle lost twice and conceded ten goals to Manchester City and Grimsby Town. He quickly returned to the 'A' side and played out the remainder of his short Newcastle career in the Northern Alliance before joining Darwen, then a Second Division side. He later headed back to a reformed Rotherham set-up.

(Note: Previously the only data referring to his Christian name showed a 'O', however it has now been established his name is William.)

Appearances & Goals:
Debut v Manchester City (a) 4 January 1896
FL: 2 app 0 gls
Total: 2 app 0 gls

REID William 1899-1900

Inside-left
5'6"
b. Mauchline, Ayrshire, 2 May 1876
d. Scotland, 1923

Career: Stevenston Thistle/Kilmarnock Ath 1894/Kilmarnock Aug 1897 (UNITED loan March 1899 to early 1900)/Partick Thistle Dec 1900 £30/Galston cs 1902/Thornhill Aug 1906/Kilmarnock Oct 1906/Galston Nov 1906.

Nicknamed 'Roggie' in his native Ayrshire, Billy Reid was a classy inside-forward. He had caught the eye of United's directors when an influential member of Kilmarnock's Scottish Cup final and Second Division title side just before the turn of the century. Always being able to create an opening with his skill on the ball, he was a deadly shot and on the verge of international recognition at one stage in his career. Reid arrived on Tyneside after scoring 12 goals in 16 outings for Killie during season 1898-99, initially on loan, a trial period which, if he fitted into the Magpies' line-up, would earn a long term contract. He began well, netting on his debut, however his form never matched his displays in the Scottish League. Reid returned north and continued his football career with both senior and local clubs, appearing in 68 games for Kilmarnock all told scoring 30 goals.

Appearances & Goals:
Debut v Derby County (h) 25 March 1899 (1 goal)
FL: 4 app 1 gl
Total: 4 app 1 gl

Honours:
Scot trial app 1898/SC final 1898/SL div 2 champs 1898, 1899.

REILLY George Gerard 1985

Centre-forward
6'4"
b. Bellshill, Lanarkshire, 14 September 1957

Career: Corby Town/Northampton Town June 1976/Cambridge Utd Nov 1979 £140,000/ Watford Aug 1983 £90,000/UNITED Feb 1985 £200,000/West Bromwich Albion Dec 1985 £150,000/Cambridge Utd July 1988 free/Barnet March 1989/Retired due to injury March 1990/Alvechurch Dec 1990/Cambridge City 1992.

Tall, strongly-built and aggressive, George Reilly learnt the game the hard way, scoring over 100 goals in the basement with Northampton and Cambridge. Moving to England from his native Scotland when two years old, the former bricklayer made an impact when he joined

Watford where he fitted into Graham Taylor's long ball game at Vicarage Road to perfection. Reilly netted the goal that sent Watford to Wembley in 1984 and became a handful to every defence he faced over his 61 outings (19 goals) for the Hornets. Joining Newcastle as the club searched for a new forward combination, he was Jack Charlton's target man, being fed by playmakers Beardsley and Waddle. But Reilly never grabbed enough goals to become a big hit at Gallowgate, only three in his first season and seven during 1985-86. Although fairly popular with the terrace masses, at one stage being given the nickname of 'Rambo' for his honest and wholehearted displays, George was replaced by new boss Willie McFaul with Billy Whitehurst and he moved to The Hawthorns where he was unlucky to be sidelined for eight months with a cruciate ligament injury. He was eventually forced to quit the football scene due to more injury, this time a back problem. Standing at 6'4", he remains one of the tallest players ever to appear for the Magpies, while he has a Geordie bloodline, his mother being from Tyneside. Reilly later ran a building business in Ely, then at Corby, specialising in hard landscaping works.

Appearances & Goals:
Debut v Luton Town (h) 23 February 1985
FL: 31 app 10 gls
FAC: 2 app 0 gls
Total: 33 app 10 gls

Honours:
FAC final 1984.

REMY Loic 2013-2014

Striker
6'2"
b. Rillieux-La-Pape, near Lyon (France), 2 January 1987

Career: ASPTT Lyon (Fr) 1993/Olymp Lyonnais (Fr) jnr 1999, prof Oct 2006 (RC Lens (Fr) loan 2007-08)/OGC Nice (Fr) June 2008 £7m/Olymp Marseille (Fr) Aug 2010 £13.6m/Queens Park Rangers Jan 2013 £8m (UNITED loan Aug 2013 to May 2014)/Chelsea Aug 2014 £10.5m.

French international striker Loic Remy was poised to join the Magpies during the January 2013 transfer window but somewhat controversially chose Loftus Road and QPR instead. Almost eight months later with the Londoners relegated to the Championship, Remy eventually signed for United on a season-long loan deal for 2013-14. Tall, lithe and swift, Remy showed in his short period with Rangers he could become a top Premier League striker netting six goals in 14 games, including a couple of spectacular efforts. He gave United's flagging strike-force a much needed boost, without a regular partner for Cisse since the departure of Demba Ba. Immediately Remy continued where he had left off at Loftus Road, netting eight goals in his first 10 matches for the Magpies. In France and on the European stage, Loic was especially successful with Nice (28 goals in 74 games) this after struggling to claim a place at Lyon, in a squad which included for a period Ben Arfa and Benzema. Earning a big move to French champions Marseille, Loic is able to play as a main striker or raiding from the flanks and totalled 39 goals in 95 matches for the Provence giants. He ended the season with 14 goals for United, one of the Premier League's best, but decided to return to London following participating in the World Cup in Brazil.

Appearances & Goals:
Debut v Fulham (h) 31 August 2013 (sub)
PL: 24(2) app 14 gls
FAC: 0(1) app 0 gls
Total: 24(3) app 14 gls

Honours:
27 France caps 2009-date/WdC 2014/11 Fr u21 app 2008-09/Fr sch-youth app/Fr Lg champs 2007 (6 app), 2008 (6 app)/Fr LC winner 2012.

RENDELL Thomas (John) 1894-1895

Left-half
5'8"
b. probably Seghill, Northumberland, March 1873
d. [Co Durham, December 1957]

Career: Shankhouse Black Watch/UNITED Aug 1894/Shankhouse Black Watch cs 1895.

A former member of the top-ranked local side Shankhouse Black Watch, Tom Rendell joined the United staff during the close-season of 1894 and was used as a utility player through the 1894-95 programme. Operating mainly at left-half, he also turned out at left and right-back, as well as centre-half. A regular for that Second Division campaign, the Daily Journal noted Tom as "a worthy sub for Jeffrey". He remained for the season before returning to local Tyneside soccer. Rendell assisted Shankhouse to Northumberland Senior Cup victories before joining United. From 1891 census information it is likely Rendell was working as a 19-year-old miner, living in the Seghill and Cramlington area of the region.

Appearances & Goals:
Debut v Darwen (a) 1 September 1894
FL: 23 app 0 gls
FAC: 2 app 2 gls
Total: 25 app 2 gls

RICHARDSON George Edward 1922-1923

Outside-left
5'9"
b. Easington, Co Durham, 4 July 1902
d. [New Kyo, Co Durham, 9 November 1960]

Career: Easington CW Sept 1919/South Shields April 1920/UNITED Aug 1922 free/Easington CW cs 1923/Huddersfield Town Dec 1923/Sheffield Wed Nov 1924 to 1925/South Shields 1925/York City Feb 1926/Bradford City Sept 1926 £100/Easington CW Oct 1928/Ashington Oct 1928/Easington CW by March 1930/Whitburn 1932/Easington CW by April 1933.

One of the club's reserves to Stan Seymour on the left wing, Eddie Richardson made a name for himself in South Shields' eleven over 35 games when they featured in the Football League's Second Division. At Gallowgate though, he rarely pushed the consistent Seymour for a first-team place, deputising for the legendary figure twice during season 1922-23. After spells at Leeds Road and Hillsborough, where he also struggled to claim a regular spot, Richardson returned to his roots and played local football. On Huddersfield's staff when the Yorkshire club won the League Championship titles in both 1923-24 and 1924-25, Richardson was a stand-in to Town's many stars of the period. He enjoyed a good period with Bradford City for two seasons, claiming 53 games (13 goals), while he played in Ashington's Football League campaign, appearing in the Northumbrian's very last fixture at senior level, against Halifax during April 1929.

Appearances & Goals:
Debut v Preston North End (h) 23 September 1922
FL: 2 app 0 gls
Total: 2 app 0 gls

Honours:
FL champs 1924 (5 app), 1925 (1 app).

RICHARDSON James Robert 1928-1934, 1937-1938

Inside-right
5'9"
b. Ashington, 8 February 1911
d. Bexley, London, 28 August 1964

Career: Blyth Spartans 1925/UNITED April 1928 £200/Huddersfield Town Oct 1934 £4,000/UNITED Oct 1937 £4,500/Millwall March 1938 £4,000 (Fulham war-guest 1941-42)(Aldershot war-guest 1941-42)(Charlton Ath war-guest 1942-43)(Leyton Orient war-guest 1944-45)/Resumed with Millwall/Leyton Orient player-trainer Jan 1948, becoming trainer June 1951 to June 1955/Millwall trainer Nov 1956 to 1957.

A motor engineer when he joined United's staff, Jimmy Richardson had displayed a special talent as a schoolboy international and when appearing for Blyth Spartans as a 14-year-old teenager, one that was richly developed by the Magpies. Very fast over ten yards, he had tremendous close control of the ball and his dribbling one-man runs attacking defenders were a feature of United's play during the early Thirties. A workhorse as well, Richardson became a popular character and one of the central figures of Newcastle's FA Cup victory in 1932, at the centre of attention when he crossed the ball for the infamous 'Over the Line' goal against Arsenal at Wembley. At his peak with United the following season, 1932-33, he was capped by England, netting twice on his two appearances for his country. With the club's relegation in 1934, Jimmy however, soon moved on, to Huddersfield where he again proved a good servant, claiming 32 goals in 125 games for the Tykes. Following a brief second stint at Gallowgate, at the end of his career Richardson settled in London and was Millwall's trainer until ill health forced him to leave his post. His brother, John Richardson appeared for Oldham.

Appearances & Goals:
Debut v Blackburn Rovers (h) 4 September 1929 (1 goal)
FL: 150 app 44 gls
FAC: 13 app 7 gls
Others: 1 app 0 gls
Total: 164 app 51 gls

Honours:
2 Eng caps 1933/Eng sch-youth app/1 FL app 1937/FAC winner 1932/FL div 3(S) champs 1938.

RICHARDSON Joseph 1929-1975

Right-back & Trainer
5'8"
b. Bedlington, Northumberland, 24 August 1908
d. Newcastle upon Tyne, 14 June 1975

Career: New Delaval Villa/Blyth Spartans cs 1928/ UNITED May 1929 joint deal £250/Retired 1945, becoming asst-trainer to his death in 1975.

Devoted to United's cause for most of his adult life, Joe Richardson became one of the real Geordie characters of St James' Park for over 46 years. A former blacksmith and strong as the proverbial ox, as a full-back, he was a gritty defender, possessing all the traditional tenacity of his local Bedlington terrier. Unruffled and robust, but fair in his play, he took no prisoners in the tackle and rivalled Alf Maitland as a youngster, then was a reserve to Jimmy Nelson before claiming the shirt for himself during season 1934-35. Throughout the years leading up to the outbreak of war, Richardson was a permanent fixture in the side, capped by England against Scotland in December 1939. Always well groomed on and off the field, he skippered United for a period during the war seasons, then turned to coaching the reserve and younger players through three decades. He was a shrewd judge of emerging talent and in his later years a father-figure to many up and coming teenagers at Gallowgate. Joe was a jovial figure, a popular backroom aide at Gallowgate. His service as a player and trainer of over 46 years is bettered only by Andy McCombie.

Appearances & Goals:
Debut v Brighton (h) 15 February 1930 (FAC)
FL: 208 app 1 gl
FAC: 15 app 0 gls
War: 114 app 0 gls
Total: 337 app 1 gl

Honours:
1 Eng war app 1940.

R

RICHARDSON Ord 1902-1903

Inside-right
5'10"
b. Newcastle upon Tyne, 1875 (Q2)
d. Gosforth, Newcastle upon Tyne, 24 February 1958

Career: Wallsend Park Villa Jan 1902/UNITED May 1902 to 1903/Morpeth Harriers Aug 1904/Wallsend Park Villa Feb 1905/Coxlodge Villa Oct 1906.

Tynesider Ord Richardson stood in once for Scottish international forward Ronald Orr during season 1902-03. It was Richardson's only taste of senior action, his remaining time at St James' Park being restricted to Northern League football. He once netted six goals for the United 'A' side when they defeated Darlington St Augustine's at St James' Park on Christmas Day 1903. Ord was more prominent on the cricket field, a well known local cricketer who appeared for Northumberland on 63 occasions between 1904 and 1919 as a talented right-hand batsman, often scoring 1,000 runs a season. Richardson turned out for several cricket clubs in the region over a lengthy period between 1888 to 1941, including Benwell, Chester-le-Street, South Northumberland and Armstrong Works.

Appearances & Goals:
Debut v Wolverhampton Wanderers (a) 1 November 1902
FL: 1 app 0 gls
Total: 1 app 0 gls

RIDLEY James 1907-1911

Outside-left
5'9"
b. Wallsend, 1889

Career: Byker East End/Willington Ath/UNITED Feb 1907 £50/Nottingham Forest Feb 1911 £150/Newcastle City Aug 1911/Ashington Feb 1912/North Shields Ath Aug 1912/Hartlepools Utd June 1914/Chesterfield 1915-16/Wallsend Sept 1919.

James Ridley was an efficient member of the United 'A' side which dominated local football during the Edwardian era. Winning the North Eastern League title on four occasions, Ridley was reserve to George Wilson during his time on United's staff. He appeared on a handful of occasions on each of his four years with the club, having five outings when Newcastle lifted the Championship trophy in 1909. He always gave a good display, being very fast with what were noted as, "electric dribbles" being a feature of his game. The swiftest man on the Magpies' books at the time, Ridley once won the Morpeth Handicap and other prominent races of the day. A reserve at Forest too, claiming only four appearances, he later joined the Newcastle City club in 1911, a team based at Brough Park in Byker that made a failed bid to move from the North Eastern League to the Football League at the end of his first season there.

Appearances & Goals:
Debut v Everton (h) 7 December 1907
FL: 17 app 2 gls
Total: 17 app 2 gls

Honours:
FL champs 1909 (5 app).

ROBERT Laurent Pierre 2001-2005

Outside-left
5'9"
b. Saint-Benoit (La Reunion, France), 21 May 1975

Career: US Benedictine (Reunion) (Fr)/FC Brest (Fr) 1990/Montpellier HSC (Fr) 1994/Paris St-Germain (Fr) cs 1999/UNITED Aug 2001 £9.2m (Mauritius national XI guest June 2005)/ Portsmouth July 2005 £1.5m/SL Benfica (Ptg) Jan 2006 free/Levante UD (Sp) July 2006 free/Derby Co Jan 2008 free/Toronto (Can) April 2008/ AE Larissa (Gr) Aug 2008/PSV Eindhoven (Neth) Sept to Nov 2009.

Born on the French Pacific island of La Reunion, 26-year-old Laurent Robert was purchased from Paris St-Germain during August 2001 for a hefty £9.2m transfer fee, one of Newcastle's biggest ever acquisitions. A French international with nine appearances to his name, his play down the left wing was at times a delight, able to skip past defenders and whip in a vicious cross, often capitalised on by Alan Shearer. Part of Sir Bobby Robson's outstanding United side which did well in the Champions League of 2002-03, he struck the ball true and hard, and with swerve. The Frenchman could be quite brilliant, yet infuriatingly mediocre in the space of a few moments. But Laurent was a match-winner; a player who could turn the course of a game with a piece of virtuoso skill that only a select few can produce. He followed David Ginola to St James' Park on the flank, and both could get the crowd roaring and both had the ability to whip the ball in from the touchline. Ginola perhaps had more flair and razzmatazz, Robert was not so stylish, yet he not only made goals, he scored them too, over 30 in total for United. And often he made the net bulge with stunning shots which swerved and dipped. Laurent scored a number of spectacular goals from outside the box much recalled by Toon supporters and he was always a danger from dead-balls. A spectacular double-strike against Tottenham was notable; a dipping volley at the Leazes End and wonderful screamer at the Gallowgate. Yet Robert in the end enjoyed an enigmatic four-year stay on Tyneside, his best campaigns being 2001-02 (10 goals) and 2003-04 (12 goals) while he was occasionally sent off, being petulant on the field at times. A temperamental and difficult character to manage, he had the talent to have joined the elite, but too often was inconsistent and moody. Bobby Robson confirmed that he was "my greatest challenge since Romario". After a fall-out with new boss Graeme Souness, Laurent moved south during the summer of 2005 to join Portsmouth (17 app) but soon headed to Lisbon with Benfica. Robert had a brief spell back in England with Derby County then played in Spain, North America and in Greece. His early career saw him appear for Montpellier (124 app) while he developed through the highly rated French national coaching system, appearing at youth and Under-21 level before reaching the 'A' and full sides. The Frenchman appeared in the Champions League for three different clubs; United, PSG and Benfica. Laurent had two brothers in the game; Fabien with Lorient and Doncaster, while Bertrand assisted PAOK in Greece. On retirement he lived in the South of France involved in various charity games and indoor football.

Appearances & Goals:
Debut v Chelsea (a) 19 August 2001
PL: 110(19) app 22 gls
FAC: 10 app 3 gls
FLC: 6(1) app 2 gls
Euro: 29(6) app 5 gls
Total: 155(26) app 32 gls

Honours:
9 Fr caps 2000-02/5 Fr A app 1999-2001/5 Fr u21 app 1997-98/Fr sch-youth app.

ROBERTS Richard James Hollis 1901-1904

Outside-left
5'7"
b. Bromsgrove, near Redditch, 30 March 1878
d. Birmingham, 5 March 1931

Career: Redditch Excelsior/West Bromwich Albion April 1899/UNITED May 1901/Middlesbrough April 1904 £450/Crystal Palace cs 1905/Retired due to injury 1909/Worcester City Sept 1910.

Joining Newcastle from the Midlands, Richard Roberts very quickly became a favourite of United's supporters. He was a fast and direct winger who proved he could score goals from the flank, claiming 12 in his first campaign for the Magpies. Consistent over two seasons for the club, he was surprisingly replaced by Bobby Templeton, a move to start with that caused dismay among the Newcastle crowd. However, when Scottish international Templeton began to turn on his magic, the furore over Roberts' loss was soon forgotten. He later concluded his career briefly on Teesside, then as part of Crystal Palace's Southern League line-up and as renowned FA Cup giant-killers, including helping to defeat the Magpies in a fêted 1907 giant-killing act. Roberts totalled 99 matches (25 goals) for Palace and 52 games for Albion, including the very first contest at The Hawthorns in 1900. Just before joining United, he reached the FA Cup semi-final, but was also part of a Throstles' team relegated from Division One, hence his move to Tyneside.

Appearances & Goals:
Debut v Blackburn Rovers (a) 7 September 1901
FL: 51 app 17 gls
FAC: 4 app 0 gls
Total: 55 app 17 gls

ROBERTSON John Grant 1988

Striker
5'7"
b. Edinburgh, 2 October 1964

Career: Tartan BC/Salvesen BC/Edina Hibs/ Heart of Midlothian jnr Sept 1980, prof Jan 1981/UNITED April 1988 £750,000/Heart of Midlothian Dec 1988 £750,000 (Dundee loan 1997-98)/Livingston player-coach July 1998, retiring playing, becoming coach cs 2000/ Inverness Caledonian manager Dec 2002/ Heart of Midlothian manager Nov 2004 to May 2005/Ross Co manager June 2005 to Oct 2005/Livingston manager Feb 2006 to April 2007/Derry City manager July 2007 to Dec 2007/Dundee Utd, Hearts & Kilmarnock part-time 'striker coach'/East Fife manager Oct 2010 to March 2012/Heart of Midlothian asst-coach July 2013.

John Robertson was tracked by a host of clubs as a schoolboy and had trials at Arsenal, Manchester City, Nottingham Forest and Leeds, before signing for his home team at Tynecastle where former United skipper Bob Moncur was manager. Very quickly the small, compact and lightning fast striker began to show why he was in demand. With Hearts, Robertson became one of the top goal-poachers in Scotland. Possessing a natural touch in front of goal, he had netted almost 150 goals for Hearts in five years when United paid out a club record fee to bring him to Tyneside. But at St James' Park he was never played in his preferred free role up front by manager Willie McFaul, his style clashing with that of Mirandinha, at Gallowgate at the same time. Many followers of the club were totally perplexed at why such a quality player only managed seven league starts in a black-and-white shirt before returning north. He was out of action for a period with a persistent muscle problem, but Newcastle's side at the time was crying out for a player of Robertson's ability in front of goal. When he returned to Scotland, John immediately started to bang the ball in the net again, eventually winning full caps for his country and scoring on his international debut. Robertson scored 300 senior goals by the time he moved into coaching, 222 for Hearts over his two spells. His brother Chris also appeared for the Tynecastle club, as well as for Rangers. John was later employed as Business Development Manager in Scotland for the recruitment consultants Orion.

Appearances & Goals:
Debut v Everton (a) 27 August 1988
FL: 7(5) app 0 gls
FLC: 0(2) app 0 gls
Others: 2 app 0 gls
Total: 9(7) app 0 gls

Honours:
16 Scot caps 1991-96/1 unoff Scot app 1990/3 Scot B app 1990-96/5 Scot u21 app 1984-85/Scot sch-youth app/SL div 1 champs 1998 (4 app)/SL div 2 champs 1999/SC winner 1998 (sub no app)/SC final 1986, 1996/SLC final 1997/Scot YPoY 1984.

ROBINSON David John 1984-1992

Sriker
6'0"
b. Walkergate, Newcastle upon Tyne, 27 November 1969

Career: Walkergate Jnrs/Wallsend BC/UNITED jnr Dec 1984, prof June 1988 (Peterborough Utd loan 1990-91)/Reading March 1992 free/Blackpool July 1992/Gateshead Aug 1994/Bishop Auckland June 1995/Lincoln City trial Nov 1995/Cambridge Utd Dec 1995/Berwick Rangers July 1996/Whitley Bay Feb 1997 to Sept 1997/Later appearing in local minor football, including for Heaton Hussar.

After overcoming a serious knee ligament injury as a junior, Dave Robinson was a live-wire centre-forward in Central League football for United. He was on the fringe of United's first eleven over four seasons, but never made the starting line-up except in friendly contests. Once netting six goals in six games during a pre-season tour of Sweden, much was expected of the tall and orthodox target man. Robinson netted as a substitute on his second outing against Reading in a FA Cup tie, but didn't break into the team in a sustained way, making all of his 10 outings from the bench for United. Robinson tried his luck with Peterborough, Reading and Blackpool, but rarely made headlines. His best period was with the Tangerines, totalling 33 games over seasons 1992-93 and 1993-94. He later joined the police force on Tyneside.

Appearances & Goals:
Debut v Arsenal (h) 12 November 1988 (sub)
FL: 0(8) app 0 gls
FAC: 0(1) app 1 gl
FLC: 0(1) app 0 gls
Total: 0(10) app 1 gl

Honours: FL div 4 prom 1991 (7 app).

ROBINSON John Allan 1942

Inside-right
5'10"
b. Shiremoor, Newcastle upon Tyne, 10 August 1917
d. Shiremoor, Newcastle upon Tyne, 30 July 1972

Career: Newbiggin Jnrs/West Wylam CW/Shiremoor/ Sheffield Wed Oct 1934 (Hartlepools Utd war-guest 1939-40)(Darlington war-guest 1939-40) (Middlesbrough war-guest 1940-41) (UNITED war-guest 1941-42)(Colchester Utd war-guest 1945-46)/ Resumed with Sheffield Wed 1945-46/Sunderland Oct 1946 £5,000/Lincoln City player-trainer Oct 1949 to 1950.

One of several full England internationals to pull on the Magpie strip during wartime soccer, Jackie Robinson burst onto the football stage as a gifted teenager during season 1935-36 and was capped on four occasions during the late-Thirties, making his debut for his country as a 19-year-old. Remembered for his pace and graceful play, Robinson could go past defenders, pass well and shoot with menace. A great all-round forward, including wartime games, he totalled more than 228 games for the Owls, netting 130 goals, one of the Tykes finest players of that era. Returning home to Tyneside for a few months during 1942, he pulled on Newcastle's colours for a wartime home fixture with Middlesbrough during February. Jackie was rated highly, but was unfortunate that the best years of his football career coincided with World War Two when he served with an Anti-Aircraft battery in the North East. On being demobbed he returned to Hillsborough, however Jackie longed to return closer to his Shiremoor home and a deal with Sunderland (85 app) was concluded. Robinson also appeared for the Football League side and when on full England duty in 1938, was in the line-up which gave the Nazi salute in Berlin. As a veteran with Lincoln City he was forced to quit the game due to a badly broken leg, an injury which stopped him entering coaching and which affected him for the rest of his life. He later worked in the construction industry in the region then became a publican at The Ship in Gateshead.

Appearances & Goals:
Debut v Middlesbrough (h) 28 February 1942 (FLN)
War: 1 app 0 gls
Total: 1 app 0 gls

Honours:
4 Eng caps 1937-39/Eng trial app 1937/1 FL app 1939/FLWC(N) final 1943.

ROBINSON James Walter 1931

Centre-half
6'0"
b. Ryton, near Gateshead, 1901 (Q3)

Career: Stargate Rovers/Burnley July 1923/Nelson July 1925/Llandudno Jan 1926/ Bradford City Nov 1926/Workington cs 1927/Doncaster Rovers Aug 1929/ Scarborough 1930/UNITED Jan 1931 £300 to May 1931/Crawcrook Albion Aug 1931/ Bristol City Sept 1931/Crawcrook Albion 1932/Aberavon Feb 1932.

A former soldier with the Grenadier Guards, James Robinson was a deputy to the injured Dave Davidson and out of favour skipper Jack Hill for a few months during season 1930-31. With a reputation as a tough and rugged centre-half, typical of the pivot's role during the Thirties era, he had learned his trade in the gritty lower divisions. After an unspectacular senior career, Jimmy then performed well for non-league Scarborough in front of watching United scouts, part of their FA Cup side to progress and catch the headlines. However, Robinson didn't stay long on Tyneside, moving after only five months. The Journal's 'Castellion' made the comment on his appearance as part of United's side in the absence of Hill that "there is very little room for comparison", while Colin Veitch wrote in his column that he was "far from being impressive". The policy of leaving out Hill was not a popular one and Robinson was perhaps unfairly compared with the England pivot. The transfer deal from Scarborough was the second transaction within a week by the Magpies, Alec Betton (another centre-back) having already arrived from the Yorkshire club.

Appearances & Goals:
Debut v Manchester United (h) 17 January 1931
FL: 1 app 0 gls
Total: 1 app 0 gls

R

ROBINSON Mark James 1993-1994

Right-back
5'9"
b. Rochdale, 21 November 1968

Career: West Bromwich Albion jnr 1985, prof Nov 1986/Barnsley June 1987 free/UNITED March 1993 £450,000/Swindon Town July 1994 £600,000/Chippenham Town July 2002/ Retired due to injury cNov 2002.

Following an unsuccessful spell at The Hawthorns where he made a teenage debut, Mark Robinson spent six seasons in the ranks of Barnsley totalling 159 matches before being given the chance of a big-time career at St James' Park. Stockily-built, Mark was solid in the tackle and fast in recovery, and performed at full-back, as cover for Barry Venison, as well as occasionally in midfield. Helping United in the final push for promotion during 1992-93, Robinson was unluckily injured in a pre-season friendly before the Geordies began their march on the Premiership. Against Hartlepool he was the victim of a dreadful tackle which broke his leg; Mark was out of action for most of the season and by the time he returned to something like full fitness Robinson had several players ahead of him in the first-team pecking order. Kevin Keegan released the defender, making a good short term profit for the Magpies. With Swindon the full-back totalled 316 games, a stalwart player in the Robins' defence for seven seasons. On leaving the game he later opened a fitness gym.

Appearances & Goals:
Debut v Charlton Athletic (h) 10 March 1993
FL/PL: 14(11) app 0 gls
FAC: 1 app 0 gls
Total: 15(11) app 0 gls

Honours:
FL div 1 champs 1993 (9 app)/FL div 2 champs 1996.

ROBINSON Paul Derrick 1998-2000

Striker
5'11"
b. Seaburn, Sunderland, 20 November 1978

Career: Roker Rookies/Redby CA 1993/Darlington jnr Nov 1995, prof July 1997/UNITED March 1998 £500,000 joint deal (Crook Town loan 1997-98)/ Wimbledon Aug 2000 £1.5m (Burnley loan 2000-01)(Dundee Utd loan 2000-01)(Hull City trial March 2002)(Grimsby Town loan 2001-02, 2002-03)(Carlisle Utd loan 2002-03)/Blackpool March 2003/ Hartlepool Utd July 2003 free/York City July 2004 (Grimsby Town loan 2004-05)/Aberdeen, Ross Co & St Johnstone all on trial July 2005/Whitley Bay Aug

2005/Torquay Utd Nov 2005 to May 2006/Horden CW July 2006/Sunderland RCA Aug 2007/Sunderland Nissan/Darlington trial July 2008/Consett Feb to May 2009/Maidenhead Utd April to May 2010/Hayes & Yeading Utd trial Aug 2010/ Hendon trial Sept 2010/Windsor & Eton Nov 2010/Beaconsfield SYCOB Jan 2011/ Chesham Utd Jan to May 2011/Jarrow Roofing Aug 2011/Chesham Utd Sept 2011/ Didcot Town Nov 2011/Jarrow Roofing player-coach Feb 2012/Newton Aycliffe July 2012/Jarrow Roofing Sept 2012/South Shields Dec 2012/Hebburn Town July 2013.

Newcastle United spent £500,000 in a joint deal to bring Darlington's promising teenage pair, James Coppinger and Paul Robinson to Tyneside in the spring of 1998. Both were raw teenagers who had shined for the Quakers in limited outings. Once a trialist at Gallowgate and at Sunderland during 1995, Robinson possessed lovely close control of the ball and enjoyed running at defenders, able to slip past opponents. A flair player, at reserve level he scored plenty of goals either as an out-and-out striker or moving forward from a wide midfield position. Given an extended chance by Ruud Gullit during the pre-season of 1999-2000, Paul scored three goals and reached the fringe of the senior eleven. Robinson though only starting twice for the Black'n'Whites and one infamous occasion was against his boyhood favourites Sunderland at Gallowgate, when Gullit selected him ahead of both Shearer and Ferguson, his last game in charge of the club. Bobby Robson's arrival saw the new boss have a close look at Paul for a season, giving the skilled striker a hint of a chance during 1999-2000, mainly fleeting appearances from the bench. Yet United's coaching staff had unanswered questions; if he could fit into a team plan and could he develop as a team player. The answer was eventually 'no' and Robinson was allowed to leave,

United accepting a surprise £1.5m offer from Wimbledon. He couldn't make an impression in London either, and afterwards bounced around Britain with a succession of clubs. His best spells were with Hartlepool (39 app), Torquay (21 app) and with Darlington (34 app) where he had made a 16-year-old debut. Drifting into non-league circles, all told Robinson pulled on the kit of over 30 different sides. The Wearsider ran into financial difficulties during 2008, being declared bankrupt, but Paul recovered his lifestyle and continuing his nomadic football career. Robinson also started coaching locally and at times acted as a personal trainer.

Appearances & Goals:
Debut v Aston Villa (h) 7 August 1999 (sub)
PL: 2(9) app 0 gls
FLC: 0(1) app 0 gls
Euro: 0(4) app 1 gl
Total: 2(14) app 1 gl

ROBINSON Raymond Wilson 1919-1920

Outside-right
5'7"
b. Blaydon, near Newcastle upon Tyne, 1895 (Q3)
d. Newcastle upon Tyne, 6 January 1964

Career: Scotswood (Grimsby Town war-guest 1915-16)/ UNITED May 1919 £400/Sunderland Aug 1920 £750/ Grimsby Town May 1921/Sunderland June 1922/Eden CW Oct 1922/Lancaster Town/Liverpool Police July 1924/ Shirebrook/Silverwood Colliery Sept 1928.

At around 13 stones in weight, Ray Robinson was quite a hefty looking winger, but nevertheless the Tynesider made a big impact on the club's side during the first season of action after World War One. A regular at outside-right that campaign, for most of the programme he performed well, able to penetrate defences from the flank. Yet for all his efforts it wasn't enough to stop United's directors bringing in Scot Billy Aitken to take over his role. Robinson moved to Wearside (10 app) and onto Blundell Park (9 app), but never gained an automatic place in either side. During World War One Ray had been attached to the Cyclists Corps then was a corporal in the Tank Corps in France. A miner before he joined United, Robinson returned to the coalface in the Nottingham and Yorkshire mines before retiring to the Newcastle area, living in Ryton.

Appearances & Goals:
Debut v Arsenal (a) 30 August 1919
FL: 27 app 4 gls
FAC: 2 app 0 gls
Total: 29 app 4 gls

ROBINSON Robert 1952-1954

Goalkeeper
5'11"
b. Newbiggin-by-the-Sea, Northumberland, 23 June 1921
d. Newcastle upon Tyne, January 1975

Career: Burnley amat/Newbiggin/ Sunderland Feb 1947/UNITED Aug 1952 £2,500 to June 1954 free/Local football.

Sunderland's reserve goalkeeper, United purchased Bobby Robinson when senior guardian Ronnie Simpson was on 'Z Training' duty as part of his National Service. He only filled in for the Scot on a handful of occasions during the 1952-53 season and with rivals John Thompson and Stuart Mitchell in the wings, left the club after two years to return to local football. Bobby did appear against Sunderland during first few days with the Black'n'Whites after moving from Wearside, a derby match during September 1952. At Roker Park he was also deputy to another noted goalkeeper in John Mapson, although Robinson totalled 20 occasions in a good run during season 1951-52 and registered 33 games for the Wearsiders. He was later a landlord at The Queen's Head in Newbiggin on the Northumberland coast.

Appearances & Goals:
Debut v Burnley (a) 6 September 1952
FL: 5 app 0 gls
Total: 5 app 0 gls

ROBINSON Stuart Alan 1975-1980

Outside-left
5'9"
b. Middlesbrough, 16 January 1959

Career: Murton Colliery/UNITED jnr June 1975, prof July 1977/Aldershot July 1980 free to cs 1983.

Slim-line winger Stuart Robinson gained a fine youth record, appearing for his country and developing through United's junior structure. He was given a chance in the first-eleven during season 1977-78, unfortunately his break in senior company coincided with a torrid relegation year for the Magpies. Newcastle dropped from the First Division and Robinson's long term opportunities thereafter were limited. He attempted a career with Aldershot in Division Four but after 89 games left the Football League scene, later running a sports centre complex.

Appearances & Goals:
Debut v Leicester City (h) 3 December 1977
FL: 11(1) app 2 gls
FAC: 2 app 1 gl
Total: 13(1) app 3 gls

Honours:
Eng sch-youth app.

ROBLEDO Edward Oliver 1949-1953

Left-half
5'9"
b. Iquique (Chile), 26 July 1928
d. Persian Gulf, 6th December 1970

Career: Barnsley 1943/UNITED Jan 1949, joint deal with G Robledo (£3,500)/Colo-Colo (Ch) May 1953 joint deal with G Robledo/Notts Co Sept 1957 to 1958.

The younger of the two Robledo brothers at St James' Park during the immediate post-war years, Ted's career in the game followed the same path as his more famous counterpart. Nevertheless, while he was something of a makeweight in the substantial deal that brought George to Gallowgate, having claimed only five games for Barnsley, Ted became a valued squad player and earned a regular position in midfield during season 1951-52. Honest and hardworking at left-half, he was a steady performer rather than brilliant and rivalled Charlie Crowe for a place in Newcastle's engine-room, Robledo gaining a place for the FA Cup final team in 1952, taking part in all of the ties during the noted run to Wembley. Dark-haired and handsome, like his brother, Ted returned to Chile at the end of the 1952-53 season and enjoyed success in his native country, again playing with his brother for top club Colo-Colo. Ted also won international honours for Chile alongside George. He attempted a comeback in the Football League with the other Magpies, alongside the Trent in Nottingham during 1957. But that didn't last long, Robledo eventually leaving the game being employed for an American company in the oil industry. His untimely death during 1970 was surrounded in controversy, Ted was assumed dead after being reported missing overboard in the Persian Gulf from a tanker, the Al Sahn, when on his way home to Lowestoft from a Dubai oil rig. Following an investigation by Interpol, the West German captain of the boat was later arrested for murder after it had been claimed a fight took place. He was charged with "wilfully and unlawfully causing the death of Robledo in a brutal and savage manner". Ultimately the captain was acquitted. No trace of Robledo's body was ever found.

Appearances & Goals:
Debut v Aston Villa (a) 31 December 1949
FL: 37 app 0 gls
FAC: 8 app 0 gls
Others: 2 app 0 gls
Total: 47 app 0 gls

Honours:
9 Ch caps 1954-55/SthA champ final 1955/FAC winner 1952/Ch Lg champs 1953, 1956.

ROBLEDO George Oliver 1949-1953

Inside-forward
5'9"
b. Iquique (Chile),
14 April 1926
d. Vina Del Mar (Chile),
1 April 1989

Career: Dearne Valley Old Boys/ Brampton Welfare/Barnsley amat 1942/Huddersfield Town amat 1943/Barnsley April 1943 (Lincoln City war-guest 1943-44)/UNITED Jan 1949 joint deal with E Robledo £23,000/ Colo-Colo (Ch) May 1953 joint deal with E Robledo £15,000/ O'Higgins (Ch) 1959/Retired 1961, later becoming a director of both Colo-Colo and O'Higgins clubs.

George Robledo was brought up in Yorkshire of an English mother after the family had emigrated from South America following the Chilean revolution in 1932. A pit worker at Wath, the stocky inside-forward-cum-striker gained a place in Barnsley's wartime side in friendly action as a 15-year-old and scored twice, quickly becoming a regular when 17 and building a reputation as a deadly goal-getter. George, who netted a hat-trick on his Football League debut, was admired and coveted by Newcastle's Stan Seymour and manager George Martin, the pair succeeded in acquiring his services once the club had gained promotion into Division One. Recording an impressive strike-rate at Oakwell of over 90 goals, he teamed up with Jackie Milburn as well as Bobby Mitchell, and the forward combination became one of the most feared in the country. A perfect foil for Milburn, Robledo was the grafter, always chasing for the ball, tackling, and lethal whenever an opening came his way. Hitting the ball true and hard, Bobby Mitchell once remarked: "He used to blast them in from all directions, and they went like a bullet." While Robledo was a huge success, everything did not go as planned, during 1949-50 United were ready to cash-in on a £25,000 offer from Sheffield Wednesday. But once that deal fell through, the South American flourished quickly in a Magpie shirt. During season 1951-52, when he netted a late winner in the FA Cup final against Arsenal, George equalled Hughie Gallacher's scoring record of 39 goals and was Division One's leading scorer. Extremely popular on Tyneside, he was a regular for his country taking part in the 1950 World Cup finals in Brazil. A hero back home in Chile, on several occasions George was nearly enticed back to his native country to help develop the game, eventually leaving Tyneside for a hefty financial package when 27 years old and at his peak. He went onto guide his club to championship titles in Chile, while in 1962, Robledo acted as liaison officer to England and was on the organising committee during the World Cup in his country. Nicknamed 'Pancho' by his colleagues, George was later employed for a mining company, and was head of sport at St Peter's school in Vina Del Mar where he resided to his death. Robledo netted seven times for the Magpies against Border Province on tour of South Africa during July 1952, while he scored four for the FA XI in October 1948. A sketch of his 1952 FA Cup winning goal was drawn by John Lennon as a child and featured on the 'Walls & Bridges' album in 1974.

Appearances & Goals:
Debut v Charlton Athletic (h) 5 February 1949
FL: 146 app 82 gls
FAC: 18 app 9 gls
Others: 2 app 0 gls
Total: 166 app 91 gls

Honours:
31 Ch caps 1950-58/WdC 1950/SthA champ final 1955/FA app 1949/FAC winner 1951, 1952/Ch Lg champs 1953, 1956/[Ch Cup winner 1958].

ROBSON Bryan Stanley 1962-1971

Striker
5'8"
b. Sunderland, 11 November 1945

Career: Clara Vale Jnrs/UNITED Nov 1962 £75/West Ham Utd Feb 1971 £120,000/ Sunderland July 1974 £145,000/West Ham Utd Oct 1976 £80,000/ Sunderland June 1979 £45,000/Carlisle Utd player-coach March 1981 £10,000/Chelsea player-coach Aug 1982 (Carlisle Utd loan 1982-83)/ Sunderland player-coach Aug 1983 free, becoming caretaker-manager March 1984/ Carlisle Utd July 1984, later becoming asst-manager and manager Aug 1985/ Gateshead Oct 1985/Newcastle Blue Star Sept 1986/ Manchester Utd scout 1987, becoming School of Excellence coach 1988/Hartlepool Utd asst-manager Oct 1988/Sunderland community officer Nov 1988/Hartlepool Utd coach 1989/Manchester Utd asst-coach July 1991/Sunderland asst-coach 1995, becoming Director of Youth Development Aug 1997 to May 2000/Leeds Utd asst-Academy Director cs 2000 to May 2004/Scouting for various clubs including Chelsea, Birmingham City & Blackburn Rovers/Sunderland chief-scout July 2011 to May 2013.

Joining United after trials at Leicester and Northampton, Bryan Robson netted the winner on his debut against Charlton as a teenager, but it took the small and chunky forward several seasons to become a deadly goal-poacher who would later be rated as the best uncapped striker in England. A fixture in Joe Harvey's plans from 1964 to 1967, Robson never found the net too often in that period, and was even set for a transfer away from Tyneside when out of the side. With Albert Bennett injured, Robson was given another opportunity and he stepped up from the Central League to team up with Welshman, Wyn Davies for the 1968-69 season. The partnership clicked and 'Pop', as he was known, started to bang the ball into the net, striking 30 for United in that season. The little and large duo combined perfectly as the Magpies stormed Europe. Robson was sharp, quick on the turn and revelled in the space that Davies created. He also could strike the ball sweetly from long range, hitting several quite spectacular efforts often in a big match atmosphere, and especially in European ties. Bryan was tipped for full England honours, but then had a controversial war of words with his manager Joe Harvey over a new contract and the lack of professionalism within the corridors of St James' Park. As a result Robson was off to Upton Park for a club record fee. The Wearsider enjoyed two marvellous spells at West Ham, scoring 104 goals in 255 matches, while Pop also served Sunderland with distinction too, over three different periods as a player when he recorded 182 appearances and 68 goals. He was the Football League's leading scorer during season 1972-73 (28 goals), and by the time Bryan had retired when into his 40's, had scored 305 goals. A fine golfer, Robson is a past winner of the footballers' championship; he ran a newsagency on Tyneside before concentrating on a career in scouting and coaching. Bryan is Sunderland's second oldest player, appearing for the red-and-whites when over 38 years of age; only another ex-Magpie player, Tommy Urwin has played for Sunderland when older. Although born in the Roker area of Sunderland, Robson left when three years of age and was raised in the Tyne Valley, at Prudhoe.

Appearances & Goals:
Debut v Charlton Athletic (a) 1 September 1964 (1 goal)
FL: 205(1) app 82 gls
FAC: 10 app 4 gls
FLC: 4 app 2 gls
Euro: 24 app 9 gls
Total: 243(1) app 97 gls

Honours:
3 Eng u23 app 1967-69/1 FL app 1970/FL div 2 champs 1965, 1976/FL div 2 prom 1980/FL div 3 prom 1982/ICFC winner 1969/PFA ToS (d2) 1979.

ROBSON Keith 1971-1974

Striker
5'11"
b. Hetton-le-Hole, Co Durham, 15 November 1953

Career: UNITED jnr, prof May 1971/West Ham Utd Sept 1974 £60,000 (Team Hawaii (USA) loan May 1977)/Cardiff City Aug 1977 £25,000/ Norwich City Feb 1978 £25,000/Leicester City Sept 1981 £30,000 (Carlisle Utd loan 1982-83)/ South China AA (HK) Sept 1983/Wroxham (Norwich) Aug 1984/Norwich Busmen/ Corinthians (Norwich)/Wroxham 1986/ Mackintosh (Norwich)/Wroxham Aug 1988, becoming asst-manager 1993 to 1998.

Tall and well-built, Keith Robson was a promising striker developed by the Magpies. However, he was unlucky to be at Gallowgate at the time of the Macdonald-Tudor partnership up front and consequently his chances of first-team duty were limited, although he did manage 16 games during season 1973-74 when Supermac was out injured. Robson was a good deputy and on moving to Upton Park, provided the Hammers with a skilful left-sided attacker. He totalled 89 games for West Ham, hitting 19 goals, including taking part in a number of successful cup runs during the mid-Seventies, although he missed out on the 1975 FA Cup final. Keith did however, figure in the Londoner's European final the following year, netting in the showpiece with Anderlecht after scoring a spectacular effort in the semi-final that clinched victory over Eintracht Frankfurt. Sometimes aggressive and temperamental on the field, at Carrow Road Keith gave some exuberant performances too in 75 outings. Robson later settled in the Norfolk area being heavily involved in local football as well as a match-day host at Carrow Road. For a lengthy period he worked as a machinist with Impress Metal Packaging before moving to Norwich Airport as an apron hand, guiding planes to their resting point. He is the only United player to have sampled football life at the idyllic Aloha Stadium in Honolulu on the island of Hawaii.

Appearances & Goals:
Debut v Chelsea (h) 24 March 1973
FL: 14 app 3 gls
FLC: 1 app 2 gls
Others: 3 app 1 gl
Total: 18 app 6 gls

Honours:
FL div 2 prom 1983 (1 app)/ECWC final 1976.

ROBSON Ralph 1939-1942

Inside-left
5'4"
b. Walkergate, Newcastle upon Tyne, 30 January 1922

Career: Parsons Works Jnrs/UNITED amat May 1939/Chopwell CW 1942.

Signed on amateur forms from local engineering works' line-up, CA Parsons in the Heaton area, Ralph Robson was a diminutive player at only 5'4" tall. Able to play wide on the left touchline, or in midfield, he found the promise of a professional career in soccer destroyed by the declaration of war four months after joining the Gallowgate staff. Robson was selected on a handful of occasions during seasons 1939-40 and 1941-42.

Appearances & Goals:
Debut v Bradford City (h) 8 June 1940 (FLNE)
War: 5 app 1 gl
Total: 5 app 1 gl

ROBSON Thomas Henry 1966-1968

Outside-left
5'8"
b. Gateshead, 31 July 1944

Career: Redheugh BC 1958/Northampton Town amat July 1959, prof Aug 1961/Chelsea Dec 1965 £30,000/ UNITED Dec 1966 £13,000/Peterborough Utd Nov 1968 £20,000/Nuneaton Borough May 1981/Stamford June 1982/Northampton Town Oct 1984/Chatteris Town Aug 1985/Peterborough Utd Nov 1986 asst-coach to 1989.

Having been at St James' Park, as well as at Old Trafford, on trial as a promising former England youth player, Tynesider Tommy Robson struggled to get a start in football and began a career as a garage mechanic in Bensham. He was given another opportunity though and started his sporting life in earnest with Northampton (82 app) before joining Chelsea following the Cobblers' rise to the top level during the Sixties. He had limited opportunities at Stamford Bridge due to the sparkling form of Bobby Tambling and an unfortunate bout of jaundice which kept him out of selection for six months. But when he was brought home by manager Joe Harvey as a wide player to replace Alan Suddick, Robson began to sparkle himself in a black-and-white shirt. A dedicated professional, Tommy always gave the side total effort, nimble and quick on the left wing, remembered for his tip-toe sorties at the opposition. Robson had one excellent season for the Magpies, during 1967-68, when he scored 11 goals in 40 games, helping the club into European football for the first time. But then he unluckily damaged a foot when gardening at home, a set-back which allowed in Geoff Allen. Robson lost his place, Harvey discarding the cheery winger and Robson moved to Peterborough where he became something of an institution for the next decade and more. The Geordie flanker clocked up a record total of 559 matches for the Posh and scored an impressive 128 goals. Tommy settled in Peterborough and played on in local minor football until 1994. He worked for the local newspaper, the Herald & Post, as well as being involved at London Road as a match-day host, later also covering the Posh for local radio.

Appearances & Goals:
Debut v Tottenham Hotspur (a) 31 December 1966
FL: 46(2) app 11 gls
FAC: 1 app 0 gls
FLC: 1 app 0 gls
Total: 48(2) app 11 gls

Honours:
Eng sch-youth app/FL div 2 prom 1965/FL div 4 champs 1974/FAV final 1984.

ROCHE David 1986-1993

Midfield
5'11"
b. Daisy Hill, Wallsend, 13 December 1970

Career: Walkergate Jnrs/Wallsend BC/UNITED jnr 1986, prof Aug 1988 (Gateshead loan 1992-93) (Peterborough Utd loan 1992-93)/Doncaster Rovers Oct 1993 £25,000/Southend Utd March 1995 £55,000 to March 1996.

As a juvenile, David Roche played in front of a 30,000 crowd at St James' Park during a pre-match schools six-a-side game. And, after being chased by Arsenal, Sunderland and Leicester, he was soon to be appearing for Newcastle United in a similar atmosphere. A tough tackling midfield player, David was the club's youth team skipper and was rapidly given a first-team debut as a teenager, then a regular place by Ossie Ardiles on the departure of ex-Scotland captain Roy Aitken. Roche gained valuable experience in the Argentinean's eleven, a side however which plummeted down the Second Division table. The Tynesider went through a torrid few months as Newcastle struggled and by the time Kevin Keegan had been installed at St James' Park, David was destined for a career in the game elsewhere. With Doncaster he totalled 56 matches before moving south to Roots Hall. Off the field Roche went through several controversial moments; he was once shot in the leg and sprayed with ammonia in a Tyneside night-spot, then at Newcastle Crown Court in March 1996 was convicted of wounding with intent following a city-centre attack. Roche was sentenced to four years imprisonment which effectively ended his football career. On release he resided in Wallsend, but found himself in trouble again, during July 2002 being arrested as part of a Northumbria Police operation code-named 'Hard Hit', convicted and jailed for eight years for his part in a drug dealing racket.

Appearances & Goals:
Debut v Arsenal (a) 15 April 1989 (sub)
FL: 23(13) app 0 gls
FAC: 1 app 0 gls
FLC: 2 app 0 gls
Others: 1(2) app 0 gls
Total: 27(15) app 0 gls

RODGER Thomas 1893-1895

Left-back
5'9"
b. Perth, 17 August 1871
d. Newcastle upon Tyne, 13 March 1946

Career: Perth Jnrs/St Johnstone 1888/ UNITED amat Jan 1893, prof Sept 1893/ Seaham Harbour March 1895.

Tom Rodger arrived on Tyneside during January 1893 from Perth, joining the club initially as an amateur player. Moving south to take up a position with the Newcastle Chronicle & Journal, having trained as a print compositor, he was a part-time player with United. Described in the Newcastle Daily Chronicle as "a young Scotch player", Rodger had played for St Johnstone as a 17-year-old. It was noted that he had "favourably impressed the committee with his powers". Tom was soon made skipper of the Alliance eleven and then became first choice left-back, Rodger having a good run in the club's senior eleven during season 1893-94, gaining notable praise during that first programme of Football League action. After six outings the following term though, he lost his place and decided to concentrate on his career in printing, remaining with the local newspaper for over 40 years. He retired in 1936, residing in Heaton. Tom was also a noted bowls player on the greens, as well as a proficient golfer.

(Note: Some sources have his name as, 'Rogers', but the family archive confirms Rodger.)

Appearances & Goals:
Debut v Liverpool (h) 25 November 1893
FL: 22 app 0 gls
FAC: 2 app 0 gls
Total: 24 app 0 gls

ROEDER Glenn Victor 1983-1989, 2005-2007

Centre-half, Coach & Manager
6'1"
b. Woodford, London, 13 December 1955

Career: Gidea Park Rangers/Arsenal jnr Dec 1969 to Feb 1972/Orient jnr Aug 1972/Queens Park Rangers Aug 1978 £250,000 (Notts Co on loan 1983-84)/UNITED Dec 1983 £120,000 to May 1989 free/Watford July 1989, becoming player-asst-coach July 1990 to Aug 1991/ Millwall late 1991/Leyton Orient player-coach Jan 1992/Purfleet Oct 1992/Gillingham player-manager Nov 1992/Watford coach June 1993, becoming manager July 1993 to Feb 1996/ Burnley asst-manager July 1997 to cs 1998, & England asst-coach 1997 to 1998/West Ham Utd asst-coach Feb 1999, becoming caretaker-manager May 2001, then manager June 2001 to Aug 2003/Scout for various clubs 2004 & 2005/UNITED Academy manager June 2005, becoming caretaker-manager February 2006, then manager May 2006 to May 2007/Norwich City manager Oct 2007 to Jan 2009/Aston Villa scout/Millwall scout June 2013.

Stylish, assured on the ball and tinged with a touch of arrogance, Glenn Roeder was Arthur Cox's final piece in his team building which ensured United's promotion to the First Division during 1984. An injury to Jeff Clarke forced United to pay out for the QPR defender and it proved a master signing. Originally a midfield player, early into his career Glenn moved into the back line and became a central figure in defence. Establishing himself over 158 games with Orient as an elegant, upright footballer, Roeder could always use the ball well and move forward in almost Continental style to make menacing progress forward. Having a crowd pleasing double-shuffle in possession of the ball which confounded opponents, he was a past skipper of Orient and QPR, leading out the Loftus Road club at Wembley in 1982. But Glenn unluckily

R

had to sit out the replayed final due to suspension following a dismissal in a league game. Totalling 181 matches for Rangers and on the fringe of a full England cap, he was also captain of the Magpies and served United with credit for six seasons. Entering management with Gillingham and Watford, he later took charge of West Ham and during the latter weeks of the 2002-03 season was rushed to hospital with what was later diagnosed as a brain tumour that required major surgery. Recovering from that set-back, Roeder returned to the North East during 2005 to take the post of leading Newcastle United's Academy. At the time of managerial upheaval at St James' Park he was on hand to become caretaker-boss alongside Tommy Craig in February 2006 on the departure of Graeme Souness. United's former skipper ended up being in charge for the rest of the 2005-06 season and such was the impression he made, guiding a struggling side from relegation worries into a final seventh place, he earned the manager's job outright in the summer. Like many ex-Magpies, Glenn had a burning enthusiasm for the club and its supporters, however season 2006-07 did not go well, although far from disastrous. Rocked by injuries to senior men like Owen, Duff and Parker, Newcastle's 13th place finish though was not good enough and Roeder was replaced during the close-season by a big-hitter, Sam Allardyce. Glenn departed in May 2007 and shortly afterwards took charge of Norwich City for a period then worked as a consultant and scouted for various clubs. Glenn had a period as Paul Gascoigne's minder and confidant when Gazza was in Italy. His father appeared in semi-professional football in the Southern League.

Appearances & Goals:
Debut v Blackburn Rovers (h) 26 December 1983
FL: 193 app 8 gls
FAC: 11 app 1 gl
FLC: 11 app 1 gl
Others: 2 app 0 gls
Total: 217 app 10 gls

In Charge: 73 games
Debut v Portsmouth (h) 4 February 2006

Honours:
6 Eng B caps 1978-80/FL div 2 champs 1983 (9 app)/FL div 2 prom 1984/FAC final 1982/PFA ToS (d2) 1982.

ROGERS Ehud 1936-1939

Outside-right
5'6"
b. Chirk, 15 October 1909
d. Chirk, 25 January 1996

Career: Weston Rhyn/Llanerch Celts/Chirk/Oswestry Town 1933/Wrexham May 1934/Arsenal Jan 1935 £2,600/UNITED June 1936 £2,500/Swansea Town May 1939 £700 (Wrexham war-guest 1939-41) (Lovell's Ath war-guest 1942-43)(Everton war-guest 1943-44)(Aberaman Ath war-guest)/Wrexham Dec 1945/Oswestry Town Feb 1947/Later, Chirk coach c1962.

Ehud Rogers was a Welsh amateur international before he caught the eye of Arsenal in 1935 after shining for Wrexham. He was light and fast, once described as "plucky", the Welshman possessed more than a touch of finesse on the ball. At Highbury Rogers was confined to largely being a reserve to the Gunners' famous stars, but grabbed five games in the 1935 title winning season. Whenever he did get a chance though he performed well, including netting twice on his debut in an 8-0 victory. His record of 16 games and five goals for Arsenal was form which alerted United. Joining the Magpies' Second Division attack, he was lively and dangerous for two seasons before fading due largely to injury just before the outbreak of the Second World War, replaced by another former Highbury reserve, Ralph Birkett. At St James' Park, as well as in North London, he often treated his colleagues to a Welsh song, tunefully rendered before leaving the dressing-room. Rogers served with the RAF in Egypt for a time during the fighting, while he also appeared for his country at full level in wartime football. He continued his career with Wrexham after the hostilities, registering a total of 97 games (34 goals) for the Dragons. Known as 'Tim', because apparently his colleagues could not pronounce his biblical Christian name, on leaving the game Rogers resided in Chirk and ran a newsagency. His brother, Joe, appeared for Manchester City and Shrewsbury.

Appearances & Goals:
Debut v Barnsley (h) 29 August 1936
FL: 56 app 10 gls
FAC: 2 app 0 gls
Total: 58 app 10 gls

Honours:
2 Wales war app 1941-45/1 Wales amat app 1934/1 WsL app 1935/1 Wales & Ireland combined app 1935/FL champs 1935 (5 app).

ROGERS Joseph James 1898-1901

Outside-right
5'11"
b. Macclesfield, 5 November 1874

Career: Stoke Utd/Macclesfield 1894/Southampton St Mary's Dec 1894/Grimsby Town May 1896/UNITED May 1898 £110/Preston North End Jan 1901 to cs 1902/ Germany playing and coaching c1903/Tivoli (Grimsby) c1906.

Joe Rogers was attracted to Newcastle United after a spell with the Mariners in which he bagged 24 goals in 57 outings. Joining United for the 1898-99 season, the Magpies first in Division One, Joe became a popular player, effective when in sight of goal and good enough to become the club's first international player. Joe was chosen to represent the FA eleven to tour Germany at the turn of the century, in all but name an international appearance. Joe had a field day on the Continent, netting seven goals on the tour, five in one fixture against a German XI. Following a stint with Preston (42 app) and then time spent coaching in Germany, he returned to England and resided in the Grimsby area for a period. At the beginning of his career with the Saints, Joe once netted 10 goals in a single game during 1895, but was afterwards strangely used in the full-back position!

(Note: There is some doubt over a recorded death in Meriden during 1955, this may be a different person.)

Appearances & Goals:
Debut v Stoke (a) 24 September 1898
FL: 54 app 10 gls
FAC: 3 app 1 gl
Total: 57 app 11 gls

Honours:
3 unoff Eng app 1900.

ROSS Eric William 1967-1969

Midfield
5'9"
b. Belfast, 19 September 1944

Career: Boyland Jnrs/Glentoran 1962 (Detroit Cougars (USA) loan cs 1967)/UNITED Aug 1967 £5,250/Northampton Town Aug 1969 £15,000 (Hartlepool Utd loan 1971-72) to cs 1976/ North Shields Oct 1976/Vancouver Whitecaps (Can) coach c1977.

As a youth star, standing out for Northern Ireland in the so-called 'Mini-World Cup' of 1963, Eric Ross developed into a great favourite in Ulster with Glentoran where he totalled over 150 games. Ross showed he was a probing midfield player with an accurate pass and shot. Joe Harvey gave him a chance to establish himself in England, but Eric struggled to make an impact on the First Division scene. Registering two appearances in each of seasons 1967-68 and 1968-69, Ross was capped by Northern Ireland when in United's reserve side, but failed to make the grade and push for a more regular place. He was transferred to Northampton where he totalled 70 games, far more effective at a lower level of football where he had time and space on the ball. Ross was on the field when Manchester United's George Best fired home six goals against the Cobblers in a famous 8-2 FA Cup victory. Bespectacled, Ross wore contact lenses on the field and later moved to Canada. He resided in Delta, British Columbia, employed as a travel agent with Uniglobe.

Appearances & Goals:
Debut v Lincoln City (a) 13 September 1967 (FLC)
FL: 2 app 0 gls
FLC: 2 app 0 gls
Total: 4 app 0 gls

Honours:
1 NI cap 1969/1 NI u23 app 1967/NI sch-youth app/1 NIL app 1967/NIL champs 1964, 1967/NIC final 1967.

ROSSI Giuseppe 2006-2007

Striker
5'9"
b. Clifton, New Jersey (USA), 1 February 1987

Career: Clifton Stallions (USA)/Parma AC (It) 2000/Manchester Utd jnr July 2004 £200,000, prof Nov 2004 (UNITED loan Aug 2006 to Jan 2007)(Parma AC (It) loan 2006-07)/Villareal CF (Sp) Aug 2007 £6.6m/ACF Fiorentina (It) Jan 2013 £8.2m.

Manager Glenn Roeder secured the loan signing of Manchester United's promising 19-year-old striker Giuseppe Rossi as the 2006-07 season began. Without the services of icon Alan Shearer, by then just retired, and Michael Owen due to injury, Newcastle's forward options were limited and Rossi boosted the manager's strike-force. Born in the USA of Italian parents, the small, compact and swift striker was highly thought of but arguably under-used by the Magpies. Strangely too often he was on the bench when he should have been on the pitch, Rossi only receiving five starts in black-and-white colours. He managed one goal wearing a Magpie shirt, against Portsmouth in a League Cup contest. Giuseppe returned to Old Trafford at the end of the year and found it difficult to push his way into Sir Alex Ferguson's line-up, only totalling 14 games, ultimately moving to Spain in search of regular action. Rossi flourished in La Liga as the little known Spanish club Villareal reached the Champions League. Favouring a role on the left alongside a main striker, he was an Owen-like predator, quick to take a snap-shot, and was soon capped by Italy going onto skipper the Azzurri in 2010. He rapidly became hot property, a player United could have potentially secured and developed. Despite a cruciate knee injury which wrecked his 2011-12 season, Giuseppe still made a big move to join Fiorentina, although he suffered more knee problems which put him on the sidelines again. Nevertheless, Rossi was part of the Italian squad and included in their 30-man pool for the 2014 World Cup, but for a second tournament running, unluckily missed the final selection.

Appearances & Goals:
Debut v Fulham (h) 9 September 2006 (sub)
PL: 3(8) app 0 gls
FLC: 2 app 1 gl
Total: 5(8) app 1 gl

Honours:
30 It caps 2009-date/OG 2008/16 It u21 app 2006-08/6 It u23 app 2008/It sch-youth app.

ROUTLEDGE Wayne Neville Anthony 2010-2011

Outside-right or Midfield
5'7"
b. Sidcup, London, 7 January 1985

Career: Crystal Palace jnr 2001, prof July 2002/Tottenham Hotspur July 2005 £1.25m (Portsmouth loan 2005-06)(Fulham loan 2006-07)/Aston Villa Jan 2008 £1.25m (Cardiff City loan 2008-09)/Queens Park Rangers Jan 2009 £600,000/UNITED Jan 2010 £2m (Queens Park Rangers loan 2010-11)/Swansea City Aug 2011 £1.8m.

Wayne Routledge could be described as the archetypal winger to have run the touchline for generations; small, tricky, fast and at times, alas, inconsistent. The Londoner began his football career with Crystal Palace, making his senior bow as a 16-year-old, and he totalled 123 games before stepping up a level when he joined Spurs in 2005 following the Eagles' relegation. Routledge then struggled to establish himself at White Hart Lane and also at Villa Park before landing in the North East. Chris Hughton (his ex-coach at Spurs) brought Routledge north to Tyneside from QPR during the January 2010 transfer window for an undisclosed fee of around £2m, in a bid to consolidate United's promotion campaign. Wayne played his part in the club's 2010 Championship victory, although was never an automatic choice down the right flank. On his day he could be direct and able to get in a match-winning cross, however that decisive ability was scarcely witnessed with Routledge more often becoming a player who for periods of

the game rarely made an impact. He was deemed surplus to requirements as Newcastle returned to Premiership football for 2010-11 and Wayne headed to Wales, joining newly promoted Swansea City. He then figured in the Swans top level revival and being more consistent, was a regular in Michael Laudrup's fine attacking line-up which secured the Football League Cup then entered the Europa League.

Appearances & Goals:
Debut v Crystal Palace (h) 27 January 2010 (sub)
FL/PL: 25(9) app 3 gls
FAC: 1 app 0 gls
FLC: 1 app 0 gls
Total: 27(9) app 3 gls

Honours:
12 Eng u21 app 2005-07/Eng sch-youth app/FL ch winner 2010, 2011/FL div 1 prom 2004/FLC winner 2013.

ROWLANDSON Thomas Sowerby 1905-1906

Goalkeeper
5'11"
b. Darlington, 1880 (Q2)
d. Becourt (France), 15 September 1916

Career: Charterhouse School/Preston North End amat 1900/Bishop Auckland amat Sept 1901/Trinity College, Cambridge University 1903/Sunderland amat Dec 1903/Darlington amat Dec 1904/UNITED amat Oct 1905 to 1906/As an amateur also served at various times; Old Carthusians & The Corinthians 1903-1910.

Tall and moustached in the style of Edwardian Britain, Tom Rowlandson was a typical gent of the era. A distinguished scholar, he was a noted amateur international player of the establishment, public-school educated at Charterhouse and a Cambridge Blue, Tom was a Corinthian personality. At St James' Park only briefly as an amateur, he deputised for Jimmy Lawrence just once, but did claim 12 outings in Sunderland's senior line-up. Also a full-back, Tom played for the Corinthians on 75 occasions, once against the Magpies in the 1906-07 FA Charity Shield fixture. He toured far and wide with England as well as Corinthian combinations, and like colleague James Raine, was a footballer with traditional amateur values, once described as "the finest type of Englishman". Residing in Yorkshire at Newton Morrell near Darlington, Tom practised as a solicitor and was a Justice of the Peace for the North Riding of the county. When the Great War started he was quick to help, handing his substantial country home over to the Red Cross to act as an Auxiliary Hospital. Tom soon joined up and was commissioned during September 1914 being awarded the Military Cross for his gallant exploits as a captain with the Yorkshire Regiment. He was afterwards a victim of the conflict, tragically killed in action in France during the Somme offensive, in the Battle of Flers at Courcelettes. Rowlandson was only 36 years of age, losing his life at the parapet of a German trench when leading his men from the very front. He is buried at Becourt Military Cemetery in France.

Appearances & Goals:
Debut v Bury (h) 21 October 1905
FL: 1 app 0 gls
Total: 1 app 0 gls

Honours:
2 Eng amat app 1907/Eng trial app 1906.

ROXBURGH Robert 1920-1924

Right-back
5'11"
b. Morpeth, Northumberland, 5 February 1896
d. Leeds, 20 November 1974

Career: Morpeth Comrades/UNITED Nov 1920 £50/Blackburn Rovers May 1924 £375/ Netherlands coaching c1935/Leeds Utd asst-trainer 1938 to Nov 1957, becoming asst-physio to June 1960.

During four seasons at St James' Park, Bob Roxburgh was resigned to be the great Bill McCracken's deputy. Appearing on 24 occasions during those campaigns, Bob performed well, especially in season 1922-23 when he was part of the side on 11 occasions. A safe defender who rarely took risks, however he had little option but to depart in order to guarantee first-team action; this he achieved at Ewood Park, claiming 128 matches for Blackburn when Rovers were a top First Division side. One Football Annual of the era summed up Bobby's play as "though quiet, and a neat kicker, he tends to limit his game by over attention to safety first tactics". Afterwards Roxburgh had a lengthy spell on the Elland Road backroom staff.

Appearances & Goals:
Debut v Arsenal (h) 30 April 1921
FL: 24 app 0 gls
Total: 24 app 0 gls

ROZEHNAL David Sebastian Klement 2007-2008

Centre-half
6'3"
b. Sternberk (Czechoslovakia), 5 July 1980

Career: Sokol Kozusany (Cz) 1988/SK Sigma Olomouc (Cz) 1989/Sokol Kozusany (Cz) 1997/SK Sigma Olomouc (Cz) 1998/Club Brugge KV (Bel) 2003/Paris St-Germain (Fr) July 2005/UNITED July 2007 £2.9m/SS Lazio (It) loan Jan 2008, pmt June 2008 £2.9m/Hamburg SV (Ger) July 2009/Lille OSC loan Aug 2010, pmt June 2011.

David Rozehnal was an experienced Czech Republic international defender who arrived on Tyneside in a £2.9m deal from French club PSG, one of several players to wear United's colours from the Paris giants. Tall and lean, Rozehnal wasn't the meaty and tough type of centre-back; more a cultured and positional defender who liked to read the game. He was smart and tidy on the ball, but lacked a physical presence to cope with many of the quality strikers in English football on the Premier League stage. David started out in United's 2007-08 rearguard alongside Cacapa or Abdoulaye Faye under Sam Allardyce's management, but lost his place as the year turned and Kevin Keegan arrived as a new boss. Rozehnal perhaps lacked a robust edge for English football, and he was disappointed when he wasn't given an extended chance in the side, this after turning down moves to Dortmund and Seville to join the Magpies. A league title winner with FC Bruges earlier in his career, after only five months at Gallowgate, the Czech moved back across the English Channel, initially on loan with Lazio then later with Hamburg and Lille where he played alongside Johan Cabaye and Mathieu Debuchy as they secured the French double in 2011. He was respected on the Continent and a regular performer at all his clubs.

Appearances & Goals:
Debut v Bolton Wanderers (a) 11 August 2007
PL: 16(5) app 0 gls
FAC: 1(2) app 0 gls
FLC: 1 app 0 gls
Total: 18(7) app 0 gls

Honours:
60 Cz caps 2004-09/WdC 2006/8 Cz u21 app/Euro u21 ch winner 2002/Bel Lg champs 2005/Fr Lg champs 2011//It Cup winner 2009/Fr Cup winner 2006, 2011 (sub no app)/Bel Cup winner 2004.

RUSH Ian James MBE 1997-1998

Centre-forward
6'0"
b. St Asaph, Denbighshire, 20 October 1961

Career: Hawarden Rangers/Chester jnr Aug 1977, prof Sept 1979/Liverpool May 1980 £350,000/Juventus (It) July 1986 £3.2m (Liverpool loan 1986-87)/Liverpool Aug 1988 £2.8m/Leeds Utd May 1996 free/UNITED Aug 1997 free (Sheffield Utd loan 1997-98)/Wrexham Aug 1998, becoming player-coach July 1999/Sydney Olympic (Aus) Nov to Dec 1999/Barnsley asst-coach Jan 2001/Total Network Solutions Non-Exec Director Sept 2001/Liverpool part-time asst-coach Jan 2003 & Wales FA coach 2003-04/Chester City manager Aug 2004 to April 2005/Wales Football Trust Elite Performance Director Sept 2007.

As the 1997-98 season began, manager Kenny Dalglish found himself with a striker headache. Having controversially sold Les Ferdinand to Tottenham, he then lost Number 9 Alan Shearer following a bad injury in pre-season action. To boost his limited options up front, Dalglish turned to his former team-mate at Liverpool, veteran striker Ian Rush, then with Leeds United. One of the country's all-time greats, Welshman Rush had seen it all at Anfield, winning 14 major trophies. In a glittering career which saw the deadly marksman net an astonishing 345 goals in 660 senior appearances for Liverpool and another 28 goals at international level, aged 36 years old his best years were clearly behind him by the time Ian settled at St James' Park. Although highly experienced, the sharpness and cutting edge was not quite there in a black-and-white shirt, Rush converting only two goals for the Magpies, although he did play Champions League football for United during their debut season in the competition. As a teenager Ian had trials with Wrexham and Burnley, and it was against Newcastle during 1979-80 that Rush had made a big impression as an 18-year-old striker for Chester, netting 18 times and helping knock out the Geordies from the FA Cup. He soon moved to Merseyside and on the road to 15 seasons at Anfield and a wonderful track record in the game where he became renowned as an incisive striker with speed, expert timing, positional awareness and deadly finishing. On retirement the Welshman settled in Cheshire and apart from his coaching appointments, carries out media work and is often seen back at Anfield. At the peak of his career Rush made a record move to join Juventus, but had an unhappy period in Turin, soon brought back to Merseyside by Dalglish. Ian twice witnessed football tragedy first hand; at Heysel in 1985 and Hillsborough four years later during 1989.

Appearances & Goals:
Debut v Aston Villa (h) 23 August 1997
PL: 6(4) app 0 gls
FAC: 0(1) app 1 gl
FLC: 2 app 1 gl
Euro: 1 app 0 gls
Total: 9(5) app 2 gls

Honours:
73 Wales caps 1980-96/2 Wales u21 app 1981-82/1 FL app 1991/Wales sch-youth app/FL champs 1982, 1983, 1984, 1986, 1990/FAC winner 1986, 1989, 1992/FAC final 1996/FLC winner 1981, 1982, 1983, 1984, 1995/FLC final 1987/EC winner 1984/EC final 1985/ESC final 1984/ICC final 1984/FoY 1984 (FWA)/PoY 1984 (PFA)/YPoY 1983 (PFA)/PFA ToS (d1) 1983, 1984, 1985, 1987, 1991/Eng HoF/FL Legend/MBE 1996.

RUSHTON George Robert 1944-1946

Outside-right
5'8"
b. Coxhoe, Co Durham, 11 February 1927

Career: Shotton CW Jnrs/UNITED amat Sept 1944/Horden CW/ UNITED prof Nov 1945 £100 to c1946/Horden CW.

Stan Seymour's scouting network during the latter years of the Second World War made sure a steady stream of young North Eastern talent ended up at St James' Park. George Rushton was one of many teenagers to try and earn a long term contract. Standing in on the wing for another of those budding soccer stars, Jack Milburn, during December 1945, Rushton never quite made the grade and left the scene during the 1946-47 season.

Appearances & Goals:
Debut v Blackburn Rovers (a) 1 December 1945 (FLN)
War: 1 app 0 gls
Total: 1 app 0 gls

RUSSELL Samuel R 1920-1925

Full-back

5'8"

b. Downpatrick, Co Down, 2 January 1900

Career: Oldpark Corinthians/Distillery (Belfast)/ UNITED trial Aug 1920, prof Sept 1920 £300/ Shelbourne May 1925/Bradford City Dec 1926/Derry City June 1931/Newry Town Oct 1932.

A hard-tackling defender, Sam Russell operated at both right and left-back positions for the Magpies. After crossing the Irish Sea to give a good showing on trial at Gallowgate during 1920, he earned a contract. Sam stepped in for established players, Hudspeth, Hampson or McCracken over five seasons for Newcastle before moving back to Ireland to claim honours and then onto Bradford City where he also found conspicuous success.

At Valley Parade, Sam made 145 appearances and helped City to the Third Division title and was chosen for his country. He was once selected for the English FA side, but had to withdraw when officials became aware of his Irish nationality. Russell served with the Royal Irish Fusiliers in World War One.

Appearances & Goals:

Debut v Manchester City (a) 2 May 1921

FL: 28 app 0 gls

FAC: 3 app 0 gls

Total: 31 app 0 gls

Honours:

3 NI caps 1930-32/2 IoI app 1926/FL div 3(N) champs 1929/EL champs 1926.

RUSSELL Thomas 1934-1937

Left-back

5'9"

b. Cowdenbeath, 23 November 1909

d. Cowdenbeath, February 1975

Career: Cowdenbeath Wed/Cowdenbeath Feb 1929/Rangers Feb 1933 £1,000/UNITED Aug 1934 £650/Horden CW May 1937 to 1939.

Having made an impact with Cowdenbeath over seasons 1930-31 and 1931-32 and totalling 67 games in Fife, Tom Russell was picked up by Rangers. A reserve fixture at Ibrox, Tom nevertheless still took part in a small way as Rangers lifted title silverware in both 1933 and 1934 before he headed for England. Russell moved to Tyneside hoping to break into United's side and make an impression in the Football League. However, even with Newcastle in the Second Division, he still found gaining a regular place difficult. Second choice to David Fairhurst, the Scot appeared during the 1934-35 season before moving into North Eastern League soccer with Horden.

Appearances & Goals:

Debut v Plymouth Argyle (a) 22 September 1934

FL: 7 app 0 gls

Total: 7 app 0 gls

Honours:

SL champs 1933 (5 app), 1934 (3 app).

RUTHERFORD John 1902-1913

Outside-right

5'9"

b. Percy Main, near Newcastle upon Tyne, 8 October 1884

d. Neasden, London, 21 April 1963

Career: Percy Main 1897/Willington Ath 1900/ UNITED Jan 1902 £375/Woolwich Arsenal Oct 1913 £800 (Chelsea war-guest 1918-19)/Stoke player-manager March to Aug 1923/Arsenal Sept 1923/Retired cs 1925/Arsenal Jan 1926/Clapton Orient Aug 1926/ Retired May 1927/Tunbridge Wells Rangers trainer Sept 1928/Tufnell Park trainer 1929.

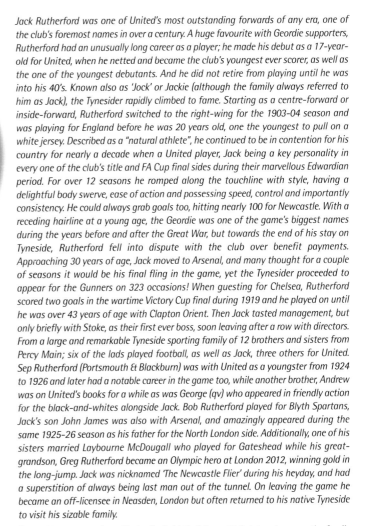

Jack Rutherford was one of United's most outstanding forwards of any era, one of the club's foremost names in over a century. A huge favourite with Geordie supporters, Rutherford had an unusually long career as a player; he made his debut as a 17-year-old for United, when he netted and became the club's youngest ever scorer, as well as the one of the youngest debutants. And he did not retire from playing while he was into his 40's. Known also as 'Jock' or Jackie (although the family always referred to him as Jack), the Tynesider rapidly climbed to fame. Starting as a centre-forward or inside-forward, Rutherford switched to the right-wing for the 1903-04 season and was playing for England before he was 20 years old, one the youngest to pull on a white jersey. Described as a "natural athlete", he continued to be in contention for his country for nearly a decade when a United player, Jack being a key personality in every one of the club's title and FA Cup final sides during their marvellous Edwardian period. For over 12 seasons he romped along the touchline with style, having a delightful body swerve, ease of action and possessing speed, control and importantly consistency. He could always grab goals too, hitting nearly 100 for Newcastle. With a receding hairline at a young age, the Geordie was one of the game's biggest names during the years before and after the Great War, but towards the end of his stay on Tyneside, Rutherford fell into dispute with the club over benefit payments. Approaching 30 years of age, Jack moved to Arsenal, and many thought for a couple of seasons it would be his final fling in the game, yet the Tynesider proceeded to appear for the Gunners on 323 occasions! When guesting for Chelsea, Rutherford scored two goals in the wartime Victory Cup final during 1919 and he played on until he was over 43 years of age with Clapton Orient. Then Jack tasted management, but only briefly with Stoke, as their first ever boss, soon leaving after a row with directors. From a large and remarkable Tyneside sporting family of 12 brothers and sisters from Percy Main; six of the lads played football, as well as Jack, three others for United. Sep Rutherford (Portsmouth & Blackburn) was with United as a youngster from 1924 to 1926 and later had a notable career in the game too, while another brother, Andrew was on United's books for a while as was George (qv) who appeared in friendly action for the black-and-whites alongside Jack. Bob Rutherford played for Blyth Spartans, Jack's son John James was also with Arsenal, and amazingly appeared during the same 1925-26 season as his father for the North London side. Additionally, one of his sisters married Laybourne McDougall who played for Gateshead while his great-grandson, Greg Rutherford became an Olympic hero at London 2012, winning gold in the long-jump. Jack was nicknamed 'The Newcastle Flier' during his heyday, and had a superstition of always being last man out of the tunnel. On leaving the game he became an off-licensee in Neasden, London but often returned to his native Tyneside to visit his sizable family.

(Note: Most sources have Rutherford's birth date as 12 October; however the family archive confirms this is his baptism date, Jack being born on 8 October.)

Appearances & Goals:

Debut v Bolton Wanderers (h) 1 March 1902 (1 goal)

FL: 290 app 78 gls

FAC: 44 app 14 gls

Others: 2 app 2 gls

Total: 336 app 94 gls

Honours:

11 Eng caps 1904-08/Eng trial app 1907-08/2 FL app 1904-22/FL champs 1905, 1907, 1909/FAC winner 1910/FAC final 1905, 1906, 1908, 1911/FAVC winner 1919/NU HoF.

RUTHERFORD Robert Edward 1905-1907

Centre-half

5'10"

b. Gateshead, 1878 (Q2)

Career: Birtley/UNITED trial Nov 1905, later amat April 1906 to cs 1907/ Later, Shildon Ath Feb 1909 to cs 1911/Birtley Nov 1912.

One of Tyneside footballs promising youngsters who was given a trial with United during the 1905-06 campaign, joining the club as an amateur towards the end of the season. Robert Rutherford was handed a single opportunity in Football League action at Anfield when United's team committee had problems with six senior men on international duty. Pushed up front in an inside-forward role, 'Ixion' in the Daily Journal remarked: "This was carrying the experimental game to extremes." Rutherford had just played reserve football against Bishop Auckland, then two days later faced the First Division leaders on Merseyside. Although the Magpies lost 3-0, and despite the comments of Ixion, Rutherford applied himself well according to contemporary reports of the match.

Appearances & Goals:

Debut v Liverpool (a) 9 April 1906

FL: 1 app 0 gls

Total: 1 app 0 gls

R

RUTHERFORD Robert 1943-1945

Inside-left
5'10"
b. South Shields, 20 April 1922
d. North Tyneside, 2004 (Q4)

Career: Wallsend St Luke's/UNITED amat Nov 1943, prof March 1944 (Hartlepools Utd war-guest 1944-45)/Gateshead Nov 1945 free to 1953.

Tynesider Bobby Rutherford's highlight during two years on the Gallowgate staff was a derby fixture with Sunderland when he scored twice in a 3-0 victory. In and out of the side during seasons 1943-44 and 1944-45, Rutherford later joined Gateshead where he accumulated 12 games in the Third Division North and FA Cup. On leaving football he became a draughtsman in the North East.

Appearances & Goals:
Debut v Darlington (h) 27 November 1943 (FLN)
War: 19 app 2 gls
Total: 19 app 2 gls

RUTHERFORD Thomas Victor 1938-1944

Goalkeeper
5'10"
b. Dunston, Gateshead, 18 July 1919
d. Wardley, Gateshead, 19 August 2000

Career: Scotswood/UNITED amat May 1938/Ashington 1940/ UNITED prof Dec 1942 to 1944 (Hartlepools Utd war-guest 1944-45).

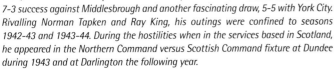

Tom Rutherford's brief period as United goalkeeper coincided with some remarkable results in wartime football. His debut against Gateshead on Christmas Day 1942 ended in a 6-6 draw, while he also took part in a 9-0 victory over Leeds, a 7-3 success against Middlesbrough and another fascinating draw, 5-5 with York City. Rivalling Norman Tapken and Ray King, his outings were confined to seasons 1942-43 and 1943-44. During the hostilities when in the services based in Scotland, he appeared in the Northern Command versus Scottish Command fixture at Dundee during 1943 and at Darlington the following year.

Appearances & Goals:
Debut v Gateshead (h) 25 December 1942 (FLN)
War: 25 app 0 gls
Total: 25 app 0 gls

RYAN John Bernard 1983-1984

Left-back
5'10"
b. Ashton under Lyne, near Manchester, 18 February 1962

Career: Mancunian BC/Oldham Ath jnr June 1978, prof Feb 1980 (Seattle Sounders (USA) loan 1979-80)/UNITED Aug 1983 £225,000/Sheffield Wed Sept 1984 cash-exch for P Heard plus £40,000/Oldham Ath Aug 1985 £25,000/Mansfield Town Oct 1987 £25,000/Chesterfield June 1989 £12,500/Rochdale June 1991 free/Bury Dec 1993/ Stalybridge Celtic July 1994/Radcliffe Borough Aug 1996.

Reports by several football commentators considered John Ryan to be a future England full-back after a string of impressive displays for Oldham. Reaching the Under-21 side in an international at Gallowgate before he moved to Tyneside, Ryan possessed lovely ball skills and attacking flair, characteristics of the modern style of full-back. Nicknamed 'Rhino' in the dressing-room, Arthur Cox swooped to bring him to St James' Park in a double full-back signing, John joining United's staff at the same time as Malcolm Brown. While Brown was unluckily injured almost immediately, Ryan stepped into Cox's promotion chasing side looking potent in attack, but occasionally fragile in defence. He was replaced by Kenny Wharton half way through the 1983-84 season, then Wes Saunders took over his role when Newcastle started a new spell at the top

level. Ryan faded dramatically from the top after that, moving to Hillsborough and back to Boundary Park where he totalled 112 games for Oldham. A double fracture of his leg in 1986 interrupted a career that had promised much, but he did go onto total 91 games for Chesterfield, 91 for Rochdale and 77 with Mansfield before a cruciate ligament injury halted his football days. John later became a partner in North Mancs Estates, a construction and development company in Greater Manchester then sold his share-holding during 2003. He was also a director of local side Radcliffe Boro for a period. His brother David Ryan appeared for Port Vale and Southport.

Appearances & Goals:
Debut v Leeds United (a) 27 August 1983
FL: 28 app 1 gl
FAC: 1 app 0 gls
FLC: 2 app 0 gls
Total: 31 app 1 gl

Honours:
1 Eng u21 app 1983/FL div 2 prom 1984/PFA ToS (d2) 1983.

RYDER Isaac James 1892-1895

Inside-left
b. Newcastle upon Tyne, 23 December 1871
d. Fenham, Newcastle upon Tyne, 26 May 1960

Career: Villa Association Jnrs, becoming secretary by 1887/ Newcastle West End 1891/EAST END cs 1892 to 1895.

From a popular local footballing family, Isaac Ryder was, with Joseph (qv), one of four brothers to feature in the early Tyneside game. Living in Westgate, Isaac was the younger of two brothers to play for the club and broke into the East End line-up during season 1891-92. A Victorian footballing stalwart of Newcastle, Ryder came into the side only once, but in what was to become a historic fixture, United's first Football League victory, 6-0 over Arsenal at Gallowgate. During his stay with the club, Isaac was restricted mainly to Northern Alliance football and once earned criticism from local reporters for "dilly-dallying" on the ball. Suffering a bad knee injury, he was a "moulders apprentice" when with the club, afterwards Isaac remained in the city employed at the Vickers engineering complex. His older brother William played for both West End and East End at reserve level, while the eldest of the family, Henry (qv), was East End's trainer. A younger brother, George, appeared with Bolton Wanderers between 1906 and 1908.

Appearances & Goals:
Debut v Woolwich Arsenal (h) 30 September 1893
FL: 1 app 0 gls
Total: 1 app 0 gls

RYDER Joseph 1892-1897

Goalkeeper
5'10"
b. Newcastle upon Tyne, 15 August 1873
d. Newcastle upon Tyne, 19 November 1945

Career: Villa Association Jnrs 1887/Elswick Rangers 1889/Newcastle Albion 1890/Newcastle West End 1890/EAST END cs 1892/Hebburn Argyle 1895/ UNITED Sept 1896/South Shields July 1897/ [Later possibly with Southwick & Willington 1895].

Joining United's founder club, Newcastle East End, Joe Ryder had to compete with several players for the goalkeeper's position during those early days at St James' Park. Newcastle tried four other custodians, Whitton, Lowery, Ramsay and Ward, and Ryder only managed two matches for the club. He was though a respected local character, good enough to appear for Northumberland County when he was on rivals West End's books. One of 14 children and brother of Isaac Ryder (qv) and trainer Henry Ryder (qv), he later served other Tyneside clubs with distinction. Joe hailed from the Westgate area of the city like the rest of the Ryder family and worked as a "plater's helper" on Tyneside.

Appearances & Goals:
Debut v Burton Swifts (a) 23 September 1893
FL: 2 app 0 gls
Total: 2 app 0 gls

SAHA Louis Laurent 1999-2000

Striker
6'1"
b. Paris (France), 8 August 1978

Career: FC Soisy (Fr)/INF Clairefontaine (Fr) 1991/FC Metz (Fr) cs 1995 (UNITED loan Jan 1999 to May 2000)/Fulham June 2000 £2.1m/ Manchester Utd Jan 2004 £12.83m/Everton Sept 2008/Tottenham Hotspur Jan 2012 free/ Sunderland Aug 2012 free/SS Lazio (It) Feb 2013 free/Retired Aug 2013.

Louis Saha's career in football reached the very top, winning the Premier League title and being part of the French squad which reached the World Cup final. Before all that dazzling success, as a young French striker at Metz with a French-Caribbean background, he landed on Tyneside on a loan deal in January 1999 when United's forward options were limited. With Duncan Ferguson injured and both Andersson and Maric almost ineffective as a partner for Alan Shearer, an extended loan deal was completed to last for the rest of the campaign. Saha was then a raw talent at 20 years old with only 31 games to his name, but with huge potential as he showed in his limited outings for Les Grenats. Wearing a black-and-white shirt he filled in when needed and went onto score a vital goal as a stand-in for Shearer in United's FA Cup run to Wembley; a Fifth Round replay winner at Ewood Park against Blackburn. Louis unluckily picked up a hamstring injury then a fractured cheek-bone, mishaps which followed him throughout his career, and was unfortunate not to be on the bench for the final against Manchester United. Manager Ruud Gullit wanted to sign him permanently in the summer but did not take up the option, judgement which proved a missed opportunity. He was disappointed and was determined to succeed elsewhere and noted his period on Tyneside in his biography: "Newcastle and its Geordies made me fall in love with England and its football." Not long after, Saha got the permanent move to the Premier League though, joining Fulham, initially in Division One, but firing the Londoners to the top with 32 goals in all competitions during season 2000-01. Often to appear with flamboyant hairstyles, after 63 goals in 143 games for the Londoners he earned a near £13m move to Manchester United with a series of merited displays and several picture goals. Saha had developed into a first-rate striker with a great first touch; he was quick, elusive, able to turn and shoot in a flash. His big negative though was a tendency to pick up injuries, notably persistent knee problems, and he was regularly on the treatment table throughout his fine career, notably missing the Champions League final of 2008 although his record of 124 outings and 42 goals for the Reds was still a good one. A decent spell at Everton (115 app 35 goals) followed then brief stays at White Hart Lane and on Wearside. Saha scored after only 25 seconds in the 2009 FA Cup final for Everton, the fastest in any final. Although he would have played in the 2006 World Cup final for France, he collected a yellow card in the semi-final and agonisingly was forced out of the FIFA showpiece against Italy. Saha became a football agent and consultant for the Stellar Group focussing on new French talent then in April 2014 he set up AXIS 10, a football solutions and player advisory company based in Luxembourg.

Appearances & Goals:
Debut v Chelsea (h) 9 January 1999 (sub)
PL: 5(6) app 1 gl
FAC: 1 app 1 gl
Total: 6(6) app 2 gls

Honours:
20 Fr caps 2004-13/WdC 2006/13 Fr u21 app 1998-2000/Fr sch-youth app/PL champs 2007, 2008/FL div 1 champs 2001/FAC final 2009/FLC winner 2006/PFA ToS (d1) 2001.

SALES Ronald Duncan 1941-1947

Centre-half
5'11"
b. South Shields, 19 September 1920
d. South Shields, 12 August 1995

Career: South Shields Town/ South Shields Ex Schoolboys/ Reyrolle Works/UNITED amat Oct 1941, prof July 1942 (Middlesbrough war-guest 1944-45)/Leyton Orient May 1947 £100/Colchester Utd Oct 1949 (Chelmsford City loan 1949-50)/ Hartlepools Utd Aug 1950/South Shields Aug 1951.

Ron Sales possessed a good left foot and started in the same line-up as Stan Mortensen at South Shields then with Johnny Dixon in the Reyrolle works side, two formidable post-war stars. Taking over from Tot Smith in the pivot's role for an extended period during season 1942-43, Sales showed he could develop into a good defender, being strong and positive. It was in London though that he made a breakthrough, recording 48 senior games for Leyton Orient before moving to the Victoria Ground, Hartlepool. He was forced to retire due to injuries with United later financing an operation on his knee complaint. Playing on in local football, he lived at Westoe and returned to the Reyrolle complex, working as a fitter. Ron was a self-confessed Newcastle supporter before and after his time on the St James' Park staff.

Appearances & Goals:
Debut v Huddersfield Town (a) 12 September 1942 (FLN)
War: 42 app 0 gls
Total: 42 app 0 gls

SALTHOUSE William 1940-1941

Outside-left
5'9"
b. probably Tyneside

William Salthouse was forward who joined United as an amateur during December 1940 from local football and who was only briefly at Gallowgate. He made a single outing for the Magpies, in a Tyne-Tees derby fixture on Christmas Day 1940. Salthouse came into the side for Laurie Nevins and had an ineffective afternoon as United fell 3-1.

Appearances & Goals:
Debut v Middlesbrough (h) 25 December 1940 (FLN)
War: 1 app 0 gls
Total: 1 app 0 gls

S

SANSOM Kenneth Graham 1988-1989

Left-back
5'7"
b. Camberwell, London, 26 September 1958

Career: Crystal Palace jnr 1975, prof Dec 1975 (Croydon loan 1996-97)/Arsenal Aug 1980 £1.35m/UNITED Dec 1988 £300,000/Queens Park Rangers June 1989 £340,000/Coventry City March 1991 £100,000/Everton Feb 1993 free/Brentford March 1993/Barnet Aug 1993/Petersfield Town Aug 1993/Partick Thistle trial Sept 1993/Wycombe Wand Sept 1993/Luton Town Oct 1993/Bromley Nov 1993/Chertsey Town Dec 1993/Watford player-coach Aug 1994, becoming asst-manager to Feb 1996/Sydenham Sports Oct 1995/Slough Town March 1996.

Former England skipper Kenny Sansom joined Newcastle as an accomplished 30-year-old defender with almost 700 senior games to his name. Short and compact, Sansom boasted a great left foot, was accurate in his distribution of the ball and a tough little competitor. The former Arsenal favourite provided experience and leadership for United's struggling line-up as they battled to steer away from the drop into Division Two. But Sansom's purchase was too late to save the Magpie's hide, although Kenny himself showed the qualities that had the Cockney recognised as one of the country's top players. Appearing in both the 1982 and 1986 World Cup finals, Bobby Robson once noted that he possessed "a dextrous left foot that could cuddle and cosset the ball". The Londoner made a name with Crystal Palace after being handed a debut as a 16-year-old and totalled 197 games for the Eagles before a multi-exchange deal saw him move to Highbury where he went onto play in 394 games for the Gunners, being a regular selection for the PFA's Team of the Season awards. Sansom had trials with Leeds before joining the Selhurst Park set-up, while he remains one of England's most capped players with 86 full internationals to his credit. After concluding his playing career Sansom entered the media in London, a co-presenter of LBC and Capital Radio's afternoon football programme, as well as a regular celebrity speaker at dinners and talk-ins. He went through a difficult period with self-confessed drink and gambling addictions, but recovered to become a popular host of the Arsenal Legends' Tour at the Emirates' Stadium and later in 2013 a coaching judge at Glenn Hoddle's Zapstarz soccer school. During the 1986 World Cup, Kenny was in the heart of England's defence when Maradona scored that infamous and illegal 'Hand of God' goal for Argentina. His brother played in non-league football in the south.

Appearances & Goals:
Debut v Sheffield Wednesday (a) 26 December 1988
FL: 20 app 0 gls
FAC: 4 app 0 gls
Total: 24 app 0 gls

Honours:
86 Eng caps 1979-88/WdC 1982, 1986/2 Eng B app 1979/1 Eng unoff app 1988/8 Eng u21 app 1979-80/Eng sch-youth app/1 FL app 1988/FL div 3 prom 1977/FL div 2 champs 1979/FLC winner 1987/FLC final 1988/FAYC winner 1977/PFA ToS (d3) 1977, (d2) 1978, 1979, (d1) 1980, 1981, 1982, 1983, 1984, 1985, 1986, 1987.

SANTON Davide 2011-date

Left-back
6'0"
b. Portomaggiore (Italy), 2 January 1991

Career: RC Mesola (It) 1997/US Ravenna (It) 1999/Internazionale (It) 2005 (AC Cesena (It) loan 2010-11)/UNITED Aug 2011 £5m.

Italian full-back Davide Santon was rated highly when he arrived on the scene in his native country as a teenage prospect during 2008-09. Joining Internazionale's youth system when 14 years of age and making his debut when he was 18, Davide quickly made an impact wearing Inter's blue-and-black stripes. He caught the eye for the Nezzarari, twice part of the squad which claimed the Scudetto. He was also a member of Jose Mourinho's squad which lifted the Champions League in 2010, although did not take part in the final. He was soon in contention for a place in the Italian national side, winning his first cap when still a raw teenager.

Playing usually at left-back, but also on the opposite flank or in a midfield role, Santon's rapid progress to the top was then put on hold when he suffered a knee injury playing for his country and was out for a lengthy period. He joined United after 51 games for the Milan giants during August 2011 when 20 years old, keen to make an impression and put his injury anguish behind him. Unluckily he suffered another knee injury in pre-season training and had to wait two months for his first outing for the Magpies. Once settled on Tyneside, Davide eventually found a slot at left-back in Alan Pardew's resurgent Magpie eleven and showed an urge to get forward, being quick, alert and dangerous in attack. Tall and athletic, he found life on Tyneside to his liking and became a popular Premier League player. Santon had a spell on loan with Serie A club Cesena in 2010-11 and skippered the Under-21 side before heading to England.

Appearances & Goals:
Debut v Tottenham Hotspur (h) 16 October 2011 (sub)
PL: 76(6) app 1 gl
FAC: 4 app 0 gls
FLC: 1 app 0 gls
Euro: 6 app 0 gls
Total: 87(6) app 1 gl

Honours:
8 It caps 2009-date/14 It u21 app/It sch-youth app/It Lg champs 2009, 2010/It Cup winner 2010.

SAUNDERS Wesley 1979-1985

Left-back or Centre-half
5'11"
b. Sunderland, 23 February 1963

Career: UNITED jnr Oct 1979, prof June 1981 (Bradford City loan 1984-85)/Carlisle Utd loan Aug 1985, pmt Nov 1985 £20,000/Dundee Feb 1988 £100,000/Torquay Utd July 1990 £60,000, becoming caretaker-manager April 1991/Retired due to injury cs 1993/Spennymoor Utd Sept 1993/Jarrow Roofing Aug 1997/Torquay Utd manager July 1998 to March 2001/Later, Jarrow Roofing asst-manager 2008.

United brought Wes Saunders, one of the region's top schoolboy players, through their junior ranks to replace Davies and Johnson at left-back as Arthur Cox was building the side to regain First Division status. Despite a few misdemeanours as a teenager, he impressed as a tall and powerful player. And Wes effectively switched to centre-half for the 1983-84 promotion season playing a part in that successful campaign. To many Newcastle supporters Saunders looked a sound player in the centre of the defence, however he fell from favour following a succession of managerial changes. Wes proceeded to have excellent spells in a lower grade of football, with Carlisle (116 app), Dundee (55 app) and Torquay (74 app), but a series of knee problems necessitating five operations forced him to quit the game. Saunders later returned to East Boldon, playing local football and employed in the family clothing business in County Durham. For a period Wes gained FIFA registration as a player agent and acted with the Grassroots Management and First Artists organisations. Saunders was a Roker Park regular as a kid, from a family of Sunderland fans.

Appearances & Goals:
Debut v Chelsea (a) 7 November 1981
FL: 79 app 0 gls
FAC: 6 app 1 gl
FLC: 8 app 0 gls
Total: 93 app 1 gl

Honours:
Eng sch-youth app/FL div 2 prom 1984/FL div 3 champs 1985 (4 app)/FL div 4 prom 1991.

SAWERS Alexander 1889

Full-back
b. Kilmarnock, 13 November 1865
d. Burnley, 2 March 1925

Career: Kilmarnock Nov 1885/Clyde/EAST END April 1889 to Nov 1889/Third Lanark by 1890/Clyde by Dec 1890/Burnley Sept 1892 to Aug 1893.

One of several Scots to head to Tyneside as football was developing fast during the late Victorian era, Alex Sawers was a member of a good Kilmarnock team which lifted the Ayrshire Cup in 1886 and noted as a "Scottish Corinthian". Described in the Northern Echo during 1889 as possessing "carthorse proportions", he was skilled and practised defender. Sawers' inaugural season of 1889-90 with East End saw the club enter league competition for the first time in the newly formed Northern League. The club needed his experience but he did not remain long in Heaton, it was reported that when playing for the Northumberland County eleven in Lanarkshire he remained in his native Scotland and did not return. Alex later had a spell back south with Burnley, in their line-up for a handful of both FA Cup and Football League matches. He was the elder brother of Bill Sawers who was capped by Scotland and served several clubs including Blackburn, Stoke and also Kilmarnock. The siblings played alongside each other for Clyde, while as a teenager Alex worked as a tailor, a trade he returned to when he settled in Burnley.

(Note: Newspaper reports have his name spelt both as Sawers and Sawyers, family history data also noting both.)

Appearances & Goals:
Debut v Darlington (h) 7 September 1889 (NL)
NL: 7 app 0 gls
FAC: 2 app 0 gls
Total: 9 app 0 gls

SCANLON Albert Joseph 1960-1962

Outside-left
5'10"
b. Hulme, Manchester, 10 October 1935
d. Salford, 22 December 2009

Career: Hulme BC/Manchester Utd amat 1950, prof Dec 1952/UNITED Nov 1960 £17,500/Lincoln City Feb 1962 £2,000/Mansfield Town April 1963/Belper Town Aug 1966 free to Oct 1966.

A survivor of the Munich Air Disaster in 1958, Albert Scanlon recovered from multiple injuries sustained in the crash; a badly broken leg, a fractured shoulder and skull, as well as kidney damage. And this after having just established a place in the Reds' line-up a few weeks before that fateful February day in Germany. He was 22 years old then, one of Matt Busby's famous Babes, Scanlon being twice an FA Youth Cup winner with Manchester United. Albert showed he was a direct and fast winger, part of the Old Trafford club's title victories in 1955-56 and 1956-57 as deputy to David Pegg. Totalling 127 games (35 goals) for the Old Trafford side, he was rated as one of the country's top young stars being perky and full of go on the flank. Once Albert recovered from his injuries, he got back into the Reds' line-up during season 1958-59, having a good season netting 16 goals and reaching the England Under-23 side. But afterwards his blossoming career stagnated due to a lack of consistency while he appeared to lose his spark and by the time Scanlon joined Charlie Mitten's squad on Tyneside, he was in need of a career boost. St James' Park though, never really suited the player; United were on their way into Division Two and when he played, Albert was often starved of the ball. After only one-and-a-half seasons contesting the Number 11 shirt with Liam Tuohy, Scanlon moved on. Afterwards he played on 116 occasions for the Stags at Mansfield before leaving the first-class game. He was later employed in a number of roles including dock worker at Salford for 15 years, security officer, bakery worker and warehouseman for Colgate Palmolive in the Manchester area. A road in Pendleton, Scanlon Lane, is named after him.

(Note: Although recorded in the Empire News Who's Who of 1955 as being Charlie Mitten's nephew, Scanlon later confirmed this was an error which endured for over 50 years. He has no family relationship with United's manager.)

Appearances & Goals:
Debut v Blackburn Rovers (h) 26 November 1960
FL: 22 app 5 gls
FAC: 4 app 1 gl
FLC: 1 app 0 gls
Total: 27 app 6 gls

Honours:
6 Eng u23 app 1959/1 FA app 1961/1 FL app 1960/FL champs 1956 (6 app), 1957 (5 app)/FL div 4 prom 1963/FAYC winner 1953, 1954.

SCARR Raymond 1942-1944

Inside-forward
5'6"
b. Chester-le-Street, Co Durham, 30 August 1921

Career: Chester-le-Street Old Boys/UNITED prof Nov 1942/Consett 1944/Murton CW 1944/Annfield Plain 1946 to c1956.

A regular in the Northern Combination League during season 1942-43, Ray Scarr was promoted to first-team action in the wartime Football League North, filling in across the forward line during seasons 1942-43 and 1943-44 when senior players were out of action. He later served Annfield Plain with distinction, registering 366 games for the Derwentside club over a decade.

Appearances & Goals:
Debut v Leeds United (a) 20 March 1943 (FLN)
War: 7 app 0 gls
Total: 7 app 0 gls

SCOTT David 1883-1889

Forward
b. Newcastle upon Tyne, c1866

Career: EAST END Oct 1883/Newcastle West End Nov 1887/Rendel 1888-89/EAST END 1888-89/Also Elswick Leather Works.

As a teenager David Scott joined the Newcastle East End set-up during season 1883-84 and made his debut in the first-eleven against Prudhoe Rovers. As a forward he became more a regular fixture in 1885-86 as East End took part in a programme of numerous friendlies before a league format arrived. Scott totalled almost 80 games (21 goals) in addition to his single first-class outing. He was good enough to appear for both the City of Newcastle and Northumberland representative sides. Dropping out of senior recognition shortly after his only senior outing, in the club's FA Cup debut at South Bank in 1887, David appeared for rivals West End and Rendel as well as continuing to turn out for the East Enders reserve combination. Scott lived in Byker during those years before the turn of the century.

Appearances & Goals:
Debut v South Bank (a) 15 October 1887 (FACQ)
FAC: 1 app 0 gls
Total: 1 app 0 gls

SCOTT Frederick Hind 1945

Outside-right
5'6"
b. Fatfield, Co Durham, 6 October 1916
d. Nottingham, September 1995

Career: Fatfield Jnrs/Bolton Wand Jan 1935/ Bradford Park Avenue May 1936/York City Feb 1937 (Gateshead war-guest 1941-43)(Charlton Ath war-guest 1943-44)(UNITED war-guest 1944-45) (Hartlepools Utd war-guest 1944-45)/Nottingham Forest Sept 1946 £3,000, player-coach 1954 to 1957, becoming trainer/Later scout for various clubs including Sunderland, Sheffield Wed, Blackpool, becoming Southampton chief-scout c1970.

An England schoolboy international during 1931, Fred Scott hailed from a mining background in County Durham. He joined Bolton then Bradford Park Avenue as a teenager and developed as an exciting winger with pace and a telling cross, but who struggled to find a regular place and had to move to York City. Serving in the RAF during World War Two, Scott took part in several wartime matches for United towards the end of the fighting on the Continent in 1945 and later served Nottingham Forest well, this after 167 outings for York. At the City Ground he became the oldest player to turn out for Forest, wearing the red shirt 20 days short of his 40th birthday. In all, Fred registered 322 games for the Trent club as they climbed from the lower reaches of the Football League. Later in his career, Scott became a noted scout, connected with football until 1983. He resided in Nottingham to his death.

Appearances & Goals:
Debut v Gateshead (a) 17 March 1945 (FLN)
War: 6 app 1 gl
Total: 6 app 1 gl

Honours: Eng sch-youth app/
FL div 3(S) champs 1951/FL div 2 prom 1957 (1 app).

S

SCOTT George 1929-1930

Outside-left
5'6"
b. Blackhill, Co Durham,
14 August 1904

Career: Crawcrook Albion/White-le-Head Rangers/Durham City amat 1923-24/Tottenham Hotspur trial 1924-25/South Shields March 1927/UNITED April 1929 £1,250/Crawcrook Albion Sept 1930/Gillingham Feb 1931/North Shields March 1932/Wigan Ath June 1933/Ashington July 1936/Crawcrook Albion March 1937.

George Scott began his career as a teenage winger in the Northern Alliance with Crawcrook and caught the eye of scouts. He was given a brief chance at White Hart Lane but soon returned north and then made a name for himself at Horsley Hill in 68 games for South Shields during their Football League era. He joined United's staff as cover on the flank for either Tommy Lang or Tommy Urwin. All his outings for the Magpies were during season 1929-30 before moving south to join Gillingham where he clocked up 39 matches. Slightly-built, he was like many of the touchline fliers of the era, tricky and fast. At Wigan, he played under Charlie Spencer's management and at Springfield Park scored plenty of goals in the Cheshire League; 101 in a little over 120 appearances.

Appearances & Goals:
Debut v Middlesbrough (h) 25 December 1929
FL: 7 app 2 gls
FAC: 3 app 0 gls
Total: 10 app 2 gls

SCOTT James 1967-1970

Midfield or Outside-right
5'9"
b. Falkirk, 21 August 1940

Career: Denny Rovers/Falkirk/Bo'ness Utd/Hibernian Oct 1958 (Toronto City (Can) loan cs 1967)/UNITED Aug 1967 £35,000/Crystal Palace Feb 1970 £20,000/Falkirk Jan 1972/Hamilton Acc July 1973 to 1975.

Jim Scott came from a noted footballing family. His father turned out for Falkirk and Burnley, while his brother, Alex appeared for Rangers and Everton; both Jim and Alex were also capped by Scotland. Scott was a player with a delicate touch, able to operate on the flank or in midfield. After establishing himself as a noted craftsman over nine campaigns at Easter Road (257 app, 75 goals), Jim gave United two very good seasons, as Newcastle qualified for Europe in 1967-68 and the following term when the Inter Cities Fairs Cup was secured. He is credited netting the club's first ever goal in European competition, against Feyenoord and during that memorable year Jim linked with Bryan Robson and Wyn Davies to good effect. He often struck important goals, one in the Fairs Cup semi-final and another in the final against Ujpesti Dozsa. Following a period in London with Palace, Jim moved back to Scotland, a broken leg when playing for Hamilton at Montrose brought an end to his career. Scott then settled in Central Scotland and teamed up with his brother to run the Hurlet pub then Aitken's Bar in Falkirk until his retirement during 2008.

Appearances & Goals:
Debut v Southampton (h) 19 August 1967 (1 goal)
FL: 70(4) app 6 gls
FAC: 4(1) app 1 gl
FLC: 4 app 0 gls
Euro: 14(1) app 5 gls
Total: 92(6) app 12 gls

Honours:
1 Scot cap 1966/Scot jnr app/ICFC winner 1969.

SCOTT James Adamson 1976-1980

Midfield
5'8"
b. Newcastle upon Tyne, 28 February 1960

Career: UNITED jnr July 1976, prof March 1978 (Carlisle Utd loan 1979-80)/Berwick Rangers Sept 1980 free/Ashington Dec 1980/Blyth Spartans c1981/Yeovil Town cs 1981 to cs 1982/Brandon Utd Nov 1982.

Known as Jamie and possessing plenty of stamina, grit and effort, Scott was introduced into United's midfield during a time of crisis as Newcastle slipped nearer to the relegation trapdoor during season 1977-78. With new blood needed, the Tynesider was given a chance, but while he was committed giving full effort, could not change results. Scott remained a squad player for another season before being released. As a youngster Jamie moved to Cannock as a six-year-old when his pitman father had to find new work in the Staffs coalfield, then headed back to Tyneside to join United. He was a fine athlete as a schoolboy, a proficient pole-vaulter; a sport he returned to once his footballing career was over. Scott became a noted pole-vault coach in the region, based at Gateshead International Stadium, being handed a UK Athletics award in 2006. His daughter, Sally Scott, also took up the sport, reaching the GB team. Jamie lives in Northumberland and also ran a stone supply business in Morpeth.

Appearances & Goals:
Debut v Chelsea (a) 18 March 1978
FL: 9(1) app 0 gls
Total: 9(1) app 0 gls

SCOTT John George 1910-1913

Outside-left
5'6"
b. Rosehill, Wallsend, 1890 (Q1)

Career: Wallsend Slipway/UNITED May 1910 £25/Grimsby Town May 1913 £50 to 1915/Grimsby Town war-guest 1917-19/Cleethorpes Town Nov 1919/Charltons (Grimsby) 1920.

A reserve to 'Wee Geordie' Wilson at outside-left, John Scott deputised for United during three seasons. Lifting the North Eastern League title with the Magpies' reserve outfit, he appeared on six occasions in 1911-12, one outing being a derby meeting with Sunderland at Roker Park. A late replacement, the press recorded his appearance, "with timidity trepidation"! Yet Jack, as he was more commonly known, was the hero of the day; he netted a late winner, scoring with the "essence of coolness", lobbing the Sunderland 'keeper from 12 yards with only three minutes left on the referee's watch. Small, yet well-built, he grabbed a chance of regular soccer at Blundell Park, being prominent during 1913-14, but events afterwards did not turn out as expected and after only 49 games he was given a free transfer on the condition he moved, as it was noted, to "any club but a league outfit". He then joined the army and served in World War One before returning to Humberside where he settled.

Appearances & Goals:
Debut v Woolwich Arsenal (h) 1 April 1911
FL: 8 app 1 gl
Total: 8 app 1 gl

SCOTT Kevin Watson 1984-1994

Centre-half
6'2"
b. Easington, Co Durham,
17 December 1966

Career: Easington
Jnrs/Middlesbrough jnr
1983/Sherburn 1984/Eppleton
CW/UNITED Dec 1984/Tottenham
Hotspur Feb 1994 £850,000 (Port Vale
loan 1994-95)(Charlton Ath loan
1996-97)/Norwich City Jan 1997
£250,000 (Darlington loan 1998-99)
to May 1999/Guisborough Town Jan
2000/ Consett 2001/Crook Town Nov
2001/ Middlesbrough asst-coach.

*Rejected at Ayresome Park and Filbert
Street and working in various jobs
including at a timber mill, Kevin Scott
was handed a lifeline by Jack Charlton and the youngster went onto to prove that he
was worth another chance in the game. A key figure alongside Gazza in Newcastle's
FA Youth Cup victory, on his senior debut for the Black'n'Whites Kevin found the net,
but then was promptly dropped and had to wait a couple of seasons before being
able to claim a regular place in defence. Under firstly Jim Smith, then Ossie Ardiles,
Kevin became United's first choice centre-half and skipper. Built for the position, he
could be a positive and dominating defender, but sometimes lacked the finer skills to
set attacks going. Although he played well during the Magpies First Division title
success, Scott then found himself replaced as Kevin Keegan fashioned a side to
challenge for the Premiership. He earned a big move though, to rejoin Ardiles at White
Hart Lane and his career looked to be taking off. But Scott found a place in
Tottenham's side difficult to hold down, especially when the South American was
sacked and he only registered 19 games in a Spurs shirt, his position taken by two
future United personalities, Sol Campbell and Colin Calderwood. Hampered by a knee
injury at Carrow Road, he moved back to County Durham on retirement. Scott worked
as a driving instructor with Loxley Driving Training in Billingham as well as coaching
at Middlesbrough's Academy.*

Appearances & Goals:
Debut v Sheffield Wednesday (h) 6 September 1986 (1 goal)
FL/PL: 229 app 8 gls
FAC: 15(1) app 1 gl
FLC: 18 app 0 gls
Others: 10(2) app 2 gls
Total: 272(3) app 11 gls

Honours:
FL div 1 champs 1993/FAYC winner 1985.

SCOTT Malcolm Ernest 1954-1961

Centre-half
6'1"
b. Westhoe, South Shields, 8 May 1936

Career: Redhead Works/Cleadon Jnrs Sept
1951/UNITED amat 1954, prof Sept 1955 £15
(Northampton Town loan 1961-62)/Darlington
Oct 1961 £2,200/York City Oct 1963 to cs
1965/Rugby Town Sept 1964 to Sept 1966.
(Northamptonshire County cricketer Oct 1959
to Sept 1969).

*Malcolm Scott had to play second fiddle to Bob
Stokoe for five seasons at St James' Park. A solid
defender nevertheless, Scott was big, somewhat
ungainly and recorded his first outing when still
a part-timer at the club. Sharing his football
with a career as an apprentice marine fitter at
John Redheads on the Tyne, Scott made his
debut as a 20-year-old in an emergency after
Stokoe had dropped out just before a game at Old Trafford. Travelling through the
night, Malcolm arrived in time to face England leader Tommy Taylor and had a
harrowing baptism, the Reds winning 6-1. His best season was 1958-59 (16 games);*

*while Scott was also tried at centre-forward on a few occasions, once against Leeds
he netted twice when up against Jack Charlton. The press of the day noted he "proved
well worthy of a prolonged run as leader of the attack". Malcolm missed a good slice
of football due to National Service and later moved to York and Darlington where he
registered 52 appearances before calling it a day. However, that was not the end of
Scott's athletic career. He was also a talented cricketer, a sport he played alongside
his football. Malcolm was an exceptional all-rounder, initially with club side South
Shields and with Durham at 17 years of age. He played for the county from 1953 to
1956 (29 matches), progressing to join Northants, a regular player alongside Colin
Milburn at first-class level for a decade. Once in 1956, when still on United's books as
a footballer, he played against the Aussie touring side, against the likes of Keith Miller
and Ritchie Benaud. He scored over 2,000 runs and took 461 wickets in his 185 county
matches, just missing out on the County Championship during 1965 and tipped for
an England place the following year. A spin bowler, he was once banned in August
1967 for an unorthodox action which contravened the rules. Also playing club cricket
for Walsall, for a period Malcolm also worked as a cricket coach for Queen's College
in South Africa during 1966, afterwards becoming a sports coach at the Royal
Wolverhampton School. He then was employed with outfitters Gray's of Cambridge
before looking after the sporting activities at St John's Community Home near
Towcester and then being in charge of St Gilbert's Community Home near
Kidderminster. Scott resides in Stourport in Worcestershire, his father, Ernest Scott
once scored five goals for QPR in a reserve trial against Tottenham during 1933.*

Appearances & Goals:
Debut v Manchester United (a) 12 January 1957
FL: 25 app 2 gls
FAC: 1 app 0 gls
Total: 26 app 2 gls

SCOTT Matthew 1889-1892, 1895

Goalkeeper
b. Newcastle upon Tyne, 1867 (Q3)
d. Newcastle upon Tyne, 27 December 1897

Career: Boundary/Elswick Rangers/EAST END Oct
1889/Sunderland Nov 1892/UNITED trial 1895/
Willington Ath March 1896/South Shields May 1897/
Elswick Leather Works.

*A prominent goalkeeper for Newcastle East End who
was signed from Elswick Rangers as the 1889-90
Northern League season was underway. Replacing
Duncan Henderson between the posts, Matt Scott was
a well-known local player and proceeded to become
the first East End player to face a penalty-kick, introduced for season 1890-91. Against
Darlington he saw the spot-kick sail over the bar. Scott was captured by Sunderland
in 1892, a club then with top-level status, joining the Newcastle Road staff in
November 1892. He made a single appearance against Wolves for the red-and-whites
in Football League action during season 1893-94 when they finished in runners-up
spot. He departed Wearside to join South Shields after a long period as a reserve to
the famous Ted Doig. With East End he was a sound 'keeper, Scott played on several
occasions for the Northumberland County XI and also represented the Newcastle &
District combination. Matt had a brief spell back with the club, on Newcastle United's
staff in 1895 when he appeared for the 'A' side, while apart from his 50-odd matches
in the first-class record book, totalled another half-century friendly and miscellaneous
games.*

Appearances & Goals:
Debut v Darlington St Augustine's (a) 26 October 1889 (FACQ)
NL: 42 app 0 gls
FAC: 9 app 0 gls
Total: 51 app 0 gls
(Void NL: 3 app 0 gls)

S

SCOTT Matthew McLintock 1900-1901

Left-back
5'10"
b. Airdrie, 11 July 1872
d. Milton, Glasgow, 14 August 1941

Career: Airdrieonians Sept 1890/UNITED Oct 1900/ Airdrieonians May 1901/Albion Rovers Oct 1901/ Stevenston Thistle Nov 1901/ Airdrieonians June 1904 to 1907.

A strapping and experienced full-back, Matt Scott spent six seasons in Airdrie's ranks before heading to Tyneside. A defender who kicked the ball long and with purpose, as well as specialising in off the line clearances, he was a valued player on the Scottish circuit, Northern Gossip magazine noting that "he has distinguished himself many a time, oft in the land of oatmeal and whisky"! At his peak with Airdrie, Scott played in the blue shirt of his country and was signed by United's directors as cover for Dave Gardner for the 1900-01 season. He infrequently gained a place in the side, by accounts of the day being a touch slow when against a winger with pace. His brother Robert was also a Scottish international with Airdrie. Matt was forced to semi-retire from the game after a severe injury when playing for Albion Rovers against Renton during February 1903, although he did attempt a comeback with Airdrie. He later lived in that Lanarkshire town.

Appearances & Goals:
Debut v Sheffield United (a) 8 December 1900
FL: 5 app 0 gls
Total: 5 app 0 gls

Honours:
1 Scot cap 1898/Scot trial 1890-98.

SCOTT William 1938-1946

Centre-forward
5'10"
b. Bucksburn, near Aberdeen, 10 October 1916
d. Bridge of Don, August 1994

Career: Woodside/Aberdeen July 1934/UNITED Sept 1938 £3,750 (Linfield war-guest 1941-42)/Consett July 1946 free.

United officials were suitably impressed when they watched Willie Scott net five goals for Aberdeen reserves as a 21-year-old. Not a regular with the Dons, claiming only 27 appearances in three seasons, a deal was settled on the spot with the Pittodrie club, and Willie travelled to Tyneside to bid for one of the forward positions. Rivalling Cairns and Stubbins, tragedy struck for the tearaway striker when he soon broke a leg and by the time he was fit again, war had been declared and his career was curtailed. Scott did, however, go onto play wartime football for the Magpies. He joined up with the local Tyneside Scottish battalion and was one of the many caught up in the evacuation at Dunkirk, captured and imprisoned in Germany. It is recorded by the club that the directors sent him "a parcel of comforts" during his incarceration. He returned to St James' Park in 1946 as a 29-year-old on peace being restored, but found that his near five-year detention had taken its toll. He was released and soon called a day to his footballing career. On retiring, Willie worked at Consett steelworks, before moving to Kincorth and Bridge of Don, near Aberdeen. He was for the latter part of his life a 'lollipop man' in Aberdeen. His son Jocky Scott, was a noted Scottish League player, coach and manager to several clubs including Dundee and Aberdeen.

Appearances & Goals:
Debut v Brentford (a) 7 January 1939 (FAC)
FL: 6 app 2 gls
FAC: 3 app 0 gls
War: 7 app 3 gls
Total: 16 app 5 gls
(Void FL: 3 app 1 gl)

SCOTT William Hill 1923-1926

Centre-forward
5'8"
b. Caldervale, near Airdrie, 22 December 1900
d. 25 January 1974

Career: Cleland Jnrs/Larkhall Thistle/Airdrieonians Feb 1923/UNITED March 1923 £800/Retired due to injury May 1926/Armadale Oct 1928.

A star of junior football north of the border, William Scott possessed all the qualities to become a hit in England. The Scot had pace, ball control and a shoot-on-sight instinct. A reserve to Neil Harris, he became a popular forward in the club's North Eastern League line-up, but was out of action for several months with a bad leg injury he picked up during season 1923-24. Willie actually called a halt to his career in October 1924, but made a comeback only for the injury to break down again, finally forcing Scott out of football. He did resume with Armadale in the Scottish Second Division for a brief period, but his contract was cancelled after a single game. United claimed compensation for his loss from the Football League's Mutual Insurance Federation in place at the time.

Appearances & Goals:
Debut v West Bromwich Albion (a) 14 March 1923
FL: 4 app 0 gls
Total: 4 app 0 gls

Honours:
Scot jnr app.

SCOULAR James 1953-1961

Right-half
5'7"
b. Livingston, West Lothian,
11 January 1925
d. Cardiff, 19 March 1998

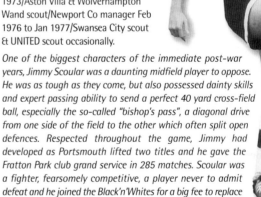

Career: Livingston Station/Edinburgh Waverley/Gosport Borough 1943/ Portsmouth Dec 1945/UNITED June 1953 £22,250/ Bradford Park Avenue player-manager Jan 1961 £1,300 to May 1964/ Cardiff City manager June 1964 to Nov 1973/Aston Villa & Wolverhampton Wand scout/Newport Co manager Feb 1976 to Jan 1977/Swansea City scout & UNITED scout occasionally.

One of the biggest characters of the immediate post-war years, Jimmy Scoular was a daunting midfield player to oppose. He was as tough as they come, but also possessed dainty skills and expert passing ability to send a perfect 40 yard cross-field ball, especially the so-called "bishop's pass", a diagonal drive from one side of the field to the other which often split open defences. Respected throughout the game, Jimmy had developed as Portsmouth lifted two titles and he gave the Fratton Park club grand service in 285 matches. Scoular was a fighter, fearsomely competitive, a player never to admit defeat and he joined the Black'n'Whites for a big fee to replace Joe Harvey as skipper. With the same driving qualities as his noted predecessor, Scoular was injured on his debut against Sunderland, wrenching a knee, but soon returned to lead United to Wembley in 1955 when he dominated the game against Manchester City and snuffed out the menace of the much vaunted 'Revie Plan'. On that occasion Charlie Buchan recorded, "I have never previously seen a wing-half display as good as that of Scoular in any big game". Jimmy was a formidable friend and foe; he had a pugnacious reputation and fell out with colleagues, opponents and referees along the way. Bob Stokoe made the comment he could be "obnoxious" at times and the cause of "friction" in the dressing-room. Often labelled as a "dirty so-and-so" by rivals, on the other hand described as "robust but fair" by United and Pompey fans, no-body though could argue with his contribution to the game, clocking up over 600 matches. After a fluctuating spell in management with Bradford Park Avenue and Cardiff, Jimmy was employed for a chemical firm as well as running a guest-house in Cardiff before retiring to live in the South Wales area. Before turning to football, Scoular worked at a steel foundry while during the war years he served in the Royal Navy, on HMS Dolphin at Gosport then as a submarine engineer. His father, Alec appeared for several Scottish clubs from 1915 to 1933.

Appearances & Goals:
Debut v Sunderland (h) 22 August 1953
FL: 247 app 6 gls
FAC: 24 app 0 gls
Others: 1 app 0 gls
Total: 272 app 6 gls

Honours:
7 Scot caps 1951-53/FL champs 1949, 1950/FAC winner 1955/FL div 4 prom 1961(m)/WsC winner 1965(m), 1967(m), 1968(m), 1969(m), 1970(m), 1971(m)/WsC final 1972(m).

SELLARS Scott 1993-1995

Midfield
5'7"
b. Sheffield, 27 November 1965

Career: Brunsmeer Ath/Leeds Utd jnr Dec 1981, prof July 1983/Blackburn Rovers July 1986 £25,000/Leeds Utd July 1992 £800,000/ UNITED March 1993 £600,000/Bolton Wand Dec 1995 £750,000/Huddersfield Town July 1999 free/AGF Aarhus (Den) April 2001/Port Vale Jan 2002/Mansfield Town March 2002/ Kettering Town July 2002 briefly/Mansfield Town Aug 2002, becoming asst-coach/ Sheffield Utd asst-coach Aug 2003/ Chesterfield asst-manager Feb 2008 to June 2009/Manchester City Head of Academy Oct 2009 to April 2014/ Wolverhampton Wand asst-coach July 2014.

Scott Sellars arrived on Tyneside as a replacement for the aging Kevin Sheedy. With a left foot as sweet as the former Everton midfielder, Sellars had not seen regular first-team action for a year, having been unable to break fully into a Leeds side during his second spell at Elland Road, despite being a substantial purchase from Ewood Park. Slipping into Newcastle's left flank, the Yorkshireman quickly began to show the Geordie crowd that his delicate skills could give United's promotion side balance as well as vision. The slightly-built Sellars became an influential figure as the Magpies entered the Premiership. He was accurate with his passing and always a danger at pulling the ball back for Andy Cole to pounce. A bad cartilage injury just when he was on top form though, put Scott out of action for nine months, and by the time he was fully fit he had the presence of David Ginola to contend with; he subsequently moved to Burnden Park in search of regular action. During the early part of his career, Sellars was chased by both Sheffield Wednesday and Manchester United as a teenager, and made his Football League debut as a 17-year-old for Leeds. A dead ball expert around the box, he was one of a handful of modern players to become heroes of the Toon Army by scoring a much recalled goal against rivals Sunderland; hitting a superb match-winning free-kick during United's promotion campaign. Scott appeared in four promotion play-offs with Blackburn, succeeding at Wembley in 1992. He enjoyed a first-class stay at Ewood Park, recording 245 games (41 goals) later becoming a noted coach to youngsters and landing the top Academy job at Manchester City. During 2012 Sellars was involved in a fatal motor accident.

Appearances & Goals:
Debut v Charlton Athletic (h) 10 March 1993
FL/PL: 56(5) app 5 gls
FAC: 3 app 0 gls
FLC: 6(1) app 2 gls
Euro: 4 app 1 gl
Total: 69(6) app 8 gls

Honours:
3 Eng u21 app 1988/FL div 1 champs 1993, 1997/PL runners-up 1996 (6 app)/FL div 2 prom 1992/FL div 3 prom 2002 (6 app)/PFA ToS (d2) 1990, 1992.

SERRANT Carl 1998-2001

Left-back
6'0"
b. Bradford, 12 September 1975

Career: FA Lilleshall Academy/Oldham Ath jnr, prof July 1994/UNITED July 1998 £500,000 (Bury loan 1998-99)(Sheffield Utd 2000-01)/ Retired due to injury May 2001/Bradford Park Avenue trial July 2003/Droylesden Aug 2004/ Farsley Celtic Jan 2005/Crystal Palace fitness-coach Nov 2007/Sheffield Utd fitness-coach cs 2008/Queens Park Rangers fitness-coach July 2010.

Newcastle United tried several players in an attempt to fill the void left by John Beresford at left-back when he departed during February 1998. One of those footballers was Oldham Athletic's Carl Serrant, purchased for what was a modest £500,000 in the summer close-down. Having recovered from a back injury as a youngster which put him on the sidelines for over a year, Serrant then picked up bad thigh and knee complaints. Carl bounced back though and was a regular at Boundary Park in the Latics' Division Two side. Totalling just over 100 games for Oldham, Serrant warranted good reviews and reached both the England Under-21 side and England 'B' line-up during season 1997-98. A positive overlapping full-back, he was a player tipped for the full eleven, called up for senior England training just after joining the Magpies, and Kenny Dalglish saw the 22-year-old as a United star of the future. Competing for selection at Gallowgate with Domi, Griffin, Quinn and veteran Stuart Pearce as well as Pistone, the Yorkshireman managed only a handful of games for the Magpies, unfortunate that Dalglish's replacement, Ruud Gullit, did not share the Scot's positive assessment of him. Carl's career was wrecked by another serious knee injury, tearing his medial ligament against Southampton as the 1999-2000 season began. Serrant struggled to regain fitness with his knee not being strong enough to stand the rigours of first-class football. He officially retired from first-class action during May 2001 when only 25 years of age, but played on in non-league for a period. Serrant then took up fitness training, having much real-life experience, and studied for a degree in sports science at Leeds University during 2002. He was appointed as part of the Crystal Palace backroom team, later moving onto QPR.

Appearances & Goals:
Debut v Liverpool (h) 30 August 1998
FL/PL: 5(1) app 0 gls
Euro: 0(1) app 0 gls
Total: 5(2) app 0 gls

Honours:
1 Eng B app 1998/2 Eng u21 app 1998/Eng sch-youth app/1 FL app 1997.

SEYMOUR Colin Matthew 1940-1943

Inside-left
5'9"
b. Newcastle upon Tyne, 1921 (Q4)
d. Bedale, Yorkshire, 9 October 1943

Career: Heaton Stannington 1939/Gateshead amat 1939/ North Shields amat//UNITED amat March 1940 to death.

The son of United's former star winger, and director, Stan Seymour (qv), Colin was a former Royal Grammar School pupil and a schoolboy international at rugby and cricket. Taking part in a few wartime games during the 1939-40 and 1942-43 seasons, as well as more frequently in the club's reserve outfit, Seymour's debut for the club was a resounding 6-1 victory over Halifax Town at Gallowgate. He later tragically lost his life during a training flight in Yorkshire. Joining the RAF as a wireless operator and air gunner, he became a pilot officer during 1943 and served in bombing operations over Germany. On a practice run his aircraft crashed in Wensleydale when returning to his base in Lossiemouth and at 22 years of age was killed. His brother Stan (junior) (qv) later became a United director.

Appearances & Goals:
Debut v Halifax Town (h) 29 May 1940 (FLNE)
War: 3 app 0 gls
Total: 3 app 0 gls

S

SEYMOUR George Stanley 1920-1929, 1938-1978

Outside-left, Manager, Director & Chairman
5'7"
b. Kelloe, Co Durham, 16 May 1893
d. Newcastle upon Tyne, 24 December 1978

Career: Kelloe Church/Sacriston Utd (Trimdon Grange guest)/Shildon Town (UNITED trial Aug 1911)/Coxhoe/Bradford City Sept 1911 £150/ Morton Feb 1913 £300/UNITED May 1920 £2,500/Retired June 1929/UNITED director June 1938 to April 1976, becoming Chairman 1953 to 1955, Honorary Manager Sept 1939 to March 1947 & Dec 1950 to Dec 1954/Vice President April 1976 to death.

One of the most distinguished names in United's history, Stan Seymour was associated with the club for almost 50 years and was known throughout the football community as 'Mr Newcastle'. On trial as a teenager with the Magpies, he arrived for the run-out without boots; Stan hardly touched the ball and was sent packing, told he was "too young and small". Seymour continued his trade as an apprentice joiner at a local pit before joining Bradford City where he made an impact. He then moved to Cappielaw with Morton where Stan flourished, a noted winger over eight seasons and 242 games, showing he could frequently score from the flank, netting 88 goals in Scotland. Working in a torpedo factory on the Clyde during the First World War, Stan returned to Gallowgate bigger and stronger and as an established footballer. Seymour went on to dominate the outside-left position in a black-and-white shirt for eight seasons as a goalscoring winger of merit. He linked stylishly with Tom McDonald, then also with Hughie Gallacher, as the Geordies lifted the FA Cup as well as Football League silverware three years later, an ever-present in both successes, scoring at Wembley as well as grabbing 18 goals in the title campaign. On the fringe of a full England cap, Seymour did win unofficial honours during a tour of Australia in 1925 but was unlucky not to gain a senior call up. His retirement was surrounded in controversy; Stan being in dispute with the club over benefit payments leaving United with some bitterness and acrimony. Thereafter he concentrated on a tobacconist and confectionary shop in Byker then later a sports outfitter's business, as well as becoming a journalist in the city covering Gateshead's Football League matches for the Evening Chronicle and Sunday Sun. Yet in 1938 with United in a dire situation, he was surprisingly invited to join the board to give the club fresh zest and the benefit of his experience as a top player. Despite being a rarity in football then for a star footballer to become a director, Seymour began to fashion the next great United line-up. After World War Two, the Magpies became one of the top attractions in the country and much of the credit was down to Seymour's vision. He was for many of those successful years during the Fifties, manager in all but name, often seen in suit and trilby hat, achieving the 'double' of playing in and managing a FA Cup winning eleven. And even when the club did have a boss, Seymour possessed tremendous influence on team affairs. Having unrivalled contacts in the game both north and south of the border, Seymour was a director who didn't appear a world apart from the players or spectators, occasionally even standing on the terraces to gauge supporters' opinions. A formidable figure, Stan could be frank and direct, sometimes controversial, and he did have well publicised differences with fellow board members. He continued to run his well-known sports shop in Newcastle, on what was known as "Seymour's Corner", while his son, Stan (junior) (qv) also took the Chairman's position at St James' Park. Another son, Colin (qv), appeared for United in wartime football and his brother-in-law, Bobby Fisher appeared for Durham City in Football League action during the 1920s. Before Stan was at St James' Park for a trial as a youngster, he was offered a chance at his boy-hood favourites Sunderland, but the future Magpie doyen never turned up at Roker Park.

Appearances & Goals:
Debut v West Bromwich Albion (h) 28 August 1920 (1 goal)
FL: 242 app 73 gls
FAC: 24 app 11 gls
Total: 266 app 84 gls

Honours:
2 unoff Eng app 1925/1 Eng unoff war app 1918/Eng trial app 1921-26/2 FL app 1925-28/1 FL war app 1918/FL champs 1927/FAC winner 1924, 1951(m), 1952(m)/NU HoF.

SHACKLETON Leonard Francis 1946-1948

Inside-forward
5'8"
b. Bradford, 3 May 1922
d. Kendal, 28 November 2000

Career: Bradford Park Avenue amat 1937/Kippax Utd/Horton Banktop (Bradford)/Arsenal amat Aug 1938 (London Paper Mills loan 1938-39)(Enfield loan 1938-39)(Dartford loan)/Bradford Park Avenue amat April 1940, prof Dec 1940 (Huddersfield Town war-guest 1940-45)(Bradford City war-guest 1940-42)/UNITED Oct 1946 £13,000/Sunderland Feb 1948 £20,050/ Retired May 1958 due to injury.

Many supporters, as well as ex-players, who watched and played with Len Shackleton consider there has never been a player quite like Shack before or since. A complete showman who could perform every trick in the book, and many never seen at all, Shackleton was a truly brilliant inside-forward. Possessing skills galore, Len made a name with his home town club, Bradford after being rejected by Arsenal as a youngster. With a tremendous record in wartime football and the immediate peacetime seasons, 24 year-old Shackleton joined United for a record fee after 21 outings and 171 goals for Bradford. And what a debut awaited the Yorkshireman at St James' Park against Newport. Newcastle won 13-0 to create a Football League record and Shack netted a double hat-trick, including three goals within five minutes to make headlines throughout the country. But Len's relationship with Newcastle management was never to be too fruitful, recording that his period on Tyneside was a "stormy couple of seasons". He only stayed for 18 months before moving to Roker Park for another record fee. Yet in that time he still became a crowd favourite on Tyneside for his playmaking in midfield and up front. With Sunderland he bedded in well, staying at Roker Park until retiring through an ankle injury and after totalling 348 senior games, scoring 100 goals, becoming part of Wearside folklore. A sorcerer of a player, he at times destroyed opponents with dribbling and passing ability, Jackie Milburn noting "when in the mood he made the ball talk". Yet, like many of his vision and style, he often confounded team-mates who were not on his wave-length while he had little time for tactics, plans and formations. Len played the game his way being also something of a rebel and many judges considered he won only five caps for his country because of his defiant nature. Yet he had his days for England, once setting off on a 50 yard dribble against Wales showing his distinctive body swerve as he weaved in and out of defenders with the ball before laying on a goal for Jack Milburn. He later settled in the region, for almost 30 years a sports journalist for the Daily Express then Sunday People. Once when commenting on his old club at St James' Park, Len noted, "I've heard of players selling dummies, but this club keeps buying them". Shackleton had a way with words and a quick humour, producing one of the most famous books on the game, his autobiography, 'Clown Prince of Soccer', which had a chapter entitled, "The average director's knowledge of football", and the page was left blank! On leaving the newspaper world in 1983, Shackleton semi-retired and later resided in Grange-over-Sands. A fine cricketer too, he appeared for both Northumberland (4 app) and Durham (1 app) at Minor County level, as well as club cricket for Benwell, Wearmouth and for Yorkshire clubs at various times. On the soccer field during 1940, he played for two different teams on the same day; for Bradford Park Avenue in the morning, then for Bradford City in the afternoon! During World War Two, Shackleton worked initially on aircraft wireless production, then as a 'Bevan Boy' in the coal pits until the late 1940s, at Gosforth Colliery when with Newcastle United.

Appearances & Goals:
Debut v Newport County (h) 5 October 1946 (6 goals)
FL: 57 app 26 gls
FAC: 7 app 3 gls
Total: 64 app 29 gls

Honours:
5 Eng caps 1949-55/1 Eng unoff app 1946/1 Eng B app 1950/1 FA app 1946/Eng sch-youth app/1 Eng over-30 app 1954/2 FL app 1949/FL div 2 prom 1948/FLN1(WLg) champs 1945 (4 app)/Eng HoF/FL Legend.

SHANKLY Robert 1934-1935

Inside-forward

5'7"

b. Douglas, Lanark, 11 February 1909

Career: Douglasdale Jnrs/Douglas Water Thistle July 1930/Hull City May 1931/Carluke Rovers Sept 1932/Brechin City Sept 1932/Rutherglen Glencairn June 1933/UNITED June 1934/Aldershot July 1935 free/Barrow June 1936/Clapton Orient July 1937 Bristol City war-guest 1940-41)(Blackburn Rovers war-guest 1940-41) to 1943.

Developed initially at Hull City by former United favourite Bill McCracken when in charge at Anlaby Road, Bob Shankly didn't break fully into the Football League on Humberside and returned to Glasgow. But with noted junior club Rutherglen Glencairn he impressed United scoring 29 goals in 47 games and he was given a second chance in England at St James' Park. Deputising in midfield, on the right or left of the field, during season 1934-35, Shankly couldn't gain a regular place but was a force in the club's Central League line-up. He moved to Aldershot (30 app) Barrow (32 app) and then Clapton Orient, where he gained a regular place infrequently, mainly at centre-forward, appearing on 14 occasions for the Londoners. He did flourish for Orient during wartime football, netting 29 goals in only 32 matches.

Note: Although sometimes noted as one of the famous Shankly family, he is not one of Bill Shankly's brothers, his namesake Bob and brother to Bill, being a different footballer of the same era. From Lanarkshire also, he could though be related to the wider family).

Appearances & Goals:

Debut v Nottingham Forest (a) 25 August 1934

L: 6 app 0 gls

Total: 6 app 0 gls

SHEARER Alan OBE 1996-2006, 2009

Centre-forward

& Manager

6'0"

b. Gosforth, Newcastle upon Tyne, 13 August 1970

Career: Cramlington Jnrs/ Wallsend BC 1983-86/ Cramlington Jnrs 1985-86/ Southampton jnr Sept 1984, prof April 1988/ Blackburn Rovers July 1992 £3.6m/ UNITED July 1996 £15.6m to May 2006 when he retired, becoming United sporting ambassador May 2006 to Sept 2008, returning as manager April 2009 to May 2009.

One of the finest centre-forwards of all time, Alan Shearer's career record of 422 club and international goals speaks for itself. The Tynesider was recognised as one of the best strikers in the world during the decade between 1995 and 2005 and a model professional on and off the field. The world record £15.6m purchase of Alan Shearer during the summer of 1996 took United's commitment to establish the Magpies as one of the top clubs in Europe to a different level. Newcastle saw off the challenge of their rivals, Manchester United, to sign the Blackburn and England striker with the advantage of knowing that he very much wanted to play for his home-town side, and in the famed Number 9 shirt. A supporter of the Black'n'Whites from a schoolboy, and of

Kevin Keegan, Alan was once at Manchester City, West Bromwich Albion and United for trials, but ended up in goal at St James' Park for part of the time and his talent was lost to Southampton. But a dramatic homecoming 12 years later awaited the Gosforth-born striker. At The Dell he developed quickly and netted a spectacular hat-trick on his first full league outing for the Saints against Arsenal, when only 17 years old, the youngest player to do so in the top flight. By the time he had scored 13 goals for the England Under-21 side Shearer was in demand. United tried, and failed, to bring him to Gallowgate during 1992, but Keegan never lost his admiration for the player described as the ultimate all-round centre-forward. It was Kenny Dalglish who secured his signature for Blackburn in a record £3.6m deal during July 1992. At the time that was a huge sum, but over the next four seasons Alan became the Premier Leagues most devastating striker and the fee was judged a bargain. Alan was strong, courageous, committed and intelligent leading the attack. Blackburn reaped the reward through his goals; 130 all told for Rovers, almost a goal a game over four seasons. He was very much the key man who won the Premier League crown for the Ewood Park club in 1995 and rapidly the Geordie became a regular for the England side. Netting on his debut for his country, Shearer went onto be top scorer in the hugely successful Euro 96 tournament and later captained his country in the World Cup of 1998. His reputation as Europe's best striker was cemented further and United stepped in to smash the previous highest transfer fee paid for Lentini and Ronaldo. It was time for Shearer to return home to a rapturous welcome and immediately he started hitting the net for the Black'n'Whites. Alan pulled on the Number 9 shirt with immense pride and passion and over the next ten seasons he became Newcastle's talisman, becoming the club's all-time record goalscorer with 206 goals. Voted the Premier League's Player of the Decade, he is also the competition's goal-king with 260 goals. And all this despite several bad injuries which both kept him out of action and threatened his career, showing his strength of character. Alan was perhaps the perfect old-fashioned centre-forward in the mould of a modern Lofthouse or Lawton; a tough competitor, able to hold the ball and bring colleagues into play. He was deadly in the air, clinical in the box and possessed a stunning long-range shot, often striking spectacular efforts. Shearer was a runner-up in the Premier League with United, reached two FA Cup finals and led the charge on the Champions League during 2002-03. Although he had a less than good relationship with manager Ruud Gullit, he saw off that low point to flourish again when Bobby Robson arrived at Gallowgate, soon firing home five goals against Sheffield Wednesday in September 1999. He also went onto score arguably United's fastest ever first-class goal, after only 10.5 seconds against Manchester City during 2003. Alan is one of only three players in both United's top-ten appearances and top-ten goals charts while he is the only player to record over 400 games and reach 200 goals in league and cup matches for the club. Capped on 63 occasions (30 goals), he was also England and United skipper for much of his stay at St James' Park while Shearer collected the Footballer of Year and Player of the Year awards on three occasions. By the time he called time on his career, appropriately scoring against Sunderland at the end of the 2005-06 season, Shearer had won no silverware with the Magpies, Newcastle under-achieving when they should have capitalised on Shearer's presence. Had he moved to Old Trafford, he could have won much with Manchester United, yet preferred the chance to wear the black-and-white striped shirt. Despite the lack of medals Shearer became a Geordie icon to his own people and that in many ways made up for a lack of trophy success, as he said: "I have lived my dreams". His testimonial match in May 2006 against Celtic (52,275) raised £1.64m for charity, and Shearer continued doing much work for good causes being a patron of the Sir Bobby Robson Foundation, launching his own Alan Shearer Foundation during 2012. After he retired Alan became one of the BBC's resident experts, a controlled and sensible voice on the game in England, while he had a brief eight match spell as United's boss when the club were in trouble at the end of the 2008-09 season, a mission impossible task in a bid to halt United's relegation. He was appointed Deputy Lieutenant of Northumberland during September 2009, a prestigious and centuries-old ceremonial role for the region. Living in Ponteland, he was deservedly honoured with the Freedom of Newcastle and OBE.

Appearances & Goals:

Debut v Everton (a) 17 August 1996

(v Manchester United (n) 11 August 1996 (CS))

PL: 295(8) app 148 gls

FAC: 36 app 21 gls

FLC: 15(1) app 7 gls

Euro: 49 app 30 gls

Others: 1 app 0 gls

Total: 396(9) app 206 gls

In Charge: 8 games

Debut v Chelsea (h) 4 April 2009

Honours:

63 Eng caps 1992-2000/WdC 1998/1 Eng unoff app 1996/1 Eng B app 1992/11 Eng u21 app 1991-92/Eng sch-youth app/PL champs 1995/PL runners-up 1997/FAC final 1998, 1999/FoY 1994 (FWA)/PoY 1995, 1997 (PFA)/PoD 2003 (PFA)/PoD & ToD (PL) 2003/PFA ToS (d1) 1992, (PL) 1993, 1994, 1995, 1996, 1997, 2003/Eng HoF/NU HoF/FL Legend/Freeman of Newcastle upon Tyne 2000/OBE 2001.

S

SHEEDY Kevin Mark 1992-1993

Midfield
5'9"
b. Builth Wells, Breconshire, 21 October 1959

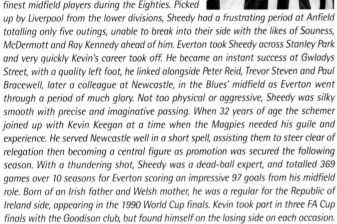

Career: Hereford Lads Club/Hereford Utd jnr April 1975, prof Oct 1976/Liverpool July 1978 £80,000/ Everton Aug 1982 £100,000/UNITED Feb 1992 free to May 1993/Blackpool July 1993 free to May 1995/Blackburn Rovers asst-coach Aug 1995/ Tranmere Rovers asst-coach June 1996, becoming asst-manager cs 1999, caretaker-manager March 2001/Hartlepool Utd asst-coach Dec 2002 to June 2003/Everton asst-coach Aug 2006.

After a modest start in the game, by the time Kevin Sheedy retired he was recognised as one of the finest midfield players during the Eighties. Picked up by Liverpool from the lower divisions, Sheedy had a frustrating period at Anfield totalling only five outings, unable to break into their side with the likes of Souness, McDermott and Ray Kennedy ahead of him. Everton took Sheedy across Stanley Park and very quickly Kevin's career took off. He became an instant success at Gwladys Street, with a quality left foot, he linked alongside Peter Reid, Trevor Steven and Paul Bracewell, later a colleague at Newcastle, in the Blues' midfield as Everton went through a period of much glory. Not too physical or aggressive, Sheedy was silky smooth with precise and imaginative passing. When 32 years of age the schemer joined up with Kevin Keegan at a time when the Magpies needed his guile and experience. He served Newcastle well in a short spell, assisting them to steer clear of relegation then becoming a central figure as promotion was secured the following season. With a thundering shot, Sheedy was a dead-ball expert, and totalled 369 games over 10 seasons for Everton scoring an impressive 97 goals from his midfield role. Born of an Irish father and Welsh mother, he was a regular for the Republic of Ireland side, appearing in the 1990 World Cup finals. Kevin took part in three FA Cup finals with the Goodison club, but found himself on the losing side on each occasion.

Appearances & Goals:
Debut v Barnsley (h) 22 February 1992
FL: 36(1) app 4 gls
FAC: 2(1) app 1 gls
FLC: 4 app 0 gls
Others: 4 app 1 gl
Total: 46(2) app 6 gls

Honours:
46 Eire caps 1984-93/WdC 1990/Eire u21 app/Eire sch-youth app/FL champs 1982 (2 app), 1985, 1987/FL div 1 champs 1993/FL div 3 champs 1976 (1 app)/FAC final 1985, 1986, 1989/FLC final 1984/ECWC winner 1985/ICC final 1981 (sub no app)/PFA ToS (d1) 1985, 1987.

SHEPHERD Albert 1908-1914

Centre-forward
5'8"
b. Great Lever, Lancashire, 10 December 1885
d. Bolton, 8 November 1929

Career: Bolton St Marks 1900/Bolton Temperance/Bolton Wand amat 1901-02/ Blackburn Rovers amat 1902-03/Bolton Wand amat cs 1902 (Bolton St Luke's loan 1903-04), prof Sept 1904/UNITED Nov 1908 £850/Bradford City July 1914 £1,500/Retired 1916.

An unselfish, astute leader of the attack who became noted for his rip-roaring dashes through the middle, Albert Shepherd possessed lightning speed off the mark and a lethal shot. Not a big man for the centre-forward's role and often weighing at around 12 to 13 stone, he had a one way to goal approach to the game and following a big transfer to St James' Park, very quickly became a crowd hero. An international when he moved to Tyneside, scoring on his England debut, Shepherd for some unknown reason was never a hit with the national side's committee, although Charlie Buchan rated him as the best player in the leader's role before 1925. Described as a "rough diamond", he was top scorer in the First Division during 1905-06 (26 goals) as well as 1910-11 (25 goals) and arrived at Gallowgate with an impressive record of 90 goals in 123 senior games for Bolton.

Albert continued in that vein for the Magpies until a ligament injury against Blackburn during April 1911 put him on the sidelines for almost two years and forced him to miss that season's FA Cup final. Shepherd recorded the fateful moment in his own words: "I was doing one of my mad rushes, as some people call them, when I collided with the Rovers custodian, and had to be carried from the field." Colleague Scott Duncan described the clash as "the worst I have ever seen". In his stride and in possession of the ball, Albert was strong and difficult to stop, he scored four goals for the Football League in a single match against the Scots, as well as on five occasions for United, while his home debut for the Black'n'Whites coincided with the remarkable 9-1 reverse at the hands of neighbours Sunderland. Shepherd was also a colourful character, often in the news for one reason or another, once agreeing with United's directors that if he netted a hat-trick, he could leave the field early to catch a train; this he duly did after 80 minutes in a match at Trent Bridge against Notts County during 1909! A title and FA Cup winner for the club, his performance in the 1910 final victory over Barnsley was outstanding, Shepherd netting twice, including the very first penalty in a FA Cup final. As a youngster Shepherd started his working life at a local Lancashire mill, after leaving the scene Albert resided in Bolton and became a well known landlord at the Crown & Cushion public-house.

Appearances & Goals:
Debut v Nottingham Forest (a) 28 November 1908 (1 goal)
FL: 104 app 76 gls
FAC: 19 app 16 gls
Total: 123 app 92 gls

Honours:
2 Eng caps 1906-11/Eng trial app 1911/2 FL app 1906-11/FL champs 1909/FL div 2 champs 1909/FL div 2 prom 1905/FAC winner 1910.

SHIEL John 1936-1938

Centre-forward
5'11"
b. Seahouses, Northumberland, 13 May 1917
d. Ashington, 30 November 2013

Career: North Sunderland/UNITED trial Aug 1935, amat Nov 1936, prof Dec 1936 £10/North Shields May 1938 free/Huddersfield Town Oct 1938 (Blyth Spartans war-guest 1939-40) to c1940/North Sunderland to 1949.

Jack Shiel was a teenage fisherman who began playing football with his local club of North Sunderland in the Northumberland non-leagues and caught United's attention, subsequently being handed a chance at professional football. At St James' Park for less than two seasons, he was given a single opportunity in United's senior eleven, as a stand-in for centre-forward Jack Smith during the 1937-38 campaign. Jack did well in reserve football for the Magpies, scoring a hat-trick on his debut against Huddersfield Town, but the striker had Smith or Cairns ahead of him in United's attack. Following a spell with North Shields, Shiel later had another chance at Football League action, this time at Leeds Road when he was signed by Geordie boss Clem Stephenson. Again though he was a reserve player and only managed a single appearance for Huddersfield. During World War Two, Jack served on Royal Navy minesweepers, and after leaving football he resided in Seahouses running a fishing boat on the Northumberland coast where his family have for many generations worked the North Sea. He also operated a tourist cruise boat to the Farne Islands. For a long period Shiel was United's oldest surviving player, living into his nineties.

Appearances & Goals:
Debut v Barnsley (a) 6 September 1937
FL: 1 app 0 gls
Total: 1 app 0 gls

SHINTON Robert Thomas 1980-1982

Striker
5'10"
b. West Bromwich, 6 January 1952

Career: Lye Town/Walsall March 1972/Cambridge
Utd March 1974 £22,000/Wrexham July 1976
£15,000/Manchester City July 1979 £300,000
(Millwall loan 1979-80)/UNITED March 1980
£175,000/Millwall loan Jan 1982, pmt March
1982/Worcester City player-manager Aug 1983
free/Weymouth Feb 1985/Malvern Town player-
manager 1986/Lodge Cottrell 1986/Willingham
player-manager 1991/Newmarket Town manager
Sept 1997 to 2001/Willingham manager.

Bobby Shinton was a slightly-framed striker who rose to prominence with Wrexham
during seasons 1977-78 and 1978-79; the Welsh club's historian noted that Shinton
had, "mesmerised the opposition" in many of his 175 games for the Robins. With good
close control of the ball, Bobby fired in 56 goals before heading for Maine Road in a
record deal. However, he never quite lived up to his top billing when he pulled on
Manchester City's blue shirt alongside international names and following only six
outings he ended up at St James' Park with his career needing to recapture its earlier
zest. With Newcastle searching for a new strike-force combination, Shinton teamed
up with Ray Clarke for the 1980-81 season, but the duo failed miserably, Shinton
ending up top scorer with a mere seven goals, the equal lowest total for a season in
United's history. A bit of a joker in the dressing-room, the genial Brummie suffered a
medial ligament injury and moved on soon after recovering, later playing in non-
league into his forties. He also set up his own glazing business in Worcester, a trade
in which Bobby had trained as before turning professional with Walsall. For a period
he also worked for Aspinall's Building Supplies in Willingham, Cambridge where he
lived. When with Wrexham, he was part of their side which first knocked out the
Magpies from the FA Cup in 1978, then faced Blyth Spartans in a famous Fifth Round
clash. Playing minor football as a veteran, Bobby was a FA Sunday Cup victor in 1987
with Lodge Cottrell.

Appearances & Goals:
Debut v Cambridge United (a) 8 March 1980
FL: 41(1) app 10 gls
FAC: 3(1) app 0 gls
FLC: 3 app 0 gls
Total: 47(2) app 10 gls

Honours:
FL div 3 champs 1978/WsC winner 1978/WsC final 1979/PFA ToS (d3) 1978.

SHORT John David 1940-1943

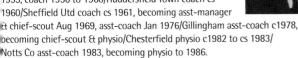

Inside-right
5'0"
b. Gateshead, 25 January 1921
d. Nottingham, June 1986

Career: St Hilda's/Leeds Utd amat Feb 1937, prof Jan 1938
(Halifax Town war-guest 1939-40)(UNITED war-guest 1940-
43)(Sunderland war-guest 1942-43)(Bradford Park Avenue
war-guest 1942-43)(Hartlepools Utd war-guest 1943-
46)(Middlesbrough war-guest 1944-45)/ Resumed with
Leeds/Millwall Nov 1948 £4,000, becoming asst-coach Dec
1955, coach 1956 to 1960/Huddersfield Town coach cs
1960/Sheffield Utd coach cs 1961, becoming asst-manager
& chief-scout Aug 1969, asst-coach Jan 1976/Gillingham asst-coach c1978,
becoming chief-scout & physio/Chesterfield physio c1982 to cs 1983/
Notts Co asst-coach 1983, becoming physio to 1986.

One of the mainstays of United's early wartime seasons, John Short was a blond-haired,
strapping half-back or inside-forward who possessed a quick football brain. Of stylish
appearance and with a battling never-say-die attitude, Short crashed home plenty of
goals for the Magpies over three wartime seasons, claiming 35 in only 43 matches. He
once netted four times against Middlesbrough during December 1941. And with
Hartlepool he also scored frequently in the war leagues, claiming 41 goals in 69 outings.
He was prolific with Leeds as well; before, during and after World War Two, John
totalling 54 goals in 120 games, while at The Den, Short recorded 272 appearances
over eight seasons before moving into a long spell as a coach, physio and scout.

Appearances & Goals:
Debut v Chesterfield (h) 12 October 1940 (1 goal) (FLN)
War: 43 app 35 gls
Total: 43 app 35 gls

SHOULDER Alan 1978-1982

Striker
5'5"
b. Bishop Auckland,
4 February 1953

Career: Leeholme
Jnrs/Byers Green
St Peter's/Bishop
Auckland 1972/ Blyth
Spartans Dec 1977/
UNITED Dec 1978
£20,000/Carlisle Utd
Aug 1982 free/
Hartlepool Utd June
1985 free/Retired Feb
1988 due to injury/
Ferryhill Ath Dec 1988/
Gretna asst-manager
c1990/Newcastle
Blue Star coach June
1992/Coundon
manager/Crook Town
player-coach cs 1993, then manager Dec 1993 to cs 1997/Gateshead asst-coach
June 1997/Blyth Spartans manager May 1998 to Oct 1998/Crook Town manager
Oct 1998 to June 2000/Bishop Auckland manager Jan 2002 to Sept 2002/Willington
manager Dec 2002/West Auckland Town manager Sept 2004/Brandon Utd to Nov
2005/Occasional player for Stanley Utd, Willington and Coundon, 2000-2003 & at
the beginning of his career, for Langley Park Ram's Head.

Alan Shoulder was a brilliant short term purchase by United. Exchanging a career as
a Deputy at Horden pit for the comparative luxury of a footballer's lifestyle, Alan
arrived from non-league football with Blyth Spartans at a late age of 25 and his
spirited play captured the hearts of United's crowd. Having become something of a
star name during Spartan's FA Cup run to the Sixth Round FA Cup draw in 1978, Alan
was signed by manager Bill McGarry after relegation from Division One and
immediately stepped up from the non-league to successfully partner Peter Withe for
two seasons. A breath of fresh air to United's flagging side, he scored 21 goals in
season 1979-80, many through sheer persistence and a lethal shot from penalties,
Alan striking nine spot-kicks home during season 1979-80, a club record. But once
his partner had returned to the top level, Shoulder's influence faded dramatically. He
soon joined Carlisle United where he was also popular to the Brunton Park crowd in
his 122 games (33 goals) and with Hartlepool (76 app 26 goals) always showing his
trademark infectious enthusiasm. On picking up a bad eye injury, Alan later returned
to local football, assisting several clubs in an equally wholehearted fashion. When at
Gretna, Shoulder helped guide the border side to the First Round of the FA Cup, the
first Scottish club to play in the competition for 100 years. Alan continued to be
involved on the North East non-league circuit as a well known and respected coach
and manager, while he also occasionally played until into his 50th year, turning out as
a 53-year-old for Brandon against Dunston in the Northern League, his last match.
Shoulder entered the family timber business near Bishop Auckland, as well as having
an interest in AMS Poultry and a small-holding nearby. Like many football enthusiasts
he played Sunday league football at the start of his career, man-of-the-match in the
FA Sunday Cup final of 1977 as Langley Park Ram's Head lifted the trophy. When he
moved from the local colliery into football with the Magpies, Alan's wages jumped
from £14/week to at times £300/week.

Appearances & Goals:
Debut v Stoke City (h) 9 December 1978
FL: 99(8) app 35 gls
FAC: 3(1) app 1 gl
FLC: 4(2) app 2 gls
Total: 106(11) app 38 gls

S

SIBIERSKI Antoine Christian 2006-2007

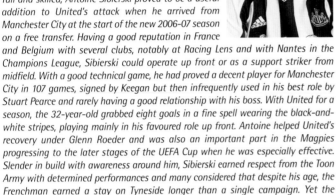

Striker
6'2"
b. Lille (France), 5 August 1974

Career: Lille OSC (Fr) 1992/AJ Auxerre (Fr) July 1996/ FC Nantes (Fr) July 1998/RC Lens (Fr) July 2000/ Manchester City Aug 2003 £700,000/UNITED Aug 2006 free/Wigan Ath June 2007 free (Norwich City loan 2008-09) to June 2009 free/Later, RC Lens (Fr) Sporting Director July 2012.

Tall and skilled, Antoine Sibierski proved to be a useful addition to United's attack when he arrived from Manchester City at the start of the new 2006-07 season on a free transfer. Having a good reputation in France and Belgium with several clubs, notably at Racing Lens and with Nantes in the Champions League, Sibierski could operate up front or as a support striker from midfield. With a good technical game, he had proved a decent player for Manchester City in 107 games, signed by Keegan but then infrequently used in his best role by Stuart Pearce and rarely having a good relationship with his boss. With United for a season, the 32-year-old grabbed eight goals in a fine spell wearing the black-and-white stripes, playing mainly in his favoured role up front. Antoine helped United's recovery under Glenn Roeder and was also an important part in the Magpies progressing to the later stages of the UEFA Cup when he was especially effective. Slender in build with awareness around him, Sibierski earned respect from the Toon Army with determined performances and many considered that despite his age, the Frenchman earned a stay on Tyneside longer than a single campaign. Yet the Frenchman was allowed to depart in the close-season of 2007, the player ending up in disagreement with the club officials over contract terms. Following retirement, Antoine was briefly a player agent before returning to Lens in a management role.

Appearances & Goals:
Debut v Levadia Tallin (a) 14 September 2006 (UEFAC) (1 goal)
PL: 14(12) app 3 gls
FAC: 2 app 0 gls
FLC: 1(1) app 1 gl
Euro: 8(1) app 4 gls
Total: 25(14) app 8 gls

Honours:
1 Fr A app 2000/OG 1996/14 Fr u21 app 1994-96 incl 3 Olym u23 app/Fr Cup winner 2000.

SIBLEY Albert 1947-1950

Outside-right
5'10"
b. West Thurrock, Essex, 6 October 1919
d. Southend, 20 February 2008

Career: Anglo Sports/Barking/Southend Utd Aug 1937 (Arsenal war-guest 1940)(Fulham war-guest 1941-42)(Tottenham Hotspur war-guest 1941-42) (Aldershot war-guest 1941-42)(Chelsea war-guest 1941-42)(Crystal Palace war-guest 1941-42)(Millwall war-guest 1941-42)(Queens Park Rangers war-guest 1941-45)/ Resumed with Southend/UNITED Feb 1947 £6,500 plus E Brown/Southend Utd July 1950 £2,000/ Retired May 1956.

Known as 'Joe' throughout his football career, Sibley had been a favourite in Essex before heading north to Tyneside. Scoring six goals in 24 games for Southend in curtailed first-class action before and after World War Two, Joe had a good track record, but took time to settle at Gallowgate. Jockeying for the outside-right position with Tommy Walker, he had a good run in the side during United's promotion campaign of 1947-48, then was recognised as second choice to Walker. He also was in the treatment room for many weeks due to a succession of knocks. Described by one pen-picture of the day as "purposeful and fast", he returned to Roots Hall and by the time he had retired from football his total games for Southend had risen to a respectable 226, netting 44 goals. Sibley afterwards resided in the Essex coastal town and worked at a local boy's school for 40 years. Due to footballing injuries, he underwent three hip replacement operations in later life. Joe served in Nigeria during World War Two.

Appearances & Goals:
Debut v Southampton (h) 15 February 1947
FL: 31 app 6 gls
FAC: 1 app 0 gls
Total: 32 app 6 gls

Honours: FL div 2 prom 1948.

SIMM William 1893-1894

Outside-right
b. Newcastle upon Tyne, 1872 (Q2)
d. Newcastle upon Tyne, 27 January 1950

Career: Portland (Newcastle)/Newcastle West End/Newcastle Albion 1892-93/ Trafalgar (Newcastle) 1893/UNITED Oct 1893/Trafalgar 1894/Newcastle Wed.

William Simm was a prominent Geordie player during the developing years of the sport on Tyneside. Capped by Northumberland County, Simm was described by the Daily Journal in 1893 as being, "one of the best local forwards". At St James' Park for only a short period, he assisted the club once in Football League action before returning to local competition. Later working as a commercial clerk on Tyneside, his brother, Richard Simm was also a distinguished Tyneside player during the same era and was on United's books in 1899-1900 without breaking into the senior eleven.

Appearances & Goals:
Debut v Small Heath (h) 28 October 1893
FL: 1 app 0 gls
Total: 1 app 0 gls

SIMPSON Daniel Peter 2009-2013

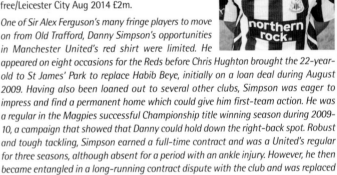

Right-back
5'9"
b. Eccles, Salford, 4 January 1987

Career: Manchester Utd jnr July 2003, prof Jan 2006 (Royal Antwerp (Bel) loan 2006-07)(Sunderland loan 2006-07)(Ipswich Town loan 2007-08)(Blackburn Rovers loan 2008-09)/UNITED loan Aug 2009, pmt Jan 2010 £500,000/Queens Park Rangers June 2013 free/Leicester City Aug 2014 £2m.

One of Sir Alex Ferguson's many fringe players to move on from Old Trafford, Danny Simpson's opportunities in Manchester United's red shirt were limited. He appeared on eight occasions for the Reds before Chris Hughton brought the 22-year-old to St James' Park to replace Habib Beye, initially on a loan deal during August 2009. Having also been loaned out to several other clubs, Simpson was eager to impress and find a permanent home which could give him first-team action. He was a regular in the Magpies successful Championship title winning season during 2009-10, a campaign that showed that Danny could hold down the right-back spot. Robust and tough tackling, Simpson earned a full-time contract and was a United's regular for three seasons, although absent for a period with an ankle injury. However, he then became entangled in a long-running contract dispute with the club and was replaced when French international Mathieu Debuchy arrived on Tyneside in January 2013. Simpson was released at the end of the season and joined the QPR set-up at Loftus Road, helping the Londoners to a quick return to Premier League football.

Appearances & Goals:
Debut v Sheffield Wednesday (h) 19 August 2009
FL/PL: 122(1) app 1 gl
FAC: 4 app 0 gls
FLC: 4 app 1 gl
Euro: 7 app 0 gls
Total: 137(1) app 2 gls

Honours:
PL champs 2008 (3 app)/FL ch winner 2010/FL ch prom 2007, 2014.

SIMPSON Neil Alexander 1990-1991

Midfield
5'10"
b. Hackney, London, 15 November 1961

Career: Middlefield Wasps/Newmachar BC/Aberdeen Aug 1978/UNITED July 1990 £100,000/Motherwell Aug 1991/Cove Rangers player-commercial manager June 1993/Elgin City commercial-manager/SFA development officer Oct 1993/Aberdeen senior community coach May 2001, caretaker-manager Dec 2010, becoming Head of Youth July 2011.

With a robust and competitive style in midfield, Neil Simpson joined his former Scotland skipper Roy Aitken at

St James' Park in readiness for a promotion assault in season 1990-91. However Neil's stay on Tyneside was anything but productive; he was dogged by injury and in the end only made a single appearance from the kick-off for the Magpies, and one that lasted only 36 minutes. Neil never showed the rich talent he had displayed in 310 games for Aberdeen. With a determined attitude, Simpson was a formidable player in Scotland, helping the Dons to much success including European glory under Alex Ferguson at Pittodrie. Although remembered for his battling powerhouse qualities, he also displayed a delightful touch on the ball, but after a headlining tackle on Ian Durrant of Rangers and an injury which kept him on the sidelines, his Scottish career was turned upside down and an exit south followed. An Englishman by birth but raised near Aberdeen of Scottish parents, he is one of only a few players to have been capped by the Scots although born across the border. Simpson has served Aberdeen as a player and coach for over 20 years.

Appearances & Goals:
Debut v Port Vale (a) 15 September 1990 (sub)
FL: 1(3) app 0 gls
FLC: 0(1) app 0 gls
Total: 1(4) app 0 gls

Honours:
5 Scot caps 1983-88/1 Scot B app 1987/11 Scot u21 app 1982-85/Scot sch-youth app/SL champs 1984, 1985/SC winner 1982, 1983, 1984/SLC winner 1986/SLC final 1988, 1989/ECWC winner 1983/ESC winner 1983.

SIMPSON Ronald Campbell 1951-1960

Goalkeeper
5'10"
b. Glasgow, 11 October 1930
d. Edinburgh, 19 April 2004

Career: Queen's Park amat June 1945 (Rangers trial April 1947)/Third Lanark June 1950/UNITED Feb 1951 £8,750/Hibernian Oct 1960 £2,100/Celtic Sept 1964 £3,000/Retired May 1970 due to injury becoming Celtic asst-coach/Hamilton Acc manager Oct 1971 to Sept 1972/St Johnstone asst-coach 1990/Partick Thistle asst-coach 1990/Dunfermline Ath asst-coach.

Brought up in the Hampden area of Glasgow, Ronnie Simpson was a player with a quite remarkable career. Making his debut in the senior game when still at school aged 14 years 304 days old for Queen's Park against Clyde in 1945, he became a noted goalkeeper for United during the Fifties decade, then after injury threatened his career, bounced back to win everything on the Scottish scene, as well as the coveted European Cup and a Scotland cap. He was by then 36 years 196 days old, the oldest international debutant for his country. Not a tall and imposing 'keeper at 5'10" tall and barely 11 stones, Simpson though possessed cat-like agility with spectacular reflexes which made up for his small stature. Ronnie took over from Jack Fairbrother between the Magpies' posts for the 1951-52 season and was an automatic choice for seven campaigns, including runs to Wembley in 1952 and 1955. Then a knee injury followed by a problematic thigh complaint and broken jaw put him on the sidelines. Following many months of treatment new boss Charlie Mitten brought in Bryan Harvey and it appeared Ronnie would hang up his gloves. But Simpson didn't give in and moved back to Scotland to start the second part of his rewarding career. Linking up with Jock Stein, he became a veteran 'keeper at Parkhead as Celtic gathered every trophy they competed for in 1966-67 proceeding to total 188 senior games for the Bhoys. Retiring due to a persistent shoulder injury when over 40, Ronnie then began on a life which took in several occupations in Edinburgh from publican to local councillor, sports shop owner and running a post-office, as well as a part-time specialised goalkeeper coach. During 1972 he became a member of the Pools Panel, a regular attendee at meetings on match-days to 2001. His father Jimmy appeared for Rangers and for Scotland, making the Simpsons a rare family international pair. A fine golfer too, Ronnie was a past winner of the footballers' championship; he resided in Scotland's capital becoming a popular match-day host at Parkhead. A marvellous character, Simpson once recorded his unique way of preparing for any post-match interviews, noting: "Before a match I take out my false teeth, and stick them in my cap which I keep in the back of the net. It's a habit I have adopted in important matches, just in case I have to meet someone at short notice or at the end of the game. Then I can always pop my teeth in!"

Appearances & Goals:
Debut v Bolton Wanderers (h) 29 August 1951
FL: 262 app 0 gls
FAC: 33 app 0 gls
Others: 2 app 0 gls
Total: 297 app 0 gls

Honours:
5 Scot caps 1967-69/2 Scot B app 1953-57/3 Scot amat app 1950/Scot sch-youth app/1 SL app 1969/4 OG (GB) app 1948/FAC winner 1952, 1955/SL champs 1966, 1967, 1968, 1969/SC winner 1967/SC final 1966/SLC winner 1966, 1967, 1968/EC winner 1967/ICC final 1967/Scot FoY 1967 (SFWA)/Scot HoF.

SIMPSON Thomas Graham 1942-1943

Centre-forward
5'10"
b. probably Tyneside

Tom Simpson signed forms for United from Tyneside football as a young professional during January 1942 and was a deputy for the potent attacking skills of Albert Stubbins. Simpson found himself in the centre-forward role on a handful of occasions during seasons 1941-42 and 1942-43, his debut being against Rotherham United during February 1942.

Appearances & Goals:
Debut v Rotherham United (a) 7 February 1942 (FLN)
War: 4 app 0 gls
Total: 4 app 0 gls

SINCLAIR John Evans Wright 1967-1969

Outside-right or left
5'6"
b. Culross, Fife, 21 July 1943
d. (Dunfermline), 2 September 2010

Career: Blairhall Colliery 1959/Dunfermline Ath July 1960 £100/Leicester City May 1965 £25,000/UNITED Dec 1967 £67,500/Sheffield Wed Dec 1969 exch for D Ford (Chesterfield loan 1972-73)(Durban Utd (SA) loan May 1973)/Dunfermline Ath July 1973/ Stenhousemuir July 1975 to cs 1976.

Jackie Sinclair cost the Magpies a near record fee when he was purchased to solve a problem wing position with the hope of giving service to the menace of Wyn Davies at centre-forward and forming a powerful front trio with Pop Robson. Sinclair could hit goals, having earned a move to England after striking 18 during season 1964-65 for Dunfermline under the guidance of Jock Stein. He had a good record at Filbert Street too, alongside Derek Dougan, totalling 53 goals in 113 matches. His pedigree was a good one, yet the little Scot never quite reached the heights expected of him and in the final analysis disappointed many. Possessing killing pace and a telling shot, though rarely used on Tyneside, Jackie had a good spell in a black-and-white shirt as the Fairs Cup was secured during 1969, netting a crucial goal in the semi-final battle with Rangers. Joe Harvey, however, exchanged the Scot for David Ford the following season and Sinclair did well at Hillsborough (109 games) before returning to his roots in Fife and serving Dunfermline again, totalling 167 games for the Pars. He later was employed for the National Coal Board at Solsgirth pit. Residing in Dollar, he afterwards worked at Stirling University and was Dunfermline golf club's steward. Jackie was a nephew of Sunderland's Tommy Wright, also a Scottish international, while his brother Willie turned out for Falkirk and Huddersfield and a cousin, another Tommy Wright also appeared for Leicester. Sinclair's son was on Dunfermline's books and took part in the 1991 Scottish League Cup final. Jackie died when on holiday during 2010 on board a cruise liner and was cremated in Dunfermline.

Appearances & Goals:
Debut v Nottingham Forest (h) 13 January 1968
FL: 42(1) app 6 gls
FAC: 1(1) app 0 gls
FLC: 1 app 1 gl
Euro: 4(2) app 1 gl
Total: 48(4) app 8 gls

Honours:
1 Scot cap 1966/ICFC winner 1969/SC final 1965.

S

SINCLAIR Thomas S 1907-1912

Goalkeeper
5'11"
b. Dunkeld, Perthshire, 8 June 1880

Career: Rutherglen Glencairn 1900/Morton May 1903/Rangers Oct 1904 (Celtic loan 1906-07)/UNITED March 1907 £375 to May 1912/(Dumbarton Harp Dec 1912)/Dunfermline Ath April 1913/Stevenston Utd July 1916/Kilmarnock Feb 1917/Stevenston Utd March 1917/Retired cs 1919.

Scot Tom Sinclair was a fine custodian and one of the many deputies to United stalwart Jimmy Lawrence. Having totalled 56 games for Rangers and played in the 1905 Scottish Cup final, Sinclair became one of the few players to appear for both Glasgow giants when he helped out Celtic after their regular 'keeper Davie Adams had been injured at the start of the 1906-07 season. Tom in fact never conceded a goal and won a Glasgow Cup medal with the Hoops then made the trip to Tyneside, United's scouts being suitably impressed with his form for the Old Firm. After helping Celtic to a Scottish Championship triumph with early season appearances, Sinclair made it a double victory in the same 1906-07 campaign with his three games for Newcastle during their English title victory. But he deputised only rarely thereafter during six seasons on the St James' Park payroll. Tom later settled in Glasgow and ran a billiard's hall in the city and in Paisley.

Appearances & Goals:
Debut v Stoke (h) 29 March 1907
FL: 8 app 0 gls
Total: 8 app 0 gls

Honours:
FL champs 1907 (3 app)/SL champs 1907 (6 app)/SC final 1905/SJC winner 1902.

SISSOKO Moussa 2013-date

Midfield
6'1"
b. Le Blanc-Mesnil, near Paris (France), 16 August 1989

Career: Esperance Aulnay (Fr) 1995/ AS Red Star (Fr) July 1999/Esperance Aulnay (Fr) Sept 2001/Toulouse jnr July 2003, prof July 2007/UNITED Jan 2013 £2.2m.

Newcastle United pulled off a bargain deal when they captured 23-year-old Moussa Sissoko during the January 2013 transfer window. Rated a £10m player only a few months before when courted by several clubs, the Magpies brought him to Tyneside for a fraction of that amount and immediately the tall, powerful midfielder showed the Premiership that he was a quality player. Netting three goals in quick succession, including two on his Gallowgate debut against Chelsea, his surging runs to support the attack earned rave reviews and while his performances dipped after that five-star beginning as he came to grips with the faster Premier League, Moussa settled in the North East and became a solid performer. A box-to-box midfield player who models himself on Patrick Viera, he can make things happen in the top third of the field, at his best accelerating from midfield where his power can take him past defenders at ease. Strong on the ball when in full flow, he started his career with United operating in an advanced role, quick to support Cisse or Remy in attack. Sissoko totalled 191 games (23 goals) for Toulouse, a regular for Les Pitchouns over five seasons and was highly rated in France. With a Mali background, his tall and rangy style saw him elevated to the French national side during October 2009 going onto feature on the Brazil 2014 World Cup stage.

Appearances & Goals:
Debut v Aston Villa (a) 29 January 2013
PL: 47 app 6 gls
FAC: 1 app 0 gls
FLC: 1(1) app 0 gls
Euro: 6 app 0 gls
Total: 55(1) app 6 gls

Honours:
21 Fr caps 2010-date/WdC 2014/20 Fr u21 app 2009-11/Fr sch-youth app.

SLOAN James 1945-1946

Centre-forward
5'11"
b. Newcastle upon Tyne, 22 February 1924
d. South Shields, 28 November 1990

Career: North Shields/Parsons Ath/UNITED amat Jan 1945, prof Feb 1945 (Middlesbrough war-guest 1944-45)/Hartlepools Utd Nov 1946 exch to cs 1952.

A product of St Aloysius School in Newcastle, Jimmy Sloan was a young leader who was blooded in United's line-up against Middlesbrough during January 1945. He had a great start wearing a Magpie shirt; in the first minute he sped off on a penetrating run and made a goal for Charlie Wayman. Reserve to Albert Stubbins for his stay at Gallowgate, Sloan moved to Hartlepool in an exchange deal involving Joe Brown and he proceeded to total 88 first-class matches scoring 32 goals for the Division Three North club.

Appearances & Goals:
Debut v Middlesbrough (a) 13 January 1945 (FLN)
War: 7 app 0 gls
Total: 7 app 0 gls

SLOAN Scott Mark 1990-1991

Forward
5'10"
b. Wallsend, 14 December 1967

Career: Ponteland Utd/Berwick Rangers Nov 1988 £1,000/UNITED July 1990 £65,000/Falkirk Nov 1991 £50,000 (Cambridge Utd loan 1993-94)/Hartlepool Utd Aug 1994 free to May 1995/Kalmar FF (Swd) Feb 1996/Berwick Rangers Aug 1997/Whitley Bay Sept 1997 to Dec 1998.

A United supporter as a lad, Scott Sloan swapped a reps career with Cadbury's to join the professional staff at St James' Park. A part-timer for Berwick Rangers, Newcastle had followed Sloan's progress after he struck 17 goals in the Scottish League during season 1989-90. Appearing in various forward positions for the Magpies, on the right and left flank especially, Sloan found the substantial jump from Berwick to English Second Division football too much and never came to terms with the faster pace. He moved to Brockville Park where Scott helped Falkirk to promotion and later appeared on 42 occasions for Hartlepool before he had another spell with Berwick increasing his career total to 70 games and 23 goals at Shieldfield. On leaving the game, Scott became a fireman on Tyneside for a period and ran a sandwich shop on the Team Valley Trading Estate in Gateshead.

Appearances & Goals:
Debut v Oxford United (a) 13 October 1990 (sub)
FL: 11(5) app 1 gl
FAC: 1 app 0 gls
Others: 1 app 0 gls
Total: 13(5) app 1 gl

Honours:
SL div 1 champs 1994.

SMAILES Andrew 1919-1922

Forward
5'9"
b. Radcliffe, near Amble, Northumberland, 21 May 1895
d. Shepton Mallet, Somerset, October 1978

Career: Ashington trial 1919/Blyth Spartans cs 1919/UNITED Oct 1919 £300/Sheffield Wed Oct 1922 £1,500/Bristol City Oct 1923/Rotherham Utd Aug 1929, becoming trainer Aug 1934 and manager Aug 1952 to Oct 1958/Middlesbrough scout/Scarborough manager Feb 1959 to Feb 1961.

Well-built and strong, but very fast too, Andy Smailes scored goals on a regular basis throughout his career. In either the central or inside roles, he was direct and possessed an ever dangerous first-time shot. Newcastle picked up Andy from Blyth straight after World War One after impressing United officials in two fixtures against the Magpies. Having netted 11 goals in nine matches for the Spartans, he was quickly offered a deal. In rapid time Smailes was elevated to the senior line-up and became a regular in the Geordies' attack. The barrel-chested striker was first choice during seasons 1919-20 and 1920-21 and was voted best inside-left in the country by Topical Times magazine during 1920. Smailes hit two goals against Sunderland in October 1920, but the combined arrival of Tom McDonald and Billy Aitken pushed him from the limelight and he moved to Yorkshire, then to Bristol where he appeared on 169 occasions for City. Later joining the Millmoor set-up at Rotherham, Andy spent 30 years in their service, guiding the Tykes to their highest ever position in the Football League during 1954-55. Related to the famous Milburn and Charlton footballing dynasty through his wife, Hannah, Andy lived in Shepton Mallet on retiring.

Appearances & Goals:
Debut v Sheffield United (a) 6 December 1919
FL: 73 app 30 gls
FAC: 4 app 0 gls
Total: 77 app 30 gls

Honours:
FL div 3(S) champs 1927.

SMALLWOOD Frederick 1943

Outside-left
5'5"
b. Brynteg, near Wrexham, 16 September 1910
d. Sunderland, December 1965

Career: Llanerch Celts/Wrexham amat Sept 1933/Chester amat Sept 1934, prof Oct 1934/Macclesfield Town 1935/Southampton June 1936/Reading June 1938 £500 (Wrexham war-guest 1939-42)(Sunderland war-guest 1941-43) (UNITED war-guest 1942-43)(Hartlepools Utd war-guest 1943-45)/Retired 1945.

A former pit worker in the Wales coalfield, Fred Smallwood was a small and quick flanker, typical of the pre-war style of winger. Resident in the North East for much of the 1939-1945 war era, Smallwood appeared frequently for the region's clubs, twice for Newcastle in a double meeting with York City during March 1943. A Welsh amateur international, he started well in his Football League career after joining Southampton, but was sidelined due to injury. Fred totalled 49 games for the Saints and was something of a dressing-room joker. On match days it was said he carried a lucky rabbit's foot in his football shorts! Fred recorded nearly 100 games for Reading in league, cup and wartime action, later Smallwood performed in a dance-band in the region, settling in the Sunderland area.

Appearances & Goals:
Debut v York City (h) 6 March 1943 (WC)
War: 2 app 0 gls
Total: 2 app 0 gls

SMELLIE Richard David 1896-1897

Centre-forward
5'10"
b. Scotland, c1861

Career: Pollokshields Ath/Albion Rovers/ Nottingham Forest Aug 1895/UNITED May 1896/ Clyde June 1897/Beith Oct 1897/Motherwell Dec 1897/Albion Rovers Dec 1897/Eastville Rovers March 1898/Albion Rovers Feb 1900.

A cool-headed and determined goal-poacher, Davie Smellie spent one terrific season on Tyneside when he led the attack with spark and determination. Replacing Willie Thompson as the club's centre-forward, during his term of action Smellie struck 15 goals and looked to be a brilliant capture. He was noted in the Newcastle Daily Journal as a "sturdy athlete", who was "fast, a good shooter, and will be a dangerous opponent". He scored four goals in a match against Darwen, but by the summer had surprisingly left the Magpies and didn't appear in Football League soccer again although he continued action in his native country. With Forest he only claimed three goals in 17 outings while in lowland Scotland he served Albion Rovers to good effect.

Appearances & Goals:
Debut v Small Heath (a) 5 September 1896
FL: 26 app 15 gls
FAC: 1 app 0 gls
Total: 27 app 15 gls

SMIRK Alfred Henry 1940

Outside-right
5'10"
b. Penshaw, near Chester-le-Street, 14 March 1917
d. Southend, November 1996

Career: Sunderland Bus Co/Sheffield Wed amat 1935/Sunderland Bus Co/Southend Utd May 1938 (UNITED war-guest 1940-41)(Colchester Utd war-guest 1945-46)/Brush Sports player-manager Feb 1946/Gateshead March 1948/Chingford Town 1949/Tonbridge March 1950.

A product of Chester-le-Street schools and an England international at that level in 1931, former Sunderland bus driver Alf Smirk was once targeted by Stan Seymour and Tom Mather as a United acquisition just prior to the Second World War. But with a £6,000 fee quoted, United backed off and the fast and furious winger remained in Essex only to find himself at St James' Park as a war-guest during the autumn of 1940 when stationed in Corbridge with the Essex Regiment. Smirk had a rewarding spell with Southend, claiming 114 games in which he scored 32 goals as part of their Division Three South line-up. A prisoner-of-war on the Continent during the hostilities, after the war he again headed back north when he signed for Gateshead where he proceeded to total 11 matches for the Redheugh club. After leaving the game, Alf settled in the south and entered the world of journalism, later becoming a denizen of football's press box for the Southend Times and Southend Standard, later becoming editor of the Laindon Recorder in Essex.

Appearances & Goals:
Debut v Chesterfield (h) 12 October 1940 (FLN)
War: 1 app 0 gls
Total: 1 app 0 gls

Honours:
Eng sch-youth app.

SMITH Alan 2007-2012

Midfield
5'10"
b. Rothwell, near Leeds, 28 October 1980

Career: Leeds Utd jnr, prof March 1998/Manchester Utd May 2004 £7m/UNITED Aug 2007 £6m/MK Dons loan Jan 2012, pmt July 2012 free/Notts Co player-coach May 2014.

At the peak of his career with Leeds and Manchester United, Alan Smith was highly rated as an elusive and dangerous forward who liked to operate between midfield and the penalty box. In a fine, young side at Elland Road alongside the likes of future Newcastle players Bowyer, Woodgate and Viduka, Smith tasted much European action, reaching the semi-final of the Champions League during 2001. Netting for the Tykes with his first touch on his debut against Liverpool as an 18-year-old, Alan went onto score 56 goals in his 228 games, being a huge favourite at Elland Road over six seasons. He showed desire to reach the top and a fiery style before moving to Old Trafford in a substantial £7m deal. The Yorkshireman had some good days in Manchester United's red over 93 outings, but often could not secure a permanent place and also suffered a career threatening leg break and ankle dislocation during February 2006 against Liverpool. That injury put Smith out of action for over 12 months and his bright career lost much momentum. Indeed, Alan later conceded that the set-back affected him for the remainder of his footballing days, losing sharpness, pace and unable to reach a top level of performance. He was picked up by Sam Allardyce at Newcastle in August 2007 for a £6m fee when 26 years old with the hope Alan could recapture his earlier sparkling form. That never quite happened at St James' Park, but Smith did produce some good performances in a much deeper enforcer midfield role where his feisty character on the field often brought him into conflict. Captain of United on occasion, a series of injuries though put him out of action for lengthy periods at Gallowgate and over his five year spell on Tyneside, Alan claimed only 77 starts during that period. He missed much of 2008-09, then was out of favour for two more campaigns as the club returned to the Premiership. Although a clinical striker earlier in his career, Smith managed just one goal for United, that in a friendly contest against Sampdoria.

Always professional in his manner and a key figure in the dressing-room, especially following relegation, Alan was influential as the club lifted Championship silverware during 2010. However, in the final analysis for such a high wage-earner over a lengthy period, he was an expensive luxury for the Magpies. But for that injury at Old Trafford Smith's career may have taken a very different path. Alan was loaned to MK Dons as 2012 opened and gave the League One club much needed experience. He was given a free transfer during the summer joining the set-up at the Stadium MK permanently.

Appearances & Goals:
Debut v Bolton Wanderers (a) 11 August 2007
FL/PL: 68(16) app 0 gls
FAC: 5 app 0 gls
FLC: 4(1) app 0 gls
Total: 77(17) app 0 gls

Honours:
19 Eng caps 2001-08/1 Eng B app 2007/10 Eng u21 app 2000-02/Eng sch-youth app/PL champs 2007 (9 app)/FL ch winner 2010/FAC final 2005 (sub no app), 2007/FAYC winner 1997.

SMITH Anthony 1975-1979

Defender or Midfield
5'11"
b. Sunderland, 20 February 1957

Career: UNITED July 1975/Peterborough Utd March 1979 joint deal with A Guy £10,000/Halifax Town Aug 1982 free/Colchester Utd trial cs 1984/Hartlepool Utd Aug 1984 to May 1989/Newcastle Blue Star.

Tony Smith was introduced into Newcastle's line-up by caretaker-boss Willie McFaul during the Magpies' relegation season in 1977-78, a year the club used a record number of players. A past England Under-19 schoolboy captain, Tony Smith was tall and dark, a powerful and composed defender in Central League football. He wasn't given a run in the side, although was on the bench for the UEFA Cup contest with Bastia. After rupturing ankle ligaments which set back his United career, Tony drifted into the lower divisions where he made over 400 appearances, Peterborough (76 app), Halifax (91 app) and Hartlepool where he was especially prominent in 233 games, captain for a period. On leaving the football scene, Smith returned to the North East and was employed at the Nissan complex in Sunderland.

Appearances & Goals:
Debut v Wolverhampton Wanderers (a) 12 November 1977 (sub)
(v Ayr United (a) 15 September 1976 (ASC))
FL: 1(1) app 0 gls
Others: 1 app 0 gls
Total: 2(1) app 0 gls

Honours:
Eng sch-youth app.

SMITH David 1935-1936

Outside-right
5'7"
b. South Shields, 12 October 1915
d. Derby, 26 November 1997

Career: South Shields YMCA/Middle Docks/Reyrolle Works/UNITED amat May 1935, prof Oct 1935 £35/South Shields May 1936 free (Rangers war-guest)(Derby Co war-guest 1942-43)/Northampton Town war-guest 1943, pmt cs 1945, becoming secretary 1951 and manager July 1954/Aldershot manager July 1959, becoming secretary-general manager March 1967 to 1972.

Newcastle United were impressed with Dave Smith's performances as an amateur playing for the Reyrolle works side on Tyneside. He was given a trial in the Magpies' reserve eleven and Smith helped to secure six goal victories in each of his two games. A stand-in for Wilf Bott during the Second Division programme of 1935-36, Smith was granted only a single game in senior company, and was out of action due to injury for 12 months. Dave was, though, a permanent fixture with Northampton despite suffering cartilage damage. He played for the Cobblers over 150 times before moving into the managerial side of the game.

Appearances & Goals:
Debut v Burnley (h) 8 February 1936
FL: 1 app 0 gls
Total: 1 app 0 gls

SMITH Jack 1934-1938

Centre-forward
5'11"
b. Batley, Yorkshire, 17 February 1915
d. 1975

Career: Whitehall Printers (Leeds)/Dewsbury Moor Welfare/Huddersfield Town amat June 1932, prof Oct 1932/UNITED Sept 1934 £2,500/Manchester Utd Feb 1938 £6,500 (Burnley war-guest)/Blackburn Rovers March 1946 £3,000/Port Vale May 1947 £1,200 to cs 1948/Macclesfield Town cs 1948/Buxton cs 1951/Macclesfield Town manager Oct 1951 to Nov 1955.

An astute piece of transfer business was recorded by Newcastle United when Jack Smith arrived at St James' Park for a modest £2,500 fee after making quite an impression in Huddersfield Town's line-up, striking 24 goals in 46 matches. But he was not first-choice at Leeds Road, then challenging for the Football League title, and the Black'n'Whites purchased him as a goal-hungry 19-year-old. Jack was immediately plunged into the Second Division fray and showed an energetic ambition. He scored the winning goal on his debut, then netted another 14 times over the next four months to establish himself as a new hero at Gallowgate. The young Yorkshireman totalled 16 goals in his first season, then another 26 and 24 in subsequent programmes. Smith was quick off the mark, could use both feet to hit shots with power and once scored four goals in a single match for United against Doncaster. By the time he moved into the First Division by signing for promotion-bound Manchester United, Jack had 65% goals per game strike-rate for the Magpies, only a handful of strikers in the club's history can better that. His transfer from St James' Park when at the peak of his goal prowess was not taken kindly by the Geordie faithful and there was much uproar at the time. At Old Trafford, Smith did not hit the net with the same authority, striking only 15 goals in 42 matches before war called a halt to his career. He lost six years of action on the field and although he appeared for Blackburn and Port Vale afterwards was not the same deadly goal-poacher he had been in black-and-white stripes for over four seasons.

Appearances & Goals:
Debut v Plymouth Argyle (a) 22 September 1934 (1 goal)
FL: 104 app 69 gls
FAC: 8 app 4 gls
Total: 112 app 73 gls

Honours:
Eng sch-youth app/FL div 2 prom 1938.

SMITH James 1969-1976

Midfield
5'11"
b. Glasgow, 20 January 1947

Career: Benburb/Aberdeen Aug 1965 (Washington Whips (USA) loan cs 1967)/UNITED Aug 1969 £80,000 (Celtic loan 1975-76)/Retired due to injury July 1976/Whitley Bay Aug 1976 briefly.

A master craftsman, 'Jinky' Jimmy Smith could send the crowd into raptures when he was in the mood, and infuriate his manager when not. The Scot had a languid, lazy style but also a tantalising right foot featuring the piece de resistance of the Smith 'nutmeg', slipping the ball through his opponents legs, a showpiece which was the talk of Tyneside. Making a name for himself at Pittodrie, Jimmy played on 140

occasions (37 goals) in Aberdeen's red before moving to Tyneside for what was reported as a £100,000 deal, the first six figure fee paid by United. However, details indicate the basic transfer was much less, with only add-ons increasing the amount to the much publicised sum. At 22 years old and already capped by Scotland, Smith was brought, as boss Joe Harvey noted, to give "an extra touch of class" to his hard working combination which did so well in lifting the Fairs Cup. Jinky made quite an impact when he arrived in Newcastle, a crowd of 7,800 turning up for his first outing in a Central League contest against Aston Villa. He took time to adapt to the different English game and was in and out of the side, but by season 1971-72 had settled and become the darling of the fans, able to hit a match-winning pass with delicate through balls and chips. Missing a year with a cartilage injury, on his return he enjoyed two-and-a-half seasons displaying a succession of magical performances before another knee complaint put him on the sidelines. And after new manager Gordon Lee had sent the mercurial Scot on loan to Parkhead, his knee broke down again and Smith was forced to halt his career. Jinky was once sent-off for a rash challenge in a Texaco Cup fixture against Birmingham after only 53 seconds during December 1973, one of the fastest dismissals of all time. In 1978 he had a testimonial which attracted a crowd of 17,428; afterwards Jimmy went into a trophy business in Newcastle, one that failed controversially, while Smith also went through a difficult period with a betting addiction. A hero to a generation of supporters, including Peter Beardsley, Smith lives on Tyneside and was a taxi driver for a spell. His brother Joe, also turned out for Aberdeen

Appearances & Goals:
Debut v Sheffield Wednesday (a) 20 August 1969 (sub)
FL: 124(5) app 13 gls
FAC: 13(1) app 0 gls
FLC: 9(1) app 0 gls
Euro: 5 app 0 gls
Others: 18(2) app 3 gls
Total: 169(9) app 16 gls
(Void FAC: 1 app 0 gls)

Honours:
4 Scot caps 1968-74/1 Scot u23 app 1967/Scot jnr app/1 SL app 1968/FAC final 1974/SC final 1967.

SMITH John 1887-1889, 1894-1896

Forward
5'9"
b. Ayrshire, 1866 (Q1)
d. Byker, Newcastle upon Tyne, 3 February 1911

Career: Kilmarnock cs 1885/EAST END Oct 1887 briefly/Kilmarnock 1887/EAST END Aug 1888/ Sunderland June 1889 £75 (EAST END guest 1889-90)/ Liverpool May 1893 £100/Sheffield Wed Aug 1893 £100/UNITED May 1894 £50 to May 1896 when he retired.

A well known and popular early player in the North East, 'Jock' Smith arrived in the region having been a regular for Kilmarnock during season 1886-87. He served United's pioneers, Newcastle East End as skipper before moving into the Football League with Sunderland (32 app), Liverpool (0 app) and Sheffield Wednesday (18 app). Tricky and hardworking, he returned to Tyneside for the 1894-95 season as an experienced campaigner and was used as a utility player; he operated in every forward position for the club, as well as at right-half during that season. Smith left the following year and later became a licensee in Byker. The Scot appeared for both the Northumberland and Durham county sides as an early footballer and when on Wearside, Smith played in Sunderland's first Football League campaign then helped them to the Football League title. On the news of his sudden death due to illness during 1911, the Magpies gave his widow permission to stage a benefit match at St James' Park.

Appearances & Goals:
Debut v Port Clarence (h) 6 October 1888 (FACQ)
FL: 25 app 10 gls
FAC: 5 app 0 gls
Total: 30 app 10 gls

Honours:
FL champs 1892.

SMITH Stephen 1918-1919

Outside-left or Wing-half
5'7"
b. Byker, Newcastle upon Tyne, c1898
d. Newcastle upon Tyne, c1965

Career: St Peter's Albion/UNITED amat 1918, prof Feb 1919/St Peter's Albion 1919/Chelsea Jan 1921/ Merthyr Town June 1923 to Feb 1925.

From the St Peter's area of Byker, Stephen Smith had been just de-mobbed from the Great War serving with the Northumberland Fusiliers when he joined the United staff as an amateur during 1918, graduating with the club as a professional in February 1919. He soon pushed his way into the club's senior side at the time, for a Northern Victory League fixture with Darlington Forge Albion. Deputising for Ed Cooper on the wing, he was unconvincing in attack and wasn't part of the pool of players when the club's directors were drawing up their retained list for the new 1919-20 season. Returning to local Tyneside football, Smith gained another opportunity at the top level when he was spotted by Chelsea, moving south to Stamford Bridge as 1921 opened. He operated as a half-back in the First Division (23 app) before moving to Merthyr Town (50 app) and becoming a regular in the Welsh club's Division Three South line-up for two seasons until he was dismissed for what was described as a breach of rules.

Appearances & Goals:
Debut v Darlington Forge Albion (h) 1 March 1919 (NVL)
War: 1 app 0 gls
Total: 1 app 0 gls

SMITH Thomas 1941-1952

Centre-half
6'0"
b. Horden, Co Durham, 2 February 1923
d. Durham, 31 March 1993

Career: Horden CW/UNITED March 1941/Annfield Plain Aug 1952 free, becoming trainer and manager/ Horden CW manager 1956 to 1957.

Although at Gallowgate for over a decade, 'Tot' Smith only managed 10 senior games, seven of which were during season 1946-47. The purchase of Scottish international Frank Brennan saw Smith as his deputy and chances were few and far between due to his rival's consistency. Nevertheless, Smith was a good defender, big and powerful and likened to a strapping boxer. He skippered United's side to the Central League championship trophy in 1948, the only occasion the Black'n'Whites have lifted what was the principal reserve title. In wartime football, Smith was a regular and only Albert Stubbins played more for the club during those years. His footballing days at Newcastle saw Tot suffer with a knee injury, the player having an artificial cartilage inserted into his knee, one of the first operations of its kind at the time. He played at both Luton and Wolves briefly, on trial, before joining United, while Smith had two other brothers in the game, George and Robert, who both also signed for the Magpies during World War Two. On leaving local football, Smith ran a betting shop near Durham.

Appearances & Goals:
Debut v Barnsley (h) 5 January 1946 (FAC)
(v Bradford City (a) 6 September 1941 (FLN))
FL: 8 app 0 gls
FAC: 2 app 0 gls
War: 145 app 0 gls
Total: 155 app 0 gls

S

SMITH William 1898-1899

Inside-left
5'9"
b. Scotland, 1873
d. 1914

W. SMITH

Career: Hibernian May 1893/UNITED Jan 1898
to 1899/Eastville Rovers/Swindon Town
June 1899 to cs 1901.

*Willie Smith was signed in time for United's
promotion run-in during season 1897-98, and
the noted Scot had a major say in the outcome
of the season. With lots of experience for Hibs
over five seasons north of the border, he
registered 87 games and 49 goals, taking part in the Edinburgh club's first Scottish
League season when he ended as top scorer for 1895-96. Smith fitted in well at St
James' Park and netted six important goals in his 19 outings, including two strikes
during Test Matches which decided the club's elevation to the First Division. The Daily
Journal commented in 1898 that he could "dribble past several opponents in a
meritorious style", although he carried a hefty frame, and was described as a, "heavyweight". Smith remained on Tyneside for part of the following season, running out in
the Magpies inaugural fixture in Division One, but then was replaced by the talent of
Willie Wardrope. Smith settled with Swindon Town and recorded good stats for the
early Robins; 75 app 20 goals. He took part in the Scottish Cup final of 1896 at Logie
Green in Edinburgh; the game with Hearts was the first, and only, final to be played
outside Glasgow.*

Appearances & Goals:
Debut v Luton Town (a) 19 February 1898
FL: 19 app 6 gls
Total: 19 app 6 gls

Honours:
FL div 2 prom 1898/SC final 1896.

SOLANO Nolberto Albino Todco 1998-2004, 2005-2007

Midfield
5'9"
b. Callao (Peru), 12 December 1974

Career: Palomino Jnrs (Pu)/Allianza Lima (Pu)
1987/Sporting Cristal (Pu) 1992 £6,000
(Deportivo Municipal (Pu) 1993 loan)/CA Boca
Juniors (Arg) Aug 1997 £600,000/UNITED Aug
1998 £2.76m/Aston Villa Jan 2004 £1.75m/
UNITED Aug 2005 £1.5m/West Ham Utd Aug
2007 free/AE Larissa (Gr) Aug 2008/
Universitario (Pu) Jan 2009/Colchester Utd &
Sheffield Utd trial Jan 2010/Leicester City Jan
2010/Hull City July 2010/Hartlepool Utd July
2011/Newcastle Benfield coach Jan 2012/
Universitario (Pu) coach June 2012 to Dec
2012/Internacional de Toronto (Can) manager
May 2014.

*The first footballer from Peru to make a big impact in England, Nolberto Solano was
an experienced player in South America by the time he found his way to Gallowgate.
Having won championship titles in his native Peru, he joined Newcastle as a 23-year-
old international midfielder during August 1998 from Argentinean giants Boca Juniors
where he played alongside Diego Maradona and Claudio Caniggia. Nicknamed by
Maradona as the 'Little Maestro', he was soon known as 'Nobby' and costing £2.76m
the talented midfielder took a year to settle then quickly developed as one of the best
creative players in the Premier League. Although Solano often played at full-back for
Peru, with a gifted right boot, Nobby could place the ball in the danger area with
precision and was always on hand to grab goals himself, notably from free-kicks or
fierce drives. There were several much recalled efforts that hit the net; a dazzling solo
50-yard run in Munich especially took the eye. He coped with the rigours of the English
game well considering Nobby was of slight build, but due to his wonderful technical
ability, intelligence with the ball and appetite for hard work, became one of the Premier
League's top performers and one of the most reliable footballers United fielded in the
era. A match-winner for the Black'n'Whites, the little Peruvian was consistently high
in the stats ranking for assists, making goals for his teammates time and time again,
from accurate crosses, deft through balls and exquisite free-kicks and corners. Skipper*

*of his country, he appeared in the 1999 FA Cup final for United and had his best spell
between 2001 and 2004, but the immensely popular Solano was controversially sold
to Aston Villa by Bobby Robson during January 2004 only to return less than two
years later during in a £1.5m deal for a second spell on Tyneside. Aged 32, he moved
to London during August 2007 and ran down his long career with West Ham United,
then in Greece with Larissa, as well as back in Chile with Universitario before settling
again in England with Leicester City, Hull City and Hartlepool. During 2011 Solano ran
into financial difficulties and was declared bankrupt, yet was as popular as ever on
his return visits to the North East. Winning several titles in South America, he is one
of the most celebrated Peruvian sportsmen, featured on postage stamps and
telephone cards. During his period on Tyneside he formed a salsa band, the Geordie
Latinos, showing off his skill as a trumpet and conga musician. Nobby won almost a
century of caps for his country and remains one of United's premium foreign imports.*

Appearances & Goals:
Debut v Chelsea (a) 22 August 1998 (sub)
PL: 210(20) app 37 gls
FAC: 25 app 2 gls
FLC: 15(3) app 2 gls
Euro: 37(5) app 7 gls
Total: 287(28) app 48 gls

Honours:
95 Peru caps 1994-2009/Peru u23 app/Peru sch-youth app/Peru Lg champs 1994, 1995,
1996, 2009/FAC final 1999/LibC final 1997/Peru PoY 1997.

SOO Frank (Hong Ying) 1941

Left-half
5'8"
b. Buxton, 12 March 1914
d. Cheadle, 25 January 1991

Career: West Derby BC/Prescot Cables/Stoke City
amat Jan 1933, prof Nov 1933 (UNITED war-
guest 1941-42)(Millwall war-guest 1941-
46)(Blackburn Rovers war-guest 1941-42)
(Everton war-guest 1941-42)(Reading war-guest
1942-44)(Chelsea war-guest 1942-43) (Brentford
war-guest 1943-45)(Shrewsbury Town war-guest
1945-46)(Burnley war-guest 1945-46)(Crewe
Alex war-guest 1945-46)(Port Vale war-guest
1945-46) (Colchester Utd war-guest)(Norwich
City war-guest)/Leicester City Sept 1945 £4,600/
Luton Town July 1946 £5,000/Chelmsford City asst-player-manager cs 1948/AC
Padova (It) manager April 1951 to June 1952/Norway national manager 1952/IFK
Eskilstuna (Swd) manager 1953/Orebro SK (Swd) manager 1953-54/Djurgardens IF
(Swd) manager 1954-55/IK Oddevold (Swd) manager 1956-57/Koping IS (Swd)
manager 1957/AIK (Swd) manager 1958/Scunthorpe Utd manager June 1959 to May
1960/St Albans City manager 1960/Koping IS (Swd) manager 1962/IFK (Swd) manager
1963/Fredrikstad FK (Nor) manager 1964/AB Copenhagen (Den) manager
1965/coaching various minor clubs around Copenhagen and Malmo 1966 to
1971/Hoganas BK (Swd) coach 1972 to 1973/Also Israel national manager.

*One the outstanding players of the late Thirties and throughout wartime soccer, Frank
Soo was capped on nine occasions by England during the hostilities and was
something of a wing-half artiste. Discovered by future United boss Tom Mather when
he was in charge of Stoke City, Soo was a player with plenty craft and vision, and also
full of confidence. Of mixed decent, his father originated from China, Frank grew
up on Merseyside before joining Stoke then was garrisoned at Whitley Bay for a period
in the RAF and took to the St James' Park field as a replacement for Norman Dodgin
during the 1941-42 wartime season. Skipper of Stoke and totalling over 250 matches
in all games for the Potters, on peace being restored Soo helped both Leicester (2 app)
and Luton (78 app) displaying a style which frequently pleased the watching crowd.
He then started a much travelled career as a Continental coach of repute, notably in
Scandinavia. With Djurgardens he lifted the Swedish title and his team appeared in
the first European Cup tournament of 1955-56, while Frank also coached Norway in
the 1952 Olympic Games.*

Appearances & Goals:
Debut v Bradford City (a) 6 September 1941 (FLN)
War: 2 app 0 gls
Total: 2 app 0 gls

Honours:
9 Eng war app 1942-46/3 FA app 1945-47/OG 1952(m)/Swd Lg champ 1955(m).

SORLEY John 1891-1893

Inside-left or Centre-forward
5'10"
b. Muirkirk, Ayrshire, 12 February 1870
d. Paisley, 10 July 1945

Career: Newmilns/EAST END Jan 1891/
Middlesbrough Sept 1893 briefly/Blackburn Rovers
Sept 1893/Burton Swifts May 1895/Hebburn Argyle
May 1896 to Aug 1899/East Stirlingshire.

'Jock' Sorley was a prominent member of the
Newcastle East End club, both at their previous home
of Chillingham Road, and when they moved to St
James' Park. The son of a master tailor, when he
arrived in the region his occupation was noted as
being a "shipyard labourer", while he caused some
confusion by using two surnames; McSorland and
Sorley, although his birth certificate shows the latter.
One of three new players to arrive from the Ayrshire
club of Newmilns, he was described in the Daily Chronicle as being "popular amongst
the followers of football during his residence in Newcastle" and when he left the club
he was awarded, "a handsome gold medal". Captain of the side for a period, Jock was
a regular goal-getter in season 1891-92 as United played Northern League football
and is recorded as the first player to miss a penalty for the club, against Stockton
during February 1892, although he converted with the rebound. The Scot took part in
United's first game at the Barrack Road venue and also their inaugural Football League
match, scoring against Arsenal, and only left the region because of a financial crisis
at St James' Park; Sorley wouldn't take a reduction in wages and moved to further
his career on Teesside. When on form, few defenders could cope with his darting runs
and eye for goal, a frequent scorer for the Geordies in every season with the club.
Later returning to Tyneside, Jock assisted Hebburn Argyle to the Northern Alliance
title in 1897 netting 30 goals by the season's end. He once scored five goals for
Newcastle in a friendly against Annbank during 1893 and in addition to his first-class
statistics registered over 40 goals in more than 50 sundry games. Around the turn of
the century, Sorley returned to Scotland and worked as a coal miner and railway
surfaceman.

Appearances & Goals:
Debut v Middlesbrough Ironopolis (h) 31 January 1891 (NL)
NL: 28 app 21 gls
FL: 1 app 1 gl
FAC: 6 app 5 gls
Total: 35 app 27 gls
(Void NL: 1 app 1 gl)

SOULSBY James 1914-1919

Centre-forward
5'10"
b. Trimdon Grange, Co Durham, 1895 (Q3)

Career: Gateshead Institute/Rodsley
(Gateshead)/West Stanley April 1914/UNITED
amat May 1914, prof Aug 1914/Blyth Spartans
Aug 1919, prof Sept 1921/Ashington July
1922/Blyth Spartans June 1923.

A rival to Bob Pailor and Tom Hall for the
leader's role at Gallowgate, James Soulsby
moved from Trimdon Grange to Low Fell during
Edwardian years and was spotted scoring goals
for Rodsley and West Stanley in local football and
given a contract with the Magpies. The First World
War put a stop to his progress, joining up with the
Northumberland Fusiliers then King's Own Yorkshire Light
Infantry and serving as a corporal in the trenches in France. He didn't gain a chance
on peace being restored, although he was a quick and skilful striker with Blyth. His
form at Croft Park gave Soulsby an opportunity to join Wolves and enter the big-time
for a second chance. But he decided to remain in Northumberland concentrating on
a teaching career. He did move to neighbouring Ashington, Soulsby helping during
the Portland Park club's short Football League era making 33 appearances for
Northumberland's other black-and-whites from the inside-right or outside-right
positions. His elder brother Robert was with United as an amateur in 1914-15 and
through the war years.

*(Note: There are other footballers by the name of Soulsby to have played in the North
East during the same era, their career paths being sometimes difficult to identify. John
Norman Soulsby appeared for Darlington, Carlisle and Spennymoor, while it is likely
a different J Soulsby turned out for South Shields, Whitburn, Wallsend, Ravensworth
and Chester-le-Street.)*

Appearances & Goals:
Debut v Middlesbrough (h) 10 March 1915
FL: 1 app 0 gls
Total: 1 app 0 gls

SOYE James 1906-1909

Inside-left
5'8"
b. Govan, Glasgow, 14 April 1885
d. Lurgan, Co Armagh, October 1975

Career: Rutherglen Glencairn/Belfast Celtic trial/
Hibernian trial/Distillery (Belfast) 1903/
Southampton cs 1905/UNITED May 1906/
Aberdeen May 1909 exch deal for W Low/
Distillery (Belfast) cs 1915/Glenavon cs 1917.

An electrical engineer by trade, Jimmy Soye
appeared at centre-forward and in both inside
channels for United, including a single
appearance as a deputy for Bill Appleyard during
the title winning season of 1906-07. Always
considered a reserve at St James' Park, Soye
found a regular place with the Dons, moving north as part of the deal that brought
Wilf Low to Tyneside. In Scotland he developed into a potent outside-left, with flair
and the habit of scoring spectacular goals. Totalling 201 senior matches for Aberdeen
over six seasons, runner-up in the title race during 1910-11, he netted on 25 occasions
reaching the fringe of the Scotland side. In Ireland with Distillery over two spells, Soye
also racked up a fine games to goals ratio, scoring 22 goals in 89 outings. He once
faced the Magpies in a friendly against the Irish before joining the Saints and scored
a hat-trick.

Appearances & Goals:
Debut v Everton (h) 15 September 1906
FL: 7 app 2 gls
Total: 7 app 2 gls

Honours:
1 SL app 1912/FL champs 1907 (1 app)/IC winner 1905/Irish City Cup winner 1905.

SPEED Gary MBE 1998-2004

Midfield
5'11"
b. Mancot, near Chester, 8 September 1969
d. Huntington, Cheshire, 27 November 2011

Career: Everton jnr/Leeds Utd jnr April 1986, prof
June 1988/Everton July 1996 £3.5m/UNITED Feb
1998 £5.5m/Bolton Wand July 2004 £750,000 (&
Wrexham part-time asst-coach July 2006 for a
period), becoming Bolton Wand player-coach
May 2007 to Oct 2007/Sheffield Utd Jan 2008
£250,000, retired playing cs 2010, becoming
coach, then manager Aug 2010/Wales manager
Dec 2010 to death.

When Welsh international Gary Speed joined the Magpies, it took the commanding
midfield player several months to settle and display the form that had earned him
the reputation of being one of the best all-round competitors in the business. Initially
given an unfamiliar role on the left of midfield, when Gary was pushed into the heart
of the action, and a central role, Newcastle fans saw the real Gary Speed and he
rapidly became one of United's blue-chip footballers at the core of the club's top rated
line-up. Powerful in the air and always a threat in the opponent's box, he began his
career at Elland Road, Speed helping Leeds to promotion and to the League
Championship during 1992 alongside David Batty before moving to Everton four years
later after 65 games. At Goodison Park, the Welshman never quite took root on
Merseyside and he made a somewhat fractious exit and controversial move to
Tyneside for a £5.5m fee during February 1998. Appearing in two FA Cup finals for
the Black'n'Whites as well as in the Champions League, Speed became an important
cog in Sir Bobby Robson's Magpie eleven, giving the side
balance in midfield with his all-action, combative style.

S

Frequently able to hit the net, Speed had the ability to arrive in the box at the right moment and was a danger at set pieces while he was also capable of many a long range efforts with his favoured left foot. He scored 40 goals for the Magpies and was skipper on occasion of the club. A top level athlete, and professional in every manner, 'Speedo' as he was nicknamed, was an immensely popular character on Tyneside. After seven seasons of worthy service, Gary joined Bolton Wanderers during July 2004 when 34 years old and then moved to Sheffield United. He played on until he was over 40 then in the summer of 2010 concentrated on a career in coaching. He became the Blades' manager as the 2010-11 season got underway then took charge of Wales. Captain of his country with 85 caps, only a handful of players have appeared more for the Welsh, while Speed clocked up over 800 senior appearances and also held for a period the record for most games played in the Premiership (535 app). His father Roger was a part-time player with Wrexham while his son Ed Speed started a career with the Red Dragons and reached the Wales youth squad. Tragically, during November 2011, all of football was stunned with the news that 42-year-old Speed had committed suicide at his home in Cheshire, although the Inquest returned a 'narrative' verdict, the Coroner being unable to determine if he killed himself intentionally, or as an accident.

Appearances & Goals:
Debut v West Ham United (h) 7 February 1998
PL: 206(7) app 29 gls
FAC: 22 app 5 gls
FLC: 9(2) app 1 gls
Euro: 39 app 5 gls
Total: 276(9) app 40 gls

Honours:
85 Wales caps 1990-2005/3 Wales u21 app 1990-92/Wales sch-youth app/FL champs 1992/FL div 2 champs 1990/FAC final 1998, 1999/FLC final 1996/PFA ToS (PL) 1993/PL Award most app 1992-2002/MBE 2010.

SPEEDIE Finlay Ballantyne 1906-1908

Inside-left
5'9"
b. Dumbarton, 18 August 1880
d. Dumbarton, 5 February 1953

Career: Artizan Thistle (Dumbarton)/Dumbarton 1895/Duntocher Hibs/Strathclyde Jnrs/Rangers Oct 1900/UNITED Sept 1906 £600/Oldham Ath June 1908 joint deal with W Appleyard/Bradford Park Avenue April 1909/Dumbarton Sept 1909, becoming asst-trainer Sept 1919 to 1920/Dumbarton Harp 1922/Dumbarton trainer 1933.

Although Finlay Speedie usually operated at inside-left, he appeared in all areas of the field for United; in defence, midfield and in attack, comprising seven different roles. Used as the club's utility man, Speedie was a distinguished player having won several Scottish honours at Ibrox in 121 games, including netting two goals in the 1904 Scottish Cup final. He was cool, assured and steady, appearing to cruise through a match with superb nonchalance, yet still be a star performer. Only at St James' Park for two seasons, Speedie became a crowd favourite after scoring twice on his debut, but was allowed to leave when the club had a mini rebuilding period during the summer of 1908. Scoring on his debut for Scotland as well, Finlay served with the Argyll & Sutherland Highlanders during World War One and was wounded during battle in France, being awarded the Military Medal in August 1918. A witty and buoyant character, described by one teammate as an "incorrigible joker", Speedie came from a footballing family; his brother Willie, and nephew, Bobby, both played for Dumbarton too. A marine engineer by profession, Finlay later worked for the Water Commissioners in the Dumbarton area. He is a celebrated name in that town, appearing for the Sons on 133 occasions and later at Boghead Park as trainer. He is described in their annals as being "idolised by the Dumbarton public".

Appearances & Goals:
Debut v Sheffield Wednesday (h) 29 September 1906 (2 goals)
FL: 52 app 13 gls
FAC: 7 app 1 gl
Others: 1 app 0 gls
Total: 60 app 14 gls

Honours:
3 Scot caps 1903/1 unoff Scot app 1903/Scot trial app 1903/1 SL app 1905/FL champs 1907/FAC final 1908/SL champs 1901, 1902/SL div 2 champs 1911/SC winner 1903/SC final 1904, 1905.

SPENCE John 1891-1892

Half-back
b. Scotland, c1865

Career: Kilmarnock/Sunderland Oct 1889/EAST END July 1891 to 1892.

John Spence arrived to boost Newcastle East End's line-up from Sunderland during the summer of 1891 after totalling just five games for the Wearsiders as they started life in the First Division. But Spence had a good return of goals, claiming three altogether, including two on his debut against Burnley, Sunderland's inaugural game in senior league action during September 1890. He is noted in the club's annals as a historic figure, one of his strikes being Sunderland's first registered goal. A Scot, he landed on Wearside from Kilmarnock but after losing his place, headed for Tyneside and gave East End some needed top-level know-how, albeit John stayed only for the season. His second first-class appearance wearing the then red shirt of East End was in a Novocastrian derby with rivals West End at St James' Park, a 2-0 victory.

Appearances & Goals:
Debut v Tow Law Town (a) 3 October 1891 (FACQ)
NL: 12 app 2 gls
FAC: 5 app 1 gls
Total: 17 app 3 gls

SPENCER Charles William 1921-1928

Centre-half
5'11"
b. Washington, 4 December 1899
d. York, 9 February 1953

Career: Glebe Rovers (Washington) 1915/Washington Chemicals 1919/UNITED amat Aug 1921, prof Oct 1921 £10/Manchester Utd July 1928 £3,250/Tunbridge Wells Rangers player-manager May 1930/Wigan Ath player-manager Aug 1932/Grimsby Town manager March 1937 to April 1951/Hastings Utd manager 1951/York City manager Nov 1952 to his demise.

During his early days at St James' Park, Charlie Spencer was a creative half-back. However, on the advent of the stopper centre-half role following the offside rule change in 1925, he was switched to a commanding defender, arguably the first exponent of the new tactic. Never showy, but consistent at his game, Charlie was a players' player, colleague Stan Seymour once noting that he was "a magnificent clubman". With a temperament for the big occasion, auburn-haired Spencer was a solid performer in both the Magpies' FA Cup and title victories during the Twenties. He was described as "lithe and graceful", reaching the England set-up at his peak in 1925 and captaining the Football League eleven two years later. Entering management, Charlie was a respected boss being in charge of Grimsby for a lengthy period, but suffered from illness at various times. He became Wigan's first ever manager and helped hugely develop the fledgling club, at that time also owning a confectionary shop in Blackpool. He started his career in football as a goalkeeper with colliery side, Glebe Rovers, and during World War One served in the Royal Engineers Signals.

Appearances & Goals:
Debut v Bolton Wanderers (h) 11 March 1922
FL: 161 app 1 gl
FAC: 14 app 0 gls
Total: 175 app 1 gl

Honours:
2 Eng caps 1924-25/5 unoff Eng app 1925/Eng trial app 1926/2 FL app 1926-28/FL champs 1927/FAC winner 1924.

SPIKE Septimus 1940-1942

Right-back
5'8"
b. Willington Quay, near Newcastle upon Tyne, 17 March 1921
d. Leicester, 1979 (Q1)

Career: Willington Ath/UNITED amat April 1940 to 1942
(Leeds Utd war-guest 1940-42).

An apprentice engineer, Septimus Spike was an automatic selection for United's reserve line-up in the wartime Northern Combination during season 1941-42. He was upgraded to take Joe Richardson's full-back shirt during September 1941 for a few games before having a handful of outings with Leeds in the Football League North competition.

Appearances & Goals:
Debut v Bradford City (a) 6 September 1941 (FLN)
War: 3 app 0 gls
Total: 3 app 0 gls

SPINK James 1913-1919

Right-half
5'8"
b. Dipton, near Consett, 1890 (Q3)
d. Lintz, near Consett, 13 August 1943

Career: Dipton Utd/Craghead Utd/UNITED March 1913 (Hartlepools Utd war-guest 1915-16)(Grimsby Town war-guest 1916-17)/Hartlepools Utd July 1919/Dipton Utd cs 1920.

Youngster Jimmy Spink emerged from the strong Northern League and showed up well for United in the seasons prior to the Great War. Promising much, he was a rival to Bob Hewison in midfield, Spink made excellent progress and earned a rapid elevation to Newcastle's Division One and FA Cup side, selected on 19 occasions during season 1914-15. Having a good and sure touch on the ball, he was destined for a bright future until war clouds put a stop to football at the end of that programme. With the Durham Light Infantry during the hostilities, Spink later appeared for Hartlepool during their North Eastern League days just before the club entered the Football League action in 1921, but he suffered bad injuries which forced him back to the non-league scene. James afterwards lived in Derwentside, his brother Tom appeared for Fulham, Rochdale and notably Grimsby.

Appearances & Goals:
Debut v West Bromwich Albion (h) 17 January 1914
FL: 20 app 0 gls
FAC: 4 app 0 gls
Total: 24 app 0 gls

SPUHLER John Oswald 1944

Outside-right
5'8"
b. Fulwell, Sunderland, 18 September 1917
d. Stockton on Tees, 7 January 2007

Career: Sunderland amat May 1932, prof Sept 1934 (Hartlepools Utd war-guest 1939-40)(Carlisle Utd war-guest 1939-40)(Middlesbrough war-guest 1940-41)(UNITED war-guest 1943-44)/Middlesbrough Oct 1945 £1,500/Darlington June 1954 £750/Spennymoor Utd player-manager cs 1956/Stockton manager 1957/ Shrewsbury Town manager Feb 1958 to May 1958/ Later becoming West Auckland Town manager to c1963/Stockton manager cs 1965.

A good servant to North East football, Johnny Spuhler appeared on nearly 190 occasions (84 goals) for Sunderland, over 250 times for Middlesbrough and over 70 for Darlington. And he wore the Black'n'White of United briefly during April 1944. An England schoolboy international during 1932, he started as an office junior at Roker Park and had just emerged as a new find in Sunderland's talented line-up before war was declared. Claiming 21 appearances in the Reds 1937-38 campaign, he was described by one colleague as being fast and direct, "like a whippet". At Ayresome Park, Spuhler was converted into an effective centre-forward, the mainstay of Boro's immediate post-war line-up, scoring almost 100 goals before he moved to Feethams. Having a period in management when he guided West Auckland to the FA Amateur Cup final in 1961, on retiring from the game, Johnny ran a post-office in Yarm, later residing in Barnard Castle and Fishburn.

Appearances & Goals:
Debut v Sheffield United (a) 1 April 1944 (FLWC)
War: 2 app 1 gl
Total: 2 app 1 gl

Honours:
Eng sch-youth app/FL WC final 1942/FAAC final 1961(m).

SRNICEK Pavel 1990-1998, 2006-2007

Goalkeeper
6'2"
b. Bohumin, near Ostrava (Czechoslovakia),
10 March 1968

Career: TJ Victorie Bohumin Jnrs (Cz)/TJ ZD Bohumin (Cz)/Tabur VTJ (Cz) 1986/Dukla Prague (Cz) 1987/Banik Ostrava (Cz)/Leicester City trial Oct 1990/UNITED trial Dec 1990, pmt Feb 1991 £350,000 (Olym Marseille (Fr) trial June 1992) to June 1998/Wolverhampton Wand trial Aug 1998/Banik Ostrava (Cz) Aug 1998/Sheffield Wed trial Oct 1998, pmt Nov 1998/Brescia (It) July 2000/Cosenza (It) 2002-03/Wolverhampton Wand trial Aug 2003/Portsmouth Sept 2003/West Ham Utd trial Jan 2004, pmt Feb 2004/Coventry City trial Aug 2004/SC Beira Mar (Ptg) Aug 2004 to May 2006/UNITED Oct 2006 to June 2007/Banik Ostrava gkp-coach/AC Sparta Prague gkp-coach Jan 2012.

A former Eastern Bloc soldier, Pavel Srnicek's arrival on Tyneside at the end of 1990, initially on trial, coincided with some of the poorest Newcastle performances on record as the Magpies struggled in Division Two. The tall goalkeeper who had impressed boss Jim Smith playing for Banik against Aston Villa in the UEFA Cup, could speak little English at first, and had a torrid early period in Newcastle's side. However, Pavel was determined to succeed. He gradually settled in the North East, learnt the language and improved his all-round goalkeeping skills immensely, especially at collecting crosses safely. His progress was such that when Kevin Keegan took charge at Gallowgate, Srnicek claimed the Number 1 shirt, even though Mike Hooper was soon purchased as first choice. Acrobatic with exceptional shot-stopping ability, but occasionally prone to error, Pavel earned something of a cult following with United's Toon Army; the Czech making a series of spectacular saves as United lifted the First Division title trophy then famously and proudly wearing a T-shirt noting, "Pavel is a Geordie" as the celebrations began. Srnicek then was part of the squad which embarked on a bid for Premier League silverware, twice being runners-up. He could make fabulous stops, one such save against Everton in which he twisted in mid-air to palm away a Limpar 25 yard deflected drive prompted Gordon Banks to note that it was in his "all time top ten great saves". Srnicek was Ludek Miklosko's deputy in the Banik team in Czechoslovakia and Pavel followed the path of Miklosko to England, and into his country's side too being part of the eye-catching Euro 96 squad in England. But he always had a constant battle to keep the first-team shirt at St James' Park. After he saw off Hooper, in came Shaka Hislop and then Shay Given, Pav finding himself third choice. That competition was frustrating for Srnicek and he wasn't favoured by Kenny Dalglish so reluctantly departed Tyneside, serving several clubs in England and in Europe before he made a return to Gallowgate on an injury to Given in 2006 for a short swansong when 38 years of age. Pavel returned to the Czech Republic where he started a career in goalkeeper coaching. Srnicek also at times commentates on Premier League football for Czech television and remains a hugely popular personality on Tyneside, often making a visit to St James' Park. In July 2014 he was made Vice-President of Dunston UTS and started a regular newspaper column in the Tyneside press.

Appearances & Goals:
Debut v Sheffield Wednesday (h) 17 April 1991
FL/PL: 149(2) app 0 gls
FAC: 11 app 0 gls
FLC: 10(1) app 0 gls
Euro: 10 app 0 gls
Others: 7 app 0 gls
Total: 187(3) app 0 gls

Honours:
49 Cz caps 1995-2002/ECh final 1996 (sub no app)/3 Cz u21 app/PL runners-up 1996, 1997/FL div 1 champs 1993.

S

STARLING Ronald William 1930-1932

Inside-forward
5'9"
b. Pelaw, Gateshead, 11 October 1909
d. Sheffield, 17 December 1991

Career: Usworth CW Jan 1924/Washington CW Sept 1924/Hull City amat June 1925, prof Aug 1927/UNITED May 1930 £3,750/Sheffield Wed June 1932 £3,250/Aston Villa Jan 1937 £7,500 (Walsall war-guest 1939-42) (Nottingham Forest war-guest 1939-42) (Northampton Town war-guest 1939-40) (Sheffield Wed war-guest 1940-41)/Nottingham Forest trainer July 1948 to June 1950/Beighton Miners Welfare Feb to April 1951.

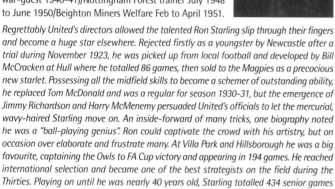

Regrettably United's directors allowed the talented Ron Starling slip through their fingers and become a huge star elsewhere. Rejected firstly as a youngster by Newcastle after a trial during November 1923, he was picked up from local football and developed by Bill McCracken at Hull where he totalled 86 games, then sold to the Magpies as a precocious new starlet. Possessing all the midfield skills to become a schemer of outstanding ability, he replaced Tom McDonald and was a regular for season 1930-31, but the emergence of Jimmy Richardson and Harry McMenemy persuaded United's officials to let the mercurial, wavy-haired Starling move on. An inside-forward of many tricks, one biography noted he was a "ball-playing genius". Ron could captivate the crowd with his artistry, but on occasion over elaborate and frustrate many. At Villa Park and Hillsborough he was a big favourite, captaining the Owls to FA Cup victory and appearing in 194 games. He reached international selection and became one of the best strategists on the field during the Thirties. Playing on until he was nearly 40 years old, Starling totalled 434 senior games plus well over 100 matches in wartime football before he retired. Ron afterwards lived in Sheffield and ran a newsagents shop close to Hillsborough.

Appearances & Goals:
Debut v Sheffield Wednesday (a) 30 August 1930
FL: 51 app 8 gls
FAC: 2 app 0 gls
Total: 53 app 8 gls

Honours:
2 Eng caps 1933-37/Eng trial app 1933/FL div 2 champs 1938/WC(N) winner 1944/FAC winner 1935.

STEEL William 1941-1942

Outside-left
5'9"
b. Newcastle upon Tyne, 1920

From the Walker district of the city, Billy Steel was an apprentice engineer at the giant Parson works during the Second World War. Joining the club as an amateur during July 1941 with a reputation of "middling a ball", his only match for the Magpies was a trip to Leeds Road to face Huddersfield Town in September 1941. United, and Steel, didn't have a happy afternoon as the Magpies fell heavily by 5-0.

Appearances & Goals:
Debut v Huddersfield Town (a) 13 September 1941 (FLN)
War: 1 app 0 gls
Total: 1 app 0 gls

STENHOUSE Henry Whiteman 1902-1905

Outside-right
5'7"
b. Blyth, Northumberland, 1882

Career: Blyth Spartans 1901/UNITED May 1902/Ashington May 1905/Blyth Spartans late 1905.

Harry Stenhouse was considered by the local media of the day as the first Blyth Spartans player to turn out in the Football League. Joining United as a direct winger who possessed a big reputation in local football, he had a cracking shot and following a series of good displays in the club's Northern League side, was elevated to the first-team in place of Willie Stewart. His debut however was not a memorable afternoon; United lost 7-0 to Villa, one of the club's heaviest defeats on record in the top flight. Stenhouse was described as "one of those speedy dashing forwards with great control of the ball". He later continued to live and work in south Northumberland, at Cowpen, originally a joiner's machinist.

Appearances & Goals:
Debut v Aston Villa (a) 29 November 1902
FL: 6 app 0 gls   Total: 6 app 0 gls

STEPHENSON Paul 1982-1988

Outside-right
5'10"
b. Wallsend, 2 January 1968

Career: Wallsend BC/St Marys BC/UNITED jnr Feb 1982, prof Jan 1986/Millwall Nov 1988 £300,000 (Gillingham loan 1992-93)/Brentford March 1993 £30,000/York City Aug 1995 £35,000/Hartlepool Utd March 1998 free to March 2003 when he became asst-coach, then caretaker-manager Feb 2006/Norwich City asst-coach Dec 2007/Huddersfield Town asst-coach Feb 2009, becoming coach Nov 2010/Accrington Stanley coach Jan 2012, becoming asst-manager July 2013 and caretaker-manager briefly Sept 2014.

A youth international, Paul Stephenson made his debut for the Magpies as a 17-year-old and almost capped a sparkling display with a goal, only for his headlining effort to be controversially chalked off by the referee. With pace and skill, the Geordie appeared to be heading in the right direction for stardom, but following two seasons as a new hopeful on the First Division scene during 1985-86 and 1986-87, Stephenson damaged ligaments and lost his momentum and place in the side. Moving to London, he had a useful stay at the Den, providing service for the noted combination of Sheringham and Cascarino to feed off in his 118 matches. Following a good stint with York (117 app) he returned to the North East with Hartlepool and proceeded to became a favourite during his 170 games for the Victoria Ground club. Starting a coaching career, Paul later was part of Lee Clark's staff at Huddersfield. During his teenage days with the Magpies the Tynesider was part of the squad which lifted the FA Youth Cup in 1985, although he missed out on selection for the final against Watford. Paul's father Peter Stephenson played for Gateshead, Middlesbrough and Ashington.

Appearances & Goals:
Debut v Southampton (h) 14 December 1985
FL: 58(3) app 1 gl
FAC: 2 app 0 gls
FLC: 3(1) app 0 gls
Others: 2 app 0 gls
Total: 65(4) app 1 gl

Honours:
Eng sch-youth app.

STEVENSON James W 1898-1900

Inside-right
5'8"
b. Paisley, 1 February 1877
d. (Thiepval), France, 3 July 1916

Career: Ashfield/Clyde June 1894/Derby Co Jan 1895/UNITED Oct 1898 £225/Bristol City June 1900/Grimsby Town Sept 1901/Leicester Fosse Jan 1902/Clyde Sept 1902 £27/[St Mirren Sept 1904].

Jimmy Stevenson was a raider who possessed plenty of craft and ball control. With Derby County, Stevenson played alongside Steve Bloomer and had a good record as a marksman with the Rams, scoring 32 goals in 84 games. He appeared in the 1898 FA Cup final before United made a bid to sign the diminutive Scot. Noted as a master dribbler, Jimmy was, as one contemporary report claimed, "a wizard with the leather". After a good season for the Black'n'Whites during 1898-99, United's first in the top division, he was unlucky with injury at St James' Park and was replaced by the emergence of Alex Gardner. Stevenson almost gained a Scotland cap on several occasions, but had to be content with trial game outings. James later went into business in Glasgow and fell in the Great War, a victim of the Battle of the Somme when serving with the Highland Light Infantry. He is remembered at the imposing Thiepval Memorial in northern France.

Appearances & Goals:
Debut v Liverpool (h) 5 November 1898
FL: 33 app 12 gls
FAC: 4 app 1 gl
Total: 37 app 13 gls

Honours:
Scot trial app 1897-1903/FAC final 1898/SJC winner 1894.

STEWART Alan Victor 1938, 1944

Centre-half
5'11"
b. Newcastle upon Tyne, 24 July 1922
d. Acomb, York, 13 July 2004

Career: UNITED amat Aug 1938 briefly/Huddersfield
Town April 1940 (UNITED war-guest 1943-44)/
Resumed with Huddersfield 1945/York City Aug 1949
to cs 1957.

*Alan Stewart was a teenage trialist with United at the
start of the 1938-39 season but wasn't retained, soon
gaining another chance at a top ranked club with
Huddersfield Town. Stewart only totalled 15 games for
Huddersfield in first-class football due to the war
ruining his early career, although he played for the Terriers during wartime and clocked
up another 85 games. He returned to St James' Park a good bit older and wiser in
1944, appearing at left-back for United during March of that Football League North
season. On signing for York City for the start of the 1949-50 programme, Alan found
a home as a solid lower division defender. Tall and commanding at the centre of York's
defence, he took part in City's famous FA Cup run to oppose Newcastle in the FA Cup
semi-final of 1955 when he tamed the likes of Stan Mortensen and Len Duquemin on
the way. Alan went onto register 231 appearances over seven seasons for the
Minstermen, one of their finest post-war servants. Stewart later became a
representative for a York brewery living in the historic city to his death.*

Appearances & Goals:
Debut v Darlington (a) 18 March 1944 (FLWC)
War: 2 app 0 gls
Total: 2 app 0 gls

STEWART Ian Edwin 1985-1987

Outside-left
5'7"
b. Belfast, 10 September 1961

Career: Cregagh Swifts/Queens Park Rangers
May 1980 (Millwall loan 1982-83)/UNITED Aug
1985 £150,000/Portsmouth July 1987
(Brentford loan 1987-88) to Nov
1988/Leicester City trial Dec 1988/Aldershot
Jan 1989/ Colchester Utd Feb 1992 to May
1992/Harrow Borough Nov 1992/Later
Northern Ireland FA Development Officer June
1995, becoming Northern Ireland FA
Grassroots Development Manager.

*Early impressions at St James' Park of Ian
Stewart's talent were most favourable. With
control and a clever, but direct style, the
Irishman looked a good purchase by manager
Willie McFaul. Stewart had turned heads with his performances in 82 games for
Rangers and could provide a dangerous cross while he was able on occasion hit a
powerful shot. However by the time of his last outing for United, during season 1986-
87, he had been labelled with the inconsistent tag, frustratingly too often on the
fringe of the action instead of making an impact on the match. Taking part in the
1986 World Cup finals for Northern Ireland, Ian never fulfilled his potential after a
bright opening for QPR, United and Northern Ireland; once hitting a stunning goal
against West Germany during an early international outing. Once he left Tyneside
Stewart's career declined, and he rarely showed the skill in senior company which had
taken him almost to the top level of football. He did though serve Aldershot well in
lower divisions of the game, totalling 131 appearances at the Recreation Ground. He
afterwards resided back in his native Ulster, working for the local Football Association
in youth development.*

Appearances & Goals:
Debut v Luton Town (h) 21 August 1985
FL: 34(8) app 3 gls
FAC: 2(1) app 0 gls
FLC: 4(1) app 0 gls
Total: 40(10) app 3 gls

Honours:
31 NI caps 1982-87/WdC 1986/NI sch-youth app/FL div 2 champs 1983.

STEWART James 1908-1913

Inside-left or right
5'9"
b. Gateshead, 7 June 1883
d. Gateshead, 23 May 1957

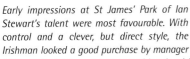

Career: Todd's Nook (Newcastle)/Gateshead NER/
Sheffield Wed April 1902 £32/UNITED Aug 1908
£1,000/Rangers Sept 1913 £600/North Shields
Ath player-manager May 1914/Later scouting
for Derby Co during 1920s & 1930s.

*Known as 'Tadger' from his early days in local
Tyneside football, Jimmy Stewart delighted many
fans during his career with a repertoire of delicate
skills and an ability to regularly hit the back of the
net. Another of United's many international stars of
the Edwardian era, Stewart returned to his area of birth
after a rewarding period at Hillsborough. In 141 games for Sheffield Wednesday he
scored 60 goals, including lifting league silverware and a run to FA Cup glory in which
he bagged vital strikes in both the semi and final rounds. That form earned Jimmy an
England cap and a big move back to Tyneside. Replacing Ronald Orr in United's ranks,
Stewart operated in both schemers' positions as well as at centre-forward on occasion.
Although not a six-footer, he was a formidable player in the air, renowned for his
prodigious leaps for high balls. Winning another title medal with the Magpies, he
missed the 1910 final but played in the showpiece a year later. The local favourite, did
though have his differences with United's hierarchy, once suspended indefinitely for
using bad language at club officials. Stewart moved to Scotland as a veteran at the
start of the 1913-14 seasons and had an enjoyable few months at Ibrox showing the
Glasgow public his skills by netting 13 goals in 21 matches. On retiring from the game,
Stewart resided in Gateshead and was employed as a commercial traveller before
becoming a licensee in Northallerton for a period, then working in accountancy back
in Newcastle. His younger brother Tom was on United's books during 1910-11.*

Appearances & Goals:
Debut v Bradford City (h) 2 September 1908
FL: 121 app 49 gls
FAC: 17 app 4 gls
Total: 138 app 53 gls

Honours:
3 Eng caps 1907-11/Eng trial app 1907-11/4 FL app 1910-11/FL champs 1903 (1 app),
1904, 1909/FAC winner 1907/FAC final 1911.

STEWART George Thomas 1896-1898

Right-back
5'10"
b. Lanarkshire

Career: Glasgow Perthshire/Partick Thistle Aug
1895/Motherwell April 1896/UNITED Dec 1896
joint deal with J Ostler £200/Grimsby Town July
1898 to 1899.

*Stout defender George Stewart came into
United's side half-way through the 1896-97
campaign. Hard and physical with little finesse
to his game, Stewart was described in the
Newcastle Daily Journal as a "full-back with
excellent credentials" who "tackled with resolution
and coolness, and kicked with great power and
judgement". Despite this glowing report though, he was
replaced by Billy Lindsay as Newcastle embarked on their final push for promotion
during the following season. With Grimsby, the Scot played on only a single occasion.*

Appearances & Goals:
Debut v Grimsby Town (a) 26 December 1896
FL: 27 app 0 gls
FAC: 3 app 0 gls
Total: 30 app 0 gls

Honours:
FL div 2 prom 1898.

S

STEWART William (Garven) 1901-1903

Outside-right
5'8"
b. Govan, Glasgow, 29 February 1876

Career: Queen's Park Aug 1900 (Third Lanark loan 1900-01)/UNITED June 1901 to cs 1903/ Queen's Park to 1907.

Forward Willie Stewart boasted a first-class reputation in Scotland, capped by his country and a Scottish Cup finalist during 1900. Working as an electrical engineer and an amateur footballer at first, he had played alongside Bob McColl in the Queen's Park eleven and was a fine athletic-looking player who combined admirably with his team-mates for a season at St James' Park. An automatic choice in United's ranks during 1901-02, he was left out of the side for patches during the following campaign and was eventually replaced by Turner and Rutherford. Thinning on top, Willie possessed an excellent turn of speed and had ability to cut in or go outside his full-back. When he was attached to Third Lanark, his loan agreement with amateurs Queen's Park meant he played in only Scottish Cup fixtures. Stewart later was employed for the White Star Line shipping company out of Liverpool. He is one of very few United players to have been born on the 29th February, a leap year.

Appearances & Goals:
Debut v Stoke (h) 14 September 1901
FL: 37 app 4 gls
FAC: 4 app 1 gl
Total: 41 app 5 gls

Honours:
2 Scot caps 1898-1900/SC final 1900.

STIMSON Mark Nicholas 1989-1992

Left-back
5'11"
b. Plaistow, London, 27 December 1967

Career: Orient jnr/Queens Park Rangers jnr/ Tottenham Hotspur jnr July 1984, prof July 1985 (Orient loan 1987-88)(Gillingham loan 1988-89)/UNITED June 1989 £156,000/ Portsmouth loan Dec 1992, pmt July 1993 £95,000 (Barnet loan 1995-96)/Southend Utd March 1996 £25,000/ Leyton Orient March 1999 free/ Gillingham trial cs 1999/Canvey Island Aug 1999/Grays Ath player-coach June 2002, becoming player-manager Sept 2002 & part-time England National XI coach/ Stevenage Borough manager May 2006/Gillingham manager Nov 2007/Barnet manager June 2010 to Jan 2011/Dagenham & Redbridge coach 2011/ Kettering Town manager Sept 2011 to Jan 2012/Thurrock manager May 2012.

Blond-haired Mark Stimson was unheard of by most United supporters when Jim Smith signed him from the fringe of the Spurs team. An attacking left-back, Stimson claimed the left-back role for three seasons as the Magpies strove to get out of the Second Division. A resilient character, he had his highs and lows at Gallowgate, both chastised and hailed by the fans during a mediocre period in United's history. As a schoolboy, Mark was offered opportunities by no fewer than six London clubs before choosing White Hart Lane, but found that manager Terry Venables would never give him a run in the first-team despite being on the bench several times. Possessing a good shot and turn of pace, he followed Jim Smith to Fratton Park and made 77 appearances for Pompey then had 62 outings for Southend. Mark began a coaching career in the south with Grays Athletic, notably reaching Wembley on three occasions as a boss in the FA Trophy and winning silverware in consecutive years. His son, Charlie Stimpson, started his footballing career with Gillingham.

Appearances & Goals:
Debut v Leicester City (a) 26 August 1989
FL: 84(4) app 2 gls
FAC: 7 app 1 gl
FLC: 5 app 0 gls
Others: 4 app 0 gls
Total: 100(4) app 3 gls

Honours:
1 Eng Nat XI app 2002/FL div 1 champs 1993 (2 app)/FL div 2 prom 2009(m)/FAT winner 2001, 2005(m), 2006(m), 2007(m).

STOBBART George Campbell 1946-1949

Forward
5'7"
b. Pegswood, Northumberland, 9 January 1921
d. Newcastle upon Tyne, 3 January 1995

Career: Netherton Jnrs/Middlesbrough May 1939 (North Shields war-guest)(Darlington war-guest 1943-44)/UNITED Sept 1946 £4,650/Luton Town Oct 1949 £12,500/Millwall Aug 1952/Brentford May 1954 to Dec 1956.

Versatile in any forward position, George Stobbart was purchased to fill the striking gap when Albert Stubbins headed for Liverpool. The Northumbrian became a valuable member of United's promotion side during 1947-48 netting several crucial goals in the finale to the season. Strong and stocky, George was a tremendous grafter up front, and had good pace over a 20 or 30 yard chase for the ball. Scoring plenty of goals for Middlesbrough during, and just after, the war, 125 in total, Newcastle paid what was a big fee for his all round ability. George had an eventful start for the Magpies, netting twice on his debut against Coventry, but he also soon picked up an ankle injury which kept him on the sidelines for a few weeks. He was also somewhat frustrated at being played out of his best position of centre-forward in a black-and-white shirt. With George Robledo arriving during 1949, Stobbart found himself out of the picture and he moved south to Kenilworth Road for a sizable £12,500 fee. Stobbart became Luton's most expensive signing and during his 116 matches once scored four goals in an eight-minute burst for the Hatters against Blackburn during 1949. On leaving the game, he resided in the Forest Hall district of Newcastle to his death.

Appearances & Goals:
Debut v Coventry City (h) 11 September 1946 (2 goals)
FL: 66 app 21 gls
FAC: 6 app 1 gl
Total: 72 app 22 gls

Honours:
FL div 2 prom 1948.

STOKOE Robert 1947-1961, 1989

Centre-half & Coach
6'0"
b. Mickley Square, near Gateshead, 21 September 1930
d. Hartlepool, 1 February 2004

Career: Wylam Boy's Brigade 1944/Army cadets 1945/Spen Jnrs 1945/UNITED Sept 1947 £10/ Bury Feb 1961 cash-exch deal for J McGrath, becoming player-manager Dec 1961/ Charlton Ath manager Aug 1965/ Leyton Orient asst-coach 1967/Rochdale manager Oct 1967/Carlisle Utd manager Oct 1968/Blackpool manager Dec 1970/ Sunderland manager Nov 1972 to Oct 1976/Bury manager Nov 1977/Blackpool manager May 1978 to Aug 1979/Carlisle Utd scout/Rochdale manager Nov 1979/Carlisle Utd manager Sept 1980 to May 1985, returning Oct 1985 to May 1986/Sunderland caretaker-manager April to May 1987, becoming consultant to May 1989/UNITED part-time asst-coach June 1989/Bury part-time asst-coach 1991/Chelsea scout 1991/Swindon Town scout Dec 1993 to cs 1994/Bury consultant to May 1996.

Bob Stokoe grew up in the coal-mining village of Mickley, embedded in a strong footballing breeding ground and had a dream like most local youngsters of playing for Newcastle United. Scoring three goals in two trial games as a forward for the Magpies, he was signed as a teenager and switched to a half-back role. Although he made his first appearance for United in the centre-forward shirt, when he found the net against Middlesbrough, he developed into a midfielder who liked to attack, but Bob found it difficult to break into the side in that role. Stokoe soon became more of a utility defender during the first four seasons of the Fifties decade and was 12th man at Wembley during 1951. With the club for almost 14 years, Stokoe was often frustrated at his lack of opportunities during the first half of his Magpie career, and he made more than one transfer request for a move. But Bob eventually switched from the half-back position to centre-half and claimed the pivot's role in season 1954-55 and at last gained the regular role he aspired to. Stokoe was outstanding at the centre of the defence as Newcastle lifted the FA Cup that year, becoming a sound and dependable backline anchor for the next five seasons. Fiercely competitive on the field, determined in the tackle and good in distribution, Stokoe skippered the side on many occasions during that period and when he left approaching 31 years of age to start a long career in management at Bury, Stokoe had served the club with distinction. One of only a handful of men to have played in a winning FA Cup team, then to manage a side to victory, with Sunderland in 1973, Stokoe became one of the modern games most travelled managers, and most respected. Having a gentle, quiet-spoken manner off the field, his character was one of steely determination to win, yet he never got the opportunity to be boss of the Magpies, despite being linked with the job several times. Bob resided in Carlisle until the summer of 1991 when he moved to Lancashire, although in 1996 he returned to his native Tyne Valley to live in Hexham. A statue of Stokoe is located at the Stadium of Light on Wearside, recognition of his achievement of lifting the FA Cup for Sunderland.

Appearances & Goals:
Debut v Middlesbrough (a) 25 December 1950 (1 goal)
FL: 261 app 4 gls
FAC: 26 app 1 gl
Others: 1 app 0 gls
Total: 288 app 5 gls

Honours:
2 FA app 1958-59/FAC winner 1955, 1973(m)/FL div 3 champs 1961/FL div 2 champs 1976(m)/FL div 3 prom 1982(m)/FL Long Service medal 1984/Freedom of Sunderland 1974.

STONES S 1887-1889

Full-back
b. unknown

Career: Guisborough/EAST END March 1887 to 1889.

Arriving from North Yorkshire, after a period in the team's second-string, Stones became Newcastle East End's regular full-back during season 1887-88 just prior to joining action in the Northern League. He was also part of the club's inaugural FA Cup game on Teesside in October 1887. When he made his first appearance for the club it was noted the newcomer "made the usually weak defence of East End strong". The full-back recorded only a single fixture for the club, but appeared in around 30 other games as East End played friendly and local football. Stones was also a noted cricketer during the summer and was once described as a "capital all rounder".

(Note: Local press reports also note his initials as E, G, J and W!)

Appearances & Goals:
Debut v South Bank (a) 15 October 1887 (FACQ)
FAC: 1 app 0 gls
Total: 1 app 0 gls

STOTT James 1895-1899

Left-half
5'10"
b. Darlington, 1870 (Q4)
d. Gosforth, Newcastle upon Tyne, 8 October 1908

Career: South Bank/Middlesbrough c1891/Liverpool Aug 1893/Grimsby Town June 1894/UNITED Aug 1895 £15/Middlesbrough Sept 1899 to 1900.

Appointed captain of Newcastle United shortly after arriving on Tyneside, Jimmy Stott was an inspiring half-back. Clever and swift, he was a good player in all departments, and especially, afraid of no man in the tackle. Stott could be tough as they come, and relished duels on the field, even censored by the club Board in 1896 for "continual fouling of his opponents"! Part of Liverpool's first promotion line-up, he repeated the feat at St James' Park, one of the stalwarts in that successful 1897-98 season. Said to be something of a snappy dresser, he often wore a top-hat on Sundays and on leaving football became a popular publican at The Star Inn on Westgate Road. He was a United shareholder but by August 1907 had been admitted to Newcastle Lunatic Asylum at Coxlodge. He died just over a year later, a tragic victim of a brain tumour when only 37 years old.

Appearances & Goals:
Debut v Loughborough (h) 7 September 1895
FL: 117 app 9 gls
FAC: 14 app 2 gls
Total: 131 app 11 gls

Honours:
FL div 2 champs 1894/FL div 2 prom 1898.

STUBBINS Albert 1936-1946

Centre-forward
5'11"
b. Wallsend, 13 July 1919
d. North Shields, 28 December 2002

Career: Sunderland amat 1935/Whitley & Monkseaton 1935/UNITED amat March 1936, prof May 1937 (Sunderland war-guest 1941-42)/ Liverpool Sept 1946 £12,500/Ashington Sept 1953/ Retired 1954/Liverpool scout 1954/New York Americans (USA) coach 1960/Trenton Grade School (USA) coach 1960 returning to Tyneside the same year.

A legendary figure of the game, flame-haired Albert Stubbins was brought up in the States as a youngster, moving in 1923 to New York and later Detroit. He returned to the North East though, and developed into a promising inside-forward. Joining Sunderland initially, Albert though always favoured the Magpies and had an agreement to leave the red-and-whites should United be interested in him. He switched clubs during 1936 and Albert was quick to gain a first-team opportunity in attack with United. By season 1938-39 such was his progress that pundits championed him for an England place. Tall and forceful, he would run at defenders, and scare them to death with his ability, possessing frightening pace and a mighty shot from his size 11 boots. Yet Stubbins was most unfortunate to be on the brink of stardom when war intervened. Remaining in the area on essential work in local shipyards at Deptford as a draughtsman, Albert made the best of a raw deal by becoming the country's most potent goalscorer. Stubbins bagged goals by the hatful. He scored over 230 goals for the Magpies over seven seasons; 42 in 1942-43, and 43 during both 1943-44 and 1944-45. Included were 29 hat-tricks, and Albert on five occasions netted five goals in a single match, while he grabbed 13 goals in six consecutive outings during 1942. His overall total for the Magpies is bettered only by Jack Milburn. Defenders had no answer to this scoring power and by the time peace was restored and football was back to normal in 1946, Stubbins was a big name, capped by England and the Football League, later netting five times against the Irish League during 1950. Albert then 27 years old, decided he needed to play top-level football and a move would be in his best interests. Despite Stan Seymour trying his utmost to make him stay, a record sale to Liverpool was arranged. At Anfield Stubbins again became a personality player, winning title and FA Cup honours with the Reds. Lean and lithe, Albert scored more goals, 83 in 180 games before leaving the first-class game. Once nicknamed 'The Smiling Assassin', Stubbins was a gentleman of the game. He is featured on The Beatles' famous album cover, Sergeant Pepper's Lonely Hearts Club Band, while he was honoured by a special luncheon at the House of Commons in 1987. Afterwards Albert returned to Tyneside, becoming a well known journalist for The People, as well as a local broadcaster, to his retirement in 1984. Stubbins resided in Wideopen on the outskirts of Newcastle, then in Cullercoats to his death.

Appearances & Goals:
Debut v Luton Town (a) 7 May 1938
FL: 27 app 5 gls
FAC: 3 app 1 gls
War: 187 app 231 gls
Total: 217 app 237 gls
(Void FL: 1 app 0 gls)

Honours:
1 unoff Eng app 1946/2 FA app 1947/4 FL app 1947-51/FL champs 1947/FAC final 1950/WC final 1942.

SUDDICK Alan 1960-1966

Forward
5'11"
b. Chester-le-Street, Co Durham, 2 May 1944
d. Manchester, 15 March 2009

Career: Chester-le-Street Old Boys/UNITED jnr June 1960, prof Oct 1961/Blackpool Dec 1966 £63,000/ Stoke City Dec 1976 (Southport loan 1977-78)/Bury Sept 1977/Barrow Sept 1978/Lancaster City Nov 1979/Blackpool April 1982/Workington 1984/ Runcorn April 1985/Morecambe/Wren Rovers 1994.

Introduced as a 17-year-old teenager during season 1961-62, one of the club's youngest ever players, Alan Suddick became the golden boy of St James' Park.

NEWCASTLE UNITED
The Ultimate Who's Who 1881-2014

S

During his opening games in a black-and-white striped shirt, Suddick ran the show as the Magpies won 4-1, 7-2 and 5-0 in quick succession. Manager Joe Harvey saw the special talent of Suddick as a player with a top class international future, but alas in the end not to reach that lofty pinnacle. Tall and slim, Suddick was versatile across the forward-line, appearing in the Number 7, 8 or 11 shirt, but always with freedom to roam up front and display his ball talents and stunning shooting ability. An entrancing player who possessed a football brain and the ability to glide past opponents, Suddick was a sorcerer with the ball at his feet and often whipped in a dangerous cross, using the 'banana' technique as it was referred to back then. When in the mood he could be brilliant, and was cheeky and mischievous at times on the pitch too, once famously pulling down the shorts of a Bury defender as he lined up for a free-kick at St James' Park. Yet he was erratic, like many of his kind. Alan had a huge terrace following, often inspiring headlines, but was an enigma to boss Harvey, who agonisingly couldn't get the best from his genius week in, week out. Sold to raise funds at a time of relegation crisis, Alan's departure to Blackpool caused huge outcry. He remained at Bloomfield Road for a decade and was equally popular, registering 371 games (81 goals) for the Seasiders. His two sons Jarryd and Fraser both played local football in the North East, while Alan had a succession of occupations after football; he ran a hotel, was a retailer and later became a decorator. Alan's father, George, was with Barnsley in 1931-32, while his grandson Lewis Suddick joined Newcastle United's junior ranks in June 2014.

Appearances & Goals:
Debut v Charlton Athletic (h) 7 October 1961
FL: 144 app 41 gls
FAC: 4 app 1 gl
FLC: 4 app 1 gl
Total: 152 app 43 gls

Honours:
2 Eng u23 app 1963/Eng sch-youth app/FL div 2 champs 1965/FL div 2 prom 1970/FAYC winner 1962.

SUGGETT Colin 1978-1994

Midfield & Coach
5'8"
b. Washington, 30 December 1948

Career: Sunderland jnr Aug 1964, prof Jan 1966 (Vancouver Royals (Can) loan cs 1967)/West Bromwich Albion July 1969 £100,000/Norwich City Feb 1973 £75,000/UNITED Aug 1978 £60,000 to June 1981, becoming asst-coach, then coach Sept 1985, caretaker-manager Oct to Dec 1988, asst-coach Dec 1988 to Feb 1994/ Various scouting posts/Ipswich Town Director of Youth March 1995, becoming Director of Coaching, then chief-scout cs 1999/ Carlisle Utd chief-scout cs 2006 to June 2007/ Norwich City scout.

The first North East player to be transferred for a six figure sum, Colin Suggett began his career as a striker with lightning speed and reflexes around the box. He had good positional sense and very quickly became a teenage star at Roker Park, having a tendency to score against the Magpies; five goals in four Tyne versus Wear contests. Colin totalled 93 appearances and scored 25 goals for the Black Cats before his big move to the Midlands. At the Hawthorns, Colin switched roles to become a midfield player, without losing the knack of putting the ball in the net. He was highly efficient in more than 150 outings for the Baggies before Suggett settled at Carrow Road where he became a firm favourite. Suggett was the Canaries' Player of the Year in 1974-75 and totalled over 250 games, having an eventful time with Norwich, experiencing both relegation and promotion, while he also reached Wembley. Bill McGarry brought him back to his native region when United were in need of experience and solidity after the turmoil of relegation in 1978. Suggett though was past his best and an ankle ligament injury towards the end of the 1978-79 season ended his career. Always keen to work with youngsters, he then moved into the coaching side of the game at St James' Park. At Gallowgate for over ten years in that capacity, although he was in charge of first-team affairs for a while after McFaul departed, Colin saw his kids win the FA Youth Cup in 1985 and players like Gascoigne, Howey, Clark and Watson all develop into international talent. Leaving the club following a dispute over youth policy with Kevin Keegan, Suggett took up a similar appointment with Ipswich Town. He later scouted for over 20 years for various clubs including Norwich, Rangers, Bolton as well as senior appointments at both Ipswich and Carlisle.

Appearances & Goals:
Debut v West Ham United (h) 23 August 1978
FL: 20(3) app 0 gls
FLC: 1 app 0 gls
Total: 21(3) app 0 gls

In Charge: 9 games (caretaker)

Honours:
Eng sch-youth app/FL div 2 prom 1975/FLC final 1970, 1975/FAYC winner 1967.

SURTEES John W 1941-1942

Inside-right
5'11"
b. Percy Main, near Newcastle upon Tyne, 1 July 1911
d. Percy Main, near Newcastle upon Tyne, 16 July 1992

Career: Percy Main amat/Middlesbrough March 1930/ Portsmouth June 1932/Bournemouth June 1933/ Northampton Town May 1934/Sheffield Wed Dec 1934 free/Nottingham Forest Oct 1936 £2,500 (York City war-guest 1940-41)(UNITED war-guest 1941-42)/Darlington manager 1943/Sheffield Wed scout Nov 1948/ Spennymoor Utd coach 1958/West Auckland Town c1960/Also in Germany coaching.

Following short periods at a trio of senior clubs and an unhappy stay with Northampton, Jack Surtees was about to turn his back on the game and head for America before being giving another chance at Hillsborough. Within six months of joining Sheffield Wednesday he was an FA Cup winner with the Owls against West Bromwich Albion in 1935. Surtees was a big, strong schemer from the Tyne community of Percy Main and had an eventful debut for Newcastle in wartime football, scoring two goals on his first outing against Leeds, yet the Magpies still fell by 5-2. Jack later resided in North Shields following a career with the Owls (50 app) and Forest (99 app) had seen him take part in 175 senior matches. His brother Albert had a spell with Aston Villa.

Appearances & Goals:
Debut v Leeds United (a) 29 November 1941 (2 goals) (FLN)
War: 2 app 2 gls
Total: 2 app 2 gls

Honours:
FA Cup winner 1935.

SWAN Christopher Samuel 1919-1923

Inside-forward
5'8"
b. Byker, Newcastle upon Tyne, 4 December 1900
d. Bournemouth, 1979 (Q3)

Career: Heaton 1919/UNITED May 1919/ Stockport Co July 1923 free/Hull City Aug 1925/Crystal Palace May 1929 to 1931/ Waterford Sept 1931/Scarborough July 1932 to cs 1933.

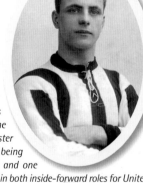

A bright schoolboy product who reached his country's side in 1915 before the close-down due to the First World War, Chris Swan was given a contract at St James' Park on the resumption of soccer. But the Tyneside youngster struggled to claim a first-team opportunity, being restricted to three games during April 1920 and one single outing two seasons later. Swan appeared in both inside-forward roles for United as well as outside-right and later had a productive stay with Hull City, claiming 77 games for the Humberside club at Second Division level. He also did well at a lower grade in the Midland League with Scarborough, scoring 20 goals in his first season, enjoying a FA Cup run with the non-leaguers during 1932-33.

Appearances & Goals:
Debut v Burnley (a) 2 April 1920
FL: 4 app 0 gls
Total: 4 app 0 gls

Honours:
Eng sch-youth app/1 EL app 1932.

SWEENEY Paul Martin 1989-1991

Left-back
5'8"
b. Glasgow, 10 January 1965

Career: St Kentigern's/Tynecastle BC/Raith Rovers July 1980/UNITED March 1989 £100,000/ St Johnstone March 1991 £100,000/Gateshead July 1993 free/Hartlepool Utd Aug 1994/Gateshead Sept 1994/Durham City Dec 1994/Morpeth Town 1995, becoming coach 1996/South Shields Sept 1996.

With a fiery style, the flame-haired Glaswegian Paul Sweeney landed on Tyneside as an unknown in England although he had proved to be a tenacious and noted defender in the hustle and bustle of lower division Scottish football. He was given the backing of the fans at St James' Park during season 1989-90 due to his all action style, determination and committed attitude, but Sweeney lacked the finer skills, a factor which manifested itself when in better quality company. Surviving a nasty car crash when on United's books, the Scot later suffered a bad knee injury which put him out of action for many weeks. Nicknamed 'Toddy' by his colleagues, as a part-timer in Scotland, Sweeney was a regular at Stark's Park from 1983-84 to joining United during 1988-89 and totalled 227 games for Raith.

Appearances & Goals:
Debut v Southampton (a) 1 April 1989 (sub)
FL: 28(8) app 0 gls
FAC: 3 app 0 gls
FLC: 2(1) app 0 gls
Others: 2 app 0 gls
Total: 35(9) app 0 gls

Honours:
Scot sch-youth app/SL div 2 prom 1987.

SWINBURNE Thomas Anderson 1934-1947

Goalkeeper
5'9"
b. East Rainton, Co Durham, 19 August 1915
d. Durham, 1969 (Q4)

Career: East Rainton/Hull City & West Ham Utd trial March 1932/Herrington Colliery/UNITED amat Jan 1934, prof April 1934 (Grimsby Town war-guest 1940-41)(Notts Co war-guest 1940-41)(Bolton Wand war-guest 1941-42)(Rochdale war-guest 1941-42)(Southport war-guest 1941-42)/Resumed with United 1945/Consett June 1947 free/Horden CW Sept 1951.

Tom Swinburne appeared for the Black'n'Whites both before and after World War Two, during an era when the Magpies had three or even four senior goalkeepers chasing for the Number 1 jersey. A pipe-smoking goalkeeper, he had as rivals for the position Tapken, McPhillips and Theaker before war, then Garbutt, Theaker and Fairbrother after the fighting had ended. He was a sound and trusty guardian at times; although it was noted he could lose the occasional soft goal, while he also had problems with repeated finger dislocations. Serving with the RAF during the war years, Tom was capped by England during the hostilities, at St James' Park against Scotland during December 1939. His two sons also played football between the posts, Alan, on United's staff in 1964-65 and later with Oldham, and Trevor (qv) for principally Carlisle, afterwards turning out for the Black'n'Whites as a guest in 1974.

Appearances & Goals:
Debut v Blackpool (h) 12 September 1934
FL: 77 app 0 gls
FAC: 7 app 0 gls
War: 48 app 0 gls
Total: 132 app 0 gls
(Void FL: 3 app 0 gls)

Honours:
1 Eng war app 1940.

TAIT Alexander 1951-1960

Centre-forward
5'11"
b. West Sleekburn, near Ashington, 28 November 1933

Career: UNITED jnr 1951, prof Sept 1952/ Bristol City June 1960 £5,000/Doncaster Rovers June 1964/Burton Albion cs 1965, later becoming manager 1966 to 1968.

Auburn-haired, described as "carroty-mopped", Alex Tait was skilful and full of dash, a bright teenage star who chose to become a part-time professional at Gallowgate when training to become a sports teacher at Loughborough College. The first North East player to appear for the England youth side, Tait netted four goals in a 6-0 victory over Wales during March 1952. Making his debut in season 1954-55, Alex had a few outings the following campaign then really made a big impression during 1956-57. Given a run of games in place of Vic Keeble, he displayed first class anticipation around the penalty area and always gave tenacious performances which thrilled the Gallowgate crowd. Also operating on the right wing, he scored a well remembered hat-trick (the first Newcastle player to do so) for the Magpies in a floodlit and fog-bound derby match with Sunderland during December 1956 and much was expected of this new find. Yet Tait was to drift from the scene, although he became a great favourite many miles south at Ashton Gate. Totalling 136 games and scoring 44 goals for Bristol City, Alex concluded his career in non-league football with Burton Albion. Residing in Tutbury, the Northumbrian became a teacher in the Trentside town, eventually appointed a Deputy Head in Derby before retiring. He was also for a spell Loughborough College sports coach.

Appearances & Goals:
Debut v Everton (h) 11 April 1955
FL: 32 app 8 gls
FAC: 2 app 2 gls
Total: 34 app 10 gls

Honours:
Eng sch-youth app.

TAPKEN Norman H 1932-1938, 1942-1943

Goalkeeper
5'10"
b. Wallsend, 21 February 1913
d. Stoke on Trent, June 1996

Career: Wallsend Thermal Welfare/UNITED amat Aug 1932, prof May 1933 £25/ Manchester Utd Dec 1938 £850 (Sunderland war-guest 1942-43)(UNITED war-guest 1942-43)(Darlington war-guest 1943-46) (Aldershot war-guest 1944-45) (Brighton war-guest 1944-45)(Chester war-guest 1944-45)/Darlington April 1947/Shelbourne 1948 to 1949/Stoke City asst-trainer July 1952 to c1960.

Although not a spectacular goalkeeper, Norman Tapken was a safe and confident teamster to have as the last line of defence. His judgement as well as anticipation was good and he took over from Micky Burns for the 1934-35 season at St James' Park. Newcastle's first choice 'keeper for three years, he had been a black-and-white fan as a schoolboy who fulfilled an ambition of playing for the Magpies, this after an early injury had threatened his career. Losing his place to Tom Swinburne, Tapken was later at Old Trafford (16 app), then returned to Gallowgate as a wartime guest player when serving in the RAF at Acklington, near Morpeth. After the war Norman totalled 32 games at Feethams then crossed the Irish Sea to appear in the Republic with Shelbourne, a short but rewarding stay which brought him plenty of honours in Ireland. Apart from reaching the Republic's cup final, he also helped win the Irish Shield and regional Leinster Cup during 1949. His brother Oswald Tapken was on United's books as an amateur in 1935-36 and 1936-37 without breaking through.

Appearances & Goals:
Debut v Bradford City (h) 17 November 1934
FL: 106 app 0 gls
FAC: 7 app 0 gls
War: 9 app 0 gls
Total: 122 app 0 gls

Honours: 2 EL app 1949/Eire Cup final 1949.

T

TATE Isaac Holliday 1923-1927

Goalkeeper
5'7"
b. Gateshead, 21 July 1906
d. Doncaster, February 1986

Career: Marley Hill/UNITED Aug 1923 £5/West Ham Utd May 1927 free/Doncaster Rovers July 1929, becoming asst-trainer Sept 1935.

From the Teams district of Gateshead, Isaac Tate became the youngest goalkeeper in the Football League at the time when he was plunged into United's side during season 1924-25. At 18 years old he stood in for the injured Bill Bradley when experienced rival Alex Mutch was also on the sidelines. Known as 'Ike' to his colleagues, he did well against West Ham United, but only managed a handful of games for the club thereafter. Despite his small build at only 5'7" tall, the Hammers' directors had been suitably impressed and promptly signed the Tynesider. At Upton Park, Tate became a deputy to international goalkeeper Ted Hufton appearing on only 14 occasions for the Londoners. Returning north with Doncaster he gained more regular first-team action, helping Rovers to a Third Division title success during 1935. All told Isaac made 135 outings for the Yorkshiremen.

Appearances & Goals:
Debut v West Ham United (h) 17 September 1924
FL: 4 app 0 gls
Total: 4 app 0 gls

Honours:
FL div 3(N) champs 1935.

TAVERNIER James Henry 2006-2014

Centre-half or Full-back
5'9"
b. Bradford, 31 October 1991

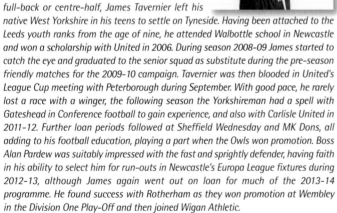

Career: Farsley Celtic BC/Leeds Utd jnr 2001/ UNITED jnr 2006, prof July 2009 (Gateshead loan 2010-11)(Carlisle Utd loan 2011-12)(Sheffield Wed loan 2011-12)(MK Dons loan 2011-12)(Shrewsbury Town loan 2013-14)(Rotherham Utd loan 2013-14)/Wigan Ath June 2014.

A lively and versatile defender, able to operate at full-back or centre-half, James Tavernier left his native West Yorkshire in his teens to settle on Tyneside. Having been attached to the Leeds youth ranks from the age of nine, he attended Walbottle school in Newcastle and won a scholarship with United in 2006. During season 2008-09 James started to catch the eye and graduated to the senior squad as substitute during the pre-season friendly matches for the 2009-10 campaign. Tavernier was then blooded in United's League Cup meeting with Peterborough during September. With good pace, he rarely lost a race with a winger, the following season the Yorkshireman had a spell with Gateshead in Conference football to gain experience, and also with Carlisle United in 2011-12. Further loan periods followed at Sheffield Wednesday and MK Dons, all adding to his football education, playing a part when the Owls won promotion. Boss Alan Pardew was suitably impressed with the fast and sprightly defender, having faith in his ability to select him for run-outs in Newcastle's Europa League fixtures during 2012-13, although James again went out on loan for much of the 2013-14 programme. He found success with Rotherham as they won promotion at Wembley in the Division One Play-Off and then joined Wigan Athletic.

Appearances & Goals:
Debut v Peterborough Utd (a) 22 September 2009 (FLC)
FL/PL: 0(2) app 0 gls
FAC: 1 app 0 gls
FLC: 3 app 0 gls
Euro: 3(1) app 0 gls
Total: 7(3) app 0 gls

Honours:
FL div 1 prom 2012 (6 app), 2014.

TAYLOR Allan 1924-1926

Goalkeeper
5'11"
b. North Shields, 1 December 1905
d. Whitley Bay, 11 April 1981

Career: Preston Colliery (North Shields)/UNITED amat April 1924, prof Aug 1925/South Shields June 1926/Tottenham Hotspur July 1929/ Hartlepools Utd May 1937/Retired May 1938.

A rival to Isaac Tate for the reserve goalkeeper's position at St James' Park, Allan Taylor made an impression in local football. Representing Northumberland during February 1924, his outstanding displays giving him a chance to join the Gallowgate staff towards the end of that 1923-24 season. He was another Tynesider who had a teenage baptism for the Magpies, and, like Tate, couldn't break into the senior eleven fully. Standing in only once for first choice Billy Bradley and just before new 'keeper Willie Wilson arrived, during season 1925-26 Taylor moved to South Shields where he became a regular at Horsley Hill during their days as a Football League force, including a spell in the Second Division. Despite having one or two harrowing experiences with Shields, conceding eight goals to Darlington and seven against Preston, Allan was in demand. Joining Spurs after a trial, he remained in North London for eight years claiming 70 appearances. Over three campaigns Taylor enjoyed promotion success at White Hart Lane, then was also part of a relegation outfit in 1934-35 when six goals flew past him in a sequence of matches against Wolves, Arsenal and Leicester. Following 27 outings at the Victoria Ground, he returned to his native Tyneside and resided in North Shields for the remainder of his days.

Appearances & Goals:
Debut v Notts County (h) 5 September 1925
FL: 1 app 0 gls
Total: 1 app 0 gls

Honours:
FL div 2 prom 1933 (5 app).

TAYLOR Colin 1963-1964

Outside-left
5'8"
b. Stourbridge, 24 August 1940
d. Dudley, 29 June 2005

Career: Stourbridge/Walsall Feb 1958/ UNITED June 1963 £20,000/Walsall Oct 1964 £10,000/Crystal Palace May 1968/Walsall Sept 1969/Kidderminster Harriers Aug 1973 to 1975.

A ginger-haired, thick-set winger, Colin Taylor is remembered for his deadly left-foot. Known as 'Cannonball' for the power of his shooting, he had a reputation as a goalscorer despite a role on the flank, netting 33 strikes for Walsall from the outside-left position during season 1960-61 and having been top scorer for the last four seasons. The 23-year-old Taylor took over from Jimmy Fell in United's ranks and for a season entertained the Geordie crowd with his occasional shots of thunder. He appeared to be a good purchase, but during the opening weeks of the 1964-65 programme manager Joe Harvey allowed the bustling player to return to the Midlands in a surprise move, remodelling his eventual promotion winning squad. Pulling on Walsall's shirt once more, Taylor became a noted servant at Fellows Park, and by the end of his career had totalled over 500 senior games. He also continued to bag plenty of goals, holding the Saddlers' aggregate goals record with 189 strikes. On retiring from the game, Colin resided in the Midlands becoming a decorator for a period and later a representative with Banks Brewery. His brother Brian also appeared for Walsall as well as Shrewsbury and Rotherham.

Appearances & Goals:
Debut v Derby County (h) 24 August 1963 (1 goal)
FL: 33 app 7 gls
FLC: 3 app 0 gls
Total: 36 app 7 gls

Honours:
FL div 2 prom 1965 (9 app), 1969/FL div 4 champs 1960/FL div 3 prom 1961.

TAYLOR Ernest 1942-1951

Inside-forward
5'4"
b. Sunderland, 2 September 1925
d. Birkenhead, 9 April 1985

Career: Hylton Colliery Jnrs/UNITED amat Aug 1942, prof Sept 1942 £10 (Distillery (Belfast) war-guest 1943-44)(Plymouth Argyle war-guest 1945-46)/Blackpool Oct 1951 £25,000/ Manchester Utd Feb 1958 £6,000/Sunderland Dec 1958 £6,000/Altrincham Sept 1961/Derry City Nov 1961/Retired Feb 1962/Carshalton Ath 1963/New Brighton (NZ) coach Feb 1964/Later, Heswall FC (Cheshire) consultant.

Known as the 'Tom Thumb' of football during the Fifties, Ernie Taylor was barely 10 stones and at only 5'4" tall was a titch among giants on the football field. With long baggy football shorts and wearing only size four boots, Taylor though had the skill and eye for a telling pass which made him one of the most productive schemers in the country. Growing up in the Pallion district of Wearside, he was a submariner during the hostilities and one of Stan Seymour's bright hopefuls as war ended. He made his debut in 1942 and soon grabbed a treble against Leeds when he had just turned 17 years of age, the club's youngest player to register a hat-trick. Taylor only figured in a handful of games when the Magpies won promotion in 1948, but was given a place for the club's rebirth in the First Division. Described as "cheeky" on the field, he was also noted as a "court jester", sometimes playing to the crowd by going past a defender, then stopping, and repeating a skilful shuffle to applause. Taylor was quick-witted and continually prompted attacks from his central midfield position. For three seasons he was an influential member of the side that attempted to lift the title trophy. And in season 1950-51 Ernie had his best season with the Black'n'Whites, reaching Wembley and setting up a marvellous Jack Milburn goal with a gloriously deft back-heel, now a famous moment in the competition's history. But after the joy of FA Cup glory, Taylor's ability was largely overlooked. At odds with Stan Seymour and often the player to drop out if the team did badly, many supporters were perplexed when he was sold to Blackpool for a large fee, despite several senior members of the side trying to reverse the decision to let him go. Teaming up with Mortensen and Matthews, Taylor quickly showed off his talent at Bloomfield Road. Totalling 237 games (55 goals) for Blackpool over seven seasons, he reached Wembley again with the Seasiders, then amazingly did it for a third time when with Manchester United, signed by the Old Trafford club as a short term move after the fateful Munich crash in 1958. Ernie deservedly won an England call-up too, in the infamous 6-3 defeat by the Hungarians during 1953. Ending his senior days with Sunderland in 71 games, Taylor was frequently among the goals as well, netting almost 100 during his career. On returning from a period in New Zealand, Taylor later settled on Merseyside, employed at the Vauxhall car plant at Hooton. His brother Eddie appeared for Willington as part of their 1950 FA Amateur Cup final line-up.

Appearances & Goals:
Debut v Barnsley (a) 9 January 1946 (FAC)
(v Huddersfield Town (h) 19 September 1942 (FLN))
FL: 107 app 19 gls
FAC: 10 app 2 gls
War: 26 app 7 gls
Total: 143 app 28 gls

Honours:
1 Eng cap 1954/1 Eng B app 1956/1 unoff Eng app 1956/FL div 2 prom 1948 (8 app)/FAC winner 1951, 1953/FAC final 1958.

TAYLOR James Davies 1939-1945

Centre-forward
5'7"
b. Sunderland, 30 November 1920

A shipwright on Tyneside, Jim Taylor joined United from the Hylton Colliery Juniors side during April 1939 for the sum of £25 and only claimed a single game for United's first-eleven as a replacement for Billy Cairns. However, in a good performance against Bradford City at the end of the wartime 1939-40 season, he netted twice as the Magpies lost narrowly 4-3 to the Yorkshire club. Described as a clever ball player with a constructive urge, he remained on United's staff until the end of the war but was not retained thereafter.

Appearances & Goals:
Debut v Bradford City (h) 8 June 1940 (FLNE) (2 goals)
War: 1 app 2 gls
Total: 1 app 2 gls

TAYLOR John Henry 1951-1960

Outside-right
5'7"
b. Crawcrook, near Gateshead,
5 October 1935
d. Sunderland, February 2002

Career: Crawcrook/UNITED jnr 1951, prof Nov 1952 (Fulham loan 1956-57 & 1957-58)/Chelmsford City June 1960 free/ Cambridge Utd 1962 to 1963.

Harry Taylor was on United's books for all of seven seasons after arriving from junior football in the Tyne Valley with Crawcrook. His career at Gallowgate started as a deputy to Len White, but was interrupted by a spell in London when on National Service with the Corps of Royal Electrical & Mechanical Engineers at Shepherd's Bush. Joining Fulham on an extended loan deal, Taylor made four appearances for the Cottagers before returning to Tyneside. And in the following season he had his best year in a Magpie jersey; Taylor claimed 17 outings on the wing during 1958-59 when a rival to Gordon Hughes for the Number 7 shirt. However, in the final reckoning he lost out to Hughes for the position and moved to non-league football in the south joining up at Cambridge with another former Newcastle reserve, Jimmy Gibson. Taylor later returned to the area, being employed for Newcastle Breweries. He was an uncle of Howard Kendall, of Preston and Everton fame.

Appearances & Goals:
Debut v Sheffield United (a) 1 January 1955
FL: 28 app 5 gls
FAC: 1 app 0 gls
Total: 29 app 5 gls

TAYLOR Philip Henry 1941-1942

Right-half
5'10"
b. Bristol, 18 September 1917
d. Liverpool, 1 December 2012

Career: Bristol Rovers amat cs 1932, prof March 1935/Liverpool March 1936 £5,000 (Bristol Rovers war-guest 1939-40)(Brighton war-guest 1940-44)(UNITED war-guest 1941-42)(Leeds Utd war-guest 1942-43)(Distillery (Belfast) war-guest 1943-44)/Resumed with Liverpool 1946, becoming coach July 1954, caretaker-manager May 1956, manager April 1957 to Nov 1959. (Gloucestershire County cricketer 1938).

A polished half-back who was a pass master in midfield, Phil Taylor was a highly sought after schoolboy, captain of the England side in 1932. He joined his local club at Eastville but made a name for himself with Liverpool after the Second World War. He was influential in the Reds' title victory during 1947 and then was skipper in their 1950 FA Cup final appointment. Phil was recognised as one of the top names of the immediate post-war boom. Capped by his country at school, 'B', Football League and full level, he also was a commanding figure at Anfield and totalled 442 games, including wartime, for the Reds. Cool and composed, Taylor was a stylist and he took part in a string of United games during the wartime season of 1941-42. He was also a fine cricketer, turning out in one first-class county fixture for Gloucestershire during 1938. Taylor took over the reins at Anfield in 1956 and was succeeded by Bill Shankly as boss. He later became a sales representative and resided in the North West into his nineties.

Appearances & Goals:
Debut v Huddersfield Town (a) 13 September 1941 (FLN)
War: 7 app 0 gls
Total: 7 app 0 gls

Honours:
3 Eng caps 1948/3 Eng B app 1947-50/FL app 1947-48/Eng sch-youth app/FL champs 1947/FAC final 1950/FLN2(WLg) champs 1943 (5 app).

T

TAYLOR Ryan Anthony 2009-date

Full-back or Midfield
5'8"
b. Liverpool, 19 August 1984

Career: Tranmere Rovers jnr, prof April 2002/
Wigan Ath July 2005 £1.25m/
UNITED Feb 2009 £2m.

*Merseysider Ryan Taylor made a name for himself
with United's supporters by scoring four goals in
six matches against the Magpies, rifling in two
brilliant long range efforts for Wigan to the
anguish of the Toon Army during his 122 games
for the Latics. Appearing in various roles, he found
himself out of the reckoning at the JJB Stadium
under Steve Bruce and moved to Tyneside when
24 years of age in 2009 as part of the deal which
took Charles N'Zogbia to Wigan. A Joe Kinnear
signing, he again became something of a utility player at Gallowgate, in midfield or
at full-back, and looked to be destined for a career on the bench with United. But on
the departure of Jose Enrique to Liverpool Ryan was handed the left-back position as
United consolidated life in the Premier League following promotion in 2010. Although
right-footed and out of position, Taylor gradually warmed to the position and won
over many sceptical supporters with gutsy performances. And he was always liable
to score the spectacular goal, being an expert at free-kicks, including a beauty against
Sunderland. Taylor though was unlucky with injuries before and during his period at
St James' Park. Breaking his metatarsal, then his leg in 2006, Ryan picked up a
succession of knocks and at the start 2012-13 suffered a serious cruciate ligament
injury and was out for several months only to damage the same knee again in training
when nearing fitness, missing over a year of action.*

Appearances & Goals:
Debut v West Bromwich Albion (a) 7 February 2009
FL/PL: 53(25) app 6 gls
FAC: 3(2) app 0 gls
FLC: 6 app 3 gls
Euro: 2 app 1 gl
Total: 64(27) app 10 gls

Honours:
4 Eng u21 app 2006/Eng sch-youth app/FL ch winner 2010/PFA ToS (d1) 2005.

TAYLOR Steven Vincent 1994-date

Centre-half
6'2"
b. Greenwich, London, 23 January 1986

Career: Whitley Bay BC/Wallsend BC/
Cramlington Jnrs 1995/UNITED jnr 1994,
prof Jan 2003 (Wycombe Wand loan 2003-04).

*Although born in London, Steven Taylor settled
on Tyneside within weeks of his birth and was
brought up in Whitley Bay, very much as a
Geordie. As a schoolboy he was soon part of the
club's Centre of Excellence and his progress at St
James' Park was quick, capped by England at
school and youth level on a regular basis.
Skippering his country too, Steven showed a
stature and mature confidence, rare for such a
youngster. He was fast-tracked at Gallowgate
and made a teenage debut during season 2003-04 against Real Mallorca in the UEFA
Cup. A strapping 6'2" centre-back, positive in the air and in the tackle, Taylor became
a regular for the England Under-21 eleven winning 29 caps all told, going onto captain
the Three Lions at that level on occasion as well. Gaining a regular slot in United's
line-up for 2004-05, he also got into his country's 'B' team during 2007 and was tipped
for a full call-up. However, injury and then relegation halted his bright progress. Also
to operate occasionally at right-back, Taylor missed a large slice of the Championship
title winning campaign in 2009-10 due to further knocks then was out of action again
before United consolidated a position back in the Premier League. He returned to the
side and began to recapture the form that had him in contention for full international
recognition; in 2007 and 2013 being called up to the full squad and getting onto the
bench against San Marino without claiming a first cap for his country. Positive and
quick, dominant in the air, Taylor's use of the ball is good while he has a deep desire*

*to see his local club do well. Steven played with both Cramlington and Whitley Ba
juniors as well as Wallsend Boy's Club, three notable Tyneside nursery sides. He als
had a spell at Wycombe Wanderers on loan in season 2003-04 under the guidance o
Tony Adams during the early part of his career, a period when he made his Footba
League bow as a 17-year-old teenager. He wears the Number 27 shirt of his boyhoo
idol Philippe Albert.*

Appearances & Goals:
Debut v RCD Mallorca (a) 25 March 2004 (UEFAC) (sub)
FL/PL: 184(11) app 12 gls
FAC: 10 app 1 gl
FLC: 8(1) app 0 gls
Euro: 26(6) app 1 gl
Total: 228(18) app 14 gls

Honours:
29 Eng u21 app 2004-09/1 Eng B app 2007/Eng sch-youth app/FL ch winner 2010.

TEMPLETON Robert Bryson 1903-1904

Outside-left
5'9"
b. Coylton, near Ayr, 29 March 1880
d. Kilmarnock, 2 November 1919

Career: Irvine Heatherbell/Westmount Juveniles/
Kilmarnock Roslin 1896/Neilston Victoria/
Kilmarnock 1897/Hibernian April 1898/Aston
Villa March 1899 £250/UNITED Feb 1903
£400/ Woolwich Arsenal Dec 1904
£375/Celtic May 1906 £250/Kilmarnock Oct
1907/Fulham July 1913 £50/ Kilmarnock April
1915/Retired May 1915.

*One of the biggest characters of soccer before
the Great War, Bobby Templeton became a legend
on and off the field, mesmerising defenders, as well
as spectators, with his graceful and potent play down
the wing. Tall and handsome, he also became a fashionable
Edwardian dandy, often in the news with his extrovert antics, once in 1908 entering
a lion's cage for a wager at Bostock & Wombwell's menagerie in Glasgow and, as the
story goes, stroked the animals head then twisted its tail! But first and foremost,
Templeton was a football artiste. He could be a match-winner when in the mood, the
type of skilful entertainer who could make the ball talk, once described when in full
flow as "a cross between a gazelle and greyhound". Often impetuous, inconsistent and
at times selfish with the ball, Bobby still delighted the Tyneside crowd over three
seasons and on his day was dazzling. William Pickford wrote in 1905: "To watch
Templeton at his best is a sight for the gods, to watch him at his worst to see at
a glance the frailty of things human." After being a regular selection for a season-
and-a-half, then appearing in 10 games of United's 1905 title season, Bobby moved
on, always finding it hard to remain at one club for long. United's fans were not happy,
especially when his replacement, Bert Gosnell, possessed a style in direct contrast to
the Scot's flamboyant showmanship. Scoring on his Scotland debut against England,
it has been claimed that the appalling Ibrox disaster of 1902 was indirectly
attributable to the crowd's swaying to watch one of Templeton's weaving dribbles.
Bobby had three spells with his home club of Kilmarnock, initially with the Kilmarnock
Rugby side, the club's reserve outfit which were confusingly termed 'Rugby' after the
ground Rugby Park. He totalled 177 games for Killie and later became a publican in
the Ayrshire town. Bobby died of heart failure following the fierce epidemic of
influenza that spread throughout the country at the end of World War One. He was
also the footballer's billiards champion when on Tyneside, along with team-mate Bill
Appleyard.*

Appearances & Goals:
Debut v Liverpool (a) 7 March 1903
FL: 51 app 4 gls
FAC: 1 app 1 gl
Total: 52 app 5 gls

Honours:
11 Scot caps 1902-13/1 unoff Scot app 1902/Scot trial app 1900-12/Scot jnr app/3 SL
app 1910-11/FL champs 1899 (1 app), 1900, 1905/SL champs 1907/SC winner 1907.

THAIN John William 1921-1922

Outside-right
5'9"
b. Pelaw, Gateshead, 3 February 1903
d. Peterborough, 1977

Career: Bill Quay/Pelaw Jnrs/UNITED Nov 1921 £10/
Brentford May 1922 free/Peterborough & Fletton
Utd 1923/Grimsby Town May 1924/
Peterborough & Fletton Utd cs 1925.

*Young forward John Thain found claiming a place in
United's side immediately after World War One
extremely difficult. He deputised only once, for Jimmy
Low during season 1921-22 and played the majority
of his football for the club in the North Eastern
League. Thain did resurrect his career when he joined Grimsby Town after a standing
out in non-league football for Peterborough as they lifted the Eastern Section trophy
of the Southern League in 1923-24. He made 26 appearances for the Mariners during
season 1924-25 before heading back to the Posh.*

Appearances & Goals:
Debut v Aston Villa (h) 17 December 1921
FL: 1 app 0 gls
Total: 1 app 0 gls

THEAKER Clarence Alfred 1938-1947

Goalkeeper
6'0"
b. Spalding, Lincolnshire, 8 December 1912
d. Hartlepool, 7 February 1992

Career: Spalding Utd 1931/Grimsby Town amat
Feb 1934, prof May 1934/UNITED Nov 1938 £1,250
(Darlington war-guest 1939-40)(Lincoln City war-
guest 1942-43)(St Mirren war-guest 1942-43)/
Hartlepools Utd June 1947 free to May 1948.

*Known as 'Cam' during his career, Theaker was
signed by United to rival Tom Swinburne at
St James' Park just before the outbreak of World
War Two. A reserve fixture at Blundell Park, deputising for the celebrated George
Tweedy on occasion, he turned out in 15 games for Newcastle before the hostilities
put a halt to first-class soccer. Theaker continued between the posts for the club
during wartime football and returned to the fold for the resumption of Football League
action in 1946-47. Then aged 33, he found no fewer than seven other custodians on
the club's staff and Swinburne was selected ahead of him, Theaker being soon
transferred to Hartlepool where he concluded a career ravished by war. He later resided
in the Durham coastal town to his demise, running a hardware business.*

Appearances & Goals:
Debut v Cardiff City (a) 21 January 1939 (FAC)
FL: 13 app 0 gls
FAC: 3 app 0 gls
War: 65 app 0 gls
Total: 81 app 0 gls

THOMAS Andrew Mark 1986-1988

Midfield
6'0"
b. Eynsham, near Oxford, 16 December 1962

Career: Oxford Utd jnr 1978, prof Dec 1980
(Fulham loan 1982-83)(Derby Co loan
1982-83)/UNITED Sept 1986
£100,000/Bradford City June 1988
£80,000/Plymouth Argyle July 1989
£80,000/Retired due to injury 1991/Thame
Utd 1992/Oxford City cs 1993, becoming
player-manager, then manager 1995 to Nov
1996/ Chesham Utd manager Dec 1996 to
Sept 1997/Brackley Town manager.

*A midfielder with a reputation for scoring
goals, Andy Thomas became a noted player
with Oxford, totalling 150 games and scoring*

*45 goals as the Headington club became a force during the 1980s, for a period under
Jim Smith's management. But a broken leg in 1984 hindered his progress and by the
time United made a move to bring him to Tyneside, Andy was ready for a new
challenge. Tall and slimly built, he operated just behind a front duo for Newcastle and
during his first season, 1986-87, looked very effective at times. He started with a bang
by hitting seven goals in five outings in United's eleven, but the following season
turned into an injury nightmare and Thomas did not figure in manager Willie McFaul's
plans as new faces arrived. He moved to Bradford City at the end of the campaign,
later being forced to retire from the first-class scene when at Home Park aged 28 due
to a degenerating disc back injury. Thomas returned to his native Oxfordshire where
he served Oxford City, reaching the FA Vase final at Wembley. For a period he later
worked for a printing company in Oxford.*

Appearances & Goals:
Debut v Wimbledon (h) 20 September 1986
FL: 24(7) app 6 gls
FAC: 3 app 1 gl
FLC: 1 app 0 gls
Others: 1 app 2 gls
Total: 29(7) app 9 gls

Honours:
FL div 2 champs 1985 (4 app)/FL div 3 champs 1984/FLC winner 1986 (sub no app)/FAV
final 1995.

THOMAS Ernest Barrie 1962-1964

Centre-forward
5'10"
b. Measham, Leicestershire, 19 May 1937

Career: Measham Imperial/Leicester City July
1954/Mansfield Town June 1957 free/Scunthorpe
Utd Sept 1959 £20,000/UNITED Jan 1962 cash-
exch deal £45,000/Scunthorpe Utd Nov 1964
£20,000/Barnsley Nov 1966/Retired due to injury
May 1968/Measham Social Welfare & Measham
Swifts manager May 1968.

*A formidable goalscorer, Barrie Thomas netted 220
goals in his career, boasting a tremendous 61%
ratio of goals per games. Thomas was a natural
goal-poacher, no great artist with the ball, but a
hearty leader who tore into defences. After being
jettisoned by Leicester following a 17-year-old
debut in the First Division and an early hat-trick
against Bolton, he developed a regular scoring habit with first Mansfield (49 goals in
73 app) then at Scunthorpe. In Lincolnshire he established a club best for a season,
31 in 1961-62, all before he joined the Magpies during January, proceeding to grab
another 10 to record an impressive 41 for the campaign. Barrie cost United a record
fee when he moved to the North East and although the leader was often in and out
of the treatment room at Gallowgate, he still managed to hit the net week-in, week-
out and only a handful of other centre-forwards in United's history claim a better
strike-rate of his 64% when at Gallowgate. Sometimes erratic in front of goal, Thomas
was nevertheless selected for the full England squad training session at Lilleshall
during 1962, only for injury to prevent his appearance. Barrie possessed high energy
and chased for everything up front, eager to get the ball. After hitting the net on 21
occasions during season 1963-64 for United, Thomas was surprisingly released to
rejoin Scunthorpe as the Magpies embarked on their promotion winning programme
the following year, Harvey remodelling his squad. At the Old Show Ground he grabbed
more goals, scoring five in a single game against Luton during 1965 and increasing
his total for the Irons to 96 in 153 matches. Retiring due to cruciate knee damage,
Thomas suffered with old footballing injuries in later life, being disabled and needing
braces for both his knees for a period. He remained in the Barnsley area running a
transport business before moving to Netherseal near Burton on Trent.*

Appearances & Goals:
Debut v Huddersfield Town (h) 20 January 1962
FL: 73 app 48 gls
FAC: 2 app 1 gl
FLC: 3 app 1 gl
Total: 78 app 50 gls

Honours:
Eng sch-youth app/FL div 2 champs 1965 (7 app)/FL div
4 prom 1968.

T

THOMAS John William 1911-1912

Inside-right
5'9"
b. Sacriston, Co Durham, 30 September 1889
d. Newcastle upon Tyne, 12 November 1947

Career: Spennymoor Utd/Brighton cs 1910/ UNITED June 1911 £25/Spennymoor Utd May 1912.

At United's Gallowgate headquarters for only the 1911-12 season, Jack Thomas played once for the first-eleven, stepping in when the Magpie forward-line was disrupted due to injury. A rival to Tommy Lowes in the battle to deputise for United's international first-teamers, the local press noted when Jack moved back to the region that he "has the reputation of being very speedy". However, Thomas made little impression at St James' Park and headed to North Eastern League football with Spennymoor on the conclusion of that season's programme. A teenager at the Goldstone Ground with Brighton, Thomas suffered will ill health on the south coast and managed only a single appearance. During the Great War, Jack had a remarkable and inspiring period serving his country. He joined the Durham Light Infantry and saw action during the early months of the conflict, captured at the Battle of Ypres during 1915. He was imprisoned in various German camps and involved in several freedom attempts, including a successful break out by means of a 'Great Escape-like' tunnel during 1916. Thomas managed to get back to England with the help of a smuggled compass in a cake sent from his Durham home and then having shown much ingenuity and resilience was soon engaged as an intelligence agent back on the Continent. His service earned him a Meritorious Service Medal and Thomas later recorded his marvellous war stories, titled "In the Hands of the Huns" in much detail in his local church magazine. After Jack's noteworthy exploits during World War One, he settled near Sacriston and worked at the local pit as a Master Weighman. He emigrated to Australia for a period, but returned to live in his native County Durham at Kibblesworth.

Appearances & Goals:
Debut v Manchester City (a) 27 January 1912
FL: 1 app 0 gls
Total: 1 app 0 gls

THOMAS Martin Richard 1983-1988

Goalkeeper
6'1"
b. Senghenydd, near Pontypridd, 28 November 1959

Career: Senghenydd Imps 1970/Aber Valley YMCA 1974/Senghenydd Swans/Bristol Rovers amat 1975, jnr July 1976, prof Sept 1977 (Cardiff City loan 1982-83)(Tottenham Hotspur loan 1982-83)(Southend Utd loan 1982-83)/ UNITED loan March 1983, pmt July 1983 £50,000 (Middlesbrough loan 1984-85)/ Birmingham City loan Oct 1988, pmt Nov 1988 (Aston Villa loan 1992-93)(Crystal Palace loan 1992-93) to June 1993 free/Cheltenham Town player-coach Aug 1993/Later becoming a

specialist gkp-coach for several clubs including Wolves, Birmingham City, Norwich City, Swindon Town & Hereford Utd/Also with the FA at Lilleshall, becoming full-time FA coach June 1998 as Regional Director then involved with the England youth and Under-21 sides, later appointed as FA Head of Goalkeeping/Also Team GB gkp-coach for the 2012 Olympics.

Established as a goalkeeper of quality with Bristol Rovers, Martin Thomas totalled a century of matches for Rovers before he was 20 years old and went onto become a noted Eastville custodian before losing his place due to a badly dislocated finger which kept him out of action for almost a year. Tall and positive, Thomas recorded 187 games for Rovers then went on a series of loan deals around the country. During season 1982-83, he unusually appeared for five different clubs, one of which eventually earned him a contract at St James' Park during the summer of 1983, this following an impressive display as the club lifted the Japan Cup on tour. A rival to Kevin Carr, Newcastle possessed two goalkeepers of similar style and ability. The pair jockeyed for the position, including sharing the role during the Black'n'Whites promotion success in 1983-84. But as Newcastle reached the First Division, Thomas soon became first choice. Capped by Wales and nicknamed 'Bud' at Gallowgate, he was understudy on the international scene to Everton's Dai Davies. Thomas had a career often disrupted by injury, but showed the Tyneside public that on his day he could be a

splendid goalkeeper. It was one of those injuries, a shoulder complaint, which forced him onto the sidelines for a long period and when he was fit, United had signed Dave Beasant as a replacement. Martin then enjoyed a good period at St Andrew's, recording 176 matches for Birmingham and following a knee injury he decided to move into coaching. Thomas became highly regarded, attached to the Football Association set-up for over 15 years, being involved more than 300 England games at various levels. He resided in Tamworth for several years before relocating to his original Aber Valley in South Wales. Both his father and brother appeared for Cardiff rugby club, brother David also playing for the Wales 'B' side at rugby union. Martin himself tried the rugby code as a youngster, but decided to concentrate on football.

Appearances & Goals:
Debut v Barnsley (a) 4 May 1983
FL: 118 app 0 gls
FAC: 5 app 0 gls
FLC: 7 app 0 gls
Others: 1 app 0 gls
Total: 131 app 0 gls

Honours:
1 Wales cap 1987/2 Wales u21 app 1979-81/Wales sch-youth app/FL div 2 prom 1984/FL div 3 prom 1983, 1992/FLT winner 1991.

THOMPSON Alan 1988-1993, 2008-2010

Midfield & Asst-coach
6'0"
b. Newcastle upon Tyne, 22 December 1973

Career: Wallsend BC/UNITED jnr Feb 1988, prof March 1991/Bolton Wand July 1993 £250,000 (+£1m later)/Aston Villa June 1998 £4.5m/Celtic Sept 2000 £3.25m/Leeds Utd loan Jan 2007, pmt Aug 2007, becoming asst-manager briefly Oct 2007 (Hartlepool Utd loan 2007-08)/Retired May 2008/ UNITED asst-coach July 2008/Celtic coach June 2010 to June 2012/Birmingham City asst-coach June 2014.

Alan Thompson made a remarkable recovery after sustaining injuries in a car accident travelling back to Tyneside which placed five of United's youth stars in hospital during 1990. Thompson suffered a broken neck and back, undergoing two operations which threatened a promising career before it had really started. However, the Tynesider battled to fitness and showed he possessed a cultured left foot, able to cross a dangerous curling ball into the box or hit a vicious shot. Appearing at full-back for the Magpies as well as in his more accustomed midfield role, Alan took part in the European youth tournament for England and had also captained his country's school eleven. Following a few outings in Newcastle's senior line-up during season 1991-92, he was replaced by more experienced professionals in Kevin Sheedy then Scott Sellars, but was always recognised as a future star. Manager Kevin Keegan though, found it increasingly difficult to satisfy the youngster's ambition and allowed Thompson to leave when he was still a teenager, for Burnden Park where he became a noted midfielder reaching the England Under-21 set-up during his 198 matches. Maturing as a footballer, he was a valuable asset on the left of midfield and he made a move to Villa Park for a substantial fee during 1998. Alan headed north to Glasgow after being excluded from Villa's 2000 FA Cup final. He enjoyed a successful period with Celtic in 231 games (52 goals), not only earning medals at Parkhead, but also a full England cap when 30 years of age. Thompson was very much a player the Magpies should have kept and given an extended opportunity. He attended school with Steve Watson and on one occasion played for three different United sides within three days; the junior eleven, the club's reserve team and the senior line-up. Following a period back at Gallowgate on the coaching staff, then a stint also returning to Parkhead, Alan settled back in the region, living in Ponteland until he joined up with Lee Clark and Steve Watson at Birmingham.

Appearances & Goals:
Debut v Swindon Town (a) 2 November 1991 (sub)
FL: 13(3) app 0 gls
FAC: 1 app 0 gls
Others: 3 app 0 gls
Total: 17(3) app 0 gls

Honours:
1 Eng cap 2004/2 Eng u21 app 1995-96/Eng sch-youth app/FL div 1 champs 1993 (2 app), 1997/FL div 1 prom 1995/FLC final 1995/SL champs 2001, 2002, 2004, 2006/SC winner 2001, 2004, 2005/SC final 2002/SLC winner 2003, 2006 (sub no app)/SLC final 2003/UEFAC final 2003/PFA ToS (d1) 1997.

THOMPSON Frank 1923-1925

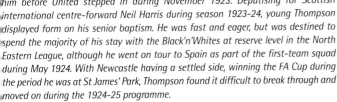

Centre-forward
5'8"
b. Birtley, near Gateshead, c1897

Career: St Peter's Albion 1921/UNITED Nov 1923
£150/Bedlington Utd Sept 1925/Exeter City Aug
1926/Workington Aug 1927/Stalybridge Celtic June
1928/Bedlington Utd/St Peter's Albion Aug 1930.

A prominent local player, Frank Thompson was described as being "a consistent performer in the Tyneside League" and several clubs were eager to sign him before United stepped in during November 1923. Deputising for Scottish international centre-forward Neil Harris during season 1923-24, young Thompson displayed form on his senior baptism. He was fast and eager, but was destined to spend the majority of his stay with the Black'n'Whites at reserve level in the North Eastern League, although he went on tour to Spain as part of the first-team squad during May 1924. With Newcastle having a settled side, winning the FA Cup during the period he was at St James' Park, Thompson found it difficult to break through and moved on during the 1924-25 programme.

Appearances & Goals:
Debut v Birmingham (a) 5 April 1924
FL: 2 app 1 gl
Total: 2 app 1 gl

THOMPSON George Alfred 1903-1905

Outside-right
5'9"
b. Wolverhampton, 1878 (Q1)
d. North Shields, 17 October 1943

Career: Halesowen Town/UNITED May 1903/Crystal
Palace May 1905 £50/Carlisle Utd May 1906/Blyth
Spartans Aug 1907/Newcastle City July 1909,
becoming secretary cs 1911.

Arriving on Tyneside from the Midlands, George Thompson found himself in the shadows of the great Jack Rutherford on Tyneside. He did appear once during the club's Football League Championship season of 1904-05, albeit in a FA Cup tie, and took part in two reserve title successes in the Northern League. It is recorded that George lodged with Bill McCracken during his time at Gallowgate, in Leazes Crescent close to the stadium, and possessed a "jovial nature". A local athlete of merit too, he had excellent sprinting ability, but didn't have any chance of dislodging England international Rutherford from his wing position on the football field. Thompson moved to London and assisted Crystal Palace during their Southern League campaign but suffered from rheumatic fever in London which forced his retirement. Later George returned to the North East settling in Tynemouth, for many years a sign and poster writer in Newcastle.

Appearances & Goals:
Debut v Nottingham Forest (a) 9 April 1904
FL: 1 app 0 gls
FAC: 1 app 0 gls
Total: 2 app 0 gls

THOMPSON (Iley) Henry 1908-1910

Left-back
5'10"
b. South Hetton, Co Durham, 1886
d. Richmond, London, 1930 (Q2)

Career: Boldon Colliery/Independent Order of Good
Templar's/North Shields Ath Jan 1906/UNITED May
1908 £50/Crystal Palace Oct 1910 £25/Horden Ath
Sept 1912 to 1915.

A solid defender for North Shields in local football, Harry Thompson was added to the staff as cover in the full-back role. One of nine brothers and sisters from a pit family at Boldon, he deputised for Tony Whitson during season 1909-10, but found the competition in

front of him overwhelming. Apart from the cultured play of Whitson, the Magpies also had on the staff Carr, McCracken, Pudan, Waugh and another up and coming youngster, Frank Hudspeth. Thompson moved to Crystal Palace where he took part in their 1910-11 Southern League campaign (4 app). During World War One he served with the Durham Light Infantry and was badly wounded in action during 1918, doctors advising Harry that he needed to have his leg amputated. But Thompson refused to undergo surgery and his wounded leg affected him for the rest of his life. Partly recovering, Thompson later worked at Horden Colliery and was treasurer of the local miners' union. Harry originally used the surname of 'Iley' but once his mother had remarried switched to Thompson. He eventually retired to the Star & Garter Home for wounded servicemen in Richmond and died there at a relatively young age.

Appearances & Goals:
Debut v Preston North End (h) 3 January 1910
FL: 2 app 0 gls
Total: 2 app 0 gls

THOMPSON John Henry 1948-1957

Goalkeeper
5'10"
b. Newcastle upon Tyne, 4 July 1932
d. Beadnell, Northumberland, 29 December 2006

Career: UNITED jnr March 1948, prof Sept 1950/
Lincoln City May 1957 £2,500/Horden CW cs 1960/
Annfield Plain/Retired 1964.

Learning much from Jack Fairbrother when a teenager at St James' Park, John Thompson then found himself as second choice to Ronnie Simpson when Fairbrother departed. His chances were limited to a handful of games during seasons 1954-55 and 1955-56, although he did get on the team-sheet for the FA Charity Shield contest with Chelsea in September 1955. Like Simpson, he was not a tall or imposing 'keeper, John being relatively small, yet agile. Thompson was a regular at Sincil Bank with Lincoln during season 1957-58 and totalled 43 games for the Imps. On leaving the game, he became self-employed, running a betting outlet on Tyneside and residing in Forest Hall, Newcastle, then later on the Northumberland coast at Beadnell.

Appearances & Goals:
Debut v Manchester United (a) 23 October 1954
FL: 8 app 0 gls
Others: 1 app 0 gls
Total: 9 app 0 gls

THOMPSON Matthew 1939-1941

Outside-right
5'9"
b. Bedlington, c1922

Matt Thompson signed amateur forms for Newcastle United during April 1939 and was on the club's books as war was declared during September. A winger, Thompson only twice received a call to appear for the senior team, once in 1939-40 and again on a single outing the following term. He was employed at a local coal-mine in Bedlington for a period. Thompson's contract was cancelled during October 1941.

Appearances & Goals:
Debut v Bradford City (h) 8 June 1940 (FLNE)
War: 2 app 0 gls
Total: 2 app 0 gls

T

THOMPSON Thomas 1946-1950

Inside-right
5'6"
b. Fence Houses, Co Durham, 10 November 1928

Career: Lumley YMCA/UNITED amat Jan 1946, prof
Aug 1946 £15/Aston Villa Sept 1950 £15,000/
Preston North End July 1955 £25,000/Stoke City
June 1961 £10,000/Barrow March 1963 £5,000/
Retired due to injury Aug 1964/Later, Preston North
End asst-coach briefly Aug 1975.

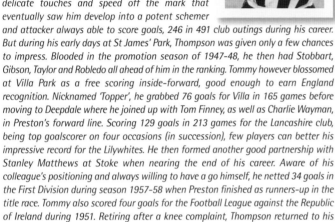

*Small but strongly-built, Tommy Thompson developed
into one of the Fifties most outstanding inside-
forwards. With plenty of stamina, he possessed
delicate touches and speed off the mark that
eventually saw him develop into a potent schemer
and attacker always able to score goals, 246 in 491 club outings during his career.
But during his early days at St James' Park, Thompson was given only a few chances
to impress. Blooded in the promotion season of 1947-48, he then had Stobbart,
Gibson, Taylor and Robledo all ahead of him in the ranking. Tommy however blossomed
at Villa Park as a free scoring inside-forward, good enough to earn England
recognition. Nicknamed 'Topper', he grabbed 76 goals for Villa in 165 games before
moving to Deepdale where he joined up with Tom Finney, as well as Charlie Wayman,
in Preston's forward line. Scoring 129 goals in 213 games for the Lancashire club,
being top goalscorer on four occasions (in succession), few players can better his
impressive record for the Lilywhites. He then formed another good partnership with
Stanley Matthews at Stoke when nearing the end of his career. Aware of his
colleague's positioning and always willing to have a go himself, he netted 34 goals in
the First Division during season 1957-58 when Preston finished as runners-up in the
title race. Tommy also scored four goals for the Football League against the Republic
of Ireland during 1951. Retiring after a knee complaint, Thompson returned to his
original joinery trade, developing a family business and living in Fulwood, Preston.*

Appearances & Goals:
Debut v Coventry City (a) 21 February 1948
FL: 20 app 6 gls
Total: 20 app 6 gls

Honours:
2 Eng caps 1952-57/1 Eng B app 1957/2 FL app 1952-57/1 FA app 1957/1 combined
Eng & Scot app 1956/FL div 2 champs 1963/FL div 2 prom 1948 (4 app).

THOMPSON William 1957-1967

Centre-half
5'11"
b. Bedlington, Northumberland, 5 January 1940
d. Ashington, 30 September 2011

Career: UNITED jnr, prof Jan 1957/Rotherham Utd June
1967 £15,000/Darlington Jan 1968 to cs 1970.

*Making his debut for the Magpies during the relegation
season of 1960-61, Bill Thompson shared the centre-half
role with John McGrath during his early years in first-
team action at Gallowgate. A former miner, Bill was long
legged and a tall, commanding defender at his best. In
fact he had developed a top reputation during 1961-62
and 1962-63, gaining a call-up to the England Under-
23 squad only for a leg knock to prevent his appearance for his country. Plagued by
injury, the fearsome Northumbrian was on the club's staff for a decade, Thompson
though never quite established himself as a first-eleven regular season after season,
having later added competition from McNamee and Moncur. Bill also had an outing
at centre-forward for Newcastle before moving to Millmoor in 1967. Concluding his
career back in the North East with Darlington (31 app), he intended to move to non-
league level with South Shields but a deal fell through and the tall stopper left the
game altogether. He returned to his native Northumberland, to Stakeford, being
employed at the Wilkinson Sword complex nearby.*

Appearances & Goals:
Debut v Chelsea (a) 5 November 1960
FL: 79(1) app 1 gl
FAC: 6 app 0 gls
FLC: 3 app 0 gls
Total: 88(1) app 1 gl

THOMPSON William Nesbit 1940-1941

Outside-right
5'8"
b. Bedlington, 31 October 1918
d. Winlaton, near Gateshead, 7 November 1986

*A former Ashington player, Bill Thompson joined the United wartime roll-call during
August 1940, but only remained for a little over 12 months, leaving due to service
commitments in October 1941. A pit-lad in the Ashington coalfield, he took part in a
single match for the Magpies, against Barnsley at Oakwell.*

*(Note: It is possible that Thompson is the same player who appeared for Gateshead
during 1946-47 and 1947-48, also from the Bedlington and Ashington district.)*

Appearances & Goals:
Debut v Barnsley (a) 5 October 1940 (FLN)
War: 1 app 0 gls
Total: 1 app 0 gls

THOMPSON William Pringle 1889-1897

Centre-forward
5'7"
b. North Seaton, Northumberland, October 1867
d. Newcastle upon Tyne, September 1928

Career: Bedlington Burdon 1882/Ashington Rising
Star c1886/Shankhouse Black Watch Aug 1886/
EAST END Dec 1889/Jarrow July 1897/Ashington
c1898 to c1900.

*Working as a blacksmith, Willie Thompson was a
dashing goal-getter during the early years of
Tyneside football. Popular with all his clubs, he was
an especially renowned striker with a powerful
Shankhouse line-up before he joined Newcastle East
End's set-up. Willie won Northumberland Challenge
Cup medals with the noted Black Watch combination and took part in one of the
biggest games staged in the north during those pioneering years, when his side faced
Aston Villa in the FA Cup at St James' Park during 1886-87. Thompson wasn't too big,
but he was swift and possessed a sure shot in either foot, as well as a magnificent
moustache in the style of the day. Working also as a miner in the Northumberland
coalfield, he became a Northumberland County player and took part in United's first
St James' Park fixture and initial Football League match against Arsenal during
September 1893, while he is registered as scoring the club's first senior hat-trick, also
against the Londoners later in the same month. A formidable player, firstly as East
End developed, then in United's first three years of Football League action, Thompson
grabbed 65 goals, a goal every second match for the Tynesiders. In addition, Willie
played in the many friendly and miscellaneous fixtures programmed during the era,
passing 230 games and registering almost 125 goals for the club overall, a admirable
record. He later suffered from injury, being described as having, "a dodgy knee" by the
local press. Willie is also recorded as scoring the very first penalty for East End during
January 1892 in a friendly against Middlesbrough. He played on in the local scene
well into his thirties as a veteran in the East Northumberland League. On retiring from
the full professional game, Thompson returned to his trade as a blacksmith, by 1911
working at one of Northumberland's pits.*

*(Note: Family research has established his middle name being Pringle, his initials being
WP rather than WK or WR as in the press. He was baptised at Woodhorn in 1867.)*

Appearances & Goals:
Debut v Darlington (a) 11 January 1890 (NL)
FL: 80 app 34 gls
NL: 36 app 18 gls
FAC: 19 app 13 gls
Total: 135 app 65 gls
(Void NL: 3 app 2 gls)

THOMSON James Arnott 1968-1971

Midfield
5'6"
b. Glasgow, 28 June 1948

Career: Petershill Jnrs/UNITED Aug 1968 (Barrow loan 1970-71)/Grimsby Town July 1971 free/Morton July 1972 briefly/South Shields 1972 (Gateshead Utd)/Petershill July 1973/Evenwood Town Sept 1976/Newcastle Blue Star/playing on in minor Tyneside football, including Usworth to c2000.

A fierce competitor in midfield, small and well-built, Jimmy Thomson was spotted playing for Scottish junior side, Petershill by United's Glasgow scouts. During season 1969-70, he rivalled Dave Elliott as the reserve anchor man to Benny Arentoft in the middle of the park, then was transferred to Blundell Park where he recorded 32 appearances for the Humberside black-and-whites. Under the guidance of Geordie boss Lawrie McMenemy, he was part of the side which won Fourth Division title honours. Converted to full-back and returning to the North East with Blue Star, Thomson reached Wembley in the 1978 FA Vase. He resided on Tyneside, for a period a publican at the Blue Bell in Felling and later employed by Vaux Breweries. Jimmy continued taking an active part in local football, playing into his forties, during 1998 turning out for Usworth.

Appearances & Goals:
Debut v Burnley (a) 1 November 1969
FL: 4(1) app 0 gls
Total: 4(1) app 0 gls

Honours:
FL div 4 champs 1972/FAV winner 1978.

THOMSON Robert W 1928-1934

Left-back
5'9"
b. Falkirk, 23 September 1903

Career: Laurieston Villa/Falkirk amat Aug 1923, prof May 1925/Sunderland April 1927 £5,000/UNITED Oct 1928 exch for R McKay/Hull City July 1934 £340/Olymp Marseille (Fr) Aug 1934/Racing Club de Paris (Fr) cs 1935/[Olymp Marseille (Fr) Aug 1935]/Ipswich Town July 1936/Retired due to injury 1937, becoming Ipswich Town asst-trainer 1937, then trainer to June 1950/Ajax (Neth) coach Dec 1950 to early 1953.

Originally a half-back, Bob Thomson moved into a full-back's role and found conspicuous success. With Falkirk he won Scotland honours against the Auld Enemy, England, before earning a big move to the First Division south of the border at Roker Park. Small but tough and persistent in defence, he also showed a grace when on the ball, even to the point where at times he appeared rather languid in style. Wearing the red-and-white of Sunderland on only 22 occasions, he then moved to Tyneside in an exchange deal with Bob McKay. Replacing Frank Hudspeth in United's rearguard, Thomson was first choice for two-and-a-half seasons before losing out to Dave Fairhurst. He then spent a long period in Newcastle's reserve line-up as the club strived for membership of the Central League. During a period in France afterwards, Bob was on the Racing Club's staff when they won the French league and cup double in season 1935-36 but did not make an appearance, and may have joined Marseille, perhaps on loan. Retiring due to a broken leg when at Ipswich, he subsequently helped out behind the scenes at Portman Road for several years. During World War Two, the Scot served with the RAF in the Middle East and was linked to the RAF's Eagle Squadron.

Appearances & Goals:
Debut v Leeds United (h) 6 October 1928
FL: 73 app 0 gls
FAC: 7 app 0 gls
Total: 80 app 0 gls

Honours:
1 Scot cap 1927/1 SL app 1927.

THORN Andrew Charles 1988-1989

Centre-half
6'0"
b. Carshalton, London, 12 November 1966

Career: Wimbledon jnr, prof Nov 1984/UNITED Aug 1988 £850,000/Crystal Palace Dec 1989 £650,000/Wimbledon Oct 1994 free/Heart of Midlothian Sept 1996/Tranmere Rovers Sept 1996 free/Retired due to injury Jan 1998/Nottingham Forest asst-coach 1998/Everton asst-coach 2004/Various scouting posts/Fulham chief-scout 2006/Coventry City chief-scout April 2008, becoming caretaker-manager March 2011, manager April 2011 to Aug 2012/Kidderminster Harriers manager Jan 2014 to Feb 2014.

Andy Thorn became Newcastle's joint record purchase at £850,000 along with his Wimbledon colleague Dave Beasant during 1988. Moving to Tyneside as a 21-year-old defender who had shown he possessed all the qualities to reach the top, Thorn was to be a key figure in manager Willie McFaul's rebuilding programme at Gallowgate. Quick and strongly framed, Andy replaced fellow Londoner Glenn Roeder in United's ranks and began his United career with a 4-0 drubbing at Goodison Park, but then netted on his home debut. Although the team failed to knit together, dropping into Division Two, Thorn's own performances were sound if not spectacular. With a new manager taking charge in the shape of Jim Smith, the Londoner was part of his side for the early weeks of the 1989-90 season, but was sold back to the capital in a bid to raise cash to fund another restructuring programme in the dressing-room. At Selhurst Park, despite being affected by knee injuries, Thorn became the cornerstone to Palace's defence for seven seasons, appearing on 168 occasions. He reached Wembley with the Eagles, repeating the feat he had achieved as a member of the celebrated Wimbledon success story, when they defeated Liverpool in the FA Cup final of 1988, the pinnacle of his 166 games for the Dons.

Appearances & Goals:
Debut v Everton (a) 27 August 1988
FL: 36 app 2 gls
FLC: 4 app 1 gl
Others: 3 app 0 gls
Total: 43 app 3 gls

Honours:
5 Eng u21 app 1988/FAC winner 1988/FAC final 1990/FL div 1 champs 1994/FL div 2 prom 1986.

TILDESLEY James 1903-1906

Right-back
5'11"
b. Halesowen, near Birmingham, 7 October 1881
d. Newcastle upon Tyne, 6 January 1963

Career: Cradley Hill St Luke's/Halesowen St John/UNITED Feb 1903/Middlesbrough Sept 1906 £200 to 1907/Luton Town Nov 1908/Middlesbrough Oct 1909/Leeds City Jan 1910/Luton Town cs 1910/West Stanley Sept 1910/Gosforth Oct 1910/Later, UNITED 1930s scout.

Picked up from local football in the Midlands, Jimmy Tildesley acted as a reserve to Jack Carr, Andy McCombie or Bill McCracken, three international backs at St James' Park. A more than able defender himself, he claimed 17 games in season 1903-04 and took part in two Northern League title successes for the Magpies' reserve side. Broad-shouldered and a tough competitor, the local press of the day recorded he tackled with, "astounding power and success". His brother Thomas Tildesley (qv) was also on the club's books at the same time and appeared once in senior action in a friendly during January 1905. Registering 25 games for Boro, after retiring from the playing side of the game, Jim became a noted scout, uncovering Micky Burns and Robert Roxburgh for the club. He later settled in Newcastle.

Appearances & Goals:
Debut v Wolverhampton Wanderers (h) 31 October 1903
FL: 21 app 0 gls
FAC: 1 app 0 gls
Total: 22 app 0 gls

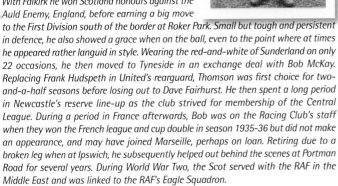

T

TINLIN Charles 1887-1893

Forward & Secretary
b. Kelso, 2 March 1869

Career: Argyle (Newcastle) 1882/North Eastern 1884/Cheviot 1885/Jesmond Ramblers Oct 1886 (all Newcastle clubs)/EAST END Sept 1887 to c1893, also acting as Match Secretary 1887-88, Financial Secretary to 1893, Secretary Jan 1890 to 1891/Also, Victoria Wednesday 1891/Newcastle Wednesday 1891/East End Wednesday 1893.

Living in Byker, originally Charles Tinlin was a player as well as administrator for the Cheviot club, and when they merged with East End during 1887, his services were captured by the Byker side before they moved the short distance to Heaton. More often than not as a player the Scot featured in the club's reserve teams, operating no more than occasionally for the senior eleven as a forward. Tinlin however also acted in administrative positions over a period including a spell in the prominent post of club Secretary. As a commercial clerk, he was well suited to office roles and was a determined individual behind the scenes in developing East End into a football force. Charles was a leading figure when the club became a public company in February 1890. It was Tinlin who suggested forming a company based on a share issue of 2000 shares valued at 10 shillings (50p) each. Charles once scored a hat-trick against Elswick Rangers in the Northumberland Challenge Cup during 1891 while he is noted in official club Minutes as still being involved during 1893 by which time East End had developed into Newcastle United. In both the 1901 and 1911 census he is registered as a "Commercial traveller" residing in Heaton Road.

Appearances & Goals:
Debut v Middlesbrough (a) 27 December 1890 (NL)
NL: 1 app 0 gls
Total: 1 app 0 gls

TINN W (William John) 1889

Full-back
b. Newcastle upon Tyne, [c1867]

Career: White Rose/Newcastle West End 1888/EAST END cs 1889 to cDec 1889/ Victoria Wednesday 1890.

A full-back who was largely selected for rivals Newcastle West End in their reserve set-up, and then after switching camps was also chiefly in East End's Swifts line-up, the club's second-string. Tinn was called up for two Northern League fixtures during season 1889-90, in Darlington, then against Elswick Rangers. He also appeared for White Rose cricket club during the mid-1880s. Census data for 1891 shows only one person of that name in the same age group, William John Tinn born in Newcastle and living in Elswick.

Appearances & Goals:
Debut v Darlington St Augustine's (a) 9 November 1889 (NL)
NL: 2 app 0 gls
Total: 2 app 0 gls

TINNION Brian 1982-1989

Left-back
6'0"
b. Burnopfield, Co Durham, 23 February 1968

Career: Dunston Jnrs/UNITED jnr March 1982, prof Feb 1986/Bradford City March 1989 £150,000/Bristol City March 1993 £180,000, becoming player-manager June 2004 to Sept 2005/Cheltenham Town trial Oct 2005/ Aldershot Town Nov 2005/Western-super-Mare Feb 2006/Team Bath player-coach Jan 2007 to cs 2007/Bristol City Director of Youth June 2013.

Making his senior debut for United in midfield, Brian Tinnion slipped into the left-back role for a long spell during season 1987-88. Fired with a determined attitude, he was a member of United's FA Youth Cup winning side then rivalled both John Bailey and Kenny Wharton at

Gallowgate and looked like seeing off his more experienced colleagues. Manager Jack Charlton rated Brian and once noted that if Tinnion "had an extra two yards of pace, he'd play for England". He continued to develop well until United went through a bad patch of results which affected his confidence. With a quality left foot, at the peak of his early development Tinnion was elevated to the England Under-21 squad during May 1988, but had to unluckily withdraw from a tour of Brazil due to injury. With new boss Jim Smith bringing in experienced players, notably Kenny Sansom, Brian moved to Bradford City and then to Bristol City, making a major contribution at both clubs, especially at Ashton Gate. Nicknamed the 'Tinman' and reverting back to midfield, he was very effective at a lower level and netted the goal which gave the Robins a memorable FA Cup giant-killing knock-out over Liverpool at Anfield in 1994. Tinnion totalled more than 170 games for the Bantams and a substantial 546 with Bristol City where he was captain and later manager. Following a spell in management and in non-league football in the South West, Brian managed a soccer school and scouted in Spain, before opening his own 'Costa Futbol Academy' in San Pedro during 2007. He eventually rejoined Bristol City in 2013.

Appearances & Goals:
Debut v Everton (a) 20 April 1987
FL: 30(2) app 2 gls
FLC: 5 app 0 gls
Others: 1(1) app 0 gls
Total: 36(3) app 2 gls

Honours:
FL div 2 prom 1998/FLT winner 2003/FLT final 2000/FAYC winner 1985/PFA ToS (d2) 2001, 2004.

TIOTE Cheick Ismael 2010-date

Midfield
5'11"
b. Yamoussoukro (Ivory Coast), 21 June 1986

Career: FC Bibo (IC)/RSC Anderlecht (Bel) 2005 (Roda JC (Neth) loan 2007-08)/FC Twente (Neth) July 2008 £2.2m/UNITED Aug 2010 £3.5m.

On many occasions players from overseas who arrived on the Premiership scene took months to adapt to both the pace and new way of life, but Cheick Tiote settled as if he had been raised on Tyneside as a kid. At 24 years old and largely unknown to football fans in England, the Ivorian cost United £3.5m from Dutch champions FC Twente in the summer of 2010 and from his debut in a black-and-white shirt against Everton impressed judges, quickly growing in stature. Operating in the protector and spoiler midfield role, he received praise from almost every quarter. Energetic, forceful and athletic with good distribution of the ball, Tiote moved to Europe from Africa when he joined Anderlecht during 2005. He was in the senior team when 19 years of age and tasted Champions League football before crossing the border to join FC Twente after a stint on loan at Roda. Under the guidance of Steve McLaren, Tiote was part of an emerging Twente side which lifted the Eredivisie title in 2009-10 before switching to Tyneside. With a style which sees Cheick continually snapping at opponents, he breaks up moves and wins the ball like few in England, although at times being over-eager, being booked no less than 14 times and sent-off in his first season. Tiote was one of the best at his role in the Premier League, the level-headed and likable African was taken to heart by the Toon fans, especially after netting a dramatic 87th minute volleyed equaliser against Arsenal in 2011 to complete a remarkable fight back from a four-goal half-time deficit. Cheick possesses a thundering shot from distance, he appeared in the 2010 World Cup in South Africa and reached the final of the African Cup of Nations with the Ivory Coast during 2012, a teammate of Didier Drogba. Although born in his country's capital, Cheik was brought up in the coastal city of Abidjan. During 2013 Tiote was given a suspended seven month sentence for admitting fake driving licence offences.

Appearances & Goals:
Debut v Everton (a) 18 September 2010
PL: 103(4) app 1 gl
FAC: 1(1) app 0 gls
FLC: 3(1) app 0 gls
Euro: 5(1) app 0 gls
Total: 112(7) app 1 gl

Honours:
47 IC caps 2009-date/WdC 2010, 2014/ACN final 2012/IC u23 app/Neth Lg champs 2010/Neth Cup final 2008, 2009/Bel Lg champs 2006 (2 app), 2007 (2 app).

TODD Kevin 1981-1983

Striker
5'9"
b. Sunderland, 28 February 1958

Career: Grindon WMC/Ryhope CA/UNITED trial March 1981, prof Aug 1981 (Darlington loan 1981-82)/Darlington Feb 1983 £5,000/Newcastle Blue Star July 1985/Kuusysi Lahti (Fin) 1987/Humbledon Plains Farm 1988/Whitley Bay Oct 1988/Berwick Rangers Aug 1990 £18,000/Bishop Auckland July 1992/Spennymoor Utd Sept 1996/Durham City Aug 1997, becoming player-coach Oct 1997, then asst-manager/Gateshead Sept 1999/Retired playing Nov 1999.

Scoring almost 200 goals in local football within three seasons was form which spurred United to offer Wearsider Kevin Todd a trial period at St James' Park; he impressed and was handed a full-time contract at the start of the 1981-82 season. Although Kevin wasn't a tall or battling type of striker, he had a good touch and liked to use his pace and ability on the ball, as well as intelligent positioning. Netting twice in his first full game for the Magpies against Watford, he rubbed shoulders with the likes of Kevin Keegan and Terry McDermott during his stay at St James' Park. Todd made a handful of appearances just before United gained promotion in season 1983-84, but snapped ankle ligaments forced him out for over six months, losing his chance in the big-time. Moving to Darlington once fit in search of regular action, Kevin did well for the Quakers in 120 games. Todd played in a lower grade of football until he was over 40 years old where he became a distinguished player for a decade and more; Scotland's Player of the Year for the Second Division in 1991 during a stint with Berwick. He reached international selection at non-league level and while briefly in Finland lifted that country's domestic cup as well as experiencing the Champions League during 1987-88 alongside Kenny Mitchell. During 1988 Kevin was part of the Humbledon Plains eleven which lifted the FA Sunday Cup. He also entered business in the North East, running a trophy shop in Sunderland.

Appearances & Goals:
Debut v Derby County (h) 10 October 1981 (sub)
FL: 5(2) app 3 gls
FAC: 2(1) app 0 gls
FLC: 1 app 0 gls
Total: 8(3) app 3 gls

Honours:
Eng (non-lg) app 1988-91/FA (non-lg) app 1990/FL div 4 prom 1985/Fin Cup winner 1988.

TOMASSON Jon Dahl 1997-1998

Striker
5'11"
b. Solrod, near Copenhagen (Denmark), 29 August 1976

Career: Solrod BK (Den) 1982/Koge BK (Den) 1985/SC Heerenveen (Neth) Dec 1994/UNITED July 1997 £2.2m/SC Feyenoord (Neth) June 1998 £2.5m/AC Milan (It) May 2002 free/VfB Stuttgart (Ger) July 2005 £5m/Villareal (Sp) loan Jan 2007, pmt July 2007/SC Feyenoord (Neth) July 2008 free/Retired June 2010/SBV Excelsior (Neth) asst-coach June 2010, becoming asst-manager, then manager June 2013/Roda JC Kerkrade (Neth) manager Dec 2013 to May 2014.

Many noted football judges in Denmark and Holland rated the talent of Jon Dahl Tomasson very highly as Newcastle United took a close interest in the young forward. The 20-year-old had just broken into the Danish national side and after almost three years in Dutch football with Heerenveen had proved to be an exciting new talent on the scene. Kenny Dalglish was determined to bring him to St James' Park to play alongside Alan Shearer and he arrived on Tyneside during the summer of 1997. Tall, skilful and with coolness of a seasoned professional on the ball, Tomasson liked to operate just behind the front striker and combined effectively in both attack and midfield. Newcastle saw off stiff competition from the likes of Real Madrid, Ajax, Barcelona and Monaco but Tomasson had a difficult period in United's black-and-white colours. In his limited outings for the Magpies, and due to injury necessity, he was pushed up front in a role he largely disliked. Tomasson later confirmed that he

"only played in two matches in my own position". Thrown into Premier League action perhaps too soon, Jon didn't get the sort of luck every striker needs early into a new career; missing a glorious chance on his debut after only 45 seconds against Sheffield Wednesday. The Dane was a touch bitter and disappointed that his chance at St James' Park did not go well. United's staff, and the fans, needed to give him time to settle and adapt. He wasn't given that phase of adjustment and was sold back to Holland within 12 months. Tomasson then rapidly showed a football audience he was a clinical finisher, developing into that top striker many had thought he could be. The Black'n'Whites watched on with frustration as Jon progressed to the top of the European and international stage, notably with Feyenoord (195 app) and AC Milan (113 app). With great movement, at his best joining the attack from deep, he became Denmark's record goalscorer with 52 goals, captain of his country as he totalled a century of caps. With a sharp footballing brain, Tomasson could hold the ball and link colleagues while he possessed a sure shot when the posts were in sight, netting almost 300 goals in his career.

Appearances & Goals:
Debut v Sheffield Wednesday (h) 9 August 1997
FL/PL: 17(6) app 3 gls
FAC: 2 app 0 gls
FLC: 2(1) app 1 gl
Euro: 6(1) app 0 gls
Total: 27(8) app 4 gls

Honours:
112 Den caps 1997-2010/WdC 2002, 2010/1 Den B app/10 Den u21 app/Den sch-youth app/Neth Lg champs 1999/Neth Cup final 1997, 2010/It Lg champs 2004/It Cup final 2003/CL winner 2003 (no app)/CL final 2005/UEFAC winner 2002/ESC winner 2003 (sub no app)/WCC final 2003/Den PoY 2002, 2004.

TOZER Ben Peter Anthony 2008-2011

Centre-half
6'1"
b. Plymouth, 1 March 1990

Career: Plymouth Argyle jnr 2005/Plymouth College FC/Swindon Town July 2007/Everton trial Nov 2007/ UNITED Jan 2008 £250,000 (Leyton Orient trial Aug 2010)(Yeovil Town trial Sept 2010)/Northampton Town loan Nov 2010, pmt June 2011 free (Colchester Utd loan 2013-14).

Ben Tozer began his career as a youngster with his local club Plymouth Argyle when he was studying for a National Diploma in Sport. When his Pilgrims coach moved to Swindon Town, Ben soon followed him to Wiltshire and he quickly made a senior debut in a League Cup match during August 2007 as a 17-year-old. Tall and mobile, he could play across the back four and his football stock was on the rise. Everton gave him a four-day trial during November 2007 and other clubs had taken notice of his progress too, including Newcastle United. Within a few weeks he was a Magpie player, joining the Black'n'Whites in the January 2008 transfer window for a fee of £250,000 when still 17 years old, one of several up and coming prospects purchased by the club at the time. Ben was included in pre-season action during 2008-09, suffered a cartilage set-back and then was on the first-team bench on several occasions. In season 2009-10 the Cornishman started in a Toon shirt for the first time, part of a young line-up against Peterborough in the League Cup, and he appeared once from the bench as United lifted the Championship trophy on their way back to the Premier League. The following season Tozer headed on loan to Northampton Town and immediately was part of the side which famously knocked out Liverpool from the League Cup at Anfield. Ben was a regular for the Cobblers and when Newcastle decided to release him, Tozer moved permanently to the Keepmoat Stadium during June 2011. He became more and more a midfield player, developing an effective Delap-like long-throw in his armoury. Ben has totalled over 150 games for the Cobblers.

Appearances & Goals:
Debut v Peterborough United (a) 22 September 2009 (FLC)
FL: 0(1) app 0 gls
FLC: 1 app 0 gls
Total: 1(1) app 0 gls

Honours:
Eng sch-youth app/FL ch winner 2010 (1 app).

T

TREWICK John 1980-1984

Midfield
5'9"
b. Stakeford, Northumberland, 3 June 1957

Career: West Bromwich Albion jnr July 1972, prof July 1974/UNITED Dec 1980 £234,567 (Oxford Utd loan 1983-84)/Oxford Utd Aug 1984 free/Birmingham City Sept 1987 £30,000/Bromsgrove Rovers Aug 1989/ Hartlepool Utd Oct 1989/Barnet, briefly 1989/ Gateshead Oct 1990 to Jan 1991/ Tamworth/ West Bromwich Albion community-officer June 1992, becoming asst-coach 1992, then caretaker-manager Oct 1994 & Dec 1997, reverting to coach to 2000/Derby Co asst-manager July 2001 to Jan 2002/Cradley Town manager 2002-03/Minnesota Thunder (USA)

asst-coach 2003/Wolverhampton Wand asst-coach/Hereford Utd coach 2004, becoming manager April 2009 to March 2010/Shrewsbury Town coach June 2010 to Jan 2014.

From a footballing family, John Trewick's father, George, and cousin, Alan, both played for Gateshead during their Football League days. Developed from a schoolboy at the Hawthorns, John was an England player at both school and youth level then after becoming a regular midfielder for Albion, assisting in a promotion success during 1975-76, he moved back to the North East for a record club fee. Possessing good vision in midfield with the capacity for hard work, Trewick kept his game simple, rarely hit a bad pass and was in many ways an ideal anchor man, although he also possessed an urge to take up good positions when going forward. But John did not settle quickly at St James' Park. He was injured for a long spell and United's fans did not see the best of his talent until after a loan spell at Oxford. Arriving back at Gallowgate for a promotion run-in during 1983-84, Trewick was lodged in a midfield role alongside McDermott and McCreery and he played an important part in regaining the club's First Division status during the second half of the season. Surprisingly though, Trewick was then released by new boss Jack Charlton, going back to the Manor Ground (142 app), where he yet again won promotion from the Second Division as well as taking part in Wembley glory. On hanging his boots up, Trewick linked up with West Bromwich Albion once more where he totalled 131 games, serving at the Hawthorns in various capacities, including a spell as caretaker manager. He then continued on a coaching career, predominantly in the Midlands.

Appearances & Goals:
Debut v Bristol City (h) 20 December 1980
FL: 76(2) app 8 gls
FAC: 7 app 0 gls
FLC: 2 app 0 gls
Total: 85(2) app 8 gls

Honours:
Eng sch-youth app/FL div 2 champs 1985/FL div 2 prom 1976, 1984/FL div 3 champs 1984 (3 app)/FLC winner 1986.

TUDOR John Arthur 1971-1976

Striker
5'10"
b. Ilkeston, Derbyshire, 24 June 1946

Career: Ilkeston Olympic YC/Stanley Common Miners Welfare/Cotmanhay Utd/ Notts County jnr/Chesterfield jnr/ Middlesbrough amat Dec 1963/Ilkeston Town Sept 1964/Coventry City jnr Jan 1965, prof Jan 1966/Sheffield Utd Nov 1968 £58,500/UNITED Jan 1971 exch deal for J Hope & D Ford/Stoke City Oct 1976 £30,000/KAA Gent (Bel) Aug 1977 £10,000/ Retired due to injury May 1978/Southend Utd trial 1978/North Shields player-coach July 1978, becoming manager Oct 1979/ Gateshead player-coach Dec 1980/

Bedlington Terriers coach Nov 1982/ Derbyshire FA Director of Coaching 1983/Minnesota Thunder (USA) coaching school June 1994 & Tonka Utd Soccer Association (USA) Director of Coaching, as well as Chan-Chaska Utd (USA) coach.

As a teenager John Tudor had trials with various clubs including Derby, Forest and Sheffield United while he was on the junior books of Notts County, Chesterfield and Middlesbrough for short periods. Moving back to non-league football without breaking through, he grabbed another chance at Highfield Road. After serving both Coventry (77 app 15 goals) and Sheffield United (78 app 33 goals) in an honest and professional manner, Tudor arrived at St James' Park to boost United's strike-force. His first season was unspectacular and at times he fought a running battle with sections of the crowd. But on the signing of Malcolm Macdonald in readiness for the start of the 1971-72 season, Tudor's career was ready to explode as a near-perfect partner to Supermac. Blond-haired, John had aerial power, worked intelligently at his game being able to bring players into the attack, and proved to be an ideal foil for Macdonald. For the next four seasons the duo formed United's cutting edge, and few partnerships in the top division could better their potency. Newcastle's previously critical fans now accepted the likable Tudor who showed cunning and courage as well as dedication in abundance. He became a genuine favourite with a terrace song to go with his popularity; "Hallelujah John Tudor"! The striker was a regular until suffering a knee ligament injury, then a change in manager and the arrival of Alan Gowling led to his transfer. Retiring from the first-class game due to his persistent knee problem, Tudor later returned to the North East when he became a publican in Bedlington at the Millfield Inn for a spell before moving back to his native Ilkeston employed as a house-manager for Shipstones Brewery. He started to become involved in coaching schools in Derbyshire, then made the switch to the States during 1994 where he has developed a successful coaching career in Minnesota. Settling in Excelsior, his son also started on a coaching career in the Mid-Western States with the Chan-Chaska club. A late developer in the game, John had worked as a welder, truck driver and tile maker before turning professional with Jimmy Hill's modern revolution at Coventry.

Appearances & Goals:
Debut v Burnley (a) 30 January 1971
FL: 161(3) app 53 gls
FAC: 14 app 3 gls
FLC: 8 app 1 gl
Others: 32(1) app 15 gls
Total: 215(4) app 72 gls
(Void FAC: 1 app 1 gl)

Honours:
FL div 2 champs 1967/FL div 2 prom 1971/FAC final 1974.

TUOHY William 1960-1963

Outside-left
5'7"
b. East Wall, Dublin, 27 April 1933

Career: St Mary's (Dublin)/Shamrock Rovers Aug 1951 (St Mary's loan 1953)/ UNITED May 1960 £9,500/ Shamrock Rovers Aug 1963 free, becoming player-coach, then player-manager cs 1964 to 1969 (Boston Rovers (USA) loan cs 1967)/ Dundalk manager 1969/Eire manager Sept 1971 to Nov 1972 & Shamrock Rovers manager 1972-73/Dublin University FC coach 1975 to 1981/ Shelbourne manager July 1981 to June 1982 & Eire youth manager 1981 to Feb 1986/Home Farm

Director of Coaching Dec 1989 to April 2008 when he retired/ Also occasional UNITED scout & Milltown player-manager 1960s.

One of the top performers in the Republic of Ireland, Liam Tuohy arrived in England as a 27-year-old with a big reputation as a skilful winger who could score goals. Switching from a part-time player in Dublin, having a job with the Guinness empire, he was purchased as Bobby Mitchell's successor in the Number 11 shirt. The Irishman made a good start with the Magpies, showing plenty of spirit, but then suffered, like many of his colleagues, when the side became entangled in a relegation dog-fight during 1960-61. Tuohy was a regular for the following season, but lost his place to Jimmy Fell and he returned to Dublin. Rejoining Shamrock Rovers, for a period he reverted to a part-time footballer also working for the HB Ice-cream company as a sales manager. Liam remained associated with Irish soccer in several roles, a prominent figure in the game for more than 50 years.

Appearances & Goals:
Debut v Preston North End (a) 20 August 1960
FL: 38 app 9 gls
FAC: 1 app 0 gls
FLC: 3 app 0 gls
Total: 42 app 9 gls

Honours:
8 Eire caps 1956-65/3 Eire B app 1958-59/24 EL app 1955-66/EL champs 1954, 1957, 1959, 1964/Eire Cup winner 1955, 1956, 1964, 1965, 1966, 1967, 1968, 1969(m)/Irish PoY 1966.

TURNER Arthur 1903-1904

Outside-right
5'8"
b. Hartley Wintney, near Farnborough, June 1877
d. Farnborough, 4 April 1925

Career: Aldershot North End 1892/South Farnborough/Camberley St Michaels/Brentford trial/Reading trial/Southampton St Mary's May 1899/Derby Co May 1902/UNITED Jan 1903/Tottenham Hotspur Feb 1904 £150/Southampton May 1904 /Bristol City loan 1904-05)/Retired cs 1905/South Farnborough Ath to 1913.

Arthur Turner was an opportunist player, quick to capitalise on an opening. Known as 'Archie' during his career (pronounced 'Arkie' as confirmed by the family), he possessed an excellent turn of speed and showed a flair which excited supporters. Playing his best football for Southampton in the Southern League, Turner totalled 98 games for the Saints and netted 30 goals, many alongside his brother, Harry. He appeared in two FA Cup finals for Southampton and was chosen for the England side on two occasions at his peak during the turn of the century. Turner was a noted footballer in the south, in 1900 becoming the first wax-work figure of a professional player to appear in Madame Tussauds, standing alongside cricket legend WG Grace. Following a brief stay at the Baseball Ground in Division One, Archie ended up on Tyneside, although he again found his stay at the top level a short one. He only managed 13 games for the Magpies suffering with illness and a desire to be back in the south. The emergence of Jack Rutherford saw Archie move on again, to White Hart Lane with Spurs, then members of the Southern League. On leaving the game, Turner entered his family's business in Farnborough, he was also a fine cricketer at club level in Hampshire.

(Note: Several sources note Turner with a middle name of 'Docwra', but it appears this is mixed with another player of the same era, Alfred Docwra Turner of Forest. There is evidence from Tottenham's archive though that the two players may be linked, and Arthur may also have the family name of Docwra.)

Appearances & Goals:
Debut v Notts County (a) 31 January 1903
FL: 13 app 1 gl
Total: 13 app 1 gl

Honours:
2 Eng caps 1900-01/Eng trial app 1900/1 SnL app 1900/FAC final 1900, 1902/SnL champs 1901.

TURNER David John 1960-1963

Right or Left-half
5'9"
b. Retford, 7 September 1943

Career: UNITED amat May 1960, prof Oct 1960/Brighton Dec 1963 £4,500 (Portsmouth loan 1971-72)/Blackburn Rovers Aug 1972 free/Sheffield Utd asst-coach cs 1974 to Jan 1978/Aldershot coach 1978, becoming asst-manager/Toronto Blizzard (Can) coach 1979/Aldershot coach Sept 1990.

On the Barrack Road staff from school football, Dave Turner helped the Magpies lift the FA Youth Cup for the first time in 1962, but found claiming a Football League place near impossible during his four seasons on Tyneside. A tough-tackling

player who could look after himself on the field, Turner was a competent wing-half and was given chances in the last fixtures of the programme for both seasons 1961-62 and 1962-63. At the time he was noted in The Journal as being a "top class prospect". Apart from a League Cup outing, Dave couldn't find a place thereafter and moved to Brighton where he did prove a capable midfield player, skipper of the Seagulls in many of his 338 games. He was a stalwart footballer at the Goldstone Ground for nine seasons. Turner then had a long period associated with Aldershot with a ten-year stint living in Canada. Latterly he resided in his native Nottinghamshire.

Appearances & Goals:
Debut v Leeds United (h) 28 April 1962
FL: 2 app 0 gls
FLC: 1 app 0 gls
Total: 3 app 0 gls

Honours:
FL div 4 champs 1965/FL div 3 prom 1972/FAYC winner 1962.

URWIN Thomas 1924-1930

Outside-right
5'6"
b. Haswell, Co Durham, 5 February 1896
d. Tynemouth, 7 May 1968

Career: Fulwell/Lambton Star/Shildon Ath 1913/Middlesbrough amat Feb 1914, prof May 1914 £100 (Fulham war-guest 1915-16)(Scotswood war-guest 1919)/UNITED Aug 1924 £3,200/Sunderland Feb 1930 £525/Retired cs 1936/Sunderland asst-trainer & scout.

Tom Urwin is one of only a handful of players to have received loyalty payments from all three of the North East's senior clubs. A great servant to the region, he was a noted schoolboy footballer, winning the English Schools Shield then capped by England in 1909-10. Urwin was working at a Wearside colliery when he signed for Middlesbrough. At 18 years of age Tom found a place in the Ayresome Park line-up quickly and appeared on 200 occasions for Boro before heading to Tyneside after a row over benefits. Bill McCracken actually poached him at Newcastle Central Station when the player was on his way to meet Manchester United officials. A midget winger full of craft, one pen-picture of the Twenties described him as being, "little but good, he has the speed and cunning and puts centres in the right place every time". Tom was part of United's first-eleven for six seasons and an influential forward in the club's title success during 1926-27 while he was also capped for his country when at Gallowgate. Operating mainly on the right-wing, Urwin also played on the left touchline in a sprightly fashion too. Moving to Wearside as a veteran in 1930 on the last leg of his regional crusade which spanned 15 seasons, all in the top flight, he totalled 55 matches for the red-and-whites becoming the club's oldest ever player when he turned out during April 1935 aged 39 years 76 days old. Tommy was later connected with the Roker side for many years as trainer to the red-and-whites' youngsters. He afterwards was employed as an accounts clerk in Sunderland Royal Infirmary and lived at Monkseaton. During World War One, Urwin served with the Royal Artillery as a battery fitter in India and Turkey.

Appearances & Goals:
Debut v Blackburn Rovers (h) 10 September 1924
FL: 188 app 22 gls
FAC: 12 app 1 gl
Total: 200 app 23 gls

Honours:
4 Eng caps 1923-26/Eng trial app 1921-26/Eng sch-youth app/10 FA app 1931-32/1 FL app 1927/FL champs 1927.

V

VAN AANHOLT Patrick John Miguel 2010

Left-back
5'9"
b. s-Hertogenbosch (Netherlands), 29 August 1990
Career: FC Den Bosch (Neth) 2003/PSV Eindhoven
(Neth) July 2005/Chelsea jnr July 2007, prof Sept
2007 (Coventry City loan 2009-10)(UNITED loan Jan
2010 to Feb 2010)(Leicester City loan 2010-11)
(Wigan Ath loan 2011-12)(Vitesse (Neth) loan 2011-
12, 2012-13, 2013-14)/Sunderland July 2014 £3m.

*Patrick van Aanholt arrived at Gallowgate as one of
Chelsea's promising youngsters on a short-term
loan deal following an injury to Jose Enrique during
2009-10. The youth and Under-21 Netherlands
international was on the fringe of the Londoner's first-team squad and was given the
United full-back shirt for a five week period as the Spaniard recovered. Quick to get
forward in the modern style, the 19-year-old Dutchman played a small part in the
club's 2010 title victory before moving back to Stamford Bridge. Making his debut for
the Blues in the same 2009-10 season, he later moved on loan again, this time to
Leicester and afterwards Wigan Athletic. With Ashley Cole and Ryan Bertrand blocking
his path at Stamford Bridge, Patrick headed back to Holland on a long term loan
arrangement with Vitesse. During 2013-14 he was called up to the full Dutch squad
after impressing with Vitesse and was included in their preliminary Brazil 2014 World
Cup roster, although unluckily missed final selection. He did though win his first cap
for Holland against Colombia during November.*

Appearances & Goals:
Debut v Leicester City (a) 30 January 2010
FL: 7 app 0 gls
Total: 7 app 0 gls

Honours:
2 Neth caps 2014-date/Neth u21 app/Neth sch-youth app/PL champs 2010 (2 app)/
FL ch winner 2010 (7 app).

VARADI Imre 1981-1983

Centre-forward
5'9"
b. Paddington, London, 8 July 1959
Career: Letchworth Town/FC 75 (Hitchin)/
Sheffield Utd jnr July 1975, prof April 1978/
Everton March 1979 £80,000/SL Benfica (Ptg)
trial July 1981/UNITED Aug 1981 £125,000/
Sheffield Wed Aug 1983 £150,000/West
Bromwich Albion July 1985 £285,000/
Manchester City Oct 1986 £100,000/Sheffield
Wed Sept 1988 exch deal/Leeds Utd Feb 1990
£50,000 (Luton Town loan 1991-92)(Oxford
Utd loan 1992-93)/Rotherham Utd loan Feb
1993, pmt March 1993/Boston Utd May 1995/
Mansfield Town Aug 1995/Scunthorpe Utd

Sept 1995/Matlock Town player-manager Nov 1995/Guiseley player-coach Dec
1996/Denaby Utd player-coach Jan 1997/Stalybridge Celtic asst-manager Dec 1997,
becoming manager Feb 1998, then player-coach March 1998/Universal Drilling Aug
1998/Sheffield FC Feb 1999.

*Well travelled, and a favourite at all his ports of call, Imre Varadi scored goals
throughout his career. Quicksilver fast, and always snapping at defenders heels, he
joined United after impressing Arthur Cox in limited opportunities for Everton (35
app). Swarthy, dark-haired and known as 'Ray', he in fact almost joined Benfica (one
trial game) before heading for Tyneside, but that spectacular deal fell through and he
pulled on the black-and-white shirt for the start of the 1981-82 season. Although
sometimes erratic in his finishing, Varadi was quick-footed, had an explosive shot and
still bagged 20 goals in his first year for United, then another 22 the following
campaign when he partnered Kevin Keegan in attack. He also once hit five goals in a
friendly against Hartlepool for the Magpies. To the shock of all United's supporters
though, Cox then sold the striker to Sheffield Wednesday to fund a replacement,
bringing in the more skilful Peter Beardsley, a player to knit better with Keegan. Born
of a Hungarian father and Italian mother, Varadi continued to find the net
nevertheless and by the end of his career in the first-class game had scored 178 goals
with his best spells away from Tyneside being with Manchester City (81 app 31 goals),
Sheffield Wednesday (121 app 46 goals) and Rotherham (79 app 28 goals). When at*

*Elland Road he appeared on a handful of occasions in Leeds' title winning season of
1991-92. Playing on until past his 40th year, Varadi then coached in Yorkshire and
became a FIFA registered player agent based in Sheffield, joining the Stellar Group
Ltd. His brother Fernando was on Fulham's staff, and as a youngster Ray had brief
spells on trial with Tottenham and Cambridge United.*

Appearances & Goals:
Debut v Watford (h) 29 August 1981
FL: 81 app 39 gls
FAC: 5 app 2 gls
FLC: 4 app 1 gl
Total: 90 app 42 gls

Honours:
FL champs 1992 (3 app)/FL div 2 champs 1990/FL div 2 prom 1984, 1989 (3 app).

VARTY Thomas Heppell 1939-1944

Outside-left
5'8"
b. Hetton-le-Hole, 2 December 1921
d. Enfield, April 2004

Career: Crook Town/Vickers Works/UNITED amat May
1939/Darlington April 1944/Watford Sept 1950 to 1951.

*Employed in the giant Vickers armament factory on
Tyneside, Tom Varty was given a chance at Gallowgate
during season 1941-42. Although appearing often for
United's wartime second-string, he was handed only one
game in senior company, against Leeds United at Elland
Road in November 1941. Later Varty made a name for
himself within Darlington's ranks, claiming 173 matches
for the Quakers. He afterwards went into business in that
town before relocating to the south.*

Appearances & Goals:
Debut v Leeds United (a) 29 November 1941 (FLN)
War: 1 app 0 gls
Total: 1 app 0 gls

VEITCH Colin Campbell McKechnie 1899-1926

Half-back & Trainer
5'6"
b. Newcastle upon Tyne, 22 May 1881
d. Berne (Switzerland), 27 August 1938

Career: Larkspur Jnrs (Newcastle)
1891/Dalton Jnrs (Newcastle)/Malcolm Jnrs
(Newcastle) 1894/Portland (Newcastle)/
Rutherford College Nomads (Newcastle)
1895/Rutherford College (Walker Parish,
Cambois, Allendale Park, all briefly)/UNITED
amat Jan 1899, prof April 1899/Retired June
1915, becoming asst-trainer to cs
1926/Bradford City manager Aug 1926 to Jan
1928.

*One of the most eminent names, not only in United's past, but in the game's history,
Colin Veitch was a true great. He was a complete footballer, able to operate in any
position, appearing for United in every role apart from goalkeeper, left-back and
outside-left. He also turned out for England in four different positions and was the
most versatile player in the country before World War One, a factor which went
against him in international selection, often leaving Veitch a constant reserve for a
decade. An outstanding schoolboy player raised in the Byker and Heaton area of the
city, the first captain of the Newcastle Boys combination, Veitch though had little
support from his family to progress a footballing career, his parents being totally
opposed to their son's involvement in what was then far from a favoured profession
and what Veitch described as "not socially acceptable". He later confirmed: "I had to
go through many months of agony before I could finally admit to the monstrous truth
that I had signed professional." He had been focussed on a teaching career, but the
lure of the game was too great for Veitch. Appearing also for United under the
pseudonym of 'Colin Hamilton' when at college, the Tynesider took part in 16 seasons
of football for the club and was a central figure in all of Newcastle's Edwardian
success; three titles and five FA Cup finals. Veitch preferred midfield, at centre-half*

here he could dictate the play, and was a player of few tricks, yet controlled the game with his straightforward ability. Ivan Sharpe noted that "Veitch played with the supreme ease of a man who is the master of his job". He was a thoughtful player, an expert tactician and invariably had control of the ball, using it to purpose. He also often found the net for the Magpies and can be recognised as perhaps the leading spirit behind the club's Edwardian success. Captain of the side on occasion, as well as England's Football League XI, he was the first United skipper to lift the FA Cup, in 1910. A man of many talents, Colin was an articulate scholar, musician, actor, playwright and from a staunch socialist family, was very politically aware, once nominated to stand for Parliament. He was also a leading activist of the Players' Union's cause at a time when they struggled to survive, the organisations Chairman from 1911 to 1918 and a sensible peace-maker during a period of much conflict with the game's rulers. At that time Colin was described as "a man of outstanding intellectual attainments and a charming personality". Married to an actress, he was heavily involved in the Newcastle Playhouse and People's Theatre, Newcastle Operatic Society and Clarion Choir, and counted George Bernard Shaw among his acquaintances. Colin's association with Newcastle United came to a bitter end in 1926 when he was sacked as manager of the club's recently formed junior set up, the Newcastle Swifts. Afterwards living in Gosforth he became a shrewd, and at times, highly critical journalist with a gifted pen for the Tyneside newspaper stable of the Chronicle, North Mail and Sunday Sun. He was once banned from St James' Park for his stinging remarks at the club. Veitch died when convalescing in Switzerland after having contracted pneumonia. During World War One, Colin rose to the rank of 2nd Lieutenant with the Royal Garrison Artillery, his brother Gerald Veitch (qv) also joined United and played friendly action for the club while a nephew, William Park appeared for York and Blackpool.

Note: Colin's death is officially registered as 26th August 1938, but extensive reports contained in a family album note he died "early" on 27th August.)

Appearances & Goals:
Debut v Wolverhampton Wanderers (h) 28 October 1899
FL: 276 app 43 gls
FAC: 45 app 6 gls
Others: 1 app 0 gls
Total: 322 app 49 gls

Honours:
6 Eng caps 1906-09/Eng trial app 1906-07/4 FL app 1906-11/FL champs 1905, 1907, 1909/FAC winner 1910/FAC final 1905, 1906, 1908, 1911/NU HoF.

VENISON Barry 1992-1995

Defender or Midfield
5'10"
b. Consett, 16 August 1964

Career: Sunderland jnr May 1979, prof Jan 1982/Liverpool July 1986 £250,000/UNITED July 1992 £250,000/Galatasaray SK (Trk) June 1995 £750,000/Southampton Oct 1995 £850,000/Retired due to injury Oct 1997.

A product of school football at Roker Park, Barry Venison was a teenage star for Sunderland (205 app), skippering the Wearsiders at Wembley in 1985 when only 20 years of age. Moving in a big deal to Anfield, Venison took part in title and FA Cup victories with Liverpool in 158 games before returning to the North East for a bargain fee. One of manager Keegan's inspired signings during the summer of 1992, Venison marshalled United's defence from the right-back spot as the Magpies stormed to claim the First Division title. Also stepping in at centre-half, he was comfortable on the ball, able to distribute passes accurately, and was also totally committed, showing determination and inspirational qualities that rallied both his colleagues and supporters. Barry quickly became a favourite and as the club tackled Premiership football he developed into an international player. Moving into a holding midfield role, Venison was selected for a deserved England cap showing the talent to cover ground, win the ball with steely aggression and release a pass from a position just in front of the defence. Venison played with pride in his shirt during a three year spell on Tyneside, during which time he skippered the side, as he had done at Roker Park and for the England youth and Under-21 elevens. A dedicated follower of fashion, the blond-haired Venison was characterised by his trade-mark flowing locks and at times flamboyant attire during

his period at Gallowgate. Barry was forced to retire from playing with a persistent back injury and afterwards worked as a television presenter then relocated to the USA in 2003. Settling in Orange County, California, he carved out a career in property development, later running Vantage Financial Solutions, "a boutique firm that buys and sells discounted Real Estate".

Appearances & Goals:
Debut v Southend United (h) 15 August 1992
FL/PL: 108(1) app 1 gl
FAC: 11 app 0 gls
FLC: 9 app 0 gls
Euro: 1 app 0 gls
Others: 3 app 0 gls
Total: 132(1) app 1 gl

Honours:
2 Eng caps 1995/10 Eng u21 app 1983-86/Eng sch-youth app/FA PL app 1994/FL champs 1988, 1990/FL div 1 champs 1993/FAC winner 1989/FLC final 1985, 1987.

VIANA Hugo Miguel Ferreira 2002-2006

Midfield
5'9"
b. Barcelos (Portugal), 15 January 1983

Career: Sporting Clube (Ptg) 2001/UNITED July 2002 £8.2m (Sporting Clube (Ptg) loan 2004-05)/Valencia CF (Sp) loan Aug 2005, pmt March 2006 £1.2m/CA Osasuna (Sp) July 2007/SC Braga (Ptg) loan cs 2009, pmt Aug 2010/Al-Ahli Club (UAE) July 2013.

Hugo Viana stood out as a top prospect in Sporting Lisbon's double winning line-up of 2001-02 and then Portugal's successful Under-21 side during the summer's European Championships in Switzerland, indeed voted Young Player of the Year in Europe. Newcastle eyed his smooth and cultured touch of the ball in midfield and splashed out a considerable £8.2m fee for his services at the end of the tournament when he was only 19 years old. At such a high fee, that deal was something of a gamble, one to end as an expensive failure. Viana's career never got going at St James' Park and his footballing destiny headed for mediocrity instead of stardom. Always displaying silky confidence about the way he played the game, Hugo struggled to come to terms with the velocity and energy of the Premier League. In his defence, manager Bobby Robson gave him little opportunity to gain experience in United's side which did well during the late 1990s and early years of the Millennium. With Solano, Speed, Dyer as well as Jenas, Robert and Bowyer competing for the midfield places, Viana was more often than not on Robson's bench (with 33 limited outings as substitute). Yet the dark-haired Portuguese showed fine technique and vision at times with a skilled left foot, scoring an important goal in the Champions League epic at the De Kuip in Rotterdam against Feyenoord during 2002. He did claim 17 starts in that 2002-03 season and 11 the following campaign, but Hugo should have recorded twice that number to develop as a top midfielder. Frustrated at his lack of opportunity, especially in a favoured central midfield role rather than out wide, he moved to Valencia during 2006 after a loan deal with United taking a substantial £7m loss on the transaction. While Viana perhaps moved to the Premier League in England too early, later confirming he "had difficulties in adapting", he did prove, in Portugal especially, that he was a gifted midfielder. Occasionally also found at left back, Hugo was capped when only 18 years of age by his country and reached two World Cups as well as playing in two European finals once he left Tyneside. Viana first appeared for Portugal against Angola in November 2001, a controversial match which saw his opponents reduced to six players and the game being abandoned.

Appearances & Goals:
Debut v NK Zeljeznicar (a) 14 August 2002 (CLQ)
PL: 16(23) app 2 gls
FAC: 0(1) app 0 gls
FLC: 2 app 0 gls
Euro: 10(9) app 2 gls
Total: 28(33) app 4 gls

Honours:
29 Ptg caps 2002-13/WdC 2002 (no app), 2006/OG 2004/Ptg u21 app/ECh u21 winner 2002/Ptg Lg champs 2002/Ptg Cup winner 2002/UEFAC final 2005/EpL final 2011/EYPoY 2002.

V

VIDUKA Mark Anthony 2007-2009

Striker
6'2"
b. St Albans, Melbourne (Australia),
9 October 1975

Career: Australian Institute of Sport/ Melbourne Knights 1992/NK Croatia Zagreb cs 1995/Celtic Dec 1998 £3.5m/Leeds Utd July 2000 £6m/Middlesbrough July 2004 £4.5m/ UNITED July 2007 free/Retired July 2009.

For over 10 seasons Mark Viduka was rated as one of the best strikers in Europe, this after banging in 35 goals on the Scottish scene for Celtic in a short but productive spell at Parkhead. Moving to the UK from a quality Croatia Zagreb combination which had faced the Magpies in a dramatic Champions League qualifier during 1997, the well-built Australian, born in Melbourne of Croatian parents, possessed a wonderful first touch of the ball and could hold up play in the centre-forward role perfectly. And his inter-play around the box was of match-winning class. Following a successful period in English football with both Leeds (166 app 72 gls) and Middlesbrough (101 app 42 gls), Viduka joined United's roster on a free transfer during the close-season of 2007 when 31 years of age and approaching the veteran stage of his career. Yet he had netted 19 goals for Boro in the season just concluded, showing he could still be a major asset. Although often on the sidelines with knocks, when he was fit and in the side, Mark was a good strike partner to Oba Martins, who needed his experience and ability to bring colleagues into the game. Season 2007-08 was a decent one for Viduka, but the following term, as United headed for relegation, he was out of the side and the pairing was fielded too infrequently. He struggled with a succession of knocks, just when the Magpies needed his guile in attack. With Newcastle cutting wages in the summer, Viduka departed and decided to call a day to his first-rate career in which he captained his country to the 2006 World Cup. One of Australia's top sportsmen, he returned to Melbourne opening a well-known eating-house, the 'Mark Viduka Bar & Grill' at Warrnambool Beach where it is boasted visitors can get "the best bbq cuckoo skewers and wampa-wampa steaks in town". He is a cousin of Luka Modric.

Appearances & Goals:
Debut v Bolton Wanderers (a) 11 August 2007
PL: 25(13) app 7 gls
FAC: 2 app 0 gls
Total: 27(13) app 7 gls

Honours:
43 Aus caps 1994-2007/WdC 2006/OG 1996, 2000/18 Aus u23 app/Aus sch-youth app/SLC winner 2000/Aus Lg champs 1995/UEFAC final 2006/SPoY 2000 (SPFA)/Oceania PoY 2000/'Alex Tobin medal' for services to Australian football.

VUCKIC Haris 2009-date

Midfield
6'2"
b. Domzale (Slovenia), 21 August 1992

Career: NK Domzale (Sln) 1993/UNITED Jan 2009 £50,000 (Cardiff City loan 2011-12)(Bradford City trial Aug 2013)(Rotherham Utd loan 2013-14).

In recent years Newcastle United have operated a policy of trailing Europe-wide to hunt out young foreign talent, with the hope they could develop new stars through the ranks of St James' Park. Haris Vuckic was one of a group of overseas teenage imports and one of only a handful to really succeed on Tyneside. The strapping youngster arrived at Gallowgate as a 16-year-old as 2009 opened from Slovenian club Domzale, near the capital Ljubljana. Having represented his country at school and youth level, his credentials fitted United's criteria. All that was to be done was to develop the skills Vuckic displayed. Tall and upright, in midfield Haris had the look of a natural footballer. He often caught the eye at Newcastle's junior and reserve level and when he received an opportunity in senior company at 17 years of age, at first in friendly contests, did not look out of place. Dark-haired, Vuckic could unleash a terrific shot from distance, becoming part of Alan Pardew's wider first-team squad in 2010. At the same time he made his full debut for his country against Scotland during

February of that year. To gain much needed experience the Slovenian had a month's loan spell with Cardiff City during 2011-12 but then suffered knee ligament damaged the following season and was out of action for a lengthy period. Once fit, he again went out on loan, this time to Rotherham where he enjoyed a successful period, a promotion winner in the Wembley Play-Off in 2014.

Appearances & Goals:
Debut v Huddersfield Town (h) 26 August 2009 (FLC) (sub)
FL/PL: 2(4) app 0 gls
FLC: 6(3) app 0 gls
Euro: 1(1) app 1 gl
Total: 9(8) app 1 gl

Honours:
1 Sln caps 2012-date/Sln u21 app/Sln sch-youth app/FL ch winner 2010 (2 app)/FL div 1 prom 2014.

WADDLE Christopher Roland 1980-1985

Forward
6'0"
b. Heworth, Gateshead,
14 December 1960

Career: Pelaw Jnrs/ Whitehouse SC/Mount Pleasant SC/HMH Printing Co/Pelaw SC/Leam Lane SC 1977/Clarke Chapman 1977/ Tow Law Town cs 1978/ UNITED July 1980 £1,000/ Tottenham Hotspur July 1985 £590,000/Olym Marseille (Fr) July 1989 £4.25m/Sheffield Wed July 1992 £1m/Falkirk Sept 1996/Bradford City Oct 1996 free/ Sunderland March 1997 £75,000/ Burnley player-manager July 1997 to May 1998/Hollinsend Aug 1998/ Torquay Utd Sept 1998/ Brunsmeer Ath 1998/Hill Top Nov 1998/Davy Sports Nov 1998/Sheffield Wed asst-coach Dec 1998 to June 2000/Worksop Town July 2000/ Parkgate Nov 2001/Staveley Miner's Welfare April 2002/Glapwell Aug 2002/South Normanton Ath March 2003/Stocksbridge Park Steels April 2003/Staveley 2003/Also occasional appearance for Belford (2002), Tow Law Town (2002) and Worksop Parramore (2012).

After being connected to the Magpies as well as Sheffield United, Sunderland and Coventry City as a youngster, Chris Waddle exchanged a labourer's job at Cheviot Seasoning, a factory making sausages and pies for a chance in professional football at St James' Park. Raised in Pelaw, the down to earth Tynesider caught the eye in Tow Law's black-and-white, netting 23 goals during 1979-80 and then made rapid progress with the Magpies, eventually becoming one of the game's biggest names, commanding at the time, the fourth highest transfer fee ever paid (behind Maradona and Gullit) when he moved to France. Yet at first, Waddle never looked to be that quality footballer. He possessed an awkward, lumbering style, but under the guidance of Arthur Cox and Kevin Keegan at Gallowgate, a hidden talent was developed. With rare ability to go past defenders using a body-swerve and deceptive pace, Chris quickly claimed a regular place in United's first-eleven. At centre-forward or on either wing, Waddle roamed across the front line and during the Magpies' promotion to Division One during 1983-84, he became a noted player. Along with Keegan and Beardsley up front, United had a forward trio of style. Waddle could place a dangerous swerving cross and had an eye for goal too, producing a vicious bend on shots. Chris could beat men in tight situations and became a match-winner, soon to be in his country's Under-21 and full squads. But with Newcastle's lack of ambition and success forcing him to move south, it was with Tottenham that Waddle became a regular for England. He appeared in the 1986 and 1990 World Cup finals, missing a crucial penalty kick in the semi-final shoot-out with West Germany in Italy. After 177 games (42 goals) for Spurs, he then made that record move to Marseille where Waddle's career flourished even further. He became a megastar in Provence alongside stars like Papin and Boli. The Geordie's showmanship and magic on the ball was adored by the French, being nicknamed 'Le Dribbleur Fou'. Chris won Le Championnat medals with Marseille as well as reaching the European Cup final in 1991. Returning to England, he joined up with Sheffield Wednesday where Chris again showed his native public what a splendid player he was over 147 games. Although at times he was dogged by injury at Hillsborough, Chris became a huge favourite, making a double Wembley appearance during 1992-93, the season he also lifted the Footballer of the Year trophy. During April 1987 Waddle had a hit record alongside Glenn Hoddle entitled Diamond Lights, then three years later cut another single with Basil Boli when at The Velodrome. Settling in Yorkshire, he often supported local clubs, appearing for a number of non-league sides and being an ambassador for Gedling Miner's Welfare FC. Chris entered the football media, becoming an appreciated analyst and commentator for the BBC and ESPN as well as a newspaper columnist. A cousin, Alan Waddle appeared for a number of clubs notably Liverpool and Swansea, while his son Jack Waddle plays for Worksop Town.

Appearances & Goals:
Debut v Shrewsbury Town (h) 22 October 1980
L: 169(1) app 46 gls
AC: 12 app 4 gls
LC: 9 app 2 gls
Total: 190(1) app 52 gls

Honours:
62 Eng caps 1985-92/WdC 1986, 1990/1 unoff Eng app 1988/1 Eng u21 app 1985/1 L app 1988/FL div 2 prom 1984/FAC final 1987, 1993/FLC final 1993/Fr Lg champs 1990, 1991, 1992/Fr Cup final 1991/EC final 1991/FoY(FWA) 1993/PFA ToS (d1) 1985, 1989.

WAKE Henry Williamson 1919-1923

Right-half
5'7"
b. Seaton Delaval, near Newcastle upon Tyne, 27 January 1901
d. Durham West, 1979 (Q3)

Career: Bigges Main CW/Birtley/UNITED jnr 1919 (Durham City war-guest 1919) prof May 1919/Cardiff City May 1923 £200/ Mansfield Town June 1931 £250/Gateshead July 1932 briefly/Wigan Ath cs 1932 to cs 1933.

A prominent youth footballer on Tyneside, an England schoolboy player and captain of the club's junior set-up, Newcastle Swifts, Harry Wake was introduced into United's senior eleven towards the end of the 1919-20 season. But the youngster always had fierce competition for a half-back place at St James' Park, with Finlay, Curry, Mooney and McIntosh all ahead of him in selection. Wake wasn't big and tough, rather a waif-like figure in midfield. Harry possessed lots of honest endeavour, ability when on the ball and found a good home at Ninian Park, breaking through into regular first-team soccer. He helped Cardiff to reach two FA Cup finals in 1925 and 1927, and made headlines on both occasions. Against Sheffield United during 1925 he unfortunately lost the ball on the edge of the box for Fred Tunstall to net the only goal of the game, while two years later he scored in the semi-final but had to miss the final due to a kidney injury. Wake also helped the Welshmen to a runners-up spot in the First Division during 1923-24 and totalled 166 appearances for Cardiff. Wake later took part in Mansfield's first Football League fixture during 1931. Harry was related to William Wake, on United books during 1906-07 and later with Exeter, Plymouth and QPR.

Appearances & Goals:
Debut v Manchester City (h) 17 April 1920
(v Hartlepools Utd (h) 11 January 1919 (NVL))
FL: 3 app 0 gls
War: 1 app 0 gls
Total: 4 app 0 gls

Honours:
Eng sch-youth app/1 WsL app 1927/FAC final 1925/WsC winner 1930/WsC final 1929.

WALKER Andrew Francis 1991

Striker
5'8"
b. Glasgow, 6 April 1965

Career: Eastercraig/Baillieston Jnrs June 1983/ Motherwell July 1984/Celtic July 1987 £375,000 (UNITED loan Sept 1991)/Bolton Wand Jan 1992 £160,000/Celtic July 1994 £550,000/Sheffield Utd Feb 1996 £500,000 (Hibernian loan 1997-98) (Raith Rovers loan 1997-98)/Ayr Utd Aug 1998/ Carlisle Utd trial July 1999, pmt Aug 1999/Partick Thistle Sept 1999/Isernia (It) briefly 1999/ Kilwinning Rangers 1999/Alloa Ath Jan 2000/ Retired June 2000.

Only at St James' Park for a brief spell on loan, Andy Walker didn't solve Ossie Ardiles' problem of finding a dangerous front man. The Scot never recaptured the form which had made him a potent attacker in Scotland, one of Celtic's heroes during their double victory in 1988 when he was Scotland's top goal-getter with 32 strikes. Joining the Hoops after a productive spell for Motherwell in 93 outings, at his peak, Walker was an excellent striker; small, yet quick and with positioning sense as well as the finish of a natural marksman. Andy held the ball up well and could bring others into the game. He scored nearly 70 goals in almost 200 games for the Parkhead club, before moving to Bolton after his unsuccessful stay on Tyneside. At Burnden Park, the Scot returned to his best, hitting 33 goals during season 1992-93 and in aggregate 55 in 87 games. Unfortunately, injury halted his exciting progress and Walker found himself back in Glasgow, but in a second spell with the Celts couldn't reproduce his earlier sparkle. After retiring from the game, Walker became a media pundit in Scotland, for Sky and STV as well as a columnist for the Sunday Mail. He also acted as a football agent.

Appearances & Goals:
Debut v Millwall (a) 21 September 1991
FL: 2 app 0 gls
FLC: 1 app 0 gls
Total: 3 app 0 gls

Honours:
3 Scot caps 1988-95/1 Scot u21 app 1988/FL div 2 prom 1993/SL champs 1988/SL div 1 champs 1985/SC winner 1988/SC final 1990/SLC final 1995/SJC final 1984/PFA ToS (d2) 1993.

WALKER Leonard 1963-1964

Right-half
5'11"
b. Darlington, 4 March 1944

Career: Middlesbrough amat 1959/Spennymoor Utd 1962/UNITED May 1963 £250/Aldershot July 1964 free/ Charterhouse School part-time coach/Darlington player-coach Aug 1976, becoming coach 1977, manager Oct 1978 to June 1979/Aldershot coach 1980, becoming caretaker-manager Jan 1981, manager April 1981 to Nov 1984, and, June 1985 to March 1991, then appointed general-manager to March 1992/Fulham asst-manager July 1994, becoming Youth Development Officer/ Later scouting for various clubs.

After making only a single Football League appearance, plus a League Cup outing, for Newcastle during season 1963-64, Len Walker moved south to become one of the lower divisions most noted players during the Sixties and Seventies. He was given little scope to impress under Joe Harvey's regime at Gallowgate, being in the shadows at half-back to Jim Iley, Stan Anderson and Ollie Burton. But joining Aldershot was the break Walker needed and the gritty, competitive midfielder proceeded to total 489 senior games over 12 seasons for the Hampshire club. Also playing at full-back, Len became the Shots' record appearance holder and was club skipper for several seasons. On retiring from the playing side of the game Walker became a highly respected coach in the basement of professional football. As boss of Aldershot, he guided the club to promotion during 1987 and remained at the Recreation Ground until they went out of business in 1992, an association for nearly 30 years. As a youth, Len was also a fine local cricketer in the Durham leagues, Walker settled in Hampshire.

Appearances & Goals:
Debut v Preston North End (h) 25 September 1963 (FLC)
FL: 1 app 0 gls
FLC: 1 app 0 gls
Total: 2 app 0 gls

Honours: FL div 4 prom 1973, 1987(m).

W

WALKER Nigel Stephen 1976-1982

Midfield
5'10"
b. Gateshead, 7 April 1959
d. Gateshead, 2 February 2014

Career: Whickham/UNITED jnr Nov 1976, prof July 1977 (Plymouth Argyle loan 1981-82)/San Diego Sockers (USA) May 1982 free/Sunderland trial Dec 1982/Crewe Alex Jan 1983/Sunderland July 1983 (Blackpool loan 1983-84)/Chester July 1984/ Hartlepool Utd July 1985 free/Blyth Spartans Aug 1987, becoming asst-coach 1991, joint manager Feb to March 1992/Dunston Fed Nov 1992/RTM Newcastle Aug 1995.

A skilful midfield player, Nigel Walker was blooded as an 18-year-old in United's relegation season from the First Division during 1977-78. With flair and style on the ball, despite the test of playing in an ordinary side, Nigel proved to Geordie supporters in 14 outings that he was very much a discovery who had the potential to become a quality player. Walker developed further in United's Second Division line-up over the next three seasons, but again in a mediocre side. He did show flashes of genius, able to glide past two or three defenders in some exciting runs from midfield. However, United's coaching staff could never quite develop the Tynesider into a midfielder who, after this brilliant approach play, could deliver the final pass or shot. Under Arthur Cox's management, he was discarded and Walker drifted around the country, and across the Atlantic, before returning to the region to appear on 92 occasions for Hartlepool then concentrating on local football. During his loan period with Blackpool, Nigel scored a hat-trick on his debut against Northampton, while the Tynesider's stay with Sunderland was decidedly short, all of eight minutes or so, making a single substitute appearance against Watford during November 1983. Nigel appeared on 216 occasions for Blyth Spartans where he oozed class at that level. He also studied technology & design through the Open University then computer sciences at Northumbria University gaining a first-class honours degree. He became a mathematics' teacher in the region living in Whickham. As a schoolboy, Walker captained the County youth side at rugby union.

Appearances & Goals:
Debut v Bristol City (h) 5 November 1977
FL: 65(5) app 3 gls
FAC: 3 app 0 gls
FLC: 1 app 0 gls
Total: 69(5) app 3 gls

WALKER Thomas Jackson 1941-1954

Outside-right
5'10"
b. Esh Winning, Co Durham, 14 November 1923
d. Middleton, Lancashire, 13 June 2005

Career: Netherton Jnrs/UNITED Oct 1941 (West Ham Utd war-guest 1942-43)/ Oldham Ath Feb 1954 £2,500/Chesterfield Feb 1957 £1,250/Oldham Ath July 1957/ Retired April 1959, later becoming Oldham Ath scout for a period.

As a schoolboy Tommy Walker played in the English Schools final for Blyth, then began his senior career at centre-half, but as wartime football came to a close had developed into a pacy winger who could operate on both flanks. On his first senior wartime outing, Walker was part of a United side which won 7-0 at Boro in 1941. Fast and direct, he tended to pick the ball up deep and storm down the touchline and proved a very effective forward, especially when in direct contrast to the tricky ball-play of Bobby Mitchell on the opposite wing. During season 1946-47 he was a rival to Jackie Milburn for the Number 7 shirt, then had competition from Sibley, Stobbart, McCall and Hair at outside-left or right. Tommy only managed eight games during United's promotion campaign the following season due to a broken arm, but by the start of the 1949-50 season was installed as a regular at outside-right. Able to deliver near inch-perfect crosses, Walker was at his peak as the Magpies reached Wembley twice in 1951 and 1952 when his penetrating sorties into the opponents' box were a feature of United's play. On leaving Tyneside, Tommy also served Oldham well, turning out in 164 matches (23 goals) for the Latics during two spells. On retiring Walker settled in the Manchester area, running a newsagency in Middleton. A Methodist lay preacher for a period, Walker took part in several sprint handicaps as a teenager, including the

famous Powderhall meeting in Edinburgh. When Tommy joined United as a 16-year-old, he was working in an insurance office in Blyth. Walker's grandson, Andy Walker was with United juniors during the late 1990s without breaking through.

(Note: Several sources have his birthplace varying from Cramlington, Esh Winning and Lanchester. In a published interview with Tom, he indicates he was from Cramlington, however genealogy data and family information shows his birthplace as Esh Winning in County Durham, being raised on the outskirts of Newcastle, at Cramlington)

Appearances & Goals:
Debut v Coventry City (h) 11 September 1946
(v Middlesbrough (a) 6 December 1941 (FLN))
FL: 184 app 34 gls
FAC: 20 app 3 gls
War: 29 app 2 gls
Others: 2 app 0 gls
Total: 235 app 39 gls

Honours:
FAC winner 1951, 1952/FL div 2 prom 1948 (8 app).

WALL(S) George Henry 1918-1919

Inside-right
5'10"
b. Nettlesworth, Co Durham, 30 March 1897
d. Newcastle upon Tyne, 28 September 1919

Career: Ouston Utd/Perkinsville/UNITED amat Jan 1918, prof May 1919 to death in Sept 1919.

An England schoolboy international forward during 1912, George Wall had been the star of a bright Perkinsville junior line-up near Chester-le-Street which had gone 83 games unbeaten. It was noted that George had netted a remarkable 216 goals at school and junior level over four seasons. He came into United's First World War Victory League side during February 1919 against Middlesbrough and was regarded as "a promising player" by the local press. Deputising for Ed Dixon, Wall had an unhappy afternoon on Teesside as the Magpies fell 3-0, but he still impressed in local football and was highly rated. After being given a contract for the 1919-20 First Division season, George died suddenly after a short illness when only 22 years of age which saddened everyone at the club. Having been on holiday in Blackpool, he gashed and broke his arm on a water-chute, and injury which developed infection. Six of his team-mates acted as underbearers at his funeral in Pelton near his birthplace.

(Note: Although club and Football League details show his surname as Wall, death registration information reveals he was named Walls. Newspaper cuttings of the time show both Wall and Walls.)

Appearances & Goals:
Debut v Middlesbrough (a) 8 February 1919 (NVL)
War: 1 app 0 gls
Total: 1 app 0 gls

Honours:
Eng sch-youth app.

WALLACE John L 1942

Centre-forward
5'10"
b. Glenbuck, Ayrshire, c1917

Career: Saltcoats Victoria/Cumnock Jnrs/Partick Thistle Nov 1935 (UNITED war-guest 1942-43)/Ayr Utd Aug 1946 to 1947.

Taking part in a single wartime fixture for United when on army service, deputising for Albert Stubbins at centre-forward in a 4-0 defeat at Huddersfield during September 1942, John Wallace had been a prominent striker north of the border. In the three seasons up to the declaration of war at Fir Park, Wallace netted 26, 23 and 28 goals in each campaign for Thistle during their Scottish League programme. Had it not been for Hitler's invasion, a bright career would no doubt have followed for this Caledonian sharp-shooter.

Appearances & Goals:
Debut v Huddersfield Town (a) 12 September 1942 (FLN)
War: 1 app 0 gls
Total: 1 app 0 gls

WALLACE Joseph 1891-1895

Forward
5'4"
b. Hurlford, Ayrshire, c1870
d. [Newcastle upon Tyne, September 1941]

Career: Glenbuck Cherrypickers/Newmilns 1888/ EAST END Jan 1891/Rendel cs 1895.

Joe Wallace was formidable little Scot who commenced his career with the marvellously named Glenbuck Cherrypickers side in Ayrshire. Enticed to Tyneside by East End's management at the same time as two other Scots (Watson and Sorley), he soon became a firm favourite to the small crowds that watched Newcastle United's embryo club. He was noted in the press of the day as "Wee Wallace", at 5'4" tall, one of the club's shortest footballers on record. Employed as a labourer in the shipyards, Wallace was a play-anywhere forward, appearing on either flank as well as in both inside-forward roles. One of the mainstays of the club's first Football League season during 1893-94 (25 league app), Joe netted six goals in the first six league matches and ended top scorer with 17 goals for the campaign. He not only took part in the club's inaugural fixture against Arsenal, but also the club's debut at St James' Park with Celtic. In all fixtures (including the profusion of friendly and miscellaneous matches) Joe scored almost 50 goals in nearly 130 outings for Newcastle, a respected goalscorer. Moving to Benwell club Rendel, he remained on Tyneside for much of his life after leaving the football scene. Wallace later ran into financial difficulties. It is recorded in the club's official Minutes of Meetings that during March 1933 he was in dire straits living on Tyneside, the club purchasing clothes and gifting him money. Joe is possibly related to several footballing Wallace's from the Glenbuck district; Alec, Bert and John also playing in the senior game.

Appearances & Goals:
Debut v Newcastle West End (a) 10 January 1891 (NL)
NL: 27 app 11 gls
FL: 42 app 19 gls
FAC: 8 app 3 gls
Total: 77 app 33 gls
(Void NL: 3 app 1 gl)

WALSHAW Kenneth 1941

Outside-left
5'9"
b. Tynemouth, 28 August 1918
d. Blyth, 16 May 1979

Career: North Shields/Sunderland amat 1939, prof Aug 1944 (UNITED war-guest 1941-42)(York City war-guest 1944-45)(Watford war-guest)/Resumed with Sunderland/Lincoln City Aug 1947/Carlisle Utd Dec 1947/Bradford City Aug 1950 to 1951/North Shields manager cs 1954.

Although he failed to make the Football League side at Roker Park, Ken Walshaw did appear in the FA Cup competition for the Wearsiders during 1946. He was small and crafty on the wing, also operating in the centre-forward's shirt for United during season 1941-42. At Lincoln he claimed 17 outings, helping the Imps to the Division Three North title, while at Brunton Park, Walshaw did better, totalling 50 games and netting 15 goals for Carlisle.

Appearances & Goals:
Debut v Bradford Park Avenue (a) 8 November 1941 (FLN)
War: 4 app 0 gls
Total: 4 app 0 gls

Honours:
FL div 3(N) champs 1948.

WARBURTON John 1894-1895

Left-back
b. Newcastle upon Tyne [1873 (Q3)]
d. [Newcastle upon Tyne, March 1922]

Career: UNITED Aug 1894/Hebburn Argyle 1895 (UNITED guest Jan 1898)/Wardley June 1898/ Hebburn Argyle Feb 1899/Morpeth Town June 1899/Hebburn Argyle Oct 1899/Prudhoe Sept 1900/Gravesend Utd Sept 1900.

Hailing from a popular local footballing family, John Warburton came into United's side for three games in succession during the New Year period of season 1895-96. Deputising for international defender Bob Foyers, he didn't receive a further opportunity in Football League soccer, but gave the club's reserve side in the Northern Alliance good service. He joined another Alliance side, Hebburn Argyle during 1895 helping them win the title in 1896-97. Warburton left Hebburn before the end of 1899 and afterwards appeared for several other local combinations. Information from census data shows it is likely he lived in Jesmond and worked as an engine fitter.

Appearances & Goals:
Debut v Leicester Fosse (h) 1 January 1896
FL: 3 app 0 gls
Total: 3 app 0 gls

WARD Edward 1920-1922

Inside-right
5'7"
b. Whitehaven, 16 June 1896
d. [Northumberland Central, 1971 (Q3)]

Career: Blyth Shamrock/Blyth Spartans April 1913/ Bedlington Utd June 1913/New Hartley Rovers/Blyth Spartans cs 1914/UNITED May 1920 £300/Crystal Palace June 1922 £250/Nelson June 1923 free/ Darlington trial Nov 1924, pmt Dec 1924/Ashington Aug 1925/Workington Aug 1927/West Stanley Aug 1928/Blyth Spartans player-trainer Oct 1930, becoming trainer Aug 1931 to c1939.

Ted Ward's family moved from the west coast to the village of Cowpen colliery near Blyth where his father and brother found work. Ted himself also worked down the pit and Newcastle United were attracted to his ability as a footballer after he impressed for Blyth in a local Aged Miners cup final against the Magpies' reserve eleven. United's directors quickly snapped the inside-forward up and he just as rapidly made a name for himself on the First Division stage. Ward rivalled Ed Dixon at inside-right, but received the nod for much of the 1920-21 programme as the club challenged for title silverware. Possessing pace and a good touch of the ball, as well as a stinging shot, Ward looked to be a find. However, within 12 months Ted had been despatched south to join Crystal Palace where he recorded only four games for the Londoners. He quickly returned north to appear with Nelson during their Football League sojourn and later in Ashington's senior eleven in Division Three North, totalling his best return of games, 26 appearances (10 goals) for the Colliers. Ward's stay in London resulted in Palace requesting a refund on the transfer fee of £250 due to Ward being sidelined with a persistent knee complaint. His younger brother Walter also appeared for Ashington.

Appearances & Goals:
Debut v West Bromwich Albion (h) 28 August 1920
FL: 21 app 5 gls
FAC: 4 app 0 gls
Total: 25 app 5 gls

Honours:
FL div 3(N) champs 1925 (5 app).

W

WARD W A 1894-1896

Goalkeeper
b. [Loughborough, c1871]
6'2"

Career: Loughborough/UNITED Sept 1894 to 1896.

A one-time inside-forward who began his career with the Loughborough club, Ward arrived at St James' Park during September 1894 for the opening games of what was only the club's second programme in the Football League. A giant of a man at 6'2" and 13 stone, he was installed as first choice goalkeeper and at one stage was described by the Newcastle Daily Journal as being "safe as the proverbial bank". Ward took over from Lowery and Ryder, but took part in both Newcastle's worst Football League defeat (9-0 to Burton Wanderers) and heaviest FA Cup reverse (7-1 to Aston Villa). By the end of the season United's team committee decided he was not the answer to a goalkeeping problem that continued for some years. Ward lost his place to Dave Henderson and left the club in 1896.

(Note: Hard information on Ward is scarce, but census data shows he is probably William A Ward, born around 1871 in Loughborough. A Walker Ward also appeared for the Leicestershire club during the same era, but he was a winger.)

Appearances & Goals:
Debut v Grimsby Town (h) 15 September 1894
FL: 18 app 0 gls
FAC: 3 app 0 gls
Total: 21 app 0 gls

WARDROPE William 1895-1900

Outside-left
5'6"
b. Wishaw, Lanarkshire, 14 February 1876
d. USA, 1911

Career: Dalziel Rovers/Motherwell amat 1895/ Linthouse amat/UNITED Aug 1895/ Middlesbrough loan April 1900, pmt May 1900 £50/Third Lanark May 1902/Fulham May 1904/ Swindon Town June 1906/Hamilton Acc Aug 1907/Third Lanark Sept 1907/Raith Rovers Sept 1908/USA & Canada coaching 1910 to death.

Willie Wardrope hit the scene in a major way during season 1895-96. With United's side just starting to develop after a couple of seasons of struggle, it was players like Wardrope who took the club onto a different level of football. The Scot netted 22 goals in 36 games in his first season, all from the left-wing position, and proved a formidable opponent. Weighing in at 12 stone, Wardrope was small yet decidedly well-built; it was noted that "his weight might embarrass many a player, but not so Wardrope who has the natural appetite of a clever forward". He was astute and skilful as well as having a terrific shot. During his opening campaign of 1895-96 Willie struck 13 goals in nine successive matches, the best by any United player. For the next four seasons Wardrope continued to be a key forward to United's cause, helping the Black'n'Whites to promotion during 1898. He was an international trialist just before the turn of the century, although later Willie was suspended by the Scottish FA for alleged irregularities. On leaving Tyneside, he appeared for Middlesbrough (73 app 24 goals) and then notably for Third Lanark where he starred as the Glasgow club won the Scottish title in 1904. Wardrope helped Fulham during their Southern League days, netting 43 goals in 91 appearances in all matches for the Cottagers and winning another title medal. Wardrope's relation, Alex, turned out for Middlesbrough, Portsmouth and Airdrie. In 1910 Willie emigrated to the USA, residing for a period in Pittsburgh before his early death.

(Note: Certain sources have Wardrope's birthplace as West Calder, however it is considered to be an error. A namesake from the West Lothian village is recorded in the 1901 census data as a shale miner when the footballer was listed in the same census with Middlesbrough.)

Appearances & Goals:
Debut v Loughborough (h) 7 September 1895 (1 goal)
FL: 131 app 48 gls
FAC: 14 app 7 gls
Total: 145 app 55 gls

Honours:
Scot trial app 1899/1 SL app 1903/1 Scot jnr app/FL div 2 prom 1898, 1902/SL champs 1904/SnL champs 1906.

WARE Harry 1935-1937

Inside-right
5'10"
b. Birmingham, 22 October 1911
d. Stoke on Trent, 28 October 1970

Career: Hanley St Luke's/Cobridge Celtic/Stoke St Peter's/Stoke City amat Dec 1927, prof Dec 1929/UNITED Sept 1935 £2,400/Sheffield Wed May 1937 £1,700/ Norwich City Nov 1937 £2,000 (Port Vale war-guest 1939-40)(Northampton Town war-guest 1940-42)(Nottingham Forest war-guest 1940-41)(Stoke City war-guest 1940-41)(Crystal Palace war-guest 1942-43)(Watford war-guest 1942-44)(Lovell's Ath war-guest 1944-45)/Northwich Victoria manager Sept 1946/EDO Haarlem (Neth) trainer Aug 1948/Northwich Victoria manager Aug 1950 to Jan 1951, and again 1952 to 1953/Port Vale trainer Nov 1956/Crewe Alex manager June 1958 to May 1960/Stoke City asst-trainer June 1960, later becoming physio and scout to his demise.

A play-anywhere midfielder, Harry Ware arrived at St James' Park as a schemer to provide quality service for centre-forward Jack Smith. Winning a promotion medal with Stoke under the guidance of Tom Mather, his new boss at Barrack Road, Harry was a slim playmaker who could create an opening. Totalling 57 matches for the Potters, he made an impact during season 1935-36 when he rivalled Billy Leighton for the inside-right channel. But after that early promise, the Brummie was injured, lost form and faded from the scene, soon moving to Hillsborough. During World War Two, Ware served as a sergeant in an anti-tank platoon and was wounded in the chest during the Overlord Normandy invasion, an injury which eventually forced his retirement from the first-class game. The son of a former boxing British and European bantamweight champion, Harry competed as a useful middleweight himself and worked in the Potteries before turning professional with Stoke. He later became an American citizen after marrying into a New Jersey family.

Appearances & Goals:
Debut v Fulham (h) 28 September 1935 (1 goal)
FL: 44 app 9 gls
FAC: 5 app 0 gls
Total: 49 app 9 gls

Honours:
FL div 2 champs 1933.

WATKIN George 1960-1963

Centre-forward
6'0"
b. Chopwell, near Gateshead, 14 April 1944

Career: Chopwell/UNITED jnr Sept 1960, prof April 1962 £25/Kings Lynn July 1963 free/Cambridge (City) 1964 to May 1964/Chesterfield July 1964 £250/Gateshead June 1965 free/Swalwell & other local sides.

George Watkin joined the Magpies from a local junior club and proceeded to impress in the club's youth and reserve line-ups. A member of United's successful FA Youth Cup side in 1962, he was quick off the mark at that level and a threat up front. Deputising once for Barrie Thomas in Newcastle's centre-forward shirt, Watkin came into a much changed front line and faced former United stalwart, Bob Stokoe at Gigg Lane. Watkin was up against it all afternoon, Ivor Broadis reporting in The Journal noted George "had the sort of debut that could well set him back a bit". The raw youth showed bags of guts but could get nowhere against the experienced Stokoe. Manager Joe Harvey found little requirement for the youngster thereafter and George moved into non-league football, re-appearing in the Football League for Chesterfield. He had eight outings for the Spireites before returning to Tyneside and joining up with Gateshead. He later resided near Consett, in Bridgehill, working for Clarke Chapman then in the National Coal Board's scientific department.

Appearances & Goals:
Debut v Bury (a) 1 December 1962
FL: 1 app 0 gls
Total: 1 app 0 gls

Honours:
FAYC winner 1962.

WATSON John 1902-1903

Right-back
5'11"
b. Newarthill, Lanarkshire, 1882

Career: Holytown Thistle/Clyde May 1902/
UNITED Nov 1902 £200/New Brompton 1903/
Brentford May 1903/Leeds City July 1908/ Clyde
cs 1910.

With a growing reputation in Scotland, Jock
Watson was a popular character and bright
prospect with Clyde and it was reported that
there was much unrest at the Shawfield Stadium
when he moved to England. Appearing for the
Glasgow select eleven, Watson was a well built and powerful defender who was
purchased in an attempt to fill a problem right-back position. Newcastle had tried
Davidson, Benson, Andy Aitken, Bennie, Wilson and Tildesley as well as Watson, but
couldn't find a consistent player until Scottish international Andy McCombie arrived
on the scene. Jock managed only a handful of games during season 1902-03 before
he tried his luck south, one of a trio of Magpies players to join Brentford, with Caie
and Davidson. A success with the Bees, he played on 170 occasions at Southern League
level for the London club, also running a public-house for a period, The New Inn, not
far from Griffin Park which he kept until the years up to World War One. Later Watson
turned out in 49 matches for Leeds City before continuing his career back on Clydeside.

Appearances & Goals:
Debut v Sheffield United (a) 15 November 1902
FL: 3 app 0 gls
Total: 3 app 0 gls

WATSON John Fox 1941

Centre-half
5'11"
b. Hamilton, 31 December 1917
d. Southend on Sea, 15 April 1976

Career: Douglas Water Thistle/Bury June 1936 (Southport
war-guest 1939-40)(UNITED war-guest 1941-42)(Fulham
war-guest 1942-46)(Brighton war-guest 1942-43)
(Hamilton Acc war-guest 1942-43)(Aldershot war-guest
1943-44)(Luton Town war-guest 1943-44)(Brentford
war-guest 1943-44)/Fulham Aug 1946/Real Madrid CF
(Sp) player-coach cs 1948/Crystal Palace July 1949/
Canterbury City Aug 1951.

A stopper centre-half from the football hotbed of Lanarkshire, Jock Watson turned out
on six occasions for Bury before war interrupted his progress. Taking the inside-
forward's shirt for the Magpies during 1941-42 when in the region, he was a regular
with Fulham from 1944-45 and continued his career with the Londoners once peace
was restored, recording 127 games at the Cottage. Tall and strong, Jock moved to Spain
when his former colleague Mike Keeping was installed as manager of Real Madrid. He
appeared once in their famous white shirts, against Celta Vigo, the Scot experiencing
a campaign with the Los Blancos albeit a decade before they reached the top of the
European game. A season later he was appointed Crystal Palace skipper and he totalled
63 matches for the Londoners before leaving the Football League circuit.

Appearances & Goals:
Debut v Bradford Park Avenue (a) 8 November 1941 (FLN)
War: 1 app 0 gls
Total: 1 app 0 gls

WATSON John Ian 1988-1993

Forward
5'9"
b. South Shields, 14 April 1974

Career: Wallsend BC/UNITED jnr Oct 1988, prof April
1992 to May 1993 free/West Bromwich Albion trial July
1993/Scunthorpe Utd July 1993/ Gateshead Feb 1994 to
April 1997/Stalybridge Celtic Dec 1997/Whitley Bay Jan
1998/Gateshead July 1998/Whitley Bay Oct 1998/Atlanta
(USA) coaching May 1999/Gateshead 2002/Durham City
c2003, becoming caretaker-manager 2005/Whitley Bay
2006/Bedlington Terriers 2006, becoming caretaker-
manager 2007/Newcastle Benfield 2008/Also appeared
for Annfield Plain and Bishop Auckland.

A friend and contemporary of his namesake Steve Watson at both Burnside School
and the renowned Wallsend Boy's Club, both players joined United's School of
Excellence as kids then developed through the junior ranks at St James's Park, but went
very different ways. While Steve became a noted star, John found it difficult to break
into the first-eleven following a brief appearance against Hull City as substitute for
rival teenager Robbie Elliott and another flirtation during the Anglo-Italian Cup during
1992-93. A utility forward, operating in the centre-forward's role originally, Watson
was handed a free transfer and managed only a handful of games for Scunthorpe
before heading back to the region when he signed for Vauxhall Conference side
Gateshead. John proceeded to become a regular fixture in the Tyneside club's line-up
totalling over 150 games in three different spells while he served several other non-
league sides as well. When a junior with the Magpies in 1990, John was injured in car
accident along with his United colleagues on the A1 when returning from a match.
Watson later worked for Gateshead Council.

Appearances & Goals:
Debut v Hull City (h) 11 May 1991 (sub)
FL: 0(1) app 0 gls
Others: 0(1) app 0 gls
Total: 0(2) app 0 gls

WATSON Peter 1891-1893

Right-back
b. Scotland

Career: [Lugar Boswell 1889-90]/Newmilns/
EAST END Jan 1891/Rotherham Town Feb 1893/
Mansfield Nov 1893.

Peter Watson was a capable full-back who arrived on
Tyneside at the same time as two other Scots, Wallace
and Sorley, as East End boosted their ranks in the
opening month of 1891. First choice until the arrival
of Harry Jeffrey, he was then reserve to the new arrival
during the club's earliest period at St James' Park.
Peter had little hope of dislodging Jeffrey from the
first-eleven and he moved to join up with Rotherham's pioneer set up, Watson taking
part in Town's first ever Football League season and faced Newcastle United as they
entered senior action too, during 1893-94. Rotherham though, failed miserably in that
testing debut campaign; they ended next to bottom of the table and had to seek re-
election. When on Tyneside, Peter had become something of a local hero when he
rescued a policeman in Byker from a gang of thugs in 1892.

Appearances & Goals:
Debut v Newcastle West End (a) 10 January 1891 (NL)
NL: 16 app 0 gls
FAC: 2 app 0 gls
Total: 18 app 0 gls
(Void NL: 3 app 0 gls)

WATSON Robert 1889-1890

Forward
b. Liverpool, c1866

Career: Everton Aug 1887/Gorton Villa 1889/EAST END Aug 1889 to cs 1890.

Robert Watson was a spritely forward who appeared on 18 occasions as an Everton
player during the very first Football League competition during 1888-89, a historic
year in football. After losing his place on Merseyside to Welsh international Charlie
Perry, his capture by Newcastle East End was a keynote signing, giving the Tynesiders
much expertise as they aspired to reach the higher ranking set-up too. He fitted in to
their side for the launch of the Northern League during September 1889 and was a
regular for the first half of the programme. His opening foray for Everton was
embroiled in a bitter FA Cup match against Bolton during 1887-88, a marathon tie of
four games which ended in much controversy, with Everton being found guilty of
"providing financial inducements" to seven players, including Watson. Everton were
disqualified from the tournament as a result.

Appearances & Goals:
Debut v Darlington (h) 7 September 1889 (NL)
NL: 9 app 0 gls
FAC: 1 app 0 gls
Total: 10 app 0 gls

W

WATSON Stephen Craig 1989-1998

Right-back
6'1"
b. North Shields, 1 April 1974

Career: Wallsend BC/UNITED jnr Sept 1989, prof April 1991/Aston Villa Oct 1998 £3.75m/Everton July 2000 £2.5m/ West Bromwich Albion July 2005 free/ Sheffield Wed loan Feb 2007, pmt July 2007, retired May 2009 due to injury, becoming asst-coach/ Huddersfield Town asst-coach Nov 2010 to Feb 2012/ Birmingham City asst-coach Aug 2012, becoming asst-manager March 2014.

On many occasions Steve Watson held his own in United's side of internationals. A versatile player who was linked with the Magpies since a 10-year-old schoolboy at the club's Centre of Excellence, Watson was a versatile player who looked comfortable in any role and operated in midfield, at right-back, in central defence or even in attack. He was also a more than competent goalkeeper in emergency. Brought up in Wallsend, Steve possessed height and was powerfully-built, the Tynesider showed much skill on the ball and ability to find the net, striking more than one spectacular effort for United. An England Under-21 regular, Watson was introduced to senior football as a teenager, the club's youngest ever player at 16 years and 223 days, when he appeared against Wolves during 1990. Energetic with loads of enthusiasm, he also possessed a dangerous long throw, in his younger days executed with a spectacular somersault! Before he was 20 the born and bred Geordie had made almost 100 appearances for the club he supported since a schoolboy at Burnside. Steve though had to take a back seat for the first period of Keegan's resurgence of the Magpies, but soon claimed a permanent place on the bench, then at times the popular local product enjoyed long and impressive runs as part of the first-team in a number of roles, more and more settling into a right-back spot where he rivalled big money signing Warren Barton. Watson was on the fringe of a full England call up by Glenn Hoddle during 1996-97, but was sold by boss Ruud Gullit to raise funds as the new manager started to fashion his own side. Watson enjoyed decent periods at both Villa Park (54 app) and Goodison Park (137 app) before being forced to quit playing due to a persistent hip injury. Steve then joined up with his teenage colleague at Gallowgate, Lee Clark, at both Huddersfield and Birmingham. As a youngster Watson also had trials with Sunderland and Huddersfield before signing forms for United, while as a youth international represented his country in two World Cup tournaments. Curiously, Steve once played for England's Under-21 eleven during the same week as he turned out in Newcastle's Northern Intermediate League line-up!

Appearances & Goals:
Debut v Wolverhampton Wanderers (a) 10 November 1990 (sub)
FL/PL: 179(29) app 12 gls
FAC: 13(4) app 0 gls
FLC: 10(6) app 1 gl
Euro: 14(3) app 1 gl
Others: 4(1) app 0 gls
Total: 220(43) app 14 gls

Honours:
12 Eng u21 app 1993-96/1 Eng B app 1998/Eng sch-youth app/PL runners-up 1996, 1997/FL div 1 champs 1993 (2 app)/FAC final 1998.

WATTERS John 1941

Inside-forward
5'9"
b. Waterside, near Dumbarton, 5 September 1919
d. Sunderland, 12 August 2012

Career: Celtic jnr 1935/St Roch's Oct 1936/Celtic Jan 1937 (Third Lanark war-guest 1939-41) (Airdrieonians war-guest 1940-42) (St Mirren war-guest 1941-42)(UNITED war-guest 1941-42)/Airdrieonians Sept 1947 free/Pollock trainer-physio April 1949/Sunderland physio 1956 to 1983.

Johnny Watters netted on his debut in a 5-3 victory for United against York City when he was stationed at a Royal Navy centre in the North East. During the Second World War the Scot took part in the D-Day invasion, serving on HMS Warspite as a medic and by the time he had returned to peacetime football, couldn't claim a regular place at Parkhead. Playing for the Celts on only 10 occasions, he had though appeared in front of the biggest league attendance in Britain when 118,730 watched the Rangers versus Celtic contest during January 1939. Having studied physiotherapy when his playing days were over, he returned to the region and for almost 30 years was connected to Sunderland as a respected physiotherapist.

Appearances & Goals:
Debut v York City (h) 27 September 1941 (FLN) (1 goal)
War: 2 app 1 gl
Total: 2 app 1 gl

WATTS Charles 1896-1908

Goalkeeper & Asst-trainer
5'9"
b. Middlesbrough, 1875
d. Newcastle upon Tyne, 23 November 1924

Career: South Bank 1891/Middlesbrough Ironopolis 1892/Blackburn Rovers June 1893/Burton Wand 1894 (Blackburn Brooks loan 1895-96)/UNITED May 1896 £60, retired cs 1906, becoming asst-trainer to April 1908/Burton Utd Oct 1908.

Taking over from John Henderson in United's goal, Charlie Watts can be recognised as the club's first custodian of note. A regular for two seasons as the Magpies claimed a First Division place; he was a robust 'keeper, agile for his era, with a reputation for punching the ball a long distance in the style of the day. He created several headlines; once in October 1897 at Turf Moor, Charlie faced three Burnley penalty kicks and never conceded a goal. Yet like many goalkeepers of the early years, Watts was prone to error and as a consequence United's directors made a wide search for a new rival, signing Matt Kingsley in readiness for Newcastle's debut in the top flight. Watts though, remained at Gallowgate for another eight seasons, a loyal servant, rarely being given an extended run, especially when Jimmy Lawrence entered the action. He did however appear on a handful occasions during the Magpies' title winning season in 1904-05. On retirement Watts assisted on the training staff at St James' Park, but then left the game, afterwards being a noted racing enthusiast on Tyneside. A loveable personality, it was remarked that he won and lost three fortunes as both a race-horse owner and turf advisor while he was well known for selling tips on the Quayside every Sunday morning. Charlie was also a gambler during his playing career, in 1898 winning a then huge amount of £600 in prize money in a Sporting Chronicle racing skills competition. His death occurred under tragic circumstances, reports indicating he committed suicide in the back lane of his home after being in a desperate state following an unsuccessful bet to win £3,000 in order to clear mounting debts. His son was also found with wounds and a fractured skull, injuries received in an apparent domestic dispute. At the inquest, Newcastle's former goalkeeper's sad demise was recorded as "suicide during temporary insanity".

Appearances & Goals:
Debut v Small Heath (a) 5 September 1896
FL: 93 app 0 gls
FAC: 8 app 0 gls
Total: 101 app 0 gls

Honours:
FL champs 1905 (4 app)/FL div 2 prom 1898.

WAUGH Kenneth 1951-1956

Right-back
5'6"
b. Newcastle upon Tyne, 6 August 1933
d. Melbourne (Australia), 1 June 2001

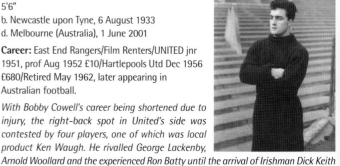

Career: East End Rangers/Film Renters/UNITED jnr 1951, prof Aug 1952 £10/Hartlepools Utd Dec 1956 £680/Retired May 1962, later appearing in Australian football.

With Bobby Cowell's career being shortened due to injury, the right-back spot in United's side was contested by four players, one of which was local product Ken Waugh. He rivalled George Lackenby, Arnold Woollard and the experienced Ron Batty until the arrival of Irishman Dick Keith settled the issue in no uncertain terms. Waugh was given a run in the team during season 1955-56, but wasn't considered First Division quality at that time. Ken was transferred soon after, moving down the east coast to the Victoria Ground where he totalled 206 senior matches for Hartlepools. On retiring from the game, he later emigrated to Australia.

Appearances & Goals:
Debut v Arsenal (a) 15 October 1955
FL: 7 app 0 gls
Total: 7 app 0 gls

WAUGH Robert 1907-1912

Right-back
5'8"
b. Heaton, Newcastle upon Tyne, 1888 (Q4)
Career: Newcastle Bentonians/UNITED amat June 1907, prof Jan 1908/Derby Co Aug 1912 £100 to 1915 (Hartlepools Utd war-guest 1918-19)/Palmers Jarrow Sept 1919/West Stanley Dec 1920.

An engineer by trade, Bob Waugh rendered useful service to the Magpies without ever threatening his rival in the senior side. That was the great Bill McCracken, so it wasn't unexpected that Waugh only collected a handful of games for the club, his best haul being eight matches during 1909-10. But on the odd occasion he did win a place on McCracken's absence through injury or international duty, Waugh pleased the crowd immensely; one local press report making the comment that he "has the ability and the temperament to reach the heights". Moving to Derby, Bob appeared on 29 occasions for the Rams, part of their Second Division title side just before the Great War. He then returned to the North East, initially with Hartlepools in the Northern Victory League immediately after World War One, then for a lengthy spell in North Eastern League football.

Appearances & Goals:
Debut v Aston Villa (h) 11 December 1909
FL: 11 app 1 gl
Total: 11 app 1 gl

Honours:
FL div 2 champs 1915.

WAYMAN Charles 1941-1947

Centre-forward
5'6"
b. Bishop Auckland, 16 May 1922
d. Bishop Auckland, 26 February 2006
Career: Chilton 1935/Chilton CW/Spennymoor Utd 1938/UNITED amat & prof Sept 1941 (Portsmouth war-guest 1944-45)/Southampton Oct 1947 £10,000/Preston North End Sept 1950 £10,000 plus E Brown/Middlesbrough Sept 1954 £8,000/Darlington Dec 1956/Retired April 1958 due to injury/Evenwood Town coach briefly 1959.

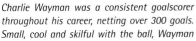

Charlie Wayman was a consistent goalscorer throughout his career, netting over 300 goals. Small, cool and skilful with the ball, Wayman developed through wartime football at St James' Park after writing to Stan Seymour for a trial. Beginning as an inside-forward, Charlie was switched to the leader's role when Albert Stubbins left and was an instant hit. He was to quickly become a feared striker as United attempted to gain promotion as soon as peacetime soccer returned in 1946. With a lethal left foot, he was mobile with pace to burn the turf and frequently was able to glide past defenders with the ball. Charlie twice scored four goals in a single match for the Magpies. During season 1946-47 he grabbed 34 goals, but was at the centre of an unsavoury dispute with club officials, notably trainer Norman Smith, on the eve of Newcastle's FA Cup semi-final with Charlton Athletic. Top scorer Wayman was dropped, United lost 4-0 and afterwards also missed a promotion place. Then Charlie was reluctantly transferred south for a club record fee, to Southampton where he became a most popular centre-forward, hitting 77 goals in only 107 senior outings. In one match against Leicester during 1948 the explosive and quick-thinking Number 9 struck five goals. And at Deepdale with Preston, Wayman again registered a first-class record of 117 goals in 171 games, netting in every round of their run to Wembley in the FA Cup of 1954. Several observers of the era reckoned it was only his lack of inches that stopped him winning an England cap,

while Wayman was the Football League's divisional top goal-getter in 1946-47, 1948-49 and 1952-53. During wartime service, Charlie served as an able seaman in the Royal Navy then entered essential work in the Durham coalfield at Chilton colliery. On retiring from the game due to a knee injury, Wayman was employed by Scottish & Newcastle Breweries, residing in his native area of Bishop Auckland, at Coundon. His brother Frank appeared for Chester while his son Paul had a period on Darlington's books.

Appearances & Goals:
Debut v Barnsley (h) 5 January 1946 (FAC)
(v Huddersfield Town (h) 20 September 1941 (FLN))
FL: 47 app 32 gls
FAC: 6 app 4 gls
War: 71 app 35 gls
Total: 124 app 71 gls

Honours:
FL div 2 champs 1951/FL div 2 prom 1948 (6 app)/FAC final 1954.

WEAVER Samuel 1929-1936

Left-half
5'9"
b. Pilsley, Derbyshire, 8 February 1909
d. Basford, Derbyshire, 15 April 1985
Career: Pilsley Red Rose/Sutton Junction trial/Sutton Town amat 1924, prof Feb 1926/Hull City March 1928 £50/UNITED Nov 1929 £2,500/Chelsea Aug 1936 £4,166 (Southampton war-guest 1939-40)(Fulham war-guest 1939-44)(Notts Co war-guest 1942-43)(Derby Co war-guest 1942-43)(Clapton Orient war-guest 1943-44)(West Ham Utd war-guest 1943-44)(Leeds Utd war-guest 1944-45)(Mansfield Town war-guest 1945-46)(Wrexham war-guest 1945-46)/Stockport Co Dec 1945/Retired cs 1947/Leeds Utd ass-trainer July 1947/Millwall trainer June 1949/Oxo Sports Club (Bromley) Jan 1954/Mansfield Town trainer Sept 1955, becoming manager June 1958 to Jan 1960 when he reverted to asst-trainer to May 1967, being caretaker-manager Nov to Dec 1971, then scout to Oct 1980 (Somerset County cricketer (1939) and Derbyshire County cricketer (1934), becoming masseur in 1956 to 1972).

Sam Weaver was a polished and powerful wing-half who became a household name during the Thirties. Although remembered in football's history as a player who mastered a prodigious long-throw, considered the longest in the game at the time, Weaver's ability was much more than producing a touch-line fling. He was a formidable midfielder who established himself as an England player as Newcastle lifted the FA Cup at Wembley in 1932. Developed at Hull by ex-Magpie Bill McCracken, he made the move to Tyneside in 1929. Sam netted on his debut at Highbury for United, then also on his first home appearance and immediately made an impact. He possessed a marvellous engine coupled with stamina and a driving power that ran the Magpies' midfield for seven seasons. And when his flowing black head of hair reached the penalty area it always meant problems for the opposition. Captain of the club on many occasions, Weaver tumbled with United into the Second Division during 1933-34, but remained loyal to the Magpies in a bid to regain their top flight status. But after two seasons of failure, Weaver's undoubted talent was stagnating and no-one was surprised when he moved back into the First Division following a big move to Stamford Bridge. At Chelsea he again became a popular character, totalling 128 games for the Blues, also skippering the Londoners before the Second World War halted his career. Weaver though remained connected with the game for many years thereafter. Associated with his local club, Mansfield Town for over 25 years, he was a noted football personality right up to his death. Sam was also a fine cricketer, although due to his football commitments, only managed two first-class games in the County Championship as a lower order batsman and left-arm bowler. When he died in 1985, Sam Weaver's ashes were scattered over the Field Mill pitch at Mansfield.

Appearances & Goals:
Debut v Arsenal (a) 30 November 1929 (1 goal)
FL: 204 app 41 gls
FAC: 25 app 2 gls
Others: 1 app 0 gls
Total: 230 app 43 gls

Honours:
3 Eng caps 1932-33/Eng trial app 1932-34/FA app 1934/2 FL app 1933-34/FAC winner 1932.

W

WESTWOOD Raymond William 1939

Inside-left
5'7"
b. Kingswinford, near Brierley Hill, 14 April 1912
d. Brierley Hill, January 1982

Career: Stourbridge/Brierley Hill Alliance/Aston Villa trial 1928/Bolton Wand amat May 1928, prof March 1930 (UNITED war-guest 1939-40)/Chester Dec 1947 £2,400/Darwen 1949.

Like his Bolton colleague Don Howe, inside-forward Ray Westwood also had a noted single appearance for the Tynesiders during wartime football. When stationed at Alnmouth he came into the side against York City and the England international crashed home a marvellous hat-trick as United won 9-2. Selected for the Football League too, Westwood was a swift mover and was remembered for his direct runs at goal. A delicate and skilled player, but very effective at the same time, he was always willing to work and could frequently bag goals. A wonderful servant to Bolton, Ray netted over 150 for the Wanderers in 358 matches, and on many occasions was a match-winner. Nephew to David Stokes, also a celebrated player for Bolton, Ray served in the army at Dunkirk and in Egypt, one of several of the squad that enlisted almost en-masse during 1939. Later he ran a fishmongers then a newsagency in his home town in Staffordshire.

Appearances & Goals:
Debut v York City (h) 28 October 1939 (FLNE) (3 goals)
War: 1 app 3 gls
Total: 1 app 3 gls

Honours:
6 Eng caps 1935-37/1 unoff Eng app 1935/Eng trial app 1934-37/6 FL app 1935-38/FL div 2 prom 1935.

WHARTON Kenneth 1978-1989, 1999-2010

Left-back, Midfield & Asst-coach
5'8"
b. Blakelaw, Newcastle upon Tyne,
28 November 1960

Career: St Mary's BC/Duke of Northumberland/Dodds' Arms/Hull City trial/Grainger Park BC/UNITED jnr Jan 1978, prof Jan 1979/Retired due to injury May 1989/Middlesbrough trial July 1989/Carlisle Utd Aug 1989/ Bradford City trial Aug 1989/West Bromwich Albion trial Oct 1989/Berwick Rangers Oct 1989/Whitley Bay Dec 1989/Winnipeg Fury (Can) April 1990, later becoming player-manager/Gateshead Jan 1992/Whitley Bay Dec 1992/St Johnstone coach Dec 1992 to Nov 1993/Middlesbrough asst-coach June 1994/UNITED asst-coach June 1999,

becoming asst-Academy Director, then Academy Director May 2002, reverting to asst-coach June 2003 to May 2010/Winnipeg Fury (Can) coach Aug 2010/Halifax City (Can) Director of Coaching Oct 2010/Also appeared in local Tyneside Sunday football, for Blakelaw SC.

A former captain of Newcastle schoolboys, Kenny Wharton was nicknamed 'Bones' due to his slight frame. Although he was not a physically imposing footballer, Kenny was a furious competitor, never shirking a challenge against a much bigger opponent. Wharton also possessed talent on the ball, able to operate in the left-back position as well as in midfield, roles in which he played in equal parts for United. With skill to deliver accurate passes and ability to find the net, Wharton proved a valuable player for the club over the 11 seasons he was a member of the first-team squad, surviving six changes in manager during that period. A regular from season 1980-81, he filled both defensive and midfield positions as Newcastle won promotion in 1983-84, while Kenny had his best season under the guidance of Jack Charlton the following year. Wharton is etched into United folklore when against Luton during April 1988 with United cruising to a 4-0 victory, he famously sat on the ball during play as United started to showboat, now captured by YouTube for all to see. A cartilage injury ended his career in the first-class game and Kenny was granted a testimonial in 1989 when a crowd of 20,899 turned up at Gallowgate. Afterwards he assisted several clubs in a bid to get back into football before settling in a role at Ayresome Park coaching juniors.

Kenny returned to the Black'n'Whites during 1999 and spent another decade on the coaching staff, predominantly with the youngsters. He then moved to North America to manage and coach the Halifax club in Nova Scotia. His son, Paul, an England youth player was with Leeds United and Hull City, while he is married to the grand-daughter of United pioneer, Tommy Ghee (qv).

Appearances & Goals:
Debut v West Ham United (a) 24 March 1979 (sub)
FL: 268(22) app 26 gls
FAC: 22 app 0 gls
FLC: 13(2) app 1 gl
Others: 6 app 0 gls
Total: 309(24) app 27 gls

Honours:
FL div 2 prom 1984.

WHITE Alexander Henry 1884-1892

Centre-half, Secretary & Director
5'10"
b. Glamis, Forfarshire, 1860
d. Newcastle upon Tyne, 18 May 1940

Career: Newcastle Rangers cOct 1880 (Chester College when temporarily away 1883-84)/EAST END Dec 1884, retired cs 1889, to return as a player occasionally to June 1891, returning again Feb 1892, finally retiring cs 1892/Was also East End Secretary June 1889 to Dec 1889, East End Committee c1888, Director Feb 1890 to cs 1891 (The Corinthians Dec 1887, Newcastle West End guest 1987-88)/Northumberland FA in various capacities, becoming Treasurer 1913 to May 1938, and an Honorary Life Member as well as FA Council Member.

Alec White (left) presented with a plaque by the Northumberland FA

The most prominent individual during the early pioneering years of Newcastle United was Scot, Alexander Henry White. A school-teacher who hailed from the district around Airlie and the historic village of Glamis near Dundee, White settled in the Heaton area of Tyneside. He started playing the fledgling game of football with Newcastle Rangers as they switched base from Gateshead to Newcastle and soon became the strongest club on Tyneside, twice winning the Northumberland & Durham Challenge Cup in its earliest years of 1881 and 1882. Although the footballers present are not recorded, White was probably on the field when they played the first game of football at St James' Park, a practice match during October 1880. When Rangers folded in 1884, Alec, by then a Northumberland County player, joined East End and was to become their leading figure. A frequent selection for the County eleven and Newcastle & District side, White operated in various roles, at the back or as a tough and clever midfielder from the old-style centre-half position, once described by one journalist of the day as showing "effective rushes" in attack. White was soon appointed captain and reached national recognition by being selected as reserve for the 1886 North versus South match, an unofficial international trial contest, while he also the following year appeared for the celebrated Corinthians eleven, both tremendous accolades considering that football on Tyneside was still very much in its infancy. Always able to score goals, once playing at centre-forward he scored seven in a 19-0 romp over Point Pleasant during 1888 in the club's highest ever victory, White did much to develop the East Enders into Newcastle's foremost club. By the time they had switched to St James' Park the Scot had guided them in two Northumberland Challenge Cup victories (1885 and 1889) as well as the prestigious Northumberland (East End) versus Durham (Sunderland Albion) inter-county title during 1889, and seen off rivals West End. That highly successful 1888-89 season when they also won the Tyne Charity Shield, was to be Alec's last as a regular. By then aged almost 30 and concentrating more on his profession as a teacher, he retired firstly in that summer, but then returned to the field, to bow out once more in 1892 shortly before East End were to change their name to Newcastle United. White clocked up over 100 appearances for the club in all matches and received a marvellous send-off at the time, portrayed as being "the life and soul of the club". Alec was afterwards often to be seen at St James' Park over the following decades and was associated with the Northumberland FA as an administrator and distinguished local character for over 50 years. He was also awarded the FA's Long Service medal. White was one of the original shareholders in the East End (and Newcastle United) company when equity was launched in 1890, a signatory to the first Articles of Association, and was also elected as one of the club's first directors. He also acted for a short time as East End Secretary. White additionally played cricket in his younger days, for White Rose and East End, acting as Secretary of both clubs for periods. His son Alex H White (junior) died in a Luftwaffe air-raid on Newcastle a year after his father's death.

Appearances & Goals:
Debut v South Bank (a) 15 October 1887 (FACQ)
NL: 8 app 3 gls
FAC: 3 app 1 gl
Total: 11 app 4 gls
(Void NL: 1 app 1 gl)

WHITE Jonathan 1896-1898

Right-back
5'10"
b. Galston, near Kilmarnock, 1870

Career: St Mirren 1892-93/Bury cs 1894/
Galston Dec 1894/Clyde June 1895/UNITED May
1896 to cs 1898/Dundee March 1899/
Leicester Fosse Sept 1899 to 1900.

*A strong and sturdy full-back, Jonathan White had
the experience of helping Bury to the Second Division
title before finding his way to Gallowgate following
a good season with Clyde in 1895-96. He turned out
on both flanks for United during his two seasons of service and once more assisted
in promotion success. Following Newcastle's elevation into the First Division, White
moved back to Scotland appearing in Dundee's first game at Dens Park during August
1899. He later had a brief excursion with Leicester Fosse, without making their Football
League side.*

Appearances & Goals:
Debut v Small Heath (a) 5 September 1896
FL: 48 app 1 gl
FAC: 5 app 0 gls
Total: 53 app 1 gl

Honours:
FL div 2 champs 1895/FL div 2 prom 1898.

WHITE Leonard Roy 1953-1962

Centre-forward
5'7"
b. Skellow, near Doncaster, 23 March 1930
d. Huddersfield, 17 June 1994

Career: Upton Colliery/Rotherham Utd amat 1947,
prof May 1948/UNITED Feb 1953 £12,500/
Huddersfield Town Feb 1962 exch for J Kerray plus
£10,000/Stockport Co Jan 1965 £4,000/Altrincham
cs 1966/Sligo Rovers/Ossett Town/Brown Tractors/
Elland Utd/Huddersfield YMCA and other local
Yorkshire non-league sides/Bradford City
asst-coach briefly.

*Initially purchased by United as cover for Tommy
Walker on the right wing, during the first few
seasons of his career at St James' Park, Len White operated as a versatile forward,
playing across the front line. While he had a few games in the Number 9 shirt up to
season 1957-58, it was the departure of Jackie Milburn and Vic Keeble that led to a
permanent switch for White into the leader's role. And what a success the stocky
Yorkshireman made of the opportunity. In his first season Len netted 25 goals, then
hit the target on a regular basis thereafter, scoring 25, 29, and 29 times in the next
three campaigns. Once grabbing four goals in a single game for United (and five in a
friendly) as well as once netting nine goals in a seven match sequence, he possessed
terrific strength on the ball, weaving in and out of challenges at speed and able to
finish with a power-packed shot. White loved to attack defences on his own and sent
the Gallowgate crowd roaring with many a spectacular goal. No-one on Tyneside
doubted his quality, and there was much resentment when Len was continually
overlooked for the England side, especially after he had shown top form in his
country's shirt at Football League level, striking an eight minute hat-trick against the
Irish during November 1958. A former plate-layer at Bullcroft and Burradon pits,
White's Newcastle career was halted as the Magpies battled for points in their
relegation season of 1960-61. In a clash with Dave Mackay of Spurs, Len was carried
from the field following a nasty and foul tackle from behind and was left on the
sidelines with ankle ligament trouble for almost six months. By the time he returned
to the fray United were in Division Two and former team-mate Joe Harvey was
installed on a rebuilding programme. Now with a weakened ankle, White was not part
of his plans and he moved to firstly, Huddersfield (110 app 39 goals), then Stockport*

*(58 app 25 goals), where he enjoyed a fruitful swansong to his career, totalling 232
first-class goals by the time he left senior football. In fact, White didn't stop playing
the game he loved until well into his fifties, appearing for several pub and works'
teams in the West Yorkshire area. Len resided in Huddersfield and was employed in
manufacturing to his death. Several brothers of his large family also played soccer to
a good level; Fred, Albert and John all appearing in the Football League. With only the
legendary Alan Shearer and Jackie Milburn scoring more league and cup goals than
Len in United's past, White can be recognised in Newcastle's history as the finest
forward not to gain a full England cap. He was worshipped during the late 1950's
almost as much as Wor Jackie had been in the years before, and then Shearer
afterwards.*

Appearances & Goals:
Debut v Liverpool (h) 21 February 1953
FL: 244 app 142 gls
FAC: 22 gls 11 gls
FLC: 3 app 0 gls
Others: 1 app 0 gls
Total: 270 app 153 gls

Honours:
2 FL app 1959-60/2 FA app 1953/FL div 3(N) champs 1951/FAC winner 1955.

WHITEHEAD Robert 1954-1962

Right-back
5'9"
b. Ashington, 22 September 1936

Career: Fatfield/UNITED jnr 1954, prof Dec 1954
(Cambridge City loan 1961-62)/
Darlington Aug 1962 £600 to c1964.

*Bob Whitehead spent eight seasons on United's
staff after signing for the club as a youngster. He
was though, only considered for selection in
Football League action for three of those years,
making his debut during 1957-58. With rival Bill
McKinney called up by the army on National
Service, he stepped in for Dick Keith in the right-
back role on 19 occasions during the next two
seasons. Bob was a capable and sound reserve, but
had little chance of permanently dislodging the
Northern Ireland international. After a period in non-league football with Cambridge
City, he returned north to serve Darlington in 59 matches. After leaving the game,
Whitehead settled in Stakeford, employed with an electronics manufacturer in
Bedlington.*

Appearances & Goals:
Debut v Burnley (a) 28 September 1957
FL: 20 app 0 gls
Total: 20 app 0 gls

WHITEHURST William 1985-1986

Centre-forward
6'1"
b. Thurnscoe, near Barnsley, 10 June 1959

Career: Hickleton Mains/Retford Town/
Bridlington Trinity/Mexborough Town
Ath/Hull City Oct 1980 £1,800/UNITED
Dec 1985 £232,500/Oxford Utd Oct 1986
£187,500/Reading Feb 1988 £120,000/
Sunderland Sept 1988 £100,000/Hull City
Dec 1988 £150,000/Sheffield Utd Feb
1990 £35,000 (Stoke City loan 1990-91)/
Doncaster Rovers Feb 1991 free (Crewe
Alex loan 1991-92)/Stafford Rangers
1992/St George Saints 1992/Hatfield
Main 1992/Kettering Town 1992/Goole
Town Nov 1992/Mossley 1992-93/St George-Budapest (Aus) 1992/South China
AA (HK) 1992-93/Voicelink (HK) 1993/Glentoran Jan 1993/Frickley Ath July 1993,
becoming manager Nov 1994 to May 1995/Preston Makedonia (Aus) c1996/
Also appeared for Stalybridge Celtic & minor Yorkshire clubs.

W

A whole-hearted striker with a powerful physique at 6'1" and over 14 stones, Billy Whitehurst caught the eye of manager Willie McFaul when United's boss was hunting for a new centre-forward to replace George Reilly. In his first spell with Hull City, he twice won promotion and Whitehurst scored 69 goals in 271 games for the Tigers. The ex-bricklayer was given a chance in First Division football at St James' Park as Christmas approached during 1985. Although not the most subtle or mobile striker the club has fielded, Billy stuck to his task in a short period wearing the black-and-white shirt. But scoring seven goals in 21 appearances during season 1985-86 wasn't deemed good enough for Division One action while during his latter days on Tyneside he fell foul of critical sections of the Geordie crowd, ending up giving them a V-sign against Bradford City as he was subbed. Whitehurst was on his way after that and he was replaced by Paul Goddard for the next campaign. Playing the game hard, Whitehurst then moved around the circuit, helping Oxford during their historic period in the top flight. Whitehurst continued his lengthy career with many clubs and tried management in the Unibond League as boss of Frickley Athletic. Since leaving the game Billy has sampled various occupations from training greyhounds, running pubs, working back in the building trade as well as at BP Saltend refinery and Drax Power Station. The Yorkshireman was also found guilty of benefit fraud while by the end of 2009 he was employed by a construction training organisation in Castleford. Recently Whitehurst has been residing in Hull.

Appearances & Goals:
Debut v Luton Town (a) 7 December 1985
FL: 28 app 7 gls
FAC: 1 app 0 gls
FLC: 1(1) app 0 gls
Total: 30(1) app 7 gls

Honours:
FL div 2 prom 1990/FL div 3 prom 1985/FL div 4 prom 1983/FLT winner 1984.

WHITSON Thomas Thompson 1905-1919

Left-back
5'8"
b. Cape Town (South Africa), 1885
d. Walker, Newcastle upon Tyne, 10 January 1945

Career: Walker Ath/Walker Parish/UNITED Feb 1905 £65 (Durham City war-guest 1919)/ Carlisle Utd player-trainer Oct 1919 free to 1924.

Nicknamed 'Tony' and born in South Africa when his Geordie parents were working in Cape Town, Whitson was a lightweight defender, something of a rarity on United's books during the glory years up to World War One. But he was tough and durable and, once he had claimed a place for the 1908-09 title winning season when he was voted best left-back in the country, became difficult to dislodge from the full-back position until Frank Hudspeth entered the fray. Bill McCracken described Tony as "reliable in everything he did", Whitson had accurate distribution from defence and as a consequence fitted into United's classical passing style with ease. He was remembered for a well timed sliding tackle, a feature of his play, whilst at his peak during 1910 and 1911, Tony reached the fringe of the international set-up. He unluckily missed the 1910 FA Cup final replay due to injury, although he appeared in six of the earlier games and the initial clash with Barnsley at the Crystal Palace. As war approached in 1914, Whitson had the distinction of winning the first army training session at St James' Park; a rifle range competition set-up on the pitch! During a period at Carlisle, he coached and skippered the Cumbrians to a North Eastern League title win in 1922. During the inter-war years, Tony resided in Walker, employed as an engineer at the Swan Hunter and Parson works on the Tyne. On his debut for United, he unluckily broke his wrist.

Appearances & Goals:
Debut v Notts County (a) 14 April 1906
FL: 124 app 0 gls
FAC: 21 app 0 gls
Others: 1 app 0 gls
Total: 146 app 0 gls

Honours:
Eng trial app 1911/1 FL app 1909/FL champs 1909/FAC final 1910 (first game), 1911.

WHITTLE Ernest 1944-1946

Inside-left
5'6"
b. Lanchester, 25 November 1925
d. Lincoln, 8 May 1998

Career: Quaking Houses Jnrs/UNITED amat May 1944, prof Nov 1944 £10 to 1946/Seaham CW cs 1947/West Stanley/Lincoln City Jan 1950 £300/ Workington March 1954 £3,200/Chesterfield Nov 1956 £1,000/Bradford Park Avenue Aug 1957/ Scarborough June 1958 free/Ruston Bucyrus (Lincoln) cs 1961/Lincoln Claytons March 1966/ Lincoln City asst-coach June 1966.

After leaving St James' Park when peacetime football resumed after the Second World War, Ernie Whittle developed into a snappy midfielder of some note in the lower divisions. Claiming 151 games (64 goals) for Lincoln, and 115 matches (46 goals) at Workington, he won a Third Division North title medal when at Sincil Bank during 1952 when he netted 19 goals. With a stocky, compact frame, he was a talented sharp-shooter who possessed a terrific shot in either foot. As a teenager during World War Two, Whittle worked down the Durham coalfield at Billy Pit near West Stanley and was given a chance with the Magpies during 1944. However, he received little opportunity when at Gallowgate, stepping in once for Charlie Wayman during February 1945 against Hartlepools. Later residing in Lincolnshire, Whittle's son and grandson were both on Lincoln's books. After his football career, Ernie for a period worked at the local liberal club in the cathedral city.

Appearances & Goals:
Debut v Hartlepools United (h) 10 February 1945 (FLN)
War: 1 app 0 gls
Total: 1 app 0 gls

Honours:
FL div 3(N) champs 1952.

WHITTON David 1892-1893

Goalkeeper
b. Scotland, c1868

Career: Dundee Wand 1889/Newcastle West End Aug 1889/EAST END May 1892 £10/Shankhouse Black Watch cs 1893/Blyth Sept 1895.

Small in stature for a goalkeeper, Dave Whitton was the club's first guardian following the change in venue from Heaton to St James' Park during the summer of 1892. An established goalkeeper on Tyneside during the Victorian pioneering days of the game, Whitton was described by the local press as a "bundle of energy". He appeared for the club during the 1892-93 Northern League programme just prior to the club's entry into the Football League, while he also took part in the first game on the Leazes' turf, against Celtic. By the time Newcastle were voted into the Second Division, Dave had departed for local rivals, Shankhouse. Whitton additionally took part in Newcastle West End's first Northern League contest in 1889 and their initial FA Cup Proper fixture against Grimsby Town during 1890.

Appearances & Goals:
Debut v Sheffield United (a) 24 September 1892 (NL)
NL: 10 app 0 gls
FAC: 1 app 0 gls
Total: 11 app 0 gls

WILKINSON Jack 1930-1932

Outside-left
5'7"
b. Wath upon Dearne, Yorkshire, 13 June 1908
d. Mexborough, April 1979

Career: Dearne Valley Old Boys/Wath Ath Feb 1925/Sheffield Wed Oct 1925 £450/UNITED May 1930 £3,000/Lincoln City Sept 1932 £600/ Sunderland Jan 1935/Hull City Oct 1936/ Scunthorpe & Lindsey Utd Aug 1937/Burton Town Aug 1939/Ransome & Marles manager Dec 1947.

Fast, small and only nine stones in weight, Jack Wilkinson was a noted schoolboy player in Yorkshire, a trialist for his country at that level. He netted 100 goals from the wing in non-league football with a celebrated Wath combination (alongside another Sheffield Wednesday and United player Tony Leach), form which alerted the attention of Yorkshire clubs. Known as 'Ginger', he entered senior football with Wednesday as a teenager and scored on his debut during season 1925-26. In that year Jack inspired the Owls in a successful promotion run-in but, following a bright opening at a higher level, faded from the scene as the Owls lifted the title in successive years. After 79 games (17 goals), Newcastle stepped in and gave Wilkinson an opportunity to rival Tommy Lang for the outside-left position. He claimed the shirt during 1930-31 with crafty displays in Newcastle's forward line, then suffered a cartilage injury and lost his place to the Scot. Moving to Sincil Bank, Wilkinson assisted Lincoln (97 app) to the Midland League championship trophy. He later worked for the Ransome & Marles company in Newark, then ran his own business in Halifax and Thurnscoe. Jack then managed a grocer's shop in the village of Staniforth near Doncaster.

(Note: Newcastle United's Player Ledger notes Jack being 23 years of age when he joined the club. His previous recorded birth of 1902 in some places is not correct, and now established as June 1908.)

Appearances & Goals:
Debut v Sheffield Wednesday (a) 30 August 1930
FL: 30 app 7 gls
FAC: 2 app 0 gls
Total: 32 app 7 gls

Honours:
FL champs 1929 (6 app), 1930 (1 app)/FL div 2 champs 1926 (7 app).

WILKINSON Jonathan 1927-1929

Centre-forward
5'8"
b. Esh Winning, Co Durham, 18 July 1908
d. Gosforth, Newcastle upon Tyne, 19 September 1979

Career: Esh Winning/Kelloe CW/Sunderland trial 1924-25/Durham City cs 1925/Crook Town Feb 1927/UNITED May 1927 £250/Everton June 1929 £675/Blackpool March 1931/Charlton Ath Feb 1933 £550 (Portsmouth war-guest 1939-40) to 1945 when he retired.

Auburn-haired and from a large coal-mining family of seven children, local starlet Jonathan Wilkinson was hot property as a youngster in Durham football. He stood out as a noted goal-getter for Crook as they lifted the league and cup double during 1926-27 and embarked on both FA Cup and FA Amateur Cup runs. Nimble of foot, after a trial with Middlesbrough, he was quickly captured by Newcastle's scouts and entered action at St James' Park as an understudy to Hughie Gallacher. The ex-pit boy was given the nickname of 'Monty' and showed delightful touches in attack when he was given an opportunity, stepping in for Gallacher during his periods of international action, injury and suspension. In 1927-28 Wilkinson grabbed nine goals in 16 outings, and on occasion switched to inside-right, linking up with 'Wee Hughie' to good effect. He once netted a treasured hat-trick in 1928 against Aston Villa during one of the most captivating tussles seen at Gallowgate, a fixture which ended in United's favour by 7-5! Supporters considered Monty deserved a better deal at St James' Park, but he was sold to Everton where he amazingly found himself as reserve to the game's other legendary centre-forward of the time, Dixie Dean! With Charlton, Jonathan at last claimed a regular place and netted more than 50 goals in over 250 senior matches. He played an important part in the Londoner's rise from Division Three to runners-up spot in the First Division during 1936-37. Wilkinson served in Burma and India with the RAF for a period during World War Two, and played for the Tea Planters Club of Calcutta. He later resided in Lincoln for a while before returning to the North East. He became a cinema manager in Washington. Jonathan is related to long-serving goalkeeper Steve Harper (qv).

(Note: Although several sources record a middle name of Montague, hence the nickname of 'Monty', birth records and his family archive do not confirm this, although he was always referred to as Monty by relatives.)

Appearances & Goals:
Debut v Aston Villa (a) 29 October 1927
FL: 27 app 11 gls
Total: 27 app 11 gls

Honours:
FL div 2 champs 1931 (5 app)/FL div 3(S) champs 1935/FL div 2 prom 1936.

WILLIAMS Ronald 1933-1935

Centre-forward
5'8"
b. Llansamlet, near Swansea, 23 January 1907
d. Swansea, 30 March 1987

Career: National Oil Refinery (Skewen)/Bethel Jnrs/Llanelli 1927-28/Swansea Town May 1929/UNITED Nov 1933 £1,500/Chester April 1935 £800/Swansea Town May 1936/Lovell's Ath Aug 1938/Llanelli Jan 1939/Milford Utd Feb 1939/Aberamen Ath Aug 1939/Bristol City 1942-43/Haverfordwest Ath Nov 1946.

Ron Williams was purchased by Newcastle in a bid to get United out of First Division relegation trouble after FA Cup hero Jack Allen had lost pace and form during season 1933-34. Williams also played on the wing at the Vetch Field and proved to be a dashing leader with a robust style in Division Two. He was difficult to knock off the ball and arrived on Tyneside after hitting plenty of goals in South Wales, including a hat-trick on his debut on Christmas Day 1929. Ronnie was one of the earliest Welshman to pull on a Newcastle shirt and he started off like a man inspired, striking 10 goals in 10 games. But then the Magpies became bogged down in a tense relegation struggle and the goals dried up. Capped by Wales when at St James' Park, Williams in fact had appeared for the club's 'A' team against local works' outfit Reyrolles, before travelling to play for his country against England a few days later. He departed from the North East soon after the club's First Division status was lost, later returning to the Swans where he totalled 196 games and 58 goals. Also a fine cricketer, Ronnie appeared for the Swansea club, while during the Second World War, he served as a policeman. Williams resided in Glamorgan, employed by Swansea Council housing department. Ronnie was also a bowls player of some note in later life, being capped by Wales in 1976.

Appearances & Goals:
Debut v Aston Villa (a) 25 November 1933 (1 goal)
FL: 35 app 14 gls
FAC: 1 app 0 gls
Total: 36 app 14 gls

Honours:
2 Wales caps 1935/3 WsL app 1930-33/WsC winner 1932.

WILLIAMSON Michael James 2010-date

Centre-half
6'4"
b. Stoke on Trent, 8 November 1983

Career: Torquay Utd jnr 1999/Southampton Nov 2001 £100,000 (Torquay Utd loan 2003-04) (Doncaster Rovers loan 2003-04)/Wycombe Wand loan July 2004, pmt May 2005/Watford Jan 2009 £150,000/Portsmouth Sept 2009 £2m/UNITED Jan 2010 £1m.

Having wasted almost six months at financially troubled Fratton Park with Portsmouth, when he wasn't given a game, Mike Williamson was delighted to move north as Newcastle made a bid for his defensive qualities during the January 2010 transfer window. At 6'4", the Stoke-born centre-back was ideally built for the position and impressed as United cruised to the Football League title in 2009-10. Some critics considered he was not quite good enough to handle Premier League strikers, but Williamson proved at times he could cope with the best, having a strong 2013-14 campaign, arguably player of the season. He became an important defender, challenging Steven Taylor for the second centre-half spot in United's line-up as a partner to Fabricio Coloccini. Making a name for himself with Wycombe in 167 games, then during a brief stay with Watford, his £2m transfer to Premier League Portsmouth looked to be a springboard to his career. But Pompey went into free-fall and Williamson found himself a victim of a crisis club unable to afford further instalments on the transfer fee if he played senior football.

Appearances & Goals:
Debut v Crystal Palace (h) 27 January 2010
FL/PL: 116(3) app 0 gls
FAC: 4 app 0 gls
FLC: 5(1) app 0 gls
Euro: 7 app 0 gls
Total: 132(4) app 0 gls

Honours:
FL ch winner 2010/FL div 2 prom 2009/
FL div 3 prom 2004.

W

WILLIS David Lalty 1907-1913

Right or Left-half
5'7"
b. Byker, Newcastle upon Tyne, July 1881
d. New Southgate, London, 26 May 1949

Career: Jarrow Ath/Gateshead NER/
Sunderland Oct 1901/Reading May 1903/
Sunderland May 1904/UNITED May 1907
£100/Reading May 1913 to 1915/Palmers
(Jarrow) player-manager 1919/Raith Rovers
trainer June 1921/Nottingham Forest
trainer July 1925/Derby Co trainer June
1933 to June 1947 (Derbyshire County
cricket masseur May 1949 to death in
May 1949).

*One of only a handful of players to have
joined United from Sunderland where he
made 52 appearances, Dave Willis returned
to his native Tyneside as a utility half-back, able to operate in any midfield role. With
plenty of talent at St James' Park already, Willis still managed to claim conspicuous
success, gaining regular selection in seasons 1907-08, 1908-09, when the title was
secured, and also 1911-12. He also came into United's FA Cup final side on an injury
to Peter McWilliam during 1911 while Dave was reserve for the 1908 final, unlucky
not to claim a starting position. Cool-headed with a broad Tyneside accent, Dave gave
plenty of effort on the field for six seasons. On retiring from the game after the First
World War, he began a coaching career in football. At Raith, the Byker-born Geordie
notably was associated with the early development of the great Alex James, the
famous Scot marrying his daughter, and once installed at the Baseball Ground he
trained the Rams to a Wembley FA Cup victory over Charlton in 1946. Additionally,
when based in the Midlands and living at Littleover, Willis was masseur to the Indian
cricket side when they visited Trent Bridge and he died shortly after a match at The
Oval in London. He passed away at the home of his son-in-law, Alex James in Finchley.
His son, Robert Willis, assisted Blyth Spartans before joining Dundee then later
Rochdale and Halifax Town.*

*(Note: Probate records show his death as 27 May 1949, a day after the generally
published date.)*

Appearances & Goals:
Debut v Nottingham Forest (h) 28 September 1907
FL: 95 app 3 gls
FAC: 12 app 1 gl
Others: 1 app 0 gls
Total: 108 app 4 gls

Honours:
FL champs 1909/FAC final 1911.

WILLIS Robert 1893-1895

Inside-right
5'10"
b. Cramlington, Northumberland, 1871

Career: Shankhouse Black Watch/Newcastle West End March 1892/Blyth cs 1892/
UNITED amat Dec 1893/Shankhouse Black Watch late 1895/
Shankhouse Sept 1896/(Ashington Nov 1899).

*The Newcastle Daily Chronicle described Bobby Willis as a "well known forward" when
he joined United's staff for the Christmas programme of 1893. A noted amateur player,
he had already appeared for the Northumberland County side and as the local press
recorded, "proved a great acquisition" for the side. Coming into United's forward line
during the Tyneside club's first Football League season, Willis struck a goal on his
debut and in a derby encounter with Middlesbrough Ironopolis over the New Year
celebrations, scored twice as United hammered the Tees' club 7-2. Bobby did well the
following season too, hitting 13 goals in only 20 games, then left the club to return
to non-league football.*

Appearances & Goals:
Debut v Small Heath (a) 16 December 1893 (1 goal)
FL: 34 app 18 gls
FAC: 2 app 0 gls
Total: 36 app 18 gls

WILLITTS Joseph 1940-1943

Right-back
5'7"
b. Shotton, Co Durham, 12 July 1924
d. Co Durham, 1980 (Q3)

Career: Shotton CW/UNITED amat Dec 1940,
prof Nov 1941/Hartlepools Utd Aug 1943/
Horden CW cs 1956.

*An apprentice electrician at Shotton colliery, Joe
Willitts came into United's side for Joe Richardson in
defence for a journey to face Sheffield Wednesday
during December 1941. A regular in the Northern
Combination side that season, he wasn't promoted
to the Magpies' first-eleven again. Like several of
United's wartime players, he moved to the Victoria Ground in search of senior action
and totalled over 250 games for Hartlepool. He was described as "a model of
consistency" for the Poolies, Joe being also recognised as a penalty king, once netting
three times from the spot in a derby match against Darlington on Good Friday 1951.
He later worked as a social club steward and driver in County Durham.*

Appearances & Goals:
Debut v Sheffield Wednesday (a) 20 December 1941 (FLN)
War: 1 app 0 gls
Total: 1 app 0 gls

WILLIS Thomas 1903-1906

Left-back
5'9"
b. Newton, Ayr, 15 October 1877
d. Johannesburg (South Africa),
24 February 1912

Career: Ayr/UNITED Nov 1903/Ayr, briefly/ Crystal
Palace May 1906 £50/Carlisle Utd March 1907 to
c1910/Rangers (Johannesburg, SA) player-coach to
death.

*After showing up well in Scottish football, several
clubs were interested in the defensive qualities of Tom Wills when he moved across
the border to sign for Newcastle. Replacing the experienced William Agnew at left-
back during the 1903-04 season, he wasn't an immediate success and the club's team
committee soon elevated local product Jack Carr to the position within a few months,
then signed international Andy McCombie. Wills though, did appear twice in United's
title winning season the following year, but moved to Crystal Palace soon after, joining
a band of players with North East connections south of the Thames. With Carlisle for
only a brief period before emigrating to South Africa, he played and coached the game
in Johannesburg. He worked with the Consolidated Langlaate Mining Company to his
death following a mining accident when only 34 years of age.*

Appearances & Goals:
Debut v Bury (h) 28 November 1903
FL: 18 app 0 gls
FAC: 1 app 0 gls
Total: 19 app 0 gls

Honours:
FL champs 1905 (2 app).

WILSON Carl Alan 1955-1960

Centre-forward
6'0"
b. Lanchester, Co Durham, 8 May 1940

Career: Crookhall CW Jnrs/Derwent Valley Jnrs/
Delves Lane Jnrs/UNITED jnr Oct 1955, prof Feb 1958/
Gateshead Jan 1960 £410/Doncaster Rovers July 1960/
Millwall July 1961/Sparta Rotterdam (Neth) July 1962/ Rot-
Weiss Essen (WG) cs 1963 to cs 1964.

*A strong, muscular centre-forward and the son of United's
Twenties centre-half Joe Wilson (qv). Carl Wilson was handed
a Football League baptism when 18 years old as a late
replacement for Len White. That match against Blackpool was
Wilson's only taste of senior football for United and the
robust leader was given a good report, The Journal noting "all*

credit went to Wilson for the fighting effort". Carl had an unlucky career as a youth at Gallowgate, breaking his wrist as well as his ankle and finding another opportunity difficult. Appearing for Gateshead (17 app) during their final days as a Football League club, Carl struggled to find consistent form at any of his English based clubs, although he managed five appearances for Millwall when they lifted the Fourth Division title silverware in season 1961-62. But when he moved to the Continent for two seasons he developed into a decent striker, once scoring a hat-trick for Sparta in a European Cup Winners' Cup tie during 1962. After his career, Wilson returned to the area of his birth, settling in Hurbuck near Lanchester. He became involved in a haulage business as well as having an involvement in a landholding.

Appearances & Goals:
Debut v Blackpool (a) 25 August 1958
FL: 1 app 0 gls
Total: 1 app 0 gls

Honours:
FL div 4 champs 1962 (5 app).

WILSON George Williamson 1907-1915

Outside-left
5'6"
b. Lochgelly, Fife, 1884
d. Vancouver (Canada), 2 June 1960
Career: Buckhaven Utd/Thomson Rovers/Lochgelly Rangers 1901/Lochgelly Utd/Cowdenbeath Aug 1902/Heart of Midlothian May 1903/Everton May 1906 £800 (Distillery (Belfast) loan 1907-08)/UNITED Nov 1907 £1,600/Raith Rovers Sept 1915 £250/East Fife 1920/Albion Rovers 1922/Raith Rovers manager June 1926 to Dec 1927/St Andrews (Vancouver, Can).

George Wilson was one of the country's biggest names when he signed for United for a new nationwide record fee of £1,600 in 1907. Known as 'Smiler', he was a dour Scot, cunning on the ball and making up for his lack of inches with extra pounds. Wilson made a name for himself at Tynecastle in Edinburgh playing 80 games (31 goals), winning Scotland caps before a joint move to Everton along with his brother, David, developed his career further. His stay at Goodison Park was a stormy one though, George never hitting it off with the Everton directors, and following vehement remarks concerning the team's style of play, he was dropped from their FA Cup final side after starring in six successful games leading up to the final. He was disciplined and loaned to appear for Distillery in Belfast. Newcastle stepped in and thereafter began a marvellous association with the Magpies. Noted by one commentator as a, "purest football gem", for eight seasons "Wee Geordie" served the club at outside and inside-left, and the chunky little Scot became a much admired personality at Gallowgate. Newcastle's attractive style of play suited his talent; he was tricky, fast and became an important figure in the Black'n'Whites terrific side that won the title in 1909 and reached three FA Cup finals. Towards the end of his career, younger wingers Goodwill and Booth pushed him hard for a place as the First World War approached and Wilson moved back to Fife. Serving in the navy during the Great War, George is one of only a few footballers to have won both a Scottish and English cup winners' medal. He netted Hearts' goal of the 1906 Scottish Cup final against Third Lanark, while he was also influential as United lifted the FA Cup for the first time in 1910. Wilson later emigrated to Canada where he died in 1960.

Appearances & Goals:
Debut v Liverpool (a) 14 December 1907 (2 goals)
FL: 176 app 25 gls
FAC: 41 app 8 gls
Others: 1 app 0 gls
Total: 218 app 33 gls

Honours:
6 Scot caps 1904-09/1 SL app 1906/Scot trial app 1905/1 IL app 1908/FL champs 1909/FAC winner 1910/FAC final 1908, 1911/SC winner 1906.

WILSON James 1959-1962

Outside-left
5'6"
b. Newmains, Lanarkshire, 20 April 1942
Career: Shotts Bon Accord/UNITED Sept 1959 £750/Morton July 1962 £1,500/Aberdeen May 1965 £10,000 (Washington Whips (USA) loan cs 1967)/Motherwell Dec 1967/Dundee June 1970 exch deal (Maritzburg (SA) loan May 1973)/Falkirk March 1975 free/Elgin City Feb 1976 to Feb 1977/Keith asst-manager, then manager 1983/Later, Cove Rangers manager June 1996.

When Jimmy Wilson was purchased from junior football north of the border, he was described by one journalist as a "bony braw Scotsman". A raw talent, Wilson came in on the right flank for Gordon Hughes during Newcastle's relegation battle in season 1960-61, but it was the following year that the Scot had his best spell for United. Now on the left-wing, he rivalled Liam Tuohy and for a few weeks claimed a place before the arrival of Jimmy Fell and emergence of teenager Alan Suddick put both Wilson and Tuohy in the shade and led to their joint departure. Jimmy returned to Scotland where he became a good club player for 17 seasons and totalled over 500 senior games. Wilson was especially prominent for Morton (123 app) and Dundee (124 app) where he took part in European football. Wilson helped Morton, Motherwell and Falkirk to the Scottish Second Division title, while he reached his country's inter-league line-up during season 1966-67. He also assisted Aberdeen (110 app 35 goals) again showing that he was a solid and effective forward. Wilson later settled in the Aberdeen area and ran a public-house for a period before managing a guest-house in the Granite city. He also became involved in hospitality at Pittodrie, an active member of the Aberdeen Former Players' Association.

Appearances & Goals:
Debut v Cardiff City (h) 1 October 1960
FL: 12 app 2 gls
FLC: 1 app 0 gls
Total: 13 app 2 gls

Honours:
1 SL app 1967/Scot jnr app/SLC final 1964/SL div 2 champs 1964, 1969, 1975.

WILSON James H 1911-1914

Goalkeeper
5'9"
b. Newcastle upon Tyne, 1890
d. Newcastle upon Tyne, 1964 (Q4)
Career: Newcastle Bentonians/UNITED amat June 1911, prof May 1912 £10/North Shields Ath June 1914 free.

The son of a distinguished Newcastle policeman, Chief Superintendant Robert Wilson from Jesmond, James Wilson impressed almost everyone that watched him play for amateur side Bentonians. Included were Newcastle officials and they signed the local goalkeeper as an understudy for Jimmy Lawrence and Syd Blake. Making his debut in a New Year's Day clash with Liverpool as 1913 opened, Wilson only rarely was given a chance due to Lawrence's consistency. He was between the posts when the club's record FA Cup defeat was recorded at St James' Park against Sheffield United during 1914, a 5-0 reverse. Joining North Shields in the summer of 1914, he was still registered with United after World War One, but did not return to senior football. For several years afterwards, Wilson was involved in local football on Tyneside.

Appearances & Goals:
Debut v Liverpool (h) 1 January 1913
FL: 3 app 0 gls
FAC: 1 app 0 gls
Total: 4 app 0 gls

WILSON John Thomas 1919-1920

Centre-forward
5'9"
b. Leadgate, Co Durham, 8 March 1897

Career: Leadgate St Ives/Leadgate Utd Dec 1918/
UNITED May 1919/Leadgate Park player-manager May
1920/Durham City Feb 1922 £50/Stockport Co May
1922/Manchester Utd Sept 1926 £500/Bristol City June
1932 to May 1933.

*Known as Jack and from the footballing heartland of the
County Durham coalfield, Wilson served as a bombardier
during the hostilities and began the new era of football
after World War One as a promising centre-forward,
given a chance for the opening games of the 1919-20
season. At the time United had a problem in finding an adequate replacement for
pre-war star Albert Shepherd and Wilson filled the role along with several others until
Neil Harris landed on Tyneside. The highlight of Jack Wilson's brief flurry with the
Magpies was a two goal strike against Arsenal at St James' Park during September
1919, but he was soon relegated to North Eastern League football. Jack was unlucky
with injuries during his period with the Black'n'Whites, twice breaking a leg. Aged 24,
his senior career appeared to be over when he moved back to Leadgate football, but
Wilson received another chance when he joined Durham City's line-up at a time when
they were in the Third Division North, their first taste of league soccer. Moving to
Stockport County (134 app), he eventually ended up at Old Trafford, captaining
Manchester United from the left-half position. By then Jack had developed into a
rugged half-back who served the Reds well during six seasons in which he totalled
140 games. On leaving the game, Wilson resided in Leadgate and for a period was
employed in the licensing trade around Tynemouth.*

Appearances & Goals:
Debut v Arsenal (a) 30 August 1919
(v Hartlepools United (a) 21 April 1919 (NVL))
FL: 7 app 2 gls
War: 2 app 1 gl
Total: 9 app 3 gls

WILSON Joseph Alexander 1933-1936

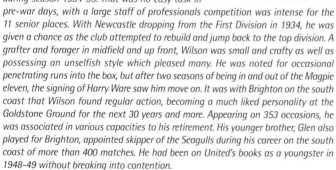

Inside-right
5'6"
b. Wylam, Northumberland, 23 March 1909
d. Brighton, 3 April 1984

Career: Spen Black & White/Winlaton Celtic/
Tanfield Lea Institute/UNITED amat May 1933, prof
Sept 1933/Brighton May 1936 £450 (Tottenham
Hotspur war-guest 1943-44)/Resumed with
Brighton, retired May 1947, becoming trainer,
asst-manager, chief-scout, caretaker-manager
Feb to April 1963, to May 1974 when he retired.

*Joe Wilson worked his way through United's junior
and reserve elevens to claim a first-team place
during season 1934-35. That was no easy task in
pre-war days, with a large staff of professionals competition was intense for the
11 senior places. With Newcastle dropping from the First Division in 1934, he was
given a chance as the club attempted to rebuild and jump back to the top division. A
grafter and forager in midfield and up front, Wilson was small and crafty as well as
possessing an unselfish style which pleased many. He was noted for occasional
penetrating runs into the box, but after two seasons of being in and out of the Magpie
eleven, the signing of Harry Ware saw him move on. It was with Brighton on the south
coast that Wilson found regular action, becoming a much liked personality at the
Goldstone Ground for the next 30 years and more. Appearing on 353 occasions, he
was associated in various capacities in his retirement. His younger brother, Glen also
played for Brighton, appointed skipper of the Seagulls during his career on the south
coast of more than 400 matches. He had been on United's books as a youngster in
1948-49 without breaking into contention.*

*(Note: Official birth and death registration information notes Joe's birth as 28 March,
however the family confirms this is an error and should be 23 March.)*

Appearances & Goals:
Debut v Hull City (h) 25 December 1934 (1 goal)
FL: 28 app 5 gls
FAC: 2 app 0 gls
Total: 30 app 5 gls

WILSON Joseph William 1927-1930

Centre-half
5'11"
b. West Butsfield, Co Durham, 29 September 1910
d. Shotley Bridge, Co Durham, 4 April 1996

Career: Crook Town/Annfield Plain/Stanley Utd/
UNITED Dec 1927 £50/Southend Utd Aug 1930
£500/Brentford July 1935/Reading Aug 1939
(York City war-guest 1941-45)/Barnsley July 1945
to April 1947/Blyth Spartans player-coach 1947,
becoming player-manager March 1948/
Consett trainer cs 1950.

*A formidable defender in his prime, Joe Wilson
played the game hard, and sometimes rough. A
County Durham schoolboy player during 1923-24,
he joined United's staff following a noted career in
local football where his father had appeared for Tow
Law Town. Joe was on the club's payroll for the first
time when United were reigning Football League Champions, it took Wilson a while
to make his senior debut, with firstly Charlie Spencer, then England skipper Jack Hill
ahead of him in selection for the defensive anchor role. Joe stepped in for a single
outing during season 1929-30, but then moved south to Southend soon after his only
appearance. Noted as "one of the finest pivots in Division Three", Wilson gave his all
in the slog of basement football. He clocked up 175 games for Southend, many as
captain, then 63 for Brentford, being a most popular character at Griffin Park during
their period in the top level, the Bees finishing in a high placing for three seasons in
a row from 1935-36 to 1937-38. Nicknamed 'Farmer Joe' by his colleagues, he was
once fined £1 at Chelmsford Police Court for poaching during his days living in Essex,
while Joe was also a somewhat radical Players' Union committee man in the years
leading up to World War Two. A PE instructor during the conflict, Wilson was stationed
in Yorkshire for much of the time where he assisted York City in over 100 games. After
retiring Wilson had a colourful life back in the North East, employed in various
occupations from insurance salesman, horse-trainer (at Alnwick), small-holding
farmer and Consett steel worker. The charming Joe resided in Crookhall near Consett
to his death, and had no fewer than 10 children, including seven boys of which six
played football and one son, Carl Wilson (qv) appeared for Newcastle United's senior
side too.*

Appearances & Goals:
Debut v Aston Villa (h) 7 December 1929
FL: 1 app 0 gls
Total: 1 app 0 gls

WILSON Terence 1992

Midfield
6'0"
b. Broxburn, West Lothian, 8 February 1969

Career: Whitburn BC/Nottingham Forest jnr
July 1985, prof April 1986 (UNITED loan Jan
1992)(Honefoss BK (Nor) loan 1992)/Retired
due to injury March 1994/Gresley Rovers/
Dunfermline Ath trial July 1996/Rushden &
Diamonds Aug 1996/Ilkeston Town Dec
1996/Later, Whitburn Jnrs July 1999/ Spartans
(Edinburgh) Nov 2000/Sunderland asst-
coach/Heart of Midlothian asst-coach/ Fulham
asst-coach/Atlanta (USA) coaching/ Total Soccer
Institute (USA) Director of Football 2006.

*Terry Wilson's short period at Gallowgate coincided with a historic moment in the
club's annals. Making his debut at Oxford on the first day of February 1992, his loan
period was perhaps manager Ossie Ardiles' last attempt to turn the tide of bad results.
Wilson, and his manager, did not have a happy 90 minutes at the Manor Ground,
United losing 5-2, a dire result which very soon marked the end for the Argentinean
and a dramatic entry of Kevin Keegan to St James' Park. Newcastle's new supremo
immediately wielded the axe and Wilson was relegated to the bench, a decision he
did not like and as a consequence Terry was quickly despatched back to Forest. Prior
to his trial at St James' Park, the Scot had been a bright youngster under Brian Clough
at the City Ground, capped at Under-21 level by his country. A regular when the Reds
finished in third spot in the title race during 1987-88 and 1988-89, he was continually
hampered by injury though, and after 145 games had to call a halt to his career*

following a bad knee complaint when only 25 years of age. Following a period in lower football, winning the Scottish Junior Cup, Wilson started on a coaching career earning a UEFA 'A' license and eventually set-up base in the USA, for several years running coaching schools in California, latterly in Santa Clara.

Appearances & Goals:
Debut v Oxford United (a) 1 February 1992
FL: 2 app 0 gls
Total: 2 app 0 gls

Honours:
4 Scot u21 app 1988-90/Scot sch-youth app/FLC winner 1989, 1990 (sub no app)/SJC winner 2000.

WILSON William 1925-1929

Goalkeeper
5'10"
b. Port Seaton, Edinburgh, 7 September 1900
d. Innerleithen, near Peebles, 24 June 1973

Career: Musselburgh Bruntonians 1922-23/Peebles Rovers Nov 1923/UNITED trial then pmt Sept 1925 £600/Millwall June 1929 £700 to cs 1934/Vale of Leithen/Duns Aug 1935/Dunfermline Ath Sept 1935/Peebles Rovers 1936/Penicuik Ath Aug 1937 (Dunfermline Ath war-guest).

Having played 60 games in Scottish senior football for borders club, Peebles Rovers, then in Scotland's Division Three, Willie Wilson joined Newcastle on a month's trial and had the opportunity to impress and earn a contract at St James' Park. United were on the verge of splashing out for Stockport's custodian Harry Hardy, but Wilson saved the club a hefty cheque of £3,500. With Bill Bradley's goalkeeper's position up for grabs, Wilson had a most remarkable start for the Magpies. On his debut against Blackburn, United fell on home soil by the amazing scoreline of 7-1. Nevertheless, Wilson was not blamed and he went onto gain a professional contract and develop into a safe 'keeper, a near perfect ever-present as the Magpies won the First Division title the following season. With plenty of confidence, the ex-miner was Newcastle's regular custodian for three campaigns, until Micky Burns and the arrival of Albert McInroy led to his departure to Millwall. At The Den he again performed well for a period, registering over 100 consecutive games for the Lions and all told 158 appearances throughout his five seasons. On leaving the game, Willie settled in the Borders, living in Innerleithen, working as a bolierhouse-man at one of the local mills.

Appearances & Goals:
Debut v Blackburn Rovers (h) 9 September 1925
FL: 127 app 0 gls
FAC: 7 app 0 gls
Total: 134 app 0 gls

Honours:
FL champs 1927/SJC winner 1923.

WILSON William 1898-1903

Right-back
5'9"
b. Durham, 1880
d. South Shields, 1921

Career: South Shields Adelaide May 1898/UNITED amat 1898, prof May 1900/Bradford City Aug 1903 £50/West Stanley Sept 1905/Allenby Park Jan 1907/West Stanley June 1907/South Shields Adelaide July 1908/West Stanley April 1913/North Shields Ath Dec 1913.

A miner in the County Durham coalfield, Billy Wilson joined United as an amateur teenager and lifted the Northern Alliance trophy with the club's 'A' side in 1898-99. He was later one of several players tried in a problem right-back role during the early campaigns of the twentieth century. Given a trial opening run-out in season 1902-03, the club's directors considered Billy Wilson "promising", but quickly put him back in the Northern League 'A' team. With the headline signing of Scottish international Andy McCombie, he didn't get another opportunity in the side and moved to join Bradford City. Taking part in the Bantams' first ever Football League match, against Grimsby during 1903, Wilson proceeded to appear on 63 occasions for City as they entered senior action in Division Two during 1903-04 and 1904-05.

Appearances & Goals:
Debut v Bury (a) 13 December 1902
FL: 4 app 0 gls
Total: 4 app 0 gls

WILSON William Arthur 1913-1922

Forward
5'9"
b. Newcastle upon Tyne, 17 March 1896
d. High Heaton, Newcastle upon Tyne, 12 March 1996

Career: UNITED jnr 1913, amat 1918 (Annfield Plain 1918), prof May 1919/Merthyr Town May 1922 free/West Stanley Aug 1923/Carlisle Utd Sept 1925/Retired Oct 1925.

Connected with Newcastle's early junior development programme for several years, Billy Wilson although not tall, was well-built and powerful, at 14 stone. An apprentice turner at the nearby Bulmer's Engineering site on Barrack Road when he joined United's Swifts, Billy was a play-anywhere forward, once noted during 1920 in the Newcastle Daily Chronicle, "as one of the finest youngsters on the club's books....and if given the chance could blossom out as England's winger". Unfortunately Wilson was rarely given an opportunity, appearing twice during the Victory League in 1919, and in a handful of friendly contests, including a tour to Spain and France during the close-season of 1921. A regular for the Magpies' reserve side from 1917 to 1922, Billy had severe competition for places as the immediate post-war years unfolded, both in attack and at half-back where he also figured. A celebrated sprinter too, he served in the Royal Navy as a Chief Petty Officer during the war. Moving to Wales to appear for Merthyr's Football League side, Wilson soon returned to Tyneside where he ran a furniture making business and then being employed as a turner at Vicker's and Parson's works. From a large family, his younger brother Arthur was also on United's books in 1926-27 without making the grade, but who had a fine career with Southampton and West Ham United. Billy is recognised as becoming the oldest United footballer on record, residing to a few days before his 100th birthday. He died in High Heaton during March 1996.

Appearances & Goals:
Debut v Scotswood (h) 15 March 1919 (NVL)
War: 2 app 0 gls
Total: 2 app 0 gls

WILSON WA 1889-1892

Full-back
b. probably Scotland

Career: Morton/[Renton]/Vale of Leven/ EAST END Aug 1889/Newcastle West End Sept 1889/ EAST END Aug 1890 to cs 1892.

A unyielding defender who had played the game to a high standard north of the border, Wilson settled on Tyneside for the start of inaugural Northern League competition during 1889-90, initially to appear in East End's blue shirts. But rivals West End poached his services and he ended up playing in the black-and-red quarters during the new season. The Scot though moved from St James' Park to join the Heaton outfit the following summer as the East Enders were winning the Tyneside rivalry. Wilson became an ever-present for East End in 1890-91 and was a dependable player for the club. At times the centre of attention and during December 1891 against Sheffield United colleague Bobby Creilly walked off the field in protest after a row with Wilson, who apparently, was showing no interest and giving little support to his team-mates. Wilson was suspended afterwards and left the club as they moved across the city during the summer of 1892.

Appearances & Goals:
Debut v Darlington (h) 13 September 1890 (NL)
NL: 29 app 0 gls
FAC: 6 app 0 gls
Total: 35 app 0 gls
(Void NL: 3 app 0 gls)

W

WILSON William Sykes 1960-1962

Right-half
5'8"
b. Walkerburn, near Peebles, 16 March 1943

Career: Walkerburn Jnrs/UNITED March 1960 to June 1962 free/Carlisle Utd trial/Gala Fairydean/ Vale of Leithen/Selkirk/Retired 1970.

A young Scot, Billy Wilson stood in for Duncan Neale in one of the club's earliest Football League Cup matches against Sheffield United at Gallowgate during 1961. Although the Magpies lost, Billy was described as being "competent and cool" and "fully justified his senior baptism".
However reporters also commented after his debut that the midfield position he filled was, "a tough teenage role, and Wilson will be best off as a Central League regular for most of this season". With Jimmy Scoular coming to the end of his Gallowgate career, the right-half spot was up for grabs. Wilson was in contention along with Neale, Wright and Franks, but the youngster lost out and by the end of the 1961-62 season was appearing in United's third-eleven. He didn't remain in Football League soccer and moved from St James' Park during the close-season of 1962 afterwards continuing to play the game in the East of Scotland league. At that level, Wilson stood out, winning titles with Gala and even facing the French 1966 World Cup side as they prepared for the tournament in the district. Billy gave up football when 27 years of age to move to a career with Prudential. Later he also ran a pub in Fife for a period, then his own business in the Borders, WSW Telecoms.

Appearances & Goals:
Debut v Sheffield United (h) 11 October 1961 (FLC)
FLC: 1 app 0 gls
Total: 1 app 0 gls

WINSTANLEY Graham 1964-1969

Centre-half
5'11"
b. Croxdale, Co Durham, 20 January 1948

Career: UNITED jnr July 1964, prof Dec 1965/ Carlisle Utd Aug 1969 £7,000/Brighton Oct 1974 £20,000/Carlisle Utd July 1979 to May 1980, becoming asst-coach/Penrith, becoming manager May 1982.

Bespectacled off the field, slim and with a quiet nature, Graham Winstanley showed considerable promise as an ice-cool defender during his period at St James' Park. Arriving at the club from school football, Graham had plenty of competition ahead of him, notably seniors, Burton, McNamee, McGrath and Moncur. But he pushed for contention during season 1966-67 and thereafter was in Joe Harvey's squad, often on the substitute's bench without getting onto the field. Winstanley appeared in European football for the Magpies, against Sporting Lisbon in Portugal and was up to the task, having a fine game against some of the Continent's top forwards. Moving to Brunton Park, Graham became a key figure in Carlisle's rise to the First Division, totalling 240 matches for the Cumbrians in his two spells with the club. Winstanley afterwards settled in Carlisle, involved in a variety of occupations from having a building supply business, working for the Cumberland News, to being a milkman, insurance salesman, as well as running a post-office and electrical wholesaler.

Appearances & Goals:
Debut v Leeds United (h) 24 December 1966 (sub)
FL: 5(2) app 0 gls
FAC: 1 app 0 gls
Euro: 1 app 0 gls
Total: 7(2) app 0 gls

Honours:
FL div 2 prom 1974, 1979 (4 app)/FL div 3 prom 1977 (4 app).

WITHE Christopher 1979-1983

Left-back
5'10"
b. Speke, Liverpool, 25 September 1962

Career: Liverpool jnr/UNITED jnr 1979, prof Oct 1980/Bradford City June 1983 free/Notts Co Oct 1987 £20,000/Bury July 1989 £40,000 (Chester loan 1990-91)/Mansfield Town loan Jan 1991, pmt March 1991 exch deal/Shrewsbury Town Aug 1993 free/Boston Utd July 1996 free/Afterwards appearing in local football around the East Midlands, including for Hucknall Town (2003), Notts Police Veterans (2007) and Kimberley Miner's Welfare (2013).

Chris Withe was briefly with Liverpool as a schoolboy and made his Football League debut only 11 days after turning professional with United during 1980. Brother of England international Peter Withe (qv) who was also on the club's books at the same time, Chris didn't possess his more famous relation's height and built, but had neat skills on the ball and when he first pulled on black-and-white colours during season 1980-81 appeared to have the qualities to become an established defender. As a rival to Peter Johnson and Ian Davies, Withe however, didn't develop as envisaged, allowing another junior product, Wes Saunders, to leap ahead of him for first-team action. Chris was transferred to Bradford City where he claimed a regular place in lower division football. Winning promotion with the Tykes, Chris made 170 outings for City, at Valley Parade on the day of the tragic fire in May 1985 which cost the lives of 56 supporters. Withe also made an impression at his other ports of call too, notably at Notts County where he was Player of the Year during 1888-89, recording 101 matches for the other Magpies. Chris totalled 116 games for Shrewsbury and 84 with Mansfield. He settled in the Nottingham area, for a period running a window-cleaning business.

Appearances & Goals:
Debut v Shrewsbury Town (h) 22 October 1980
FL: 2 app 0 gls
Total: 2 app 0 gls

Honours:
FL div 3 champs 1985, 1994/FL div 4 prom 1992/FLT final 1996.

WITHE Peter 1978-1980

Centre-forward
6'2"
b. Toxteth, Liverpool, 30 August 1951

Career: Smiths-Coggins (Liverpool) 1966/Southport amat Nov 1970, prof Aug 1971 (Skelmersdale Utd loan 1971-72)/ Barrow Dec 1971 free/Port Elizabeth City (SA) 1972/Arcadia Shepherds (SA) 1973/ Wolverhampton Wand Nov 1973 £13,500/ Portland Timbers (USA) May 1975/ Birmingham City Aug 1975 £40,000/ Nottingham Forest Sept 1976 £42,000/UNITED Aug 1978 £200,000/ Aston Villa May 1980 £500,000/ Sheffield Utd July 1985 (Birmingham City loan 1987-88)/ Huddersfield Town asst-player-manager July 1988/Power Dynamos (Zam) 1989/Aston Villa asst-manager Jan 1991/ Wimbledon manager Oct 1991 to Jan 1992/ Evesham Utd Feb 1992 /PFA Area Manager 1992-93/Birmingham City community officer 1993/ Aston Villa youth development officer Aug 1994, becoming chief-scout Oct 1996, then Head of European Scouting/Thailand FA coach Oct 1998 to Sept 2003/Indonesia FA national manager & Technical Director June 2004 to Sept 2007/Stockport Sports manager June 2012 to November 2012/PTT Rayong (Th) manager Jan 2014 to May 2014/Nakhon Pathom Utd (Th) coach Sept 2014.

A much travelled striker, Peter Withe didn't reach great heights in the game until he teamed up with Brian Clough at Nottingham Forest. Brave and strong, Withe was an unselfish target man up front, expert at holding and laying the ball off. All left foot, the Number 9 was a menace in the box, his aerial prowess always able to cause problems for defenders. At the City Ground he helped Forest to the First Division title trophy before surprisingly dropping a division to join Bill McGarry's rebuilding plans at St James' Park after running into dispute with Clough. With a record of 39 goals in 99 games for Forest he was United's record purchase and Withe immediately became a big favourite with his never-say-die attitude. Peter was undoubtedly too good for Second Division football and his continued presence in a black-and-white shirt rested on United's quick promotion. In 1978-79 and 1979-80 that didn't materialise and

Withe soon moved back to Division One, joining Aston Villa where he again helped win the title (netting 20 goals), as well as the European Cup in 1982; Peter firing home the trophy winner during an epic against Bayern Munich in Rotterdam. Goals flowed for Withe at Villa Park, registering 92 in 233 games, form which also earned him England recognition. A bubbly personality, Withe later assisted Villa on the coaching staff after a brief spell in management at Wimbledon, while he also was an occasional BBC radio summariser until moving to the Far East. For almost ten years he guided both the Thailand and Indonesian national sides, notably twice lifting the ASEAN championship, the Tiger Cup. Peter relocated to Connolly in Australia for a period, setting up a football academy in Joondalup in 2007 before returning to the UK during 2012 where he settled in the Midlands. Apart from scouting, Peter is co-host of a football show on BBC Radio in the West Midlands and a local commentator. As a teenager Withe worked as an apprentice electrician in Liverpool's dockside before turning to professional football. His brother Chris (qv) also appeared for Newcastle, while his son, Jason, had spells with Huddersfield Town and West Bromwich Albion and later served Burnley.

Appearances & Goals:
Debut v Luton Town (h) 26 August 1978
FL: 76 app 25 gls
FAC: 4 app 2 gls
FLC: 3 app 0 gls
Total: 83 app 27 gls

Honours:
11 Eng caps 1981-85/WdC 1982 (no app)/FL champs 1978, 1981/FL div 2 prom 1977/FLC winner 1978/EC winner 1982/ESC winner 1982/ICC final 1982/ASEAN ch winner 2000(m), 2002(m)/PFA ToS (d2) 1979, 1980.

WOOD Edmund Eli 1928-1930

Centre-half
6'0"
b. Stirchley, near Solihull, 10 February 1903
d. Northampton, June 1986

Career: Bourneville/Nuneaton Town/Redditch/Northampton Town March 1923/Bromsgrove Rovers May 1925/Birmingham April 1926/Rhyl Ath Oct 1927/UNITED May 1928 £950 to May 1930/Wellington Town cs 1930/Runcorn cs 1931/Rhyl Ath.

Tall and solid, Ted Wood was raised in the Stirchley and King's Norton area of the Midlands and arrived at St James' Park as a defender who had failed to break through with Birmingham, at a time when the centre-half position was up for grabs. Impressing in Rhyl's FA Cup run during 1927-28, he was tried in the pivot's role for a brief period during seasons 1928-29 and 1929-30. Coming into the side for Ossie Park when the Magpies had defensive problems, Wood did not have a memorable debut for the club. At St James' Park he faced Burnley and United lost 7-2 with the visitor's prolific centre-forward George Beel scoring a hat-trick, Wood chasing his shadow all afternoon. The defender's unfortunate display prompted United's directors to splash out a record fee for Burnley's England captain Jack Hill and Ted was destined to spend the rest of his career in Newcastle's second-team as one of his deputies. Wood started his career under the guidance of former United player Bob Hewison at Northampton and he totalled 49 games at the County Ground, for three seasons part of their Division Three South line-up. Ted later returned to Northampton, employed as a fireman in that town. He lived there for over 40 years.

Appearances & Goals:
Debut v Burnley (h) 29 August 1928
FL: 9 app 0 gls
Total: 9 app 0 gls

WOOD George Andrew 1945-1946

Goalkeeper
5'10"
b. Gateshead, 11 April 1923
d. Gateshead, 2001 (Q1)

Career: Blucher Utd/UNITED amat March 1945, prof April 1945 to 1946.

George Wood filled the boots of regular goalkeeper Dave Cumming in wartime football only occasionally during the 1944-45 and 1945-46 seasons. His debut for the Magpies was in a derby tussle with Sunderland during April 1945 and although United lost 3-0, Wood's highlight was the return meeting the following month. Newcastle thrashed the Wearsiders 5-0 while George was also on the field for one of the easiest games any United 'keeper has taken part in, an 11-0 mauling of Middlesbrough during May 1945. He was one of eight goalkeepers on the club's staff for the 1945-46 season but wasn't retained when normal Football League action returned for the following campaign.

Appearances & Goals:
Debut v Sunderland (h) 2 April 1945 (FLN)
War: 7 app 0 gls
Total: 7 app 0 gls

WOOD Littleton 1889-1890

Forward
b. Glasgow, 3 June 1870
d. Newcastle upon Tyne, June 1940

Career: Science & Art (Newcastle)/EAST END Oct 1889/Science & Art 1890.

Moving to Tyneside from Glasgow by the start of the 1880s and a product of the Science & Art college side on Bath Lane, Littleton Wood impressed East End's committee men as a teenager and was signed as the 1889-90 season began. He was chiefly a reserve player, appearing regularly for East End Swifts, but managed one senior outing in the first-eleven during November of that season. He was included in the side which made the trip to south Durham to meet Darlington St Augustine's, to be crowned the Northern League's inaugural champions that season. Wood was good enough to also represent Northumberland and was noted as a splendid athlete, a proficient runner with the Newcastle Harriers club. He trained to be a mechanical engineer and worked as a designer and draughtsman living in Gateshead.

(Note: Newspaper reports spell his Christian name as both Lyttleton and Littleton, birth and death records note the latter.)

Appearances & Goals:
Debut v Darlington St Augustine's (a) 9 November 1889 (NL)
NL: 1 app 0 gls
Total: 1 app 0 gls

WOODBURN James 1935-1948

Right or Left-half
5'9"
b. Rutherglen, Glasgow, 29 January 1917
d. Leeds, 2 January 1978

Career: Kilsyth Emmet/Coltness Utd/UNITED amat 1935, prof Feb 1938 £100 (Third Lanark war-guest 1939-41) (Liverpool war-guest 1940-41) (Wrexham war-guest 1940-41) (Aberdeen war-guest 1941-42) (Northampton Town war-guest 1941-42) (Dundee Utd war-guest 1942-43) (Hibernian war-guest 1942-44) (Bolton Wand war-guest 1943-44) (Doncaster Rovers war-guest 1944-45) (Dundee war-guest 1945)/Resumed with United 1946/Gateshead player-trainer Sept 1948 £750/Retired June 1952.

United discovered former electrician Jimmy Woodburn in Scotland on one of their many scouting trips north of the border. Purchased as a teenager to groom for the future, Woodburn developed in the years just before the outbreak of the Second World War and was most unlucky to have broken through into United's senior eleven only to suffer a cartilage injury then saw the clouds of war descend. With exceptional positional sense on the field, he worked tirelessly and read the game well, appearing in all half-back roles for Newcastle, as well as in inside-forward positions too. After serving in the Cameronians (Scottish Rifles) during the war, for part of the conflict in Belgium, Poland, France and Germany including taking part in the D-Day landings, Jimmy returned to the fold in 1946 and competed along with Joe Harvey and Duggie Wright as United strived for a promotion spot. He was used largely as a utility player in midfield, appearing on 17 occasions as the Magpies returned to the First Division during 1948. Remaining in the region after a spell with Gateshead (147 app), Jimmy coached for the Newcastle Education Authority then became a house-master with an approved school at Axwell House near Blaydon. Woodburn's father turned out for St Mirren in Scottish football, while throughout his period in the services during wartime, Woodburn took part in many representative games at home and abroad, part of combined line-ups containing a rich collection of star footballers.

Appearances & Goals:
Debut v Coventry City (a) 1 October 1938
FL: 44 app 4 gls
FAC: 3 app 0 gls
War: 45 app 4 gls
Total: 92 app 8 gls
(Void FL: 3 app 0 gls)

Honours:
FL div 2 prom 1948/SLC(S) winner 1944.

W

WOODGATE Jonathan Simon 2003-2004

Centre-half
6'2"
b. Middlesbrough, 22 January 1980

Career: Marton/Leeds Utd jnr 1996, prof May 1997/UNITED Jan 2003 £8m/Real Madrid (Sp) Aug 2004 £13.65m/Middlesbrough loan Aug 2006, pmt April 2007 £7m/ Tottenham Hotspur Jan 2008 £8m/ Stoke City July 2011 free/ Middlesbrough July 2012 free.

Since joining the Premier League elite for its second year of competition in 1993-94, the Black'n'Whites continually searched for an imposing centre-back who could both organise and command United's back-line, as well as have the ability to move from defence with the ball. During January 2003 Bobby Robson signed 23-year-old Jonathan Woodgate from Leeds United for a sizeable £8m fee, a tall North Easterner from Teesside who had shown the very qualities United needed, Robson describing Jonathan as a "footballing defender". Woodgate was the answer to a position where most others had failed. Indeed many reckoned he was the best defensive organiser in a black-and-white shirt since the days of Bob Moncur. Yet the cool-headed, silky and thoughtful Woodgate was continually struck by injury, unfit when he arrived then suffering an ongoing problem with hamstring tears and thigh muscles which ruined his career and stopped Jonathan becoming a huge star. When he was fit though, Woodgate made a big difference to United's trophy chasing eleven at home and abroad. The Magpies looked top quality when Woodgate was available, forming a good looking partnership with Bramble. However during his short stay at Gallowgate, the longest run in the side the Teessider managed was a dozen or so games, fit for around 50% of Newcastle's fixtures. Despite this nagging problem, Real Madrid also admired his defensive attributes and elegant calm in the back line and offered United what was a staggering £13.65m for his services. Although not wanting to lose the player, the bid was too good to refuse and he moved to the Bernabeu at the start of the 2004-05 season, a club record sale after less than two years at Gallowgate. As it turned out for United it was an astute piece of business. Woodgate continued to endure injury misery, breaking down soon after arriving in Madrid and being on the sidelines for almost 18 months. When fit, he made his Real debut and was bizarrely ordered off against Athletic Bilbao after scoring an own-goal! He moved back to England joining Spurs (65 app) during 2008, but again was destined to be in the treatment room too often. Capped by England, that recurring injury nightmare halted his international career while Jonathan attempted to recapture his lost years in a Stoke City shirt during 2011-12. As a young professional with Leeds, Woodgate was one of several bright new stars to shine in the Tykes' line-up. Connected to the Elland Road club from 13 years of age, Jonathan was part of their talented side which finished in the top four of the Premier League on three seasons in a row and did well in the Champions League, registering just short of 150 games and reaching his country's eleven as a teenager before moving to Tyneside. Woodgate though, was embroiled in a distasteful episode when Leeds players, including Lee Bowyer, were involved on an attack on an Asian student. A long-running court saga followed which disrupted his early career.

Appearances & Goals:
Debut v Chelsea (h) 1 March 2003
PL: 28 app 0 gls
FAC: 2 app 0 gls
Euro: 7 app 0 gls
Total: 37 app 0 gls

Honours:
8 Eng caps 1999-2009/1 Eng u21 app 2000/Eng sch-youth app/FLC winner 2008/FAYC winner 1997.

WOODS Charles Morgan Parkinson 1958-1962, 2000-2004

Inside-right & Chief-scout
5'7"
b. Whitehaven, 18 March 1941

Career: Keels BC/Cleator Moor Celtic 1956/UNITED jnr Nov 1958, prof May 1959 £25/Bournemouth Nov 1962 £5,000/Crystal Palace Nov 1964/Ipswich Town July 1966/Watford June 1970 £9,000 (Colchester Utd loan 1971-72)/Blackburn Rovers asst-coach July 1972 briefly/Ipswich Town asst-coach March 1973, becoming coach Aug 1982 and asst-manager 1991, then scout and chief-scout 1995/Tottenham Hotspur scout May 1998/UNITED chief-scout April 2000 to Aug 2004/Eire FA scout 2006/Ipswich Town advisor & scout 2007 to June 2009/Tottenham Hotspur scout 2010.

After being rejected by Aston Villa as a youngster, Charlie Woods was given a contract by United, exchanging a job at Haigh pit in Whitehaven for a professional footballer's career at St James' Park. Woods soon made an impression although he had the daunting task of filling George Eastham's boots when the future England player ran into dispute with United. Then only a raw youngster, Woods was plunged into United's side for a relegation fight during season 1960-61 but coped well. Small and compact, he dazzled on his first outing in a high profile friendly against Barcelona (scoring a beauty) then did the same on his full debut against Fulham, a terrific contest at Craven Cottage which ended in a 4-3 defeat. Woods scored one goal and made another, the press noting he was "irrepressible" during the 90 minutes. Charlie was a fixture at inside-right, and showed plenty of talent with the ball and could wallop a stinging shot. But United's overall performances in that programme were dire, and the young Woods suffered as a consequence. Newcastle fell into Division Two and a change in management saw Jimmy Kerray arrive and Charlie move south, eventually becoming a loyal servant at Portman Road. As a player he appeared on 89 occasions, then turned to coaching, being associated with the East Anglia club for more than 20 years. Brought to Portman Road by Bobby Robson, he was a long-term confident of Robson and later returned to St James' Park as his chief-scout.

Appearances & Goals:
Debut v Fulham (a) 31 August 1960 (1 goal)
FL: 26 app 7 gls
FAC: 3 app 3 gls
FLC: 1 app 0 gls
Total: 30 app 10 gls

Honours:
FL div 2 champs 1968.

WOODS Harold 1922-1923

Inside-right
5'8"
b. St Helens, Lancashire, 12 March 1890

Career: Parr Holy Trinity/St Helens Town Sept 1910/Ashton Town/Norwich City June 1911/ South Shields Aug 1919/UNITED trial May 1921, pmt Jan 1922 £2,800/Arsenal June 1923 £575/ Luton Town Aug 1926/North Shields Oct 1930.

A versatile player, Harry Woods could play in any forward position and appeared across the front line for United. Having shined for Norwich City's pre-league line-up in the Southern League, he then took part in South Shields' first Football League game against Fulham during August 1919. Harry also made an impression at Horsley Hill and his ability was noticed a few miles up the Tyne at St James' Park. He joined United as a reserve with plenty of experience, 151 outings for Norwich and 95 for Shields. Well balanced, tricky on the ball and able to use possession to advantage, he was one of several forwards tried in the months immediately after World War One. But the purchase from Scotland of Billy Aitken pushed Woods out of the picture and he moved to Highbury. In London, Harry played some of his best football, top scorer for the Gunners in 1923-24 and 1924-25. He scored 22 goals in 75 fixtures, making his debut for Arsenal against Newcastle. Harry ended his senior career with Luton and again returned good statistics, 27 goals in 105 matches at Kenilworth Road. Woods was a glass worker before turning to football, and served in the Tank Corps in France during the First World War.

Appearances & Goals:
Debut v Arsenal (a) 4 February 1922
FL: 14 app 2 gls
FAC: 2 app 0 gls
Total: 16 app 2 gls

WOODS Patrick Bede 1943-1945

_eft-half
5'10"
b. South Shields, [5 September 1921]
d. [Jarrow, 1986 (Q2)]

Career: Bedewell/UNITED amat & prof Nov 1943
(York City war-guest 1944-45)/Hartlepools Utd
war-guest 1943-44, pmt Oct 1945 free to c1946.

*Joining United from local football during November
1943, Pat Woods gained a run in United's Football
League North line-up in each of three seasons up
to 1946. His debut was marked with a 3-1 derby
victory over Sunderland at Gallowgate. Pat also
guested for York City and Hartlepools United,
joining the Victoria Ground set-up permanently in
October 1945. Woods didn't graduate to Football League status once a peacetime
programme was restored, but did appear for Hartlepool in FA Cup action, against
Gateshead at Redheugh Park during November 1945.*

Appearances & Goals:
Debut v Sunderland (h) 13 November 1943 (FLN)
War: 16 app 0 gls
Total: 16 app 0 gls

WOOLLARD Arnold James 1952-1956

Right-back
6'0"
b. Pembroke (Bermuda), 24 August 1931

Career: Hamilton (Bmd)/Bermuda Ath Ass/
Northampton Town June 1949/Peterborough
Utd June 1952/UNITED Dec 1952
£5,000/Bournemouth June 1956
£2,000/Northampton Town March 1962 to cs
1963/Bermuda Ath Ass to 1967 when he
retired.

*Arnold Woollard was initially an outside-right
but switched to defensive duties once he had
moved to England from his home in Bermuda
during 1949. His career took off when he caught the eye of Newcastle officials
following outstanding performances for Peterborough in a giant-killing FA Cup run
during 1952-53. A fine all-round defender, Woollard stepped into United's back-line,
initially as deputy to Frank Brennan at centre-half during 1952-53, but had an
uncomfortable debut against Portsmouth; United lost 5-1 and Arnold netted an own-
goal. Afterwards he was more often as a reserve to Bobby Cowell and when the full-
back was badly injured, Arnold had the opportunity of a more regular place in the
Magpies' side, but lost out to Ron Batty. He did though, become one of the soundest
right-backs in the lower divisions appearing for Bournemouth over six campaigns
(174 app) and then returning to Northampton where he appeared on 34 occasions.
Woollard helped the Cobblers to the Third Division title in 1962-63. On leaving the
professional game, Arnold resided on his home island of Bermuda for a period, where
he was recognised as one of his country's finest sportsmen, included in their Hall of
Fame. Woollard was employed with the Bank of Bermuda before returning to England
during 1988 and residing in Buckinghamshire.*

*(Note: Woollard's birth is noted in United's official records as 1931, while other data
shows 1930.)*

Appearances & Goals:
Debut v Portsmouth (a) 18 April 1953
FL: 8 app 0 gls
FAC: 2 app 0 gls
Total: 10 app 0 gls

Honours:
1 Bmd cap 1965/FL div 3 champs 1963.

WOOLLETT Charles 1941-1946

Outside-left
5'7"
b. Dawdon, Co Durham, 25 November 1921
d. [Co Durham], 16 July 2011

Career: Murton CW Jnrs 1938/Hetton Jnrs 1939/
Eppleton CW 1940/UNITED amat Dec 1941, prof Nov
1942 (Middlesbrough war-guest 1944-45)
(Hartlepools Utd war-guest 1945-46)/Bradford City
Aug 1946 £600/Murton CW player-coach June
1948/York City Feb 1949 to cs 1949/Blyth Spartans.

*One of the mainstays of wartime football at St James'
Park, Charlie Woollett ran the touchline with distinction.
Very fast, he linked with Stubbins at centre-forward in
a highly productive way over four seasons. Scoring on
his debut against Middlesbrough during December
1941, a 7-0 victory, Woollett later also guested for Boro against the Magpies, such
was the strange format of wartime soccer. Working at Easington and Murton pits
during the war, Tommy Pearson was preferred on the wing once football was restored
to normal, and Woollett was deemed surplus to requirements. He later made 44
appearances for Bradford City, costing the Tykes a fee of £600 when he moved from
Gallowgate. He afterwards lived in Easington and was a publican at several hostelries
as well as being a keen pigeon racer and greyhound owner in true County Durham
tradition.*

Appearances & Goals:
Debut v Middlesbrough (a) 6 December 1941 (FLN) (1 goal)
War: 75 app 13 gls
Total: 75 app 13 gls

WRIGHT George Brian 1956-1963

Right-half
5'11"
b. Sunderland, 19 September 1939

Career: UNITED jnr, prof Sept 1956/Peterborough Utd May
1963 £7,500/Scarborough July 1972 to cs 1973.

*Brian Wright joined United's junior set-up from school
football and quickly made an impression as he worked
his way through the ranks. Tall and sturdy, he skippered
the Magpies' youth team and when he first appeared for
the senior eleven at the City Ground against Forest,
turned on a grand performance, "inspiring bite and
insistence" noted one report. Strong, forceful and
industrious, with control of the ball in midfield, he also
possessed a full-bodied tackle. Wright was given a few outings at half-back during
season 1960-61 and after the club's relegation that year, received an extended run
for the following term. But the appointment of Joe Harvey as boss saw wholesale
changes to the playing staff. Duncan Neale took his place, then Ollie Burton became
a big purchase and Wright was frozen out. Brian moved to Peterborough where he
proceeded to appear for the Posh for the next nine seasons, totalling 324 matches in
Division Three and Four. Only a handful of players have topped that figure for
Peterborough, one being another ex-Newcastle man and a teammate in their blue
shirt, Tommy Robson. Wright started off with Posh under the management of Jack
Fairbrother and took part in the London Road club's shock League Cup victory over
the Magpies at St James' Park in season 1965-66. Brian later resided on Wearside
after hanging up his boots.*

Appearances & Goals:
Debut v Nottingham Forest (a) 23 April 1960
FL: 45 app 1 gl
FAC: 1 app 0 gls
FLC: 1 app 0 gls
Total: 47 app 1 gl

W

WRIGHT John Douglas 1938-1948

Left-half
5'11"
b. Rochford, near Southend on Sea, 29 April 1917
d. Bedlington, Northumberland, 28 December 1992

Career: Chelmsford City 1935/Southend Utd Aug 1936/UNITED May 1938 £3,250 (Southend Utd war-guest 1939-40)(Swansea Town war-guest 1942-43)(Hamilton Acc war-guest 1943-44)/Lincoln City Dec 1948 £600/Blyth Spartans player-trainer Dec 1954, becoming player-manager cs 1955, then secretary May 1957 to Nov 1960.

A player who possessed captivating artistry on the ball, Doug Wright graced United's midfield for only two Football League seasons, immediately before and after the Second World War, but made a huge impact on both colleagues and spectators who watched him play. Slimly framed with a mop of wavy hair, he possessed a master's touch of the ball and distinguished poise on the field. Wright had a rapid climb to fame, signing for the Black'n'Whites after only 34 games with his first senior club, Southend. Recommended to United by ex-captain, Jimmy Nelson, Doug made such an impact in Newcastle colours that he became Newcastle's playmaker-in-chief in a Seymour-led resurgence. Rarely to tackle fiercely, Wright was the entertainer on the field and had a superb range of passing, especially long and accurate balls to the wing. Former colleague Len Shackleton once wrote in a moment of generous praise that Wright was "twice as good as Bobby Moore". Wright was picked for his country, in a game against Norway at St James' Park, but then his whole career was wrecked by Hitler's invasion of Poland. Like many footballers, Wright served abroad, with the Durham Light Infantry then as part of the noted Tyneside Scottish regiment. He was wounded in the leg, nearly losing his life at Dunkirk and later took part in Operation Overlord during 1944. A sergeant in the artillery, he was mentioned in dispatches for his "heroic" exploits. Wright regained his place in Newcastle's ranks for season 1946-47, but damaged his cartilage and was a long term casualty. By then it was clear perhaps too many years had passed and despite being highly praised for his ice-cool contribution by other team-mates like Joe Harvey, he was discarded to Lincoln, rather too hastily according to many fans. At Sincil Bank, Wright played a major part in their promotion during 1952, an inspirational skipper of the Imps. The midfielder totalled 246 outings for Lincoln before returning to the North East when he joined the Blyth Spartans staff. Afterwards Doug settled in that town, at Newsham, a noted personality to his death. He worked at Blyth power station for nearly 25 years before retiring. Wright's father Jocky appeared for several clubs, including Bolton and Sheffield Wednesday, while his brother Bill was Reading's captain.

Appearances & Goals:
Debut v Plymouth Argyle (h) 27 August 1938
FL: 72 app 1 gl
FAC: 10 app 0 gls
War: 23 app 0 gls
Totals: 105 app 1 gl
(Void FL: 2 app 0 gls)

Honours:
1 Eng cap 1939/FL div 3(N) champs 1952.

WRIGHT John William 1958-1959

Outside-left
5'11"
b. Blackpool, 4 March 1931

Career: Blackpool May 1950/Leicester City Aug 1955 £1,500/UNITED July 1958 £7,500/Plymouth Argyle Aug 1959 £5,150/Hull City Aug 1961 briefly/Millwall Aug 1961/Tonbridge cs 1962.

Fair-haired, Billy Wright was a direct winger who played in any forward position. Understudy to the great Stanley Matthews at Bloomfield Road, he moved to Leicester in search of more regular action and for a season did well at Filbert Street, helping City to promotion from the Second Division. A record of 10 goals in 29 games from the flank was first-class and Newcastle picked him up for a small fee during the summer of 1958. He was given a chance at the start of the following season, at centre-forward as well as on the touchline and in a schemer's role. Scoring twice in an amazing match which took place with Chelsea that ended 6-5 in the Blues' favour,

Wright picked up an injury and couldn't hold his place, being transferred before the new season started. He afterwards drifted around the lower divisions without making a huge impact, a player whose potential was never fulfilled. Wright's best spell was with Plymouth in Division Two, totalling 46 games over two seasons. He later lived in Blackheath in South London.

Appearances & Goals:
Debut v Blackpool (a) 25 August 1958
FL: 5 app 3 gls
Total: 5 app 3 gls

Honours:
FL div 2 prom 1957/FL div 4 champs 1962.

WRIGHT Thomas James 1988-1993, 1999

Goalkeeper
6'1"
b. Ballyclare, near Belfast, 29 August 1963

Career: Grange Rangers/Brantwood/Linfield 1984/ UNITED trial Jan 1988, pmt March 1988 £30,000 (Hull City loan 1990-91)/ Nottingham Forest Sept 1993 £450,000 (Reading loan 1996-97)/ Manchester City loan Jan 1997, pmt March 1997 £450,000 (Wrexham loan 1998-99)(UNITED loan Aug 1999 to Oct 1999)/Northern Ireland gkp-coach Sept 1999 to June 2000/Bolton Wand loan Jan 2001, pmt March 2001/ Ballymena Utd Aug 2001/ Linfield gkp-coach Jan 2002 to April 2003/Northern Ireland FA development officer April 2003 to Nov 2003/Ballyclare Comrades Nov 2003/ Limavady Utd manager Nov 2003/ Ballymena Utd manager May 2005/ Norwich City gkp-coach May 2008/ Shamrock Rovers gkp-coach March 2009/Lisburn Distillery manager Sept 2009/St Johnstone asst-manager Nov 2011, becoming manager June 2013 & Northern Ireland gkp-coach Feb 2012 to June 2013.

Tommy Wright followed the path of former Northern Ireland international goalkeeper Willie McFaul to St James' Park. A highly rated 'keeper from Linfield, like McFaul, Tommy took time to claim a regular place on Tyneside, arriving initially to compete for the vacant Number 1 jersey when Martin Thomas was injured. Rivalling fellow Irishman Gary Kelly, then Dave Beasant and also John Burridge, Wright gained the shirt for season 1989-90 then was sidelined through a knee injury. Bouncing back, he again claimed the position for season 1991-92 but was once more injured after a string of brilliant displays and Tommy saw Pavel Srnicek take-over the position as United won promotion the following year. When Newcastle started life in the Premier League, Wright made only a fleeting appearance before the purchase of Mike Hooper saw his departure to Forest. Between the posts as Frank Clark guided the Reds into the Premier League, Wright experienced an unlucky career, constantly battling against injury both at Gallowgate and at the City Ground in Nottingham. Yet Wright played on for a lengthy period, as a veteran returning to Gallowgate in a short-term loan during 1999-2000 when Given and Harper were both injured. Winning promotion from tier-two of football on four occasions, Tommy was over 37 years of age when he played his last top level fixture, against the Magpies for Manchester City in Premier League action. As a teenager, he was also a proficient athlete, chosen for his country at the cross-country event; he was All-Ireland champion in 1978 and was offered a lucrative athletics scholarship in the States, but chose to stay in Northern Ireland, employed as a publican before starting on a career in the game. After retirement Tommy began coaching during 2002 and led St Johnstone to Scottish Cup victory in 2014, their first in the competition for over 130 years.

Appearances & Goals:
Debut v Aston Villa (a) 14 January 1989
FL/PL: 75(1) app 0 gls
FAC: 4 app 0 gls
FLC: 6 app 0 gls
Others: 1 app 0 gls
Total: 86(1) app 0 gls

Honours:
31 NI caps 1989-2000/1 NI u23 app 1989/NI u21 app/NI jnr app 1986/NI B Lg app/NI sch-youth app/1 FL app 1993/FL div 1 champs 1993/FL div 1 prom 1994, 2000 (1 app), 2001 (4 app)/FL div 2 prom 1999 (1 app)/SC winner 2014(m)/NILC winner 2011(m).

WRIGHTSON Jeffrey George 1984-1987

Midfield
5'11"
b. Walker, Newcastle upon Tyne, 18 May 1968

Career: Wallsend BC/UNITED jnr July 1984, prof May 1986/Preston North End July 1987 free/Darlington trial July 1992/Blackpool trial Aug 1992/Gateshead Aug 1992 to April 1997/Bishop Auckland Aug 1997/ Kingstonian 1997-98/Stalybridge Celtic Dec 1997/ Yeovil Town Jan 1998/Spennymoor Utd Aug 1998 to 1999/Blyth Spartans Jan 2000 to 2001 /Walker Central 2004, becoming asst-manager/ Gateshead asst-manager April 2007 to April 2010.

With United as a schoolboy during 1982, as a junior Jeff Wrightson helped United lift the FA Youth Cup alongside Paul Gascoigne in 1985. Tall and positive, he was called up to the senior eleven at a time of near panic in United's ranks. With the Magpies fighting at the bottom of the First Division during season 1986-87, the young Tynesider was thrown into the battleground during the Christmas and New Year programme. Stepping into David McCreery's anchor role in midfield, Wrightson was up against it and saw Everton inflict a heavy defeat on his Football League baptism. Nevertheless, Wrightson gave his all, but was unlucky to be given his opportunity in senior football at the wrong time. He later spent five seasons in Preston's ranks, a noted defender in the Third and Fourth Divisions. Wrightson clocked up almost 200 games for the Deepdale club, once netting a goal from the centre-circle in a match against Scarborough; a stunning volley from the opposition goalkeeper's kick up field. Jeff then joined Gateshead where he became a commanding player in the Vauxhall Conference. He totalled over 200 games for the Tynesiders, captain for a period, before returning as coach and assistant-manager. Wrightson settled on Tyneside for a period working as a housing officer in Walker, latterly appointed as Operations Manager for Your Homes in the city. His son Kieron had a spell on Newcastle's junior staff and later moved into local non-league football.

Appearances & Goals:
Debut v Everton (h) 26 December 1986
FL: 3(1) app 0 gls
Total: 3(1) app 0 gls

Honours:
FAYC winner 1985.

XISCO (Jimenez Tejada) Francisco 2008-2013

Centre-forward
6'2"
b. Palma de Mallorca (Spain), 26 June 1986

Career: CD Atletico Baleares (Sp) 2003/Deportivo La Coruna (Sp) July 2003 (UD Vecindario (Sp) loan 2006-07)/UNITED Sept 2008 £5.7m (Racing Santander (Sp) loan 2009-10)(Deportivo La Coruna (Sp) loan 2010-11, 2011-12)/Cordoba (Sp) Jan 2013 free.

Amidst the takeover of Newcastle United and several managerial changes as the opening decade of the Millennium came to a close, United brought Spanish centre-forward Xisco to Tyneside for a £5.7m fee from Deportivo La Coruna, a club United did three substantial deals with during the era. Kevin Keegan was boss at the time of his arrival but the player was not a Keegan choice, instead brought to the club by others behind the scenes. The tall Xisco had only a modest curriculum-vitae with Deportivo, 12 goals in 44 games, but helped the Galicians to qualify for the UEFA Cup. In Magpie colours he rarely showed enough in training to prompt any United manager, all five men in charge, to give him an extended run in the side. While perhaps Xisco was never talented enough on the ball to be a Premier League striker, he was unlucky to be at Gallowgate during a period of such upheaval. Managing only four starts for the club, all in his debut season of 2008-09, Xisco scored once, a tap-in against Hull City. He was rarely in contention for a place after that, on the bench on four occasions during the Magpies' Championship winning season. From the Balearic Islands, the Spaniard was loaned out to Racing Santander for 2009-10 and Deportivo in 2010-11 then again for 2011-12 when he assisted in their promotion back to La Liga, netting two crucial goals in the final two games of the season. On a five-year contract with high wages, Newcastle struggled to offload the striker, never mind recoup part of the substantial outlaw, but he agreed an exit during January 2013 and returned to Spain. In all, Xisco pulled on the black-and-white

stripes for 441 minutes of football over his four-and-a-half year period with the club.

Appearances & Goals:
Debut v Hull City (h) 13 September 2008 (1 goal)
FL/PL: 3(6) app 1 gl
FAC: 1 app 0 gls
FLC: 0(1) app 0 gls
Total: 4(7) app 1 gl

Honours:
11 Sp u21 app 2007-09/FL ch winner 2010 (2 app)/Sp div 2 champs 2012/Sp div 2 prom 2014.

YANGA-MBIWA Mapou 2013-date

Centre-half
6'0"
b. Bangui (Central African Republic),
15 May 1989

Career: Port-De-Bouc (Fr)/Montpellier HSC (Fr) jnr 2005, prof July 2007/ UNITED Jan 2013 £6.7m (AS Roma (It) loan 2014-15).

Mapou Yanga-Mbiwa skippered Montpellier to the French title for the very first time in season 2011-12 and was highly rated in Le Championnat as a defender of quality. The versatile centre-back joined the United rollercoaster during the January 2013 transfer window with more than 200 appearances to his name for La Paillade in France, a regular in their line-up for five seasons. At 23 years of age, Mapou had been capped by his adopted country alongside his Magpie teammates Cabaye, Debuchy and Ben Arfa. Born in the Central African Republic, a former French territory, Yanga-Mbiwa was raised in Marseille, moving to Provence when a youngster. A commanding figure, he soon was given an opportunity in United's side with Coloccini's absence and for a period impressed all with assured and cool displays for a player not used to the rigours and pace of English football. With first-class technical ability and good distribution of the ball, the athletic centre-back cemented his talent on the Premier League during the 2013-14 season but could not hold a regular place in United's line-up. He also appeared at full-back for the Magpies.

Appearances & Goals:
Debut v Aston Villa (a) 29 January 2013 (sub)
PL: 28(9) app 0 gls
FAC: 1 app 0 gls
FLC: 2 app 0 gls
Euro: 6 app 0 gls
Total: 37(9) app 0 gls

Honours:
3 Fr caps 2013-date/8 Fr u21 app 2010/Fr Lg champs 2012/Fr div 2 prom 2009.

YEATS John 1939-1942

Centre-half
5'11"
b. Gateshead, 14 January 1920
d. [Newcastle upon Tyne, 1974 (Q1)]

Career: Whitehall Jnrs/UNITED amat April 1939, prof Aug 1940 to 1942 (Middlesbrough war-guest 1941-42).

Appearing for the Magpies during the first three seasons of the wartime football, John Yeats slipped into Newcastle's side as a deputy pivot for Jimmy Denmark and Tot Smith. A frequent member of the second eleven, he worked as a turner at the Parson engineering works on Tyneside.

Appearances & Goals:
Debut v Bradford City (h) 8 June 1940 (FLNE)
War: 4 app 0 gls
Total: 4 app 0 gls

Y

YOUNG David 1963-1973

Midfield
5'10"
b. Newcastle upon Tyne, 12 November 1945

Career: UNITED amat May 1963, prof Sept 1964/Sunderland Jan 1973 £20,000/Charlton Ath Aug 1974 £27,000/Southend Utd Sept 1976 free/Dartford Dec 1978 to May 1980.

Lean and leggy, David Young grew up in Walker and was first connected with Newcastle as a schoolboy in 1961, becoming an amateur, then part-time professional, when he was undecided whether to follow a football career or a path in accountancy, before taking the plunge to go full-time pro during April 1967. He spent almost a decade on United's staff as a somewhat underrated professional without ever really commanding a first-team place. David did have one productive season in 1970-71 when he appeared on 29 occasions, mainly in a midfield marker role. A players' player, Young rarely caught the eye, was efficient rather than spectacular and went through a game giving plenty of effort as he covered lots of defensive ground. Also able to play at centre-half, but he found his path blocked by Bob Moncur, Young was skipper at Central League level and took part in United's Inter Cities Fairs Cup campaigns of 1969-70 and 1970-71 before heading for Roker Park. With rivals Sunderland (41 app), David found himself part of the famous Wearside FA Cup march on Wembley during 1973, a substitute as the red-and-whites defeated Leeds United in the final. Young went onto make 89 appearances for Charlton, mainly at centre-half alongside another former United player, Arthur Horsfield. He was captain at the Valley when the Londoners gained promotion to Division Two, Young then recorded 67 games for Southend. After retiring from the game, he remained in the south, employed in sports centre management in Orpington, Bexleyheath and Gillingham for 30 years. Young settled in retirement in Kent.

Appearances & Goals:
Debut v Southampton (a) 14 January 1970 (ICFC)
FL: 41(2) app 2 gls
FLC: 4 app 0 gls
Euro: 5(1) app 0 gls
Others: 2(1) app 0 gls
Total: 52(4) app 2 gls

Honours:
FL div 3 prom 1975/FL div 4 prom 1978/
FAC winner 1973 (sub no app).

YOUNG Philip 1890-1892

Full-back or Half-back
b. Newcastle upon Tyne, 1868 (Q4)
d. Newcastle upon Tyne, 1916 (Q3)

Career: EAST END cs 1890 (Doncaster Rovers loan Nov 1891) to Jan 1892.

Philip Young was a reserve full-back who made his bow in the first-eleven during a high-profile friendly contest with top Scottish side Renton in December 1890. From Heaton, Phil did show up well for East End Swifts and graduated to the Northern League side during the spring of 1891 coming in for Wilson when St Augustine's visited Chillingham Road. The following season though saw Young at full-back for East End Amateurs, the club's second-eleven, until they were disbanded in January 1892. He was one of two East End men that headed to Yorkshire to help out Doncaster at the time of crisis in 1891. During his Twenties, Young worked as a decorator on Tyneside.

Appearances & Goals:
Debut v Darlington St Augustine's (h) 21 March 1891 (NL)
NL: 1 app 0 gls Total: 1 app 0 gls

YOUNG William 1888-1889

Half-back
b. probably Scotland

Career: Kilmarnock area/EAST END Aug 1888 to June 1889 & again Aug 1890 briefly.

Several of East End's early footballers hailed from Ayrshire, including Willie Young. He wasn't automatic choice when he arrived on Tyneside, but found a role in the half-back line during season 1888-89 appearing in the FA Cup qualifying matches against the likes of Port Clarence and Stockton. Young also took part in the Northumberland Challenge Cup final at the end of that season, but retired hurt at half-time and had to watch his colleagues complete a victory over Elswick Rangers. He returned to East End for training in August 1890 but appears not to have remained with the club long. Apart from his four senior matches for East End, Young totalled another 40 games in sundry fixtures.

Appearances & Goals:
Debut v Port Clarence (h) 6 October 1888 (FACQ)
FAC: 4 app 1 gl Total: 4 app 1 gl

New Arrivals

CABELLA Remy Joseph 2014-date

Midfield
5'7"
b. Ajaccio, Corsica (France), 8 March 1990

Career: Gazekec FC Ajaccio (Fr)/Montpellier HSC (Fr) jnr 2004, prof July 2009 (AC Arles-Avignon (Fr) loan 2010-11)/UNITED July 2014 £12m.

Following a transfer chase for several months, Newcastle United landed the signature of 24-year-old midfield talent Remy Cabella as the World Cup in Brazil came to its conclusion during the summer of 2014. Part of the French squad, Cabella showed with Montpellier that he was an exciting, flair player, with lots of attacking intent, making things happen on the field where it matters. A supporter favourite at Stade de la Mosson, the slender Corsican possesses plenty of energy and totalled 133 senior games (31 goals) in France and on the European stage before moving to Tyneside. Able to go past defenders in a one-to-one situation and always looking to make a telling pass, Cabella also has a fearsome shot. Having an Italian and French bloodline, he recovered from a cruciate knee injury and missed the 2009-10 season recovering with a spell at Arles-Avignon the following campaign. Remy then came to prominence in the south of France during season 2011-12 and was an influential member of the Montpellier side alongside Mapou Yanga-Mbiwa to lift the Ligue 1 title that season for the first time in the club's history.

Appearances & Goals:
2014-15 on

Honours:
1 Fr cap 2014-date/WdC 2014 (no app)/17 Fr u21 app 2010-14/Fr Lg champs 2012.

COLBACK Jack Raymond 2014-date

Midfield
5'9"
b. Killingworth, near Newcastle upon Tyne, 24 October 1989

Career: Sunderland jnr, prof cs 2009 (Ipswich Town loan 2009-10, 2010-11)/UNITED June 2014 free.

Raised a Newcastle supporter, Jack Colback secured a chance in football with the Black'n'White's deadliest rivals Sunderland as a youngster. Having been with the Wearsiders since he was 10 years of age, Jack gained experience over two loan spells at Ipswich Town and became a regular choice in Sunderland's line-up during 2011-12. Colback totalled 135 matches for the Black Cats, usually in a central midfield role, but also at full-back, and showed an ease of passing, coolness in possession and stamina to keep going for the full 90 minutes. At 24 years of age he took the opportunity when out of contract to make a controversial switch from Wear to Tyne in June 2014 and join his boyhood favourites. Sunderland were not happy, having developed the player since a schoolboy, but Newcastle had acquired a midfielder with drive and plenty of top-level experience, having reached the Football League Cup final at Wembley in 2014, and one with a crucial desire to play in a black-and-white shirt. Jack recorded an eventful debut for Sunderland against Wolves during May 2010, being dismissed after a few minutes on the pitch as a late substitute. Colback was included in the England squad as the 2014-15 season began.

Appearances & Goals:
2014-15 on

Honours:
Eng sch-youth app/FLC final 2014.

DE JONG Siem Stephan 2014-date

Midfield
6'1"
b. Aigle (Switzerland), 28 January 1989

Career: SV DZC 68 (Neth)/De Graafschap (Neth) 2001/Ajax (Neth) 2005/UNITED July 2014 £5m.

Following an option to purchase striker Luuk De Jong at the end of the 2013-14 season was not taken up by United, the Magpies brought his elder brother Siem De Jong to Tyneside before the new season began. The 25-year-old Ajax captain had established himself as one of Holland's top performers, totalling almost 250 games for the Amsterdam club and lifting four consecutive Eredivisie titles, twice as skipper. De Jong also has experience of playing Champions League, Europa League and international football, while he featured alongside Vernon

...nita at the Ajax Arena. A midfield creator and occasional striker, he filled the void of the departed Cabaye in United's midfield, being an attack-minded playmaker who frequently could find the net, recording 78 goals in Dutch football. Favouring a role just behind a striker, like his brother, Siem was born in Switzerland but raised in Doetinchem and came through the Ajax academy, making his senior debut during September 2007. Tall and imposing on the field, he immediately impressed to become a stand-out player, but then was out of action with an injury.

Appearances & Goals:
2014-15 on

Honours:
5 Neth caps 2011-date/3 Neth B app 2008-09/12 Neth u21 app 2008-10/Neth sch-youth/Neth Lg champs 2011, 2012, 2013, 2014/Neth Cup winner 2010/Neth Cup final 2011.

FERREYRA Facundo 2014-date

Striker
5'1"
b. Lomas de Zamora (Argentina),
4 March 1991

Career: CA Banfield (Arg) jnr, prof Jan 2011/CA Velez Sarsfield (Arg) July 2012 £3m/Shakhtar Donetsk (Ukr) July 2013 £5m (UNITED loan 2014-15).

Nicknamed 'Chucky', Newcastle United acquired the services of 23-year-old Argentine striker Facundo Ferreyra at the start of August 2014 on a season loan deal. With civil war erupting in Ukraine, the Shakhtar Donetsk forward moved to the Premier League, United having an option to purchase the player outright as the season developed. Starting his career with Buenos Aries club Banfield, Ferreyra moved to Velez Sarsfield in 2012 and quickly made an impression, scoring 17 goals in season 2012-13 as they won the title. He moved to Ukraine for the following season for a substantial fee and the tall, quick South American enjoyed another trophy winning season in 2014 and experienced Champions League and Europa League action. An up and coming forward in Argentina's ranks, Facundo has appeared for his country's Under-20 line-up and in the South American Youth Championship as well as Under-20 World Cup. Ferreyra has Italian heritage and was given his nickname from the Child's Play horror film character as a youngster.

Appearances & Goals:
2014-15 on

Honours:
Arg u20 app/Arg Lg champs 2013/Ukr Lg champs 2014.

JANMAAT Daryl 2014-date

Right-back
5'1"
b. Leidschendam (Netherlands),
22 July 1989

Career: VSV Tonegido (Neth)/Feyenoord (Neth) jnr 1995/ADO Den Haag (Neth) July 2007/SC Heerenveen (Neth) July 2008/Feyenoord (Neth) July 2012 £1.5m/ UNITED July 2014 £5m.

Dutch international full-back Daryl Janmaat joined a growing band of footballers with experience at the top level in Holland to settle in the North East during the summer of 2014. Taking part in the Netherlands' line-up alongside Tim Krul which lifted the bronze medal in the Brazil World Cup, at right-back Daryl was a ready replacement for Debuchy who moved to Arsenal. At Feyenoord, Janmaat was a regular and consistent performer over two seasons following a move from Heerenveen. With an assured and confident style and similar attacking qualities as the departed Frenchman, he was a popular defender at the De Kuip arena in Rotterdam and covers well in defence. At 25 years of age, the Dutchman has much to offer the Black'n'Whites, first capped against Turkey in September 2012 for his country and being a regular member of the squad thereafter, totalling 21 caps before moving to England.

Appearances & Goals:
2014-15 on

Honours:
21 Neth caps 2013-date/WdC 2014/11 Neth u21 app/Neth sch-youth app/Neth Cup winner 2009.

PEREZ Gutierrez Ayoze 2014-date

Striker
5'11"
b. Maria Jimenez, near Santa Cruz de Tenerife (Spain), 29 July 1993

Career: San Andreas (Sp)/CD Tenerife (Sp) jnr (San Adreas (Sp) loan), prof 2012/UNITED June 2014 £1.6m.

Making a name for himself as a striker with Tenerife, and known as Ayoze (although his surname is Perez Gutierrez), the Canary Islander possesses a style up front with close control of the ball, sharp movement and eager anticipation. He has shown versatility to any role in attack and netted 16 goals during the 2013-14 season in Spain's Segunda Division. His form and with it, rise to prominence attracted scouts from several clubs, a young starlet in Spanish football. Ayoze showed a maturity in his game for a 20-year-old and he invoked a release clause in his contract with CD Tenerife, the Magpies stepping in to bring the Spaniard to Tyneside during the close-season of 2014. Perez quickly made an impression and was included in Spain's Under-21 squad as the new 2014-15 season started. His brother Samuel played in the lower leagues in Spain and travelled to the North East with him, joining Blyth Spartans in Northern League football.

Appearances & Goals:
2014-15 on

Honours:
Sp div 3 prom 2013.

RIVIERE Emmanuel José 2014-date

Centre-forward
6'0"
b. Le Lamentin, Martinique (France), 3 March 1990

Career: Espoir Saint-Luce (Fr) 1996/AS Saint-Etienne (Fr) jnr 2005, prof cs 2008/Toulouse (Fr) July 2011 £4.7m/AS Monaco (Fr) Jan 2013 £3m/UNITED July 2014 £6m.

Newcastle United's search for striking reinforcements which saw on loan Loic Remy and Luuk de Jong fill a gap, was resolved with the reported £6m purchase of Emmanuel Riviere. The 24-year-old Monaco centre-forward had shown he was one of the brightest forwards in French football having scored 46 goals in 182 outings. Making his professional debut in January 2009 with Saint-Etienne, the tall and lithe Riviere became a regular from season 2009-10 possessing a lightning quick style. Born on the island of Martinique, a French region in the Caribbean Antilles, he can operate both as a lead strike or raid from the flanks. On the fringe of a full call up for the French national side, and known as 'Manny', he was a colleague of Moussa Sissoko at Toulouse.

Appearances & Goals:
2014-15 on

Honours:
15 Fr u21 app/Fr sch-youth app/Fr div 2 champs 2013.

LASCELLES Jamaal 2014-date

DARLOW Karl 2014-date

United purchased Nottingham Forest pair, centre-back Jamaal Lascelles (left) and goalkeeper Karl Darlow (right) during August 2014 for a combined fee of around £7m. The up and coming players were immediately loaned back to Forest for the 2014-15 Championship season and therefore will not make their United debuts until 2015-16. Darlow is the grandson of ex-Newcastle and Wales centre-forward Ken Leek (qv).

Players to have appeared (including as substitute) in any supplementary first-team match and who was not selected for a first-class appearance. Included are the many pioneer players who took part during the formative years of Stanley FC and Newcastle East End FC before league competition flourished and when a multitude of friendlies were played each season. Also incorporated are those players who have not taken part in a first-eleven fixture but who reached the substitute's bench without being selected to take the field (see Introduction for further classification).

In Section 2 it should be noted that appearance and goal totals for players who featured in friendly and miscellaneous games for Stanley and East End between 1881 to around 1893, as well as thereafter for United in certain overseas tour matches, are incomplete, team details being untraced and contradictory. Games and goals for each player during this era are totalled where known and notated by an asterisk * indicating the player's record is potentially incomplete. Appearances and goals also include 'Newcastle United XI' games where players also made an outing in a secondary fixture. Players to have only been selected for these subsidiary contests are included at the end of this section.

The following members of United's Support Staff also appeared in miscellaneous fixtures, biographies being included in Section 4 ref: Bayles W, Carver JW, Galvin A, Herd G, Irvine JA, Morris P, Pickering J, Sadler A, Smith STG, Tunks RW, Wright D. In addition managers who were not also United players occasionally appeared in such matches as well, usually as a substitute, biographies contained in Section 3 ref: Gullit R, Dalglish K, Mitten C.

United hopeful Liam Atkin takes the field at Norwich in place of Nicky Butt during a friendly at Carrow Road in 2006. Manager Glenn Roeder (right) looks on.

AARONS Rolando James 2012-date

Outside-left 5'9"
b. Kingston (Jamaica),
16 November 1995
Career: Bristol City jnr/UNITED jnr
July 2012, prof April 2014.

Described as a fleet-footed outside-left, Rolando Aarons registered his first outing with senior company as an 18-year-old in the opening friendly of the 2014-15 pre-season – at Oldham during July. Joining United during the close-season of 2012 following a trial and a spell in Bristol City's junior ranks, his early days with the Magpies were affected by injury but during the latter weeks of the 2012-13 season and then following campaign, the winger started to make an impact at reserve level as well as in the FA Youth Cup. Possessing a good turn of pace and tricks on the ball, Aarons signed his first professional contract in April 2014. He moved to the South East of the country from the Caribbean as a youngster.

Misc App & Goals: 3(4) app 1 gl.

Postscript: Aarons made his senior debut against Manchester City as a substitute on the opening day of the 2014-15 season. He was also included in the England Under-20 squad.

ADJEI Samuel 2009-2012

Striker 6'1"
b. Eksjo (Sweden), 18 January 1992
Career: Waggeryds IK (Swd)/
Jonkopings Sodra IF (Swd)/UNITED
Feb 2009 (Hartlepool Utd loan-trial
Feb 2012) to June 2012 free/
Jonkopings Sodra IF (Swd) Jan 2013.

With plenty of pace up front, 17-year-old Swedish youth international Sam Adjei was given an opportunity with the Magpies as one of an influx of young football prospects from the Continent. Able to play in attack or as a wide striker, Sam was unfortunate with injury on Tyneside which restricted his progress. He only took part in a single friendly encounter in first-team colours, against Huddersfield Town during July 2009 before being told to find another club. Adjei briefly turned out for Hartlepool in Division One (1 app) then headed back to Scandinavia and continued to play for Second Division club, Sodra.

Misc App & Goals: 0(1) app 0 gls.

ALLISON William Scott 1924

Outside-right 5'9"
b. Camelon, Falkirk, August 1905
Career: Dunipace Jnrs/UNITED trial Oct to Nov 1924/
Kettering Town 1925/Raith Rovers Dec 1925 to cs 1933.

Willie Allison joined United on a month's trial from the Central Belt of Scotland having impressed appearing on the wing for his local club Dunipace Juniors, near Falkirk. Appearing once for the senior line-up in a fixture with South Shields, in the Ingham Cup final in aid of hospital charity, the Scot didn't show enough to earn a contract and returned north. After a spell south with Kettering, he found a place in the Raith Rovers line-up, a frequent goalscorer when they were promoted from Division Two during 1926-27. He appeared as a regular for three seasons totalling 71 games (30 goals).

Misc App & Goals: 1 app 0 gls.

ALNWICK Jak 2008-date

Goalkeeper 6'1"
b. Hexham, 17 June 1993
Career: Prudhoe YC/Sunderland jnr/
UNITED jnr 2008 (Gateshead loan
2011-12).

The younger brother of Ben Alnwick, another goalkeeper on the football circuit, Jak Alnwick was recognised as a promising all-round custodian who joined the Magpies after leaving the Sunderland junior set-up. Jak initially found his way up the ladder at St James' Park blocked by other 'keepers, but the departure of Foster and veteran Harper gave him an opening to challenge to become one of United's three senior goalkeepers. Having appeared for England at age groups from Under-16 to Under-20, Alnwick appeared in friendly matches for Newcastle during 2012-13, 2013-14 and 2014-15 while he was named on the bench on eight occasions for league and cup fixtures. He is an athletic shot-stopper.

Misc App & Goals: 2(2) app 0 gls.

ANDERSON Cecil 1953-1957

Goalkeeper 6'2"
b. Burnopfield, Co Durham,
28 June 1936
d. Gateshead, 4 November 2006
Career: Hyndly Jnrs/Leslie's Works/
Hebburn Argyle/UNITED amat 1953,
prof Sept 1954 (Ashington loan
1956-57)/West Stanley 1957/North
Shields 1958/South Shields 1959/Eppleton CW/Later various local clubs including Hylton CW 1964.

Born in Burnopfield, Cec Anderson moved to Hebburn when his family relocated in 1938. He was a noted juvenile player, representing Jarrow, Hebburn and Felling schoolboys and while employed as a welder at the Leslie Works, Cec was spotted by United scouts. Immediately after joining the Black'n'Whites, Anderson was thrown into first-team action in a friendly at Doncaster Rovers during October 1954 when the Magpies couldn't field regular goalkeepers Ronnie Simpson and Stewart Mitchell, nor Chris Harker. It wasn't a good evening at Belle Vue for the new guardian, Newcastle losing 7-2 to the Second Division club, Anderson being kept busy for most of the 90 minutes. He didn't remain long at Gallowgate, his career being disrupted by National Service in 1955 and 1956 when he served with the Royal Signals at Moenchengladbach. When in Germany he was watched by Bayern Munich playing services football and offered a deal in Bavaria, only for his wife to reject any move from Tyneside. He also had the opportunity to play in North America but decided to remain in the region. After leaving United in 1957 Cec appeared in local football, once being ordered off for Ashington after only five minutes as the referee did not like his modern Continental style boots he brought from Germany! Anderson ran a welding and fabrication company, Glenn Welding on Tyneside.

Misc App & Goals: 1 app 0 gls.

ARCHIBALD [Andrew] 1902

Half-back
b. unknown

Only with United briefly on trial during March 1902, Archibald was in United's midfield for an exhibition fixture against Celtic played at Berwick, a 4-2 defeat. It is likely he is Andrew Archibald who returned to Gallowgate and was offered terms in September 1900.

Misc App & Goals: 1 app 0 gls.

ARMSTRONG John 1881-1891

Half-back & Committee-Director
b. Sunderland, c1863

John Armstrong joined Newcastle United's pioneer club Stanley FC when the cricketers from the St Peter's area of the city decided to form an association football club during November 1881. Armstrong can be recognised along with William Coulson as being instrumental in forming Newcastle United. He played cricket for Woodbine CC, then Stanley and was one of the earliest of the fledgling club's Committee members and a director when East End became a limited company in 1890, serving on the Board until 1891. At half-back, he was a regular for Stanley during the historic first season of 1881-82, playing in eight of the 11 opening fixtures, including the club's very first game against Elswick Leather Works 2nd XI. Skipper of the side during 1883-84, John was the first captain to lead the club to silverware when, as East End, the club won the Northumberland Challenge Cup during 1885. He then took part in the region's top contest, the Northumberland-Durham Inter-County challenge final, when East End faced Darlington but lost 1-0. The half-back was still playing for the club lower down the ranks at reserve level as a veteran during 1888-89. Armstrong was a ship's joiner at the Tyne yards and lived originally in Stanley Street (from which the club's name was derived) then in Walbottle Street in the heart of Byker. His father, also a joiner, was an original shareholder of the club too.

Misc App & Goals: 59 app 5 gls.*

ARMSTRONG Keith Thomas 1979

Forward 5'8"
b. Corbridge, Northumberland,
11 October 1957
Career: Sunderland Jan 1975
(Newport Co loan 1978-79)
(Scunthorpe Utd loan 1978-79)/
UNITED cs 1979 (OPS (Fin) loan 1978-79)/Hong Kong FC 1979/OPS (Fin)
1980/Newport Co trial Oct 1980/Workington trial Nov 1980/OPS (Fin) 1981/Koparit (Fin) 1982/OPS (Fin) 1983/FC Kuusysi (Fin) 1984/KPV (Fin) 1985/KePS (Fin) 1986/Vasa IFK (Fin) 1987/TP-55 (Fin) 1989/IFK Mariehamn (Fin) 1990/RoPS (Fin) 1991, becoming player-manager 1993/TP-Seinajoki (Fin) manager Jan 1995 to 1996/FC Haka (Fin) manager 1998/HJK (Fin) manager 2001 to Sept 2007/SJK (Fin) Sporting Director Aug 2012.

After spells with Sunderland (11 app), Newport and Scunthorpe trying to find his way in the professional game, Tynesider Keith Armstrong worked at a local brewery when he arrived at St James' Park in a bid to impress boss Bill McGarry. He first appeared for United in a friendly match at Torquay during August 1979 then after a handful of further outings, when the boss was looking for someone to be loaned to the Oulu club in Finland, 21-year-old Armstrong was the name McGarry came up with. Although hardly an attractive move at the time, as it turned out, the adventure turned into a good step for Armstrong. He settled quickly in Finland and became a noted footballer, lifting trophies and appearing in the European Cup...even scoring at Anfield, although Liverpool netted 10 goals at the other end! Keith played for several clubs, notably for Oulu (92 app) and won the Finnish title on three occasions as a player, then as a manager was successful in five more trophy victories, Manager of the Year in 1999, 2000 and 2003. Taking his club into the Champions League, he also lifted the Finnish Cup three times. Nicknamed 'Keke' and holding dual nationality, Armstrong was a popular character in that country. After his football career, he worked as a television pundit in Finland and even took part in the local version of Strictly Come Dancing during 2006.

Misc App & Goals: 2(2) app 0 gls.

Players: other fixtures

ARMSTRONG Robin J 1976-1979

Midfield 5'10"
b. Newburn, Newcastle upon Tyne
Joining United as a junior from schools football in July 1976, Robin Armstrong turned professional during May 1978 and was a midfielder who could make little progress against such talent as established names Hibbitt, Connolly and Martin, as well as locals Walker and Cartwright at Gallowgate at the time. He appeared in a testimonial fixture for the Black'n'Whites at Blyth as the 1979-80 season started but was not retained and left the club in October 1979.

Misc App & Goals: 1 app 0 gls.

ARMSTRONG George 1965

Outside-right or left 5'6"
b. Hebburn, Co Durham, 9 August 1944
d. Hemel Hempstead, Hertfordshire, 1 November 2000
Career: Hawthorn Leslie Jnrs/Grimsby Town trial/UNITED trial 1961/Arsenal August 1961 (UNITED guest Oct 1965)/Leicester City Sept 1977 £15,000 (Philadelphia Fury (USA) loan cs 1978)/Stockport Co Sept 1978/ Retired 1979 becoming Aston Villa asst-coach/FK Mjolner (Nor) Jan 1981/Fulham asst-coach Dec 1981/ Trowbridge Town player July 1982 to June 1983/ Worcester City manager 1984-85/Kuwait national coach 1988-89/Also; Middlesbrough asst-coach, Queens Park Rangers asst-coach, FK Mjolner (Nor) manager/Arsenal asst-coach July 1990 to death in 2000.
A much gifted and decorated Tynesider, youth international George Armstrong was missed by United when working as an apprentice electrician as the Sixties began only to develop into a potent and consistent winger who lifted the league and cup double with Arsenal in 1971. Over 16 seasons (621 games 68 goals) for the Gunners, George also won the Fairs Cup and reached three other finals as well as reaching the England Under-23 side (6 app). He was a highly effective flank man, giving quality on the right or left wing. Known as 'Geordie' Armstrong in the capital, he made a return to the North East to appear in the Brian Clough testimonial fixture at Roker Park during October 1965, playing his part in a star-studded United guest forward line which hit six goals against their rivals. Following his retirement from playing, Armstrong was part of the Arsenal coaching staff and died after collapsing at their training complex in Hertfordshire when 56 years of age.

Misc App & Goals: 1 app 0 gls.

ARNISON Paul Simon 1994-2000

Right-back 5'10"
b. Hartlepool, 18 September 1977
Career: Everton jnr/UNITED jnr July 1994, prof March 1996/York City trial 2000/Hartlepool Utd March 2000 free/Carlisle Utd loan Oct 2003, pmt Feb 2004 free/Bradford City July 2008 free/Darlington Aug 2009/Celtic Nation (Carlisle) July 2012/Sunshine Coast Fire (Aus) player-coach Jan 2013.
Paul Arnison was capable of playing in defence or midfield and was on the fringe of United's first-team squad during the latter seasons of the 1990s, appearing in a senior line-up against Bishop Auckland during August 1995 when several youngsters were blooded as substitutes. But he couldn't fully break through and moved to a lower level of the game where he was a solid performer for both Hartlepool (90 app) and Carlisle (110 app). Paul helped Hartlepool to promotion from Division Three during 2003 then moved to Brunton Park where he

was influential as the Cumbrians regained their Football League status by winning the Conference title in 2005 and reaching the Football League Trophy final. Arnison was then part of Carlisle's Division Two title winning side the following year. Later appearing for Darlington, he lifted the FA Trophy at Wembley in 2011 before heading to Australia to start a coaching career.

Misc App & Goals: 1(1) app 0 gls.

ATKIN Liam 1999-2007

Midfield 6'2"
b. Ashington, 12 December 1986
Career: UNITED jnr 1999, prof Dec 2004/Carlisle Utd Jan 2007 free/ Queen of the South trial Aug 2007/ Newcastle Blue Star Sept 2007/Blyth Spartans Oct 2007/Gateshead Nov 2007/Ashington Feb 2008/Airdrie Utd trial July 2008/Cheltenham Town trial Aug 2008/West Allotment Celtic Aug 2008/Ashington May 2009/Blyth Spartans June 2011/Ashington Aug 2011 & UNITED community and later Foundation coach Jan 2009/Celtic Nation Sept 2013/Shildon Sept 2014.
Slim and tall, Liam Atkin could operate in defence or in midfield, a versatile footballer with a good engine and passing ability. Ashington born and bred, he was part of a Newcastle United XI side which travelled to Spain to face Malaga in September 2005 then was elevated to the senior squad for Newcastle's pre-season matches for the new season, in 2006-07. He took part as a substitute at Carrow Road against Norwich City when several youngsters were fielded. However, just as he was making an impression Atkin unluckily broke his leg in a training collision with James Milner. After that, he found it difficult to regain momentum at St James' Park, later moving into non-league football in the region, notably for Ashington where he appeared over 200 times. Liam also retained a link with the Magpies as a coach with the club's Foundation set-up.

Misc App & Goals: 1(1) app 0 gls.

AYRE Colin 1971-1975

Outside-right or left 5'10"
b. Ashington, 14 March 1956
Career: UNITED jnr Oct 1971, prof Sept 1973/Telstar (Neth) July 1975 free to June 1976/Torquay Utd Sept 1976/Ashington 1976/Telstar (Neth) July 1977/Wacker Innsbruck (Ast) Nov 1980/SPG Raika Innsbruck (Ast) Feb 1982/Whitley Bay/later appearing for local clubs including Stobswood March 1988.
A local winger from Ashington, Colin Ayre was part of United's junior ranks as the Seventies began. Ayre was included in a United line-up sprinkled with first-teamers for a friendly against Workington at Borough Park during August 1973, but with players like Stewart Barrowclough ahead of him on the staff, the Ashington product had little hope of breaking through. He moved to Torquay but managed two games for the Gulls before heading for Holland and Austria where he recorded a decent career. Later moving into a midfield role, Colin was part of Wacker Innsbruck's Second Division winning side in 1981.

Misc App & Goals: 1 app 0 gls.

BAILEY John 1899

Right-back
b. unknown
With the local Mickley club, John Bailey was handed a United trial during April and May 1899. The full-back was given one opportunity in first-team company, for the friendly visit of Hibernian to St James' Park during April 1899. Taking part in a 2-2 draw he wasn't retained and returned to appear for Mickley.

Misc App & Goals: 1 app 0 gls.

BALDWIN Shaun Thomas 1991-1996

Striker 5'10"
b. Newcastle upon Tyne, 16 September 1976
Part of United's junior developme[nt] squad as the club went through [a] huge transformation during the ea[rly] seasons of the 1990s, Shaun Baldw[in] joined the club in April 1991 fro[m] Benfield School and didn't receive many opportunities [to] impress. He was one of several substitutes to get on [to] the pitch during the Derek Bell testimonial at Gateshe[ad] during August 1993, however a fractured tibia set h[im] back and with big-name stars arriving at Gallowgate [on] a frequent basis during that era, he was allowed [to] depart during 1996.

Misc App & Goals: 0(1) app 0 gls.

BARNETT Charles John 2007

Midfield 5'10"
b. Liverpool, 19 September 1988
Career: Liverpool jnr, prof July 2006 to June 2007 free/UNITED trial July 2007 to Aug 2007/Nottingham Fores[t] Blackburn Rovers & Scunthorpe Utd trial Aug to Sept 2007/Tranmere Rovers Aug 2008/Falkirk trial cs 2010/ Accrington Stanley Aug 2010 to June 2013/Telford Utd Aug 2013.
On Liverpool's books as a junior, Charlie Barnett earne[d] a professional contract at Anfield and was a FA You[th] Cup winner with the Reds in both 2006 and 200[7] alongside Jay Spearing, scoring a wonderful 30 ya[rd] strike at St James' Park in a semi-final meeting. Th[e] England Under-16 player however was released and h[e] landed at a number of clubs, including the Magpies, [in] search of a new deal. A lively attacking midfielder wit[h] good strength and a strong shot, he worked well wit[h] other players and liked to get into the box. Barnett wa[s] at Gallowgate for a month as the 2007-08 bega[n] appearing from the bench against Italian giants Juventu[s] during July. With a glut of midfield players already at S[t] James' Park, he wasn't retained, Charlie finding a hom[e] with Tranmere (44 app) before moving to serv[e] Accrington where he totalled over 100 games, includin[g] a match against United in a Football League Cup ti[e] during August 2010.

Misc App & Goals: 0(1) app 0 gls.

BARNWELL John 1969

Midfield 5'8"
b. High Heaton, Newcastle upon Tyn[e] 24 December 1938
Career: Heaton Stannington/Whitley Bay/Bishop Auckland amat 1953/ Arsenal amat Sept 1955, prof Nov 1956/Nottingham Forest March 1964 £40,000 (UNITED guest Nov 1969)/Sheffield Utd April 1970 to June 1971 when he retired due to injury/ Hereford Utd coach cs 1972/ Peterborough Utd coach 1974, becoming manager May 1977 to Nov 1978/ Wolverhampton Wand manager Nov 1979 to Jan 1982/ Saudi Arabia coaching 1982-83/AEK Athens (Gr) manager Aug 1983 to Jan 1984/Notts Co manager June 1987 to Dec 1988/Walsall manager Jan 1989 to March 1990/Northampton Town managerial consultant 1992-93/Grantham Town manager Feb 1996/LMA Chief Executive Aug 1996, becoming Vice-President.
A former England youth player, John Barnwell, guested once for his hometown club during November 1969, par[t] of United's line-up which faced Sunderland in the Le[n] Ashurst testimonial at Roker Park. He could have been [a] Magpie player when a schoolboy, but United hesitate[d] and he eventually joined Arsenal (151 app) where h[e]

became a regular for the Gunners, and later also for Nottingham Forest (202 app). A talented and workmanlike midfielder, Barnwell was capped by England at Under-23 level (2 app), he won promotion with Sheffield United before retiring through injury then started on a coaching career of mixed results; boss when Wolves reached the Football League Cup final in 1980 and once banned from Greek football after making remarks about the game's standards in that country. He later did much to raise the profile of the League Managers Association, associated with the LMA for many years.

Misc App & Goals: 1 app 0 gls.

BARRETT Paul David 1994-1999

Midfield 5'10"
b. Newcastle upon Tyne, 13 April 1978
Career: Montague & N Fenham BC/ Walker Central BC 1988/UNITED jnr cs 1994, prof June 1998 (York City trial 1999)/Wrexham March 1999 free/ Blyth Spartans 2004 free/Gateshead/ Dunston Fed.

As a schoolboy in Newcastle's West End, Paul Barratt appeared for England at Under-18 level and was offered a place at the FA's School of Excellence at Lilleshall, but decided to stay on Tyneside with United. Paul was a busy midfielder, fast and accurate when using the ball, as well as having an eye for goal. As a teenager, Barratt impressed many showing good strength and as a leader from midfield. Although restricted by two long-term injuries, he reached contention as the 1996-97 season began and was selected to take part in a friendly against Gateshead during July, appearing from the dug-out for Darren Huckerby in attack. He was also on the bench for the UEFA Cup-tie with Monaco. Barratt found a home on the Welsh border with Wrexham, totalling over 130 games and winning promotion from Division Three in 2002-03.

Misc App & Goals: 0(1) app 0 gls.

BARRON Charles William 1916

Right-back 5'9"
b. Prudhoe, near Gateshead, 1889 (Q3)
Career: Durham City/Leicester Fosse Sept 1914 (UNITED war-guest 1915-16)/Scotswood cs 1919.

Returning home to Tyneside for part of the hostilities during World War One, Charles Barron played local football and pulled on United's black-and-white striped shirt once during April 1916, in an entertaining contest with Blackburn Rovers at Ewood Park, won 5-4. Although normally a right-back for Leicester, Barron appears to have operated in midfield during that game. Never a regular at Filbert Street, totalling 22 games, he experienced a woeful season in the Fosse ranks during 1914-15 when the Foxes were forced to apply for re-election.

Misc App & Goals: 1 app 0 gls.

BARTLETT Adam James 2001-2005

Goalkeeper 6'0"
b. Newcastle upon Tyne, 27 February 1986
Career: UNITED jnr 2001, prof July 2002 to May 2005/Trials at various clubs during cs 2005; Rochester Rhino's (USA), Vasteras SK (Swd), Dunston Fed, Doncaster Rovers, Dundee Utd, Rotherham Utd, Boston Utd, Aberdeen, Leeds Utd, Rushden & Diamonds/Blyth Spartans Sept 2005 (Vancouver Whitecaps briefly)/Consett July 2006/ Kidderminster Harriers July 2008 (Cambridge Utd loan 2008-09)/Hereford Utd June 2009/Gateshead June 2012/Also brief periods at Blackpool, York City, Hartlepool Utd & Burton Albion.

Connected with United since a nine-year-old at the club's Academy, Adam Bartlett was a tall and agile goalkeeper. He was strong on shot-stopping and able to pick crosses out of the air with ease at junior level. But with Shay Given and Steve Harper dominating the 'keeper places at Gallowgate, there was little opportunity for the Geordie at his home-town club. He reached United's Premier League squad during the 2003-04 season and sat on the bench for a visit to face Sheffield Wednesday in friendly action. Adam was also part of the party which travelled for a huge Champions League clash with Internazionale in Milan during March 2003. Released at the end of the 2004-05 season, Bartlett travelled far and wide to earn a contract, but eventually settled with Blyth Spartans where his form over almost 100 games caught attention. Adam played for the England 'C' team on five occasions, first capped when at Croft Park in May 2007. He moved to Kidderminster then Hereford where he totalled 127 games in the Football League. Adam was part of the Gateshead eleven which took part in the 2014 Conference Play-Off in a bid to reach Football League status once more. He also coaches locally in the North East.

Misc App & Goals: 0 app 0 gls (1 sub no app).

BEATTIE William 1894-1895

Right-back
b. Newcastle upon Tyne, [1873]
William Beattie was at St James' Park during season 1894-95 just after the club had progressed to Football League status. Having appeared for Science & Art in 1889, he joined United from the associated Rutherford College side during October 1894. Beattie became one of Newcastle's earliest recorded substitutes, coming on for Harry Jeffrey during a friendly with Sunderland in January 1895, a derby contest lost by 4-1.

Misc App & Goals: 0(1) app 0 gls.

BELL [Thomas] 1891-1892

Half-back
b. [Newcastle upon Tyne, c1872]
With Newcastle East End during the 1891-92 season, Bell made a friendly appearance for the club against Victoria Wednesday and was largely a reserve in the Heatonites second-string, then known as East End Amateurs. He is probably the same footballer who appeared for Rendel, Newcastle West End and afterwards Newcastle Wednesday and Heaton Rovers. Bell was recognised as a good footballer and represented Northumberland County's line-up. It is likely to be the Bell who lived on Heaton Road and purchased shares in the East Enders during 1891 when an apprentice pattern-maker.

Misc App & Goals: 1 app 0 gls.*

BERTRAM Mark Joseph 2005-2008

Right-back 5'10"
b. Newcastle upon Tyne, 2 April 1990
Career: UNITED jnr 2005, prof c2007, to March 2008 free/Gateshead June 2008/Team Northumbria Dec 2009 to c2014 & UNITED Foundation asst-coach.

Operating at full-back or occasionally in midfield, Mark Bertram was of small build, but very lively in any position. He possessed good mobility, able to pass the ball and carry it, linking the play effectively. Along with several other young professionals he was given a chance from the bench in a handful of pre-season warm-up games at the start of 2007-08. Mark developed alongside Andy Carroll in Newcastle's junior squad, but was hindered by a cartilage injury and was out of action for several months. Leaving the professional game, he took a Sports Development degree at Northumbria University in Newcastle. Bertram was a keen cricketer in the summer months and played for the Benwell & Walbottle club.

Misc App & Goals: 0(3) app 0 gls.

BETTS Arthur Charles 1911

Left-back or Left-half 5'11"
b. Gainsthorpe, near Scunthorpe, 2 January 1886
d. Scunthorpe, 1967 (Q2)
Career: N Lindsey/Gainsborough Trinity May 1905/Watford May 1907/ Gainsborough Trinity May 1910 free/ UNITED July 1911 trial, pmt Sept 1911 £500/Derby Co Oct 1911 £450/Hull City May 1914/ Scunthorpe & Lindsey Utd June 1920/Normanby Park Steelworks player-coach May 1923/Lysaght Sports coach.

A stonemason by trade, Charlie Betts impressed United officials in outings for Gainsborough Trinity during 1910-11, then a Second Division outfit. Totalling 102 games for the Lincolnshire club over three seasons, he moved to Tyneside for a £500 fee; £350 to Gainsborough and £150 to his previous club, Southern League Watford where he had totalled 100 matches. But he didn't settle at Gallowgate, Betts appearing once for the Magpies in senior company, at Saltburn during September 1911 when he partnered Bill McCracken at full-back. He soon moved to Derby and was part of the Rams' Division Two title side in 1912, recording 74 games for County. Calm headed and plucky, he was described at the time as a "dashing and enthusiastic performer".

Misc App & Goals: 1 app 0 gls.

BISHOP Simon Thomas 1987-1990

Goalkeeper 6'0"
b. Middlesbrough, 12 March 1971
Career: UNITED jnr Aug 1987 to cs 1990/Later with Barrow Jan 2000/Gateshead July 2006/Spennymoor Utd Jan 2007/Stalybridge Celtic Feb 2007/Guisborough Town July 2007/Tow Law Town July 2008/Spennymoor Town July 2009/Bishop Auckland 2011-12/Also appeared for; Whitby Town, Northallerton Town, Dunston Fed & Sunday league team Hetton Lions (2009-10).

Simon Bishop was a young 'keeper at Gallowgate when Gary Kelly and Martin Thomas held the first-team shirt. Rarely to be given any hint of a chance, he was once handed the senior jersey for a friendly with Alnwick Town during March 1988, Simon having an easy afternoon in Northumberland as United won 6-1. Bishop later found a career on the North East non-league scene with various clubs over a period of more than 20 years.

Misc App & Goals: 1 app 0 gls.

BLACK William Hardy 1881-1883

Full-back
b. Newcastle upon Tyne, 1863 (Q2)
d. Newcastle upon Tyne, 1932 (Q2)
Born and raised in the suburb of Byker like many of the club's earliest trail-blazers as the game developed, Willie Black was also a cricketer in the district, appearing for the Stanley club during the summers of 1880 and 1881. He joined Stanley FC when it was formed in November 1881 when he was a teenager and was with the new club when they changed their name to Newcastle East End the following year. A regular full-back for a period, he lived in Conyers Road then Headlam Street and like many of United's pioneers worked in Tyneside's shipyards, as a riveter.

Misc App & Goals:
11 app 0 gls.*

Players: other fixtures

BLACKETT John Thomas 1883-1888

Full-back

b. St Peter's, Newcastle upon Tyne, 1861 (Q4)

d. Newcastle upon Tyne, 8 February 1936

One of four Blackett brothers to play football during the embryo Victorian years of the game's development on Tyneside, John Blackett appeared for East End over three seasons. Joining the club in 1883, he was originally raised in St Peter's, Newcastle United's birthplace, not far from Stanley Street. A wherryman, Blackett was the older brother of William (qv) and Frank (qv) and played for the East Enders for three seasons, good enough to be selected for the Newcastle & District XI that faced The Corinthians in 1887. John occasionally operated as a goalkeeper, and like most players of the era, played in various outfield positions, notably half-back as well as full-back. He unluckily broke his leg during the Temperance Festival matches of the summer 1887 and was unable to work for many months, the club playing benefit matches to keep him financially secure. By the time of the 1911 census, he was living in Raby Street and still working as a waterman on the Tyne.

Misc App & Goals: 5 app 0 gls.*

Footnote: The youngest of the Blackett brothers, Joseph (b 20 June 1875) did not appear in senior football for United or their pioneers, but he was the most successful of the noted Tyneside footballers. With Newcastle's reserve squad, he joined Wolves in 1897 and totalled 103 games, also appearing for Derby, Sunderland, Middlesbrough, as well as Leicester, Luton and Rochdale where he became manager.

BLOOMER Stephen 1918

Inside-right 5'7"

b. Cradley Heath, 20 January 1874

d. Derby, 16 April 1938

Career: Derby Swifts 1888/Derby Midland March 1891/Derby Co amat June 1891, prof Aug 1892 (Tutbury Hawthorn guest April 1892)/Middlesbrough March 1906 £750/Derby Co Sept 1910 to retirement in 1914/FC Britannia (Ger) coach July 1914 (Ruhleben FA during internment 1914-18)/FC Blauw-Wit (Neth) coach May 1918/UNITED war-guest 1918-19/Derby Co asst-trainer & occasional player Aug 1919, retiring playing Jan 1920, becoming trainer Aug 1921/Grenadier Guards (Can) coach April to Aug 1922/Real Union (Sp) manager Oct 1923 to April 1925/Derby Co asst-trainer & groundsman to demise in 1938.

The biggest name in English football in the years before World War One, Steve Bloomer had a brief run out in United's colours at the end of his illustrious playing career, in a wartime friendly against Sunderland at St James' Park during December 1918. A match in aid of war charities, Bloomer was outstanding and scored in a 4-0 victory. Capped on 23 occasions for England, he scored a remarkable 28 goals for his country and was recognised as the finest striker in the business. Although described as a "pale, thin, ghost-like, almost ill-looking" individual, he possessed a rich footballing talent, a natural in touch and movement, penned as being "as crafty as an Oriental, and as slippery as an eel". Bloomer was cool-headed, had a direct style, a wonderful body-swerve to go past defenders and a terrific shot, always quick to see an opening. With Derby (527 app over 18 seasons) and also for Middlesbrough (130 app), Bloomer graced the football field and netted 333 goals for the Rams and 62 for Boro. Apart from his England caps, Steve was a regular for the Football League XI (15 app) and reached two FA Cup finals. During World War One, Steve was confined to the Ruhleben civilian detention camp in Berlin, along with United player Ed Dutton. During a flirtation as a coach and manager afterwards, in Spain he led the Real Union club of the Basque region to a Copa

del Rey victory in 1924. Steve was inducted into the country's football Hall of Fame and noted as a Football League Legend while a bust of Bloomer stands next to the home dug-out at Pride Park. He was related by marriage to Alf Quantrill, Derby and England, while Steve's brother Philip was briefly on Derby's books also.

Misc App & Goals: 1 app 1 gl.

BOSWELL William 1887

Forward

b. Winsford, Cheshire, December 1864

Career: Durham University 1885/Gateshead Ass 1886 (EAST END guest Feb 1887)/Newcastle West End 1886-87/Gateshead NER 1889 to 1891.

William Boswell made a single guest appearance for the East Enders against a Durham University side during February 1887 when he was a player with the Gateshead club. Noted as a bricklayer's apprentice then afterwards as a "Locomotive Burner" in the 1891 census, Boswell by then worked at the giant North Eastern Railway complex in Gateshead. He later became an engine-driver residing in Hexham. William was a decent footballer, good enough to represent Durham County during 1886-87 and 1887-88. His brother also appeared for Gateshead Association after the pair had settled on Tyneside following a move from Cheshire.

Misc App & Goals: 1 app 0 gls.*

BRADY J 1890-1891

Forward

b. Scotland

Career: Renton Thistle to 1889/EAST END Aug 1890/Rendel [Renton] 1891 to 1892.

A Scottish forward, Brady turned out for Newcastle East End in friendly action during September 1890 after arriving with another Renton player J Ward at the start of the new season. He was also a noted runner during his time on Tyneside. It is possible that he is Joseph Brady who appeared with Renton in 1891-92 then joined Sheffield United for the following campaign before returning to Scotland with Edinburgh St Bernard's in August 1893. He turned out in a Scottish trial match during March 1894.

Misc App & Goals: 2 app 0 gls.*

BRENNAN Stephen 1998-2005

Right-back 5'8"

b. Dublin, 26 March 1983

Career: St Joseph's BC (Dublin) 1994/UNITED jnr cs 1998, prof 2000 (Shelbourne loan 2004-05)/St Patricks Ath Aug 2005 to Nov 2008/Bray Wand Feb 2009 to Jan 2012.

A bright Irish full-back, Stephen Brennan was brought to Tyneside as a 15-year-old after United had created a scouting network in Dublin. Described as a prodigious talent as a teenager, he was capped by Ireland at youth and Under-21 level when in United's ranks. Fast down the right touchline, he was unlucky with injury at St James' Park though, having problems with a persistent hamstring and dislocated shoulder. Brennan took part in a Newcastle United XI fixture with Gateshead during August 2002, then was an unused substitute for a friendly with Sheffield Wednesday a year later. But those injuries cost him opportunities just when he was at the right age and when both first-teamers Griffin and Hughes were out of action. Stephen was also unfortunate not to win a first outing for the Republic's senior international side, again injured when he was lined up to deputise. Later playing in midfield and operating at centre-half, Brennan continued his career back in Ireland.

Misc App & Goals: 0(1) app 0 gls.

BROOKS David 1917

Left-half

b. unknown

Career: Belfast Celtic/Distillery (Belfast)(UNITED war-guest 1917-18)/Newcastle Munition Wand manager 1918/Wallsend manager 1919.

David Brooks turned out for United at left-half in a sing[le] fixture, against South Shields at Horsley Hill durin[g] October 1917. A player with Distillery in Northern Irelan[d] he remained in the region with local clubs on Tyneside[.]

Misc App & Goals: 1 app 0 gls.

BROUGHTON Frederick 1888-1890

Full-back

b. Newcastle upon Tyne, June 1869

d. Newcastle upon Tyne, 1945 (Q1)

Fred Broughton became a Newcastle East End playe[r] during September 1888, in the reserve Swifts eleven the[n] on the senior's team-sheet for the friendly wit[h] Edinburgh University during January of the followin[g] year. One of several early footballers born and raised i[n] Byker, Fred worked in the shipyards, by the 1891 censu[s] being noted as a "Holder Up". From research it has bee[n] ascertained he also played for the North Sands Rover[s] eleven in 1888 as a guest. He was the younger brothe[r] of John Broughton (qv) who appeared in the club[s] Northern League side. In 1901, Fred was living in the S[t] Peter's district, still working in the shipyards, now as [a] riveter.

Misc App & Goals: 1 app 0 gls.*

BROWELL Thomas 1916

Centre-forward 5'8"

b. Walbottle, Newcastle upon Tyne, 19 October 1892

d. Fylde, October 1955

Career: Newburn Grange/Hull City amat April 1910, prof Oct 1910/Everton Dec 1911 £1,650/Manchester City Oct 1913 £1,780 (West Stanley war-guest 1915-16)(UNITED war-guest 1915-16)/Blackpool Sept 1926 £1,150/Lytham player-coach June 1930 to cs 1933/Morecambe Dec 1933 to May 1934.

One of three brothers to start their careers in footba[ll] with Hull City, Tommy Browell became a potent striker i[n] the game before and after World War One. He first mad[e] an impact as a teenager at Anlaby Road in Hull (52 ap[p], 32 gls) where his high energy levels provided muc[h] excitement up front. Tom's ability as a cut and thrus[t] goal-poacher earned a move to Manchester City durin[g] 1913 and at Maine Road he soon became a terrac[e] favourite. Back in his native Tyneside during th[e] hostilities, Browell guested for the Magpies in attack fo[r] a double-header with Blackburn Rovers during April 191[6] in aid of war charity. The Geordie netted an impressiv[e] 139 goals in 247 games for City over nine seasons, at hi[s] peak immediately after war, during season 1920-2[1] grabbing 31 goals. He was close to an England cap; [a] trialist in 1911-12 while he also appeared for the Footba[ll] League and FA combinations after the hostilities. Browe[ll] reached the FA Cup final in 1926, City's ace up front i[n] that run with seven goals, and later played a brief par[t] in Blackpool's Second Division title victory during 1929-30. After leaving the game, Tommy settled on the wes[t] coast, a tram driver for Lytham St Annes Corporatio[n.] Such was his popularity a street was named after hi[m] near to Maine Road in Manchester.

Misc App & Goals: 2 app 0 gls.

BRYCE 1889-1890

Half-back

b. unknown

A player with Newcastle East End during season 1889-90, Bryce made his debut appearance towards the end of the campaign in a friendly against Elswick Rangers at Chillingham Road, a convincing 5-0 victory. It is possible the player was James Bryce who appeared for Kilmarnock during the previous season of 1888-89, a time when many largely amateur Scottish footballers crossed the border in an attempt to fix up a professional contract.

Misc App & Goals: 2 app 0 gls.*

BUNYAN Charles 1901-1903

Goalkeeper 5'10"
b. Brimington, near Chesterfield, April 1878
d. Ixelles, Brussels (Belgium), 3 August 1922
Career: Chesterfield Old Horns/Spital Olympic/Chesterfield Town 1886/ Hyde Utd 1887/Derby Co 1890/ Chesterfield Town Aug 1892 (Sheffield Utd guest Nov 1892)/Sheffield Utd Feb 1894/Derby Co March 1894/ Ilkeston Town Aug 1895/Heanor Town/Walsall Nov 1896/New Brompton June 1898/UNITED Jan 1901/ Ripley Ath March 1903/Willenhall/Bloxwich Strollers/ Canadian football c1905/Grassmoor Red Rose Aug 1906/Brimington Ath player-trainer Aug 1908/Racing Club de Bruxelles (Belg) coach 1910/Sweden Olympic Council coach 1912/Orgryte IS (Swd) coach 1912/ Standard Liege (Belg) coach/RSC Anderlecht (Belg) coach 1916.

An England amateur player, Charles Bunyan had a colourful career and was a larger-than-life character in football. During the early part of his footballing days as a 'keeper with Hyde United he was between the sticks as Preston famously fired 26 goals past him during an FA Cup-tie in October 1887. Sometimes erratic as a last line of defence, he also once conceded another 12 goals as Walsall lost heavily to Darwen during the 1896-97. Bunyan would use occasional venture up field himself leaving the posts unguarded in bizarre forays. For a period when in Derbyshire he combined his footballing career with that of a publican at The Poplar and Marquis of Hartington, near to Chesterfield's ground. Charles was well-known in the district, dabbling as a theatrical impresario bringing many acts to his pubs, music-hall style, while he developed a somewhat lucrative sideline of selling home-made shin-guards to local players. Strong-willed and often with a short fuse, his relationship with club officials was sometimes strained. Although he was in the game for a lengthy period, Bunyan rarely had a sustained period with a top club; playing as a regular in Walsall's Second Division line-up (47 app) just before the turn of the century. With United on the lookout for goalkeeping cover he joined Black'n'Whites as 1901 opened. Charles took part in one senior fixture for the Magpies; a home friendly contest with Derby County during February of that year. Bunyan was reserve to Kingsley and Watts and was part of the reserve team which lifted the Northern Alliance trophy during 1900-01. After retiring from playing, Charles began a coaching career on the Continent where he was involved in organising the Olympics in Stockholm during 1912. Escaping from German occupation as war broke out and returning to England, Bunyan joined the noted Middlesex Footballer's Battalion in 1915 only to be forced out of the fighting due to shell-shock. He afterwards lived in Belgium to his death. His brother George appeared once for Walsall, while his son Maurice played in Belgium and later coached in the Low Countries, manager of Bordeaux during the Forties. Bunyan's second offspring, Charles (junior), appeared for the Great Britain team at the 1920 Olympics when an amateur with Chelsea.

Misc App & Goals: 1 app 0 gls.

BURN Steven R 1976-1979

Left-back 5'6"
b. Newcastle upon Tyne, 1959
Steven Burn joined United initially as a schoolboy during the summer of 1975 earning a contract the following year in July 1976. He took part in a friendly encounter with Gateshead in August 1978, arriving on the field from the substitute's bench after 70 minutes. Burn though was not considered again and was released in the close-season of 1979.

Misc App & Goals: 0(1) app 0 gls.

BURNS John G 1887-1888

Half-back or Forward
b. Newcastle upon Tyne, c1871
With the Cheviot junior club of Byker, John Burns teamed up with the rapidly developing Newcastle East End line-up during the 1887-88 season. A prominent player with Cheviot, he was a Byker man employed as a labourer in one of the local engine-works. Burns gained a call-up from the reserve side for two games in 1887-88 before departing, probably during the close-season.

Misc App & Goals: 2 app 0 gls.*

BURT Jamie Paul 1994-1997

Striker 5'11"
b. Blyth, 29 September 1979
Career: UNITED jnr cs 1994 to cs 1997 free/Carlisle Utd 1997/Whitby Town Aug 2001/Chesterfield Dec 2001 (Carlisle Utd loan 2002-03)/ Scarborough Aug 2003 free/Whitby Town Sept 2003/Blyth Spartans Oct 2003/Bedlington Terriers Sept 2006/Also appeared for; Bridlington Town, FC Aberdeen (Scarborough), Edgehill Mere (Scarborough)/Later returned to the North East and appeared in minor football, including for Blyth Joiners Arms and Blyth Sports & Social.

Raised in Blyth, Jamie Burt at one point in his junior career looked to have a bright future. Highly rated by United's coaches at the time, he was even tipped for the very top after appearing for his country at school and youth level. Jamie played alongside Michael Owen as England faced Scotland at St James' Park in 1995, yet while Owen's career went to the very top, Burt's never really took off. He only managed one appearance in United's senior side, as a substitute during a friendly against Bishop Auckland in August 1995. He found the net when alongside Paul Kitson in attack during the 4-3 victory but then was soon caught up with a disastrous drug addiction. Arrested by police as part of Operation Elbe to drive out the heroin menace around Blyth, Burt was convicted for conspiring drugs in March 1999. As a result his football career was in tatters. He moved into non-league football with Whitby where after impressing in a good FA Cup run during 2001-02 gained another chance in senior football with Chesterfield, cementing a regular spot the Spirerite's line-up, totalling 46 games. Jamie's brother David Burt was also on United's books.

Misc App & Goals: 0(1) app 1 gl.

CAIG Antony 2002-2006

Goalkeeper 6'1"
b. Whitehaven, 11 April 1974
Career: Carlisle Utd July 1992/ Blackpool March 1999 £5,000/ Charlton Ath loan Nov 2000, pmt Jan 2001/Hibernian July 2001/UNITED trial Oct 2002, loan Jan 2003, pmt June 2003 (Barnsley loan 2003-04)/ Vancouver Whitecaps (Can) April 2006 free/Gretna loan June 2007, pmt Oct 2007/Houston Dynamo (USA) Jan 2008/New York Red Bull (USA) April 2008/Chesterfield March 2009/Workington July 2009 & Carlisle Utd gkp-coach/Carlisle Utd June 2010, retaining the role as gkp-coach.

Newcastle added goalkeeper Tony Caig to their squad during 2002-03 essentially as cover to the established Shay Given and Steve Harper. Having tasted promotion success in the Third Division during 1995, 1997 and 2001, Tony had good experience having played 56 games for Blackpool and almost 300 for Carlisle where he twice reached the Football League Trophy final in 1995 and 1997. As third choice custodian, Caig was rarely in the limelight, appearing in a handful of pre-season friendlies as well as being selected on 16 occasions over four seasons for the substitute bench in first-class action, all without getting between the posts for real. It was frustrating for the Cleator Moor raised 'keeper who had started his football at Brunton Park. Tall and ideally built for the goalkeeper role, after his stint in the shadows, Tony completed a switch to Canada. Returning to Carlisle at the end of his career, he again reached the final of the Football League Trophy in 2011. Caig began a specialised coaching role with goalkeepers.

Misc App & Goals: 0(4) app 0 gls.

CALDWELL Gary Robert 1998-2004

Centre-half 6'1"
b. Stirling, 12 April 1982
Career: Celtic BC/UNITED jnr June 1998, prof April 1999 (Darlington loan 2001-02)(Hibernian loan 2001-02)(Coventry City loan 2002-03) (Derby Co loan 2003-04)/Hibernian Jan 2004 free (SBV Vitesse (Bel) trial July 2004)/Celtic June 2006 free/Wigan Ath Jan 2010 becoming asst-player-coach July 2014.

Within 12 months of his elder brother Steven's arrival at Gallowgate, Gary Caldwell also made the trip from his home in Stirling to join Newcastle's junior ranks. A centre-back like his brother, Gary had appeared for the Scotland school and youth side and was a much coveted youngster. He had loan spells to gain experience in competitive football and some at St James' Park rated Gary highly, but he struggled to get any opportunity in Newcastle's senior line-up. There was plenty of defensive competition for the centre-back role; Goma, Marcelino, Dumas, Aaron Hughes as well as Dabizas, Beharall and of course his own brother. Many considered he should have been given a chance by Bobby Robson, yet the closest Gary came to first-class action was a couple of outings on the bench early in the 1999-2000 campaign and a similar non-playing role in a tough UEFA Cup trip to face Roma during the same season. Reaching Scotland's line-up as a United reserve at Under-21, 'B' and full level, Caldwell did appear in United's first-team during an end-of-season trip to face a Trinidad XI and Tobago side in May 2001 then afterwards in a friendly with Hull City and for a testimonial fixture against West Bromwich Albion (when he played alongside his brother for the Magpies). A tough competitor with decent distribution of the ball from the back line, Gary became frustrated at Gallowgate and was allowed to leave to find a new club, moving to Easter Road in Edinburgh were his career took off. Caldwell became a regular for the

Players: other fixtures

Scots for a period, while he secured medals in the Scottish title race, Scottish Cup and Scottish League Cup. Gary was highly rated with Hibs and Celtic, voted his country's Footballer of the Year for 2008-09 and twice selected for the Team of the Year award. As 2010 opened and after 265 games north of the border, Caldwell moved back to the top level in England, joining Wigan where he showed that he could make a career in one of the world's best leagues. In over 100 games, he became a lynchpin at the back for the Latics for a period and was central to their survival battles to stay in the Premier League, always a committed skipper for Roberto Martinez. Due to a persistent hip injury he unluckily missed out on their Wembley glory in the 2013 FA Cup, a non-playing substitute, but as captain lifted the trophy. Steve played alongside his brother in the blue shirt of his country, a rarity for the Scots and totalled 18 games at Under-21 level, four at 'B' level and more than 50 caps for the full national side.

Misc App & Goals: 0(4) app 0 gls.

CAMPBELL Thomas 1887-1888

Full-back
b. probably Tyneside
Career: Rosehill 1884/Boundary 1885/EAST END March 1887/Rendel 1888, becoming trainer 1894.

Tom Campbell was a defender who took part in a handful of first-team fixtures for Newcastle East End during season 1886-87 including the record 19-0 walkover of Point Pleasant. Starting playing the game on a regular basis with local clubs Rosehill and Boundary, he appeared for Northumberland and the Newcastle & District eleven during 1887-88. After Campbell left the East Enders, Tom had a lengthy stay with Benwell club, Rendel on the other side of the city. At their Mill Lane ground, he was a stalwart player and reached the Northumberland Challenge Cup final with Rendel.

Misc App & Goals: 20 app 0 gls.*

CARNIE 1904

Inside-forward
b. probably Scotland
When United travelled to face Kilmarnock in a friendly match during April 1904, they gave an opportunity at inside-forward to a player noted in the press of the day by the name of Carnie. Virtually nothing is known about this footballer, only that he played for a club "south of Ayr". It is likely he was a local Ayrshire junior given a trial by Newcastle officials in the 4-1 defeat.

Misc App & Goals: 1 app 0 gls.

CARR John James 1913-1914

Forward 5'9"
b. Seaton Delaval, Northumberland, 1894 (Q4)
Career: Bedlington Utd/UNITED April 1913 £50/Ashington 1914/Blyth Spartans Sept 1914 (Ashington loan 1914-15) to c1920.

Watched by United scouts when playing local football in the Northern Alliance, John Carr was given a contract at St James' Park towards the end of the 1912-13 season but found it impossible to push his way through a very talented first-team squad of players. Carr took part in the match against a Player's Union XI during September 1913 at Gallowgate to raise funds for the organisation. He soon returned to football in Northumberland with Ashington and Blyth Spartans.

Misc App & Goals: 0(1) app 0 gls.

CARTER Graeme 1986-1990

Centre-half 6'0"
b. Wheatley Hill, Co Durham, 18 November 1969
Career: UNITED jnr June 1986, prof June 1988 to 1990/Gateshead Sept 1990/Local North East football including Brandon Utd 2002-03, Newcastle Blue Star/Bishop Auckland coach/Darlington asst-coach at Elite Advanced Development Centre 2010.

A tall defender from the Castle Eden and Wheatley Hill district, Graeme Carter spent four years with United after being offered an apprenticeship with Middlesbrough. Carter started once and totalled three games for the Magpies, all as substitute outings, in 1988-89 and 1990-91. He moved to Gateshead but only played briefly at the International Stadium. Carter's footballing career was disrupted by a dislocated shoulder injury and he later coached in County Durham. Graeme set up a paper recycling company in 2000, selling the concern then creating a new venture, Shred Direct in 2013 based in Shotton Colliery.

Misc App & Goals: 1(3) app 1 gl.

CAVE Philip Adam 2001-2007

Left-back 5'8"
b. Newcastle upon Tyne, 12 May 1987
Career: Walker Central BC/UNITED jnr 2001, prof July 2003 to May 2007 free/Darlington trial May 2007/LA Galaxy (USA) trial 2007/Scunthorpe Utd trial 2007/Gateshead Aug 2007/Livingston July 2008/Gateshead loan Feb 2009, pmt cs 2009/Blyth Spartans July 2010/Whitley Bay March 2012/Ashington May 2012/Bedlington Terriers Sept 2012.

One of four young fringe players to be given a run-out in a friendly against Norwich during July 2006, Phil Cave was a gritty defender during the early part of his career, although later switched to a more midfield flanking role. In Newcastle colours at left-back, he showed good overlapping strengths that complemented his ability to contain most wingers at reserve level. Strong in the tackle, Cave found it difficult to break through into United's experienced first-team squad and like many junior products ended in Scotland or on the North East non-league scene. With Gateshead, Phil enjoyed two promotion successes which took the Tynesiders into the Conference. He appeared almost 100 times for both Gateshead and Blyth.

Misc App & Goals: 0(1) app 0 gls.

CHAMBERS Henry 1918-1919

Centre-forward 5'10"
b. Willington Quay, near Newcastle upon Tyne, 17 November 1896
d. Shrewsbury, 29 June 1949
Career: Rosehill Villa 1910/Willington Utd Methodists 1912/North Shields Ath 1913/Liverpool April 1915 (Distillery (Belfast) war-guest) (Glentoran war-guest)(UNITED war-guest 1918-19)/West Bromwich Albion March 1928/Oakengates Town player-manager July 1929/Hereford Utd Jan 1933/Later occasional player for Oakengates Town to 1949.

From Tyneside and a past England schoolboy international, Harry Chambers took part in three games for United during 1918 and 1919, all derby encounters against Sunderland and Middlesbrough, and scored a brace against the Teessiders. A noted player with Liverpool at the time, after the Great War the Geordie striker was to enrich his reputation even further as he became one of the country's best attackers, at centre-

forward or inside-forward. He was capped on eight occasions by England and played six times for the Football League during a period when he bagged goals galore for the Reds at the top level. Nicknamed 'Smiler', he was Liverpool's goal threat as they lifted the title crown in 1922 and 1923, topping their goal charts for the opening five post-war seasons. With a big frame, yet possessing delightful touches with the ball, he registered an impressive 151 goals in 338 matches over nine seasons. Chambers had a left-foot shot of power and with his bow-legged style on the field was one of the characters of the years between the wars. Chambers played in Shropshire local leagues until he was over 50 years of age.

Misc App & Goals: 3 app 2 gls.

CHARLTON Robert Sir OBE, CBE 1974

Centre-forward 5'9"
b. Ashington, 11 October 1937
Career: Manchester Utd amat Jan 1953, prof Oct 1954/Retired April 1973/Preston North End manager June 1973 (returning as a player 1974-75)(UNITED guest May 1974) to Aug 1975/Waterford player Jan 1976 briefly/Wigan Ath director c1980, becoming caretaker-manager April to June 1983/Manchester United director June 1984 to date.

One of England's greatest sporting names; Bobby Charlton won 106 caps (49 goals) for his country, played in three World Cups (1962, 1966 as a winner, and 1970 as well as being part of the squad in another during 1958. A legend to Manchester United fans, as firstly a lively winger then a power-packed centre-forward or midfielder, Charlton was at the core of everything successful at Old Trafford during the 1950s and 1960s, totalling over 750 games (253 goals). Recovering from injuries sustained in the Munich Air Disaster, Bobby won three titles with the Reds, played in three cup finals and capped a marvellous career by lifting the European Cup as skipper at Wembley in 1968. Footballer of the Year and European Footballer of the Year, he holds a special place in football, honoured by being a Football League Legend, member of the Hall of Fame and lifting the UEFA Presidents Award, as well as the OBE, CBE and Knighthood in 1994 for services to the game. He is also a Freeman of Manchester. From the celebrated Ashington footballing family and brother to Jack Charlton (qv) as well as related to Jack Milburn (qv), Bobby made a somewhat nostalgic appearance for Newcastle in Tony Green's testimonial match during May 1974. Pulling on United's Number 9 shirt and playing alongside John Tudor, Charlton gave a wonderful display as United won 5-3; directly facing his brother Jack in Boro's ranks for the first 45 minutes. When boss of Preston, he controversially resigned after his star defender, John Bird, was sold to the Magpies against his wishes.

Misc App & Goals: 1 app 0 gls.

CHIRNSIDE James 1886

Goalkeeper
b. Newcastle upon Tyne, 1858 (Q3)
d. Byker, Newcastle upon Tyne, 24 August 1921
One of several noted local cricketers to briefly appear for the early Newcastle United line-up, James Chirnside took up the goalkeeper role once as a guest for the club during November 1886 when he played for East End against the Newcastle FA side. He had the easiest time between the sticks as the East Enders won 6-0. As a cricketer, Chirnside was a prominent player appearing for a number of local clubs between 1875 and 1898; Jesmond, Newcastle, Ryton, Heaton, Brunswick, Wallsend, North Durham as well as Friends Trinity, North Eastern Berwick, Walker, Wallsend Wednesday and the Northumberland cricket club. He played for the Northumberland County side against the MCC in July 1883 at Lords. A true Victorian sportsman in the region, James was also a first-

te rugby player with the Newcastle rugby club between 876 and 1884. It appears Chirnside lived all of his life in e Byker suburb; from census records, in 1881 he was oted as a debt collector, then a decade later was escribed as a shipyard clerk living in Dalton Street near st End's old football ground, while by the time of the 101 and 1911 national tally he was still living in the strict, in the Byker area remaining employed in the Tyne ipyards.

Misc App & Goals: 1 app 0 gls.*

CHRISP James 1883

Forward
b. unknown

A player who was likely a guest footballer for Newcastle East End for the match against a Sunderland 'A' line-up during November 1883. Played in Byker, that fixture was the very first Tyne versus Wear derby contest.

ensus information reveals two possible locals by the ame of James Chrisp, one from Newcastle and living ear St Nicholas' cathedral, or a future cricketer from the lonkwearmouth district. It is possible the Wearside-orn Chrisp was a guest player. He later appeared for shbrooke CC, Durham Colts and represented Durham ounty (1891-94). Chrisp was a notable Wearsider, ecoming a solicitor and local councillor.

Misc App & Goals: 1 app 0 gls.*

CLARK Joseph Walter 1918

Inside-left or Outside-left 5'8"
b. Willington Quay, near Newcastle upon Tyne, 15 February 1890
d. 1960
Career: Wallsend Elm Villa/Wallsend Park Villa/Hull City Jan 1912/Hebburn Argyle Sept 1912/Cardiff City May 1913 (UNITED war-guest 1918-19)

Durham City war-guest 1919)(South Shields war-guest 919)/Aberaman Ath April 1921/Southampton May 922/Rochdale June 1923 free to 1924.

Vith United all but closing down during much of World Var One, when the club did organise a few friendly or harity raising matches, they had to call on guests from he ranks of the footballing professionals back on yneside during the hostilities. Joe Clark was one who ulled on his boots for his local club, taking part in three ames during 1918, all against Wearside rivals underland. Joining Cardiff City during 1913 after npressing in an FA Cup-tie for Hebburn, and just before he Welsh club joined Football League membership, he vas on the staff as they entered the big-time although hiefly as a reserve winger or inside-forward. Joe totalled 6 games for City and was part of the Bluebirds' promotion side of 1920-21.

Misc App & Goals: 3 app 1 gl.

CLARKE David Leslie 1967-1969, 1986

Goalkeeper 5'8"
b. Newcastle upon Tyne, 24 July 1949
Career: Montague & N Fenham BC/UNITED June 1967/Doncaster Rovers Aug 1969 free (Darlington loan 1969-70)/Gainsborough Trinity c1970/South Shields-Gateshead Utd 1974/Blyth Spartans cs 1977, becoming coach lov 1985 (& UNITED briefly March to April 1986), etired playing 1986, becoming asst-manager, then manager May 1988 to Nov 1988/Alnwick Town gkp-oach 1989-90/Gateshead coach 1994 to 1996.

A good shot-stopper, Dave Clarke was highly thought of s a teenage goalkeeper at Gallowgate, joining the staff when studying to be a motor mechanic. But at only 5'8"

tall, his lack of height and build probably stopped the Tynesider graduating to the big-time in football. During United's debut European season of 1968-69, Clarke was on the bench as Willie McFaul's deputy on five occasions en-route to the Inter Cities Fairs Cup final. However, John Hope was signed and Dave returned to becoming third choice 'keeper. He was given a free transfer at the start of the 1969-70 programme when he joined Lawrie McMenemy's Doncaster Rovers. But Dave could only manage a handful of games at Belle Vue and afterwards also at Darlington on loan before heading for the non-league circuit. Clarke then became one of the top goalkeepers to play football at that level, winning 16 England semi-professional caps for his country. With notably Blyth Spartans, he appeared over 400 times for the Northumbrians and was part of their famous FA Cup giant-killing line-up during 1977-78. Dave returned to St James' Park briefly towards the end of the 1985-86 season when United were thrown into turmoil after both Thomas and McKellar were injured. Clarke arrived as cover but, like his first period with the Magpies, couldn't get that all-important first match in the record book. Following his long and rewarding period at Croft Park as a player, coach and manager, Clarke later was employed by an electrics and fire alarm company on Tyneside living in High Heaton. He was also a keen cricketer, playing locally for Kirkley CC.

Misc App & Goals: 0 app 0 gls (5 sub no app).

COCO Francesco 2005

Left-back 6'0"
b. Paterno (Italy), 8 January 1977
Career: AC Milan (It) jnr 1993, prof 1995 (Vincenza (It) loan 1997-98) (Torino (It) loan 1999-2000)(FC Barcelona (Sp) loan 2001-02)/Internazionale (It) loan 2005-06)(Torino (It) loan 2006-07)(Manchester City trial Jan 2007)/Left Inter Sept 2007.

In what could be termed the modern era of football, several established and experienced players arrived at St James' Park on a short-term trial period, hoping to show United's manager he was worth a contract. Italian international full-back Francesco Coco was one of those footballers, landing on Tyneside when 28 years of age at the start of the 2005-06 season. With Babayaro often injured and Bernard out of favour, the Newcastle left-back spot was available. Possessing dark Latin looks and a playboy image in Milan, Coco had undoubted talent, but perhaps not the correct application while he was also unlucky with injury during his career. Having appeared at the top level in Serie A with AC Milan, playing parts in their title victories during 1995-96 and 1998-99, he also pulled on the famous shirts of Barcelona and Inter. Totalling 56 games for AC Milan, Francesco was capped at Under-21 and Under-23 level for Italy and went onto appear on 17 occasions for the Azzurri in full internationals, part of the 2002 World Cup squad. Coco had played for the very best and appeared in a friendly for the Magpies against non-leaguers Yeading, but manager Graeme Souness didn't take up the option to sign the defender and Coco continued on a trail looking for a new start but with little success. He eventually left the professional game and started to concentrate on a business empire; owning shop outlets, his own clothing label (Urban 77) as well as being involved in real estate. Something of a celebrity in Italy, Francesco is well known on the social and party scene and is often on Italian television. He also coaches youngsters.

Misc App & Goals: 1 app 0 gls.

COLLINS George Edward 1899-1904

Outside-left or right 5'9"
b. Felling, near Gateshead, 1880
d. Darlington, 6 October 1958
Career: Gateshead NER/UNITED trial May 1899, prof May 1900 & again Sept 1902/Darlington Jan 1904/Shildon/Gillingham manager July 1919 to May 1920/Darlington reserve-team manager 1920 to 1933, manager June 1933 to Oct 1936, later becoming director/Afterwards scouting in the North East.

Tynesider George Collins appears to have been at St James' Park in two or three spells at the turn of the century in between working as a brass finisher. He took part in a friendly against touring side from South Africa, the Kaffirs during September 1899, then later signed professional forms for the club. He was in the ranks again for another friendly with Dundee in December 1902 and was part of the reserve eleven which claimed Northern League silverware during 1903 then seems to have drifted from the scene. George later joined Darlington and over the next 30 years was an important part of the Quakers' set-up. Known as 'Genial George', he was a player, trainer, manager and director at Feethams, scoring their first goal as a professional club in the North Eastern League competition during 1908. As boss, he lifted the Third Division North knock-out trophy in 1934 and was runners-up in the competition two years later. Collins worked at Darlington Forge as a traffic manager.

Misc App & Goals: 2 app 0 gls.

COOK John Pryor 1881-1886

Half-back, Forward & Secretary 6'0"
b. Newcastle upon Tyne, 1863 (Q4)
d. Newcastle upon Tyne, 7 February 1904
Career: STANLEY Nov 1881, becoming Secretary July 1883, to 1886 (Also St Silas 1883 to 1887)(Addison 1884 to 1885).

One of Stanley FC's earliest enthusiasts, John Cook was a well-built man, usually playing in attack during their inaugural season of friendly games (7 app). He became one of the emerging club's most dependable players, taking part in the opening five seasons of Newcastle United's existence. He participated in the club's historic debut match against Elswick Leather Works 2nd XI then in East End's first competitive fixture during 1883 in the Northumberland & Durham Challenge Cup, also against the Elswick club. Raised in Heaton, he was a surveyor's clerk, an occupation which suited his secretarial role with East End. Like many of the early footballers, John regularly pulled on whites during the summer, playing cricket for East End CC between 1886 and 1892. Cook was also a fine bowls player, taking to the greens for the Newcastle and Armstrong Park clubs. He later became a Northumberland FA referee in the region. The Tynesider was employed with the City Engineering Department and at the time of his death resided at Cardigan Terrace near Heaton Park.

Misc App & Goals: 46 app 15 gls.*

COOPER 1885

Full-back
b. unknown

With East End briefly during the 1885-86 season, it appears Cooper was a substitute defender when Berwick Rangers arrived in Heaton during October. East End were two men down and reports indicate officials looked to the crowd to fill the gap, Cooper stepping forward (with Walker, qv) and taking part in a goalless draw.

Misc App & Goals: 1 app 0 gls.*

Players: other fixtures

CORMACK Peter Robert 1992-1994

Centre-half 6'0"
b. Southport, 8 June 1974
Career: Hutchison Vale 1989/Meadowbank Thistle Aug 1990/UNITED Aug 1992 £10,000 (St Johnstone trial Jan 1994)(Brighton trial)/Morton Aug 1994 free/Raith Rovers loan then pmt Feb 1999/ Stirling Albion loan then pmt March 1999/Clydebank Aug 1999/Ross Co Jan 2000 free/Stenhousemuir July 2000/Albion Rovers July 2002/Bo'ness Utd 2004/ Arbroath July 2005 to 2006.

The son of noted Liverpool and Scotland midfielder Peter Cormack who had appeared alongside United boss Kevin Keegan at Anfield, Peter Cormack (junior) operated both as a midfielder and defender. However, the strapping utility player failed to make an impression after arriving with good reports. Hard-working, Cormack appeared against Crook Town then claimed a place on the bench when Keegan selected a weakened side for the Anglo-Italian Cup match during December 1992 against AS Bari in Italy. Peter though didn't get the nod to play and headed for Scotland at the end of the 1993-94 season. With Morton he assisted in their Division Two title success during 1995, being a regular selection and totalling 91 games for the Greenock club. On leaving the full-time professional game, Peter worked in finance in Edinburgh with the Royal Bank of Scotland before joining National IFA Towry during 2012 as a sport advisor. He continued with part-time football for a period and also covered the game in the Central Belt for the Press Association.

Misc App & Goals: 0(1) app 0 gls.

COULSON William Armstrong 1881-1888
CLUB FOUNDER

Forward, Committee, Secretary & Club Founder
b. Byker, Newcastle upon Tyne, August 1862
d. Stamford, near Rennington, Northumberland, 7 February 1948

Recognised as Newcastle United's Founder, William Coulson was captain of the Stanley Cricket Club and skipper of Stanley Football Club when they were formed in November 1881, leading the decision making process to form a new football organisation. He played in nine of the 11 opening fixtures during 1881-82, not surprisingly appearing in the very first game. He was also skipper of the club's initial competitive line-up in January 1883. As East End developed Coulson left the scene during the summer of 1883, being given a "gold scarf pin" as a token of his service, but William continued on the periphery, occasionally returning as a player and having a spell with North Eastern, then becoming Secretary of the East End club during the close-season of 1886 until 1888. Coulson also continued his involvement with Stanley's cricketers and was linked to the Newcastle CC as early as 1876, an active member of the committee. As a teenager, Coulson trained to become a teacher in the district, at the time of Newcastle United's formation he was registered in census data as an "Assistant Teacher" living on Raby Street near to St Peter's, the Stanley club's base. By 1891 William was recorded as a "School Master" residing at Fell Street in Byker. His younger brother Robert Coulson was also with Stanley in that first season, but only appeared at reserve level before also playing for Argyle and North Eastern, as well as on the cricket field for North Durham in Gateshead. William moved to Rennington village near Alnwick and was by 1901 Head Teacher at the local school, remaining in that area of Northumberland for the rest of his life. During 2014 Coulson was inducted into United's Hall of Fame, 133 years after the foundation of the Club.

Misc App & Goals: 15 app 0 gls.*

COULTHARD Thomas DeArr 1921-1924

Right-back 5'9"
b. Cockerton, Darlington, 12 February 1900
d. Newcastle upon Tyne, 16 September 1971
Career: Darlington Forge Jnrs/Darlington Railway Ath/UNITED March 1921 £125/Norwich City May 1924 £200/Ebbw Vale Nov 1926 £250/Carlisle Utd June 1928/Wallsend Aug 1931/West Stanley July 1935.

Tom Coulthard was third choice understudy to Bill McCracken when at St James' Park, challenging Russell, Roxburgh and Hampson for a first-team place whenever the famous Irish international was missing. He travelled with the first-team for a six-match tour of Scandinavia at the end of the 1921-22 season and took part in three of the fixtures. Winning a North Eastern League title medal with the reserve line-up in 1922-23, Coulthard got another chance to shine as the Magpies faced a Corinthians side in an exhibition match at New Year during the following season. But it was perhaps inevitable he would move on, joining Norwich at the end of 1923-24. He was a steady and solid player in Division Three South for City (42 app), and later for Carlisle United (105 app) at Division Three North level. Tom had the misfortune to register two own-goals for Norwich against Charlton during October 1925. His younger brother William totalled 120 games for Darlington. Born in Cockerton village, he was the son of a local shoe-maker.

Misc App & Goals: 4 app 0 gls.

COUPER William 1892-1893

Forward
b. unknown
Career: Middlesbrough Ironopolis 1891/Newcastle West End 1891/EAST END Oct 1892 to c1893.

With Ironopolis at the time of what was a bitter amateur versus professional dispute with Teesside rivals Middlesbrough, William Couper (or Cooper) appeared for the Irons in season 1891-92 during a period when they dominated the newly formed Northern League competition, title winners in that season. Couper soon moved to Tyneside and initially was with the Newcastle West End club. He switched to East End in October 1892 and made his debut against Boro on Teesside, appearing up front during the 1892-93 season, but more often for the 'A' side. Couper appears to have departed in the early months of 1893.

Misc App & Goals: 1 app 0 gls.*

COURT 1907

Inside-forward
b. unknown

A promising footballer with Southern League club Sheppey United, inside-forward Court was handed a United trial opportunity during April 1907 when the Magpies travelled to Scotland on an end-of-season break. He was part of the line-up in Edinburgh for a fixture against Leith Athletic. Given the inside-left berth, he played in a benefit game staged at Easter Road and also when the Magpies faced Aberdeen. Although netting at Pittodrie, Court was not retained when the party returned to Tyneside.

Misc App & Goals: 2 app 1 gl.

COX 1919

Half-back or Forward
b. unknown

A player who arrived on Tyneside from the "sou country" during May 1919, on what is suspected, was short trial period. Cox was included in the party wh. faced a Middlesbrough side during May 1919, a w funds charity match. He scored in the 2-2 draw afte "clever solo run" but wasn't signed by the Magpies.

Misc App & Goals: 1 app 1 gl.

COXALL Philip 1984-1989

Centre-half 5'10"
b. Sunderland, 29 January 1969
Career: UNITED jnr cs 1984, prof Au 1987 to cs 1989 free/Later with Durham City Aug 2000/Gretna Aug 2001/Bedlington Terriers 2002/Esh Winning 2003/Washington Aug 200

Raised on Wearside and a Sunderla supporter as a lad, Phil Coxall appeared for Durha County schools and was on the fringe of an England ca up as a youngster. He had been to several clubs as a k Sunderland, Tottenham, Watford, Manchester Ci Nottingham Forest and Leicester. Newcastle United w another team which offered him a chance and accepted schoolboy terms during the summer of 198 Coxall developed through the ranks and was part of mini-tour of the Caribbean with the first-team at t end of the 1987-88 season. Reading the game well fro the back and powerful in the air, he was in the side wh the Black'n'Whites faced a Jamaica XI and may ha played against a Trinidad & Tobago combination (r record exists of the line-up). Ultimately though, he w not considered good enough and was released, Pl afterwards appearing on the non-league scene where was described as a "class-act" in that level of footba He later coached at Sunderland Academy.

Misc App & Goals: 2 app 0 gls.

COXON Frederick James 1887-1888

Full-back & Half-back
b. Newcastle upon Tyne, 1868 (Q4)

Another player with local Cheviot juniors from 1885, Fr Coxon joined the club when the Byker team merged wi Newcastle East End during September 1887. He wc raised in the All Saint's district of the city and was 1891 living in Heaton employed as a chemical agent. committee member of the Cheviot club at Byker Vicarag Fred broke into the East End line-up briefly during seaso 1887-88, but was normally found in the second-strin ranks.

Misc App & Goals: 1 app 0 gls.*

CRAWFORD Robert 1884-1888

Goalkeeper & Half-back, Trainer & Committee
b. Glasgow, c1853
d. [Newcastle upon Tyne, 1926]
Career: Newcastle Rangers 1881/EAST END Oct 1884, also becoming trainer to 1886, Committee 1885 to 1888/Science & Art 1889 to 1891.

The younger brother of David Crawford (qv), also a playe for Rangers and later Newcastle United Chairman, Sc Robert Crawford was usually found in midfield or th forward line but occasionally also played as a goalkeepe Having been part of the Newcastle Rangers combinatio which appeared in the early Northumberland & Durha Challenge Cup finals of 1882 and 1884 as well as bein part of the Rangers eleven which featured in the fir Northumberland Senior Cup final during 1884, Crawfor was a prominent pioneer footballer. He played fo

orthumberland County in 1883 and 1884 and joined
ast End when Rangers ran into difficulties along with
is brother and noted players White and Hoban.
rawford had a short-lived playing career with East End,
s a 'keeper against Morpeth Harriers in December 1884
hile he was also considered in reserve fixtures. Robert
as described in one pen-picture that year as having
proved a useful half-back – by no means showy, but
orks hard". Robert remained connected with the club as
    trainer and umpire (in days before referees and
nesmen) as well as an active Committee member.
rawford officiated at other games around Tyneside and
ecame one of the club's original shareholders when the
amily purchased a stake in the new limited company
uring 1890. Robert was employed as a foreman in a
hemical works, initially living at Addison Street, then
ynemouth Road. He was also recorded as having resided
t Leazes Terrace next to St James' Park.

Misc App & Goals: 1 app 0 gls.*

CRETNEY John Thomas 1901-1902

Left-half 5'10"
b. Harrington, near Workington, 1879
d. Manchester, 1954
Career: Workington/UNITED trial
April 1901, prof May 1901/
Workington Aug 1902/Burnley June
1905/Gainsborough Trinity July 1911/
Croydon Common Nov 1911/
adiham March 1912.

reserve half-back at St James' Park during seasons
900-01 and 1901-02, John Cretney was close to a first-
lass outing, but had to be content with a handful of
ppearances for the Magpies in friendly contests. A
lacksmith's striker as a teenager, he first appeared in
he senior ranks against Rangers during April 1901 as
he club headed across the border at the end of the
eason. He faced Hearts as well before returning to
yneside but the Sporting Man recorded, "Cretney was
ot a great success". With the like of Jack Carr as
referred left-half at Gallowgate, Cretney continued in
he club's second-string (winning the Northern Alliance
itle in 1902) then moved back to Workington at the start
f the 1902-03 season. John received another chance
hough at the big-time, with Burnley during 1905. At Turf
Moor he managed to find a regular slot, mainly at right-
half, totalling 177 games over six campaigns in Division
Two. One reporter described Cretney as putting "his heart
nto his work, tackles well, and knows how to place the
ball to advantage".

Misc App & Goals: 5 app 0 gls.

CROOKS Albert 1899

Right-back
b. unknown
Facing Everton in a friendly match at St James' Park
during March 1899, trialist Albert Crooks featured as
United won 2-1, but didn't end up with a professional
contract from the Magpies. No further reports have been
traced of the player.

Misc App & Goals: 1 app 0 gls.

CUGGY Francis 1917

Right-half 5'9"
b. Walker, Newcastle upon Tyne,
16 June 1889
d. Walker, Newcastle upon Tyne,
27 March 1965
Career: Walker/Willington Ath Dec
1907/Sunderland March 1909 (South
Shields war-guest 1915-16)(UNITED
war-guest 1917-18)/Wallsend player-manager May
1921 to cs 1922/Celta Vigo (Sp) manager Nov 1923 to
1928.

Capped twice by England before the First World War,
Frank Cuggy played all his senior football for Sunderland,
a formidable right-half United let slip from under their
noses when a noted Newcastle schoolboy. He did pull on
United's shirt for a brief period during October 1917, in
a double-header against South Shields in aid of hospital
charity. Modestly built and rather lightweight, Cuggy was
part of the red-and-whites line-up which lifted the
Football League title in 1913 and battled through to the
FA Cup final in the same year, only to lose to Aston Villa
when the double was in reach. Frank formed a great
triangle for Sunderland with Charlie Buchan and Jackie
Mordue; he was an attacking but versatile midfielder
who possessed superb ball control with a tenacious edge
to his game despite his slight appearance. Also winning
Football League representative honours, Frank was cool
on the field, smooth and precise with the ball and
appeared on 187 occasions for the Wearsiders being
described in Sunderland annals as "an early version of a
utility player". The Great War arrived at the wrong time
for Cuggy, the Tynesider losing a large chunk of his career
when at his peak. Later he coached Celta Vigo to the
Galician championship in 1923 and afterwards worked
in the Tyne shipyards, returning to his Walker roots.
Throughout his days with Sunderland, Frank resided at
Bigges Main.

Misc App & Goals: 2 app 0 gls.

CURRY Thomas (No. 2) 1926-1928

Inside-left 5'7"
b. Newcastle upon Tyne
Career: Clarence Wesleyans/Barnsley
Jan 1920/Jarrow 1920/Scotswood
Aug 1920/Pandon Temperance/
Aberdare Ath June 1923/UNITED trial
Oct 1925, prof April 1926 to May
1928 free.

To avoid confusion with his first-eleven namesake, Tom
Curry, the club and Football League officials gave Curry
the suffix of "No 2" in official ledgers. During the early
years of his career after World War One, the Tynesider
only managed fleeting appearances in Football League
action with Barnsley (1 app) and in Aberdare's Division
Three South line-up (4 app) before returning to his native
region. He was given another opportunity with the
Magpies and featured in one match, a friendly against
Hull City in the Hull Hospitals Cup tournament during
April 1927. Although part of United's title winning squad
in 1927, Curry was behind Tom McDonald as well as
Halliday and McCurley in selection and left the club at
the end of the 1927-28 campaign.

Misc App & Goals: 1 app 0 gls.

CURTIS John Joseph 1918

Outside-right 5'6"
b. South Bank, 13 December 1888
d. Wimbledon, London, 8 March 1955
Career: Eston Utd/South Bank St
Peter's/South Bank/Sunderland April
1907/Shildon Ath Dec 1907/
Gainsborough Trinity May 1908/
Tottenham Hotspur April 1909/
Fulham cs 1913/Brentford June 1914/Stockport Co Jan
1915 (UNITED war-guest 1918-19)/Middlesbrough Aug
1919/Shildon Ath Oct 1920/Netherlands coaching 1927
to 1939, including for HFC Haarlem.

Jack Curtis appeared as a guest for the Magpies as World
War One came to a close during December 1918 against
Sunderland, this after serving in the conflict as a gunner
in the Royal Field Artillery. A fast and "nippy" winger,
Curtis managed a single game for the red-and-whites
on Wearside, but afterwards established a place with
Tottenham, playing a small part in their Division Two
promotion during 1908-09 then becoming a regular for
two seasons, totalling 89 matches for Spurs. Not tall, but
solidly built, his rise to prominence at White Hart Lane
was good enough to get Curtis into England reckoning,

appearing in a trial fixture at Anfield during January
1910. Unluckily though he suffered injury and lost his
footballing momentum. Jack married into a Dutch family
and was living in Holland when Germany threatened the
country in 1939, leaving quickly after the Blitzkrieg.

Misc App & Goals: 1 app 0 gls.

DANQUAH Frank Wiafe 2006-2010

Striker 5'11"
b. Amsterdam (Netherlands),
4 October 1989
Career: Ajax (Neth) jnr 2004/FC
Omniworld (Neth) 2005/UNITED jnr
July 2006, prof cs 2008 (Stockport Co
trial April 2010)(Bournemouth trial
April 2010)/Ferencvaros (Hng) July
2010 free to Dec 2010/Waasland-Beveren (Bel) Feb 2011
to April 2011/Kayseri Erciyesspor (Trk) trial July 2011/
Elche CF (Sp) trial Aug 2011/Gateshead trial Sept 2011/
Newcastle Benfield Dec 2011/PEC Zwolle (Neth) trial
July 2012/FC Chabab (Neth) Aug 2012/FC Brasov (Rom)
Jan 2013 to late 2013.

A past Under-15 international for Holland, Frank
Danquah was one of several teenage prospects brought
to Tyneside during the opened decade of the Millennium
from the Continent, most never developing as hoped. A
strong and forceful striker, he was highly tipped for
stardom upon arrival at Newcastle, but suffered from a
run of injuries. Frank picked up a bad knee tendon knock
and was out for almost a year, then when he was fit
again suffered an ankle problem. The tall and slim Dutch
youngster with Ghanaian roots pulled on United's shirt
three times in friendly action, off the bench at the start
of 2007-08 and 2008-09. Although he was selected as a
substitute in the Premier League against Hull City, he
couldn't force his way into the manager's team selection.
After his period with the Magpies, Danquah travelled
Europe in search of a contract, without settling at any
club for long.

Misc App & Goals: 0(3) app 0 gls.

DARK Alfred James 1920-1921

Half-back 6'0"
b. Keynsham, Gloucestershire,
21 August 1893
d. St George's, Bristol, 3 August 1964
Career: Seaton Delaval/Wallsend Feb
1920/UNITED March 1920 £352/Leeds
Utd May 1921 £100/Port Vale June
1923/Halifax Town June 1924/Barrow
May 1928/Sittingbourne Aug 1929/North Shields Oct
1930 to Jan 1931.

Alf Dark became a United professional during March
1920 after good displays for Wallsend on Tyneside. With
Newcastle looking for fresh talent after World War One,
the half-back was one of many new faces at Gallowgate
during that period. Although he got a chance in the
Black'n'Whites' first choice eleven for a friendly with
Edinburgh St Bernard's during April 1920...and scored a
goal in a 5-0 romp...Dark wasn't retained. He moved onto
Leeds, making his senior debut when aged 29, then was
a regular at both Port Vale (26 app) and Halifax (133 app)
as his career kept going until nearing 39 years of age.

Misc App & Goals: 1 app 1 gl.

Players: other fixtures

DAVISON John Edward 1915

Goalkeeper 5'7"
b. Gateshead, 2 September 1887
d. Wortley, Yorkshire, 1 February 1971
Career: Gateshead St Chad's/Gateshead Town/Sheffield Wed April 1908 £300 (UNITED warguest 1915-16)(South Shields warguest 1915-16)/Mansfield Town player-manager June 1926, retired playing 1927/Chesterfield manager Feb 1928/Sheffield Utd manager June 1932/Chesterfield manager Aug 1952 to May 1958, becoming chief-scout.

Not tall for a goalkeeper at only 5'7" in height, Teddy Davison nevertheless was a top-class custodian, good enough to appear for England during March 1922 and tour Australia with the FA party in 1925. The Gateshead product was noted as being of "placid and gentle character" but on the pitch showed "razor-sharp reflexes" and much "courage and determination" which made up for his small build. A stalwart figure for Sheffield Wednesday, Teddy worked as a compositor in one of Newcastle's newspaper rooms before getting a break at Hillsborough. He went onto register all of 424 games (plus 11 wartime fixtures) for the Owls before and after the First World War, first choice for almost 13 seasons. As the conflict started to have a major impact on football, Davison guested for Newcastle during November 1915, against South Shields in a fund raising fixture. He afterwards quickly joined up and served with the Royal Field Artillery in France before continuing his career in Yorkshire on peace being restored. As a manager Teddy successfully led Chesterfield to the Division Three North title in 1931 before switching to Bramall Lane. He guided Sheffield United to Wembley in the 1936 FA Cup final then to promotion just before war again broke out during 1939. Davison remained with the Blades for 20 years, winning the wartime Football League North crown in 1945-46. During an off-day with Wednesday, he once conceded 10 goals against Aston Villa during season 1912-13. Davison was given a Football League Long Service award in 1950.

Misc App & Goals: 1 app 0 gls.

DAWES Ian Michael 1982-1985

Centre-half 5'10"
b. Aldershot, 5 January 1965
Career: Trimdon Jnrs 1979/Queens Park Rangers jnr/Washington Jnrs/UNITED jnr April 1982, prof June 1983 to cs 1985/Northampton Town loan 1985, pmt June 1985/Gateshead July 1986/North Shields cs 1988/Ponteland Utd 1989 to 1991 when he retired.

Ian Dawes was born in the south when he father was in the army, but returned to the family's native County Durham when he was a two-year-old. He joined United from school football in April 1982 after a brief period with QPR and came through the club's junior development programme of the Eighties. A former England Under-19 international, he was handed a senior debut in a friendly at Hartlepool during the pre-season preparations of season 1984-85 and took part in a number of other matches at that time. Versatile, Ian started as a centre-back but also operated in midfield and even up front. With stamina and high fitness levels, he could run all day but perhaps lacked that short burst of speed to reach the very top level. Dawes moved to Northampton but struggled to hold a first-team position, totalling six matches for the Cobblers in season 1985-86. He appeared for Gateshead but was sidelined through an ankle ligament injury then continued as a part-time player in the North East. Dawes joined Northumbria Police in 1986 initially as a uniformed constable quickly moving through the ranks to be appointed a Detective Inspector then becoming one of the region's top officers; Area Commander for South Tyneside during 2011 and Chief Superintendent in 2013. For a period he also

appeared for the Northumbria Police football side. His uncle, Malcolm Dawes, appeared notably for Hartlepool and Aldershot.

Misc App & Goals: 2(4) app 1 gl.

DAWSON Percival Hall 1915

Centre-forward 5'11"
b. Cullercoats, near Tynemouth, 4 December 1889
d. Cullercoats, near Tynemouth, 1974 (Q1)
Career: Whitley Ath/North Shields Ath/Heart of Midlothian Jan 1911 £100/Blackburn Rovers March 1914 £2,500 (UNITED war-guest 1915-16)(Dumbarton warguest 1918-19)/Preston CW (North Shields) cs 1923/Barrow Feb 1924, retiring during the season.

Making eight outings in Blackburn's Football League title victory during 1914, Percy Dawson hailed from the North East coast and made his mark in Edinburgh with Hearts. Joining the Tynecastle set up half way through the 1910-11 campaign, Percy became a hot-shot in Scotland and netted 72 goals in only 92 matches, a tremendous record over his four seasons with Hearts as they twice finished in third place. Possessing classy touches on the ball and an eye for goal, Blackburn brought him back to the English game and Dawson was a hit at Ewood too, a danger up front scoring 73 times in 151 appearances. His arrival late in the 1913-14 season made a difference to Rovers' title push as the trophy was secured. He was unfortunate to be at the peak of his game, grabbing 20 goals in 28 games during the following campaign, just as war escalated. When he returned to senior action in 1919, he was older and not the same potent forward, but Percy still gave good service to a Rovers line-up much changed since the days of pre-war trophy glory. With United effectively in the process of closing down in 1915 as war affected the country, Dawson helped United out in November 1915 when a fixture with South Shields in aid of war charities was arranged. Once retired, he settled in the North East going into the licensing trade. Percy ran several pubs until he fully retired during the late Fifties.

Misc App & Goals: 1 app 0 gls.

DICKINSON Stuart John 1984-1987

Defender 5'8"
b. Whitby, 29 May 1968
Career: UNITED jnr July 1984, prof June 1986 to May 1987 free/Later appearing in local football.

Stuart Dickinson was part of Newcastle's talented squad of junior players which reached the FA Youth Cup final in 1984-85, alongside Paul Gascoigne, Kevin Scott and Joe Allon. A versatile defender, he was a regular in that run but while others progressed to gain much experience on senior duty, Dickinson was restricted to an outing in a secondary first-team match at Durham, a testimonial for City's Paul Main during August 1986. He left Gallowgate at the end of that season and played on the non-league circuit. Afterwards Dickinson ran a pub-restaurant in Cleveland. His son later joined the Newcastle Academy without breaking through.

Misc App & Goals: 0(1) app 0 gls.

DINNING Tony 1989-1994

Midfield 5'11"
b. Wallsend, 12 April 1975
Career: Wallsend BC/UNITED jnr July 1989, prof Oct 1993 (Djurgardens IF (Swd) loan)/Stockport Co June 1994 free/Wolverhampton Wand Sept 2000 £600,000/Wigan Ath Sept 2001 £750,000 (Stoke City loan 2001-02) (Walsall loan 2003-04)(Blackpool loan 2003-04)(Ipswich Town loan 2004-05)/Bristol City loan, pmt Oct 2004 free/Port Vale loan March 2005, pmt June 2005/Stockport Co July 2006/Chester City trial Sept 2007, pmt Oct 2007 (Inverness Cal Thistle trial Jan 2009)(Gray Ath loan 2008-09)(Gateshead loan 2008-09)/Hednesford Town May 2009/Stafford Rangers 2009/Bridgnorth Town player-coach July 2010, retired playing cs 2011, becoming coach then asst-manager June 2011.

On the fringe on Newcastle's first-eleven selection as h developed from United's junior and reserve sides, Ton Dinning was a contemporary of the likes of Lee Clark Robbie Elliott and Steve Watson as the club wa completely remodelled during the early seasons of th Nineties. The midfielder or defender was only handed Magpie first-team shirt as a substitute for the contes with Gateshead during August 1993, a testimonial fo ex-United player Derek Bell. The Wallsend lad found regular place at Edgeley Park with Stockport, going ont total over 250 matches for County in two spells Although he suffered from a broken leg, his form ther earned a move to Wolves (37 app), then to Wigan (9 app). Dinning was always able to find the net, claimin 61 goals during his senior career. Tony had a degree o success in the lower divisions being part of Wigan's ris to the top, Division Two title winners in season 2002-03 He also won promotion with Stockport (1996-97) an Stoke City (2001-02). Later in his career he skippered Por Vale and when with Blackpool lifted the Football Leagu Trophy at Wembley in 2004.

Misc App & Goals: 0(1) app 0 gls.

DIXON Henry 1892-1893

Forward
b. Newcastle upon Tyne, 1869 (Q4)
Joining the East End club on the demise of his own club Newcastle West End, during the summer of 1892, Henry Dixon originally appeared for White Rose, joining the S James' Park set-up during the 1889-90 season. Not regular with East End, he afterwards assisted the Science & Art College eleven. As a cricketer Dixon appeared fo White Rose and Bath Lane cricket clubs. He worked as a railway clerk on Tyneside.

Misc App & Goals: 2 app 0 gls.*

DIXON John 1881-1882, 1888-1893

Full-back, Committee-Director & Secretary
b. Newcastle upon Tyne, c1860
Career: STANLEY Nov 1881/Heaton Ass 1882 to 1884/EAST END 1888, becoming 'A' Team Secretary and Committee member, then Director March 1890 to July 1893 ,acting as Secretary Jan 1893 to July 1893.

An important figure in the rise of Newcastle United, John Dixon played cricket on Tyneside before moving into the new association football scene. He was a first choice selection in Stanley's inaugural campaign of 1881-82 (9 app), scoring twice in the very first match against Elswick Leather Works 2nd XI. As a player he operated in all areas of the field; defence, midfield, attack and even as goalkeeper. On the club's Committee during those formation years, when Newcastle East End decided to become a limited company in the spring of 1890, Dixon was one of the first directors, also being a shareholder from the outset. At that time he resided in Addison Street in Byker, working as a compositor in the printing trade Dixon also acted as Secretary for periods, while he also played cricket for Woodbine and Heaton.

Misc App & Goals: 11 app 2 gls.*

DIXON Stephen 1895-1898

Left-half
b. Newcastle upon Tyne

Joining the Magpies during November 1895, the local newspapers of the day record little on the player who appeared once for the club, in a friendly with Stockton at Gallowgate during January 1897. On the staff for around two seasons, he appeared in United's Northern Alliance title winning eleven of 1898.

Misc App & Goals: 1 app 0 gls.

DOUGLAS 1903

Goalkeeper
b. probably Scotland

When Newcastle travelled on a three-match end-of-season trip to Scotland they gave a trial outing to a player by the name of Douglas. As recorded by the Glasgow Times in the match report for a clash against Rangers at Ibrox during April 1903. Douglas had an uneventful single outing as United drew 2-2. No further information is recorded on the player in United's archive, or in either the Scottish or English database.

Misc App & Goals: 1 app 0 gls.

DOBSON Colin 1965

Outside-left or Inside-forward 5'8"
b. Eston, near Middlesbrough, 9 May 1940

Career: South Bank/Sheffield Wed amat 1955, part-time prof Nov 1957, prof July 1961 (UNITED guest Oct 1965)/Huddersfield Town Aug 1966 £25,000 (Brighton loan 1971-72)/Bristol Rovers July 1972 free, becoming player-coach/Coventry City asst-coach May 1976 to Aug 1983/Port Vale asst-manager Dec 1983 to March 1984/West Riffa Club (Bhn) coach 1985/Al-Rayyan SC (Qt) coach Aug 1985/Aston Villa asst-coach June 1986 to June 1987/Sporting Clube (Ptg) asst-coach 1988 to Nov 1988/Gillingham asst-coach & chief-scout 1988/Coventry City asst-coach/Al-Arabi SC (Kwt) coach 1994/Port Vale asst-coach Sept 1995 to May 1996/Oman national youth coach 1996/Coventry City asst-coach Jan 1999/Stoke City chief-scout 2000 to 2005/Later scouting for various clubs before rejoining Stoke City.

One of five guest players to pull on United's colours in a testimonial match for Brian Clough at Roker Park during October 1965, Colin Dobson scored in a convincing 6-2 victory. A talented Teessider, Dobson was a prominent forward during the Sixties, doing well for both Sheffield Wednesday (195 app) and Huddersfield Town (175 app), always hitting the net, over 100 for his Yorkshire clubs. Colin was capped by England at Under-23 level (2 app) and appeared for the Football League as well as the FA on tour, just missing out on a full cap when at the top of his game with the Owls. Small and direct with a skilled left foot, Dobson was disappointed at being sidelined from Wednesday's 1966 FA Cup final line-up. He soon left Hillsborough and was then part of three promotion winning line-ups during the early Seventies when he operated in a modern midfield role before starting on a varied period in coaching. At the beginning of his fine career, Colin worked as an apprentice at a ship-building company on Teesside.

Misc App & Goals: 1 app 1 gl.

DOBSON Richard Lawrence 1937-1939

Inside-right 5'8"
b. Barrington, Northumberland, 1 May 1916
d. Northumberland Central, 2000 (Q4)

Career: Barrington/UNITED amat May 1937/North Shields/UNITED prof May 1938/North Shields May 1939 £200/Chester May 1939 free.

Richard Dobson had shown enough in local football with first, Barrington, then North Shields, to be coveted by the Magpies during the years before the Second World War. A schemer who didn't quite make it with the club, he made his first outing for the Black'n'Whites during August 1938, at Gallowgate, in The Football League Jubilee fixture with Gateshead. He then faced the Tynesiders again as the season opened, in a testimonial match at Redheugh Park.

Misc App & Goals: 2 app 1gl.

DONINGER Mark 2005-2009

Midfield 5'11"
b. Gosforth, Newcastle upon Tyne, 19 October 1989

Career: Walker Central BC/UNITED jnr 2005, prof cs 2008 to May 2009 free/Darlington trial July 2009/Blyth Spartans Aug 2009/Team Northumbria/Derby Co, Hartlepool Utd, Grimsby Town, Burton Albion & S-Lg (Sing) 2009-10, all on trial/Sligo Rovers Feb 2010/IA Akranes (Ice) Feb 2011/UMF Stjarnan (Ice) July 2012/Bedlington Terriers Nov 2012/Shildon Sept 2013/Perth SC (Aus) Jan 2014.

Mark Doninger was United's reserve-team captain whose attacking play from midfield brought him many goals at that level. However, he never did quite enough to get promoted into the first-team and record his full debut. Nicknamed 'Dozzi', Mark did play in a Newcastle United XI match against Hull City during August 2007. He was in the squad for other friendlies, then got close to his first appearance by sitting on the Premier League bench, also for a contest with Hull City then for a handful of games to follow. Preferring a central berth in midfield, the fair-haired Geordie was released in May 2009 and tried unsuccessfully to find a new club for many weeks. Mark eventually moved to Ireland, then to Iceland to continue playing the game before returning to the North East and joining Bedlington Terriers in the Northern League.

Misc App & Goals: 0(1) app 0 gls.

DOYLE Daniel 1888

Left-back 5'11"
b. Paisley, 16 September 1864
d. Glasgow, 8 April 1918

Career: Darngavil/Hurlford/Rawyards Jnrs/Slamannan Barnsmuir/Broxburn Shamrock/Hibernian 1886 (Heart of Midlothian loan 1888)/East Stirlingshire 1888/Sunderland Aug 1888/EAST END Sept 1888/Grimsby Town Dec 1888/Bolton Wand April 1889/Everton Aug 1889/Celtic Aug 1891 to April 1899/Mossend Hibs Aug 1899/Celtic player-asst-trainer to 1904.

One of the early greats of Scottish football, Dan Doyle was something of an errant traveller during his youthful days, calling at a number of clubs briefly as he crossed the border to capitalise on England's professional status as a so-called "soldier of fortune". A pit worker in Central Scotland, he was one of several distinguished Scots to appear in Newcastle in fleeting bursts during the game's formative years. He landed on Tyneside and had a short period with the East Enders between September and

December 1888, apparently going by the pseudonym of McCrinnon (or McCrinnons, or McCrinnond), probably in an attempt to avoid sanction by the Scottish FA for playing with professional clubs. Due to this, factual information on his transitory period with Newcastle East End is limited. It is confirmed he did play for the East Enders in a published life story from the 1930s and it appears he pulled on their blue shirt against Bishop Auckland. He had an eventful period in England, with Grimsby involved in a heavy tackle which injured Will Cropper of Staveley, who later tragically died as a result of the clash. Dan moved on and eventually settled on Merseyside with Everton (45 app) where he helped the Goodison club to secure the Football League title in 1891. Some judges recognised Doyle as arguably the greatest defender of his time, a good all-round athlete with powerful and accurate kicking. Noted as dealing with troublesome wingers in an uncompromising manner, Doyle moved back to Glasgow during 1891 causing some controversy when he broke his contract, the Merseysiders raising an action against the player. With Celtic (133 app) he became a celebrated figure, being capped on eight occasions by his country (including as captain) and nine by the Scottish League XI. He won plenty of medals at Parkhead; four Scottish League crowns included while he also appeared in three Scottish Cup finals. Doyle became a spirit merchant in the Glasgow area after football.

Misc App & Goals: 1 app 1 gl.

DOYLE Stephen Charles 1982

Midfield 5'9"
b. Neath, Glamorgan, 2 June 1958

Career: Preston North End jnr, prof June 1975/UNITED trial July 1982/Huddersfield Town trial Sept 1982, pmt Oct 1982 free/Sunderland Sept 1986 £75,000/Hull City Aug 1989 £75,000/Rochdale Nov 1990 to March 1995/Chorley 1995, becoming caretaker-manager Nov 1996.

Steve Doyle had clocked up 238 games for Preston when he arrived at St James' Park along with his Deepdale colleague John Anderson on a six-week trial during the summer of 1982, after the pair had been released by new boss Gordon Lee. While Anderson earned a contract and flourished with the Magpies, Doyle was rejected despite scoring a picture goal in his first outing at Morton; a crisply struck volley from the edge of the box. As a ball-winning anchor man in midfield, he did impress at Leeds Road with Huddersfield and started on a career with the Terriers which saw the midfielder claim 187 games before moving back to the North East to join Sunderland. With the red-and-whites Doyle was again a consistent performer, although at times far from being a Wearside favourite in his 115 matches. Often fiercely competitive, he ended his Football League days with Rochdale, totalling almost 150 games. Doyle was capped by Wales at youth and Under-23 level (2 app) and came close to a full cap, selected for the squad without making his debut. He played in a trio of Third Division promotion winning sides spanning a decade, including when at Roker Park. Steve totalled over 700 appearances in professional football.

Misc App & Goals: 6 app 2 gls.

Players: other fixtures

DRYSDALE Jason 1994-1995

Left-back 5'10"
b. Bristol, 17 November 1970
Career: Watford jnr March 1985, prof Sept 1988/UNITED Aug 1994 £425,000/Swindon Town March 1995 £425,000/Northampton Town March 1998/Forest Green Rovers May 1998/Aberystwyth Town 2001/Bath City 2001/Mangotsfield Town 2003/Paulton Rovers 2004.

While Kevin Keegan made several marquee signings, he also often brought largely unknown talent to St James' Park, such as Huckerby, Holland and Guppy, with the aim of developing top footballers. Jason Drysdale was another player from the lower divisions who was given a chance to prosper, moving to Tyneside in August 1994 from Watford after he had graduated to appear for the Football League eleven during 1992. An ex-England youth full-back who had become a regular choice over four seasons (160 app) in the Hornet's line-up, being something of an attacking full-back who could hit the net. Drysdale though never showed enough to threaten regular full-backs Beresford or young Rob Elliott. He appeared against Manchester United at Ibrox during August 1994 in a friendly and then faced a Northern Ireland XI. He was also named as substitute on six occasions during 1994-95 without getting onto the field to record his first-class debut for the Black'n'Whites. Towards the end of that season, Jason took up a deal with Swindon and moved south for a fee of £425,000, the Magpies recouping their initial outlay. He was part of the Robins' Division Two Championship winning eleven in 1995-96 and recorded 54 games at the County Ground while at the beginning of his career Drysdale lifted the FA Youth Cup with Watford. His parents hailed from the North East and Jason's father, Brian Drysdale, turned out for several clubs and topped 500 games, including prominently for Hartlepool and Bristol City. Jason settled in the Bristol area, reported as working as a driver for UPS.

Misc App & Goals: 1(1) app 0 gls.

DUTTON Edwin 1910-1912

Inside-forward 5'10"
b. Mittenwalde (Germany), 8 April 1890
d. Wilmslow, Cheshire, 24 May 1972
Career: FC Britannia (Ger)/BFC Preussen (Ger) 1903/UNITED trial Sept 1910, pmt Oct 1910/Newburn Steelworks Sept 1912/[Bristol City Nov 1912]/FC Britannia 92 (Ger) Jan 1913 (Ruhleben FA (Ger) Nov 1914 to 1919 when interned)/Stuttgarter Kickers (Ger) manager 1924 to 1926/South Shields trainer/Ipswich Town trainer cs 1927 to Aug 1932.

With family connections in Germany, his English father Tom Dutton spent much of his life on the Continent and settled in Berlin running a sports outfitters shop, noted as being a "sporting pioneer" who did much to introduce both football and cricket to the German capital. Not surprisingly his son, Edwin had sporting genes, and played a number of activities but who concentrated on football as the game developed in that country with Berlin clubs Britannia and Preussen. He was selected for the German national side as a teenager during April 1909 and took part in a 3-3 draw against Hungary in Budapest. Edwin was spotted by United when on tour to Denmark and Germany in May of that year and was eventually offered a deal on Tyneside. Dutton had little opportunity of breaking into United's international line-up at either insider-right or outside-right during those Edwardian years, but he was a regular with the Magpies at reserve level, winning the North Eastern League title in 1910-11 and Northumberland Senior Cup during 1912. Edwin travelled with United's first-team party to the Continent during May 1911 and took part in the six-match tour of Germany and Switzerland. Although the

team line-ups have not been traced, Newcastle won all their fixtures handsomely and Dutton appears in one newspaper photograph prior to a contest. He probably appeared in more than this single outing*. Dutton remained registered with United until 1913, although subsequently had played for other clubs. By the time the Great War started, Dutton was back in Germany working at his father's retail business. He was arrested in November 1914 as a British national and interned at the Ruhleben civilian detention centre at Spandau in the capital, one of several footballers in the camp, alongside such noted names as Steve Bloomer and Fred Spiksley. When released, he returned to Tyneside and married the daughter of United trainer Jimmy McPherson. After a spell with Ipswich he settled in Newcastle, following his McPherson relations as a chiropodist and masseur, opening a practice during the Thirties, Dutton & Fawcett on Osborne Road, later residing in the Bucklow district in Wilmslow.*

(Note: Dutton's birth and death for a long period had not been firmly established, however a copy of his death certificate acquired by the McPherson family confirms the data.)

Misc App & Goals: 1 app 0 gls.*

EDEN James Samuel 1886-1892

Full-back
b. Newcastle upon Tyne, 1866 (Q2)

An early footballer between 1883 and 1885 with the Heaton Association club, neighbours of Newcastle East End, James Eden switched to his rival's camp during 1886. By season 1887-88 he was skipper of the reserve-eleven, and took part in senior fixtures during the programme, leaving around 1892. Additionally, Eden played cricket for the Gloucester CC in Newcastle. He lived in the Byker suburb and worked as an engine-fitter.

(Note: Another early footballer, John R Eden, appeared for Elswick during the same era, it is not thought they were the same player, or related.)

Misc App & Goals: 1 app 0 gls.*

EDMUNDSSON Joan Simun 2009-2012

Midfield 5'9"
b. Totfir (Faroe Islands), 26 July 1991
Career: B68 Toftir (Fls) 2008/Manchester City trial 2009/UNITED trial Dec 2009, loan Jan 2010, pmt June 2010 (Gateshead loan 2010-11)/Viking FK (Nor) loan Feb 2012, pmt March 2012 free (FC Fredericia (Den) loan 2012-13)/AB Argja (Fls) Feb 2014.

United's only footballer from the Atlantic's Faroe Islands, Joan Edmundsson settled on Tyneside as an 18-year-old after a period in England attempting to earn a professional contract with colleague Christian Mouritsen. The Black'n'Whites gave the attacking midfielder a chance, but like most of the foreign youngsters at the club during this era never progressed suitably and wasn't given any sort of sustained opportunity to impress in senior company. Joan appeared from the bench against Norwich in friendly action during July 2010, but moved to Scandinavia to find a club able to give him regular playing time. Having gained international caps at youth and Under-21 level, Edmundsson moved up to became a regular for the Faroe Islands full line-up with over 25 caps.

Misc App & Goals: 0(1) app 0 gls.

ELLIOTT Stuart Thomas 1994-2000

Midfield 5'9"
b. Willesden, London, 27 August 1977
Career: Forest Utd (Kingsbury)/Arsenal jnr 1993/UNITED jnr Aug 1994, prof Aug 1995 (Hull City loan 1996-97)(Wigan Ath trial Feb 1997)(Swindon Town loan 1997-98)(Gillingham loan 1998-99) (Hartlepool Utd loan 1998-99)(Wrexham loan 1998-99)(Bournemouth loan 1999-2000)(Stockport Co loan 1999-2000)/Darlington July 2000 free/Plymouth Argyle March 2001 free/Crewe Alex, Scunthorpe Utd, Kidderminster Harriers all on trial cs 2001/Carlisle Utd Aug 2001/Durham City Oct 2001/Scarborough Oct 2001/Exeter City trial Jan 2002, pmt Feb 2002/Merthyr Tydfil April 2002/Halifax Town Aug 2002/Harrogate Town March 2003/Harrow Borough Aug 2003/Waltham Forest Jan 2004/Gateshead April 2005, also a period as UNITED Academy coach/Northwich Victoria June 2005/York City July 2007/Grays Ath May 2008 (Crewe Alex loan 2008-09)/Durham City June 2009/Bedlington Terriers Sept 2009/Walker Technology College coach.

Stuart Elliott was given a second chance by United after being released by Arsenal as a 16-year-old. A wholehearted midfield player or central defender and a good organiser on the field, he was strong in the air and a hard tackler on the ground. Much travelled in his career, the flame-haired Elliott reached the fringe of United's side during the pre-season preparations of 1995-96, appearing against Rushden & Diamonds and Gateshead from the bench. He spent several periods on loan when on United's staff, returning for other outings with senior company in friendly action, however apart from substitute places for Premier League and Champions League matches (including v Barcelona) during 1996-97 and 1997-98, could never claim a place and joined Darlington in the close-season of 2000. He then proceeded to have a solid if unspectacular career in the lower divisions and at non-league level with 20 different clubs. Stuart once scored a remarkable 50-yard strike from the centre-circle for the Quakers against Nottingham Forest in 2000.

Misc App & Goals: 0(4) app 1 gl.

ENGLISH John Cogal 1918

Left-back 5'8"
b. Hebburn, Co Durham, 13 December 1886
d. Northampton, 21 January 1953
Career: Hebburn Argyle Sept 1907/Wallsend Park Villa 1910/Preston North End May 1910/Watford Aug 1912 £100/Sheffield Utd April 1913 £500 (UNITED war-guest 1917-18)(South Shields war-guest 1919)(Darlington Forge Albion war-guest 1919)/Darlington player-manager July 1919, retired playing Jan 1921, to May 1928/Nelson manager June 1928/Northampton Town manager Jan 1931/Exeter City manager Oct 1935 to 1939/Darlington manager June 1940 to May 1946.

Part of Sheffield United's FA Cup winning line-up in 1915, Jack English was most unlucky to be at the peak of his footballing ability when war escalated. At the time he was described as a "hardy man of the North", Jack had been honoured by the Football League side and was on the fringe of a full cap just as the game closed down at the end of the 1914-15 season. Small, neat and tidy at full-back, he used the ball well and possessed a fine sense of anticipation. English helped United out, as he did with other local clubs, during May 1918 for a game against Sunderland at Gallowgate. He went onto face the Wearsiders once more, as well as lining up twice against Middlesbrough, partnering Bill McCracken in defence on all four appearances. At the time of appearing for United, he also played for an unofficial England XI. After the war, Jack was embroiled in a contract dispute when he did not want to continue with Sheffield United.

Instead English desired a return to the North East with Darlington; the Blades though wouldn't release him and when he left in any event, the Tykes debarred him from playing in Football League action. He entered management in the lower leagues, leading the Quakers to first the North Eastern League title and then into Football League action when they finished as runners-up of Division Three North at the end of their first season. Jack then guided Darlington to the title in 1924-25 and to taste Second Division football for the first and only time, arguably the club's finest ever period. His son Jack (junior) appeared for Northampton Town and remains the Cobblers' record goalscorer.

Misc App & Goals: 4 app 0 gls.

FAIRLESS Stephen 1977-1980

Full-back 5'8"
b. Peterlee, Co Durham
Career: UNITED jnr July 1977, prof March 1979 to cs 1980/Later with Peterlee.

Stephen Fairless joined United as a youngster from St Bede's School in Peterlee. A regular in the junior side, he was called up as part of Bill McGarry's United eleven which faced Gateshead in August 1978. It was noted in the press match report that "in Steve Fairless United have a great young prospect". However the defender didn't progress and he left the club soon afterwards.

Misc App & Goals: 1 app 0 gls.

FEATHERSTONE Henry Wilson 1917-1918

Full-back & Forward 5'9"
b. Wallsend, 20 June 1885
d. Bill Quay, near Gateshead, 23 February 1956
Career: Wallsend Park Villa/St Mirren May 1909/Cardiff City cs 1911/ Ashington June 1914 (UNITED war-guest 1917-18)/Linfield Oct 1918/ Belfast Utd Sept 1920/Ashington Nov 1920/Halifax Town Aug 1923/Victoria Garesfield CW Jan 1925/ Stanley Utd c1926.

Harry Featherstone was a Tynesider who started his senior career unusually in Scotland with St Mirren, moving to Paisley with Park Villa colleague Harry Harvey (qv), also to guest for United. Strangely, Featherstone who was a more than competent full-back, also played up front and saw regular action at Love Street (37 app) before moving to Wales with Cardiff City. He started in the centre-forward shirt at Ninian Park and made an immediate impact, netting four goals against Cwm Albion on only his third outing, continuing as a regular scorer for City in their pre-Football League days. During World War One, Harry pulled on Newcastle's black-and-white striped shirt when back on Tyneside in the local Newcastle & District United League as well as on four occasions in senior friendlies over two spells during 1917 and 1918, all in the forward-line. On peace being restored, Featherstone settled back in the North East and turned out for Ashington. He was restored at full-back by then, helping the Colliers in their debut season as a Football League club during 1921-22. The Geordie totalled 71 first-class games when at Portland Park. Harry won both the Welsh Cup (1912) and Irish Cup (1919) during his travels.

Misc App & Goals: 4 app 0 gls.

FENWICK Alfred Randolph 1916

Left-half & Centre-forward 5'11"
b. Hamsterley, Co Durham, 26 March 1891
d. Hamsterley, Co Durham, 22 March 1975
Career: Craghead Utd/Hull City Oct 1911/West Ham Utd April 1914 (UNITED war-guest 1915-16)(South Shields war-guest 1919)(Hartlepools Utd war-guest 1919)/Coventry City Dec 1919 £325/Craghead Utd Aug 1921/Blyth Spartans Aug 1921/Ashington May 1924/ Blyth Spartans Dec 1924/Halifax Town 1925/Bedlington Utd Aug 1926/Blyth Spartans trainer Feb 1929, becoming director Nov 1946 to c1959.

When back in the North East during the First World War, West Ham United's Alf Fenwick played twice for the club in April and May 1916, against Blackburn Rovers and Sunderland. He also featured in the Northern Victory League during 1919 for both Hartlepools and South Shields. A very effective half-back later in his career, described as a "combative North-Easterner" and "as strong as a horse", Alf was a fringe player at both Hull and West Ham, once scoring five goals in only four games as a stand-in centre-forward for the Tigers during 1913. He appeared in the Hammers' first season of Football League action before moving to Coventry after the war and finding a regular position. In midfield he totalled 53 games in City's Second Division line-up before being part of Ashington's days as a senior club during 1924-25 (12 app). He is recorded as being the first Collier to be sent-off as a Football League club, against Barrow during September. Fenwick afterwards played on in non-league football and for many years was associated with Blyth Spartans as a player then trainer and director. His son, also Alfred, was a reserve with Sheffield Wednesday and Reading while he is related to both England international Austen Campbell and Burnley's Alan Brown, later Sunderland manager. Raised in Medomsley, before he joined Hull City, Alf worked as a "hewer" in Hamsterley Colliery nearby.

Misc App & Goals: 2 app 0 gls.

FENWICK Joseph 1881-1887

Full-back, Forward & Committee
b. Newcastle upon Tyne, 1864 (Q1)
d. Newcastle upon Tyne, 1928 (Q1)

A Stanley and East End man through and through, Joe Fenwick was one of the St Peter's cricketers, alongside skipper William Coulson, who started a new football club under the title of Stanley FC. Playing in six of the opening season's fixtures, he remained with the club as it changed to Newcastle East End and was on the managing committee in the days before a Board of Directors. Having trials for the Northumberland County side during 1883-84, Fenwick was part of the East Enders line-up which lifted the Northumberland Senior Cup in 1885 and took part in the final of the prominent Northumberland & Durham Inter-County Challenge decider against Darlington. A coppersmith by trade, he lived on Chapel Street then Raby Street, near to Stanley's original pitch off Walker Road. By the time of the 1911 census he was still a resident of St Peter's in Byker. Fenwick also played cricket for the Guild of St John cricket club.

Misc App & Goals: 47 app 2 gls.*

FERGUSON J 1885-1887

Full-back
b. unknown
Career: North Eastern Oct 1884/Tyne Association 1885/ EAST END guest April 1885, then cs 1886/Newcastle West End 1886-87.

A noted sportsman on Tyneside, playing not only football, but also rugby for the Northern rugby club, Ferguson was

an unyielding defender who was selected on several occasions for the Northumberland County side between 1884-85 and 1886-87. With East End in two spells after a period with Tyne Association, the region's original pioneer club, Ferguson was in the Heatonites line-up against Darlington in the 1885 Northumberland & Durham Inter-County Challenge final.

Misc App & Goals: 11 app 0 gls.*

FINLAY Robert 1881-1884

Half-back or Full-back
b. Berwick upon Tweed, c1866

With Stanley FC from inception in November 1881, Robert, together with his elder brother William Finlay (qv), were on the field for Newcastle United's very first game that November against Elswick Leather Works 2nd XI. As a 15 or 16-year-old teenager, he took part in eight games of that historic debut season and also went onto appear in the club's first competitive fixture. Good enough to be selected for Northumberland in trial matches during 1883, the first such representative games in the region, Finlay lived in Byker, originally a clerk then as a fitter. Robert remained with East End until around 1884, while he also appeared as a guest for Newcastle West End during season 1883-84. He was also a bright cricketer appearing for the Rosewood, Guild of St John, St Luke's and Armstrong clubs.

(Note: Although the Tyneside newspapers of the day note the brothers as both Finlay and Findlay, from census returns their surname is recorded as Finlay.)

Misc App & Goals: 20 app 4 gls.*

FINLAY William 1881-1884

Forward & Secretary
b. Scotland, c1864
Career: STANLEY Nov 1881, becoming Secretary to c1883/Newcastle West End 1884/Science & Art 1886-87/St Peter's 1886-87/Newcastle Wed 1889 to 1891.

Billy Finlay was only a teenager, like many of Stanley's footballers when the club was formed during November 1881. The elder brother of Robert Finlay (qv) in the club's pioneer line-up as well, Billy was appointed the first Secretary of the new organisation. Also Stanley's cricket secretary, he was a regular in that original football season for the fledgling outfit, appearing in eight matches, including the historic first outing when he was a goalscorer. He was Stanley captain during 1882 when they changed title to Newcastle East End and took part in the club's first competitive fixture. Then a clerk living in Belvedere Street in Byker, a decade later Finlay was still a resident of the district, in Hotspur Street, working as a Brewer's agent. Like his younger brother, he was a trialist for Northumberland and played cricket for a number of other clubs apart from Stanley; Guild of St John, Armstrong, West End, St Luke's and Woodbine.

(Note: Census returns show the brothers' surname as Finlay rather than Findlay.)

Misc App & Goals: 27 app 1 gl.*

FINNIGAN Carl John 2000-2006

Centre-forward 5'11"
b. Jarrow, 1 October 1986
Career: Jarrow BC/UNITED jnr 2000, prof July 2003 to 2006/St Mirren trial/Falkirk Jan 2007 free/St Johnstone June 2011/Dundee loan Feb 2012, pmt June 2012/Chippa Utd (SA) Aug 2013/Gateshead Sept 2014.

Having trials at both West Ham and Bolton as a schoolboy, Carl Finnigan was with the Magpies' Academy set-up during 2000. Having reached the England Under-

Players: other fixtures

17 squad, he was a highly rated striker. Lively up front at junior and reserve level, Carl was a centre-forward with good awareness and the ability to find space in the area and snap up half-chances. Scoring plenty goals (over 50) in United's shadow squad, Finnigan appeared from the bench in a friendly contest with Norwich at Carrow Road during the 2006-07 pre-season. But that was as far as the Tynesider reached with the Magpies. In Scotland, despite being injured with cartilage problems, he fashioned a respectable career, reaching the Scottish Cup final during 2009 with Falkirk and playing in the Bairns' first ever European match, although his evening's work was marred by a red card. He had totalled 150 games on the Scottish beat before heading for Cape Town in South Africa.

Misc App & Goals: 1(1) app 0 gls.

FITZGERALD Peter Joseph 1959

Forward 5'10"
b. Waterford, 17 June 1937
d. Waterford, 29 June 2013
Career: Bohemians (Waterford)/St Patrick's Ath 1955-56/Waterford Utd 1956 (UNITED trial May 1959)/Sparta Rotterdam (Neth) May 1959 £5,000/Leeds Utd Aug 1960 £7,000/Chester July 1961 £3,000/Waterford Utd Sept 1963 (Cork Hibernians loan 1965) to Aug 1967/Hyde Utd to cs 1970/Later becoming Ferrybank (Waterford) manager/Bolton (Waterford) manager/Waterford Crystal manager/Waterford Utd caretaker-manager 1996.

When Charlie Mitten took United on a short end-of-season trip to Ireland in May 1959, he gave 21-year-old Waterford forward Peter Fitzgerald a run-out in the first-half of a testimonial friendly with Evergreen in Cork. Young Fitzgerald was a bright and ambitious talent, but in his 45 minutes wearing United's black-and-white shirt was deemed not quite good enough by the Magpies to earn a contract. Yet Peter did make a name for himself in the game. One of six Waterford brothers to play football, a legendary sporting family in Munster, he was soon given the opportunity by Dutch champions Sparta, going onto play in the European Cup for the Rotterdam club with fellow Irishman Johnny Crosson. Peter moved to Elland Road for the start of the 1960-61 season and while he never commanded a regular spot in the Tykes' line-up, claiming only eight matches, Peter figured in Don Revie's first line-up, playing alongside emergency centre-forward Jack Charlton against Portsmouth. A versatile forward, in seasons 1961-62 and 1962-63 he recorded 89 games for Chester in Division Four and by that time had become an international player for the Republic of Ireland (5 app) adding to his amateur and League caps. Fitzgerald won the league title in his native country in 1965-66 and reached the cup final during 1959, both with the Blues of Waterford.

Misc App & Goals: 1 app 0 gls.

FLYNN T 1884-1887

Forward
b. unknown

A reserve player with Newcastle East End during season 1884-85, Flynn recorded a single outing for the senior eleven over two years later in January 1887 when the club faced Shankhouse Black watch, but fell 3-0. It is likely he was the same player who appeared for the Jesmond club.

Misc App & Goals: 1 app 0 gls.*

FORD Arthur 1902-1904

Right-half 5'10"
b. Newcastle upon Tyne, c1880
d. Newcastle upon Tyne, 1922 (Q2)
Career: Elswick Harriers/UNITED May 1902/Scotswood c1904.

Arthur Ford was one of several fringe and trial players given a chance in a friendly contest against Shaddongate United (later Carlisle United) during April 1904. He joined the Magpies from the Elswick Harriers outfit, a club United had a close link with at the time, at the end of the 1901-02 season. The midfielder though rarely threatened Scottish first-teamers Gardner and Caie for a place in United's senior line up and moved back to local football. Ford worked as a pattern-maker and resided in the Elswick, then Benwell, suburbs of Newcastle.

Misc App & Goals: 1 app 0 gls.

FORSTER Fraser Gerard 2004-2012

Goalkeeper 6'6"
b. Hexham, 17 March 1988
Career: Stocksfield BC/Wallsend BC/UNITED jnr Oct 2004, prof July 2007 (Stockport Co loan 2008-09) (Bristol Rovers loan 2009-10)(Norwich City loan 2009-10)(Celtic loan 2010-11, 2011-12)/Celtic pmt July 2012 £2m (plus £2.2m of later fee)/Southampton Aug 2014 £10m.

Fraser Forster had trials at Liverpool, Leicester, Rangers and Hibs before he joined his boyhood favourites at St James' Park after a period in the Academy ranks. The well-built teenager was unfortunate during his stay at Gallowgate, Fraser's time with his local club coinciding with the development of goalkeeping rival Tim Krul. Had it not been for the brilliance of the Dutchman between the sticks, United's Number 1 position in succession to Shay Given and Steve Harper could have been Forster's. As it was the likable giant of a keeper, standing at 6'6", United's tallest ever footballer, had to be content with a series of friendly appearances and a position on United's senior bench as substitute 'keeper; 24 games over five seasons. Fraser also had to go out on loan to gain experience and ultimately the towering custodian was forced to move away from Tyneside to progress a senior career. At Norwich he impressed many and was the Canaries' regular 'keeper as they won the Championship prize in 2010, then Fraser spent two seasons in Scotland with Celtic where he won more silverware in both league and cup competition north of the border. Fraser was a wanted man. Not only did the Parkhead club require him permanently but so did other teams. Born and bred in the Tyne valley, Fraser was educated at the Royal Grammar School and joined the Hoops in a £2m permanent deal during the summer of 2012, quickly winning more trophies during 2012-13 and enjoying an extended run in the Champions League. Fraser rapidly made progress as an emerging goalkeeper, selected for the full England squad. He made his debut for the Three Lions during November 2013 and was part of the World Cup squad for the trip to Brazil the following year. During the 2013-14 season Fraser became the Scottish League's record holder for clean sheets, recording 1,256 minutes and 13 games without conceding a goal. Not surprisingly he was selected in the Team of the Year for that campaign. His father Brian Clive Forster QC was appointed a Circuit Judge in 2007.

Misc App & Goals: 3(5) app 0 gls.

FORSTER Stephen 1982-1986

Midfield 5'10"
b. Tynemouth, 18 November 1967
Career: UNITED jnr Nov 1982, prof Nov 1985 to cs 1986/Local football.

An FA Youth Cup winner with United during 1985, Stephen Forster was one of several young players from that squad of juniors who promised much at St James' Park. For a couple of seasons he provided the midfield guile alongside Paul Gascoigne and when pushed forward, with Joe Allon in attack. While others flourished in senior company though, Forster was only handed a single opportunity to shine at the end of the 1985-86 season. Steve was in the line-up when United sent a team to appear in the David Mills testimonial at Ayresome Park against Middlesbrough. He later coached local football in the North Shields area, becoming a teacher on Tyneside.

Misc App & Goals: 1 app 0 gls.

FRANCIS Alex James 2005-2008

Midfield 5'11"
b. Low Fell, Gateshead, 7 January 1990
Career: Redheugh BC/UNITED jnr 2005, prof July 2005 to March 2008 free/Gateshead June 2008 (Gateshead College Sept 2008 to Dec 2009)(Blyth Spartans loan 2009-10)/Spennymoor Town Oct 2010/West Auckland Town Aug 2011 (Seaham Red Star loan 2013)/Darlington trial July 2013.

An all-action midfielder with strength in the tackle and quality on the ball, Alex Francis showed up well during his days as a junior with the club. A versatile player and a very good team-man, he could score from midfield too. With Gateshead, Francis appeared on 66 occasions while he also turned out for the England College's FA XI during 2009 when playing and studying at Gateshead College Academy of Sport. During that time he also reached the national college final and netted the winning goal. Featuring on a regular basis in the Northern League, the Tynesider suffered a double fracture of his leg playing for West Auckland Town against Whitley Bay in a FA Vase match during 2012. Working at the Nissan complex in the region, he appeared as a midfield substitute in United's pre-season games of 2007-08.

Misc App & Goals: 0(3) app 0 gls.

FRASER Alexander 1903-1904

Inside-left 5'7"
b. Inverness, 1883
d. Newcastle upon Tyne, 1958 (Q2)
Career: Inverness Thistle/UNITED trial Dec 1903, pmt Dec 1903 £20/Fulham Oct 1904/Bradford Park Avenue April 1908/Darlington Oct 1909/Middlesbrough Feb 1912/Newcastle City Sept 1913/Hartlepools Utd trainer July 1924.

Described as a thoughtful and clever inside-forward, Alex Fraser was an intricate playmaker of the Scottish school. Given a chance by United as he turned 20 years of age, he arrived on Tyneside with Inverness colleague Charles Urquhart. The Highlander showed up well in reserve football, and on occasion during his brief taste of first-team football. In a friendly against Shaddongate United (soon Carlisle United) during April 1904 he scored a hat-trick in a 4-1 victory, while he found the net four times in other contests with Bradford City and the Corinthians. Fraser was part of the Magpie second-eleven to lift the Northern League title in the same season. His performances deserved a least a call-up to the league or cup side, but the Scot couldn't press for a regular position and moved south to join Southern League Fulham. He became an important creative midfielder at the Cottage as the Londoners lifted two Southern League crowns and moved to become a Football League club in season 1907-08. Totalling 114 games, he was also in the side when Fulham defeated Manchester United in the FA Cup quarter-final, yet missed out when they met the Black'n'Whites in the semi-final. Fraser moved back to the North East during the later years of his career, at Middlesbrough picking up a bad injury against Bolton which finished his senior career. He continued for a brief period with the ambitious Newcastle City club at a time when they had sights on becoming a rival in the senior game to United. Alex settled on Tyneside and was a boilermaker with the North Eastern Railway company.

Misc App & Goals: 4 app 7 gls.

FRASER R 1920

Inside-forward
b. unknown
Little is known about R Fraser, at St James' Park for a match with South Shields during September 1920, a testimonial fixture for long-serving ex-player and trainer Tommy Ghee. Fraser doesn't appear to have been registered on United's books or with the Football League and may have been a local trialist.

Misc App & Goals: 1 app 0 gls.

FRASER Thomas John 1924-1925

Goalkeeper 5'10"
b. Glencairn, Dumfriesshire, 26 February 1900
d. Wynnewood, Pennsylvania (USA), January 1973
Career: Hurlford 1921 (Kilmarnock loan 1921-22)(Dundee loan 1921-22)/Dumbarton Harp Dec 1921/Beith 1921-22/Dundee 1922-23/Beith July 1923 (UNITED trial Aug 1923 briefly)/UNITED May 1924/Clyde Aug 1925/Bethlehem Steel (USA) 1929/Newark Americans (USA) c1930.

Newcastle United twice had a look at goalkeeper Tom Fraser, firstly when he was thought to be an amateur with Beith only for the Magpies to be told he was a professional, the player having to leave St James' Park promptly. But the club kept a track of his progress and at the second opportunity they signed the Scot towards the end of the following season. With veteran 'keeper Sandy Mutch injured just before United lifted the FA Cup in 1924, Newcastle needed goalkeeper cover. Fraser arrived and soon travelled to Spain as deputy to Bill Bradley for the club's nine-game tour at the end of that successful 1923-24 season. While all match line-ups are not traced, he did play in a handful of fixtures, including against Barcelona and Real Madrid during May 1924. He also took part in a fixture with South Shields as the new 1924-25 season progressed. Fraser returned to Scotland with Bill Bradley claiming the shirt, becoming a respected last line of defence with Clyde in 163 games. Fraser was part of the Bully Wee's Division Two promotion side in 1925-26 and represented the Glasgow combination during 1926-27 as he took part in top flight football north of the border. In 1927 he sailed from Glasgow to ply his trade in North America, residing in the USA for the rest of his life. Tom lived in New York state then Philadelphia and became a naturalised US citizen.

Misc App & Goals: 3 app 0 gls.*

FULLER Robert 1964-1967

Centre-forward 5'10"
b. Gateshead, 26 June 1947
Career: Whickham/Wrekenton Welfare/UNITED Oct 1964/Brighton May 1967 £2,000 to c1968/South African football 1969.
A solid, fair-headed centre-forward, Bob Fuller was a young reserve

competing with Peter Noble and Kit Napier behind the likes of Ron McGarry, Bryan Robson and Albert Bennett at St James' Park. A regular scorer at Central League level for the Magpies, Fuller was handed a single run-out in senior company as the 1966-67 season began, in a game at Brunton Park against Carlisle. Then he was unlucky to badly injury an ankle in a reserve clash with Manchester United's Harry Gregg. With United eyeing much more high profile leaders as they consolidated their top-level status as the mid-Sixties unfolded, Bob moved to Brighton in a deal which also took George Dalton south. However, Fuller had to be content with a place on the bench and never appeared in a senior shirt for the Seagulls. Bob was forced to retire due to injury and out of football found conspicuous success in the corporate dealings of telecommunications. Firstly, training as an accountant with the National Coal Board and British Gas where he was appointed as an auditor, Bob moved to the Far East to join Hong Kong Electricity where in 1982 he moved into the rapidly growing telecoms sector with Hutchison. Under a new Orange brand, Fuller become Chief Executive of the UK company in 1997. Described in the business world as a "hard-edged Geordie", Bob then successfully managed 3 Mobile both in Italy and back in Britain. He retired during June 2007 after a distinguished career developing the mobile phone industry.

Misc App & Goals: 1 app 0 gls.

GALBRAITH James 1888

Inside-forward
b. Scotland
Career: Dumbarton Ath (Newcastle West End guest Jan 1887 & Jan 1888) (EAST END guest April 1888)/Dumbarton by cs 1889 (Celtic guest May 1890)/Middlesbrough cs 1892 briefly.

As an amateur Dumbarton Athletic footballer, James Galbraith faced Newcastle West End twice in exhibition friendly matches on Tyneside at New Year 1887 and 1888. During January 1887, the Scottish visitors remained in Newcastle for a few days and Galbraith guested for the West Enders against Albion Rovers. He must have enjoyed Tyneside life as he was back again the following year, spending a period in the North East during 1888. This was at a time when, as the Dumbarton club history notes, "approaches by English clubs stepped up", agents attracting Scots with professional contracts south of the border. He was given an opportunity in Newcastle East End's line-up against Elswick Rangers during April and reports noted the Scot showed up well. However, he did not remain with the Chillingham Road club and Galbraith returned to the west of Scotland. He became a notable member of a historic Dumbarton eleven, part of the side which lifted the title north of the border (shared with Rangers) in the very first season of the Scottish League, 1890-91. He also reached the Scottish Cup final that year as runner-up to Hearts. Galbraith, who appeared for the Dunbartonshire eleven, made a move back to England as a professional with Middlesbrough during the summer of 1892. But his stay in Cleveland was short, appearing only once in senior action for Boro, in the opening game of the 1892-93 Northern League programme – when he was sent-off and not to play again on Teesside.

Misc App & Goals: 1 app 0 gls.

GALLAGHER 1889-1890

Half-back
b. unknown
Gallagher was a half-back who turned out during season 1889-90 against Blackburn Rovers, when the Ewood Park club travelled to Heaton for an exhibition fixture in the opening game of the season. That was a prestige match against the Lancastrian club, three times winners of the FA Cup at the time. Gallagher played in midfield as the much more experienced visitors won by 2-1. Likely a trialist, he was handed other opportunities but not given a contract.

Misc App & Goals: 3 app 0 gls.*

GARDNER James 1881-1883

Full-back & Half-back
b. unknown
With trailblazers Stanley FC during their first season of 1881-82, James Gardner took part in what was Newcastle United's very first fixture against the Elswick Leather Works 2nd XI during November 1881. Gardner recorded four games in that gateway campaign and also played in East End's first match of competitive action. He guested for Newcastle Rangers during 1883-84 and was with the Heaton Association club from 1883 to 1886. It is likely the player is James H Gardner, born in Leeds (c1866) and during 1881 living on Molyneux Street in Heaton.

Misc App & Goals: 8 app 1 gl.*

GARDNER William Marr 1882-1883

Full-back
b. Newcastle upon Tyne, 1860 (Q4)
d. Newcastle upon Tyne, 29 September 1907
An engine-fitter who was with Newcastle East End between 1882 and 1883, like many of the working-class members of the early Stanley and East End footballers, he lived in Byker. As a teenager, William played alongside namesake James Gardner (qv) who was possibly a relation. He also was a cricketer with Guild of St John CC. Gardner remained as a resident of the city's eastern district, noted as a marine-engineer.

Misc App & Goals: 2 app 0 gls.*

GATE Kris 2001-2007

Midfield 5'7"
b. Walker, Newcastle upon Tyne, 1 January 1985
Career: Walker Central BC/UNITED jnr July 2001, prof March 2004 (Grimsby Town trial Nov 2005) to May 2007 free/Gretna & Darlington trial May 2007/St Mirren & Bradford City trial July 2007/Newcastle Blue Star July 2007/Gateshead Sept 2007/Harrogate Town June 2012/Bedlington Terriers July 2012/Perth SC (Aus) March 2013.

Fair-haired Kris Gate was part of the Black'n'Whites successful Premier League Under-17 title side in 2002 and reached first-team contention between 2004 and 2006. He first appeared from the substitute's bench for a friendly with Rangers in July 2004 then took part in a pre-season friendly two years later against Norwich. In between, the Walker-born player reached United's Premier League team-sheet as sub during 2005-06. Skipper of the club's reserve eleven, Gate was a slight but determined full-back or midfielder with good passing ability and vision. He dictated the game from the heart of the action and was industrious but couldn't push further for a senior position, dogged by a cartilage problem when at a stage in his development he should have been pressing strongly. Moving into non-league level in the region, Kris did well for Gateshead, clocking up over 130 games over five seasons at the International Stadium.

Misc App & Goals: 2(1) app 0 gls.

Players: other fixtures

GIBBON Henry 1924-1925

Outside-right 5'9"
b. Hetton-le-Hole, Co Durham, 19 April 1906
d. Barrow, 15 January 1972
Career: Houghton/UNITED trial Sept 1924, he took part in the two-legged Ingham Cup Aug 1925 free/Sunderland amat May 1926, prof Sept 1926/Notts Co July 1927/Seaham Harbour Sept 1928 to 1929.

Noted as a fine footballer and cricketer as a schoolboy and youth in County Durham, Harry Gibbon was a young miner at the local pit at Hetton before being given an opportunity by the Magpies. With the club for season 1924-25, he took part in the two-legged Ingham Cup final with South Shields at St James' Park during October 1924. But Harry wasn't retained and the winger tried again to claim a professional career with Sunderland. Again he had no joy, but did have marginal better success with Notts County where he made his Football League bow in Second Division action during 1927-28. Gibbon managed only three games for the Trent club before returning to County Durham to appear in the North Eastern League. In between his football, he continued to play cricket, and with a football career on the wane, started to concentrate on the summer game. Gibbon was a celebrated Minor County player for Durham between 1925 and 1938 (97 app, 3,334 runs, 57 wickets), a fine all-rounder for Eppleton, New Seaham Park and Sunderland cricket clubs, as well as later, in Lancashire for Bacup. He lifted the Minor County title during 1926 and once took seven wickets for only 16 runs in a county game against Denbighshire during 1935. He also played against top level opponents; against South Africa, Australia and the West Indies. In later years Gibbon worked in a warehouse, as a local council clerk and resided in Barrow.
Misc App & Goals: 1 app 0 gls.

GIBSON Barry Jon 1993-1998

Outside-right 5'10"
b. Wallsend, 30 March 1979
Career: Wallsend BC/UNITED jnr March 1993, prof 1997 to cs 1998/ Morpeth Town 1998/North Shields 2000/Heddon 2005/North Shields 2007 to 2009 when he retired.

Raised in Walkerville and from the football breeding ground of St Cuthbert's School in Newcastle, Barry Gibson represented both the City and Northumberland schoolboy side. As a young player he started as a centre-forward, then ended up playing on the right flank of midfield before developing into a winger at St James' Park. Barry was noted as being fast and having a boxful of tricks who specialised in the 'Johan Cruyff step-over'. A player who loved to go head-on at defenders around the box, he could be mesmerising at times. Nicknamed 'Trigger', the quality of United's first-team squad at a time when the club challenged for the Premier League title probably stopped the Tynesider making the grade, Barry managing only one outing in senior ranks, as a substitute in a part first-team match with Bishop Auckland during August 1995. He afterwards joined the Northumbria Police, joining the force in 2000 and latterly working as an officer in Gosforth.
Misc App & Goals: 0(1) app 0 gls.

GILLIEAD Alex Nicholas 2011-date

Forward 6'1"
b. Shotley Bridge, Co Durham, 11 February 1996
Career: Swalwell Jnrs/UNITED trial 2011, jnr July 2012, prof July 2013.

England youth international forward Alex Gilliead joined United on a scholarship deal during the close-season of 2012 after being attached to the Magpies as a 15-year-old. A pacy forward able to play across the front line and also on the wing, as well as raid from midfield, he quickly made an impression in Newcastle's junior line-up. His ability and versatility was noticed and he was signed as a professional in July 2013. Alex made his senior bow for the last six minutes of the friendly with Sheffield Wednesday at Hillsborough at the start of the 2014-15 campaign. Gilliead is a former season-ticket holder at St James' Park, from a family of Toon supporters, and is one of several bright hopefuls from the club's Development squad which includes with Adam Armstrong and Jonathyn Quinn, a rich striking talent. When he was only eleven years of age, Alex somewhat reluctantly had a trial at Sunderland which came to nothing.
Misc App & Goals: 0(1) app 0 gls.

GILMARTIN J 1888-1889

Full-back
b. Scotland

Arriving on Tyneside from Rangers in August 1888, Gilmarton took part in the first game of the season alongside Clydeside colleague Smith, both players being given a chance by Newcastle East End in a benefit match. Against Elswick Rangers, they lost 4-0 and neither Glasgow imports stayed long thereafter.
Misc App & Goals: 1 app 0 gls.*

GOLDING George D 1886-1887

Half-back
b. Prescot, Lancashire, c1863

Born and raised in the Prescot area near Liverpool, George Golding moved to Tyneside by the start of the 1880s, living in Byker with his uncle. One of several Newcastle East End players to be associated with the adjacent Heaton Association side, Golding was with the friendly neighbours between 1883 and 1886. He made the short trip to wear East End's blue shirts for the start of the 1886-87 season and was a regular in midfield during that campaign before departing at the end of the programme.
(Note: Newspaper reports also express his surname as Goulden, but national registration and census information confirm Golding.)
Misc App & Goals: 16 app 0 gls.*

GORMAN Charles 1884-1885

Forward
b. Norwich, 1865

A member of the early Newcastle East End team during the 1884-85 season, Charles Gorman appeared for the Northumberland County side towards the end of that campaign as well as representing the City of Newcastle XI. From Norfolk, he settled on Tyneside living in Byker. Gorman scored the winning goal for the club as the Northumberland Challenge Cup was secured in 1885, and Charles was a runner-up during the same campaign in the Northumberland & Durham Inter-County final, his one season with East End being thoroughly eventful. After his days with the East Enders, Gorman appeared for the St Mary's & St James' club in Newcastle.
Misc App & Goals: 10 app 5 gls.*

GRAY Charles 1883-1887

Half-back & Secretary
b. Byker, Newcastle upon Tyne, 1864 (Q4)
d. Newcastle upon Tyne, 21 January 1907

Secretary of Newcastle East End for seasons 1885-86 and 1886-87, Charles Gray also occasionally pulled on the club's shirt, initially in November 1883 against Whitburn, captain for a period in 1885. Living in Burton Street and working as a shop-assistant in Byker, when he relinquished the administrative post during the summer of 1886 he was heavily criticised for not informing the local press of East End's team line-ups. Charles later appeared for Rendel on the other side of the city, joining the Benwell club in 1887. He appears to have been connected with the West Road outfit into the 1890s. Gray was for a period also a member of the Northumberland FA committee. When the 1901 census was completed, Charles was employed as a rent-collector living in Gosforth.
Misc App & Goals: 7 app 2 gls.*

GREEN Stuart 1996-2002

Midfield 5'10"
b. Whitehaven, 15 June 1981
Career: Marchon 1993/Carlisle Utd jnr 1996/UNITED jnr cs 1996, prof June 1997 (Carlisle Utd loan 2001-02, 2002-03)/Hull City loan July 2002, pmt Dec 2002 £150,000 (Carlisle Utd loan 2002-03)/Crystal Palace Aug 2006 £75,000/Blackpool Jan 2008 free (Crewe Alex loan 2008-09)/Wycombe Wand July 2009 free/Carlisle Utd trial July 2011/Workington July 2011/Whitehaven Amateurs July 2012 player-manager to July 2013.

A former England youth trialist, Stuart Green was a lively attacking midfielder or striker, capable of carrying the ball and putting incisive passes into the box. Somewhat famously, Green was caught up in Gallowgate controversy when boss Ruud Gullit selected both Alan Shearer and Duncan Ferguson for the bench instead of starting against rivals Sunderland during August 1999, Green being captured in the pictures beamed around the country as an unused substitute in the dug-out with United's £23m strike-force. Overcoming a bad heel injury, Stuart was included by new boss Bobby Robson on the end-of-season trip to play two games in the Caribbean during May 2000. He appeared with the seniors from the bench, then again at the start of the following campaign against Burnley. Stuart was on the fringe of a call-up before a shoulder injury curtailed his season. After a brief look-in as sub during season 2001-02, Green was released after loan spells at Carlisle United. With Hull City, the Cumbrian appeared on 146 occasions and took part in promotions from Division Three in 2004, and Division One (Two) the following year. Stuart reached the final of the Football League Trophy when at Brunton Park in 2003.
Misc App & Goals: 1(3) app 0 gls.

GREENUP 1886-1887

Half-back
b. [Alnwick]

Little is known about Greenup, a midfielder who appeared once in the colours of East End, against Durham College during October 1886. It is probable that the player was a trialist and is one of two brothers from Alnwick; Joseph Greenup (b. c1868) or Andrew Greenup (b. c1866).
Misc App & Goals: 1 app 0 gls.*

GUDJONSSON Bjarni Eggerts 1997-1998

Midfield 5'8"
b. Akranes (Iceland), 26 February 1979
Career: IA Akranes (Ice) jnr Jan 1995, prof March 1996 (Real Madrid & Liverpool trials 1996)/UNITED trial Dec 1996, pmt April 1997 £250,000/ KRC Genk (Bel) Nov 1998 £125,000 /Stoke City March 2000 £250,000/VfL Bochum (Ger) May 2003 free/Coventry City loan Jan to May 2004, pmt July 2004 free/Plymouth Argyle Dec 2004 free/Watford trial Aug 2005/IA Akranes (Ice) Jan 2006/KR Reykjavik (Ice) July 2008/Fram Reykjavik (Ice) manager 2013.

During United's resurgence in the 1990s the Geordies purchased many high-profile players, but also took a punt on several up and coming youngsters from home and abroad. During 1996-97 Icelandic teenager Bjarni Gudjonsson was twice given the opportunity to show United's coaching staff he had potential to become a top footballer after shining playing for the Iceland Under-21 side. Having also been at Real Madrid (where he netted a hat-trick in a junior match) and looking very much the school leaver, slight and boyish, Gudjonsson displayed much talent for his age and was offered a deal at the end of his second period on Tyneside in April 1997. Bjarni operated in midfield with vision, was highly-skilled with plenty of tricks and despite his size and build, was well-equipped to keep the ball moving in the centre of the field. From a family of footballers, he had the sport in his blood. His father Gudjon played and coached the game, while brothers Thordor and Johannes appeared in Europe as well. Gudjonsson developed through Newcastle's reserve set-up and reached senior company for friendlies during July 1997 with a place on the substitute's bench but without getting on the field. Although he appeared for his country when a United player he never reached serious first-team action. Ruud Gullit released him during season 1998-99 and Bjarni went onto have a respectable career elsewhere; first establishing himself as a play-maker with Genk, lifting the Belgian title in 1999. He returned to England to play second-tier football with Stoke City, a key factor in their Second Division promotion combination during 2002 as well as Football League Trophy victory. Totalling 161 matches for the Potters, he also made 23 full appearances for Iceland, skippering his country on occasion.

Misc App & Goals: 0 app 0 gls (2 sub no app).

GUINAN Stephen Anthony 1996

Striker 6'1"
b. Birmingham, 24 December 1975
Career: Nottingham Forest jnr 1991, prof Jan 1993 (Greensboro Dynamo (USA) loan 1995)(Darlington loan 1995-96)(UNITED guest May 1996) (Burnley loan 1996-97)(Crewe Alex loan 1997-98)(Halifax Town loan 1998-99)(Plymouth Argyle loan 1998-99)(Scunthorpe Utd loan 1999-2000)/Cambridge Utd Dec 1999/ Plymouth Argyle March 2000/Shrewsbury Town March 2002/Hereford Utd cs 2002/Cheltenham Town May 2004/Hereford Utd loan Jan 2007, pmt June 2007/ Northampton Town July 2009 (Forest Green Rovers loan 2010-11)/Kidderminster Harriers May 2011, becoming player-coach Sept 2012, then coach & Academy Manager.

A solid journeyman footballer who travelled the lower leagues after leaving Nottingham Forest, Steve Guinan guested for United as a substitute for Tino Asprilla when Kevin Keegan took a strong side to play in Stuart Pearce's testimonial towards the end of the 1995-96 season. Tall and powerfully built, he was with Forest for seven years but totalled only nine games and rarely received a chance, being sent on a succession of loan deals. He played a brief part of Forest's promotion side during 1998 then later was also successful in 2006 (Cheltenham) and 2008 (Hereford). His best periods were at Whadden Road

and Edgar Street, claiming 111 games for Cheltenham and 94 for Hereford. Guinan could find the net, scoring 29 for the Bulls during season 2003-04 at Conference level and recorded almost a century in his lengthy career. He was capped by England's non-league 'C' National Game XI on four occasions before he began a coaching career with Kidderminster. Steve also coached the British Universities squad.

Misc App & Goals: 0(1) app 1 gl.

HAFEKOST Charles Henry 1917

Right-half 6'0"
b. Sunderland, 22 March 1890
d. December 1967
Career: Sunderland Royal Rovers/New Brompton July 1912/Liverpool May 1914 (UNITED war-guest 1917-18) (Darlington Forge Albion war-guest 1919)(Sunderland war-guest 1919).

Charlie Hafekost topped the New Brompton (soon to be renamed Gillingham), scoring list for season 1913-14 in the Southern League and earned a move to Anfield at the end of the campaign. Unfortunately the 24-year-old Wearsider's big move coincided with the outbreak of World War One and his opportunity was wrecked by the conflict. He made only a single appearance for Liverpool before football was halted, while during the hostilities when back in the North East during 1917, guested for United in two fixtures during October against South Shields. He also appeared for Sunderland and for the Darlington Forge Albion club during the Northern Victory League programme in the early months of 1919. Before starting out on a football career in Kent, Hafekost was employed as a plumber at Williamson's Quarry on Wearside.

Misc App & Goals: 2 app 0 gls.

HALLAM David 1986-1989

Forward 6'0"
b. Newcastle upon Tyne, 18 October 1969
Career: UNITED jnr June 1986, prof June 1988 to cs 1989 free/Later with Blyth Spartans cs 1993.

David Hallam was a tall striker and a strong front man whose physical presence gave him an advantage in the air. He also had good feet and was at home in most forward positions. On United's books as a schoolboy as early as 1984, Hallam reached Newcastle's first-team squad during season 1987-88, and earned a place on the bench for the trip to play Portsmouth at Fratton Park during May. The Geordie striker didn't get into the action and was released the following summer when he moved into non-league football. He lifted the Northumberland Senior Cup with Blyth, scoring the only goal of the 1994 final against Blue Star.

Misc App & Goals: 0 app 0 gls (1 sub no app).

HANN Ralph 1930-1932

Wing-half 5'9"
b. Whitburn, Co Durham, 4 July 1911
d. Derby, 17 July 1990
Career: Marsden CW/Whitburn St Mary's/Sunderland amat April 1929, prof Jan 1930/UNITED Aug 1930 free/ Derby Co March 1932 joint deal with D Hutchison/Crystal Palace Sept 1946, becoming trainer/Luton Town trainer July 1947/Derby Co trainer Nov 1953 to May 1967.

Ralph Hann failed to make the grade at Roker Park and was given another chance when he joined the Magpie staff as the 1930-31 season began. In midfield he was a reserve contender to regulars Weaver and MacKenzie as

well as their main deputy Jimmy Naylor. He made one senior appearance for the Geordies, Ralph travelling to Edinburgh with United's first-eleven to play in a testimonial fixture against Hearts at Tynecastle during September 1931. Hann caught the eye of Derby County then managed by ex-United player George Jobey. When he took Duncan Hutchison to the Baseball Ground, Ralph was added as part of the deal. His move south is well recorded; not aware of the proposed transfer, Ralph was found in a Newcastle cinema when he needed to be at Gallowgate to meet officials, apparently as the story goes, located by a policeman and brought to St James' Park. With the Rams, Hann totalled 122 games over seven seasons in a solid and unspectacular manner, part of County's line-up which ended as runners-up in the title race for 1935-36. During the Second World War, he worked at the Carriage & Wagon Works in the Midlands and returned to the Baseball Ground as part of the backroom team until the arrival of Brian Clough saw a mass clear-out. He then started a private physiotherapy clinic in Derby. His daughter, Judith Hann, became a well-known television personality during the Seventies and Eighties, presenting the long-running BBC programme Tomorrow's World.

Misc App & Goals: 1 app 0 gls.

HARKER Richard 1904-1905

Inside-forward 5'10"
b. Wardley Colliery, near Gateshead, 20 May 1883
d. Arras (France), 9 April 1917
Career: Hebburn Excelsior/Swalwell/ UNITED trial Aug 1903 briefly/ Washington Utd Aug 1903/Wardley CW/UNITED April 1904/Crystal Palace May 1905/Hibernian July 1907 £75/ Heart of Midlothian June 1909/Crystal Palace June 1911/Darlington July 1912 to c1914.

The New Year 1905 holiday exhibition match with famed amateur combination, The Corinthians marked the only appearance of inside-forward Richard Harker. Respected in local football for two seasons before joining the Magpie staff permanently, Harker was at Gallowgate just as the club began to embark on a period of mastery in the game. At inside-forward he was a contemporary of the emerging Peter McWilliam and was never considered good enough to challenge the likes of Howie and Orr as well as McWilliam. After securing a Northumberland Senior Cup medal and Northern League title with the club's reserve side in 1904-05, Richard headed to London, joining Southern League Crystal Palace where several exiles from the region were based. He was one of those local footballers to take part in the era's biggest FA Cup giant-killing as Palace knocked out United, then League Champions, from the competition in 1906-07. Richard afterwards had a very productive stay in Scotland's capital, scoring plenty of goals for both Hibs and Hearts at the top level. In two seasons at Easter Road he netted 29 in 68 matches, then across the city at Tynecastle returned 20 in 67 appearances. Joining the Tyneside Scottish Pals battalion of the Northumberland Fusiliers, Harker was killed in action in Flanders during the First World War. He is remembered at the Arras Memorial, Pas de Calais.

Misc App & Goals: 1 app 0 gls.

Players: other fixtures

HARRISON Anthony Leslie 1983 & 1986-1987

Goalkeeper 6'1"
b. Gateshead, 9 January 1954
Career: Whitburn CA 1972/Boldon CW 1973/Whitley Bay Jan 1974/ Southport Feb 1977/Carlisle Utd June 1978/North Shields cs 1982 (UNITED trial Feb 1983)/Newcastle Blue Star cs 1984/Gateshead cs 1985/(UNITED loan April 1986 to 1987)/Bishop Auckland cs 1986/ Durham City 1988/ Hartlepool Utd Aug 1988/Whitley Bay 1989-90/Durham City asst-manager 1994, becoming manager/Blyth Spartans asst-manager Oct 1999 to July 2000/Prudhoe Town manager c2002/ Ashington manager cs 2003/ Consett manager Dec 2004/Prudhoe Town manager 2005 to cs 2006/Dunston UTS coach 2006, becoming asst-manager Aug 2009/ Also Middlesbrough asst-coach for a period at the School of Excellence.

As a young non-league goalkeeper with North Shields, Tony Harrison had a brief period with the club during February 1983 attempting to impress the coaching staff. Harrison worked in the local Land Registry office before he enjoyed two seasons of regular action in Southport's Division Four line-up during 1976-77 and 1977-78, registering 54 games, alas taking part in the Haig Avenue clubs last season in senior membership. Tony looked a solid 'keeper at that level until he fractured his arm, an injury followed by more misfortune just after he joined Carlisle when he broke a leg in a pre-season friendly during 1978. At Brunton Park he was destined to be reserve to Trevor Swinburne so only totalled 14 games over four seasons. He returned to Gallowgate on April 1986 when the Magpies went through a goalkeeping crisis. Shortly after a bizarre 8-1 reverse at West Ham United when they fielded three different 'keepers (including two emergency outfield players), senior custodian Martin Thomas was in the treatment room and the club brought in locals Harrison and Dave Clarke to support on loan Dave McKellar as cover. Harrison took part in one match for United's senior line-up, against Middlesbrough in the David Mills testimonial fixture during April 1986 and featured in FA Youth Cup games during 1986-87. Harrison later became a well-known player and coach in local non-league football for 25 years. In 2014 he was part of the Dunston coaching team which guided the Tynesiders to FA Vase success at Wembley. Tony also worked for Tyne & Wear local authority and for Gateshead Council.

Misc App & Goals: 1 app 0 gls.

HARRISON George 1913-1914

Centre-half
b. unknown
Career: Hexham Ath/UNITED May 1913/Gateshead July 1914.

George Harrison was one of a long line of local footballers to enter St James' Park in search of fame, and a degree of fortune. An outstanding talent at half-back in the Tyne valley with Hexham, he joined the club on a year-long contract at the end of the 1912-13 season. Harrison was selected in midfield alongside Colin Veitch and Jock Finlay for a match played in aid of Players Union funds during September of the new campaign. He was released in the summer of 1914 and war put an end to any further chance of football in the big-time.

Misc App & Goals: 1 app 0 gls.

HARRISON James [John] 1887-1890

Full-back & Half-back
b. Newcastle upon Tyne

With Heaton Association and Cheviot before becoming a Newcastle East End player, James Harrison was part of the Cheviot junior set-up which was merged into the East Enders during September 1887. Raised as a lad in Byker, Harrison was still a teenager when he became an East End reserve and was handed an outing in December 1888 against Port Clarence, a 5-1 victory. Harrison continued as a regular reserve player with East End Swifts before leaving during the summer of 1890. Likely to be referred to as John as well, a John Harrison purchased shares in East End in 1891, residing at Wilfred Street in Byker.

Misc App & Goals: 1 app 0 gls.*

HARRISON Peter Michael 1982

Centre-half 5'11"
b. Newcastle upon Tyne,
14 August 1959
Career: Redheugh BC/Nottingham Forest jnr 1977-78/Gateshead Aug 1978 (UNITED trial May 1982)/RSC Charleroi (Belg) July 1982/Gateshead July 1987/Barrow 1987-88/Gateshead 1989-90, 1990-91/Later coaching in the North East becoming Hebburn manager/Blyth Spartans manager Nov 1995 to March 1997.

As a youngster Peter Harrison was part of Nottingham Forest's youth ranks before moving back to Tyneside to appear for Gateshead. He was given a trial with the Magpies during Arthur Cox's reign during May 1982, in a 6-2 victory at Hartlepool, and while he was told to return for further review wasn't immediately offered a full-time contract. Instead, soon after Peter headed for Belgium when he joined Charleroi for a spell, teaming up with a young Philippe Albert before the future United centre-half moved to Anderlecht. Described as a "footballing centre-back", Harrison spent five seasons with the Ardennes club, promoted from the second-tier in 1985 and later appointed captain for a period. Returning to the North East, he joined Gateshead once more and by the time he had rejoined for a third occasion, brought his total of games at the International Stadium to over 200. Peter set up a sportswear retail business in Gateshead and also created a FIFA licensed football agency, MPH Soccer Management. He represented several high profile clients including Andy Carroll's early career, although by 2011 his venture floundered. Harrison made headlines shortly afterwards by revealing all in the media on the sometimes murky world of football transfers.

Misc App & Goals: 1 app 0 gls.

HARRISON William 1903-1904

Outside-left 5'9"
b. probably Tyneside
Career: Elswick Harriers (UNITED trial Aug 1902)/ UNITED Sept 1903/Morpeth Harriers Aug 1904.

Newcastle United gave six fringe players a chance in a part senior line-up against Shaddongate United during April 1904, Billy Harrison appearing on the left wing in Cumberland. Like his colleague Arthur Ford, another promising Elswick Harriers footballer on Tyneside, Billy was given a short-term contract following trials with the Magpies, but never developed in a manner good enough for a club shortly to become the country's finest. According to the Carlisle press, Harrison netted twice on his only outing however, the Newcastle reports do not confirm this, giving the goals to his inside partner Alex Fraser.

Misc App & Goals: 1 app 0 gls.

HART Thomas 1884-1886

Forward
b. Newcastle upon Tyne, c1872

A teenager in the ranks of Newcastle East End juniors Tommy Hart was elevated to the first-team company for a friendly against Sunderland in Byker during November 1885, a prestigious fixture billed as the holder of the Northumberland Challenge Cup versus holder of the Durham Challenge Cup. The Wearsiders won narrowly by a single goal. Hart didn't feature again and it appears he left the club in 1886.

Misc App & Goals: 1 app 0 gls.*

HARVEY Henry 1918

Left-half 5'10"
b. Wallsend, April 1888
Career: Wallsend Park Villa/St Mirren May 1909/Cardiff City Aug 1912 (UNITED war-guest 1918-19) to c1920
Nicknamed 'Kidder' during his career Harry Harvey was one of several guests to wear the Newcastle black-and-white striped shirt in friendly matches during the later years of the First World War. A former St Mirren and Cardiff player, Harvey appeared twice for the Magpies in a double-header against Wearside rivals Sunderland over the Christmas period of 1918. With Park Villa colleague Harry Featherstone, the Tyneside pair joined St Mirren together and Harvey registered 20 games over two seasons in Scotland's top level. He then joined Cardiff and appeared in City's pre-Football League days, alongside Featherstone who ventured to Wales too. In Southern League fare, Harry was a regular for three campaigns before the First World War halted action and once peace was restored he struggled to claim a position at Ninian Park as Cardiff entered the Football League in 1920.

Misc App & Goals: 2 app 0 gls.

HARVEY George 1902-1903

Centre-forward
b. unknown
Career: UNITED trial April 1902, pmt Sept 1902 to 1903.
George Harvey played alongside the likes of Jack Rutherford, Jock Peddie and Ronald Orr in United's forward line which faced minnows Workington Black Diamond during April 1902. A local player who joined the club following a trial, he netted the only goal of the game on the west coast, but only stayed at the club for a season getting close to a senior call-up again only once more.

Misc App & Goals: 2 app 2 gls.

HATELEY Anthony 1965

Centre-forward 6'1"
b. Derby, 13 June 1941
d. Preston, 1 February 2014
Career: Normanton Sports April 1954/Derby Co jnr April 1955/Notts Co amat May 1956, prof June 1958/ Aston Villa Aug 1963 £25,000 (UNITED guest Oct 1965)/Chelsea Oct 1966 £100,000/Liverpool July 1967 £96,000/Coventry City Sept 1968 £80,000/Birmingham City Aug 1969 £72,000/Notts Co Nov 1970 £20,000/Oldham Ath July 1972 £5,000/Boston Minutemen (USA) cs 1974/ Bromsgrove Rovers Aug 1974/Prescot Town July 1975/ Keyworth Utd Dec 1978/Retired Aug 1979.
Centre-forward Tony Hateley was one of several big-name leaders who appeared at the top level during the Sixties and Seventies. At the time when he guested for

the Black'n'Whites in a testimonial during season 1965-66, the club was in dire need of his type of threat up front. The big and robust Number 9 was linked with a move to United along with Ron and Wyn Davies as well as John Ritchie. But Hateley headed for Chelsea and onto Liverpool in big-money moves. Tony's brief appearance in a Toon shirt saw him lead an attack of noted guests as United won 6-2 in a match against Sunderland to mark Brian Clough's playing career. Tall, powerful in the air and in the old-fashioned leader mould, Hateley netted 86 goals for Villa before less successful stints at Stamford Bridge and Anfield. Appearing for the FA XI on tour in 1969, Tony took part in the 1967 FA Cup final while during the early and later part of his career, he twice won promotion out of Division Four with Notts County (207 app 114 goals). On retiring Hateley worked for a period in the Everton lottery office at Goodison Park, then as a representative of Nottingham brewers, Thwaites, and for a Midland soft drinks company. His son, Mark Hateley, was another excellent centre-forward, conspicuously for Rangers and England.
Misc App & Goals: 1 app 1 gl.

HAYTON Tony 1981-1986

Midfield 5'8"
b. Ashington, 7 February 1967
Career: UNITED jnr Nov 1981, prof Feb 1985 to cs 1986/Later appearing and coaching in local football and Blyth Spartans asst-coach.

A former captain of the Northumberland schoolboy side, Tony Hayton soon became a promising midfielder with United at teenage level. One of several youngsters of the mid-Eighties at St James' Park to be highlighted as potential stars, the diminutive Hayton was known for his ferocious tackling and high energy in midfield. Part of the club's 1984-85 FA Youth Cup winning side, Tony graduated to first-team company, first as a substitute in a friendly match at the Victoria Ground in Hartlepool during August 1984. Unlucky to be dogged by a knee injury, he was released by the Magpies and afterwards coached youngsters in the South Northumberland area, notably for Blyth Spartans. He worked for a period at the Alcan complex in Lynmouth.
Misc App & Goals: 0(2) app 0 gls.

HENDERSON (Jameson) 1898

Inside-right
b. probably Scotland
It was noted by the contemporary press that a forward by the name of "Jameson" arrived at St James' Park during February 1898 for a trial from the "Glasgow area". The Daily Chronicle and Daily Leader newspapers recorded that he used a false name as he was an amateur with Queen's Park called Henderson. It was also noted he was a "Scotland player", but not an international; rather it is likely that Henderson is the Queen's footballer who also appeared for the Scottish amateur combination (similar to England's famed Corinthians line-up). He took part in an entertaining 4-4 draw with Derby County at Gallowgate during the same month but was not deemed good enough and was not retained. He later signed for South Shields in November 1898.
Misc App & Goals: 1 app 0 gls.

HENDERSON Crosby Gray 1906-1907

Full-back 5'10"
b. South Hylton, Sunderland, 12 May 1885
d. Sunderland, 27 April 1970
Career: Hylton Rangers/Hylton Star May 1906/UNITED May 1906/Morpeth Harriers Aug 1907/Grimsby Town May 1908/Birmingham May 1910/Brighton Aug 1911/Luton Town July 1912/Houghton Rovers Sept 1913/West Stanley Oct 1913.

A stand-out player in the Wearside League before joining Newcastle at the end of the 1905-06 season, Crosby Henderson worked as a ship-plater in Sunderland and was described as a "solid full-back". He played on both the right and left flanks and operated alongside Bill McCracken and then Dick Pudan in United's defence for two friendly encounters during October 1907, the first a social fund raising match against Sunderland at West Stanley. The Wearsider appeared for the Magpies as the reserve eleven secured the North Eastern League title in 1907-08. Unable to challenge for a first-eleven position with such high quality players ahead of him at Gallowgate, he moved back to local football before getting a chance with the other black-and-whites of Grimsby. Still registered as a Magpie player, he was part of a treble deal which saw United reserve Harry Leonard also move to Blundell Park and Bob Blanthorne end up at Barrack Road. Henderson was first choice for two seasons, totalling 67 games for the Mariners. He also had a short spell in the Second Division with Birmingham during 1910-11. His son, Charlie Henderson later played for Sheffield United, Bolton and Wolves.
Misc App & Goals: 2 app 0 gls.

HENDERSON George Alan 1937-1940

Right-half 5'8"
b. South Shields, 10 June 1916
d. [South Shields, 1970 (Q4)]
Career: South Shields/UNITED trial Dec 1937, amat Feb 1938, prof May 1938 to cs 1940.

A South Shields lad, George Henderson performed well in front of United's officials during the winter of 1937-38, earning a professional contract with the Geordies. George took part in an end-of-season Hospitals Cup match with Grimsby during May 1939. A rival to Gordon, Woodburn and Garnham for the right-half position, Henderson was unlucky to be an up and coming footballer when the ill-fated 1939-40 season started. Just 23-years-old, his career was left in ruins as war was declared with only three matches played. When United's wartime roster was published in the summer of 1940 he was not listed.
Misc App & Goals: 1 app 0 gls.

HENDERSON Jeffrey 2005-2012

Centre-half 6'1"
b. Ashington, 19 December 1991
Career: Ellington Jnrs/UNITED jnr 2005, prof July 2008 (Gateshead loan 2011-12)(Bradford City trial March 2012)/Sligo Rovers July 2012 free.

Hailing from the traditional football heartland of Ashington, former Northumberland Boys player Jeff Henderson was a strong centre-half, powerful in the air and a solid tackler on the ground. With the club's Academy since the age of 13, he became skipper of the youth side and was an unused substitute for a Football League Cup-tie with Nottingham Forest in September 2011. Jeff also made two appearances from the bench in friendlies at the start of the 2010-11 and 2011-12 campaigns. Playing his football afterwards in Ireland, Henderson was described as a "no-nonsense centre-back" and was part of the

Sligo team which lifted the League of Ireland title during 2012-13 and then took part in Champions League qualifiers.
Misc App & Goals: 0(2) app 0 gls.

HENRY James 1881-1882 & 1886

Half-back & Forward
b. probably Tyneside
Although James Henry was with Stanley FC when the club was formed in November 1881, he appeared just twice in the senior eleven, his debut a late season fixture in March 1882 against Derwent Rovers at their South Byker pitch – and against visitors that could only field eight men. He joined the newly formed Heaton Association club for the 1882-83 season and was a customary name on their team-sheet over four seasons, recognised by Northumberland's selectors, a trialist for the County in 1883 and 1884. Guesting for Newcastle West End in January 1885, Henry joined North Eastern during 1886 and appeared for East End during September 1886.
Misc App & Goals: 2 app 0 gls.*

HERON Samuel 1885-1887

Full-back
b. unknown
A former Jesmond footballer from 1883 to 1885, Sam Heron joined Newcastle East End for the 1885-86 season and was in the club's reserve line-up during that campaign. He made the first-team for East End the following season, recording his debut outing against West End in October 1886, the re-opening of St James' Park after the West Enders had taken residence. Following a trio of games during October he appears to have left the Chillingham Road set-up in the close-season.
Misc App & Goals: 3 app 0 gls.*

HETHERINGTON James 1887-1888

Half-back
b. Jarrow [or Newcastle upon Tyne], c1861
One of the region's earliest footballers with the ground-breaking Newcastle Rangers combination, James Hetherington spent almost four years between 1880 and 1884 with the club who were the original tenants of St James' Park. Skipper of the side for a period, Hetherington was a boiler-maker from Byker and was part of the Rangers' side which secured the Northumberland & Durham Challenge Cup during 1882 and afterwards took part in the first Northumberland Challenge Cup final in 1884. Hetherington was rated highly in those early years of the game and he played in the very first representative fixture in the region, for a Northumberland & Durham XI against Cleveland during February 1881. He afterwards represented Northumberland, in their inaugural County side during 1883-84. James joined Gateshead Association at the end of that season and moved to Newcastle East End's Chillingham Road during 1887. Hetherington gave the team much needed experience in the season but only managed two first-eleven outings, during February 1888, games in which he scored in each contest.
Misc App & Goals: 2 app 2 gls.*

Players: other fixtures

HIGGINS Steven 1983

Right-back 5'11"
b. Tyneside
Career: Redheugh BC/Gateshead 1979 (UNITED trial March 1983)/ Barrow c1987/Newcastle Blue Star briefly Aug 1988/Barrow Aug 1988/ Gateshead/Newcastle Blue Star 1992, later becoming manager.

One of two players in Gateshead's team to be given a run-out for Newcastle, Steve Higgins, along with future colleague Keith McNall, impressed appearing in local non-league football. Steve was given an opportunity with senior company for a fixture at Hull City during May 1983, arriving as a replacement for Ray Clarke during the contest. Although United needed a boost to their reserve squad, Higgins wasn't retained and moved back to Gateshead where he continued as a top-rated defender at that level. Described as an elegant full-back, he appeared almost a decade for the other Tynesiders, totalling 319 matches. In between spells with Gateshead where he lifted the Northern Premier League title in 1986, Steve had a successful spell at Holker Street in Barrow colours, claiming more silverware, this time at Wembley in the FA Trophy during 1990. Residing in Whickham, he later worked as a lorry driver before opening a sports trophy business.

Misc App & Goals: 0(1) app 0 gls.

HILL 1904

Inside-forward
b. unknown

A Scottish trialist for United during April 1904 when the club played a series of games north of the border at the end of season 1903-04, Hill figured at inside-forward alongside Jimmy Howie in a clash with St Mirren. It is noted in the Glasgow Times he was from "Ayrshire Juniors".

Misc App & Goals: 1 app 0 gls.

HISCOCK Charles Arthur 1882-1888

Full-back & Half-back
b. Lyndhurst, Hampshire, c1855

One of three noted members of the Hiscock family to appear for Newcastle East End, Charles was brother to Matt Hiscock (qv) and cousin of 'Ned' Hiscock (qv). With the Rosewood junior club originally, as a teenager he became part of the East End camp from late in 1882 when they were taken over. Remaining on East End's roll-call until 1888, Charles served the club well, as did his other relations, but he appeared for East End's first-team only on a handful of occasions, making his bow during February 1883 against Heaton Association. According to census information, Charles had an interesting path of employment, perhaps typical of the day. He was a "footman" and "servant" working on an estate in Warwickshire in 1881, moving to Tyneside for a period, then by 1891 was in service in Mayfair, London, to return to Heaton as a "Superintendant". He was later to move to Gloucestershire by 1911.

Misc App & Goals: 3 app 0 gls.*

HISCOCK Matthew Kerley 1883-1891

Full-back, Secretary & Committee-Director
b. St Peter's, Newcastle upon Tyne, c1865
d. Whitley Bay, 11 May 1940

A solid performer for Newcastle East End, joining the club in 1883 as a teenager, Matt Hiscock became a prominent figure of the emerging organisation, a Committee member running the new club. He also was appointed Secretary during the summer of 1884 when he largely stopped playing, although Matt did appear for

Hawthorns Apprentices during February 1884 when working for the Tyne yard as a shipwright. As an East End player, playing alongside relation Ned Hiscock, he lifted the Northumberland Challenge Cup in 1885. Matt retained an affinity with the club through those early developing years and was one of East End's first 13-man Board of Directors when they changed to limited company status in March 1890, also becoming a shareholder at that time. He was cousin of 'Ned' Hiscock (qv) and brother to Charles Hiscock (qv).

Misc App & Goals: 26 app 0 gls.*

HOBSON John Thomas 1881-1882, 1888-1892

Full-back, Goalkeeper & Forward
b. Satley, near Lanchester, Co Durham, 1867
d. Heaton, Newcastle upon Tyne, 27 February 1930
Career: STANLEY Nov 1881/Heaton Ass 1882 (Newcastle Rangers guest March 1884)/North Eastern 1886/St Silas/EAST END 1888 to 1892.

As a youth, John Hobson trained to be a plumber in Byker; later becoming a sanitary and gas engineer, running his own business and residing for a period near to Alec White in Mowbray Street. Part of Stanley FC's first squad of players, he was one of the mainstays of the club's landmark season in the game, appearing in nine of the 11 matches during the inaugural 1881-82 programme, including the opening match. John appeared in a number of roles for East End like many of their early players. He operated as a goalkeeper, full-back and up front in the forward line. Hobson moved to the neighbouring Heaton Association club during 1882, frequented by many East Enders, and was appointed skipper for their first season of action in 1882-83. John made a return to his first club, Stanley, now titled as Newcastle East End based at Chillingham Road, during 1888 but was not a regular in the senior side. A keen cricketer in the summer, Hobson played for Woodbine, Heaton and East End cricket clubs.

Misc App & Goals: 9 app 0 gls.*

HOFFMAN (Holt) Ernest Henry 1918

Goalkeeper 5'7"
b. South Shields, 16 July 1892
d. Hebburn, 20 January 1959
Career: Hebburn Wesleyans/Hebburn Old Boys/Hebburn Argyle 1914/South Shields amat 1914 (Bradford Park Avenue war-guest 1915-16) (Tottenham Hotspur war-guest 1917-18)(UNITED war-guest 1917-18)/Resumed with South Shields 1919, prof March 1920/Derby Co April 1923/ Ashington Aug 1923/Darlington Aug 1924/Wood Skinner's (Hebburn) Oct 1925/Jarrow manager Sept 1926/York City Aug 1929/Blyth Spartans manager May 1933 to 1937/Birmingham City chief-scout/South Shields manager April 1939 to Oct 1946.

Although not tall for a goalkeeper at only 5'7" in height, Ernie Hoffman nevertheless became a respected custodian. An England amateur international player when with Hebburn Argyle, Hoffman stood in for Jimmy Lawrence when United entertained Middlesbrough in a wartime friendly during May 1918. He also appeared for the club in the local Newcastle & District United League as well as for Spurs as a late replacement during the First World War. After the hostilities, Hoffman appeared for both South Shields (24 app) and Ashington (39 app) when they were Football League clubs. He took part in the Tyneside's first fixture against Fulham during 1919. Rather bizarrely when between the posts for the Colliers, Ernie conceded a goal scored by his opposite number; a spot-kick against New Brighton taken by Irish international goalkeeper Bert Mehaffy. During the late-Thirties, he also scouted for clubs, notably Birmingham and was connected with Jarrow, Blyth Spartans and South Shields in the old-style secretary-manager role, guiding the Croft Park Spartans to the North Eastern League title in 1935-36. Of part German decent and

raised in South Shields, due to the First World War and with it anti-German feeling, for a time he was also known by the surname of Holt. Ernie was also interned during the fighting.
(Note: Some sources note Hoffman was born in Wakefield, but registration records show South Shields.)
Misc App & Goals: 1 app 0 gls.

HOGG William 1915-1919

Centre-forward 5'9"
b. Hendon, Sunderland, 29 May 1879
d. Sunderland, 30 January 1937
Career: Walkergate Rangers/ Rosehill/Willington Ath 1897/ Sunderland Oct 1899 £65/Rangers May 1909 £100/Dundee May 1913/ Raith Rovers player-manager cs 1914 (UNITED war-guest 1914-15, 1917-19)(Hartlepools Utd war-guest 1915-16)/Dundee Hibs May 1921/Montrose loan 1921, pmt Dec 1921/Dundee c1921/Sunderland trainer Oct 1927 to 1934.

Billy Hogg was one of football's top forwards in the years of Edwardian Britain, capped by England on three occasions in season 1901-02 and also by the Football League XI during those early years of the century. Born on Wearside, following the Victoria Hall disaster in the town in which his younger brother was killed, Hogg's family moved to Newcastle and from four years of age was brought up a Geordie in the Walker area of the city. As a schoolboy he faced Colin Veitch on the football field and like his contemporary soon was a highly coveted teenager. With Sunderland, Billy was part of the Roker Park line-up which challenged strongly at the top of the First Division. Lifting a title medal in 1902, Hogg was a potent centre-forward who claimed 84 goals for the Wearsiders in 303 games. Stockily framed, he was spritely for a big man; Billy possessed skill and finishing ability and was also to operate at both inside-forward or on the right wing. Hogg moved to Scotland during 1909 and did exceptionally well for Rangers too, almost 50 goals in 107 games, lifting Scottish League silverware three times in a row between 1911 and 1913. During World War One, Hogg was back on Tyneside where he grew up, employed in an engineering works and taking part in the Magpies' local Newcastle & District United League programme. He was also a star name in something of a patched up Magpie senior eleven on two occasions. Billy was later involved in the hotel and pub trade in the region, his brother Jack also appeared for Sunderland, while his son turned out for Bishop Auckland and Bradford City. Hogg famously scored a hat-trick for Sunderland when the Wearsiders sensationally won 9-1 at Gallowgate during December 1908.

Misc App & Goals: 2 app 1 gl.

HOLFORD Thomas 1917

Half-back 5'5"
b. Hanley, Stoke, 28 January 1878
d. Blurton, Stoke, 6 April 1964
Career: Stoke Cobridge 1896/Stoke May 1898/Manchester City July 1908/ Port Vale player-manager May 1914 (UNITED war-guest 1917-18) (Nottingham Forest war-guest 1918-19)/Resumed with Port Vale 1919, becoming trainer May 1923, manager June 1932 to Sept 1935, then trainer July 1939 to July 1946, and scout to 1950.

Although only a diminutive figure at around nine stones and 5'5" tall on the field, Tom Holford was a respected and inspirational midfielder in the years before and after the Great War. Capped by England during February 1903 when with the original Stoke club, Holford served the early Potters with distinction, appearing on 269 occasions in senior action. Often belligerent in the midfield battleground, at one time nicknamed "Dirty Tommy", he also excelled at distribution of the ball and was captured by Manchester City (184 app) taking part in their Second Division title success during 1910. Serving with the Royal Artillery and on Tyneside for a period during World War One, Tom teamed up in midfield with another celebrated guest for Newcastle, Frank Cuggy, as United twice defeated South Shields in war fund matches during October 1917. He also was a wartime league title winner appearing for Nottingham Forest. Holford played on for a lengthy career of over 25 years, featuring also in defence or even up front, once netting four goals against Everton for City. A veteran with Port Vale, he later continuing to serve the Valiants as trainer and manager. His cousin Wilf Kirkham also pulled on the shirt of both Stoke and Port Vale.

Misc App & Goals: 2 app 1 gl.

HOLLIDAY Albert 1937-1946

Right-back 5'9"
b. Tow Law, Co Durham, 16 October 1916
d. Durham West, 1987 (Q4)
Career: Brandon Utd/UNITED amat May 1937/ Spennymoor Utd/UNITED prof April 1938 (Spennymoor Utd loan 1939-40)(St Mirren war-guest 1941-42)/ Resumed with UNITED March 1946/Consett April 1946 free.

Living in Sunniside, Albert Holliday first arrived at St James' Park as a young amateur full-back during 1937, but was told that the club would keep an eye on him and invite him back. Gaining more experience in the strong and tough North Eastern League with Spennymoor, Holliday was signed at the end of the following campaign and he became one of several backs in contention for a first choice place at senior level, rivalling notably Craig and Richardson. Albert faced Gateshead, took part in a testimonial match at York during May 1939 then had his professional contract suspended as war was declared in September 1939. Appearing for Spennymoor again during the war years, and for St Mirren when relocated to Scotland as part of the Forces, Holliday was demobbed and returned to Gallowgate at the end of the 1945-46 season. By then he was 29 years of age, and the club had too many young defenders coming through the ranks, prominently Bobby Cowell and Bobby Corbett. Holliday was released and he joined Consett back in the North Eastern League.

Misc App & Goals: 3 app 0 gls.

HOPKINSON William 1917-1919

Half-back
b. unknown

Part of United's scratch pool of footballers during a period of almost close-down in the years of the First World War, Billy Hopkinson took part in the local Newcastle & District United League for the Magpies. He appeared in what could be classed as a reserve eleven during seasons 1917-18 and 1918-19, but didn't get a call up to Newcastle's senior squad for the Northern Victory League as 1919 opened. Serving in the early air force, he did though gain an outing for a match against Sunderland in aid of war funds during May 1918, although the line-up was a patched up eleven.

Misc App & Goals: 1 app 0 gls.

HOUTSONEN Leo 1980

Left-back or Centre-half 5'9"
b. Pieksamaki (Finland), 25 October 1958
Career: KuPS (Fin) 1975/OPS (Fin) 1978/UNITED trial July 1980/Norwich City trial 1980/KuPS (Fin) 1981/ Caroline Hill (HK) 1981/OPS (Fin) 1982/KuPS (Fin) 1984/KINGS (Fin) 1991/KuPS (Fin) 1992/KINGS (Fin) 1993 to retirement in 1993.

Attached to Newcastle for a trial period before the start of the 1980-81 season when the club prepared in Scandinavia with five matches, Leo Houtsonen wasn't retained by boss Bill McGarry, but developed into a highly experienced international defender afterwards. A youth international as a teenager, he went onto be capped on 47 occasions for Finland between 1978 and 1986, a fine player for his country during that period. Failing to win a contract in England with United and later Norwich, the centre-back spent his career in his native country, notably with Oulu (134 app) and Kuopio (over 170 app). Leo won three Finnish titles and on retirement Houtsonen became a well-known Finnish businessman. He gained a MSc degree at the University of Tampere and was for a time President and Chief Executive of Veraventure, a state-owned investment company. His younger brother Jyrki also appeared for the KuPS outfit.

Misc App & Goals: 5 app 0 gls.

HUDSPETH William 1882-1883

Goalkeeper
b. unknown

William Hudspeth was a Victorian footballer on Tyneside who appeared for Newcastle East End during season 1882-83. He took over the 'keeper's position initially during February 1883 and two games have been traced featuring Hudspeth in the line-up; against Heaton Association and Newton.

Misc App & Goals: 2 app 0 gls.*

HUNTER R 1887-1889

Forward
b. unknown

A reserve player with Newcastle United's pioneers, East End, Hunter was elevated to senior action during season 1887-88 and 1888-89. His debut occurred in the final of the Northumberland FA Charity Shield during April 1888, a 2-0 defeat to arch rivals West End.

Misc App & Goals: 2 app 0 gls.*

HUNTLEY S 1884-1886

Half-back
b. unknown

Part of Newcastle East End's shadow squad for seasons 1884-85 and 1885-86, Huntley made only a single appearance in the first-team. He pulled on the club's blue shirt in the years before the black-and-white arrived against Wearmouth during January 1886.

Misc App & Goals: 1 app 0 gls.*

HUTCHINSON William 1901-1903

Outside-left
b. unknown

Hailing from Alston, Billy Hutchinson made the journey from the Northumberland Pennines for a trial period with United during February and March 1901. He was selected on the touchline for a tough friendly outing against Everton during March with the task of providing service to centre-forward Jock Peddie. He did reasonably well as United won 2-1, but didn't get close to another promotion to the first-team squad. He was still registered with United for season 1902-03.

Misc App & Goals: 1 app 0 gls.

INGRAM 1902

Centre-forward
b. probably Tyneside

Described by the local press as a young South Shields lad who was given a trial with Newcastle during December

1902. Ingram was included in the Black'n'Whites' selection for the Boxing Day friendly against Dundee at St James' Park. While not a full senior line-up, Ingram played alongside young stars-to-be Peter McWilliam and Jack Rutherford in the 1-1 draw but wasn't retained, the Daily Leader described his performance in senior company as "poor".

Misc App & Goals: 1 app 0 gls.

INMAN Bradden 2008-2013

Midfield 5'9"
b. Adelaide (Australia), 10 December 1991
Career: UNITED July 2008, prof July 2009 (Crewe Alex loan 2012-13)/ Crewe Alex pmt Aug 2013 £100,000.

Brad Inman arrived at St James' Park as a 16-year-old after settling on Tyneside two years earlier. A skilful midfielder who liked to support the strikers, he followed the path of James Troisi, but like his fellow Australian wasn't really given an opportunity, although showing much promise and talent. He found breaking into United's side hard, despite showing up well at reserve level. The Aussie got a chance against Carlisle during July 2010 after twice sitting on the first-team bench in seasons 2008-09 and 2009-10. With Scottish blood, Brad was capped by the Scots at youth and Under-21 level (2 app) and moved to Crewe on a long-term loan deal for much of the 2012-13 season. At Gresty Road he was a hit; the Aussie linked the play and had a good eye for goal. Dubbed the "new Tim Cahill" by sections of the Aussie media, Inman helped the Railwaymen to a Wembley victory in the Football League Trophy final during 2013 then concluded a permanent deal to move to the Cheshire club.

Misc App & Goals: 1 app 0 gls.

IRVINE J C 1887-1888

Half-back
b. probably Scotland

A former Motherwell player, Irvine was one of an influx of Scottish footballers to arrive on Tyneside at both Newcastle East End and rivals, West End during the late-1880s. He joined the Chillingham Road set-up during 1887 and was described in the local press that he was a sprinter as well as a footballer. However, he failed to make an impact.

Misc App & Goals: 7 app 0 gls.*

ISAAC William James 1935-1939

Inside-left 5'10"
b. East Cramlington, near Newcastle upon Tyne, 4 September 1918
d. Maidstone, 14 April 1941
Career: Seaton Delaval Amateurs/ UNITED amat Aug 1935, prof Sept 1936 £5 (Whitley Bay Ath loan 1937-38)/Brighton May 1939 £200 to demise in 1941.

Billy Isaac was a bright teenager who joined the club after a period as an amateur. With vision as a schemer, United officials had a close look at player in senior company during a testimonial fixture at Redheugh Park, Gateshead in October 1938 and once more against York City at the end of the season. Described as a forward of the "thrustful type" being "stout-hearted", the decision though was not to retain Isaac and he moved to Brighton for a £200 fee. The Northumbrian was unable to hold down a first-team role at the Goldstone Ground either before war put an end to his prospects. Joining the army in 1939 and serving with the Royal Artillery, tragically

Players: other fixtures

Billy died suddenly of meningitis in Shorncliffe Military Hospital during the early years of the hostilities in April 1941. He was only 22 years of age.

Misc App & Goals: 2 app 1 gl.

JAMESON 1898

(See Henderson)

JEFFERSON James William Wood 1937-1945

Outside-right 5'6"
b. Felling, Gateshead, 7 November 1918
d. Felling, 5 May 1977
Career: Chopwell CW Jnrs/UNITED amat Sept 1937/ Gateshead trial Aug 1939/UNITED prof Aug 1939 £10 (North Shields war-guest 1939-40) to Oct 1945 free/ West Stanley 1946.

Taking part in two fixtures for United just when the Second World War erupted in the autumn of 1939, James Jefferson could count himself as being very unfortunate. Having earned a professional contract with the Magpies after playing for the Chopwell Colliery junior side, he found his career ruined within two weeks of the 1939-40 season's start, the programme being cancelled by government decree. Jefferson then played in Newcastle's team for hastily arranged friendlies against Barnsley and Preston before a wartime structure was put in place. After the conflict, he returned to Gallowgate and went through a trial period in October 1945 but was not retained. A miner at Chopwell pit, he served in the Royal Navy during the Second World War.

Misc App & Goals: 3 app 0 gls.

JENKINS William G 1887-1889

Forward
b. unknown

With Burslem Port Vale Rovers, William Jenkins played the sport in the Potteries before joining Newcastle East End during the summer of 1887. He occasionally received a call during 1887-88, but more often than not was in the reserve line-up. Jenkins departed during 1889 and indication is that he played briefly for Sunderland, although he did not record a senior appearance for the Wearsiders. William was also a noted athlete, a member of the Sunderland Harriers Athletic Club.

Misc App & Goals: 3 app 1 gl.*

JOHNSON Terence 1967-1971

Striker 5'9"
b. Benton, Newcastle upon Tyne, 30 August 1949
Career: Longbenton YC/UNITED jnr, prof May 1967 (Darlington loan 1969-70)/Southend Utd Jan 1971/ Brentford Nov 1974 £10,000/Blyth Spartans cs 1977 to 1983.

One of a number of talented juniors who wasn't given much of a chance at St James' Park during the latter years of the Sixties, Terry Johnson was a quick and nimble striker at youth and Central League level, scoring over 30 goals in his first season. Johnson was picked to sit on the bench for a First Division match with Stoke City at the Victoria Ground in December 1968, but wasn't called into play and only reached the fringe of the side when on tour to North America in 1970. He moved to Southend in search of more frequent action and proved he could be a dangerous striker registering 170 games (38 goals). Terry helped the Shrimpers to promotion into Division Three during season 1971-72 while the Tynesider also made a name in Brentford colours, described in the London club's history as a "human dynamo, equally at

home out on the wing, or inside, creating or scoring chances". Terry totalled over 100 matches for the Bees (30 goals) before returning to the North East. A tough character on the field, Johnson was part of the Blyth Spartans success story during the late Seventies, joining the Croft Park set-up in time for a headlining FA Cup run in season 1977-78. Up front with another United player, Alan Shoulder, Johnson scored some important strikes as the non-leaguers reached the latter stages of the competition. Johnson netted the goal which knocked out Stoke City, then in the Fifth Round against Wrexham found the net again and almost put the Spartans through to the quarter-final, only for a debatable equaliser to force a reply. On retiring from the game, Terry at times ran a fruit & veg stall at Blyth Market and resided in the Killingworth district of Tyneside.

Misc App & Goals: 1(2) app 0 gls.

JOHNSON (Johnston) J 1919

Forward

It is noted in the local press that United fielded a Clapton Orient player by the name of Johnson (or Johnston) for the fixtures against Middlesbrough and Wallsend during April 1919. There are two possibilities for this footballer; Joseph Johnson or James Johnston. Joseph John Johnson hailed from Rossendale (b. 1882) in Lancashire and appeared as a winger with Rossendale United before moving to Grimsby Town (1905), Carlisle United (1906), Millwall Athletic (1907), Luton Town (1908) then Clapton Orient (1912) and Brentford (1913). Alternatively, and more likely due to his birthplace being Sunderland (b. 1882), the player being back home during the war years, James Thompson Johnston began his career with Wearside club Sunderland Royal Rovers. After a brief spell at Middlesbrough he joined Clapton Orient in 1908 and became a stalwart player at full-back. A consistent and dependable defender for seven seasons, he totalled 224 games for the Londoners. He appeared for the Football League XI during 1910-11 while Jim was tipped for an England place before the Great War. There is also a Johnson who appeared for Darlington Forge Albion, South Shields, Hebburn CW and Hartlepool in the war seasons and he could be the same player, or be Joseph Johnson (b Felling) who appeared with Sunderland in the Northern Victory League and later at Ebbw Vale.

Misc App & Goals: 2 app 1 gl.

JONES Gary 1992

Centre-forward 6'1"
b. Huddersfield, 6 April 1969
Career: Rossington Main Colliery/ Doncaster Rovers Jan 1989/Grantham Town Nov 1989 £8,500/Kettering Town Jan 1990 £17,500/Boston Utd Aug 1991 £3,000 (UNITED trial July 1992)(Manchester Utd trial)/
Southend Utd June 1993 £25,000 (Lincoln City loan 1993-94)/Notts Co March 1996 £140,000 (Scunthorpe Utd loan 1996-97)/Hartlepool Utd March 1999 £60,000/Halifax Town loan March 2000, pmt June 2000/Nuneaton Borough cs 2002/Hucknall Town 2002-03/Gainsborough Trinity 2002-03/Armthorpe Welfare cs 2003/Selby Town Nov 2006/Armthorpe Welfare Jan 2008/Winterton Rangers July 2009/Retired Nov 2009.

Following a period with struggling Doncaster Rovers, Gary Jones moved into non-league football and started to impress in the Conference with Boston United. He showed Football League scouts he had talent in front of goal, netting almost 50 goals in a little over 70 matches. Newcastle gave the tall and lively striker a trial during July 1992, appearing in a match against Gateshead just before the new season began. Jones however wasn't retained but he claimed another opportunity at a lower level when he joined Southend a year later. With Notts County, Gary was a key asset to the Trent Magpies lifting the Division Three title during 1997-98, scoring 28 goals in the season. He was unstoppable during that promotion success, although he rarely recaptured that

form in front of goal elsewhere at Football League level. He totalled 136 matches and 46 goals for County undoubtedly the best period of his senior career which recorded in aggregate 394 games.

Misc App & Goals: 1 app 0 gls.

KEEN Peter Alan 1993-1999

Goalkeeper 6'0"
b. Middlesbrough, 16 November 1976
Career: UNITED jnr cs 1993, prof Aug 1995/Carlisle Utd Aug 1999 free (Darlington loan 2000-01)/ Scarborough Sept 2004 free/ Gateshead cs 2005/Horden CW cs 2006/Gateshead Feb 2007/Billingham Synthonia/Bedlington Terriers July 2009.

Peter Keen was an agile goalkeeper and good shot-stopper but found himself unable to break into the first-team at a time when a number of top goalkeepers were on the books. Keen replaced Steve Harper from the bench for friendly contests with Hartlepool and Rushden & Diamonds during July 1995, then appeared against Bishop Auckland. He also reached the Premier League dug-out during 1998-99 before joining Carlisle United. At Brunton Park the Teessider did well, claiming 66 games over five seasons in Division Three and even once scored for the Cumbrians; a kick-out from his own penalty area against Blackpool during 2000 which sailed straight into the Tangerines' net! Peter returned to the North East to play non-league football, recording 70 games for Gateshead. Keen was embroiled in an investigation over the sale of FA Cup final tickets when the Magpies reached the Wembley showpiece in 1999.

Misc App & Goals: 1(2) app 0 gls.

KEIDEL Ralf 1997-1999

Midfield 5'10"
b. Wurzburg (Germany), 6 March 1977
Career: ASV Rimpar (Ger)/ Wurzburger Kickers (Ger)/FC Schweinfurt (Ger) 1996/UNITED trial Oct 1997, pmt Nov 1997 £150,000/ MSV Duisburg (Ger) cs 1999 free/Rot-Weiss Oberhausen (Ger) July 2004/LR Ahlen (Ger) July 2005/FC Ingolstadt (Ger) July 2006.

Born near Frankfurt, Ralf Keidel started his football career in the lower pyramid of the German game. He was a midfielder who worked from the heart of the pitch and got forward to advantage whenever the chance arose. Joining Newcastle, Ralph was selected in friendly encounters with Bohemians and Benfica during July and August 1998, appearing from the bench for cameo outings in a black-and-white shirt. Reaching the German Under-21 side during his period with the Magpies, skippering his country's line-up, Ralph was however often in the treatment room during his stay on Tyneside. Boss Kenny Dalglish elevated him to the first-team squad and to the substitute bench for the Premier League match against Sheffield Wednesday in 1997-98, but that's as close as the German got to a senior outing for the Magpies. The necessity to return to Germany for National Service in April 1999 did not help his progress with the Magpies and Ralph was released during the summer of that year. Keidel returned to Germany where he appeared for Bundesliga side Duisburg (over 100 app) before playing for lower ranked clubs over more than a decade, notably for Ingolstadt.

Misc App & Goals: 0(2) app 1 gl.

KELLY 1888

Centre-forward
b. Scotland

A striker who initially arrived on Tyneside as the 1887-88 season closed, Kelly was given a run-out in a match with Elswick Rangers. He returned for the start of the following programme at the same time as other reserve Scots, Gilmartin and Smith of Rangers. He made an appearance in a Newcastle East End shirt during August, also against Elswick Rangers. It was noted he was the brother of a Renton footballer, probably James Kelly a noted Scottish international who later became a distinguished servant to Celtic with a long family connection at Parkhead. James had two brothers, twins John and Charles. Born in Cardross in Dunbartonshire, Kelly is likely to be one of them.

Misc App & Goals: 2 app 0 gls.*

KELLY Patrick 1997-1999

Midfield 6'0"
b. Kirkcaldy, 26 April 1978
Career: Northern Colts (Glasgow)/ Celtic East 1990/Celtic BC 1992/Celtic Aug 1995/UNITED Aug 1997 £20,000 (Reading loan 1997-98)/Livingston July 1999 free/Raith Rovers Feb 2001/Partick Thistle Aug 2001/East Fife Aug 2003/Cowdenbeath Feb 2005/Retired due to injury/Newburgh Utd coach.

A past Scottish youth international and highly rated by United's manager Kenny Dalglish and coach Tommy Burns, Paddy Kelly joined United as a 19-year-old having turned down a further contract with Celtic after making his debut for the Hoops in 1996-97. At Gallowgate he rejoined his mentor from Parkhead, ex-Scotland international Burns, while he was also known to boss Dalglish, having played alongside his son in Celtic's youth team where Kelly had skippered the side. Paddy was given a brief opportunity in United's first-team from the bench during a friendly with Bohemians during pre-season preparations for 1998-99. However when the managerial regime changed at Barrack Road, new manager Ruud Gullit cleared out many of Dalglish's players, including Kelly. The Fifer continued his career in Scotland, prominently with Livingston and East Fife. With Partick Thistle, Kelly helped the Jags to the Scottish Division One title in 2001-02. He made only three senior appearances in England, all when at loan to Reading where Burns had been appointed as manager.

Misc App & Goals: 0(1) app 0 gls.

KENNEDY H 1888-1889

Half-back
b. unknown

With Newcastle East End from the close-season of 1888, Kennedy was a reserve player at Chillingham Road who was called upon for a single outing at the start of the 1888-89 campaign against Ashington.

Misc App & Goals: 1 app 0 gls.*

KENNAIR Edward 1895-1898

Goalkeeper
b. Birtley, near Gateshead, January 1871
d. Birtley, near Gateshead, 9 January 1936

From the local Birtley club, Edward Kennair joined Newcastle United during August 1895 and came in for regular 'keeper Charlie Watts for a friendly against Derby County in the 1897-98 season, during February. He

conceded four goals on that afternoon but did make some good saves in an action-packed 4-4 draw. He and was one of several custodians at the club around that time as the Black'n'Whites looked for goalkeeping cover. Winning the Northern Alliance title with United's second-string in 1898, Edward did not stay long after his senior debut. He worked as a joiner at a local colliery.

(Note: Family history data and contemporary reports show his surname spelt in various ways from Kennair, Kannair, Kinnair to Kinnear.)

Misc App & Goals: 1 app 0 gls.

KIRKLAND J 1892-1893

Half-back
b. Co Longford, Ireland, 1873
Career: Duntocher Hibs 1889/UNITED Aug 1892/Bootle Nov 1892/Bury 1894-95.

Moving from Scottish club Duntocher Hibs, near Clydebank, Kirkland joined Newcastle East End's squad of players in August 1892. He appeared in practice matches then was selected for the first-team for a fixture with Stockton in October 1892. He moved on and later appeared with Bootle (1892-93) and Bury (1894-95). At Gigg Lane he appeared on five occasions when Bury lifted the Division Two title in 1895.

Misc App & Goals: 1 app 0 gls.*

KNIFTON Thomas 1898-1900

Left-back
b. Wolstanton, Staffordshire, 1876 (Q2)
d. Whitley Bay, 28 November 1926

Appearing for Heaton Science and Willington Athletic on Tyneside, Tom Knifton joined United during May 1898 after winning the Northumberland Senior Cup. When in United's reserve combination he secured the trophy again during April 1899, the month he was also elevated to Newcastle's first-team line-up for a friendly against Hibernian. Tom also played against Dundee the following season but with James Jackson and Dave Gardner in the left-back role did not progress to league and cup football for the Magpies. Although noted as having a period with Notts County, this hasn't been confirmed while he was described as a "clever exponent" at full-back. Born in Staffordshire, during the 1880s his father moved his family to Tyneside after he had found work as a pottery manufacturer. Living in Heaton, Tom worked as a copperplate engraver.

Misc App & Goals: 2 app 0 gls.

LACEY Thomas 1899, 1902-1903

Full-back 5'9"
b. [Newsham, Northumberland, 28 March 1879]
d. [Newcastle upon Tyne, 1976 (Q3)]
Career: Burradon/UNITED trial April 1899, pmt May 1899/Bristol City Nov 1899/UNITED Sept 1902 to c1903.

Tom Lacey had two spells with United, before and after a sojourn in the south with Bristol City. Noted as a good local defender, he appeared for a Northumberland XI against Durham in the Northern Alliance County fixture during 1899. As a reserve Newcastle player he rarely got a look in at first-class action, Lacey appeared once in superior company for a friendly against Derby County during April 1899, a 4-1 victory. He did little at the early Bristol club either, making no first-eleven appearances at a time just after they moved to professional status and changed their name from Bristol South End. From census information it is probable that Lacey was born near Blyth and later ran the Killingworth Arms public-house for a period before World War One.

Misc App & Goals: 1 app 0 gls.

LEE Bernard James 1896-1897

Inside-forward 5'10"
b. Scotland [Alloa or Edinburgh], 1873
Career: Leith Ath June 1893/Bury Sept 1894/UNITED Oct 1896/Luton Town April 1897/Nelson Aug 1898/ Bo'ness Feb 1899/Dartford Aug 1899/King's Park Sept 1900/Brighton Aug 1902/Broxburn Utd Aug 1903.

Known commonly as Barney Lee, the Scot moved south to join Bury for season 1894-95 and did well at Gigg Lane for a short period. Recording 25 games and netting 11 goals, Lee was part of the Shakers' Second Division title line-up in 1894-95 while during the following season had a good day against the Magpies when he scored twice. Newcastle brought the schemer to St James' Park when they were looking for experience as they tried to fashion a side to make a bid for promotion from the Second Division in 1896. With Aitken or Connell claiming the inside-forward roles in a Magpies shirt, Barney had to be content with only two friendly outings for the club, against Burnley and Stockton during 1896-97. It was no surprise when he was transferred to Luton at the end of the season and later became a regular with Brighton during their pre-Football League era, lifting the Southern League Division Two trophy.

Misc App & Goals: 2 app 0 gls.

LEE George Thomas 1941

Outside-left 5'8"
b. York, 4 June 1919
d. Norwich, 1 April 1991
Career: Acomb (York) 1934/ Tottenham Hotspur trial April to May 1935/Scarborough Aug 1935/York City amat June 1936, prof July 1937 (UNITED war-guest 1940-41) (Bradford Park Avenue war-guest 1941-42)(Lincoln City war-guest 1943-44)(Chester war-guest 1943-44)/ Nottingham Forest Aug 1947 £7,500/West Bromwich Albion July 1949 £12,000/Lockhead Leamington June 1958 free/Vauxhall Motors March 1959/West Bromwich Albion trainer June 1959/Norwich City trainer May 1963 to May 1987.

An FA Cup winner with West Bromwich Albion in 1954, George Lee was a free-scoring winger, a touchline player who could always cut towards the goal and be a danger. With a thumping shot in his left foot, he was nicknamed 'Ada' and began to show his talent with York City during the seasons before the outbreak of the Second World War. Remaining in the area with the Army, his record for the Minstermen was first-class, netting 101 goals in 195 matches in all games. When with City during the hostilities he guested for the Magpies once, in a contest against an Army & RAF XI during May 1941. Moving to Forest when peacetime football returned, he soon became a West Bromwich Albion player and at the Hawthorns was a hugely popular winger who varied his game and style to good effect. In a quality side, apart from winning silverware at Wembley, he almost claimed a title medal as well when the Baggies ended runners-up in the Championship chase during the same season. George totalled 295 games (65 goals) as first choice for almost seven seasons. Lee afterwards was connected with Norwich City for almost 25 years as trainer and scout.

Misc App & Goals: 1 app 0 gls.

Players: other fixtures

LEMMENS Erwin 1999

Goalkeeper 6'0"
b. Brussels (Belgium), 12 May 1976
Career: KSK Beveren (Bel) 1995 (UNITED trial July 1999)/RRC Santander (Sp) July 2002/RCD Espanyol (Sp) Aug 2003/Olympiacos (Gr) Nov 2005/RKC Waalwijk (Neth) Jan 2007 free/FCV Dender EH (Bel) July 2007 to 2008/KSK Beveren (Bel) July 2009 to July 2010/KSC Lokeren (Bel) gkp-coach & Belgian national gkp-coach.

With manager Ruud Gullit on the hunt for a new 'keeper at the start of the 1999-2000 season, Erwin Lemmens was given an opportunity to impress during a short pre-season tour in Holland. He appeared in a contest against Den Bosch, replacing Perez between the posts for part of the game. But the 'keeper wasn't retained and he afterwards continued to appear for Beveren in Belgian football before moving to Spain during 2002. When with Espanyol in Barcelona, Erwin reached his peak of performance and he was capped by Belgium during 2004. Moving into coaching, Lemmens became a well-known goalkeeper coach in Belgium, looking after his national side at the very top level and with the party to the World Cup in Brazil during 2014.

Misc App & Goals: 0(1) app 0 gls.

LIDDLE James Frederick 1931-1932

Outside-left 5'7"
b. Mickley, Northumberland, 1911 (Q1)
Career: Crawcrook Albion/Queens Park Rangers 1927/Huddersfield Town cs 1929/Rotherham Utd Oct 1929/Crawcrook Albion/UNITED trial April 1931, prof June 1931 £100/Gillingham June 1932 free/Coventry City May 1934/ Exeter City cs 1937 to 1939.

Ex-miner Jim Liddle resurrected a flagging career after spells with QPR, Huddersfield and Rotherham went nowhere. Handed a trial outing against a Yeovil & Petters line-up during April 1931, he did enough in the 3-2 victory in Somerset to warrant a contract. Being a former sprinter in his teens, he was a fast raiding winger, but with Tommy Lang ahead of him at Gallowgate had little opportunity to claim a senior position. Liddle moved to Southern League Gillingham during the summer of 1932 and then found a place on the touchline at both Coventry (71 app) and Exeter City (48 app). He was part of the Coventry side which lifted the Division Three South knock-out trophy in 1935-36.

Misc App & Goals: 1 app 0 gls.

LIGHTFOOT Robert 1882-1889

Half-back
b. Newcastle upon Tyne, 2 April 1867
d. Newcastle upon Tyne, 17 February 1932

A member of the Rosewood club of Byker, Robert Lightfoot joined the emerging Newcastle East End organisation when they took over his club late in 1882. He made his first appearance against Hamsterley Rangers during November and remained with the new footballing set-up through their development and as the East Enders became a force in Tyneside football. Lightfoot lived in Byker, at the time of the club's formation, at The Cumberland Arms, then a teenager, the son of the publican. He was versatile, appearing in defence, midfield and attack for the early Stanley and East End clubs. Lightfoot was captain of the reserve team for much of his five season period with East End, but found a regular place during season 1885-86 and 1886-87. Robert also turned out on occasion for Newcastle West End (appearing in their first season of 1882-83) and North Eastern, before joining the West Enders at St James' Park in the summer of 1889 for a longer period. By 1891 Lightfoot was employed as an iron-moulder on Tyneside.

Misc App & Goals: 62 app 1 gl.*

LINFORD Frederick 1917-1918

Inside-forward 5'11"
b. Whitley Bay, March 1901
d. Old Hartley, Whitley Bay, 10 April 1979
Career: UNITED jnr 1917/Smith's Dock 1918/Leeds City Dec 1918/Lincoln City Oct 1919 £250/Chelsea July 1920/Fulham March 1924/Blyth Spartans April 1926/Shiremoor Albion Oct 1928/Colombia (London) Oct 1929/Dorman Long Aug 1932/Ashington Sept 1934.

Fred Linford was part of the club's junior Newcastle Swifts set-up in the final months of World War One, wearing United's black-and-white stripes in the Newcastle & District United League. The teenager was called-up for a senior fixture against Sunderland at the end of the 1917-18 season and took part in a 3-1 defeat to the Wearsiders during May. Linford wasn't retained when Newcastle decided on their squad and he found a place in the Leeds City pool of players although quickly was embroiled in the illegal payment scandal which rocked the club during 1919. With City folding, he was part of the entire playing staff which was auctioned off, and Fred (with two colleagues) were purchased by Lincoln City (30 app). A sprightly forward who normally appeared on the wing, Linford was a member of the Imps side demoted from the Football League, but his talent was good enough to bounce back with Chelsea (41 app) in the top flight. He enjoyed a good season during 1922-23 for the Londoners but was usually a reserve at Stamford Bridge. The Tynesider moved the short distance to Craven Cottage where he totalled another 41 games for Fulham.

(Note: Fred is also referred to as Linfoot, but all local information notes Linford.)

Misc App & Goals: 1 app 0 gls.

LOCKHART 1887

Half-back
b. unknown

According to contemporary reports, Lockhart was a footballer who came into Newcastle East End's line-up as a late replacement for William Blackett during February 1887 in a game with Berwick Rangers. No other information has been traced.

Misc App & Goals: 1 app 0 gls.*

LOGAN John William 1941

Half-back 5'7"
b. Horden, Co Durham, 16 August 1912
d. Barnsley, October 1980
Career: Horden CW/Middlesbrough trial March 1933/Charlton Ath July 1934/Darlington May 1935/Barnsley March 1937 £750 (Hartlepools Utd war-guest 1939-40)(UNITED war-guest 1940-41)(Huddersfield Town war-guest 1942)(Bradford City war-guest 1942-44)(Bradford Park Avenue war-guest 1943-44)(Everton war-guest 1944-45)(Darlington war-guest 1944-45)/Resumed with Barnsley/Sheffield Wed Jan 1947 £2,000, retired playing 1951, becoming asst-trainer and trainer to Feb 1967.

Before the outbreak of World War Two, Johnny Logan was a part of Barnsley's Division Three title winning line-up in 1939. At 27 years of age, his career was seemingly on the rise, yet Hitler put an end to all that. Raised in the pit village of Horden, he made an impression at Darlington in 78 outings before switching to Yorkshire. With Barnsley he was a tough tackling midfielder, stocky and strong, having a forceful and direct style. Logan continued appearing for the Tykes through the war years when working in the County Durham and Yorkshire coalfields and during May 1941 travelled to Tyneside with his Barnsley colleague John Steele (qv), to take part in a United fixture against a combined Army & RAF XI. Guesting for several other clubs too, Logan remained with Barnsley (347 app) until he was purchased by Sheffield Wednesday in the twilight of his career, later becoming trainer for a lengthy period. He left Hillsborough in 1967 and worked at the Wilson & Longbottom foundry in Barnsley as well as coaching local teams.

Misc App & Goals: 1 app 0 gls.

LORD Daniel 1881, 1885-1887

Forward
b. Jarrow, 1866 (Q4)
d. [Ponteland, near Newcastle upon Tyne, 4 February 1944]

With Stanley FC for a short period as they were formed late in 1881, Daniel Lord soon joined Heaton Association where he later became club secretary during 1884. He was at the time training to become a school-teacher in Byker, Lord represented Northumberland County and rejoined Stanley, by then renamed Newcastle East End in 1885. He made his debut during February 1886 against Bishop Auckland Church Institute, but moved to Chester for a period to continue his teacher-training. Dan was also connected with Addison, Cheviot and North Eastern football clubs on Tyneside. Lord hailed from a Scottish family, in later years becoming a school headmaster in Newcastle.

Misc App & Goals: 9 app 2 gls.*

LOUGH Darren 2006-2010

Left-back 6'0"
b. Ashington, 23 September 1989
Career: UNITED jnr July 2006, prof July 2009 to May 2010 free/Inverness Cal Thistle, Gillingham, Leyton Orient & Gateshead, all on trial cs 2010/Ashington Sept 2010/KA Akureyri (Ice) June 2012 (Ashington loan when out of season)(UNITED part-time Foundation asst-coach).

Darren Lough took part in a series of pre-season friendlies before the 2007-08 campaign including a prestige fixture against Juventus. A tall, rangy and brave defender who never shirked a tackle, Lough though suffered badly with serious injuries including recovering from a leg break during a FA Youth Cup match in 2007 when at Gallowgate. Darren eventually joined Ashington where he was skipper of the Colliers before he moved to Iceland, returning to play for the Northumbrians in the Icelandic close-season. Strong in the air and good at set-pieces, Darren was a solid player at that level of football but again suffered mishap, fracturing his skull in FA Cup action. Thankfully he made a full recovery.

Misc App & Goals: 1(4) app 0 gls.

MACK Patrick 1888-1889

Centre-forward
b. unknown
Career: Hastings c1883/Hibernian 1888/EAST END Dec 1888/Darlington St Augustine's cs 1889.

During the Victorian pioneering years, many Scottish footballers crossed the border to spend a period in the North East as the game developed. Patrick Mack was one, a goal-getter who had a productive if short period in Newcastle East End's blue shirt. The Scot netted 13 goals in just less than 30 games for the Heatonites during season 1888-89 alongside fellow Scots Mulvey and Collins. He turned out for Hibs in the Scottish Cup against Mossend Swifts during September 1888.

Misc App & Goals: 28 app 13 gls.*

MADDEN James 1901-1902

Goalkeeper
b. unknown

With South Shields in season 1900-01 as a bright and able goalkeeper, United signed James Madden during April 1901 at a time when the club were searching for talent. He was selected between the posts for one senior fixture, a New Year's Day clash with Third Lanark at St James' Park in 1902, but did not remain at the club long after that.

Misc App & Goals: 1 app 0 gls.

MAHON Michael John 1964

Outside-right 5'8"
b. Manchester, 17 September 1944
Career: North Shields/Preston North End trial/UNITED amat Jan 1964/ Loughborough College cs 1964/North Shields/Loughborough College/Port Vale amat May 1966, prof April 1967/ York City July 1969 free/Colchester Utd May 1970 free/Wimbledon Dec 1973 £3,000/ Rowhedge (Colchester) player-manager cs 1976.

Mick Mahon was a 19-year-old amateur when he pulled on United's shirt in Central League football as 1964 opened yet showed much promise and was quickly plunged into a first-eleven friendly with Middlesbrough during January. In a 4-3 victory, young Mahon found the net with a fabulous strike and he was set for a bright future in the game. Mick though planned to train as a teacher at Loughborough College and left the Gallowgate scene. He was capped by England when still an amateur (3 app) and also featured for the national University line-up. Mahon had talent as a winger and once he had concluded his training returned to football in a professional capacity, signing for Port Vale. Mick was a regular at Vale Park totalling 99 games before heading for York (33 app) and Colchester (158 app). He was part of the Essex club's notable FA Cup giant-killing triumph over Leeds United in 1971. Later Mahon became a popular forward with Wimbledon and was part of the Dons' dramatic rise from the very basement of the game, in the side which won back-to-back Southern League titles as well as part of more FA Cup giant-killing. He was afterwards employed as a teacher in the Colchester area, becoming a school examination officer.

Misc App & Goals: 1 app 1 gl.

MARKEY Brendan 1995

Striker 5'10"
b. Clondalkin, Dublin, 19 May 1976
Career: Cherry Orchard (Dublin)/ Bohemians (Dublin) 1994 (UNITED trial May 1995)/Millwall cs 1996 £60,000 (Dundalk loan 1996-97) (Bohemians (Dublin) loan 1997-98)/ Shamrock Rovers cs 1998/Waterford Utd 1999/Newry Town 2000/Bohemians (Dublin) 2000/ Dublin City 2001/Glenavon Feb 2003/Dundalk 2003/ Athlone Town 2003/Monaghan Utd 2004/St Patrick's Ath July 2004/Mount Merrion 2007/Malachide Utd 2009/Bangor Celtic 2010.

Irishman Brendan Markey was given a trial opportunity with the Magpies after catching the eye playing for Bohemians in UEFA's Intertoto Cup. In the party when United played Rushden & Diamonds at Nene Park during July 1995, he entered the action on the field as a substitute for Les Ferdinand. Markey had a short period with the Magpies trying to earn a contract but the Dublin-born striker wasn't retained, although it is noted in some quarters that boss Kevin Keegan offered him a contract but the Irishman turned it down. Described as a quick, darting type of forward, he was picked up by Millwall and joined the Lions for the 1996-97 season but never played a game in their first-team. Brendan

returned to Ireland where he appeared on the local scene for the next decade, including experiencing more football on the European stage.

Misc App & Goals: 0(1) app 0 gls.

MARR Alexander 1881-1884

Half-back & Forward
b. Newcastle upon Tyne, 28 November 1865
When Stanley FC were born during November 1881, Alex Marr was a 15-year-old school-master's monitor in Byker, and he joined up with the new football club. Even at such a young age, the teenager took part in the future Newcastle United's first season of action, totalling seven games in that 1881-82 programme of friendlies. Included was the historic first match for Newcastle United. Alex continued with East End in seasons 1882-83 and 1883-84 and was on the field for the club's first competitive match. Later Marr was with Elswick Leather Works in the west of the city between 1885 and 1887. He also played cricket for Brunswick.

Misc App & Goals: 14 app 0 gls.*

MASON Philip 1986-1992

Midfield 5'6"
b. Consett, 3 December 1971
Career: UNITED jnr April 1986, prof May 1990 to cs 1992 free/Blyth Spartans 1992/Gateshead 1992-93 /Kettering Town 1993/Worcester City 1994/Spennymoor Utd 1995/ Worcester City 1996/Oxford City 1997/Brackley Town 1997/Aylesbury Utd Jan 1999/ Boreham Wood 2001/Banbury Utd 2002/Woodford Utd 2003, becoming asst-manager, player-manager 2006, then manager/Wellingborough Town manager Sept 2012 to Nov 2012/Long Buckby manager July 2013 to cs 2014.

A combative midfielder, Phil Mason developed through the Magpie junior and reserve teams alongside Lee Clark, Steve Watson and Steve Howey. Manager Ossie Ardiles always gave youth a chance and handed Mason an outing in a strong United side which faced a North East Non-League XI during May 1990. A combination of injury (being one of the five United juniors injured in a car crash during September 1990) and the departure of Ardiles saw Phil released when Kevin Keegan pruned his staff for the start of a new era at Gallowgate. Mason carried on successfully in non-league football for over 15 years, after spells with Blyth and Gateshead moving south, notably with Woodford United for a decade. He later entered management and set up a personal fitness business in the Daventry area.

Misc App & Goals: 2(1) app 0 gls.

MAXWELL James Morton 1904

Outside-right 5'7"
b. New Cumnock, Ayrshire, 10 January 1882
d. Mesopotamia, 21 April 1917
Career: Kilmarnock Shawbank/UNITED trial April 1904/ Petershill Jnrs June 1904/Kilmarnock Dec 1904/Sheffield Wed March 1907 £500/Arsenal May 1908 £350/Hurlford Sept 1909/Galston 1909-10/Carlisle Utd 1910-11/ Lanemark Aug 1911/Kilmarnock Dec 1912/Nithsdale Wand Aug 1913 to April 1914.

With Newcastle on a five-game end-of-season tour of Scotland during April 1904, James Maxwell was part of United's line-up to face his local club Kilmarnock at Rugby Park. Playing alongside fellow Scots McWilliam and Howie, he didn't have a great afternoon as United fell 4-1. Newcastle didn't pursue a deal but Maxwell showed he was a decent player on the wing, good enough to appear for the Scottish League eleven in March 1907 and reach the fringe of a full call-up by his country, playing in the official trial matches. After 57

games for Killie, Sheffield Wednesday offered him a contract where United didn't, and at Hillsborough the Scot enjoyed a brief period in the top flight (27 app), netting during an early outing in a Sheffield derby. A pacy forward with good ball control, he only appeared twice for Arsenal before heading back north. Joining the forces in World War One, Maxwell was killed on active duty with the Seaforth Highlanders during the fighting in Mesopotamia (now Iraq). His name is remembered on the Basra Memorial. Maxwell's son 'Bud' appeared for several clubs, including Kilmarnock, as well as Preston and Barnsley.

Misc App & Goals: 1 app 0 gls.

MELLING Terence 1965-1966

Striker 6'0"
b. Haverton Hill, Co Durham, 24 January 1940
Career: Slough Town Sept 1958/ Maidstone Utd/Tow Law Town/ UNITED amat Dec 1965, prof Dec 1965/Watford May 1966 free/ Newport Co Feb 1967 £2,000/ Mansfield Town Nov 1967 £3,000/Rochdale Sept 1968 £1,000/Darlington March 1969/Scarborough Oct 1969 to 1970/Tow Law Town.

A soldier in the Coldstream Guards serving in various countries including East Africa, Terry Melling returned to his native North East after his period in the army, standing out for Tow Law Town in Northern League football as a 25-year-old striker. With dark curly hair, he was a powerful footballer with the build expected of a Guardsman at that time. With limited striking options during season 1965-66, manager Joe Harvey selected Melling as his attack-minded substitute for three top level games; against Arsenal, Everton and Leicester. Terry never got the call onto the pitch and continued his career elsewhere, dropping to a lower rank of football with a series of clubs. Noted as a "rumbustious striker" at that level, Melling had short and productive periods with Watford (30 app), Darlington (22 app) and Mansfield (35 app). When he appeared in Rochdale's colours, Melling won promotion from Division Four in 1969. He also clocked up 37 games for Newport and is described in County's annals as a "fearsome Northerner", once netting a hat-trick in a Welsh derby with Wrexham.

Misc App & Goals: 0 app 0 gls (3 sub no app).

MELVILLE Darren 1980-1985

Midfield 6'1"
b. South Shields, 25 September 1965
Career: UNITED jnr Jan 1980, prof June 1984/Whitley Bay cs 1985 free/Claudelands Rovers (NZ) Jan 1986/Waikato Utd (NZ) 1986 (and Ngaruawahia Utd coach 1993) to April 1996/Dunedin Technical (NZ) player-coach May 1996/Melchester Rovers (NZ) player-coach 1999 to 2000.

A former England Under-18 schoolboy captain, Darren Melville joined Newcastle as a star in the making, a tall and commanding centre-half. Moving to a midfield slot as his career developed through United's junior set up, Darren showed he was a good passer of the ball and was strong in the tackle. He was on the fringe of Newcastle's line-up as season 1984-85 began and took part in a handful of friendly matches at that time. Yet, Melville had the likes of McDonald, Megson, McCreery and new star Paul Gascoigne as rivals for the central midfield role and didn't manage to push a way into the league or cup line-up. Following a spell with Whitley Bay, Melville moved to New Zealand and enjoyed a lengthy career on the other side of the world. With the Waikato club of Hamilton, he appeared in the National League and was

Players: other fixtures

a stand-out player, lifting the Chatham Cup twice (the New Zealand equivalent to the FA Cup) and reaching two further finals. He returned to the UK during 2000 and settled on Tyneside, initially running Carpet Line Direct Ltd then creating NUTEX UK Ltd based in South Shields, a textile wholesale business. Latterly Darren has coached local Sunday league football on South Tyneside.

Misc App & Goals: 1(4) app 0 gls.

MELVIN Thomas 1886-1887

Half-back

b. Ballast Hills, Northumberland, c1859

Career: Heaton Ass 1882 (Newcastle Rangers guest March 1884)/North Eastern 1886/St Silas/EAST END 1886 to c1887.

Also a noted cricketer for the Heaton, North Eastern and St Silas cricket clubs, Tom Melvin combined both sports at all those Tyneside associations. On the football field he operated in the three areas of outfield play; defence, midfield and attack, appearing for Newcastle East End as a substitute for the injured Muir against Elswick Rangers during March 1887. Employed in the manufacture of boiler equipment for the shipyards, Melvin was another Byker resident.

Misc App & Goals: 0(1) app 0 gls.*

MIDDLETON Henry [William] 1906-1909

Centre-forward 5'10"

b. Newcastle upon Tyne, c1885

d. [Newcastle upon Tyne, 1945 (Q4)]

Career: Hamsterley/Scotswood/UNITED amat July 1906, prof Feb 1907 £5/Brighton cs 1909/Watford Feb 1911/Darlington June 1912/Blyth Spartans July 1913 to Jan 1914.

Harry Middleton caught the attention of the Black'n'Whites playing for the strong Scotswood line-up in local football. Joining Newcastle for the 1906-07 season, United's international array of talent at St James' Park made it extremely hard for any local player to break into the side. Normally a forward, he gained one opportunity, Middleton playing out of position in the half-back line for a social fund raising fixture at West Stanley against Sunderland during October 1907. Harry did well at reserve level for the Magpies, twice part of North Eastern League title sides in 1907-08 and 1908-09. Heading for Watford, he totalled 23 games for the Hornets in the Southern League but after impressing during his early matches faded from the scene at Cassio Road.

Misc App & Goals: 1 app 0 gls.

MILLER C 1881-1882

Full-back

b. unknown

With United's founding team in St Peter's, joining Stanley FC during 1881, Miller registered one game in the club's significant opening season of 1881-82, the final match with Burnopfield, described as a "very pleasant game". Miller soon joined a new club which had been formed on the opposite side of the community, Newcastle West End, to be great rivals in the future to the newly titled East End. He arrived at St James' Park during 1882 and pulled on West End's colours to 1886.

Misc App & Goals: 1 app 0 gls.*

MILLER George 1888

Full-back

b. probably Scotland

George Miller crossed the England-Scotland border during August 1888 having appeared for Hurlford in East Ayrshire. He featured for Newcastle East End for the first time against Ashington during September but did not figure in any match at senior or reserve level afterwards.

Misc App & Goals: 1 app 0 gls.*

MILLER John Joseph 1884-1886

Forward

b. Newcastle upon Tyne, c1863

During the 1880s East End field several players with the surname of Miller, reports confusingly noting various initials during the era. In seasons 1884-85 and 1885-86, Newcastle East End used reserve forward Jack Miller. Living in Byker, Miller worked in the local shipyards as a riveter and remained a United supporter all his life.

Misc App & Goals: 2 app 0 gls.*

MILNE Alexander James 1917-1918

Full-back 6'2"

b. Hebburn, Co Durham, 29 September 1889

d. Doncaster, March 1970

Career: Hebburn Old Boys/West Stanley/Hebburn Argyle 1909/Stoke Oct 1912 (Sunderland Rovers war-guest 1915-16)(South Shields war-guest 1915-16)(UNITED war-guest 1917 & 1918) (Wallsend war-guest)/Resumed with Stoke/Doncaster Rovers May 1926/Retired May 1930.

Working back on his native Tyneside in a munitions factory during World War One, Stoke's Alex Milne guested for several clubs when in the area. The resourceful full-back teamed up with the Magpies for three fixtures, in October 1917 and again at the start of the following season during August 1918. Moving to the Victoria Ground after working as a ship riveter, Milne was a good servant to the Potters; he was a rugged and no-nonsense defender who claimed 276 games in all games for Stoke, just before and after they rejoined the Football League set-up. Lifting the Southern League title in 1915, then promotion to the top level during 1922, Milne played on after the conflict until into his forties, having an end-of-career run with Doncaster which extended to 77 games.

Misc App & Goals: 3 app 0 gls.

MONTAGUE Thomas K 1902-1903

Right-half

b. unknown

With the Black'n'Whites on trial during December 1902 and over the Christmas holiday period, Tom Montague is recorded as a "south countryman" who arrived from Army service in the Royal Artillery. In games against Dundee and Third Lanark, he showed enough in midfield to be given a short-term contract. Tom was attached to the club until September 1903 when archive material notes his contract was cancelled, and it appears he returned to serve with the 12th Brigade Royal Artillery. Montague was still registered with the Magpies as late as 1904-05. He didn't appear in professional football for any other club.

Misc App & Goals: 2 app 0 gls.

MONTGOMERIE Raymond Samuel 1980-1981

Forward 5'11"

b. Irvine, Ayrshire, 17 April 1961

Career: Saltcoats Victoria July 1979/UNITED January 1980/Dumbarton Aug 1981 free/Kilmarnock Aug 1988/Partick Thistle July 1999/Retired cs 2000/Saltcoats Victoria manager and later Chairman.

Picked up from the Saltcoats Victoria junior side, Ray Montgomerie was only a teenager when he arrived on Tyneside, and as he later recorded, was soon home sick for Ayrshire. The youngster certainly had talent up front and was part of the Magpies' tour party for pre-season matches in Scandinavia during July 1980. However, the Scot never settled and Ray headed back north as the 1981-82 season began when he joined Dumbarton. He learnt the essentials of football with the Sons of the Rock, claiming a promotion prize in 1984. Montgomerie then showed United he was a good footballer by switching to defence and becoming a redoubtable player for Kilmarnock for a decade. Totalling over 300 games for Killie, he was strong and aggressive; a defender who played with passion and never shirked a challenge. Montgomerie was a key player as the Ayrshire club won promotion to the top level through Division Two and Division One. He then led them to a Scottish Cup victory in 1997, claiming the trophy as skipper and subsequently tasting European action. Ray totalled over 600 games north of the border and on retirement headed back to his roots with Saltcoats, Montgomerie becoming manager and later Chairman of the Ayrshire non-leaguers. He also kept an association with Kilmarnock in hospitality and by looking after Rugby Park's match-day arrangements.

Misc App & Goals: 2(5) app 3 gls.

MOORE James 1890

Forward

b. probably Scotland

Career: Edinburgh St Bernard's/Aston Villa/Newcastle West End Jan 1890/EAST END April 1890/Sunderland Albion 1890-91.

With Newcastle East End briefly as well as at rivals West End, James Moore had a more fruitful stay on Wearside in the colours of Sunderland Albion. He appeared on 10 occasions in their FA Cup and Football Alliance line-up during season 1890-91 when they were runners-up in the league race to Stoke. A lively attacker, when at West End he represented Northumberland County before making the short trip to Wearside. Moore played once for East End, a match with Sheffield United during April 1890.

Misc App & Goals: 1 app 0 gls.*

MORRIS Callum Edward 2005-2010

Centre-half 6'0"

b. Newcastle upon Tyne, 3 February 1990

Career: UNITED jnr 2005, prof March 2009 (Leeds Utd trial April 2010) to June 2010 free/Inverness Cal Thistle trial July 2010/Gateshead trial July 2010/Blyth Spartans Aug 2010/Jerez Industrial CF (Sp) Feb 2011/Hayes & Yeading Nov 2011/Morpeth Town March 2012/Dunfermline Ath Aug 2012/Dundee Utd June 2014.

Callum Morris possessed the right qualities for a centre-back role; he was tough and with stamina and strength in the air as well as on the ground. Always consistent, Morris was good enough to appear for the Republic's youth and Under-21 line-up, having Irish ancestry, and took part in Newcastle's friendly match against Hartlepool during July 2008, replacing Brazilian Cacapa in defence. He also faced Shamrock on United's short trip to Ireland the following season. Despite his potential at junior and reserve level, Callum never got the break on Tyneside and moved to non-league football then to Spain, joining Glenn Hoddle's venture in Jerez. But he soon moved back to Britain and was described as an "inspirational defender" during 2012-13 for Dunfermline, although he had to endure much at the cash-stricken Fife club. He was included in Scotland's PFA Team of the Year for Division One in both 2012-13 and 2013-14.

Misc App & Goals: 1(1) app 0 gls.

MURDOCH Charles 1906-1907

Right-half 6'0"
b. Edinburgh, c1885
Career: Edinburgh St Bernard's/ UNITED Aug 1906/ Edinburgh St Bernard's cs 1907 to cs 1908.

When Newcastle faced distinguished amateurs The Corinthians in a New Year 1907 holiday exhibition, they gave a run out to Charles Murdoch who had arrived as a young player from St Bernard's at the start of the season. Working as a plumber in Scotland's capital and residing in the Calton Hill district, although not part of the Edinburgh club's regular line-up, he had much potential and Charles became one of several lads in United's second string eyeing a chance at the big-time. Participating in United's 1906-07 reserve North Eastern League title side, Murdoch though wasn't quite good enough and he returned to Scotland's capital at the end of the season where he went onto make his senior debut in the Scottish League. As a powerful and strapping half-back, he played a handful of games for St Bernard's during season 1907-08.

Misc App & Goals: 1 app 0 gls.

MURRAY R 1881-1882

Half-back or full-back
b. unknown

A junior player with Rosewood, Murray also acted as secretary to the Byker club during the opening years of the 1880s decade. He was also attached to neighbours Stanley FC in their first season of 1881-82, chiefly in second-string action, being elevated the following season for one senior match against Hamsterley Rangers during November 1882.

Misc App & Goals: 1 app 0 gls.*

MURRAY Nathan Andrew 1991-1995

Centre-half 6'1"
b. South Shields, 10 September 1975
Career: FA Lilleshall Academy 1990/ UNITED jnr Nov 1991/Middlesbrough trial March to April 1995/Carlisle Utd cs 1995/Portsmouth cs1996.

Nathan Murray was a star schoolboy footballer, captaining the young England side in 1991 and a student footballer at the Football Association's elite academy. He joined United during the 1991-92 season and quickly stood out in the FA Youth Cup and reserve line-up. An unused substitute in United's first-team squad during season 1992-93, Nathan was on the bench for two Anglo-Italian Cup fixtures against Ascoli and Cesena when boss Keegan rested his promotion chasing seniors and fielded a squad-based line-up. He didn't get into the play and was unlucky to break an ankle during March 1993 in a reserve outing, an injury which curtailed his career. Murray was soon released as Newcastle moved into the Premier League and big stars on Tyneside. He tried to make an impression with Carlisle at Brunton Park, then at Portsmouth but without success.

Misc App & Goals: 0 app 0 gls (2 sub no app).

McCABE Frank T 1890-1893

Goalkeeper
b. unknown

Frank McCabe was Newcastle East End's reserve goalkeeper for season 1890-91 when Matt Scott held the first-team position. Described as an experienced hand at the time, one local scribe promoted Frank as "one of the best goalkeepers that has ever played for a Northumberland club". He appears to have departed for a period, then returned as a trialist during March 1893 when the goalkeeper was part of the side in friendlies with Derby County and Nottingham Forest. He wasn't retained and McCabe later played for East End Wednesday and the Newcastle Barmen combination on Tyneside.

Misc App & Goals: 8 app 0 gls.*

McCLEN Edward J 1884-1886

Goalkeeper
b. Newcastle upon Tyne, c1866

One of Newcastle East End's back-up goalkeepers over seasons 1884-85 and 1985-86, McClen was employed as an apprentice boiler-smith and lived on Headlam Street in Byker. Making his debut in a friendly contest with Berwick Rangers during October 1885, Edward soon tasted competitive action in the Northumberland Charity Shield tournament against Elswick Leather Works.

Misc App & Goals: 17 app 0 gls.*

McCOLL Donald 1890-1891

Forward
b. Scotland, c1867

Part of the Newcastle East End reserve set-up during the season 1890-91 season, when the club competed in the Northern League, Donald McColl had enjoyed a productive three seasons as part of the rival West End line-up from 1887 to 1890 playing in their first Northern League fixture. Lodging with William Swinburne (also to appear for both clubs), McColl did not feature often at Chillingham Road being reserve to Thompson, Sorely and McInnes. He may have been a former Renton and Darlington footballer who also played once in FA Cup action for Sunderland during 1884-85 – the club's debut in the competition, McColl scoring their only goal in a 3-1 defeat against Redcar. McColl worked as a machine-man on Tyneside.

Misc App & Goals: 2 app 0 gls.*

McCOLL Thomas 1902-1903

Inside-left
b. Cathcart, Glasgow, c1885

With Queen's Park and brother of celebrated Scottish centre-forward Bob McColl (qv) who also appeared as an amateur with the famous combination in Glasgow, Tom McColl arrived at St James' Park during October 1902 on a trial. With his more famous elder kin one of the biggest names in football at the time, he had a good mentor during his short period as an amateur at Gallowgate. Tom figured in three games for the club, friendlies against Scottish opponents Dundee, Rangers and minnows Moffat. He played alongside Bob in all matches including at Dens Park in October, and at Ibrox during January 1903. Not long after Tom moved back to Glasgow and it appears he did not play any professional football, although may have continued as an amateur. He largely ran the family confectionary business in the city when his brother focussed on football, Tom originally creating a small scale enterprise from his hobby of making sweets. By 1916 the RS McColl business had a factory supplying 30 branches, later becoming a limited company in 1925. The two brothers sold their controlling interest in what was a nationwide retail company to Cadbury in 1933,

although both stayed on in a management capacity before retiring fully in 1946. The brothers were brought up in Mount Florida, close to Hampden Park.

Misc App & Goals: 3 app 0 gls.

McCOY Peter Joseph 1946-1949

Right-back 5'9"
b. Thornley, Co Durham, 31 July 1923
d. Peterlee, Co Durham, 31 July 1986
Career: Shotton Jnrs/UNITED Sept 1946/Norwich City Feb 1949 £5,000/ Murton CW Oct 1950.

Peter McCoy hailed from County Durham and joined the United playing staff as football returned to normality following the Second World War. Peter travelled with the first-team squad for a four-match tour of Ireland at the end of the 1947-48 season after taking part in the club's Central League title victory. He was selected at full-back to partner Ron Batty against Ballymena but with Bobby Cowell and Benny Craig ahead of him in the right-back position was picked up by Norwich City for a £5,000 fee in February 1949. His stay at Carrow Road wasn't too fruitful though, McCoy appearing on only six occasions before returning to local football in the North East. He later lived and worked in the Peterlee area of County Durham.

Misc App & Goals: 1 app 0 gls.

McCRINDLE Robert 1888-1889

Half-back
b. Probably Scotland

Newcastle East End's committee brought two new Scottish players to Tyneside during the Christmas and New Year period of season 1888-89, Richardson and Robert McCrindle, both of Ayrshire club Hurlford. Having experience playing the game around Kilmarnock, McCrindle was given an outing in a fixture with Mossend Swifts during December 1888, a 3-1 defeat at Chillingham Road. Nothing is recorded thereafter about the player and it is likely he departed during January 1889.

Misc App & Goals: 1 app 0 gls.*

McDONALD J 1887-1888

Forward
b. unknown

On Newcastle East End's books for the 1887-88 campaign, McDonald received a single call-up as a guest player during December against Darlington, a 5-2 defeat. He was attached to rivals Newcastle West End and had joined the St James' Park club during the 1886-87 season remaining at Barrack Road until around 1891.

Misc App & Goals: 1 app 0 gls.*

McDOUGALL Alexander Leod 1885-1888

Goalkeeper
b. Byker, Newcastle upon Tyne, July 1857

A Tyneside shipyard worker, described being employed as a "riveter" in the 1881 census and living near St Peter's in Byker, Alex McDougall spent almost three years with Newcastle East End between 1885 and 1888. A proficient 'keeper, he was selected for the Northumberland County representative eleven during 1886. Two years later McDougall left Chillingham Road, afterwards appearing for Gateshead Association for a period in 1888 and 1889. He remained associated with East End though, like many of the Byker residents (then living in Glasshouse Street).

Players: other fixtures

When the club became a limited company in 1890, Alex was one of the early share-holders.

(Note: His surname spelling varies from McDougall to McDougal, but baptism records note the former.)

Misc App & Goals: 11 app 0 gls.*

McFARLANE [George] 1882-1884

Half-back & Forward
b. [Newcastle upon Tyne, c1864]

A former Rosewood junior, George McFarlane found himself part of the larger Newcastle East End association when the two neighbours merged late in 1882. McFarlane was chiefly a reserve player in seasons 1882-83 and 1883-84, but he did get the call-up during October 1883 for a game with Birtley as a deputy for Alex Marr.

Misc App & Goals: 1 app 0 gls.*

McGOVERN Philip 1970

Striker 5'9"
b. Partick, Glasgow, 29 March 1948
Career: St Anthony's July 1967/ Albion Rovers April 1968/UNITED Feb 1970 £15,000/Ayr Utd Nov 1970 £10,000/Kilmarnock Nov 1972 £6,000/ Clydebank Feb 1974/Albion Rovers Aug 1976/Perthshire July 1977.

With the Magpies in need of striking back-up as the Seventies opened, boss Joe Harvey gave a chance to Phil McGovern, a comparatively raw striker from Albion Rovers and at the time a part-time decorator. Watched by both Joe Richardson and Stan Seymour, the Magpies took a gamble with the inexperienced Scot who had displayed potential with 30 goals in Scotland's Division Two during 1968-69 and 1969-70. First wearing United's colours in a friendly with Dundee United during February 1970, Phil also went on the club's end-of-season tour to North America and took part in the seven match programme. Yet with Davies, Robson and Dyson all in front of him for selection, the tall and dark-haired McGovern returned to Scotland during the 1970-71 season and finished his senior career where he started, in Coatbridge with Albion Rovers. His Scottish career record was a decent one; 184 games and 52 goals.

Misc App & Goals: 5(1) app 1 gl.

McGUFFIE Ryan 2000-2002

Full-back 6'0"
b. Dumfries, 22 July 1980
Career: Calside BC/St Johnstone, Rangers & St Mirren trial/Queen's Park Feb 1999/Annan Ath July 1999/ UNITED Aug 2000 £5,000 to July 2002/Carlisle Utd, Macclesfield Town & Queen of the South trial cs 2002/ Gretna Aug 2002 free (Shamrock Rovers guest-trial July 2005)/Morton Jan 2008/Queen of the South May 2010/ St Albans Saints (Aus) player-coach Feb 2014.

Ryan McGuffie impressed watching United coaches at a pre-season tournament in Scarborough and was offered the opportunity to join the Magpies' set-up for the start of the 2000-01 season. Ryan was a versatile player with the ability to defend and attack, getting forward down the flanks to provide the extra man. Playing for United against Exeter City in May 2001, he wasn't considered good enough for the top level and was allowed to return north of the border. Settling with Gretna as an influential defender or midfielder, Ryan was part of their rise from the bottom of the Scottish game to the very top, reaching the Premier League through three successive promotions as well as progressing to the Scottish Cup final. They lost only on penalties in 2006, Ryan netting at Hampden Park. He topped 150 games for the club and

also briefly experienced UEFA Cup football with the Anvils of Raydale Park. After their decline, he continued to be a respected player with Morton and Queen of the South and totalled over 400 games in Scottish football. Before joining the Black'n'Whites, McGuffie attended University in Glasgow, where he played for Queen's Park, while the Scot continued his studies on Tyneside.

Misc App & Goals: 0(1) app 0 gls.

McGUINESS J 1888-1890

Forward
b. probably Scotland

A forward who arrived on Tyneside from Clydebank as part of a Scottish influx of players as the 1888-89 season got underway, McGuiness played a few games during September but did not appear with the seniors again. He was with the reserve side, East End Swifts for season 1889-90.

Misc App & Goals: 4 app 0 gls.*

McINTOSH James 1892

Outside-left
b. Scotland
Career: East End (Dundee) 1888 to 1890/Strathmore/ UNITED Dec 1892 briefly/Dundonians Jan 1894.

As Newcastle East End were in the process of changing their name to Newcastle United, Jimmy McIntosh was brought from Scotland. Yet when United's officials tried to register the player with the Football Association, the governing body refused to do so because they had never heard of the new title of Newcastle United...the change in title having being made only two days earlier! The former East End (the Tayside version, later Dundee FC) footballer only spent a few weeks with the Tynesiders, playing two friendly games, including the very first under the title of Newcastle United against Middlesbrough during December 1892. He scored in that match at St James' Park but never completed his transfer to East End and was recorded as playing with Strathmore and Dundonians afterwards.

Misc App & Goals: 2 app 2 gls.

McKENZIE George 1881-1882

Forward
b. South Shields, 1863 (Q3)

One of Stanley Cricket Club's players and with Stanley's football venture from the outset in November 1881, George McKenzie played in the club's inaugural fixture and totalled seven appearances in the 11-match opening programme of friendlies. Additionally, McKenzie holds the distinction of scoring the club's (and Newcastle United's) historic first goal against Elswick Leather Works 2nd XI, the Tyneside Daily Echo recording the effort as follows: "the Stanley men, with the wind in their favour, made a rush with the ball to the opposite goal, when Coulson passed to Findlay and during a scrimmage in front of goal it was put through the posts by McKenzie." George took part in trials for Northumberland County and was employed as a coal-merchant's clerk, living in Byker. He played for Newcastle Rangers and Heaton Association in season 1882-83 and remained with the latter club for almost four years to 1886, for a period as captain. He also had a period with St Silas, a team based in Byker and was noted as being one of the Temperance Festival (The Hoppings) football tournament organisers, a popular summer event in Newcastle.

Misc App & Goals: 8 app 1 gl.*

McLACHLAN Ian Morton 1920-1925

Left-back 5'9"
b. Wooler, Northumberland, 7 March 1901
d. Portsmouth, 9 March 1974
Career: Blyth Spartans 1919/UNITED amat May 1920 (Blyth Spartans occasionally 1920-21)(Queen's Park loan 1921-22)/Blyth Spartans March 1923/UNITED amat cs 1924/Also appeared for Leadgate Park/Later became Portsmouth club doctor and director July 1952, appointed Chairman May 1959 to 1966.

A noted local amateur footballer, Ian McLachlan represented Northumberland in the years after World War One and also the North Eastern League XI. He was a solid full-back for Blyth Spartans where his father was a director and when at Durham University Ian appeared for United as an amateur in reserve football on and off over a period of five years. Described as having a touch of class with the ball, he pulled on a senior shirt once against The Corinthians during December 1921, an entertaining match in the snow which ended after 80 minutes due to the weather with United leading 5-4. During those years as an amateur, he also turned out frequently for Blyth and in first-class Scottish football for Queen's Park (5 app) in Glasgow when studying medicine at University. With the Spartans he appeared in their early FA Cup glory, when they faced Stoke City during season 1922-23. United held his registration should Ian choose to turn professional, however that never happened with McLachlan concentrating on a profession as a doctor, following his father into medicine. He settled in the Portsmouth area becoming a noted medical practitioner, Medical Officer of Heath for a period and Chairman of Pompey when they lifted the Division Three title in 1962. He was also associated with NALGO cricket club in Portsmouth.

Misc App & Goals: 1 app 0 gls.

McLAUGHLIN Patrick Joseph 2007-2011

Midfield 5'11"
b. Larne, 14 January 1991
Career: UNITED jnr July 2007, prof July 2008 (GAIS (Swd) trial March 2011)/York City July 2011 free/ Grimsby Town June 2013.

Paddy McLaughlin showed much talent and flair in United's junior side, having an eye for a pass and vision in midfield. However, the Irish youngster suffered with a groin problem when on Tyneside and he found it tough going to step forward. He did reach the fringe of first-team selection as an unused substitute as the Magpies faced Carlisle in a pre-season encounter during 2010-11. While McLaughlin could make little headway in the search for a place at Newcastle United, he did graduate through Northern Ireland's international age groups; from Under-15, youth and Under-21 level (10 app) for his country. Eventually Pat had to move on to find some regular action, dropping down to York City in the summer of 2011. He played a big part in City returning to the Football League and securing the FA Trophy, then had a good season with the Minstermen in 2012-13, claiming 33 games. McLaughlin moved to Grimsby for the following campaign.

Misc App & Goals: 0 app 0 gls (1 sub no app).

McLEAN Robert 1905-1906

Half-back 5'9"
b. Alexandria, Dunbartonshire, 26 April 1884
Career: Rutherglen Glencairn/Vale of Leven Aug 1900/Millwall Aug 1904/UNITED June 1905/Carlisle Utd March 1906/Southampton cs 1906/Dumbarton Aug 1907/Vale of Leven Aug 1908.

On arriving at Gallowgate during the summer of 1905, Rob McLean found himself way down the pecking order in terms of a first-team place with Newcastle. At half-back there was a rich pool of talent already at the club and the bustling and vigorous Scot hadn't much hope of claiming a place. McLean took to the field with United's seniors for a disaster fund-raising match with Blyth Spartans during November 1905, then again when the Corinthians were entertained on Tyneside at the turn of the year. Northern Gossip magazine recorded he "did not turn out the success anticipated". He appeared only four times for Southampton before moving back to Scotland.
Misc App & Goals: 2 app 0 gls.

McMAHON Kevin 1967-1969

Centre-forward 6'0"
b. Tantobie, Co Durham, 1 March 1946
Career: Dipton Jnrs/Wolverhampton Wand jnr 1961/Consett 1965/UNITED Aug 1967 £50/York City May 1969 free (Bolton Wand loan 1971-72)/Barnsley July 1972 exch/Hartlepool Utd July 1973 free/Gateshead Utd March 1976/Retired due to injury 1977.

Kevin McMahon had a brief spell with Wolves without breaking through and tried a second time to become a professional footballer with the Magpies, joining the staff in August 1967. Along with the likes of Alan Duffy and Terry Johnson in United's shadow squad during the late Sixties, Kevin McMahon again found it testing to get into the first-team picture at Gallowgate. Tall and tough in the centre-forward role, he managed two games with United's star men, friendlies against Glentoran and Barnsley during 1967-68 and 1968-69. He did though find regular action when transferred to York City. A robust and determined striker, Kevin totalled 110 games (35 goals) for the Tykes and netted 13 valuable goals as part of their 1971 Fourth Division promotion side. He combined well with another ex-United forward, Mick Mahon, for a period City fielding a duo of Mahon and McMahon up front! Kevin had another good spell with Hartlepool, claiming 34 goals in 126 games at the Victoria Ground, again showing he was a danger man in attack in the lower divisions. After retirement from the game, Kevin was employed for a period with the Eveready company, but had to reduce work-time due to an industrial injury, a legacy of knee injuries as a footballer. He also worked for the local authority in County Durham.
Misc App & Goals: 2 app 0 gls.

McMENAMIN Colin 2001-2002

Striker 5'10"
b. Glasgow, 12 February 1981
Career: Calside BC/Queen of the South jnr 1996/Annan Ath 1999/UNITED Jan 2001 £40,000 (Oldham Ath April 2002 trial)/Livingston Aug 2002 free (Falkirk loan 2003-04)/Shrewsbury Town July 2005 free/Gretna Aug 2006 free (Livingston loan 2007-08)/Dundee Jan 2008/Queen of the South Nov 2010/Ross Co June 2011/Morton Jan 2013/Celtic Nation (Carlisle) May 2013/Stenhousemuir player-coach June 2014.

After scoring plenty of goals with Annan Athletic and a colleague of Ryan McGuffie who also joined United, the Magpies gave a chance to young Scottish striker Colin McMenamin during January 2001, signing for the club after a short trial period. Hard-working in all areas, dangerous in attack, McMenamin covered a lot of ground in support of team-mates. Colin found the net at junior and reserve level for the Geordies and the Scot grabbed a first-team shirt from the bench in a friendly against Exeter City during May 2001. But with an array of expensive stars in front of him for the striking role at Gallowgate, it was of no surprise when he moved on, to Livingston at the start of the 2002-03 season. In Scotland, Colin did well, lifting First Division title medals in 2007 and 2012, for both seasons voted as that league's Player of the Year. A goal-poacher up front, he netted over 100 goals north of the border and was part of Gretna's short period of glory, claiming 26 goals during season 2006-07.
Misc App & Goals: 0(1) app 0 gls.

McMILLAN 1902

Inside-forward
b. Northumberland
From North Sunderland on the coast of Northumberland, McMillan was a trialist given a run out during a friendly at Alnwick in March 1902. Little has been recorded of the inside-forward but he wasn't signed on by the Magpies after the 4-0 victory.
Misc App & Goals: 1 app 0 gls.

McVEE Alexander 1890-1891

Forward
b. unknown
On Newcastle East End's playing staff at Chillingham Road during season 1890-91 when the club were in Northern League action, Alex McVee joined the set-up from Middlesbrough's squad during the latter weeks of the campaign. He appeared in three fixtures against Nottingham Forest, Derby County and Sheffield United, all prestigious friendlies, but had moved on by the start of the new season.
Misc App & Goals: 3 app 0 gls.*

NEWTON Conor 2002-2014

Midfield 5'11"
b. Newcastle upon Tyne, 17 October 1991
Career: Grainger Park BC 2001/UNITED jnr 2002, prof July 2008 (St Mirren loan 2012-13, 2013-14)/Rotherham Utd May 2014 free.

Raised in Whickham, Conor Newton possessed tremendous work-rate in midfield and was a strong looking footballer in United's development squad. Rarely to give the ball away in his central midfield role, he was injured in a reserve match early into his professional United career and missed most of the 2011-12 season but made an impact the following season. Newton also benefited from a five-month loan with Scottish club St Mirren during the second-half of that 2012-13 season. Under the guidance of ex-United star and coach Tommy Craig at Greenhill Road in Paisley, Conor was a regular on the field with United teammate Paul Dummett and reached the Scottish League Cup final at Hampden Park, netting what was the winning strike in a 3-2 victory over Hearts. That was his first ever senior goal and with it, the Tynesider became embedded into St Mirren's history. Conor was called onto the field for Newcastle against the Saints in a pre-season friendly during July 2013, then rejoining the Paisley club for the start of the new season. He totalled over 50 games when on loan, then decided to opt for a better chance of regular football at Championship level with newly promoted Rotherham United.
Misc App & Goals: 0(1) app 0 gls.

NGO BAHENG Wesley Christopher 2007-2010

Striker 6'4"
b. Blanc-Mesnil, Paris (France), 23 September 1989
Career: Le Blanc-Mesnil (Fr) 1997/Le Havre AC (Fr) jnr 1999/Bolton Wand trial Jan 2007/UNITED trial cs 2007, prof Jan 2008 to May 2010 free/KV Mechelen (Bel), FC Nurnberg (Ger), SC Farense (Ptg), Amiens SC (Fr) & Gateshead, all on trial July to Sept 2010/Aldershot Nov 2010/Hereford Utd Jan 2011/Le Blanc-Mesnil (Fr) July 2011/FC Dieppe (Fr) June 2012.

Wesley Ngo Baheng was a young French striker with a powerful physique who operated also as an attacking midfielder. Tracked by Sam Allardyce when he was in charge of Bolton, Wesley joined the Magpies as a 18-year-old after a spell with the Le Havre academy, taking the same route as Charles N'Zogbia to Tyneside. He had the build to become a dangerous striker though perhaps lacked the subtlety required for the top level. Injury restricted his early development on Tyneside, out with a cruciate ligament problem yet he recovered to show much promise. Wesley appeared for United's first-eleven in a friendly against Shamrock Rovers as part of training for the new 2009-10 season. He also reached the substitute bench on four occasions in that campaign without recorded his league or cup debut for the club. With a Cameroon background, Ngo Baheng struggled to secure a long term deal after he left Newcastle, returning to the Continent in 2010. He is also a musician of sorts, compiling a rap solo album under the name of F-Ikass in 2009 entitled 'Time To Smash'.
Misc App & Goals: 1 app 0 gls.

NICHOLSON Thomas 1896

Inside-left
b. Manchester
Career: West Manchester/Newcastle West End 1887/Heywood Central (Manchester) cs 1890/Newcastle West End March 1892/Blyth cs 1892/UNITED guest Sept 1896.

A former Newcastle West End star, Tom Nicholson was a first-class forward for East End's great rivals at St James' Park. Especially prominent during season 1887-88 when the West Enders became the district's top side for a short period, Nicholson operated at inside-forward as well as in the centre-forward role and once scored four times as West End registered a record 15-0 victory over North Eastern during 1888. He also converted a hat-trick as Shankhouse were defeated in the final of the Northumberland Challenge Cup during the same year, going onto figure in the Northumberland & Durham Inter County final with Sunderland. Sometime later, during September 1896, Nicholson took part in a single fixture for Newcastle United, as a guest in a benefit match for Johnny Campbell. He was by then a veteran, but still well respected on Tyneside as one of the city's early pioneer footballers. He also played cricket for the Elswick Ordnance club.
Misc App & Goals: 1 app 0 gls.

NIXON 1903

Goalkeeper
b. unknown
When the Magpies travelled to Cumberland to play the Workington Black Diamond club during April 1903, they included an unknown goalkeeper by the name of Nixon in their ranks. Probably a trialist, he played in the 3-2 defeat and wasn't retained.
Misc App & Goals: 1 app 0 gls.

Players: other fixtures

NOBLE Robert 1965-1970

Centre-half 5'11"
b. South Gosforth,
Newcastle upon Tyne, 25 May 1949
d. King's Park, Sydney (Australia),
15 May 2005
Career: Willington Quay/Howdon BC/UNITED jnr Aug 1965, prof April 1967 £1,000 (Barrow loan 1969-70)/Bury Aug 1970/Barrow Oct 1970/Colchester Utd trial July 1972, pmt Aug 1972 £1,000/Southport March 1973 £2,000/Darlington Aug 1975/Western Suburbs (Aust) Feb 1977/Inter Monaro (Aust) March 1979/Griffith City (Aust) 1982 to 1984.

Bobby Noble was a fair-haired centre-half in United's ranks for five years without fully making his mark as a Newcastle player. Noble played at the back in two friendly encounters for the Magpies; against Hearts during October 1965 and Barnsley in November 1968. With Moncur, Burton, McNamee and Winstanley all claiming the two centre-back roles for the club, he was transferred to Bury for the start of the 1970-71 season and onto Barrow where he had been on loan when at Gallowgate. Strong and rugged, he was appointed skipper at Holker Street, Bobby made 94 appearances and was at the club when they were voted out of the Football League in 1972. The Tynesider went onto play a small role in Southport's Division Four title success in 1972-73 then had a good stint at Haig Avenue (68 app) before moving to Darlington. Noble emigrated to Australia in 1977, continuing his football trade in New South Wales and playing in the very first season of the Australian National League. He remained in the Sydney area to his death in 2005.

Misc App & Goals: 2 app 0 gls.

NOGUERIA Victor 1978

Goalkeeper 6'1"
b. Mozambique, 17 July 1959
Career: Rangers (SA) 1976/UNITED trial Aug 1978/Atlanta Chiefs (USA) 1979/Montreal Manic (Can) 1982/Chicago Sting (USA) 1983/San Diego Sockers (USA) 1986/Cleveland Force (USA) 1987/San Diego Sockers (USA) 1988/Milwaukee Wave (USA) 1992/San Diego Sockers (USA) Oct 2003/Retired Jan 2005/Coached various professional and college sides in USA including Torrey Pines, West Coast, Sharks, Cederburg, Milwaukee Wave, San Diego Sockers and Cardinal Strich.

Manager Bill McGarry used his links in South Africa to bring Victor Nogueria to Tyneside on trial at the start of the 1978-79 season. He was involved in the match to celebrate the centenary of the Arbroath club during August 1978, and then in a Tyneside derby against Gateshead, sharing the match between the posts with Mick Mahoney. Nogueria didn't show enough to warrant a contract and he soon moved to the USA where he started a long career in the game Stateside, at his peak lifting the NASL championship in 1984 with Chicago Sting. He played in various indoor leagues in the States as well, securing seven indoor titles, awarded Goalkeeper of the Year on eight occasions and appearing for the USA National Futsal team (16 caps). Victor then began coaching the game extensively. His daughter, Casey Nogueria appeared for the USA women's football side.

Misc App & Goals: 0(2) app 0 gls.

NUGENT Jacobus (James) 1888-1889

Forward
b. Gateshead, 1867 (Q1)
d. Jesmond, Newcastle upon Tyne, 29 March 1958
Career: Harp FC/Elswick Rangers c1887 (Newcastle West End guest Dec 1887 to Jan 1888) (EAST END guest Nov 1888 & Nov 1889)(Sunderland Albion guest May 1890)/Also, Trafalgar 1887 to 1892, acting as junior XI secretary/Newcastle Wed 1890-91/EAST END 1892-93 briefly.

With an Irish family background, James Nugent was regarded as a top-notch striker in the early years of football's development on Tyneside, notably with Elswick Rangers where he was a big favourite at their Mill Lane ground. Nugent appeared for Northumberland and for the Newcastle & District XI, top honours in the region at that time. With Elswick Rangers, he appeared in the Northumberland Challenge Cup final of 1889, runner-up after a controversial three-match contest with Newcastle East End. In many games for the strong Rangers club he played alongside his younger brother John Nugent, another decent footballer on Tyneside then. James guested for East End on two occasions, while he did the same with West End at St James' Park. Nugent returned to join the East Enders during season 1892-93 but only as a reserve. He later resided in Jesmond into his nineties having worked as a shipyard labourer and lamplighter for a Tyneside gas company.

(Note: Although census data reveals he was born in Newcastle, birth registration records confirm he was a Gateshead man.)

Misc App & Goals: 2 app 1 gl.*

NULENS Kurt 1992

Goalkeeper
b. Belgium, c1971

Kurt Nulens was a 21-year-old trialist from Belgium's lower league structure of football who landed at St James' Park in the close-season of 1992. Kurt had been watched by Kevin Keegan and Terry McDermott when they were in the Low Countries and he played twice for the Toon eleven, in a friendly against Gateshead and in a Newcastle United XI fixture against Crook Town, both at the end of July. He was though not deemed as good as youngsters on the staff and returned to Belgium.

(Note: His surname could also be Nuelands.)

Misc App & Goals: 2 app 0 gls.

O'BRIEN Peter 1885-1889

Forward
b. Crieff, Perthshire, c1863
d. [Tynemouth district, 1927 (Q3)]

Joining Newcastle East End during January 1885, Peter O'Brien immediately became a regular for the Heaton club for the rest of season 1885-86. He continued to be on East End's playing staff until around 1889. By 1890 he was living at Corbridge Street in Byker, and when he acquired shares in East End's new limited company was working as a painter and decorator. O'Brien was recognised as a noted runner in the region too, taking part in many events, most professional competitions including the Town Moor Harriers Run, a race which he ended as victor during April 1887.

Misc App & Goals: 40 app 9 gls.*

O'DONNELL William 1895

Right-back
b. unknown

A youngster with the Newcastle Trafalgar club, United offered local defender Billy O'Donnell an opportunity in a trial outing against East Stirlingshire at St James' Park during March 1895. The full-back showed enough in a 6-1 romp to warrant a contract and he joined the Magpies permanently during July of that year. O'Donnell though didn't progress after that and little was heard of him afterwards. Census information reveals two possible William O'Donnell's living in Newcastle, both hailing from Scotland.

Misc App & Goals: 1 app 0 gls.*

ORD Roger Joseph 1895

Goalkeeper 5'10"
b. Cramlington,
near Newcastle upon Tyne, 1871 (Q2)
d. 1940
Career: Shankhouse Black Watch c1890/Middlesbrough Ironopolis 1893/Shankhouse Black Watch cs 1894 (UNITED trial April 1895)/Hebburn Argyle 1895/Arsenal July 1897/Luton Town Sept 1900/Wellingborough Town 1903.

A goalkeeper with the renowned local Shankhouse club, Roger Ord tasted Football League action with Ironopolis during season 1893-94 (28 app) and faced the Black'n'Whites. He was given a chance by the Magpies and appeared as United's custodian on trial in a single fixture against Bolton Wanderers during April 1895. He had a somewhat harrowing day against a strong outfit from Division One as Newcastle fell 6-1. Ord was a decent player nevertheless at local level, called up to represent the Northumberland Alliance League side in 1893 and who had been part of the Shankhouse team which lifted the Northumberland Challenge Cup. After his brief period at St James' Park, Ord joined Arsenal and featured in their Second Division line-up over three seasons, totalling 99 matches. Roger then served Luton at Southern League level in 71 games. The Northumbrian was also a decent cricketer and sported a distinctive moustache in the style of Edwardian England. By 1911, he was working back in his native Cramlington, at the Klondyke colliery.

Misc App & Goals: 1 app 0 gls.

ORR Bradley James 1998-2004

Midfield 6'0"
b. Liverpool, 1 November 1982
Career: Everton jnr/UNITED jnr 1998-99, prof July 2001 (Burnley loan 2003-04)/Bristol City July 2004 free/Queens Park Rangers July 2010 £500,000/Blackburn Rovers Jan 2012 free (Ipswich Town loan 2012-13) (Blackpool loan 2013-14)(Toronto (Can) loan 2013-14).

Brought up in the same district of Merseyside as Steven Gerrard and captain of United's youth and reserve side, Bradley Orr was unlucky not to get into United's league or cup line-up, on the fringe of a call-up during season 2003-04 when he sat on the bench in three UEFA Cup matches. A box-to-box player in midfield, he did get pitch-time from the bench against Gateshead during August 2002 when several youngsters were utilised, and was an unused sub for another friendly against Sheffield Wednesday. Dropping down to third-tier football with Bristol City, Orr became a regular at Ashton Gate for over six seasons when he moved to a defensive role. A rock-solid player in their red shirt, Bradley operated at right-back, was tough, quick down the flank to join the attack and totalled 255 games, enjoying promotion in 2007 with the Robins. Despite being a touch hot-tempered on and off the field, once jailed for 28 days in 2006 for a nightclub incident, Orr moved up a level when he joined QPR (43 app) where he was part of the London club's Championship title side in 2010-11. Bradley achieved Premier League status with Blackburn Rovers, but initially couldn't claim an automatic place at the struggling Ewood Park club and was loaned out. He is uncle to Liverpool and England full-back Jon Flanagan.

Misc App & Goals: 0(1) app 0 gls.

PARKINS W 1887

Half-back
b. unknown

A Gateshead Association player between 1886 and 1888, Parkins guested for Newcastle East End during April 1887. He was selected for the line-up in a joint rugby and association rules tournament at Shotley Bridge and faced a Medomsley side.

Misc App & Goals: 1 app 0 gls.*

PARKINSON H 1887-1888

Goalkeeper
b. unknown

Having appeared for Stoke in Midland's football, Newcastle East End brought goalkeeper Parkinson to Tyneside for season 1887-88 and he became one of the club's custodians at reserve level. Parkinson was promoted twice to the senior team, facing Newcastle West End then Middlesbrough during January and February 1888. He conceded nine goals in his tough outings and wasn't considered again.

Misc App & Goals: 2 app 0 gls.*

PARKINSON Michael 1985-1992

Full-back or Outside-right 5'7"
b. Newbottle, Co Durham, 8 June 1971
Career: Burnmoor Jnrs/UNITED jnr Dec 1985, prof June 1989 to cs 1992/Hartlepool Utd/Seaham Red Star/Bishop Auckland/Esh Winning.

From the Houghton-le-Spring area, Michael Parkinson rubbed shoulders with the fellow juniors Appleby, Makel and Lormor in the Newcastle dressing-room during the mid-Eighties. While several of those names progressed to have decent careers and others such as Howey, Clark and Watson flourished, Parkinson didn't get the breaks needed and ended up in local non-league football. He played as a substitute for the Black'n'Whites in a match against a North East XI to raise funds for Jackie Bell's family during May 1990 but that was the closest the full-back-cum-winger came to a first-team outing. Parkinson was a former Durham schoolboy player.

Misc App & Goals: 1(1) app 0 gls.

PARR William Henry 1884-1887

Forward
b. Tunstall, Staffordshire, 16 August 1867
d. Newcastle upon Tyne, 23 March 1946

Noted as being a potter in the traditional Victorian ceramic industry around Stoke, William Parr moved to Tyneside during the early 1880s when in his teens and joined Newcastle East End around March 1884. Initially playing in the club's junior side, he was elevated to the first-eleven during 1884-85, part of the team against Brunswick Villa Athletic, an 8-1 victory in the Northumberland Challenge Cup. Parr left Chillingham Road during the close-season of 1887 and remained in the North East turning out for Heaton Wanderers. By the turn of the century, William was still on Tyneside, recorded in the 1901 census as a "flint miller" living in St Peter's, while some 30 years he later resided at Willington Quay. The local press ran a feature on Parr when he was remarried for the third time when aged 70 having something of a remarkable family; William fathered all of 16 children and had 30 grand-children!

Misc App & Goals: 2 app 2 gls.*

PATTINSON J 1890-1893

Half-back
b. unknown

Chiefly a reserve midfield player with Newcastle East End, Pattinson was called upon to face London Casuals and Sunderland during April 1893, then rarely figured after that despite being able to get on the scoring list. It is possible he is the same person as the J Patterson (qv) who briefly was a club director in 1891 and 1892.

Misc App & Goals: 3 app 3 gls.*

PATTISON John William 1920

Outside-left 5'8"
b. Pity Me, Co Durham, 10 April 1897
d. Bristol, 11 April 1970
Career: Leadgate Park/Framwellgate Moor/Durham City Jan 1920/UNITED April 1920 £100/Durham City Nov 1920 free/Derby Co July 1921/Bristol Rovers Sept 1922/Leadgate Park June 1924/South Shields Jan 1925/Durham City Aug 1925/South Shields Oct 1925/Torquay Utd July 1926/Taunton Town Aug 1928/Grays Thurrock Utd cs 1929/Dunston Utd Sept 1929/West Stanley trial/Durham City amat Dec 1929/Bath City amat Jan 1930/Grays Thurrock Utd Sept 1930/Frenchay Utd Dec 1932/Glastonbury Sept 1933/Warminster Town Nov 1936.

Very fast down the flank, John Pattison shined in Durham City's North Eastern League side just after World War One and was picked up by United at the end of the 1919-20 season. One of several wingers on the club's books, he could play on either flank and was short and sturdy in build. John ran the left touchline for the Black'n'Whites against St Bernard's during April 1920 at Gallowgate, a match in which he did well as United won 5-0. But that's as far as his senior career went at St James' Park and he moved on to make his Football League debut with Derby County during 1921, scoring the winner for the Rams against Blackpool and totalling 15 outings in Division Two. Much travelled after leaving United, Pattison rejoined Durham City when they were members of the Football League and was part of Torquay's pre-Football League line-up which took Southern League silverware in 1927. He was also in the Devon side which made their bow in the Third Division South during the following season. All told, Pattison had a modest senior career of 62 senior games (10 goals), his best return with any club was at Plainmoor with 28 appearances, a record boosted by his Southern League outings.

Misc App & Goals: 1 app 0 gls.

PENNINGTON Charles Edward 1897-1898

Left-back
b. Bishop Auckland, 1873
d. Co Durham, September 1929

A noted amateur footballer with Bishop Auckland at either half-back or full-back, Charles Pennington was on United's staff for a short period as an amateur around the same time as his colleague from Kingsway, John Allen. Part of the Bishop's line-up as they lifted the FA Amateur Cup in 1896, he was highly rated as an amateur footballer when employed as a "Coke Drawer" at a County Durham colliery. Charles joined Newcastle in November 1897 after a short period with Northfleet and spent a few months with the Magpies, although a controversy blew up, United's officials being censored for 'poaching' and the club fined. Pennington played in a strong line-up which took on South Shields during January 1898, but he returned to Bishops during the early part of that year and continued playing the game with the noted Durham side. He reached the FA Amateur Cup final once more in 1900, again a victor as his side defeated Lowestoft Town. Charles also lifted the Northern League title with Bishop

Auckland. Pennington had a short period in South Africa at the turn of the century and died in 1929, killed in a motor accident when he was knocked down by a charabanc.

Misc App & Goals: 1 app 0 gls.

PENNY Alexander 1890-1891

Forward
b. Kemback, Fife, 7 June 1866
d. Arbroath, 4 March 1939
Career: Gateshead NER/Newcastle West End cs 1890/EAST END Oct 1890/Newcastle Wednesday 1891/Arbroath Wand June 1893/Dundonians Jan 1894/Arbroath c1895 to 1897.

From a Fife village near Cupar, Alex Penny left his job as a flax mill worker to settle on Tyneside during the 1880s. He appeared for railway works side Gateshead NER then Penny moved across the River Tyne to join Newcastle West End during the summer of 1890. Remaining with the St James' Park side for only a few months, he soon was on his travels again, but not far, barely the two miles or so across the city to sign for Newcastle East End. Appearing for both rivals in the 1890-91 season, Penny never settled at Chillingham Road either. He went on to turn out for lesser club Newcastle Wednesday in 1891 then returned to Scotland. He settled in Forfarshire and was for a long period associated with Arbroath, a player and later supporter. He ran a tailoring business in the coastal town and died watching a First Division match at Gayfield Park in 1939.

Misc App & Goals: 3 app 1 gl.*

PEPPER G 1885-1886

Full-back
b. unknown

Defender Pepper signed for Newcastle East End during December 1885 and had a run of appearances in the blue shirt of the Heatonites during the winter of 1885-86, making a debut against Gateshead Casuals in December. He did not remain long with the club, leaving at the end of the season.

Misc App & Goals: 5 app 0 gls.*

PEPPER Graham Anthony 1991-1996

Centre-half 5'11"
b. Newcastle upon Tyne, 19 August 1977
Career: UNITED jnr Nov 1991 to cs 1996/Gateshead Aug 1998/Blyth Spartans July 2001/Whitley Bay Aug 2003.

With big stars beginning to flock to St James' Park as the Black'n'Whites became a Premiership force, Graham Pepper found it impossible to push his way into the reckoning at first-team level. Sidelined with injury for a spell, he managed a single appearance as a substitute, in Derek Bell's testimonial match at Gateshead during August 1993. And with boss Kevin Keegan virtually dismantling the club's reserve set-up he had no alternative but to ply his trade in the local part-time non-league scene. Over a three season spell with Gateshead, Pepper totalled 65 games. He played alongside his brother Carl at both Whitley Bay and Blyth.

Misc App & Goals: 0(1) app 0 gls.

Players: other fixtures

PEREZ Lionel Pierre Antoine 1998-2000

Goalkeeper 5'11"
b. Bagnols-sur-Ceze (France),
24 April 1967
Career: Nimes Olymp (Fr) 1989/FC Bordeaux (Fr) 1993 (Stade Lavallois (Fr) loan 1995-96)/Sunderland Aug 1996 £250,000/UNITED July 1998 free (Scunthorpe Utd loan 1999-2000) (Cambridge Utd loan 1999-2000)(Olym Lyonnais loan 1999-2000 briefly)/Cambridge Utd July 2000 free/ Enfield cs 2002/Chelmsford City Jan 2003/Stevenage Borough Feb 2003, retiring in 2004, becoming goalkeeper & fitness coach 2005 to 2007/FC Chusclan Laudin (Fr) coach 2007/SO Cassis Carnoux (Fr) asst-coach 2009 to 2010.

The departure of Pavel Srnicek and Shaka Hislop during the close-season of 1998 resulted in the Black'n'Whites bringing in a new goalkeeper, essentially as third choice behind two emerging custodians in Newcastle's squad; Shay Given and Steve Harper. Provence-born Lionel Perez had for the previous two seasons been with neighbours Sunderland and in the summer of 1998 moved from Wear to Tyne. A somewhat flamboyant and eccentric character, Perez appeared on 84 occasions for the Black Cats and often gave a mix of brilliant and bizarre performances. He was something of showman and a crowd favourite despite the odd lapse on Wearside. The Frenchman played a huge part in the Red'n'Whites' failed bid for promotion through a dramatic penalty shoot-out at Wembley in 1998. In French action, the blond-haired Perez began with Nimes (alongside Eric Cantona) where he won promotion from the French Second Division in 1991 then joined Bordeaux before heading for Wearside. At St James' Park he saw little first-team football, playing in several friendly games and sitting on the bench for the opening three months of the 1998-99 season before Harper took over. Sparingly used during the following campaign, Perez joined Cambridge United where he totalled 104 games, reaching the final of the Football League Trophy in 2002 before returning to France.

Misc App & Goals: 8(2) app 0 gls.

PHALP Thomas Shaw 1881-1882

Goalkeeper & Half-back
b. Newcastle upon Tyne, December 1861
d. Newcastle upon Tyne, 5 September 1943

Thomas Phalp was with Stanley FC as they started to play football for the first time during November 1881, appearing in the club's opening match on 26th November 1881 against the Elswick Leather Works 2nd XI. Operating as a goalkeeper and half-back, Phalp moved from the St Peter's area of Byker to team up with Heaton Association in 1882, a club to have close connections with East End. Thomas fulfilled the role of secretary with Heaton and was also a committee member. Phalp was another son of the Byker and Heaton districts, living during the latter years of the century at Heaton Terrace and Warkworth Street, employed as an engineering administrator and later as a chemical clerk and house agent. By 1898 he was employed by the Lansdale company in Byker then as a time-keeper at a pottery works. Thomas played cricket too, notably for Woodbine cricket club.

Misc App & Goals: 4 app 0 gls.*

PIGG Albert 1924-1925

Centre-forward 5'11"
b. Medomsley, Co Durham, 6 April 1903
d. Consett, 22 September 1944
Career: Allendale Park/UNITED trial Oct 1924, pmt Nov 1924 £10/Crewe Alex Nov 1925 £50/Carlisle Utd Aug 1926/Raith Rovers May 1927/Barnsley July 1929/Consett May 1930/Annfield Plain April 1931.

Albert Pigg was a fiery and lethal goalscorer in reserve and lower level football. The son of a coal-miner, he joined the Magpies as the 1924-25 season was underway and soon made an impression. Pigg led the line at centre-forward for Newcastle's Ingham Cup meeting with South Shields during November 1924 while in the following month, he scored a hat-trick in what could be called a Newcastle United XI line-up against a Wallsend combination. Yet, the Durham lad couldn't break fully into the club's senior line-up and had to move elsewhere to find action and it was in the Scottish League that he enjoyed a prolific period. With Raith Rovers in Scotland's Division One, he netted 37 goals in 59 matches and earned a move back to England with Second Division Barnsley. Albert scored on his debut for the Tykes, but then was switched from his favourite centre-forward role and he lost his sparkle. Oddly when with Carlisle, the Cumbrians fielded two unrelated forwards by the name of Pigg both from the North East; Albert and Billy appearing during season 1926-27. At the time of his death in 1944 he was living at the Freemasons Arms Hotel in Consett.

(Note: Albert Pigg's career should not be confused with that of namesake Billy who appeared for Ashington and QPR during the same era.)

Misc App & Goals: 2 app 3 gls.

PINAS Brian Ulrich 1997-1998

Outside-left 5'8"
b. Rotterdam (Netherlands),
29 December 1978
Career: DHC Delft (Neth)/Ajax (Neth) jnr/Feyenoord (Neth) jnr 1991/UNITED July 1997 free/Feyenoord (Neth) July 1998 free (SBV Excelsior (Neth) loan 1999-2000 to 2002-03)/FC Groningen (Neth) July 2003/Cercle Brugge KSV (Bel) July 2005/NAC Breda (Bel) Aug 2006/FC Dordrecht (Neth) Aug 2007/RVV Hercules (Neth) July 2010 to cs 2011.

Of Surinamese decent, Brian Pinas was one of a group of promising Continental youngsters brought to Tyneside during the mid-to-latter years of the 1990s decade. Snatched from Feyenoord's youth ranks, the 18-year-old Dutch youth international winger was spotted when United's juniors visited Holland for a youth tournament. Slender but a skilful and lively player, Pinas was capable of fine touches but lacked the physical strength to make it in the English game. The closest the Dutchman came to getting into United's first-eleven was under Kenny Dalglish's reign, being chosen to warm the substitute's bench on five occasions in Premier League and Champions League fixtures during the early part of 1997-98, including the Magpies' debut and epic Barcelona fixture at Gallowgate. He also appeared against Birmingham City and Bradford City in friendly action during July 1997. Brian was released at the end of the 1997-98 season when he headed back to Holland, making a name for himself with Excelsior where Brian totalled over 100 matches. Despite two bad injuries in his career, Pinas successfully continued to play for lesser clubs in the Eredivisie, and also in Belgium, always as an out-and-out old-fashioned left winger.

Misc App & Goals: 0(2) app 0 gls.

PLATT James Archibald 1974

Goalkeeper 5'10"
b. Ballymoney, Co Wexford,
26 January 1952
Career: Ballymena Utd/Liverpool trial 1970/Middlesbrough May 1970 £10,000 (UNITED guest May 1974) (Hartlepool Utd loan 1978-79)(Cardiff City loan 1978-79)/Ballymena Utd player-manager April 1983/Coleraine player-manager June 1984 to April 1990/Ballyclare Comrades manager 1991 to 1992/Assyriska (Swd) manager 1992-1993/ Northern Ireland FA coach/Darlington asst-manager Aug 1995, becoming manager Dec 1995 to Nov 1996/ Gateshead coach 1996/Middlesbrough asst-coach/ Darlington gkp-coach May 2009 to Aug 2009/ Middlesbrough community coach to 2013 & coaching local football in Cleveland.

Appearing on 481 occasions for Middlesbrough, Jim Platt was one of the game's best 'keepers during his era. Like his fellow countryman at Gallowgate, Willie McFaul, he appeared for Northern Ireland (23 caps) but had the enduring Pat Jennings ahead of him although Jim did appear in the 1982 World Cup. Platt guested for the Magpies in a testimonial fixture for fellow custodian Jimmy Montgomery during May 1974 at Roker Park. A good find by Boro manager and ex-United skipper Stan Anderson when a teenager in Ulster, Platt became first-choice at Ayresome Park over 12 seasons being a consistent and at times brilliant shot-stopper. He was a key figure in Boro's Second Division title success during 1973-74. Back in Northern Ireland for a period during the Eighties and Nineties, Platt reached two Irish Cup finals before returning to the North East to settle. After leaving the senior game, Jim resided near to Middlesbrough, coaching local youngsters, running 'Jim Platt Coaching' as well as being instrumental in setting up Boro's Former Players Association. He also is a club host at the Riverside Stadium. His father and brother both played football in Northern Ireland.

Misc App & Goals: 1 app 0 gls.

POUTON Alan 1991-1995

Midfield 6'0"
b. Newcastle upon Tyne,
1 February 1977
Career: UNITED jnr March 1991, prof July 1993/Oxford Utd Nov 1995 free/York City Dec 1995 free/Grimsby Town loan July 1999, pmt Aug 1999 £150,000/Gillingham Jan 2004 £30,000 (Hartlepool Utd loan 2004-05)/Retired due to injury Jan 2007/Dover Ath June 2007/Maidstone Utd cs 2009/Sutton Utd Aug 2009/Retired cs 2010/Maidstone Utd asst-manager March 2011 to Jan 2012.

Although Alan Pouton wasn't retained by Newcastle or Oxford United, he went onto still accumulate 311 senior matches in Divisions One and Two. A tall midfielder with a powerful shot, he was also the proverbial tough-tackling competitor. With York City (103 app) and Grimsby Town (137 app), Pouton became a good club player in the lower leagues. At Blundell Park he was especially popular due to his never-say-die attitude and stylish step-over on the ball. At Gallowgate, Alan was one of several young professionals to be given a run out in what was a first-team match to some extent against Bishop Auckland during August 1995.

Misc App & Goals: 1 app 0 gls.

PRATT Thomas 1919

Half-back
b. unknown

As football returned to something like normal following the Great War, United arranged a series of friendly contests to supplement their Northern Victory League programme. Several trialists were included in these games, Thomas Pratt being one such footballer who was part of the squad against Middlesbrough in May 1919. He was unlucky not to score, The Journal noting that "one shot in particular severely tested Williamson, and might possibly beaten any other keeper". From Lancashire he wasn't signed by the club afterwards.

Misc App & Goals: 1 app 0 gls.

PURVIS Alexander 1906-1910

Goalkeeper 5'11"
b. Scotland
Career: Bute Wand/UNITED trial Aug 1906, pmt Sept 1906/Clyde Dec 1910 to cs 1911.

Alex Purvis made the lengthy journey from Rothesay on the Isle of Bute for a trial on Tyneside as the 1906-07 season began. Recommended by United's Scottish scouting team, he earned a contract and was one of the club's reserves to Jimmy Lawrence. Apart from Lawrence, he had Kelsey, Sinclair and Blake as rivals and consequently received very little opportunity, custodian for the seniors once, in a match to raise social funds against Sunderland at West Stanley in October 1907. Returning to Scotland, he later appeared on six occasions for Clyde in the Scottish League.

(Note: In the Scottish football archive the player is noted by the name of Purves.)

Misc App & Goals: 1 app 0 gls.

PURVIS Joseph W 1887-1891

Forward
b. Newcastle upon Tyne, c1866
Career: Newcastle FA 1882/Cheviot 1886/EAST END Sept 1887/Rendel 1891-92/Harp FC/Newcastle Wed 1891-92/Also, Jesmond FC.

A teenager from Jesmond when he was playing football on Tyneside, Joe Purvis found himself part of the Newcastle East End set up when his junior club Cheviot was taken over in September 1887. Making a debut in East End's line-up for a match with Bede College during October 1887, he then scored twice against Gateshead the following month. Purvis was talented enough to appear for Northumberland's County side while Joe was also a cricketer for Friends cricket club. He purchased shares in the Newcastle East End company during the 1890s and was noted as a confectioner.

Misc App & Goals: 2 app 2 gls.*

QUINN Jonathyn Stephen 2012-date

Striker 6'0"
b. Ashington, 17 September 1995
Career: Alnwick Jnrs/Wallsend BC/UNITED July 2012/(Blyth Spartans loan 2014-15).

One of a long line of footballers produced by the Wallsend Boys Club on Tyneside, Jonathyn Quinn was raised in Alnwick and formed a dangerous strike partnership in United's junior and reserve sides with Adam Armstrong. Described as a hard-working forward, technically good on both the left and right, who is effective in the opponent's penalty box. Mobile and with a sure strike of the ball, Jonathyn became a Newcastle player in 2012 and has caught the eye of United's coaching staff. He made headlines when he netted a 28 minute hat-trick against Sunderland during the 2013-14 FA Youth Cup. Quinn reached contention for a senior outing when he was named on the substitute's bench for the pre-season friendly against Sheffield Wednesday in July 2014.

Misc App & Goals: 0 app 0 gls (1 sub no app).

RAE William 1899-1900

Outside-left 5'10"
b. Kelton, near Castle Douglas, c1880
Career: 6th Galloway Rifle Volunteers FC (Dalbeattie)/Douglas Wand Dec 1898/Newton-Stewart Ath March 1899/6th Galloway Rifle Volunteers (Dalbeattie) May 1899/Douglas Wand Sept 1899/UNITED Sept 1899/Douglas Wand Aug 1900/Glossop May 1901/Douglas Wand April 1902/Royal Albert Aug 1904/Douglas Wand Sept 1904/Linfield Aug 1905/Douglas Wand Sept 1907/5th King's Own Scottish Borderers FC Sept 1909/[Dalbeattie Star Dec 1911].

Described at the time as being speedy and with good ball playing ability, Willie Rae was a star player in the south-west of Scotland. With the Magpies for short period at the turn of the century, Rae did not venture too long from his native Galloway and moved to and from Castle Douglas over a seven year period. Rae was selected in a strong Newcastle forward line including Jock Peddie and Joe Rogers to face Dundee in December 1899. However that was the closest the Scot came to achieving a Football League or FA Cup debut for United. Joining Glossop in Lancashire for a period between his trips back to Castle Douglas, Rae totalled 14 games in first-class action during 1901-02. He was employed as a plumber when not playing football and appeared for the pioneers of Queen of the South, the King's Own Scottish Borderers.

Misc App & Goals: 1 app 0 gls.

REED Ebor 1922-1925

Half-back 5'9"
b. Quarrington Hill, Co Durham, 30 November 1899
d. Co Durham, 14 November 1971
Career: Spennymoor Utd/UNITED Feb 1922 £200/Cardiff City May 1925 £200/Nottingham Forest July 1926/Rotherham Utd May 1927/Derry City July 1929/Portadown June 1932/[Dundalk].

The son of a pork butcher and born near Coxhoe in central Durham, Ebor Reed was able to operate in the centre or on the flanks of midfield's half-back line. He spent over three years at St James' Park without breaking through fully. With stars like Mooney, McIntosh, Curry as well as Gibson and MacKenzie ahead of him in selection, the Durham product managed three games with the first-team including against The Corinthians in January 1923, then against South Shields during November 1924. A strong tackler in the North Eastern League, winning the title in 1922-23, Reed then joined Cardiff and Nottingham Forest but again found it tough to claim a place. However with Rotherham, Ebor was an automatic choice for two seasons during 1927-28 and 1928-29, taking part Third Division North football and totalling 65 games. Reed had a rewarding stay in Ireland after leaving the English game during 1929, capped by the Irish League during his period there.

Misc App & Goals: 3 app 0 gls.

REID Brian Robertson 1994

Centre-half 6'2"
b. Paisley, 15 June 1970
Career: Renfrew Waverley/Morton July 1988/Rangers March 1991 £350,000 (UNITED loan March 1994 to June 1994)/Morton March 1996/Burnley Sept 1998/Dunfermline Ath July 1999/Blackpool Oct 2000/Falkirk Jan 2003/Queen of the South Aug 2003/Ayr Utd Sept 2006, becoming manager Oct 2007 to May 2012/Bristol City & Falkirk match analyst/Global (Plp) manager Jan 2013 & Philippines Under-23 coach/Nuneaton Town manager April 2014.

A former Rangers and Scotland Under-21 centre-half, Brian Reid played a small part in title victories at Ibrox during 1990-91 (3 app) and 1992-93 (2 app) and was unlucky with his early career due to a cruciate ligament injury. A mishap to England stopper Steve Howey in 1993-94 prompted Kevin Keegan to bring Reid to Tyneside as back-up, although the Scot hardly figured in senior activity; once on the substitute's bench for the Premier League visit to face Manchester City at Maine Road during April 1994. Reid liked to play the ball out of the back-line and had the opportunity to claim a deal at Gallowgate if he could prove his fitness. But he did not do enough and Keegan's squad was soon strengthened by the arrival of Philippe Albert during the close-season so Reid was not retained. Thereafter he pulled on the shirt of Morton over 150 times and had spells back in England with Burnley (33 app) and Blackpool (69 app) where he helped the Seasiders to promotion from Division Three in 2001. Before moving into management with Ayr United, Reid was also a promotion winner in Scotland during 2000 and 2003. As boss at Somerset Park, he twice succeeded with promotion bids too, in 2009 and 2011. Reid moved to the Far East during 2013, in charge of the Global club of Leyle in the Philippines for a year. As a teenager, he had a brief spell with Chelsea as a junior player.

Misc App & Goals: 0 app 0 gls (1 sub no app).

RICHARDSON J 1888-1889

Forward
b. probably Scotland

One of two players to arrive from Hurlford near Kilmarnock, and noted as J Richardson, he settled with Robert McCrindle in Newcastle during December 1888. He was given an opportunity in an attractive friendly on Tyneside against Mossend Swifts, Richardson scoring in a 3-1 defeat. It is likely the player is one of two footballers from Hurlford, Robert or A Richardson. The former was with Sheffield Wednesday from March 1891 to April 1892 and had a good season with the Owls, claiming 17 goals in the 1890-91 Football Alliance competition just before they joined the Football League.

Misc App & Goals: 1 app 1 gl.*

RICHARDSON Michael Scott 2010-2014

Midfield or Striker 5'10"
b. Newcastle upon Tyne, 17 March 1992
Career: Cramlington Jnrs/Walker Central BC/UNITED Aug 2010 (Leyton Orient loan 2011-12)(Gillingham loan 2012-13)(Birmingham City loan 2012-13)(St Mirren trial July 2013) (Accrington Stanley loan 2013-14) to June 2014 free/Hibernian trial July 2014.

Brought up in a household of United supporters in Kingston Park, Michael Richardson worked as an apprentice electrician before catching the attention of United scouts playing for Walker Central. Ginger-haired, Richardson possessed good pace and quick thinking from an attacking role in midfield. Sent out on loan to a number of clubs to gain experience, Richardson played a small part (2 app) in Gillingham's Division Two trophy success during 2012-13. He sat on the bench for United in senior matches on four occasions during 2010-11 and took part in a pre-season friendly for the Magpies against Darlington in July 2011, replacing Ben Arfa from the bench. A broken ankle hindered his bright progress the following season when he had a spell with Accrington Stanley (18 app) and then was released during the summer of 2014.

Misc App & Goals: 0(2) app 0 gls.

Players: other fixtures

RILEY 1882-1883

Half-back
b. unknown

Registering a single match for Newcastle East End during April 1883, a friendly contest with Tyne Valley club Newton, half-back Riley has not been traced playing again.

Misc App & Goals: 1 app 0 gls.*

ROBERTSON E W 1899

Outside-left
b. unknown

Although EW Robertson (or Robinson) was described in the local newspaper columns as being a scholar at Oxford University, no record exists of the man in the comprehensive University archive. He played two trial games for Newcastle during January 1899. Selected on the left flank for contests with Burnley and Hearts over the New Year holiday programme, the athletic youngster had experienced players Macfarlane then Smith alongside him for each outing. Nothing is recorded as to his performance, other than the Black'n'Whites kept his registration until 1903 although it appears he wasn't at Gallowgate after his trial appearance.

Misc App & Goals: 2 app 0 gls.

ROBINSON William 1919-1921

Centre-half 5'8"
b. Walker, Newcastle upon Tyne, c1897
Career: Walker Parish Church/UNITED amat Dec 1919, prof Jan 1920 £10/Retired due to injury 1921.

Billy Robinson served as a sergeant with the Royal Engineers during the First World War and saw action in Mesopotamia (now Syria/Iraq). Returning to his native Tyneside after the conflict, Robinson was signed by the Magpies from his local Walker church team as the club built very much a new squad of players containing several eager and new youngsters, like Robinson. After making good progress, appearing for the seniors against South Shields during September 1920, Billy was unlucky to sustain a bad foot and knee injury in reserve colours, serious enough to force him out of the game the following year. By September 1922 the injury was severe enough that he lost his job and the player asked the club for medical assistance.

Misc App & Goals: 1 app 0 gls.

ROBSON Edward Riddell 1913, 1918

Goalkeeper 6'0"
b. Allendale, near Hexham, 21 August 1890
d. Hexham, 2 February 1977
Career: Dinnington/UNITED amat April 1913/Gateshead/Watford June 1914 (Sunderland war-guest)(UNITED war-guest 1918-19) Portsmouth July 1919/Sunderland May 1922 £250/Swansea Town May 1924 £250/Wrexham June 1926/Grimsby Town July 1928/Rochdale March 1929 to cs 1929/Hexham trainer.

Ted Robson had a respectable career in the game during the inter-war era, several years after first being at Gallowgate in 1913 as a young amateur player when employed as a postman in the Tyne valley. He wasn't retained then Robson headed south to start his goalkeeping occupation in earnest. Back in the area during the First World War, Ted was a guest for the Magpies in December 1918 against his future club Sunderland. Robson started to breakthrough at a relatively late age after World War One, appearing on 112 occasions for Portsmouth and helping Pompey to the Southern League title during 1920, then into the Football

League, taking part in their first ever match in senior company. Robson secured a big move back to the North East when he joined Sunderland where he made 40 appearances. At Roker Park he was a regular choice in 1922-23, ending the season as runners-up in the title race, but afterwards losing his place to future United star Albert McInroy. As a veteran with Swansea and Wrexham he became a Division Three South champion (1925) as well as Welsh Cup finalist (1926) and being capped by the Welsh League side.

Misc App & Goals: 1 app 0 gls.

ROBSON George Chippendale 1925-1927

Inside-right 5'9"
b. Newcastle upon Tyne, 17 June 1905
d. London, March 1982
Career: Dene Villa/St Peter's Albion/UNITED May 1925 £150/West Ham Utd May 1927 £250/Brentford Feb 1931/Heart of Midlothian Dec 1935 £2,400 to 1943/Later becoming a West Ham United scout to 1971.

A former lorry driver on Tyneside before he turned professional with the Magpies, George Robson was a talented footballer. Wearing United colours, he faced Rangers when they visited Gallowgate during September 1925, but with the Magpies having a rich selection of forwards to choose from as the title trophy was secured, his opportunities were limited. Robson was dubbed the best of United's reserves not to gain a call up and George was too good to play North Eastern League football, winning the title in 1925-26. As a consequence he joined West Ham United (the first of three Robson's to make that move south). George ironically made his Football League debut against the Magpies in the last fixture of the 1927-28 season. He was though in and out of the Hammers' line-up (18 app) and moved across London in search of more playing time. With Brentford he eventually achieved that, although not until he spent a period languishing in the reserve team. But promoted, he made his mark, becoming a first-class schemer for the Bees with skill and vision on the ball. Totalling 131 games and scoring 34 goals, Robson was part of Brentford's finest side as they rose to the top flight in the years before World War Two. He was a Division Three South (1933) and Division Two (1935) winner with the Griffin Park club and was described in the London club's annals as a footballer who was at times "a joy to behold". Robson was also popular 400 miles north in Edinburgh, a regular inside-forward for Hearts during four seasons up to the outbreak of the war and runner-up in the Scottish title race in 1937-38. He played on during the hostilities at Tynecastle recording 173 games all told. George appeared in the prestigious British Empire Exhibition tournament in Glasgow with Hearts during 1938.

Misc App & Goals: 2 app 0 gls.

ROCHE Thomas R 1883-1892

Forward
b. Newcastle upon Tyne, 1865 (Q3)
d. Newcastle upon Tyne, 8 May 1908

Born and raised in the St Peter's area around Raby Street, the son of an Irish publican at the Jack Tarr Inn, Thomas Roche joined up with the renamed Newcastle East End club during 1883. He was only a teenager when he first appeared for the Byker club, but he spent a lengthy period with the East Enders although connected to the closely linked Cheviot organisation between 1884 and 1887 until they merged. Roche reached East End's first eleven during season 1885-86 against Newcastle West End in a Christmas city derby. By the time he purchased shares when East End became a limited company late in 1890, Thomas was recorded in the club's surviving share-ledger as a "Publican" at the "Glendale Inn, Potts Street, Byker". He afterwards resided in Heaton.

Misc App & Goals: 6 app 2 gls.*

ROCHFORD William 1939

Full-back 5'10"
b. Newhouse, Co Durham, 23 May 191?
d. East Headleyhope, Co Durham, 9 March 1984
Career: Cuckfield/Esh Winning Jnrs/Portsmouth amat July 1931, prof Aug 1931 (UNITED war-guest 1939-40)/Southampton July 1946 £550, becoming player-coach Aug 1949/Colchester Utd July 1950 £1,000/Retired 1951, afterwards scouting for various clubs based in the North East, including Southampton & Sheffield Wed.

On the outbreak of the Second World War many player. born and bred in the North East returned home, either to work in essential occupations or on periods of training and leave from the services. Country Durham man Bi Rochford was one who headed back to his native Newhouse and Esh Winning area for a period. Bill donnec United's black-and-white colours in a Tyne-Tees wartime derby during October 1939 and also for a few reserve matches. On the south coast, firstly with Portsmouth and later Southampton, he performed with credit. The tough full-back who could operate both on the right or left flank, was an automatic choice for Pompey, talented enough to be on the fringe of the England set-up during 1935-36 and 1936-37 when he appeared in trial fixtures and pulled on the Football League Xl shirt. Bill was known as 'Rocky' Rochford and skippered the Blues to FA Cup victory in 1939. He played football for Pompey through the conflict when he worked in aircraft manufacture reaching the London (& South) War Cup final during 1942. Rochford totalled over 300 in all matches for the Fratton Park club; Bill then moved to the Dell as something of a veteran, captain of the Saints too in his 134 games. Rochford settled back in the North East, taking up farming near Tow Law, but also keeping his links with the game, being an active scout, notably spotting Bobby Robson at Langley Park Juniors.
(Note: Birth and death registration documents show a conflict in Rochford's birth, on either 23 or 27 May.)

Misc App & Goals: 1 app 0 gls.

ROWE 1902

Right-back
b. probably Scotland

A trialist from a Perth junior club, Rowe arrived at St James' Park during December 1902, Newcastle officials giving the youngster a run-out in back-to-back friendlies with Hibs and Dundee on Christmas Day and Boxing Day. Little is recorded of the player, but the Daily Leader noted that he was "very capable and daring at close quarters", but added he wasn't "very good with his kicking". Rowe wasn't offered a contract and returned to Scotland where it appears he did not play in first-class football.

Misc App & Goals: 2 app 0 gls.

ROWLANDS John 1882-1886

Half-back & Forward
b. Newcastle upon Tyne, 1864 (Q1)
d. Newbiggin by the Sea, Northumberland, 20 March 1941

A member of the Rosewood junior set up in the Byker area, when his club merged with the Newcastle East End late in 1882 he found himself a young teenager in a rapidly developing football organisation. Rowlands is registered in the national census data of 1881 as a 17-year-old boiler-worker from Parker Street close to the St Peter's area. John was elevated to East End's first choice eleven for friendlies with Heaton and Newton in the second half of season 1882-83, playing as a half-back and a forward. Afterwards he was part of the club's reserve eleven for a couple of seasons to 1886. Rowlands continued working in the shipbuilding yards as a boilermaker, remaining in Byker to his death on the Northumberland coast.

Misc App & Goals: 2 app 0 gls.*

RUSSELL F 1886-1890

Defender

[Scotland, c1863]

With local Byker side Raby Rovers, Russell joined the Newcastle East End staff in 1886 and remained with the club until around 1890, although only rarely reaching first-team contention. He was selected for the match against Medomsley in April 1887, a 4-2 defeat. It is probable that the player was shareholder Frank Russell who lived on Heaton Road. At the time he was a young trainee doctor, born in Scotland. He later practised as a physician and surgeon on Tyneside from a Heaton base.

Misc App & Goals: 2 app 0 gls.*

RUTHERFORD George Thompson 1908-1912

Inside-right 5'10"
b. Percy Main, near Newcastle upon Tyne, September 1892
d. Percy Main, near Newcastle upon Tyne, 29 September 1913
Career: Willington Ath/UNITED Feb 1908 to May 1912/Local football to demise in 1913.

The younger brother of the great Jack Rutherford (qv) and starting his career with the same local Tyneside club as his famous relation, George Rutherford showed enough talent on the ball to be given a contract during the 1907-08 campaign when he was a teenager. With United at the peak of their Edwardian prowess, obtaining senior opportunities was always going to be difficult for the young schemer. But he did get a chance against Carlisle United in September 1908, partnering Jackie on the right flank. George secured the North Eastern League crown appearing for the second-string during 1908-09 and 1910-11 then was released at the end of the 1911-12 season. Working as a printer, tragically, Rutherford died after a cycling outing in prolonged wet weather to the Borders during September 1913. He contracted pneumonia and tuberculosis and died at his home on Tyneside.

Misc App & Goals: 2 app 0 gls.

RUTHERFORD Jonathan Paul 1984-1987

Centre-forward 5'10"
b. Sunderland, 23 February 1967
Career: Sunderland jnr/UNITED jnr c1984, prof July 1985 to May 1987 free/Alloa Ath Sept 1987/Falkirk Sept 1988/Hartlepool Utd trial July 1992/Meadowbank Thistle Oct 1992/ Scarborough Sept 1994/Berwick Rangers Dec 1994/ Billingham Synthonia 1997.

Although Paul Rutherford did not make the grade in English football with the Magpies, the Wearsider carved out a decent career in Scotland after leaving United. Following a single match for Newcastle, as substitute against Middlesbrough in a testimonial for David Mills during April 1986, Rutherford was handed a free transfer and move to Alloa. The striker assisted the Wasps to promotion from Division Two in 1989 then moved the short distance to Falkirk, where he was part of the Bairns' Division One title winning squad of 1991. Paul totalled 205 games (59 goals) north of the border while he also had a short period with Scarborough's Division Three side during 1994-95.

Misc App & Goals: 0(1) app 0 gls.

RUTHERFORD William 1914-1920

Forward 5'9"
b. Gateshead
Career: Rodsley (Gateshead)/UNITED Jan 1914 £40 to July 1920 free.

Born and raised in Gateshead, Billy Rutherford impressed United officials appearing for his local club Rodsley in Bensham during season 1913-14. The Black'n'Whites offered the Tynesider a contract and he joined what was a substantial staff of professionals. A versatile forward able to operate in the leader's role or in an inside berth, he was some way from selection for United's Football League line-up in the years before World War One, but gained a brief chance in senior company at the end of the conflict as the club were reassembling their squad. Facing Sunderland and Blackburn in 1916 then South Shields during July 1919 Rutherford was retained for the new season but left during the summer of 1920.

Misc App & Goals: 3 app 0 gls.

RYDER Stephen 1884-1889

Half-back & Forward
b. Scotland, c1863

Operating in both defence and attack in his appearances for Newcastle East End, Stephen Ryder first pulled on the blue shirt during the end-of-season Temperance Festival on the Town Moor during June 1884. He had a good run in the side as the new 1884-85 season unfolded, and was often seen the following campaign too, occasionally captaining the line-up. Ryder continued with East End in 1887-88 and 1888-89, but now as a reserve, skippering the second-eleven. It is likely he his related to both Isaac Ryder (qv), Joseph Ryder (qv) and trainer Henry Ryder (qv), although this has not been confirmed. He was described as being employed as a "house painter".

Misc App & Goals: 18 app 0 gls.*

SAMPSON R 1887-1889

Forward
b. unknown

Deputising for David Scott in the final games of season 1887-88, and again in a rare outing during 1888-89, Sampson was a regular in attack for the second-string during his period at Chillingham Road.

Misc App & Goals: 2 app 1 gl.*

SCOPE John William 1887

Full-back
b. Newcastle upon Tyne, 1 October 1865
d. Newcastle upon Tyne, [1911]

An early Tyneside footballer with North Eastern in Heaton between 1884 and 1887, John Scope only appeared once for Newcastle East End as a guest, during March 1887 for a fixture with Elswick Rangers. He hailed from the St Michael's area of Byker and played with credit for North Eastern, one of the region's earliest clubs. John later also turned out for Victoria Wednesday in 1892. During the decade before the turn of the century and then up to World War One, Scope worked as a tailor. He was also an early shareholder of the club.

Misc App & Goals: 1 app 0 gls.*

SATKA Lubomir 2012-date

Centre-half 6'0"
b. Ilava (Slovakia), 2 December 1995
Career: MFK Dubnica (Slv)/UNITED jnr May 2012, prof March 2014.

Lubomir Satka was offered a deal at St James' Park when he was only 16 years of age, a highly rated and promising centre-back in his home country of Slovakia. Impressing in the 2012 Northern Ireland Milk Cup tournament and known as Lubo, he is a towering defender being quick and cultured on the ball with vision to place a pass. An Under-15 and Under-16 international, he was captain of the Slovakian Under-17 team and graduated to play at Under-19 as well as Under-21 levels, destined to go through all age groups to gain a full cap for his country. Following the path of Liverpool's Martin Skrtel to the English game, such was Lubo's progress on Tyneside that he was included in the senior squad to travel for the final Premier League fixture of the 2013-14 season at Liverpool. He was handed a place on the bench at Anfield as cover for Coloccini, Williamson and Steven Taylor. Lubo made his bow for the Magpies in the friendly with Oldham during the pre-season of 2014-15.

Misc App & Goals: 1(5) app 0 gls.

SCOTT William Reed 1939

Inside-left 5'7"
b. Howdon, near Newcastle upon Tyne, 6 December 1907
d. Hammersmith, London, 18 October 1969
Career: Howdon BL/Middlesbrough May 1927/Brentford May 1932 £1,500 exch deal (UNITED war-guest 1939-40)(Darlington war-guest 1939-40)(Gateshead war-guest 1941-42)(Hartlepools Utd war-guest 1943-45)(Sunderland war-guest 1944-45)/Resumed with Brentford/Aldershot July 1947/Dover Aug 1948.

Capped by England against Wales in October 1936, Billy Scott was regarded as a creative mastermind on the field, something of an unorthodox player but very effective. He was described in one contemporary report as "a strategist and roamer in the Alex James mould". Having joined Brentford after a treble signing from Boro during 1932, with the Bees, Scott was instrumental in midfield as the Londoners climbed from the lower divisions to a place in the top-six of England's elite. He was part of title sides in 1933 (Division Three South) and 1935 (Division Two) and totalled almost 300 matches and nearly 90 goals, for a period alongside two other Newcastle players George Robson and Joe Wilson. Scott played on after World War Two until he was 40 years of age. During a period at home on Tyneside just after war had been declared, Scott appeared for Newcastle on two occasions, against Middlesbrough and Preston during October 1939.

Misc App & Goals: 2 app 1 gl.

SHAW A 1888-1890

Forward
b. unknown

A stand-in forward during season 1888-89, Shaw played for Newcastle East End's reserve line-up but initially received a call up for the friendly contest with Ashington in September 1888. After leaving the Heatonites during the 1889-90 season he teamed up with the Birtley club on the outskirts of Gateshead.

Misc App & Goals: 3 app 1 gl.*

Players: other fixtures

SIMM John Thomas 1881-1883

Forward
b. Seaham Harbour, Co Durham, 1863 (Q4)
d. Newcastle upon Tyne, 1946 (Q2)

Briefly with Stanley FC as they kicked off the association game late in 1881, John Simm played once for the new club as a teenager against Newcastle FA during that opening campaign. At that time he was living at Clifford Street in Byker, working as a "Pattern Maker". Being a reserve with Stanley, he soon joined Newcastle West End, another new organisation, for the 1882-83 season and can claim to have played in each clubs very first season of action. Simm did not stay at St James' Park long either, after playing in the new side's first ever match he switched to Heaton Association during 1883 where he remained for almost four years. He also played for Rosehill and Elswick Rangers. Ten years on from the 1881 census, Simm is recorded as still residing in Byker, employed as a "Post Master".

(Note: Reports have his surname as Simms and Simm, family history information confirms the latter.)

Misc App & Goals: 1 app 0 gls.*

SIMPSON Joseph Pattison Hetherington 1881-1882

Half-back
b. Berwick upon Tweed, 1860 (Q2)
d. Tynemouth, 9 May 1886

Joe Simpson was one of Stanley's cricketers who tried the developing game of football when his club formed Stanley FC during November 1881. Treasurer of the cricket club, Simpson was an enthusiastic figure of the new venture along with Coulson and Finlay. He took part in five of the pioneering games in that first season of 1881-82 before moving the short distance up the Tyne slopes of Byker to join Heaton Association. Joe remained connected with Heaton for nearly four years, although he also turned out for North Eastern in 1882-83 and it is likely he is the same player who also pulled on the colours of Newcastle FA and West End reserves. Joe died as a result of a tragic bathing accident in Tynemouth during May 1886; noted in the press as an "untimely death". Simpson was employed as a railway telegraph clerk as a goods yard.

Misc App & Goals: 5 app 0 gls.*

SMITH 1888

Half-back
b. probably Scotland

Like most developing North Eastern clubs, Newcastle East End began to raid Scotland for footballers during the latter years of the 1880s and Smith was one of several to populate Tyneside. He arrived for the 1888-89 season, noted as being a Rangers player, landing at Chillingham Road with a colleague from Glasgow, J Gilmartin in August 1888. Neither stayed long at the Heaton ground, Smith wearing East End's colours only once, in a benefit match against Elswick Rangers during that August, a 4-0 defeat. Smith appears to have departed soon after.

Misc App & Goals: 1 app 0 gls.*

SMITH Benjamin James 2001-05, 2006

Goalkeeper & Gkp-coach 6'0"
b. Newcastle upon Tyne, 5 September 1986
Career: UNITED jnr 2001, prof July 2003 (Middlesbrough loan 2005-06) to Dec 2005/Leeds Utd trial Dec 2005/ Stockport Co March 2006/UNITED asst-gkp-coach July 2006/Doncaster Rovers player Aug 2006 (Lincoln City loan 2007-08) (Morecambe loan 2009-10)/Shrewsbury Town July 2010/Rochdale Aug 2012/Southport March 2013.

The son of ex-United goalkeeper and coach Simon Smith (qv), Tyneside-born Ben Smith had a similar time at St James' Park as his father. With two quality custodians ahead of him in Given and Harper, and budding 'keeper rivals in Caig and Karelse, Smith had very limited opportunities to break through. He was part of the first-team squad due to goalkeeper absentees for a high-profile visit to play Celtic at Parkhead during August 2004, sitting on the bench for the 2-1 defeat. Despite his lack of progress at Gallowgate, Smith was a brave goalkeeper at reserve and junior status, good at getting down to shots, and he moved on to carve a livelihood in the lower divisions. Making his Football League debut during 2006-07 with Doncaster (29 app), Ben was later with Shrewsbury, being one of their 'keepers as the Shropshire side won promotion from Division Two in 2012. He totalled 43 games for the Shrews. Ben opened a trendy cafe, bar and spa with his wife in the Welsh border town and acted as a sports consultant to law firm Beeston & Shenton.

Misc App & Goals: 0 app 0 gls (1 sub no app).

SNOWBALL Thomas 1899-1900

Left-back 5'9"
b. Broomhill, Northumberland
d. Blyth, 5 July 1955
Career: Broomhill/Shankhouse/UNITED trial April 1899, pmt 1899/Shankhouse 1900/UNITED trial Jan 1900/ Shankhouse July 1902/Ashington May 1904.

Tom Snowball was a well respected local footballer with the prominent Shankhouse club near Cramlington. A miner at Isabella pit, he was at Gallowgate in two spells trying to earn a senior place, the full-back played on three occasions for the Magpies. Firstly, during April 1899 and then again at the end of the year in December after a dispute over his permanent release from Shankhouse which involved the Northern Alliance and Football Association. But with Scott, Davidson and Dave Gardner also competing for the two full-back places, he returned to the south Northumbrians before returning during 1900 for a short period. After his footballing years, Snowball continued to work in the Northumberland coalfield, an underground colliery Deputy during the years leading up to World War One. Tom lived in Blyth.

Misc App & Goals: 3 app 0 gls.

SODERBERG Ole Petter 2008-2012

Goalkeeper 6'4"
b. Norrkoping (Sweden), 20 July 1990
Career: Viking FK (Nor)/BK Hacken (Swd) 2003/UNITED Jan 2008 (Darlington loan 2011-12) (Chesterfield loan 2011-12)(Leicester City trial Feb 2012)/Molde FK (Nor) April 2012 free/Kalmar FF (Swd) Jan 2014.

Capped at school and youth level for Sweden, then with his country's Under-21 side, Ole Soderberg was a tall, strong goalkeeper and good shot-stopper. Settling on Tyneside when 17 years old as 2008 opened, he suffered due to the quality of the 'keepers ahead of him in the St James' Park pecking order, notably Harper, Krul, Elliot as well as Fraser Forster. The blond-haired Swede was called to sit on United's first-team bench on more than 20 occasions, 19 during season 2010-11, but never got onto the field. He joined Molde in Norway during 2012 and has since moved back to Sweden with Kalmar. His elder brother Tom also played in Swedish football and later in Greece.

Misc App & Goals: 0 app 0 gls (22 sub no app).

SPEARS Alan Frederick 1954-1960

Centre-forward 5'8"
b. Amble, 27 December 1938
Career: UNITED jnr May 1954, prof Feb 1956/Millwall June 1960 free/ Lincoln City July 1963 free/Cambrid City Feb 1964.

Former England schoolboy Alan Spea took part in two friendlies for Unit against Scottish opponents, Morton and Partick Thisi during season 1956-57. On the edge of selection Newcastle's Football League line-up, Spears was qu and nimble in attack, but couldn't leapfrog over a lo list of forwards available during the late Sixties, due part to his call-up to National Service when he had serve in Germany and Hong Kong. Moving to the low divisions, Alan appeared at outside-left and played small part in Millwall's Fourth Division title victory 1961-62 then after 32 games for the Lions headed f Lincoln and afterwards for Cambridge City in non-leag football.

Misc App & Goals: 2(1) app 1 gl.

SPEIGHT John 1881-1887

Goalkeeper, Forward & Committee
b. Gateshead, 1866 (Q2)
d. Gateshead

A stalwart for the early Stanley and Newcastle East En teams, John Speight was a reserve player as the club wo formed for season 1881-82, then became a first-tea choice in the seasons which followed with his first outir a friendly against Hamsterley Rangers during Octob 1882. He operated as a forward and as a last line defence, taking part in friendly or local cup matches ov five years. Speight was also in the line-up for the club first competitive fixture during January 1883, Northumberland & Durham Challenge Cup matc against Elswick Leather Works. John won a Challeng Cup winner's medal in 1885 when East End defeate Sleekburn Wanderers and was also a Northumberland Durham Inter-County Challenge Cup finalist. He joine the club's Committee around 1886 and also playe cricket for Woodbine CC of Heaton. When Speight firs appeared for the club he was employed as a "messenge boy" and by 1911 was recorded as working as a "Catt Drover" living at Hawks Yard in Gateshead.

Misc App & Goals: 30 app 2 gls.*

ST JOHN Ian 1965

Centre-forward 5'8"
b. Motherwell, 7 June 1938
Career: Motherwell Bridge Works/ Douglas Water Thistle/Motherwell jnr Aug 1956, prof 1957/Liverpool April 1961 £37,500 (UNITED guest Oct 1965)/Coventry City Sept 1971, becoming asst-manager Dec 1971 to March 1972 (Hellenic (SA) loan Feb 1971)(Cape Town City (SA) loan 1972)/Tranmere Rovers Oct 1972/ Motherwell manager June 1973/Portsmouth manager Sept 1974 to May 1977/Sheffield Wed asst-coach July 1978 to cs 1979.

Once on the verge of joining United in October 195 when boss Charlie Mitten moved for the Scot as he wa banging in the goals for Motherwell (105 in 144 app), Ia St John soon joined Liverpool instead and began rewarding period at Anfield. Although slightly built, a centre-forward the Scot was a razor-sharp and skilled front man who led Liverpool's attack superbly well durin the Sixties as they were rebuilt by Bill Shankly. He wa the ace goalscorer (18 goals in 40 app) during thei Second Division victory of 1962, then was a title winne in 1964 and 1966, and FA Cup victor during 1965 wher he netted the deciding goal. St John also reached the European Cup Winners Cup final with the Reds an gistered over 420 games (118 goals) in a Liverpool shirt ver nine seasons. Nicknamed 'The Saint', he did pull on ewcastle's shirt eventually, as a guest striker in the rian Clough testimonial during October 1965, artnering other noted guests like George Armstrong and ony Hateley in United's forward selection, scoring in a -2 victory. St John appeared for Scotland on 21 ccasions and was also part of the Under-23 (3 app) and cottish League line-ups, while Ian was inducted into cotland's Hall of Fame. On leaving the game after a spell n management, St John entered the media with Radio Merseyside then moved to a high-profile role in 1984 ith ITV's hugely popular Saint & Greavsie Show. He was lso a presenter and pundit covering football for World f Sport during the Eighties. Latterly St John has been n after-dinner speaker and Radio City (Liverpool) roadcaster, as well as a columnist for the Sunday Post. le lives on Merseyside.

Misc App & Goals: 1 app 1 gl.

STEELE Eric Graham 1971-1974

Goalkeeper 5'11"
b. Wallsend, 14 May 1954
Career: Wallsend Rising Sun/Wallsend BC/UNITED jnr Feb 1971, prof July 1972/Peterborough Utd loan Dec 1973, pmt July 1974 £10,000/Brighton Feb 1977 £19,000/ Watford Oct 1979 £100,000 (Cardiff City loan 1982-83)/Derby Co July 1984 free/Southend Utd July 1987 £10,000 (Mansfield Town loan 1987-88)/ Notts Co Oct 1988/Wolverhampton Wand March 1989/ Retired becoming gkp-coach for various clubs, part-time and full-time; Derby Co, Aston Villa, Blackburn Rovers, Barnsley, Wolves, Manchester City, Huddersfield Town & the FA since 2001/Manchester Utd gkp-coach Aug 2008/Shrewsbury Town gkp-coach July 2013/Derby Co gkp-coach Oct 2013.

Eric Steele was a top-ranked schoolboy goalkeeper, capped by England at Under-18 level. He was part of United's junior squad during the early years of the Seventies, on the fringe of Newcastle's line-up but unluckily had the consistent and durable Willie McFaul ahead of him. Steele's opportunities were limited to 11 substitute outings on the bench as cover for McFaul in Texaco Cup and Anglo-Italian Cup matches during 1972-73 and 1973-74. And with Martin Burleigh as second choice, Steele headed south in a bid to find a regular position between the posts. The Wallsend product found that with Peterborough (151 app) and then had spells with a number of clubs, notably Brighton (98 app), Southend (35 app), Watford (65 app) and Derby (53 app). Agile and brave, Eric was part of promotion winning line-ups on no fewer than seven occasions. Concluding his playing career with Wolves, Eric commenced on a long stint as a goalkeeping coach, setting up a goalkeeping school and being attached to several clubs, latterly with Manchester United in a full-time capacity over five years. Before concentrating on coaching, for a period Steele ran a pub-restaurant in Derbyshire.

Misc App & Goals: 0 app 0 gls (11 sub no app).

STEELE John 1941

Inside-left 5'9"
b. Camlachie, Glasgow, 24 November 1916
d. [Barnsley], 23 January 2008
Career: Barony Parish Church/ Lesmahagow 1934/East Fife 1934 (Raith Rovers loan 1935-36)/Ayr Utd 1935 (Raith Rovers loan 1936-37)/ Barnsley June 1938 £2,500 (Aberdeen war-guest) (UNITED war-guest 1940-41)/Resumed with Barnsley, becoming asst-trainer 1951, manager March 1960, then General Manager Sept 1971 to retirement in 1982 (acting as caretaker-manager Nov 1972 to April 1973), becoming Director 1982 to 1984, thereafter Life Vice-President.

Barnsley stars Johnny Steele and John Logan both guested for Newcastle in a wartime fixture against a combined eleven from the RAF and Army during May 1941. Both were grand servants for the Tykes and Steele became a household name at Oakwell, connected with the club for almost 70 years as player, trainer, manager, and director then Vice-President. Having moved south following a successful period in Ayr United's line-up during which time he secured the Scottish Division Two prize in 1937, when 22 years of age during 1938-39, Steele went onto lift the Division Three North title with Barnsley then was unfortunate to see his up-and-coming career shattered by war. A potent schemer and striker, Johnny continued to appear for the Tykes when he worked in the Yorkshire coalfield for a period during wartime football, Steele later serving in Air-Sea Rescue with the RAF in Burma and India. All told claiming 74 goals in 130 matches for Barnsley, he possessed dash on the ball and was renowned for what were described as "surging runs and corkscrew dribbles". As a boss of the Tykes, Steele guided Barnsley to promotion in 1968 and was in charge for a lengthy period of 549 games.

Misc App & Goals: 1 app 0 gls.

STOKOE Graham Lloyd 1991-1992

Midfield 6'0"
b. Newcastle upon Tyne, 17 December 1975
Career: UNITED jnr cs 1991 to 1992/ [Birmingham City]/Stoke City jnr April 1992 free, prof July 1994/Hartlepool Utd loan Feb 1996, pmt Aug 1998 free/Blyth Spartans June 1999 to 2000.

Graham Stokoe was only briefly with United after joining the club as a schoolboy in 1991, this after a chase with Middlesbrough, Manchester United and Aston Villa for his footballing services. Stokoe possessed a bright juvenile record and was part of a United side to face Gateshead during August 1993 in a testimonial match for Derek Bell. He soon moved on, joining the Stoke City youth set up where he graduated through the Potters' ranks to make his senior debut during season 1996-97. A tall and rangy midfielder, Stokoe though managed only two outings but did total 31 matches for Hartlepool United.

Misc App & Goals: 1 app 0 gls.

STOREY A 1887-1889

Forward
b. unknown

Storey was a junior player with Cheviot in 1885, and witnessed his club consumed by the growing Newcastle East End outfit during 1887. Becoming a reserve at the bigger organisation, Storey impressed East End's committee men playing in the Town Moor Temperance Festival during June of 1887 and was given a senior debut the following season. In November 1887 he appeared against Morpeth Harriers, then received another call-up during February 1888 when the strong Middlesbrough eleven were the opposition, the Teessiders winning 6-0. That was however his last appearance at senior level.

(Note: His Christian initial could also be T or W, while it is likely that the player is the same person as a 1891 East End shareholder W Storey who worked as a fireman and lived in Raby Street in Byker.)

Misc App & Goals: 3 app 0 gls.*

STREETE Remi 2009-date

Centre-half 6'2"
b. Aylesbury, 2 November 1994
Remi Streete joined United as a junior in 2009 and turned professional during November 2011. Having a footballing background, being the son of former Cambridge United, Wolves and Derby defender Floyd Streete, who appeared on 425 games during his overall career, he moved from the south to Tyneside as a youngster. Brought up in South Shields and attending school in Boldon, Remi developed well at Gallowgate. Well-built and commanding as a centre-back, Streete quickly made an impression in a Toon shirt being elevated to the senior squad during 2012-13, on the Premier League bench for a visit to face Arsenal and in the reckoning for a debut in the Europa League that season. Streete recovered from a bad ankle injury and played at the back for part of the friendly with Motherwell during July 2013 before continuing to get close to a first-class debut. He also took part in the pre-season friendlies for 2014-15.

Misc App & Goals: 0(5) app 0 gls.

SWINBURNE Trevor 1974

Goalkeeper 6'0"
b. East Rainton, Co Durham, 20 June 1953
Career: East Rainton Jnrs/Sunderland jnr July 1968, prof June 1970 (UNITED guest May 1974)(Sheffield Utd loan 1976-77)/Carlisle Utd May 1977/ Brentford Aug 1983 £12,000/Leeds Utd June 1985 (Doncaster Rovers loan 1985-86)/Lincoln City Feb 1986/Retired May 1987.

From a noted footballing family of goalkeepers, Trevor Swinburne was the son of ex-United star Tom Swinburne (qv) and brother to Alan, who was on Newcastle's books during 1964 and later played for Oldham. An FA Youth Cup winner with Sunderland in 1969, Trevor played a small part in the Black Cats promotion to the top level in 1976 as a deputy to Jimmy Montgomery before moving to Cumbria after only 13 matches at Roker Park. He found a sound home at Brunton Park, totalling 286 games and rarely missing a fixture over six campaigns. He was a popular 'keeper and won promotion from Division Three with Carlisle in 1982. Trevor followed in his father's footsteps by wearing the Magpie jersey during May 1974 in a testimonial for Montgomery at Roker Park, arriving from the bench for the second-half. After leaving the football scene, Swinburne worked as a prison-officer in Leicester.

Misc App & Goals: 0(1) app 0 gls.

SWINBURNE William 1887

Half-back
b. Benwell, Newcastle upon Tyne, 1863 (Q1)
d. [Low Fell, Gateshead, 14 December 1929]
Career: Hawthorn Rovers/South Elswick/Newcastle West End 1886 (EAST END guest Dec 1887)/ Newcastle Pelicans cs 1891.

Billy Swinburne was raised in the Benwell and Elswick district of the city and became a prominent sportsman in Newcastle during the years leading to the turn of the century. A proficient rugby and cricket player, he appeared for Newcastle Rangers, North Durham and Northern (as skipper) at the rugby code, as well as for Northumberland, and for several Tyneside cricket clubs during the summer years; including West End, Gloucester,

Players: other fixtures

Bath Lane, Elswick Ordnance, Clavering and the City of Newcastle. He even also turned his athletic talent to the game of baseball too, then a popular sport in the region, playing for the Pelicans. On the football field, Swinburne also represented Northumberland at County level, captain of the side, at the time being arguably the highest honour local players could attain. Swinburne appeared for Newcastle East End as a guest during December 1887 against Darlington, but was a far more prominent West Ender. Tom lifted the Northumberland Challenge Cup, was captain of the St James' Park club and took part in their first Northern League fixture during 1889, against great rivals East End. It was recorded that he was employed as a model-maker.

Misc App & Goals: 1 app 0 gls.

TAYLOR James 1887

Full-back
b. South Shields, 1863 (Q4)
d. Newcastle upon Tyne, 28 October 1928
Career: Drysdale (Newcastle) c1884/ Newcastle West End Dec 1884 (EAST END guest Dec 1887) to cs 1892/ Rendel.

James Taylor was a prominent player on Tyneside, appearing for Newcastle East End's rivals, Newcastle West End. Taking part in over 100 times for the St James' Park outfit as a dependable full-back, he became a regular in their red-and-black colours for season 1885-86 and remained with the club until their demise in the summer of 1892. At his peak, Taylor was capped by the County while he also represented the Newcastle & District XI. James also lifted the Northumberland Challenge Cup in 1888 with the West Enders. Along with some of his colleagues from the Gallowgate base, Taylor guested for East End against Darlington in a Christmas fixture during December 1887. He was also a regular cricketer in the area, playing for West End, Bath Lane and Newcastle Working Men's Club teams. Taylor was employed as a clerk and resided in Elswick.

Misc App & Goals: 1 app 0 gls.

TELFORD B 1886-1887

Forward
b. unknown

A footballer and cricketer for Newcastle East End in 1886 and 1887, Telford was called up from the reserve ranks for a single outing against Morpeth Harriers during September 1886. He also appeared in whites for the City of Newcastle cricket eleven during the mid-1880s. Telford is likely the same footballer who appeared for St Silas FC.

Misc App & Goals: 1 app 0 gls.*

TERRIER David 1998

Right-back 5'11"
b. Verdun (France), 4 August 1973
Career: Verdun (Fr) jnr/FC Metz (Fr) jnr 1987, prof 1992/West Ham Utd trial June 1997/UNITED Jan 1998 to June 1998 free/OGC Nice (Fr) May 1999/AC Ajaccio (Fr) 2001/US Creteil-Lusitanos (Fr) 2005 to 2007.

With Newcastle United searching far and wide for footballing talent as the 1990s unfolded, versatile defender David Terrier was one of several players from the near-Continent to enrol with the Magpies after more than 130 games for FC Metz. Having faced the likes of Shearer and Asprilla as a defender with Metz against United in the UEFA Cup during 1996, Terrier performed well. Following a deal with West Ham that turned sour following an ankle injury, a period in which he made only a single appearance as substitute, David travelled north

to join the Magpies. Yet the French Under-21 international saw little action wearing a black-and-white senior shirt, limited to a place on United's bench in season 1997-98, against Liverpool during January. With Barton, Watson and Hughes ahead of him in the reckoning, David moved back to France where he added to the League Cup final appearance with Metz by lifting the Second Division title in 2002 as part of Ajaccio's line-up. On retirement Terrier coached locally in Belleville-sur-Meuse near Metz, setting up his own soccer school entitled 'Foot de bonheur'....'Foot of Happiness'. He also opened a retail outlet selling watches and jewellery and was a regional representative of the French equivalent of the PFA.

Misc App & Goals: 0 app 0 gls (1 sub no app).

THOMPSON 1886-1887

Half-back
b. unknown

Thompson was part of the Newcastle East End team which took part in an unusual combined association and rugby code tournament at Shotley Spa in April 1887. He faced Medomsley, but was not a selection again.

Misc App & Goals: 1 app 0 gls.

THOMPSON George Alexander 1911 & 1918

Outside-right 5'6"
b. South Shields, 23 March 1884
d. County Durham
Career: South Shields Bertram 1904/ South Shields Adelaide 1905/North Shields Ath Oct 1906/Sheffield Utd Oct 1906/Derby Co Sept 1908/UNITED briefly cs 1911/South Shields Parkside Aug 1911/South Shields Albion Sept 1912/Crewe Alex June 1914 (UNITED war-guest 1917-18)/Later becoming Luton Town manager Feb 1925 to Oct 1925.

George Thompson was part of a patched up United line-up full of guest players to face a Sunderland eleven in a wartime match at St James' Park during May 1918. With core players still serving in the Great War, United officials turned to any professional in the area, and locally born Thompson was one. A former Derby County outside-right, Thompson had begun his career playing for both South Shields and North Shields when a boiler-maker on Tyneside, joining Sheffield United (42 app) during 1906 after starring as a teenager in the Tyneside League. A busy, darting forward, Thompson was the archetypical small winger. At the Baseball Ground he appeared alongside Steve Bloomer, totalling 55 games for the Rams and was for two seasons a consistent flanker in Second Division action. After the Great War, Thompson became Luton Town's first manager, but his stay at Kenilworth Road only lasted eight months. On leaving football he became an on-course bookmaker.

Misc App & Goals: 1 app 0 gls.

THORNLEY Irvine 1918

Centre-forward 5'9"
b. Hayfield, near Glossop, 1883 (Q4)
d. South Shields, 24 April 1955
Career: Glossop Villa/Glossop St James/Glossop Jan 1902/Manchester City May 1904 £750/South Shields Aug 1912 (Clydebank war-guest 1917-18)(Smith High Docks war-guest 1917-19)(Elswick Works war-guest 1918)(UNITED war-guest 1918-19)/Hamilton Acc May 1919/Houghton Rovers cs 1920.

With players of the calibre of Billy Hogg, Tom Holcroft and Steve Bloomer, United fielded several top ranked names in their friendly fixtures during World War One. Irvine Thornley was another exceptional player, a star with Manchester City and capped by England during

March 1907 as well twice by the Football League. After a period in Glossop's Division Two line-up (82 app, goals), he became instrumental on the field for City, thrustful and lively centre-forward, not big, but sma and fast with a pin-point finish. A touch controversial times, he was once suspended for a year over an illeg payment scandal at Maine Road. Originally a butcher his father's business, Irvine won the Second Division tit in 1910 and totalled an impressive return of 93 goals 204 games for City. With links to South Shields, Thornle joined the non-league club during 1912 and at that lev of football was a sensation. He grabbed over 150 goo in three seasons, merciless when he faced North Easte League defenders and the key factor as Shields won t title in 1913-14 and 1914-15. Thornley guested f Newcastle on a single occasion, against Sunderland in match for war charities during August 1918, forming dangerous attack with fellow guest, Liverpool's Har Chambers. He was one of the Manchester City playe who missed three penalties in one fixture against th Magpies during January 1912, Thornley's in the fin minutes, although from the rebound City grabbed c equalising goal. On retirement after the First World Wc Irvine settled on Tyneside, managing a local theatre fe a period then running a grocer's shop near to the Horsle Hill stadium. His two brothers, Hartley and Jack, als played for Glossop in Football League action. During th Great War, Thornley served with the Royal Field Artiller

Misc App & Goals: 1 app 0 gls.

THORNTON Mark David 1993-1996

Defender 6'0"
b. Newcastle upon Tyne, 17 November 1976
Career: Cramlington Jnrs/UNITED jnr July 1993 to cs 1996 free/Oxford Utd Gateshead 1996.

One of two brothers in United's junic ranks, Mark Thornton reache contention during the pre-season matches of seaso 1995-96, taking part in friendlies against Rushden & Diamonds, Hartlepool and Bishop Auckland. Thornto was released though and like many young United player ended up in non-league football. His brother Stev suffered the same fate, unable to reach the senior elever Mark later joined Northumbria Police.

Misc App & Goals: 1(2) app 0 gls.

TIKVA Shalom 1990

Midfield 5'10"
b. Netanya (Israel), 8 May 1965
Career: Maccabi Netanya (Is) 1982/ Standard Liege (Bel) June 1988 (UNITED trial May 1990)/RC Lens (Fr) July 1991/K Boom (Bel) July 1992/ Maccabi Netanya (Is) July 1993/ Neuchatel Xamax (Switz) July 1994/ Standard Liege (Bel) July 1995/Hapoel Tel Aviv (Is) July 1996 to c2000.

The only footballer of Israeli nationality to play fo. Newcastle, Shalom Tikva appeared on 23 occasions fo. his country and won both the title and domestic cup ir Israel. After a string of impressive displays in Belgium': top league, he was given an opportunity to make ar impact during a trial at the end of the 1989-90 season The midfielder appeared when United took part in c testimonial against Derry City during May 1990 However, United boss Jim Smith did not decide to keep hold of the Israeli midfielder. Tikva spent a productive period with Standard Liege in over 50 games and reache the Belgian Cup final during 1989.

Misc App & Goals: 1 app 0 gls.

TILDESLEY Thomas 1905

Right-back

b. Halesowen, near Birmingham, 1886 (Q3)

Career: UNITED 1905/Later with Selby Utd/Falkirk Sept 1909.

Tom Tildesley was the younger brother of Newcastle's James Tildesley (qv), at the club during the same period. With not only his brother as a rival, but players of the calibre of internationals McCombie and McCracken, it was extremely hard for the youngster to impress. Thomas claimed a single outing, against amateur touring combination, The Corinthians, over the New Year 1905 holiday programme. He played for the Magpies' second-eleven when they lifted the Northern League trophy in 1904-05. Tildesley didn't remain long at St James' Park and later was registered with Falkirk until the close-season of 1913, but didn't appear for the club, or for any other senior outfit. Before moving to Tyneside, he worked in the family fruit and vegetable business, an occupation he returned to by the time of the 1911 census.

Misc App & Goals: 1 app 0 gls.

TROISI James 2005-2008

Midfield 5'10"

b. Adelaide (Australia), 3 July 1988

Career: West Torrens Birkalla (Aus) 1999/Burning Ambition Academy (Aus)/Adelaide City (Aus) 2001/UNITED jnr July 2005, prof Nov 2006 (Roda JC Kerkrade (Neth) loan 2006-07) to May 2008 free/Genclerbirligi SK (Trk) Aug 2008/Kayserispor (Trk) July 2009/Juventus (It) Aug 2012 (Atalanta BC (It) loan 2012-13)(Melbourne Victory (Aus) loan 2013-14).

A young Australian midfielder with an Italian and Greek background, James Troisi arrived on Tyneside in 2005 and quickly caught the eye as a stylish, attacking midfielder who liked to run at defenders at pace. In the club's junior ranks he was coached by Academy boss Glenn Roeder and when the former United skipper was appointed manager, Troisi was one of a handful of Newcastle's kids to quickly climb the ladder. He was fast as well as skilful, did well on the flanks and from deep, but suffered from inconsistency. During season 2006-07 James reached the Premier League substitute's bench for the trip to White Hart Lane to face Spurs, and also sat out four games of the Magpies UEFA Cup campaign. He was again introduced the following season but was not called upon apart from substitute outings in pre-season friendlies during July 2007 then a change in manager signalled his departure from St James' Park. Troisi proceeded to make an impression in Europe, with Turkish clubs Genclerbirligi and Kayserispor. His flair play earned a big move to Juventus where he was loaned out to Serie A side Atlanta to gain experience. Part of Australia's youth and Under-23 team, appearing in the Beijing Olympics during 2008, he also reached the senior squad in 2006 as an 18-year-old then made his debut during March 2008 just before he left United. James was part of his country's World Cup squad for Brazil in 2014 appearing in two games, and by the end of the summer had collected 13 caps.

Misc App & Goals: 1(4) app 0 gls.

URQUHART George 1903-1905

Goalkeeper 6'0"

b. Inverness, c1881

Career: Inverness Thistle/UNITED trial Dec 1903, pmt Jan 1904 £20 to c1905.

Highlander George Urquhart took part in two friendly matches for the Magpies during season 1903-04 after being signed from Inverness Thistle when the club were looking for a replacement for Matt Kingsley. Urquhart twice won the Northern League title with the Black'n'Whites, in 1903-04 and 1904-05, however he wasn't the long term answer to Newcastle's

---

goalkeeping position, the club soon bringing another Scot to Gallowgate, Jimmy Lawrence. George left Tyneside and did not appear in senior football for any other club.

Misc App & Goals: 2 app 0 gls.

URWIN George S 1887-1892

Full-back

b. Newcastle upon Tyne, c1867

A defender who took part in a handful of fixtures for Newcastle East End during 1887-88, George Urwin featured in two visits to Chillingham Road by strong Scottish clubs, Abercorn and Partick Thistle – both to end in defeats with 10 goals conceded. By season 1889-90 he was a reserve back with East End Swifts and remained with the club until 1892. Urwin lived in Byker and was a tailor by trade based on Percy Street.

Misc App & Goals: 4 app 0 gls.*

VEITCH Gerald Kidd 1903-1904

Left-half

b. Newcastle upon Tyne, 1875 (Q2)

d. Hexham, 4 April 1968

Career: Rutherford College (Newcastle)/UNITED Sept 1903 to c1904.

Coming through the ranks of Rutherford College like his younger brother Colin Veitch (qv), the Tyneside half-back was at the centre of a storm when he joined the Magpie staff. The College staff was most unhappy, complaining that United had signed an amateur without going through the proper procedure. Nevertheless, Gerald became a Newcastle player and with the pedigree of his famous relation always had a chance of succeeding. A member of the reserve line-up which secured the Northern League crown in 1903-04, Veitch was selected for a senior match to face The Corinthians at Barrack Road during December 1903, however, Gerald didn't progress at St James' Park and left the scene around 1904. Working as a commercial clerk, during the inter-war years he resided on Bentinck Road and Gerald, like his brother Colin, was long associated with the Newcastle Operatic Society as performer, coach, stage manager and producer. He was also a keen supporter of the Gosforth Presbyterian Musical Society. He later lived in Hexham into his nineties.

Misc App & Goals: 1 app 0 gls.

WAKEFIELD William 1887-1891

Forward

b. Newcastle upon Tyne, 31 December 1866

A Cheviot player in the Byker heartland, William Wakefield became part of the larger Newcastle East End ranks when both clubs decided to combine during September 1887. In season 1890-91 he was playing for the club's reserve side and received a chance with the seniors during February 1888 against Gateshead. Census information shows he started working as a sail-maker then became a cooper.

Misc App & Goals: 2 app 1 gl.*

WALKER 1885

Half-back

b. unknown

When Newcastle East End faced Berwick Rangers in a friendly contest at Chillingham Road during October 1885, the Heaton club found themselves two men short. It was noted that officials found two bystanders from the crowd at late notice to fill the gap, one being Walker (the other Cooper, qv). It is not known if Walker was a known footballer or just an enthusiastic supporter, given a surprise run-out in the East End shirt, a match which ended in a scoreless draw.

Misc App & Goals: 1 app 0 gls.*

WALTON Robert William 1905-1907

Right-back 5'10"

b. Low Law, Co Durham, 1886

Career: Tow Law/Newton/North Shields Ath/UNITED amat July 1905, pmt May 1906/Bradford Park Avenue Oct 1907 £200/Wallsend Park Villa Nov 1911.

Occasionally United's hierarchy selected young fringe players to join the senior party on the club's pre-war tours to the Continent. Local lad, Bob Walton was in the group which travelled at the end of the 1906-07 season to play four matches in Germany. A right-back, he partnered Bill McCracken in three of the tour games; against Mannheim, Freiburg and Karlsruher. After that though, Walton wasn't considered for first-team duty although he operated as a solid defender when the Black'n'Whites lifted North Eastern silverware in 1906-07 and 1907-08. He joined Bradford Park Avenue during that last season, in October 1907 to boost their ranks. He totalled over 30 games and was part of the Yorkshire club's inaugural season in the Football League during 1908-09. On joining the Magpies as a teenager, Walton was living in Burradon and working at the nearby pit.

Misc App & Goals: 3 app 0 gls.

WATSON Thomas H 1881-1882

Half-back

b. Newcastle upon Tyne, 1866 (Q4)

A player to operate in all outfield positions for Newcastle's pioneers; in defence, midfield and in the forward line, Tom Watson was one of the earliest footballers with the club, attached with Stanley as the club kicked off in November and December 1881. The national census in that year recorded Watson as living in Elizabeth Street in Byker, employed as a marine engine-fitter. He only appeared once during the inaugural season, against Burnopfield, but was a regular in the club's second-eleven in a half-back role. During the summer of 1882 Watson made the switch to neighbours Heaton Association where he appeared for two years during which time he was captain. Watson was also a cricketer in the summer months; for Rosewood, Woodbine and Heaton cricket clubs on Tyneside.

Misc App & Goals: 2 app 0 gls.*

WEBSTER Keith 1962-1966

Right-half 5'6"

b. Stockton on Tees, 6 November 1945

Career: Stockton Jnrs/UNITED Dec 1962 £25/Darlington Nov 1966 £2,000 to c1968/Juventus (Aus) 1973/Alexander (Aus) 1975/Box Hill (Aus) asst-coach by 1983.

Nicknamed 'Curly' due to his curled hair; Keith Webster spent nearly four years at Barrack Road and only rarely managed to push his way into the first-team squad. A small, busy and compact half-back, Keith got into the starting line-up for a friendly encounter with Hearts during September 1966. That evening at Gallowgate was a gloomy night for the Magpies as they fell 7-2 to the Scots and Webster didn't get another opportunity. With players such as the experienced Stan Anderson dominating the right flank of midfield, Webster headed to Darlington. After a period at Feethams (10 app), Webster moved to Australia where he enjoyed over a decade in the game around Victoria State.

Misc App & Goals: 1 app 0 gls.

Players: other fixtures

WHARRIER Percy 1905-1907

Goalkeeper 6'2"
b. Longbenton, Newcastle upon Tyne, September 1888
d. Newcastle upon Tyne, 30 August 1966
Career: UNITED amat Nov 1905, trial Jan 1906 to cs 1907/Blyth Spartans 1908-09/Sheffield Wed trial/ Dumbarton Harp 1910/Third Lanark Nov 1912/Renton 1913/Third Lanark 1914 (Vale of Leven loan 1915-16) (Ayr Utd loan 1917-18)/Dumbarton Harp 1919-20/ Dumbarton June 1920/Helensburgh loan 1922-23, pmt Aug 1923.

For a period Percy Wharrier was deputy with Crumley and Rowlandson, then Kelsey and Sinclair, to goalkeeper Jimmy Lawrence at St James' Park. A tall and striking 'keeper, he took part in the regular meeting with amateurs The Corinthians over the Christmas and New Year holiday programme of 1906. Wharrier moved to Scotland after being released by United and found himself reserve to another notable Scottish goalkeeper Third Lanark's Jimmy Brownlie. Over eight seasons at Cathkin Park, Percy did total 25 games for the Glasgow club as he received call-ups to cover for his international rival.

Misc App & Goals: 1 app 0 gls.

WHIGHAM William Murdoch Morrison 1969

Goalkeeper 6'2"
b. Airdrie, 9 October 1939
Career: Shotts Bon Accord June 1959/Albion Rovers/Falkirk July 1960/ Middlesbrough Oct 1966 £10,000 (UNITED guest Nov 1969)/Dumbarton July 1972/Darlington Aug 1974 to 1975.

The second prominent Middlesbrough goalkeeper with Jim Platt to appear in a testimonial fixture for the Black'n'Whites, Willie Whigham made a name as a top shot-stopper with Falkirk as the Sixties began. The Scot had trained as a motor mechanic before concentrating on football then was part of a promotion winning side during 1961. A popular custodian at Brockville Park, Willie appeared on 244 occasions for Falkirk before heading to Teesside. Whigham had his ups and downs at Ayresome Park in 214 games, was at times a quite brilliant last line of defence and brave at diving at forward's feet, although remembered also for a few costly lapses, like most goalkeepers. A promotion winner with Boro, the Scot was also a touch explosive, once suspended after he clashed with ex-United trainer Jimmy Greenhalgh in the Boro dressing-room. For the Len Ashurst testimonial match during November 1969, Willie replaced regular custodian Willie McFaul at Roker Park.

Misc App & Goals: 1 app 0 gls.

WHITE J 1881-1882

Full-back
b. unknown

As Stanley FC started playing the game in November 1881, White appears to have been a guest player for the club. One appearance has been traced, against Newcastle FA 2nd XI during December 1881. The Victorian footballer may have been James White who played for Birtley FC between 1882 and 1887.

Misc App & Goals: 1 app 0 gls.*

WILDE 1942

Outside-left
b. unknown

Newcastle United fielded a line-up including an unknown trialist by the name of Wilde, for a fixture against a Northumberland Army XI during September 1942. Facing a strong services combination, United's somewhat patched up line-up fell 2-0 and Wilde wasn't noted again.

Misc App & Goals: 1 app 0 gls.

WILSON John 1882-1883, 1885-1887

Half-back
b. Newcastle upon Tyne, c1866

An engineering fitters' apprentice from Byker and brother to William Wilson (qv) who also featured for Newcastle East End, John Wilson began playing football in 1882 with Rosewood. He joined the Newcastle East End squad towards the end of that year when his club was amalgamated into the East Enders set-up. He appeared in season 1885-86 and 1886-87 for the senior combination, his debut taking place against Sunderland in February 1886 at the Fulwell Ground. Wilson also played with Jesmond and North Eastern.

Misc App & Goals: 5 app 0 gls.*

WILSON Neil 1985-1987

Forward
b. Bishop Auckland, 4 August 1969
Career: UNITED jnr Oct 1985, prof July 1986 to May 1987 free/Later appeared in North East local football, including for Thornaby 2000/Minor football including Shildon Grey House.

One of a stock of junior products in the mid-Eighties, Neil Wilson was at Gallowgate when the likes of Stephenson, Scott, Tinnion and Bogie came through United's youth development programme. With a good touch of the ball up front, Wilson had a promising beginning as the Player of the Tournament in the respected Northern Ireland Milk Cup of 1985 which has also seen Lee Clark and Keith Gillespie win the award. Although he was called up for a part senior outing in a friendly with Durham City during August 1986, appearing as a substitute, Neil drifted into the local non-league scene where he performed for several years.

Misc App & Goals: 0(1) app 0 gls.

WILSON William 1882-1887

Half-back, Forward & Committee
b. Newcastle upon Tyne, c1863

A teenage player with juniors Cheviot and Rosewood, Billy Wilson became part of the Newcastle East End club when they amalgamated with their Byker neighbours late in 1882. Wilson graduated from the reserve side to become especially prominent during season 1883-84 as the club rapidly developed. The Tynesider was also a Committee member from as early as that season. Leaving the East Enders in 1887, by the time he purchased shares in the newly formed limited company during March 1890, Billy was still an avid supporter and was registered as a "confectioner" residing in Raby Street, later noted in census records as a "baker" by 1911 and residing on Heaton Road. He also played cricket for Drysdale during the summer season. His brother John Wilson (qv) also appeared for East End during the same era.

Misc App & Goals: 20 app 0 gls.*

WINN C 1885

Forward
b. unknown

Taking part in the prestigious Northumberland & Durham Inter-County Play-Off final with Durham champions Darlington during April 1885, Winn may have been a guest player for Newcastle East End. He doesn't appear to have played in any other fixture for the club and possibly could be E Winn who appeared for Newcastle West End as well as Elswick Rangers and Elswick Leather Works between 1884 and 1886.

Misc App & Goals: 1 app 0 gls.*

WINSKILL Neil 1993-96, 1998-06, 2011-date

Full-back & Coach 5'7"
b. Wallsend, 4 February 1978
Career: Wallsend BC/UNITED jnr 1993, prof July 1994 to June 1996/ Newcastle Blue Star July 1996 to May 1998/Whickham 1999 to 2000 when he retired playing/Newcastle upon Tyne City Council football development coach Jan 1997/UNITED Development Officer & asst-coach 1998 to 2006, as well as part-time Northumberland FA coach Jan 2003/West Allotment Celtic coach 2006/Ashington asst-manager 2009 to Sept 2012/UNITED Foundation Development Manager Sept 2011 & asst-coach 2013 to date.

A modern attack-minded full-back in the mould of John Beresford, Tynesider Neil Winskill found the likes of Hottiger, Watson, Elliott and the stylish Beresford a big hurdle to get past as he developed through Newcastle's junior and reserve squads. And when Kevin Keegan controversially disbanded the second-string opportunities became almost non-existent at St James' Park. Neil did pull on United's first-team shirt for a single fixture when several fringe players were given a run-out against Bishop Auckland during August 1995. He inevitably moved to non-league football where Winskill played well enough for local sides Blue Star and Whickham despite an injured knee, before beginning a successful career as a football coach in the North East. Earning UEFA standard coaching badges and a degree in Applied Sports Science, Winskill returned to Newcastle United as part of the Academy and Foundation set-up, as a modern forward-thing coach to age groups from under-10 through to under-15. In 2013 Neil won a FA Elite Coaching Award then was honoured at Buckingham Palace for his contribution to grassroots football as part of the Football Association's 150th celebration.

Misc App & Goals: 1 app 0 gls.

WOOD Samuel Philips 1887

Half-back & Forward 5'10"
b. Greencroft, Co Durham, 1869 (Q1)
d. Morpeth, 20 December 1945
Career: Heaton Ass 1882/Elswick Leather Works 1884/Boundary 1884/ Rendel 1887 (EAST END guest April 1887)/Newcastle West End 1889/ Newcastle Wed 1890/Middlesbrough 1891 to c1893/Also Elswick Ordnance Works.

Sam Wood was a well-known figure in the North East during the Victorian era, especially with the city's western district football clubs. Wood crossed the city divide to turn out for East End as a guest player during April 1887, facing Medomsley in what was called the Shotley Spa Tournament. Living in Elswick then nearby Benwell, Wood was employed as a milling machinist and was once described in the sporting news columns as a "dashing forward with good shooting power". He played for Northumberland at County level and moved to Teesside towards the end of his career, with Middlesbrough in seasons 1891-92 and 1892-93. Wood was also a prominent cricketer in the region for a lengthy period, a wicket-keeper with a number of clubs, notably Boundary where he was also secretary. Sam also appeared for local clubs during the summer into the 1920s; for East End, Rendel, Elswick Ordnance, Stanley & District as well as Morpeth, Hartford Hall, Longhirst and even the County Asylum cricket club. He also represented Northumberland, playing seven matches between 1884 and 1887. Sam's brother, Thomas Wood, also played both sports on Tyneside. Later in life Wood became a school-attendance officer living in Morpeth.

Misc App & Goals: 1 app 0 gls.*

WOODMAN Frederick John 2011-date

Goalkeeper 6'3"
b. Croydon, London, 4 March 1997
Career: Warlingham Colts/Crystal Palace jnr/UNITED jnr Aug 2011, prof March 2014/(Hartlepool Utd loan 2014-15).

Teenage England youth international Freddie Woodman followed his father, United coach Andy Woodman (qv), to become a professional goalkeeper, and is highly regarded in the game as a top prospect. Courted by a string of clubs when a schoolboy in London, Newcastle secured the talented and tall stopper in 2011 as a 14-year-old from Crystal Palace's academy. He experienced a taste of first-team football as part of United's pre-season preparations in 2014-15, on the bench for the friendly against Oldham during July when both Tim Krul and Rob Elliot were unavailable then also on tour to New Zealand. Woodman had just helped England to victory in the European Under-17 Championship in Malta; Freddie saving a penalty against Holland in the deciding shoot-out, man-of-the-match in that final. First capped at Under-16 level, he signed professional forms with United during March 2014 after battling back from a nasty ankle ligament injury. Woodman's god-father is ex-England defender Gareth Southgate, who struck up a close friendship with his father Andy at Crystal Palace.

Misc App & Goals: 0 app 0 gls (3 sub no app).

WRIGHT 1895

Outside-right
b. unknown

With United on trial during April 1895, described as an "amateur from the County of Durham", outside-right Wright had a stunning outing for Newcastle during April 1895. Against Preston North End he grabbed two goals in a 5-3 victory at Gallowgate, but then wasn't heard of again. He came with "very high credentials" and despite his good show no trace can be found of why the Magpies did not sign the forward, while it doesn't appear from Football League registration records Wright appeared for any other senior club.

Misc App & Goals: 1 app 2 gls.

WRIGHT 1904

Right-back
b. unknown

Another trial player for Newcastle by the name of Wright, he appeared against Shaddongate United during April 1904. Operating at full-back against the future Carlisle United at their Millholme Bank pitch, a 4-1 victory, like his earlier namesake, Wright wasn't retained by the Geordies.

Misc App & Goals: 1 app 0 gls.

YOUNG John Bell 1903-1905

Inside-right 5'7"
b. Hurlford, Ayrshire, 2 November 1883
Career: Kilmarnock Shawbank/Hurlford/UNITED trial Jan 1903, pmt June 1903/Kilmarnock July 1905/Bristol Rovers May 1906/Hurlford cs 1906/Norwich City May 1907/Kilmarnock Feb 1908 £50/Hurlford Oct 1908/Crystal Palace Oct 1909/Hurlford Aug 1910 to 1919.

A play-maker in midfield, John Young had stiff competition at Gallowgate during his short period with the Magpies. With United the leading side in the country, the Scot had little hope of moving international Jimmy Howie from the inside berth in Newcastle's line-up. Only once was he selected with senior company, for a friendly at Carlisle against Shaddongate United during April 1904. Young was

part of the successful United reserve side to win the Northern League title in 1904-05. He later managed to carve out a career with several clubs north and south of the border, being described when with Norwich as being "wonderfully quick on his feet" and "one of the prettiest of dribblers". John totalled 26 games for City during their pre-Football League days, and also claimed 15 goals in 38 matches for Kilmarnock. During 1906 Young is noted as a reserve for Scotland's eleven to play Wales.

Misc App & Goals: 1 app 0 gls.

ZIEGLER Marc 1999

Goalkeeper 6'4"
b. Blieskastel, Zwilling (West Germany), 13 June 1976
Career: FC Saarbrucken (Ger)/SV Webenheim (Ger)/VfB Stuttgart (Ger) 1993 (UNITED trial July 1999)(DSC Arminia Bielefeld (Ger) loan 1999-2000)/Bursaspor (Trk) July 2000/FC Tirol (Ast) Jan 2001/FK Austria Wien Jan 2002/Hannover 96 (Ger) June 2003/Austria Vienna June 2004/FC Saarbrucken (Ger) July 2005/DSC Arminia Bielefeld (Ger) July 2006/FC Saarbrucken (Ger) June 2007/Borussia Dortmund (Ger) July 2007/VfB Stuttgart May 2010 to cs 2013.

A German youth and Under-21 player at national level, Marc Ziegler had appeared in the 1998 UEFA Cup Winners Cup final with Stuttgart by the time he arrived in Newcastle's camp on trial during the pre-season of 1999-2000. Manager Ruud Gullit wanted another 'keeper for his squad and the German was one of a handful of Continental-based custodians looked at (along with Lemmens, De Vlieger and Karelse). Marc was given a run-out in warm-up games with Celtic at Parkhead and Stoke City in the Potteries. Gullit decided against signing the big 6'4" goalkeeper, instead moving for John Karelse. Ziegler went onto have a valued career in both Germany and Austria. He was twice a title winner in Austria, during 2001 and 2002 and found success in his native country too, reaching four finals. In a sequence of outstanding defensive play with Tirol, he went unbeaten for all of 1,007 minutes of football.

Misc App & Goals: 2 app 0 gls.

ZOLA-MAKONGO Calvin 2000-2004

Striker 6'3"
b. Kinshasa (Zaire/Congo), 31 December 1984
Career: Walker Central BC/Newcastle College/UNITED jnr cs 2000, prof Jan 2002 (Oldham Ath loan 2003-04)/Tranmere Rovers July 2004 free/Crewe Alex July 2008 £200,000/Burton Albion loan Jan 2011, pmt July 2011/Aberdeen Jan 2013 free/Stevenage June 2014.

Calvin Zola fled the war-torn Congo in 2000 and settled on Tyneside being spotted by United playing for Walker Central and the Newcastle College team. A towering, rangy striker with great skill and the confidence to try every trick in the book to beat a defender, Zola was part of the Magpie junior side which lifted the Premier League Under-17 title in 2002. He was elevated to the first-team squad at the start of the 2003-04 season and took part in the new campaign's preparations with a friendly at Hull City, coming off the bench for Michael Chopra. Calvin had periods when he looked like he was going to be a top player, especially when on loan with Oldham in 2003-04, but the striker failed to progress and the tall African joined Tranmere during the summer of 2004. At Prenton Park, Zola developed, although he had to overcome an immigration investigation and was forced to cease playing for a period until his visa was resolved. Calvin claimed 108 games (18 goals) for the Mersey club before doing well with Crewe in 79 games (24 goals). Zola became a good lower division striker and with Burton Albion netted 34 goals in 96 outings before moving to Pittodrie.

Misc App & Goals: 0(1) app 0 gls.

The following players appeared in "Newcastle United XI" fixtures but did not progress to a higher level. These matches comprised a mix of first-team squad players and fringe reserves.

BARNETT 1926

Right-back
b. unknown

A player who was on United's staff in season 1926-27, Barnett joined the club during August. He appeared in a Newcastle United XI fixture in the following month against York City at Fulfordgate, but didn't remain with the Magpies.

Misc App & Goals: 1 app 0 gls.

BENNETT Ian Michael 1989-1991

Goalkeeper 6'0"
b Worksop, 10 October 1971
After a spell with QPR as a youngster, Ian Bennett signed forms with United in March 1989 yet couldn't break through at St James' Park either. He did manage a fringe match against Durham City during August 1990 before heading south again to join Peterborough United in March 1991. From there Bennett's career started to develop, eventually becoming a noted 'keeper to taste Premier League action with Birmingham City. The Brummies paid £325,000 to take Ian to St Andrew's in December 1993 and they received good service from the tall and slimly built custodian over his 354 games. He won promotion twice with the Blues and was a League Cup finalist in 2001 as well as claiming the Football League Trophy. Bennett also appeared for Dagenham & Redbridge during his early years, then for Coventry City on loan as well as a trio of Yorkshire clubs; Leeds, Sheffield United and Huddersfield Town as his career lengthened into his forties. With the Terriers he achieved promotion success again during 2012 before retiring in the close-season of 2014. During July Bennett was then appointed Academy goalkeeping-coach at the John Smith's Stadium.

Misc App & Goals: 1 app 0 gls.

BEWICK James 1932-1935

Centre-half 5'10"
b. Southwick, Sunderland, 31 December 1906
d. Sunderland, 1979
A former Herrington Swifts product, Jimmy Bewick joined United's reserve squad during March 1932 and spent a couple of seasons at St James' Park before joining Port Vale. In United's line-up to face a Rest of Northumberland County XI during May 1933, he never challenged Davidson or Betton, then Tony Leach for the centre-half role during his stay. Moving to Vale Park in May 1935, he failed to hold down a place, and with Walsall it was a similar story, claiming three senior games at each port of call. He afterwards played non-league football for Yeovil & Petters United and back in the North East for South Shields.

Misc App & Goals: 1 app 0 gls.

Players: other fixtures

BRODIE John 1968

Full-back 5'9"

b. Ashington, 8 September 1947

A guest defender for United in a contest with Whitley Bay during May 1968, John Brodie was an ex-Bay player who had earned a professional contract with Carlisle United, moving to Brunton Park during December 1967. Described as a "ball playing full-back", Brodie represented Northumberland during his teenage days and collected a handful of outings in Cumberland for Carlisle (9 app). John was picked up by Port Vale during January 1971 after a spell with Bradford Park Avenue and became a regular in the Potteries over seven seasons at Third Division level. Despite three times breaking his leg, he totalled 193 games at Vale Park until the last of those mishaps forced his retirement during 1978.

Misc App & Goals: 1 app 0 gls.

BROWN Thomas Frank 1924-1926

Right-back 5'7"

b. [Sunderland, 1906 (Q3)]

Tommy Brown played with minor local clubs East Mount and Rocket Athletic before stepping up to appear for Crook Town in 1923. It was from the Durham club that United saw him perform with gusto and he joined the Newcastle staff during January 1924 for a £125 fee. *Brown faced stiff competition for a first-team place with Hudspeth, Russell and Chandler at Gallowgate and once reached the fringe of senior action when he faced a Wallsend XI during December 1924. After winning the reserve North Eastern League title in 1925-26, he joined Fulham on a free transfer during June and experienced Second Division fare in 13 appearances before switching across London with Charlton. That move did not go well and he headed north to be a regular in York City's last season as a non-league club during 1928-29 (48 app) before joining the Football League. He also took part in a memorable FA Cup qualifying tie against Jarrow during that campaign; three close games eventually settled at St James' Park with a 3-2 victory for York.*

(Note: There has been some difficulty in confirming Brown's place and date of birth with various sources noting Darlington, Prudhoe and Sunderland.)

Misc App & Goals: 1 app 0 gls.

CAIZLEY Kevin 1984-1988

Midfield 5'10"

b. Jarrow, 2 December 1968

First joining the Magpies as a schoolboy in the summer of 1984, Kevin Caizley turned pro during August 1987 and jostled with a group of youngsters trying to claim a midfield place at St James' Park. Described once by Glenn Roeder as a "second David McCreery", he was part of the squad which faced non-leaguers Worksop Town during August 1987 but didn't reach contention again. Released at the end of the 1987-88 season, Caizley had a short period with Darlington (18 app) before playing on the local non-league scene with Blyth Spartans and Hebburn. He moved to North America during the 1990s and became a coach to a number of clubs including Kingwood, Albion Hurricanes and at the Kettle Soccer School. Kevin also began to practise as a chiropractor in the States.*

Misc App & Goals: 1 app 0 gls.

COLE Anthony Richard 1988-1992

Centre-half 6'0"

b. Gateshead, 18 September 1972

Developing through United's junior ranks as the Nineties unfolded, Anth Cole joined United as a kid in June 1988 turning pro during December 1990. He had a most unlucky career, being in line for senior debuts at both Newcastle, and later at Middlesbrough, but missed out due to injury. As an 18-year-old starlet at Gallowgate, boss Jim Smith told him he would mark the dangerous Steve Bull for his United debut against Wolves during November 1990, but in a warm-up match against Barnsley Reserves suffered torn medial ligaments and instead was on the sidelines for a lengthy period. Then after he left United and had made a fresh start with Boro in the summer of 1992, the same happened again, this time breaking his foot three days before a planned league bow against Nottingham Forest. When fit the Gateshead product was an assured defender and he did receive one senior call-up for the Magpies, in a testimonial match for Warren Teasdale against Whitley Bay during May 1991. He didn't get to experience league and cup action in England, but moving to Scotland during 1993, Cole totalled nine matches for St Johnstone and 34 for Berwick. He also turned out for Blyth Spartans and on retirement following persistent injury, he initially worked in a warehouse before entering sales, excelling with the JMF Print Group in Swalwell. He became Sales Director then Managing Director during 2007. Cole kept in touch with the game though, founding and running a local coaching organisation S20 – Soccer 20 Skills as well as coaching Low Fell Juniors and having a period as an assistant at Gateshead.*

Misc App & Goals: 1 app 0 gls.

COMINELLI Lucas Ariel 1999-2000

Midfield 6'1"

b. Buenos Aires (Argentina), 25 December 1976

Beginning his senior career with Spanish club Grenada CF in August 1999, midfielder Lucas Cominelli was one of several overseas players given the opportunity as youngsters to blossom at Gallowgate during the modern era. Few did so, and within a year the Argentine was looking for a new club. Arriving at Gallowgate during October 1999, the tall and well-built South American received one call-up with a side comprising several seniors for a match at Blyth during February 2000. He moved to Carlisle during March 2000 but didn't earn a contract, heading back to Grenada and onto a long list of clubs around Europe and beyond; US Avellino, UD Las Palmas, Pahang (Malaysia), St Pauli, AD Ceuta, AO Ayia Napa, Ethinikos and UD Vecindario as well as several on trial including SK Brann and Fortuna Dusseldorf. Cominelli did make a return to England when he joined Oxford United during January 2005 and totalled 16 games at the Kassam Stadium club. He later became a football agent with players such as Ali Faurlin (QPR) on his books.*

Misc App & Goals: 1 app 0 gls.

CONLON Bryan 1961-1962

Centre-forward 6'1"

b. Shildon, Co Durham 14 January 1943

d. Shildon, Co Durham, October 2000

Bryan Conlon developed as a noted striker in the lower divisions after he left the St James' Park set up as a youngster in June 1962. Having joined the Black'n'Whites during May 1961 from the Shildon Works team which had won the Durham Junior Cup, the tall and bustling centre-forward appeared in junior action with the likes of Suddick, Craig and Moncur at United's Hunter's Moor ground. After graduating to a Newcastle United XI line-up to face Hartlepool United during August 1961, Conlon was part of a cull at Gallowgate in the summer of 1962 when Joe Harvey took over as boss. He moved to South Shields but resurrected his career with Darlington during August 1964 where he was part of the Quakers' Division Four promotion side in 1966. Described as a "craggy centre-forward", after 91 games (35 goals) Millwall paid £17,000 for his services in November 1967 where he totalled another 45 matches (13 goals). Conlon moved on to Norwich City and Blackburn Rovers with limited success and during the Seventies wound down his career with Crewe, Cambridge United and Hartlepool United before having a spell back at Shildon in 1974-75 and 1975-76. He settled in that town where he coached local sides for a period.*

Misc App & Goals: 1 app 0 gls.

DUNBAR Stuart 1980

Midfield

b. Sunderland, 1962 (Q1)

A former Sunderland junior, Stuart Dunbar was a young product who arrived at Barrack Road on a non-contract basis during July 1980 after impressing with United's Northern Alliance and Northern Intermediate line-ups in 1979-80. Only at Gallowgate for a short time, he appeared in the junior side for the first few games of the 1980-81 season and was part of a Newcastle United XI side which faced Consett in August before leaving the scene. After his football career, he ran a successful business in the North East.

Misc App & Goals: 1 app 0 gls.

GALLON John William 1939

Inside-forward 5'8"

b. Burradon, Newcastle upon Tyne 12 February 1914

d. Surrey, 1993 (Q3)

One of the many unfortunate footballers to have their careers disrupted when at their peak, Jack Gallon had just been signed by Swansea Town when war broke out after showing he could be a telling inside-forward with Bradford clubs; City (23 app) and Park Avenue (32 app). Back on Tyneside when contracts were cancelled, Jack guested for the Magpies in a match in October 1939 against a services combination from the 53rd Royal Field Artillery. During the early part of his career Gallon played for Blyth Spartans, Bedlington United and Carlisle United before joining Bradford City in June 1936. After World War Two, he ended his football days with Gateshead during 1945-46 and 1946-47 and totalled 30 games.*

Misc App & Goals: 1 app 0 gls.

GARBUTT Peter 1968

Centre-half 6'1"

b. Corbridge, Northumberland, 28 December 1939

d. 2009

Twice a winner of the FA Amateur Cup with Crook Town, Peter Garbutt also played for the England amateur line-up during his successful non-league career during the early 1960s. He was part of the Crook defence alongside Frank Clark which first lifted the trophy in 1962, then Peter skippered the Millfield club to a second triumph two years later. The centre-back showed enough at amateur and non-league level, as well as in the FA Cup, to prompt Carlisle United to sign Peter during August 1964 and he quickly found more success as part of a good Cumbrian side which lifted the Division

Three title during 1964-65. Garbutt became a regular at Brunton Park after that, facing the Magpies in a famous FA Cup-tie victory at Gallowgate during January 1968, the star of the show as he blotted out Wyn Davies. Registering 151 games for Carlisle, he guested for United, with his Carlisle colleague John Brodie, against Whitley Bay during May 1968.

Misc App & Goals: 1 app 0 gls.

GODSMARK Jonathan 2005-2010

Outside-right 5'6"

b. Guidepost, Northumberland,
3 September 1989

Extremely fast and skilful, nicknamed in local football as the "Guidepost Speed Demon", Jonny Godsmark loved to dribble with the ball at speed on the wing and regularly turned defenders to set up chances from all areas of attack. He joined United's youth set-up from Bedlington Juniors in 2005 and was given a professional contract during July 2008 but couldn't claim a spot in the first-team squad. The closest the diminutive winger came was getting a chance from the bench was in a Newcastle United XI fixture with Hull City during August 2007 while he also sat in the dug-out without appearing in other pre-season games. He left Gallowgate during May 2009 on a loan deal to Hereford United (13 app), but soon returned to the region to appear for Ashington in 2010-11 once he had been released by the Magpies.

Misc App & Goals: 0(1) app 0 gls.

GRIGG Paul 1979-1980

Outside-left

b. Corbridge, Northumberland, 1962 (Q3)

Paul Grigg signed associated schoolboy forms with Newcastle during June 1979. A slightly-built left winger, he took part in two sundry United fixtures, both victories, against Spennymoor United and Consett during August 1980 when he was on a non-contract basis with the Magpies. Showing a traditional style on the wing, Grigg moved into non-league football in the region and appeared notably for Whickham, Gateshead (two spells), Whitley Bay, North Shields and Blyth Spartans during the Eighties. With Gateshead, Paul was part of their Northern Premier League title squad in 1982-83. It was reported he ran an import business in Newcastle for a period.

Misc App & Goals: 2 app 0 gls.

HARBACH Peter Colin 1982-1987

Midfield 5'6"

b. Carlisle, 30 April 1967

Joining the club as a 15-year-old from Trinity School in Carlisle during November 1982, Peter Harbach was a diminutive midfield player who often got forward in attack. In the club's 1985 FA Youth Cup squad, Peter became a professional at Gallowgate after that success and appeared for a Newcastle United XI which visited Scarborough during August 1985 but didn't progress to the first-team squad again. He moved back to Carlisle in May 1987 and signed for the Brunton Park club, making his Football League debut but only remained a season (7 app) before joining Barrow and Workington in non-league football. He afterwards was associated with Carlisle City for a long period as a lively and influential player at that level, still playing for the Cumbrians into his forties. He settled in Carlisle and became an IT consultant, for a time sponsoring City in the Northern Alliance.

Misc App & Goals: 0(1) app 0 gls.

HERBERTSON Brian 1952-1957

Inside-forward 5'8"

b. Bamburgh, Northumberland
4 February 1936

From the historic Northumberland coastal village of Bamburgh, Brian Herbertson was tied to Newcastle as an amateur in June 1952, turning professional the following year during February. He spent over three seasons as a part-time pro, but rarely came into the club's reckoning for a first-team place, appearing once in a testimonial match at Annfield Plain during September 1955 when he played alongside Alan Monkhouse, Bill Curry and, unusually, Frank Brennan in attack. Brian left Gallowgate during the 1956-57 season and later appeared for Blyth Spartans as the Fifties came to a close.

Misc App & Goals: 1 app 0 gls.

HERON Thomas 1987-1992

Midfield 5'9"

b. Wallsend, 31 March 1973

Enrolled in United's School of Excellence and a former pupil at High Farm School, Tommy Heron signed schoolboy forms with the club in September 1987 and stepped up to full professional level during June 1991. Heron played and scored in a 5-2 victory at Durham City during August 1990 but couldn't break into the first-team squad like contemporaries Lee Clark, Alan Thompson and Steve Watson. Heron favoured the left midfield slot and was described as having a "nice touch and elegant, flowing style". He spent the 1992-93 season with Carlisle United, but managed only a single appearance for the Blues before playing non-league football.

Misc App & Goals: 1 app 1 gl.

JONES 1910

Right-half

b. unknown

The Sporting Man newspaper recorded that Jones was a trialist at St James' Park who had travelled north in August 1910 from a Southern League club. He appeared for the Magpies in a match at Annfield Plain during October, however soon after departed. It is possible the player was Joseph Jones who became a United professional a year later in November 1911 and later joined Blackpool.

Misc App & Goals: 1 app 0 gls.

KENDRICK Joseph 2000-2003

Left-back 5'11"

b. Dublin, 26 June 1983

Joining United's junior squad in 2000-01, Joe Kendrick was offered professional terms during July 2002 and reached the Republic's youth and Under-21 line-up. One of several defenders trying to make the grade with the Magpies, the closest the Irishman came to first-team action was a run out from the bench in a United XI fixture with Gateshead during August 2002. Despite his lack of progress with the Black'n'Whites, he was a purposeful defender who possessed strength and mobility. After a trial at Hartlepool, Kendrick made an unusual move to join TSV Munich 1860 during July 2003. But he did not remain long in Bavaria, most unlucky to break his leg on his debut. He had trials with Dunfermline, Torquay, Mansfield Town as well as linking

with Darlington back in the North East where he registered 57 games. Joe appeared for several clubs afterwards; Tamworth, Workington, Drogheda (playing Champions League football), Bray Wanderers as well as Sligo Rovers (reaching the Irish Cup final in 2010) and Mansfield again while Kendrick spent a few months with Azerbaijan club, Neftchi Baku PFK in 2008-09. He joined Blyth Spartans during February 2012 and with good attacking quality and a strong shot, he was a valuable member of the Croft Park team to the summer of 2014 then joined Bedlington Terriers, while Joe also had a spell with Durham City. His great uncle, Joe Kendrick (senior) was a noted footballer for Everton and Ireland in pre-war years.

Misc App & Goals: 0(1) app 0 gls.

KILFORD Brian G 1981-1986

Full-back 5'8"

b. Jarrow, 1 February 1967

Part of Newcastle's FA Youth Cup winning line-up which defeated Watford during 1984-85, Brian Kilford had joined the club as a schoolboy in November 1981. Attending Springfield School in Jarrow, the compactly framed full-back was the proverbial tough-tackling defender however didn't progress sufficiently after that Youth Cup success. Following one outing at Scarborough during August 1985, he departed in the close-season of 1986 into local football with a period at South Shields. Later Kilford became a noted amateur runner in the region.

Misc App & Goals: 1 app 0 gls.

LABONTE Aaron M 2001-2003

Centre-half 5'11"

b. Middlesbrough, 27 November 1983

Attached to United between 2001 and 2003, Aaron Labonte operated at centre-back and after turning professional in August 2002 was used as a substitute for a Newcastle United XI which faced Gateshead during the same month. Released at the end of the 2002-03 season, he spent short periods on trial at Hartlepool United and Sheffield Wednesday before trying his luck in Scotland with Livingston. It was with Dunfermline Athletic though that saw Aaron grab an opportunity and after signing for the Pars in July, he went onto total almost 100 games for the Fife club. Quick and athletic at centre-half, Aaron could also appear at full-back, he took part in both the 2004 Scottish Cup final and 2006 Scottish League Cup final, both defeats at Hampden Park. Labonte moved to Ireland during January 2008 when he linked up with Finn Harps but only remained a year in County Donegal.

Misc App & Goals: 0(1) app 0 gls.

LAMBTON Colin George 1959-1963

Full-back 5'8"

b. Newcastle upon Tyne,
21 February 1942

*With Chester Moor juniors, Colin Lambton caught the eye of United's local scouts and joined the Magpie N's ranks during November 1959, turning professional in February 1960. At full-*back or wing-half, Lambton was a contemporary of several talented teenage backs at Gallowgate then; Colin Clish, David Craig and Frank Clark. Playing one fixture with senior company against Hartlepools United in August 1961, progress of his rivals prompted the club to

Players: other fixtures

release Lambton and he joined Doncaster Rovers during July 1963. He made his Football League bow in Division Four but managed only six games for Rovers before moving back to Tyneside when he joined South Shields the following summer.

Misc App & Goals: 1 app 0 gls.

MARTIN Ian 1997-2000

Goalkeeper 6'0"

b. Ballymoney, Northern Ireland, 22 October 1980

Although born in Ulster, Ian Martin moved with his family to Western Australia when he was a year old. He learnt the goalkeeping trade at John Curtin College then appeared between the posts for Aussie clubs Sorrento and Joondalup in Perth. Ian returned to Northern Ireland as a 15-year-old, being coached by ex-Magpie 'keeper and manager Willie McFaul. Martin had trials at Darlington before he signed for the Magpies as a junior during the summer of 1997. He claimed a place in Northern Ireland's youth side and then reached United's starting line-up for the friendly with Hartlepool during August 1999 but rarely came close to challenging senior 'keepers Given and Harper while Martin also faced competition from Caig, Perez and Peter Keen. He moved to Coleraine following his release during the summer of 2000, then after a spell back in Oz with Adelaide City Force, joined Leigh RMI during August 2003 where he appeared until October 2004.

Misc App & Goals: 1 app 0 gls.

MILLER Mark John 1979-1980

Midfield 5'6"

b. Tynemouth, 22 September 1962

Joining the Black'n'Whites during November 1979 as a teenager, Mark Miller was fast and skilful, something of a tiny-tot at only 5'6" tall. Mark took part in two victories for the Magpies against Spennymoor United and Consett during August 1980, when several youngsters were given run-outs in Newcastle United XI fixtures. He left United during 1980 and briefly appeared for Whitley Bay before moving to Gillingham in October 1981 but soon was back at Hillheads. Belle Vue at Doncaster was his next port of call and Mark had a good season with Donny, claiming 37 games for Rovers, his best return in England as he enjoyed Fourth Division promotion success. He played a small part in Darlington's 1985 promotion as well as heading for a Mediterranean climate on the island of Malta. Miller started a long and rewarding period on the historic island in 1985, firstly as a player with Rabat Ajax, then as coach and manager. Subsequently with Floriana as player-coach, Mark moved into full coaching and managerial roles with Sliema Wanderers, Hibernians and as Valletta boss during May 2012, as well as for a period the island's youth and Under-21 coach. Mark found success too, winning the Maltese title as both a player and manager and tasting European football, including the Champions League.

Misc App & Goals: 2 app 0 gls.

McMAHON David 1997-2001

Striker 6'1"

b. Dublin, 17 January 1981

Brought to Tyneside from Tolka Rovers during the summer of 1997 as a youngster, David McMahon earned a professional contract at Gallowgate in February 1998. The Irishman then impressed for his country in the

European Under-16 championships held in Scotland later in the year. Strong and direct in attack, although perfectly built for a leader's role, he couldn't break through at St James' Park, recording a single outing against Hartlepool during August 1999. David totalled a few appearances for both Darlington and Falkirk as part of loan deals, scoring on his debut for the Bairns, but was given a free transfer in May 2001. Afterwards, David resided on Tyneside for a period, appearing in local football for Durham City, Blyth Spartans, Whitley Bay as well as Bedlington Terriers, Ashington, Newcastle Blue Star and Ryton. The Irishman also had brief spells in Scotland with Peterhead and Queen of the South. He also worked for a company of wine importers.

Misc App & Goals: 1 app 0 gls.

McNALL Keith 1982

Striker 5'10"

b. Gateshead, 8 May 1962

Blond-haired, Keith McNall had a limited window to impress United's boss Arthur Cox when he joined the club on a week-long trial during August 1982. The Crook Town striker had proved a dangerous front man on the local scene and he scored in a 6-0 victory with a close-in header in his one trial appearance against Workington during August 1982. But Keith wasn't retained, perhaps Newcastle being too hasty to send him back to Crook without giving the youngster a longer opportunity. McNall joined Gateshead in 1983 and was watched again by the Magpies as he became a stalwart forward for the other Tynesiders in two spells with a period at Bishop Auckland in between. A tough striker with lots of guts on the field, he appeared on 259 occasions for Gateshead and netted 95 goals, part of the side which lifted the Northern Premier League title during 1985-86. Also with Barrow after playing for Gateshead, McNall ended his playing career with Whitley Bay, Eppleton CW and Dunston Fed. McNall settled in Low Fell and for 31 years was employed in financial services with Northern Rock before becoming a postman. He also started coaching with Low Fell Juniors then Gateshead as Junior Development officer to 2014. As a youngster Keith appeared alongside Chris Waddle for Clarke Chapman Juniors when he started out in 1978.

Misc App & Goals: 1 app 1 gl.

NEWSON William John 1956-1960

Right-back 5'9"

b. Blyth, 27 December 1938

Bill Newson came through United's junior N's ranks during 1956 and signed professional forms with the Geordies in May 1957. With other full-back rivals such as Keith, McKinney and Whitehead, his chances were limited wearing the black-and-white stripes, claiming a single outing in a fringe line-up against North Shields during April 1959. He moved to Ashington on a free transfer during March 1960 and continued to play in local football.

Misc App & Goals: 1 app 0 gls.

NICHOLSON Frederick 1925-1928

Inside-left 5'10"

b. Willington, Co Durham, 19 August 1904

d. Co Durham, 1992

Aged 19 when he joined United as an amateur during November 1925 from Hunswick Villa, Fred Nicholson, like many of the club's players on the periphery of first-team action, had several established seniors ahead of him in the pecking order, in Nicholson's case the dependable and almost ever-present, Tom McDonald. The schemer was

offered a professional contract during January 1926 and faced York City the following September for a friendly encounter, scoring in a 3-2 victory. Part of the Magpies shadow squad which secured the North Eastern League trophy in 1925-26, he soon moved on, joining Durham City during August 1927 initially on loan, then permanently the following summer. Nicholson featured for City in their Football League era, in Division Three North during 1927-28 (9 app).

Misc App & Goals: 1 app 1 gl.

OLSON Daniel M 1985

Outside-left 5'9"

b. Tyneside, 1966

Arriving at St James' Park as a bright trialist from local football, Danny Olson appeared in a wide midfield role for Newcastle's reserve eleven in August 1985 but couldn't secure a professional deal with the Magpies. He returned to the non-league scene and later became a coach in the North East, for a period associated with Monkseaton High School Football Academy where his team lifted the English Schools trophy. For periods he was associated with Sunderland's coaching staff and at Morpeth, North Shields (2003), Cramlington Town, as well as being Alnwick Town manager (2011-12). Danny was then coach at West Auckland Town when he visited Wembley for the 2014 FA Vase final as well as being with Gateshead College. Latterly Olson resided in Whitley Bay.

Misc App & Goals: 1 app 0 gls.

PEAKE Jason William 1992

Midfield 5'11"

b. Coalville, near Leicester, 29 September 1971

Released by Leicester City in the summer of 1992 after a loan spell with Hartlepool United, Magpie boss Kevin Keegan handed Andy Peake a trial period with the Tynesiders. As a young and eager playmaker at Filbert Street, he had been tipped as a new star, however the ex-England school and youth midfielder lost his way with the Foxes after only 10 appearances. Peake had a neat passing game but after an outing against Crook Town for the Magpies during July 1992 wasn't retained and he continued looking for a new club, eventually joining Halifax Town. Peake also turned out for Brighton, Bury, Rochdale and Plymouth before moving into non-league football with Nuneaton Borough during December 2000. In two spells with Rochdale between 1994 and 2000, Andy totalled 208 matches at Division Three level. He later played minor soccer in the Leicester Senior League and became a chiropodist in the East Midlands.

Misc App & Goals: 0(1) app 0 gls.

ROBSON Damon 1995-2003

Midfield 5'7"

b. Chester-le-Street, Co Durham, 19 September 1983

Ex-England Under-17 player Damon Robson was a diminutive footballer, but strong and mobile, always able to switch midfield into attack with powerful runs. Connected to United as a schoolboy since 1995, he became a professional for the 2000-01 season and although he progressed to appear in a United XI match against Gateshead during August 2002 along with a few of his reserve colleagues, Damon was unable to break into the strong first-team pool of midfielders. Robson was released during the summer of 2003 and began a career in local non-league football, notably with Chester-le-Street, Spennymoor United,

Bishop Auckland, Horden and, especially Whitley Bay where he took part in their FA Vase success. He gained three winners' medals with the Seahorses, enjoying glory at Wembley in 2009, 2010 and 2011 when he was skipper. Robson also coached local teams for Gateshead Schools FA and Lumley FC when employed as a teacher on Tyneside.

Misc App & Goals: 0(1) app 0 gls.

SNOWDON Thomas Henry 1908-1911

Outside-right 5'8"
b. Jarrow, 1887 (Q1)
d. South Shields, 13 January 1950
Noted as a "promising find" when he signed for Newcastle United during February 1908, Harry Snowdon had shined for South Shields clubs, Albion, Parkside and Athletic before settling at St James' Park. A popular footballer in that Tyneside town, Snowdon could be classed as one of the touchline fliers; small, tricky and fast. On three occasions he was a member of the Newcastle reserve squad which secured North Eastern League silverware between 1908 and 1911. But at Gallowgate, United already had Rutherford and Duncan on the right flank so after a single outing against Annfield Plain in October 1910, Harry returned to South Shields during the close-season of 1911. His performances at that level though remained terrific and Burnley gave him another go at the Football League. Joining the Turf Moor staff in October 1911 for a £50 fee, this time he did make the big-time, turning out on 15 occasions in the Second Division before once more moving back to Shields, this time with the Albion club in August 1912. Off the football pitch, Snowdon worked in a foundry as an iron-moulder, living in South Shields to his death.

Misc App & Goals: 1 app 0 gls.

TALBOT Paul Michael 1997-2000

Left-back 5'10"
b. Gateshead, 11 August 1979
Tyneside full-back Paul Talbot made two appearances for the Black'n'Whites during season 1999-2000, in loosely termed senior games against Hartlepool United and Blyth Spartans. Reaching the England Under-16 squad, Talbot was a highly rated teenage player with a great left-foot at Chester-le-Street and Hilda Park juniors, targeted by Kenny Dalglish when in charge of Blackburn, then only to find Paul at Gallowgate when the Scot took charge. He had been attached to Newcastle's School of Excellence and became a trainee during July 1997 then a professional in August 1999. But Talbot didn't break through fully at United, and joined York City during March 2000 where he registered six games in Division Three before signing for Gateshead at the end of the season. Paul thereafter appeared for a number of clubs in a career which stretched into 2014; Queen of the South, Burton Albion, Spennymoor, Newcastle Benfield, Durham City as well as Blue Star, Bedlington Terriers, Sunderland RCA, Harrogate Town and South Shields. In two spells with Gateshead he totalled over 150 matches.

Misc App & Goals: 1(1) app 0 gls.

WALTON Gary 1979-1984

Centre-forward 5'11"
b. Coundon, Co Durham, 23 December 1962
d. Coundon, Co Durham, 17 July 2000
Spotted by United's Alan Shoulder playing minor soccer in County Durham with Coundon Three Tuns where he had twice been prominent winning the Durham Challenge Cup, Gary Walton was given a six month trial period during May 1979 with the hope that his powerful centre-forward play at local level could be nurtured by the United coaching staff. Thrustful and dangerous, Walton scored goals galore for the club at junior level and was handed a professional deal in December 1980. Gary continued to stand out as part of Newcastle's second-string, scoring 39 goals in one season for the club and at one stage he was much championed for a place in United's first-team line-up. Walton did pull on Newcastle's senior shirt for a friendly at Ashington during August 1984 but Walton departed soon after and reverted to local football, notably appearing for Coundon Working Men's Club. Nicknamed 'Hoss' by his friends, he settled in his native former mining village of Coundon near Bishop Auckland and worked as a window-cleaner. Tragically Gary was killed at his local village pub during July 2000; murdered after a sustained attack by a young Irish jump-jockey who worked at nearby stables. An annual football tournament pays tribute to Walton; the Gary Walton Memorial Trophy.

Misc App & Goals: 1 app 0 gls.

WHITFIELD Thomas 1956-1960

Half-back 5'7"
b. Fatfield, Co Durham, 1 November 1937
Tommy Whitfield was a part-timer professional with the Magpies, joining the set up during May 1956 after impressing with Shiney Row Boy's Club. A half-back, he rarely got a look in as part of United's substantial playing staff of over 40 professional footballers, although did gain one outing in a friendly at South Shields during April 1957. Whitfield joined the strong Horden Colliery Welfare side in January 1960 on a free transfer.

Misc App & Goals: 1 app 0 gls.

The following Sunderland players appeared in a combined "Newcastle United & Sunderland XI" in Jack Milburn's testimonial fixture during May 1967, as did Magpie coach George Herd (qv).

IRWIN Cecil 1967

Right-back 6'1"
b. Ellington, Northumberland, 8 April 1942
Raised in Ashington, Cec Irwin was a 16-year-old debutant for Sunderland (the youngest at the time) during September 1958 and was capped for England at youth level before he became a regular fixture in the red-and-whites line-up during 1961-62. Totalling 352 matches, he was a tall, imposing full-back with a receding hairline who loved to maraud down the flank to support the attack. Cec was a popular character at Roker Park for a decade winning a Second Division title medal in 1964. Jack Milburn was his favourite when a lad growing up in South East Northumberland and he guested for Newcastle in Milburn's testimonial fixture during May 1967 facing an International XI at St James' Park. Following his long stint with the Black Cats, Irwin became Yeovil boss between

1972 and 1975 then briefly played for Ashington before concentrating on the managerial role at Portland Park. He was in charge of the Colliers on three occasions before bowing out in 2002. Irwin for many years ran a newsagency on Woodhorn Road, living in Ellington village.

Misc App & Goals: 1 app 0 gls.

KINNELL George 1967

Centre-half 5'11"
b. Cowdenbeath, 22 December 1937
Although noted as a centre-back during his later days with Sunderland and when he guested for United in Jack Milburn's testimonial during May 1967, George Kinnell was a versatile footballer. With Aberdeen (164 app) he operated in midfield and even up front, netting almost 50 goals in his career total. Captain of the Dons for a time, George moved to Stoke City for a £27,000 fee during November 1963 and had three good years in the Potteries. At the Victoria Ground he reached the 1964 Football League Cup final during his 111 games. Following a brief sojourn with Oldham, Kinnell ended up at Roker Park in October 1966, joining his celebrated relation, cousin Jim Baxter on Wearside. A move to Middlesbrough followed where George did not find the favour of the Boro support, a target of the boo-boys on occasion. Kinnell headed to Australia in June 1969 where he played for the Juventus club of Melbourne. His brother Andy Kinnell also played in Scotland.

Misc App & Goals: 1 app 0 gls.

MARTIN Neil 1967

Centre-forward 6'0"
b. Tranent, East Lothian, 20 October 1940
Serving his apprenticeship as a mining engineer when with Alloa Athletic, Neil Martin developed as a top-rated striker after learning the game at Recreation Park and then with Queen of the South. A £7,500 deal in July 1963 took him to Hibernian and at Easter Road Neil flourished, initially under the guidance of Jock Stein. He scored plenty of goals for Hibs, 86 in 114 games and earned a call-up to firstly the Scotland Under-23 eleven, then the full national team in May 1965, the first of three caps. Rated highly, he also appeared twice for the Scottish League side. Martin soon attracted suitors and moved to England for a £45,000 fee when he joined a strong Scottish contingent at Roker Park during October 1965. Tall and slim, Martin took knocks manfully and was always a threat, especially in the air. With Sunderland his record of 46 goals in 99 games was first-class and he enjoyed a fine period with Coventry City too (122 app 45 gls). Another good spell with Nottingham Forest was next for the Scot (139 app 34 gls) but then he was discarded by Brian Clough and Martin ended his career with short spells at Brighton, Crystal Palace and St Patrick's Athletic before retiring during 1978. Neil then moved into coaching in Kuwait, followed by a brief period in charge of Walsall, before returning to the Middle East where he spent a decade alongside Dave Mackay. Martin afterwards was a licensee in the Midlands before returning to his native East Lothian.

Misc App & Goals: 1 app 0 gls.

SECTION 3 | Managers

United's dedicated managers since the first appointment, that of Andy Cunningham in 1930. Where managers were also players, biographies can be found in 'Players', Section 1 ref: Cunningham A, Harvey J, Keegan JK, McFaul WS, Roeder GV, Seymour GS, Shearer A (see Introduction for further classification).

They played for & managed United ...

CUNNINGHAM Andrew 1930-1935

SEYMOUR Stan 1939-1947, 1950-54

HARVEY Joe 1962-1975, 1980

McFAUL Willie 1985-1988

KEEGAN Kevin 1992-1997, 2008

ROEDER Glenn 2006-2007

SHEARER Alan 2009

Boss Kevin Keegan watches from the sidelines alongside Scott Sellars and kitman Ray Thompson (left), with assistant Terry McDermott (right).

ALLARDYCE Samuel 2007-2008

Manager
6'2"
b. Dudley, 19 October 1954

Career: Bolton Wand jnr, prof Nov 1971/Sunderland July 1980 £150,000/ Millwall Sept 1981 £95,000/Tampa Bay Rowdies (USA) June 1983/ Coventry City Sept 1983/ Tampa Bay Rowdies (USA) 1984/ Huddersfield Town July 1984/Bolton Wand July 1985 £10,000/Preston North End Aug 1986 free/West Bromwich Albion player-coach June 1989/Limerick manager cs 1990/Preston North End asst-coach Aug 1992, becoming caretaker-manager Sept to Dec 1992, as well as occasional player/ Blackpool manager July 1994 to May 1996/Sunderland Director of Youth Sept 1996/Notts Co manager Jan 1997/Bolton Wand manager Oct 1999/UNITED manager May 2007 to Jan 2008/Blackburn Rovers manager Dec 2008 to Dec 2010/West Ham Utd manager June 2011.

A former powerfully-built centre-back of the tough and no-nonsense school of defending; Sam Allardyce had a decent playing career notably for Bolton where he totalled 244 games. Following a short period at Roker Park with Sunderland as a player (27 app) and coach, he entered management in England at one of his former clubs, Preston North End. Rejoining Bolton during October 1999, 'Big Sam' as he was to be nicknamed in football, guided the unfashionable Trotters to become an established Premier League club, defying the odds season after season. In nine campaigns of relative success, he also took them into Europe and to the Football League Cup final. Allardyce's success revolved around preparation, hard work by all, as well as thorough organisation on and off the field. Sam was rated highly, tipped even as a future England manager. But his style of play on the pitch was sometimes termed dour, yet was highly effective. And that did not go down well with Newcastle supporters when he was appointed boss by Chairman Freddy Shepherd in place of Glenn Roeder during May 2007. Bringing with him an array of backroom staff to embrace modern technology and sports science thinking, from fitness experts to body analysts, as well as a batch of new players, few of which impressed, Allardyce also found that within a month of his arrival the club was in new ownership with his Chairman on his way out of St James' Park. Sam not only had to develop a team on the pitch but also had to impress the incoming owner. He began well, a 3-1 victory at his previous home of the Reebok Stadium in Bolton and his side was comfortably placed in fifth spot. However by December the Magpies had slipped to mid-table and the Toon's entertainment value had plummeted with a series of bleak performances which had both fans and the new regime disgruntled. The manager needed two to three years to rebuild Newcastle United his way, but after a mere 24 matches and less than eight months in charge he was sacked during January 2008. Allardyce had hardly been given the time to imprint a new way for the Magpies. Out of the game for a while, he landed the Blackburn post and afterwards moved to take charge of West Ham United, taking the Hammers to promotion. His son Craig Allardyce appeared notably for Mansfield Town.

In Charge: 24 games
Debut v Bolton Wanderers (a) 11 August 2007

Honours:
FL div 2 champs 1978/FL div 3 champs 1998(m)/FL div 1 prom 2001(m)/FL ch prom 2012(m)/FL div 4 prom 1987/FLC final 2004(m)/PFA ToS (d4) 1987.

ARDILES Osvaldo Cesar 1991-1992

Manager
5'6"
b. Cordoba (Argentina),
3 August 1952

Career: Junior (Arg)/Estrella Roja Cordoba (Arg)/Instituto de Cordoba (Arg) 1971/Atletico Belgrano 1974/ Atletico Huracan (Arg) 1975/ Tottenham Hotspur July 1978 £325,000 (Paris St-Germain (Fr) loan 1982-83)(St George Saints (Aust) 1985)(Blackburn Rovers loan 1987-88)/Queens Park Rangers Aug 1988 free/Fort Lauderdale Strikers (USA) June 1989/Swindon Town July 1989, becoming manager/UNITED manager April 1991 to Feb 1992/West Bromwich Albion manager May 1992/Tottenham Hotspur manager June 1993 to Nov 1994/Chivas-Guadalajara (Mex) manager June 1995 to Oct 1995/Shimizu S-Pulse(Jap) manager June 1996 to Dec 1998/Croatia Zagreb (Cr) manager June 1999 to Oct 1999/Yokahama F-Marinos (Jap) manager Jan 2000 to June 2001/Al-Ittihad SC (Sy) manager Sept 2001 to Nov 2001/Racing Club (Arg) manager July 2002 to May 2003/Tokyo Verdy (Jap) manager June 2003 to July 2005/Beitar Jerusalem (Is) manager May 2006 to Nov 2006/Atletico Huracan (Arg) manager Sept 2007/Cerro Porteno (Pg) manager May 2008 to Aug 2008/Machida Zelvia (Jap) manager Jan 2012 to Nov 2012.

An established star with Argentina, winning the World Cup in 1978, Ossie Ardiles collected over 50 caps for his country and had a marvellous career as a small and slight looking midfielder, but one who combined skill with non-stop work-rate to perfection. Brought to White Hart Lane for a substantial fee by former United coach Keith Burkinshaw, he was a huge favourite with Spurs' fans, totalling 314 senior games and winning FA Cup, League Cup and European honours with the Londoners. The conflict with his country Argentina over the Falklands saw Ardiles move to France, but he returned to England thereafter, soon moving into management. He proved himself as a young boss with Swindon, with a football ethic of playing a possession style game with an attacking flair. And the Robins gained a place in the First Division only for financial irregularities to rob Ardiles of his triumph. Arriving at St James' Park in the customary blaze of publicity, 38-year-old Ossie began the task of getting Newcastle into Division One by discarding Jim Smith's experienced players and bringing in youth, in part due to having no cash to buy new blood. While supporters liked his fresh approach to the game with a passing movement from defence to get forward, Ardiles could never develop a rearguard. Without a solid defence, Newcastle struggled. And without experience in the side they stumbled to the bottom of the Second Division in 1991-92 and Ossie found the Magpies staring England's third-tier of football in the face. United's boardroom had to act and as Sir John Hall took control, Ardiles was sacked after only 10 months in the post with Kevin Keegan brought in to save the club from disaster. The Argentinian proceeded to do a good job at The Hawthorns, but faced similar problems when in charge of Tottenham and did not last long. He then was in charge of several clubs around the world and later opened his own soccer school in the UK retaining a home in Hertfordshire. Taking part in the 1981 Escape to Victory film, Ossie also became an after-dinner speaker and regular television pundit, notably covering Sky's Spanish football coverage. When at St James' Park, Ardiles pulled on United's Toon shirt for non first-class matches with Blyth Spartans and Dunston Fed during 1991-92.

In Charge: 46 games
Debut v Bristol Rovers (h) 1 April 1991

Honours:
53 Arg caps 1975-82/WdC 1978 winner, 1982/2 FL app 1988/FL div 2 prom 1990(m) (annulled), 1993(m)/FAC winner 1981/FAC final 1987/FLC final 1982/UEFAC winner 1984/Eng HoF/FL Legend/PFA ToS (d1) 1979.

CHARLTON John OBE 1984-1985

Manager
6'2"
b. Ashington,
8 May 1935

Career: Ashington YMCA/Ashington Welfare/Leeds Utd amat July 1950, prof May 1952/ Middlesbrough manager May 1973/ Sheffield Wed manager Oct 1977 to May 1983/ Middlesbrough caretaker-manager March 1984 to May 1984/ UNITED manager June 1984 to August 1985/Eire manager Jan 1986 to Dec 1995.

A member of the North East's most famous sporting family, Jack Charlton was recommended to Leeds by his uncle Jim Milburn. Tall, leggy and tough, after working at Linton pit and completing National Service in the Royal Horse Guards, Charlton developed into a formidable centre-half who played at Elland Road for 20 seasons creating a record appearance total of 772 games. He was always capable of scoring goals from set-pieces and Charlton netted almost 100 for the Tykes. Success came to Jack late into his career as part of Don Revie's resurgence at Elland Road. Winning title (and being runners-up on five occasions), League Cup, FA Cup and European honours, he also reached England's side alongside his brother Bobby, winning 35 caps. A member of the immortal 1966 World Cup winning eleven, he was Footballer of the Year in 1967. Jack then entered management where he became a demanding boss with a formidable will to win as he had displayed as a player, taking both Middlesbrough and Sheffield Wednesday to promotion. Manager of the Year in 1974, Charlton had always been a Newcastle United supporter, often tipped as taking over the Magpie hot-seat. That occurred when Arthur Cox departed and 'Big Jack', as he was known, had a short and stormy period in charge of affairs at Gallowgate. An earthy and forthright character, Charlton was never keen to use the transfer market as a manager, and when United's fans clamoured for new blood on the departure of star Chris Waddle, Charlton resisted any use of limited transfer funds. He sensationally quit on the eve of the 1985-86 season after being taunted by the crowd during a pre-season friendly. Yet Charlton had consolidated the Magpies on their return to the First Division, heading the table early into the programme and few knew of the financial problems of the club, which in fact restricted any big name purchases. In addition, his tactical style of play, so successfully employed at Ayresome Park and Hillsborough, was not liked by many of United's support. Charlton spent time working for television, including presenting programmes on his other love of angling, before taking the Republic of Ireland manager's position during 1986. Again he adopted the same tactics on the field and Jack successfully guided the country to both the World Cup and European Championship finals, becoming a hugely admired figure in Ireland, honoured with the Freedom of Dublin. Residing near Newcastle, Charlton remained associated with the game as a media expert and popular after-dinner speaker until retirement and was appointed Deputy Lord Lieutenant for Northumberland for a period. Despite his experience in charge of United, Jack still holds a deep affection for the club he supported as a kid. He once said of the Black'n'Whites: "There's only one club in the world that I'll leap off my seat for if they score." Jack remained equally as popular with Newcastle supporters who hold no grudge against one of their own local heroes.

In Charge: 48 games
Debut v Leicester City (a) 25 August 1984

Honours:
35 Eng caps 1965-70/WdC 1966 winner, 1970, 1990(m), 1994(m)/1 Eng B app 1970/1 FA app 1961/1 unoff Eng app 1969/6 FL app 1965-68/Rest of UK app 1969/FL champs 1969/FL div 2 champs 1964, 1974(m)/FL div 2 prom 1956/FL div 3 prom 1980(m)/FAC winner 1972/FAC final 1965, 1970/FLC winner 1968/ICFC winner 1968, 1971/ICFC final 1967/FoY 1967 (FWA)/MoY 1974 (LMA)/FL Long Service medal 1972/Eng HoF/Freedom of Dublin 1994/OBE 1974.

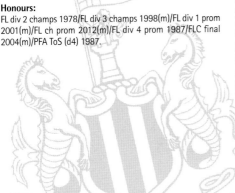

COX Arthur 1980-1984, 1994-1997, 2008

Manager & Assistant-coach
5'7"
b. Southall, Warwickshire, 14 December 1939

Career: Coventry City 1954/Retired due to injury, becoming asst-coach 1958/Walsall asst-coach 1964/ Aston Villa asst-coach 1967, caretaker-manager Nov to Dec 1968/Halifax Town coach 1969/ Preston North End coach cs 1969/Sunderland coach 1973, becoming asst-manager/Galatasaray SK (Trk) coach 1976/Chesterfield manager Oct 1976/UNITED manager Sept 1980/ Derby Co manager June 1984 to Oct 1993/UNITED asst-coach May 1994, becoming Director of Coaching & chief-scout, caretaker-manager Jan 1997/Fulham chief-scout Sept 1997, becoming Director of Football Nov 1999 to Sept 2000 & England asst-coach Feb 1999 to Oct 2000/ Manchester City chief-scout May 2001, becoming asst-manager April 2002 to June 2004 when he retired/ UNITED asst-coach Jan 2008 to Aug 2008.

Arthur Cox's early career in the game was wrecked due to a broken leg when he was only 18 years of age playing for Coventry's 'A' side against Cheltenham. The injury was bad enough to force his retirement without breaking into City's senior eleven. But a door was opened for the youngster to enter coaching at Highfield Road and following a learning period with a number of clubs, Arthur started to become recognised after being assistant to Bob Stokoe as Sunderland lifted the FA Cup in 1973. In charge of Chesterfield, Cox further enhanced his reputation by building a good side in the lower divisions and when United were searching for a new manager to replace Bill McGarry during 1980, Cox was the choice. Not a big name and not flamboyant, Cox was to many a surprise appointment, but his workmanlike, no-nonsense attitude slowly produced the goods at St James' Park. And above all he will be remembered as the manager who brought Kevin Keegan to Gallowgate, arguably one of the club's greatest ever signings. That transfer coup was a master stroke of business. Keegan's influence attracted other players to Cox's squad and United gained promotion to Division One with a style of football that was attractive and entertaining. In the process Arthur also brought into the line-up two more huge Newcastle stars to be, Peter Beardsley and the rapidly developing Chris Waddle. Described by Keegan as possessing "old fashioned virtues", that success should have been the start of a long association for Cox as Newcastle's manager, but just as the promotion celebrations had died down, a week later he sensationally quit after a dispute over contract terms and the direction of the club's strategy. Moving to the Baseball Ground, two divisions lower than United, Arthur spent almost a decade with Derby, steering them from the Third Division to Division One, but also tasting relegation. He departed after being troubled by a back injury, later returning to the game as one of Kevin Keegan's trusted aides at St James' Park, Craven Cottage, Maine Road and with England. He also came out of retirement in Derbyshire and settled back at Gallowgate as one of Keegan's assistants for a short period in 2008.

In Charge: 181 games
Debut v Queens Park Rangers (a) 13 September 1980

Honours:
FL div 2 champs 1987(m)/FL div 2 prom 1984(m)/FL div 3 prom 1986(m).

DALGLISH Kenneth Mathieson MBE 1997-1998

Manager
5'8"
b. Dalmarnock, Glasgow, 4 March 1951

Career: Possilpark BB/Possilpark YMCA 1962/ Glasgow Utd/Drumchapel Amat/Celtic jnr May 1967 (Cumbernauld Utd loan July 1967), prof April 1968/Liverpool Aug 1977 £440,000, becoming player-manager June 1985 to Feb 1991/Blackburn Rovers manager Oct 1991 to June 1995, becoming Director of Football/ Rangers consultant Dec 1996/UNITED manager Jan 1997 to Aug 1998/Celtic consultant May 1999, becoming Technical Director June 1999 to June 2000, caretaker-manager Feb 2000 to June 2000/Liverpool ambassador July 2009, becoming caretaker-manager Jan 2011, manager May 2011 to May 2012/Liverpool director (non-executive) Oct 2013.

If one man in football had the pedigree to replace Kevin Keegan as boss of Newcastle United it was Kenny Dalglish, ironically his replacement at Liverpool as a player 19 years earlier. The Scot possessed a track record to rank with the best, both as a cunning, quite brilliant striker and cautious, shrewd manager with Celtic, Liverpool and latterly Blackburn Rovers, winning domestic and European trophies as well as a century of caps for his country. Yet the substitution as a boss on Tyneside was far less fruitful than as a player in the red shirt of Liverpool. After he made a name for himself in the hoops of Celtic (320 app 167 goals), Dalglish became one of Europe's top strikers on Merseyside, possessing the special ability to both create and score goals, many in a dazzling fashion. He was also determined and unselfish playing up front or in midfield with much skill and flair, netting 172 goals in 515 matches at Anfield. Kenny collected an amazing medal haul as well as becoming Scotland's most honoured international (102 app 30 goals) before moving into a full-time management role with the Reds. With a somewhat dour personality when in the limelight, but always admired by his players, Dalglish was appointed Gallowgate boss as 1997 opened after a period out of football having led Blackburn to a surprise Premier League win in 1995. Then 45 years old, he inherited a marvellous side packed with internationals, including spearhead Alan Shearer from his Ewood Park glory days. Many reckoned with an astute couple of signings added to the squad, especially in defence, Dalglish could fashion Keegan's Entertainers into Dalglish's champions. The Scot started well, guiding the Magpies into runners-up spot in the table by the end of 1996-97 for the second successive campaign, and as a bonus, into the Champions League for the very first time. In the process though the Scot ravaged Keegan's squad, changing personnel with crowd favourites heading out of the door and new men arriving, many not as good as the players to have departed. Newcastle fans, and the club's directorate, soon became increasingly disgruntled. Unlucky to lose Shearer with a lengthy injury, by the time Kenny had led United to the 1998 FA Cup final, the Black'n'Whites' style of football had changed dramatically. Gone were the days of gorgeous total football. The Magpies were much more of a lacklustre outfit, heading the wrong way in the table and were criticised for it. They lost convincingly at Wembley and more disapproval came the manager's way. A bad start to the 1998-99 programme saw Dalglish leave St James' Park following a bitter fall-out after only 20 months in charge. Supporters were exasperated at how the club had fallen from their lofty position challenging the very best. Later Kenny returned to Celtic to become Director of Football. However that appointment was not a success either and he left football during 2000. Following a decade out of the game, a return to Liverpool beckoned in 2011 and after taking the club to two Wembley finals in 2012, as well bringing United's Number 9 Andy Carroll to Anfield for a record fee, he was rather surprisingly dismissed during the summer of 2012, for evidently not doing enough to revitalise an ailing super-club. Over his long career Kenny witnessed at first hand football heartbreak; at both the Heysel and Hillsborough tragedies. His son Paul Dalglish (qv) was in United's squad from 1997 to 1999, while Kenny made a brief appearance for the Magpies as a substitute in a testimonial during 1999.

Misc App & Goals: 0(1) app 0 gls

In Charge: 77 games
Debut v Southampton (a) 18 January 1997

Honours:
102 Scot caps 1972-87/WdC 1974, 1978, 1982/5 Scot u23 app 1972-76/Scot sch-youth app/PL champs 1995(m)/PL runners-up 1997(m)/FL champs 1979, 1980, 1982, 1983, 1984, 1986(pm), 1988(pm), 1990(pm), 1995(m)/FAC winner 1986(pm), 1989(m)/FAC final 1988(m), 1998(m), 2012(m)/FLC winner 1981, 1982, 1983, 1984, 2012(m)/FLC final 1978, 1987(pm)/FL div 2 prom 1992(m)/SL champs 1972, 1973, 1974, 1977/SC winner 1972, 1974, 1975, 1977/SC final 1973/SLC winner 1975, 2000(m)/SLC final 1972, 1973, 1974, 1976, 1977/EC winner 1978, 1981, 1984/EC final 1985/ESC winner 1977/ESC final 1978/ICC final 1981, 1984/PoY (PFA) 1983/FoY (FWA) 1979, 1983/MoY 1986, 1988, 1990, 1995/PFA ToS (d1) 1979, 1980, 1981, 1983, 1984/Eng HoF/Scot HoF/FL Legend/Freeman of Glasgow 1986/MBE 1985.

DINNIS Richard Ramsey 1975-1977

Coach & Manager
5'10"
b. Blackburn, 11 December 1942

Career: Great Harwood/Blackburn Rovers amat 1957 to 1959/Bishop Auckland trial Feb 1961/Burnley asst-coach 1965/ Blackburn Rovers asst-coach 1969, becoming coach 1971, caretaker-manager Dec 1974 to Jan 1975/UNITED coach June 1975, becoming manager Feb 1977 to Nov 1977/Philadelphia Fury (USA) coach 1978/ Blackburn Rovers coach 1979/Vancouver Whitecaps asst-coach 1979 to 1981/Bristol City chief-scout, becoming asst-manager 1982/Middlesbrough asst-coach March 1985/Al-Ittihad (SAr) coach Aug 1985 briefly/Accrington Stanley part-time coach 1992/Barrow manager Dec 1992 to 1993/ Burnley CoE Director 1993 to 1995/Bolton Wanderers CoE asst-director 1995 to 1997.

A former England grammar schoolboy player, Richard Dinnis had a period on the books of Blackburn Rovers as a youngster, but never graduated to first-team football. A school-teacher, dividing his time between geography and PE, Dinnis had a short-lived and turbulent reign as Newcastle's manager. Without the experience of playing the game to any high standard, Dinnis nevertheless developed into a coach who was held in high regard by the players, holding a UEFA coaching badge. Teaming up with Gordon Lee at Ewood Park, the partnership landed on Tyneside during 1975 and started to bond quickly with United's squad. When Lee walked out on the club, Richard was the dressing-room choice as United's new boss and there started a stormy period of power struggle of player against director at Gallowgate. The club's hierarchy wanted to appoint a big name, as did most supporters, but United's footballers backed Dinnis to the point that even strike calls were made. Although inexperienced at that level, as Alan Gowling recorded: "He listened, observed, learned and gained the respect of the players." Newcastle's directors had to back down and offer Richard control, albeit a temporary position. And Dinnis led the club to a lofty place in the First Division and into the UEFA Cup for season 1977-78. At that point Dinnis perhaps should have moved quicker into the transfer market to reinforce his squad, instead more contract wrangling followed, but Richard was still in charge as the Magpies started the new season, yet the opening weeks of that campaign proved to be a disaster. Newcastle were knocked out of the UEFA Cup and had slumped to bottom of the division after 10 defeats in a row. He was sacked after a less than 12 months in the job. Afterwards Dinnis acknowledged that he "wasn't ready to become manager of Newcastle United". He stayed in the game with various coaching appointments including a spell in the States, a coach when Vancouver Whitecaps won the NASL title. Richard returned to teaching at Canon Slade School in Bradshaw near his birthplace. Dinnis resides in Blackburn and for a lengthy period worked with BBC Radio Lancashire covering football.

In Charge: 41 games
Debut v Bristol City (a) 5 February 1977

GULLIT Ruud (Rudi Dil) 1998-1999

Manager
6'3"
b. Jordaan, Amsterdam (Netherlands), 1 September 1962

Career: ASV Meerboys (Neth) 1970/DWS Amsterdam (Neth) Aug 1978/FC Haarlem (Neth) July 1979/Feyenoord (Neth) April 1982 £300,000/ PSV Eindhoven (Neth) July 1985 £400,000/AC Milan (It) March 1987 £5.5m/UC Sampdoria (It) July 1993 free/AC Milan (It) July 1994 free/UC Sampdoria (It) Nov 1994 free/Chelsea June 1995 free, becoming player-manager May 1996 to Feb 1998/UNITED manager Aug 1998 to Aug 1999/ Amsterdam Football School Jan 2000/Netherlands Under-21 manager March 2003/Feyenoord manager cs 2004 to May 2005/LA Galaxy (USA) manager Nov 2007 to Aug 2008/Terek Grozny (Rs) manager Jan 2011 to June 2011.

For a period, Newcastle United went through a spell of appointing high-profile managers to go with the club's big ambition and huge support. And after the likes of Ardiles, Keegan and Dalglish, another celebrity of the world stage landed on Tyneside, Ruud Gullit. A footballing master with notably AC Milan and Holland where he skippered the Netherlands to glory in the 1988 European Championship, Gullit had forged a decent side when boss of Chelsea in his first taste of management before falling out with the Stamford Bridge hierarchy. Tall, multi-lingual and respected, the 36-year-old Gullit faced a big job at St James' Park, to revitalise a super-team that had been ripped apart by his predecessor. United wanted to claim back their Entertainers tag, lost under Dalglish, however the new boss found the task too hot to handle. One of the world's greatest players during his era, Gullit was a past winner of the World and European Footballer of the Year award and lifted trophy after trophy. A midfield player who loved to join the attack, Gullit had few peers during the 1980s and early 1990s. Stylish and cool, he quickly became a noted footballer with Feyenoord and PSV before heading for Italy, joining AC Milan for what was at the time a world record fee. At the San Siro, Ruud was part of a fabulous Milan eleven to twice lift the European Cup. Coping with a string of knee injuries, the Dutch ace ended his playing career in England with Chelsea, becoming boss at Stamford Bridge during 1996. The media dubbed his style of play as 'Sexy Football'; fast and fluid on the pitch. Departing after a contract dispute, Gullit was one of the candidates for the manager's office at St James' Park when United's own brand of Sexy Football in the form of The Entertainers was kicked into touch by Kenny Dalglish. The self-assured and almost arrogant Gullit arrived in a blaze of publicity during August 1998 and immediately watched his new charges steam-rolled 4-1 by Liverpool. The Dutchman needed time and money to remodel the squad and build a new side. He brought in quality in the shape of Ferguson as well as Dyer, and in the process of rebuilding guided the Magpies from a lowly position then to a second successive FA Cup final. Although the Black'n'Whites again fell to a top side at Wembley, it appeared the Geordies were heading in the right direction. But few on the outside quite knew that the relationship between the manager and his top players, and there were many, was not good. That all came to a head as the new season got underway - in a white-hot derby atmosphere against Sunderland on Tyneside during August 1999. Gullit did not get on too well with a core of United's senior men, notably Lee, Dabizas, Barnes, Albert, Pearce and above all Alan Shearer. Newcastle started the Tyne-Wear contest with their £23m strike-force on the bench, Shearer and Ferguson both overlooked. Newcastle lost 2-1 and Gullit resigned after one year and one day in charge of the Geordies. Marrying the niece of Johan Cruyff and always elegant and well spoken, Ruud returned to Holland and later took up various posts on the fringe of the game as well as managerial roles in the Netherlands, USA and Russia without success. He was also often to be seen on UK television as an expert pundit joining BBC's Match of the Day line-up for 2014-15, while it was reported in 2013 that Gullit had relocated to Miami in Florida often coaching youngsters. For a period when a player, he was part of a reggae band called Revelation Time. His father turned out for the Real Sranang club in Holland and for Surinam, while Ruud appeared as a player for United in friendly action against Reading and Stoke during the pre-season of 1999.

Misc App & Goals: 0(2) app 0 gls

In Charge: 51 games
Debut v Aston Villa (a) 9 September 1998

Honours:
66 Neth caps 1982-94/WdC 1990/4 Neth u21 app/Neth sch-youth app/ECh winner 1988/FAC winner 1997(m)/FAC final 1999(m)/Neth Lg champs 1984, 1986, 1987/Neth Cup winner 1984/Neth div 2 champs 1981/It Lg champs 1988, 1992, 1993/It Cup winner 1994/EC winner 1989, 1990/ESC winner 1990/ICC winner 1990/World FoY 1987/Euro FoY 1987/Neth FoY 1984, 1986/PFA ToS (PL) 1996.

HUGHTON Christopher William Gerard 2008-10

Coach & Manager
5'7"
b. Forest Gate, London, 11 December 1958

Career: Tottenham Hotspur amat, part-time prof June 1977, prof June 1979/West Ham Utd loan Nov 1990, pmt Dec 1990 free/Brentford March 1992 free/Retired due to injury cs 1993/ Tottenham Hotspur asst-coach June 1993, becoming coach, caretaker-manager Nov 1997, then asst-manager 2001 (Eire coach & asst-manager Feb 2003 to Oct 2005) to Oct 2007/ UNITED coach Feb 2008, becoming caretaker-manager Sept 2008, and again Feb to Sept 2009, pmt manager Oct 2009 to Dec 2010/Birmingham City manager June 2011/Norwich City manager June 2012 to April 2014.

In almost 550 games at club and international level, Chris Hughton was a first-class left-back, with Spurs (398 app) for 11 seasons making his debut during August 1979. Having completed training as a lift engineer before signing full-time at White Hart Lane, Chris soon became recognised as a bright, attack-minded defender. A regular spot and full international call-up quickly came his way, as did honours, lifting the FA Cup and UEFA Cup with Tottenham. After a short period away from White Hart Lane at the end of his playing career and when knee problems forced him to quit playing, he rejoined the club he started with as a coach in 1993. Of Irish descent, Chris worked with several different managers in North London and learnt much of the football world of management. It was the ideal preparation for his own elevation to a club boss. That education continued when he joined the topsy-turvy world of Newcastle United in 2008, Hughton soon being handed the caretaker-manager role as Allardyce departed and Chris subsequently took the temporary post on two further occasions as the Magpies went through an unsteady period. On relegation from the Premier League in 2009, Chris held the fort during the close-season and was placed in control as Newcastle kicked off the Championship campaign, earning the manager's job for himself, appointed permanently during October 2009. Despite all the gloom of relegation, much player unrest and several high-profile departures, Hughton knuckled down, stabilised the dressing-room and did a remarkable job in making sure the Black'n'Whites returned to the Premier League at the first attempt. With a galvanised camp, United cruised through the campaign and totalled a club record 102 points in the process of lifting silverware. Although Chris had given United a trophy, like many managers elevated from within, his reign did not last long. He was replaced during December 2010, being rather unfortunate as the Magpies had started well on their return to Premier League action, being in a healthy position. But the club wanted a change in direction. Hughton soon found a new appointment, his reputation being high. The Londoner was installed as boss of troubled Birmingham City where he just missed out on a promotion double, then took charge of Norwich City in the Premier League. His elder brother Henry appeared for Orient, Crystal Palace and Brentford, while his son, Cian, started a career on Tottenham's books as well, going onto make his senior debut with Lincoln City.

In Charge: 78 games
Debut v West Bromwich Albion (a) 8 August 2009

Honours:
53 Eire caps 1980-92/WdC 1990 (no app)/FL div 2 prom 1991/FL ch winner 2010(m)/FL div 3 champs 1992/FAC winner 1981, 1982/FAC final 1987/FLC final 1982/UEFAC winner 1984.

KINNEAR (Reddy) Joseph Patrick 2008-09 2013-14

Manager & Director of Football
5'9"
b. Dublin, 27 December 1946

Career: St Albans City Aug 1962/Tottenham Hotspur trial June 1963, amat Aug 1963, prof Feb 1965/Brighton Aug 1975 £40,000/Retired due to injury 1977/Woodford Town player-coach/Nepal national coach 1984/Al-Sharjah SC (UAE) July 1985/Al-Shabab SC (UAE) coach cs 1987/India & Nepal coaching Oct to Nov 1987/Malaysia FA national coach/Doncaster Rovers asst-manager 1987, becoming caretaker-manager March to June 1989/Wimbledon coach Sept 1989, becoming manager Jan 1992 to March 1999/ Oxford Utd Director of Football 2000 to Jan 2001/Luton Town Director of Football 2001, becoming manager Feb 2001 to May 2003/Nottingham Forest manager Feb 2004 to Dec 2004/UNITED manager Sept 2008 to Feb 2009, returning as Director of Football June 2013 to Feb 2014.

Newcastle United were in something of a crisis when Kevin Keegan surprisingly departed for a second time in September 2008. With the new season barely four weeks old, the Black'n'Whites needed an experienced head to steady a wobbling ship until a succession plan could be considered and put in place. United turned to 61-year-old Joe Kinnear, out of the game for almost four years following his departure as boss of Nottingham Forest. Immediately the sometimes brusque and belligerent Kinnear swung into action, in his opening press conference having a running battle with sections of the media famously broadcast to the football world. After that rash and headline beginning, events settled down and Joe, officially an 'Interim Manager', attempted to make sure Newcastle did not slip into a relegation battle. A former Tottenham and Republic of Ireland full-back, he had burst onto the scenes as a teenager in a fine Spurs line-up during the mid-Sixties. Quick and hard-tackling, Kinnear won domestic and European honours at White Hart Lane despite a broken leg and was part of the Republic of Ireland eleven for a decade. Following 265 games for Spurs and a brief period with Brighton, Joe moved into coaching when his playing days were restricted by a cruciate ligament injury. It was at Wimbledon that Kinnear made an impact as a manager, guiding the unfancied Dons to a high league placing until a heart complaint during 1999 forced him to the sidelines. Spells at Luton and Forest followed before needing the battling qualities Joe showed when in charge of the famous Crazy Gang to halt a Newcastle slide. At times controversial and in disagreement with football's authorities, his direct and down-to-earth approach did the trick for a period. Kinnear though still suffered from a recurring heart problem and being the high-profile manager of Newcastle United was perhaps not suited to a person with that condition. Joe took ill prior to a fixture against West Bromwich Albion at the Hawthorns in February 2009. He subsequently had to undergo surgery and his time as Newcastle's boss came to an end after just four months. To the surprise of many, Kinnear returned to Gallowgate during the summer of 2013 on the departure of Derek Llambias, taking control of playing affairs as Director of Football for a short and controversial period, again creating plenty of colourful and negative newspaper headlines. Although born in Dublin, Joe moved to England as a seven-year-old and was raised very much a Londoner, taking his mother's maiden name of Kinnear when she remarried.

In Charge: 22 games
Debut v Blackburn Rovers (h) 27 September 2008

Honours:
26 Eire caps 1967-76/FL div 3 prom 2002(m)/FAC winner 1967/FLC winner 1971, 1973/UEFAC winner 1972/MoY 1994 (LMA).

LEE Gordon Francis 1975-1977

Manager
5'10"
b. Pye Green, Hednesford, 13 July 1934

Career: Girton Road Gasworks/Hednesford Town 1953/Aston Villa Oct 1955 £250/Shrewsbury Town player-coach July 1966/Port Vale manager May 1968/Blackburn Rovers manager Jan 1974/UNITED manager June 1975/Everton manager Feb 1977 to April 1981/Preston North End manager Dec 1981 to Dec 1983/Saudi Arabia coaching 1984/KR Reykjavik (Ice) coach March 1985 to Sept 1987/ Leicester City asst-manager Jan 1988, becoming caretaker-manager Jan 1991 to May 1991.

A resourceful left-back or left-half with Aston Villa, Gordon Lee totalled 142 games for the Midland side over six seasons and appeared in two Football League Cup finals, a victor with the claret-and-blues in the first ever competition during 1961. Tall and angular faced with the twang of the Midlands, Lee took to coaching at Shrewsbury and eventually found his way to Tyneside after guiding both Port Vale and Blackburn to promotion success on limited budgets. Rated the best young manager out of the First Division with a strong-minded and sometimes hard-nosed streak, after a bitter dispute between United and Rovers when he moved to Tyneside, Lee's reign at Gallowgate was tinged with controversy from start to finish. His appointment was the centre of a tug of war between United and Rovers, then he fashioned United into a hardworking, modern combination to the joy of supporters who had for years struggled with an apparent lack of professionalism within the camp. As a manager he could foster and motivate players, yet Lee never found a place for panache and artistry in his team, and disliked the star system. And that brought him into conflict with one of the biggest of that breed, Malcolm Macdonald. In the process a string of famous Lee quotes have been recorded...."I've heard of supermarkets but what's a Supermac?"...."They say he's got flair, for me flares are what a tailor puts on the bottom of trousers"...."They say he's a star, well stars are what you see in the sky"! Although the club reached Wembley in the League Cup during 1975-76 and made a good challenge for both the FA Cup and a European place, there was an undercurrent of feuding within the inner sanctum. Supermac was sensationally sold to Arsenal and soon after Lee sold himself to Everton in mid-season, leaving the club stunned. At Goodison he initially did well taking the Toffees to another League Cup final and third and fourth placing in the table, but then Gordon's regime fell apart and he was dismissed. After that, Lee struggled to land a top job. Perhaps unfairly maligned for his periods in charge of both United and Everton, Lee had undoubted qualities a manager and as time passed, his work was judged in a better light. He latterly has resided in Lytham St Annes.

In Charge: 84 games
Debut v Ipswich Town (a) 16 August 1975

Honours:
FL div 3 champs 1975(m)/FL div 4 champs 1970(m)/FL div 4 prom 1971/FLC winner 1961/FLC final 1963, 1976(m), 1977(m).

LIVINGSTONE Dugald 1954-1956

Manager
5'7"
b. Alexandria, near Dumbarton, 25 February 1898
d. Marlow, Buckinghamshire, 15 January 1981

Career: Parkhead 1915/Ashfield July 1916/Celtic Jan 1917 (Dumbarton Harp war-guest 1917-21)(Clydebank war-guest 1918-19)/Everton April 1921/ Plymouth Argyle Feb 1926/Aberdeen Aug 1927/Tranmere Rovers June 1930/Retired playing 1933/Exeter City trainer 1935/Sheffield Utd trainer June 1936 to Oct 1949/ Sparta Rotterdam (Neth) coach Nov 1949/Eire national coach Aug 1951/Belgium national coach Sept 1953/ UNITED manager Dec 1954/Fulham manager Jan 1956/Chesterfield manager May 1958 to 1962.

As a player, Duggie Livingstone was regarded as a model professional, a cool and calculated full-back who did well at Everton (100 app) and Tranmere (95 app) after starting with Celtic where he totalled 47 games. Switching to coaching at Exeter, Livingstone spent a long period at Bramall Lane with Sheffield United and almost joined rivals Wednesday as boss as 1947 began but at the last moment pulled out of the deal. Livingstone made a name for himself when he was in charge of the Belgian national side for the 1954 World Cup, his side recording a memorable victory over the holders West Germany. Newcastle's directors, not too keen at the time to enter the modern style of appointing a manager, nevertheless had been considering a change from the old way of a Team Committee. Livingstone was appointed just before the club embarked on another FA Cup run which ended at Wembley in 1955. He arrived at St James' Park bristling with modern coaching techniques, and his stay was not a happy one. Attempting to bring in Continental methods, now quite accepted, but then unheard of in the North East, caused many raising of eyebrows. Described as a "school-teacher manager", he tried to coach United's established stars and once famously attempted to tell Bobby Mitchell how to side foot the ball, drawing a chalk-mark on his boot. Jackie Milburn remarked, "Frankly we needed new training like a hole in the head". Yet some players appreciated Livingstone's ideals. With a calm and laid-back style, he was a sound tactician and always tried new ways of undoing opponents. Bob Stokoe noted that Duggie "was first-class and of great benefit". Livingstone disliked director meddling in team affairs and at St James' Park had the formidable Stan Seymour to contend with. United's supremo made sure he had a say in just about everything and Livingstone was even obliged to submit his team selections to the Board for approval. His 1955 FA Cup final line-up was suitably changed by Seymour when it did not contain Milburn. After that success, Livingstone's role was diminished. He was told to look after the juniors and it was no surprise when he moved to Fulham seven months later. Ahead of his time for the many football clubs in England still being run on a pre-war model, especially at Gallowgate, Livingstone can be regarded as a trailblazing boss. On leaving the game, he resided in Marlow alongside the Thames to his death. His brother Alan also had a career in football during the inter-war years, prominently at Merthyr and Mansfield.

In Charge: 58 games
Debut v Sheffield United (a) 1 January 1955

Honours:
WdC 1954(m)/FAC winner 1955(m)/SL champs 1919.

MARTIN George Scott 1947-1950

Manager
5'9"
b. Bothwell, near Hamilton, 14 July 1899
d. Luton, 6 November 1972

Career: Cadzow St Anne's/ Hamilton Acc Aug 1920 (Bo'ness loan 1921-22)(Bathgate loan 1921-22)/Bo'ness Sept 1922/Hull City Oct 1922/Everton March 1928 £1,750/Middlesbrough May 1932 £1,800/Luton Town Aug 1933, becoming asst-trainer 1937, then trainer Aug 1939, manager Dec 1944/UNITED manager May 1947/Aston Villa manager Dec 1950 to Aug 1953/ Luton Town chief-scout 1960, becoming manager Feb 1965 to Nov 1966.

Smart and elegant, George Martin took control of Newcastle to lead a determined push to reclaim the club's First Division status immediately after World War Two. Having done wonders in charge of Luton Town, Martin was United's highest paid boss at the time, earning a salary of £1,250 per year and a £250 bonus for achieving promotion. His early months in charge of a somewhat dissenting dressing-room was difficult and he received wholesale criticism after a succession of player changes, including the sale of record signing and terrace favourite Len Shackleton to Sunderland. Yet Martin had to take control of his playing staff and quickly developed a new side. Promotion was secured the following season, in 1948, and success brought a new crop of heroes to the field; Milburn, Brennan, Mitchell included. An astute boss, Martin though didn't remain long on Tyneside afterwards. Aston Villa lured him south, but again it was a short period in charge and after a spell out of football he returned to Luton Town, a club where he was always held with affection. As a player George was a stylish inside-forward who performed well for Hull City in 218 games before getting a big move to join Everton (86 app). He was part of First and Second Division title sides at Goodison Park, appearing as a forward alongside Dixie Dean. A cunning schemer, he was a sharp-shooter, Martin concluding his playing career with Boro (6 app) and Luton (106 app). Also skilled at bowls, tennis and golf, Martin was an interesting character famed for his sculpting as well as tenor singing and a liking for Italian opera, making broadcasts away from the football scene. At one point during his younger years, George even considered a career on the stage, training in London as a singer before switching to the football field.

In Charge: 154 games
Debut v West Ham United (h) 26 May 1947

Honours:
FL champs 1928 (10 app), 1932 (2 app)/FL div 2 champs 1931/FL div 2 prom 1948(m)/FL div 3(S) champs 1937 (3 app).

MATHER Thomas 1935-1939

Manager
5'7"
b. Chorley, 1888
d. Stoke on Trent, 29 March 1957

Career: Bolton Wand asst-secretary 1910, becoming secretary and later manager cs 1915/Manchester City asst-secretary 1919/Southend Utd manager May 1920 to Jan 1922/Stoke City manager Oct 1923/UNITED manager June 1935 to Oct 1939/Leicester City manager June 1945 to March 1946/Kilmarnock manager June 1947 to March 1948.

A genial personality, Tom Mather built a fine side at Stoke with little or no resources, winning the Third and Second Division titles and introducing Stanley Matthews to senior football. Arriving at St James' Park on a yearly package of £750 in a bid to revive the club's sagging fortunes, he soon attempted to sign Matthews for the Magpies, a deal that fell through, although plenty of other noted players did end up at Gallowgate. Mather was just beginning to forge a successful partnership with new director Stan Seymour when war was declared and he soon moved on. Frequently to be seen with a bowler hat and impeccably dressed, Mather was from the old school of managers, brought up in office administration, yet he knew his football and held much tactical discussion at St James' Park while Tom always gave confidence to youngsters. Albert Stubbins was one such teenager he gave an opportunity to at Gallowgate. Away from football, Mather later worked in the catering industry in the Potteries. During World War One, he served in the navy, narrowly escaping death when a u-boat struck his ship in the Atlantic. Before moving into football full-time, Mather was employed as a clerk in a Bolton tannery works.

In Charge: 179 games
Debut v Bradford Park Avenue (h) 31 August 1935

Honours:
FL div 2 champs 1933(m)/FL div 3 champs 1927(m).

MITTEN Charles 1958-1961

Manager
5'8"
b. Rangoon (Burma), 17 January 1921
d. Stockport, 2 January 2002

Career: Dunblane overs/Strathallan Hawthorn 1935/Manchester Utd amat Aug 1936, prof Jan 1938 (Tranmere Rovers war-guest 1939-41)(Cardiff City war-guest 1941-42) (Southampton war-guest 1943-44) (Chelsea war-guest 1943-45)(Wolverhampton Wand war-guest 1944-45)/Independiente Sante Fe (Col) June 1950 to July 1951/Fulham Jan 1952 £22,000/ Mansfield Town player-manager Feb 1956 £3,500/ UNITED manager June 1958 to Oct 1961/Altrincham manager Nov 1962.

One of the most controversial characters of post-war football, Charlie Mitten was also one of the top wingers of his day. Born on a British army base in Burma where his father served with the Royal Scots, Charlie was raised in Dunblane in Perthshire. At outside-left, he was a strong and forceful player, once selected by Sir Matt Busby in his greatest ever team. Flamboyant and a larger than life character, his Old Trafford career was severed by war, but he still managed to total 220 matches (including wartime) and has a noteworthy return of goals, 80 from the flank. He netted four goals, including a hat-trick of penalties in one game against Aston Villa. Winning an unofficial England cap at the start of the 1946-47 season and a FA Cup medal at Old Trafford as well as being three times title runners-up, Mitten caused headlines when he walked out on Manchester United and moved to Bogota, in the process breaking the maximum wage rule and earning a small fortune. Contravening rules, Mitten was handed a lengthy six-month FA suspension and on his return to Britain appeared for Manchester Sunday League club, The Spinners Arms for a spell. After 160 games for Fulham and 106 for Mansfield Town, Charlie was rated as an up and coming young boss and was soon heading towards St James' Park as an appointment to bring United into a rapidly modernising football world. At 37 years of age Mitten's management started with a bang...a 5-1 home defeat to Blackburn. Yet Charlie was bright, innovative and full of ideas. A tracksuit boss, he was on the training ground and even turned out for the Black'n'Whites in friendly action during 1958-59. His colourful style and sharp wit brought freshness to Gallowgate. Mitten changed many things; from training methods, junior development (his kids winning the FA Youth Cup just after he left) to streamlining the club's kit. Some of the changes were for the better, some controversial, and always he never quite got the backing of a feuding boardroom, split in support of the manager. His mentor William McKeag defending him to the hilt, but others, notably Stan Seymour did not have the same view. And that was never to the good of the team, Mitten once commenting that, "Newcastle was unmanageable because of the boardroom intrigue". He attempted to buy several youthful big names of the future for the Magpies; Denis Law, Ian St John, George Herd, Charlie Cooke and Jimmy Greaves. He did land some good players, Ivor Allchurch included, but had to contend with many problems, not least George Eastham's dramatic stand which ended in the High Court. And by the start of the new Sixties decade, United struggled to avoid the drop from Division One. Mitten could not stop a slide and he was dismissed, interestingly at a time when the powerful McKeag was out of the country. Charlie found it difficult to claim a top job in football after that and he ran the White City greyhound stadium in Manchester for a period, being a dog racing enthusiast, once being said to have moved Len White off the medical table at Gallowgate to allow one of his valuable dogs treatment! He also was a UEFA licensed agent for a while, organising soccer tours around the world. Mitten settled in Stockport, his two brothers played football for Ballymena, his sons, John (qv) was at Newcastle, while Charles (junior) was in United's youth ranks and operated on the Football League circuit too, with Halifax then at non-league Yeovil. His grandson, Paul Mitten, was on Manchester United's books and later with Crewe and Coventry City.

Misc App & Goals: 0(6) app 1 gl

In Charge: 150 games
Debut v Blackburn Rovers (h) 23 August 1958

Honours:
2 Eng unoff app 1947-55/1 Col unoff app 1950/FAC winner 1948/FL(WLg) champs 1942/FL WC(S) final 1944.

McGARRY William Harry 1977-1980

Manager
5'8"
b. Goldenhill, Stoke on Trent, 10 June 1927
d. Pretoria (South Africa), 15 March 2005

Career: Northwood Mission/ Port Vale amat April 1945, prof June 1945/ Huddersfield Town March 1951 £12,000/ Bournemouth player-manager March 1961/Watford manager July 1963/Ipswich Town manager Oct 1964/ Wolverhampton Wand manager Nov 1968 to May 1976/ United Arab Emirates coach 1976/Saudi Arabia national coach June 1976 to Oct 1977/UNITED manager Nov 1977 to Aug 1980/Brighton scout 1980/Power Dynamos (Zam) coach/Zambia national coach 1982 to 1983/South African FA Director of Coaching 1984/Wolverhampton Wand manager Sept 1985 to Nov 1985/Bophuthatswana (SA) coach 1985 to 1989/Botswana coaching 1993.

United needed a tough figure to stabilise the club after the turmoil left in the wake of successive managements of Gordon Lee and Richard Dinnis. That man was former England international wing-half Bill McGarry. Portrayed as a disciplinarian with a rather direct and brusque manner, he joined the Magpies as they were destined for the Second Division and wasn't able to halt the slide. McGarry underwent a massive rebuilding process, falling out with many along the way, discarding those players at the centre of the player-power controversy and bringing in experienced pros from around the country. For one season Bill appeared to have blended a decent team together, spearheaded by his marquee signing, Peter Withe during 1979-80. But after heading the table the Magpies fell away and a promotion chance was lost. As a player, McGarry was robust and aggressive, and revelled in a hard-man tag. He made 381 appearances for Huddersfield over 11 seasons when they were a top side, winning caps for England and reaching the World Cup quarter-final in the 1954 Swiss hosted tournament. During his early days as a manager Bill enjoyed good periods at Portman Road and Molineux, reaching domestic and European finals. McGarry settled in South Africa and neighbouring Botswana and died in the former British protectorate during 2005.

In Charge: 126 games
Debut v Arsenal (h) 19 November 1977

Honours:
4 Eng caps 1954-56/WdC 1954/1 Eng B app 1954/1 FL app 1956/1 FA app 1955/13 FA tour app 1956/FL div 2 champs 1968(m)/FL div 2 prom 1953/FLC winner 1974(m)/UEFAC final 1972(m).

PARDEW Alan Scott 2010-date

Manager
5'11"
b. Wimbledon, London, 18 July 1961

Career: Whyteleafe 1980/Epson & Ewell cs 1981/Morden Nomads/ Corinthian Casuals/Dulwich Hamlet Sept 1984/Yeovil Town Feb 1986 £5,000/ Crystal Palace March 1987 £7,500/Charlton Ath Nov 1991 free (Tottenham Hotspur loan 1995-96)/ Barnet player-coach July 1995/ Reading asst-coach June 1997, then caretaker-manager March 1998/Aston Villa scout 1998/Dulwich Hamlet Sept 1999/Reading caretaker-manager again Sept 1999, becoming manager Oct 1999/ West Ham Utd manager Sept 2003/ Charlton Ath manager Dec 2006 to Nov 2008/Southampton manager July 2009 to Aug 2010/UNITED manager Dec 2010.

When former Charlton, Reading, West Ham United and Southampton manager Alan Pardew was appointed boss to replace Chris Hughton in December 2010 eyebrows were raised by many. Although in the hot-seat for over 10 years, Pardew was not one of the high-profile names the Magpies were used to. Yet, as was to be shown, the Londoner made a relative success of the job as compared to his latter-day predecessors and won over the doubters, and there had been many in the game, media and Toon Army. The club wanted a change in direction following the successful 2009-10 promotion campaign, someone experienced and comfortable, as Pardew is, presenting all things Newcastle United to the media, at the time often quickly to deride the Magpies. As a player Pardew came up through the grass-roots game, becoming a hard-working midfielder of some merit after starting on the non-league scene in Sunday League and with clubs in the south of London, then at Yeovil. Working as a apprentice glazier and cab driver for periods, he was given a chance by Crystal Palace during 1987 and later was an integral part of a successful Selhurst Park eleven which reached the 1990 FA Cup final, netting the goal which took the Eagles to Wembley in a semi-final victory over Liverpool. Alan totalled 168 games for Palace and 124 outings for Charlton, then following a brief spell with Tottenham in which he appeared in the Intertoto Cup during 1995, entered full-time coaching with Reading. A strong character, confident and a man-motivator, when in charge at Upton Park, he returned to the FA Cup final as a boss, and was agonisingly close to victory, losing to Liverpool after a penalty shoot-out in 2006. Pardew also took the Hammers to promotion then a cull saw him move on. He was ousted at Southampton too before heading north to Tyneside. At St James' Park the Londoner enjoyed a wonderful start as boss, defeating Liverpool 3-1, then he consolidated the good work already in place by securing United's Premier League status. Pardew started to fashion his own Magpie side with astute signings under a very different transfer policy as compared to the big-spending past. During 2011-12, his new squad found balance with a cutting edge and their progress was such that the Black'n'Whites had a chance of Champions League qualification, eventually missing out by five points and qualifying for the Europa League instead. United's improvement was eye-catching and the silver-haired Pardew lifted both the Premier League and League Managers Association Manager of the Year award, the first honour won by any United boss at St James' Park. The following season of 2012-13 was a disappointment as was the next campaign, despite a good first half of the programme when United rose to sixth by Christmas. At Hull, later in the season, an emphatic United win was marred by a touchline altercation which led to the Newcastle manager receiving a five-match stadium ban and a further three-match touchline ban, in addition to a heavy fine. That aside, Pardew is an excellent communicator in front of the television cameras, so vital in modern football. Alan gave the Magpies much needed stability after a long period of upheaval.

In Charge: 162 games (to cs 2014)
Debut v Liverpool (h) 11 December 2010

Honours:
FL div 1 prom 2005(m)/FL div 2 prom 2002(m)/FL div 2 prom 1989/FAC final 1990, 2006(m)/FLT winner 2010(m)/MoY 2012 (PL)/MoY 2012 (LMA).

ROBSON Robert William Sir CBE 1999-2004

Manager
5'10"
b. Sacriston, Co Durham, 18 February 1933
d. Urpeth, Co Durham, 31 July 2009

Career: Chester-le-St Jnrs/Langley Park Jnrs 1944/ Middlesbrough jnr 1948/ Southampton trial 1948/ Fulham May 1950/ West Bromwich Albion March 1956 £25,000/ Fulham Aug 1962 £20,000/FA staff coach 1965/Oxford Univ coach & Surrey Football Coaches Ass coach 1965-66/ Vancouver Royals (Can) player-coach May 1967/Fulham manager Jan 1968 to Nov 1968/Chelsea scout Dec 1968/ Ipswich Town manager Jan 1969 & part-time England 'B' manager Jan 1978 to July 1982/England manager July 1982 (effective Sept 1982)/PSV Eindhoven (Neth) manager July 1990/Sporting Clube (Ptg) manager July 1992 to Dec 1993/FC Porto (Ptg) manager Feb 1994 to May 1996/FC Barcelona (Sp) manager July 1996 to July 1997 becoming Technical Director/PSV Eindhoven (Neth) manager July 1998/FA coach July 1999/UNITED manager Sept 1999 to Aug 2004/Eire national consultant Jan 2006 to Nov 2007/ Also Ipswich Town President July 2006.

Bobby Robson was hailed the returning local hero when he was appointed United boss soon after the 1999-2000 season began as a veteran 66-year-old manager, famously of England, and recently at Barcelona. In an age of high profile managers, few were as more respected than Bobby Robson. A fine inside-forward, then wing-half as a player, reaching England recognition during the Fifties, he was an apprentice electrician in the Durham coalfield before he served Fulham (after interest from a long list of clubs, including the Magpies) then West Bromwich Albion with distinction. Robson totalled 370 matches when alongside the Thames, then 257 at the Hawthorns before moving into management back at Craven Cottage during 1968. He became a noted boss with Ipswich, lifting the FA Cup and UEFA Cup, then with England where he led the country to the World Cup quarter-final in 1986 and semi-final during 1990. His standing was such that Bobby continued with a successful career on the Continent, in charge of Porto, Sporting Clube, PSV and at the Camp Nou. From a household of Newcastle United supporters, although he left the region as a teenager, Robson never forgot his roots and was delighted when appointed United manager during September 1999, previously linked with the post in 1975 and 1998. Bobby was immensely proud to manage the side he supported as a lad growing up around Sacriston and Langley Park, once noting: "I bleed black and white just like my dad." He had to quickly repair a broken club. Where Gullit failed, Robson succeeded in getting United back to their previous high status in England and Europe. With immense passion for the game and the Magpies in particular, he had a remarkable start, winning his opening fixture at Gallowgate by all of 8-0 against Sheffield Wednesday. Knighted when in charge at Gallowgate for his long service to football; over 650 matches as a player and over 1,000 as a manager, it took the experienced and wily boss almost three years of hard work to re-model the Geordie super-team. But Robson did so in marvellous style, taking the Black'n'Whites back to the upper reaches of the Premier League and into the Champions League with an attractive line-up full of star quality. He was able to get the best out of his players and handle sometimes difficult characters and United finished in fourth, third and fifth positions as the club became respected again. For five years he guided the Magpies, becoming revered and distinguished, yet, the axe fell on Sir Bobby too. Robson in the end failed to step Newcastle up to the trophy-winning level. Given a bit longer at the helm he may have achieved that, but Bobby was not helped by a brat-pack of millionaire players that at times failed to earn their rich pickings. In the end he paid the penalty with the sack. Robson should have gone out a hero. But that is not football, or Newcastle's way. In August 2004 he was controversially dismissed after a poor start to the new season. History shows that the decision was a disastrous one as the Magpies stumbled through a succession of regimes over the next decade, and out of the Premiership. Remarkably, following his exit from St James'

Managers

Park, Sir Bobby's popularity became even greater, especially on Tyneside. Robson received much backing afterwards and became the game's iconic father figure. Although Robson was later involved in the Republic of Ireland international set-up, the Newcastle post was his last in the game. On several occasions during his life he battled against cancer, sadly in 2009 the Geordie icon died of the disease. Tributes were overwhelming, the sign of his immense standing in football. His name lives on, The Bobby Robson Foundation, a well-known and active charity raising substantial sums. He also earned the CBE, as well as the Freedom of Newcastle, Ipswich and the City of Durham. Statues of Bobby stand at Portman Road and St James' Park, while Sir Bobby Robson Way can be found in Newcastle Great Park and an East Coast train is named after the footballing legend.

In Charge: 255 games
Debut v Chelsea (a) 11 September 1999

Honours:
20 Eng caps 1958-62/WdC 1958, 1962 (no app), 1986(m), 1990(m)/3 unoff Eng app 1960-62/1 Eng B app/1 Eng u23 app 1956/4 FL app 1960-62/14 FA app 1955-62/FAC winner 1978(m)/Neth Lg champs 1991(m), 1992(m)/Ptg Lg champs 1995(m), 1996(m)/Ptg Cup winner 1994(m)/Sp Lg champs 1998(m)/Sp Cup winner 1997(m)/UEFAC winner 1981(m)/ECWC winner 1997(m)/Euro MoY 1997/PFA Merit Award 2003/Eng HoF/NU Hall of/Freeman of Newcastle upon Tyne 2005/Freeman of Ipswich 2008/Freeman of Durham City 2008/Knighthood 2002/CBE 1991.

SMITH James Michael 1988-1991

Manager
5'8"
b. Sheffield,
17 October 1940

Career: New Cross Utd/Oaksfield/Sheffield Utd amat 1956, prof Jan 1959/Aldershot July 1961 free/Halifax Town July 1965 free/Lincoln City March 1968 £500/Boston Utd player-manager June 1969/Colchester Utd player-manager Nov 1972/Blackburn Rovers manager June 1975/ Birmingham City manager March 1978/Oxford Utd manager March 1982/Queens Park Rangers manager June 1985/UNITED manager Dec 1988 to March 1991/Middlesbrough asst-coach March 1991/Portsmouth manager May 1991/ LMA chief-executive Feb 1995/Derby Co manager June 1995 to Oct 2001/ Coventry City advisor 2001, becoming asst-manager Jan 2002 to April 2002/ Portsmouth asst-manager June 2002/Southampton asst-manager Nov 2004 to May 2005/Oxford Utd manager March 2006 to Nov 2007, becoming Director of Football, and caretaker-manager Dec 2008 to Jan 2009.

As a teenager in Sheffield, Jim Smith was good at most sports; cricket, boxing and football. Without reaching lofty heights as a player, totalling over 300 games in the lower leagues notably with Halifax Town (128 app), Jim Smith developed into one of the most highly respected managers on the circuit, one that tasted football throughout the top and lower divisions. A hardworking and enthusiastic wing-half as a player, he guided Colchester, Birmingham and Oxford to promotion, and then steered QPR to a good position in the First Division and to Wembley in the League Cup. Joining United on the departure of Willie McFaul, 48-year-old Smith's wheeling and dealing style of management immediately went into action. Fond of the transfer market, he brought in many faces during his period in charge, Mick Quinn and Roy Aitken included. And the 'Bald Eagle' as he was nicknamed, very nearly succeeded in taking Newcastle back into the First Division, missing promotion in the play-off of 1990. Tough and outspoken at times, but with a cheery Yorkshire character, Smith could explode on occasion and many players talked about his blood and thunder sessions in the dressing-room when things did not go as planned. During his period in office, he found the minefield of politics at St James' Park and the immense pressure to succeed a struggle. With a corporate revolution brewing in the background, Jim resigned, taking up a much more relaxed position at Fratton Park. He later described his time in charge of Newcastle as "two years of heartache". Smith afterwards led Derby County into the Premier League during 1996 and

spent a period working with Harry Redknapp before returning to Oxford United where he had enjoyed much earlier success. Smith belongs to a select group of managers to have registered over 1,000 games as a boss.

In Charge: 121 games
Debut v Wimbledon (h) 10 December 1988

Honours:
FL div 1 prom 1996(m)/FL div 2 champs 1985(m)/FL div 2 prom 1980(m)/FL div 3 champs 1984(m)/FL div 4 prom 1974/FLC final 1986(m).

SMITH Norman 1938-1962

Trainer & Manager
5'8"

b. Newburn, Newcastle upon Tyne, 12 December 1897
d. Newcastle upon Tyne, 18 May 1978

Career: Mickley Ath/Ryton Utd/Mickley Ath/Bolton Wand 1921/Newburn 1921/Huddersfield Town May 1923/Sheffield Wed Dec 1927/Queens Park Rangers Aug 1930/Retired 1932/FC Kreuzlingen (Swtz) player-trainer 1932/FC St Gallen (Swtz) trainer/ UNITED trainer July 1938, becoming manager Nov 1961 to June 1962.

Norman Smith was a highly promising schoolboy player on Tyneside, appearing for Northumberland and reaching England trial matches. During a playing career as a wing-half for Huddersfield on 24 occasions during the Twenties, then with Sheffield Wednesday (23 app) and QPR (27 app), Norman remarkably was involved in seven title chases yet was always classed as a reserve. At Huddersfield Town, the Terriers claimed three trophies and were runners-up twice, then with the Owls, he was in the squad when the Hillsborough club lifted two titles. The Tynesider was Stan Seymour's choice to become his right-hand man at St James' Park when the club was being overhauled from top to bottom just before World War Two. Speaking German fluently, he had a successful spell coaching in Switzerland before settling back in his native Tyneside and immediately after the war, his influence was such that United's side developed into one of the nation's best. However, with a fearsome growl at times, Norman occasionally fell out with players, notably Charlie Wayman. At the very heart of the Magpies for over 20 years, he stepped into the managerial role when 64 years of age on the dismissal of Charlie Mitten, very much as a short term caretaker. That temporary role was concluded when Joe Harvey walked through the St James' Park gates in 1962. Afterwards Norman retired from the game and watched United from the stand, tragically dying suddenly after a visit to Gallowgate, collapsing on his way from the stadium. During his career Smith had trained both the England and Football League sides. United player Duggie Graham was his son-in-law.

In Charge: 25 games
Debut v Stoke City (a) 25 November 1961

Honours:
FL champs 1925 (1 app).

SOUNESS Graeme James 2004-2006

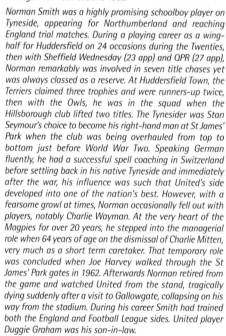

Manager
5'11"

b. Edinburgh, 6 May 1953

Career: Tynecastle BC/Tottenham Hotspur jnr April 1969, prof May 1970 (Montreal Olym (Can) loan cs 1972)/Middlesbrough Jan 1973 £32,500 (Adelaide West (Aus) guest 1977)/Liverpool Jan 1978 £352,000/UC Sampdoria (It) June 1984 £650,000/ Rangers player-manager April 1986 £300,000, becoming manager May 1989/Liverpool manager April 1991 to Jan 1994/Galatasaray SK (Trk) manager June 1995 to May 1996/Southampton manager July 1996/Torino (It) manager June 1997 to Sept 1997/SL Benfica (Ptg) manager Nov 1997 to May 1999/Blackburn Rovers manager March 2000/UNITED manager Sept 2004 to Feb 2006.

Graeme Souness was the third ex-Liverpool superstar to sit in the Newcastle United managerial hot-seat. Like Keegan and Dalglish before him, Souness boasted a huge array of success with Liverpool, and later at Ibrox with Rangers. The former Scotland enforcer had lifted over 20 major trophies, including four European Cups. Souness was a midfielder who more often than not dictated and dominated games with the air of authority, both with exquisite footballing skills and a stamp of robust power. As a young Scot in Edinburgh, Graeme turned down local clubs to head for London but failed to settle and break through at Tottenham (1 app). He then made the grade on Teesside with Middlesbrough (216 app) under the reigns of Jack Charlton. Tough and uncompromising in midfield possessing a power shot and a will to win, Graeme impressed many as he flourished at Ayresome Park. Indeed, the Magpies tried to sign him as a player in 1977, but it was Liverpool who secured his signature as the following year opened. Souness quickly grew in stature, becoming skipper of Scotland as well as at Anfield and totalled 359 games in the red shirt. Moving back north of the border, Souness then proceeded to win more trophies with Rangers, initially as a player but then as boss, transforming the somewhat insular Scottish game into a far more cosmopolitan one. By the time he landed on Tyneside, Souness had been through it all as a manager (including a triple heart bypass operation in 1992), experiencing the ups and downs as boss back at Liverpool, of Southampton, Galatasaray, Torino, Benfica and Blackburn Rovers where he both secured promotion and the Football League Cup in 2002. Arriving at Gallowgate during September 2004 as the 51-year-old successor to Sir Bobby Robson, Graeme found he had a tough job on his hands. Following Robson did not help and he needed to make sure the Magpies kept in touch with the likes of Arsenal, Manchester United and the nouveau riche Chelsea. Souness inherited a vulnerable defence but still had the Shearer ace up front and plenty of talent to blend. Always smart, presentable and eloquent, he got Newcastle out of a slump and took the Magpies close to two cup finals in 2004-05; losing in the semi-final of the FA Cup and quarter-final of the UEFA Cup. Boosted by the substantial outlay of nearly £28m on forwards Michael Owen and Albert Luque for the new season, as well as the arrival of Scott Parker and Emre for another £10m, much was expected from his new squad. Yet that huge expenditure did not bring reward, Graeme later noting never wanted Luque, prompting suspicion of Boardroom interference. United's play was mediocre on the field while he also had to cope with a long list of injuries as well as running feuds with top players Craig Bellamy and Laurent Robert which did not help. Souness was sacked after a little over 16 months in charge during February 2006. He left Tyneside noting the United position was "the most difficult job I ever head". Graeme didn't return to football management and always able to communicate well, the Scot became a regular television pundit and summariser with Sky. When at Anfield and at the peak of his playing days, Souness made a cameo appearance in the cult television drama Boys from the Blackstuff, while as boss at The Dell he was the subject of an infamous hoax, bringing on Ali Dia as a substitute, supposedly a Senegalese player, but a business studies student at Newcastle University.

In Charge: 83 games
Debut v Hapoel BS (h) 16 September 2004 (UEFAC)

Honours:
54 Scot caps 1974-86/WdC 1978, 1982, 1986/2 Scot u23 app 1974-76/Scot sch-youth app/FL champs 1979, 1980, 1982, 1983, 1984/FL div 1 prom 2001(m)/FL div 2 champs 1974/FAC winner 1992(m)/FLC winner 1981, 1982, 1983, 1984, 2002(m)/FAYC winner 1970/SL champs 1987(pm), 1989(pm), 1990(pm), 1991(m)/SC final 1989(pm)/SLC winner 1987(m), 1988(m), 1989(m), 1991(m)/SLC final 1990(m)/It Cup winner 1985/Trk Cup winner 1996(m)/EC winner 1978, 1981, 1984/ESC final 1978/ICC final 1981/Scot MoY 1989/PFA ToS (div 1) 1981, 1982, 1983, 1984/Eng HoF/Scot HoF/FL Legend.

Individuals appointed to support either the Manager or Board of Directors in terms of playing affairs: Assistant Manager & Director of Football, Trainers & Coaches; first-eleven, reserve team, Academy leaders as well as senior coaches to the youth team. Additionally, senior physiotherapists are included (see Introduction for further classification). Honours noted at the end of each biography are those achieved as a player or manager only.

Biographies of the majority of the club's Support Staff who were also United players are included in 'Players', Sections 1 or 2. There are exceptions, individuals who appeared in friendly action for the club but who were predominantly linked to the Magpies as a coach ref: Bayles W, Carver JW, Galvin A, Herd G, Irvine JA, Morris P, Pickering J, Sadler A, Smith STG, Tunks R, Wright D. Support staff who also became United managers are included under 'Managers', Section 3.

Keeping players in the peak of condition was rather different over a century ago;
Jimmy McPherson puts Jack Carr through his paces in a St James' Park training room around 1908.

Support Staff

BARRON Paul George 2007-2010

Goalkeeper-coach
6'2"
b. Woolwich, London,
16 September 1953

Career: Welling Utd 1971/ Wycombe Wand 1973/Slough Town Aug 1975/Plymouth Argyle July 1976/Arsenal July 1978 £70,000/Crystal Palace Aug 1980 £300,000 player-exch/West Bromwich Albion Dec 1982 £60,000 (Stoke City loan 1984-85)/Queens Park Rangers March 1985 £35,000 (Reading loan 1986-87)/Welling Utd Aug 1988 to May 1989/Cheltenham Town Aug 1990/Welling Utd Nov 1990 to Jan 1991 (Birmingham City loan 1991-92)/Cheltenham Town 1993/part-time gkp-coach for various clubs including Coventry City, Queens Park Rangers & West Bromwich Albion/Aston Villa gkp-coach 1993/Middlesbrough gkp-coach 2001/UNITED gkp-coach Nov 2007 to Dec 2010/ Nottingham Forest gkp-coach June 2011 to cs 2013/ Crawley Town gkp-coach Dec 2013.

When goalkeeping coach Terry Gennoe departed during the 2007-08 season manager Sam Allardyce looked around for a new specialist to look after United's 'keepers Shay Given, Steve Harper and rising youngsters Krul and Forster. Paul Barron was appointed in November, a former Arsenal and Crystal Palace goalie. Tall and athletic, during his playing days he was distinguished by a full head of blond, curly hair noted as a competent and at times brilliant last line of defence. Moving to South London to join Crystal Palace as part of the big deal that took future United full-back Kenny Sansom to Arsenal, Barron had only managed to get eight games for the Gunners, but then went onto turn out on 110 occasions for Palace and 73 for West Bromwich Albion. Paul was a trusted confident to Chris Hughton when he took over and left St James' Park when his boss was dismissed as 2010 came to a close.

Honours:
FLC final 1986.

BAYLES William 1883 & 1891-1894

Half-back & Trainer
b. Barton, Yorkshire,
24 September 1851
d. Byker, Newcastle upon Tyne,
16 February 1903

A veteran trainer of United's pioneers, Newcastle East End, Billy Bayles was born and raised near Darlington before settling in the Byker district of Tyneside. He took charge of the fitness routines during the club's days at Chillingham Road in Heaton, joining the East Enders in February 1891 for a salary of, "10 shillings per week". Described in the contemporary press as being an "old footballer" and also having been an athlete of distinction, noted as "the well known ped who held the title of Champion of England". Billy won the All-England 140 yard handicap in 1870 and the following year the All-England £50 handicap, in years when professional running (and betting) was extremely popular. Bayles went onto lift national titles in 1872 as well. He moved across the city to a new St James' Park base along with the rest of East End in the summer of 1892 and continued looking after the players until the arrival of Harry Kirk in December 1894. When the club moved base, Bayles also took over the groundsman's duties, while in his younger days he appeared at the Byker ground in a Tyneside derby for Newcastle East End against Newcastle West End during November 1883.*

Misc App & Goals: 2 app 0 gls.

BOERSMA Philip 2004-2005

Assistant-coach
5'11"
b. Kirkby, near Liverpool,
24 September 1949

Career: Liverpool amat 1965, prof Sept 1968 (Wrexham loan 1969-70)/Middlesbrough Dec 1975 £72,500/Luton Town Aug 1977 £35,000/Swansea City Sept 1978 £35,000 to April 1981 when he retired due to injury, becoming

coach, asst-manager, then physio/ Lincoln City coach March 1984, becoming asst-manager 1985 to Dec 1985/Doncaster Rovers physio cs 1986/ Rangers physio cs 1986, becoming coach/Liverpool coach April 1991, becoming asst-manager/Oldham Ath asst-coach 1994/Galatasaray SK (Trk) coach June 1995/Southampton coach July 1996/Torino (It) coach Aug 1997 to Sept 1997/SL Benfica (Ptg) coach Nov 1997 to June 1999/Blackburn Rovers coach March 2000/UNITED asst-coach Sept 2004 to April 2005/ Llangefni Town asst-manager Dec 2007 to Jan 2008.

Graeme Souness brought a three-man back-room team with him to St James' Park he was familiar with when he arrived as boss for the start of the 2004-05 season. Alongside Dean Saunders and Alan Murray, Phil Boersma was one of his coaches, an ex-Liverpool player like his boss. As a striker or midfielder with the Reds, he was for a period understudy to the formidable pairing of Toshack and Keegan during the Seventies, once walking out on Liverpool when he wasn't chosen in the FA Cup final side against United in 1974. Despite his disappointment at times, Phil enjoyed good and effective spells with his pacy style over seasons 1972-73 to 1974-75. Totalling 120 appearances (29 goals) for the Reds, he then headed for Middlesbrough (55 app) and Swansea City (22 app) where he sustained an ankle fracture in 1979 which ended his playing career. Moving to a role behind the scenes at the Vetch Field as the Swans climbed up the league structure, the Merseyside joined the coaching staff at Ibrox and rekindled the friendship with Souness which had been formed on Teesside; Boersma afterwards following the Scot on his managerial travels. With Newcastle, Phil largely looked after the club's reserve set-up until he made headlines for the wrong reasons during a night out on the eve of United's FA Cup semi-final in Cardiff during 2005. Leaving the club shortly afterwards, later Boersma worked briefly with Welsh League side Llangefni Town.

Honours:
FL champs 1973, 1976 (3 app)/FL div 3 prom 1979/FL div 4 prom 1970 (7 app)/UEFAC winner 1973 (sub no app).

BOND Kevin John 2006

Assistant-manager
6'0"
b. West Ham, London,
22 June 1957

Career: Bournemouth jnr July 1972/Norwich City jnr July 1974, prof April 1976/Seattle Sounders (USA) Feb 1981 £200,000/ Manchester City Sept 1981 £350,000/ Southampton Sept 1984 £60,000/ Bournemouth Aug 1988 £50,000/Exeter City Aug 1992/ Sittingbourne March 1994/Dover Ath/Manchester City asst-coach/ Wrexham coach/ Altrincham coach/ Stafford Rangers manager Oct 1997/Portsmouth asst-manager May 1998 to Dec 1999/Salisbury City coach/ Portsmouth coach/Southampton coach Dec 2004/ Portsmouth asst-manager Dec 2005/UNITED asst-manager June 2006 to Sept 2006/Bournemouth manager Oct 2006/Tottenham Hotspur asst-manager Oct 2008 to June 2012/Queens Park Rangers asst-manager Dec 2012.

The son of John Bond, a noted player for West Ham and later manager (notably for Norwich and Manchester City), Kevin Bond's career began alongside his father as a young professional at Norwich, then later at Maine Road. Although having to cope with the sometimes difficult position of being the boss's son, Kevin showed he was a good player in his own right and more than justified a place in his father's line-up. A central defender who read the game well and anticipated moves, he registered 166 games for the Canaries and reached the England 'B' eleven before having a few months in the States. Then he headed for Moss Side when he joined Manchester City, being reunited with his father for season 1981-82. With 124 games to his name at Maine Road, afterwards Bond again was a solid performer with Southampton (174 app) where he was skipper for a period. Having a varied coaching career, when aged almost 49 Kevin arrived at Gallowgate as Glenn Roeder's right-hand man, described as a "modern pro-active coach" by his new boss. Remaining on Tyneside for only five months, Bond took charge of his ex-club Bournemouth before teaming up with Harry Redknapp at Tottenham when Kevin was appointed as Redknapp's assistant at White Hart Lane in 2008, and later with QPR.

Honours:
2 Eng B app 1980-81/FL div 2 prom 1985 (3 app).

BONETTI Peter Phillip 1996-1997

Goalkeeper-coach
5'11"
b. Putney, London,
27 September 1941

Career: Worthing YC 1956/ Chelsea trial Jan 1958, amat May 1958, prof April 1959 (St Louis Stars (USA) loan 1975) to May 1975, returning Oct 1975/ Dundee Utd June 1979 to Sept 1979/Retired Aug 1980/ Chelsea asst-coach/Specialist gkp-coach to a number of clubs at various times; Wolves, Leicester City, Queens Park Rangers, Watford, Manchester City, Birmingham City, England, and including UNITED Dec 1996 to cs 1997.

As Newcastle United were completely overhauled and revamped to cope with the modern football world, the club's coaching staff expanded substantially and Kevin Keegan appointed former England colleague Peter Bonetti as part-time goalkeeping coach to replace John Burridge as 1996 came to a close. Having a headlining career with Chelsea, nicknamed 'The Cat' due to his celebrated feline agility between the posts, Bonetti was the master of the reflex save and produced many a spectacular and acrobatic stop. He was rated highly alongside Gordon Banks and Pat Jennings as the Football League's best at the time. Banks kept him out of the England side on most occasions, but Peter did appear in the 1970 World Cup and won seven caps all told to add to his 700-plus senior games for Chelsea accumulated over 20 seasons at Stamford Bridge. At St James' Park, Bonetti was something of a travelling goalkeeper mentor, also at the time linked with several clubs in a similar capacity. He helped develop Magpie custodians Srnicek and Hislop as well as youngster Steve Harper. The son of a Swiss-born restaurateur, for a period Bonetti left football completely and set up home on the Isle of Mull in Scotland, opening a guest-house and working as a postman.

Honours:
7 Eng caps 1966-70/WdC 1970/1 unoff Eng app 1965/1 Eng B app 1970/13 Eng u23 app 1962-65/5 FL app 1963-70/2 FA app 1962-67/1 RoW app 1968/FL div 2 prom 1963, 1977/FAC winner 1970/FAC final 1967/FLC winner 1965/FLC final 1972/ECWC winner 1971/FAYC winner 1960/FL Long Service medal 1978.

BUNN Frank Stephen 2011

Assistant-coach
6'0"
b. Birmingham,
6 November 1962

Career: Luton Town jnr April 1979, prof May 1980/Hull City July 1985 £40,000/Oldham Ath Dec 1987 £90,000, retired due to injury Dec 1991/ Stalybridge Celtic Aug 1992/ Wigan Ath community officer/Radcliffe Borough Dec 1994/Manchester City asst-coach 1998/ Coventry City coach Feb 2007, becoming caretaker-manager Feb 2008/UNITED asst-coach March 2011/ Rochdale asst-manager June 2011/Huddersfield Town asst-coach July 2012.

Frankie Bunn joined United towards the end of the 2010-11 season to look after the Magpies Under-18 youth squad. A striker prominently with Luton and Hull, totalling 269 games (77 goals) before a knee injury cut short his playing career before he was 30 years of age, Bunn once netting all of six goals in a Football League Cup fixture for Oldham against Scarborough in October 1989. Having spent a period with Wigan, Manchester City and Coventry, he arrived on Tyneside to nurture United's budding graduates from the club's Academy. However he only remained at the club's Benton complex for a matter of four months, leaving to take up a post at tier-three Rochdale. Bunn's son, Harry, totalled over 100 games for Bury before joining Stockport County.

Honours:
FL div 2 champs 1982 (2 app)/FLC final 1990.

BURKINSHAW Keith Harry 1968-1975

Assistant-coach & Coach
5'11"
b. Higham, near Barnsley,
23 June 1935

Career: Wolverhampton Wand amat 1951-52/Denaby Utd/ Liverpool Nov 1953/ Workington Dec 1957 £3,500, becoming player-manager Nov 1964/ Scunthorpe Utd March 1965 £3,000 to cs 1968 when he retired/UNITED asst-coach July 1968, becoming coach cs 1971 to May 1975/Tottenham Hotspur coach July 1975, becoming manager July 1976 to May 1984/ Bahrain national coach June 1984 to Aug 1986/ Sporting Clube (Ptg) manager 1986 to Feb 1988/ Gillingham manager Oct 1988 to April 1989/England asst-coach 1990/Swindon Town chief-scout March 1991/West Bromwich Albion asst-manager May 1992, becoming manager June 1993 to Oct 1994/Aberdeen Director of Football May 1997 to July 2001, becoming caretaker-manager Nov 1997/PL delegate & assessor/ Watford asst-manager March 2005 to Dec 2007, returning as consultant Nov 2008 to Dec 2008.

A much respected and noted coach raised in the Higham and Darton district near Barnsley, Keith Burkinshaw was all set for a coaching position in Zambia before landing the job at St James' Park as part of his former Workington manager, Joe Harvey's staff. He did a good job at St James' Park working alongside Harvey, developing a flamboyant and exciting side when he was elevated to the senior position during the summer of 1971. Keith took responsibility for most of the tactical and coaching of the squad which took United to Wembley in 1974. A straight talking Yorkshireman, he was inventive in a much changing era for football. United's directors were heavily criticised on Burkinshaw's dismissal following the departure of Harvey, many players and the majority of supporters seeing him as a figure who could have served the club well over a sustained period. Keith proceeded to be appointed boss at White Hart Lane and the Yorkshireman brought in players like Argentineans Villa and Ardiles to Tottenham. He fashioned a side to reach Wembley on three occasions, twice as winners of the FA Cup, as well as a team good enough to lift the UEFA Cup. But after that success Burkinshaw's career took a downward spiral, surprisingly not being able to maintain another top position in England despite a first-class track record. As a player Keith exchanged life at Dodworth Colliery to become a professional footballer and was a solid wing-half who spent seven years at Anfield claiming only a single outing. He then appeared over 300 times in the lower divisions for Workington, Joe Harvey's first signing as a boss, then topped 100 games at Scunthorpe.

Honours:
FL div 2 prom 1978(m)/FL div 4 prom 1964/FAC winner 1981(m), 1982(m)/FLC final 1982(m)/UEFAC winner 1984(m).

BURNS Thomas 1997-1998

Coach
5'11"
b. Glasgow, 16 December 1956
d. Glasgow, 15 May 2008

Career: St Mary's Boy's Guild/ Eastercraigs YC 1970/Celtic jnr 1970, prof Aug 1973 (Maryhill Jnrs loan) (Salisbury CSC (Rhd) loan cs 1975) (Blackpool loan 1982-83)/ Kilmarnock Dec 1989, becoming player-asst-manager Sept 1991, then player-manager April 1992/Celtic manager July 1994/UNITED coach June 1997 & Scotland B coach March to April 1998/Reading manager March 1998 to Sept 1999/Celtic player-development officer Feb 2000 to demise & Scotland asst-manager March 2002, becoming caretaker-manager Nov 2004 to Jan 2007.

Born in the Calton district of Glasgow, Tommy Burns became a legendary figure for Celtic appearing 500 times in senior action for the Hoops. A midfield player with poise and plenty of drive and skill, he won trophies in abundance with the Glasgow giants. With a fabulous left-foot and impeccable control of the ball, Tommy also appeared for his country, collecting eight caps during the Eighties. He entered coaching with Kilmarnock, becoming manager in 1992 and was always destined to return to Kerrydale Street in Parkhead. A former teammate of Kenny Dalglish, he became boss of Celtic Park for three years then moved south to rejoin Dalglish as a senior coach at Newcastle during the close-season of 1997. Dalglish's stay at Gallowgate was though to be a brief one and Burns moved on, taking charge at Reading in 1998. That move did not work out for the Scot and he moved back to Glasgow, rejoining the Bhoys as development officer during 2000. He also continued to be involved with the Scotland set-up which began when he was at Gallowgate, as assistant-manager, later having a long spell as caretaker-boss. Tragically, Burns succumbed to cancer during 2008 and died in his native Glasgow when only 51 years of age.

Honours:
8 Scot caps 1981-88/5 Scot u21 app 1977-82/1 SL app 1979/Scot sch-youth app/SL champs 1977, 1979, 1981, 1982, 1986, 1988/SL div 1 prom 1993(m)/SC winner 1977 (sub no app), 1980, 1985, 1988, 1989, 1995(m)/SC final 1984/SLC winner 1983/SLC final 1977, 1978, 1984, 1995(m).

CALDERWOOD Colin 2009-2010

Coach & Assistant-manager
6'0"
b. Stranraer,
20 January 1965

Career: Ayr Utd jnr/Mansfield Town jnr June 1980, prof March 1982/Swindon Town July 1985 £30,000/Tottenham Hotspur July 1993 £1.25m/Aston Villa March 1999 £225,000/ Nottingham Forest March 2000 £70,000 (Notts Co loan 2000-01), retired due to injury May 2001/Tottenham Hotspur asst-coach/Northampton Town manager Oct 2003/Nottingham Forest manager May 2006 to Dec 2008/UNITED coach Jan 2009, becoming asst-manager Oct 2009/Hibernian manager Oct 2010/Birmingham City asst-manager Nov 2011/ Norwich City asst-manager June 2012 to April 2014.

Colin Calderwood was manager Chris Hughton's assistant as United regained their Premier League status at the first attempt in season 2009-10. A former Scottish international centre-half, Calderwood made a name for himself as a player with Swindon Town, appearing on more than 400 occasions for the Robins. When a scandal erupted in 1990, Colin was arrested with others during the investigation into illegal payments at the County Ground, soon being released without charge, although the club was found guilty and demoted. His form for Swindon earned a big move to Tottenham for the start of the 1993-94 season, playing alongside Hughton who he was later to team up with as a coach. Also to appear at full-back, Colin progressed to the full Scotland line-up even though he had passed 30 years of age, going onto win 36 caps for his country. Following 199 games for Spurs, Calderwood moved from the dressing-room to the coaches' room when he returned to White Hart Lane having played on with periods at Aston Villa and Nottingham Forest. He had spells as manager at Northampton and Forest before joining United's staff half-way through the 2008-09 season. Colin was soon appointed assistant-manager in October 2009. Following the successful Championship winning campaign, Calderwood was given the opportunity to manager Hibernian, and he moved the 120 miles north to Edinburgh. However his stay at Easter Road did not last long before teaming up again with Hughton at St Andrews, then at Carrow Road.

Honours:
36 Scot caps 1995-2000/WdC 1998/Scot sch-youth app/1 FL app 1993/FL div 4 champs 1986/FL div 1 prom 1993, 2008(m)/FL div 2 prom 1990 (annulled), 2006(m)/FL div 3 prom 1987/PFA ToS (d2) 1992.

CARVER John William 1979-85, 1992-05, 2011-date

Left-back, Assistant-coach, Coach & Assistant-manager
5'8"
b. Newcastle upon Tyne,
16 January 1965

Career: UNITED jnr 1979, prof Jan 1983/Cardiff City July 1985/ Retired due to injury late1985/Newcastle Blue Star 1985-86/ Gateshead 1987, becoming player-manager/Whitley Bay 1990 & FA Regional coach/ UNITED part-time asst-coach, becoming CoE Director 1992, then asst-coach Jan 1997, coach Nov 1998, caretaker-manager Sept 2004, Academy Director Oct 2004 to June 2005/Leeds Utd coach July 2005, becoming asst-manager May 2006, caretaker-manager Sept 2006 to Oct 2006/Luton Town asst-manager April 2007 to Jan 2008/Toronto (Can) manager Dec 2008 to May 2009/Plymouth Argyle asst-manager Dec 2009/ Sheffield Utd coach Aug 2010 to Dec 2010, becoming caretaker-manager Dec 2010/UNITED asst-manager Jan 2011.

Born and bred in Newcastle's West End, as a teenager John Carver was one of United's junior footballers, a promising full-back who signed associated schoolboy forms in October 1980. He reached first-team selection in three friendly matches during the preparations for season 1984-85. But with the likes of Wharton, Saunders and Ryan ahead of him in the pecking order, during the close-season of 1985 Carver headed to Wales in search of a regular position with Third Division Cardiff City. Unluckily the Tynesider was injured in his first season with the Bluebirds, a recurrence of a thigh knock picked up in a United reserve match against Wolves during 1982-83. It was a bad set-back, serious enough to force Carver to quit playing when still only 20 years old after only 15 senior appearances to his name. John was on the proverbial scrapheap. However with determination and traditional Geordie grit, he played non-league for a period (113 app for Gateshead) and started a new career in the coaching side of the game. The Tynesider secured a role with the Football Association in the region and Carver slowly began to make an impression as a dedicated coach. The dream job with Newcastle United came his way as the Nineties opened, returning to Gallowgate as assistant-coach. He soon moved up the ladder at St James' Park, John enjoying a close and trusted relationship with Bobby Robson and was stunned by his departure like many. He was handed the caretaker's role during September 2004, for a brief period in charge of his boyhood heroes, for one game against Blackburn Rovers. Carver soon moved on having to make way for a new managerial team and he was afterwards at several clubs over the next five years. The local lad once more though settled at St James' Park, appointed assistant-manager in 2011, becoming again a steadfast right-hand man, this time to Alan Pardew, importantly with much local knowledge. John is brother-in-law to United player Peter Haddock (qv).

Misc App & Goals: 0(4) app 0 gls

In charge: 1 game (caretaker).

CAVANAGH Thomas Henry 1981-1982

Assistant-manager
5'8"
b. West Derby, near Liverpool,
29 June 1928
d. Driffield, Yorkshire,
14 March 2007

Career: Preston North End amat, prof Aug 1949/Stockport Co Jan 1950/Huddersfield Town May 1952/Doncaster Rovers May 1956 £1,500/Bristol City July 1959 £2,000/Carlisle Utd June 1960/ Cheltenham Town player-manager April 1961 to Aug 1961/Brentford coach c1962, becoming manager Jan 1965 to March 1966/Nottingham Forest coach April 1966/Hull City coach July 1971/Manchester Utd coach Dec 1972, becoming asst-manager 1977 to 1980 & Northern Ireland asst-manager 1976 to 1979/UNITED asst-manager July 1981 to Oct 1982/Rosenborg BK (Nor) coach Oct 1982 to Sept 1983/Burnley asst-manager cs 1985, becoming manager Oct 1985 to May 1986/FA coach Lilleshall/Wigan Ath coach March 1988 to 1989.

One of football's errant travellers, Tommy Cavanagh possessed a no-nonsense attitude, yet was a witty and jovial character. With a wealth of experience in the game, firstly as a wing-half or inside-forward who totalled almost 350 games, then as a coach reaching the heights of success at Old Trafford and guiding Forest to runners-up position in the First Division, Tommy moved to Gallowgate as Arthur Cox was attempting to restructure the club. With a colourful personality, once sacked at Cheltenham for swearing during matches, Cavanagh only stayed on Tyneside for a little over a year before continuing his journey around the football scene. During his playing days, Tommy tasted relegation with Huddersfield, Bristol City and twice at Doncaster where he was skipper during his 124 matches. He was also a team-mate of Bill McGarry at Leeds Road when the Terriers won promotion in 1953 and recorded 98 matches (29 goals) for the Yorkshire club.

Honours:
FL div 2 prom 1953.

Support Staff

CLARKE Stephen 1998-2000

Coach
5'10"
b. Saltcoats, 29 August 1963

Career: Beith Jnrs/St Mirren jnr Oct 1979, prof Feb 981/Chelsea Jan 1987 £422,000, retired playing cs 1998, becoming asst-coach/UNITED coach Sept 1998, becoming caretaker-manager Aug 1999 to May 2000/Chelsea scout Aug 2000, becoming asst-coach, then coach 2004/West Ham Utd asst-manager Sept 2008 to June 2010/Liverpool coach Jan 2011/West Bromwich Albion manager June 2012 to Dec 2013.

A one-time target of the Magpies in his younger years as a player and a teammate of Ruud Gullit at Stamford Bridge, Steve Clarke had been with Chelsea for 12 seasons before he arrived on Tyneside to become the Dutchman's chief aide in September 1998. Over his period of 421 games for the Pensioners, Clarke had displayed a Scottish tenacity and total professionalism at left-back, as well as on occasion right-back and in central defence. His top-level know-how was invaluable as a new side was formed at St James' Park, coach of the Black'n'Whites as they reached the 1999 FA Cup final. Yet Gullit left within three months of that Wembley appearance and Clarke was a legacy of the Dutchman's command, departing soon afterwards, but not before he was caretaker-boss for a single fixture against Manchester United in August 1999, a 5-1 defeat. Steve's coaching ability was in demand though and he settled back at Stamford Bridge before moving across London to Upton Park. Always respected, the Scot joined up with his fellow countryman Kenny Dalglish in a new Liverpool set-up as 2011 began and then took charge of a Premier League club himself at The Hawthorns. He proved he could do a job in charge during 2012-13 but was somewhat unlucky to be discarded by Albion's ownership mid-way through the following campaign.

In charge: 1 game (caretaker)

Honours:
6 Scot caps 1988-94/2 Scot B app 1987-90/8 Scot u21 app 1984-85/Scot sch-youth app/1 FL app 1988/FL div 2 champs 1989/FAC winner 1997/FAC final 1994/FLC winner 1998/ECWC winner 1998.

DODDS Thomas J 1887-1891, 1897-1903

Trainer
5'9"
b. North Shields, 1849
d. Darlington, 24 January 1909

Career: EAST END trainer 1887/Sunderland trainer 1891/ Liverpool asst-trainer Feb 1897/ UNITED trainer May 1897/Leyton trainer May 1903/Liverpool asst-trainer for a period.

Originally with the Newcastle East End club in Byker and Heaton, Tom Dodds was a major influence on Sunderland's formidable side before the turn of the century, but he left Wearside following rows with Chairman John Henderson over a lack of player discipline. A bearded and zealous character usually seen in a bowler or cap, he was in charge of the Magpie players as they moved into the First Division for the first time in 1898, described in The Journal as having "expert skill as a professor of physical culture". Dodds went onto play his part in the club's consolidation as a major force in the game during the following years. Being dismissed in May 1903 with a £25 pay off, he spent a period in London before teaming up with Tom Watson at Liverpool. He later resided in Tyne Dock for a period and died of pneumonia. Originally Dodds was an athlete of note, moving into training and described as "one of the most popular and deservedly respected members of our North of England Sporting fraternity".

DONACHIE William 2010-2014

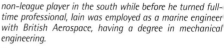

Assistant-coach
5'9"
b. Castlemilk, Glasgow, 5 October 1951

Career: Glasgow Utd/Celtic BC/ Manchester City jnr, prof Dec 1968/Portland Timbers (USA) March 1980 £200,000/ Norwich City Sept 1981 £200,000/Portland Timbers (USA) March 1982 £200,000/ Burnley Nov 1982/Oldham Ath July 1984, becoming player-asst-manager, retired as a player 1991/Everton asst-manager Nov 1994/Sheffield Utd coach cs 1997/ Manchester City coach Feb 1998/Sheffield Wed asst-manager Nov 2001/Ipswich Town asst-manager Oct 2002 to June 2006/Millwall asst-manager cs 2006, becoming manager Nov 2006 to Oct 2007/Antigua & Barbuda manager 2008/ UNITED asst-academy-manager Jan 2010, becoming asst-coach Oct 2011 to Feb 2014.

Willie Donachie, like several of Newcastle's backroom staff during modern years, has an impressive track record as a player and coach. One of the best full-backs around during the 1970s, Willie was in the Scotland side at an early age and was an admirable servant at left-back to Manchester City for 11 seasons, a regular by 1971-72. He faced the Black'n'Whites in the 1976 Football League Cup final and totalled 436 matches for the Maine Road club. Having a productive spell in North America also, Willie played on until he past his 39th year, then joined the backroom team at Oldham after 192 games at Boundary Park. The Scot linked up with United's Academy at Benton as 2010 opened and when Alan Pardew organised his staff in that year, Donachie got the job of looking after the Magpies' reserve team as well as up and coming kids from the junior ranks. He also briefly had a spell with the senior squad, Donachie left Tyneside following an altercation with one of his young charges.

Honours:
35 Scot caps 1972-79/WdC 1974 (no app), 1978/2 Scot u23 app 1972/FL div 2 champs 1991/FL div 2 prom 1982/FLC winner 1976/FLC final 1974.

DOWIE Iain 2009

Assistant-manager
6'1"
b. Hatfield, Hertfordshire, 9 January 1965

Career: Baldock Town/Hertford Town/Cheshunt 1983/St Albans City March 1985/Hendon Oct 1986/ Luton Town Dec 1988 £30,000 (Fulham loan 1989-90)/West Ham Utd March 1991 £480,000/Southampton Sept 1991 £500,000/Crystal Palace Jan 1995 £400,000/West Ham Utd Sept 1995 £500,000/Queens Park Rangers Jan 1998 exch deal, becoming caretaker-manager Sept 1998, then player-coach to March 2001/Oldham Ath coach Nov 2001, becoming manager June 2002/Crystal Palace manager Dec 2003/Charlton Ath manager May 2006 to Dec 2006/Coventry City manager Feb 2007 to Feb 2008/Queens Park Rangers manager May 2008 to Oct 2008/UNITED asst-manager April 2009 to May 2009/Hull City manager March 2010 to cs 2010.

Former Northern Ireland international centre-forward Iain Dowie was appointed to the role of Alan Shearer's coach and assistant at a time of crisis. With Newcastle facing the Premier League trapdoor in 2008-09, Dowie joined forces with his ex-colleague at Southampton in an attempt to steer United clear of the drop. It was a late gamble by Newcastle's ownership, one in the end to fail, but Dowie knuckled down to the tough ask in the last eight matches of the season. Entering the senior game at a relatively late age during 1988-89, being spotted in non-league circles with Hendon, Dowie joined Luton Town when he was 23 years of age and was a full-bodied striker, never brilliant or silky-smooth, but extremely effective up front. He found the net for Southampton (143 app 32 goals) as the proverbial old-fashioned target man – for a season alongside Shearer – and was captain of his adopted country. Iain's first appointment in coaching was with QPR and when he joined Charlton as boss during 2006 had to face a High Court challenge from Crystal Palace. In between coaching and manager appointments, like many ex-players, Iain has been part of the Sky team covering the game. His brother Bob was also a fine

non-league player in the south while before he turned full-time professional, Iain was employed as a marine engineer with British Aerospace, having a degree in mechanical engineering.

Honours:
59 NI caps 1990-2000/1 NI u21 app 1990/1 NI u23 app 1989/NI sch-youth app/FL div 1 prom 2004(m)/FL div 2 prom 1991.

EASTICK Brian 2003-2004

Academy Head Coach
6'0"
b. Balham, London, 27 January 1951

Career: Crystal Palace jnr/ Plymouth Argyle/Chelsea asst-coach/Queens Park Rangers asst-coach 1975/Brighton asst-manager cs 1981 to Dec 1982/ Sporting Club (Kwt)/Charlton Ath coach 1987/Newport Co manager Sept 1987 to March 1988/Leyton Orient asst-manager 1988 & FA part-time coach Lilleshall Academy 1988 to 1995/Coventry City asst-coach Dec 1990/Crewe Alex 1993/Sheffield Utd coach 1994 to Dec 1995/ Northern Ireland part-time asst-manager 1995 to 1998/Birmingham City Director of Youth 1996/UNITED Academy Head Coach June 2003 to Sept 2004/Eire u21 asst-coach May 2005/FA coach Aug 2005 to Oct 2013/ Nottingham Forest asst-coach May 2014.

A former England teenager, Brian Eastick's playing career as a goalkeeper with Crystal Palace and Plymouth did not reach first-team level and he began a coaching career at Stamford Bridge and Loftus Road. Joining United as a 52-year-old highly experienced coach of over 30 years, Eastick was poached from St Andrew's to look after the club's youth development. However Eastick's time on Tyneside was unproductive, the Londoner leaving within four months. With the Football Association, Brian looked after England's Under-18, Under-19 and Under-20 sides as well as assisting Stuart Pearce at Under-21 level. He was also part of the ex-United full-back's GB Olympic coaching team for London 2012. Eastick had a brief taste of management when in charge of Newport County during 1987-88, a period when the Welsh club were heading out of the Football League. He rejoined Pearce as part of his coaching team at Forest in 2014.

Honours:
Eng sch-youth app.

FAZACKERLEY Derek William 1990-1995

Assistant-coach & Coach
5'11"
b. Preston, 5 November 1951

Career: Blackburn Rovers jnr May 1969, prof Oct 1969/ Chester City player-coach Jan 1987/York City player-coach July 1988/Bury player-coach Dec 1988, becoming caretaker-manager April 1989/Workington coach Sept 1989/Darwen/Kumu (Fin) player-coach May 1990/ UNITED asst-coach Oct 1990, becoming coach Feb 1992/Blackburn Rovers coach Sept 1995 to Dec 1998/ England asst-coach Feb 1999 to Dec 2000 & Bolton Wand coach April 1999/ Barnsley coach Jan 2001/ Manchester City coach Nov 2001 to July 2008/Huddersfield Town coach Dec 2008/Leicester City coach Oct 2010, becoming asst-manager Oct 2011/ Birmingham City coach June 2012 to Feb 2014/Oxford Utd asst-manager July 2014.

A great favourite at Ewood Park, Derek Fazackerley spent the majority of his playing career with Blackburn, totalling a record 689 senior games over 17 seasons for the Lancashire club. A tough central defender, quick and forceful, he played alongside two ex-United defenders in John McNamee and Glenn Keeley and was twice linked with a move to St James' Park, deals that never came to fruition. Fazackerley was a near perfect professional and brought those qualities to the coaching side of the game. Given an opportunity at St James' Park by Jim Smith, he was promoted to look after the first-team squad by Kevin Keegan and assisted in the development of the Magpies as one of the Premier League's top sides. Derek only departed due to a wish to reside in his native Lancashire and afterwards continued to be a valuable tactician at several clubs, again with Keegan at Maine Road, then with Lee Clark at Huddersfield and Birmingham. Latterly he has been an

analyst and commentator for BBC Radio Lancs before joining Oxford United.*

Misc App & Goals: 0(1) app 0 gls

Honours:
FL div 3 champs 1975/FL div 3 prom 1980.

GALVIN Anthony 1991-1992

Assistant-manager
5'9"
b. Huddersfield, 12 July 1956

Career: Hull University/Goole Town/Tottenham Hotspur Jan 1978 £30,000/Sheffield Wed Aug 1987 £140,000/Swindon Town Aug 1989 free, becoming asst-manager Feb 1991/ UNITED asst-manager March 1991 to Feb 1992/ Gateshead occasionally as a player 1991/Later Royston Town manager to May 1996/ Buntingford Town coach.

Tony Galvin became Newcastle United's assistant-manager under Ossie Ardiles, the pairing originally bonding together during their successful spell at White Hart Lane as players, then with Swindon Town in management. A graduate in Russian Studies at Hull University, Galvin enjoyed nine seasons with Spurs, claiming nearly 300 games as a winger who operated in a deep lying position with an endless appetite for work up and down the touchline. He was one of the Londoners unsung heroes as Tottenham twice lifted the FA Cup as well as the UEFA Cup, a very effective player who appeared on 29 occasions for the Republic of Ireland. Tony was actually on United's books as a player, but didn't see first-class action although he did turn out in a friendly against Whitley Bay. After football Galvin gained another degree and became a college lecturer in Leisure & Tourism, running a department at Uxbridge College for a period. Tony was also an account manager at the government Skills Funding Agency and helped out his son at Potton United where he was player-boss. He also coached at football academies with his brother Chris (Leeds, Hull, York City and Stockport) in the Royston area.

Misc App & Goals: 0(1) app 0 gls

Honours:
29 Eire caps 1983-90/Eng sch-youth app/FL div 2 prom 1990/FAC winner 1981, 1982/FLC final 1982/UEFAC winner 1984.

GEDDIS David 2001-2004

Assistant-coach
5'11"
b. Carlisle, 12 March 1958

Career: Ipswich Town jnr June 1973, prof Aug 1975 (Luton Town loan 1976-77)/Aston Villa Sept 1979 £300,000 (Luton Town loan 1982-83)/Barnsley Sept 1983 £50,000/Birmingham City Dec 1984 £80,000 (Brentford loan 1986-87)/ Shrewsbury Town Feb 1987 £25,000/ Swindon Town Oct 1988 £25,000/ Darlington March 1990 free to May 1990/Middlesbrough asst-coach 1991 to cs 2001/ UNITED asst-coach Nov 2001 to Sept 2004/Leeds Utd asst-coach cs 2006 to Dec 2006, becoming caretaker-manager Oct 2006/FA coach.

David Geddis was part of Bobby Robson's accomplished Ipswich Town line-up during the 1970s, back then he was a strong and determined striker with long flowing blond hair who played alongside many talented players up front such as Paul Mariner and Eric Gates. He was part of Robson's team which lifted the FA Cup in 1978, creating the winning goal by laying on the chance for Roger Osborne against Arsenal. Dave's playing career took him to Aston Villa where he was part of the squad which lifted the Football League title and European Cup, although he didn't play in the final victory. Remarkably, David totalled 56 games at Villa and Birmingham as well as for Ipswich. Nearly joining the Magpies in 1983, after heading to the lower divisions where he began coaching at Middlesbrough during 1991, Dave earned a UEFA Pro Licence. Robson brought the Cumbrian-born Geddis into his coaching set-up during November 2001 and he spent three seasons on United's roster from 2001-02 to the start of 2004-05, largely looking after the Magpie reserve squad. Afterwards Geddis had a spell at Elland Road before joining the Football Association set-up. When a young footballer at Portman Road, David survived a fatal car accident which claimed the life of a colleague, Peter Canavan.

Honours:
1 Eng B app 1978/Eng sch-youth app/FL champs 1981 (9 app)/FL div 2 prom 1985/FL div 4 champs 1991/FAC winner 1978/EC winner 1982 (sub no app)/FAYC winner 1975.

GENNOE Terence William 1997-99, 2006-07

Goalkeeper-coach
6'2"
b. Shrewsbury, 16 March 1953

Career: Shrewsbury Town jnr 1969/ Bricklayer's Arms (Shrewsbury)/ Bury June 1973 (Blackburn Rovers loan 1973-74) (Leeds Utd loan 1974-75)/ Halifax Town May 1975 £3,000/ Southampton Feb 1978 £35,000 (Everton loan 1980-81)(Crystal Palace loan 1980-81)/Blackburn Rovers Aug 1981 £60,000, retired May 1992 becoming education officer & gkp-coach/UNITED gkp-coach June 1997/ Celtic gkp-coach July 1999/UNITED gkp-coach July 2006 to Oct 2007/Aston Villa gkp-coach Sept 2011.

After employing part-time goalkeeping coaches since the dedicated role became vogue during the early 1990s, United opted for a full-time appointment when ex-Blackburn Rovers custodian Terry Gennoe arrived on Tyneside in the summer 1997, having like Alan Irvine, worked with United boss Kenny Dalglish at Blackburn. A tall and imposing figure and extremely likable, Gennoe had a long period as a commanding 'keeper at Ewood Park, totalling a record 334 games between 1981 and 1992, signed by ex-United coach Bobby Saxton after an earlier loan period under Gordon Lee. He retired during the close-season of 1992, moving onto the Ewood coaching staff. A popular character within St James' Park, Gennoe worked with Steve Harper and Shay Given for two seasons before leaving during the summer of 1999 to join Celtic, once more teaming up with Dalglish for a period. Gennoe returned to Gallowgate for the 2006-07 campaign, to again coach seniors Harper and Given as well as emerging youngsters Forster and Krul. A long term back injury restricted Gennoe and he was forced to give up active coaching, leaving the Magpies during October 2007 although he returned with Aston Villa in 2011.

Honours:
Eng sch-youth app/FL div 4 prom 1974 (2 app)/FLC final 1979/PFA ToS(d2) 1985.

GREENHALGH James Radcliffe 1962-1966

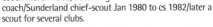

Coach
5'9"
b. Manchester, 25 August 1923
d. Darlington, 31 August 2013

Career: Newton Heath Loco/ Hull City Aug 1946/ Bury Dec 1950 £13,000/ Wigan Ath cs 1955/Gillingham asst-player-coach July 1956/Lincoln City asst-coach Feb 1959/UNITED coach June 1962/Darlington manager July 1966/Middlesbrough asst-coach March 1968, becoming coach/Sunderland chief-scout Jan 1980 to cs 1982/later a scout for several clubs.

An uncompromising wing-half as a player, predominately with Hull (167 app) and Bury (125 app), Jimmy Greenhalgh was a tough tackler in the lower divisions. He was an ever-present as the Tigers lifted the Third Division North title in 1949 and cost Bury a club record fee when he moved to Gigg Lane. Greenhalgh was appointed as Joe Harvey's club marshall as the Magpies made a sustained bid to regain their First Division status. Jimmy was something of a fitness fanatic and hard task master, but Greenhalgh also had an astute tactical appraisal of the game and linked well with Harvey's motivation qualities. It was a partnership that took United to the Second Division title in 1965. After spells as manager and coach elsewhere, Greenhalgh became a respected scout residing in County Durham.

Honours:
FL div 3(N) champs 1949.

HARDY George 1906-1910

Assistant-trainer
5'10"
b. Newcastle upon Tyne, 20 February 1877
d. Southend, 2 January 1947

Career: UNITED asst-trainer 1906/Arsenal trainer July 1910 to Feb 1927/Tottenham Hotspur trainer cs 1927 & Northfleet Utd trainer 1931 (Tottenham nursery club) to demise/Also occasional trainer to England between 1923 and 1937.

Born and bred in Byker, George Hardy was a local runner of note, winning several sprint handicaps in the north. However, his athletic career was ended when an industrial accident at a local saw-mill resulted in him losing his left eye during January 1905. Hardy was appointed as an assistant to Sandy McPherson at St James' Park soon after and he was a valuable part of the backroom staff until he relocated to capital in the summer close down of 1910 to join Arsenal. Appointed trainer to the London club it was the start of a lengthy period of over 40 years serving the Gunners, then rivals Tottenham. At Arsenal, George worked closely with the great Herbert Chapman during the building of a celebrated side at Highbury. But during the mid to late Twenties the relationship deteriorated between manager and trainer, and following a FA Cup match against Port Vale during 1927, Hardy, in his chief's eyes, appeared to interfere too much in tactics on the field; Chapman sent the trainer to the dressing-room, quickly afterwards to be sacked. Hardy though was a respected figure in London, on occasion being in charge of the England eleven while he was described like many old-style trainers as "a firm and kindly friend". George was not out of work long, joining neighbours Tottenham within a few weeks and remaining at White Hart Lane until the immediate post-war years. During the early days of Arsenal's tenure at Highbury during 1913 and when dressing-rooms had yet to be completed, George had to carry off fellow Tynesider George Jobey when he was injured then wheel him in a borrowed milk cart to his own house for treatment! Another ex-United player, Bob Benson was treated by Hardy after collapsing when playing wartime football for the Gunners; he died "in the arms of the Arsenal trainer". Hardy himself passed away when preparing Spurs for a match against West Bromwich Albion during January 1947. Tottenham's club tribute in the match programme noted that Hardy had a "comprehensive knowledge of anatomy, and he applied that knowledge to the great advantage of the players who were in his charge".

HERD George 1976

Assistant-coach
5'8"
b. Gartcosh, Glasgow, 6 May 1936

Career: Gartcosh Thistle/ Inverness Thistle/Queen's Park Aug 1956/Clyde May 1957/ Sunderland April 1961 £42,500 (Vancouver Royals (Can) loan cs 1967) becoming asst-coach Jan 1968/Hartlepool Utd player-coach June 1970 to 1971/Gateshead coach 1973/UNITED asst-coach July 1976 to Oct 1976/ Sunderland asst-coach cs 1977 to cs 1980/Queen of the South manager June 1980/Darlington coach cs 1981/ Middlesbrough asst-coach 1982/Sunderland youth development officer cs 1983 to cs 1985/Kuwait coaching c1993/Sunderland asst-coach July 1993 to Aug 1994/Sunderland Red Star coach Aug 2007/ Sunderland RCA asst-manager Sept 2007 to Sept 2013 when he part-retired.

When George Herd moved south and crossed the border to England as a highly rated inside-forward of the old style, the Scot nearly landed at St James' Park. Instead, he joined neighbours Sunderland in a £42,500 deal during 1961. Newcastle boss Charlie Mitten had watched Herd shine with Clyde as part of a side which lifted the Scottish Cup. Small and stocky, George was a consistent and productive servant at Roker Park, a huge favourite over nine seasons and 318 games (55 goals). Capped by Scotland, he was a central figure to the Wearsiders during the Sixties, having vision to make an opening and ability to net himself. Some 15 years later in the summer of 1976, Herd did join the Magpies, appointed assistant-coach as part of Joe Harvey's last set-up at Gallowgate. Looking after United's Central League line-up, he

Support Staff

departed after only three months. As a coach, Herd was associated with all the North East's senior clubs, also attached to Middlesbrough, Darlington and Hartlepool, as well as his principal club as a player Sunderland. He remained in the region, involved in non-league and grass-roots football and was coaching into his 70th year with Wearside club RCA until he decided to semi-retire in 2013. George also once pulled on the United shirt appearing for Jackie Milburn's testimonial side, a combined United and Sunderland team in 1967.

Misc App & Goals: 1 app 0 gls

Honours:
5 Scot caps 1958-61/2 Scot u23 app 1958/1 Scot amat app 1957/3 SL app 1960-61/FL div 2 prom 1964/SC winner 1958.

HUGHES Edward 1948-1962

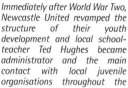

Youth Manager
5'11"
b. Newcastle upon Tyne, 1900
d. Newcastle upon Tyne, 27 November 1966

Immediately after World War Two, Newcastle United revamped the structure of their youth development and local school-teacher Ted Hughes became administrator and the main contact with local juvenile organisations throughout the region. The club's principal junior team was the NNNNs (Northumberland, North Durham and Newcastle Nursery), created soon after World War Two although initially the link to the parent club was rather informal but was to be integrated fully for season 1948-49, soon with a shortened title of the 'Ns'. Hughes managed this set-up and as the club developed what could be considered a modern-type youth policy, the Ns became increasingly important, joining the Northern Intermediate League for 1950-51 to compete with the junior sides of other senior clubs. At an even lower level, there was another Ns team, often referred to as Ns Juniors, which played in the local Newcastle & District Junior League. Hughes had a hand in bringing local schoolboys to the club and alongside coach Benny Craig, Ted looked after United's successful FA Youth Cup winning squad in 1962. Residing in Jesmond, he was for a long period a teacher at St Aloysius School in Newcastle.

HUGHES Ian James 1985-1986

Assistant-coach
5'9"
b. Sunderland, 24 August 1961

Career: Sunderland jnr Aug 1977, prof Aug 1979/Barnsley July 1981/Sunderland cs 1982, retired due to injury, becoming asst-coach to June 1985/ UNITED asst-coach Sept 1985 to June 1986/Later scouting for various clubs including West Ham Utd.

When ex-player and then coach Willie McFaul was elevated to become United's manager he needed extra bodies on the coaching staff. One of his recruits was Ian Hughes, a former Sunderland full-back who unluckily was forced to give up playing due to a bad knee injury picked up in a pre-season friendly. Hughes was given a role to look after the Geordies' youth squad for season 1985-86. Originally joining the Roker Park staff as a talented schoolboy in 1977, Ian forced his way into the first-eleven during the Black Cat's promotion season of 1979-80 as a replacement for Rob Hindmarch and made a single appearance for the Rokerites. With a Welsh background the Wearsider also reached the young Wales squad and had a bright future before injury wrecked his career. Hughes only remained at Gallowgate for one season, Ian resided on Wearside, later employed with a pharmaceutical company as well as continuing working in football as a scout, notably with West Ham United.

Honours:
FL div 2 prom (1 app).

IRVINE James Alan 1997-2002

Assistant-coach, Coach & Director of Youth
5'9"
b. Glasgow, 12 July 1958

Career: Glasgow Utd/Queen's Park amat Sept 1977/Everton May 1981/Crystal Palace Aug 1984 £50,000 (Albion Rovers loan 1985-86)(Alloa Ath loan 1985-86)/Dundee Utd June 1987/Blackburn Rovers loan Oct 1989, pmt Nov 1989 £30,000, retired May 1992, becoming asst-coach/UNITED asst-coach March 1997, becoming coach March 1997, then Director of Youth, caretaker-manager Aug 1998/Everton asst-manager May 2002/Preston North End manager Nov 2007/Sheffield Wed manager Jan 2010 to Feb 2011/Everton Academy manager July 2011, becoming director/West Bromwich Albion manager June 2014.

A product of Glasgow junior football and the amateur Queen's Park set-up, Alan Irvine made a dream move to Goodison Park in 1981 to join Everton as a 22-year-old player, turning professional having completed his chartered insurance exams. A forward with traditional Scottish sorcery to the fore, he also possessed a blast of pace to get past defenders. Alan's playing career never reached the very top, due in part to a succession of unfortunate injuries, but after wearing the blue shirt of the Toffees on 80 occasions, Irvine had good periods as a talented wing man or midfielder with Palace (127 app), back in Scotland with Dundee United then at Blackburn (62 app). The Scot arrived at St James' Park during March 1997, one of Dalglish's first appointments having worked alongside his fellow Scot at Ewood Park. He was soon in charge of Newcastle United's Academy, in control of the club's overall youth development programme which was resurrected under the pair's leadership. Highly thought of in the game as a coach, Alan remained on Tyneside for almost five seasons and was caretaker-boss with Tommy Craig during August 1998 (one game v Liverpool) before stepping up to become assistant to David Moyes at Everton, who also came through the ranks of Glasgow's junior game. Irvine's stock in football was on the up and he was offered the manager's job at Preston in 2007, but his first role as outright boss did not go well. Alan was sacked although he was not out for work long, having another chance at Hillsborough before returning to Goodison Park to look after the Finch Farm Everton Academy. He then returned to the hot-seat as West Bromwich Albion's boss in the close-season of 2014.

Misc App & Goals: 0(1) app 0 gls

In charge: 1 game (caretaker)

Honours:
FLC final 1984/FL div 2 prom 1992 (6 app)/SL div 2 champs 1981.

JOYCE Joseph Patrick 2006-date

Academy Manager
5'9"
b. Consett, Co Durham, 18 March 1961

Career: Barnsley jnr Nov 1979, prof Sept 1980/Scunthorpe Utd Feb 1991 free/Carlisle Utd Aug 1993 player-coach/Darlington Sept 1993/Carlisle Utd coach 1993, becoming asst-manager Aug 1996/York City asst-coach 1997/ PFA coaching staff 1998, becoming Head of Coaching/ UNITED Academy manager Sept 2006.

As a player, Joe Joyce was a thorough professional with Barnsley for 11 seasons, a quick tackling right-back who recorded 388 games for the Tykes. Having turned down offers from Nottingham Forest and Blackburn to settle at Oakwell, Joyce became skipper and a consistent and influential figure in Barnsley's Division Two line-up. A bad leg break at the end of the 1988-89 campaign set the Consett-born player on the road to a career in coaching and following a long period with the PFA, becoming chief of their coaching team, he joined United's Academy as the 2006-07 season began. Joe took over from Glenn Roeder when he was given first-team control.

Honours:
FL div 3 champs 1995/FL div 3 prom 1981.

KIRK Harry 1894-1897

Trainer
5'6"
b. unknown

Career: Notts Co trainer 1890 to 1893/UNITED trainer Dec 1894 to June 1896, becoming asst-trainer to May 1897.

A former trainer at Notts County, Harry Kirk was appointed in December 1894 after a period alongside the Trent. Kirk was sacked from his position at Meadow Lane following the Notts Magpies relegation from Division One at the end of the 1892-93 season. Kirk spent his period at St James' Park during the building of a side good enough for Football League soccer. He was replaced by Leach in the close-season of 1896, although Kirk remained connected with the club in other capacities to the end of the 1896-97 season. He later was a pavilion attendant at the Trent Bridge cricket ground.

LAWRENSON Mark Thomas 1996-1997

Assistant-coach
6'0"
b. Preston, 2 June 1957

Career: Preston North End jnr 1971, prof Aug 1974/Brighton July 1977 £100,000/Liverpool Aug 1981 £900,000, retired due to injury March 1988/Thame Utd 1988/Barnet 1988/Oxford Utd manager April to Oct 1988/ Tampa Bay Rowdies (USA) 1989/ Peterborough Utd manager Sept 1989 to Nov 1990/Corby Town player 1991/Chesham Utd player 1992/UNITED asst-coach Nov 1996 to June 1997.

Newcastle United's Entertainers line-up was often criticised due to a frailty in defence, usually as a result of an inability of not shutting up shop at key moments in games. However, when statistics are analysed United had one of the best defensive records in the division for 1995-96 and 1996-97, but crucially lost goals at critical moments. Kevin Keegan wanted an experienced defender on his coaching staff to stiffen his side's defending and following the departure of Derek Fazackerley he brought in former Liverpool centre-back Mark Lawrenson as the 1996-97 season was underway. With a dedicated 'defensive coach' remit, the much honoured Lawrenson knew all about the art of stopping other teams scoring, having a resolute partnership with Alan Hansen in Liverpool's shirt. A record signing for the Reds from Brighton (174 app), Mark totalled 355 outings for the Anfield club and collected five titles and the European Cup as well as winning domestic cups and almost 40 caps of the Republic of Ireland. Once his career was effectively cut short by an Achilles tendon injury, Lawrenson had a brief spell with struggling Oxford then Peterborough as he tried football management. Mark's stay on Tyneside was short, only seven months before leaving his position in the summer of 1997 when new boss Kenny Dalglish reshaped his backroom team. His father Tommy Lawrenson was, like his son, on Preston's books and appeared for Southport. After leaving the Black'n'Whites, Mark concentrated on a career in the television and radio media, a regular BBC expert pundit and summariser.

Honours:
39 Eire caps 1977-88/FL champs 1982, 1983, 1984, 1986, 1988/FL div 2 prom 1979/FAC winner 1986/FLC winner 1982, 1983, 1984/EC winner 1984/EC final 1985/ESC final 1984/ICC final 1981/PFA ToS (d1) 1983, 1984, 1985, 1986, (d2) 1979.

LEACH William 1896-1897

Trainer
5'10"
b. unknown

Career: Derby Co trainer/ UNITED trainer June 1896 to cs 1897/Grimsby Town trainer May 1897 to Nov 1897/ Luton Town trainer 1903 to 1904.

At St James' Park for only a brief period, Billy Leach arrived to succeed Harry Kirk for the start of the 1896-97 programme from Derby County. Leach had a sound reputation at the time and 'Ixion' of the Newcastle Daily Journal wrote that he had been instrumental in taking the Rams from the bottom of the table to runners-up spot in the First Division during 1895-96. It was noted that Leach would get the players "in the pink of condition". He didn't remain long on Tyneside though, departing during the close-season of 1897 and being replaced by Tom Dodds.

LEWIN Ronald Denis 1966-1968, 1974-1976

Assistant-coach
5'9"
b. Edmonton, London,
21 June 1920
d. Cockermouth,
24 September 1985

Career: Enfield Town amat 1936/Bradford City Sept 1943 (Stockport Co war-guest 1943-44)/ Fulham June 1946/ Gillingham June 1950/ Chatham Town May 1955/Skeid (Nor) coach/Norway national coach Jan 1956 to Dec 1957/Cheltenham Town manager 1958 to 1960/Wellington manager 1962/Everton asst-coach Sept 1962/UNITED coach Aug 1966/Walsall manager July 1968 to Feb 1969/UNITED asst-coach July 1974 to July 1976/Reykjavik (Ice) coach 1976/Prottur (Ice) coach 1980/Brandon Utd manager 1981/Gateshead youth-officer July 1983/Workington coach 1985 to death/Also coached in Greece and Kuwait.

A member of Fulham's Second Division title winning side during 1948-49, Ron Lewin couldn't claim a place at a higher level at the Cottage, but was a good club player, a sound right-back who also did well at Gillingham where he totalled 204 matches in Division Three South. On retiring from the playing aspect of soccer, Lewin began a long and varied coaching career which took him to Europe and beyond, and to all levels of the game. He was brought into Joe Harvey's organisation on the departure of Jimmy Greenhalgh, and was prominent as the club qualified for Europe for the very first time. Lewin took up the manager's job at Fellows Park in 1968 before the Black'n'Whites embarked on that inaugural and successful season in the Inter Cities Fairs Cup. During the Second World War, Lewin spent six years as a physical training and parachute instructor.

Honours:
FL div 2 champs 1949 (6 app).

MILNE Gordon 1999-2004

Assistant-manager &
Director of Football
5'8"
b. Preston, 29 March 1937

Career: Preston Amateurs/ Morecambe/Preston North End Jan 1956/Liverpool Sept 1960 £16,000/Blackpool May 1967 £30,000/Wigan Ath player-manager Jan 1970 & England youth manager Aug 1971/

Coventry City manager June 1972, becoming Executive Manager May 1981/Leicester City manager Aug 1982, becoming General Manager June 1986/Besiktas JK (Trk) manager Aug 1987 to Dec 1993/Grampus 8 (Jp) manager 1994 to June 1995/LMA Chief Executive 1995/Buraspor (Trk) manager Aug 1996 to May 1997/Trabzonspor AS (Trk) manager Aug 1998 to June 1999/UNITED asst-manager Nov 1999, becoming Director of Football 2000 to Aug 2004/Besiktas JK (Trk) Technical Director 2004-05, becoming caretaker-manager Oct 2005.

Vastly experienced as a player, coach and manager, Gordon Milne joined Bobby Robson's newly installed back-room team in November 1999, initially as assistant-manager. Another of the many Liverpool connections to be at St James' Park, 62-year-old Milne had been one of Bill Shankly's midfield anchormen following a move from Preston to Anfield in 1960. He lifted the League Championship under Shanks and played for England as a tireless, stocky midfielder with a cultured touch of the ball in the old-style half-back role. Totalling 282 games for the Reds, he was included in Alf Ramsay's 40-man World Cup squad for the 1966 tournament, but dropped out in the final cut. As a manager and coach, Gordon was well travelled. He found much success in Turkey, lifting trophies with Besiktas and working for a season with Les Ferdinand. During 2000 Milne moved into a Director of Football role at St James' Park, assisting Robson handling the vast amount of organisation needed on the playing side of a Premier League club, including much needed scouting around the UK and Continent. He remained Bobby's closest ally throughout his time as manager, leaving soon after Robson was sacked at the start of the 2004-05 season. With a football pedigree, Gordon's father Jimmy Milne also enjoyed a respected career with Preston. Remarkably both father and son missed a FA Cup final for their respective clubs due to injury, for Preston in 1938 and then Liverpool in 1965.

Honours:
14 Eng caps 1963-65/3 unoff Eng app 1963-66/2 FL app 1964/1 FA app 1960/FL champs 1964, 1966/FL div 2 champs 1962/FL div 2 prom 1983(m)/Trk Lg champs 1990(m), 1991(m), 1992(m)/Trk Cup winner 1989(m), 1990(m)/ECWC final 1966.

MONEY Richard 2008-2009

Director of Academy & Coach
5'11"
b. Lowestoft, 13 October 1955

Career: Lowestoft Town/ Scunthorpe Utd July 1973/ Fulham Dec 1977 £50,000/ Liverpool April 1980 £333,333 (Derby Co loan 1981-82)/Luton Town March 1982 loan, pmt April 1982 £100,000/ Portsmouth Aug 1983 £55,000/ Scunthorpe Utd player-coach Oct 1985, becoming caretaker-manager Feb to April 1987/Retired playing 1989/Aston Villa asst-coach Sept 1989/Scunthorpe Utd manager Jan 1993 to March 1994/Nottingham Forest asst-manager June 1994/Manchester City asst-coach, becoming asst-manager Jan 1997/Coventry City Academy Manager May 1998, becoming coach Nov 2001 to June 2002/AIK (Swd) coach Jan 2003 to April 2004/Vasteras (Swd) coach May 2004/Singapore coaching/Newcastle Jets (Aus) coach/Walsall manager May 2006 to April 2008/UNITED Director of Academy & Youth June 2008, becoming coach Sept 2008 for a period/Luton Town manager Oct 2009 to March 2011/Cambridge Utd manager Oct 2012.

Richard Money was one of several ex-footballers to have taken charge of the club's Premier League Academy following the opening of the complex in 1999. A former Liverpool right-back, Money made his name as a player with Fulham (121 app) and was purchased by Bob Paisley at Anfield during April 1980. But Richard found breaking through on Merseyside difficult and he totalled only 17 games in a red shirt, although he did turn out in the European Cup semi-final during 1980-81 and was on the bench for the final against Real Madrid. Money went onto enjoy a productive period with the Irons of Scunthorpe, amassing 324 appearances in the Fourth Division. Joining the Magpies as a 52-year-old with a wealth of coaching experience, he remained at the Benton Academy for two seasons, Richard departing to take on the manager's role at troubled Luton Town in October 2009. That appointment lasted less than two years and afterwards Money took control at Cambridge United, leading them to Wembley victory in the FA Trophy and then defeating Gateshead in the Conference Play-Off during 2014 as his side returned to the Football League.

Honours:
1 Eng B app 1980/FL div 2 champs 1982, 2007(m)/EC winner 1981 (sub no app)/FAT winner 2014(m).

MONTGOMERY James 1992-1993

Goalkeeper-coach
5'11"
b. Sunderland, 9 October 1943

Career: Burnley trial/ Sunderland amat June 1958, prof Oct 1960 (Vancouver Royals (Can) loan cs 1967) (Southampton loan 1976-77)/ Birmingham City loan Feb 1977, pmt March 1977/ Nottingham Forest Aug 1979/ Birmingham City asst-coach July 1980/Sunderland player-coach Aug 1980 to July 1982/Later coaching locally in North East having various part-time roles including as UNITED gkp-coach 1992 to cs 1993/ Sunderland Director of Youth 1993 to 1995/Darlington asst-coach & gkp-coach, becoming coach Feb 2001/ reverting to part-time roles including for Scarborough, Bradford City (2004) and RCA Sunderland.

One of several first-class goalkeepers to ply his trade in England during the Sixties and Seventies era, Jimmy Montgomery was a long serving and popular last line of defence for Newcastle's great rivals Sunderland. Following a swansong as a player with Birmingham City and Forest, 'Monty' as he was known in the game, began a career in coaching during 1980. After a period on the Roker Park staff he became the Magpies first dedicated goalkeeper-coach when that role became a requirement for all top clubs. That was a part-time appointment, Kevin Keegan bringing in the former Wearside favourite to United's training set-up to work with 'keepers Pavel Srnicek and Tommy Wright. As a player Montgomery spent the greater part of his exceptional playing career with the Wearsiders, a 17-year-old debut and going onto rack up a record 627 appearances in senior football for the red-and-whites over a period of 16 seasons. Agile and spectacular, he often pulled off stunning saves including famously a double stop in the 1973 FA Cup final against Leeds United; first from a Trevor Cherry header then a follow up Peter Lorimer rocket. With several top notch 'keepers in English football at the time, Jimmy was unlucky not to win an England cap, tipped several times but always overlooked, although he was an unused substitute for the England versus France clash in 1969. Jimmy left Newcastle as the 1993-94 season began and afterwards rejoined the Black Cats. He also worked at the Meadowfield Sports Centre in Durham for a period; Montgomery remains a legendary figure in Sunderland's history and is a personality host at the Stadium of Light and was appointed a club ambassador in February 2012.

Honours:
6 Eng u23 app 1964-67/Eng sch-youth app/FL div 2 champs 1976/FL div 2 prom 1964/FAC winner 1973/EC winner (sub no app) 1980/ESC winner 1979 (sub no app).

MORRIS Peter John 1978-1979

Assistant-manager
5'8"
b. New Houghton, Derbyshire,
8 November 1943

Career: New Houghton/ Ladybrook Colts/ Langwith BC/ New Houghton Baptists/ Ladybrook Colts/ Mansfield Town jnr Jan 1959, prof Nov 1960/Ipswich Town March 1968 £15,000/Norwich City June 1974 £60,000, becoming asst-coach/ Mansfield Town player-manager July 1976 £20,000/UNITED asst-manager Feb 1978/Peterborough Utd manager Feb 1979 to May 1982/Crewe Alex manager Nov 1982/ Southend Utd manager Aug 1983 to Feb 1985/ Nuneaton Borough manager June 1985/El Hajar (SAr) coach/Leicester City coach Jan 1987, becoming caretaker-manager Nov to Dec 1987 and asst-coach 1988/Kettering Town manager June 1988 to May 1992/Boston Utd manager June 1992/Northampton Town asst-manager Sept 1993/Kings Lynn manager Aug 1995/Kettering Town manager Aug 1998 to Feb 2001/Kings Lynn manager May 2002 to Nov 2003.

Peter Morris was more than once linked with a transfer to St James' Park during his career as a player. A strong midfielder, he tasted promotion success with Mansfield, Ipswich and Norwich and totalled 366 games for the Stags as well as 258 at Portman Road at a higher level under Bobby Robson. Skipper before he was 20 years of age at the Field Mill Ground, Morris was a non-stop worker in midfield and was a highly respected professional who once he retired linked up with Bill McGarry at Gallowgate during 1978. At that time Peter was still registered as a player, but only took part in friendly action for the Magpies against Gateshead and in Jinky Smith's testimonial. Like many of United's modern coaches, Morris landed at many ports of call on his travels, later being in charge of several clubs in the East Midlands. Morris was also a scout for several clubs, including for Manchester City and Newcastle during recent years, latterly part of Graham Carr's team at Gallowgate.

Misc App & Goals: 1(1) app 0 gls

Honours:
FL div 2 champs 1968, 1972/FL div 2 prom 1975/FL div 3 champs 1977(m)/FL div 4 prom 1963/FLC final 1975.

MURRAY Alan 2004-2006

Assistant-manager
5'8"
b. Newcastle upon Tyne,
5 December 1949

Career: Wolverhampton Wand trial 1966/ Howdon BC/ Willington Quay/Middlesbrough Sept 1967 (York City loan 1971-72)/ Brentford June 1972/ Doncaster Rovers July 1973 to 1977/Middlesbrough commercial manager 1988/Hartlepool Utd commercial manager 1990, becoming manager March 1991 to Feb 1993/ Billingham Synthonia manager 1993/Darlington manager Oct 1993 to Feb 1995/Southampton asst-manager July 1996/SL Benfica (Ptg) asst-manager Nov 1997, becoming caretaker-manager June 1999/ Blackburn Rovers asst-manager March 2000/UNITED asst-manager Sept 2004 to Feb 2006.

A Tynesider from Walker, Alan Murray was appointed as assistant-manager to Graeme Souness shortly after he arrived at St James' Park during September 2004. Having worked alongside the former Liverpool star at Southampton, in Portugal and at Ewood Park, Murray was a dependable confidant to the Scot. Being a Geordie who knew all about the close link between the community and football club, Alan's local connection was an added bonus for the new manager. As a player, Murray never reached the heights of stardom; a midfielder or winger, he began with Middlesbrough but only appeared 10 times with the Teesside club. Strong and stocky, Murray did have a decent period with Doncaster Rovers in Division Four, appearing on 164 occasions at Belle Vue. He entered coaching at Hartlepool, being elevated to the manager's chair from a commercial role in 1991 on the departure of Cyril Knowles due to illness. Murray made an exit from Gallowgate on the sacking of his boss in February 2006.

Honours:
FL div 4 prom 1991(m).

McMENEMY Christopher 1993-1999

Assistant-coach, Coach & Director of Youth
6'1"
b. Gateshead, 1 August 1961

Career: Southampton jnr June 1977, prof June 1979/ Retired due to injury Nov 1979/ Salisbury 1981/ Romsey Town/ Southampton asst-coach 1982/ Sunderland asst-coach 1985/ Chesterfield coach 1988, becoming asst-manager Nov 1988 and manager Jan 1991 to Feb 1993/Tottenham Hotspur scout/UNITED chief-scout July 1993, becoming asst-coach Feb 1994 & Director of Youth, then coach Sept 1995, asst-coach cs 1997, chief-scout Nov 1998 to cs 1999.

Chris McMenemy took control of Newcastle's youth development at Gallowgate during February 1994 following a period in charge of Chesterfield when he was recognised as the youngest manager in the game at 29 years of age. From a family with a rich footballing pedigree, his father Lawrie is celebrated in Southampton's history, while he also had a brief spell on United's books as a player. Chris is also distantly related to the famous pre-war Scottish McMenemy clan of which Harry appeared for Newcastle in the 1932 FA Cup final. Starting his career as an apprentice under his father's influence at The Dell, he never made the senior eleven, his career wrecked when 18 years of age with an ankle injury and Chris moved into coaching. On the departure of Derek Fazackerley, Chris moved into the senior position at Barrack Road but then returned to other roles before departing in the close-season of 1999. He later also acted as a United scout under Sam Allardyce. On leaving the top-level coaching scene, McMenemy formed a FIFA registered sports agency and worked with several clubs in England and Spain as a scouting consultant. He joined the Sillsport organisation during 2011 in a similar role.

McPHERSON James Quar (senior) 1903-1932

Trainer
5'9"
b. Cupar, Fife, 1 September 1862
d. Newcastle upon Tyne, 6 December 1932

Career: Berliner (Ger)/ Kilmarnocktrainer 1889/ UNITED trainer July 1903/ Retired Jan 1928, becoming masseur to his death.

A former athlete in Victorian Britain, James McPherson was a successful professional runner over various distances when the sport of 'pedestrianism' was a popular pastime in the country. Moving to Ayrshire from Fife as a youth, he worked as a printer and joined Kilmarnock during 1889 as a part-time trainer, using his athletic skills to keep the Killie players in shape. McPherson had entered football by way of a position in Berlin for a period, keeping players fit and ready for action. Known as 'Sandy', he arrived at St James' Park just as the club was ready to take off and become Edwardian England's top side. Possessing a jolly nature, with an abundance of tact and spirit, he became an important backstage aide at Gallowgate for the next 25 years. Much admired by his players, Bill McCracken recorded in his memoirs that he had "never met another man so blessed with the gift of keeping men together, and making them feel they were on top of the world". Inside Gallowgate he was affectionately known as 'Auld Jimmy' and many other famous names of the era reaped praise on the Scot. McPherson created a cheerful atmosphere at St James' Park for over a decade and was influential in ensuring the Magpies had a first-class team spirit during their greatest period of success. He was also remembered for ever smoking a pipe, even taking it into the bath after a game; it was said he always "left a trail of smoke where ever he went"! Hailing from a noted sporting family, several of the McPherson clan played football and became accomplished trainers. James, David and John were with Kilmarnock, the latter, known as 'Kytie' being capped by Scotland. And Jimmy's son, James (junior) (qv) also carried on the McPherson name within the corridors of St James' Park, while his brother John was to sadly to die at an early age. Jimmy's third son, Robert, appeared for United in local football during 1917-18 and 1918-19 then followed in the family tradition, being a trainer in Holland with the HBS club, then with Ipswich Town during the Thirties. Additionally, United's long-serving trainer was also related by marriage to Edwin Dutton (qv), on United's staff and who appeared for the German national side in 1909. McPherson was at the core of much success with the Magpies; four title wins and seven FA Cup finals. Sandy also trained both the England and Scotland teams during his career, looking after the England amateur tour to Belgium during May 1923. Residing in Jesmond, when he died in 1932, one obituary noted that, Jimmy had been at the very heart of Newcastle United and had, "lived for the club".

(Note: Another Kilmarnock footballer, Hugh McPherson, may also be related but is not confirmed.)

McPHERSON James Quar (junior) 1927-1938

Trainer
5'10"
b. Kilmarnock, 13 April 1891
d. Newcastle upon Tyne, 12 August 1960

Career: North Shields Ath/ UNITED trial Aug 1911/ Houghton Rovers Feb 1914/ Vitesse (Neth) c1920/Norway manager Aug 1920/Merthyr Town trainer cs 1921, becoming manager April 1922 to cs 1923/UNITED asst-trainer c1927, becoming trainer July 1930 to May 1938.

Son of United's celebrated trainer Sandy McPherson (qv) and a 'chip of the old block', James (junior) tried a career as a professional footballer, at Gallowgate for trials in 1911. But he took a trainer's route in the game, briefly looking after Norway for the 1920 Olympics in Antwerp. He returned to Gallowgate during the late 1920s as an assistant to his father, this after being in charge of Football League side Merthyr Town for a period. He took control of United's first-team squad of players when Andy Cunningham arrived as manager of the club. Jimmy became his principal aide as the Magpies reached Wembley in 1932 and lifted the FA Cup. Yet the club didn't progress after that success and McPherson left St James' Park following relegation and on the arrival of a new management team at Board level in the shape of Stan Seymour. After the Second World War he became a chiropodist and masseur on Osborne Road in Newcastle. His son, the third James Q McPherson to be connected with the club, was on the Magpies' books between 1935 and 1938 without reaching first-team football, later being killed in 1942 serving in the Second World War as a sergeant-observer with the RAF.

NELSON James Frederick 1977-date

Assistant-coach & Head of Education & Welfare
5'11"
b. Newcastle upon Tyne, 4 November 1943

Career: Whitehall Jnrs 1959/ Gateshead 1961/Sunderland Aug 1962/Ipswich Town July 1963/ Barrow Jan 1965 to cs 1966/Northern Counties College FC/Northumberland Schools FA coach/UNITED asst-coach 1977, becoming Academy Head of Education & Welfare.

For over 35 years Jimmy Nelson has been associated with United behind the scenes, both coaching and looking after the interests of the club's junior players. The Tynesider started his career in the game as a full-back with Gateshead and was given an opportunity at Roker Park with Sunderland as the 1962-63 season began. Nelson though couldn't break into the red-and-whites' first-eleven with players like Irwin, Ashurst and his namesake Colin Nelson ahead of him. Taken to Portman Road by Jack Milburn, he also found it difficult getting a first-team place with Ipswich Town, but joining Division Four club Barrow during January 1965, Jimmy secured a spot in their Football League line-up. Nelson totalled 15 games at Holker Street over two seasons before a fall-out with the boss led to Jimmy returning to Tyneside and focussing on becoming a teacher. Training at Benton's Northern Counties College, he found a post at Walbottle School and later Gosforth High School. Jimmy kept in touch with football, coaching the school game and was given the opportunity to join the United staff in a part-time role by Richard Dinnis during 1977. Nelson became a full-time coach when the United Academy was up and running becoming Education Officer. During his lengthy period with the Magpies, Jimmy coached the club's junior side with Colin Suggett to FA Youth Cup victory in 1985 and guided a rich line of future stars; Paul Gascoigne, Lee Clark, Steven Taylor and Andy Carroll, to name a handful of many. He also helped Robbie Elliott, Alan Shearer and Michael Chopra on the road to stardom at Gosforth High School. His son James (junior) was in United's junior ranks for a period and later became a tennis player, one-time USA Open Boys doubles champion, rated the best player the North East has produced.

NELSON H 1890

Trainer
b. unknown

Little is known about Nelson, a trainer at Chillingham Road in Heaton to the Newcastle East End team during 1890. He remained less than a season with the club.

OLIVER Kenneth 1971-1974

Assistant-coach
5'10"
b. Pelton, Co Durham, 26 November 1938

Career: Birtley ROF/ Lumley Jnrs/ Sunderland May 1958/ South Shields cs 1959 free/ Barnsley Feb 1960/ Watford July 1963 £10,000/ Workington Feb 1965 exch deal/ Bournemouth Jan 1967 £3,500, retired due to injury Jan 1968/Bradford City coach 1970/UNITED asst-coach cs 1971/Crook Town coach May 1974 to 1976/Birmingham City asst-coach, then coach 1977/Walsall coach cs 1979/Tottenham Hotspur asst-coach 1982 to 1984/Qatar & Saudi Arabia coaching/Carlisle Utd coach Oct 1986/Walsall physio April 1987 briefly.

The departure of first-team coach Dave Smith saw boss Joe Harvey reshuffle his support team and a new addition to the backroom staff was County Durham-born Ken Oliver, a former inside-forward and centre-forward, notably with Barnsley in the lower divisions. Having failed to make the senior eleven at Roker Park, Ken did well elsewhere with a career total of 109 goals in 284 games. He became a regular over four seasons at Oakwell, described as a dogged and durable forward, especially good in the air and having a "quick eye for goal". He became a popular footballer in Yorkshire and was top scorer for two seasons, claiming 54 goals in 113 matches. Afterwards doing well with Watford (63 app) and Workington (94 app), Oliver started on a varied coaching career following a kneecap injury. He landed at St James' Park in the close-season of 1971 and remained as assistant-coach to Harvey and Keith Burkinshaw over three seasons; 1971-72 to 1973-74, largely looking after United's Central League line-up. After as stint with Carlisle and Walsall during the Eighties, Oliver left the touchline of football and became a consultant for KAM Sports, also being a self-employed taxi operator in Tamworth.

PEARS John 1893-1896

Assistant-trainer & Trainer
5'7"
b. probably Northumberland

Career: UNITED asst-trainer 1893, becoming trainer Aug 1895 to March 1896.

First appointed to Newcastle's staff in 1894, John Pears was elevated to the post of first-team trainer as the new 1895-96 campaign began at a salary, according to the club's Minutes, of "35 shillings per week". However, within a year United's directors were expressing dissatisfaction with the methods of Pears and he was sacked during the spring of 1896, being replaced in a temporary role by Willie Thompson. Pears had become an early shareholder of the club during his period at St James' Park, at the time in 1895 living on Pitt Street, off Barrack Road. Census information is not conclusive identifying the trainer, but two candidates living on Tyneside were both born in Northumberland, one in the city, the other in Alston, and living in the Benwell and Elswick districts.

(Note: Some contemporary newspaper and photograph captions note Pears as Pearce.)

PEARSON Nigel Graham 2006-2008

Assistant-manager
6'1"
b. Nottingham, 21 August 1963

Career: Heanor Town/ Shrewsbury Town Nov 1981 £5,000/ Sheffield Wed Oct 1987 £250,000/ Middlesbrough July 1994 £750,000 to May 1998 when he retired/ Carlisle Utd manager & Director of Coaching Dec 1998 to May 1999/Stoke City asst-manager 1999/FA coach to England youth & u21 side 2001/West Bromwich Albion asst-manager Nov 2004, becoming caretaker-manager Sept to Oct 2006/UNITED asst-manager Oct 2006 (England u21 coach Feb 2007 to Aug 2007), becoming caretaker-manager May 2007 and again Jan to Feb 2008/Southampton manager Feb 2008/Leicester City manager June 2008/Hull City manager June 2010/ Leicester City manager Nov 2011.

When Glenn Roeder landed the Newcastle manager's job on a permanent basis, his choice of assistant went to former Middlesbrough and Sheffield Wednesday centre-back Nigel Pearson. Arriving at St James' Park for the start of the 2006-07 programme, Pearson had much experience on the sidelines. Like Roeder, he was a respected ex-defender having caught the eye of bigger clubs when at Shrewsbury (184 app). Despite twice breaking his leg, Nigel went onto play 224 games for the Owls then 139 for Boro. He reached four Wembley cup finals and missed another two due to injury, an inspired leader on the field, Nigel was described as "the heart and soul" of Wednesday for five seasons. Pearson was twice the man United turned to as a caretaker boss; in May 2007 when Roeder departed, then again in January 2008 as Sam Allardyce left. In total he managed the Magpies over four games during those periods. Pearson was offered the role of manager at the St Mary's Stadium during February 2008 although he moved on quickly to take charge of Leicester City then Hull, before moving back to the Foxes in 2011 and guiding them to the Premier League in 2014 for a second time. Form football stock, his grandfather Percy Mills made over 400 games for Notts County while great-uncles Bertie Mills and Arthur Mills also appeared in the senior game during the inter-war years. When at Carlisle, Nigel was in charge when the Cumbrians dramatically scrambled clear of demotion from the Football League on the very last day in 1998-99, thanks to goalkeeper Jimmy Glass netting a famous last minute goal. His son James Pearson made his debut for Leicester in 2014.

In charge: 4 games (caretaker)

Honours:
FL ch winner 2009(m), 2014(m)/FL div 1 champs 1995/FL div 1 prom 1998/FL div 2 prom 1991/FAC final 1997/FLC winner 1991/FLC final 1997, 1998/PFA ToS (d1) 1998, (d2) 1991.

PICKERING John 1962-1965, 1986-1988

Centre-half, Assistant-coach & Coach
6'0"
b. Stockton on Tees, 7 November 1944
d. North Yorkshire, 30 May 2001

Career: Stockton Jnrs/ UNITED jnr Nov 1962, prof April 1963/ Halifax Town Sept 1965 £1,250/ Barnsley July 1974/Blackburn Rovers asst-coach June 1975, becoming asst-manager April 1978, caretaker-manager Oct 1978, then manager Feb 1979 to May 1979/Bolton Wand coach 1979/ Carlisle Utd coach April 1980/Lincoln City asst-manager Nov 1981, becoming manager July 1985 to Dec 1985/ Queens Park Rangers scout 1986/Cambridge Utd scout 1986/UNITED asst-coach June 1986, becoming coach Sept 1987/Lincoln City asst-manager Nov 1988/ Middlesbrough coach May 1990, becoming asst-manager 1992, caretaker-manager May 1994, then asst-coach cs 1994 to demise.

A noted schoolboy footballer on Teesside, captain of the Stockton Boys line-up, John Pickering was on United's books as a young player, but couldn't break into the Magpies first-eleven as a centre-back apart from a single appearance in a friendly against St Johnstone during February 1964. He had tough competition for a central defender's position in the shape of Moncur, Burton, McGrath and Thompson. As a 20-year-old John moved to Halifax in search of regular playing time for a modest £1,250 fee and he became the cornerstone of Town's defence for almost a decade, making a record 402 appearances over nine seasons for the Shay club. Progressing into the coaching scene under Jim Smith and Jim Iley at Blackburn, he was respected by his players and when at Carlisle, Peter Beardsley once remarked that he was the best coach the England player had worked with. Pickering made a sentimental return to St James' Park during the summer of 1986 under Willie McFaul's management. At that time John was out of football and the chance at Gallowgate allowed the Teessider to return to soccer, although his stay on Tyneside was to be a short one. Initially looking after the club's junior players, he exchanged roles with Colin Suggett and became first-team coach for a period. Pickering stood in as caretaker-manager at both Blackburn (1978) and Middlesbrough (1994), having a short period as boss in his own right with Rovers. He was given the honour of leading the Boro side out at Wembley in the 1998 Football League Cup final.

Misc App & Goals: 1 app 0 gls

Honours:
FL div 4 prom 1969.

ROUND Stephen John 2007-2008

Coach
5'10"
b. Burton upon Trent, 9 November 1970

Career: Derby Co jnr cs 1988, prof July 1989/ Retired due to injury 1996/ Nuneaton Borough March 1996/ Derby Co coach March 1996/ Middlesbrough coach June 2001 & part-time England coach cs 2006/England coach Dec 2006/UNITED coach July 2007/Everton asst-manager July 2008/Manchester Utd asst-manager July 2013 to April 2014.

As a player Steve Round was a promising full-back at Derby County, joining the Rams as a kid when Arthur Cox was in charge. He had just reached first-team action with nine outings during 1991-92 and 1992-93 in the second-tier of the game when he was injured. It was a bad knock, a cracked patella injury forcing him to retire when only 25-years-old in 1996 and with only a handful of senior appearances to his name. Round joined County's coaching staff and soon worked with future Middlesbrough and England boss Steve McClaren. When he moved to Teesside, Round joined him and followed McClaren into the England set-up too. Steve remained with the Tees club having a duel role at Boro, but with new boss Gareth Southgate arriving Round left in December 2006. With a growing reputation as a progressive coach, he then moved to St James' Park when 36 years of age during the summer of 2007 as Sam Allardyce's first-team mentor. Young, enthusiastic and respected in the game, Round stayed a season at Gallowgate before becoming second in command to David Moyes at Everton during the close-season of 2008. He followed the Scot to Old Trafford and a dream job with Manchester United, alas to depart before the 2013-14 season was completed when the new managerial team was discarded.

RYDER Henry Joseph 1896-c1901

Assistant-trainer
5'10"
b. Newcastle upon Tyne, 15 October 1868
d. Newcastle upon Tyne, 1 September 1929

One of a well-known footballing family on Tyneside during the Victorian years, Harry Ryder was brought up around Spring Garden Lane near Gallowgate. By the time of the 1891 census he was working as a "slater" on Tyneside, an occupation he was still employed as when the 1911 poll took place, then residing in Byker. Nicknamed 'Hen', he was part of the club's staff as assistant-trainer between 1896 to around 1901, looking after the Magpies' 'A' side as they lifted the Northern Alliance title in 1898 and 1901, as well as the Northumberland Senior Cup on three occasions. One of 14 children, two younger brothers appeared for the club, Joseph (qv) and Isaac (qv). When he died in 1929, Harry was still living in Byker.

SADLER Adam 1990-1996, 2000-2008

Goalkeeper, Goalkeeper-coach & Assistant-coach
5'10"
b. Seghill, Northumberland, 9 January 1980

Career: UNITED jnr 1990/ Manchester Utd jnr 1996/ Barnsley 1998 to 1999/ Gretna c1999/ Gretna c1999/West Allotment Celtic (Newcastle) 2004/UNITED asst-coach July 2000, becoming gkp-coach Feb 2006, Academy asst-coach July 2006, then asst-coach Nov 2007 to Sept 2008/Norwich City asst-coach Dec 2008 to Jan 2009/Team Northumbria coach 2009/Blyth Spartans asst-manager June 2009/Gateshead asst-coach May 2010/Plymouth Argyle asst-coach & Head of CoE Sept 2010/Manchester City asst-coach July 2011/SC Tavriya (Ukr) asst-coach July 2013.

When Roy Tunks departed Tyneside as Graeme Souness was dismissed, Adam Sadler stepped up to look after goalkeeping duties in 2006. From North Tyneside and a product of the Astley school in Seaton Delaval, Adam was a former junior with the Magpies, having first joined the club's development programme when aged nine. He made though, little headway within United's ranks and he tried to progress at both Old Trafford and Oakwell. However, being told at 5'10" his height would always make it difficult for Adam to succeed as a 'keeper, he concentrated on a football career in coaching when 21 years of age. Holding a UEFA Pro Licence, Sadler was involved at United's Academy then replaced Lee Clark as assistant-coach when he moved on, and under Glenn Roeder's management the Seghill-raised coach was highly regarded. But as is common within football, as one manager moves on, his coaching team are forced to do likewise. Sadler headed for Norwich before being appointed alongside ex-United midfielder Scott Sellars as part of Manchester City's set-up. He afterwards took up a post in Ukraine for a period.

SAUNDERS Dean Nicholas 2004-2006

Coach
5'8"
b. Swansea, 21 June 1964

Career: Swansea City jnr June 1980, prof June 1982 (Cardiff City loan 1984-85)/Brighton Aug 1985 free/Oxford Utd March 1987 £60,000/Derby Co Oct 1988 £1m/Liverpool July 1991 £2.9m/Aston Villa Sept 1992 £2.3m/Galatasaray (Trk) July 1995 £2.35m/Nottingham Forest July 1996 £1.5m/Sheffield Utd Dec 1997 free/SL Benfica (Ptg) Dec 1998 £500,000/Bradford City Aug 1999 free to July 2001 when he retired/Blackburn Rovers coach 2001/ Derby Co coach 2002, becoming caretaker-manager May 2003/UNITED coach Sept 2004 to Feb 2006/Wales asst-manager June 2007 & Wales u21 manager/ Wrexham manager Oct 2008 & Wales u21 manager/ Doncaster Rovers manager Sept 2011/Wolverhampton Wand manager Jan 2013 to May 2013.

At the peak of his playing career as a quicksilver forward, Dean Saunders commanded a record £2.9m fee when he moved from the Baseball Ground to Anfield during the close-season of 1991, having scored 57 goals in 131 outings for Derby. Following an uncertain early career, Arthur Cox at Derby did much to develop Saunders into a top goal-getter for the Rams, a nimble, quick and ever-dangerous striker. Saunders only stayed for a little over a season on Merseyside with Liverpool (61 app) before joining Aston Villa where he again recorded good stats on the pitch; 49 goals in 144 matches. Dean was an exciting front man with flair and a sure strike in front of goal. With Graeme Souness at Anfield, as well as in Turkey when he scored the winning goal in the Turkish Cup final, then at the Estadio da Luz in Lisbon, the Welshman joined United's staff as part of the Souness regime during the summer of 2004. Noted as first-team coach, he possessed a lively personality around St James' Park. When his boss was edged out of Gallowgate half way through the 2005-06 campaign, Saunders followed him out the door. Dean wasn't left on the sidelines for long, soon teaming up with the Welsh FA before trying management himself, at Wrexham, Doncaster and Wolves. Winning 75 caps for Wales, Saunders had football blood-line, his father Roy Saunders also pulling on the shirt of Swansea and Liverpool as a half-back. During 1994, Dean had to defend an action in the High Court when Paul Elliott of Chelsea claimed a tackle effectively ended his career. It was determined that Saunders had made an honest attempt to play the ball and he was cleared. His son Callum began a career at Crewe Alexandra.

Misc App & Goals: 0(1) app 0 gls

Honours:
75 Wales caps 1986-2001/1 FL app 1991/FL div 1 champs 1998 (9 app)/FAC winner 1992/FLC winner 1994/Trk Cup winner 1996.

SAXTON Robert 1988-1991

Assistant-manager
5'10"
b. Bagby, near Thirsk, 6 September 1943

Career: Wolverhampton Wand jnr 1960/ Denaby Utd/ Derby Co Feb 1962/ Plymouth Argyle Feb 1968 £12,000/ Exeter City Sept 1975 £4,000, becoming player-manager Jan 1977/Plymouth Argyle manager Jan 1979/ Blackburn Rovers manager May 1981 to Dec 1986/ Preston North End coach Jan 1987/York City manager June 1987/Blackpool coach Sept 1988/UNITED asst-manager Dec 1988, becoming caretaker-manager March 1991/Manchester City chief-scout Oct 1991/ Blackpool chief-scout, becoming asst-manager 1994/ Sunderland asst-coach June 1995, becoming asst-manager Aug 1998 to Oct 2002, later returning July 2006/Plymouth Argyle asst-coach briefly 2010-11.

Bobby Saxton had a respectable if not spectacular playing career in the lower divisions. A wing-half or centre-half with resolve, he played on over 450 occasions, captain at Plymouth in many of his 256 outings for the Pilgrims. Wholehearted and enthusiastic, he brought those qualities to St James' Park when he was appointed as Jim Smith's aide in December 1988. Described by one player at St James' Park as a "bubbly, enthusiastic character", Saxton almost helped guide United back into the First Division on the club's relegation, but a play-off disappointment was the runners-up prize for a season of hard work in 1989-90. He was caretaker-boss at Gallowgate for one match during March 1991 when Smith departed. Saxton later though assisted Peter Reid in taking Sunderland into the Premier League for the first time in 1996. As a manager with Exeter during 1977, Saxton won the Fourth Division championship trophy.

In charge: 1 game (caretaker)

Honours:
FL div 3 prom 1975/FL div 4 prom 1977(pm).

SMITH David Bowman 1967-1971

Assistant-coach & Coach
5'10"
b. Dundee, 22 September 1933

Career: Ashdale/ East Craigie/ Burnley jnr cs 1950, prof Sept 1950/Brighton July 1961/Bristol City July 1962/Burnley asst-coach c1962/Libya FA national coach/Sheffield Wed asst-coach 1965, becoming coach/UNITED asst-coach June 1967, becoming coach July 1968/Arsenal asst-coach cs 1971/ Mansfield Town manager April 1974/Southend Utd manager May 1976 to June 1983/Plymouth Argyle manager Dec 1984/Dundee manager June 1988 to Jan 1989/Torquay Utd manager Oct 1989 to April 1991/ Cyprus coaching 1993/afterwards local coaching in the South West.

A former Scottish youth and amateur international, as a player Dave Smith was a promising full-back with Burnley, a regular during 1957-58 and 1958-59, but unlucky to be on the sidelines when the Turf Moor club won the title in 1959-60. Dave had the misfortune to fracture his leg on no fewer than five occasions and as a consequence had a career on the field which never fully developed. As a coach Smith became a likable and jovial character, popular with his players, but tough and forceful with a competitive Scottish edge. Replacing Ron Lewin as United's first-team coach in the close-season of 1968, he was meticulous in method and on the bench throughout the clubs Inter Cities Fairs Cup success during the following season. But Dave soon afterwards departed for Highbury after a dispute over wages...and having to include painting the dressing-rooms to his coaching duties, such was life at Gallowgate then. Smith later was in charge of lower division clubs, having success at Southend, Mansfield and at Plymouth where he was within a whisker of taking Argyle into the top division. Smith returned to his native Dundee as boss of the Dark Blues after nearly 40 years south of the border, however that move was only to last seven months. Later Dave settled in the Plymouth area and moved into grass-roots football, coaching local youngsters in the Devon area as well as an occasional scout for senior clubs.

Misc App & Goals: 0(1) app 0 gls

Honours:
Scot sch-youth app/Scot amat app/FL div 4 champs 1975(m), 1981(m)/FL div 3 prom 1986(m)/FL div 4 prom 1978(m).

SMITH Simon Timothy Gordon 1978-82, 1993-04

Goalkeeper & Goalkeeper-coach
5'10"
b. Newton Aycliffe, 16 September 1962

Career: UNITED jnr Nov 1978, prof Oct 1980 to June 1982 free/ Whitley Bay July 1982/ Gateshead cs 1985/ Blyth Spartans Jan 1988/ Gateshead again to 1995/ Specialist part-time gkp-coach to a number of clubs including UNITED 1993, Sunderland, Carlisle Utd (being also a non-contract player to all three clubs), Wigan Ath, Manchester Utd, Sheffield Wed, Hull City and Hartlepool Utd/UNITED gkp-coach cs 1999 to Sept 2004/Canada FA & LA Galaxy (USA) gkp-coach 2006/ Carlisle Utd part-time gkp-coach July 2007 to Aug 2008/FA gkp-coach 2009, becoming national gkp-coach & manager.

On Newcastle United's books as a teenager, Simon Smith was a young rival to the likes of Steve Hardwick and Kevin Carr at St James' Park. Opportunities though were virtually non-existent for the youngster and Simon decided to play non-league, with notably Gateshead, where he totalled 501 games. He also focussed on a career as a specialist goalkeeper coach where in due course Smith became a well respected expert, obtaining the top UEFA Grade A licence as well as earning a BSc in sports studies. He set up his own goalkeeping coaching school during 1995 and joined the adidas national coaching programme in 2000. Simon held sessions far and wide, from the North East to Vancouver, also being at varying times a part-time coach with a string of professional clubs. Following a full-time role with United during the early years of the Millennium (when he appeared once on tour against Trinidad in May 2000), Smith joined the Football Association set-up and apart from coaching various levels of England teams, was appointed head of all goalkeeping coaching. Based in Whitley Bay, he was also a consultant to the Canadian Soccer Association. His son Ben Smith (qv) was also on United's books and tasted friendly action with the Black'n'Whites.

Misc App & Goals: 1(1) app 0 gls.

SPRAGGON Frank 1977-1978

Assistant-coach
5'9"
b. Newcastle upon Tyne, 27 October 1945

Career: Middlesbrough jnr, prof Nov 1962 to April 1976/ Minnesota Kicks (USA) 1976/ Hartlepool Utd Nov 1976/ Retired due to injury/UNITED asst-coach Feb 1977 to Nov 1978/KR Reykjavik (Ice) manager 1977/ Later coaching in County Durham and Teesside, including Middlesbrough asst-coach.

Although Tynesider Frank Spraggon spent the majority of his playing career with Teesside rivals Middlesbrough, the left-back and occasional central defender, had been raised a Magpie supporter in his youth, growing up in the Marley Hill and Whickham area of Tyneside. Frank could have joined United, Preston or West Bromwich Albion as a teenager, however he decided to settle in Cleveland soon developing a bond with notably, trainer Harold Shepherdson (marrying his daughter), being a 17-year-old debutant for Boro. It was at Ayresome Park that Frank played the majority of his football, a regular from 1967-68. Over 13 years with Boro, Frank totalled a substantial 332 haul of games despite being hindered by a cartilage operation which went wrong during season 1971-72 and left him with partly blurred vision. Part of Newcastle's backroom team in 1976-77 and 1977-78, Spraggon was appointed when Richard Dinnis took control, but he left St James' Park after a dispute. Afterwards Frank was involved in coaching at Middlesbrough's Centre of Excellence and Community scheme, as well as more generally in Cleveland and County Durham. He is also involved in Boro's Former Players Association.

Honours:
FL div 2 champs 1974/FL div 3 prom 1967 (1 app).

STONE Steven Brian 2009-date

Assistant-coach & Coach
5'9"
b. Gateshead, 20 August 1971

Career: Cleveland Hall Jnrs (Gateshead)/Nottingham Forest jnr June 1987, prof May 1989/ Aston Villa March 1999 £5.5m/ Portsmouth loan Oct 2002, pmt Dec 2002 free/Leeds Utd June 2005 to Dec 2007 when he retired/UNITED part-time asst-coach May 2009, becoming asst-coach March 2010, then coach Dec 2010, briefly caretaker-manager Dec 2010.

When Alan Pardew was installed as boss the Londoner made sure he was surrounded by staff that not only knew their football, but also understood what the club meant to the local public. Two were Tyneside-born and bred; John Carver and former England international Steve Stone. To have a first-rate career as a midfield player who loved to raid down the right flank, Stone was at the peak of his game during the mid to late Nineties. As a teenager he wrote to Newcastle and other clubs for a trial and it was with Nottingham Forest, for a period under Frank Clark's management, that he blossomed. At the City Ground for over 15 years (229 app), reaching the England line-up as a forceful, workaholic midfielder nicknamed 'Bulldog' by some. After suffering knee problems, Stone was transferred to Aston Villa towards the end of the 1998-99 season and although he recorded over 100 games, was often on the sidelines due to injury. He was affected by a troublesome back complaint then unluckily Steve then suffered a persistent Achilles injury. From Gateshead, after retiring Steve settled in Northumberland and couldn't be more pleased to land a coaching position with United during 2010, the club he supported since a schoolboy, initially at the club's Academy and later as assistant-coach to the reserve eleven. When Pardew arrived, he soon recognised Stone's experience at the top level would be an asset to the senior pool, elevating the Geordie to first-team coach during the 2010-11 season. Steve was joint caretaker-boss with Peter Beardsley when Chris Hughton departed, but never selected the side.

Misc App & Goals: 0(1) 0 gls

Honours:
9 Eng caps 1995-96/1 unoff Eng app 1996/FL div 1 champs 1998, 2003/FL div 1 prom 1994/FAC final 2000/PFA ToS (PL) 1996.

TUNKS Roy William 1974, 2004-2006

Goalkeeper & Goalkeeper-coach
6'0"
b. Wuppertal (Germany),
21 January 1951

Career: Lancing/Rotherham Utd jnr Nov 1966, prof March 1968 (York City loan 1968-69) (Ipswich Town loan 1973-74) (UNITED loan Aug 1974)/ Preston North End Nov 1974 £7,000/Wigan Ath Nov 1981, becoming player-coach 1984, then asst-manager 1986/Hartlepool Utd July 1988/Preston North End Nov 1988 to 1990 when he retired/FA coach, also coaching England women's team/Blackburn Rovers gkp-coach June 1997/UNITED gkp-coach Oct 2004 to Feb 2006/ Tranmere Rovers gkp-coach July 2009/USA coaching c2010/Manchester City Academy gkp-coach 2011/Also various coaching activities between appointments, including Premier Soccer Academies.

Roy Tunks had two spells at St James' Park, once as an emergency goalkeeper at the start of the 1974-75 season, then some 30 years later when he arrived as a specialist coach to Newcastle's goalkeepers. The Magpies pre-season preparation during August 1974 was based around the Texaco Cup tournament and with regular deputy to Willie McFaul, reserve Martin Burleigh in dispute with the club, United were left with untried youngsters Bell and Edgar. Boss Joe Harvey called for Roy Tunks, then with Rotherham United and a noted 'keeper in the lower divisions, with the Millers in 158 games. He wanted a move up the football pyramid and the Newcastle crisis was his opportunity to impress and seal a deal. Tunks caught the eye in training and was an unused sub in a Texaco fixture against Middlesbrough. But United would not pay the quoted fee of £70,000, at the time a substantial amount. Born on a British Army complex in Germany and raised in Sussex, Roy never got a move to the big-time. But he continued to show up well during 10 seasons with Preston (355 app) and later for Wigan (302 app), totalling over 800 games in league and cup football as he played on until he was nearly 40 years of age. Roy turned to coaching, joining the Football Association set-up in Lancashire. Tunks became Blackburn's coach under Graeme Souness and he moved to Tyneside for a second time when his Ewood boss was newly in charge for the 2004-05 season. Roy's stay on Tyneside was longer this time around, for 16 months instead of a few weeks. When Souness departed, Tunks left too, afterwards continuing to be a valued coach in the UK and abroad described as having a "unique and acerbic wit".

Misc App & Goals: 0 app 0 gls (1 sub no app)

Honours:
FL div 3 prom 1978/FL div 4 prom 1982/FLT winner 1985.

VEITCH D 1893

Trainer
b. unknown

Briefly noted as one of the club's trainers during season 1893-94, no hard information on Veitch has been discovered in the contemporary news press. He appears to have left the club's new base at St James' Park as quickly as he arrived.

WADSWORTH Michael 1999-2001

Assistant-manager & Coach
5'10"
b. Barnsley, 3 November 1950

Career: Worsbrough Bridge Miners Welfare c1971/ Gainsborough Trinity/ Scunthorpe Utd Aug 1976/ Frickley Ath cs 1977, becoming player-coach/ Mossley 1978-79/ FA North West Regional coach, becoming FA asst-coach 1982 to 1991, in various roles including technical co-ordinator, match observer, non-league FA manager/ Matlock Town manager 1985-86/ Barnsley asst-coach 1992, becoming caretaker-manager May 1993 to cs 1993/Carlisle Utd manager & Director of Coaching Aug 1993/Norwich City asst-coach Jan 1996/ Scarborough manager June 1996 to Jan 1999/Colchester Utd manager Jan 1999 to Aug 1999/St Kitts & Nevis part-time coach cs 1999/Crystal Palace asst-coach Sept 1999/UNITED coach Sept 1999, becoming asst-manager/Southampton asst-manager July 2001/ Oldham Ath manager Nov 2001/Huddersfield Town manager July 2002 to March 2003/DR Congo national manager Nov 2003 to Jan 2004/SC Beira Mar (Ptg) manager May 2004 to Sept 2004/Shrewsbury Town asst-manager Jan 2005 to March 2006/Gretna Director of Club Development Dec 2006, becoming asst-manager cs 2007, then caretaker-manager Feb 2008 to March 2008/Chester City manager June 2009 to Sept 2009/Hartlepool Utd manager Aug 2010 to Dec 2011/ Celtic Nation manager April 2013 to Sept 2013/ Sheffield Utd coach Oct 2013/Sheffield FC manager May 2014.

Without any real pedigree as a player, Mick Wadsworth carved out a career in football coaching and management which spanned over 30 years. A centre-forward in non-league, he had a spell with Scunthorpe appearing on 31 occasions as a striker during season 1976-77 when they battled near the bottom of Division Four. Wadsworth began coaching with Frickley in Yorkshire then spent several years on the Football Association's coaching staff, for a period being an official "match observer" for England managers Bobby Robson and Graham Taylor. Mick was in charge at Carlisle when they lifted the Third Division title in 1995 and guided the Cumbrians to Wembley in the Football League Trophy. Trusted by Bobby Robson, United's boss appointed 45-year-old Wadsworth as assistant-manager at St James' Park in September 1999. The Yorkshireman spent two seasons as Bobby's aide during 1999-2000 and 2000-01. But he moved on during the summer of 2001, being offered the assistant-manager's job at Southampton. Numerous appointments followed for Mick; from Oldham to the African Cup of Nations with Congo, but rarely did he find any degree of success. In 2014 he joined the world's oldest football club, Sheffield FC.

Honours:
FL div 3 champs 1995(m)/FLT final 1995(m).

WATSON David 2011-date

Assistant-coach
5'11"
b. Liverpool, 20 November 1961

Career: Liverpool jnr April 1977, prof May 1979/ Norwich City Nov 1980 £200,000/ Everton Aug 1986 £1.23m, becoming caretaker-manager March to May 1997, retired playing March 2001, becoming asst-coach/ Tranmere Rovers manager April 2001 to Sept 2002/Liverpool schools coach 2004/Wigan Ath asst-coach April 2008/UNITED asst-coach Nov 2011.

A formidable centre-half when at his prime with Everton, Dave Watson was the archetypical English centre-back, consistent and committed. He joined Newcastle's highly experienced coaching team in November 2011 with a remit of looking after the club's Under-18 line-up. Some 30 years earlier and working as a metal worker, as a teenager at Anfield he didn't get the break to appear for the all-conquering Reds in senior football and had to move to Norwich to get the start he wanted. At Carrow Road in 261 games, Dave became an established central defender, much coveted by top sides. Watson returned to Merseyside to pull on Everton's blue shirt, becoming a lynchpin as the club lifted league and cup honours, skipper when they won the FA Cup in 1995. A leader from the back and disciplined on the field, Watson also became an England centre-back. By the time he moved into coaching at Goodison Park at the end of the Nineties, Watson had totalled almost 530 games for the Toffees over 14 seasons. His younger brother Alex played a handful of games for Liverpool then notably with Bournemouth and Torquay.

Honours:
12 Eng caps 1984-88/7 Eng u21 app 1984/FL champs 1987/FL div 2 champs 1986/FL div 2 prom 1982/FAC winner 1995/FAC final 1989/FLC winner 1985/PFA ToS (d2) 1986.

WISE Dennis Frank 2008-2009

Director of Football
5'7"
b. Kensington, London, 16 December 1966

Career: Bellevue Jnrs/ Southampton nursery (Slough) 1979, jnr 1981, prof 1982/ Wimbledon March 1985/ Chelsea July 1990 £1.6m/ Leicester City June 2001 £1.6m/ Millwall Sept 2002 free, becoming player-manager Nov 2003 to May 2005/ Southampton Aug 2005 to Dec 2005, becoming player-coach then caretaker-manager Dec 2005/Coventry City coach Jan 2006/Swindon Town manager May 2006/ Leeds Utd manager Oct 2006/UNITED Director of Football Jan 2008 to March 2009/Chalfont St Peter development role Oct 2009.

One of the celebrated Crazy Gang of fast-rising Wimbledon during the 1980s and recording 165 games at Plough Lane, Denis Wise developed into a player rated as one of the country's best midfield men; determined and a real competitor on the field. He lifted the FA Cup alongside Andy Thorn and Dave Beasant for the Dons before making a big move to Stamford Bridge in 1990. With Chelsea for 11 seasons (445 app 75 gls), he skippered the Blues to trophies and became one of football's characters. Small, aggressive and chirpy in action, Wise reached the England side too. He was often involved in skirmishes on the field and occasionally made headlines for the wrong reasons off the pitch; involved later in his career in a brawl when at Leicester with teammate Callum Davidson. Following Mike Ashley's takeover of the club during the summer of 2007, Wise was appointed to an important boardroom role of Director of Football. He commanded a powerful position with a place on the Club's Board advising the new ownership as well as appointed boss, as it was noted, to "aid the quest for talent", assisting in signing and developing players, as well as controlling reserve and junior set-ups. Never too popular with the Geordie support as a player, he wasn't accepted on Tyneside, especially when he seemingly was at odds with Kevin Keegan over transfer policy, once the former United icon had been installed as manager for a second time. Wise's stay with Newcastle United was never going to last long and he departed during March 2009 following the acrimonious dispute between Keegan and club. Wise twice successfully defended court actions; once in 1995 following a dispute with a taxi driver, then during 2013 after a financial dispute with ex-Newcastle associate and Charlton co-owner Tony Jimenez. His son Henry Wise started a career with QPR.

Honours:
21 Eng caps 1991-2001/3 Eng B app 1989-90/1 Eng u21 app 1988/FL div 2 prom 1986 (4 app)/FAC winner 1988, 1997, 2000/FAC final 1994, 2004/FLC winner 1998/ECWC winner 1998/ESC winner 1998.

WOODFIELD David 1979-1980

Assistant-coach
5'11"
b. Lemington Spa, 11 October 1943

Career: Manchester Utd trial/ Wolverhampton Wand amat Jan 1959, prof Oct 1960 (Los Angeles Wolves (USA) loan cs 1967)/Watford Sept 1971 £30,000, becoming player-coach June 1973, retired playing 1974, then coach May 1975/ Qatar national asst-coach cs 1975/Saudi Arabia national coach 1976/ UNITED coach July 1979 to June 1980/Afterwards coaching in Oman, Kuwait and Malaysia with Sabah FC to 2011.

When Bill McGarry took over the managerial reigns in November 1977 the former England wing-half reorganised his coaching staff and later brought in trusted lieutenant David Woodfield as assistant-coach. Having worked with McGarry in the Middle East and as a player for Wolves, a close working relationship existed. As a footballer Woodfield had been a tall and positive centre-half for the Molineux club, a popular and regular defender in the gold shirts from season 1962-63. He played on 276 occasions, occasionally at full-back too, showing a determined, dogged and honest attitude

Support Staff

in the traditional style of the centre-half. David's stay on Tyneside was not a long one, less than a year, departing in the summer of 1980. Later Woodfield continued on what was a varied career around the globe, in 1990 having to flee Kuwait as a result of Iraq's invasion. For a period David resided in Suffolk running a traditional country pub and by 2013 had settled in Burwell, Cambridgeshire where he did a bit of coaching for the local Burwell Tigers.

Honours:
FL div 2 prom 1967.

WOODMAN Andrew John 2010-date

Goalkeeper-coach
6'3"
b. Camberwell, London,
11 August 1971

Career: Selsdon Jnrs 1982/ Crystal Palace jnr 1986, prof July 1989 (Bognor Regis loan)/ Exeter City July 1994/ Northampton Town March 1995/Brentford Jan 1999 (Peterborough Utd loan 1999-2000)(Southend Utd loan 2000-01)/Colchester Utd loan Nov 2000, pmt cs 2001/ Oxford Utd loan Jan 2002, pmt March 2002/Redbridge Aug 2004/Stevenage Borough Jan 2005/Torquay Utd trial/Thurrock April 2005/ Rushden & Diamonds July 2005 player-gkp-coach, becoming asst-manager 2006/West Ham Utd gkp-coach 2006/Charlton Ath gkp-coach cs 2007/UNITED gkp-coach Dec 2010.

Having worked with United's boss Alan Pardew as a player at Crystal Palace then on his coaching staff at West Ham and Charlton, Andy Woodman moved to the North East from his London base as 2010 closed to look after the fitness and development of the club's goalkeepers. Replacing Paul Barron, the Londoner had been a lower division stopper for 17 years (468 app) after starting as an apprentice with his local club at Selhurst Park. He was an understudy to Nigel Martyn, on the bench for most of the season without getting a game when Palace won promotion to the Premier League in 1993-94 – then being handed a free transfer. Woodman did well at Northampton, appearing on almost 200 occasions for the Cobblers including two successive Play-off finals at Wembley. When with Rushden & Diamonds an ankle ligament injury curtailed his playing career. Possessing an effervescent personality, the imposing Woodman quickly became a popular character on the sidelines at Gallowgate. Andy co-wrote Woody & Nord with Gareth Southgate, a football book with an interesting twist; relating the very different career journeys of the two Palace juniors, one to the very top, and the other in the game's professional basement. With a family background steeped in boxing, his father was a sparring partner to champion Terry Downs, while his grandfather was a noted bare-knuckle fighter in London, a training partner in the ring to another celebrated champion, Tommy Farr. Andy's goalkeeping son, Freddie Woodman, joined United in 2011 and reached the young England set-up.

Honours:
FL div 3 champs 1999/FL div 3 prom 1997.

Physio Team

In addition to regular appointments of trainers and coaches over Newcastle United's history, in post-war years the club employed a dedicated physiotherapist. At first ex-players and trainers took over the role, but then specially trained and qualified professionals looked after United's squad of players.

COLLINS Brian 1977-1982

Physiotherapist
5'10"
b. unknown

United's first specialist physiotherapist, taking over from ex-trainer Alex Mutch during the close-season of 1977, Brian Collins remained at St James' Park for five years before leaving during the summer of 1982 following a fall-out with boss Arthur Cox. He remained in the North East out of football, later a clinical educator in Wansbeck's physiotherapy department.

LIVERSEDGE Ian 1982-1984

Physiotherapist
5'7"
b. Orrell, near Wigan

A junior player with Everton and amateur with Blackpool as well as Crewe, Ian Liversedge went to Chester College to train as a PE teacher. He later taught at a Birkenhead school for a period and began to pursue a career in physiotherapy, obtaining a degree at Salford. Liversedge entered senior football for a second time when he became part-time physio with Tranmere Rovers before landing the Newcastle United job in July 1982. When on Tyneside Ian also played occasionally for Whitley Bay before settling back in the North West. He was attached to Oldham, Manchester United, Stoke City, Burnley and Accrington Stanley at various times, also setting up a Sports Physio Therapy service in the Greater Manchester area. Liversedge continued to be involved with clubs in that region, latterly with Altrincham, Fleetwood Town and across the Pennines with Huddersfield.

MUTCH Alexander Christopher Pusey 1929-1983

Assistant-trainer &
Physiotherapist
5'9"
b. Inverurie, Aberdeenshire,
11 July 1913
d. Newcastle upon Tyne,
January 1987

The son of United goalkeeper Sandy Mutch (qv), young Alex joined the club in 1929 and was a teenage amateur player, this after his father's move from Huddersfield Town to become the Magpies' regular 'keeper then on retirement, club groundsman. Initially on the groundstaff, Mutch (junior) was a teenager with aspirations as a footballer having played for Newcastle Boys when at Atkinson Road school and visited Liverpool as a trialist. However, he never made it as a player and in 1932 joined United's training staff as an assistant to ex-player Andy McCombie, at varying times looking after the club's junior line-ups. Alex was to remain a bright and breezy character in the corridors of Gallowgate for nearly six decades; witnessing much glory in league, cup and even Europe during his time with the Magpies. Mutch began to also look after the ailments of players and when football clubs decided to appoint a dedicated physio during the 1950s,

the Scot became Newcastle's first such appointment, described initially as "Treatment Specialist", although his role was far removed from the highly sophisticated fitness and injury teams now in place. Then heat-lamp treatment, rub-downs and the 'magic sponge' were the order of the day, and when a bad knee or ankle injury often ended a player's career. Alex, more often than not clad in an old-style white medical coat, was an important part of the Black'n'Whites renowned spirit during the Fifties and Sixties; one of several old-hands within St James' Park steeped in the tradition of the club. He was a jovial figure, nicknamed within St James' Park as 'The Great Claude' after a television character Claude Snudge from the Bootsie & Snudge comedy series. Having worked with the good and great of United for a lifetime, Mutch knew his football. His 57 years of service is one of the longest on record. Alex retired in 1983 and afterwards resided in Newcastle. During World War Two, he served with the Medical Corps and was at the famous battle of El Alamein.

WRIGHT Derek 1984-date

Physiotherapist
5'10"
b. Stanley, Co Durham,
10 October 1958

Derek Wright is another long-time member of United's backroom staff, serving as physiotherapist in the treatment-room for more than 30 years, one of the club's longest serving figures behind the scenes. Born and raised in Stanley, Derek was a more than decent full-back as a teenager with Durham Boys and earned a contract with Arsenal, joining the Gunners in 1975. A stocky and solid defender, Wright brushed shoulders with many of football's top stars at Highbury; Alan Ball, Liam Brady and former United idol Malcolm Macdonald included. Derek appeared for Arsenal's junior and reserve side, and in friendly action for the first-eleven, but an injury to his ankle before he was 20 wrecked his career. That unfortunate set-back was bad enough to end his top-class playing days in the game although the disappointment and experience served him well by the time he had returned as a physio. Leaving North London in 1976, Derek tried to play again at a lower level with York City, while he also turned out for non-league Durham City. But by then Wright concentrated on a path in physiotherapy, initially training and working at Pinderford Hospital in Wakefield from 1977 and then back in the North East at a Bedlington rehabilitation centre, Hartfield Hall. Derek joined Fulham as physio in 1984 when Malcolm Macdonald was in charge before landing the post at St James' Park during October 1984. It was a dream move for the likable Wright, having supported the Magpies as a kid. Involved in day-to-day team matters with the Magpies, Derek worked under 16 different managers during his lengthy period in the Gallowgate treatment room. Wright was also physio to England Under-21 set-up for six years covering three European Championships. Derek actually turned out in Newcastle colours on six occasions, in friendlies between 1986 and 1992.

Misc App & Goals: 1(5) app 0 gls

Club Doctors

From earliest times, Newcastle United have appointed a Club Doctor to oversee medical issues. In addition, certain directors of the club also were respected medical men and took an active interest in the players' well being. While a full list of all doctors associated with the Magpies is incomplete, the following individuals have held the position at various times over the years.

As Director: *Braithwaite F, Nevin RW, Rutherford R, Rutherford RJ, Salkeld DV, Simpson RW.*

As Club Doctor: *Appleby EP, Beveridge K (pictured), Catterson P, MacKay J, McDonald R, McGuiness I, Stevenson G.*

SECTION 5 Directors & Officials

Individuals to have served the club at Board of Director level including Chairmen as well as other modern posts. Included are the pioneering Committee men of Stanley FC and Newcastle East End FC in the years before the club turned professional during 1890 (see Introduction for further classification).

Included are all those personalities to be formally appointed a Director of Newcastle United as well as, where traced, the early Committee men of the Magpies' pioneers. When Stanley FC kicked off in the Byker area of Newcastle late in 1881, the football club was run by an organising Committee, with a President elected by 1885 if not before. Under the title of East End, they became a Limited Company during February 1890 with a shareholding of 2,000 ten-shilling shares. A formal Board of Directors was created and over much of the period which followed, ownership and control of the Magpies has been restricted to holders of those shares, with the Board empowered to accept or reject the transfer or sale of such shares. It was in many respects a closed-shop until Sir John Hall's takeover as the 1990s opened, when, ironically the new ownership of Newcastle United was held by substantially one family.

During the last 30 years the club's corporate structure and titles has varied, confusingly being renamed Newcastle United PLC between 1990 and 1992 although directors over this short period were the same as for the football club. Generally spans in the boardroom are the first and last with all corporate entities. The club was listed on the Stock Exchange as a PLC during April 1997 and the organisation created a separate PLC Board, from the latter months of 1996 (formally in February 1997) to July 2007 (formally to February 2008), those Directors and Officials are included, notated 'PLC Director'.

At the heart of Newcastle United for a century and more has been the Club's Secretary, the man who held the administrative controls and managed day-to-day business. These important individuals are also included as are modern posts of Managing Director, Chief Executive, President and Sole Owner.

Biographies of Directors and Officials who were also United players, managers or support staff are included Sections 1-4 ref: Armstrong J, Auld JR, Bennie RB, Broughton J, Cook JP, Coulson WA, Crawford R, Dixon J, Fenwick J, Finlay W, Gray C, Hiscock MK, Seymour GS, Speight J, Tinlin C, White AH, Wilson W, Wise DF.

Not included are employee 'directors' who were not registered with Companies House or noted in official AGM Reports.

Delight for Board members Wilf Taylor (left) and Stan Seymour (right) as the FA Cup is hoisted by skipper Jimmy Scoular in 1955.

Directors & Officials

ANTONOPOULOS Allison

PLC Director:
Feb 2004-June 2007
b. Alnwick, 1960

The daughter of Sir John Hall (qv), and sister of fellow director Douglas Hall (qv), Allison Antonopoulos became a PLC director during February 2004 to enhance the Hall's representation with the family having a significant stake in Newcastle United. With the Cameron Hall property company, Allison took up an executive role once Wynyard Park became part of the family portfolio in 1987, becoming Managing Director of the luxury hotel and leisure complex which opened on the former Marquis of Londonderry estate near Billingham. She has been credited with much of the historic mansion's restoration into one of the North's top venues.

ARCHIBALD George Greig

Chairman: 1913-1915
Director: June 1897-July 1920
b. Inveresk, near Edinburgh,
15 December 1844
d. Rye Hill,
Newcastle upon Tyne, 1927

Joining United's Board in June 1897, George Archibald was, like the majority of Newcastle's Chairmen, a distinguished Tyneside figure. An engineer in his younger days, he was an enthusiastic supporter of the club's cause during the earliest days of the game in the city, and by the time he was appointed to the directorate had switched trades, becoming a successful wine and spirit merchant also described as a "brewer", in 1890 running the Green Tree on St Lawrence Road in Walker. The elaborately moustached and well-dressed Archibald was also a local politician, being elected to the city corporation in May 1894 and becoming Alderman during 1914. He had a keen interest in municipal matters and was Chairman of the city's Fire Brigade Committee. George was appointed Chairman of the Magpies during 1913 and held the post until the First World War put a stop to football in 1915. Archibald left the Board in the summer of 1920 after 24 seasons, part of the management which had established the club on the football map. He resided in the Rye Hill district of Newcastle to his death.

ARCHIBALD W

Committee: 1888-1889
b. unknown

Recorded in the Tyneside press of the day as being an active Newcastle East End Committee member during the latter years of the 1880s, further information on Archibald has not been traced. He was more than likely a resident of Heaton and Byker.

ARNOLD Andrew Paige

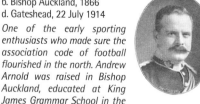

Committee: Oct 1886-1887
b. Bishop Auckland, 1866
d. Gateshead, 22 July 1914

One of the early sporting enthusiasts who made sure the association code of football flourished in the north. Andrew Arnold was raised in Bishop Auckland, educated at King James Grammar School in the town then at Wharfedale boarding school and Durham University as he qualified to be a medical practitioner, following in his father's profession as a surgeon. Along the way to becoming a doctor he played most sports, including football prominently with Tyne and Gateshead as well as for Durham and Northumberland, being secretary of the Durham University FC. He was also a rugby player and talented cricketer, turning out for the Rockcliffe, Northumberland and North Durham clubs. Arnold became a Committee member of Newcastle East End for a short period during the mid-1880s accepting an invitation to join the Heaton club in October 1886. By 1891 he was living in Gateshead, later having a medical practice at Regent House on Bensham Road while he was also Surgeon-Major to the 5th Volunteer Battalion of the Durham Light Infantry for a period as well as Accident Surgeon at Redheugh Colliery in Gateshead.*

ASHLEY Michael James Wallace

Sole Owner: July 2007-date
Director: 2014-date

b. Burnham, Buckinghamshire, 1964

When Mike Ashley purchased the 41.6% share-holding of the Hall family then swiftly acquired the 28% held by Freddy and Bruce Shepherd in Newcastle United during the summer of 2007 for just over £134m, few in the North East had heard of the London-based entrepreneur and billionaire. The headlining deal was a shock to everyone concerned with Magpies and very quickly officials, players and supporters had to come to terms with a new way of running their famous institution. Ashley had become one of the wealthiest businessmen in the country during the Nineties, described by the BBC when he took control as the "the UK's 25th richest man". Creating a sports retail venture with a single shop in Maidenhead during the 1980s, his chain of stores grew rapidly and he floated the Sports Direct business in 2007 and earned a fortune. Living in North London, although an avid football supporter, he arrived at St James' Park with limited knowledge of how the football industry worked. With a new management structure, his team completely overhauled the way United were run, much more on a lean and affordable basis rather than high spending on marquee players with big wages that rarely produced. The initial months and years were at times difficult while the much publicised relationship between owner and supporters become fractious, to an extent that he placed the 'for sale' notice on the club during the autumn of 2008. But Ashley stuck with the Magpies and gradually, his financial model, so different to the previous Hall and Shepherd regime, started to bring dividends. Despite relegation for a season, stability was established at Gallowgate and a strategy rolled out to ensure a step-by-step progression as a Premier League club. Away from St James' Park, Ashley's Sports Direct empire based at Shirebrook in Derbyshire went from strength to strength, becoming a major UK concern which moved into the FTSE 100 during September 2013 as one of the country's most successful companies.

BARKER John Denis

Secretary: May 1959-Aug 1971
b. Norton on Tees,
4 February 1923
d. Newcastle upon Tyne,
1976 (Q3)

Denis Barker followed a longstanding United staff plan from office clerk to assistant-secretary to become Secretary on the demise of Frank Watt (junior) then Ted Hall. Described as an amiable man having worked in a Tyne accounting office, he learnt the ropes of football administration over a period of more than a decade before being elevated to the senior post. Barker joined the club as an office clerk in November 1948 but quickly found himself second-in-command when Watt passed away as 1950 ended. On being appointed Secretary during May 1959 he soon had to cope with first, the shock of relegation at St James' Park, then a headlining High Court case with former player George Eastham which went to a high profile trial. The pipe-smoking Barker, a Benton resident of the city, resigned as the 1971-72 season began following a clash with coaching staff.

BARNES Justin Douglas William

PLC Director: Sept 2007-2008
b. Surrey, 1965 (Q1)

When Mike Ashley acquired Newcastle United in the summer of 2007, a new management team arrived led by Chris Mort. He was supported by short-term appointments of Sports Direct executives Steve Hayward and Justin Barnes. Noted as a United Non-Executive Director, Barnes ran Ashley's various brands such as Lonsdale, Donnay and Slazenger and was described as a "Trade Mark attorney". Justin did not remain at St James' Park for long, making an exit as the club stabilised. He was also noted as Company Secretary of St James Holdings, the company which purchased the Magpies in 2007. Barnes held various positions as a director over a successful business career, since 1992 running The Brandson Partnership Ltd, a management consultancy based in the south.

BATES Stuart Frederick

Director: 1905-Dec 1929
b. Gosforth,
Newcastle upon Tyne, 1861 (Q1)
d. Gosforth, Newcastle upon Tyne, 5 December 1929

As a young man on Victorian Tyneside, Stuart Bates played rugby for the Northumberland club and cricket for South Northumberland. Always a keen sports enthusiast, he tried football too and later became a keen supporter of Newcastle United, joining the director list for the 1905-06 season. That was just as the Magpies began a period of dominance in the English game, Bates being on the Board as the club lifted three Football League titles and reached five FA Cup finals. A solicitor in Newcastle, he spent 25 seasons with the club and had a period on the Management Committee of the North Eastern League, recognised as an advocate of the local game. Living in Gosforth, he was also a keen golfer, one of the founders of the City of Newcastle golf club at Chimney Mills.

BELL Joseph

Chairman:
Aug1908-March1909
Director: 1891-March 1909

b. Newcastle upon Tyne, c1862
d. Newcastle upon Tyne,
22 March 1909

Chairman of the Magpies for a short period at the height of the club's Edwardian mastery, Joseph Bell was an extremely popular character at St James' Park. Nicknamed 'Uncle Joe', he was at the very heart of United's formidable set-up, striking a rare player-director relationship in the days before managers became commonplace. Often leading the team out onto the pitch during that successful era, Bell was seldom away from the playing staff and was a hugely positive factor in the club's development as a top-

ranked side. Colin Veitch wrote of Bell: "He occupied a unique position among the players and was an invaluable aid." With a jovial personality, the well-built Novocastrian hailed from Heaton where he was described as owning a grocery business as well as having an interest in a local building business with his relation John Bell. One of the earliest supporters of the East Enders, he purchased shares as the club became a Limited Company in 1890 and during those formative years loaned the club much needed funds. It was at Bell's residence on Rothbury Terrace during the summer of 1892 that the now historic meeting took place between officials of East and West End which led to the Heatonites moving to St James' Park and being the city's sole principal club. Bell was an early director, but left the Board for a brief period in 1897 only to swiftly return. A liberal, he also served on Newcastle upon Tyne's Board of Guardians. Appointed to the Chair in August 1908, Joseph died when in post during 1909 when the Black'n'Whites were recognised as the best side in the country. At the time Bell lived in Jesmond, he was related to John W Bell (qv) also to serve in the boardroom.

BELL John William

Director: 1905-1907
b. Newcastle upon Tyne, 1860 (Q2)
d. Newcastle upon Tyne, 15 December 1907

A well-known figure on Tyneside, John Bell ran a building business and grocer shop like his elder brother Joseph Bell (qv). He was a freemason in the city, attached to the Byker Holmes Lodge. The family held a powerful shareholding in the club during the early years of United's development. Living in Jesmond, Bell suffered injury after a gas explosion at St James' Park during January 1906 just prior to a United 'A' match when a heating geyser leak ignited. After watching the black-and-whites play Liverpool in December 1907, a wonderful 5-1 victory at Anfield, he died suddenly.

BELL Thomas

Director: 1891-1895

The identity of Newcastle East End director Thomas Bell remains to be verified. There were several Bells living in the district at this time. A Heaton teenager (aged around 19) did purchase shares in the Newcastle East End football venture during January 1891 shortly after the club became a Limited Company, Thomas Bell resided in the core support base of Heaton and Byker, on Heaton Road. Census information shows he was a pattern-maker's apprentice at this time, but he looks to be too young to be on the club's Board and more likely to be the player who appeared once in season 191-92 (qv). It is suspected that East End's Thomas Bell is the same individual who was connected with rival club Newcastle West End a few years earlier. He is the most likely candidate. When West End moved to a new ground at St James' Park, he was noted as a "patron" of the club, Bell kicking off the opening game during September 1886 in his capacity as Sheriff of Newcastle upon Tyne. He may well have become involved with the East End club during 1891, by then having served as Lord Mayor of the city (1889-90) and living in Jesmond, close to several other East End directors at that time. Indeed, by 1891, he resided next door to Stuart Bates. Born in Topcliffe, Yorkshire (7 December 1841), Thomas settled on Tyneside during 1864 becoming a successful shipbroker, senior partner with Quayside-based Pyman, Bell & Co. Pictured,

he was a prominent figure in the community, a local councillor while Thomas was also a director of the North Eastern Bank. He died in his Northumberland country home of Hesleyside in Bellingham on 19 September 1914. It is not thought he was related to Joe or John Bell, on the Board during the era.

BENNETT Lionel Trevor MBE

Director/Associate Director: Jan 1991-Aug 1996
President: March 1993-Dec 1997
Patron: Dec 1997-Jan 2007
b. Blaina, Monmouthshire, 20 June 1921
d. Leicester, January 2007

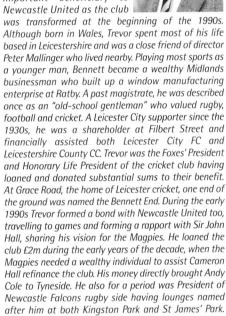

Trevor Bennett was an important beneficiary to Newcastle United as the club was transformed at the beginning of the 1990s. Although born in Wales, Trevor spent most of his life based in Leicestershire and was a close friend of director Peter Mallinger who lived nearby. Playing most sports as a younger man, Bennett became a wealthy Midlands businessman who built up a window manufacturing enterprise at Ratby. A past magistrate, he was described once as an "old-school gentleman" who valued rugby, football and cricket. A Leicester City supporter since the 1930s, he was a shareholder at Filbert Street and financially assisted both Leicester City FC and Leicestershire County CC. Trevor was the Foxes' President and Honorary Life President of the cricket club having loaned and donated substantial sums to their benefit. At Grace Road, the home of Leicester cricket, one end of the ground was named the Bennett End. During the early 1990s Trevor formed a bond with Newcastle United too, travelling to games and forming a rapport with Sir John Hall, sharing his vision for the Magpies. He loaned the club £2m during the early years of the decade, when the Magpies needed a wealthy individual to assist Cameron Hall refinance the club. His money directly brought Andy Cole to Tyneside. He also for a period was President of Newcastle Falcons rugby side having lounges named after him at both Kingston Park and St James' Park. Living in Newtown Linford, Bennett was appointed Newcastle's President and was later a patron of Mallinger's Kettering Town. He also did much for charitable causes and two years before he died, Trevor was honoured with the MBE in 2005 as recognition of his generous donations to an abundance of causes and charities over a number of years.

BIRKETT James

Committee: c1885-1890
Director: Feb 1890-1891

b. unknown

Local Heaton councillor James Birkett became one of the club's first directors when a company was created during February 1890 chairing the inaugural public meeting in Heaton when the new organisation was established. Also a city magistrate, he was on Newcastle East End's Committee in the years preceding the switch to company status. James was an iron-founder and a resident of Heaton and Byker, on Heaton Park Road. Birkett was elected a Vice-President of the club for season 1885-86 to 1887-88.

BLACK John

Director: cs 1892-cs 1899
b. Newcastle upon Tyne, c1839
d. Forest Hall, Newcastle upon Tyne, 13 June 1909

One of the pioneers of football's development on Tyneside, John Black lived in Buckingham Street not far from St James' Park and had interests in the licensing trade. From a Scottish family, he was associated with the running of the Duke of Buckingham, one of several pubs in proximity of the ground. He was also linked with the Lord Hill Inn close by and was described in census records up to his death in 1909 as an "innkeeper". During the sport's early days on Victorian Tyneside, the Lord Hill was a popular location in football circles, associated with what was even then a fervent supporter base. Newcastle West End used the Lord Hill as a headquarters (1 Barrack Road) for a period when the club was based at St James' Park. They changed in the pub before games, walked across Barrack Road in full kit before taking to the field. They were even nicknamed the 'Lord Hill Men' for a time by certain members of the local press. Black was initially very much a Newcastle West End man becoming a committee member and then a director as the club became one of the game's earliest limited companies in July 1890. John was a key figure in the West Ender's cause, and financially more than once helped keep the club afloat in those difficult fledgling years, once in 1890 offering to pay for the erection of a stand at the early St James' Park. Yet the struggle for cash brought about West End's collapse at the end of the 1891-92 season and on his club's demise Black joined up with Newcastle East End, purchasing shares almost immediately and helped forge a single football identity of Newcastle United, supporting his new organisation with cash when needed. Indeed, during October 1893 it is recorded in the club's official Minutes that he paid debts owning to Derby, Liverpool and West Bromwich Albion totalling £18 6s 8d to halt a storm with the Football Association. And a year later it was his gratitude which loaned the club £7 10s (£7 50p) to purchase Bob McDermid. He remained on the United's early hierarchy until 1899. His son, noted as "John Black the younger" also managed public-houses around Tyneside.

BOWMAN George Sir

Director: March 1981-Aug 1990
b. Newcastle upon Tyne, 2 July 1923
d. Newcastle upon Tyne, 3 August 1990

A life-long supporter of Newcastle United, when Sir George Bowman joined the Board in 1981 he broke a tradition of family succession in the Magpies' order. The son of Sir James Bowman, a noted trade unionist on Tyneside and past Chairman of the National Coal Board who was knighted during January 1961, George took the Baronet title on his father's death. A self-made businessman who did not suffer fools gladly, he operated a well-known landscape and garden-centre business, O'Hare & Bowman, on Whitley Road in Shiremoor. George was a down-to-earth Tynesider who gave the club directorate a fresh outlook. An enthusiastic fan at heart, he remained in the boardroom for a decade and was well respected by players and staff for being able to interact successfully with the club's employees.

Directors & Officials

BRAITHWAITE Fenton OBE

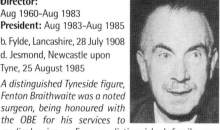

Director:
Aug 1960-Aug 1983
President: Aug 1983-Aug 1985

b. Fylde, Lancashire, 28 July 1908
d. Jesmond, Newcastle upon Tyne, 25 August 1985

A distinguished Tyneside figure, Fenton Braithwaite was a noted surgeon, being honoured with the OBE for his services to medical science. From a distinguished family near Blackpool, educated at Baines Grammar School, then university in Manchester before taking up medicine at St Bartholomew's Hospital, Braithwaite became a specialist in reconstructive techniques, prominent during World War Two with the RAF. He held the rank of Squadron Leader then Acting Wing Commander and cared for injured and burned pilots. Based at RAF Rauceby, much of his work was pioneering and his patients were to be known as the "Guinea Pigs", yet his specialism was hugely successful and the servicemen treated formed a post-war club called the "Guinea Pig Club" in recognition of his, and others, work. Fenton then moved to Tyneside and became Head of Plastic Surgery at the Royal Victoria Infirmary, a leading expert in cleft lip and palate deformities. Braithwaite was elected to the United boardroom as the Sixties began. He possessed a great passion for the game and was to spend 24 seasons as an active member of the Magpies, the highlight of his period at Gallowgate being the club's entry into European competition and subsequent glory in Budapest at the end of 1968-69. Slightly-built, the Lancastrian had a sharp mind and was described as "a man of great wisdom". Living in Jesmond and highly articulate, Fenton spent much of his time with United setting up and establishing the club's pioneer Development Association, his brainchild which was to financially assist the club enormously, funding many ground improvement projects when cash was in short supply. Following retirement from medicine, Fenton attended St James' Park almost daily and was a regular traveller with both the first-team and reserve sides in his capacity as a director. Braithwaite perhaps typified Newcastle's part-time and unpaid directorate for almost a century; one of the region's luminaries, from the elite of the city being eminent in his own particular field.

BRAMWELL William

Director: cs 1892-1906
Jan 1908-June 1924

b. Elswick, Newcastle upon Tyne, 1866 (Q1)
d. Newcastle upon Tyne, 5 June 1924

When William Bramwell purchased shares in the Newcastle East End company during the 1890s he was living at Brighton Grove in the city's West End. Described as a "principal traveller and departmental buyer" for a firm of wholesale grocers, Bramwell was initially a follower of East End's local rivals Newcastle West End. A football enthusiast from earliest days of the game on Victorian Tyneside, he did not allow the demise of the St James' Park club to colour his affection for the sport, becoming immediately a director of the rival Heaton outfit when they relocated to Barrack Road. He remained in the boardroom for all of 32 seasons one of the longest on record (with a short break during 1906 and 1907, returning to service when John Bell died). William saw days of financial struggle as a new Football League member, then helped guide Newcastle to win promotion and develop into the country's top outfit within a decade. An enthusiastic Freemason in Newcastle, so popular and very influential during that era, he was an active member of the Fenham Lodge and a past Master of the Commercial Lodge. William was also linked with the Wesleyan Church and

occupied every office open to a layman. Residing in Fenham, he died just after the Black'n'Whites lifted the FA Cup at the new Wembley stadium in 1924.

BROWN W

Committee: 1888-1889

b. unknown

Recorded in the contemporary press as being a Newcastle East End Committee man during the years of 1888 and 1889, no further details on Brown have been identified. He was though in all probability a football enthusiast living in Heaton or Byker.

CAMERON John

Chairman: Oct 1894-May 1895
& June 1904-Aug 1908
Director: 1891-July 1916

b. Aberfeldy, Perthshire, 14 May 1857
d. Jarrow, 23 July 1916

John Cameron came south from Scotland as a youth with his family to seek work and settled on Tyneside during the 1870s, employed in the clothing business on an apprenticeship with Bainbridge & Company in Market Street. He later worked as a "commercial traveller", a representative for a Leeds based clothier and then developed his own business, residing in the East End heartland of Heaton and later in Jesmond. A supporter of East End's cause, his family was original shareholders possessing one of the biggest stakes in Newcastle United's pioneers. Cameron joined the club's Board a year before the move from Chillingham Road to St James' Park and soon became an influential figure. John was heavily involved forming an infrastructure of local football; he founded the North Eastern League and encouraged the Northern Alliance competition, while he became the first Newcastle director to sit on the country's governing body, the Football League Management Committee, from 1907 to 1916. Appointed Chairman of the Magpies in two spells, briefly before the turn of the century, and then from 1904 to 1908 when the Magpies possessed the nation's top side. Serving 26 seasons in the boardroom, the Newcastle Daily Journal noted Cameron as being "largely responsible for cultivating the scientific game which has characterised the career of Newcastle United". A well known lay preacher too, Cameron died in July 1916 only months after taking over the management of the County Hotel in Jarrow. He left a widow and eight children, the club assisting their well-being by raising a substantial sum of £768. Two other members of the family, James (qv) and Daniel were also shareholders.

CAMERON James

Director: 1893-1894

b. probably Aberfeldy, Perthshire

Related to Chairman John Cameron (qv), the family were the largest equity holders in the Newcastle East End club from the outset in 1890, John, James and Daniel Cameron acquiring 20 shares. James resided with his relation at that time, at Jesmond Vale Terrace and was in the clothing business on Tyneside. A director of the club only briefly, he left most of the football association to John.

CARMICHAEL Michael

Director: 1891-1898

b. Auchterarder, Perthshire, November 1845
d. Oak Bay, British Colombia (Canada), 13 February 1926

A Scot from Perthshire, Michael Carmichael settled on Tyneside, living in North Shields from the 1870s where he built up a successful brewing concern. By the time he spent a substantial sum on a 50 share investment in Newcastle East End during May 1892, Carmichael had lived in Byker and Sunderland then was a resident of Jesmond, on Sandyford Road. On that acquisition he became one of the clubs largest and most powerful shareholders. Appointed a director soon after East End became a limited company, the Scot remained a part of the early Magpie management until he decided to head overseas in 1908. From family history information, Carmichael moved to Canada, living in Montreal, Quebec and by 1911, in Saskatchewan. When he died aged 80, he was residing in Oak Bay near Vancouver.

CASSIDY Denis Patrick

PLC Chairman:
July 1998-Dec 1998
PLC Director:
Feb 1997-Dec 1998

b. Newcastle upon Tyne, 2 February 1933
d. London, 29 June 2014

An enduring supporter of the Black'n'Whites first watching United in 1943, Denis Cassidy was raised in Elswick on Tyneside but moved south during the late 1950s becoming an experienced businessman with a varied career. Beginning his time at the top echelons of British industry with the Dunlop company, he joined British Home Stores in 1969 where he became Chairman and Chief Executive of what later became Storehouse PLC. Cassidy then joined the Boddington Group during 1987 and was appointed Chairman until he retired from the Board in 1995. He was also associated with several other companies including being Chairman of Gillow PLC and at major concerns BAA, Seeboard, Compass, Headway, Liberty as well as Ferguson International Holdings and the Oliver Group. Described as a "City veteran" his calibre fitted the requirement of the club's PLC boardroom as a non-executive director perfectly, joining his boyhood heroes in February 1997. Denis took the PLC Chair on the resignation of Sir Terry Harrison enjoying an excellent working relationship with Freddie Fletcher. But Cassidy left the club at the end of 1998 and later published a book revealing much of his period as a club director, 'The Day the Promises Had to Stop'. He resided in Oakham, Rutland.

CATESBY William Peter

Director: March 1981-Jan 1984

b. Oxford, September 1940

Peter Catesby was described as a "new breed" of director when he was elected to United's Board in 1981. A respected member of the North East business community, Catesby had a hotelier background, a director with the Swallow Hotel Group, a Vaux company which included in their portfolio the Gosforth Park Hotel. Peter was an operator with a modern viewpoint described as a "larger than life character", just what the club's somewhat old-style leadership needed at the time. He was instrumental in setting up a thorough budgeting model for the club, Catesby however, remained one of the Magpies' executives for less than four years. After leaving St James' Park due to disagreements over certain financial decisions in player acquisition as 1984 opened, Peter continued a successful career, becoming Managing Director of Swallow Hotels, then Chief Executive until the company was acquired by Whitbred later in 1999. He then was an advisor to Friendly Hotels for a period, becoming a non-executive director during 2001. Peter was appointed Chairman of The Real Hotel Company the following year and is a past Chairman of the British Hospitality Association. For much of his time in the north Catesby was based in Sedgefield.

CHARNLEY Lee

Director: Dec 2008-date
Managing Director: April 2014-date
Football Secretary: Oct 2007-date
b. Blackpool, November 1977

Working as an administrator with the Football League governing body at their headquarters at Lytham St Annes, Lee Charnley moved across the Pennines to join Newcastle United in 1999 as assistant to Russell Cushing. On the club's takeover by Mike Ashley during the summer of 2007, Cushing soon departed and Lee was appointed Football Secretary in October of that year. Charnley then cemented a position with the new regime being a hardworking as well as thorough administrator and became a director at the end of 2008. Essentially running the weekly business of the Black'n'Whites, with almost 20 years working in football, Charnley did much to transform the Magpies into a club with a stable and healthy financial status. He became Managing Director during 2014.

CLARK William

Committee: 1888-1889
b. unknown

Probably a resident of Heaton and Byker, William Clark is noted in the newspaper columns as serving on Newcastle East End's Committee shortly before the club became a Limited Company in 1890. The 1891 census records three Clarks living in the city; all living in the Byker and Heaton districts. It is likely William is one of these residents.

COOK R

Committee: 1883-1884
b. unknown

Cook was one of the Victorian men of the Byker and Heaton suburb to assist in the early development of Newcastle United. Recoded as being Chairman of Stanley Cricket Club at the time they decided to venture into football, he was also a Committee member of the East End club prior to the formation of a limited company. Cook was certainly engaged with the running of the club during 1883-84 and probably was involved before and after, records being untraced for that period.

CORBIDGE Mark Andrew

Director: July 1996-July 1997
PLC Director:
April 1997-July 1997
Joint Chief Executive:
Nov 1996-July 1997
b. Sheffield, December 1963

Mark Corbidge was one of several high-profile businessmen to be associated with Newcastle United as the club had a short and somewhat ill-fated period as a public company between 1997 and 2007. He joined the club from NatWest Markets prior to becoming a director to oversee the "strategic and business development of the Group" including leading the PLC floatation preparations. Handling the club's transformation to PLC status, Mark gained a degree at Middlesex University then studied in France before joining the corporate finance wing of Rothschild & Sons during 1987. He moved to Warburg & Company then Solomon Brothers in Germany for a period before returning to the UK to run NatWest Markets corporate finance office in Leeds. Mark was appointed Joint Chief Executive with Freddie Fletcher and as Newcastle United converted to PLC ranking in November 1996, he allegedly had disagreements with boss Kevin Keegan over the path the club were heading...Keegan eventually departing. Corbidge himself moved on soon after, during the close-

season of 1997, and subsequently held various appointments in the world of finance. He was with Daughty Hanson and the TMF Group while for a period as the Millennium opened was Chief Executive of Umbro.com, the on-line part of the UK sports company. Corbidge also was involved in the United Soccer League in Florida. He joined the Canada Pension Plan Investment Board during December 2013 as a senior principal, one of the world's largest investors in private equity.

CRAWFORD David

Chairman: Dec 1928-1929
Committee: c1885-1888
Director: June 1904-1929

b. Scotland, c1845
d. Newcastle upon Tyne,
7 February 1930

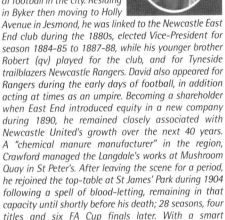

David Crawford was another local dignitary to be associated closely with the rise of football in the city. Residing in Byker then moving to Holly Avenue in Jesmond, he was linked to the Newcastle East End club during the 1880s, elected Vice-President for season 1884-85 to 1887-88, while his younger brother Robert (qv) played for the club, and for Tyneside trailblazers Newcastle Rangers. David also appeared for Rangers during the early days of football, in addition acting at times as an umpire. Becoming a shareholder when East End introduced equity in a new company during 1890, he remained closely associated with Newcastle United's growth over the next 40 years. A "chemical manure manufacturer" in the region, Crawford managed the Langdale's works at Mushroom Quay in St Peter's. After leaving the scene for a period, he rejoined the top-table at St James' Park during 1904 following a spell of blood-letting, remaining in that capacity until shortly before his death; 28 seasons, four titles and six FA Cup finals later. With a smart appearance and neatly trimmed grey beard, he was described as possessing "persuasive eloquence". Chairman of the Black'n'Whites briefly, David was also Northumberland FA President from 1886 to 1889.

CUSHING Russell

Director: Nov 1989-Sept 2007
Chief Operating Officer:
June 2001-Sept 2007
Secretary: July 1973-Sept 2007
PLC Secretary:
July 2000-Sept 2007
b. Norwich, 1947 (Q2)

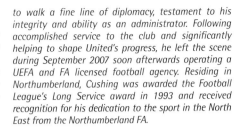

From East Anglia, Russell Cushing left school to become a trainee accountant and first became involved in football as part of Norwich City's office staff, appointed Assistant Secretary in the summer of 1965. When the same Newcastle United post became vacant he was tipped off by ex-United striker Albert Bennett (then at Norwich) and travelled north to land the job during June 1971. Appointed to the Secretary role two years later, Cushing soon became a valued official within football and saw it all happen at St James' Park. He worked through many highs and lows during more than 36 years at Gallowgate, a rollercoaster which took him from the depths of the second-tier, to the top of the Premiership, into the Champions League and dealing with multi-million pound transfers and super-star players from home and on the Continent. Cushing was appointed to the Board initially in 1989 and held executive positions in addition to the traditional Company Secretary post; General Manager and Chief Operating Officer. Although at times he stepped down from the Board at points of restructuring only to quickly return, he ran day to day operations during the turbulent Magpie Group's takeover, and then was at the heart of the club's resurgence afterwards, Russell having at times

to walk a fine line of diplomacy, testament to his integrity and ability as an administrator. Following accomplished service to the club and significantly helping to shape United's progress, he left the scene during September 2007 soon afterwards operating a UEFA and FA licensed football agency. Residing in Northumberland, Cushing was awarded the Football League's Long Service award in 1993 and received recognition for his dedication to the sport in the North East from the Northumberland FA.

DAVIS Harry

Director: Dec 1954-April 1960
b. Newcastle upon Tyne, c1888
d. Newcastle upon Tyne,
3 April 1960

Initially purchasing shares in the club during 1928, Harry Davis like many of United's directorate was a fervent Magpie supporter since childhood. A dental surgeon who resided in Gosforth, he was at the forefront of his profession in the North East, being appointed as President of the British Dental Association for 1957-58. He was a colleague and friend of Chairman Wallace Hurford who was also a prominent member of the dentistry fraternity on Tyneside.

DICKSON Henry Hirst

Director: Oct 1971-Nov 1977
b. Tynemouth, 23 June 1916
d. Newcastle upon Tyne,
13 November 1977

A Tynesider and resident of Jesmond, Harry Dickson was a major shareholder of the club when he joined the Board during October 1971. Related to the Rutherford side of United's boardroom by marriage, Dickson was a prominent civil servant at the extensive government complex in Benton. His son, George Dickson (qv), also became a Newcastle director.

DICKSON George Rutherford

Director: Nov 1984-May 1989
b. Newcastle upon Tyne,
1947 (Q4)
d. Newcastle upon Tyne,
10 February 2010

The son of Harry Dickson (qv) and another within the Rutherford family dynasty at Gallowgate, George Dickson replaced Peter Catesby on the club's top-table during November 1984. A major shareholder thanks to his family inheritance, Dickson was an ardent and fervent United supporter in the family tradition. His holding in the company was the largest at the time and when the share-war for control of Newcastle United erupted, he soon became a significant figure to the success of the Magpie Group. George sold out to John Hall in November 1988 giving the takeover added momentum as a result. For much of his working life, Dickson was employed at Thermal Syndicate and at the civil service centre in Longbenton.

Directors & Officials

DIXON Josephine

Director: May 1995-May 1998
PLC Director:
Dec 1996-May 1998

b. Newcastle upon Tyne, 1959 (Q3)

Appointed Finance Director in 1995 and elevated to the club's Board Jo Dixon remains Newcastle United's first and only female executive in over 130 years to sit in the football boardroom (as distinct to the PLC table). A former graduate of London University, Dixon worked at accountants Deloitte, Touche & Ross in the capital, merchant bank Shire Trust, then investment company County NatWest Ltd. As Newcastle United moved into corporate business during the mid-1990s, Dixon joined United when the club moved towards a PLC flotation. At St James' Park, she took the responsibility of finance as well as information technology and personnel, all as the organisation headed into a new world of football as the decade progressed, leading the due diligence process in the run up to floatation. Raised in Gosforth and educated at the Sacred Heart Grammar School, Dixon held various director appointments after her United post, being involved in the Eden Project as Finance Director for a period. Also having appointments with Standard Life's Equity Income Trust, the Worldwide Healthcare Trust, Baring and Serco companies, latterly Jo settled at Allendale in the Northumberland Pennines running the local Post Office as sub-postmistress, the hub of the community.

DUNN Edward

Director: 1981-May 1989

b. Westerhope, Newcastle upon Tyne, 2 June 1934

From the West End of Newcastle and a supporter since a 12-year-old lad, Eddie Dunn became a club director as the 1980s decade opened, bringing fresh ideas and enthusiasm to an aging boardroom. Running a longstanding and well-known coaching business in the region between which ferried the clubs' players and supporters around the country, Eddie was Managing Director of both Armstrong Coaches and Moordale Coaches until 1969. At that time, Moordale separated from Armstrong's and continued as an independently run company by Eddie and his long-standing business partner Bob Armstrong. Curtis coaches was added to the business in 1971, followed by Rochester & Marshall in 1976, making it the largest private coach operator in the North East, with a 55 vehicle fleet. Dunn was a determined character and during his time on the Board, took a positive role, working closely with the club's finance team and visiting the office from his Moordale base in Old Eldon Square. As the Magpie Group began to assert their influence at the end of the Eighties, Dunn stepped aside. He continued to run his family business until the Proudmutual Group (now Arriva) acquired Moordale in 1990, then Eddie took on a Ford car franchise, Cramlington Ford, before largely retiring, the business now part run by his son. Living in Ponteland, he remains a United supporter through the ups and downs of the Magpie rollercoaster, a season-ticket holder in the Milburn Stand. He was for a number of years a keen supporter of local side Westerhope FC, assisting in the team's administration. Dunn plays bowls for the Portland Bowling club in Newcastle.

ELLIOTT E

Committee: c1883-c1889

b. unknown

Probably involved with the Newcastle East End club prior to, and after, the established membership of the club's Committee in 1883-84, Elliott would have been an acquaintance of the likes of William Coulson in Byker. At the AGM of the club in November 1888, Elliott was named as East End's Treasurer.

FENDER John Lawrence

PLC Chairman:
May 2000-May 2002
PLC Director:
May 1998-May 2002

b. (Greenwich, London,1943 (Q1))

A chartered surveyor, property consultant and fund manager, John Fender was involved in the financing of several high-profile projects over a successful career in the City. Included were the Broadgate complex in London and Sir John Hall's MetroCentre on Tyneside. His association with Cameron Hall, where he was also a non-executive director for a period, led to Fender being brought into the Newcastle United boardroom during the second year of the club's PLC status. A respected financial guru with the National Westminster bank's offshoots; County Nat West, Greenwich Nat West, Nat West Markets and Nat West Securities, John was also a keen supporter of Newcastle Falcons rugby club. He was appointed Chairman of the PLC following the departure of Freddie Fletcher. John left the club during the spring of 2002 after what was described as being unable to agree to "new conditions". Fender continued his valued profession in the corporate banking world and was a director with Black Country Properties, one of many other appointments in his business career.

FENTON Thomas

PLC Director: May 1998-Dec 1998

b. [Lanchester, Co Durham, 1932 Q1]

A director of several companies during his business life including high-profile posts with the Tyne & Wear Development Corporation which did much to transform the regions old industrial riverside, Tom Fenton was also active with the North East based Smith Print Group. Fenton was invited to join the club's PLC executive during May 1998. Residing in Ponteland, he spent less than a year as a director before quitting following the controversy surrounding Douglas Hall and Freddy Shepherd.

FENWICK Charles W

Committee: c1885-1888

b. Newcastle upon Tyne, c1832

Purchasing shares in the new Newcastle East End company when they moved to become a limited company, Charles Fenwick was one of the small group of enthusiastic supporters of the game in the Byker and Heaton district. He was appointed to the Committee certainly for season 1885-86 onwards, and maybe before. Living in South View, then later Malcolm Street, Fenwick was noted as a joiner in surviving share ledger and helped organise the club prior to the first Board of Directors being established in 1890.

FERGUSON J S

Secretary: May 1895-Oct 1895

b. Motherwell

Appointed to the important post of Newcastle United Secretary during May 1895, the Scot was described as the club's first professional and paid administrator. A former Secretary of Motherwell as well as the Referee's Association of Scotland, he did not remain long in the post, only a period of six months. He found the position difficult at times, when he departed during October 1895 it was described in the club's Minutes of Meetings that he left due to having "too many masters", remarks pointed at the 12-man Board of Directors at the time. It was also noted that when Ferguson was in charge of the club party for games at Liverpool and Newton Heath, he had allowed players to play cards in his bedroom to the early hours. The Secretary was reprimanded, while there was also a dispute with the club over gateman's wages, which had been allegedly kept by the Scot, and not paid. He was replaced by a man who rarely courted controversy and could cope with the sometimes frustration and complexity of football administration, fellow Scot Frank Watt.

FLETCHER Alfred Olding

Director: July 1996-April 2000
Chief Executive:
Jan 1992-June 2000
PLC Chairman:
Dec 1998-June 2000
PLC Director:
Dec 1998-July 2000
PLC Chief Executive:
Nov 1996-July 2000

b. Greenock, 20 March 1941
d. Ponteland, near Newcastle upon Tyne, 27 August 2012

A cheery and tenacious Scot, Freddie Fletcher was an influential personality in turning Newcastle United from a club living in the past into a giant fit for the modern football world of the Premier League, Europe and television dominance. From Greenock, Fletcher had already been involved in the game with his local club Morton and at Ibrox with Rangers, as well as with the Scottish Football League and Scottish FA before he joined Sir John Hall's team. He was in the background as a consultant during the corporate battle for control of Newcastle and then formally joined the club in December 1991, soon becoming Chief Executive as the Magpies were transformed at the beginning of the 1990s; one of his first tasks being to sack Ossie Ardiles and bring in Kevin Keegan as boss. With a degree from Strathclyde University and much experience in business development, he helped overhaul Rangers as Commercial Director from 1986 to 1989 when employed by club owners the Lawrence Group. A resourceful character, Fletcher was a shrewd operator and at the forefront of developing the Black'n'Whites for the new football scene. The Scot had the foresight to visualise how the game was changing and benefit from United's loyal support and strong brand in parallel to Keegan's revolution on the pitch. The club's turnover rocketed as Fletcher negotiated major corporate sponsorship deals with Asics, adidas and Newcastle Breweries, and very quickly the Magpies became not only one of England's biggest clubs, but also in Europe. He never shied away from making difficult or unpopular decisions, notably the controversial change in seating arrangements at St James' Park, which in hindsight was the right thing to do, capitalising on premium and corporate areas. As a result he was nicknamed the 'Jockweiller', yet his forthright, focused and at times abrasive methods were just what United needed at the time. Freddie was heavily involved in player acquisitions too and was an influential member of the directorate which brought many a famous name to Gallowgate as the Entertainers were born. During the spring of 2000 Fletcher resigned from the boardroom yet remained in the region he had grown to love. Freddie then had various business interests in the North East, as a director of several companies including the Esh Group and being involved in football's expansion in the media as part of the NTL Group. He also was a director with Home Housing Association, the Protector Group, Mercer Street consultancy and Metnor. Retaining his support of Newcastle United, being a regular at St James' Park, Freddie was a past Lord Provost of his hometown in the West of Scotland and a noted liberal councillor for almost 20 years during his younger years. The silver-haired Scot lived in Darras Hall and was a well-known and respected member of the Tyneside business community.

FORBES George Robert

Chairman: Dec 1990-Dec 1991
Director: Oct 1983-July 1992

b. Duns, Berwickshire,
9 October 1944

Appointed Chairman of Newcastle United at the height of combat between rival factions to control the Black'n'Whites as the Nineties opened, George Forbes hailed from the Borders and took over from Gordon McKeag once the Magpie Group gained a foothold in the boardroom. Acting as something of an intermediary between the two warring factions, Forbes had the difficult, if not impossible, task of pulling the club together. At the time Newcastle United was in turmoil; a poor side on the pitch, increasing debts off it, and a split directorate. Despite working tirelessly and unobtrusively to find a compromise between rivals, Forbes was no match for John Hall's determination and financial muscle and eventually stepped down from the Chair in December 1991 as the Cameron Hall empire took control in all but name. As a youngster George played football for noted border club Chirnside United while his uncle, John Johnston, was on United's books as a centre-forward during the mid-Thirties. A noted rally driver in the 1960s and 1970s and friend of the Seymour family, he was invited to join the boardroom in 1983 but left the club completely during the summer of 1992 as the Hall regime took full occupation, although Forbes continued afterwards to be a supporter from his Milburn Stand seat. With a mild-mannered nature but tough interior, Forbes continued to run a large farm complex, Georgefield near Coldstream, as well as business interests ranging from livestock auctions and property in the Borders. He was also a member of British Cereal Exports, Chairman for a period between 2006 and 2012.

FORSTER George

Director: 1891-1892

b. unknown

A director of the Newcastle East End club for a single season, in 1891-92, George Forster was part of the establishment just prior to the Heatonites moving to St James' Park across the city. A shareholder from 1891, he was employed as a "manager" living initially at Kingsley Place in Newcastle, later moving to South Shields.

FOX Alfred

Director: 1898-1904

b. Newcastle upon Tyne,
20 December 1841
d. Newcastle upon Tyne,
7 September 1905

The son of a city publican and furrier, Alfred Fox was educated at Robinson's Academy and followed his father into the retail fur trade as a teenager before going his own way with a boot and shoe business. He ran an outlet on Pilgrim Street, then Fox worked in the tobacco trade, described at the turn of the century as a "cigar merchant". From the Elswick district of the city, he resided in Maple Street then Belgrave Parade and had a tobacconist business on Collingwood Street in the heart of the city. An enthusiast of most sport in his younger days, he was a keen oarsman in the popular Tyne races, connected to the Northern Rowing Club. Alfred also was a prominent member of the Bentinck Athletic Club. Fox joined the United boardroom during 1898 after purchasing a substantial holding in the club in 1895. He was for a time a local councillor for the St John's ward on Newcastle Corporation, first elected in 1890 and serving until 1904.

GILCHRIST Adam Brown

Chairman: May 1890-cs1891
Director: Feb 1890-cs 1891

b. Friar's Goose, Gateshead, January 1845
d. Dartford, 4 April 1915

Adam Gilchrist was described as a traditional "wherryman" and ran a boat company on the River Tyne. Born alongside the river at Friar's Goose and later living in Harbottle Street in the heart of Byker, when he became a Newcastle East End shareholder during 1890, Gilchrist had been heavily involved when a limited company was set up during February at the Leighton Schoolrooms on Heaton Road. By the time of the new companies first Annual General Meeting during May, Adam was elected Chairman. He remained only for a short period formally with the East Enders, leaving the boardroom at the end of the 1890-91 season. Gilchrist managed his business from 23 Side in Newcastle and later relocated to Dartford in the south, employed as a commercial clerk.

GOLDING Walter Heathcote

Secretary: Aug 1890-1891,
May 1892-July 1893
& Oct 1895-Dec 1895

b. King's Lynn, 18 March 1865
d. Newcastle upon Tyne,
4 January 1918

An East End supporter from earliest years, residing in Heaton's Chillingham Road and later Mowbray Street, Walter Golding was associated with the club in various administrative roles during the early years of development. A solicitor's clerk at the time (later qualifying as a lawyer), Golding was noted as a painstaking and enthusiastic official, initially working as Financial Secretary before being appointed Secretary during August 1890 noted as possessing "excellent business qualifications, in addition to having a thorough knowledge of the game". The trials and tribulations of keeping East End's matters in check forced his resignation during January 1893 in the wake of a bribery scandal following a match with Middlesbrough, but he was quickly persuaded to return only to quit once more in July of that year. Walter, though, was back at the helm two years later,

re-appointed in October 1895 as the club went through a revolving door period of appointments. On Ferguson's departure, he stood in briefly before he handed over the key role to Frank Watt as 1895 closed. When Golding left Newcastle United he was handed a "gold purse" as a token of his service to the club. From King's Lynn originally, he settled on Tyneside when his father moved north serving in the army. Walter later resided in Monkseaton, his family being shareholders of the club until the Magpie Group's takeover during the modern era. Golding afterwards concentrated on his legal career, becoming a partner with Watson, Burton & Corder and was well-known in Newcastle's liberal association, secretary for a period of the Heaton ward. During 1917 he was appointed to the title of District Grand Master of the Manchester Unity of Oddfellows, a friendship and social organisation. He was given the middle name of Heathcote after a certain Colonel Heathcote who saved the life of his father during the Boer War.

GRAHAM John

Chairman: 1915-1919
Director: cs 1892-Oct 1893
& 1895-May 1934

b. North Sunderland,
Northumberland, 9 June 1863
d. Newcastle upon Tyne,
28 July 1948

One of the keenest supporters of local football during the formative Victorian years, John Graham appears to have been a Newcastle West End man when football kicked off with much zest during the years of the 1880s. He was at the summit meeting between East End and West End during the summer of 1892 and once the Heaton club had relocated to St James' Park, Graham became both a shareholder and director of East End, thereafter spending no fewer than 40 seasons with the club (the second longest in United's history). He acted as secretary to the club's 'A' team for a period and was associated with junior football as well as being elected Chairman of the Magpies during the First World War. Known as 'Jack' by his family, he was a postmaster, following in the footsteps of his mother's occupation, moving to Tyneside from North Northumberland and working in the Civil Service for over 40 years. He was appointed Postmaster of South Shields after the Great War, then Postmaster across the Tyne at North Shields. Graham would have been a friend of the MacKenzie family, from the same Northumbrian village of North Sunderland-Seahouses, and eventually became a fellow director of RW MacKenzie (qv). He was also related by marriage to the wider family.

HALL Douglas Stuart

Director: Nov 1990-May 1991,
Nov 1991-March 1998 &
July 1998-June 2007
PLC Director:
April 1997-March 1998,
Dec 1998-June 2007

b. Alnwick, Northumberland,
July 1958

The son of knighted Tyneside tycoon John Hall whose family held the majority shareholding in Newcastle United from 1991 to 2007, Douglas Hall first joined the club's Board at the height of the share-war for ownership of the Magpies at the beginning of the 1990s decade. With a full takeover in their sights, father and son became directors at the end of 1990, but their stay lasted only six months before resigning only to claim a place at St James' Park once more when the acquisition was assured as the following

Directors & Officials

year closed. Born in the heart of Northumberland and to have a spell at Manchester University, Hall worked alongside his father as Cameron Hall grew into one of the region's most active property developers. He became Chairman of the company when Sir John stood down. At St James' Park, Douglas relished the opportunity to develop Newcastle United from a sleeping giant and he was influential, if controversial at times, as the Black'n'Whites became one of Europe's biggest clubs, often scouting across Europe for star names. When his father retired from day-to-day activities Douglas worked closely with Chairman Freddy Shepherd as the Hall families' stakeholder and as the club's account documents reveal, he instilled an entrepreneurial culture, "initiating ideas which have contributed to the Group's rejuvenation". Duped by a notorious fake sheik with Shepherd in a News of the World sting during March 1998, he was forced to step-down from the Board of both the football club and PLC in the wake of the 'Toongate' scandal but as the major shareholder with his father, soon returned, although his reputation was tarnished. Nevertheless Douglas continued to be directly involved in the Newcastle United decision making until the Cameron Hall investment was sold to Mike Ashley during June 2007. For many years residing in Low Fell, Hall decided to move to the Mediterranean, settling in Gibraltar where he headed Newcastle United International Ltd. Later his family opened a visionary exclusive club, Fifty Five in the British enclave.

HALL Edward

Secretary: Oct 1950-May 1959

b. [Newcastle upon Tyne], c1901

d. Newcastle upon Tyne, 5 May 1959

First joining Newcastle United's office staff to a post of what was described as a "confidential clerk" during February 1927, Teddy Hall worked alongside the Frank Watt father and son duo for over 20 years before being appointed to the Secretary post in his own right during October 1950. Graduating to the assistant role in 1932, Hall spent the majority of his adult career with the Magpies, becoming an experienced administrator, at the helm as the club lifted the FA Cup treble during the Fifties. Living in Gosforth, for his services to the game he was awarded the Football League Long Service medal in 1951.

HALL John Sir

Chairman: Dec 1991-Dec 1997
Director: April 1990 to Dec 1990 & Nov 1991-Dec 1997
President: Dec 1997-date

b. North Seaton, Northumberland, 21 March 1933

Sir John Hall is recognised in the Magpies' long history as the Chairman who made the biggest impact on Newcastle United Football Club. For a time, perhaps the most powerful man in the North East, Sir John stepped in and rescued an ailing institution during 1990 and 1991 with his financial backing, business acumen and enthusiastic drive.

Loaning the club various sums at critical times, he turned the club into an organisation to rival not only the best in Britain but also in Europe. When he stepped down from the Chair at the end of 1997 the club were on the crest of something special, however by the time he sold his controlling stake in the Black'n'Whites a decade later during 2007, much of that impetus had been squandered. Before Sir John Hall became connected with Newcastle United, the club was in a grim state. Turnover was a mere £4m, they had little capital, a stadium in need of vast improvement, and a team languishing in the second-tier of English football going nowhere fast, and if anywhere, towards the old Division Three for the first time. Becoming the figurehead for change as the Magpie Group started a takeover bid in 1988, the Northumberland-born entrepreneur, property developer and former National Coal Board surveyor was determined to make Newcastle United one of the powers in football. As soon as his company Cameron-Hall took full control during 1992 the club was rapidly transformed. Funds were provided, almost without limit; St James' Park rebuilt, the team changed beyond recognition with big-name stars galore. As a result United's status changed spectacularly with turnover approaching £100m. They challenged at the top of the Premier League and became one of Europe's foremost and progressive clubs. Knighted in July 1991, Sir John takes the credit of making it all happen and few individuals in United's history has achieved as much. Yet one thing Hall did not accomplish, was to bring a principal trophy to St James' Park before he retired from the scene. He also attempted to build a Newcastle United Sporting Club on a Barcelona model, comprising not only football but also rugby (Falcons), ice hockey (Cobras) and basketball (Eagles). Away from sport, Hall had made headline news and a multi-million fortune by transforming a wasteland in Gateshead into the MetroCentre, at the time Europe's largest retail complex. Acting very much as a visionary and strategist, Sir John was a Millennium Commissioner for the North and developed the Wynyard Estate, the former home of the Londonderry family. With a miner's background he was raised in the Ashington area and after working at local pits, moved into estate management before creating his own development company during 1969. His son Douglas (qv) was also a director of the club during the same period while his daughter Allison (qv) became a PLC member of the Board. To mark the contribution he made to the club, the Leazes End stand was renamed the Sir John Hall Stand in 1993 while he became Club President. He was also awarded the Freedom of Gateshead during 2011. Sir John resides on part of the Wynyard Estate in County Durham.

HARRISON Terence Sir

PLC Charman: Feb 1997-May 1998
PLC Director: Feb 1997-May 1998

b. [Co Durham], 7 April 1933

One of several respected businessmen with a local background to be associated with the club's PLC structure, albeit for a short period. Terry Harrison made a name in industry with NEI, formally Clarke Chapman and Parsons, two of Tyneside's most prominent companies. Educated at Durham University and trained as an engineer, he rose to become Chief Executive then Chairman of NEI. He was later Chief Executive of Rolls Royce up to retirement in 1996 while Terry also had various other non-executive roles with such companies as Alfred McAlpine and T&N. For his work as a distinguished industrialist, Harrison was knighted in 1995. A supporter of the Magpies from a young age, Harrison was appointed as Newcastle United's PLC Chairman during February 1997 after a troubled first six months as a listed company, the club receiving a far from easy ride within the City. Living at Whalton in Northumberland, Harrison remained as the club's figurehead for just over a year.

HATTON Leonard Thomas OBE

Director: Jan 2002-June 2007

b. London, September 1928

Len Hatton was involved in various sporting ventures before he joined the club's executive in 2002; Chairman of the Sports Aid Foundation and on the British Athletics Federation working party. An athlete in his younger days, the London-born businessman began his career in the construction industry as a quantity surveyor, forming his own practice, Shaw & Hatton. Acquainted to Sir John Hall and Cameron Hall, Hatton took a stake in Newcastle United and remained a director for five years. He was also involved in property development around the UK and Europe, residing in homes situated in Ascot, Monaco and Le Touquet. Always taking a keen interest in the development of sporting activities, Len was associated with the Polytechnic club in London, also becoming a patron of the European PGA and President of the Sports Aid Trust. During June 2013, Hatton was honoured with the OBE for nearly five decades of services to sport.

HAYWARD Steven J

PLC Director: Aug 2007-2008

b. unknown

A senior manager in Mike Ashley's Sports Direct empire, Steve Hayward became a Non-Executive Director of United when the club was purchased in the close-season of 2007. With a background in international marketing, being involved with such names as Universal and Coca Cola, Hayward latterly specialised in the sports and leisure sector. Having a long-time role with Sports Direct, he remained with the Black'n'Whites for nearly a year, largely behind the scenes. He later ran a consultancy titled, The Ideas Generator.

HENRY William

Director: Feb 1890-cs 1891

b. Newcastle upon Tyne, November 1859

One of Newcastle East End's original directors when a company was created in February 1890, William Henry lived in the Heaton and Byker area and was a keen devotee to the fledgling organisation. He was probably on the club's Committee for part of the time prior to the issue of a shareholding while afterwards as East End developed, he stepped aside during the summer of 1891 and continued in his occupation as a stationer and printer, living on Heaton Park Road.

HOOLE Malcolm George

Secretary: Aug 1971-July 1973

b. unknown

Malcolm Hoole joined the Magpies staff as office clerk in October 1948, and like several officials of the club over the years, worked his way through the ranks behind the scenes to be appointed to the post of Secretary. Moving to the assistant's role during 1964, he succeeded Denis Barker on his resignation, but only stayed in the club's top management position for two years before departing in July 1973. Hoole resided in the Stakeford and Choppington area of Northumberland.

HUDSON William Robinson

Director: Feb 1890-1895

b. Newcastle upon Tyne, 1862 (Q2)

Recorded in the club's hand-written Victorian share ledger as a "clerk" living initially in Mowbray Street in Heaton, then Bond Street, William Hudson was a supporter of the Newcastle East End club which had such a strong following from the Newcastle district. He is recorded in the original Articles of Association as one of the club's first directors, remaining on the directorate until 1895 assisting through the difficult years of development as a football club, and as East End changed title to become Newcastle United. A hotel and inn proprietor, he was later running an establishment in Middlesbrough by 1911. Purchasing shares during February 1890 at the outset, remarkably after more than a century one of his actual share documents still exists from that era.

HURFORD Wallace Edwin

Chairman: Oct 1959-Oct 1964
Director: April 1950-Jan 1967

b. Newcastle upon Tyne, 1891 (Q2)
d. Jesmond, Newcastle upon Tyne, 26 January 1967

A dental surgeon by profession, Wallace Hurford's family had links with the club going back to the days of Newcastle East End. From a teenager he was a supporter of the Magpies and a season-ticket holder in the old West Stand. He also played football himself for Armstrong College and when at Durham University. A shareholder too, Hurford was first nominated for a position on the Board during 1930, but it took Wallace another 20 years to achieve an ambition of entering the boardroom, in April 1950. With a friendly manner and common sense approach, Hurford was largely responsible for developing the club's post-war youth set-up under the banner of the N's. He was elected Chairman during October 1959 but had to preside over a difficult period in the club's history; relegation from the top-tier, the sacking of Charlie Mitten and a rebuilding period thereafter, as well as a High Court appearance in the George Eastham saga. He suffered ill-health during 1964 and Lord Westwood took over the Chair in October of that year. Hurford remained a director to his death in Jesmond during 1967. During the First World War he served in the Royal Medical Corps, while Wallace was also a prominent bridge player, once winning the North of England championship.

IRVING John Andrew

Director: Feb 2008-date
Secretary: Sept 2007-date

b. Newcastle upon Tyne, June 1978

Educated at Dame Allan's School in Newcastle, John Irving joined the club's staff as Financial Controller during 2007 shortly after the club's purchase by Mike Ashley. Becoming Company Secretary during September 2007 and a Director the following year, Irving had previously been employed in accountancy at Procter & Gamble on Tyneside having studied business, economics and finance at Loughborough. Managing the club's day-to-day financial business, John is also a Patron of the Newcastle United Foundation.

JOHNSON Robert

Director: cs 1892-1893

b. unknown

Living in Wallsend, Robert Johnson worked as a joiner on Tyneside and was a supporter of the Newcastle East End club as they grew in stature in Byker and Heaton during the latter years of the century. On the club's Board for only a single season, that of 1892-93, immediately after moving from Chillingham Road to St James' Park, Johnson stood down before the club changed name to Newcastle United.

JONES Russell

Director: July 1992-July 2002
PLC Director: April 1997-2004

b. Oldham, 1944 (Q4)

Russell Jones relocated to the North East of England from Lancashire when he was only five years of age. The family settled in Blackhall and Jones followed a career path in architecture, becoming a director with a local practice before teaming up with Sir John Hall in his development company during 1986, at one stage in the 1990s being Managing Director. Having much experience in property construction and development, being an integral part of the Gateshead MetroCentre scheme, Russell joined Newcastle United's boardroom with the specific responsibility to oversee the vast overhaul of the club's historic site at Gallowgate. Described once as a "modest mastermind behind St James' Park's transformation", he expertly managed the initial development of the ground from the drawing-board to a finished all-seater stadium in a rapid timescale, then focussed on a planned enlargement - and alternative proposed move to a brand new showpiece close by on Castle Leazes. What would have been an eye-catching and magnificent new base fell through, and the existing site was then further developed during 2000 into the present-day arena, being a notable feat of design and construction, expanding the stadium without losing any capacity during the building programme. Once United's headquarters was complete, Jones left the football scene, remaining in the region living at Wynyard, County Durham.

JOSEPHS John Irving

PLC Director: July 1998-Dec 1998

b. Newcastle upon Tyne, 1939

Born and bred in Newcastle, John Josephs was an economics graduate of King's College, Durham becoming a Chartered Accountant. A partner with an accountancy firm, Josephs also joined the new Metro Radio Group in the Seventies becoming a founder shareholder in the Tyneside radio station when it was floated. He became Chief Executive of the media organisation during January 1993 and when the company was sold, he spent nearly another decade in broadcasting with Forever Broadcasting PLC and the Radio Partnership Ltd before retiring in 2004. Josephs had played an integral part in changing the face of the radio media in the North East and elsewhere. During this period he was also a director of Newcastle United PLC, but like many of that era, for only a brief period, between July and December 1998. An enduring Magpie supporter, he joined the fold with Denis Cassidy when Freddy Shepherd and Douglas Hall were forced to resign, both new members themselves departing when Shepherd and Hall returned. A prominent personality on Tyneside, among his other appointments were as a non-executive director and Chairman of

Mincoffs Solicitors, being associated with the law firm for over 40 years. John was also a governor of the University of Northumbria, treasurer of the United Hebrew Congregation of Newcastle and director of Train Fitness as well as the North East Theatre Trust. Josephs was a keen athlete, a member of Heaton Harriers and continued running into his later years.

LEE John Walton

Chairman: Dec 1949-Nov 1951
Director: June 1934-Nov 1954

b. Whitley Bay, 1887 (Q3)
d. Newcastle upon Tyne, 30 November 1954

John Lee was a successful Tynesider who ran an egg importing and poultry merchant's business. Possessing a vibrant personality he was an inspiration and a tonic within United's ranks, Stan Seymour once remarking that he "created an atmosphere of welcome and fellowship". Becoming a director of the club during the summer of 1934 after being first nominated four years earlier, Lee reached the Chairman's seat at the end of 1949 and was in charge for two years, including a period when the Magpies lifted the FA Cup in 1951. He was also a director of several other companies in the region as well as Chairman of the Crown Building Society. Residing in Whitley Bay, Lee died when still a director of the Black'n'Whites during 1954.

LEWIS John

Director: 1924-Jan 1925

b. Darwen, Lancashire, c1870
d. Newcastle upon Tyne, 14 January 1925

John Lewis held a post within Newcastle United's executive for less than a year, during the mid-Twenties. From Lancashire, he moved to the region and by 1901 was residing in Heaton, employed as a superintendent with the Newcastle upon Tyne Gas Company. He remained a manager with that utility for several years, later living at The Grove in Gosforth before his death when still a director of the club.

LIDDLE Thomas Teasdale

Committee: c1889-Feb 1890
Director: Feb 1890-cs 1891

b. Gateshead, 11 September 1865
d. Newcastle upon Tyne, 26 December 1948

From a family involved in what was then an extensive glass-making industry around Tyneside, Thomas Liddle was initially a reserve player with East End during their earliest days. He later appeared with Heaton and became one of Newcastle East End's Committee members, then one of the new company's first directors during 1890. When he acquired shares in that year, Thomas was based at the Ouseburn Glass Works, while his father, John Liddle, also purchased equity, both residing at Addison Street in Jesmond. He was later a manufacturer at the Clayton Glass Works in Gateshead. Thomas remained a director only for a year, departing in the summer of 1891 becoming afterwards a clerk for an engineering works on Tyneside. Also playing cricket in the district, Liddle later lived in Walkerville to his death.

Directors & Officials

LILBURN William

Director: April 1908-May 1923

b. Holy Island, Northumberland, c1870

At the time when William Lilburn purchased a share-holding in Newcastle United during 1904, he ran a fishmongers business in Cullercoats, later also developing that concern to include retailing poultry. Living at Netherton on Heaton Road, Lilburn filled a vacancy on the Board when Joe Bell died. Census information reveals a clear path of his life from birth into his fortieth year by 1911. The son of a Holy Island fisherman, William followed his father on the North Sea boat working off the Northumberland coast and by 1891 was a 21-year-old fishmonger. Ten years later he had moved down the coast to reside in Cullercoats and started his business which was still going strong by the start of World War One. It appears Lilburn later moved to Australia while his son, William junior, became the third generation to be a fishmonger, with shops on Chillingham Road and Heaton Road.

LLAMBIAS Derek David

Deputy Chairman: May 2008
Managing-Director: June 2008-June 2013

b. Chelsea, London, 1957 (Q1)

Taking over the executive management of Newcastle United following Chris Mort's return to his law firm at the end of the 2007-08 season, Derek Llambias was a self-confessed West Ham United supporter and long-time acquaintance of owner Mike Ashley. Over the five years in charge of the Magpies, Llambias developed a firm liking for the Black'n'Whites as he was at the heart of the up and down fortunes of the Tynesiders. Derek previously had a career record in entertainment and hospitality, in London and the States, latterly managing the capital's swanky club, Fifty, one of London's oldest casinos. He oversaw a difficult period at St James' Park as the Magpies tumbled out of the Premier League, but guided the club straight back into the elite then onto a European stage. Llambias was astute and carried through his actions, but during the close-season of 2013 the Londoner decided to step aside when Joe Kinnear was appointed Director of Football. His son Warren, an actor, appeared in 'The Shouting Man' during 2012, a comedy drama based loosely around a fictional FA Cup-tie between Gillingham and Newcastle United.

LUNN James

Chairman: 1909-1911
& Dec 1928-March 1941
Director: July 1896-March 1941

b. Newcastle upon Tyne, 3 October 1859
d. Gosforth, Newcastle upon Tyne, 2 March 1941

Associated with Newcastle United as a shareholder and Board member for over 45 years, James Lunn was perhaps typical of the club's directorate for a century. From a distinguished Newcastle family, he was related to Sir George Lunn who was a prominent Novocastrian too, a liberal politician and Lord Mayor of Newcastle. James ran a Building Contracting business, was a councillor, and purchased shares in 1895, joining the Board of Directors a year later. Lunn was a prominent voice in all things Newcastle United during much of the club's pre-war

success story, with record service as a director of 45 seasons. He became Chairman over two spells, firstly in 1909 for a short period before the Great War, then again in 1928 for a much longer spell of unbroken seasons up to the Second World War. On the Board as the club lifted four Football League titles and reached no fewer than seven FA Cup finals, he was then in the Chair when the Magpies were relegated for the first time during 1934. James was elected to the Newcastle Council in 1909 and held the position of Sheriff of Newcastle during 1921-22 and as an Alderman in 1927. He was also a Justice of the Peace, Freeman of the City and Chairman of the Royal Arcade Building Society. James resided initially in Eldon Square, then in Gosforth. Lunn remained connected with the Black'n'Whites to his death. He married the sister of fellow director, John P Oliver ensuring a substantial powerbase in the club's hierarchy.

MALLINGER Peter Charles

Director: Feb 1989-July 1992

b. Tynemouth, 1936 (Q3)
d. Leicester, 7 January 2011

Although Peter Mallinger lived for many years out of the North East region, in Leicestershire, he was born in Tynemouth and raised in Jesmond, a Newcastle United supporter as a young lad attending many games during the Forties and Fifties, including the club's record 13-0 hiding of Newport County. Living in Montreal, Canada for a short period, he was also a budding footballer as a youth with Oadby Town having trials with Coventry, Derby and Leicester City, on their books for two years. Mallinger by then had settled in the Midlands creating a successful retail business selling fabrics and the like, Newarke Wools Ltd, which he sold for £4m during 1987. Peter always kept in touch with the Magpies and was invited by friend, United Chairman George Forbes, to join the Board during 1989 when the club was in a fierce struggle over control of the club. Mallinger was in charge of growing retail operations, opening outlets in Eldon Square and the MetroCentre. He also introduced Trevor Bennett to the United fold. A likable character, tall and coherent; he tried to manoeuvre a middle ground during a very difficult period as the club edged close to financial collapse. On the eventual takeover by Cameron Hall, being part of the losing camp, it was no surprise when Peter was ousted from his place at the table during 1992. Mallinger remained in football, acquiring a controlling stake in Kettering Town near to his home in the East Midlands during 1993. He managed the Poppies for over a decade until 2005, reaching Wembley in the FA Trophy. Peter later had a period with Corby Town, another local non-league club. He lived in retirement in Leicestershire until his death during 2011. Mallinger is one of a handful of football directors to tell his story from the boardroom, publishing 'So You Think You Want To Be a Director of a Football Club'.

MAYO John Charles CBE

PLC Director:
Feb 1997-May 1998

b. unknown

City gent John Mayo became a non-executive member of the club's PLC during February 1997 bringing his considerable experience as an investment banker to the St James' Park table. Graduating from Loughborough University, he qualified as an accountant and started a career with Arthur Anderson during 1981. Within three years Mayo had joined the corporate finance division of SG Warburg & Co and was appointed to their Board in 1990. John afterwards held senior positions within ICI and Zeneca,

the Pentland Group, as well as electronics giants Marconi and GEC. He then formed Beehive Capital and became Chief Executive of Pro-Bono-Bio, an international health-care company, as well as active in Bermudian based biotech Celtic Pharma. A director and non-executive director of many companies during his successful career, Mayo was honoured with the CBE for services to industry during 1999.

MILNE George Taylor

Chairman: 1911-1913
Director: cs 1892-Sept 1917

b. Alnwick, 12 March 1845
d. Newcastle upon Tyne, 17 September 1917

Father of United player William Milne (qv) and a senior representative of the well known John Sinclair cigarette and tobacco company on Tyneside, George Milne was a director of Newcastle United for 26 seasons. From the historic Northumberland town of Alnwick, Milne first joined the club's executive for the 1892-93 season and remained a valued member of the Magpies to his death in 1917. Very well respected in North East sporting circles, he was also an enthusiastic follower of Northumberland cricket, his three sons playing for Benwell CC and appearing for the County side. George (junior) was an especially prominent player for Northumberland from 1901 to 1928 (152 app) also appearing for Benwell Hill as well as being on United's playing staff between 1903-04 and 1904-05 without breaking through. His brother James also had a period with the United 'A' line-up. A Newcastle West End supporter originally, George had been connected with the St James' Park rivals for some years before their liquidation in 1892 and attended the meeting in Heaton to decide upon the move to take over the Barrack Road ground. Chairman at Gallowgate from 1911, he was also President of the Northumberland FA, a member from 1902 to 1917, while George was also a life Governor of the Royal Victoria Infirmary. He died after attending a Newcastle Swifts match during 1917, contracting pneumonia which proved fatal.

MOLINEUX Walter

Director: Sept 1929-Feb 1944

b. Walkden Worsley, Lancashire, c1875
d. Newcastle upon Tyne, 23 February 1944

One of several solicitors to have taken a seat in United's hierarchy, Walter Molineux was a well-known Newcastle worthy and was elected to the Board following three deaths of the directorate in quick succession during 1929. He moved from Lancashire to reside on Tyneside and was articled with Sinton, solicitors; Walter then set up his own law practice around 1906, based on Pilgrim Street, then Grey Street and Eldon Square. A colleague of William McKeag, he formed a new company, Molineux, McKeag and Cooper during the inter-war years. Walter often acted for Newcastle United at that time and was for a period Under-Sheriff of Newcastle upon Tyne in 1940. Apart from having a passion for football, Molineux was also President of the Northumberland County Bowling Club as well as a member of Northumberland Golf Club. During his period on Tyneside, he resided in Heaton then Jesmond, at the time of his demise, at Fernwood Court.

MORT Christopher Andrew

Chairman: June 2007-June 2008
Director: June 2007-June 2008
b. Abergavenny, 1965 (Q3)

A solicitor with the high-profile Freshfields Bruckhams Deringer law firm in London, Chris Mort acted for Mike Ashley on various transactions and when the London-based businessman purchased the club during 2007, Mort was seconded to the club as Chairman for 12 months. Overseeing the acquisition and transition, with much experience in sport and leisure deals, Mort undertook a full review of the Newcastle United organisation. He was the voice of the Magpies for a year, at times having a difficult task in trying to bond the new regime with factions of the Toon Army. Mort oversaw the creation of the charitable Newcastle United Foundation during his period at Gallowgate and handed over to Derek Llambias when he stepped aside in the summer of 2008. Chris returned to his role as a partner with Freshfields in the capital and is recognised as a top-rated lawyer in the City.

MURAS William A

Committee: 1881-1883
b. Newcastle upon Tyne, February 1866
d. Newcastle upon Tyne, 20 December 1937

Appearing for Newcastle's original pathfinders of association football, Tyne Association from 1881, William Muras was raised in the All Saints district of the city and also played football with Stanley during their first season of 1881-82 as a reserve. It is recorded that William was a Stanley and Newcastle East End Committee member for a period, then Muras moved to the Jesmond club in 1883 while he also was linked to Tyne Pilgrims and played cricket for North Eastern. He is registered as being employed as a "ticket writer" and "clerk" and by the time of the 1911 census was noted as being a "manager of works", still involved in the production of tickets and posters. After World War One William settled in Jesmond.

MURTON Henry Angus

Committee: 1888-1889
b. Berry Edge, Co Durham, 16 February 1848
d. Riding Mill, Northumberland, 3 April 1927

By the Edwardian era Henry Murton was a well known businessman on Tyneside, having a successful retail enterprise to eventually become one of Newcastle's first department stores. Born near Consett, Murton followed the trade of his father as a "waterproof and India Rubber merchant". Living in Jesmond, he developed the family retail business which became well known on Tyneside with shops on Market Street, Grey Street and later Grainger Street in Newcastle's heart which provided goods from surgical appliances, rubber mats to waterproof garments. Murton also specialised in all forms of sports outfitting, supplying a wide range of equipment throughout the country; kit for football, cricket and rugby as well as selling his own specialised products of fishing gear and snooker cues, one being branded as The Murton Meteor. Also having outlets in Sunderland, Murton's became a well established name on the High Street until the later years of the 1950s when the company was taken over by the Co-op. At the time of Henry's involvement with Newcastle East End on Victorian Tyneside, he was 40 years of age, a Committee member for a short period. The Tyneside entrepreneur also became a shareholder of the club, purchasing equity during 1890 and 1891. Murton moved to Riding Mill along the Tyne valley in his later years.

MacKENZIE Robert William

Director: 1905-Aug 1929
b. Seahouses, Northumberland, May 1866
d. Gosforth, Newcastle upon Tyne, 22 August 1929

A Newcastle councillor for a period who joined the Board when John Auld stepped down during 1905, Robert MacKenzie went onto serve the Magpies for 25 seasons. With a family home in Seahouses on the Northumberland coast, he ran a decorating business, described in the national census as a "House decorator and painter". The son of a local publican, Robert also became a licensee for a period, at the King Street Inn, in addition being heavily involved in the running of North Sunderland FC. Also serving with the Seahouses lifeboat, his wife was a great niece of Northumbrian heroine Grace Darling. MacKenzie served with the Artillery regiment of the Volunteer Force and later lived in Gosforth. The family were probably introduced to Newcastle United by director and one-time Chairman John Graham (qv) who also came from the Seahouses-North Sunderland village and whose nephew married into the wider family. The MacKenzie's soon became fervent United supporters through generation after generation. Two other relations of the family also subsequently became directors; his son Roderick R MacKenzie (qv) and Ronald MacKenzie (qv).

(Note: An early shareholder, Thomas MacKenzie of Byker, a builder, who purchased shares in the East End club during the 1890s could be linked, however extensive research shows no evidence.)

MacKENZIE Roderick Rose

Director: Sept 1953 to Feb 1976
b. Seahouses, Northumberland, 19 August 1893
d. Seahouses, Northumberland, 17 February 1976

The son of Robert W MacKenzie (qv), previously on the club's Board in pre-war years, Roderick continued the family and Seahouses connection with the Black'n'Whites for another 23 seasons in post-war football. He was Vice-Chairman of the Magpies between 1959 and 1963, Roderick ran the family decorating business in Northumberland. Described as a true gent of the north with a distinct Northumbrian accent, he lived his entire life in the Northumbrian fishing village and served in the Royal Engineers during World War One.

MacKENZIE Ronald

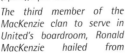

Director: Dec 1977-Feb 1989
b. Seahouses, Northumberland, October 1926
d. Benitachell, near Alicante (Spain), April 1994

The third member of the MacKenzie clan to serve in United's boardroom, Ronald MacKenzie hailed from Seahouses like his relations. His uncle was Roderick Rose MacKenzie (qv) and Ron joined Newcastle's hierarchy during December 1977, replacing Harry Dickson after failing to gain election the year before on the death of his senior. An astute businessman, MacKenzie became an influential figure at St James' Park, possessing a significant shareholding in the club. When the Magpie Group started a bid to oust the closed Boardroom at the

end of the Eighties, MacKenzie sold out to John Hall in March 1989, this following his brother's sale of shares which were originally purchased by the family way back during the Edwardian era. It was a vital coup for the Magpie Group and a significant step-forward in the takeover of the Magpies. Ronald was also Vice-Chairman, between 1980 and 1987, and at times had Board disputes with other powerful factions at the top-table, notably the Rutherford's. A tough but fair Northumbrian, he settled in Stannington and like other members of the family ran the family decorating business in Northumberland which still operates presently. On leaving the Gallowgate scene, Ronald retired and moved to the Mediterranean coast on the Costa Brava where he died in 1994.

McCONACHIE George

Director: cs 1892-1898
b. Keith, Banffshire, 25 December 1864
d. Gosforth, Newcastle upon Tyne, 15 April 1943

One of several Scots to serve Newcastle United's directorate, George McConachie hailed from the far north of Scotland where he worked as an agricultural hand then moved to Tyneside in his twenties. McConachie took over the tenancy of the Black Bull public-house on Barrack Road which became a popular bar with football supporters at St James' Park, as it still is some 120 years later. He remained in charge of the inn for over 50 years. Originally with the Newcastle West End faction, he was present at the meeting to discuss how rivals East End could benefit from his own club's demise during 1892, George quickly supported the new organisation by purchasing 25 shares. Joining the revamped management at that time, he remained on the club's Board for six years. George was later a Corporation councillor, representing the Westgate ward from 1914 to 1918 when he lived on Brighton Grove. The Scot was also an enthusiastic supporter of athletics on Tyneside, the founder of the Elswick Harriers club, later becoming President. At certain times during those early years both footballers and athletes used the Black Bull as a meeting point. McConachie did well for himself, the family noting that during his heyday he "lived in a manor house in Hepscott near Morpeth and had a Rolls-Royce limousine". At the time of his death during 1943 he was residing in Gosforth.

McKEAG William

Chairman: 1958-Nov 1959
Director: May 1944-Oct 1972
b. Belmont, Durham, 29 June 1897
d. Whitley Bay, 4 October 1972

The son of a pit worker in County Durham who was killed in a colliery accident, William McKeag was one of the most prominent figures to serve the region during the last century. A solicitor and initially a Liberal MP for Durham City (1931-1935), he became a Newcastle councillor during 1938 and was an outspoken local politician for the next 25 years. Alderman of the city and twice Lord Mayor (1951-52 & 1953-54), McKeag was an instantly recognisable figure, with pin-stripe suits and sporting a famous monocle as well as having the gift of colourful oratory, Churchillian style. Before he became associated with Newcastle United, William was a director of Durham City during the inter-war years and had a love of football from an early age. He was first proposed for a seat on the Magpie Board during 1930 and in fact became something of a rebel shareholder, a fierce critic of the

Directors & Officials

club as the troubled years of the mid-Thirties unfolded. Eventually settling in Jesmond, he was elected during May 1944 and together with Stan Seymour (senior), the club possessed two forthright and powerful directors. That sometimes brought conflict between the two men who did not always see eye to eye. In some quarters William McKeag was also known as 'Mr Newcastle' just as Seymour was. Possessing a fierce loyalty to the North East and Tyneside in particular, he was Chairman of the club during 1958 and 1959, while apart from running his legal practice (Molineux, McKeag & Cooper), William was also a governor of the Royal Victoria Infirmary and Royal Grammar School and was honoured by becoming a Freeman of the City in 1966 while he was also Icelandic Counsel. Father of Gordon McKeag (qv), later Chairman of the club too, he served in two world wars reaching the rank of major, awarded the Meritorious Service Medal during the Great War. As a young man in Durham, he was a useful local footballer and also took up boxing, as well as running under an assumed name in professional sprint meetings at Powderhall in Edinburgh. William McKeag died during October 1972 when still a member of United's executive and after 30 seasons with the club.

McKEAG William Gordon

Chairman: June 1988-Dec 1990
Director: Nov 1972-Nov 1991

b. Whickham, near Newcastle upon Tyne, 28 November 1927
d. Jesmond, Newcastle upon Tyne, 29 September 2005

Gordon McKeag took over the family position in Newcastle's boardroom during November 1972 on the death of his father. Educated at the Royal Grammar and Durham schools and later Cambridge University, McKeag studied law and followed in his father's footsteps at the family's Gosforth legal practice which had been associated with the club since pre-war years. Always interested in local sport, Gordon captained Percy Park rugby club and appeared for Northumberland. He also represented the county at squash and was a fine cricketer (for Tynemouth) as well as tennis player of repute. McKeag was brought up with Newcastle United in his blood, a fervent supporter who eventually became a force around the top-table, reaching the Chairman's seat on the resignation of Stan Seymour (junior) in 1988. His reign though was one of bitter feuding and determined defence against a takeover challenge from the Magpie Group and Sir John Hall. A three-year battle for control raged in which Gordon was the object of much scorn as well as insult. While he eventually conceded, on leaving the scene McKeag departed with integrity and respect, handling a difficult time admirably. Like most solicitors, Gordon had a way with words and invariably showed a vein of bulldog resistance as well as a wry sense of humour. McKeag vacated the Chair in December 1990 following a share-issue flop after 20 seasons as a director of the club, although he remained on a so-called "shadow board" until the takeover of the club was completed. He remained a supporter thereafter and also retained his post as President of the Football League (Nov 1988 & Jan 1992 to June 1997). His links with both the Football Association and Football League grew stronger as he left Gallowgate, being a member of various committees administrating the game, being appointed to the League Management Committee, FA Council as well as FA Cup Committee. The McKeag family involvement in the club spanned a period of almost half a century.

MacPHERSON David

Chairman: Oct 1893-Oct 1894
Director: 1893-c1895

b. Newcastle upon Tyne, c1863
d. Newcastle upon Tyne, 7 March 1925

David MacPherson was a prominent figure in Tyneside sporting circles and as a North East correspondent for the national Topical Times newspaper under the well-known nom-de-plume of 'TT Mac'. With a Scottish background, but born in the city, he was a follower of the new game of football since the pioneer days of the Tyne and Rangers clubs, then being a supporter of East End from earliest times. Associated with the early days of Newcastle United's development, MacPherson was only a director of the club for a short period. He was elected to the Board during 1893 after he purchased shares in the company following Newcastle East End's moved to St. James' Park. A commercial clerk for the United Alkali Company and living in the Heaton district at Cardigan Terrace, he became Chairman during October of that year, but had stepped down on his first anniversary in charge of the Magpies. However, David did not leave the football scene remaining a knowledgeable commentator in the local and national media. He also promoted all types of sport and was secretary of the National Cycling Union and prominently was involved in the wonderfully named Bumbler's Cycling & Dramatic Club on Tyneside. MacPherson was also the owner of a tobacconist and newsagents outlet on Pink Lane.

McVICKERS Derek

Director: Nov 1991-July 1992

b. Co Durham, January 1941

Appointed to the directorate at the end of 1991 as combat intensified for control of Newcastle United, Derek McVickers remained on the Board for only seven months. A colleague of Bob Young who also hailed from the same area of County Durham, McVickers added younger blood to the boardroom, but found himself embroiled in what became a bitter and highly public scrap for power. He ran several companies around Consett over the years, notably a sports outfitters and electrical business. McVickers later moved to the Far East for a period.

NESHAM William

Chairman: Aug 1895-Jan 1901
Director: cs 1892-Jan 1902

b. Newcastle upon Tyne, 4 June 1828
d. Newcastle upon Tyne, 8 January 1902

Appointed Newcastle West End's first Chairman during the summer of 1889 when the rival club became a Limited Company, William Nesham probably founded the club with Bill Tiffen and owned the lease for 5.25 acres of land on Leazes, known as St James' Park. He sold that to the West Enders in December 1890 to cement the site as a home for football. Residing in the historic Leazes Terrace overlooking the ground, he was an aficionado of the early game in the region. Along with John Black, as a Committee member then director, Nesham did much to see that West End survived for a decade and enjoyed some early success before a cash crisis eventually saw their demise. He was the club's President for a period then Nesham was then invited to join the East End directorate and for almost a decade served Newcastle United with esteem. It was noted that he assisted the early Black'n'Whites financially at times of need during the 1890s and was a man "widely known and universally respected". A wealthy local dignitary from a prominent

Tyneside family, the son of a physician and surgeon, William (senior), he paraded a marvellous set of whiskers in the fashion of the Victorian era. Nesham was a successful merchant importing various goods with a base near the Quayside, by the 1901 census, noted as dealing in "gunpowder, and other explosives". He held the Chairmanship from 1895 to the start of 1901 while William was also President of the Northumberland FA at the time of his demise. The Tynesider was also a highly respected cricketer in his youth appearing as a wicket-keeper for the pre-county Northumberland XI and for the Northumberland club. He retained a close connection with the summer game in Jesmond, officiating as an umpire on occasion. His brother Thomas also played cricket on Tyneside to a similar high standard. William was also linked with running minor local club Newcastle Wednesday. Nesham was born and died in Leazes Terrace a mere throw-in from the St James' Park pitch. On his death Northern Gossip magazine's tribute was of high praise, noting he was a "thorough English gentleman, a keen lover of sport, and had done much for the good of football in the North of England".

(Note: Several reports spell his surname as Neasham, however family history and club documentation confirm it as Nesham.)

NEVIN Robert William

Director: 1922-1944

b. Newcastle upon Tyne, 1878 (Q1)
d. Newcastle upon Tyne, 15 October 1945

Robert Nevin was the son of one of Newcastle East End's original shareholders, John Nevin, who resided in Heaton and was a supporter of the local club. Inheriting the family equity, Robert joined the club's Board for season 1922-23 and remained an influence at St James' Park until the latter years of World War Two. A doctor, he ran a medical practice on Heaton Road and was a consultant to the Magpies' physio team.

NEYLON James Joseph

Secretary: 1891-Feb 1892
& Sept 1893-May 1895

b. Caherfeenick, Co Clare, c1851
d. Newcastle upon Tyne, 2 November 1922

An Irishman from Caherfeenick on the Atlantic west coast, James Neylon left the Emerald Isle in his 'teens to join relations in Spital Tongues and during the 1880s and 1890s was employed as a "barman" living at Cook Street in Byker, then on Chillingham Road, near to Newcastle East End's ground. Records show he was employed by Robert Deuchar & Company and working as a pub "manager" as confirmed by the club's share documents. During 1890 he actually used one of the inns he controlled, The Viaduct Hotel, for a time as East End's office and meeting place. James was a keen supporter and become an early shareholder. Knowing most of the movers and shakers of the emerging club became East End's Secretary for season 1891-92, also associated with neighbours Heaton Rovers, a vice-president during 1892. He resigned in February due to illness, but remaining associated with the club, Neylon was appointed again to the post for the start of the 1893-94 campaign, the first season of Football League action. He remained in office until the summer of 1895. By then James was involved in various activities in the community, described in Northern Gossip magazine during 1900 as giving "many public services to the City of Newcastle". He was noted as a "Guardian for Byker"; a champion of the poor and under-privileged, while by the time of the 1911 national census Neylon was employed as a "Registrar of Births & Deaths" in Newcastle, residing in Benwell. He remained in the city's West End to his death.

OLIVER John Thompson

President: 1884-1888

b. Newcastle upon Tyne, 1844 (Q3)
d. Edinburgh, 30 August 1918

The club's first figurehead as pioneers Newcastle East End developed in the Heaton district of the city, John Oliver was one of the enthusiastic Committee men who ran the fledging organisation before East End became a Limited Company. Appointed President, he may have been associated with the club shortly after formation in 1881, the first traceable record being his leadership for seasons 1884-85 and 1885-86, while Oliver could have been linked with the club to the transformation into a company in 1890. The exact identity of Oliver is not conclusive, however at the time of his Presidency, during the 1880s, census information for Newcastle reveal two potential residents of the community; John Thompson Oliver, pictured (living in Elswick during 1881, but moving to the Heaton and Jesmond suburb by 1901) and James T Oliver (from Cornwall and living in North Shields, a church minister). To be such a figurehead, even of a newly developing club like East End, Oliver must have been a well-known citizen which points to the former; John Thompson Oliver, who in addition, by the end of the century was residing alongside the majority of the club's directors and officials. It is probable East End's first President was this Oliver, who hailed from a distinguished Tyneside family. He was born in the Westgate district, his father Adam being a civil engineer and grandfather, the noted architect and surveyor, Thomas Oliver, who is acclaimed for producing the well-known Oliver's map of Newcastle. John lived in Rye Hill, Elswick, St Andrews, then at Highbury in Jesmond and also became a civil engineer, joining the North Eastern Railway Company in 1857. He spent 56 years with the organisation, becoming Assistant Chief Engineer by the time of his retirement, at the heart of the huge development of the railway network in the region. Oliver was also a member of the Newcastle Board of Guardians and he took a particular interest in the well-being of what were termed the "waifs and strays" of the community, serving over 30 years as secretary of the Newcastle Ragged and Industrial Schools.

OLIVER John Peel

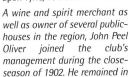

Chairman: 1919-Dec 1928
Director: cs 1902 to Dec 1928

b. Newcastle upon Tyne, 1860
d. Jesmond, Newcastle
upon Tyne, 19 December 1928

A wine and spirit merchant as well as owner of several public-houses in the region, John Peel Oliver joined the club's management during the close-season of 1902. He remained in a very active role for 27 seasons, enjoying the Edwardian Masters era and being Chairman of the club when they won the FA Cup in 1924 and the Championship three years later. Well known in football circles, he was "highly respected for his integrity" and held a position on the powerful Football League Management Committee from 1917 to his death. It was just before one of those meetings of the games' rulers, in 1921, that Oliver suffered a heart attack at the Euston Hotel and had to be rushed to hospital. His activities were restricted afterwards but Oliver remained a loyal servant to Newcastle United's cause to his demise in December 1928, shortly after visiting St James' Park. One of eight children and brother of Robert Oliver (qv) and father of Thomas Oliver (qv), both on the club's Board, the family acquiring shares in the Magpies during the Edwardian era. He was originally a joiner living in Spital Tongues then moved into the victualler's trade by 1890 being in charge of The Crown and New Burnt House inns. Living in Heaton and afterwards Jesmond, Oliver married the

sister of Newcastle East End's Secretary Tom Watson (qv), later prominent and successful boss of both Sunderland and Liverpool. In addition, Oliver's sister married James Lunn (qv) another long serving club director. It is said he is also related to Cumbrian huntsman John Peel, made famous in the celebrated folk song, "D'ye ken John Peel" written by Robert Graves, however no evidence can be found to support this.

OLIVER Robert

Director: June 1904-May 1925

b. Newcastle upon Tyne,
July 1868
d. Newcastle upon Tyne,
13 May 1925

Brother of John Peel Oliver (qv) and living for a period in Heaton, Robert Oliver became a United director during 1904 in a reshuffle and served alongside his relation for over 20 years, through a period of great success at St James' Park. Like John Peel Oliver, Robert was a wine and spirit merchant, probably in conjunction with his brother. Additionally he had a financial interest in various licensed properties in Newcastle and Hexham, it was noted that he was "personally associated" in the management of the Belle Grove Hotel in Spital Tongues not far from the Gallowgate stadium.

OLIVER Thomas

Director: May 1925-Aug 1937

b. Newcastle upon Tyne, 1889

Thomas Oliver replaced his uncle Robert Oliver (qv) on the club's Board in May 1925. The eldest son of John Peel Oliver (qv), he was the fourth member of the family to serve the club. Living in Gosforth during the 1930s, he was an engineering surveyor. At one point United's share register noted no fewer than 19 different members of the Oliver family holding the restricted shares in the company.

PATTERSON J

Director: 1891-1892

b. unknown

Having one season serving on the club's Board of Directors, J Patterson was involved when the organisation was still called Newcastle East End and just before the Heaton outfit relocated to St James' Park in the summer of 1892. An early shareholder, Patterson resided at Rothbury Terrace, the same street as fellow supporter Joseph Bell. He later lived on Jesmond Vale Terrace close by. It is possible he may have been the same individual as J Pattinson (qv) who appeared in friendly games during April 1893.

PEEL James Edward

Director: Feb 1890-Jan 1893
Secretary: Jan 1893

b. Newcastle upon Tyne, 1859 (Q1)
d. Walthamstow, London,
28 November 1920

One of Newcastle United's original shareholders and directors when the East End company was set-up during February 1890, James Peel was a legal clerk by profession, living

in Cardigan Terrace, Heaton. He stepped into the Secretary role for a short period when Walter Golding resigned and was also club Treasurer for a spell. Peel relocated to London at the beginning of 1893, taking up a post in the legal centre around Temple and the Royal High Court of Justice, becoming by 1911 a senior barrister's clerk to a group of prominent King's Counsel. He was highly regarded within East End's camp, when he departed south James was presented with a "diamond ring, a purse of gold and an illuminated album". Peel resided in Walthamstow to his death.

PRICE Andrew Brian

Director: 1996-1998
Secretary: Jan 1997-May 1998
PLC Secretary:
Jan 1997-May 1998

b. Yorkshire, c1962

Joining the club in 1996 to become Newcastle United PLC's Secretary and Director of Legal Affairs once the Magpies' had started their transition to public status, Andrew Price was a solicitor with a speciality in sport. Previously associated with Leeds United through the Dubb Lupton Alsop law firm, he was appointed to strengthen the administrative function before and after United's floatation. After his stint at St James' Park, Price returned to DLA in Leeds during January 1999, continuing to give the club advice, before joining Addleshaw Goddard as Head of Sport. In June 2009 Price took a similar role with Couchmans in London. Andrew became a recognised lawyer operating across various aspects of sport, notably media, sponsorship and commercial arrangements, working with the likes of Premier Rugby, the Football League and World Snooker. From Yorkshire he was raised supporting Leeds United.

REVILL Timothy John

PLC Director:
July 2002-June 2007

b. [Chatham, 1950 (Q3)]

Tim Revill was an experienced London based Chartered Accountant who set up his own practice, Revill & Co on the Isle of Man and then when based in Gibralter founding the successful STM Group PLC, a cross border financial services provider. An expert in his field with a reputation for straight forward talking, Tim was once described in the financial press as a "financial butler to the rich". Specialising in financial planning, he lectured widely and served on international monetary and tax steering committees. Apart from his non-executive role with Newcastle United, Revill also had several other similar appointments including directorships with Kingswalk Investments, later the European Wealth Group, and Stan James PLC. Tim stepped down on the purchase of the club by Mike Ashley in the summer of 2007.

RICHARDSON William John

Committee: c1885-Feb 1890
Director: Feb 1890-1891

b. unknown

A pattern-maker on Tyneside, living at Addison Street in Heaton, William Richardson was one of the group of keen Newcastle East End patrons who assisted in the development of what would become Newcastle United Football Club. Initially on the Chillingham Road committee from as early as 1885 (and perhaps before), Richardson was club Treasurer for 1887-88 and one of the first directors in 1890, but left the management of the club to others during the following year.

Directors & Officials

ROBERTSON Walter J

Secretary: July 1893-Sept 1893

b. unknown

Secretary of the club for only three months, Walter Robertson was one of three individuals who replaced Walter Golding in the Secretary's role for short spells during the mid-1890s. Following James Peel and John Dixon, Robertson's position was described in the Newcastle Daily Chronicle as "pro-tem". He resided on Westgate Road and was noted as an "enthusiastic supporter" of the recently titled Newcastle United. He stood down when James Neylon took over the role as the 1893-94 season began.

(Note: In certain places his surname is noted as Robinson.)

ROBINSON James

Committee: 1888-1889

b. Newcastle upon Tyne, c1856

Census records show only one James Robinson residing in the Byker and Heaton districts during 1891, he was only briefly associated with the East End club as a Committee member.

ROWATT John

Secretary: 1888

b. Scotland

John Rowatt (junior) lived in Heaton with his father, a Scottish family who had laid roots on Tyneside during the Victorian era. Working as a clerk, John played football for the Heaton Association club during the early years of the 1880s, and also pulled on the colours of Addison, Heaton Rovers, St Silas, Cheviot and North Eastern in 1885. Rowatt had a period with Newcastle East End's reserve squad as a half-back and forward, probably after his club Cheviot merged with the Chillingham Road outfit during September 1887. Robert looked after the administration of the club's second and third elevens in season 1887-88. He was then appointed Honorary Secretary soon after, for a period in 1888 when still in his teens, working alongside Charles Tinlin before John handed over the administrative reigns to Tom Watson. He remained as a player with East End Swifts for 1889-90 but never reached the first-team and also acted occasionally as an umpire. Rowatt also played with Newcastle FA on Tyneside during those early years of the game's development.

RUSH James

Director: April 1967-April 1990

b. Longbenton, Newcastle upon Tyne, 16 August 1909
d. Stannington, near Newcastle upon Tyne, 24 April 1993

A former RAF pilot during World War Two, when Jimmy Rush joined Newcastle United's executive during the spring of 1967, he was a well respected personality in the North East. Elected to the Board to replace Wally Hurford, Rush sat around the top-table throughout 24 seasons. A charismatic gentleman of the old-school; he wore a bowler hat, dressed well, drove a Daimler car and was well spoken, yet was born into a less than well off family. A self-made man, during 1947 he founded a company of glass manufacturers based on Stepney Bank, Byker where the industry had a long and proven tradition. Later setting up a factory in North Shields, the company grew

into an important export business on Tyneside. Before that corporate success, Rush had achieved a noteworthy wartime service record rising to the rank of Squadron Leader after learning to fly and gaining a pilot's licence during the early Thirties. Then based in London, he became a pilot, flying mail from Brussels and Copenhagen to the capital while he also worked as a flying instructor and started air-racing during 1935. He joined the services on the outbreak of war in 1939, Jimmy serving in the Battle of Britain as well as over Europe, the Western Desert, Eritrea, Burma, India and South Africa. During 1944 he commanded an operational squadron of Dakota's in the Far East and was awarded the Air Force Cross for distinguished service. The Tynesider resumed racing after the conflict and won the 1953 Royal Aero Club British championship and also represented Great Britain in meetings across Europe. During May 1954, Rush became the first Englishman to take part in New York's prestigious St Patrick's Day Procession, flying in and out of the skyscrapers. Top-ranked in that sport, he was one of the colourfully termed "Throttle Benders Union"! Rush was a diminutive figure, hugely likable and who possessed an entertaining personality with many a story of his intriguing life. A valued member of the club's Board with much influence, apart from possessing a passion of football and Newcastle United, Rush was also a man of wide-ranging talents and indulged in collecting artwork, a Fellow of the Royal Society of Arts. He was an expert of Beilby glass, writing a history of the notable Tynesider manufacturer William Beilby. Also a keen patron of the scout movement as well as owning and racing greyhounds at Brough Park, Jimmy was later appointed a Vice-President of the Black'n'Whites.

RUTHERFORD George Frederick

Chairman: March 1941-Dec 1949
Director: 1925-Dec 1949

b. Whitley Bay, 1883 (Q4)
d. Newcastle upon Tyne, 7 December 1949

One of three members of the Rutherford line to have held the Chairmanship of Newcastle United, George Rutherford was the first to be elected as a figurehead of the Magpies, replacing James Lunn during March 1941. A coal merchant in the North East, he held control of affairs throughout World War Two and saw the club return to the First Division in 1948. A long-standing shareholder of the club since Edwardian years, George was first nominated to become a director in 1923, joining the Board two years later. He was remembered as an unselfish individual, a steady influence around the table. Living in Gosforth, he sat on the Football League Management Committee from 1938 to 1942 and was Vice-President of the Football League thereafter to his death in 1949. The wider family included in addition Harry Dickson (qv) and George Dickson (qv), both directors illustrating the close-knit family association running the club for over a century.

RUTHERFORD Robert

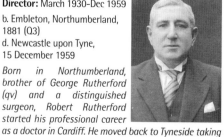

Chairman: Nov 1951-1953
Director: March 1930-Dec 1959

b. Embleton, Northumberland, 1881 (Q3)
d. Newcastle upon Tyne, 15 December 1959

Born in Northumberland, brother of George Rutherford (qv) and a distinguished surgeon, Robert Rutherford started his professional career as a doctor in Cardiff. He moved back to Tyneside taking

the post of Deputy Medical Officer of Health for Newcastle during 1911 and later moved to become Medical Officer of Health, and Schools Medical Officer for Wallsend. By that time Rutherford had been nominated to join his brother George on United's Board. He was first put forward as a candidate in 1927 but not co-opted until 1930. Noted as a "loveable character", he was known affectionately as 'Dr Bob' and was a great raconteur when on United's travels. Rutherford could be blunt and direct at times, he was a true United supporter often travelling with the team, especially after retiring from his medical post in 1947 when he also acted as the Magpies' doctor. Bob was Chairman between 1951 and 1953, but unfortunately missed the Wembley victory in 1952 having to undergo an operation in London. During World War One, Rutherford served in the Medical Corps and was honoured with the Military Cross. Residing in the Jesmond and Gosforth district, he died during December 1959 when still on the club's Board and after nearly 30 years with the Black'n'Whites. His son Robert James Rutherford (qv) went onto become Chairman as well.

RUTHERFORD Robert James

Chairman: Jan 1978-March 1981
Director: April 1950-March 1981

b. Newcastle upon Tyne, 1913 (Q2)
d. Newcastle upon Tyne, 15 August 1995

The son of past Chairman Dr Robert Rutherford (qv) and elected to Newcastle's inner sanctum during April 1950, Bob Rutherford went onto spend 31 seasons at the club's top-table. The third direct member of the family to spend a long period looking after United's business over a period of no less than 56 years of unbroken service (1925-1981), Rutherford was educated at the Royal Grammar School and Durham University. He followed his father into the medical profession, also becoming an eminent surgeon operating on many United players to rectify injuries. Although Bob witnessed all of Newcastle's victorious Fifties era, by the time he was elevated to the Chair during January 1978, the club was in rapid decline. Being Lord Westwood's deputy for over a decade prior to his appointment, Rutherford shunned the public spotlight and suffered from supporter criticism at the club's lack of professionalism and modern success. At a critical point in United's history during March 1981, he resigned both his post as Chairman and director along with Lord Westwood, when he was asked to increase a financial guarantee to the club's bankers. An outstanding golfer and enthusiastic supporter of rugby, Rutherford resided in Gosforth to his death in 1995. The Rutherford dynasty, like the Oliver family, held a widespread shareholding of the Magpies.

SALKELD David Victor

Director: March 1976-March 1981

b. Newcastle upon Tyne, September 1919
d. Gosforth, Newcastle upon Tyne, 22 April 2009

David Salkeld was attached to Newcastle United for around 10 years as club doctor before being elected to the Magpies' Board during 1976. Born and bred in the city, Salkeld was a prominent medical practitioner on Tyneside, during the Forties and Fifties based at Brighton Grove, then later on Ellison Place, setting up the Saville Medical Group, one of the largest in the region. Educated at the Royal Grammar School, then at King's College, Durham he finalised his studies at Charing Cross Medical School in London. Serving with the Territorial Army, he was also medical officer for two regiments with a rank of Major in the Royal Army Medical Corps. David possessed a fervour for rugby and cricket, playing rugby for the Old Novo's club and was selected for Northumberland, while he appeared for the Northumberland County club during the summer months as a batsman and medium pace bowler. He also turned out for the Durham University and England University sides as well as club cricket for Bamburgh, Benwell and Alnwick all during the 1940s, then for a long period with South Northumberland CC from 1949 to 1959, being later a committee member during the Sixties. He was good enough to appear for the County side in the Minor Counties Championship during 1956. Being an avid sportsman, Salkeld also followed the fortunes of the Magpies during the post-war years and spent five years with a voice in the boardroom at St James' Park.

SANDERSON William John

Director: July 1896-June 1897

b. Newcastle upon Tyne, June 1853

d. Warkworth, Northumberland, 9 March 1929

With a family home at Eastfield Hall near Warkworth in Northumberland, William Sanderson spent a single campaign in the power-room of Gallowgate, during 1896-97. Also with a base in Gosforth, Sanderson was a successful wine and spirit merchant, joining the family business at the Haymarket Brewery during 1870 but had retired by 1887 to devote time to what were called "philanthropic projects". A prominent figure in the north, William became a councillor in 1894, serving as Sheriff, then was appointed Lord Mayor of Newcastle during 1907 and 1908. He was a local member for the St Thomas' ward near St James' Park, and also an Alderman and JP for both Newcastle and Northumberland. Involved in many activities in the city, described as a man of "great public spiritedness", William was also a governor of the Royal Victoria Infirmary for 12 years while he was associated with several important organisations in the country's pre-Welfare State society; the Crippled Children's Home in Gosforth, the Deaf & Dumb Institution as well as being President of the Home Society for teaching the Blind. Sanderson was also a prominent member of the Board of Guardians.

SEYMOUR Stanley (Jnr)

Chairman: March 1981-June 1988
Director: April 1976-Nov 1991
President: Aug 1989-Nov 1992

b. Greenock, 29 May 1916
d. Birmingham, 5 November 1992

Stan Seymour was the elder of two sons of former United stalwart, 'Mr Newcastle', George Stanley Seymour (qv). He was born in Scotland when his father was playing for Morton but moved to the North East when Stan (senior) returned to his native region and signed for United during 1920. For many years Stan was involved in the family sports outfitters business, a well-known outlet in the city, indeed the location on Market Street being celebrated as 'Seymour's Corner'. Not surprisingly he was a United supporter through and through with a down-to-earth Geordie upbringing. He was first promoted for a post on the Board in 1959 but did not become a director until he replaced his father during 1976. Seymour was also a keen rugby addict, but football was his first love and apart from the day-to-day activities of Newcastle United was heavily involved in promoting local football in the area. He was keenly involved in the Northern Alliance league

as well as being a Northumberland FA executive, becoming President of the local governing body. Seymour always fought hard for the development of youngsters at Gallowgate, maintaining the club had to balance purchases with local talent. A well-built, portly and popular character, Stan took over the Chairman's post on the resignation of Bob Rutherford and presided over one of the most thrilling periods in United's modern history when he was instrumental in attracting Kevin Keegan to Tyneside during 1982. For a period Stan had a seat on the FA Council, he guided United into a new era of commercialism and sponsorship, forming a productive bond with neighbours across Barrack Road, Newcastle Breweries. Residing in Morpeth, he liked to keep a somewhat low profile, yet watched the Black'n'Whites incessantly, travelling to the majority of away fixtures and being a regular with the reserve team as well. Stan resigned in the summer of 1988 just before combat with the Magpie Group erupted. He remained connected to the club he cherished as President until he died suddenly after attending a United fixture at St Andrews, Birmingham in 1992. Together with his father, the Seymour family clocked up 54 seasons of consecutive service in the boardroom (1938-1992). His brother Colin (qv) appeared for the club during wartime football but was tragically killed in a flying accident.

SHEPHERD Bruce Stewart

PLC Director: July 2002-June 2007

b. Newcastle upon Tyne, 10 November 1946

Bruce Shepherd, the younger brother of Chairman Freddy Shepherd (qv), largely looked after the family marine enterprise on Tyneside when his brother was absorbed with the running of the Magpies for a decade. As Chief Executive of the Shepherd complex spanning over some 150 acres on the site of the Tyne's historic shipyards, Bruce is a shrewd businessman and like his brother a strong and positive voice promoting the North East region, including that of Newcastle United. A major shareholder of the club alongside his brother, Bruce was elected to the PLC Board and remained associated with the club until the sale of the family shareholding to Mike Ashley during the summer of 2007. At that point the two Shepherd brothers were prominent in developing their family business interests of marine activities and property development, especially focussed on regeneration of the East End of Newcastle and Tyne riverside.

SHEPHERD William Frederick

Chairman: Dec 1997-July 2007
Director: Nov 1991-July 2007
PLC Chairman: May 2002-July 2007
PLC Director: April 1997-March 1998 & Dec 1998-July 2007

b. Gisland, Northumberland, 29 October 1941

Freddy Shepherd hails from a local Tyneside family steeped in support of Newcastle United for generations. Born on the Northumberland and Cumberland border near Haltwhistle, his grandfather founded a well-known Shepherd scrap metal business based at Byker Bank, whose adverts were seen on United programmes throughout the Forties, Fifties and Sixties. Schooled in Australia for a few years, then raised in the Byker and Walker area of the city, as a teenager Shepherd was an apprentice marine engineer delivering plans, amongst

other duties, to the renowned Swan Hunter shipyard. Together with his brother Bruce Shepherd (qv), who was to become a United PLC director, they developed the family Shepherd Offshore company into a highly successful business dealing in warehousing, logistics, offshore services and marine fabrication based alongside the Tyne. Watching the Black'n'Whites since a child, his successful corporate ventures brought him into contact with Sir John Hall during the 1990s and as the Magpie Group came to the end of successfully bringing change to the Boardroom at St James' Park, Freddy was invited to join the directorate in November 1991 during a period of major restructuring. Forceful, at times direct and to the point, yet always with Newcastle United's interests at heart – being essentially a fan turned director – Shepherd took over from Sir John as a full-time and hands-on Chairman during December 1997 having built up a substantial shareholding himself, although some way below the majority stake held by Cameron Hall. For 10 seasons between 1997-98 and 2006-07 Shepherd held significant control of the Magpies, in charge when Bobby Robson was appointed as boss. He presided over a relatively thriving period; challenging at the top of the Premier League and bringing Champions League football to Tyneside, reaching two FA Cup finals, and always with big spending on high profile players. He was also forward thinking attempting to forge a link with China (with Dalian Shide FC) long before that country's economic surge, while Shepherd together with his son was instrumental in setting up the deal to launch the movie 'Goal' with Newcastle United the club featured to a world-wide audience. Yet Freddy had difficulties like all Chairmen; infamously caught by a News of the World sting with Douglas Hall (when he stood down from the PLC Board for a short period) and criticised for the sacking of Robson and subsequent managerial appointments as well as hefty purchases of Owen and Luque which proved less than successful. Shepherd was also a PLC director and Chairman of the PLC when the acquisition of the club by Mike Ashley took place in 2007. He was forced out of St James' Park that summer, earning a substantial multi-million pound sale from his shares. Afterwards Freddy was linked with taking control of La Liga club, Real Mallorca, but once that fell through concentrated on other activities in the region and elsewhere, back with Shepherd Offshore and including property development. He is also Chairman and majority shareholder of sports agency, Triple S. Something of a Geordie champion, in 2012 he acquired the listed Palace of Arts building in Newcastle's Exhibition Park, planned to house his collection of vintage horse-drawn carriages and cars. The Shepherd family also purchased the historic Mitford Estate in Northumberland and began a restoration programme. A keen sailor, he is a past President of Newcastle Yacht Club.

SIMPSON Robert Wilfred

Director: June 1918-Sept 1935

b. Govan, Glasgow, c1879
d. Hebburn, 6 September 1935

*During his younger days on Tyneside and having trained to be a medical practitioner in his native Glasgow, Robert Simpson was a sportsman himself, playing most activities in the region to a decent standard. He was also a keen supporter of the Magpies and by the time he had become a noted doctor in the city, was appointed as the Black'n'Whites' medical officer following service in World War One as a captain with the Royal Army Medical Corps. Becoming a director in June 1918 as the conflict came to a close, Simpson ran a surgery in the city-centre, at Prudhoe Street. He was also a prominent politician, a councillor and Deputy Lord Mayor for a period. Robert resided at Jesmond View House in Heaton for many years, then in Hebburn and was Vice-Chairman at the time of his death during 1935.

NEWCASTLE UNITED
The Ultimate Who's Who 1881-2014

Directors & Officials

SLATER Kenneth

Director: June 2001-Sept 2007

b. Blakelaw,
Newcastle upon Tyne,
25 October 1956

With Newcastle United since leaving school as a 15-year-old, Ken Slater was first attached to the club on a youth employment scheme from Newcastle College. Employed full-time with the club during May 1972, he climbed the ladder from office administrator to wages clerk, accounts clerk, Assistant Secretary in 1984, before becoming Club Accountant and Financial Controller then Group Financial Director by June 2001. In all Slater served the club for 35 years and by the time he joined the boardroom, Ken had accumulated a vast knowledge of football and had worked closely with all the eminent power-brokers of United during his long period at St James' Park; from Stan Seymour (senior and junior) to Lord Westwood, Sir John Hall, Freddie Fletcher and Freddy Shepherd. On the purchase of the club by Mike Ashley, Slater departed with fellow long serving colleague Russell Cushing. Afterwards, he was appointed to a similar Finance Director role with the Protector Group on Tyneside, becoming Joint Managing Director in 2013. Residing near Bolam in Northumberland, Slater remains a season-ticket holder in the East Stand at St James' Park.

SPITTLE Henry

Committee: 1889-1890

b. Alnwick, 1854
d. Newcastle upon Tyne, 4 May 1919

A master draper who hailed from the county seat of Alnwick, Henry Spittle was a supporter of the early Newcastle United pioneers in Byker donating new blue strips for the team during April 1887. He became a Committee member for season 1889-90, although potentially he was involved in the running of the club before then. It was recorded that one of his tasks was to draft a set of Club Rules when the East Enders had developed to an extent that regulations were required. While he purchased shares in the new limited company when it was formed during the early months of 1890, the Northumbrian didn't become one of the organisation's first directors. Spittle resided in Jesmond and lived into his eighties.

STABLEFORTH Arthur George

Director: Sept 1935-March 1952

b. Hartlepool, c1879
d. Newcastle upon Tyne,
5 March 1952

Taking the place on Newcastle United's directorate of Robert Simpson during 1935, Arthur Stableforth was brought up in Hartlepool but by the 1890s had moved to Tyneside. He lived in the Westgate district and managed a dairy locally. Younger brother of Charles T Stableforth who became Sheriff of Newcastle, he later resided in Whitley Bay being on United's Board through the years of the late Thirties and Forties.

STEEL John P

Director: Feb 1890-1891
Secretary: Dec 1889 & April 1890-Aug 1890

b. unknown

Residing in Heaton and employed as a "school attendance officer", during the latter years of the Victorian era John Steel was a keen supporter of the ambitious Newcastle East End outfit. He purchased shares when they opted to become a limited company during 1890, Steel appointed as one of the original 13-man Board of directors. John was a member of East End's Committee during the formative years before a directorate was formed, acting as Secretary for a period. He left the running of the club to others within a short period and later in life settled in the Stocksfield area alongside the Tyne.

STEPHENSON Robert Noel David OBE

Chief Executive:
Nov 1991-Jan 1992

b. Newcastle upon Tyne,
June 1932
d. Kelso district, 2006 (Q1)

A prominent member of the North East business community for more than 30 years, David Stephenson was a driving force behind one of Tyneside's flagship companies, Newcastle Breweries Ltd. As neighbours of Newcastle United, he had a close association with the Magpies alongside fellow director Alastair Wilson. David played rugby for Gosforth and trained as an accountant, having a spell working in Canada during the late Fifties before joining the Scottish & Newcastle Group in 1960. He moved to Edinburgh for a period before returning to Tyneside and possessing a high level of corporate management expertise became Managing Director of the North East concern during 1976. Living at Felton near Morpeth, Stephenson was linked to many activities which affected Tyneside life, he was a board member of the Newcastle Building Society, North Housing Ltd, The Theatre Royal, as well as Newcastle Polytechnic. David was also associated with Loretto School in Musselburgh. Stephenson sat on various forums such as the Children's Foundation and Northumbria Coalition against Crime. Apart from his close involvement as a sponsor with United, David was associated with Middlesbrough as well, in 1986 assisting greatly in the rescue plan which saved the club from financial collapse. The well-regarded and prominent Novocastrian was honoured for services to the region with the OBE during December 1990, a few months before retirement. Stephenson was a founder member of the Magpie Group in 1989 which began to challenge the ownership of Newcastle United and during the autumn of that year was invited to join the Board but declined the opportunity. Once he retired from S&N as the Nineties began, Stephenson was tempted to become the new regime's first Chief Executive. Appointed in November 1991, Stephenson though only remained at St James' Park a few weeks before handing over to Freddie Fletcher.

STEWART Robert Strother

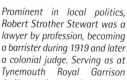

Director: Aug 1916-1927

b. Newcastle upon Tyne,
16 May 1878
d. Newcastle upon Tyne,
15 November 1954

Prominent in local politics, Robert Strother Stewart was a lawyer by profession, becoming a barrister during 1919 and later a colonial judge. Serving as at Tynemouth Royal Garrison Artillery before the Great War, he lived in Leazes Terrace then Jesmond. During World War One, Robert held a TG (Temporary Gentleman) commission with the rank of major, while he became a local councillor in the city from 1912 to 1924. Stewart also stood for the House of Commons, initially attempting election in 1918 at Workington, then Stockton after World War One, before becoming a liberal MP for the same Teesside town in 1923, winning a seat ahead of future Prime Minister Harold Macmillan. During the inter-war years he also became a United director, being an influential voice around the table. Stewart held various appointments being a past Chairman of the Pensions Appeal Tribunal and a member of the Newcastle Board of Guardians. Highly educated, he attended Durham University and Westminster College, Cambridge as well as the theological college of the Presbyterian church. During the late Twenties, Robert was offered an overseas post as part of the Government's Colonial Legal Service, leaving United's directorate during 1927 to serve in Trinidad, Malta and the Gold Coast. Stewart was married to a noted Newcastle artist, Ida Taylor.

STONEHOUSE David Coulson

Director: April 2000-June 2001
Chief Executive:
April 2000-June 2001
PLC Director:
April 2000-June 2001
PLC Chief Executive:
April 2000-June 2001

b. Newcastle upon Tyne,
April 1955

Exchanging affinity from Sunderland to Newcastle United during 2000, David Stonehouse started his business career with accountancy firm Arthur Young in 1980. The Tynesider became a partner with Price Waterhouse Cooper and joined Sunderland's top-team during September 1996 as Finance Director. Educated at Dame Allan's School in the city then Keele University, on Freddie Fletcher's departure, Stonehouse arrived at Gallowgate as Chief Executive. Described at the time as a "smooth operator", he showed good communication skills during his 14 month tenure with United, a voice of good sense, but his stay was to be short. During the summer of 2001 Stonehouse left the club noting "personal reasons" for his departure. Throughout his career David held director posts with several companies including fund managers NEL, technology company Datatrial, Parkdean Holidays and accountants UNW where he became Chairman. He was also a director for a period of St Oswald's Hospice. Following his departure from St James' Park, Stonehouse successfully developed IT company TSG with local entrepreneur Graham Wylie, becoming Chief Executive during July 2003. Living in Gosforth, he confirmed in one interview that he was a Newcastle United supporter at heart, despite his Sunderland appointment.

TAYLOR Wilfred Burns

Chairman: cs 1955-cs 1958
Director: Nov 1941-Feb 1971

b. North Shields, 13 February 1888
d. Newcastle upon Tyne, 27 February 1971

Wilf Taylor was a successful miller by trade in the region, a director of local enterprise Hindhaughs. From good Tyneside stock, Taylor's uncle was Sheriff of Newcastle upon Tyne and he became a United official during the Second World War, in November 1941. That appointment to the Board was after several years of trying to gain a seat at the table, initially with a nomination during 1936. Small and frail looking, Taylor possessed a wise head and was full of fun. He became Chairman following the 1955 FA Cup final, Wilf remaining in charge until the summer of 1958 when he stepped down at a time of boardroom feuding between the Seymour and McKeag factions. Taylor played a prominent part in the quarrel with star forward George Eastham, having sympathy with the player and attempting to find common ground, yet he ended up defending the club's stance in Court even though personally he had reservations surrounding the defence and principals at stake. Spending 30 seasons as a valuable member of the Magpies' leadership, during the Fifties decade Wilf became an influential figure in the wider administration of the game, sitting on the Football League Management Committee from 1956 to 1964, and Vice-President of the League for six years, to 1970. His reign on Newcastle's directorate ended shortly after, on his demise during February 1971. As a youth it is recorded that he played football on Tyneside to a local level, once receiving a roasting as a defender by future United star Jackie Rutherford.

TELFORD James

Chairman: Jan 1901-June 1904
Director: cs 1892-June 1904

b. Crawford, Lanarkshire,
27 December 1847
d. Newcastle upon Tyne,
28 March 1926

A shrewd businessman who was involved in the drapery trade, John Telford is credited with changing the whole outlook on football on Tyneside. The Scot can claim to have been a major influence in putting the name of Newcastle United on the soccer map in the decade which followed their move to St James' Park in 1892. The Newcastle Daily Journal noted that Telford, "established the financial success of the club" while Colin Veitch recorded that he was "the driving power in Newcastle football". Residing off Westgate Road, at Blenheim Street then Rye Hill, he was a Newcastle West End supporter, but backed the rival East Enders club once they had become the city's sole club in 1892. He became a director at that time and Chairman at the start of 1901. A powerful, eloquent character, at times even domineering, James had a personality that ensured results and courage to voice his conviction. Telford was involved in most of the club's early transfers being a good judge of a player, bringing many of Newcastle's Edwardian stars to St James' Park and building the foundations for the success that was to follow. Yet the Scot made enemies too, and with some fellow directors and shareholders opposed to his leadership, he lost his boardroom place after a coup in June 1904, a shock on Tyneside at the time. Official Minutes of the club record that there had been friction between Telford and the Bell family over voting powers by proxy. His departure was not liked in the dressing-room with Bob McColl one of several players who publically opposed his removal. Veitch wrote in his memoirs that Telford had received treatment of a "scurvy nature". At the time of his departure, James also owned the club's office at 9 St James Street. A dispute followed over a new lease and the club were forced to move to new premises on Grainger Street for a period. Despite a sour ending, he remained an important figure in the Black'n'Whites early history. Topical Times newspaper recalled in 1921 that the Scot was "without doubt the one director who can claim credit for making Newcastle United famous".

TURNBULL Alexander B

Chairman: July 1891-Oct 1893
& May 1895-Aug 1895
Director: Feb 1890-1901

b. Scotland, c1858

The club's second Chairman following a move to limited company status during early 1890, Alex Turnbull was very much an East Ender. Residing in Heaton, on Rothbury Terrace, he was one of the Chillingham

---

Road outfit's original shareholders, indeed the family which included William Turnbull (qv), also a director, held a substantial stake with 35 shares. A business representative travelling the country, he was involved in the coal trade running the Byker & Heaton Coal Company and later a local brick manufacturing enterprise. His wider family were wine and spirit merchants and also had interests in public-houses, including that of the East End Hotel, later the Chillingham Hotel near the club's ground. Involved in the meeting which took place at his neighbour, Joe Bell's house, on Rothbury Terrace which made the decision to move to St James' Park in 1892, Turnbull presided over the public gathering which changed the name of the club from East End to Newcastle United later in that year. He remained the club's figurehead until October 1893, during that year having spoken with passion for United's corner when they were seeking votes for election into the Football League. He did have another short period in the Chair during 1895, while he left the boardroom completely just after the turn of the century.

TURNBULL William

Committee: 1888-1889

b. probably Scotland

A wine and spirit merchant who purchased shares in the Newcastle East End company during May 1890, William Turnbull lived in Heaton at Meadowfield House on Chillingham Road near to the club's ground, with relations Adam and Joseph Turnbull, also recorded as being club shareholders. Related to Chairman Alex Turnbull (qv), an innkeeper as well, he ran the Egypt Tavern on City Road and The Adelaide on New Bridge Street, two popular establishments during the 1880s and 1890s.

WALLER Thomas

President: 1888-1889 **Committee:** 1888-1889

b. Newcastle upon Tyne, April 1849
d. Newcastle upon Tyne, 4 June 1898

Newcastle East End's club President for season 1888-89, Tom Waller was a well-known local councillor and one of a noted family from the city. Running a marine store situated on Ridley Terrace, his brothers Henry and George operated a construction business based in Heaton and Byker. Representing the All Saints ward on the Council (his brother Henry was councillor for Heaton), he officiated on various Corporation committees during that era and was a respected figure. Originally a "rag merchant & dealer" during the 1870s, Thomas was Newcastle East End's leader at a time of unrest and infighting at Chillingham Road. It was noted in the local press during October 1889, an open comment to Waller, that "when you have got through your electioneering work...just give the club an overhauling, and see if you can secure the perfect harmony that used to exist." Waller appeared to have achieved that, East End becoming stronger by 1890. By the time the club moved to limited company status in the early part of that year, Thomas left running the East Enders to others in the district, although he remained a supporter of the club. His brother George William Waller was a celebrated Tyneside cyclist, becoming World Champion at the popular Victorian sport in 1879.

WALTON Stephen John

Director: July 2007-Aug 2007
Chief Executive:
July 2007-Aug 2007

b. Sunderland, 1954

For several years Steve Walton had been deeply involved in the finance and risk management of many top clubs as director of Barclays Bank, known as "Mr Football" in the banking world. Amongst his clients were

---

Liverpool, Everton, West Ham United, as well as Sunderland and Newcastle United. Following a career of over 30 years with the corporate arm of the top bank, Walton arrived as Chief Executive of Newcastle United, however the timing of his new role coincided with the shock sale of the club to Mike Ashley during the summer of 2007. As a result his time in the post was brief indeed, the new owner wanting his own men in place. Walton returned to Barclays, heading the organisations relationship with large commercial clients as Corporate Director, but he soon had another go at the sometimes fractious business of football when appointed to the Chief Executive post of his home-town club, Sunderland during the early weeks of 2009. Brought up in Seaburn and a supporter of the red-and-whites for over 40 years, Steve enjoyed over two years working with the Wearsiders but left the Stadium of Light in July 2011. He afterwards joined Sunderland travel firm Hays Travel as non-executive director until February 2014.

WATSON Thomas

Secretary: cs 1888-June 1889

b. Byker, Newcastle upon Tyne,
8 April 1859
d. Liverpool, 11 May 1915

While Tom Watson never kicked a ball in anger for United's pioneers, he gave the city's top clubs fine service as Secretary and in all but name, manager, before making a huge reputation for himself in charge of Sunderland and Liverpool. Born in Byker, he appeared as a footballer and as Secretary for Rosehill alongside the Tyne, while he was also an enthusiastic cricketer for Rosehill Star CC. Tom joined Newcastle West End as Secretary during the summer of 1886, then after a period establishing the St James' Park club, Tom moved across the city during 1888 to team up with Newcastle East End at Chillingham Road. A cheery character with a Geordie twang, Watson was described as being silver-tongued and sported a large well-trimmed moustache in the fashion of the day. As a shrewd administrator, the Tynesider helped form the Northern League during 1889 which was a major catalyst in the development of soccer in the region. The Newcastle Daily Chronicle noted that he had "proved himself a true judge of style" and he did such a good job, turning a struggling East End club around, that Tom was lured to join Sunderland in the close-season of 1889 for what was described as a healthy salary of £150 per annum, at the time a club far more advanced than either East End or West End. He was a forward thinking individual and did much to build the celebrated "Team of all the Talents" on Wearside. Sunderland went onto lift the League Championship in 1892, 1893 and 1895, as well as being runner-up during 1894 under Watson's guidance, while he was also appointed to the League's influential Management Committee. Sunderland's John Grayston noted that he "could rule his team with kindness and firmness, and always made himself the chum of the rank and file". At one point in 1895, and before the appointment of Frank Watt, Watson applied for the vacant United Secretary's post, but lost out to the Scot. A year later, during July 1896 he moved to Liverpool for twice his salary and again weaved his magic, developing a fine set-up in a spell of 19 years with the Reds, the Anfield club winning title and FA Cup honours in 1901, 1906 and 1914, twice being league runners-up as well. It is recorded that he even encouraged players to drink beer and red wine as part of his master plan! At that time Athletic News noted Watson as a Secretary who had "few equals, and no superior". Also on the FA Council, Tom was an outstanding personality of the Edwardian game, being awarded the Football League's Long Service medal during 1910. He died on Merseyside in May 1915 and is buried at Anfield cemetery, a gravestone added by the family in 2014 noting the connection to East End. Watson married into the Oliver family of United directors.

Directors & Officials

WATT Francis (Frank) George (Snr)

Secretary:
Dec 1895-Feb 1932

b. Edinburgh, 1854
d. Newcastle upon Tyne,
26 February 1932

One of the trail-blazers of the game in Scotland, Frank Watt was a player with pioneer clubs Third Edinburgh Rifle Volunteers, the early St Bernard's club, and Edinburgh Swifts as well as Hearts occasionally, all during the 1870s. He then became the first Secretary of the Edinburgh FA in 1876 where he was an influential factor during football's rise in the East of Scotland over the next decade and more. Often a referee, Frank was the official in charge for what was termed the Championship of the World contest in 1883 between West Bromwich Albion and Renton at Hampden Park, while he also refereed the Hearts versus Hibernian derby. Also noted as Grange Cricket Club's scorer in the capital for a period, Frank was highly respected north of the border. He landed the post of Dundee Secretary during November 1895 before being waylaid and redirected to Tyneside by Newcastle directors Bell and Telford. He was appointed United's Secretary a month later at the end of December 1895 on a salary of £140 per year, described as he arrived to take up his post on 1st January as, "ripened in experience as a legislator, referee and team builder". That was a milestone date in the club's history. Watt was a first-class administrator and did much to create Newcastle's standing as one of the finest and most well-regarded clubs in the country. The Scot went onto serve Newcastle for the next 37 seasons, the longest period by any club Secretary. In Hereward's History of the club (the first lengthy account published in 1932-33), Frank was narrated as having "materially helped to build up one of the greatest football combinations the game has ever known", while journalist Tom Hall's version 16 years later noted that he was "the man who planned a new Newcastle United, a style that was copied far and wide". Although he shunned publicity and the limelight, Watt became the driver behind the scenes and within a decade the Magpies had narrowly missed securing the double and by the time he died when still in post, the club had lifted four Championship titles and reached six FA Cup finals. Known as 'The Guv'nor', Frank lived close to the club's headquarters in St James Street then at St Thomas' nearby; he possessed a magnificent moustache throughout his time in office at Barrack Road and was famous for his cigar and a cloud of smoke which followed him around. Watt became admired throughout football, Colin Veitch recording that he was "always approachable and ever willing to render good advice". He was acquainted with everyone worth knowing in the game north and south of the border and his portly, well-dressed frame became one of football's senior figures, a genial character who was held in great esteem. Awarded the Football League's Long Service medal during July 1918, one obituary described Watt as possessing "great tact, shrewdness, a cool-head and firmness at the right time and place". His son, Frank Watt (junior) took over the Secretary role at Gallowgate on his death in 1932, and remained with the club until 1950; nearly 55 years unbroken family service in the top administrative post with the club.

(Note: In many sources of official information FG Watt senior and junior are referred to as both Frank and Francis, both signing their name as 'Frank')

WATT Francis (Frank) George (Jnr)

Secretary: Feb 1932-Oct 1950

b. Edinburgh, 1886
d. Newcastle upon Tyne, 6 October 1950

Commonly referred to as 'Fritz' perhaps to distinguish him from his esteemed father, Frank Watt (junior) joined United's office staff as a teenage office-boy and became his father's assistant-secretary during 1904. In the backrooms during all of United's success in pre-war years, Watt became almost as popular as his father at St James' Park and in the wider football community. It is recorded he possessed a rare sense of humour, although the warm and sociable Scot did not have the striking personality of his senior, being an unassuming character. Given also the nickname of 'Honest Frank', he served in France as a gunner with the Royal Garrison Artillery during the Great War and later resided in Gosforth. On his father's death in February 1932, Fritz was elevated to Secretary and he continued in the family tradition looking after United's affairs until his own demise during October 1950. He was given the Football League's Long Service award in June 1939, an honour his father had also achieved before him.

WESTWOOD William; Baron, Lord OBE (Snr)

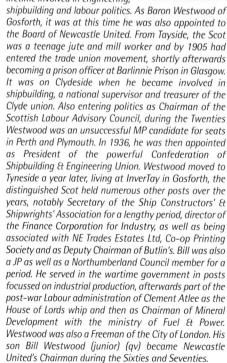

Director: May 1944-Sept 1953

b. Broughty Ferry, near Dundee, 28 August 1880
d. Newcastle upon Tyne, 13 September 1953

A prominent trade unionist between the two world wars, Bill Westwood earned firstly an OBE (in 1920) then a knighthood during January 1944 after a lifetime involved in engineering, shipbuilding and labour politics. As Baron Westwood of Gosforth, it was at this time he was also appointed to the Board of Newcastle United. From Tayside, the Scot was a teenage jute and mill worker and by 1905 had entered the trade union movement, shortly afterwards becoming a prison officer at Barlinnie Prison in Glasgow. It was on Clydeside when he became involved in shipbuilding, a national supervisor and treasurer of the Clyde union. Also entering politics as Chairman of the Scottish Labour Advisory Council, during the Twenties Westwood was an unsuccessful MP candidate for seats in Perth and Plymouth. In 1936, he was then appointed as President of the powerful Confederation of Shipbuilding & Engineering Union. Westwood moved to Tyneside a year later, living at InverTay in Gosforth, the distinguished Scot held numerous other posts over the years, notably Secretary of the Ship Constructors' & Shipwrights' Association for a lengthy period, director of the Finance Corporation for Industry, as well as being associated with NE Trades Estates Ltd, Co-op Printing Society and as Deputy Chairman of Butlin's. Bill was also a JP as well as a Northumberland Council member for a period. He served in the wartime government in posts focussed on industrial production, afterwards part of the post-war Labour administration of Clement Atlee as the House of Lords whip and then as Chairman of Mineral Development with the ministry of Fuel & Power. Westwood was also a Freeman of the City of London. His son Bill Westwood (junior) (qv) became Newcastle United's Chairman during the Sixties and Seventies.

WESTWOOD William; Baron, Lord (Jnr)

Chairman: Oct 1964-Jan 1978
Director: Aug 1960-March 1981
President: Jan 1978-1983

b. Dundee, 25 December 1907
d. Gosforth, Newcastle upon Tyne, 8 November 1991

Apart from Sir John Hall, the Second Baron Westwood is Newcastle United's most celebrated figure to have taken control of the Black'n'Whites boardroom. Son of a past director who was knighted after rising to fame as a union leader in the shipyards, Lord Westwood was a true gent, noted as being firm, but fair in his attitude to life, business and to football. Although Bill Westwood inherited his father's estate during 1953, he made his own way, very much like Sir John Hall. He started as a railway clerk at the LMSR office in Glasgow, became company secretary to a cinema group, then by the time he was appointed to the Magpie boardroom in August 1960 was a director of a host of companies, including toy manufacturing giant Dundee-Combex-Marx which included brands such as Hornby Railways. Part of Newcastle society, he possessed traditional values and was a Fellow of the Royal Society of Arts and a colourful after-dinner speaker having razor sharp humour. From Tayside originally, Westwood was both distinguished and distinctive with silvery wavy-hair and a famous black patch over one eye, the legacy of a car accident in 1956. Taking the Chair at Gallowgate on the illness of Wally Hurford during 1964, Westwood became a high-profile leader and controlled the club at a time of fluctuating fortunes; promotion, a European victory, Wembley appearances, but then slump and financial collapse. By the time of his resignation as Chairman in January 1978, his reign had turned sour and he received much criticism from disillusioned supporters. When asked to help fund mounting debts during March 1981, Westwood resigned completely from club activities. A magistrate, Lord Westwood was also a servant of the Football League, on the Management Committee from 1970, becoming President in 1974 to his departure from United's top-table. Bill Westwood died in Gosforth late in 1991, future United Chairman Gordon McKeag said on his death that he was, "a man of wit, dignity and charm". He was a director for 21 seasons, and along with James Lunn, served the longest period as Chairman, for 14 seasons. His cousin, Hal Stewart, ran Morton FC during the Sixties and Seventies.

WHEATLEY Leslie Alan

Director: May 1998-April 2000
Chief Operating Officer: July 1999-April 2000
PLC Director: May 1998-April 2000
PLC Secretary: May 1998-July 1999

b. Birkenhead, 1952 (Q3)

Raised on Merseyside and educated at Durham University, Les Wheatley like many of United's modern breed of directors possessed a finance background. He developed a career with accountant giants Arthur Young, had a period with Westland Helicopters before moving to Ernst Young. Les spent seven years with Greater Manchester Buses and led a successful employee buy-out, then became Managing Director. Appointed as the Magpies' Finance Director during the spring of 1998, when Les joined United he was described in the business press as a "people-person". As a result of a club re-shuffle during July 1999, Wheatley was elevated to the post of Chief Operating Officer. During his time at Gallowgate the Merseysider was prominent in raising finance to enlarge St James' Park to its present capacity of over 52,000. Wheatley though headed back to his native Liverpool to join the Anfield club during 2000 and enjoyed success with the Reds, witnessing the Champions League trophy end up in the boardroom. He departed in January 2009 when new owners took control and then spent time back in the North East, spearheading an expansion of security company The Protector Group. Other posts held included being Non-Executive director and Chairman of the audit committee of Printing.com. A keen rugby enthusiast too, Wheatley played the sport in his younger years.

WILLIAMSON David Craig

Director: June 2008-Dec 2008

b. Edinburgh, 1959

One of several businessmen to be only briefly in post at St James' Park during the modern era, David Williamson was appointed as the club's Operations executive during February 2008 then a director soon after following a successful period in charge of Newcastle Racecourse. Brought up in Scotland's capital, David was employed with Thistle Hotels then David Lloyd Leisure covering the North East and Scotland. He took root on Tyneside during 2002 when he began to transform what was then an ailing organisation at Gosforth Park. Brought into the club boardroom during the early months of Mike Ashley's regime, Williamson was axed as part of a swift cost-cutting measure with the Magpies facing relegation from the Premier League in 2008-09. After his time in football, the Scot was a director with Danieli Holdings which included Gosforth based Phoenix Security. He also founded Tyneside company LeisureTime operating pubs, travel and leisure activities. During 2012 Williamson returned to Newcastle Racecourse to take charge as Executive Director.

WILSON Alastair McKinnon OBE

Director: April 1998-Dec 1998

b. Stirling, 1941
d. Muckhart, Clackmannanshire, 5 January 2006

A genial Scot, Alastair Wilson was, like David Stephenson, a long-time executive of Scottish & Newcastle Breweries and had a passion for sport. For over 25 years the neighbours across Barrack Road forged a close and productive relationship, the Magpies soon adorning the famous Newcastle Blue Star on their shirt and Wilson was at the heart of that bond of mutual benefit. Joining the brewers in 1967 he worked his way up to become Managing Director of Newcastle Breweries during 1985, along the way making sure his company became United's first sponsor. Equally comfortable in the boardroom as with the public at large, he was significantly involved in bringing Kevin Keegan to Tyneside for the first time in 1982, devising an inventive deal with Stan Seymour (junior). Alastair was influential as well when Keegan returned as boss a decade later. Wilson was also the driving force as a sponsor of Durham County CC as they developed at first-class level, the likable Scot was linked to Middlesbrough too, while before that, when based in north of the border, saw his Scottish & Newcastle firm also associated strongly with Rangers. Over the Scots long period on Tyneside, Wilson did much for local causes such as the Children's Foundation while he was also a member of the Newcastle Initiative which was a catalyst for urban regeneration during the 1990s. Honoured with the OBE in June 1998, he retired from the brewery at the start of that year and took up an appointment as a

United director during April with responsibility for "communications and public affairs", this after a series of PR disasters at St James' Park. It appeared Alastair was perfectly suited to the role with his warm Caledonian personality. Wilson though, left within a year, the role at the heart of Newcastle United proving frustrating. Alastair afterwards was a director with Premium Bars & Restaurants PLC, returning to his native Scotland, residing near Gleneagles on the edge of the Highlands.

WINSKELL Ian Michael

PLC Director:
July 1999-July 2000
PLC Secretary:
July 1999-July 2000

b. Sunderland, 1957 (Q4)

Michael Winskell hailed from a family of lawyers, his grandfather founding the Tyneside company of Winskell & Winskell. Appointed a PLC director of Newcastle United during 1999, he had the responsibility to deal with the corporate and strategic planning of the Group as a whole, as well as acting as Company Secretary. In his forties, Michael took a part-time role with the Magpies, maintaining directorships with other companies including leisure operator Champneys, as well as his own family law practice which eventually merged with Blackett, Hart & Pratt. Winskell left St James' Park following a year on the PLC Board.

WOODMAN William

Director: Feb 1890-1891

b. Newcastle upon Tyne, c1860
d. Margate, 12 September 1910

Probably on Newcastle East End's early Committee, William Woodman was one of the men invited to form the club's first Board of Directors in February 1890. Purchasing shares when the club became a limited company, he is recorded in the Victorian Share Ledger as a "solicitor's clerk". Woodman lived at Cardigan Terrace in Heaton where fellow East End supporters James Peel and David MacPherson resided. By the time of the 1901 census, Woodman had become a Managing Clerk for a solicitor's practice in the city. Moving to Belle Grove Terrace in Spital Tongues, he died on the south coast when travelling on business or vacation.

YOUNG Robert

Director: May 1989-July 1992
Honorary President:
Aug 1993-date

b. Dipton, Co Durham, May 1946

Raised in the Usher Moor area of County Durham, Bob Young was a keen supporter and executive-box holder of the Magpies when he was invited to join the directorate during May 1989. A long-serving local councillor and straight-talking businessman, he arrived at the start of a headlining battle for control of the club and Young became an influential figure, helping negotiate a truce between the two controlling factions which were splitting the club apart. Young also supported the Black'n'Whites financially at a difficult period. He was something of a tough character who stood little nonsense. As Managing Director of one of the country's largest independent mining and haulage operations, Young Group PLC, Bob was a self-made man,

having started his empire as an apprentice in a civil engineering company in London before starting his own haulage and plant company back in the North East. Once described as a "wily character", Young eventually sold his 10% stake in Newcastle United to Sir John Hall and left the Board soon afterwards, but remaining as Honorary President. He also traded his share-holding in the Young Group, afterwards setting up a stud-farm and hotel enterprise in Ebchester. Always a supporter of his local community around Consett, he set up the Robert Young Scholarship Fund at Durham University, as well as the Robert Young Charitable Trust and Bob Young Grassroots Endowment Fund. As a teenager Bob began his working life at Bearpark Colliery, while his father was also an avid United fan. Young resides at Iveston near Consett.

ZOLLNER Lauritz Ludvig (Louis)

Director: cs 1899-July 1904

b. Copenhagen (Denmark), 18 April 1854
d. Whitley Bay, 20 January 1945

As a teenager Louis Zollner began working in shipping at Elsingor before moving from his home in Copenhagen to make a life for himself in England, initially in Manchester then for 50 years in Newcastle. The Dane settled on Tyneside and became a prominent member of the business community, one of the city's most respected citizens. Originally an importer of cattle and sheep from Scandinavia to England, Zollner was a keen sportsman during his younger days being a proficient athlete, rower and cyclist, once winning a novel race against a yacht from Portsmouth to Newcastle! Invited to join United's boardroom just before the turn of the century, he purchased a shareholding during 1898 and remained a member for five years. Becoming a very active merchant across the North Sea, he was appointed Danish Consul for the region for 29 years and was a Grand Knight of the Iceland Falcon as well as a Knight of the Norwegian Order of St Olaf and Commander of the Dannebrog. Louis had many hobbies, apart from supporting local sport and Newcastle United in particular, he was also a leading chess player being President of the local association. Residing in Jesmond, then at Whitley Bay, on his 80th birthday a lavish gathering was held at Newcastle's Grand Assembly Rooms with over 300 guests in attendance.

PRESENTATION COPIES

1 Newcastle United Football Club
2 The City of Newcastle upon Tyne
3 Paul Joannou
4 Alan Candlish
5 Bill Swann

6 Bob Moncur
7 Newcastle upon Tyne Central Library
8 Peter Beardsley MBE
9 Alan Shearer OBE
10 Newcastle Chronicle & Journal
11 National Football Museum

The following United enthusiasts have subscribed for the Ultimate Series; Newcastle United: The Ultimate Record and/or Newcastle United: The Ultimate Who's Who

12	Kevin Steptoe	91	Robert Rutherford	170	Kirk Leech	248	Bryan Milne
13	Frank Moyle	92	Dave, Yuko & Ko Woodrow	171	Lavender Lee-Flynn	249	Chris Urwin
14	Tom, William & James Howes	93	Jonathan Thompson	172	Leazes Jack	250	David & Jack Frame
15	Johnny Bewick	94	Julie Stanford	173	John Richards	251	David Armstrong
16	Steven O'Mara	95	Jerome Borkwood	174	Sam Brent	252	Michael Armstrong
17	James Savage	96	Adrian Borkwood	175	Peter Nelson	253	Bill Stephenson
18	Aaron Hughes	97	John Bradley	176	Stephen Hunter	254	Graeme N Gilhespy
19	Dean Paul Richardson	98	Craig Nicholson	177	Paul Ross	255	John Anderson
20	Kevin Richardson	99	David G	178	Bill Turnbull	256	Lee Cowan
21	David Haley and Sons	100	Roy Miller	179	Gary Hughes	257	One Posh Mag
22	Anthony Britton	101	Geoff Smithson	180	Gregory James Hollin	258	Louis Azzopardi
23	Gavin Duncan	102	Thomas Gordon	181	Ian Gowens	259	Michael Vinton
24	Ryan Brown	103	Robert Gordon	182	Kevin Miles	260	David Thompson
25	Keith McLellan	104	Colin McClenaghan	183	Sam Maill	261	Michael P Durham
26	Dr Nabeel Alsindi	105	Phil Mudie	184	Jamie Maill	262	Mick Whitfield
27	Andrew Morris	106	Michael Mudie	185	Dave & Jacqui Candlish	263	Peter Gibson
28	Mark Pearce	107	Jonathan Pickett	186	Karen Candlish & John Price	264	Samuel Villius
29	Barry Moyle	108	Malcolm Scott	187	Ron Wilson	265	Simon Youngson
30	Michael Hedley	109	Eamonn Byrd	188	Madeline and Edward Galvin	266	Steve Sowden
31	Oli Mussett	110	Dan & Tara Devlin	189	Charles Frederick Vickers	267	Terje Kvicksson
32	Stewart Pearson	111	Philip Dobbs	190	John Alder RIP	268	Tony Conaboy
33	Jim and Joy Farms	112	Christopher Brown	191	Bill Bruce	269	Ian Edgar
34	Stephen Faulkner	113	Jarrod Bailey	192	Anthony Hutchinson	270	David, Peter & Joseph Leech
35	John Bolam	114	Nat Mankelow	193	Craig Chalmers	271	David Low
36	David Bolam	115	Matt Mankelow RIP	194	Scott Lohnes	272	Brian White
37	Michael Bolam	116	Graeme Parkin	195	Anthony Taylor	273	Andy Gilbert
38	Terence Ross	117	John Jobling	196	Dr Keith Beveridge	274	Colin Varty
39	Gary Langley	118	Warrant Officer Frizzell	197	Keith Mason	275	David Claydon
40	Duncan Walker	119	Daniel George Frizzell	198	Kev Lambert	276	Kirsten Marsh
41	Anthony Garforth Ryle	120	Les Hancock	199	Richard Lynch	277	Nick Pearson
42	Tommy Hall RIP	121	Martin Black	200	Tom W Wales	278	Ged Clarke
43	Ross Alexander Bowman	122	Martin Roberts	201	Anthony John Nicholson	279	Christo Patsan
44	Gordon Barr	123	John W Bradley	202	Jim Jobson	280	Ian Jobson
45	Ken Pullar	124	Melvyn Hughes	203	Colin Wafer	281	Jordon Tinniswood
46	Les Wheatley	125	David Hughes	204	Eric Hogg	282	Luke Barrett
47	Christopher Langshaw	126	Richard Hughes	205	John Gordon	283	Peter Wilkinson
48	Jonathan Waller	127	Nigel Maddison	206	Dale Lang	284	Stephen Kettle
49	Jim Walker	128	Adam Lomax	207	Darren Barnes	285	Nicholas Johnson
50	Bill Burnett	129	Rob Millican	208	Gary Dodd	286	Alan Shell
51	Paul Tully	130	Trevor & Dawn Smith	209	Michael Wannop	287	Lasse Leipola
52	Gerald M Graham	131	Andrew Veitch	210	James Addison	288	Roland Archibold
53	David Taylor	132	D G Brownlow	211	Jon Steven White	289	Michael Le Hanie
54	Richard McGrill	133	Dave Greaves	212	John Paul Hardy	290	Mark Spud Smith
55	Richard Barron	134	NUFC Midland Supporters Club	213	Martin Waggott	291	Cameron Shiels
56	Peter Shiel	135	David Emmerson	214	Michael Hicks	292	Derek Nesbitt
57	Hugh Collingwood	136	David Pallister	215	Paul Rowe	293	Malcolm Jackson
58	John Edward Fitz-Gerald	137	Keith Gunning	216	Tim Bell	294	Peter Dunleavy
59	Harry Peasland	138	Lovaine & Angela Donaldson	217	Ian Harrison	295	Stephen Hurst
60	Shaun Robson	139	Rob Wallace	218	John F Yates	296	Dr Anton Lang
61	John M Hall	140	Shaun Carroll	219	William A Powell	297	Jared Robinson
62	Mick Tait	141	Tyronne Browne	220	David Garforth Ryle	298	Bill Marsh
63	Graeme Thompson	142	Adrian & Melanie Freemantle	221	Albert Robson	299	Ian Lewis
64	Matt Watson–Broughton	143	Ethan Wiley	222	Alan Price	300	David Stonebanks
65	Steve Field	144	Nicola Atkinson	223	Clive Swinsco	301	Tony Noble
66	Peter Stephenson	145	Mark Sneddon	224	Si Martin	302	John Kelters
67	Alex Wolens	146	Warren Young	225	Paul Gordon	303	Harvey Lavelle
68	Philip Hughes	147	Andrew Kirkham	226	Pete Atkinson	304	Ian Ferguson
69	Glenn Robison	148	Andy Robson	227	Simon B Pearce	305	Kev Hill
70	Tony Lister	149	Tony Talbott	228	Tony Ampleford	306	Colin Powell
71	Mattias Cal Karlsson	150	James Antonio Turner	229	Sushane Nair	307	James Dawson
72	Paul Laverick	151	Maurice Lockey	230	George Weatherstone	308	Tommy Thompson
73	Alan Alsop	152	Christopher Coulthard	231	Michael Harris	309	Selby Toon Army
74	Stephen Brennan	153	David MacLaren	232	John Howey	310	Paul Durham
75	Jake Coulson	154	Barry Barkes	233	Elwyn Jones	311	Will Potts
76	Charlie Parwani	155	Graham Armstrong	234	Jeff Wilson	312	Keith Arthur
77	Paul White	156	Ian Shanks	235	Andrew Nugent	313	Keith Bartley
78	Andy Anderson	157	Stephen & Michael Minto	236	David Dent	314	Trevor Clifford Bartley
79	Darren Reeve	158	Mark Henzell Adamson	237	Steven Cavagan	315	Roger Talbot
80	Jim Mitchell	159	Bruce Renwick	238	David Webster	316	Fen
81	Simon Harwood	160	Geoff & Michael Davidson	239	Fraser Browne	317	Fink The Fan
82	Stephen Rowan	161	James Edes	240	Krzysztof Mrózek	318	Fred Howitt
83	Liam Murphy	162	Larry Lim Gim Lee	241	Eddie Kinney	319	Brad McLeod
84	Tony Fiddes	163	Mark Oselton	242	Kevin Silver	320	Philip Haggan
85	Joe Fiddes	164	Peter Whitney	243	Gary Dodd	321	Gavin Brown
86	Anna Fiddes	165	Jake Davey	244	Ian Gregg	322	Stephen Tonge
87	Dave Hill & Alastair Hill	166	Trevor Stephenson	245	Christopher, Victoria & Rachel Jensen	323	Keith Woollard
88	Steve Dale	167	Rob Mason	246	Abhisit Vejjajiva	324	The Fegans
89	Glenn Hall	168	Whitley Bay Scorer	247	Graeme Milne	325	Glenn Carver
90	Neil Rutherford	169	Stephen King			326	Frank Carver

327	Alfonso Carver	419	Daniel Campbell	509	Nicholas Howorth	602	Michael John Little
328	Daniel Grayson	420	David Campbell	510	Callum Wilkie	603	Ian Francis Jack
329	John P Aliamus	421	David Atkinson	511	Chris Scott	604	Matthew Maxwell
330	Harry Sanderson	422	George Graham	512	Anke Chapman	605	Pat & Davie Kelly RIP,
331	Alastair FM Lambie	423	John Morrow	513	Ray Mossom		Lee Yellop RIP,
332	Simon Hill	424	Joseph Gaul	514	Phill Rochead		Terry McGlade RIP
333	Scott McBarron	425	Mark Bridgett	515	Michael Walker	606	David Edward Kelly
334	Kurt Taylor	426	Paul, Cheryl,	516	Simon Malia	607	Steven White
335	Duncan Mackay		Stacey & Samantha Bell	517	Steve Pharoah	608	Tom Mitchell
336	Peter R Foster	427	Peter Moyle	518	Stuart Hutton	609	John Anderson
337	Talal Altuwaijri	428	Edward McKenzie	519	Ed Young	610	Robin Blagburn
338	Luke Henry	429	Jeff Harper	520	James Brown	611	Colin Lisle
339	Leonie Underdown	430	Richard K Johnston	521	Eddie McCoy	612	Eddie & Kieran Richardson
340	Stephen Baird	431	Scott	522	Joe Davey	613	Geoff Green
341	alalbenandcal	432	William Gouldburn	523	Andrew Conway	614	George Mitchell
342	Michael Purdy	433	John, Laura & John	524	Andrew Hayes	615	Grainger Fenton
343	James Purdy	434	Kenneth Elliott	525	Andrew Hedges	616	Jack Ord
344	Aidan Robertson	435	Chris Kelly	526	Bob Cook	617	Keith Topping
345	Bob Carson	436	John Annett RIP	527	Colin Shield	618	Philip Brown
346	Daniel J Marshall	437	John William Wallace	528	George Shield	619	Steve Corrigan
347	David Lough	438	David Jakeman	529	David Skipsey RIP	620	Bernie Lamb
348	James Barrie Gadsden	439	Alan McNeil	530	Gareth Furlong	621	Bill Corcoran
349	Jonathan Hope	440	Chris Dixon	531	Gary Bellerby	622	Josh Guy
350	Mark Field	441	Stephen Dixon	532	Ian Weller	623	Redcar Toontone
351	Martin Wardhaugh	442	Daniel Cook	533	Paul & Helen Tilley	624	Tony Hill
352	Michael Maloney	443	Derek Younger	534	Peter Bennett	625	David White
353	Neil & Jake Robinson	444	Simon McGeary	535	Vaughann Turnbull	626	Robert Williams
354	Pat Martin	445	Kevin Burn	536	Arthur Farey	627	Stuart Wigg
355	Paul Simpson	446	William O'Driscoll	537	Barry Foster	628	Paul Rudd
356	Richard Rafeek	447	William McCartney	538	Brian James Hands	629	Oliver Smithson
357	Owen S Quigley	448	Rod Stockley	539	Dennis Flynn	630	Dennis Bryden
358	Roger M Douglass	449	David McCormack	540	Jean Barber	631	Gordon Smith
359	Stephen Glynn	450	Thomas Bell	541	Keith Mason	632	Philip Wright
360	Stephen Glynn	451	J.Q.McPherson Snr &	542	Norman Dawe	633	Nicholas Andrew Hood
361	Stephen Parkin		J.Q.McPherson Jnr RIP	543	Paul Reed	634	David Malone
362	Will Burns	452	Geoff Dixon	544	Arron Phillips	635	Michael Malone
363	Benjamin Allen	453	James Austin	545	Michael Jones	636	Kevin Nixon
364	Chris Sheridan	454	Dave, Clare, Lydia	546	Rob Norton	637	Peter Calleeuw
365	Arthur Preston		and Georgia Crawford	547	Tom Cadwallender	638	Roger Burton
366	Thomas Rodger RIP	455	Michael John Murray	548	Dave & David John Rowe	639	Simon Gardner
367	Jamie Stevenson	456	Gavin Haigh	549	David Robertson	640	Dylan Hughes
368	John Edminson	457	Joyce McKenzie	550	Joel Blakey	641	Tony Hogg
369	Gordon Mitchell	458	Tox te Boekhorst	551	Ron Renton RIP	642	Trevor Corbitt
370	James Edward Maughan	459	Simon Cruickshank	552	John Clouston	643	David Watson
371	Len & Ian Brooks	460	Alfie McKie	553	Steve & George Curry	644	Paul Wright
372	Michael Murray	461	Harry Oswell	554	Ken Stark	645	Sam James Nesbitt
373	Alan Cochrane	462	Josh Witherow	555	Duffy	646	Brian Longworth
374	David Potter	463	Mark Jensen	556	Mick & Shirley	647	Tony Farrar
375	Iain Stewart	464	Nick Embiricos	557	Ron Rickeard	648	James Odemuyiwa
376	Paul, Lesley & Lauren Gowans	465	David Dickie	558	Alistair Brett	649	John Clark
377	Bob Borthwick	466	Cliffy Ahmed	559	Jack Brett	650	Ann Mac
378	David Bowman	467	Zen Li	560	Lol Kindley	651	Jimmy Beresford
379	John Fergusson	468	Alana Miller	561	Robert Woods	652	The Brown & O'Keefe families
380	Vince Edes	469	Lawrence Cook	562	Johnny Bruce	653	Tom Lynch
381	Jonathan Edes	470	Peter Corrigan	563	Richard Howarth	654	Vincent & Lena McCormack
382	Nathan Castle	471	Sneck	564	Robin Taylor-Wilson	655	Ray Smith
383	Gary McIver	472	George & Ann Stokes	565	Bill Veitch	656	Robert F Roddham
384	Wayne Ruddy	473	Ian & Aaron Smith	566	Kevin Skinner	657	Dave Taylor
385	Malcolm Dix	474	John Campion	567	Shae Conway	658	Paul Elsender
386	Stephen Nichols	475	Paul Darling	568	The Brennans, Washington	659	Scott Jon Stewart
387	Danny Baines	476	Richard Potrzeba	569	Lawrence Brennan	660	Andrew & Julie Huddart
388	Laura Pringle	477	The Carney Family	570	Neil James Cockburn	661	Graham Gaffney
389	Martin Giles	478	William Joseph Marlon McReavy	571	John D Moore	662	Steve Wraith
390	Horold Hodgson	479	Gavin Quinlan	572	Marc Duffy	663	John Wraith
391	Pam Colyer	480	Paul Wardle	573	Christopher Hurst	664	Rob Wraith
392	Paul Winship	481	Raymond Walton	574	Bethany Alice Moreland	665	Stephen McMullen
393	John Brian Morrow	482	Paul Gluza	575	Nick Duckworth	666	John Guy
394	Leon Milner	483	Bill Stainton	576	Peter Page	667	Gurdip Singh Kambo
395	David Jones	484	Dave Maughan	577	Ben Lowans	668	George Green
396	Mr S Stapleton	485	Euan McFarlane	578	David Gunn	669	Allan, David & James
397	Frank Gilmour	486	Jason Jones	579	Robin Golding	670	Anne, Susan & Jack
398	Paul John Carlton	487	Ben Chapman	580	Colin McAllister	671	Loudfoot, Ian & Jack Ross
399	Rob Storey	488	Ian Glen	581	M Henderson	672	Nicky Jones
400	Shaune Pearson	489	Steve Tansey	582	Chris Foster	673	Anthony Stobart
401	Ross Muers	490	Malcolm Gibson	583	Peter Rae	674	Scott Muncaster
402	Brian Flinn	491	Tom Gibson	584	Les Rae	675	Ian Scott
403	Magnolia Lee-Flynn	492	Bob Hogg	585	Frank Cassidy	676	David Littlewood
404	Jules Lee	493	Steve Clark	586	Terry Cassidy	677	Iain Hindhaugh
405	Arnold Langwell	494	Eric Wilson	587	Seamus Michael Cassidy	678	Ian Gibson
406	Edward John Hogan	495	Adrian Clark	588	Steven R Milne	679	Anthony Simm
407	Barrie Wilson	496	David Dando	589	Robert W Milne	680	John Herbert
408	David Briggs	497	Iain Colquhoun	590	Les Pearson	681	Chris Shilton
409	Kevin, Brendon,	498	Kenneth Martin	591	Wayne Allen	682	Wilfred Martin Renton
	Mark & Rhiannon Stubbs	499	Phyllis Martin	592	Mark Batey	683	David Ian Renton
410	Roy Mitford	500	Greg Billington	593	Peter Glass	684	John Joseph Hackett
411	John Headley	501	Thomas Wilkinson	594	Alan Turner	685	Les Slater RIP
412	Oskar Parish	502	Bill & Norman Walker	595	The Glennie Family	686	Peter Child
413	Kevin Spence Morris	503	Councillor Michael Hood	596	Geoff, Gemma & Stuart Dick	687	Jack Mackenzie
414	Paul Hicks	504	Anthony Ainsley	597	John Wood	688	Duncan MacKenzie
415	Rachel Quinn	505	James Ainsley	598	Stewart Kirkpatrick	689	Iain MacKenzie
416	Barry	506	Morgan David Cook	599	Bryan Williams RIP	690	Niall MacKenzie
417	Alan Small	507	The Park Family	600	Matthew Valentine	691	Joseph & Daniel Moran
418	Christopher Campbell	508	Jon Leon White	601	John AJ Hurst	692	David Clarke

693 Frank Hamill	784 Joyce & Les Roadley	876 Brian Blenkinsop	969 Mark Turnbull @BFGeordie
694 Les Storey	785 Gordon Young	877 Robert Towers	970 Malc Hetherington
695 Mark Cripps	786 Stew Waters RIP	878 Barry Speker OBE DL	971 Mark Bowie
696 David Andrew Robinson	787 Paddy Fagan	879 Chris Horrocks	972 Paul Bowie
697 Gerry Allan	788 Steve Melia	880 Alexander Jackson	973 Mark Shaw
698 Trevor Hails	789 Phil Bradbury	881 Rob Sampson	974 Kay Langford
699 Aidan James Bell	790 Paul Mac	882 Sean Douglass	975 Mick Percival
700 Chris Biskupek	791 Raymond Nicholson	883 Simon Moran	976 Mick Rennison
701 Daniel Bloyce	792 Richard Gibbo Gibson	884 Mick Thomson	977 John Brent
702 Dominic Moore	793 Rob Armstrong	885 George Rowan	978 Mike Rennie
703 Paul Walker	794 Roger Jennings	886 Ian Firth	979 Chris Smith
704 Kenny Owens	795 Steve Kirby	887 Alastair Thomson	980 Harry Galsworthy
705 Paul Mooney	796 Sean Stewart	888 Steve & Simon Hilditch	981 Jeff Tate
706 Peter Collyns	797 David Waggott	889 Steve Reynolds	982 Paul Moulding
707 Stuart B McLeod	798 Philip Johnson	890 David Irving	983 Eddie Howe
708 Ian Scott	799 Steve Wilkinson	891 Lee Irving	984 Peter Sylvestersson
709 Paul Marshall Scott	800 Laurence Thompson	892 Stuart Mather	985 Steve Pringle
710 Martin Shillito	801 Sam Hall	893 Richie Gray	986 Bill Pringle
711 Ken Bell	802 Steve Evans	894 Colin Taylor	987 Paul Hundrup
712 Tommy Mackinnon	803 Ernie Wilson	895 Oscar James Aram	988 Duncan James
713 Marcus, Tony & Sean Martin	804 Graeme Robson	896 Terry Warr	989 Paul Emmerson
714 Piotr & Jakub Jozefowicz	805 Thomas McCruden	897 Thomas Joyce	990 Keith Faulkner
715 John Thomas, John William, Anthony John, Arnutchai John, Michael Nopadol Miller	806 Andrew Bush	898 Stephen Brown	991 John Faulkner
	807 Tony James	899 Mal Broon	992 Jimmy & James Burns
716 Graham Fryer	808 Trevor Lee	900 Magnus Grinde	993 Jimmy, James & Joseph Burns
717 Meg Hobson	809 Will Gibson	901 Stephen Bambrough	994 R Fletcher
718 Alski Broon	810 Alan Birbeck	902 Andrew Sproat	995 Rich Meehan
719 William Kenneth Swaddle	811 Alan Bye	903 Andrew Smith	996 Richard Greenwood
720 Michael Stephenson	812 Andrew McTernan	904 Nikita & Monty Johnson	997 Anthony Joyce
721 Jeremy Nicoll	813 The Nicholsons	905 David Kennedy	998 John Taskas
722 Stephen Wood Hutchinson	814 Brent McIver	906 Brian Robinson	999 Joseph & Samuel Buck
723 John Johnson	815 Dean McIver	907 Brian Hobson	1000 Linda Nelson
724 Ethan Gallagher	816 Mark Slater	908 Bill Reay	1001 Dave Green
725 Shaun Turner	817 Keith Hudson	909 Garry Cosgrove	1002 Lee, Matthew & Danielle Scott
726 David Dobson	818 Kenny JJ Dartnall	910 Kevin Taylor	1003 Kevin Mason
727 Alan Dormer	819 John Charles Shutt	911 Billy Taylor	1004 Andrew McQueen
728 Kevin Brown	820 James Chestney	912 John Preston (Garage)	1005 Eddie McQueen
729 Graeme Brown	821 South Shields Mags	913 Paul, Sean & Mark Donnelly	1006 David Smith
730 Gary Patterson	822 Dr Christopher Pentland	914 Paul, Mark & Sean Donnelly	1007 Peter McCartney
731 Scott Healey	823 Craig Hayton	915 Allen Convery	1008 Vince Doran
732 Thomas Logan	824 Jill Morris	916 Chris Octon	1009 Andrew Waddington
733 Jamie Lye	825 Matthew Alexander	917 Carl Greener	1010 Steve Murphy
734 Jon Lienard	826 Ruth Irving	918 Bob Greener	1011 Jimmy Florance
735 Kevin Hinds	827 Dave Ridley	919 Gary Holmes	1012 Ian Nesbit
736 Matthew Slater	828 David Jackson	920 Trevor Holmes	1013 William Nesbit
737 Michael Hogan	829 Dennis Telford	921 Bob Rayner	1014 Richard Spowart
738 Micah	830 Derek Cooper	922 Brian Harrihill	1015 Andrew Spowart
739 Trev Parker	831 Jack Luke	923 Douglas Bairstow	1016 Malcolm Spowart
740 Ann Bell	832 Jimmy, Joe, Sally & David Morgan	924 Paul Maddison	1017 Billy (William) Wilson
741 Bearsden Mag		925 Philip McCahy	1018 Harry & Paul Hewetson
742 Elle Howe	833 Paul Robinson	926 Jim McCahy	1019 Aarron Kimber
743 The Hodgson Family	834 Adam Bates	927 David Dixon-Todd	1020 John Mayne
744 Andy Griffin	835 Michael Farrow	928 Joseph Close	1021 Gary Staward
745 Mike Evans	836 David Lee	929 Alex Chun	1022 Keith Brewis
746 Rafferty family	837 Gary Davis	930 Colin Hostler	1023 Michael Murphy
747 Mike & Jean Bell	838 David G Smith	931 Charles Robertson Taylor	1024 Craig Falcus
748 Bob Holcroft	839 Christopher M Smith	932 Dave Newby	1025 Mick Hutchfield
749 Callum Woodrow	840 Geoff Bell	933 Graeme E Cross	1026 Darren Miller
750 Lee Robertson	841 Glenn Wallace	934 Malcolm A Hull	1027 David Ware
751 Ian Robertson	842 Tom McCallum	935 Derek Meehan	1028 Graeme Harwood
752 John Clark	843 Ian Johnson	936 Trevor Dunn	1029 James Smith (senior)
753 Charly Curtis	844 David Jackson	937 The Drapes	1030 Calum Heslop
754 Brian Gowens	845 Cameron Howes	938 Aidan Gifford	1031 Stuart Seaborn
755 Brian Codling	846 Harry Kidd	939 Graham Crosby	1032 George Robert Coulson
756 Colin Dixon	847 Jim Thompson	940 Richard Laidlaw	1033 Stuart Black
757 Paul Robson	848 Jim Murray	941 Gordon Small	1034 John Beavis
758 Iain Tipping	849 Robert William Sample	942 Gregor Gregorc	1035 Trevor Ross
759 Algy Sidney	850 Geoff Buffey RIP	943 Peter Holgate	1036 Terry Turner
760 John Sinclair	851 Kev Taylor	944 Don Bankier	1037 Ken Slater
761 Brian Wilkin	852 Keith N Robson	945 Hugh Macdonald	1038 Newcastle John
762 Glynn McGee	853 Kenneth Weall	946 Jessica Summers	1039 Richard Swann
763 George Michael Scott	854 Lawrence Connelly	947 Ian Archbold	1040 Mark Swann
764 George Edward Bainbridge	855 Lee Jones	948 John Ryles	1041 Karen Swann
765 Ray Duffell	856 Lee Hodgkinson	949 Jim McBurnie	1042 Mark Hannen
766 John Aitman	857 Colin Liddle	950 Andrew Allister	1043 Dave Hewson
767 Brian Jackson	858 Malcolm Bell	951 Malcolm Webb	1044 Simon Arbon
768 Paul Crozier	859 Aaron James Henderson	952 James Brown	1045 Kath Cassidy
769 Jeff Todd	860 Martyn Gray	953 Walter Scott	1046 Steve Huddart
770 Jim Lamb	861 Matt Cook	954 Lewis Brown	1047 Dag Martin Hagen
771 Jimmy Jones	862 Diddler, Wrighta & Buster	955 Jason John Facer	1048 Philip Hagen
772 Anthony Reynolds	863 Pete Murray	956 Jeremy Robson	1049 James Copner
773 Thomas James Burke	864 Michael Dunn	957 John Kidd	1050 Colin Hall
774 Ken Pollard	865 Mick & Tiffany Pilch	958 Adrian Scott	1051 Iain Rae Moir
775 Kevin Ferguson	866 Mark Mulhern	959 Michael Rochford	1052 Mitchell A Joannou
776 Steven Carr	867 Neil Thornton	960 John Rochford	1053 E Joannou RIP
777 Kathleen Irene Carr	868 Paul Connelly	961 John Williamson	1054 Lauren Katie Jenkins
778 Liam Errington	869 Peter Bainbridge	962 Gordon Lundgren	1055 The Goslings
779 Russell John Gardiner	870 Derek Ginsberg	963 Irene & Eddie Lundgren	1056 Anth Raine
780 Howard Beckett	871 Bryn Waller	964 Les Ruffell	1057 Peter McCarthy
781 Chris Baldry	872 Liam Ramshaw	965 Thomas Tomlin	1058 George Willis
782 James Palmer	873 Daniel Ramshaw	966 Alan Gibson	1059 Norman Edgar
783 Mark Ashley Roadley	874 Run Geordie Run	967 Jim Wallis	1060 Richard Stocken
	875 Oliver & Henry Smith	968 Steven Hughes	1061 Richard M Drake

1062 Yogi Brewin	1155 Ian Lambert	1248 Simon Andrew Jobling	1341 Mark Sturmey
1063 Sean Ward Ivey	1156 Stephen Gamsby	1249 Dean Carlyle	1342 Neil Edward Buckingham
1064 Graham Wallis	1157 John Herdman	1250 Kenneth J Tiffin	1343 Mike Pedley
1065 Steven Thomas	1158 Nathan James Coverdale	1251 Jamie @toonjamie Smith	1344 Michael Cryan
1066 Tom Watson	1159 Lesley Hutchinson	1252 Koko of Ruse	1345 Kirsty Fisher
1067 James Watson	1160 Debbie Whittaker	1253 David C Mills	1346 Steven Nicholas
1068 Robert Watson	1161 David Pattison	1254 William Henry Sanderson	1347 Andrew Ridley
1069 Gary Watson	1162 Paul Christian Brown	1255 Gordon Andrew Seery	1348 Brian Kyle
1070 Roger Spence	1163 Jon Henderson	1256 Andrew Rayne	1349 Alan Thomas Clark
1071 Alan Eltringham	1164 Ramon Fritschi	1257 Anthony Robert Beattie	1350 Ian Wilson
1072 Philip Walton	1165 David Irving	1258 Keith Howson	1351 Tristan Kitchin
1073 Frank Spoors	1166 Riccardo Rossi	1259 Paul Mann	1352 Colin Tait
1074 C D Carey	1167 David Evans	1260 Bruce D Reid	1353 Colin Dooley
1075 Barbara Luke	1168 Ken Sweet	1261 Steve Barrett	1354 Kieran Edward Smith
1076 Andrew Hewison	1169 Harry Rowland Scott	1262 Nigel Cowley	1355 Jordanville Mag
1077 Chris Le Grice	1170 Keith Reynolds	1263 Glen House	1356 Michael Johnson
1078 Geoffrey Hogg	1171 Andrew James Palmer	1264 Oliver Black	1357 Adrian Littlewood
1079 Harry Hall	1172 Jevon Whiteley	1265 John E Potter	1358 Benji Fleming
1080 Michael Thomas Driver	1173 Victor Gascoigne	1266 Dave Ruddock	1359 Graeme Robson
1081 Steve Hastie	1174 Stephen Taylor	1267 Nigel Sowerby	1360 Callum Robson
1082 Dominic Irving	1175 Gerry Saenger	1268 Andy Robinson	1361 Christian Mark Allen
1083 Ian Smith	1176 Jackie Bambrick	1269 Daniel Michelmore	1362 Gordon Riddle
1084 Terry Holliday	1177 Ross Mikle Penman	1270 John A Leslie	1363 Michael Parry
1085 Neil James Skelly	1178 Philip Lars Penman	1271 Dave Mitchell	1364 Mathew Jake Greenwell
1086 Michael Lee Clark	1179 Ken Kelly	1272 Malcolm Ferguson	1365 Robin McMenzie
1087 Matthew James Sharff	1180 Michael Zago	1273 David Taylor	1366 Chris Tuck
1088 Phil Robinson	1181 Paul McGuigan	1274 Barry Thompson	1367 Colin Tuck
1089 Steve Heads	1182 Mike Eames	1275 Harry William Metcalfe	1368 Billy Miller Jnr
1090 Murray Baker	1183 Mark Broomfield	1276 Matteo Tonna	1369 Bill Miller Snr
1091 Alan Beale	1184 Mark Stephenson	1277 David Scorfield	1370 Bobby Kelters
1092 James Angus Leybourne	1185 Graham Skipsey	1278 Daniel Ingram Armstrong	1371 The Oil
1093 John Joseph Lee	1186 Steve Redshaw	1279 Rod Mckend	1372 James Lowe
1094 Thomas Mc Evilly	1187 Robert M Livingston	1280 Richard T Kelly	1373 Will Hamilton
1095 Paul W Shipley	1188 Ray Brown	1281 David Brent	1374 Ali & Mike Ryan
1096 Piers Masterton Wilcox	1189 Geoff Robinson	1282 Michael Robert Parker	1375 Keith Brown
1097 Keith Wilson	1190 Robin Johnston	1283 Jason Rhodes	1376 Daniel Gullen Munro
1098 Gary Davis	1191 Thomas Lister	1284 Gary Taylor	1377 Stephen Laverton
1099 Sam Berg	1192 David Wilson	1285 Michael Boreham	1378 Robert Scott
1100 Philip Miller	1193 Connor James Lee	1286 Steven Hill	1379 George Leonard May
1101 Christopher Scott	1194 Kevin McClurey	1287 Rocky Chaddha	1380 Bill & Sylvia Blueitt
1102 Peter Drew	1195 Steven Whittle	1288 Christopher Evans	1381 Mick Johnson
1103 Michael 'Bourlotos' Knipe	1196 Richard Waugh	1289 Stanley Johnson	1382 David Morton
1104 Holler Watches	1197 Faye Sanderson	1290 Jamie Gallagher	1383 Peter Charles
1105 Paul Kiernan	1198 Michael James Openshaw	1291 Brian Stenhouse	1384 Brian Maw
1106 Matt Hutchings	1199 Pete Bond	1292 NUDSA	1385 Andrew Robert Maitland
1107 Ian Gardner	1200 Michael Wallace	1293 Leslie Florence	1386 Leon Brunt
1108 Richard G Grieve	1201 Terry Spencer	1294 Loraine Mitcheson-Smith	1387 Neil Jensen
1109 Les Butcher	1202 Tom Chapman	1295 Tom Bestford	1388 Bill McSorland
1110 Bryn Middlemass	1203 Tom Chapman	1296 Liam Bestford	1389 Eirik Thom
1111 Jonathan Edward Miller	1204 Raymond Beattie	1297 Jack Geordie Hopper	1390 Phil Robinson
1112 Anthony Thompson	1205 Charlie Rutherford	1298 Steven Holliday	1391 Matt Young
1113 Mark Thrower	1206 David Keith Coulson	1299 Brian William Middlemas	1392 Yvonne Sewell
1114 Dave Boylen	1207 Thomas Doran	1300 George Lewis-Hall	1393 Erik Andrè Rødsrud
1115 Mark Anthony Crowther	1208 David Martin Horne	1301 The Gilberts, Kettering	1394 Lewis Marriott
1116 Kevin Morgan	1209 John Leonard Tither	1302 Peter W May	1395 James Chorley
1117 Martin Rimmer	1210 Thomas Tones	1303 Alastair Conn	1396 Doug Sutherland
1118 Liam Chris	1211 Dave Burton	1304 Ian Cockbain	1397 Dave Morton
1119 Peter Clegg	1212 Colin Simpson	1305 Phil Ingoe	1398 Martin Kelly
1120 Roger Doyle	1213 Mick Rodgers	1306 Paul J Featherstone	1399 Philip McCracken
1121 Brian Daley	1214 Mrs C Armstrong	1307 Anth Carmichael	1400 JJ Moseley
1122 Daniel James Squires	1215 Mark Adam Curry	1308 Mark Bowerman	1401 John Lackenby
1123 Phil Robson	1216 Steven Hogg	1309 Ian Oliver	1402 Joseph Lackenby
1124 Steve Cole	1217 Gareth Manuel	1310 John Burton Hunter	1403 Alan Keith
1125 Barry Gibson	1218 David Sharpe	1311 Graeme Elliot	1404 Gary Mark Coates
1126 Ross Tweddell	1219 Bob Geordie Best	1312 Rolf Corneliusson	1405 Ian Coates
1127 Colin Robson	1220 Bobby Best	1313 Paul Williams	1406 Brian Love Maw
1128 Michael Newies	1221 Jimmy Gordon	1314 Leon Black	1407 Thomas Harvey Wright
1129 Harry Barron	1222 Matthew James Bedford	1315 Alan Gardner	
1130 Deborah Brown	1223 Mark Graydon	1316 Alan Gardner	
1131 Ian Sharp	1224 Paul Wood	1317 Joe Mckenzie	
1132 Danny Alan Montgomery	1225 Paul Anderson	1318 George Carter	
1133 Edwin C Tully	1226 Joe Ford	1319 David Wiseman	
1134 Connor Peter Sisk	1227 Andrew Sanderson	1320 Joe Hastings	
1135 Frankie Storey	1228 Arthur Walker	1321 Mark Richard Sowton	
1136 Dale Huey	1229 John Pace	1322 Rob Morgan, Cardiff	
1137 Michael Cowell	1230 Michael McDonald	1323 Graham Di Duca	
1138 Joan Barnes	1231 Ian Murdoch	1324 Luke Irving	
1139 Ian Hepplewhite	1232 Lynne Oates	1325 Paul Edwards	
1140 Samuel Jonathon Webster	1233 Stephen Hetherington	1326 Dave Reay	
1141 Carl Heads	1234 Paul Greener	1327 Robert Henry Smith	
1142 David Smith	1235 Paul Roadley	1328 Steven Orange	
1143 Marc Cameron	1236 Lynne Clarke	1329 Ian Kerr	
1144 Jack Heads	1237 Paul David Miller	1330 Sean Borland	
1145 Terry Fisher	1238 Neil William Devine	1331 Les Scott	
1146 Simon Cataudo	1239 Karl Jon Rickelton	1332 Mike Whittaker	
1147 Gareth Kerr	1240 David Rice	1333 Dawn J	
1148 George Wales	1241 Roger Tames	1334 Alex Innerd	
1149 Trevor Lewin	1242 Björn Scheving Aas	1335 Michael Grayson	
1150 Douglas Robert Bidgood	1243 Martin McGuinness	1336 Richard Sewell	
1151 Warren 'Waz' Black	1244 Bernard Morton	1337 Sean Kelly	
1152 Peter John Harpham	1245 Oliver Knapton	1338 Jean Shiels	
1153 Antony Nicholson	1246 Peter David Askew	1339 David Wheeler	
1154 Grant Lyon	1247 Ray Brewis	1340 Mike Jackman	

a = away fixture
ABA = Amateur Boxing Association
Acc = (Hamilton) Academicals
ACN = African Cup of Nations
AGM = Annual General Meeting
AIC = Anglo Italian Cup
Alex = Alexandra (Crewe)
amat = amateur
app = appearance
ASC = Anglo Scottish Cup
ASEAN = Association of Southeast Asian Nations
Ass = Association
asst = assistant
ATC = Air Training Corps
Ath = Athletic
b. = born
BB = Boy's Brigade
BBC = British Broadcasting Corporation
BC = Boys Club
BL = British Legion
Boro = Middlesbrough FC (in text)
BSc = Bachelor of Science degree
c = circa, about
CA = Copa America
Cal = (Inverness) Caledonian
CBE = Commander of the British Empire
CC = Copa Commebol or Cricket Club
CCC = County Cricket Club
champs = national tier-one league champions winner
CID = Criminal Investigation Department
CL = Champions League (after 1992)
Co = County or Company
CoE = Centre of Excellence
cs = close-season
CSA = Copa South America
CW = Colliery Welfare football club
CWS = Cooperative Wholesale Society
d. = died
DCM = Distinguished Conduct Medal
div = division
E or Euro = European, Europe
EC = European Cup (to 1992)
ECWC = European Cup Winners Cup
ECh = European International Championship
Eire Lg = Republic of Ireland (Eire) League
Eire Cup = Republic of Ireland (Eire) Cup
EL = League of Ireland (Eire)
EpL = Europa League
ESC = UEFA or European Super Cup
Exch = exchange deal
FA = Football Association
FAAC = FA Amateur Cup
FAC = FA Cup
FACQ = FA Cup Qualifying round
FAI = Football Association of Ireland (Eire)
FAT = FA Trophy
FAV = FA Vase
FAVC = FA Victory Cup (wartime)
FAYC = FA Youth Cup
FC = Football Club
Fed = (Dunston) Federation FC
FiC = Football in the Community
FIFA = Federation Internationale de Football Association
FL = Football League
FLa = Football League abandoned fixture
FLC = Football League Cup (and later sponsored competitions)
FL ch = Football League Championship (tier-two)
FL div 3 champs = title winning team
FL div 2 prom = promotion winning team
FLN = Football League North (wartime)
FLN2 = Football League North 2nd (or 1st) competition (wartime)
FLNE = Football League North East (wartime)
FLT = Football League Trophy
FL div 3(N) = Football League division 3 (North)
FL div 3(S) = Football League division 3 (South)
FMC = Full Members Cup
free = free transfer
FTSE = Financial Times & London Stock Exchange (index)

gl, gls = goal, goals
gkp = goalkeeper
Gp = Group
h = home fixture
HMS = Her or His Majesty's Ship
IC = Irish Cup (before nation split)
ICC = Intercontinental Cup (since 1960)
ICFC = Inter Cities Fairs Cup and later European Fairs Cup
IL = Irish League (before nation split)
incl = included
ITC = Intertoto Cup
Jnr = Junior club
jnr = signed as junior player
JP = Justice of the Peace
LC = League Cup
LibC = Libertadores Cup
Lg = League
m = (m) honours when a manager
m = (£7) million
MBE = Member of the Order of the British Empire
MerC = Mercosur Cup
MLS = Major League Soccer (North America)
MM = Military Medal
MP = Member of Parliament
MSM = Meritorious Service Medal
N = North
NASL = North American Soccer League
NER = North Eastern Railway
NG or Nat XI = National Game or National XI appearance (non-league England XI)
NIC = Northern Ireland Cup
NIGC = Northern Ireland Gold Cup
NIL = Northern Ireland League
NL = Northern League
No = Number
N's = Newcastle United junior side
NVL = Northern Victory League (wartime)
OBE = Officer of the Order of the British Empire
OG = Olympic Games
Olym = Olympic
pa = per annum/year
PFA = Professional Footballers Association
PE = Physical Education
PL = Premier League
PLC = Public Limited Company
pm = player-manager
pmt = permanent transfer
PR = Public Relations
prof = professional contract
prom = promotion
PT = Physical Training
Q3 = Quarter 3 (as in birth or death; the four quarters of the year)
QC = Queen's Counsel
qv = cross-reference to another biography
RAF = Royal Air Force
RMI = Railway Mechanics Institute
ROF = Royal Ordnance Factory
RoW = Rest of the World
S = South
SC = Scottish Cup
SC = social club or sport club, when affixed to a club
SCC = Scottish Challenge Cup
sch = school
Scot SthLC = Scottish Southern League Cup (wartime)
SFA = Scottish Football Association
SL = Scottish League
SLC = Scottish League Cup
SJC = Scottish Junior Cup
SnL = Southern League
snr = senior player
SQC = Scottish Qualifying Cup
SthA = South America (international championship)
sub = substitute
SVC = Scottish Victory Cup
TC = Texaco Cup
TTW = Tyne Tees Wear Cup (wartime)
TUC = Trades Union Congress

UEFA = Union of European Football Associations
UEFAC = UEFA Cup
unoff = unofficial
Utd = United
u21 = Under-21 international appearance (and Under-23)
v = versus
YC = Youth Club
VC = Victoria Cross
WCC = World Club Cup
WC = Football League War Cup
Wand = Wanderers
Wed = Wednesday (Sheffield)
WL or Wlg = War League
WdC = World Cup
WsC = Welsh Cup
WsL = Welsh League
WMC = Working Men's Club
YC = youth club
YMCA = Young Men's Christian Association

Annual Awards
EFoY = European Footballer of the Year award
WFoY = World Footballer of the Year award
FoY 1976 (FWA) = Footballer of the Year, Football Writers' Association award (since 1947-48)
PoY 1976 (PFA) = Players' Player of the Year, Professional Footballers' Association award (since 1973-74)
YPoY 1976 (PFA) = Players' Young Player of the Year, Professional Footballers' Association award (since 1973-74)
SFoY 1976 (FWA) = Scotland Footballer of the Year, Football Writers' Association award (since 1964-65)
SYPoY 1976 (FWA) = Scotland Young Player of the Year, Football Writers' Association award (since 2001-02)
SPoY 1976 (PFA) = Scotland Player of the Year, Professional Footballers' Association award (since 1977-78)
SPoY = Sports Personality of the Year (BBC)
PoD = Player of the Decade
ToD = Team of the Decade
ToY = Team of the Year
LMA MoY = League Managers Association, Manager of the Year award (since 1994)
Neth FoY or PoY = various nation Footballer of the Year or Player of the Year award
PFA ToS (D1) = Professional Footballers' Association, Team of the Season award (division) (since 1973-74)
Eng HoF = England Hall of Fame award (since 2002, National Football Museum)
Scot HoF = Scotland Hall of Fame (since 2004, Scottish Football Museum)
NU HoF = Newcastle United Hall of Fame award (since 2012)
FL Legend = Football League Legend (centenary award 1998)

Continental senior league & cup
Eredivisie = Netherlands tier –one
Bundesliga = Germany tier-one
La Liga = Spain tier-one
Le Championnat = France tier-one
Serie A = Italy tier-one
Scuddetto = Italy tier-one title trophy
Copa del Rey = Spanish Cup (FA Cup equivalent)
Coppa Italia = Italian Cup (FA Cup equivalent)
Coupe de France = French Cup (FA Cup equivalent)

Universal abbreviations:
The following club titles have been used in the text; PSV (PSV Eindhoven), PSG (Paris St-German), QPR (Queens Park Rangers), WBA (West Bromwich Albion).
Monthly abbreviations used; Jan, Feb, Aug, Sept, Oct, Nov, Dec

Country abbreviations:
Eng = England
Scot = Scotland
NI = Northern Ireland
Wales
Eire = Republic of Ireland
Irel = Ireland (before nation split)
GB = Great Britain
UK = United Kingdom
Alb, Albania
Alg, Algeria
Arg, Argentina
Ast, Austria
Aus, Australia
Belg, Belgium
Bm, Burma
Bmd, Bermuda
Bhn, Bahrain
Brz, Brazil
Cam, Cameroon
Can, Canada
Ch, Chile
Chn, China
Col, Colombia
Cr, Croatia
Cy, Cyprus
Cz, Czech Republic/Czechoslovakia
Den, Denmark
Fls, Faroe Islands
Fin, Finland
Fr, France
Ger, Germany
Gr, Greece
Grg, Georgia
Gy, Guyana
HK, Hong Kong
Hng, Hungary
IC, Ivory Coast
Ice, Iceland
Ind, India
Is, Israel
It, Italy
Jap, Japan
Jm, Jamaica
Kwt, Kuwait
M/Fr, Monaco
Mal, Malaysia
Mex, Mexico
Mnts, Montserrat
Neth, Netherlands
Ng, Nigeria
Nor, Norway
NZ, New Zealand
Pg, Paraguay
Plp, Philippines
Pol, Poland
Ptg, Portugal
Pu, Peru
Qt, Qatar
Rhd, Rhodesia
Rom, Romania
Rs, Russia
SA, South Africa
SAr, Saudi Arabia
Sb, Serbia
Seng, Senegal
Sing, Singapore
Sln, Slovenia
Slv, Slovakia
Sp, Spain
Swd, Sweden
Swtz, Switzerland
Sy, Syria
Th, Thailand
TT, Trinidad & Tobago
Trk, Turkey
Tun, Tunisia
UAE, United Arab Emirates
Ugy, Uruguay
Ugd, Uganda
Ukr, Ukraine
USA, United States of America
USSR, Union of Soviet Socialist Republics
WG, West Germany
Zam, Zambia